European Union Law

As the preferred choice on EU law for both teachers and students, this textbook offers an unrivalled combination of expertise, accessibility and comprehensive coverage. Written in a way which combines clarity with sophisticated analysis, it stimulates students to engage fully with the sometimes complex material, and encourages critical reflection.

The new edition reflects the challenges facing the European Union now, with dedicated chapters on Brexit, the migration crisis and the euro area, and with further Brexit materials and analysis integrated wherever relevant. Materials from case law, legislation and academic literature are integrated throughout to present the student with the broadest range of views and deepen understanding of the context of the law. A dedicated site introduces students to the wide-ranging debates found in blogs on EU law, EU affairs more generally and Brexit. A required text for all interested in European Union law.

Damian Chalmers is Professor of EU law and Law of Regional Integration at the National University of Singapore. He was previously Professor at the London School of Economics and Political Science where he was Head of its European Institute for four years. He was co-editor of the European Law Review for six years, and has held Visiting Positions at, inter alia, the College of Europe, the EUI, NYU, the CEU and the Instituto de Empresa.

Gareth Davies is Professor of EU law at the Vrije Universiteit Amsterdam. He previously worked as a barrister in London before becoming a University Lecturer at the University of Groningen until 2007. In 2006 he was an Emile Noel Fellow at New York University Law School, and in 2014 a Fernand Braudel Senior Fellow at the EUI.

Giorgio Monti is Professor of Competition Law at the European University Institute and the Ronald Coase Visiting Professor of Law and Economics at Tilburg University for 2018-19. He is the Scientific Coordinator of the Florence Competition Programme, which provides judicial and executive training in the field of competition law. Since 2017 he has been one of the Editors of the Common Market Law Review.

European Union Law

TEXT AND MATERIALS

FOURTH EDITION

Damian Chalmers
National University of Singapore

Gareth Davies
Vrije Universiteit, Amsterdam

Giorgio Monti
European University Institute, Florence

CAMBRIDGE
UNIVERSITY PRESS

CAMBRIDGE
UNIVERSITY PRESS

University Printing House, Cambridge CB2 8BS, United Kingdom

One Liberty Plaza, 20th Floor, New York, NY 10006, USA

477 Williamstown Road, Port Melbourne, VIC 3207, Australia

314–321, 3rd Floor, Plot 3, Splendor Forum, Jasola District Centre, New Delhi – 110025, India

79 Anson Road, #06-04/06, Singapore 079906

Cambridge University Press is part of the University of Cambridge.

It furthers the University's mission by disseminating knowledge in the pursuit of
education, learning, and research at the highest international levels of excellence.

www.cambridge.org
Information on this title: www.cambridge.org/9781108463591
DOI: 10.1017/9781108654173

First published 2019

Printed in Singapore by Markono Print Media Pte Ltd

A catalogue record for this publication is available from the British Library.

Library of Congress Cataloging-in-Publication Data
Names: Chalmers, Damian, author. | Davies, Gareth, author. | Monti, Giorgio, author.
Title: European Union law : text and materials / Damian Chalmers, National University of Singapore;
    Gareth Davies, Vrije Universiteit, Amsterdam; Giorgio Monti, European University Institute, Florence.
Description: Fourth edition. | Cambridge, United Kingdom : Cambridge University Press, 2019. | Includes bibliographical
    references and index.
Identifiers: LCCN 2018059108 | ISBN 9781108463591 (paperback)
Subjects: LCSH: Law–European Union countries. | European Union. | LCGFT: Textbooks.
Classification: LCC KJE947 .E883 2019 | DDC 341.242/2–dc23
LC record available at https://lccn.loc.gov/2018059108

ISBN 978-1-108-46359-1 Paperback

Additional resources for this publication at www.cambridge.org/chalmers4e

Brief Contents

Contents

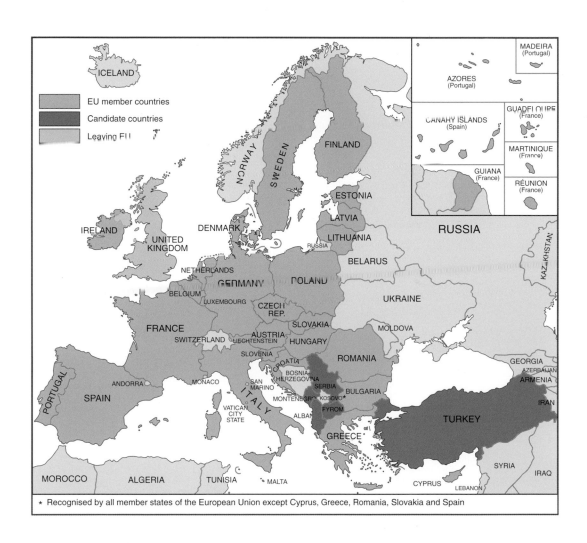

ICELAND

EU member countries

Candidate countries

Leaving EU

NORWAY

SWEDEN

FINLAND

ESTONIA

LATVIA

LITHUANIA
RUSSIA

IRELAND

UNITED
KINGDOM

DENMARK

BELARUS

NETHERLANDS

GERMANY

POLAND

BELGIUM

LUXEMBOURG

CZECH
REP.

UKRAINE

FRANCE

SLOVAKIA

SWITZERLAND
LIECHTENSTEIN

AUSTRIA

HUNGARY

MOLDOVA

SLOVENIA

ROMANIA

GEORGIA

PORTUGAL

ANDORRA

MONACO

SAN
MARINO

CROATIA

BOSNIA
HERZEGOVINA

SERBIA

AZERBAIJAN

ARMENIA

SPAIN

ITALY

MONTENEGRO

KOSOVO*

BULGARIA

IRAN

VATICAN
CITY
STATE

FYROM

TURKEY

ALBAN

GREECE

SYRIA

MOROCCO

ALGERIA

TUNISIA

MALTA

CYPRUS

LEBANON

IRAQ

RUSSIA

MADEIRA
(Portugal)

AZORES
(Portugal)

GUADELOUPE
(France)

CANARY ISLANDS
(Spain)

MARTINIQUE
(France)

GUIANA
(France)

RÉUNION
(France)

KAZAKHSTAN

* Recognised by all member states of the European Union except Cyprus, Greece, Romania, Slovakia and Spain

xix

Preface

The cover of this book portrays the *Myth of Europa*. The story has it that Europa, a Phoenician princess, was abducted by Zeus, the god of thunder, disguised as a bull. Zeus had been searching for a wife beautiful enough to become Queen of his native Crete. When he saw Europa he was smitten. Europa was gathering flowers by the seaside with her friends when she came upon the bull. Uncommonly gentle, the bull inspired no fear. Decking its horns with flowers, Europa climbed upon its back, whereupon the bull – Zeus – took off at a trot and dived into the sea. Europa was carried off to Crete, where she became the mother of Minos, the mythical King of Crete, who periodically demanded a tribute of young men and women of Athens to be sacrificed to the Minotaur.

This myth has not died with the ancients. In 1956, the six countries that were to sign the EEC Treaty appropriated her name to issue a set of Europa stamps to symbolise a community of interests and objectives. And today, Zeus's kidnap of Europa is depicted on the Greek 2 euro coin. The myth has been understood in a variety of ways. On one level it is a story of virtue, innocence and romance; on another, it is a warning of violence and exclusion. As with many of the ancient myths, misunderstanding and contestation lie at its very heart. The Roman depiction on our cover is one of the first depictions and, insofar as the human participants are depicted as Romans, reminds us too that the myth has been repeatedly appropriated and reinvented. We have also here a tale with its origins in modern Lebanon, which was told by the Ancient Greeks, and which then became a central fable of Ancient Rome. Yet Europa's myth is now seen as the origin of a territory whose cultural heartland lies somewhere in central Europe, *Mitteleuropa*, perhaps in the modern Czech Republic, perhaps in Vienna, but certainly somewhere in a nation that became a Member State of the European Union only very recently. In today's Europe, misunderstanding, contestation, appropriation and reinvention permeate not only its founding myth, but also its most modern institution, the European Union, the law of which is this book's subject. European Union law is often seen as embodying new ideals, new rights and new forms of welfare. Equally, however, it is portrayed as being intrusive, divisive and costly. On the one hand, EU law is said to bring an international comity and to provide a powerful counter to the narrow (and historically dangerous) parochialism that has marked so much of Europe's bloody past. On the other hand, critics point to an overweening, inflexible, even pernicious European-ness, that is intolerant of national diversity and that stymies local democracy.

It is exactly this anxious fragility that gives European Union law its peculiar vitality and interest. It brings both a sceptical eye to the analysis of EU law and a constant demand to revisit old assumptions. As such, as the Brexit process has well illustrated, debates about EU law have in recent years been central in reconsidering ideas of the State, political community, the market, tradition and society.

This book owes a number of large debts. The efficiency, the friendliness and patience of Cambridge University Press continue to be a hallmark of our relationship with them. We would like to thank Jem Langworthy, Marianne Nield, Dominic Stock and Marta Walowiak. We were also a blessed with a team of great research assistants. A big thank you to Cheryl, Jarrett, Jessica, Kinnari, Ning and Trinisha. They were a pleasure to work with, and the book is much better because of them. The division of responsibility for the book is as follows. Damian Chalmers wrote Chapters 1–10, 12 and 15. Giorgio Monti wrote Chapters 13, 20, 21 and 22. Gareth Davies wrote Chapters 11, 14, 16, 17, 18 and 19. Finally, there are a number of personal debts. Damian Chalmers would like to thank Juliana Cardinale once again for her love, patience and jokes. Gareth Davies wishes to thank Marjolein van Wieringen again for her tolerance and good humour during the exceptionally busy mid-2018 when he was trying to write. Giorgio Monti continues to thank Ayako for her common sense and support, and Giulia and Sofia for being constant sources of wonder and laughter. Finally, we would like to thank each other!

We have aimed to state EU law as at 1 December 2018. However, the vagaries of the Brexit process meant that it was not settled by then! We have tracked developments up until 31 March 2019. The United Kingdom is unlikely to have left the European Union in the first few months after publication of this edition. This edition is written on the assumption that it will leave and that the European Union will comprise only 27 States.

DC, GD, GM

ACKNOWLEDGEMENTS

Every attempt has been made to secure permission to reproduce copyright material in this title and grateful acknowledgement is made to the authors and publishers of all reproduced material. In particular, the publisher would like to acknowledge the following for granting permission to reproduce material from the following publications:

Chapter 1: J. Habermas and J. Derrida, 'February 15, or, What Binds Europeans Together: Plea for a Common Foreign Policy Beginning in Core Europe' in D. Levy, J. Torpey and M. Pensky (eds.), *Old Europe, New Europe, Core Europe: Transatlantic Relations after the Iraq War* (London, Verso, 2005); L. Hooghe and G. Marks, 'Cleavage Theory Meets Europe's Crises: Lipset, Rokkan, and the Transnational Cleavage' (2018) 25 *Journal of European Public Policy* 109; L. v. Middelaar, *The Passage to Europe: How a Continent Became a Union* (New Haven, Yale University Press, 2013); C. Offe, 'Europe Entrapped: Does the EU Have the Political Capacity to Overcome its Current Crisis?' (2013) 19 *European Law Journal* 595; M. Wilkinson, 'The Specter of Authoritarian Liberalism: Reflections on the Constitutional Crisis of the European Union' (2013) 14 *German Law Journal* 527; D. Chalmers, 'Brexit and the Renaissance of Parliamentary Authority' (2017) 19 *British Journal of Politics and International Relations* 663; C. Kreuder-Sonnen, 'An Authoritarian Turn in Europe and European Studies?' (2018) 25 *Journal of European Public Policy* 452.

Chapter 2: E. Mastenbroek and D. Martinsen, 'Filling the Gap in the European Administrative Space: The Role of Administrative Networks in EU Implementation and Enforcement' (2018) 25

Journal of European Public Policy 422; M. Egeberg, J. Trondal and N. Vestlund, 'The Quest for Order: Unravelling the Relationship between the European Commission and European Union Agencies' (2015) 22 *Journal of European Public Policy* 609; J. Tallberg, 'Bargaining Power in the European Council' (2008) 46 *Journal of Common Market Studies* 685; D. Grimm, 'Does Europe Need a Constitution?' (1995) 1 *European Law Journal* 282; P. Dann, 'European Parliament and Executive Federalism: Approaching a Parliament in a Semi-Parliamentary Democracy' (2003) 9 *European Law Journal* 549; M. Shackleton, 'Transforming Representative Democracy in the EU? The Role of the European Parliament' (2017) 39 *Journal of European Integration* 191; D. Curtin, 'Overseeing Secrets in the EU: A Democratic Perspective' (2014) 52 *Journal of Common Market Studies* 684.

Chapter 3: R. Kardasheva, 'The Power to Delay: The European Parliament's Influence in the Consultation Procedure' (2009) 47 *Journal of Common Market Studies* 385; C. Joerges and J. Neyer, 'Transforming Strategic Interaction into Deliberative Problem-Solving: European Comitology in the Foodstuffs Sector' (1997) 4 *Journal of European Public Policy* 609; D. Miller, 'Democracy's Domain' (2009) 37 *Philosophy & Public Affairs* 201; J. Habermas, 'Democracy in Europe: Why the Development of the EU into a Transnational Democracy Is Necessary and How It Is Possible' (2015) 21 *European Law Journal* 546; F. Cheneval and K. Nicolaidis, 'The Social Construction of Demoicracy in the European Union' (2017) 16 *European Journal of Political Theory* 235.

Chapter 4: S. Schmidt, *The European Court of Justice & The Policy Process* (Oxford University Press, 2018); G. Conway, *The Limits of Legal Reasoning and the European Court of Justice* (Cambridge University Press, 2012); M. Broberg, 'Acte Clair Revisited: Adapting the Acte Clair Criteria to the Demands of the Times' (2008) 45 *Common Market Law Review* 1383.

Chapter 5: B. de Witte, 'Direct Effect, Primacy, and the Nature of the Legal Order' in P. Craig and G. de Búrca (eds.), *The Evolution of EU Law*, 2nd edn (Oxford University Press, 2011); T. Isiksel, *Europe's Functional Constitution: A Theory of Constitutionalism Beyond the State* (Oxford University Press, 2016); N. Walker, 'The Place of European Law' in G. de Búrca and J. Weiler (eds.), *The Worlds of European Constitutionalism* (Cambridge University Press, 2012); M. Kumm, 'The Jurisprudence of Constitutional Conflict: Constitutional Supremacy in Europe before and after the Constitutional Treaty' (2005) 11 *European Law Journal* 262.

Chapter 6: D. Chalmers and S. Trotter, 'Fundamental Rights and Legal Wrongs: The Two Sides of the Same EU Coin' (2016) 22 *European Law Journal* 9; M. Cartabia, 'Europe and Rights: Taking Dialogue Seriously' (2009) 5 *European Constitutional Law Review* 5; U. Sedelmeier, 'Political Safeguards against Democratic Backsliding in the EU: The Limits of Material Sanctions and the Scope of Social Pressure' (2017) 24 *Journal of European Public Policy* 337.

Chapter 7: M. Amstutz, 'In-Between Worlds: *Marleasing* and the Emergence of Interlegality in Legal Reasoning' (2005) 11 *European Law Journal* 766; C. Harlow, '*Francovich* and the Problem of the Disobedient State' (1996) 2 *European Law Journal* 199; H. Scott and N. Barber, 'State Liability under *Francovich* for Decisions of National Courts' (2004) 120 *Law Quarterly Review* 403.

Chapter 8: G. Falkner and O. Treib, 'Three Worlds of Compliance or Four? The EU-15 Compared to New Member States' (2008) 46 *Journal of Common Market Studies* 293; T. Börzel, T. Hofmann and D. Panke, 'Caving In or Sitting Out? Longitudinal Patterns of Non-Compliance in the European Union' (2012) 19 *Journal of European Public Policy* 454; E. Chiti, 'The Governance of Compliance' in M. Cremona (ed.), *Compliance and the Enforcement of EU*

Law (Oxford University Press, 2012); M. Smith, *Centralised Enforcement, Legitimacy and Good Governance in the EU* (Abingdon, Routledge, 2009); B. Jack, 'Article 260(2) TFEU: An Effective Judicial Procedure for the Enforcement of Judgments?' (2013) 19 *European Law Journal* 404.

Chapter 9: A. Fritzsche, 'Discretion, Scope of Judicial Balance and Institutional Review in European Law' (2010) 47 *Common Market Law Review* 361; J. Mendes, *Participation in EU Rule-Making: A Rights-Based Approach* (Oxford University Press, 2011); A. Arnull 'Private Applicants and the Action for Annulment under Article 173 of the EC Treaty' (1995) 32 *Common Market Law Review* 7; C. Harlow, 'Towards a Theory of Access for the European Court of Justice' (1992) 12 *Yearbook of European Law* 213.

Chapter 10: K. Hayward, 'The Pivotal Position of the Irish Border in the UK's Withdrawal from the European Union' (2018) 22 *Space and Polity* 238; I. Loader and N. Walker, *Civilizing Security* (Cambridge University Press, 2007); J. Wiener and A. Alemanno, 'The Future of International Regulatory Cooperation: TTIP as a Learning Process Toward a Global Policy Laboratory' (2015) 78 *Law and Contemporary Problems* 103; A. Bradford, 'The Brussels Effect' (2012) 107 *Northwestern University Law Review* 1; J. Scott, 'Extraterritoriality and Territorial Extension in EU Law' (2014) 62 *American Journal of Comparative Law* 87.

Chapter 11: R. Bellamy, 'Introduction: The Making of Modern Citizenship' in R. Bellamy *et al.* (eds.), *Lineages of European Citizenship: Rights, Belonging and Participation in Eleven Nation States* (Basingstoke, Palgrave Macmillan, 2004); D. Kostakopoulou, 'European Union Citizenship: Writing the Future' (2007) 13(5) *European Law Journal* 623; A. Iliopoulou Penot, 'The Transnational Character of Union Citizenship' in M. Dougan, N. Nic Shuibhne and E. Spaventa (eds.), *Empowerment and Disempowerment of the European Citizen* (Oxford, Hart, 2012); H. Stalford, *Children and the European Union: Rights, Welfare and Accountability* (Oxford University Press, 2012); D. Kostakopoulou and N. Ferreira, 'Testing Liberal Norms: The Public Policy and Public Security Derogations and the Cracks in European Citizenship' (2014) 20(2) *Columbia Journal of European Law* 167.

Chapter 12: K. Aas and H. Gundhus, 'Policing Humanitarian Borderlands: Frontex, Human Rights and the Precariousness of Life' (2015) 55 *British Journal of Criminology* 1; E. Kofman, 'Citizenship, Migration and the Reassertion of National Identity' (2005) 9 *Citizenship Studies* 453; E. Guild, 'Seeking Asylum: Storm Clouds between International Commitments and Legislative Measures' (2004) 29 *European Law Review* 198; P. Slominski and F. Trauner, 'How Do Member States Return Unwanted Migrants? The Strategic (Non-)Use of "Europe" during the Migration Crisis' (2018) 56 *Journal of Common Market Studies* 101.

Chapter 13: H. Samuels, 'A Defining Moment: A Feminist Perspective on the Law of Sexual Harassment in the Workplace in the Light of the Equal Treatment Amendment Directive' (2004) 12 *Feminist Legal Studies* 181; B. Hepple, 'Race and Law in Fortress Europe' (2004) 67 *Modern Law Review* 1; K. Crenshaw, 'Demarginalizing the Intersection of Race and Sex: A Black Feminist Critique of Antidiscrimination Doctrine, Feminist Theory and Antiracist Politics' (1989) *University of Chicago Legal Forum* 139; C. Fagan and J. Rubery, 'Advancing Gender Equality through European Employment Policy: The Impact of the UK's EU Membership and the Risks of Brexit' (2018) 17(2) *Social Policy and Society* 297.

Chapter 14: M. Maduro, 'Reforming the Market or the State? Article 30 and the European Constitution: Economic Freedom and Political Rights' (1997) 3 *European Law Journal* 55; F. De Witte, 'Transnational Solidarity and the Mediation of Conflicts of Justice in Europe' (2012) 18

European Law Journal 694; S. Deakin, 'Legal Diversity and Regulatory Competition: Which Model for Europe?' (2006) 12 *European Law Journal* 440; F. Scharpf, 'The European Social Model: Coping with the Challenges of Diversity' (2002) 40 *Journal of Common Market Studies* 645; S. Deakin, 'Legal Diversity and Regulatory Competition: Which Model for Europe?' (2006) 12 *European Law Journal* 440.

Chapter 15: M. Dawson, 'The Legal and Political Accountability Structure of "Post-Crisis" EU Economic Governance' (2015) 53 *Journal of Common Market Studies* 976; D. Kelemen and T. Teo, 'Law, Focal Points, and Fiscal Discipline in the United States and the European Union' (2014) 108 *American Political Science Review* 355; J. Binder, 'The Banking Union and National Authorities 2 Years Down the Line: Some Observations from Germany' (2017) 18 *European Business Organisation Law Review* 401.

Chapter 16: D. Regan 'An Outsider's View of "Dassonville" and "Cassis de Dijon": On Interpretation and Policy' in M. Poiares Maduro and L. Azoulai (eds.), *The Past and Future of EU Law* (Oxford, Hart, 2010).

Chapter 17: H. Schepel, 'Constitutionalising the Market, Marketising the Constitution, and to Tell the Difference: On the Horizontal Application of the Free Movement Provisions in EU Law' (2012) 18 *European Law Journal* 177; T. Hervey, 'Buy Baby: The European Union and the Regulation of Human Reproduction' (1998) 18 *Oxford Journal of Legal Studies* 207.

Chapter 18: C. O'Brien, 'Social Blind Spots and Monocular Policy Making: The ECJ's Migrant Worker Model' (2009) 46 *Common Market Law Review* 1107; N. Nic Shuibhne, *The Coherence of EU Free Movement Law* (Oxford University Press, 2013).

Chapter 19: G. Majone, *Evidence, Argument and Persuasion in the Policy Process* (New Haven, CT, Yale University Press, 1989).

Chapter 20: M. de la Mano, 'For the Customer's Sake: The Competitive Effects of Efficiencies in European Merger Control', Enterprise Papers No. 11 (Brussels, Enterprise Directorate-General, 2002); M. S. Jacobs, 'An Essay on the Normative Foundations of Antitrust Economics' (1995–1996) 74 *North Carolina Law Review* 219; W. E. Kovacic, 'The Intellectual DNA of Modern Competition Law for Dominant Firm Conduct: The Chicago/Harvard Double Helix' (2007) 1(1) *Columbia Business Law Review* 1; E. M. Fox and L. A. Sullivan, 'Antitrust – Retrospective and Prospective: Where are We Coming From? Where are We Going?' (1987) 62 *New York University Law Review* 936; W. Möschel, 'Competition Policy from an Ordo Point of View' in A. Peacock and H. Willgerodt (eds.), *German Neo-Liberals and the Social Market Economy* (London, Macmillan, 1989); R. Wesseling, *The Modernisation of EC Antitrust Law* (Oxford-Portland, Hart, 2000); A. Wigger and H. Buch-Hansen, 'Explaining (Missing) Regulatory Paradigm Shifts: EU Competition Regulation in Times of Economic Crisis' (2013) *New Political Economy* 1; C. Harding and J. Joshua, *Regulating Cartels in Europe: A Study of Legal Control of Corporate Delinquency*, 2nd edn (Oxford University Press, 2010); L. Laudati, 'The European Commission as Regulator: The Uncertain Pursuit of the Competitive Market' in G. Majone (ed.), *Regulating Europe* (London, Routledge, 1996); Y. Svetiev, 'Networked Competition Governance in the EU: Delegation, Decentralization or Experimentalist Governance?' in C. F. Sabel and J. Zeitlin (eds.), *Experimentalist Governance in the European Union: Towards a New Architecture* (Oxford University Press, 2010).

Chapter 21: M. Marquis, 'O2 (Germany) v. Commission and the Exotic Mysteries of Article 81 (1) EC' (2007) *European Law Review* 27; J. Temple Lang, 'Some Aspects of Abuse of a Dominant

Position in EC Antitrust Law' (1979) 3 *Fordham International Law Forum* 1; D. J. Gerber, 'Law and the Abuse of Economic Power in Europe' (1987) 62 *Tulane Law Review* 57; D. A. Crane, 'Antitrust Antifederalism' (2008) 96(1) *California Law Review* 1.

Chapter 22: M. Blauberger, 'Of Good and Bad Subsidies: European State Aid Control through Soft Law and Hard Law' (2009) 32(4) *West European Politics* 719; A. Heimler and F. Jenny, 'The Limitations of European Union Control of State Aid' (2012) 28(2) *Oxford Review of Economic Policy* 347.

Abbreviations

AFSJ	Area of Freedom, Security and Justice
BIT	Bilateral Investment Treatment
CETA	EU–Canada Comprehensive Economic and Trade Agreement
CFSP	Common Foreign and Security Policy
COREPR	Committee of Permanent Representatives
CSR	Country-Specific Recommendation
DCFTA	Deep and Comprehensive Free Trade Area
DG	Directorate General
EAN	European Administrative Network
ECB	European Central Bank
ECHR	European Convention on Human Rights
ECI	European Citizens' Initiative
ECJ	European Court of Justice
ECN	European Competition Network
ECSC	European Coal and Steel Community
ECtHR	European Court of Human Rights
EEA	European Economic Area
EEC	European Economic Community
EFSF	European Financial Stability Facility
EFTA	European Free Trade Association
EMS	European Monetary System
EMU	European Monetary Union
ERM	Exchange Rate Mechanism
ERT	European Round Table
ESCB	European System of Central Banks
ESM	European Stability Mechanism
EU	European Union
EUCFR	European Union Charter of Fundamental Rights
EURATOM	European Atomic Energy Community
GATT	General Agreement on Tariffs and Trade
GATS	General Agreement in Trade in Services

GBER	General Block Exemption Regulation
GMO	Genetically Modified Organism
IGC	Intergovernmental Conference
IMF	International Monetary Fund
MEP	Member of the European Parliament
MEQR	Measure Equivalent to a Quantitative Restriction
MOU	Memorandum of Understanding
MTBO	Medium-Term Budgetary Objective
NCA	National Competition Authority
NCB	National Central Bank
NGO	Non-Governmental Organisation
OHIM	Office for Harmonization in the Internal Market
OMT	Outright Monetary Transactions
PSPP	Public Sector Assets Purchasing Programme
QMV	Qualified Majority Voting
SCF	Scientific Committee for Food
SEA	Single European Act
StCF	Standing Committee on Food Stuffs
TEU	Treaty on European Union
TFEU	Treaty on the Functioning of the European Union
TSCG	Treaty on Stability, Coordination and Governance in the Economic and Monetary Union
UNCRPD	UN Convention on the Rights of Persons with Disabilities
UNHCR	United Nations High Commission for Refugees
UPC	Agreement on a Unified Patent Court
WTO	World Trade Organisation

Table of Cases

Court of Justice of the European Union: numerical order

European Court of Justice: opinions

European Ombudsman

European Court of Human Rights

EFTA Court of Justice

World Trade Organization

National Courts

Austria

Table of Treaties, Instruments and Legislation

Treaties and Analogous Instruments

Declarations Annexed to the Lisbon Treaty Final Act

Declarations in Connection with the Lisbon Treaty

Protocols Annexed to the EC Treaty

Protocols Annexed to the Lisbon Treaty

Protocols Annexed to the TEU

Protocols Annexed to the TEU, EC, ECSC and Euratom Treaties

Protocols Annexed to the TEU and EC Treaty

EU Legislation and Policy Documents

COUNCIL RESOLUTIONS

INTER-INSTITUTIONAL AGREEMENTS

Brexit

TREATY ON THE FUNCTIONING OF THE EUROPEAN UNION

Lisbon Treaty numbers and their Amsterdam and Pre-Amsterdam equivalents (Amsterdam and Pre-Amsterdam is EC Treaty unless specified otherwise)

Lisbon	Amsterdam	Pre-Amsterdam	Lisbon	Amsterdam	Pre-Amsterdam
1			48	42	51
2			49	43	52
3			50	44	54
4			51	45	55
5			52	46	56
6			53	47	57
7	3 TEU	C TEU	54	48	58
8	3(2)	3(2)	55	294	221
9			56	49	59
10			57	50	60
11	6	3c	58	51	61
12	153(2)	129a	59	52	63
13			60	53	64
14	16	7d	61	54	65
15	255	191a	62	55	66
16	286	213b	63	56	73b
17			64	57	73c
18	12	6	65	58	73d
19	13	6a	66	59	73f
20	17	8	67	61	73i
21	18	8a		29 TEU	K.1 TEU
22	19	8b	68		
23	20	8c	69		
24	21	8d	70		
25	22	8e	71	36 TEU	K.8 TEU
26	14	7a	72	64(1)	73l(1)
27	15	7c		33 TEU	K.4 TEU
28	23	9	73		
29	24	10	74		
30	25	12	75	60	73g
31	26	28	76		
32	27	29	77	62	73j
33	135	116	78	63(1, 2), 64(2)	73k(1, 2), 73l(2)
34	28	30	79	63(3, 4)	73k(3, 4)
35	29	34	80		
36	30	36	81	65	73m
37	31	37	82	31 TEU	K.3 TEU
38	32	38	83	31 TEU	K.3 TEU
39	33	39	84		
40	34	40	85	31 TEU	K.3 TEU
41	35	41	86		
42	36	42	87	30 TEU	K.2 TEU
43	37	43	88	30 TEU	K.2 TEU
44	38	46	89	32 TFEU	K.4 TEU
45	39	48	90	70	74
46	40	49	91	71	75
47	41	50	92	72	76

Lisbon	Amsterdam	Pre-Amsterdam	Lisbon	Amsterdam	Pre-Amsterdam
93	73	77	145	125	109n
94	74	78	146	126	109o
95	75	79	147	127	109p
96	76	80	148	128	109q
97	77	81	149	129	109r
98	78	82	150	130	109s
99	79	83	151	136	117
100	80	84	152		
101	81	85	153	137	118
102	82	86	154	138	118a
103	83	87	155	139	118b
104	84	88	156	140	118c
105	85	89	157	141	119
106	86	90	158	142	119a
107	87	92	159	143	120
108	88	93	160	144	121
109	89	94	161	145	122
110	90	95	162	146	123
111	91	96	163	147	124
112	92	98	164	148	125
113	93	99	165	149	126
114	95	100a	166	150	127
115	96	101	167	151	128
116	96	101	168	152	129
117	97	102	169	153(1, 3, 4, 5)	129a
118			170	154	129b
119	4	3a	171	155	129c
120	98	102a	172	156	129d
121	99	103	173	157	130
122	100	103a	174	158	130a
123	101	104	175	159	130b
124	102	104a	176	160	130c
125	103	104b	177	161	130d
126	104	104c	178	162	130e
127	105	105	179	163	130f
128	106	105a	180	164	130g
129	107	106	181	165	130h
130	108	107	182	166	130i
131	109	108	183	167	130j
132	110	108a	184	168	130k
133			185	169	130l
134	114	109c	186	170	130m
135	115	109d	187	171	130n
136			188	172	130o
137			189		
138	111(4)	109(4)	190	173	130p
139			191	174	130r
140	121(1), 122(2), 123(5)	109j, 109k, 109l	192	175	130s
141	123(3), 117(2)	109l(3), 109f(2)	193	176	130t
142	124(1)	109m(1)	194		
143	119	109h	195		
144	120	109i	196		

Lisbon	Amsterdam	Pre–Amsterdam	Lisbon	Amsterdam	Pre–Amsterdam
197			249	218(2)	162(2)
198	182	131	250	219	163
199	183	132			
200	184	133	251	221(2), (3)	165
201	185	134	252	222	166
202	186	135	253	223	167
203	187	136	254	224	168
204	188	136a	255		
205			256	225	168a
206	131	110	257	225a	168a
207	133	113	258	226	169
208	177/178	130u/130v	259	227	170
209	179	130w	260	228	171
210	180	130x	261	229	172
211	181	130y	262	229a	172
212	181a	130y	263	230	173
213			264	231	174
214			265	232	175
215			266	233	176
216			267	234	177
217	310	238	268	235	178
218			269		
219	111(1, 3, 5)	109(1, 3, 5)	270	236	179
220	302, 303, 304	229, 230, 231	271	237	180
221			272	238	181
222			273	239	182
223	190(4, 5)	138(3)	274	240	183
224	191(2)	138(3)	275		
225	192(2)	138b	276		
226	193	138c	277	241	184
227	194	138d	278	242	185
228	195	138e	279	243	186
229	196	139	280	244	187
230	197(2)–(4)	140	281	245	188
231	198	141	282	8	4a
232	199	142	283	112	109a
233	200	143	284	113	109b
234	201	144	285	246	188a
235			286	247	188b
236			287	248	188c
237	204	147	288	249	189
238	205(1, 3)	148(1, 3)	289		
239	206	150	290	202	145
240	207	151	291	202	145
241	208	152	292		
242	209	153	293	250	189a
243	210	154	294	251	189b
244			295		
245	213	157	296	253	190
246	215	159	297	254	191
247	216	160	298		
248	217(2)	161	299	256	192

Lisbon	Amsterdam	Pre-Amsterdam	Lisbon	Amsterdam	Pre-Amsterdam
300	257/258/263	193/194/198a	329		
301	258(1), (2), (4)	194(1), (2), (4)	330		
302	259	195	331		
303	260	196	332		
304	262	198	333		
305	263(2), (3), (4)	198a(2), (3), (4)	334		
306	264	198b	335	282	211
307	265	198c	336	283	212
308	266	198d	337	284	213
309	267	198e	338	285	213a
310	268/270	199/201a	339	287	214
311	269	200	340	288	215
312			341	289	216
313	272(1)	203	342	290	217
			343	291	218
314	272(2–10)	203	344	292	219
315	273	204	345	295	222
316	271	202	346	296	223
317	274	205	347	297	224
318	275	205a	348	298	225
319	276	206	349	299(2)–(4)	227
320	277	207	350	306	233
321	278	208	351	307	234
322	279	209	352	308	235
323			353		
324			354	309	236
325	280	210	355	299(2)–(6)	227
326			356	312	240
327			357	313	247
328			358		

Informative EU Related Websites and Blogs

General EU Law

European Law Blog
  http://europeanlawblog.eu/
EU Law Analysis
  http://eulawanalysis.blogspot.com/
EJIL:Talk!
  http://eulawanalysis.blogspot.com/
European Parliamentary Research Service Blog
  https://epthinktank.eu/
Eutopia Law
  https://eutopialaw.com/
KSLR EU Law Blog
  https://blogs.kcl.ac.uk/
  kslreuropeanlawblog/#.XDnYllz7RPY
Despite our Differences
  https://despiteourdifferencesblog
.wordpress.com/
European Law Monitor
  https://www.europeanlawmonitor.org/

EU Politics and Policy

EUROPP by LSE
  http://blogs.lse.ac.uk/europpblog/
The UK in a Changing Europe
  http://ukandeu.ac.uk/
Dahrendorf Forum
  http://www.dahrendorf-forum.eu/
  dahrendorf-blog/
Journal of Common Market Studies
  https://jcms.ideasoneurope.eu/
Jon Worth

  https://jonworth.eu/
Ideas on Europe
  https://ideasoneurope.eu/
Centre for European Reform
  https://www.cer.eu/
Centre for European Policy Studies
  https://www.ceps.eu/
Bruegel
  http://bruegel.org/blog/

Brexit

University of Bristol Law School
  https://legalresearch.blogs.bris.ac.uk/?s=
  brexit
Brexit Border Blog
  http://brexitborder.com/
Chris Grey Brexit Blog
  http://chrisgreybrexitblog.blogspot.com/
Pete North
  http://peterjnorth.blogspot.com/
Brexit Central
  https://brexitcentral.com/
European Centre for International Political
  Economy
  http://ecipe.org/blog/
Open Europe
  https://openeurope.org.uk/today/blog/
Bruges Group
  https://www.brugesgroup.com/blog/
  blogger

Specialised Topics

Migration

EU Immigration and Asylum Law and Policy
  http://eumigrationlawblog.eu/
MPC Blog
  https://blogs.eui.eu/
migrationpolicycentre/
Rights in Exile
  http://rightsinexile.tumblr.com/
The Migrationist
  https://themigrationist.net/

Trade

Regulating for Globalisation
  http://regulatingforglobalization.com/
2017/11/26/welcome-to-regulating-for-
globalization-blog/
EFILA
  https://efilablog.org/

Competition

Chilling Competition
  https://chillingcompetition.com/
How to Crack a Nut
  http://www.howtocrackanut.com/
Kluwer Competition Law Blog
  http://competitionlawblog.kluwer
competitionlaw.com/

EU Law Enforcement

EU Law Enforcement
  http://eulawenforcement.com/

EU Constitutional Law

Verfassungsblog
  https://verfassungsblog.de/

Time Line

19 September 1946	Speech by Winston Churchill at University of Zurich calling for a 'United States of Europe'.
04 April 1949	Treaty establishing the North Atlantic Treaty Organisation (NATO).
05 May 1949	Treaty of London establishing the Council of Europe.
09 May 1950	Schuman Declaration.
24 October 1950	Pleven Plan proposing a European Defence Community.
04 November 1950	European Convention for the Protection of Human Rights and Fundamental Freedoms (ECHR).
18 April 1951	Treaty of Paris establishing the European Coal and Steel Community (Belgium, France, Germany, Italy, Luxembourg, Netherlands).
27 May 1952	Treaty establishing a European Defence Community (Belgium, France, Germany, Italy, Luxembourg, Netherlands).
30 August 1954	French Assembly vote down European Defence Community.
20 May 1955	BENELUX Memorandum proposing customs union presented to ECSC Heads of Government (Beyen Plan).
1–3 June 1955	Messina Conference discussing steps for further European integration.
21 April 1956	Presentation of Spaak Report to ECSC Heads of Government.
25 March 1957	Signing of Treaty of Rome establishing the European Economic Community (EEC) and European Atomic Energy Community (Euratom) (Belgium, France, Germany, Italy, Luxembourg, Netherlands).
04 January 1960	Treaty of Stockholm establishing European Free Trade Association (EFTA) (Austria, Denmark, Norway, Portugal, Sweden, Switzerland and United Kingdom).
14 January 1963	British application for EEC membership vetoed by French Government and negotiations with Denmark, Ireland, Norway and United Kingdom end.
05 February 1963	*Van Gend en Loos* judgment of Court of Justice.
15 July 1963	*Plaumann* judgment of Court of Justice.
15 July 1964	*Costa* v. *ENEL* judgment of Court of Justice.

08 April 1965	Merger Treaty creating common institutions for three Communities.
30 June 1965	'Empty chair crisis'. Refusal of French Government to take its seat in the Council.
29 January 1966	Luxembourg Accords ending 'empty chair crisis' and agreeing not to vote on any measure where any Member State raises 'very important interests'.
13 July 1966	*Consten and Grundig* judgment of the Court of Justice.
27 November 1967	Second British application to join the European Economic Community vetoed by the French Government.
31 December 1969	End of the Transitional Period.
21 April 1970	Own Resources Decision establishing independent Community Budget.
17 December 1970	*Internationale Handelsgesellschaft* judgment of the Court of Justice. 19–21 October 1972
19–21 October 1972	Paris Summit establishing social and environment policy as objectives of European integration and creating the 'snake in the tunnel', the first system of European monetary cooperation.
01 January 1973	Denmark, Ireland and United Kingdom accede to the EEC. Norway refuses to do so after referendum.
21 February 1973	*Continental Can* judgment of the Court of Justice.
29 May 1974	*Internationale Handelsgesellschaft* judgment of German Constitutional Court.
04 December 1974	*Van Duyn* judgment of the Court of Justice.
10–11 March 1975	First European Council held in Dublin.
08 April 1976	*Defrenne* judgment of Court of Justice.
06 December 1978	Brussels European Council establishing European Monetary System and Exchange Rate Mechanism.
20 February 1979	*Cassis de Dijon* judgment of the Court of Justice.
7–10 June 1979	First direct elections to European Parliament.
01 January 1981	Greece joins the European Community.
19 June 1983	Stuttgart European Council Solemn Declaration on European Union.
14 February 1984	European Parliament Draft Treaty on European Union.
01 February 1985	Greenland leaves the European Economic Community.
14 June 1985	Commission White Paper on Completing the Internal Market.
14 June 1985	Schengen Convention for the gradual abolition of checks at common borders (Belgium, France, Germany, Luxembourg, Netherlands).
8–29 June 1985	Milan European Council opening Intergovernmental Conference (IGC) which leads to Single European Act.
01 January 1986	Portugal and Spain accede to the European Economic Community.
17 and 18 February 1986	Single European Act signed committing the European Economic Community to complete the internal market by 31 December 1992.
01 July 1987	Single European Act enters into effect. The European Economic Community henceforth known as the European Community.
22 October 1987	*Foto-Frost* judgment of the Court of Justice.

27–28 June 1988	Hannover European Council asks the President of the Commission, Jacques Delors, to chair a committee comprising the national central bankers to examine practical steps to realise economic and monetary union.
20 September 1988	Speech by British Prime Minister at the College of Europe, Bruges, criticising the direction and pace of European integration.
24 October 1988	Council establishes Court of First Instance (now the General Court).
09 November 1989	Fall of the Berlin Wall.
8–9 December 1989	Strasbourg European Council agree to convene an IGC to amend the EC Treaty to enable economic and monetary union.
19 June 1990	Convention implementing the Schengen Agreement.
25–26 June 1990	Dublin European Council agree to convene an IGC on political union.
18 June 1991	*ERT* judgment of the Court of Justice.
19 November 1991	*Francovich* judgment of the Court of Justice.
07 February 1992	Treaty on European Union (TEU) signed at Maastricht.
02 May 1992	Treaty of Oporto establishing the European Economic Area between the European Community and the EFTA States.
02 June 1992	Danish referendum rejects TEU by 50 to 49.7 per cent.
20 September 1992	French referendum approves TEU by 51 to 49 per cent.
11 December 1992	Edinburgh European Council set out principles which allow second Danish referendum to be held on TEU (which approves the TEU in 1993, with 56.8 per cent of votes in favour).
22 June 1993	Copenhagen European Council sets criteria for membership for States from Central and Eastern Europe ('Copenhagen criteria').
15 October 1993	*Brunner* judgment of the German Constitutional Court on the constitutionality of the TEU.
01 November 1993	TEU enters into force. European Union comes into being.
24 November 1993	*Keck* judgment of the Court of Justice.
01 January 1995	Austria, Finland and Sweden accede to the European Union. Norway refuses to do so after a referendum.
15 December 1995	*Bosman* judgment of the Court of Justice.
02 October 1997	Treaty of Amsterdam signed establishing, inter alia, the Area of Freedom, Security and Justice.
12 May 1998	*Martinez Sala* judgment of the Court of Justice.
01 January 1999	Eleven Member States (all Member States other than Denmark, Greece, Sweden and United Kingdom) enter into the third stage of EMU, the single currency arrangements.
15 March 1999	Resignation of Santer Commission following allegations of maladministration and corruption.
01 May 1999	Treaty of Amsterdam enters into force.
12 May 2000	Speech by German Foreign Minister, Joschka Fischer, at Humboldt University, Berlin, in which he calls for a need to determine the final point ('finality') of European integration.
02 October 2000	Charter of Fundamental Rights of the European Union (EUCFR) proclaimed by European Convention drafting it.

26 February 2001	Treaty of Nice signed.
07 June 2001	Irish referendum rejects Treaty of Nice by 53.87 per cent of the votes.
25 July 2001	Adoption of Commission White Paper on European Governance.
20 September 2001	*Courage* v. *Crehan* judgment of the Court of Justice.
15 December 2001	Laeken Declaration of the European Council on the Future of the European Union establishes the Future of Europe Convention to propose treaty amendments allowing for institutional reform and constitutionalisation of the Treaties.
01 January 2002	Euro banknotes are circulated for the first time.
21 June 2002	Seville Declaration offers Ireland certain guarantees, on which basis a second referendum is held ratifying the Treaty of Nice in 2002 (with 62.9 per cent in favour).
01 February 2003	Treaty of Nice comes into force.
18 July 2003	Future of Europe Convention proposes a Draft Treaty Establishing a Constitution for Europe.
01 May 2004	Czech Republic, Cyprus, Estonia, Hungary, Latvia, Lithuania, Malta, Poland, Slovenia and Slovakia accede to the European Union.
29 October 2004	Following on from the Future of Europe Convention, the Member States sign the Constitutional Treaty.
29 May and 1 June 27 June 2005	Constitutional Treaty rejected in French and Dutch referendums by 54.68 per cent and 61.54 per cent of votes, respectively.
22 November 2005	*Mangold* judgment of the Court of Justice.
01 January 2007	Bulgaria and Romania accede to the European Union.
13 December 2007	Signing of Lisbon Treaty.
12 June 2008	Irish referendum rejects Lisbon Treaty by 53.4 per cent.
03 September 2008	*Kadi I* judgment of the Court of Justice.
19 June 2009	Declaration adopted by the European Council on the 'concerns of the Irish people' on which basis a second referendum ratified the Lisbon Treaty by 67.1 per cent.
30 June 2009	*Lisbon Treaty* judgment of the German Constitutional Court.
21 October 2009	Greek Government announces that its budget deficit is not 3.5 per cent of GDP as initially estimated but 12.5 per cent.
01 December 2009	Entry into force of the Lisbon Treaty.
02 May 2010	IMF and euro area governments agree €110 billion loan to Greece.
09 May 2010	European Financial Stability Facility (EFSF) established to provide €440 billion of conditional loans to euro area States experiencing public financing difficulties.
14 May 2010	Securities Market Programme (SMP) established by European Central Bank to purchase securities of euro area States having difficulties raising capital.
28 November 2010	€85 billion conditional loan facility provided to Ireland.
08 March 2011	*Zambrano* judgment of the Court of Justice.
04 May 2011	€78 billion conditional loan facility provided to Portugal.
31 January 2012	*Slovak Pensions* judgment of the Czech Constitutional Court.

02 February 2012	European Stability Mechanism Treaty (ESM) signed between euro area States, subsuming EFSF and offering up to €500 billion conditional loans to euro area States experiencing public financing difficulties.
02 March 2012	Treaty on Stability, Coordination and Governance in the Economic and Monetary Union (TSCG) signed by all Member States other than Czech Republic and United Kingdom.
13 May 2012	Second conditional loan facility of €130 billion provided to Greece.
09 June 2012	€100 billion conditional loan facility offered to Spanish banks.
06 September 2012	European Central Bank replaces SMP with Outright Monetary Transaction (OMT) Programme committing itself to potentially unlimited purchase of euro area government securities.
12 September 2012	*European Stability Mechanism (Temporary Injunctions)* judgment of the German Constitutional Court.
08 October 2012	ESM Treaty enters into effect.
27 November 2012	*Pringle* judgment of the Court of Justice.
01 January 2013	TSCG enters into effect.
23 January 2013	British Prime Minister, David Cameron, commits the Conservative Party, if re-elected, to renegotiate the United Kingdom's relationship with the European Union and to submit it to a referendum by 31 December 2017.
05 April 2013	*Fransson* judgment of the Court of Justice.
13 May 2013	€10 billion conditional loan facility provided to Cyprus.
01 July 2013	Croatia accedes to the European Union.
18 July 2013	*Kadi II* judgment of the Court of Justice.
08 December 2013	Ireland successfully exits its EFSF loan arrangement.
31 December 2013	Spain successfully exits the ESM loan arrangement for its banks.
14 January 2014	German Constitutional Court questions legality of Outright Monetary Transactions Program of the European Central Bank.
21 January 2014	Accession negotiations opened with Serbia.
18 May 2014	Portugal exits its ESM Programme.
27 June 2014	Albania granted candidate status for membership of the European Union.
15 July 2014	Jean-Claude Juncker appointed to be President of the European Commission on the basis of the Spitzenkandidat system.
4 November 2014	Single Supervisory Mechanism comes into effect.
11 November 2014	*Dano* judgment of the Court of Justice.
18 December 2014	Opinion of the Court of Justice on Union accession to the European Convention on Human Rights.
22 January 2015	ECB announce expansion of asset purchase programme.
12 March 2015	Iceland withdraws application for EU membership.
16 June 2015	*Gauweiler* judgment of the Court of Justice.
17 June 2015	Hungary announces construction of wall between it and Serbia to prevent non-EU nationals entering its territory.

25 August 2015	Germany announces suspension of Dublin Regulation so that it will accept asylum seekers who have transited through other Union States.
22 September 2015	Decision 2015/1601 relocating 120,000 asylum seekers from Italy and Greece to other EU States.
16 October 2015	Hungary closes its border with Croatia to non-EU migration.
19 February 2016	European Council agrees new settlement for the United Kingdom in anticipation of UK referendum on EU membership.
18 March 2016	EU–Turkey agreement on return of non-EU nationals.
31 March 2016	Cyprus exits the ESM.
23 June 2016	United Kingdom votes by 51.9 per cent of votes to 48.1 per cent to leave the European Union.
24 January 2017	UK Supreme Court judgment in *R (Miller)* v. *Secretary of State for Exiting the European Union.*
16 March 2017	European Union (Notification of Withdrawal) Act given royal assent.
29 March 2017	United Kingdom submits Article 50 TEU notice to the European Council to leave the European Union.
6 September 2017	*Slovakia and Hungary* v. *Council* judgment of the Court of Justice.
8 December 2017	Joint Report of EU and UK negotiators on Progress of Article 50 TEU Negotiations.
20 December 2017	Commission proposes action against Poland under Article 7 TEU for failure to uphold the rule of law.
17 April 2018	*Egenberger* judgment of the Court of Justice.
26 June 2018	European Union (Withdrawal) Act given royal assent.
20 August 2018	Greece exits its ESM programme.
25 November 2018	Heads of EU Governments endorse Withdrawal Agreement with the United Kingdom and Political Declaration on the Future Relationship between the United Kingdom and the European Union.
11 December 2018	*Weiss* judgment of the Court of Justice.
13 December 2018	ECB announces end of Asset Purchase Programme.
15 January 2019	The UK House of Common votes against approving the Withdrawal Agreement and Political Declaration on the Future Relationship by 432 votes to 202 votes.
11 March 2019	Agreement on Instrument relating to the agreement on the withdrawal of the United Kingdom of Great Britain and Northern Ireland from the European Union and the European Atomic Energy Community.
12 March 2019	The UK House of Common votes against approving the Withdrawal Agreement and Political Declaration on the Future Relationship by 391 votes to 242 votes.
22 March 2019	European Council Decision allows for Brexit not to take place until 22 May 2019.
29 March 2019	The UK House of Common votes against approving the Withdrawal Agreement and Political Declaration on the Future Relationship by 344 votes to 286 votes.
10 April 2019	European Council Decision allows for Brexit not to take place until 31 October 2019.

1

European Integration and the Treaty on European Union

CONTENTS

1 INTRODUCTION

This chapter sets out the central features of the European integration process, which provide the historical and political context for EU law. It also introduces some of the central concepts, ideas and developments in European Union law.

Section 2 explores how EU law is centred around an interplay between two themes. The first is the government of many contemporary problems through law. The second is the development of the ideals of Europe and European union. This interplay lays the ground for many of its debates. The European ideal conceives of Europe as the central place of progress, learning and civilisation, placing faith in humanity and her capacity to improve. Its dark side is its arrogance and its dismissal of 'un-European' ways of life or thought as violating these virtues. The idea of European union sets up a political community in competition with the nation State but one, nevertheless, through which government policy is carried out.

Section 3 considers the establishment of the three Communities, the European Economic Community (EEC), the European Coal and Steel Community (ECSC) and the European Atomic Energy Community (EURATOM). It sets out the central institutions: the Commission, the Parliament, the Council and the Court of Justice. It also considers the central policies, most notably the common market. This section also compares two developments of the 1960s that set out the two dominant models of political authority in EU law: the Luxembourg Accords which set out an intergovernmental vision with political authority and democracy vested in the nation State and *Van Gend en Loos* which set out a supranational one in which these are vested in supranational institutions and the rights of European citizens. Finally, this section evaluates the Single European Act (SEA). This established the internal market, and transformed the legislative and political culture surrounding the European Communities by setting out both an ambitious legislative programme and providing for significant amounts of legislation to be adopted free from the national veto.

Section 4 looks at the establishment and early years of the European Union. It considers the three dominant strategies used to justify the authority of the Union, and how these were deployed in the various treaty reforms. These strategies involve increasing EU competencies to allow it to offer more benefits to its subjects, attempting to generate a sense of common identity, and democratic reform of its institutions. At Maastricht, the treaty which instituted the European Union, the central elements of each were, respectively, the establishment of economic and monetary union, European Union citizenship and increased powers for the European Parliament. The Treaty of Amsterdam, signed in 1997 to deal with unfinished business from Maastricht, established the area of freedom, security and justice. Its central features were the abolition of internal border controls between all States other than the United Kingdom and Ireland; the establishment of a supranational immigration and asylum policy; and police cooperation and judicial cooperation in criminal and civil matters. Amsterdam sought to orient Union identity more strongly around fundamental rights. In terms of democratic reform, it increased the powers of both the European Parliament and national parliaments.

These strategies were only partially successful. Devices were also introduced to offset tensions generated by the increased centralisation and supranationalisation of lawmaking. The subsidiarity principle provides that the Union should only act when Member States cannot realise its objectives unilaterally and, by reason of the nature or scale of the action, these are better realised through Union action. Differentiated integration was also introduced. In some instances, such as economic and monetary union, it took the form of special regimes for individual Member States. At Amsterdam, a more general form of differentiation was adopted, enhanced cooperation, which allowed a majority of States to enact EU laws where others were unwilling.

Section 5 considers the enlargement of the Union. Initially agreed between 6 States, the Union had grown to fifteen States by the mid-1990s. Almost all were prosperous and almost all came from Western Europe. The accessions from 2004 onwards brought the number of Member States to twenty-eight with most of the new States being from Central and East Europe and having a post-communist past. This has made the Union a genuinely pan-European organisation but it has made it much more heterogencous, posing new preferences and challenges, and raising the question of whether it is possible to have a 'one size fits all' EU law.

Section 6 analyses the period of institutional reform which led up to the Treaty of Lisbon. It looks, first, at the European Union Charter for Fundamental Rights and Freedoms (EUCFR). This pioneered the convention method for institutional reform, where instead of everything being decided by governments behind closed doors a body was established meeting in open session, taking evidence from civil society, to put forward proposals. The section then goes on to consider the limited institutional reforms agreed at the Treaty of Nice in 2004 and the failure of the Constitutional Treaty. It is then given over to discussion of the Treaty of Lisbon.

The Treaty settles the European Union around two treaties, the Treaty on European Union and the Treaty on the Functioning of the European Union (TFEU). The Treaty catalogues EU competencies, for the first time. In addition, whilst special arrangements are made for foreign and defence policy, all other policies are brought within a common supranational framework. The Treaty next orients the collective identity of European Union around a particular mission, respect for democratic values and democratic identities. In this regard, the Union must now respect the values set out in the EUCFR and is to be founded on representative democracy. It must also respect the fundamental democratic structures of Member States. Finally, the Treaty of Lisbon continues the process of democratic reform with yet further powers for both the European Parliament and significant power for national parliaments, who can now police the subsidiarity principle. As a counterweight, it accelerates the process of differentiated integration, with a number of special regimes provided for both the EUCFR and the area of freedom, security and justice.

Section 7, finally, considers how the financial crisis has affected the European Union and led to its re-evaluation. It first considers the mechanisms, notably the European Stability Mechanism Treaty, set up outside the formal structures of EU law to provide financial support to those States which were no longer able to sustain their public finances. It looks at the limited controls on these, and how these have moved the Union more directly into the world of fiscal and welfare policy, albeit in an asymmetric way where some States have considerably more influence than others. It then looks at the more general vision now set out by both EU legislation (the 'six-pack') and by the Treaty on Stability, Coordination and Governance in the Economic and Monetary Union (the fiscal compact). These put in place a series of extensive controls on fiscal and macroeconomic policy for the euro area States in particular. It ponders the nature of this vision in these, and the challenges posed for democratic politics by it. Finally, the crisis has led to a re-evaluation of the Union. Some see the crisis as a reason for stronger Union institutions with wider competencies whilst others consider the crisis exposes the difficulties of the European integration and throws the project into further doubt.

2 EUROPE AND THE EUROPEAN UNION

This book is about the European Union which is an organisation that uncomfortably straddles two different agendas. It was established, on the one hand, to deal with a series of problems and realise a set of goals that individual States feel unable to manage alone. On the other, it is to lay claim to and to further a European heritage. The opening words of the Preamble of the Treaty on European Union establishing the European Union state:

> RESOLVED to mark a new stage in the process of European integration undertaken with the establishment of the European Communities,
>
> DRAWING INSPIRATION from the cultural, religious and humanist inheritance of Europe, from which have developed the universal values of the inviolable and inalienable rights of the human person, freedom, democracy, equality and the rule of law . . .

EU law involves a constant interplay between these two agendas, with elements of both permeating all the chapters of this book. If other chapters of this book focus on particular problems, which have been addressed by the European Union, it pays to reflect at the beginning of this book on the central elements of this European inheritance, so we know the sort of venture upon which the European Union is embarked.

If discussion of the Ancient Greeks and Charlemagne seems removed from that on the single currency, Brexit or the migration crisis, it is worth considering whether we discuss these topics differently because we think of them as European ones. Is it a term, therefore, which comes with cultural baggage, reflects certain values or a view of power with certain people invariably at the centre of this and others at its periphery? Also, how do the European Union's own practices contribute to our views of what Europe is about? None of these questions have easy answers but that makes them no less significant in helping to appraise what we think of EU law.[1] And if that makes EU law a little more complex, it also makes it more interesting.

(i) The Idea of Europe

The term 'Europe' has been used for a variety of purposes. The first references to 'Europe' depict it as a woman and the sun. The most famous early reference to Europe is that found in Greek mythology. Europa was a Phoenician woman seduced by the Greek god, Zeus, to come from Lebanon to Crete.[2] Europa was also, however, a Phoenician word that referred to the setting sun.

---

[1] For a good introduction to this debate see A. Triandafyllidou and R. Gropas, *What Is Europe?* (London, Palgrave Macmillan, 2015).

[2] D. de Rougemont, *The Idea of Europe* (New York, Macmillan, 1965) 6–19.

From this, Europe was associated in Ancient Greece with the idea of 'the West'. Originally used to designate the lands to the west of Greece, usage shifted as the Ancient Greek territorial centre of gravity changed with incursions into modern Turkey and Iran. In his wars, Alexander the Great used it to denote non-Persians and it became associated with the lands in Greece and Asia Minor (today's Turkish Mediterranean coastline). Following this, the term was to lie largely dormant for many centuries. The Roman Empire and Christianity dominated in the organisation of political life, and neither had much use for the term.

Europe re-emerged as an important political idea from the eighth century AD onwards. It acquired then many of the associations that we currently make when we use the word 'European'. In part, it became an expression of a siege mentality. The advance of Islam from the South and the East led to Europe being associated with resistance to the religion. An army of Franks, which fought against the Moors, was referred to as a 'European army'.[3] At this time Europe also became associated with the idea of Western Christianity. The Frankish Empire stretched across much of West Europe under the rule of Charlemagne in the ninth century AD. He styled himself as the father of Europe and sought to impose a political system across the region, based on communication between a large number of political and administrative centres. Alongside this, common economic practices were developed: shared accounting standards, price controls and a currency. Finally, he also sought to build a common Christian culture, which fostered learning, Christian morality, the building of churches and the imposition of a single interpretation of Christianity.[4]

However, it was only from the twelfth century onwards that Europe was used to refer to a place whose inhabitants enjoyed a shared way of life. This way of life was based on Christian humanism, revolving around images of God with Christ portrayed as human.[5] Alongside particular religious beliefs, Europe also became associated with a particular form of political economy, namely that of rural trade.[6] Increasingly, the rural town became the centre of the local economy. Trade relations between towns expanded across Europe, so that from the fifteenth century onwards, trade flourished between the Italian ports in the south and Flanders in the North, in which the role of the merchant was pivotal. The final feature of this European region was the persecution of non-Christians, be they pagans or followers of other faiths, such as Judaism or Islam. Those whose conduct offended the central values of Christianity were also maltreated, such as heretics and homosexuals, as were those perceived as socially unproductive, in particular, lepers.

Developments in the sixteenth and seventeenth centuries were to shape the subsequent evolution of the European idea. The establishment of the modern nation State consolidated power in centralised, impersonal bureaucracies and led to certain core policies, such as tax, law and order and foreign policy being the exclusive competence of these bureaucracies.[7] This

---

[3] D. Lewis, *God's Crucible: Islam and the Making of Europe 570–1215* (Norton, New York, 2008).

[4] R. McKitterick, *Charlemagne: The Formation of a European Identity* (Cambridge University Press, 2008); O. Phelan, *The Formation of Christian Europe: The Carolingians, Baptism and the Imperium Christianum* (Oxford University Press, 2014).

[5] J. Le Goff, *The Birth of Europe* (Oxford, Blackwell, 2005) 76–80.

[6] On the earlier origins of this in the developments of crops of rye and oats which led to new divisions of labour within agriculture, to trade and to sustaining centres of population see M. Mitterauer, *Why Europe? The Mediaeval Origins of Its Special Path*, trans. G. Chapple (Chicago University Press, 2010) ch. 1.

[7] C. Tilly (ed.), *The Formation of Nation-States in Europe* (New Jersey, Princeton University Press, 1975); G. Poggi, *The Development of the Modern State: A Sociological Introduction* (California, Stanford University Press, 1978); M. Mann, 'The Autonomous Power of the State: Its Origins, Mechanisms and Results' (1984) 25 *European Journal of Sociology*

hegemony of the nation State over political life led to Europe increasingly being identified with coordinating peaceful relations between these States. Europe became about the pursuit of peace.[8] These associations with peaceful coexistence morphed easily into Europe being identified with what human beings had in common. Europe set out what was universal, and required States to act in the light of it. Europe became, therefore, about acting in the name of humanity, science or progress.[9]

A further twist has come from the political conflicts that took place within national societies across Europe in the nineteenth and twentieth centuries. These have left a particular shared legacy across Europe in which Europe is attributed, because of this experience, with a particular approach to these conflicts.[10]

J. Habermas and J. Derrida, 'February 15, or, What Binds Europeans Together: Plea for a Common Foreign Policy Beginning in Core Europe' in D. Levy, J. Torpey and M. Pensky (eds.), *Old Europe, New Europe, Core Europe: Transatlantic Relations after the Iraq War* (London, Verso, 2005) 5, 10–12

[T]he spread of the ideals of the French revolution throughout Europe explains, among other things, why politics in both of its forms – as organizing power and as a medium for the institutionalization of political liberty – has been welcomed in Europe. By contrast, the triumph of capitalism was bound up with sharp class conflicts, and this fact has hindered an equally positive appraisal of free markets. That differing evaluation of politics and markets may explain Europeans' trust in the civilizing power of the state, and their expectations for it to correct market failures.

The party system that emerged from the French revolution has often been copied. But only in Europe does this system also serve an ideological competition that subjects the socio-pathological results of capitalist modernization to an ongoing political evaluation. This fosters the sensitivities of citizens to the paradoxes of progress. The contest between conservative, liberal and socialist agendas comes down to the weighing of two aspects: Do the benefits of a chimerical progress outweigh the losses that come with the disintegration of protective, traditional forms of life? Or do the benefits that today's processes of 'creative destruction' for tomorrow outweigh the pain of modernity's losers?

In Europe, those affected by class distinctions, and their enduring consequences, understood these burdens as a fate that can be averted only through collective action. In the context of workers' movements and the Christian socialist traditions, an ethics of solidarity, the struggle for 'more social justice', with the goal of equal provision for all, asserted itself against the individualist ethos of market justice that accepts glaring social inequalities as part of the bargain.

185; H. Spruyt, *The Sovereign State and Its Competitors: An Analysis of Systems Change* (New Jersey, Princeton University Press, 1994).

[8] M. L'Abbé de Saint-Pierre, *A Project for Settling an Everlasting Peace in Europe*, 2nd edn (Santa Venera, Midsea Books, 2009); I. Kant, *Perpetual Peace* (New York, Cosimo, 2005); J. Rousseau, 'On the Writing of the Abbé of Saint-Pierre' in J. Rousseau, *The Plan for Perpetual Peace, On the Government of Poland, and Other Writings on History and Politics*, trans. C. Kelly and J. Bush (Dartmouth, Dartmouth College Press, 2005) 23–122. On the role of this association in current debate see C. Kølvraa, 'European Fantasies: On the EU's Political Myths and the Affective Potential of Utopian Imaginaries for European Identity' (2016) 54 *JCMS* 169.

[9] E. Husserl, 'The Vienna Lecture: Philosophy and the Crisis of European Humanity' in *Crisis of European Sciences and Transcendental Phenomenology*, trans. D. Carr (Chicago, Northwestern University, 1970). R. Gasché, *Europe, or The Infinite Task: A Study of a Philosophical Concept* (Stanford University Press, 2009).

[10] J.-W. Müller, *Constitutional Patriotism* (New Jersey, Princeton University Press, 2007) ch. 3.

Contemporary Europe has been shaped by the experience of the totalitarian regimes of the twentieth century and by the Holocaust – the persecution and annihilation of European Jews in which the National Socialist regime made the societies of the conquered countries complicit as well. Self-critical controversies about the past remind us of the moral basis of politics. A heightened sensitivity to injuries to personal and bodily integrity reflects itself, among other ways, in the fact both the Council of Europe and the EU made the ban on capital punishment a condition for membership.

Europe as an idea, according to Habermas and Derrida, conveys an ambivalent attitude towards both the market and towards progress, as well as concerns about social justice and human rights.[11] However, there are a number of challenges in associating Europe with noble ideals. Many authors have noted that such interpretations airbrush too easily Europe's history of intolerance, colonialism, slavery and racism.[12] These phenomena have contributed to European thought and ways of life, and are, thus, also part of what Europe is about. They formed, moreover, the context for development of much of Europe's economic progress and its liberal ideals. Europe's idea of itself, therefore, as the cradle for universal ideals, such as liberalism and democracy, occurred, therefore, at a time when Europe thought of itself as the world, and the rest of the world as empty space to be discovered and colonised. In this worldview, Europe did not merely sit at the centre of the universe but set out what was the universe.[13]

Today, this can permeate through into a belief that European values or views are universal views,[14] Europe's role is to civilise others, and an intolerance of things 'non-European'. Such views manifest themselves in the European integration process. Time and again, the process is emphasised as a form of particularly enlightened cooperation between nations. This leads to an assumption about the desirability of its policies, with opponents of integration often dismissed as nationalistic (and thus unreasonable and chauvinistic). It may be, however, that they simply disagree with the policy or the procedure, or that they believe in values or ways of life that they think should not be appropriated by the European idea.

(ii) The Idea of 'European Union'

The idea of European union has different associations from that of Europe. After all, many self-avowed Europeans oppose European union! Independent proposals for a 'united Europe' first emerged at the end of the seventeenth century. However, they firmly vested ultimate authority in the State, with pan-European structures acting as little more than a fetter upon the autonomy of States. In 1693, the English Quaker, William Penn, wrote *An Essay towards the Present and Future Peace of Europe*. Penn suggested that a European Parliament be established, consisting of representatives of the Member States. Its primary purposes would be to prevent wars breaking

---

[11] See also the famous 1935 lecture by E. Husserl, 'Philosophy and the Crisis of European Humanity' reprinted in E. Husserl, *The Crisis of European Sciences and Transcendental Phenomenology* (Chicago, North Western University Press, 1970) Appendix I.

[12] For alternate accounts attempting to do this see P. Pasture, *Imagining European Unity since 1000 AD* (Basingstoke, Palgrave, 2015); G. Bhambra and J. Narayan (eds.), *European Cosmopolitanism: Colonial Histories and Postcolonial Societies* (Abingdon, Routledge, 2017).

[13] E. Wolf, *Europe and the People Without History*, 2nd edn (Berkeley, University of California Press, 2010); D. Guénoun, *About Europe: Philosophical Hypotheses*, trans. C. Irizarry (Stanford University Press, 2013).

[14] R. Kanth (ed.), *The Challenge of Eurocentrism: Global Perspectives, Policy and Prospects* (Basingstoke, Palgrave, 2009).

out between States and to promote justice. A more far-reaching proposal was put forward by John Bellers in 1710. Bellers proposed a system based upon the Swiss model whereby Europe would be divided into 100 cantons, each of which would be required to contribute to a European army and send representatives to a European Senate.

The first proposal for a Europe with a sovereign central body came from the Frenchman, Saint-Simon, and was published in a pamphlet in 1814, entitled *Plan for the Reorganisation of the European Society*. Saint-Simon considered that all European States should be governed by national parliaments, but that a European Parliament should be created to decide on common interests. This Parliament would consist of a House of Commons peopled by representatives of local associations and a House of Lords consisting of peers appointed by a European monarch. Saint-Simon's views enjoyed considerable attention during the first part of the nineteenth century. Mazzini, the *éminence grise* of Italian nationalism, allied himself with Proudhon and Victor Hugo in declaring himself in favour of a United Europe. Yet, the nineteenth century represented the age of the nation State and the relationship between that structure and that of a united Europe was never fully explored.

The balance was altered by the First World War, which acted as a stimulus for those who saw European union as the only way to prevent war breaking out again between the nation States and to respond to increased competition from the United States, Argentina and Japan. Most prominent was the pan-European movement set up in the 1920s by the Czech, Count Coudenhove-Kalergi.[15] This movement not only enjoyed considerable support amongst many of Europe's intellectuals and some politicians, but was also genuinely transnational, having 'Economic Councils' both in Berlin and in Paris. During the 1920s, the idea of European unity received governmental support in the shape of the 1929 Briand Memorandum. This Memorandum, submitted by the French Foreign Minister to 26 other European States, considered the League of Nations to be too weak a body to regulate international relations, and proposed a European Federal Union, which would better police States, whilst not 'in any way affect[ing] the sovereign rights of the States which are members of such an association'. This proposal, despite acknowledging the authority of the nation States, was still regarded as too radical and received only a lukewarm response from the other States.

Understandings of what European union meant took, however, an exponential leap with the coming into being of the European Communities and its transformation into the European Union in the early 1990s. The term was now identified with a powerful political organisation. This has sharpened three debates, in particular.

First, European union was, increasingly, seen as something which competes with the nation State. In some instances, this was done by replicating the symbols and tools of nationhood at a pan-European level: the (re)discovery of European flags, anthems, Cities of Culture or common passports.[16] In others, notably European citizenship,[17] it was done by setting out a model of political community which is an alternative to the nation State rather than a mimic of it.[18]

---

[15] N. Coudenhove-Kalergi, *Pan-Europe* (New York, Knopf, 1926). An excellent discussion can be found in C. Pegg, *Evolution of the European Idea 1914–1932* (Chapel Hill, University of North Carolina Press, 1983).

[16] C. Shore, *Building Europe: The Cultural Politics of European Integration* (London–New York, Routledge, 2000).

[17] See Ch. 11.

[18] In some cases, EU policies adopt elements of both models, M. Sassatelli, *Becoming Europeans: Cultural Identity and Cultural Policies* (Basingstoke, Palgrave, 2009).

The second association ran in an opposite direction to the first. The European Union is also a vehicle through which national governments pursue their interests. As such, the narrative of Europe and the European Union are deployed to justify and redefine national government policy. Bickerton has argued that this has led to a subtle and problematic shift in national government understandings of what they are about. They have moved from being nation States to Member States of the European Union.

C. Bickerton, *European Integration: From Nation States to Member States* (Oxford University Press, 2012) 60, 68–9

[W]e can point to two critical features of member statehood that stand out in terms of how they contrast with dominant assumptions and practices of modern nation states. The first is that central to member statehood is a presumed *opposition* between state and society. The purpose of limiting national power in ways that appear external to the national polity is in order that domestic populations are distanced from policymaking and decision-making. National elites seek to insulate themselves from the force and compulsion of public opinion because of the risk that 'vile people' . . . will generate vile policies. The idea of membership thus belongs to this sought-for separation between state and society. The contrast with modern nation states is striking: here the goal was to achieve a unity in what was a fractious and divided social space. Problems of economic and ideological conflict have generally been sublimated through unifying categories such as the people and the nation, even if those categories have themselves been subject to long-standing disagreements about their precise meaning.

Whilst modern nation states have sought unity, member states assume division. The state-society relationship is thus reconfigured in a way very alien from traditional thinking about the state: a presumed relationship of representation is replaced by one of insulation and separation.

The second feature is the way constraints upon the exercise of national power are based not upon a political ideal or principle but rather on an institutional and bureaucratic understanding of such limits. The picture we thus have of the member state, where its central principle of legitimization resides in the actions of public officials, is one of an administrative machine rather than a political community.

European union, for Bickerton, has, thus a couple of undesirable consequences. It allows national governments to distance themselves more easily from their citizens by adopting a 'Them' and 'Us' approach, and it results in a more managerial form of politics in which civil servants and executives are more pre-eminent.[19] Others are less pessimistic. They observe that European union provides new opportunities for other actors to advance their interests, and these can be often quite emancipatory. EU rights may provide possibilities for domestically marginalised actors to challenge that marginalisation.[20] European union can provide incentives for social movements and interest groups from across Europe to come together to identify common challenges, and to mobilise for change at both a European and a national level.[21] Finally, the

---

[19] This has led him to see Brexit as a significant democratic opportunity. C. Bickerton and R. Tuck, 'A Brexit Proposal – Bickerton and Tuck', *The Current Moment*, 20 November 2017, https://thecurrentmoment.files.wordpress.com/2017/11/brexit-proposal-20-nov-final1.pdf.

[20] D. Kelemen, *Eurolegalism: The Transformation of Law and Regulation in the European Union* (Cambridge, MA, Harvard University Press, 2011).

[21] L. Parks, *Social Movement Campaigns on EU Policy: In the Corridors and in the Streets* (Basingstoke – New York, Palgrave Macmillan, 2015); D. della Porta and L. Parks, 'Social Movements, the European Crisis, and EU Political Opportunities' (2018) 16 *Comparative European Politics* 85.

actions of the European Union can themselves mobilise protest and contestation at a domestic level, leading to greater debate and accountability there.[22]

Thirdly, the European Union, has stimulated more intense and wider forms of interaction across Europe's borders. It has led not merely to increased travel, migration, investment and trade across Europe, but also to high levels of debate about Europe and what is taking place in other European States.[23] Furthermore, in a number of ways, European States and societies increasingly imitate each other. Similar laws are often adopted across Europe on matters which have little to do with the European Union.[24] The types of culture consumed by Europeans – be it free newspapers, stuff downloaded from the Internet, or films watched at the cinema – are increasingly similar.[25]

If this has led to talk of a European society,[26] some cynicism has been expressed about its qualities. Its central advocates include transnational elites: transnational companies who trade across Europe, mobile professionals who like the increased opportunities offered by Europe for work and play, and those heavily involved in making policy who see it as providing a venue for getting what they want.[27] A culturally dislocating side to it has also been observed. It has claimed that the processes of change and movement generated by it have made people less sure of who they are, destabilised familiar reference points, and created a generic sameness with high streets across Europe having a similar look which is, nevertheless identified with nowhere in particular.[28] These wider processes of European union are, thus, marked by high levels of economic, political and cultural polarisation.[29]

L. Hooghe and G. Marks, 'Cleavage Theory Meets Europe's Crises: Lipset, Rokkan, and the Transnational Cleavage' (2018) 25 _Journal of European Public Policy_ 109, 114–15

Transnationalism also has transparent distributional consequences, biasing the gains from trade to those who have mobile assets. Losers who feel they are slipping with no prospect of upward mobility resent the dilution of the rights and protection of citizenship by a global élite that views national states and their laws as constraints to be finessed or arbitraged. As Wolf wrote in the _Financial Times_: '[t]he share of immigrants in populations has jumped sharply. It is hard to argue that this has brought large economic, social and

---

[22] D. Imig and S. Tarrow (eds.), _Contentious Europeans: Protest and Politics in an Emerging Polity_ (Lanham, Rowman & Littlefield, 2001); S. Hutter _et al._ (eds.), _Politicising Europe: Integration and Mass Politics_ (Cambridge University Press, 2016).

[23] T. Risse, _A Community of Europeans? Transnational Identities and Public Spheres_ (Ithaca, Cornell University Press, 2010).

[24] M. Gelter and M. Siems, 'Citations to Foreign Courts – Illegitimate and Superfluous, or Unavoidable? Evidence from Europe' (2014) 62 _AJCL_ 35; D. Studlar _et al._, 'Tobacco Control in the EU-15: The Role of Member States and the European Union' (2011) 18 _JEPP_ 728; A. Piatti-Crocker, 'Veil Bans in Western Europe: Interpreting Policy Diffusion' (2015) 16 _Journal of International Women's Studies_ 15.

[25] D. Sassoon, _The Culture of the Europeans: From 1800 to the Present_ (London, Harper Collins, 2006).

[26] W. Oughton, _European Society_ (Oxford, Polity, 2008); K. Eder, 'The EU in Search of its People: The Birth of a Society Out of the Crisis of Europe' (2014) 17 _European Journal of Social Theory_ 219; H.-J. Trenz, _Narrating European Society: Toward a Sociology of European Integration_ (Lanham, Rowman & Littlefield, 2016).

[27] A. Favell, _Eurostars and Eurocities: Free Movement and Mobility in an Integrating Europe_ (Oxford, Blackwell, 2008); N. Fligstein, _Euroclash: The EU, European Identity, and the Future of Europe_ (Oxford University Press, 2008).

[28] C. Rumsford, 'The Strangeness of Europe' (2016) 14 _Comparative European Politics_ 504.

[29] N. Gidron and P. Hall, 'The Politics of Social Status: Economic and Cultural Roots of the Populist Right' (2017) 68 _British Journal of Sociology_ S57.

cultural benefits to the mass of the population. But it has unquestionably benefited those at the top, including business.' Resentment can be sharp among those who value national citizenship because they have few alternative sources of self-worth. Nationalism has long been the refuge of those who are insecure, who sense they are losing status, and who seek standing by identifying with the group. The promise of transnationalism has been gains for all, but the experience of the past two decades is that it hurts many. Hence, opposition to transnationalism is for many a populist reaction against élites who have little sympathy for national borders . . .

Kriesi *et al.* have explored how European integration and immigration have structured preferences and political conflict in Britain, France, Germany, Switzerland, the Netherlands and Austria by pitting the winners of globalization who favor transnational integration against losers who seek demarcation. '[T]wo of the most important groups on the winners' side, highly educated people and socio-cultural specialists, are far more supportive of opening borders than are those with lower levels of education and those who are unskilled workers'.[30] At its nationalist pole, this cleavage connects the defense of national culture to national sovereignty, opposition to immigration and trade skepticism. These are reinforcing issues for those who feel they have suffered transnationalism– the down and out, the culturally insecure, the unskilled, the deskilled, i.e., those who lack the education needed to compete in a mobile world.

3 THE EUROPEAN COMMUNITIES

(i) From the Treaty of Paris to the Treaty of Rome

The origins of the European Union lay in a crisis. In 1949, the Ruhr and the Saar, then under the administration of the International High Commission, were due to be handed back to the Federal Republic of Germany. French fears of emerging German industrial might were compounded by Germany's increasing share of European steel production. The French response was a plan drafted by the French civil servant, Jean Monnet, which was known as the Schuman Plan, after the French Finance Minister, Robert Schuman.[31]

Robert Schuman, Declaration of 9 May 1950[32]

Europe will not be made all at once or according to a single plan. It will be built through concrete achievements which first create a *de facto* solidarity. The coming together of the nations of Europe requires the elimination of the age-old opposition of France and Germany. Any action which must be taken in the first place must concern these two countries. With this aim in view, the French Government proposes that action be taken immediately on one limited but decisive point. It proposes that Franco-German production of coal and steel as a whole be placed under a common High Authority, within the framework of an organisation open to the participation of the other countries of Europe.

---

[30] H. Kriesi *et al.*, *Political Conflict in Western Europe* (Cambridge University Press, 2012) 73.

[31] W. Diebold, *The Schuman Plan: A Study in International Cooperation* (Oxford University Press, 1959).

[32] European Parliament, *Selection of Texts Concerning Institutional Matters of the Community for 1950–1982* (Luxembourg, Office for Official Publications of the European Communities, 1982) 47.

> The pooling of coal and steel production should immediately provide for the setting up of common foundations for economic development as a first step in the federation of Europe, and will change the destinies of those regions which have long been devoted to the manufacture of munitions of war, of which they have been the most constant victims.
>
> The solidarity in production thus established will make it plain that any war between France and Germany becomes not merely unthinkable, but materially impossible. The setting up of this powerful productive unit, open to all countries willing to take part and bound ultimately to provide all the member countries with the basic elements of industrial production on the same terms, will lay a true foundation for their economic unification.

This Plan formed the basis for the Treaty of Paris in 1951, which established the ECSC.[33] This Treaty entered into force on 23 July 1952 and ran for fifty years.[34] It set up a common market in coal and steel. This was supervised by the High Authority, a body independent from the Member States, which had considerable powers to determine the conditions of production and price for coal and steel.[35] The Treaty of Paris was signed by only six States: the BENELUX States (Netherlands, Belgium and Luxembourg), Italy, France and Germany. The United Kingdom was invited to the negotiations, but refused to participate as it opposed both the idea of the High Authority and the remit of its powers.[36]

The ECSC Treaty provided only limited reassurance for the BENELUX States. These were increasingly worried by the nationalist policies of the government in France, in particular, its attempt to upgrade bilateral relations with Germany. In 1955, the Belgian Foreign Minister, Henri-Paul Spaak, suggested that there should be integration in a limited number of sectors, notably transport and energy. This displeased the Netherlands as it threatened its competitiveness, particularly in the transport sector. The Dutch Government responded by reactivating the 1953 Beyen Plan, which proposed a common market that would lead to economic union. A meeting of Foreign Ministers was held in Messina, Italy, in 1955. The British were invited but did no more than send a Board of Trade Official. Despite considerable French scepticism, a Resolution was tabled, calling for an Intergovernmental Committee under the chairmanship of Spaak, to examine the establishment of a common market. As a carrot to the French, it was agreed that this should be done in tandem with examining the possibility of integration in the field of atomic energy. British objections to the supranational elements required for a common market entailed that they did not participate in the project.

The Spaak Report, published in 1956, laid the basis for the Treaty Establishing the European Economic Community (EEC Treaty). The Report made a pragmatic distinction. Matters affecting the

---

[33] On the negotiations, see P. Gerbet, 'The Origins: Early Attempts and the Emergence of the Six (1945–52)' in R. Pryce (ed.), *The Dynamics of European Union* (London, Croon Helm, 1987); R. Bullen, 'An Idea Enters Diplomacy: The Schuman Plan, May 1950' in R. Bullen (ed.), *Ideas into Politics: Aspects of European History 1880–1950* (London, Croon Helm, 1984).

[34] The ECSC expired on 23 July 2002. Decision of the representatives of the Member States meeting within the Council on the consequences of the expiry of the European Coal and Steel Community, OJ 2002, L 194/35.

[35] A good history is D. Spiernburg and R. Poidevin, *The History of the High Authority of the European Coal and Steel Community: Supranationality in Operation* (Weidenfeld & Nicholson, 1994). See also W. Kaiser, 'Transnational Practices Governing European Integration: Executive Autonomy and Neo-Corporatist Concertation in the Steel Sector' (2018) 27 *Contemporary European History* 239.

[36] E. Dell, *The Schuman Plan and the British Abdication of Leadership in Europe* (Oxford, Clarendon, 1995); C. Lord, '"With but not of": Britain and the Schuman Plan, a Reinterpretation' (1998) 4 *JEI History* 23.

functioning of the common market would require a supranational decision-making framework and supranational supervision of Member States' compliance with their obligations. More general matters of budgetary, monetary and social policy would remain with the Member States. Where these policies had a significant effect on the functioning of the common market, however, Member States should endeavour to coordinate these policies. An intergovernmental conference (IGC) was convened in Venice, with the Spaak Report as the basis for negotiations. The result was the signing of the Treaties of Rome in 1957 between Germany, France, Italy and the BENELUX States: one establishing the EEC, the other EURATOM. The treaties duly entered into force on 1 January 1958.[37]

(ii) The EEC Treaty

The dominant aim of the EEC Treaty was the establishment of a common market. This contained four central elements:

- The *customs union* required the abolition of all customs duties (taxes levied on imports or exports for crossing a national frontier) or charges having equivalent effect on the movement of goods between Member States. It also established a common external tariff on goods coming from outside the EEC so that these were charged the same tariff wherever they entered the EEC.
- The *economic freedoms* prohibited Member States from restricting the free movement of goods, workers, services and payments or the establishment of natural persons or companies in another Member State. These prohibitions were all subject to exceptions allowing a Member State to restrict free movement if it threatened a public good (i.e. public health) protected by the Treaty.
- *Harmonisation of laws* would protect public goods, such as public health, threatened by free movement. Goods or services complying with these laws were entitled to be marketed across the EEC.
- *A common commercial policy* was to establish uniform terms and conditions for when goods produced outside the EEC could enter the EEC market.

The EEC Treaty included a number of other policies. The more significant included a competition policy to ensure that cartels and monopolies did not obscure trade between Member States as well as policies to regulate national activities, such as State aids or public undertakings, which might significantly distort competition within the common market. Arguably, the most famous policy at the time, was the Common Agricultural Policy. Agriculture accounted for about 20 per cent of the European labour force and memories of the crisis suffered by the sector during the 1930s recession had led to considerable government intervention. The common agriculture policy made this intervention and the management of agricultural markets an EEC affair. The EEC Treaty also contained a limited social policy, whose central feature was the establishment of a principle of equal pay for work of equal value for men and women.[38] Development of this principle was to shape anti-discrimination in law across Europe, however, in the generations to come.

---

[37] The literature on the negotiations is voluminous. E. di Nolfo (ed.), *Power in Europe? Britain, France, Germany, Italy, and the Origins of the EEC, 1952–1957* (Berlin – New York, de Gruyter, 1992); E. Serra (ed.), *The Relaunching of Europe and the Treaties of Rome* (Baden Baden, Nomos, 1989); W. Loth, '60 Years Ago: The Foundation of EEC and EAEC as Crisis Management' (2017) 23 *JEI History* 9.

[38] C. Barnard, 'The Economic Objectives of Article 119' in T. Hervey and D. O'Keeffe (eds.), *Sex Equality Law in the European Union* (Chichester, John Wiley, 1996) 321, 322–4.

The other remarkable feature of the EEC Treaty was its institutional arrangements. It was built around four institutions:

- The *Commission*, a body of officials independent from the Member States, was responsible, *inter alia*, for proposing legislation and checking that the Member States and other EEC institutions complied with EEC law.
- The *Assembly*, later to develop into the European Parliament, was composed, initially, of national parliamentarians. It was to be consulted in most fields of legislative activity and was the body responsible for holding the Commission to account.
- The *Council* was where national governments were represented. It had the power of final decision over almost all areas of EEC activity. It voted by unanimity or, in a few areas, by a weighted form of voting, known as Qualified Majority Voting (QMV), which gave larger States more votes but less votes than a system based purely on population would allocate to them.
- The *Court of Justice* ruled on whether Member States or EEC Institutions had complied with EEC law. It could answer questions on points of EEC law referred to it by national courts where these were necessary to decide a dispute before the latter.

This settlement was notable primarily because it could not be seen simply as a bargain between national governments, which was controlled exclusively by these. All the Institutions, other than the Council, were autonomous from national governments, and even the Council allowed for the possibility that in those areas where there was QMV individual governments had lost their veto.

(iii) The Emergence of Two Visions of EU Law: The Intergovernmental and the Supranational

1958 marked not only the coming into force of the Treaties, but also Charles de Gaulle becoming President of France.[39] De Gaulle's vision of European integration was an intergovernmental one, which saw only the nation State as capable of sustaining democracy. On such a view, the supranational features of the EEC institutional settlement – be this expressed through judgments of the Court of Justice, majority voting by national governments or proposals by the Commission – was invariably a threat to democracy insofar as it both limited the autonomy of national institutions and had insufficient authority of its own to fall back upon. At a press conference on 15 May 1962, he declared:

> These ideas (supranationalism) might appeal to certain minds but I entirely fail to see how they could be put into practice, even with six signatures at the foot of a document. Can we imagine France, Germany, Italy, the Netherlands, Belgium, Luxembourg being prepared on matters of importance to them in the national or international sphere, to do something that appeared wrong to them, merely because others had ordered them to do so? Would the peoples of France, of Germany, of Italy, of the Netherlands, of Belgium, or of Luxembourg ever dream of submitting to laws passed by foreign parliamentarians if such laws run counter to their deepest convictions? Clearly not.[40]

---

[39] An excellent overview of this period is N. Ludlow, *The European Community and the Crises of the 1960s: Negotiating the Gaullist Challenge* (Abingdon, Routledge, 2006).

[40] This can be found at D. Weigall and P. Stirk, *The Origins and Development of the European Community* (Leicester University Press, 1992) 134.

As early as 1961, de Gaulle had attempted to put this into practice through the Fouchet Plan. This proposed a European Political Community whose remit would cover not only economic, but also political and social affairs. It would be based on intergovernmental cooperation, with each State retaining a veto. This failed to gain the support of the other Member States.[41]

Matters came to a head in 1965.[42] The Commission proposed a package deal linking increased powers for the Assembly, an independent budget for the EEC and financial regulations, which would allow the common agricultural policy to make progress. When negotiations broke down, the French walked out, refusing to take part in further EEC business.[43] The crisis was eventually defused in January 1966 in Luxembourg, but in a way that would cast a shadow over the development of the EEC for the next twenty years.

The Luxembourg Accords, as they came to be known, were an 'agreement to disagree'. If a Member State raised 'very important interests' before a vote in the Council was taken, it was agreed that the matter would not be put to a vote. In essence, it gave every Member State a veto in all fields of decision-making. Whilst this veto was developed at the behest of France, once in place, it was invoked equally freely by all the Member States,[44] even where the interest in question was insignificant.[45] This veto stymied lawmaking for the next twenty years.

Some significant institutional developments, nevertheless, took place. At the signing of the Treaty of Rome, a single Court and a single Assembly were established for the three Communities.[46] In 1965, the other Institutions – the Council and the Commission – were also merged.[47] In 1970, the EEC was provided with its own Budget and autonomous revenue stream.[48] Finally, it was agreed in 1976 that there should be direct elections for the European Parliament.[49] These were first held in 1979 and have since been held at five-yearly periods.

If intergovernmentalism was taking hold as a vision of European integration amongst national governments, another vision – a supranational one – gained traction amongst the EEC's courts. This was because of a remarkable decision of the Court of Justice. If *Van Gend en Loos* is arguably the most important decision ever given by that court, the facts were arcane. Van Gend en Loos, a Dutch road haulier, was charged an import duty on chemicals imported from Germany by the Dutch authorities.[50] It considered this breached what is now Article 30 of the TFEU, which prohibits customs duties or charges having equivalent effect being placed on the movement of goods between Member States. It invoked the provision before a Dutch tax court, the

---

[41] P. Gerbet, 'The Fouchet Negotiations (1960–2)' in R. Pryce (ed.), *Dynamics of Political Union* (London, Croon Helm, 1987); N. Ludlow, 'Challenging French Leadership in Europe: Germany, Italy and the Netherlands and the Origins of the Empty Chair Crisis of 1965' (1999) 8 *Contemporary European History* 231.

[42] N. Ludlow, *The European Community and the Crises of the 1960s* (London: Routledge, 2007).

[43] On de Gaulle's Europe, see W. Loth (ed.), *Crises and Compromises: The European Project, 1963–9* (Baden Baden, Nomos, 2001); C. Parsons, *A Certain Idea of Europe* (Ithaca, Cornell University Press, 2003).

[44] W. Nicholl, 'The Luxembourg Compromise' (1984) 23 *JCMS* 35. For a modern perspective, see J.-M. Palavret *et al.* (eds.), *Visions, Votes and Vetoes: Reassessing the Luxembourg Compromise 40 Years On* (Brussels, Peter Lang, 2006).

[45] In 1985, they were invoked by Germany to prevent a 1.8% decrease in the price of colza, a cooking oil grain. M. Vasey, 'The 1985 Farm Price Negotiations and the Reform of the Common Agriculture Policy' (1985) 22 *CMLRev* 649, 664–6.

[46] This was done in a separate treaty, the Convention Relating to Certain Institutions Common to the European Communities (1957).

[47] P.-H. Houben, 'The Merger of the Executives of the European Communities' (1965) 3 *CMLRev* 37.

[48] Decision 70/243/EEC, OJ English Special Edition 1970 (I) 224.

[49] Decision 76/287/EEC OJ 1976, L 278/1. Until 1979 it consisted of representatives of national parliaments.

[50] It was no coincidence that the case came from the Netherlands. The Dutch branch of FIDE, the main European law association, had been pushing for some years for test cases on this. A. Vauchez, 'The Transnational Politics of Judicialization: Van Gend en Loos and the Making of EU Polity' (2010) 16 *ELJ* 1, 9–10.

Tariefcommissie, which asked the European Court of Justice whether a party could invoke and rely on Treaty provisions in proceedings before a national court. Historically, the justiciability of an international treaty was a matter for national law as this went to its internal effects within the latter's sovereign territory. To hold otherwise, the Court of Justice had to find that the EEC Treaty was unlike any other international treaty.[51]

Van Gend en Loos v. *Nederlandse Administratie der Belastingen*, 26/62, EU:C:1963:1

The first question . . . is whether Article [30 TFEU] has direct application in national law in the sense that nationals of member states may on the basis of this Article lay claim to rights which the national court must protect.

To ascertain whether the provisions of an international treaty extend so far in their effects it is necessary to consider the spirit, the general scheme and the wording of those provisions.

The objective of the EEC Treaty, which is to establish a common market, the functioning of which is of direct concern to interested parties in the community, implies that this Treaty is more than an agreement which merely creates mutual obligations between the contracting States. This view is confirmed by the preamble to the Treaty which refers not only to governments but to peoples. It is also confirmed more specifically by the establishment of institutions endowed with sovereign rights, the exercise of which affects Member States and also their citizens. Furthermore, it must be noted that the nationals of the States brought together in the Community are called upon to cooperate in the functioning of this Community through the intermediary of the European Parliament and the Economic and Social Committee.

In addition, the task assigned to the Court of Justice under Article [267 TFEU][52] the object of which is to secure uniform interpretation of the Treaty by national courts and tribunals, confirms that the States have acknowledged that Community law has an authority which can be invoked by their nationals before those courts and tribunals. The conclusion to be drawn from this is that the Community constitutes a new legal order of international law for the benefit of which the States have limited their sovereign rights, albeit within limited fields, and the subjects of which comprise not only Member States but also their nationals. Independently of the legislation of Member States, Community law therefore not only imposes obligations on individuals but is also intended to confer upon them rights which become part of their legal heritage. These rights arise not only where they are expressly granted by the Treaty, but also by reason of obligations which the Treaty imposes in a clearly defined way upon individuals as well as upon the Member States and upon the institutions of the Community.

If the Court was split down the middle over this judgment,[53] the most striking feature was its statement that 'the Community constitutes a new legal order of international law for the benefit of which the States have limited their sovereign rights . . . '. This parroted the language of a

---

[51] The details of the Court's rulings as regards supremacy and as regards direct effect are considered more fully in Chs. 5 and 7, respectively. See, however, M. Rasmussen, 'Law Meets History: Interpreting the Van Gen den Loos Judgment' in F. Nicola and B. Davies (eds.), *EU Law Stories* (Cambridge University Press, 2017).

[52] Article 267 TFEU enables national courts and tribunals to refer questions of the interpretation of Community law to the Court of Justice. The relationships between national courts and the Court of Justice are considered in detail in Ch. 7.

[53] M. Rasmussen, 'The Origins of a Legal Revolution: The Early History of the European Court of Justice' (2008) 14 *JEI History* 77, 93–5.

number of national constitutions which, following the Second World War, allowed sovereignty to be limited by treaties or transferred to international institutions.[54] However, it was one thing for a national constitutional court to state this, and another for the Court of Justice. National courts adopting this phrase were engaging in an act of self-limitation. They deferred to the norms of international law. By contrast, the Court of Justice was doing the opposite. It was asserting the power of EEC law over national law. Indeed, it went even further as it was constructing a new matrix for legal authority within the EEC. National legal systems no longer formed the central building block. Instead, legal authority flowed from the Treaty with national legal systems having to adapt as sub-units to it.

The judgment also makes a claim about the nature of political community within the EU. The justification for the authority of EEC law is that the EEC exists to benefit not merely the governments but also the peoples of Europe. Whilst traditional international law governs mutual obligations between States, EU law recognises other subjects: private parties, be they EU citizens, non-EU nationals, or corporations. These are to hold a direct relationship with EU law through its conferring both rights and obligations on them. These rights and obligations, in turn, set up legal relations between them independently of national law. A new legal community was thereby born generating its own mutual commitments and sense of right and wrong.

As other chapters in this book will detail, whilst the EEC legislative process struggled in the 1960s and 1970s, this vision was put into effect during that time.[55] Buoyed by *Van Gend en Loos*, networks of lawyers, academics and Commission officials burgeoned.[56] These pushed European integration forward through litigation. Prompted by their demands, the Court gave a series of integrationist judgments, which developed treaty-making powers for the Community, elaborated rights which could be invoked by individuals against national governments, and detailed the content of the economic freedoms and the competition provisions of the Treaty.[57]

(iv) The Initial Enlargements

The United Kingdom was all too aware that the establishment of a common market left it economically isolated. From 1956 onwards, it pushed for a free trade area with other European States, which culminated in its setting up of the European Free Trade Area (EFTA) with Austria, Denmark, Norway, Sweden, Switzerland and Portugal in 1960. By 1961, however, States within the EEC were experiencing faster economic growth rates than Britain and the latter's failure to prevent South Africa's expulsion from the Commonwealth, following the Sharpeville massacres,

---

[54] B. de Witte, 'The European Union as an International Legal Experiment' in G. de Búrca and J. Weiler (eds.), *The Worlds of European Constitutionalism* (Cambridge University Press, 2012) 19, 26–8; K v. Leeuwen, 'On Democratic Concerns and Legal Traditions: The Dutch 1953 and 1956 Constitutional Reforms "Towards" Europe' (2012) 21 *Contemporary European History* 357.

[55] A. Vauchez, 'Introduction: Euro-Lawyering, Transnational Social Fields and European Polity-Building' in A. Vauchez and B. de Witte (eds.), *Lawyering Europe* (London, Bloomsbury, 2013).

[56] A. Vauchez and A. Cohen, 'The Social Construction of Law: The European Court of Justice and Its Legal Revolution Revisited' (2011) 7 *Annual Review of Law and Society* 417; A. Bernier, 'Constructing and Legitimating: Transnational Jurist Networks and the Making of a Constitutional Practice of European Law, 1950–70' (2012) 21 *Contemporary European History* 399; M. Rasmussen, 'Establishing a Constitutional Practice: The Role of the European Law Associations' in W. Kaiser and J.-H. Meyer (eds.), *Societal Actors in European Integration: Polity-Building and Policy-Making 1958–1992* (Basingstoke, Palgrave, 2013).

[57] It also led to political tensions. B. Davies, *Resisting the European Court of Justice: West Germany's Confrontation with European Law, 1949–1979* (Cambridge University Press, 2012) chs. 3 and 4.

brought home Britain's relative decline on the international stage. It applied for membership in 1961 but the French President, de Gaulle, vetoed its entry in 1963. Four years later, the United Kingdom, plus Ireland, Denmark and Norway, reapplied. The application was once again vetoed by de Gaulle. This use of the veto left France isolated, and French policy changed in 1969 with the resignation of de Gaulle. The Six agreed in The Hague to open negotiations with the applicants, with a view to extending membership. The United Kingdom, Denmark and Ireland formally became members on 1 January 1973.[58] However, following a referendum, where 53 per cent voted against membership, Norway did not accede to the EEC.

The next State to join was Greece. Greece applied for membership in 1975, following its establishment of a democratic government. For the Greeks, accession was not only economically attractive, but symbolised modernisation and democratic stability. For the Member States, Greece was important geopolitically during the Cold War because of its strategic location in the Aegean. Membership was, therefore, seen as tying Greece more firmly to the West. Greece became a member in 1981. Like Greece, Spain and Portugal emerged from dictatorships and isolationism in the mid-1970s. They made applications to join the Communities only two years after Greece, in 1977. Yet, accession was more problematic in their cases. The size of the agricultural sector in Spain resulted in initial French resistance to entry due to the likely negative effects on the French agricultural sector. It was, thus, not until 1986 that Spain and Portugal became members.

(v) The Single European Act

Things changed in the 1980s. Following the recession of the early 1980s, national governments converged in their belief that economic policy-making had to focus on measures which stimulated competition and trade. Market integration fitted this consensus.[59] Alongside this, transnational pressure groups had begun to locate themselves in Brussels, leading to an organised industrial constituency that was increasingly rallying for pan-European solutions.[60] Powerful industrial organisations such as the European Round Table (ERT) and the Union of Industrial and Employers' Confederations of Europe (UNICE) lobbied aggressively across Europe, arguing for the completion of the common market as a means of promoting European competitiveness.[61] Finally, direct elections had produced a more aggressive European Parliament. Under the chairmanship of Alfiero Spinelli, it produced a draft Treaty on European Union, which proposed a fully federal Europe with common foreign, macroeconomic and trade policies and a developed system of central institutions.[62]

---

[58] U. Kitzinger, *Diplomacy and Persuasion: How Britain Joined the Common Market* (London, Thames & Hudson, 1973); C. O'Neill, *Britain's Entry into the European Community. Report on the Negotiations of 1970–1972* (London, Frank Cass, 2000); D. Gowland, *Britain and the European Union* (Abingdon, Routledge, 2016) ch. 2.

[59] On the convergence of national government preferences see K. Middlemas, *Orchestrating Europe: The Informal Politics of European Union 1973–1995* (London, Fontana, 1995) 115–35; A. Moravscik, *The Choice for Europe: Social Purpose and State Power from Messina to Maastricht* (Ithaca, Cornell University Press, 1998) ch. 5; J. Gillingham, *European Integration 1950–2003: Superstate or New Market Economy* (Cambridge University Press, 2003) ch. 9.

[60] N. Fligstein and J. McNichol, 'The Institutional Terrain of the European Union' in W. Sandholtz and A. Stone Sweet (eds.), *European Integration and Supranational Governance* (Oxford University Press, 1998) 59, 75–80; N. Fligstein and P. Brantley, 'The Single Market Program and the Interests of Business' in B. Eichengreen and J. Frieden (eds.), *Politics and Institutions in an Integrated Europe* (Berlin, Springer, 1995).

[61] W. Sandholtz and J. Zysman, '1992: Recasting the European Bargain' (1989) 42 *World Politics* 95, 116; M. Cowles, 'Setting the Agenda for a New Europe: The ERT and EC 1992' (1995) 33 *JCMS* 527; Middlemas, n. 59 above, 136–40.

[62] OJ 1984, C 77/33. For comment, see R. Bieber *et al.*, *An Ever Closer Union: A Critical Analysis of the Draft Treaty Establishing the European Union* (Luxembourg, Office for Official Publications of the European Communities, 1985).

These pressures for further European integration were fragmented. The final piece of the jigsaw fell into place with the appointment of a new Commission in 1984, headed by the charismatic, former French Finance Minister, Jacques Delors. Delors, in lobbying for the post, had already seized upon the goal of market unity as the principal task of the new Commission to be achieved by the end of 1992. In November 1984, he gave the national governments four choices for recapturing momentum: monetary policy, foreign policy and defence, institutional reform, or the internal market.[63] All agreed that the internal market was the way forward. The Commission was instructed by the Member States to consider the practical steps necessary to realise this. The idea had been kicking around the Commission since 1981 when the German Commissioner, Karl-Heinz Narjes, had looked into creating an 'internal market' in which there were no barriers to the exchange of goods, services and labour.[64] The new British Commissioner, Lord Cockfield, took up Narjes' work, and in June 1985, presented the *White Paper on Completion of the Internal Market* to the Heads of Government at Milan.[65]

The paper was a clever piece of work, suggesting that only 279 measures were necessary to realise the internal market. Member States were not, therefore, committing themselves to an open-ended set of obligations, but to a finite and limited project. The project was also cast as largely a technical mission rather than having broader panoramas of greater integration.[66] In 1985, the Italian Government called for a conference to amend the Treaties.[67] The result was the signing of the Single European Act (SEA) in 1986.

The principal achievements of the SEA appeared modest at the time.[68] Provision was made for express competencies in health and safety at work, economic and social cohesion, research and development and environmental protection. However, apart from the first of these, there were already activities in these fields, albeit under other headings. There was also codification of intergovernmental cooperation in foreign policy. A new institution, the European Council, comprising of Heads of Government, was established.[69] However, there had been regular summits from 1961 and it was agreed in 1974 that these should meet twice a year to discuss internal difficulties within the European Communities, broader issues about the future of European integration, and the place of the European Communities in the world order.

However, two reforms combined to mark the SEA as arguably the most significant treaty reform in the Union's history.

The first was the commitment to establish the internal market by 31 December 1992. The internal market is now set out in Article 46(2) TFEU:

> The internal market shall comprise an area without internal frontiers in which the free movement of goods, persons, services and capital is ensured in accordance with the provisions of the Treaties.

---

[63] Middlemas, n. 59 above, 141.

[64] N. Fligstein and I. Mara-Drita, 'How to Make a Market: Reflections on the Attempt to Create a Single Market in the European Union' (1996) 102 *American Journal of Sociology* 1, 11–13.

[65] EC Commission, 'Completing the Internal Market', COM(85)310 final.

[66] W. Sandholtz and J. Zysman, '1992: Recasting the European Bargain' (1989) 42 *World Politics* 95, 114–15.

[67] On the controversial manner in which it did this see L. v. Middelaar, *The Passage to Europe: How a Continent Became a Union* (New Haven, Yale University Press, 2013) 100–11.

[68] G. Bermann, 'The Single European Act: A New Constitution for the European Community?' (1989) 27 *Columbia Journal of Transnational Law* 529; C.-D. Ehlermann, 'The Internal Market Following the Single European Act' (1987) 24 *CMLRev* 361; A. Moravscik, 'Negotiating the Single European Act' (1991) 45 *IO* 19.

[69] Article 2 SEA.

Secondly, a new legislative procedure, the cooperation procedure, was introduced for adoption of most of the legislation necessary to establish the internal market.[70] It provided crucially for voting by Qualified Majority in the Council.

Neither reform seemed radical at the time. The internal market project seemed simply a restatement of the old dream of establishing a common market. The new voting procedures' effect was uncertain, particularly as the United Kingdom, Greece and Denmark insisted upon a Declaration being appended to the SEA that nothing within it affected Member States' rights to invoke the Luxembourg Accords. However, the SEA confounded expectations and changed both the legislative and political culture of the Union. In legislative terms, Member States became less tolerant of attempts to invoke the Luxembourg Accords.[71]

The legislative processes were energised. By the end of 1992, almost 95 per cent of the measures had been enacted and 77 per cent had entered into force in the Member States.[72] Alongside this, the Commission had vastly understated the legislative output of the European Communities. This increased to 2,500 binding acts per year by 1994.[73] Some 53 per cent of the legislative measures adopted in France in 1991 were inspired by its Treaty obligations and 30 per cent of all Dutch legislation during the 1990s implemented Union legislation.[74]

4 THE ESTABLISHMENT OF THE EUROPEAN UNION

(i) The Road to Maastricht

The transformation brought about by the SEA coincided with the end of the division of Europe, the collapse of the Berlin wall in 1989, and the relaxation of currency controls, which destabilised weaker States' currencies and public finances.[75] The uncertainty generated by the currency instability following this relaxation of controls also appeared to threaten the single market.[76] The early 1990s were, thus, marked by a curious mix of pan-European idealism,[77] increased anxiety about excessive EU legislative intervention,[78] and an uncertain economic context.

Monetary union thus fitted the aspirations of those, notably President Mitterand of France and President Kohl of Germany, who saw it as the cantilever to open the door to greater political integration and protection against currency volatility. In June 1988, the Heads of State asserted that 'the Single European Act confirmed the objective of progressive realisation of economic and

---

[70] This legislative procedure no longer exists. It has been superseded by the ordinary legislative procedure.

[71] In 1987 it was agreed, therefore, that if a majority of States wanted a vote, a vote would be taken, irrespective of the objections of individual States. Council Rules of Procedure, Article 5, OJ 1987, L 291/27.

[72] *Twenty Sixth General Report on the Activities of the European Communities 1992* (Luxembourg, Office for Official Publications of the European Communities, 1993) 35.

[73] W. Wessels, 'An Ever Closer Fusion? A Dynamic Macropolitical View on Integration Processes' (1997) 35 *JCMS* 267, 276.

[74] G. Mancini, 'Europe: The Case for Statehood' (1998) 4 *ELJ* 29, 40.

[75] K. Mcnamara, 'Consensus and Constraint: Ideas and Capital Mobility in European Monetary Integration' (1999) 37 *JCMS* 455.

[76] T. Padoa-Schipoa *et al., Efficiency, Stability and Equity: A Strategy for the Evolution of the Economic System of the European Community* (Oxford University Press, 1987).

[77] This idealism is well captured in the first lines of J. Weiler, 'The Transformation of Europe' (1991) 100 *Yale LJ* 2403, 2405–6.

[78] This is most famously captured in the speech given by Margaret Thatcher, the British Prime Minister, at the College of Europe where she expressed opposition to the ideological direction taken by the Communities and their levels of intervention. See www.margaretthatcher.org/speeches/displaydocument.asp?docid=107332. However, others expressed concern. On the worries of François Mitterand, see Middelaar, n. 67 above, 186–7.

monetary union'.[79] They mandated a committee of central bank governors chaired by the Commission President, Jacques Delors, to examine the concrete steps required for this. The report of the latter was submitted in June 1989.[80] In December, an intergovernmental conference was convened to amend the Treaties. Presidents Kohl and Mitterand considered that such a union would be unsustainable without further political integration.[81] In June 1990, it was agreed that a separate intergovernmental conference should be held on political union.[82] These parallel conferences culminated in the signing of the Treaty on European Union, at Maastricht, on 10 December 1991.[83]

(ii) Maastricht and the Union's Three Legitimation Strategies

The Treaty on European Union (TEU) was a different beast from the SEA. If the latter was presented as largely about finishing the unfinished business of the common market, the TEU, involved a project, whose central policy, monetary union, was traditionally viewed as one of the core prerogatives of the modern nation State, namely the right to print its own money. The TEU, furthermore, also proclaimed the new European Union as a political project with its own political values and political communities. This shift is reflected in the first article of the TEU, the first two paragraphs of which stand unaltered from those agreed at Maastricht.

Article 1 TEU

By this Treaty, the HIGH CONTRACTING PARTIES establish among themselves a EUROPEAN UNION, hereinafter called 'the Union' on which the Member States confer competences to attain objectives they have in common.

This Treaty marks a new stage in the process of creating an ever closer union among the peoples of Europe, in which decisions are taken as openly as possible and as closely as possible to the citizen.

The ambitious nature of these claims raised questions about the acceptability of this to the Union's citizens. To try to get these to identify with it, the European Union adopted three strategies.

L. v. Middelaar, *The Passage to Europe: How a Continent Became a Union* (New Haven, Yale University Press, 2013) 223–4

There are three basic forms, three notions that can lend credibility to a sense of 'we Europeans'. These are 'our people', 'to our advantage' and 'our decisions'. With a nod to history we might call them the 'German', 'Roman' and 'Greek' strategies. European politics has taken shape by deploying these three strategies by turns.

---

[79] Conclusions of Hanover European Council, EC Bulletin 6–1988 1.1.1–1.1.5.

[80] *Report on Economic and Monetary Union in the European Community by Committee for the Study of Economic and Monetary Union* (European Commission, Luxembourg, 1989).

[81] On the negotiations leading to Maastricht see C. Mazzucelli, *France and Germany at Maastricht: Politics and Negotiations to Create the European Union* (New York, Garland, 1997); K. Dyson and K. Featherstone, *The Road to Maastricht: Negotiating Economic and Monetary Union* (Oxford University Press, 1999).

[82] Political union was added very much as an afterthought to economic and monetary union and negotiations were not well prepared. R. Corbett, 'The Intergovernmental Conference on Political Union' (1992) 30 *JCMS* 271.

[83] The most detailed analysis of the negotiations is F. Laursen and S. Vanhoonacker, *The Intergovernmental Conference on Political Union: Institutional Reforms, New Policies and International Identity of the European Community* (Dordrecht, Martijnus Nijhoff, 1992).

The 'German' strategy relies on a cultural or historical identity shared by rulers and ruled. They speak the same language, or believe in the same values and holy scriptures, or have the same customs, or ancestors who fought the same wars. The public is supposed to feel that 'they' (the rulers) and 'we' (the ruled) belong to the same people. Around 1800, German thinkers such as Herder, Schlegel and Fichte turned nationalism (which emerged with and in the wake of the French revolution) into an intellectual narrative. They felt they were part of a single German culture, which regrettably lacked a state. In their work they wanted to arouse a sense of being a nation. State power would follow. This ideological programme found imitators all over Europe. From London to Belgrade and from Paris to Palermo people used the same strategies to make a national identity visible, or indeed to generate one. A national history, a flag and anthem, national holidays, conscription and compulsory education, the codification of an official language, monuments to heroes, the 'invention of traditions' – these are all familiar elements.

The 'Roman' strategy bases its appeal on the benefits that people derive from a functioning political system. Rulers offer protection. They create opportunities or distribute money. The public they have in mind consists of clients. The reference is therefore not to republican Rome but to imperial Rome – to the Rome in which the citizen has no voice and the populace was mollified with 'bread and circuses'. Of all the benefits that imperial Rome offered its people, security was the most fundamental. The *pax romana* – along with more material benefits such as aqueducts or baths – was a trump card for an empire attempting to bind foreign peoples to its authority.

The 'Greek' strategy, finally, rests on periodic appraisal by the population of representatives who take decisions on its behalf. Sometimes this is supplemented by a direct vote by the people on specific matters. The aim is to ensure that rules and decisions are felt to be 'our concern'. To this end, a democracy gives the public a vote. The origins of the majority principle (on which rest both direct democracy and its modern, representative version) lie in Ancient Greece. In the 'Greek' strategy, the public is allocated a remarkably powerful role, and in the long run this increases a state's political capacity to respond to an open future.

These strategies came into play at Maastricht and many subsequent treaty reforms.

The Roman strategy is adopted where the EU is granted additional competencies. These competencies allow the EU to do more things, hopefully to the advantage of its citizens. These advantages, it is hoped, will generate support for the EU.

At Maastricht, the most high-profile new competence added was that of economic and monetary union. An independent European Central Bank was to be exclusively responsible for authorising the issue of a new currency, the euro, with constraints placed on national budgetary policies to prevent these destabilising the new currency. A wide array of other competencies were also added: visas, education, culture, public health, social policy, consumer protection, the establishment of trans-European networks in transport, energy and telecommunications, industrial policy and development cooperation.

This idea of EU action being about securing benefits was reinforced by the introduction of the subsidiarity principle into the Treaty. In almost all of these fields, there was the possibility of both EU and domestic action. This principle provided that, in these cases, the EU was only to act if unilateral action by Member States could not realise the objects of the proposed action and by reason of its scale or effects the action could be better achieved by the Union.

All these competencies were governed supranationally. Maastricht also made provision for two important policies to be governed largely intergovernmentally: common foreign and security policy, and justice and home affairs, a ragbag field focused on migration of non-EU nationals, judicial cooperation and policing.

The second strategy, the German strategy, involves Treaty reforms, which are about *collective identity formation*. They establish symbols suggesting a shared European identity. The most significant innovation introduced in this regard by Maastricht was European citizenship. All Member States nationals were now to be EU citizens. EU citizenship rights were significant but much more limited than those granted by national citizenship, however. They granted new rights to free movement around the Union and to access to social benefits in other Member States as well as new possibilities for democratic participation in both local and European Parliament elections. Much of the power of EU citizenship lies, however, in its symbolism. It suggests a community of citizens whose mutual ties to one another are not confined by the national State but are rather founded on some wider sense of being European.

The third strategy, the Greek strategy, involves institutional reform. This reform goes, on the one hand, to making EU decision-making work more efficiently and, on the other, to making it more democratic. Both were addressed at Maastricht by the introduction of a new legislative procedure, which is called the ordinary legislative procedure and has since become the European Union's dominant legislative procedure. This procedure provides for QMV in the Council. Maastricht, thus, provided for much more by passing of national vetoes than previously. In terms of democracy, elected bodies were given more influence. The ordinary legislative procedure gave the European Parliament the power to veto legislation. Alongside this, there was a commitment to involve national parliaments more within the integration process.

Each of these strategies faces challenges. The Roman strategy of additional competencies allows for a wider range of EU laws to be passed. This might generate a greater array of winners from these laws, but it will also create a wider array of losers.[84] The strategy provides nothing for these losers. These effects grow with the volume of EU law as each piece of legislation creates new winners and losers. The German strategy faces the difficulty that creation of common identities can appear fake and propagandist.[85] Ethically problematic notions can lie behind these identities, and, even when they do not, these identities still create uncomfortable divisions between Europeans and non-Europeans. Finally, any sense of European identity competes with ideas of national identity, and, for better or worse, the pull of the latter on most citizens' sense of belonging is stronger.[86] The Greek strategy of securing popular engagement through institutional reform is particularly difficult to realise. European public opinion is diverse and contradictory. The assumption that granting European public opinion an institutional arena for its legislative expression will lead to strong support for that arena is fraught as this opinion is just as likely not to engage or disagree strongly with EU activities. Furthermore, democracy is not being valued for its own sake but because it might engender support for EU processes. This can lead to the European Union's democracy being seen as something provided for show rather than as a source of emancipation.[87]

Nevertheless, it was believed at Maastricht that these tensions could largely be managed within a single pan-Union framework. As they arose, EU Institutions would find common responses to them. It was assumed that where this was impossible, it was because of differences between

---

[84] F. Scharpf, *Governing in Europe: Effective and Democratic?* (Oxford University Press, 1999) 8–9.

[85] C. Shore, *Building Europe, The Cultural Politics of European Integration* (London, Routledge, 2000) chs. 1–4.

[86] Just over half of the EU's citizens are proud to see themselves as national and European, 8% as exclusively European, and 18% as exclusively national. T. Raines, M. Goodwin and D. Cutts, *The Future of Europe: Comparing Public and Elite Attitudes* (London, Chatham House, 2017) 12.

[87] Middelaar, n. 67 above, 291–307.

societies rather than because of differences within societies. The British held a different attitude on the euro from the Germans, for example. This led to tailored solutions being offered to individual Member States in discrete fields of activity. The United Kingdom and Denmark reserved the right not to participate in the euro. As the United Kingdom did not wish to extend EU social policy to all main areas of labour law, an Agreement on Social Policy was adopted which bound all other Member States. Finally, Ireland and Denmark secured protection from EU law, respectively, for their abortion law and legislation prohibiting foreigners owning second homes.

The assumption that the differences were simply between States and not within the societies of each State was not true.

L. Hooghe and G. Marks, 'A Postfunctionalist Theory of European Integration: From Permissive Consensus to Constraining Dissensus' (2008) 39 *British Journal of Political Science* 1, 8–9

Public opinion on European integration . . . is rather well structured, affects national voting and is connected to the basic dimensions that structure contestation in European societies.

With the Maastricht Accord of 1991, decision making on European integration entered the contentious world of party competition, elections and referenda. Content analysis of media in France, the Netherlands, Germany, Britain, Switzerland and Austria reveals that the proportion of statements devoted to European issues in national electoral campaigns increased from 2.5 per cent in the 1970s to 7 per cent in the 1990s. [88] In the 1990s, between a tenth and an eighth of all policy statements in a sample of British and Swiss media contained references to Europe.

Analysing a dataset of 9,872 protests from 1984 through 1997, Doug Imig and Sidney Tarrow conclude that 'European integration is highly salient to a growing range of citizens across the continent'.[89] On conservative assumptions, they find that the proportion of social movement protest oriented to Europe has risen from the 5–10 per cent range in the 1980s to between 20 and 30 per cent in the second half of the 1990s.

An expert survey conducted by Kenneth Benoit and Michael Laver finds that European integration was the third most important issue in national party competition in Western Europe in 2003, behind taxes v. spending and deregulation/privatization, but ahead of immigration. European integration topped the list in Britain, France, Cyprus and Malta. In Eastern Europe, joining the European Union was typically the most salient issue.[90] At the same time – no coincidence – conflict over Europe within national parties has intensified in almost all EU countries.

Matters exploded into the open on 2 June 1992 when the Danes voted against ratification of the TEU. To boost the credibility of the process, President Mitterand decided to hold a referendum in France. He misjudged. Only 51 per cent of the vote was in favour of ratification. The Danish referendum also signalled the beginning of a bitter legislative fight in the British Parliament, in which legislation was only adopted in July 1993 – a year and a half after the Treaty had been agreed – after the government

---

[88] H. Kriesi, 'How National Political Parties Mobilize the Political Potentials Linked to European Integration' (2007) 8 *EUP* 83.

[89] D. Imig, 'Contestation in the Streets: European Protest and the Emerging Europolity' in G. Marks and J. Steenbergen (eds.), *European Integration and Political Conflict* (Cambridge University Press, 2004) 232; S. Tarrow, *The New Transnational Activism* (Cambridge University Press, 2005).

[90] K. Benoit and M. Laver, *Party Policy in Modern Democracies* (London, Routledge, 2006) 160 and 176.

had threatened to resign if its own MPs did not vote for it.[91] The Treaty was salvaged at Edinburgh, in December 1992. A decision was adopted 'interpreting' the Treaty giving the Danish Government guarantees about EU citizenship and defence as well as setting out in more detail the subsidiarity principle.[92] This allowed the Danish Government the necessary breadth to hold a second referendum in May 1993, with 56 per cent voting in favour of ratification.

The drama of ratification now moved to the courts. Unsuccessful challenges to the Treaty were made before the British, French, Danish and Spanish courts.[93] The challenge before the German Constitutional Court was to have the most far-reaching consequences.[94] In its judgment, the German Constitutional Court placed markers on the nature and limits of European integration. It ruled that within the current state of European integration, democratic legitimacy was constituted above all at a national level. However, it argued, a stable currency was a precondition for democracy. Two things followed. Germany could constitutionally join the euro provided the disciplines associated with a commitment to currency stability were observed. In all other fields, integration would only be possible if it did not fundamentally undermine national self-government.

(iii) The Treaty of Amsterdam

The TEU entered into force on 1 November 1993 but the environment was now heavily polarised.[95] Member States had, however, committed to a further intergovernmental conference in 1996. Negotiations began in earnest in that year, and the Treaty of Amsterdam was signed on 2 October 1997.

Amsterdam adopted the same three strategies as Maastricht.

It adopted the Roman strategy of increasing the number of EU competencies. Competencies in the fields of employment and equal opportunities were added, and the Agreement on Social Policy was abolished, with social policy placed on the same footing as other EU policies. However, the central monument of the Treaty of Amsterdam was the Area of Freedom, Security and Justice (AFSJ). The AFSJ is now set out in the following terms.

Article 67 TFEU

(1) The Union shall constitute an area of freedom, security and justice with respect for fundamental rights and the different legal systems and traditions of the Member States.

(2) It shall ensure the absence of internal border controls for persons and shall frame a common policy on asylum, immigration and external border control, based on solidarity between Member States, which is fair

---

[91] R. Rawlings, 'Legal Politics: The United Kingdom and Ratification of the Treaty on European Union' [1994] *PL* 254 and 367; D. Baker, A. Gamble and S. Ludlum, 'The Parliamentary Siege of Maastricht: Conservative Divisions and British Ratification' (1994) 47 *Parliamentary Affairs* 37.

[92] D. Howarth, 'The Compromise on Denmark and the Treaty on European Union: A Legal and Political Analysis' (1994) 31 *CMLRev* 465.

[93] *R* v. *Secretary of State for Foreign and Commonwealth Affairs, ex parte Rees-Mogg* [1994] QB 552 (Britain); *Re Treaty on European Union* (Decision 92–308), Journel Officiel de la République Française 1992, No 5354 (France); *Treaty of Maastricht*, UfR (1998) 800 (Denmark); *Re Treaty on European Union* [1994] 3 CMLR 101 (Spain).

[94] *Brunner* v. *The European Union* [1994] 1 CMLR 57.

[95] Opinion polls showed that those who considered the European Union a 'good thing' had dropped from 72% in 1990 to 48% in autumn 1996. Eurobarometer, *Public Opinion in the EU, Report No. 46, Autumn 1996* (Luxembourg, Office for Official Publications of the European Communities, 1997).

towards third-country nationals. For the purpose of this Title, stateless persons shall be treated as third-country nationals.

(3) The Union shall endeavour to ensure a high level of security through measures to prevent and combat crime, racism and xenophobia, and through measures for coordination and cooperation between police and judicial authorities and other competent authorities, as well as through the mutual recognition of judgments in criminal matters and, if necessary, through the approximation of criminal laws.

(4) The Union shall facilitate access to justice, in particular through the principle of mutual recognition of judicial and extrajudicial decisions in civil matters.

To realise the AFSJ, the Treaty of Amsterdam first integrated the Schengen Agreements and their *acquis* into the legal framework of the TEU. These Agreements, signed in 1985 and 1990, between all Member States, other than Ireland and the United Kingdom, provided for the abolition of frontier checks between parties and a common external frontier. To realise this, the 1990 Convention had provided for intergovernmental cooperation in the fields of migration of non-EU nationals, crime and policing.[96] Secondly, the AFSJ brought immigration, asylum, the rights of non-EU nationals and judicial cooperation on civil matters within the first pillar of the European Communities. Policing and judicial cooperation on criminal matters remained subject to the predominantly intergovernmental procedures of the third pillar.

In terms of collective identity formation (the German strategy), Amsterdam oriented EU identity more strongly around fundamental rights. A new Article 6 TEU stated that the Union was to be founded on the 'principles of liberty, democracy, respect for human rights and fundamental freedoms, and the rule of law'. Provision was also made for a Member State to have its EU rights suspended where it was deemed to have seriously and persistently breached these ideals.

Institutional reform (the Greek strategy) took the form of significant extension of QMV so that it became the norm for EU lawmaking for the first time.[97]

Amsterdam largely followed the logic of Maastricht. Tensions were to be addressed through the choice as to whether to have common EU measures or not. Like Maastricht, it also took the view that insofar as this was not possible it was because of differences between States about the pace and direction of integration rather than because of wider social conflicts generated by this integration. It, therefore, continued the practice of special deals for Member States in particular fields. The United Kingdom and Ireland were given the right to maintain border controls on movement from other Member States and the right to decide whether to opt into individual pieces of EU legislation adopted to realise the area of freedom, security and justice. In like vein, Denmark secured agreement that it was only to be bound by such legislation under its general obligations in international law, as a Schengen signatory, rather than because this legislation was EU law. There was awareness, however, that disagreements between States about the pace and direction of integration were becoming more widespread and more difficult to predict. Provision was made, therefore, for groups of Member States to engage in 'enhanced cooperation':[98] adoption of EU laws amongst themselves.

---

[96] This is now to be found at OJ 2000, L 239/19. Iceland, Switzerland, Liechtenstein and Norway are also members.
[97] A. Maurer, 'The Legislative Powers and Impact of the European Parliament' (2003) 41 *JCMS* 227, 229.
[98] See pp. 138–43.

5 RECASTING THE BORDERS OF THE EUROPEAN UNION

The success of the SEA entailed that exclusion from the world's largest trading bloc posed significant economic risks for neighbouring States. At the same time, communism collapsed in Central and Eastern Europe. Many of these States now saw Union membership as the anchor around which changes in their societies could be made.

The process of expansion began with the EFTA States (Norway, Sweden, Finland, Iceland, Austria, Liechtenstein and Switzerland). In 1991, the Treaty of Oporto was signed, establishing the European Economic Area (EEA).[99] The EFTA States were required to adopt all EU legislation in the fields of the internal market, research and development policy, social policy, education, consumer protection and environmental protection in return for access to the internal market.

In June 1993, the European Union agreed that membership be offered to Austria, Finland, Sweden and Norway.[100] Austria, Finland and Sweden voted for membership whilst Norway voted against. The three new Member States acceded on 2 January 1995.

More challenging was the question of membership of the (predominantly) former communist States of Central and Eastern Europe. By the early 1990s, twelve of these had applied for membership.[101] This would almost double the size of the Union with a corresponding reduction of political influence for existing Member States. It would create a financial burden on current members as the applicants were poorer than the Western European States and many had large agricultural populations, which could press claims for support from the Union budget. Nevertheless, in 1993, at Copenhagen, the European Union agreed that the States of Central and Eastern Europe could become members of the European Union once able to satisfy the obligations of membership. These obligations, the 'Copenhagen criteria', required new Member States to have:

- stable institutions guaranteeing democracy, the rule of law, human rights and respect for and protection of minorities
- a functioning market economy as well as the capacity to cope with competitive pressure and market forces within the Union
- the ability to assume the obligations of membership, including both adherence to the aims of the EU and adoption of all existing Union legislation
- the legislative and administrative capacity to transpose Union legislation into national legislation and to implement it effectively through appropriate administrative and judicial structures.[102]

On 1 May 2004, the Czech Republic, Poland, Hungary, Slovenia, Estonia, Latvia, Lithuania, Malta, Slovakia and Cyprus acceded to the European Union. Bulgaria and Romania were considered not ready for membership, and could only join on 1 January 2007. The final State to become an EU member State was Croatia who acceded on 1 July 2013.

The expansion of the Union to twenty-eight Member States transformed the European Union. It could now claim to be a pan-European organisation rather than predominantly a West

---

[99] Although Switzerland signed the Treaty, following a referendum, it decided not to ratify it.

[100] M. Jorna, 'The Accession Negotiations with Austria, Finland, Sweden and Norway: A Guided Tour' (1995) 20 *ELRev* 131; F. Granell, 'The European Union's Enlargement Negotiations with Austria, Finland, Norway and Sweden' (1995) 33 *JCMS* 117.

[101] These were Bulgaria, Cyprus, the Czech Republic, Estonia, Hungary, Latvia, Lithuania, Malta, Poland, Romania, Slovenia and Slovakia.

[102] This last condition was added at Madrid in December 1995.

European one. It also led to greater variation in institutional capacity and economic performance amongst the Member States. Concerns about these, which are not exclusive to post-2004 entrants, have led to two features of the European Union.

The first has been the establishment of additional criteria for participation in some EU policies. The Schengen Convention, it will be remembered, provides for border free travel between Member States and was integrated into the area of freedom, security and justice by the Treaty of Amsterdam. However, four member States – Bulgaria, Croatia, Cyprus and Romania – are not permitted to implement the Convention, and with it border-free travel because there is lack of confidence in their capacity to police their external borders. In Cyprus, this is because of the conflict in the island. In Bulgaria and Romania, despite positive assessments by the Committee established to oversee this, implementation has been refused on the grounds of perceived corruption with the consequence that there is a lack of faith in their policing of their borders.[103]

For the euro, States have to meet tough assessments on their budgetary and economic performance prior to entry.[104] Eleven States joined the euro initially in 1999. Eight States have joined since, with the total number of euro zone States standing at nineteen in 2018.[105]

The second is additional policing by EU Institutions of Member States seen as posing particular institutional risks. On their accession, a process, the Cooperation and Verification Mechanism, was established under which the Commission monitored observance of Bulgarian and Romanian obligations under EU law and their performance against a number of further benchmarks on anti-corruption, rule of law and independence of the judiciary. If these States failed to meet these benchmarks sufficiently, measures could be taken against them including suspension of their EU rights. These benchmarks also represented, however, goals to be realised if these States were to be released from the process. They have not been successful in this. Initially established for first three years of their membership, the Cooperation and Verification Mechanism is still in both place for both States.[106]

The number of EU States is unlikely to remain stable. Following the United Kingdom's departure, membership now stands at twenty-seven. Six States have currently applied for membership: Albania, Bosnia and Herzegovina, Montenegro, Northern Macedonia, Serbia and Turkey.

All applicant States, other than Bosnia and Herzegovina, currently have candidate status. This means that they meet the Copenhagen criteria. For all Western Balkans States (so all current applicants other than Turkey), this status also reflects a commitment to cooperate with the International Criminal Tribunal for the former Yugoslavia and regional cooperation within the Western Balkans. The next step, membership negotiations, which focuses on these States transposing into national law all EU law and establishing an effective machinery to administer it, has rarely been straightforward. Northern Macedonia was granted candidate status in 2005. This did not lead to immediate accession negotiations, despite a Commission Recommendation in 2009 that they begin. As a consequence of EU State

---

[103] For excellent discussion see J. Bornemann, 'Joining Schengen: Cutting a Gordian Knot for Romania and Bulgaria?' http://eumigrationlawblog.eu/joining-schengen-cutting-a-gordian-knot-for-romania-and-bulgaria/.

[104] See p. 662.

[105] The euro area States are Austria, Belgium, Cyprus, Estonia, France, Finland, Germany, Greece, Ireland, Italy, Latvia, Lithuania, Luxembourg, Malta, the Netherlands, Portugal, Slovenia, Slovakia and Spain.

[106] Romania has gone further towards meeting the goals set for it than Bulgaria: European Parliament, *Assessment of the 10 years' Cooperation and Verification Mechanism for Bulgaria and Romania* (Policy Department Budgetary Affairs, Brussels, 2017). For criticism of the process see L. Toneva-Metodieva, 'Beyond the Carrots and Sticks Paradigm: Rethinking the Cooperation and Verification Mechanism Experience of Bulgaria and Romania' (2014) 15 *Perspectives on European Politics and Society* 534.

concerns about its domestic legal and political situation and relations with other States, it was only in 2018 that the EU indicated a willingness to start negotiations the subsequent year. The most tortuous relationship has been between the European Union and Turkey. In 1987, Turkey applied for membership, but it was not until 1999 that the Member States recognised its eligibility for membership. In December 2004, Turkey was granted candidate status, but negotiations were disrupted in December 2006, when, angered by a perception that the European Union was not doing enough to improve the lot of the Turkish Cypriot community, Turkey decided to refuse admission of ships or planes flying the Cypriot flag into its ports or airports. As a consequence, the European Union decided that there would be no negotiations in eight fields[107] and it would not consider negotiations in any field closed until this matter was resolved. Negotiations have been extremely slow since then, and have deteriorated still further with the Turkish Government's announcement of a state of emergency and arrest of over 150,000 people in response to a failed coup in 2016.[108]

6 THE ROAD TO LISBON: THE DECADE OF INSTITUTIONAL REFORM

The current EU Treaty framework is set out by the Treaty of Lisbon, which came into force on 1 December 2009. The Treaty was the culmination of over a decade of argument about institutional reform. This debate differed from those preceding the previous Treaties. Its central focus was rarely about what more the *European Union should do*. Instead, attention focused on *how the European Union went about its business* and how it could establish a political identity, which would garner greater popular support.

(i) The Road to the Constitutional Treaty

The achievements of the Treaty of Amsterdam were seen at the time as unfinished ones.[109]

First, there had been a failure to agree on whether the European Union should have its own Bill of Rights. The Member States agreed, in 1999, that an EU Charter of Fundamental Rights should be established, at least cataloguing such rights. Instead of this being left to intergovernmental negotiations, a special Convention was established.[110] Chaired by Roman Herzog, formerly the German President, the Convention was composed of fifteen representatives of national governments; thirty representatives of national parliaments; sixteen representatives of the European Parliament and one representative of the Commission. It met in open session, decided upon matters by consensus rather than by voting and received extensive representations from civil society. In October 2000, the Convention adopted the European Union Charter of Fundamental Rights and Freedoms ('the Charter'). Possibly as a consequence of the process which led to its coming into being, on the one hand the Charter recognised a wide range of rights, whilst on the other its status, and therefore the legal effects of these rights, was left undetermined.

---

[107] These are free movement of goods, right of establishment and freedom to provide services, financial services, agriculture and rural development, fisheries, transport policy, customs union and external relations.

[108] European Commission, *Turkey 2018 Report*, SWD(2018)153 final, 8–40. On the difficulties within this relationship in recent years, see G. Yilmaz, 'From Europeanization to De-Europeanization: The Europeanization Process of Turkey in 1999–2014' (2016) 24 *Journal of Contemporary European Studies* 86; M. Cebeci, 'De-Europeanisation or Counter-Conduct? Turkey's Democratisation and the EU' (2016) 21 *South European Society and Politics* 119.

[109] K. Hughes, 'The 1996 Intergovernmental Conference and EU Enlargement' (1996) 72 *International Affairs* 1; A. Teasdale, 'The Politics of Qualified Majority Voting in Europe' (1996) *Political Quarterly* 101, 110–15.

[110] G. de Búrca, 'The Drafting of the EU Charter of Fundamental Rights' (2001) 26 *ELRev* 126.

The second concerned the institutional pressures generated by enlargement. A Protocol had been signed at Amsterdam, agreeing that a conference be convened at least one year before membership of the EU reached twenty, to review the composition and functioning of the institutions. Discussions began on 1 May 1999. This task was a challenging one as reallocation of power within the EU Institutions entailed that for every winner there would be an equivalent loser. The Treaty of Nice was finally signed on 11 December 2000, after over ninety hours of acrimonious, direct negotiations between the Heads of Government.[111]

The Treaty of Nice came into force on 2 February 2003.[112] Even within governmental circles, the agreement was seen as limited and unsatisfactory. The Member States announced that there would be another IGC in 2004 to consider the unresolved issues. Dissatisfaction concerned, first, the process. There was considerable unhappiness with the closed negotiations between governments which ran up against deadlines late into the night. This seemed neither an effective nor a democratic way to secure deep-seated institutional reforms.[113] Dissatisfaction focused, secondly, on the managerial ambitions of the reforms. They appeared too concerned with technical effectiveness and the accompanying institutional tinkering. This was seen as neither ambitious enough to equip the Union for the challenges it faced nor sufficient to engender the popular affinity necessary for the Union to sustain any kind of wider authority amongst its citizenry.

In 2000, at the Humboldt University in Berlin, Joschka Fischer, the German Foreign Minister, suggested that European integration had to have an endpoint, and this should be a European constitution.[114] A number of Heads of Government picked up on this,[115] and, in December 2001, at Laeken in Belgium, the Member States decided to abandon the traditional IGC process. A draft Treaty would be formulated by a Convention modelled on that used to draft the Charter. Furthermore, that Convention was to have big ambitions. It was to be one on the *Future of Europe*. Chaired by Valéry Giscard d'Estaing, the Convention opened in February 2002.[116] At its first session, Giscard indicated that the purpose of the Convention should be a single proposal opening the way for a Constitution for Europe.[117] Sixteen months later, he presented this proposal, the Draft Constitutional Treaty, with much pomp and fanfare to the Member States. The IGC following the Convention was short. The Member States made only one significant modification to the draft Constitutional Treaty, namely on the weighting of voting rights for national governments. The Constitutional Treaty was duly signed in Rome in October 2004.

---

[111] M. Gray and A. Stubb, 'The Treaty of Nice: Negotiating a Poisoned Chalice?' (2001) 39S *JCMS* 5.

[112] The delay was because a referendum in Ireland in June 2001 rejected it. A Declaration was added that nothing in EU law affected Irish military neutrality. This was the basis for a second referendum in Ireland which adopted the Treaty by 62.89% of the vote.

[113] Declaration 23 to the Treaty of Nice on the Future of the Union.

[114] J. Fischer, 'From Confederacy to Federation: Thoughts on the Finality of European Integration', Humboldt University, Berlin 12 May 2000, available at www.cvce.eu/en/obj/speech_by_joschka_fischer_on_the_ultimate_objective_of_european_integration_berlin_12_may_2000-en-4cd02fa7-d9d0-4cd2-91c9-2746a3297773.html.

[115] P. Norman, *The Accidental Constitution: The Story of the European Convention* (Brussels, Eurocomment, 2003) 11–24.

[116] For accounts of the Convention, in addition to Norman, *ibid.*, see G. Stuart, *The Making of Europe's Constitution* (London, Fabian Society, 2002); C. Closa, *Improving Constitutional Politics? A Preliminary Assessment of the Convention*, CONWEB Paper No. 1/2003; M. Kleine, 'Leadership in the European Convention' (2007) 14 *JEPP* 1227; D. Finke *et al.*, *Reforming the European Union: Realizing the Impossible* (New Jersey, Princeton University Press, 2012) chs. 2 and 3.

[117] P. Magnette, 'In the Name of Simplification: Coping with Constitutional Conflicts in the Convention on the Future of Europe' (2005) 11 *ELJ* 432, 436.

The Constitutional Treaty sought to establish the Union as an autonomous constitutional democracy. In addition to many institutional reforms, it thus included many of the symbols associated with national constitutional democracies. There was provision for a European Union flag, anthem, motto and holiday. Union instruments were now to be known as 'laws' or 'framework laws'. There was a primacy clause asserting the precedence of Union law over national law within the limits of the Treaty. A Bill of Rights of sorts was established with the incorporation of the Charter into the Treaty, and the Union was to have its own legal personality and Foreign Minister.

To mark this spirit of constitutional democratic renewal, ten Member States arranged for referenda to determine whether to ratify it.[118] The first referendum, held in Spain, approved the Constitutional Treaty. However, the next referenda, held in France (on 29 May 2005) and the Netherlands (three days later, on 1 June 2005), rejected the Treaty, with 55 per cent voting against it in France and 62 per cent voting against it in the Netherlands. Analysis of the reasons for the 'No' vote in the Netherlands and France showed the Constitutional Treaty had little hold or meaning for public debate, despite voters being reasonably well-informed.[119]

These referenda exposed the difficulties in the strategy behind the Constitutional Treaty. Processes of collective identity-formation, making people feel more European, are difficult to formulate. They rely on co-identification, solidarity and trust developing between Europeans. Within the national context, national identification is made easier by the cultural, economic and politico-administrative boundaries of most modern States reinforcing each other.[120] There is a *national* system of law and order, a *national* community with its own myths and symbols, a *national* welfare system, a *national* economy and a *national* administration. For better or worse, this reinforcement generates common identities, and, even then, as the fraught histories of many nation States illustrate, only some of the time. This is absent within the Union, and to imagine a convention in a hall in Brussels could establish it was highly optimistic. More telling, however, was the failure of the other strategy. It might be thought that, in the absence of a common identity, Europeans might still welcome the chance offered through institutional reform to engage with each other on matters of common concern. However, Europe's publics saw themselves as, at best, a chorus for the Constitutional Treaty, who were given the chance to comment on it, but, for many people, little more.[121]

(ii) The Lisbon Treaty

By the end of June 2005, European integration had reached an impasse. Eighteen Member States had ratified the Constitutional Treaty. Of the remaining seven Member States, six (Czech Republic, Denmark, Ireland, Poland, Portugal and the United Kingdom), were scheduled to hold referenda. There was a significant chance of a 'No' vote in all bar Portugal. The popular vote was out on the European Union, and there was a deep divide in which two-thirds of Member States wished to press ahead but one-third did not or could not.

---

[118] Luxembourg held a referendum after the Dutch and French referenda which approved the Constitutional Treaty. Other States due to hold a referendum were Czech Republic, Denmark, Ireland, Poland, Portugal and the United Kingdom.

[119] Flash Eurobarometer 171 and 172 – *European Constitution: Post-Referendum Survey in France and in The Netherlands.* This was all notwithstanding that 88% of the French and 82% of the Dutch still had positive perceptions of the Union in the period after the referendum. EC Commission, 'The Period of Reflection and Plan D', COM(2006) 212, 2.

[120] S. Bartolini, *Restructuring Europe: Centre Formation, System Building, and Political Structuring between the Nation State and the European Union* (Oxford University Press, 2005) 410.

[121] On this see Middelaar, n. 67 above, 273–4 and 289–91.

In March 2007, at the fiftieth anniversary of the Treaty of Rome, the German Government obtained a commitment from the other Member States to place 'the European Union on a renewed common basis before the European Parliament elections in 2009'.[122] In other words, Member States committed to a new treaty. The process was very different from that for the Constitutional Treaty. Agreement was to be reached on the main points in confidential negotiations between Ministries, which would set out a mandate for an IGC. The starting point for discussions was the Constitutional Treaty with negotiations simply to be about what would make a revised treaty acceptable to those national governments constituting the recalcitrant third. Limited by this mandate, the tasks of the latter would be restricted to translating the political agreement into legal detail and resolving any ambiguities. The Heads of Government met between 21 and 23 June 2007 to conclude the first stage of the process: a sixteen-page mandate for the IGC. On 13 December 2007, the new text, the Treaty of Lisbon, was formally signed.

There was a lack of transparency about this process and an exclusion of national parliaments, which was never justified. Insofar as much of the substance of the Lisbon Treaty replicated the Constitutional Treaty, it opened negotiators to charges of arrogance for ignoring the referenda results in France and the Netherlands[123] and begged questions as to why referenda were not held in those States, which had promised referenda for the Constitutional Treaty. For only one State, Ireland, was to hold a referendum on the Lisbon Treaty.

The strategies informing the Lisbon Treaty differed from those preceding the Single European Act and the Treaties of Maastricht and Amsterdam. There was no significant attempt to add significant new competences under the umbrella of some flagship polices such as the single market, euro or the AFSJ. Instead, the material benefits supplied by European integration (the Roman strategy) were to be enhanced by consolidating EU competencies, setting them out more clearly but also, if possible, bringing them within a unitary supranational system. The constitutional concept was also dropped, along with the references to a pan-European flag, anthem, motto and holiday. There was, thus, little attempt at trying to make people feel more European (the German strategy). Instead, the central concern was to improve the quality of EU lawmaking and government (the Greek strategy) through formalising more clearly the range of EU powers, anchoring the EU more clearly around democratic values, and institutional reform.

(a) The Consolidation of EU Competencies and Two Treaties of Equal Value: The Treaty on European Union and the Treaty on the Functioning of the European Union

The Lisbon Treaty sought to set out what the Union was, what it did and how it did it in a manner that was both more visible and easier to understand. To that end, two treaties, the TEU and the TFEU were to replace the previous framework.[124] Each treaty was to have 'the same legal value'.[125]

---

[122] EU Council, *Declaration on the Occasion of the Fiftieth Anniversary of the Signature of the Treaty of Rome* (Brussels, 25 March 2007), para. 3.

[123] For a thoughtful comparison see House of Commons, *EU Reform: A New Treaty or an Old Constitution* (2007, Research Paper, 07/64, House of Commons, London).

[124] On the Treaty of Lisbon see House of Lords European Union Committee, *The Treaty of Lisbon: An Impact Assessment*, 10th Report, Session 2007–8; P. Craig, *The Lisbon Treaty: Law, Politics and Treaty Reform* (Oxford University Press, 2010); J.-C. Piris, *The Lisbon Treaty: A Legal and Political Analysis* (Cambridge University Press, 2010); D. Ashiagbor *et al.* (eds.), *The European Union after the Treaty of Lisbon* (Cambridge University Press, 2012).

[125] Article 1(2) TFEU.

The central items set out by the TEU are:

- the mission and values of the European Union: respect for the rule of law, the principle of limited powers, respect for national identities, democracy and fundamental rights
- the contribution of national parliaments to the functioning of the European Union
- the composition and central functions of the EU Institutions
- some of the Union's central policies in its external relations: a common foreign and security policy; common security and defence policy; and neighbourhood policy to develop special relations with nearby countries
- procedures for amendment of the two Treaties
- legal personality for the Union
- the circumstances in which a Member State may be admitted to the Union and when they may leave it.

The TFEU sets out the explicit competencies of the Union in all fields other than mentioned above on external relations, and the detailed institutional procedures to be used in each field. The competencies are catalogued at the beginning of the TFEU.[126]

Article 3 TFEU

(1) The Union shall have exclusive competence in the following areas:
    (a) customs union;
    (b) the establishing of the competition rules necessary for the functioning of the internal market;
    (c) monetary policy for the Member States whose currency is the euro;
    (d) the conservation of marine biological resources under the common fisheries policy;
    (e) common commercial policy.
(2) The Union shall also have exclusive competence for the conclusion of an international agreement when its conclusion is provided for in a legislative act of the Union or is necessary to enable the Union to exercise its internal competence, or insofar as its conclusion may affect common rules or alter their scope.

Article 4 TFEU

(1) The Union shall share competence with the Member States where the Treaties confer on it a competence which does not relate to the areas referred to in Articles 3 and 6.
(2) Shared competence between the Union and the Member States applies in the following principal areas:
    (a) internal market;
    (b) social policy, for the aspects defined in this Treaty;
    (c) economic, social and territorial cohesion;
    (d) agriculture and fisheries, excluding the conservation of marine biological resources;
    (e) environment;
    (f) consumer protection;
    (g) transport;
    (h) trans-European networks;
    (i) energy;

---

[126] On the implications of exclusive and shared competence see pp. 210–12.

(j) area of freedom, security and justice;

(k) common safety concerns in public health matters, for the aspects defined in this Treaty.

(3) In the areas of research, technological development and space, the Union shall have competence to carry out activities, in particular to define and implement programmes; however, the exercise of that competence shall not result in Member States being prevented from exercising theirs.

(4) In the areas of development cooperation and humanitarian aid, the Union shall have competence to carry out activities and conduct a common policy; however, the exercise of that competence shall not result in Member States being prevented from exercising theirs.

Article 5 TFEU

(1) The Member States shall coordinate their economic policies within the Union. To this end, the Council shall adopt measures, in particular broad guidelines for these policies. Specific provisions shall apply to those Member States whose currency is the euro.

(2) The Union shall take measures to ensure coordination of the employment policies of the Member States, in particular by defining guidelines for these policies.

(3) The Union may take initiatives to ensure coordination of Member States' social policies.

Article 6 TFEU

The Union shall have competence to carry out actions to support, coordinate or supplement the actions of the Member States. The areas of such action shall, at European level, be:

(a) protection and improvement of human health;

(b) industry;

(c) culture;

(d) tourism;

(e) education, vocational training, youth and sport;

(f) civil protection;

(g) administrative cooperation.

The Lisbon Treaty was not simply about setting out more clearly what the Union was and did. It also involved a significant extension of supranational disciplines to activities. In part, this was done through the establishment of new formal competencies in the fields of energy, intellectual property, space, humanitarian aid, sport, civil protection and climate change. However, the Union already undertook a number of measures in these fields under the umbrella of other competences. Much more significant was the bringing of policing and judicial cooperation in criminal matters within the aegis of the TFEU. Prior to the Lisbon Treaty, this field had been handled predominantly intergovernmentally. Incorporating it within the TFEU meant that this highly sensitive field, which went to how States policed their territories as well as a host of related civil liberties issues, was now to governed supranationally, and was, in principle, no different from any of the other areas of competence set out in the TFEU.

(b) The Lisbon Treaty and the Pursuit of Democratic Values

The Lisbon Treaty was also notable for anchoring Union identity much more tightly around a European heritage of democratic values. This is done in the first substantive provision of the TEU.

Article 2 TEU

The Union is founded on the values of respect for human dignity, freedom, democracy, equality, the rule of law and respect for human rights, including the rights of persons belonging to minorities. These values are common to the Member States in a society in which pluralism, non-discrimination, tolerance, justice, solidarity and equality between women and men prevail.

This shift was significant. The Union committed itself to giving the Charter the same legal value as the TEU and the TFEU, albeit that it was not to be used to expand the competences of the Union, and to acceding to the European Convention for the Protection of Human Rights and Fundamental Freedoms.[127] In addition, there was a stronger commitment to both citizenship and democracy.

Article 9 TEU

In all its activities, the Union shall observe the principle of the equality of its citizens, who shall receive equal attention from its institutions, bodies, offices and agencies.

Every national of a Member State shall be a citizen of the Union. Citizenship of the Union shall be additional to national citizenship and shall not replace it.

Article 10 TEU

(1) The functioning of the Union shall be founded on representative democracy.
(2) Citizens are directly represented at Union level in the European Parliament. Member States are represented in the European Council by their Heads of State or Government and in the Council by their governments, themselves democratically accountable either to their national Parliaments, or to their citizens.
(3) Every citizen shall have the right to participate in the democratic life of the Union. Decisions shall be taken as openly and as closely as possible to the citizen.
(4) Political parties at European level contribute to forming European political awareness and to expressing the will of citizens of the Union.

This had to be seen alongside the consolidation of the Union's supranational qualities. The Union now had the power to govern a whole host of areas supranationally, which often raised questions that were politically sensitive and involved significant civil liberties issues. These included social policy, many tax and family law matters, data protection, immigration, criminal justice, extradition, asylum and refugee policy. This raised questions over who has most authority to determine the meaning of these values. For their content will both go to important questions

---

[127] Article 6 TEU.

about what the Union and Member States are about, and will shape the content of these sensitive policies. It also raised questions about what the Union should do when other settlements claimed to be able to protect these values better than it.

The Lisbon Treaty adopted similar strategies to those used with previous treaties.

It set out, first, a common view on how a number of politically sensitive areas were to be addressed. National security was to remain the sole responsibility of each Member State. Nothing was to affect the competence of Member States to provide, commission or organise non-economic services of a general interest; namely, services seen as particularly important to citizens (such as the railways, the water or the post) which may not be provided without public intervention. A national government could insist that if an EU measure touched fundamental aspects of their social security or criminal justice systems, it should be discussed by the Heads of Government within the European Council. Following rejection of the Lisbon Treaty by Irish voters in June 2008, further guarantees were added.[128] EU law was not to prejudice the security and defence policy of any Member State, provide for the creation of a European army or conscription, or affect a State's right to decide whether or not to participate in a military operation.

Secondly, differentiated obligations were provided for States who felt that these common solutions did not sufficiently accommodate their interests and values. The right of the United Kingdom and Ireland to decide whether to participate or not in EU laws being adopted in the area of freedom, security and justice was extended to cover laws governing policing and judicial cooperation in criminal justice. The Charter was not to *extend* the ability of any court to declare Polish or British measures incompatible with EU fundamental rights law. As these States had particular concerns about the development of EU social rights, Title IV of the Charter, the section where most of these rights were set out, was only justiciable in these States insofar as they were provided for in national law. Finally, nothing in EU law was to affect the rights to life, protection of the family or to education as set out in the Irish Constitution.

However, these strategies were insufficient for the German Constitutional Court. It was particularly concerned that EU law should not be allowed to have the last word on when something was democratic or not and that the Union should be able to take over fields of activity where concerns about democracy were particularly acute, and national settlements might be able to claim that they could govern more democratically than the European Union.

These issues came to the fore when it was asked to rule on the compatibility of the Lisbon Treaty with the German Basic Law, Germany's constitutional document.

---

2 BvE 2/08 *Treaty of Lisbon*, **Judgment of 30 June 2009**

216 The principle of democracy may not be balanced against other legal interests; it is inviolable. The constituent power of the Germans which gave itself the Basic Law wanted to set an insurmountable boundary to any future political development.

217 It may remain open whether, due to the universal nature of dignity, freedom and equality alone, this commitment even applies to the constituent power, i.e. to the case that the German people, in free

---

[128] 53.4% of voters rejected the Lisbon Treaty, initially in 2008. A series of guarantees were offered which were only formally adopted into EU law when Croatia acceded in 2013: Protocol on the Concerns of the Irish People on the Treaty of Lisbon, OJ 2013, L 60/131. A second referendum was held on the basis of these guarantees in October 2009 in which 67.1% of voters voted for the Lisbon Treaty.

self-determination, but in a continuity of legality to the rule of the Basic Law, gives itself a new constitution . . . the structural principles of the state laid down in . . . the Basic Law, i.e. democracy, the rule of law, the principle of the social state, the republic, the federal state, as well as the substance of elementary fundamental rights indispensable for the respect of human dignity are, in any case, not amenable to any amendment because of their fundamental quality . . .

248 The safeguarding of sovereignty, demanded by the principle of democracy in the valid constitutional system prescribed by the Basic Law in a manner that is open to integration and to international law, does not mean that a pre-determined number or certain types of sovereign rights should remain in the hands of the state . . .

249 European unification on the basis of a treaty union of sovereign states may, however, not be achieved in such a way that not sufficient space is left to the Member States for the political formation of the economic, cultural and social living conditions. This applies in particular to areas which shape the citizens' living conditions, in particular the private sphere of their own responsibility and of political and social security, protected by fundamental rights, as well as to political decisions that rely especially on cultural, historical and linguistic perceptions and which develop in public discourse in the party political and parliamentary sphere of public politics. Essential areas of democratic formative action comprise, *inter alia*, citizenship, the civil and the military monopoly on the use of force, revenue and expenditure including external financing and all elements of encroachment that are decisive for the realisation of fundamental rights, above all in major encroachments on fundamental rights such as deprivation of liberty in the administration of criminal law or placement in an institution. These important areas also include cultural issues such as the disposition of language, the shaping of circumstances concerning the family and education, the ordering of the freedom of opinion, press and of association and the dealing with the profession of faith or ideology.

250 . . . Democracy first and foremost lives on, and in, a viable public opinion that concentrates on central acts of determination of political direction and the periodic allocation of highest-ranking political offices in the competition of government and opposition. Only this public opinion shows the alternatives for elections and other votes and continually calls them to mind also in decisions relating to individual issues in order that they may remain continuously present and effective in the political opinion-formation of the people via the parties, which are open to participation for all citizens, and in the public information area. To this extent, . . . the Basic Law also protect(s) the connection between political decisions on facts and the will of the majority constituted by elections, and the resulting dualism between government and opposition in a system of a multiplicity of competing parties and of observing and controlling formation of public opinion.

251 Even if due to the great successes of European integration, a common European polity that engages in issue related cooperation in the relevant areas of their respective states is visibly growing . . . it cannot be overlooked, however, that the public perception of factual issues and of political leaders remains connected to a considerable extent to patterns of identification related to the nation state, language, history and culture. The principle of democracy . . . therefore require(s) factually to restrict the transfer and exercise of sovereign powers to the European Union in a predictable manner, particularly in central political areas of the space of personal development and the shaping of living conditions by social policy.

If the Lisbon Treaty was an attempt to carve out a stronger democratic identity for the Union, through requiring stronger respect for democratic values or establishing more democratic processes, this judgment is quite damning. It suggests that, for many significant tasks, the Union has neither the necessary democratic pedigree nor the democratic qualities. In this, it was very much a precursor of the contestation that was to rain down on the Union in the subsequent decade. However, its ring-fencing of certain fields of activity from Union authority was also a precursor of other things to come, namely the intolerance and authoritarianism that were to beset Europe. For its limits on Union authority are premised on domestic processes both being democratic and on EU law being unable to augment the quality of domestic democratic life by either being an effective curb on undemocratic behaviour or through opening up new avenues for citizen involvement or ways of seeing things.[129]

(c) Lisbon and the Recasting of the Union Public Sphere

The central thrust of the Lisbon Treaty was institutional reform. QMV was extended to about fifty new areas. Beyond this, the central reforms were dominated by three trends. First, there was provision for greater parliamentary involvement. The ordinary legislative procedure was applied to a further forty areas. National parliaments were given additional time to consider EU legislative proposals and powers to review, although not veto, EU legislative proposals for compliance with the subsidiarity principle, the principle that only allows EU measures to be adopted if their objectives cannot be sufficiently achieved by unilateral Member State action and can, instead, be better realised through Union action. Secondly, Lisbon reformed the EU Institutions. Most centrally, a new method for weighing QMV within the Council was adopted, which looked both at the number of States adopting a measure and at their respective populations. Also, the European Council was given a more central Treaty role as a political agenda-setter. To consolidate this role, a new President of the European Council was established to drive forward and prepare its work. A further institutional innovation was made to strengthen the Union's profile and cohesion in the field of foreign policy: the High Representative. A member of both the Council and the Commission, her duty is to represent the Union in matters relating to the common foreign and security policy and ensure the consistency of the Union's external action. The final theme was greater citizen engagement. A citizens' initiative was established whereby the Commission is obliged to consider proposals for legal measures made by petitions of 1 million citizens coming from at least seven Member States.

7 THE EUROPEAN UNION AND THE ERA OF CRISIS

The Lisbon Treaty duly entered into force on 1 December 2009. Any thoughts that the Treaty marked a new equilibrium for European integration were blown away by the onset of the sovereign debt crisis, which began in October 2009. This date heralded the beginning of a period in which European Union politics was characterised by a series of crises which were of a different order from anything before. To be sure, EU policies, notably its agricultural policies, had provoked significant social conflicts and political protest since the early 1970s.[130] However, the conflicts emerging since 2009 combined a volatile mix of elements. They involved, first, challenges to EU policies, which were not confined to a particular sector, but were seen as affecting national territories more widely. Protests usually involved a far wider array of national

---

[129] See the debate between F. Mayer, 'Rashomon in Karlsruhe: A Reflection on Democracy and Identity in the European Union: The German Constitutional Court's Lisbon Decision and the Changing Landscape of European Constitutionalism' (2011) 9 *I-CON* 757; K. Nicolaidis, 'Germany as Europe: How the Constitutional Court Unwittingly Embraced EU Demoi-cracy: A Comment on Franz Mayer' (2011) 9 *I-CON* 786.

[130] D. Imig and S. Tarrow, 'Studying Contention in an Emerging Polity' in D. Imig and S. Tarrow (eds.), *Contentious Europeans: Protest and Politics in an Emerging Polity* (Lanham, Rowman & Littlefield, 2001); C. Roederer-Rynning, 'Farm Conflict in France and the Europeanisation of Agricultural Policy' (2002) 25 *WEP* 105.

actors and had a far higher political salience than previously. Secondly, protest took aim not only at EU policies but at the central institutions of national government. Traditional political parties, national representative institutions and the capacity of national administrations were put in question in a way that, certainly in Western Europe, had not happened in recent times.[131] Thirdly, the EU as a whole rather than particular institutions or actors was blamed for the consequences of these policies.[132] This led to a questioning of the need for European integration in many Member States, which reached its zenith with the United Kingdom vote to leave the European Union in June 2016. Fourthly, this political contestation generated crisis for the European Union not simply because of the social divisions and lack of trust in government that it exposed but also because, as this piece below illustrates, it has stretched the capacities of the EU settlement to deal with the problems in hand.[133]

C. Offe, 'Europe Entrapped: Does the EU Have the Political Capacity to Overcome its Current Crisis?' (2013) 19 *European Law Journal* 595, 610

We face a deep divorce between politics and policy: On the one hand, there is often populist mass politics (including identity-related 'culture wars') that has no perceptible implication for policy making on citizens' core interests and bread-and-butter issues. On the other, there is elitist policy making that has no roots in, no links to, nor legitimation through politics. This is the deepening bifurcation of those two spheres within the European polity. Political elites are increasingly unable to achieve outcomes that voters desire and to convince voters that their interests are in their, the elites', trustworthy and competent hands. What voters need and want is beyond the capacity of the political system to deliver, without the latter being able to explain the former what the hindrances are, and how they might be removed. It is as if one has mail ordered a shirt and is supplied a pair of socks. The promises and appeals by which political power is acquired (ie politics) are disjointed, under the dictate of financial markets, from the purposes to the achievement of which power resources mandated to governments are effectively employed and used for the making of policies.

To this situation, elites (as well as commentators and academic observers) respond by diagnosing and complaining about an emerging condition of 'ungovernability.' Non-elites feel cheated and follow the appeals of ever shriller and ever more antipolitical forms of fundamental opposition campaigns, such as that of Grillo in Italy who, right after winning a spectacular quarter of the popular vote in the February 2013 national elections, gleefully predicted that the Italian Republic's disintegration and exit from the Euro zone within a matter of six months due to its manifest fiscal starvation.

---

[131] K. Armingeon and K. Guthman, 'Democracy in Crisis? The Declining Support for National Democracy in European Countries, 2007–2011' (2014) 53 *EJPR* 423; H. Kriesi and L. Morlino, 'Conclusion: What Have We Learnt and Where Do We Go from Here?' in M. Ferrin and H. Kriesi (eds.), *How Europeans View and Evaluate Democracy* (Oxford University Press, 2016); W. Merkel and S. Kneip (eds.), *Democracy and Crisis: Challenges in Turbulent Times* (Cham, Springer, 2018); H. Kriesi, 'The Implications of the Euro Crisis for Democracy' (2018) 25 *JEPP* 59.

[132] S. Hobolt and J. Tilley, *Blaming Europe? Responsibility without Accountability in the European Union* (Oxford University Press, 2018).

[133] These issues were explored in greater depth in C. Offe, *Europe Entrapped* (Cambridge, Polity, 2015). For similar views see F. Scharpf, 'The Costs of Non-Disintegration: The Case of the European Monetary Union' in D. Chalmers, M. Jachtenfuchs and C. Joerges (eds.), *The End of the Eurocrats' Dream: Adjusting to European Diversity* (Cambridge University Press, 2016); W. Streeck, 'Europe under Merkel IV: Balance of Impotence' (2018) II(2) *American Affairs* 162.

(i) The Sovereign Debt Crisis

The origins of the sovereign debt crisis lay in staggering losses incurred by financial institutions as a result of fall in the price of United States housing from 2006 onwards.[134] The International Monetary Fund (IMF) estimated that write-downs on bad debts incurred by these between 2007 and 2010 were $4.1 trillion.[135] This led to the collapse of a large US bank, Lehman Brothers, in autumn 2008, which threatened, briefly, to bring the global financial system down. This shock, in turn, generated a number of threats to European Union governments' public finances. First, lending not only slowed as there was less capital, it was also redirected. Lenders re-evaluated traditional low-risk investments, such as national government debt. The consequence was that the cost of borrowing increased for governments whose public finances were perceived as weak. Secondly, the general reduction in lending led to a shrivelling of the economy, and consequently tax receipts, putting further pressure on public finances. This was particularly so for economies that relied heavily on the financial sector and expansive lending by it to sectors such as property. Thirdly, many States had to bail out a number of their commercial banks to prevent these going bankrupt, with catastrophic consequences for their economies.[136]

The first States to experience difficulties were outside the euro area. Latvia and Hungary had to seek financial support from the IMF and the European Union in 2008, with Romania doing likewise in 2009. The sovereign debt crisis only became a pan-Union crisis in October 2009 when the new Greek Government announced that its budget deficit for 2009 was not 3.7 per cent of GDP, as previously stated, but 12.5 per cent.[137] This led to lenders having increasing doubts about Greece's ability to repay its debts. By May 2010 its bonds had been rated by all major agencies as having junk status, with the consequence that it could no longer borrow on capital markets to sustain its public finances.

The central institutional responses to the crisis were to unfold over the next five years. They took three central forms. First, arrangements were put in place to offer financial guarantees to euro area States who could no longer sustain their public finances and sought financial support. Secondly, a series of EU disciplines governing public finances and economic performance were put in place with a view to prevent future crises of this sort. Thirdly, the European Central Bank was granted an increasing number of powers to manage economic performance within the euro area and protect it against future financial risks.

(a) Emergency Politics and the Salvaging of Euro Area Finances

Faced with the prospect of the Greek Government defaulting on its debts in May 2010, the European Union and IMF agreed to underwrite its debts up to €110 billion. By that date, however, it was already clear that Greece was unlikely to be the only State experiencing difficulties financing its public debt. A number of vehicles were created to provide support for States in this situation.[138]

---

[134] More detailed discussion of the response to the crisis is in Ch. 15.

[135] IMF, *Global Financial Stability Report: Responding to the Financial Crisis and Measuring Systemic Risks, April 2009* (Washington, IMF, 2009) 30.

[136] By 2012, the Commission estimated that €4.5 trillion had been spent rescuing banks in the EU. European Commission, 'A Roadmap towards a Banking Union', COM(2012)510, 3.

[137] European Commission, 'Report on Greek Government Debt and Deficit Statistics', COM(2010)1.

[138] The European Financial Stability Facility (EFSF) was established as an intergovernmental arrangement between the euro area States, www.esm.europa.eu/efsf-overview. The other was Regulation 407/2010/EU establishing a European Financial Stabilisation Mechanism, OJ 2010, L 118/1.

These were consolidated into a process, the European Stability Mechanism (ESM) in October 2012.[139] Established as a private company in Luxembourg by two treaties, one in 2011 and the other in 2012, the ESM could offer guarantees of up to €500 billion to States who sought these to sustain their public finances. Any offer of guarantees was conditional, however, on the State in question agreeing a Memorandum of Understanding (MOU) with the ESM which would set out conditions to be met to restore (in the ESM's eyes) its public finances. Invariably, these included a mixture of privatisations, tax increases, cuts in public spending, administrative reform, and measures to improve tax collection.

Between 2010 and 2015, five States sought support from the ESM: Greece, Ireland, Portugal, Spain and Cyprus.[140] Whilst this support, in all cases, prevented all these States defaulting on their debts, with all the unpredictable consequences that this would have entailed, the conditions imposed by the MoU were associated with a number of negative consequences.

First, they imposed considerable social hardship as a result of the restrictions on public spending and increases in taxes imposed. Unemployment, for example, went up in Greece, the country hardest hit, from 7.8% in 2008 to 27.5% in 2013, with over 23% of Greeks not having any health insurance in 2014.[141] The number of Greeks living in or at risk of poverty went up from 19% in 2008 to just under 45% in 2013, with social protection benefits for families declining by 25% between 2009 and 2012.[142] Secondly, there was a perception that these conditions were being imposed upon the poorer southern States by the richer northern States in the euro area. Power lay with the latter as they were not only providing the financial support but could set the terms under which it was offered. This inevitably meant that they set out the model of recovery that States receiving support should follow.[143] Thirdly, recipient States were told that they had to accept the terms of support as the consequences would otherwise be too dramatic.[144] This characterisation of the situation – as an emergency which required one to do whatever it takes – led to a corresponding marginalisation of the constitutional processes and democratic politics of these States.[145]

(b) The Disciplining of Fiscal and Economic Governance: The 'Six-Pack' and the Fiscal Compact

The second style of institutional response was to address the perceived origins of the crisis. In October 2010, a Task Force chaired by the President of the European Council, Herman van

---

[139] See www.esm.europa.eu/; M. Ruffert, 'The European Debt Crisis and EU law' (2011) 48 *CMLRev* 1790.

[140] All States have now exited the ESM with the exception of Greece.

[141] A. Kentikelenis, 'Bailouts, Austerity and the Erosion of Health Coverage in Southern Europe and Ireland' (2015) 25 *EJPub Health* 365.

[142] G. Kaplanoglou and V. Rapanos, 'Evolutions in Consumption Inequality and Poverty in Greece: The Impact of the Crisis and Austerity Policies' (2018) 64 *Review of Income and Wealth* 105.

[143] U. Beck, *German Europe* (Cambridge, Polity, 2013) 62 *et seq.*; S. Bulmer, 'Germany and the Eurozone Crisis: Between Hegemony and Domestic Politics' (2014) 37 *WEP* 1244; M. Schoeller, 'Providing Political Leadership? Three Case Studies on Germany's Ambiguous Role in the Eurozone Crisis' (2017) 24 *JEPP* 1.

[144] J. White, 'Emergency Europe' (2015) 63 *Political Studies* 300; M. Matthijs, 'Integration at What Price? The Erosion of National Democracy in the Euro Periphery' (2017) 52 *Government and Opposition* 266.

[145] On the constitutional litigation generated by this see C. Kilpatrick, 'On the Rule of Law and Economic Emergency: The Degradation of Basic Legal Values in Europe's Bailouts' (2015) 35 *OJLS* 325; D. Chalmers, 'Crisis Reconfiguration of the European Constitutional State' in D. Chalmers, M. Jachtenfuchs and C. Joerges (eds.), *The End of the Eurocrats' Dream: Adjusting to European Diversity* (Cambridge University Press, 2016).

Rompuy, and comprising all EU Finance Ministers identified these as insufficient budgetary discipline by the Member States, a lack of competitiveness in a number of national economies, and several States having imbalanced economies which were, thus, over-exposed to external economic risks.[146] The Task Force's report formed the basis for the 'six-pack': six EU laws, adopted in November 2011, which consolidated EU oversight of domestic fiscal and economic policy-making around three central goals.[147] First, States should avoid *excessive deficits*. To that end, they should avoid budget deficits of more than 3 per cent of GDP and bring their total debt down to 60 per cent of GDP.[148] Secondly, States should strive for *balanced budgets*. In principle, taking account of the place of the State on the economic cycle, only a small budget deficit should be incurred. Finally, they should avoid *excessive macroeconomic imbalances* through excessive reliance on industries or sectors that were vulnerable to external shocks.

The six-pack also included laws to monitor States' performance and to sanction euro area States. However, Germany pushed for a further Treaty amendment, whose central provision would be a new balanced budget rule. This would require euro area States to have an annual structural deficit of not greater than 0.5 per cent of GDP in the case of States with total debt of more than 60 per cent and 1 per cent in the case of States whose total debt was lower than that.[149] Furthermore, this balanced budget rule was to be enshrined in a permanent and binding domestic law preferably of a constitutional nature. The Treaty, informally known as the fiscal compact, was intended to be a formal amendment to the TFEU. However, in December 2011, the British and Czech governments indicated that they were not willing to sign it. It was, therefore signed as an international treaty, the Treaty on Stability, Coordination and Governance in the Economic and Monetary Union (TSCG), by twenty-five States in January 2012, and entered into force on 1 January 2013.[150]

This regime puts in place a pan-Union system of fiscal retrenchment and welfare reform. As a strategy for economic recovery, it was not uncontroversial with critics arguing, in particular, that it ignored the different ways euro area States generate economic growth,[151] was unlikely to reduce debt[152] and unduly impeded effective State intervention in the economy.[153] However, the disciplines put in place set out an orthodoxy which national parliaments were required to follow and which left little room for democratic consideration of alternatives.[154]

---

[146] *Strengthening Economic Governance in The EU: Report of The Task Force to the European Council, October 2010*: www.consilium.europa.eu/uedocs/cms_data/docs/pressdata/en/ec/117236.pdf.

[147] This is explored in more detail on pp. 667–77.

[148] A budget deficit is the gap between government revenue and government expenditure in a single year.

[149] A structural deficit adjusts the calculation of the budget deficit for where a State is in the economic cycle. In times of boom, this requires states to run surpluses. It can incur greater deficits at moments of recession because of the reduction in tax receipts and increases in spending.

[150] Croatia has also since signed the treaty. On the details see P. Craig, 'The Stability, Coordination and Governance Treaty: Principle, Politics and Pragmatism' (2012) 37 *ELRev* 231.

[151] P. Hall, 'Varieties of Capitalism and the Euro Crisis' (2014) 37 *WEP* 1223. However compare T. Iversen, D. Soskice and D. Hope, 'The Eurozone and Political Economic Institution' (2016) 19 *Annual Review of Political Science* 163.

[152] P. de Grauwe, 'The Legacy of the Eurozone Crisis and How to Overcome It' (2016) 39 *Journal of Empirical Finance* 147.

[153] Scharpf, n. 133 above.

[154] In like vein, W. Streeck, 'Heller, Schmitt and the Euro' (2015) 21 *ELJ* 361; I. Sánchez-Cuenca, 'From a Deficit of Democracy to a Technocratic Order: The Post Crisis Debate on Europe' (2017) 20 *Annual Review of Political Science* 351; C. Bonefeld, 'Authoritarian Liberalism: From Schmitt via Ordoliberalism to the Euro' (2017) 43 *Critical Sociology* 747.

M. Wilkinson, 'The Specter of Authoritarian Liberalism: Reflections on the Constitutional Crisis of the European Union' (2013) 14 *German Law Journal* 527, 551–2

The question of how far, for example, to socialize the economy is largely excluded from the realm of our democratic collective choices, even if imposed wholesale, in an executive manner, in order to rescue financial institutions deemed essential to the capitalist economy. The characterization of the current market liberalism in the EU as authoritarian is strongly confirmed by the language typically used in its support: '[T]here is no alternative' to monetary union. The Euro cannot fail, we are told; the consequences would be too grim for all concerned and would signal the end of the EU itself. What we are now offered by the political Messianism of European elites is not integration through law, let alone integration through concrete achievements of actual solidarity, but integration through necessity.

The point about such eschatological sentiment is that if there is truly 'no alternative,' then why bother going through the motions of political democracy at all? Beyond the instrumental utility for those in power of even a sham constitution attaining a certain level of unreflective popular support in order to increase compliance, democratic politics becomes superfluous in these circumstances. Necessity tranquilizes politics in an atmosphere where decision has become more important than judgment.

Instead of encouraging the building of a strong democracy, authoritarian liberalism is content with a weak, deracinated public, one that can be better managed and controlled by the technocratic and political elites at national and supranational level. The emergence of what might be termed a novel form of supranational Machtstaat favors, in other words, no more than a partial democracy, and is content with a limited one, in which any transnational elements of political democracy, or solidarity beyond the market are tamed, if not erased. Publics, to the extent they survive the onslaught of austerity measures, are pitted against each other rather than against the ruling elites. Core is pitted against periphery, nation against nation; it is, as certain political leaders now urge in the climate of economic austerity, sink or swim.

(c) The Increasing Government of the Euro Area by the European Central Bank

Prior to the sovereign debt crisis, the European Central Bank's central role had been authorising the printing of euros and the setting of short-term interest rates. This changed in three significant ways.

First, the bank became a lender of last resort. It soon became clear that the guarantees offered by the ESM and the instruments prior to it were insufficient to generate confidence in a number of euro area economies. From May 2010 onwards, the European Central Bank (ECB) had to intervene repeatedly to purchase securities of euro area States without which these States would have gone bankrupt.[155] Fed up with these *ad hoc* interventions, the ECB announced the establishment of the Outright Monetary Transactions (OMT) programme in September 2012.[156] It would purchase unlimited amounts of Member State securities if markets refused to purchase these, but only for States who had agreed an MoU with the ESM. For such States, it would lend to them when nobody else would, but only these were subject to the draconian conditions of an ESM programme.[157]

---

[155] Decision 2010/5/ECB establishing a securities markets programme, OJ 2010, L 124/8. The States benefiting from intervention were Italy, Greece, Spain, Portugal and Ireland.

[156] www.ecb.int/press/pr/date/2012/html/pr120906_1.en.html.   [157] OMT has so far not been used.

Secondly, the ECB was transformed into one of the world's most powerful financial regulators. The impetus was concerns about the fragility of the euro area banking system. There were concerns that many banks were barely solvent and that if a large bank went bust that this might threaten not just that bank's national banking system but also the banking system in the euro area and beyond. In 2013, the Single Supervisory Mechanism was established.[158] This put the ECB directly in charge of supervising the 118 most significant banks in the euro area, who controlled over 80 per cent of its banking assets.[159] Other banks were to be supervised by their respective national authorities but these were now to be coordinated by the ECB.

The third role is that of stimulating the wider economy. In a number of other jurisdictions, notably Japan, the United Kingdom and the United States, central banks engaged in large-scale purchases of assets from financial institutions. This was intended to restore the balance sheets of these institutions and, in turn, provide them with more capital to lend to help stimulate the wider economy. Whilst the ECB had engaged in some purchases of assets, this was limited compared to other banks. This changed in January 2015. Disturbed by the very weak levels of growth in the euro area, the ECB announced that it was establishing a 'public sector assets purchasing programme' (PSPP) under which it would be purchasing €60 billion of assets per month.[160] Intended initially for eighteen months, these purchases were continued and the programme only finished at the end of 2018.

There are concerns about the way that these powers have been acquired and the checks and balances on their use. The decisions to act as a lender of last resort and stimulate the euro area economy were taken, unilaterally, by the ECB. There was no democratic input into them and few practical legal controls on their operation.[161] The powers are also extremely wide-ranging, arguably more so than the traditional one of authorising the printing of money. This has led to concerns that the ECB was engaging in a power grab. This was raised before the German Constitutional Court. In 2014, it expressed a tentative view that the OMT programme might be illegal because, *inter alia*, the ECB did not have the powers to adopt such a programme.[162] After the Court of Justice set out limits on how the programme was to be run, the German court accepted the legality of the programme on this basis.[163] It was not so generous about the PSPP programme, ruling in 2016 that this programme was something that clearly exceeded the ECB's powers.[164] The Court of Justice has yet to respond, and the German Constitutional Court will, in turn, respond to that. How this plays out is likely to shape who makes economic policy in the euro area for the foreseeable future.

---

[158] On the political dynamics see R. Epstein and M. Rhodes, 'The Political Dynamics behind Europe's New Banking Union' (2016) 39 *WEP* 415; G. Glöckler, J. Lindner and M. Salines, 'Explaining the Sudden Creation of a Banking Supervisor for the Euro Area' (2017) 24 *JEPP* 1135.

[159] The Single Supervisory Mechanism is complemented by the Single Resolution Mechanism. This came into being on 1 January 2016, and established a Resolution Board (outside the aegis of the ECB) to manage the orderly winding-up of any significant bank which is about to fail. See p. 692.

[160] Decision 2015/774 on a secondary markets public sector asset purchase programme, OJ 2015, L 121/20.

[161] N. Scicluna, 'Integration through the Disintegration of Law? The ECB and EU constitutionalism in the Crisis' (2017) *JEPP*, early publication online

[162] 2 BvR 2728/13 *ESM/OMT I*, Judgment of 14 January 2014 (German Constitutional Court).

[163] *Gauweiler*, C-62/14, EU:C:2015:400; 2 BvR 2728/13 *ESM/OMT II*, Judgment of 21 June 2016.

[164] 2BvR 859/15 *PSPP*, Order of 15 August 2017 (German Constitutional Court).

(ii) Brexit

(a) The 2016 Referendum to Leave the European Union

The immediate history of the United Kingdom's decision to leave the European Union (Brexit) begins with the decision of the Labour government not to hold a referendum on ratification of the Lisbon Treaty. This was criticised by the Conservative opposition which stated that they sought such a referendum. However, when the Conservative Party entered into coalition government in 2010 after ratification of the Lisbon Treaty, no referendum was held on the basis that the treaty was now in force. This infuriated many Conservative MPs who felt United Kingdom citizens were still entitled to vote on it. In October 2011, in response to a petition of over 100,000 signatures a House of Commons motion was put forward for a referendum on the Treaty. Notwithstanding instructions by the government to the contrary, 60 MPs voted for it with an estimate that around 150 would have so voted but for strong government pressure. It was seen by those around the British Prime Minister as the moment when it became clear that the Conservative Party would want a referendum on EU membership sooner or later.[165] However, just over a year later he acted on it. With the United Kingdom Independence Party (UKIP), the party seeking British exit from the Union, rising to third in the polls, the British Prime Minister, David Cameron, gave his Bloomberg speech in January 2013 where he committed the United Kingdom to a referendum on EU membership if the Conservative Party was elected back into government in 2015.[166] Prior to the referendum, he would renegotiate the United Kingdom's relationship with the European Union, and, on the basis of that negotiation, would decide whether to recommend for the United Kingdom to remain a member of the European Union or not.

After winning the 2015 election Cameron was as good as his word. He began a series of negotiations with the other Member States which culminated in an agreement in February 2016. The agreement focused around four themes. First, stronger safeguards were to be put in place to ensure a level playing field between operators, particularly in the field of financial services, in non-euro area States and those in euro area States. Secondly, there was a commitment to enhance competitiveness and accelerate regulatory reform. Thirdly, it was agreed that the commitment to ever closer Union in the Treaties would not bind the United Kingdom. Largely symbolic, it was intended to signify that the United Kingdom would participate in no further political integration. Fourthly, for a period of seven years, the United Kingdom would not have to pay any in-work benefits to EU citizens during their first four years of residence.[167]

These concessions were as much as could be realistically secured without Treaty reform: something other States were unwilling to offer.[168] However, it was seen as meagre fare back in the United Kingdom. Its critics focused on two aspects. It did not directly restrict migration from other Member States, which was increasing at a fast rate,[169] and it did not curb the primacy

---

[165] T. Shipman, *All Out War: The Full Story of How Brexit Sank Britain's Political Class* (London, Collins, 2017) 7–8.

[166] www.gov.uk/government/speeches/eu-speech-at-bloomberg/.

[167] Conclusions of the Presidency of the European Council of 18 and 19 February 2016, EUCO 1/16, Annex A.

[168] On the challenges see I. Rogers, 'Cameron's Brexit Referendum', Hertford College, Oxford, 24 November 2017, www .politico.eu/article/ivan-rogers-david-cameron-speech-transcript-brexit-referendum/.

[169] Net migration by EU citizens increased from 65,000 in 2012 to 184,000 in December 2015. This was lower than migration by non-EU citizens but there was no equivalent increase for the latter, with the relevant figures being 160,000 and 189,000 respectively. www.ons.gov.uk/peoplepopulationandcommunity/populationandmigration/ internationalmigration/bulletins/migrationstatisticsquarterlyreport/february2018.

of EU law in any way at all.[170] Whilst Cameron thought this agreement was sufficient for him to campaign for the United Kingdom to remain in the European Union, 140 Conservative MPs did not and campaigned to leave. The party of government was split down the middle.

The campaign was a mendacious and bitter affair, which culminated in the murder of an MP campaigning to remain, Jo Cox, by a British fascist. It also, however, led to a very high turn-out with 33,577,342 votes cast on 23 June 2016. Of these, 51.89 per cent voted to leave the European Union. If this was a relatively narrow margin of victory, the size of the vote meant that it still represented a significant groundswell against the European Union. The vote revealed a polarised population. Those most likely to leave were the poor, the old and those without a university education, and a central driver for many was opposition to migration and multiculturalism. The reverse was true for those who were affluent, under 45 or had a university degree. Regional and national polarisation was also a feature. London, Northern Ireland and Scotland all voted to remain. The rest of England and Wales also voted to leave.[171] David Cameron immediately resigned, and was succeeded as Prime Minister by Theresa May.

She faced three particular challenges: organising the withdrawal of the United Kingdom from the European Union; agreeing a relationship between the United Kingdom and the European Union after Brexit; and managing the domestic legal implications of Brexit.

(b) The Withdrawal Negotiations

The process of leaving the European Union is governed by Article 50 TEU.

Article 50 TEU

(1) Any Member State may decide to withdraw from the Union in accordance with its own constitutional requirements.

(2) A Member State which decides to withdraw shall notify the European Council of its intention. In the light of the guidelines provided by the European Council, the Union shall negotiate and conclude an agreement with that State, setting out the arrangements for its withdrawal, taking account of the framework for its future relationship with the Union ... It shall be concluded on behalf of the Union by the Council, acting by a qualified majority,[172] after obtaining the consent of the European Parliament.

(3) The Treaties shall cease to apply to the State in question from the date of entry into force of the withdrawal agreement or, failing that, two years after the notification referred to in paragraph 2, unless the European Council, in agreement with the Member State concerned, unanimously decides to extend this period.

The article structures negotiations heavily in favour of the European Union. Two years is insufficient for the leaving State to put in place its own migration and customs capabilities. It is reliant on the Union agreeing to a longer transition period to enable it to put these in place. The size of the European Union, comprising as it does twenty-seven States, means that it is much

---

[170] Central to the decision of Boris Johnson, one of the prominent politicians to campaign to leave, was a failure of the government to agree to a Sovereignty Bill as part of these negotiations, Shipman, n. 165 above, 146–7 and 163–4.

[171] S. Hobolt, 'The Brexit Vote: A Divided Nation, a Divided Continent' (2016) 23 *JEPP* 1255; M. Goodwin and O. Heath, 'The 2016 Referendum, Brexit and the Left Behind: An Aggregate-Level Analysis of the Result' (2016) 87 *Political Quarterly* 323.

[172] This will be 72% of the Member States representing 65% of the Union's population. The leaving State is excluded from these calculations. Articles 50(4) TEU and 238(3)(b) TFEU.

more important to that State's economy than that State is to the European Union's economy. Leaving without legal arrangements in place is devastating for the sectors of that State's economy reliant on trade with the European Union. Finally, prior to exit, the State is prohibited from putting in place trade arrangements with non-EU States or arrangements with the EU on data flows or aviation. It has no legal system to allow these activities to take place on the day of exit, therefore, without some accommodation from the European Union.

Nevertheless, the United Kingdom without, it appears, forward planning, gave notice on its intention to leave on 29 March 2017, as required by Article 50(2) TEU.[173] Prior to giving that notice, on 17 January 2017, the British Prime Minister set out a 'Plan for Britain', which included certain red lines for future relations with the European Union. Amongst these was an ending to Court of Justice jurisdiction over the United Kingdom, control over migration from other EU States and, with it, an end to British membership of the single market, and the restoration of the power to conclude its own trade agreements with other States.[174] The European Union responded by setting out certain guidelines of its own for negotiations. These set out ambitions for an orderly withdrawal by the United Kingdom. As a consequence, there would be no formal agreement on anything until everything was agreed. The guidelines also set out three issues around which much of the negotiations were to focus. These were:

- the rights of EU citizens from other Member States residing in the United Kingdom prior to Brexit and the corresponding rights for UK citizens residing in the rest of the European Union
- settlement of both parties' financial obligations
- any agreement had to avoid a hard border anywhere in the island of Ireland. Whilst not formally part of the 1998 Belfast Agreement ('the Good Friday Agreement') between Ireland and the United Kingdom which secured peace in Northern Ireland, this absence of a hard border had been seen as central to underpinning it.[175]

In December 2017, a Joint Report was published by the UK and EU negotiators. This indicated general agreement on the questions of citizenship and financial obligations. The issue of no hard border on the island of Ireland was much more challenging. On the one hand, it was agreed by both parties that the absence of a hard border required no 'physical infrastructure or related checks and controls'.[176] The World Trade Organisation (WTO), the central body regulating international trade, requires, however, the United Kingdom, unless it forms a customs union with the European Union,

---

[173] Notification was delayed by a successful judicial review action requiring legislation to be enacted before this could happen. *R* v. *Secretary of State for Exiting the European Union, ex parte Miller and another* [2017] UKSC 5. This was duly done through the European Union (Notification of Withdrawal) Act 2017.

[174] 'The government's negotiating objectives for exiting the EU: PM speech', 17 January 2017, www.gov.uk/government/ speeches/the-governments-negotiating-objectives-for-exiting-the-eu-pm-speech (sometimes known as the 'Lancaster House' speech).

[175] A common travel area existed intermittently since Irish independence in 1922 up until 1952. In that year, it was formalised by a secret exchange of letters between the two governments. A joint statement referred to it as a 'fundamental public policy objective' for both governments in 2011: Joint Statement Regarding Co-Operation on Measures to Secure the External Common Travel Area Border, 20 December 2011, https://assets.publishing.service .gov.uk/government/uploads/system/uploads/attachment_data/file/99045/21197-mea-sec-trav.pdf; B. Ryan, 'The Common Travel Area between Britain and Ireland' (2001) 64 *MLR* 855; I. Maher, *The Common Travel Area: More than Just Travel* (Dublin - London, RIA & British Academy, 2017).

[176] Joint report from the negotiators of the European Union and the United Kingdom Government on progress during phase 1 of negotiations under Article 50 TEU, 8 December 2017, para. 43, https://ec.europa.eu/commission/sites/beta-political/files/joint_report.pdf.

to introduce controls on goods coming from Ireland to ensure that they pay the same tariffs and meet the same regulatory requirements as goods entering the United Kingdom from other States around the world.[177] The establishment of a customs union would require the United Kingdom to apply the same tariffs on goods coming from non European Union States and to apply no tariffs on goods coming from the European Union. This would prevent the United Kingdom making trade agreements with non-EU States, one of its red lines, on anything other than trade in services. Moreover, the establishment of such a customs union would be insufficient to ensure no hard border between Ireland and Northern Ireland. For it would not address restrictions that would occur because of different regulatory requirements, namely that the United Kingdom allowed a good to be sold whose sale was prohibited in the European Union. These restrictions could only be done away with if a single market in goods was established in which product standards between the two were aligned. On the other hand, many EU States were unhappy about an agreement being made to resolve the border issue that would allow UK goods access to EU markets whilst not requiring them to comply with EU environmental, labour or tax standards as they were worried that this would allow the United Kingdom to undercut the single market.

This issue bedevilled subsequent discussions. On 25 November 2018, the European Council endorsed a Withdrawal Agreement between the United Kingdom and the European Union.[178] The Withdrawal Agreement provided only for a temporary fix on the border question. A Protocol on Ireland/Northern Ireland was attached to the Withdrawal Agreement. In principle, it is temporary, lasting until 31 December 2020, and to be superseded by the agreement establishing the future relationship between the United Kingdom and the European Union. The Protocol provided for the creation of a single customs territory between the United Kingdom and the European Union. The central commitments within this customs territory were twofold. On the one hand, Northern Ireland would align its laws with EU law on the latter's customs union and single market in goods. The laws involved are substantial, amounting to a 75-page list within the agreement. On the other, the European Union committed to free movement of goods between it and Northern Ireland.

Any agreement replacing the Protocol must meet, however, a number of demanding conditions. It must contain safeguards, which ensure no hard border in the island of Ireland and protect the 1998 Agreement securing peace within Northern Ireland and its constitutional status. At the moment, it appears that such safeguards could only be provided if (a) just Northern Ireland or (b) the United Kingdom as a whole remained part of the European Union's customs union and its single market in goods. Both scenarios break the commitments made by Theresa May that the United Kingdom would have a fully functioning trade policy after Brexit, and the first one, the Northern Ireland only solution, raises the possibility of controls on movements of goods between Northern Ireland and the rest of the United Kingdom.

(c) The United Kingdom's Relations with the European Union after Brexit

The European Union insisted that any agreement on the United Kingdom's future relationship with the European Union could only take place after the United Kingdom had left. Alongside the

---

[177] General Agreement on Tariffs and Trade (1994), Article I(1) (most favoured nation principle) and Article XXIV(5) (customs union exception).

[178] Agreement on the withdrawal of the United Kingdom of Great Britain and Northern Ireland from the European Union and the European Atomic Energy Community, as endorsed by leaders at a special meeting of the European Council on 25 November 2018 (hereafter the 'Withdrawal Agreement').

Withdrawal Agreement, the European Union and the United Kingdom, therefore, adopted a Political Declaration setting out the framework for the future relationship between them.[179] This Political Declaration sets out guidelines for the negotiation of a treaty, which will structure future relations, and will be negotiated following Brexit and the successful ratification of the Withdrawal Agreement. There would be legal disruption if neither EU law nor this possible agreement governed relations between the Union and the UK during this period of negotiations. To counter this, the Withdrawal Agreement provides for a transition period after Brexit up until 31 December 2020.[180] The aspiration is that the new treaty will come into force then, and this will allow a seamless move from the transition period to it. However, the Withdrawal Agreement provides for the European Union and the United Kingdom to extend the transition period for up to the end of 2022, provided they agree to do by 1 July 2020.[181] Even this deadline of agreement and ratification by the end of 2022, less than four years after Brexit, will be challenging.

The reason is that the Political Declaration anticipates a very wide-ranging treaty centred on three themes.

The first, identified cryptically, as Initial Provisions, covers matters such as data protection, shared commitments to core values and rights, and UK participation in EU programmes, be these on, *inter alia*, education, space, development or science.

The Declaration envisages, secondly, a Security Partnership. This shall involve commitments and cooperation on, amongst other things, law enforcement; foreign policy, security and defence; information exchange; development and irregular migration.

Most focus has been on the third pillar anticipated by the Political Declaration: the Economic Partnership. This Partnership has been constrained by the starting points of the two parties. On the one hand, the United Kingdom has insisted that it does not include free movement of persons. On the other, the European Union excluded a sector-by-sector approach and insisted that any arrangement offer fewer benefits than full membership. This precludes an arrangement in which free movement of persons is restricted but there is full free movement of goods, services and capital. As there is free movement of capital and extensive liberalisation of trade in goods between the EU and non-EU State, this means, consequently, that the Economic Partnership can only provide for significant free movement of goods and limited free movement of services between the Union and the United Kingdom. The Political Declaration provides for this, and any negotiations will be about this about the extent and balance of this liberalisation.

The Withdrawal Agreement and Political Declaration were extremely unpopular within the United Kingdom Parliament, with the House of Commons required, in particular, to pass a resolution approving them before the United Kingdom could ratify them.[182] Much of the Conservative Party and the Northern Irish Democratic Unionist Party were unhappy, upon whom the UK government relied for its parliamentary majority, with the Protocol on Ireland/Northern Ireland. By contrast, the Labour Party saw the Political Declaration as not moving far enough towards establishing a customs union between the Union and the UK as it made no provision for negotiating one, something sought by the Labour Party.

When the United Kingdom Government brought this Resolution for approval to the House of Commons in January 2019, it was heavily defeated by 432 votes to 202 votes. In response to this, the European Union and the United Kingdom agreed an instrument interpreting the Withdrawal Agreement. This instrument emphasised the temporary nature of the Protocol on

---

[179] Hereafter the 'Political Declaration'. [180] Withdrawal Agreement, Article 126.
[181] Withdrawal Agreement, Article 132. [182] European Union Withdrawal Act 2018, section 13(1)(b).

Ireland/Northern Ireland and prioritised the search for alternatives to it that would still ensure no hard border on the island of Ireland. This had no effect. The House of Commons rejected the Withdrawal Agreement twice more. However, it also indicated that it would be unacceptable for the United Kingdom to exit the European Union without a withdrawal agreement. In the light of this impasse, the date for Brexit was pushed back from 29 March 2019 to 22 May 2019. When it became clear that matters would not be resolved by that latter date, a new deadline for reaching agreement was set of 31 October 2019. At the time of writing, the impasse remains.

(d) Managing the Domestic Legal Consequences of Brexit

A legal vacuum would be created with disastrous consequences for many economic and social relations if EU law ceased to apply on the day the United Kingdom left the European Union, and there was no law put in place to govern these relations from that moment onwards. Arrangements had to be put in place which allowed EU law which had applied directly in the United Kingdom to be replicated by domestic instruments and for British institutions to manage the application and development of this law.

The relevant legislation, the European Union Withdrawal Act 2018, was an arduous affair which took over a year to pass through the British Parliament and over 273 hours of debate. It repealed the European Communities Act 1972 so that EU laws adopted after Brexit do not have primacy over UK law.[183] It gave legal effect to all existing EU laws, other than the Treaties, which applied directly in the United Kingdom.[184] These laws were to apply after Brexit and to have primacy over all other UK law until otherwise amended by Parliament or by procedures put in place by it.[185] Central controversies raged around a number of other points, however.

First, the withdrawal treaty can only be ratified, *inter alia*, if the House of Commons passed a resolution approving it and the future framework for UK–EU relations.[186] On initial sight, this requirement seemed meaningless as the United Kingdom was going to have to pass legislation to implement that treaty in any case. However, the purpose of this resolution was to allow the House of Commons to instruct the government to renegotiate terms prior to any ratification. The vote was, therefore, to take place, where practicable before the EU had finished adopting the treaty into its law, and it required the government to set out within fourteen days how it was likely to proceed in the light of the resolution. The UK Government initially objected on the grounds that this might weaken its negotiating position as the EU would know that any agreement might have to be revisited. However, any return to negotiations leaves the United Kingdom in a difficult position. The two-year clock would have almost run out, and, according to Article 50 TEU, could only be extended with the agreement of all twenty-seven EU Member States. The United Kingdom would be in the position of either having to offer something to each one of these to extend negotiations or having to accept a take it or leave it offer from the EU.

Secondly, tension flared between the United Kingdom Government and the Scottish Parliament over how the Act affected the balance of powers within the United Kingdom. The Scottish Parliament was particularly upset that it would not have powers to amend the new retained laws, particularly as many of these fell in areas such as the environment or agriculture and fisheries, which fell within its fields of competence. The United Kingdom Government was concerned that

---

[183] European Union Withdrawal Act 2018, ss. 1 and 5(1).   [184] *Ibid.* ss. 3 and 4(1).   [185] *Ibid.* s. 7(2)–(4).
[186] The process is set out in European Union (Withdrawal) Act 2018, s. 13.

the Scottish Parliament might use these powers, however, to disrupt trade between Scotland and the rest of the United Kingdom. A compromise was adopted in the Act, which allows the Scottish Parliament to amend such laws unless a regulation is adopted by the UK Government restricting it from so doing. The Scottish Parliament would be consulted before any such regulation was adopted.[187] This did not satisfy the Scottish Parliament. It refused to consent to this. Whilst the Act still entered into force, it did so in breach of the Sewel Convention which requires the Scottish Parliament to agree to any legislation passed by the UK Parliament over its fields of competence.

The third central controversy raged around the powers granted to Whitehall, the United Kingdom executive, by the Act. The government was particularly concerned about laws that made no sense after Brexit (e.g. they relied on exercise of a power by an EU Institution). To this end, the Act provides that any deficiency of retained law or failure to operate effectively as a result of Brexit can be amended by statutory instruments for a period of two years after Brexit.[188] This power to amend laws was seen by critics as trespassing on the powers of Parliament. To address this, a draft of any proposed instrument can only become law if laid before both the House of Commons and Lords, and approved by a resolution of each.[189]

These debates generated acrimony, in part, because the issues were significant. However, they were symptomatic of a wider issue. Parliament was having to consider issues which it had not considered for a while. The system of party politics, which usually operated to structure its debates, had not developed mature positions over many of these issues, and its authority was challenged by the majority of its members having supported UK membership of the EU.

D. Chalmers, 'Brexit and the Renaissance of Parliamentary Authority' (2017) 19 *British Journal of Politics and International Relations* 663, 666–7

First, Parliament is significantly disengaged from those activities currently governed by EU law. There is weak and selective engagement with the EU legislative process, particularly by the House of Commons. In 2015, for example, whilst 57 measures were adopted under the ordinary legislative procedure . . . the House of Commons gave only eight opinions on Commission legislative proposals . . . There is even more scant involvement with the transposition of EU law into United Kingdom law . . . in the twenty one year period up until the end of 2014, just over one in twenty EU Directives were transposed by Acts of Parliament rather than statutory instruments . . .

This disengagement generates a practical problem of lack of Parliamentary slack. Parliament's business has, hitherto, been filled up with legislating other types of activity. The House of Lords European Union Committee has, thus, already talked of Brexit dominating the domestic legislative agenda for an extended period, and asked for a government strategy on this to make Parliamentary engagement manageable.[190]

Yet it is unrealistic to assume that other domestic agendas can be backgrounded. Reform of EU law will have to compete with these for Parliamentary attention. The threshold for reform of EU law will, therefore, not be whether reform is a good idea, but whether it is sufficiently important to displace other Parliamentary priorities.

Secondly, hitherto, there are weak patterns of party contestation on activities governed by the European Union. This affects the quality of debate or contestation that Parliament may be able to offer. For competing political programmes allow the different interests and perspectives interested in EU law to be brought

---

[187] *Ibid.* s. 12.   [188] *Ibid.* s. 8.   [189] *Ibid.* Sch. 7, para. 1.
[190] House of Lords European Union Committee, *Brexit: Parliamentary Scrutiny*, 4th Report, Session 2016–17, HL Paper 50, para. 80.

around principled commitments going to its retention, reform or repeal. In turn, these commitments communicate to voters central points of contestation in intelligible ways, thereby facilitating their political choices. This contestation has, however, been weak or suppressed at the macro-, meso- and micro-levels.

At the macro-level, if public opposition to EU membership has never really loitered below 30% in the last thirty years, all mainland political parties supported EU membership prior to 2015 during that period. Even the 2015 Conservative Party commitment to a referendum on EU membership was coupled with support for the single market and 'a family of nation States all part of the European Union'. This cohesiveness of views and divergence from public opinion was also reflected in the stances of individual MPs at the referendum. 76% (489/647) declared themselves in favour of Remain with only the Democratic Unionist Party and UKIP having a majority of MPs supporting Leave.

At the meso-level, this absence of party competition was reflected in the evaluation of EU performance. The *Balance of Competencies Review* of the coalition government treated the questions of the extent of EU competencies and the manner in which these had been exercised as an exercise in stakeholder democracy rather than as one in political contestation.[191] The advantages and disadvantages of EU action were, thus, treated as a matter of report, which was to structure future debate with action to be evaluated in terms of its costs and benefits as articulated by informed or engaged interests. Inevitably, this approach struggled in fields such as animal welfare, food safety, fisheries and free movement of people where political debate was already highly charged and contested ...

Finally, it carried over into the micro-level with how British governments approached the carrying over of EU obligations into UK law. Transposition was treated as a task of regulatory compliance. Gold-plating through the addition of further domestic regulatory requirements was to be avoided with copy-out of the Directive into national law treated as the default option ...

(iii) The Crisis of Liberal Values

As cited earlier, Article 2 TEU founds the European Union upon respect for liberal values, most notably human rights and democracy. Provision is, furthermore, made for the European Union to make recommendations to a Member State where there is a clear risk of a serious breach of these values.[192] It may go further and sanction it, including suspending its voting rights, where there is a persistent and serious breach of these values.[193] However, since 2010, an increasing number of States have begun to challenge these values, and the European Union's pursuit of them.

In 2010, a new government came to power, the Fidesz government of Viktor Orbán, with a large majority. Hungary was at that time emerging from the financial crisis and had had to address significant problems with its budgetary situation. The Orbán government believed that Hungary's predicament had been caused, in part, by a constitution which imposed too many checks on effective government action, and by a vision of society which was too liberal and individualistic at the expense of national citizens' commitment to one another.[194] To this end, it

---

[191] *Review of the Balance of Competences between the United Kingdom and the European Union*, Cm. 8415 (London, Foreign and Commonwealth Office, 2012).
[192] Article 7(1) TEU.   [193] Article 7(2)–(3) TEU.
[194] Orban has, therefore, stated that his ambition is to move Hungary away from being a liberal State to being a 'workfare State' marked by a stronger sense of cultural heritage, family and protecting the dignity of poor Hungarians. 'Speech at the XXV. Bálványos Free Summer University and Youth Camp' ('Tusnádfürdő speech'), 26 July 2014, https://budapestbeacon.com/full-text-of-viktor-orbans-speech-at-baile-tusnad-tusnadfurdo-of-26-july-2014/.

began a series of regular changes to the Hungarian constitution and weakened the powers and independence of the powers of the Constitutional Court. It also required all media outlets to register with a media-control body controlled by Fidesz which could subject these outlets to fines or even deregister them for imbalanced news coverage or broadcasts which violated public morality or were insulting to the majority of Hungarians.[195]

The illiberal agenda of the Orbán government moved centre stage in the European Union because of two developments outside of Hungary.

The first was the growth in undocumented migration into the Union from the Mediterranean. Significant numbers of undocumented migrants crossing the Mediterranean seeking a better life or asylum can be traced back to the early 1970s, at least. In 2014, however, there was a sharp increase in the number of those making the journey to over 216,000 persons as a result both of the ongoing conflicts in Iraq, Libya and Syria and migratory pressures from sub-Saharan African States. European public awareness of the issue rose further in 2015 as the numbers increased to over 1 million. Moreover, the majority were now taking the shorter crossing from Turkey to Greece rather than those from North African to Italy or Malta.[196] Not only did Greece not have the facilities to deal with so many people, but the crossings with their risks and deaths were being played out in front of the world's media.[197]

This led to significant tensions between Member States about where these people should be settled. Under EU law, the States of arrival – primarily Greece, Italy and Malta – were responsible for housing them whilst they considered their asylum claims.[198] However, in practice, the States receiving the most asylum seekers in 2015 were Germany (442,000), Hungary (174,000) and Sweden (156,000).[199] In September 2015, to reverse this, Hungary completed a wall along its southern border with Serbia to stop any migrants or asylum seekers entering, and took steps to close its other southern border with Croatia. In turn, whilst not building any walls, Austria, Denmark, France, Germany, Slovenia and Sweden all instigated controls at their borders to monitor and regulate those entering. There was, thus, a danger of the Schengen system of free movement of persons breaking down. Periphery States would encourage asylum seekers and economic migrants to move, whilst richer EU States, along with transit States, would erect controls to prevent this happening. The EU, consequently, attempted to come up with a system to take some of the burden off periphery States. In September 2015, a decision was taken to reallocate 120,000 asylum seekers between EU Schengen area States other than Italy and Greece.[200] The Czech

---

[195] See P. Sonnevend et al., 'The Constitution as an Instrument of Everyday Party Politics: The Basic Law of Hungary' and L. Sólyom, 'The Rise and Decline of Constitutional Culture in Hungary' in A. von Bogdandy and P. Sonnevend (eds.), Constitutional Crisis in the European Constitutional Area (Oxford, Hart, 2015).

[196] The most comprehensive report is IOM, Four Decades of Cross-Mediterranean Undocumented Migration to Europe (Geneva, IOM, 2017).

[197] These deaths were only a small fraction of the total number who have died making the crossing. On 11 November 2017, the German newspaper, the Tagesspiegel, published a moving list of the 33,293 people known to have died crossing the Mediterranean since 1 January 1993, www.tagesspiegel.de/downloads/20560202/3/ listeentireberlinccbanu.pdf. The real figure is undoubtedly much higher. To put this, in perspective, 140 people were killed crossing the Berlin wall in its twenty-eight-year history.

[198] See pp. 559–63.

[199] Pew Research Centre, Number of Refugees to Europe Surges to Record 1.3 Million in 2015, http://assets.pewresearch .org/wp-content/uploads/sites/2/2016/08/14100940/Pew-Research-Center-Europe-Asylum-Report-FINAL-August-2–2016.pdf.

[200] Decision 2015/160 establishing provisional measures in the area of international protection for the benefit of Italy and Greece, OJ 2015, L 248/80.

Republic, Hungary and Poland refused to comply with the decision, with Slovakia stating that it would take only 200 and they had to be Christian. Notwithstanding a Court of Justice judgment upholding the decision,[201] the first three States continued to refuse.[202] The political heat was lessened with an agreement between the EU and Turkey in early 2016. In return for aid, Turkey agreed to police much more effectively those crossing from its coastline for the EU.[203]

However, in the meantime, a second development emerged: the election of governments sympathetic to Orbán's vision in other Member States.[204] In 2015, the Beata Szydło government was elected in 2015. As with the Orbán government, it was unhappy with the Constitutional Tribunal in Poland and took measures to change the workings and composition of the court in a way that threatened its independence.[205] It also took measures to restrict media freedom in 2016 by passing a law allowing it to appoint the heads of all public broadcasters. In 2017, an Austrian Government entered into power which included the radical right Freedom Party, a party whose views was previously considered so unacceptable that when it last entered into power in 1999 other EU governments refused to deal with it. The Austrian Government also made clear its opposition to any reallocation of asylum seekers. Finally, in May 2018, a government was formed between the Populist Five Star Movement and the radical right party, the Norther League. The agreement between the parties indicates that they are unwilling to comply with EU budgetary powers and there is a commitment to return 500,000 irregular migrants to their country of origin.

These two developments coalesced in the summer of 2018. The arrangements with Turkey had led to a reduction in the numbers crossing the Mediterranean, so that only 172,301 crossed in 2017, but it had also led to the crossings between North Africa and Italy and Spain becoming the main points of entry.[206] The new government in Italy felt that it was taking far too high a proportion of the asylum seekers and economic migrants coming to the European Union. At the same time, Angela Merkel's coalition partner in Germany, the CSU, felt that Germany was taking too high a proportion of asylum seekers because other States were not considering asylum cases as required by EU law.[207] It wanted asylum seekers to be checked at the Austrian border and refused entry if their cases should be heard elsewhere. Austria promised a counter-response if this were done.

In June 2018, a new agreement was reached. There would be much stronger policing of the Mediterranean and more active return of those intercepted to their State of embarkation. Within the EU, Schengen area States would, on a voluntary basis, set up 'controlled centres',[208] which would process asylum seekers and economic migrants with a view to sending back the latter quickly whilst admitting the former. These centres would, in effect, be large camps. They would

---

[201] *Slovak Republic and Hungary* v. *Council*, C-643/15 and C-647/15, EU:C:2017:631.

[202] The pace of reallocation was also generally slow. In November 2017, over two years after the decision, only just over 31,500 people were relocated, http://europa.eu/rapid/press-release_IP-17-4484_en.htm.

[203] On these events see A. Niemann and N. Zaun, 'EU Refugee Policies and Politics in Times of Crisis: Theoretical and Empirical Perspectives' (2018) 56 *JCMS* 3.

[204] On this see D. Kelemen, 'Europe's Other Democratic Deficit: National Authoritarianism in Europe Democratic Union' (2017) 52 *Government and Opposition* 211.

[205] In 2017, the Commission, thus started action under Article 7(1) TEU against Poland on the basis that its judicial reforms posed a clear risk of a serious breach of the values in Article 2 TEU. European Commission, 'Proposal for a Council Decision on the Determination of a Clear Risk of a Serious Breach by the Republic of Poland of the Rule of Law', COM(2017)835 final.

[206] Up-to-date data is available at https://data2.unhcr.org/en/situations/mediterranean#.

[207] On the wider issues surrounding allocation between Member States see R. Bauböck, 'Refugee Protection and Burden-Sharing in the European Union' (2018) 56 *JCMS* 141.

[208] *European Council meeting (28 June 2018) – Conclusions*, EUCO 9/18, para. 6.

be spread across the European Union but only in States that were willing to host them. Alongside this, all States were to take measures to restrict the movement of asylum seekers around the Union. Asylum seekers arriving within the Union were to be sent to one of these centres, processed and then either returned to their State of origin or sent on to a destination within the European Union.

This crisis differed from the euro area in that it was characterised by States foisting the issues onto other States. They would either try to get other Member States to host the asylum seeker or, if possible, make this a matter for non-EU States by requiring them to police their coastlines better or host more asylum seekers.[209] However, the two crises also had shared characteristics. In both cases, whatever one thinks of the content of the measures, the EU took decisions which had a 'one minute to midnight' feel to them, evoked the spirit of there being no alternative, involved little consultation and were relatively indifferent to popular support. As this piece indicates, this has contributed to the style of political opposition to the EU.

C. Kreuder-Sonnen, 'An Authoritarian Turn in Europe and European Studies?' (2018) 25 *Journal of European Public Policy* 452, 459–60

[T]he EU's democratic deficit implies limitations for political opposition and access to contestation, inciting 'the mobilization of new – perhaps populist – opposition in principle.' European authoritarianism exacerbates this problem exponentially: EU emergency measures that are highly intrusive and side-line domestic democratic procedures quickly lead to the popular impression of disempowerment by distant and unaccountable technocrats. Coupled with the European emergency discourse continuously portraying political decisions as necessary and without alternative, dissatisfied voters develop both anti-EU sentiment and alienation from the domestic political mainstream that seems complicit in the dealings – driving them into the arms of nationalist populists . . .

Secondly, the complex configurations of postnational exceptionalism and the authoritarian structures it engenders represent perfect targets for populist denunciation. Since populism builds on the critique of self-referential élites, it feeds on opaque and hardly attributable political choices implemented by technocrats. On the one hand, populist leaders can draw on the exceptionalist power of EU institutions to shift blame to Brussels (or Frankfurt), because the delegation chain is interrupted or at least elusive for the general public. This allows them to downplay their own role in unpopular political decisions and fuel scepticism vis-à-vis Europe. On the other hand, the incomprehensibility of responsibilities and policy effects of European emergency measures opens the way for blaming Brussels for basically anything, irrespective of the degree to which one is affected by the policies. Eventually, as Schlipphak and Treib note,[210] populist leaders are even enabled to portray the EU and its political interventions as a threat to the national identity that only they are able to defend – thus bolstering their cause and position with a discrete national emergency discourse. This way, European authoritarianism may also have contributed, among other important factors, to the rise and perpetuation of nationalist authoritarianism in Eastern Europe.

Yet the consequences of European-level authoritarianism do not end with fuelling nationalist authoritarianism in response. By creating political opportunities for the exclusionary discourse of populism, it

---

[209] K. Greenhill, 'Open Arms behind Barred Doors: Fear, Hypocrisy and Policy Schizophrenia in the European Migration Crisis' (2016) 22 *ELJ* 317; F. Schimmelfennig, 'European Integration (Theory) in Times of Crisis: A Comparison of the Euro and Schengen Crises' (2018) 25 *JEPP* 969.

[210] B. Schlipphak and O. Treib, 'Playing the Blame Game on Brussels: The Domestic Political Effects of EU Interventions against Democratic Backsliding' (2017) 24 *JEPP* 352, 354.

also strengthens popular Euroscepticism and thus the constraining dissensus inhibiting further integration on conventional paths. In line with the above reasoning, this will put the EU between a rock and a hard place as institutional drift slides it into further crises of functionality that require integrative solutions. Either the EU then goes back to integration by stealth or it has to bear the (prohibitive) costs of inaction. This builds the final link in the cycle of authoritarianism: discretionary supranational governance provokes a nationalist backlash which fosters precisely those preconditions that facilitated the emergence of exceptionalism at the EU level in the first place. European and domestic authoritarianism are thus mutually reinforcing.

FURTHER READING

S. Bartolini, *Restructuring Europe: Centre Formation, System Building, and Political Structuring between the Nation State and the European Union* (Oxford University Press, 2005).

C. Bickerton, *European Integration: From Nation States to Member States* (Oxford University Press, 2012).

D. Chalmers, M. Jachtenfuchs and C. Joerges (eds.), *The End of the Eurocrats' Dream: Adjusting to European Diversity* (Cambridge University Press, 2016).

M Dawson, H. Enderlein and C. Joerges (eds.), *Beyond the Crisis: The Governance of Europe's Economic, Political and Legal Transformation* (Oxford University Press, 2015).

N. Fligstein, *Euro-Clash: The EU, European Identity and the Future of Europe* (Oxford University Press, 2008).

J. Habermas, *The Crisis of the European Union: A Response* (Cambridge, Polity, 2012).

J. Le Goff, *The Birth of Europe* (Oxford, Blackwell, 2005).

L. v. Middelaar, *The Passage to Europe: How a Continent Became a Union* (New Haven, Yale University Press, 2013).

T. Shipman, *All Out War: The Full Story of How Brexit Sank Britain's Political Class* (London, Harper Collins, 2016).

A. Vauchez, *Brokering Europe: Euro-Lawyers and the Making of a Transnational Polity* (Cambridge University Press, 2015).

J. Zielonka, *Europe as Empire: The Nature of the Enlarged European Union* (Oxford University Press, 2006).

J. Zielonka, *Counter-Revolution: Liberal Europe in Retreat* (Oxford University Press, 2018).

2

The EU Institutions

CONTENTS

1 INTRODUCTION

This chapter looks at the institutional settlement governing the European Union.

Section 2 looks at three general features of the European Union's institutional settlement. First, the EU Institutions are granted most of their powers to realise goals set out in the EU Treaties. Their mission is, thus, much more goal-oriented than with many domestic institutions, with their authority correspondingly much more tied to the legitimacy of these goals and how effectively these are realised. Secondly, many EU tasks require the Institutions to work in tandem with one another. It is, thus, often insufficient to view them in stand-alone terms. Their success and power often depends on how effective they are at managing their relations both with other EU Institutions and national administrations. Thirdly, the limits on the powers of EU Institutions are fuzzy. On the one hand, EU law operates according to the doctrine of conferred powers. The powers of EU Institutions are to be limited by what is granted by EU law. This doctrine has been eroded by Member States being allowed to grant EU Institutions wide powers to do things outside the Treaty framework.

Section 3 considers the European Commission. An independent supranational administration, the Commission has four central types of power: legislative and quasi-legislative powers; agenda-setting powers where it can propose laws, policies and the budgets; executive powers to administer EU policies; and supervisory powers to police the observance of EU law. These powers are much more extensive than those typically enjoyed by national administrations. As new tasks have fallen to the European Union, these have increasingly been granted to specialised European Regulatory Agencies, who now carry out a wide array of quasi-legislative and executive tasks alongside the Commission in an extensive range of sectors. In addition, the Commission's powers of supervision over national administrations are often used to forge a relationship whereby, whilst the latter do most of the administration of EU law and policies within national territories, they do it in liaison with the Commission. The consequence is a relatively unaccountable pan-Union executive order which carries out a large number of quasi-legislative, regulatory and executive tasks.

Section 4 looks at the Council of Ministers (Council). Comprised of national Ministers, it has the final power of decision over almost all fields of EU law. The Council sits in ten configurations with the minster responsible for a particular field representing the State in that field. It has two dominant forms of voting: unanimity, where each national government has a veto, and Qualified Majority Vote (QMV), a weighted form of voting which usually requires fifteen States representing 65 per cent of the population to vote for a measure for it to be adopted. The Council is highly dependent on the Committee of Permanent Representatives (COREPER), national civil servants based in Brussels who prepare the Council's work, and, in so doing, decide what the Council discusses and votes upon. With the Council discussing only a small minority of the items on its agenda, most items are decided through agreement within COREPER. These will not be decided by COREPER alone, however, but by Working Groups of civil servants working in and from the different national capitals. This world of COREPER and Working Groups raises questions about the balance of power between politicians and civil servants, on the one hand, and the transparency and accountability of this administrative machinery, on the other.

Section 5 considers the European Council, which comprises the Heads of Government and meets at least four times per year. Its central role is to provide political direction, and it has done this much more intensively in the last ten years. It was, thus, the central player in formulating EU policies and overseeing them in relation to both the sovereign debt and migration crises. It is less constrained by EU law than other EU Institutions. Its prominence has, thus, raised questions about both the place of EU law in European integration and the traditional checks and balances associated with EU decision-making. Its rise is associated with a new style of integration prevalent in emerging policy fields. There is less use of supranational institutions and EU law. Instead, national governments exercise more control over the process, and integrate through the coordination of policy positions rather than through enacting EU laws.

Section 6 looks at the European Parliament (Parliament). The Parliament comprises 705 Members of the European Parliament (MEPs) directly elected for five years. It is the forum where there is most open public debate about EU decision-making, but public engagement with it is limited, and its representative qualities are weakened by there being no European political parties and seats being allocated on the basis of national quotas. Its legislative powers vary according to the legislative procedure used. It can always propose amendments and, in the most common legislative procedure used, it can also veto draft EU laws. It has significant powers to hold all the other EU Institutions to account. This is particularly true of the Commission, which it can fire and which it co-appoints. It has used this power of co-appointment in recent years to engage in a form of a parliamentary government where the incoming Commission consults with it over the policy agenda for the next five years, and there is then extensive collaboration between the two institutions during that term to realise this agenda.

Section 7 considers the transparency of the institutional settlement. Institutions must keep up-to-date electronic registers to which the public should have access and individuals can also apply for documents held by EU Institutions, agencies or bodies. Parties may seek documents created by these institutions and documents passed on to them by third parties which are held by them. Institutions should refuse access for three types of document. There are, first, fields where access should always be refused if there is a risk of the protected interest being undermined (e.g. defence, financial and monetary policy and international relations). There are, secondly, fields where access should be refused if the protected interest would be specifically and actually undermined (e.g. the institution's internal deliberations, investigations and inspections, the commercial interests of third parties) unless there is an overriding public interest in favour of disclosure. Thirdly, an institution should consult with a Member State if a document originates from that State. The latter can refuse disclosure if it can provide plausible reasons which would justify non-disclosure under either of the other two headings.

2 THE EU INSTITUTIONS AND THE INSTITUTIONAL FRAMEWORK

The central EU Institutions and their collective mission are set out in Article 13 TEU.

Article 13

(1) The Union shall have an institutional framework which shall aim to promote its values, advance its objectives, serve its interests, those of its citizens and those of the Member States, and ensure the consistency, effectiveness and continuity of its policies and actions. This institutional framework comprises:
 – The European Parliament,
 – The European Council,
 – The Council,

– The European Commission,
– The Court of Justice of the European Union,
– The European Central Bank,
– The Court of Auditors.

(2) Each institution shall act within the limits of the powers conferred on it in the Treaties, and in conformity with the procedures, conditions and objectives set out in them. The institutions shall practise mutual sincere cooperation.

The first four of these institutions are considered in this chapter. They have three striking features.[1]

First, the EU Institutional framework exists to promote a particular mission: Union policies and values and the interests of the Member States and its citizens. It is, thus, a purposive association. This is different from a State where the legislature is simply engaged in lawmaking rather than promoting a particular policy. The authority of EU Institutions is tied much more strongly to the authority of these policies and the Union's success in realising them. If one does not believe in market liberalisation, for example, the establishment of a legislative machinery to realise it can never be legitimate as it curtails the debate about whether market liberalisation should take place at all.[2]

Secondly, the Treaty often requires EU Institutions to interact with each other. The legislative process, for example, involves three EU Institutions: the Commission, Parliament and Council. The power of each makes no sense without regard to the power of the other. EU Institutions should, therefore, not be seen simply in terms of their individual powers but also in terms of their relationship to one another. In some cases, cooperating with another institution can enhance their power. In other situations, they may be competing with it.

Thirdly, the limits on the power of EU Institutions are fuzzy. On the one hand, Article 13(2) TEU indicates that they operate under the doctrine of conferred powers. They only have the powers granted to them by EU law. The rationale for the doctrine is that administrative power should not only require justification and be constrained in a liberal society, but there should also be clarity about its limits. In EU law, this has been understood that the doctrine places not merely substantive limits on what the EU Institutions can do but also governs how they are to reach their decisions. Article 218(9) TEU states that, for international agreements, the Council can adopt a decision, which sets out the European Union's negotiating position and binds Member States to this position. In *World Radiocommunication Conference*, the European Union participated in the 2015 conference of the International Telecommunication Union, a UN agency, which was responsible for getting international agreement over the use of radio spectrum. Instead of adopting the decision proposed by the Commission for this conference, the Council adopted a set of Conclusions which did not bind EU Member States. The Commission challenged the legality of this.

---

[1] The Court of Justice and European Central Bank are considered in more detail in Chs. 4 and 15 respectively. The Court of Auditors comprises twenty-seven members and audits the revenue and expenditure of the Union: Article 287 TFEU.

[2] M. Bartl, 'The Way We Do Europe: Subsidiarity and the Substantive Democratic Deficit' (2015) 21 *ELJ* 23.

Commission v. *Council*, C–687/15, EU:C:2017:803 ('World Radiocommunication Conference')

40 As regards, first, the form of the contested act, it must be recalled that the Treaties set up a system of allocation of powers among the EU institutions, assigning to each institution its own role in the institutional structure of the European Union and the accomplishment of the tasks entrusted to the European Union. Accordingly, Article 13(2) TEU provides that each institution is to act within the limits of the powers conferred on it in the Treaties, and in conformity with the procedures, conditions and objectives set out therein. That provision reflects the principle of institutional balance, characteristic of the institutional structure of the European Union, a principle which requires that each of the institutions must exercise its powers with due regard for the powers of the other institutions ...

41 Accordingly, as the Court has repeatedly held, in so far as the rules regarding the manner in which the EU institutions arrive at their decisions are laid down in the Treaties and are not within the discretion of the Member States or of the institutions themselves, the Treaties alone may, in particular cases, empower an institution to amend a decision-making procedure established by the Treaties ...

42 In this case, it must, first, be emphasised that, contrary to what is suggested by the Council, the practice of the institutions, and in particular, with respect to the present case, an alleged consistent practice in relation to the preparation of the EU position for the purposes of the world radiocommunication conferences by means of conclusions, a practice which is contradicted by the position maintained by the Commission in this action, cannot alter the rules of the Treaties that the institutions are obliged to respect. In accordance with settled case-law, a mere practice on the part of the Council cannot derogate from the rules of the Treaty and cannot therefore create a precedent that is binding on the EU institutions ...

44 The fact that an institution of the European Union derogates from the legal form laid down by the Treaties constitutes an infringement of essential procedural requirements that is such as to require the annulment of the act concerned, since that derogation is likely to create uncertainty as to the nature of that act or as to the procedure to be followed for its adoption, thereby undermining legal certainty.

The institutional balance secured by the doctrine of conferred powers has been described as the guarantee for democracy within the European Union by the current President of the Court of Justice.[3] Its status in EU law is, fuzzy, however, because of a parallel doctrine which allows Member States to grant EU Institutions powers that are not provided for in the Treaties if these powers do not change the essential character of the EU Institution. In *Pringle*, a challenge was made to the EU Decision authorising ratification of the European Stability Mechanism Treaty, the agreement between seventeen euro area States which offered financial support to those euro area States otherwise unable to finance themselves. EU Institutions were central to the administration of this agreement with the Commission and European Central Bank (ECB) assessing the conditions which should be exacted in return for granting financial support and monitoring whether the State fulfilled those conditions. Pringle argued, *inter alia*, that this violated the doctrine of conferred powers in Article 13(2) TEU.

---

[3] K. Lenaerts and A. Verhoeven, 'Institutional Balance as a Guarantee for Democracy in EU Governance' in C. Joerges and R. Dehousse (eds.), *Good Governance in Europe's Integrated Market* (Oxford University Press, 2002).

Pringle v. *Government of Ireland*, C-370/12, EU:C:2012:756

155 The ESM Treaty allocates various tasks to the Commission and to the ECB.

156 As regards the Commission, those tasks consist of assessing requests for stability support (Article 13(1)), assessing their urgency (Article 4(4)), negotiating a [Memorandum of Understanding (MoU)] detailing the conditionality attached to the financial assistance granted (Article 13(3)), monitoring compliance with the conditionality attached to the financial assistance (Article 13(7)), and participating in the meetings of the Board of Governors and the Board of Directors as an observer (Articles 5(3) and 6(2)).

157 The tasks allocated to the ECB consist of assessing the urgency of requests for stability support (Article 4(4)), participating in the meetings of the Board of Governors and the Board of Directors as an observer (Articles 5(3) and 6(2)) and, in liaison with the Commission, assessing requests for stability support (Article 13(1)), negotiating an MoU (Article 13(3)) and monitoring compliance with the conditionality attached to the financial assistance (Article 13(7)).

158 In that regard, it is apparent from the case-law of the Court that the Member States are entitled, in areas which do not fall under the exclusive competence of the Union, to entrust tasks to the institutions, outside the framework of the Union, such as the task of coordinating a collective action undertaken by the Member States or managing financial assistance . . . provided that those tasks do not alter the essential character of the powers conferred on those institutions by the TEU and TFEU . . .

159 The duties allocated to the Commission and to the ECB in the ESM Treaty constitute tasks of the kind referred to in the preceding paragraph.

160 First, the activities of the ESM fall under economic policy. The Union does not have exclusive competence in that area.

161 Secondly, the duties conferred on the Commission and ECB within the ESM Treaty, important as they are, do not entail any power to make decisions of their own. Further, the activities pursued by those two institutions within the ESM Treaty solely commit the ESM.

162 Thirdly, the tasks conferred on the Commission and the ECB do not alter the essential character of the powers conferred on those institutions by the TEU and TFEU.

163 As regards the Commission, it is stated in Article 17(1) TEU that the Commission 'shall promote the general interest of the Union' and 'shall oversee the application of Union law'.

164 It must be recalled that the objective of the ESM Treaty is to ensure the financial stability of the euro area as a whole. By its involvement in the ESM Treaty, the Commission promotes the general interest of the Union. Further, the tasks allocated to the Commission by the ESM Treaty enable it, as provided in Article 13(3) and (4) of that treaty, to ensure that the memoranda of understanding concluded by the ESM are consistent with European Union law.

165 As regards the tasks allocated to the ECB by the ESM Treaty, they are in line with the various tasks which the TFEU . . . confer on that institution. By virtue of its duties within the ESM Treaty, the ECB supports the general economic policies in the Union, in accordance with Article 282(2) TFEU . . .

EU Institutions can almost have any powers that Member States want them to have. The only constraints are that these powers must be granted by an agreement between Member States and must not alter an EU Institution's essential character.[4] However, these are weak constraints. *Pringle* makes clear that not all the Member States need agree to these new powers. It can be an agreement between some of the Member States. Meanwhile, the 'essential character' of EU

---

[4] P. Craig, '*Pringle* and Use of EU Institutions outside the EU Legal Framework: Foundations, Procedure and Substance' (2013) 9 *EUConst* 263.

Institutions is understood very broadly indeed. In the case of the Commission, for example, it is deemed to be anything which promotes the 'general interest of the Union': something which allows it to be granted almost any legislative, executive or judicial power.

Pringle was tempered by *Ledra*, where the Court stated that EU Institutions acting outside the framework of the Treaties must still comply with other EU laws.[5] The Court therefore stated that in exercising its powers under the ESM, the Commission was not only bound by fundamental rights law but could be brought before the EU Courts for failures to do this. If this ensures that EU Institutions are subject to the disciplines of EU administrative law and judicial accountable, there remains the problem of institutional balance. *Ledra* does not prevent significant tasks being granted to EU Institutions, which increases the power of these vis-à-vis other EU Institutions and which these may also be poorly equipped to discharge. The grant of these tasks also changes the overall character of the European Union. They have been invariably granted to non-elected institutions, and thus contributed to a Union which is less electorally accountable and more dominated by executives.

3 THE COMMISSION

(i) The Commission Bureaucracy

Although the Commission is, legally, a single body, its institutional reality is more complex. It performs a large number of tasks, employs more than 32,000 people[6] and is composed of three tiers: the College of Commissioners, the Directorates General (DGs) and the Cabinets.

(a) The College of Commissioners

Formally, the Commission consists of twenty-seven Commissioners, with one Commissioner from each Member State.[7] These Commissioners make up the College of Commissioners: the body that, formally, takes all Commission decisions. The Commission is appointed for a five-year term.[8] Once appointed, the Commissioners are allocated portfolios by the President.[9]

---

[5] *Ledra Advertising*, C-8–10/15 P, EU:C:2016:701.

[6] https://ec.europa.eu/info/sites/info/files/european-commission-hr-key-figures_2018_en.pdf.

[7] Article 17(4) TEU. It was initially anticipated that from 1 November 2014 the Commission should comprise only two-thirds of that number, unless the European Council decided to alter this. A condition for Ireland having a second referendum on the Lisbon Treaty was that the principle of one Commissioner per Member State should continue. The European Council adopted a Decision giving effect to this principle with a commitment to review it by November 2019 at the latest, Decision 2013/272/EU concerning the number of members of the European Commission, OJ 2013, L 165/98. In February 2018, it was informally agreed that the principle of one Commission per Member State should continue for the Commission starting its term in 2019, https://verfassungsblog.de/eu-leaders-agenda-whos-afraid-of-reforms/.

[8] Article 17(3) TEU.

[9] The current portfolios are President; High Representative for Foreign Affairs and Security Policy; Better Regulation, Interinstitutional Relations, the Rule of Law and the Charter of Fundamental Rights; Digital Single Market; Energy Union; the Euro and Social Dialogue, Financial Stability, Financial Services and Capital Markets Union; Jobs, Growth, Investment and Competitiveness; Budget and Human Resources; European Neighbourhood Policy and Enlargement Negotiations; Trade; International Cooperation and Development; Climate Action and Energy; Environment, Maritime Affairs and Fisheries; Health and Food Safety; Migration, Home Affairs and Citizenship; Employment, Social Affairs, Skills and Labour Mobility; Economic and Financial Affairs, Taxation and Customs; Humanitarian Aid and Crisis Management; Agriculture and Rural Development; Transport; Internal Market, Industry, Entrepreneurship and SMEs;

The Commissioners are to be persons whose 'independence is beyond doubt'.[10] They are required not to seek or take instructions from any government or any other body and a duty is imposed on Member States to respect this principle.[11] In addition, Commissioners must not find themselves in a position where a 'conflict of interest' arises. They must not, therefore, engage in any other occupation during their period of office. If any Commissioner fails to observe these rules, the Court of Justice may, on application by either the Council or the Commission, compulsorily retire that Commissioner.[12]

This independence should not be seen in too absolute terms. Sanctions for breach of this principle can only be applied where the behaviour of the Commissioner is manifestly inappropriate.[13] Just over one-third of Commissioners become lobbyists after finishing their time in the Commission, no doubt aided in their new jobs by their old contacts in the Commission.[14] Furthermore, chosen because of distinguished and well-connected careers, Commissioners have a list of professional and political contacts with over two-thirds being from a party in government at the time of appointment.[15]

> Usually, they are members – and appointees – of the major parties in their member state and continue some involvement with national politics after becoming Commissioners. Frequent trips to speak before (and to lecture to) national audiences are common. Again, the metaphor of gatekeeping is perhaps most useful: Commissioners are an easy and efficient way for the Commission to maintain a link with member state governments and domestic political systems. They will know what legislative proposals are politically acceptable in national capitals, while at the same time being in an ideal position to communicate to national elites the requirements of efficient European policy-making.[16]

That said, this networking and gatekeeping role should not be overstated. Research has found little evidence of partisanship by Commissioners either in favour of their respective Member States or sectors with which they have an association.[17]

The other feature of the College is the principle of *collegiality*. The Commission is collectively responsible for all decisions taken and all Commission decisions should be taken collectively. In principle, these decisions should take place at the weekly meetings of the Commission by a simple majority vote of the College. Meetings of each Commissioner's Cabinet (staff) occur two

---

Justice, Consumers and Gender Equality; Education, Culture, Youth and Sport; Regional Policy; Competition; Research, Science and Innovation; the Security Union; the Digital Economy and Society.

[10] Article 17(3) TEU.

[11] There is one exception, the High Representative of the Union for Foreign Affairs and Security Policy. She has the portfolio of both the common foreign and security policy and the security and defence policy within the Commission. She has a double hat which involves her also acting under a mandate from the Council, Article 18(2) TEU.

[12] Article 245 TFEU.   [13] *Commission* v. *Cresson*, C-432/04, EU:C:2006: 455.

[14] R. Vaubel *et al.*, 'There Is Life after the Commission: An empirical Analysis of Private Interest Representation by Former EU-Commissioners, 1981–2009' (2012) 7 *Review of International Organizations* 59.

[15] A. Wonka, 'Technocratic and Independent? The Appointment of European Commissioners and its Policy Implications' (2007) 14 *JEPP* 169, 178.

[16] T. Christiansen, 'Tensions of European Governance: Politicised Bureaucracy and Multiple Accountability in the European Commission' (1997) 4 *JEPP* 73, 82. See also A. Wille, *The Normalization of the European Commission: Politics and Bureaucracy in the EU Executive* (Oxford University Press, 2013) 70–8.

[17] R. Thomson, 'National Actors in International Organizations: The Case of the European Commission' (2008) 41 *Comparative Political Studies* 169; R. Deckarm, 'The Countries They Know Best: How National Principals Influence European Commissioners and their Cabinets' (2017) 24 *JEPP* 447.

days before the weekly meeting. If there is agreement, it will be formally adopted as an 'A' item and there will be no formal discussion of the matter at the meeting. However, the reality is that there is little discussion within the College about the majority of the Commission's business.[18] There are even fewer votes, in large part because it is felt that this might lead to majority of Commissioners from smaller Member States imposing something on States representing the majority of the EU population.[19]

The only Commissioner without a portfolio, the President, is the most powerful of all the Commissioners.[20] He has six important roles.

- He is involved in the appointment of the other Commissioners. With the Heads of Government, he nominates the other Commissioners, who are then subject to a collective vote of approval by the Parliament and then appointed by the European Council.[21]
- He decides on the internal organisation of the Commission. He allocates individual portfolios at the beginning of the term, which can then be shifted by him during the term of office.
- Individual Commissioners are responsible to him. The President can request individual Commissioners to resign.[22]
- He provides 'political guidance' to the Commission. At its most formal, this involves chairing the weekly meetings of the Commission. More substantively, it means establishing the political priorities of the Commission through setting out a political agenda at the beginning of the Commissioner's five-year term.
- He has a roving policy brief. Although this causes tensions with the individual Commissioner concerned, the President may seek to take over a particular issue and drive Commission policy on that issue.
- He has a representative role. He represents the Commission at meetings involving the Heads of Government and must account to other institutions when there is a questioning of the general conduct of the institution or a particular issue raises broader questions.

As the size of the Commission has increased with the increase in Member States, so has the President's power. In a group of twenty-seven Commissioners, collective discussions are harder and it is also more difficult for individual Commissioners to take a stand as they are just one of a large group. This gives the President space to direct activities. He has greater resources than others to oversee what is going on in the different nooks and crannies of the Commission, and he can also convene informal meetings between Commissioners or set up particular project teams to get agreement on matters of importance to him.[23] He can also insist that individual Commissioners and the Commission as a whole deliver on the political agenda set out by him at the beginning of his term.[24] Experience suggests that both his effectiveness and his control over the Commission may depend on how this has been crafted. The most effective Commissioners have been ones where the agenda was clear and stable right from the beginning and focused on a

---

[18] A. Wonka, 'Decision-Making Dynamics in the European Commission: Partisan, National or Sectoral?' (2008) 15 *JEPP* 1145, 1151.

[19] Wille, n. 16 above, p. 83.   [20] The President in 2018 was Luxembourgeois, Jean-Claude Juncker.

[21] Article 17(7) TEU.   [22] Article 17(6) TEU.

[23] Wille, n. 16 above, pp. 63–6; A. Bürgin, 'The Impact of Juncker's Reorganization of the European Commission on the Internal Policy-Making Process: Evidence from the Energy Union Project' (2018) *Public Administration* (forthcoming).

[24] H. Kassim *et al.*, 'Managing the house: The Presidency, Agenda Control and Policy Activism in the European Commission' (2017) 24 *JEPP* 653.

limited number of priorities that, on the one hand, were significant and caught the public's imagination, and, on the other, were sufficiently limited that they did not overload the Commission or cause it to lose focus.[25]

(b) The Directorates General

The majority of Commission employees work for the DGs. These are the equivalent of Ministries within a national government. In 2018, there were thirty-one DGs, although the number and organisation is subject to frequent change.[26] In addition, there were sixteen service departments, which provide support to these DGs.[27] Whilst all DGs fall within the portfolio of at least one Commissioner and are answerable to (at least) that Commissioner, with thirty-one DGs and twenty-seven Commissioners, there is no neat dovetailing. Furthermore, DGs' duties are to the Commission rather than the Commissioner. Individual Commissioners have complained about the autonomy they enjoy and the lack of loyalty they show.[28] Their expertise and resources often grant them considerable leeway in deciding when to drive forward a policy and the content of that policy.[29]

The variety of Commission activities results in little cohesion between the different DGs.[30] Commission officials often identify with their DGs and the values promoted by it.[31] As a consequence, the interests and values of officials working for the Environment DG are likely to be very different from those working in the Competition DG. In addition, each DG may focus on very different tasks. The bulk of the work of the Environment DG will be concentrated around the proposal and enforcement of legislation. By contrast, in the fields of education and culture the Union has no lawmaking powers. The work of officials in that DG focuses on the development of programmes, administration of Union funding and bringing different public and private actors together.

---

[25] H. Müller, 'Setting Europe's Agenda: The Commission Presidents and Political Leadership' (2017) 39 *JEI* 129.

[26] Agriculture and Rural Development; Budget; Climate Action; Communication; Communications Networks, Content and Technology; Competition; Economic and Financial Affairs; Education, Youth, Sport and Culture; Employment, Social Affairs and Inclusion; Energy; Environment; European Civil Protection and Humanitarian Aid Operations; European Neighbourhood Policy and Enlargement Negotiations; Eurostat – European statistics; Financial Stability, Financial Services and Capital Markets Union; Health and Food Safety; Human Resources and Security; Informatics; Internal Market, Industry, Entrepreneurship and SMEs; International Cooperation and Development; Interpretation Joint Research Centre; Justice and Consumers; Maritime Affairs and Fisheries; Migration and Home Affairs; Mobility and Transport; Regional and Urban Policy; Research and Innovation; Taxation and Customs Union; Trade; Translation.

[27] Administration and Payment of Individual Entitlements; Data Protection Officer; European Anti-Fraud Office (OLAF); European Personnel Selection Office; European Political Strategy Centre; Foreign Policy Instruments; Historical Archives Service; Infrastructure and Logistics in Brussels; Infrastructure and Logistics in Luxembourg; Internal Audit Service; Legal Service; Library and e-Resources Centre; Publications Office; Secretariat-General; Structural Reform Support Service; Taskforce on Article 50 negotiations with the United Kingdom.

[28] D. Curtin and M. Egeberg, 'Tradition and Innovation: Europe's Accumulated Executive Order' (2008) 31 *WEP* 639, 657. Civil servants working in the DGs also perceive that, because of their size and expertise, they have the upper hand over Commissioners. A. Elinas and E. Suleiman, *The European Commission and Bureaucratic Autonomy* (Cambridge University Press, 2012) 65–73.

[29] M. Hartlapp, J. Metz and C. Rauh, *Which Policy for Europe? Power and Conflict inside the European Commission* (Oxford University Press, 2014) 246–56; A. Ershova, 'The Watchdog or the Mandarin? Assessing the Impact of the Directorates General on the EU Legislative Process' (2019) 26 *JEPP* 407.

[30] L. Cram, 'The European Commission as a Multi-Organization: Social Policy and IT Policy in the EU' (1994) 1 *JEPP* 195.

[31] H. Kassim *et al.*, *The European Commission of the Twenty First Century* (Oxford University Press, 2013) 115–18; M. Egeberg, 'Experiments in Supranational Institution Building: The European Commission as Laboratory' (2012) 19 *JEPP* 939, 941–4.

(c) The Cabinets

Formally appointed by the President, each Cabinet is the Office of a Commissioner. Composed of seven to eight officials,[32] the Cabinets act, first, as the interface between the Commissioner and the DGs under her aegis.[33] They enable liaison between the two, and they help the Commissioner with formulating priorities and policies. They also act as the eyes and ears for the Commissioner, keeping her informed about what is happening elsewhere in the Commission. Finally, they combine with other Cabinets to prepare the weekly meetings for the College of Commissioners.

These tasks place the Cabinets in a very strong position. Much of the negotiations between Commissioners is, in practice, done by the Cabinets. Similarly, by acting as the interface between the Commission and the DG, they inevitably become gatekeepers to the Commissioner, with DG officials having to negotiate with them to get access to the Commissioner. Their role is, thus, controversial. DGs have seen them at times as Machiavellian, by-passing normal procedures and sabotaging perfectly acceptable proposals.[34]

(ii) The Powers of the Commission

The powers of the Commission are headlined in a single article.

Article 17 TEU

(1) The Commission shall promote the general interest of the Union and take appropriate initiatives to that end. It shall ensure the application of the Treaties, and of measures adopted by the institutions pursuant to the Treaties. It shall oversee the application of Union law under the control of the Court of Justice of the European Union. It shall execute the budget and manage programmes. It shall exercise coordinating, executive and management functions, as laid down in the Treaties. With the exception of the common foreign and security policy, and other cases provided for in the Treaties, it shall ensure the Union's external representation. It shall initiate the Union's annual and multiannual programming with a view to achieving interinstitutional agreements.

(2) Union legislative acts may only be adopted on the basis of a Commission proposal, except where the Treaties provide otherwise. Other acts shall be adopted on the basis of a Commission proposal where the Treaties so provide.

The article is terse about the scope and detail of these powers, which are scattered around the rest of the Treaty. It makes sense to consider them in the light of the central roles enjoyed by the Commission.

---

[32] The President's Cabinet is larger, with thirteen officials.

[33] On the functioning and composition see M. Egeberg and A. Heskestad, 'The Denationalization of Cabinets in the European Commission' (2010) 48 *JCMS* 775.

[34] The conduct of Martin Selmayr, the Head of President Juncker's cabinet from 2014 to 2018, was, thus, the stuff of folklore, D. Herszenhorn, '"Monster" at the Berlaymont', *Politico*, 17 November 2016.

(a) Legislative and Quasi-Legislative Powers

The Commission has direct legislative powers in only two limited fields: ensuring public undertakings comply with EU law[35] and determining the conditions under which EU citizens may reside in another Member State after having worked there.[36] It has more significant quasi-legislative powers. These are powers granted to it by EU legislation to adopt general rules, which, whilst not legislative in nature, have binding legal effects. The number of such measures adopted is considerable, typically about 1,500 per annum.[37] They can also be highly significant. For example, the 1996 measure prompting the Bovine Spongiform Encephalopathy (BSE) crisis, the prohibition on the export of beef and bovine products from the United Kingdom, was instigated under powers granted to the Commission to make veterinary and zootechnical checks on live animals and products with a view to the completion of the internal market.[38] This measure had huge implications for animal welfare, public health, public finances and the livelihood of farmers across the Union, and prompted a crisis in relations between the United Kingdom and the rest of the European Union.[39]

Justifications for this are that the main lawmaking processes can be too slow, lack the necessary expertise or do not take a sufficiently long-term perspective. Quasi-legislation also liberates other institutions to spend more time on matters of greater political significance.[40] For all this, the widespread grant of such powers raises questions of democratic accountability as it supplants the legislative process.[41] It would be worrying, for example, if they allowed the Commission to rewrite an EU law or gave it *carte blanche* to determine the content of this law.

There are two forms of quasi-legislation: delegated measures and implementing measures. Delegated measures are to be used to amend or supplement non-essential elements of legislation.

Article 290 TFEU

(1) A legislative act may delegate to the Commission the power to adopt non-legislative acts to supplement or amend certain non-essential elements of the legislative act.

The objectives, content, scope and duration of the delegation of power shall be explicitly defined in the legislative acts. The essential elements of an area shall be reserved for the legislative act and accordingly shall not be the subject of a delegation of power.

By contrast, implementing measures are to provide greater uniformity to the application and implementation of EU legislation by setting out in greater detail its implications, be this through further rules or individual decisions.

---

[35] Article 106(3) TFEU.   [36] Article 45(3)(d) TFEU.

[37] 1,448 implementing measures were therefore adopted in 2016 and 1,506 in 2015. European Commission, 'Report on the Working of Committees during 2016', COM(2017)594, 7.

[38] The measure was Decision 96/239/EC, OJ 1996, L 78/47. The principal basis for it was Directive 90/425/EEC, OJ 1990, L 224/29, Article 10(4). On the subsequent political crisis see M. Westlake, 'Mad Cows and Englishmen: The Institutional Consequences of the BSE Crisis' (1997) 35 *JCMS (Annual Review)* 11.

[39] R. Brookes, 'Newspapers and National Identity: The BSE/CJD Crisis and the British Press' (1999) 21 *Media, Culture and Society* 247.

[40] G. Majone, 'Two Logics of Delegation: Agency and Fiduciary Relations in EU Governance' (2001) 2 *EUP* 103; F. Franchino, 'Efficiency or Credibility? Testing the Two Logics of Delegation to the European Commission' (2002) 9 *JEPP* 1; M. Pollack, *The Engines of European Integration: Delegation, Agency and Agenda-Setting in the EU* (Oxford University Press, 2003) 101–7.

[41] M. Cini, 'The Commission: An Unelected Legislator?' (2002) 8(4) *Journal of Legislative Studies* 14.

(2) Where uniform conditions for implementing legally binding Union acts are needed, those acts shall confer implementing powers on the Commission . . .

The first question goes to the remit of these powers. The starting point for deciding whether excessive powers have been granted is the same for both delegated and implementing powers. A prime example of its application is *DK Recycling*. An EU law, Directive 2003/87/EC, set out a trading scheme for greenhouse gas emissions in which allowances to emit these gases were auctioned off to traders. Some allowances could, however, be provided free of charge, and the Commission was granted implementing to set out criteria for allocating these, which had to be done on a sector-by-sector basis and had to be fully harmonised (i.e. exhaustive). It duly did this in 2011. The German Government allocated a free allowance to DK Recycling for an installation which recycled waste for the steel industry on the grounds that it would, otherwise, suffer undue hardship. The Commission vetoed this allocation as this ground was not amongst the criteria set out in its measure. DK Recycling challenged this, arguing that the Commission had the power to set undue hardship out as a criterion in its implementing measure. Its failure to do so violated DK Recycling's fundamental rights, namely its right to property.

DK Recycling und Roheisen v. Commission, C–540/14 P, EU: C:2016:469

47 . . . the Court has already ruled that provisions which, in order to be adopted, require political choices falling within the responsibilities of the EU legislature cannot be delegated by the legislature, and that, accordingly, implementing measures adopted by the Commission cannot amend essential elements of basic legislation or supplement it by new essential elements . . .

48 Identifying the elements of a matter which must be categorised as essential must be based on objective factors amenable to judicial review, and requires account to be taken of the characteristics and particular features of the field concerned . . .

49 As regards the elements of Directive 2003/87 which must be categorised as essential . . . it must be pointed out that, although the principal objective of that directive is to reduce greenhouse gas emissions substantially, that objective must be attained in compliance with a series of sub-objectives. As indicated in recitals 5 and 7 of that directive, those sub-objectives include the safeguarding of economic development and employment and the preservation of the integrity of the internal market and of conditions of competition . . .

50 The repeated reference to the sub-objective relating to the preservation of conditions of competition in the internal market, not only in recitals 5 and 7 of Directive 2003/87 but also in recitals 8 and 15 of Directive 2009/29, demonstrates the essential nature of that sub-objective in the scheme for greenhouse gas emission allowance trading.

. . .

52 Thus, in Article 10a(1) of Directive 2003/87, the legislature emphasised the requirement of full harmonisation by providing that 'the Commission shall adopt Community-wide and fully-harmonised implementing measures for the allocation of the allowances', and, moreover, indicated to the Commission the criteria in accordance with which harmonisation was to be undertaken, namely, in essence, on the basis of benchmarks in sectors and subsectors.

53 In providing for this method of free allocation of allowances, fully-harmonised on a sectoral basis, the legislature gave concrete expression to the essential requirement that distortions of competition in the internal market be minimised.

54 Consequently, the Commission cannot, without being in breach of that requirement, and thus without amending an essential element of Directive 2003/87, lay down rules for the free allocation of allowances that are not fully harmonised and sectoral.

55 There is no doubt that the Commission's introduction into Decision 2011/278 of a provision permitting the free allocation of allowances to certain undertakings faced with 'undue hardship' following the application of the sectoral criteria laid down by that decision would have conflicted with the principle of the harmonised and sectoral allocation of allowances free of charge, since it would necessarily have implied a case-by-case approach based on there being particular and individual circumstances peculiar to each operator affected by such 'undue hardship'. Consequently, such a provision would have been such as to amend an essential element of Directive 2003/87, thus undermining the scheme it establishes.

Powers cannot, therefore be granted to make or to amend political choices made by the EU legislature. *DK Recycling* suggests that to ascertain whether a matter is a political choice reference must not be had to some external text but to the parent legislation. The measure will be an illegal political choice if it goes to the central objectives of that parent law, as set out in the latter's Preamble.[42] The Court will usually look beyond the legislative text to find that a measure involves a political choice if it affects either the sovereign rights of non-EU States or fundamental rights.[43] However in *Europol Third Country Agreements*, it found lawful implementing powers to decide with which third countries the EU should share the personal data of those suspected of serious criminal offences.[44] It acknowledged that this raised issues of fundamental rights but argued that this had been addressed by the parent instrument as it required account to be taken of the quality of data protection ensured by the non-EU State.

There are, however, further requirements which apply to delegated acts, and not to implementing acts, for these to be found lawful. Delegated acts have a particular purpose. The EU legislature is establishing a regulatory framework through the parent law, and delegated powers are granted to adopt rules for that regulatory framework, and, accordingly, have to fall within it.[45] By contrast, the Court does not see implementing acts as being used to fill in a regulatory framework. They are rather to provide further detail on the content of an EU law to ensure that it is implemented uniformly in all Member States.[46] The anticipation is, therefore, delegated powers give a more extensive role to the Commission than implementing powers.[47]

As a consequence, the EU legislature cannot grant loosely defined delegated powers to the Commission. The parent legislation must identify the powers as delegated powers and must set

---

[42] In like vein, *Dyson* v. *Commission*, C-44/16 P, EU:C:2017:357. On the case law see M. Chamon, 'Institutional Balance and Community Method in the Implementation of EU Legislation following the Lisbon Treaty' (2016) 53 *CMLRev* 1501, 1515–16.

[43] *Parliament* v. *Council*, C-355/10, EU:C:2012:516.   [44] *Parliament* v. *Council*, C-344/10, EU:C:2015:579.

[45] *Commission* v. *Parliament and Council*, C-427/12, EU:C:2014:170; *Commission* v. *Parliament and Council*, C-88/14, EU:C:2015:49; *Czech Republic* v. *Commission*, C-695/15 P, EU:C:2017:595.

[46] *Commission* v. *Parliament and Council*, C-417/12, EU:C:2014:170. Implementing measures must be measures which can lend themselves in principle to implementation by Member States. The Court has, thus, ruled that a power to fine a Member State could not be an implementing measure, *Spain* v. *Council*, C-521/15, EU:C:2017:982.

[47] On the debate that led to this see G. Brandsma and J. Blom-Hansen, *Controlling the EU Executive?: The Politics of Delegation in the European Union* (Oxford University Press, 2017) 63–75.

out, in precise terms, the objectives, content, scope and duration of these powers.[48] In *Connecting Europe Facility*, the Court stated that the parent legislation must specify whether the delegated power is to supplement a legislative act, amend it or do both.[49] When a power to supplement a legislative act is granted, the Commission is only authorised to flesh out the act. It can, according to the Court, only develop those details which have not been specified by the EU legislature. In addition, as it has only a power to supplement the law, it has no power to amend subsequently any measure that it has adopted. By contrast, when granted the power to amend legislation, the Commission has the power to amend and repeal any non-essential parts of the law.

Subject to this, the EU legislature has considerable freedom over whether to grant implementing or delegated powers to the Commission as the distinction between when a measure is supplementing, amending (both delegating) or implementing (implementing) its parent legislation is unclear to the point of being inoperable.[50] This is all the more so as the Court has stated that it will only intervene to second-guess the legislature's choice where there is a manifest error of assessment. It will not look, therefore, at whether the choice was the right one but only at whether it was a reasonable one.[51]

This matters as the exercise of delegated powers is subject to fewer controls than the exercise of implementing powers. The controls to which the EU legislature subjects the Commission are not determined, therefore, by reference to the risks or the nature of the task but largely by how it chooses to design the powers.[52] The procedures governing how the Commission is to exercise its implementing powers are known as comitology, and are addressed in more detail in Chapter 3.[53] The procedures governing delegated powers are briefly described in Article 290(2) TFEU.

Article 290 TFEU

(2) Legislative acts shall explicitly lay down the conditions to which the delegation is subject; these conditions may be as follows:

(a) the European Parliament or the Council may decide to revoke the delegation;

(b) the delegated act may enter into force only if no objection has been expressed by the European Parliament or the Council within a period set by the legislative act.

For the purposes of (a) and (b), the European Parliament shall act by a majority of its component members, and the Council by a qualified majority.

In March 2011, a Common Understanding was agreed between the EU Institutions, which elaborated on the processes to be followed.

---

[48] *Czech Republic* v. *Commission*, C-695/15 P, EU:C:2017:595. [49] *Parliament* v. *Council*, C-286/14, EU:C:2016:183.

[50] P. Craig, 'Comitology, Rulemaking and the Lisbon Settlement: Tensions and Strains' in C. Bergström and D. Ritleng (eds.), *Law-Making by the EU Commission: The New System* (Oxford University Press 2016); Chamon, n. 42 above, pp. 1520–3. On the practice see E. Tauschinsky, 'Searching for Order: Exploring the Use of Delegated and Implementing Acts in the EU Customs Code' (2018) 6 *Theory and Practice of Legislation* 53.

[51] *Commission* v. *Parliament and Council*, C-427/12, EU:C:2014:170.

[52] For a comparison see T. Christiansen and M. Dobbels, 'Non-Legislative Rule Making after the Lisbon Treaty: Implementing the New System of Comitology and Delegated Acts' (2013) 19 *ELJ* 42.

[53] The regime is now set out in Regulation 182/2011 laying down the rules and general principles concerning mechanisms for control by Member States of the Commission's exercise of implementing powers, OJ 2011, L 55/13. See pp. 146–51.

Common Understanding – Delegated Acts, EU Council 8753/11

4 The Commission, when preparing and drawing up delegated acts, will ensure a simultaneous, timely and appropriate transmission of relevant documents to the European Parliament and the Council and carry out appropriate and transparent consultations well in advance, including at expert level ...

10 Without prejudice to the urgency procedure,[54] the period for objection defined on a case-by case basis in each basic act should in principle be of two months, and not less than that, extendable by two months at the initiative of the European Parliament or the Council.

It is difficult for the Parliament or the Council to get a measure revoked as it both generates conflict and they cannot insist on a substitute measure being adopted to take its place, with the corresponding danger of a legal vacuum if the measure is revoked.[55] Their greatest influence lies therefore in being consulted before any delegated measure is adopted. In the first few years, both felt that the Commission was not consulting sufficiently.[56] In 2016, the Commission committed, therefore, 'to gathering, prior to the adoption of delegated acts, all necessary expertise, including through the consultation of Member States' experts and through public consultations'.[57] If this seemed anodyne, the Council had wanted the Commission to consult much more systematically with national experts, with a commitment to take the 'utmost account' of the opinions of these.[58] Within this context, there is, therefore, a risk that consultation with these national experts will be emphasised at the expense of that with the European Parliament and the wider public.[59]

(b) Agenda-Setting

The Commission has responsibility for initiating the policy process in a number of ways.

First, the Commission is responsible for stimulating policy debate. In 2017, for example, as a way of trying to address the crisis of trust in the EU, it set out five scenarios for the *Future of Europe* by 2025 in order to prod Member States to reach agreement on what they wanted from the European Union.[60]

---

54 This allows for shorter periods in exceptional cases such as security matters, protection of health or humanitarian assistance. The parent act must stipulate when this procedure can be used, *Common Understanding – Delegated Acts*, EU Council Doc. 8753/11, para. 12.

55 M. Kaeding and K. Stack, 'Legislative Scrutiny? The Political Economy and Practice of Legislative Vetoes in the European Union' (2015) 53 *JCMS* 1268.

56 *Initiative to complement the Common Understanding on delegated acts as regards the consultation of experts*, EU Council Doc. 6774/14, p. 2.

57 Interinstitutional Agreement between the European Parliament, the Council of the European Union and the European Commission on Better Law-Making, OJ 2017, L 123/1, para. 28.

58 *Initiative to complement the Common Understanding on delegated acts as regards the consultation of experts*, n. 56 above, p. 5. There is significant evidence that this is only done patchily by the Commission, K. Siderius and G. Brandsma, 'The Effect of Removing Voting Rules: Consultation Practices in the Commission's Delegated Act Expert Groups and Comitology Committees' (2016) 54 *JCMS* 1265.

59 J. Mendes, 'The Making of Delegated and Implementing Acts: Legitimacy beyond Inter-Institutional Balances' in C. Bergström and D. Ritleng (eds.), *Law-Making by the EU Commission: The New System* (Oxford University Press, 2016) 233, at 236–8.

60 These were carrying on doing the same as now, focusing on the single market, allowing those States that wished to integrate further to do so but not requiring it of others, focusing more intensely on certain key policies and greater integration across the board, European Commission, *White Paper on the Future of Europe* (Brussels, European Commission, 2017).

Secondly, it has the power of financial initiative, as it starts the budgetary process by placing a draft budget before the Parliament and the Council.[61]

Thirdly, and most significantly, in most fields it has a monopoly over the power of legislative initiative.[62] On paper, this power is really significant. The Commission can prevent the adoption of new EU laws or the amendment of existing ones by simply refusing to put a legislative proposal forward. In that way, the Commission can kill off certain policy fields or force EU activity to be focused on one or two activities.[63] Indeed, the central role of elections in national democracies is to elect a government who will put an agenda to be voted upon by the national parliament. Party manifestos consist in large part, therefore, of legislative agendas that would be put forward if a party were elected. The Commission's power is further enhanced as, after making a legislative proposal, it can withdraw it at any time before the proposal is adopted as law provided it gives reasons for this which are supported by 'cogent evidence or arguments',[64] something which will not be difficult to find. In such circumstances, the other EU Institutions will not be able to adopt the law, and, thus, negotiations between these always take place under this shadow.

Practice is more nuanced. In some instances, the Commission may be little more than a technical agenda-setter. In this role, it drafts proposals at the behest of other political actors: be it national governments, other EU Institutions or even powerful industries or non-governmental organisations (NGOs), and simply translates their preferences into a legislative form. In other circumstances, it may be a political player in its own right with the proposal reflecting its own political preferences. Kreppel and Otzas found that, in general, the Commission was an important political player by looking at how much of its Annual Work Programmes between 2000 and 2011 the Commission was able to turn into law, as they assumed that these Work Programmes were more likely to reflect its own preferences.[65] Some 67.3 per cent became EU laws. The fact that nearly a third were not adopted could not be explained if the Commission were the handmaiden of the Member States. However, the figure, whilst lower than the 80–95 per cent that EU governments get adopted as laws in their own States, was still very high.

The Commission's power is influenced by a number of factors.[66] Central is institutional context. In areas where a unanimity vote by Member States is not required, the Commission can act as a broker between some actors and outmanoeuvre others.[67] In some areas, it can also induce other EU Institutions to adopt its proposal as the 'lesser evil' by threatening other powers at its disposal, such as bringing a Member State before the Court of Justice, which would lead to

---

[61] Article 314(2) TFEU.

[62] The main exception is Common Foreign and Security Policy where it has only an ancillary role. In this field initiatives or proposals may only be made by any Member State or the High Representative with Commission support, Article 30(1) TEU.

[63] On how Commission inactivity led to a tailing away of EU environmental policy, see Y. Steinebech and C. Knill, 'Still an Entrepreneur? The Changing Role of the European Commission in EU Environmental Policy-Making' (2017) 24 *JEPP* 429.

[64] *Council* v. *Commission*, C-409/13, EU:C:2015:217, para. 76.

[65] A. Kreppel and B. Otzas, 'Leading the Band or Just Playing the Tune? Reassessing the Agenda-Setting Powers of the European Commission' (2017) 50 *Comparative Political Studies* 1118.

[66] On the strategies deployed by these different actors see S. Princen, 'Agenda-Setting Strategies in EU Policy Processes' (2011) 18 *JEPP* 927.

[67] S. Schmidt, 'Only an Agenda-Setter? The Commission's Power over the Council of Ministers' (2000) 1 *EUP* 37.

more draconian consequences.[68] There is also a temporal dimension. If the Commission is impatient, its influence is weakened, as it has to accept more readily the views of the other institutions. By contrast, if the other institutions are impatient for a measure to be adopted, the Commission's power increases.[69]

Most commentators agree that a shift has happened in recent years in how the Commission exercises this power. First, national governments, national parliaments and other EU Institutions are increasingly interested in issuing instructions and limiting the Commission's discretion. It has had to become responsive to this.[70] Secondly, as public mood has hardened against the European Union, the Commission has tended to focus its priorities more sharply. Thus, it has concentrated on legislating more intensely in more narrowly focused areas (such as on the euro area crisis) at the expense of an array of proposals across an array of matters.[71] Finally, alongside this, as what the European Union does has become more politically contested, the Commission has to reach out to a wider array of actors beyond its traditional constituencies to try and get appeal. A study of EU consumer protection legislation found it much more engaged with consumer groups than previously.[72]

All this has generated incentives for the Commission to consult before adopting a proposal. As an unelected EU Institution, it can bolster its legitimacy by showing that it has listened to an array of views.[73] Furthermore, it is under a duty to consult broadly.

Article 11 TEU

(3) The European Commission shall carry out broad consultations with parties concerned in order to ensure that the Union's actions are coherent and transparent.

The Commission understands this duty as requiring adequate coverage in its consultations amongst those affected by any proposal, those implementing it, and, because of their organisation's objectives, those with a direct interest in the proposal (e.g. NGOs).[74]

These duties are very generic and three types of concern have emerged.

The first goes to the range and balance of interests consulted. The widest studies found that the overwhelming proportion of participants are commercial interests. The largest study found that business and occupational interests accounted for just over 62 per cent of all participants but

---

[68] S. Schmidt, 'The European Commission's Powers in Shaping Policies' in D. Dimitrakopoulos (ed.), *The Changing Commission* (Manchester University Press, 2004).

[69] M. Pollack, 'Delegation, Agency and Agenda Setting in the European Community' (1997) 51 *IO* 99, 121–4.

[70] J.-P. Jacqué, 'Lost in Transition' in D. Ritleng (ed.), *Independence and Legitimacy in the Institutional System of the European Union* (Oxford University Press, 2016); N. Lupo, 'The Commission's Power to Withdraw Legislative Proposals and its "Parliamentarisation", between Technical and Political Grounds' (2018) 14 *EUConst* 311.

[71] S. Becker *et al.*, 'The Commission: Boxed In and Constrained, but Still an Engine of Integration' (2016) 39 *WEP* 1011; I. Camisão and M. Guimarães, 'The Commission, the Single Market and the Crisis: The Limits of Purposeful Opportunism' (2017) 55 *JCMS* 223.

[72] C. Rauh, 'EU Politicization and Policy Initiatives of the European Commission: The Case of Consumer Policy' (2019) 26 *JEPP* 319.

[73] A. Bunea and R. Thomson, 'Consultations with Interest Groups and the Empowerment of Executives: Evidence from the European Union' (2015) 28 *Governance* 517.

[74] European Commission, 'General Principles and Minimum Standards for Consultation of Interested Parties by the Commission', COM(2002)704. See D. Obradovic and J. Alonso, 'Good Governance Requirements Concerning the Participation of Interest Groups in EU Consultations' (2006) 43 *CMLRev* 1049.

that this figure was even higher, at over 80 per cent, when the proposal concerned market regulation. By contrast, public interest groups accounted respectively for just 18 per cent and (just under) 11 per cent of participants.[75] Interests from larger, older Member States, such as France, Germany or the United Kingdom were also more likely to be engaged than those from other States.[76]

The second concern revolves around who actually influences the Commission amongst those consulted. Studies have found simple consultation insufficient. Influence, it appears, rests on supplying a number of things to the EU Institutions. These include expertise, the reputation of the participant, its ability to enlist either citizen support or economic buy-in from industry.[77] Paradoxically, this can secure greater influence for public interest participants, as commercial interests will rarely have the public support or range of expertise that allows them to have exclusive influence over the institutions.[78] However, even if this secures some plurality of views, it is still a system that rewards those who are well organised and know how to play the lobbying system.

This led to a third concern. Lobbyists were either securing undue influence through back-channelling or were being used as fronts for more secretive constellations of interests to exercise influence opaquely.[79] In 2011, the European Transparency Register, was established by the European Parliament and Commission to cover those engaged in influencing EU policy formulation or EU decision-making.[80] Membership is voluntary but neither the Commission nor the Parliament will meet with those who are not registered.[81] This has led to a high take-up with 11,612 parties registered at the end of 2017.[82] At the heart of the Register is a Code of Conduct which must be observed by those who are registered. This Code requires parties, *inter alia*, to declare the interest that they represent; provide only complete, unbiased, up-to-date information which is not misleading; not obtain information dishonestly, and not induce EU staff to breach EU rules.[83] The central challenge with the Code has been compliance. In 2017, just over 20 per cent of those checked had to be removed from the Register because of non-compliance with the Code or inaccurate information.[84] This suggests poor conduct by lobbyists is common.

These developments have eroded the traditional justification for the Commission's power of initiative, namely that its autonomy would result in the best representation of the common

---

[75] A. Rasmussen and B. Carroll, 'Determinants of Upper-Class Dominance in the Heavenly Chorus: Lessons from European Union Online Consultations' (2014) 44 *BJPS* 445, 452.

[76] C. Quittkat, 'The European Commission's Online Consultations: A Success Story?' (2011) 49 *JCMS* 653, 666–70.

[77] H. Klüver, 'Lobbying as a Collective Enterprise: Winners and Losers of Policy Formulation in the European Union' (2013) 20 *JEPP* 59; S. Arras and C. Braun, 'Stakeholders Wanted! Why and How European Union Agencies Involve Non-State Stakeholders' (2018) 25 *JEPP* 1257.

[78] A. Judge and R. Thomson, 'The responsiveness of legislative actors to stakeholders' demands in the European Union' *JEPP* (forthcoming).

[79] European Commission, 'Follow-Up to the Green Paper "European Transparency" Initiative', COM(2007)127, 3–4.

[80] Agreement between the European Parliament and the European Commission on the establishment of a transparency register for organisations and self-employed individuals engaged in EU policy-making and policy implementation, OJ 2011, L 191/29. On the background see M. Cini, 'EU Decision-Making on Inter-Institutional Agreements: Defining (Common) Rules of Conduct for European Lobbyists and Public Servants' (2013) 36 *WEP* 1143, 1146–9.

[81] There is currently a proposal for registration to be mandatory. European Commission, 'Proposal for an Interinstitutional Agreement on a Mandatory Transparency Register', COM(2016)627.

[82] Joint Transparency Register Secretariat, *Annual Report on the operations of the Transparency Register 2017*, 9. This is available at http://www.europarl.europa.eu/at-your-service/files/transparency/en-annual-report-on-the-operations-of-the-transparency-register-2017.pdf.

[83] Agreement between the European Parliament and the European Commission on the establishment of a transparency register, n. 80 above, Annex III.

[84] Joint Transparency Register Secretariat, n. 82 above, p. 12.

European interest.[85] It has been suggested that one way to address this would be to hold pan-Union elections for the President of the Commission. Candidates for the Presidency would have to put forward manifesto in the same way as parties seeking domestic government, with the consequence that voters can decide on what legislative agenda is put before the Union for the next five years.[86]

This has not happened. However, in 2014 the *Spitzenkandidat* process was adopted. The procedure for appointing the President of the Commission requires account to be taken of the preceding European Parliament elections and the Parliament to agree to their appointment.[87] In that year, all the major groupings in the European Parliament stated that they would not accept any candidate who had not been nominated by a grouping, and that the President should be the person nominated by the grouping who received the most votes.[88] Candidates were nominated by the groupings and prior to the 2014 elections, they toured most of the Union, setting out their views. The European People's Party duly secured the most votes, and their candidate, Jean-Claude Juncker, was duly put forward to be President of the Commission. The process was seen as a power grab by the European Parliament, and two States, Hungary and the United Kingdom, voted against his appointment. There were also doubts about the democratic quality of the choice before voters. Martin Schulz, Juncker's main rival, for example, never visited the United Kingdom during the campaign. Member States are split over continuing the process. Some, notably the French President Macron, believe that it leads to the process being stitched up by the European Parliament and the President being granted a status that he should not have. However, all European Parliament groupings support its use for the 2019 elections as they believe it gives the Commission President a stronger mandate.[89]

A further way opening up the process was suggested at the *Future of Europe* Convention. A network of NGOs, Democracy International, argued that there should be greater provision for participatory democracy to accommodate a broader array of public concerns and interests.[90] As a consequence, provision was made for a European Citizens' Initiative (ECI), which is now set out in Article 11(4) TEU.

Article 11 TEU

(4) Not less than one million citizens who are nationals of a significant number of Member States may take the initiative of inviting the European Commission, within the framework of its powers, to submit any appropriate proposal on matters where citizens consider that a legal act of the Union is required for the purpose of implementing the Treaties.

---

[85] K. Featherstone, 'Jean Monnet and the "Democratic Deficit" in the European Union' (1994) 32 *JCMS* 149, 154–5.

[86] A. Føllesdal and S. Hix, 'Why There Is a Democratic Deficit in the EU: A Response to Majone and Moravcsik' (2006) 44 *JCMS* 533, 554.

[87] Article 17(7) TEU.

[88] On the 2014 process see S. Hobolt, 'A Vote for the President? The Role of Spitzenkandidaten in the 2014 European Parliament Elections' (2014) 21 *JEPP* 1528; M. Goldoni, 'Politicising EU Lawmaking? The Spitzenkandidaten Experiment as a Cautionary Tale' (2016) 22 *ELJ* 279.

[89] European Parliament decision of 7 February 2018 on the revision of the Framework Agreement on relations between the European Parliament and the European Commission, A8–0006/2018.

[90] See, on this, in particular, J. de Clerck-Sachsse, 'Civil Society and Democracy in the European EU: The Paradox of the European Citizens' Initiative' (2012) 13 *Perspectives on European Politics and Society* 299.

Article 11(4) TEU has been implemented by Regulation 211/2011 which elaborates on the requirements and modalities for the ECI.[91]

Any proposed ECI must, first, be registered with the Commission and declared eligible.[92] Eligibility requires there to be an organising committee comprised of EU citizens from at least seven Member States[93] and the Commission being provided information on, *inter alia*, the title, subject matter and objectives of the ECI, and the Treaty articles under which it is proposed Union action should be taken.[94] The Commission will examine the proposal. It will not declare the ECI eligible if it is manifestly abusive, vexatious or frivolous; falls outside EU competences; or contradicts the fundamental rights and values set out in Article 2 TEU.[95] The committee, then, has twelve months from registration to obtain at least one million statements of support[96] of which there must be a minimum number of statements of support from at least seven Member States. This minimum will equate to the number of MEPs of each of those State multiplied by 750.[97] At the end of this period, the national authorities must verify and certify the signatures to ascertain whether these thresholds have been met.[98]

In its first nine years, only four ECIs successfully both met the criteria for eligibility and reached the threshold number of statements of support.[99] This low use may be driven by weak awareness of the ECI and limited popular enthusiasm for it, with those enthusiastic about European integration more ready to use it than opponents.[100] However it may be that the criteria are too exacting. Proportionate to the Union's overall population, they are less onerous than citizens' initiatives used in other jurisdictions[101] but one finds another ten ECIs which collected 100,000–300,000 statements of support and generate significant levels of awareness in at least part of the Union.[102] From the perspective of participatory democracy, the position is more depressing when one looks at the Commission action that happened as a follow-up to these four successful ECIs. The Commission is required to set out its actions and any proposed action within three months of receiving a successful ECI.[103]

(c) Executive Powers

The Commission is responsible for ensuring that the Union's revenue is collected and passed on by national authorities and that the correct rates are applied. It is also responsible for overseeing and coordinating a large part of Union expenditure. Secondly, it is responsible for administering Union aid to third countries. Thirdly, the High Representative is to represent the Union for matters relating to the common foreign and security policy. Notably, she shall conduct political dialogue with third parties on the Union's behalf and shall express the Union's position in international organisations and at international conferences.[104] To that end, she is assisted by a

---

[91] Regulation 211/2011 on the citizens' initiative, OJ 2011, L 65/1.   [92] *Ibid*. Article 4(1).   [93] *Ibid*. Article 3.
[94] *Ibid*. Article 4(1) and Annex II.   [95] *Ibid*. Article 4(2).   [96] Article 11(4) TEU.
[97] Regulation 211/2011, Article 7(1)–(2).   [98] *Ibid*. Article 8(1).
[99] http://ec.europa.eu/citizens-initiative/public/initiatives/successful.
[100] For data supporting this see A. Kandyla and S. Ghergina, 'What Triggers the Intention to Use the European Citizens' Initiative? The Role of Benefits, Values and Efficacy' (2018) 56 *JCMS* 1223.
[101] V. Cuesta-López, 'A Comparative Approach to the Regulation on the European Citizens' Initiative' (2012) 13 *Perspectives on European Politics and Society* 257, 261.
[102] J. Greenwood and K. Tuokko, 'The European Citizens' Initiative: The Territorial Extension of a European Political Public Sphere?' (2017) 18 *European Politics and Society* 166.
[103] Regulation 211/2011, Article 10(1)(c).   [104] Article 27(2) TEU.

European External Action Service comprising officials from the Council Secretariat and the Commission.[105] The High Representative occupies a unique position. Responsible for the conduct of the Union common foreign and security policy and its security and defence policy, she is both one of the Commissioners[106] and acts under the mandate of the Council.[107] The intention of this 'double hat' is to create a more integrated and coordinated external policy,[108] as well as to give the EU a more salient international profile.[109] Saddling the Commission and the Council, she is subject to a double chain of accountability. Thus, she cannot be dismissed unilaterally by the President of the Commission, who requires the agreement of the European Council, the body representing the Heads of Government, to carry this out.[110] Finally, the Commission handles applications for membership of the European Union by carrying out an investigation of the implications of membership and submitting an opinion to the Council.[111]

(d) Supervisory Powers

The Commission polices the Union. It enjoys, first, certain regulatory powers. It can declare illegal State aids provided by Member States[112] or measures enacted in favour of public undertakings which breach the Treaty.[113] It has also been granted powers to declare anti-competitive practices by private undertakings illegal and to fine those firms,[114] as well as the power to impose duties on goods coming from third States, which are benefiting from 'unfair' trade practices, such as dumping or export subsidies.[115] Secondly, it may bring Member States before the Court of Justice for breaching EU law.[116] It uses this power extensively.[117] The Commission is also responsible for monitoring compliance by Member States with judgments of the Court of Justice. It can bring those Member States, which it considers to have failed to comply, back before the Court to have them fined.[118] Its most wide-ranging supervisory powers are, arguably, over euro area States in the fields of economic and fiscal policy. The Council can sanction States in these fields on the basis of a Commission finding that they have breached EU law limits with regard to their public finances or more general state of their economy. These powers to propose sanctions give the Commission oversight over almost all areas of fiscal, welfare and economic policy in order to verify whether compliance with EU norms is taking place.[119]

There is a danger of seeing this relationship as exclusively about policing. The reality is usually different. The EU has few administrative resources on the ground of its own. It is reliant on national administrations with far greater resources to do this. Supervision of these gives the

---

[105] Article 27(3) TEU.   [106] Article 17(4) TEU.

[107] Article 18(2) TEU. She, consequently, also chairs the Foreign Affairs configuration of the Council, Article 18(3) TEU.

[108] Article 18(4) TEU.

[109] She, consequently, also takes part in the work of the European Council as a consequence of its pre-eminence in this field, Article 15(2) TEU. On the European Council see pp. 89–94.

[110] Article 18(1) TEU. However, if the Parliament passes a motion of censure over the whole Commission, she must resign with the other Commission members, Article 17(8) TEU.

[111] Article 49 TEU.   [112] Article 108(2) TFEU.   [113] Article 106(3) TFEU.

[114] Regulation 1/2003, OJ 2001, L 1/1, Articles 7 and 23 respectively.

[115] In relation to dumping see Regulation 2016/1036 on protection against dumped imports from countries not members of the European Union, OJ 2016, L 176/21.

[116] Article 258 TFEU.

[117] At the end of 2016, for example, 1,657 infringement proceedings against Member States were open. European Commission, 'Thirty-Fourth Annual Report on Monitoring the Application of EU Law', COM(2017)370, 25.

[118] Article 260(2) TFEU.   [119] For more detail see pp. 665–77.

Commission the possibility to establish an ongoing engagement with national counterparts about how to administer EU policies in which the relationship is often one of give and take.[120] Many authors have noted that this relationship establishes a European administrative network (EAN), comprising EU and national actors, which comes together to administer the Union territory.[121] The interaction within this network means that it is too simplistic to characterise this network as EU or national, as administrators are focused on making the network work as smoothly as possible and harnessing each other's resources.[122] This network raises a number of issues.[123]

E. Mastenbroek and D. Martinsen, 'Filling the Gap in the European Administrative Space: The Role of Administrative Networks in EU Implementation and Enforcement' (2018) 25 *Journal of European Public Policy* 422, 429

Most literature stresses EANs' positive contribution to European integration – their ability to harmonize rules, to create domestic change and to improve compliance. At the same time, EANs raise a set of normative issues, related to the fact that EANs are mostly made up of civil servants and experts from the national and European administrations. Mandating such administrative actors implies processes of depoliticization, devolving power towards the administration and blurring the lines of political responsibility. The increased autonomy of regulatory networks reduces the influence of formal rule-making institutions thus disempowering (supra)national majoritarian institutions and potentially the Commission as the Union's core executive. Accordingly, decision-making influence further drifts away from national constituencies. As observed by Raustiala[124] for trans-governmental networks more broadly, these developments are at odds with the thrust of legitimacy theory. While improving effectiveness and rule harmonization, EANs may seriously damage EU legitimacy.

Furthermore, accountability problems loom large. The selective composition and informality of many EAN privileges certain interests at the expense of others. Their weak visibility insulates them from public scrutiny. Their decisions are not exposed to parliamentarian involvement, let alone control. Interactions between qualified peers cannot substitute public accountability. As argued by Martinsen and Jørgensen[125], EANs

---

[120] H. Hofmann and A. Türk, 'Conclusion: Europe's Integrated Administration' in H. Hofmann and A. Türk (eds.), *EU Administrative Governance* (Cheltenham, Edward Elgar, 2006); D. Curtin, *Executive Power of the European Union: Law, Practices and the Living Constitution* (Oxford University Press, 2009) 166–72.

[121] M. Hobolth and D. Martinsen, 'Transgovernmental Networks in the European Union: Improving Compliance Effectively?' (2013) 20 *JEPP* 1406; E. Mathieu, 'When Europeanization Feeds Back into EU Governance: EU Legislation, National Regulatory Agencies, and EU Regulatory Networks' (2015) 94 *Public Administration* 25; M. Blauberger and B. Rittberger, 'Conceptualizing and Theorizing EU Regulatory Networks' (2015) 9 *Regulation and Governance* 367.

[122] On the dynamics of this see E. Matthieu, *Regulatory Delegation in the European Union: Networks, Committees and Agencies* (Basingstoke, Palgrave Macmillan, 2016) 166 *et seq.*

[123] See also M. Egeberg and J. Trondal, 'Why Strong Coordination at One Level of Government Is Incompatible with Strong Coordination across Levels (and How to Live with It): The Case of the European Union' (2016) 94 *Public Administration* 579.

[124] K. Raustiala, 'The Architecture of International Cooperation: Transgovernmental Networks and the Future of International Law' (2002) 43 *Virginia Journal of International Law* 1.

[125] D. Martinsen and T. Jørgensen, 'Accountability as a Differentiated Value in Supranational Governance' (2010) 40 *American Review of Public Administration* 742.

perform poorly from an accountability perspective: there is no forum for holding EANs accountable, they are not obliged to justify their actions and the lack of hierarchy diffuses who is to be held accountable.

Partly remedying these deficiencies, Bignami[126] has argued that EANs only will emerge if democratically elected governments agree on the underlying policy objectives. Furthermore, governance in networks may foster legitimacy by allowing affected actors to participate in decision-making, which may enhance the acceptance of outcomes and the engagement of citizens more broadly. However, such inclusiveness of EANs is still up for an empirical test.

(iii) Regulatory Agencies and the Commission

In 2001, the Commission recommended in its *White Paper on Governance*, that independent EU regulatory agencies should be established in any field marked by specialisation, complexity and where a single public interest predominates.[127] In 2018, thirty-three European regulatory agencies were in operation.[128] The remit of these agencies is wide, ranging from fundamental rights, environment, transport, financial services, and external frontiers to pharmaceuticals, intellectual property and energy.[129] Chiti has proposed a helpful threefold categorisation:[130]

- *Agencies with the power to take decisions.* The Office for Harmonisation in the Internal Market (OHIM) can grant Community trademarks and registered designs, and the Community Plant Variety Office can do the same for Community plant variety rights. The EU chemicals regime has a 'no data, no market rule' which requires manufacturers to register a dossier assessing the risks of these chemicals with the European Chemicals Agency. The Single Resolution Board can set up resolution schemes for large banks which are about to fail. These schemes can require disposal of the institution's assets, write-down of its debts or transfer of its assets to other parties. The European Banking, Insurance and Occupational Pensions and Securities and Markets Authorities can all adopt draft technical standards which the Commission can adopt or reject, but not amend, as law.
- *Agencies with instrumental powers.* These are powers to provide expert opinions to the European Commission which will be used to grant market authorisations[131] or prepare legislation.[132] In such instances, the Commission will invariably have a duty to consult the Agency, but it will be

---

[126] F. Bignami, 'Transgovernmental Networks vs. Democracy: The Case of the European Information Privacy Network' (2005) 26 *Michigan Journal of International Law* 807.

[127] European Commission, 'European Governance: A White Paper', COM(2001)428, 24.

[128] https://europa.eu/european-union/about-eu/agencies_en. There are also six Executive agencies. These are more managerial in nature, being responsible for the administration of a Union programme. Their mandate is set out in Regulation 58/200, laying down the statute for executive agencies to be entrusted with certain tasks in the management of Community programmes, OJ 2003, L 11/1. A further three agencies are involved with the Common Security and Defence Policy and another two with managing EURATOM.

[129] The most extensive overview is C. Ossege, *European Regulatory Agencies in EU Decision-Making Between Expertise and Influence* (Basingstoke, Palgrave Macmillan, 2016); M. Chamon, *EU Agencies: Legal and Political Limits to the Transformation of the EU Administration* (Oxford University Press, 2016).

[130] E. Chiti, 'European Agencies' Rulemaking: Powers, Procedures and Assessment' (2013) 19 *ELJ* 93, 94–9.

[131] Agencies with this role include the European Chemicals Agency, the European Food Safety Authority and the European Medicines Agency.

[132] Agencies doing this include the European Network and Information Security Agency, the European Maritime Safety Agency and the European Railways Agency.

for the Commission or other EU Institutions to decide what level of risk is acceptable.[133] That said, they may only depart from the Agency's views on what risks are present if they can provide an alternative, equally authoritative, contradictory opinion.[134]

- *Agencies whose responsibility is to disseminate information.* Some agencies merely disseminate information to the public. These are the least powerful of all the agencies, and include the European Environment Agency, the European Agency for Safety and Health at Work and the European Union Agency for Fundamental Rights.

Combined, these powers are substantial and wide-ranging. In *ESMA*, the Court considered the powers which may be granted to individual agencies.[135] It stated that, to be lawful, the objectives of the agency had to be set out in the parent legislation, and the powers had to be precisely delimited and amenable to judicial review. However, it took a generous view of when this was so. It allowed the agency in that case, the European Securities and Markets Authority, to have the power to set general binding norms on the grounds that the circumstances in which it could do so were set out clearly in the EU legislation, and there were a series of procedural controls requiring it to consult widely before adopting any such measure.

Agencies have largely emerged in fields where the Commission is less interested in acquiring powers of its own but is interested in there being an EU administrative capacity.[136] Egeberg, Trondal and Vestlund have, consequently, noted that the growth of these agencies and their powers is synonymous with centralisation of EU executive power and a quest for executive order at the expense of both domestic and parliamentary politics.

> **M. Egeberg, J. Trondal and N. Vestlund, 'The Quest for Order: Unravelling the Relationship between the European Commission and European Union Agencies' (2015) 22 *Journal of European Public Policy* 609, 624**
>
> From an organizational perspective, the following factors are conducive to the development of relatively close relationships between Commission DGs and EU agencies. First, both are sharing the function of being primarily executive bodies. Second, at both places, personnel from the bottom to the top, have an EU institution as their primary organizational affiliation. Third, compared to the Council and the EP, only the Commission disposes over administrative capacity to follow up work at the policy implementation stage. And fourth, and finally, legitimized templates of department–agency arrangements found at the national level point in the direction of assigning agencies to particular departments within the executive rather than to legislative chambers. This seems to be the case at least in a European context.
>
> . . . Moreover, the Commission has created its own administrative infrastructure within the affected DGs as well as across such DGs in order to follow up its agencification policy in practice. Concerning practice, we have demonstrated how the Commission has systematically allocated the agencies among its DGs according to issue area. In an overwhelming majority of cases, the DGs supervise, have regular meetings with, and

---

[133] *BASF Agro* v. *Commission*, T-584/13, EU:T:2018:279.

[134] *Pfizer Animal Health* v. *Council*, T-13/99, EU:T:2002:209.

[135] *United Kingdom* v. *Parliament and Council* ('*ESMA*'), C-340/12, EU:C:2014:18.

[136] D. Kelemen, 'The Politics of "Eurocratic" Structure and the New European Agencies' (2002) 25 *WEP* 93; M. Egeberg and J. Trondal, 'EU-Level Agencies: New Executive Centre Formation or Vehicles for National Control?' (2011) 18 *JEPP* 868; M. Scipioni, '*De Novo* Bodies and EU Integration: What Is the Story behind EU Agencies' Expansion?' (2018) 56 *JCMS* 768.

consider themselves to be parent DGs rather than partners of their respective agencies. It is also quite common for DGs to comment on the annual work programme of 'their' agencies, and increasingly so. Finally, we have shown that agency attention is directed significantly more towards the Commission than towards the Council or the EP. In sum, our interpretation is that although agencification tends to de-concentrate executive power, it nevertheless may indicate centralization of executive power at the EU level, since powers may have been delegated to agencies more often from national governments than from the Commission. The fact that agencies are geographically spread and located outside the political centre does not seem to affect the centre's actual control over agencies.

If this is troubling, the processes of accountability, to which agencies are subject, have had limited effectiveness.[137] The central form of national oversight is all agencies having a management board, which comprises national representatives, approves their work programme and budget, and ensures that they do not go beyond their mandate.[138] However, in practice, few national representatives take instructions from national governments.[139] Consequently, the central controls reinforce the influence of the Commission over these agencies. In 2012, an alert system was established which is activated when the Commission believes the agency is violating EU law, or when its mandate or its actions are in manifest contradiction to EU policy objectives. In such circumstances, it formally requests the agency to refrain. If there is no compliance with this request, it formally raises the issue with the Council and the Parliament, with a further request to the agency to refrain from any action whilst these EU Institutions discuss what to do.[140]

4 THE COUNCIL OF MINISTERS

(i) The Powers and Workings of the Council

The Council comprises a Minister from each Member State authorised to commit the government of that State on that matter.[141] Environmental Ministers will, thus, sit in the Environmental Council and Agriculture or Fisheries Ministers in the Agriculture and Fisheries Council. Since 2002, it has been agreed that more than one Minister from each Member State may sit in a Council meeting, particularly where an issue crosses different ministerial portfolios.[142] The Council sits in ten configurations:[143]

- General Affairs
- Foreign Affairs

---

[137] See, generally, M. Busuioc, *European Agencies: Law and Practices of Accountability* (Oxford University Press, 2013).

[138] On these, *ibid.* ch. 5.

[139] M. Buess, 'European Union Agencies and their Management Boards: An Assessment of Accountability and Demoi-Cratic Legitimacy' (2014) 22 *JEPP* 94.

[140] Joint Statement of the European Parliament, Council and European Commission on decentralised agencies (2012) para. 59, https://europa.eu/european-union/sites/europaeu/files/docs/body/joint_statement_and_common_approach_2012_en.pdf.

[141] Article 16(2) TEU.

[142] Decision 2002/682/EC, EURATOM adopting the Council's Rules of Procedure, OJ 2002, L 230/7.

[143] Decision 2009/878/EU establishing the list of Council configurations in addition to those referred to in the second and third subparagraphs of Article 16(6) TEU, OJ 2009, L 315/46 as amended by European Council Decision 2010/594/EU amending the list of Council configurations, OJ 2010, L 263/12.

- Economic and Financial Affairs
- Justice and Home Affairs
- Employment, Social Policy, Health and Consumer Affairs
- Competitiveness
- Transport, Telecommunications and Energy
- Agriculture and Fisheries
- Environment
- Education, youth, culture and sport.

The presence of so many configurations has been seen as fragmenting the Council and preventing it from developing sufficiently general overall visions. These weaknesses are meant to be addressed by the General Affairs Council, which comprises Foreign Ministers. It is, on the one hand, responsible for securing consistency in the work done by the other Council configurations. On the other, it also acts as a point of liaison with the Heads of Government in the European Council by preparing meetings for the latter and ensuring that decisions are followed up by the different Council configurations.[144] It is questionable whether it does either of these jobs effectively. The initial draft for the Constitutional Treaty proposed a permanent General and Legislative Affairs Council based in Brussels comprised of Ministers of Europe to do this.[145] This was rejected on the ground that these Ministers might become too autonomous and powerful. However, its very suggestion intimates that Foreign Ministers, meeting every now and then in Brussels, as is the case now, may neither have the required interest nor the resources to do the job satisfactorily.

The powers of the Council are unsatisfactorily paraphrased in Article 16 TEU.

Article 16 TEU

(1) The Council shall, jointly with the European Parliament, exercise legislative and budgetary functions. It shall carry out policy-making and coordinating functions as laid down in the Treaties.

In fact, ranged across the Treaties, the Council's powers are multifaceted and varied. It includes the following:

- It acts as a forum within which Member States can consult and coordinate their behaviour in areas of policy where responsibility lies with them, such as general economic policy.[146]
- It can take the other EU Institutions before the Court of Justice for failure to comply with EU law.[147]
- It can request the Commission to undertake studies or submit legislative proposals. The Commission can refuse to comply with this request but must provide reasons for doing so.[148]
- It prepares the work for the European Council meetings and ensures their follow-up.[149]
- It polices the fiscal and economic policies of euro area States. It can find that States are running excessive budget deficits, excessive macroeconomic imbalances or significantly deviating from

---

[144] This is done in liaison with the Presidents of the European Council and the Commission Article 16(6) TEU.
[145] Article 23(1) Draft Constitutional Treaty.   [146] Article 121 TFEU.   [147] Articles 263 and 265 TFEU.
[148] Article 241 TFEU.   [149] Article 16(6) TEU.

their commitment to secure a balanced budget.[150] If States persist, notwithstanding this finding, the Council can impose significant fines.[151]

- It frames the common foreign and security policy and takes the decisions necessary for defining and implementing it on the basis of general guidelines and strategic lines defined by the European Council.[152]
- It has power of final decision on the adoption of legislation in most areas of Union policy.

The last power, the power of final decision, is particularly significant. Whilst shared with the Parliament in certain fields, it leads to the perception of Council as the most important institution in the lawmaking process as it has to say 'yes' before any law can be adopted.

(ii) Decision-Making within the Council

The first form of voting is the *simple majority* vote. Under this, each Member of the Council has one vote, and fourteen votes are required for a measure to be adopted.[153] This is used in only a few areas, principally procedural ones, as it fails to protect national interests and undue weight is given to the interests of small States at the expense of larger ones. The only area of real significance subject to it is the decision to convene an intergovernmental conference to amend the TEU.[154] The second form of voting is *unanimity*. Every Member State has a veto on the matter before the Council, but it must actively vote against a measure for it to be vetoed; abstention is insufficient. Unanimity voting is used in the most politically sensitive areas. It is still widespread in the Treaty.[155] The most common form of voting is Qualified Majority Voting (QMV). This is a weighted system of voting in which regard is had to the number of States voting for a measure and the populations of those States voting for it.

Article 16 TEU

(4) As from 1 November 2014, a qualified majority shall be defined as at least 55% of the members of the Council, comprising at least fifteen of them and representing Member States comprising at least 65% of the population of the Union.

A blocking minority must include at least four Council members, failing which the qualified majority shall be deemed attained.[156]

The other arrangements governing the qualified majority are laid down in Article 238(2) TFEU.

---

[150] These terms are explored in more detail in Ch. 15. See pp. 667–69. See, respectively, Article 126(6) TFEU; Regulation 1176/2011 on the prevention and correction of macroeconomic imbalances, OJ 2011, L 306/25, Article 7(2); Regulation 1466/97 on the strengthening of the surveillance of budgetary positions and the surveillance and coordination of economic policies, OJ 1997, L 2091/1 as amended by Regulation 1175/2011, OJ 2011, L 306/12, Article 6(2).

[151] Article 126(11) TFEU; Regulation 1174/2011 on enforcement measures to correct excessive macroeconomic imbalances in the euro area, OJ 2011, L 306/8, Article 3; Regulation 1173/2011 on the effective enforcement of budgetary surveillance in the euro area, OJ 2011, L 306/1, Article 6.

[152] Article 26(2) TEU.   [153] Article 238(1) TFEU.

[154] This is taken by the European Council, Article 48(3) TEU. The others are adoption of the Council's own rules of procedure (Articles 240(3) and 235(3) TFEU for European Council) and request for the Commission to undertake studies or submit proposals (Article 241 TFEU).

[155] The Annex at the end of Ch. 3 contains a list of the different legislative competences of the Union and the procedures and voting requirements used.

[156] These requirements are also replicated in Article 238(3) TFEU.

> ### Article 238 TFEU
>
> (2) By way of derogation from Article 16(4) TFEU ... where the Council does not act on a proposal from the Commission or from the High Representative of the Union for Foreign Affairs and Security Policy, the qualified majority shall be defined as at least 72% of the members of the Council, representing Member States comprising at least 65% of the population of the Union.

There were two features of particular controversy about the voting requirements.

First, there was a concern that if States representing 65% of the population had to vote in favour of a measure, this could lead to a situation where Germany with the help of one other large Member State could veto a measure. To prevent this, a requirement was introduced that a measure would only be blocked if four Member States voted against it.

Secondly, Poland was unhappy with this formula as it had benefited disproportionately from the previous formula. At its insistence, a decision was agreed accompanying the Lisbon Treaty which qualified these voting thresholds.[157]

> ### Decision 2009/857 relating to the implementation of Article 9C(4) TEU and Article 205(2) TFEU ...[158]
>
> Article 4 ... if members of the Council, representing:
> (a) at least 55% of the population; or
> (b) at least 55% of the number of Member States;
> necessary to constitute a blocking minority resulting from the application of Article 9C(4), first subparagraph TEU or Article 205(2) TFEU indicate their opposition to the Council adopting an act by a qualified majority, the Council shall discuss the issue.
>
> Article 5 The Council shall, in the course of these discussions, do all in its power to reach, within a reasonable time and without prejudicing obligatory time limits laid down by Union law, a satisfactory solution to address concerns raised by the members of the Council referred to in Article 4.

In other words, if States representing 19.25% of the population or seven Member States oppose a measure, it will act as a *de facto* veto.

The type of vote required can structure the climate of negotiation. Under unanimity, Member States, aware of their veto, may be more inclined to assert their self-interest more aggressively and less willing to compromise.[159] With QMV, as there is the possibility of outmanoeuvre, Member States may be more disposed towards constructing common solutions and less protective of their initial positions.[160] Being outvoted means no influence in the final legislative text whereas a willingness to vote for an imperfect text means some influence. Equally, winning coalitions of States may be reluctant to press their advantage

---

[157] Declaration 7 to the Lisbon Treaty on Article 16(4) TEU and Article 238(2) TFEU, Article 4.

[158] OJ 2009, L 314/73. The Treaty numbers referred to here were the predecessors to Articles 16(4) TEU and 238(2) TFEU.

[159] F. Scharpf, 'The Joint Decision Trap: Lessons from German Federalism and European Integration' (1988) 66 *Public Administration* 239.

[160] D. Naurin, 'Most Common When Least Important: Deliberation in the European Union Council of Ministers' (2010) 40 *BJPS* 31.

over other States as they will be aware that they may be generate opposition which will come back to haunt them in future votes.[161]

A culture of consensus, therefore, dominates fields where QMV is the voting rule. Most of the time, a text will be sought to which everybody can agree, with individual State concerns taken on board where possible. A study found, therefore, that between 2009 and 2015, on average a State would either vote against a measure or abstain in 10.97 per cent of cases (about one in nine). Yet this figure is distorted by three States (Germany (15.5 per cent), Poland (19.23 per cent) and the United Kingdom (17.86 per cent)) withdrawing support much more frequently than other Member States.[162]

This culture of consensus shapes the content of the legislation. In some instances, legislation is kept as general as possible so as not to open up possibilities for disagreement.[163] This can obstruct EU legislation from realising the goals behind its proposal. It is more common, however, as already mentioned to incorporate individual national concerns into the text. As a consequence, as EU membership has grown, so has the length of EU law. The 2004 enlargement led, for example, to the length of legislative documents increasing by approximately 15 per cent.[164] This, of course, increases the complexity, cumbersomeness and internal contradictions within EU legislation.

This consensus has led to concerns about the quality of debate in the Council. The Lisbon Treaty opened up Council deliberations and votes on legislative acts to the public.

Article 16 TEU

(8) The Council shall meet in public when it deliberates and votes on a draft legislative act. To this end, each Council meeting shall be divided into two parts, dealing respectively with deliberations on Union legislative acts and on non-legislative activities.

National governments have tried to minimise the effects of this. In practice, the public deliberations and votes have, thus, often involved Council Ministers reading out agreed positions or texts or the Chair stating that a measure has been adopted by QMV or not.[165] Negotiations are held informally, in some cases involving just a few States, out of the public eye. More significant has been the requirement for most Member State votes on legislation to be recorded.[166] This has shifted legislative negotiations in that Member States will vote (or not vote) a particular way because of perceptions about how it will be received back home. Governments are, in particular,

---

[161] S. Novak, 'The Silence of Ministers: Consensus and Blame Avoidance in the Council of the European Union' (2013) 51 *JCMS* 1091; S. Smeets, 'Consensus and Isolation in the EU Council of Ministers' (2016) 38 *JEI* 23.

[162] D. Finke, 'Underneath the Culture of Consensus: Transparency, Credible Commitments and Voting in the Council of Ministers' (2017) *EUP* 339, 348–350.

[163] G. Tsebelis, 'Bridging Qualified Majority and Unanimity Decision-Making in the EU' (2013) 20 *JEPP* 1083.

[164] E. Best and P. Settembri, 'Legislative Output after Enlargement: Similar Number, Shifting Nature' in E. Best *et al.* (eds.), *The Institutions of the Enlarged European Union: Change and Continuity* (Cheltenham, Edward Elgar, 2008).

[165] S. Novak, 'The Surprising Effects of Transparency on the EU Legislative Process' (2014) 51 *Cuadernos* 41, 57–9.

[166] Bizarrely, the requirement only applies to legislation adopted under legislative procedures other than the ordinary legislative procedure and other legally binding acts. It does not apply to legislation adopted under other procedures, Council Decision adopting the Council's Rules of Procedure, OJ 2009, L 325/35, Articles 7 and 9. It has become increasingly difficult for this position to be maintained as whilst EU Institution's documents prepared during legislative negotiations are not published openly, parties can increasingly demand access to them, *De Capitani* v. *Parliament*, T-540/15, EU: T:2018:167. On this see pp. 127–9.

now more likely to vote against a measure whether there is strong scepticism about the issue back home or, in States where Euro-scepticism is strong, it is seen as extending the scope of EU law.[167]

(iii) The Management of the Council: The Presidency and COREPER

Any discussion of the Council must also include discussion of the Committee of the Permanent Representative (COREPER). The Permanent Representations in Brussels are the Member States' missions to the European Union. Each Permanent Representation will comprise a significant number of civil servants from that Member State. COREPER is where they formally come together to contribute to the EU institutional settlement. It is divided into COREPER I and COREPER II. The former is composed of deputy permanent representatives and is responsible for issues such as the environment, social affairs, the internal market and transport. COREPER II consists of permanent representatives of ambassadorial rank responsible for the more sensitive issues, such as economic and financial affairs and external relations. Each meets weekly.

The formal duties of COREPER seem minimal. It is merely to prepare the work of the Council and carry out any tasks assigned to it.[168] It has no power to take any substantive decisions of its own.[169] COREPER is, nevertheless, a very powerful body. This is because it decides what matters will be discussed and voted on by Ministers within the Council. Items not up for discussion will be resolved within COREPER, instead. This is done through COREPER dividing the agenda for Council meetings into 'A' and 'B' matters. 'A' items are classified as technical matters on which there is agreement within COREPER. These are adopted as approved by the Council at the beginning of the meeting without further discussion. 'B' items, by contrast, are considered more contentious, requiring discussion and possibly a vote by Ministers. An 'A' item is effectively decided by COREPER, and a 'B' item by the Ministers. Whilst there is disagreement about the precise amount, the overwhelming majority of items are 'A' items are resolved within COREPER.[170]

If the vast majority of Council business is resolved within COREPER, it does not act as a loose cannon, but as a conduit for informing national capitals of the work of the European Union and enabling national positions to be properly defended.[171] It is, thus, assisted by about 250 Working Groups of national civil servants. A Commission proposal is first passed to these Groups for analysis. These Groups provide Reports which set the agenda for COREPER meetings by indicating points on which there has been agreement within the Working Group (Roman I points) and points which need discussion within the COREPER (Roman II points). It is best to see COREPER as the tip of complex networks of national administrations working together to agree legislation.[172] Furthermore, there is evidence that, within this network of civil servants, Ministers are consulted

---

[167] S. Hagemann, S. Hobolt and C. Wratil, 'Government Responsiveness in the European Union: Evidence from Council Voting' (2017) 50 *Comparative Political Studies* 850.

[168] Article 16(7) TEU, Article 240(1) TFEU.   [169] *Commission* v. *Council*, C-25/94, EU:C:1996:114.

[170] Some have suggested that 70–85% of items are 'A' items, whilst others put it as high as 85–90%. F. Häge, 'Politicising Council Decision-Making: The Effect of European Parliament Empowerment' (2011) 34 *WEP* 18, 33–4; L. Buonanno and N. Nugent, *Policies and Policy Processes of the European Union* (Basingstoke, Palgrave Macmillan, 2013) 50.

[171] F. Hayes-Renshaw, C. Lequesne and P. Lopez, 'The Permanent Representatives of the Member States of the European Union' (1989) 28 *JCMS* 119, 129–31.

[172] D. Bostock, 'Coreper Revisited' (2002) 40 *JCMS* 215, 231–2.

on matters of political salience.[173] In this, a bigger problem might be ministerial indifference with it not being uncommon for Ministers not to sit in the Council and have civil servants sit in their place.[174]

The other issue is government by 'moonlight'. Meetings of COREPER are not public. Its minutes are not published and it is not accountable to any parliamentary assembly. To be sure, many decisions taken in any national government are taken by civil servants, but it is the unprecedented extent of COREPER's influence that raises particular concerns about accountability and transparency.

The other body central to the management of the Council is the Presidency.[175] This is held by pre-established groups of three Member States for a period of eighteen months ('trio Presidencies'). It is held on the basis of equal rotation.[176] The Presidency is responsible for chairing all configurations of the Council, other than foreign affairs,[177] with each of the three States chairing Council meetings for six months whilst being assisted by the other two.[178] The Presidency has a number of duties.

- It sets the agenda for individual Council meetings.
- It represents the Council both before the other EU Institutions and in the world more generally.
- It acts as a 'neutral broker' between other Member States in order to secure legislation.
- It sets a legislative agenda for the eighteen-month period of the trio Presidency.

Being a neutral broker prevents the Presidency from hijacking the agenda of the Council to further national priorities.[179] Equally, changes to the Presidency every eighteen months disrupts continuity, and this, in turn, limits what can be done.[180] Nevertheless, studies have found that the Presidencies can shape the direction of the European Union. Much depends on how the trio Presidencies work together with influence requiring that they work well as a team.[181] In such circumstances, whilst there is still limited scope for the Presidency to put new policies on the table, it can have significant scheduling power. It decides how much time is allocated to particular topics, and where the focus should be in discussion.[182] This allows it to exercise significant influence over the detail of legislative discussions even if it has less sway over the broader ideological direction of the Union.

---

[173] F. Häge, *Bureaucrats as Law-Makers: Committee Decision-Making in the EU Council of Ministers* (Abingdon, Routledge, 2013) esp. chs. 13 and 14.

[174] This has been calculated to happen 11% of the time overall, with it happening more than 20% of the time in the case of Cyprus, Greece, Denmark, Estonia, Latvia and Malta. C. Grøn and H. Salomonsen, 'Who's at the Table? An Analysis of Ministers' Participation in EU Council of Ministers Meetings' (2015) 22 *JEPP* 1071.

[175] The Council also has a small Secretariat of its own, which helps service it and provide it with legal and translation services Article 240(2) TFEU.

[176] Article 16(9) TEU and Article 236(b) TFEU. The sequence is set out in Decision 2009/908/EU laying measures for the implementation of the European Council Decision on the exercise of the Presidency of the Council, and on the chairmanship of preparatory bodies of the Council, OJ 2009, L 322/28, Annex I.

[177] This is chaired by the High Representative for Foreign Affairs and Security Policy, Article 18(3) TEU.

[178] Decision 2009/881/EU on the exercise of the Presidency of the Council, OJ 2099, L 315/50, Article 1.

[179] P. Alexandrova and A. Timmermans, 'National Interest Versus the Common Good: The Presidency in European Council Agenda Setting' (2013) 52 *EJPR* 316.

[180] A. Warntjen, 'The Elusive Goal of Continuity? Legislative Decision-Making and the Council Presidency before and after Lisbon' (2013) 36 *WEP* 1239.

[181] A. Batory and U. Puetter, 'Consistency and Diversity? The EU's Rotating Trio Council Presidency after the Lisbon Treaty' (2013) 20 *JEPP* 95.

[182] F. Häge, 'The Scheduling Power of the EU Council Presidency' (2017) 24 *JEPP* 695.

5 THE EUROPEAN COUNCIL

(i) The Institution of the European Council

The European Council comprises the Heads of Government of the Member States, its President and the President of the Commission.[183] It meets at least four times per year, although additional meetings can be convened if necessary.[184] There is a mismatch between this and the wide-ranging tasks of the European Council. To that end, the Lisbon Treaty created a new office: the President of the European Council.[185] Elected by the European Council by QMV for a term of two and a half years, which may be renewed once,[186] the President sits as an additional member of the European Council.[187] His most central tasks are to:

- chair and drive forward the work of the European Council whilst endeavouring to facilitate consensus and cohesion within it
- ensure the preparation and continuity of the work of the European Council in cooperation with the President of the Commission, and on the basis of the work of the General Affairs Council.[188]

This has an *ex ante* and an *ex post* dimension. *Ex ante*, he is to organise, coordinate and secure direction for the European Council, building alliances and facilitating agendas. *Ex post*, he is to see that European Council decisions are implemented. A number of features appear to constrain the President's ability to do this. He has only a very small administration, and, if the President is expected to cooperate with the Commission, the essential structure of the relationship is a competitive one with each wishing to be the agenda-setter. Notwithstanding this, the President of the European Council has carved out a role of being an honest broker between Member States. Heads of Government realise that they have to work through him if they are to build common European Council agendas rather than just leaving this to the Commission.[189]

(ii) The Powers of the European Council

The European Council enjoys a wide range of powers.

First, it makes decisions about the future membership of the European Union. It is the European Council, therefore, which takes the decision to suspend the membership of a State. It sets the criteria to be met by a State wishing to join the Union.[190] Whilst it cannot expel a State, the European Council also takes the decision as to whether a Member State has committed persistent and serious breach of the values on which the EU is founded, namely respect for democracy, human rights and the rule of law.[191] On the basis of such a decision, the Council can take sanctions against that State which can include suspension of voting rights.[192] Finally a Member State wishing to leave the Union triggers the process by notifying the European Council.[193]

Secondly, the European Council is central in any revision of the Treaties under either of the two procedures provided for this. Under the ordinary revision procedure, after consulting other

---

[183] Article 15(2) TEU.   [184] Article 15(3) TEU.   [185] The current incumbent is the Pole, Donald Tusk.
[186] Article 15(5) TEU.   [187] Article 15(2) TEU.   [188] Article 15(6) TEU.
[189] I. Tömmel, 'The Standing President of the European Council: Intergovernmental or Supranational Leadership?' (2017) 39 *JEI* 175.
[190] Article 49 TEU.   [191] Article 7(2) TEU.   [192] Article 7(3) TEU.   [193] Article 50(2) TEU.

EU Institutions, it can call, by simple majority, either a convention along the lines of the *Future of Europe* convention or an intergovernmental conference.[194] These will put forward amendments which have to be ratified by all Member States in accordance with their constitutional requirements.[195] The simplified revision procedure allows the European Council, after consulting the other EU Institutions, to amend Part III of the TFEU, the part of the TFEU comprising all the internal policies of the European Union.[196] Any such amendment must not increase EU competences, and must be ratified by all Member States in accordance with their constitutional requirements.[197] It also establishes a *passerelle* procedure, which allows, in any part of either of the TFEU or Title V TEU (which governs external action), for a requirement of a unanimity vote to be changed to QMV and any legislative procedure to be replaced by the ordinary legislative procedure.[198] Any amendment must secure the consent of the European Parliament and be notified to national parliaments. If any national parliament indicates opposition, the amendment must be dropped.[199] At the time of its introduction, there were concerns that this procedure provides for the loss of the national veto in lawmaking and increased European Parliament powers without the need for each national parliament to have to agree to it positively.[200] If they are silent, the matter goes through. However, for all that, it has not yet been used.

Thirdly, it makes appointments to the other EU Institutions and determines the composition of some of them. Within the limits set by the Treaties, it establishes the number of MEPs and Commissioners for the European Parliament and Commission, respectively.[201] It appoints its own President,[202] the President of the Commission and the Commission as a whole,[203] the High Representative for Foreign Affairs and Security Policy,[204] and the Executive Board of the ECB.[205] To be sure, this is often done in tandem with other EU Institutions but almost every non-elected office involves appointment by the European Council.[206] Even judges of the Court of Justice, while not appointed by the European Council, are appointed by common accord of the governments of the Member States.[207]

Fourthly, the European Council has a prominent role in Common Foreign and Security Policy (CFSP). It defines and identifies the strategic objectives and interests of CFSP and sets out guidelines.[208] It also acts as a forum where Member States can consult each other about matters of general interest in this field.[209]

Fifthly, the European Council resolves issues which have reached an impasse within the Council of Ministers. It can do this informally in all fields by virtue of the domestic authority

---

[194] The latter can only be convened with the consent of the European Parliament, Article 48(3) TEU.

[195] Article 48(2)–(4) TEU.

[196] It excludes common foreign and security policy common commercial policy, development policy, association policy, humanitarian aid, economic, financial and technical cooperation with non-EU States, sanctions, internal agreements and the customs union. It also excludes the flexibility provision, Article 352 TFEU.

[197] Article 48(6) TEU. The procedure has been used once to amend Article 136 TFEU.

[198] The ordinary legislative procedure is discussed at pp. 121–9.

[199] The *passerelle* procedure is set out in Article 48(7) TEU. There is an exclusion for anything with defence or military implications.

[200] E.g. 2 BvE 2/08 *Treaty of Lisbon*, Judgment of 30 June 2009, (German Constitutional Court) paras. 311–21.

[201] Articles 14(2) and 17(5) TEU respectively. [202] Article 15(5) TEU. [203] Article 17(7) TEU.

[204] Article 18(1) TEU. [205] Article 283(2) TFEU.

[206] The most significant exception is the Ombudsman, which is appointed by the European Parliament, Article 228(1) TFEU.

[207] Article 19(2) TEU. [208] Articles 22 and 26 TEU. [209] Article 32 TEU.

of Heads of Government as issues too controversial or significant for a Minister to concede can sometimes be resolved by these. In particularly sensitive fields, the European Council is deployed where a Member State feels the European Union is touching on matters of particular significance for it. 'Brake procedures' allow a member of the Council to refer a legislative proposal to the European Council for resolution if the proposal affects important aspects of its social security system[210] or fundamental aspects of its criminal justice system.[211] Equally, in CFSP, on activities where there is provision for QMV, a Member State may refer the matter to the European Council for 'vital and stated' reasons.[212] In all these instances, the European Council will only take the matter forward if there is agreement with the Head of Government of the Member State concerned.

The sixth, and the most significant, form of power is agenda-setting. In some fields this is explicitly mandated,[213] but, even where there is not the case, the European Council has a general agenda-setting power.

Article 15 TEU

(1) The European Council shall provide the Union with the necessary impetus for its development and shall define the general political directions and priorities thereof. It shall not exercise legislative functions.

As Article 15(1) TEU makes clear, the European Council cannot propose legislation. Instead, its role is to direct the course to be taken more generally. A division of labour, thus, takes place, in which it will usually set out broad principles and ask the Commission to develop an Action Plan to implement these principles. The most pre-eminent example was the Taskforce on Economic Governance comprising national Finance Ministers, whose report provided the settlement subsequent to the sovereign debt crisis, which imposed much more extensive constraints on national budgetary and economic policies.[214] The Commission then proposed a programme of legislation on the basis of this report, which was adopted as EU law by the other EU Institutions (the 'Six-Pack' and 'Two-Pack').[215]

The influence of the European Council depends, in such circumstances, on how much attention it gives an issue and how prescriptive it seeks to be. In instances where it sets out the detail and strategy to be taken, the sheer sway of twenty-seven Heads of Government requiring something to be done makes it a dominant player, even if it has no formal legislative role.[216] In the last few years, the European Council has appeared to take a much more active role in setting the European Union's agenda.[217] This has appeared to take two forms. One is selective involvement with a few high-profile issues, which are seen as placing particular intense demands

---

[210] Article 48 TFEU.   [211] Articles 82(3) and 83(3) TFEU.   [212] Article 31(2) TEU.

[213] Article 68 TFEU (freedom, security and justice); Article 148 TFEU (employment).

[214] *Strengthening Economic Governance in the EU: Final Report of The Task Force to the European Council* (Brussels, European Council, October 2010), https://www.consilium.europa.eu/media/27405/117236.pdf.

[215] On this legislation see p. 666.

[216] This was certainly the case in the sovereign debt crisis, E. Bressanelli and N. Chelotti, 'The Shadow of the European Council. Understanding Legislation on Economic Governance' (2016) 38 *JEI* 511.

[217] U. Puetter, *The European Council and the Council: New Intergovernmentalism and Institutional Change* (Oxford University Press, 2014) 91–147; S. v. Hecke and P. Bursens, 'The Council Presidency and the European Council: Towards Collective Leadership in the EU' in F. Foret and U. Rittelmeyer (eds.), *The European Council and Economic Governance* (Routledge, Abingdon, 2014).

on national leaders, rather than with more systematic engagement with long-term strategy or wider public concerns about what the EU should or not be doing.[218] The other is a much regularised monitoring of what both the EU Institutions and the Member States are doing.[219] A central example of the latter is the European Semester for Economic Policy Coordination. In spring of each year, the European Council agrees pan-Union policy orientations across a range of economic, social and environmental fields. Member States develop individual national reform plans in light of that. These are subject to evaluation and tailored recommendations by the Commission and the Council, and, then, finally, endorsed by the European Council. However, the European Semester indicates the uncomfortable relationship between EU law and the European Council. Whilst the position of other EU Institutions within the Semester is governed by EU law,[220] despite being arguably the central actor, the European Council is not.

(iii) The European Council within the EU Institutional Settlement

The emergence of the European Council has had a number of implications for the EU institutional settlement.

First, the European Council is both powerful and intergovernmental. If other EU Institutions just give effect to its directions, this raises questions about how autonomous or supranational the European Union is. Decisions will be taken by just a few Heads of Government with the supranational institutions' role reduced to deciding how to implement these. To be sure, this characterisation is an inaccurate caricature. The European Council's agenda-setting is neither so aggressive nor so expansive as to warrant this description nor the other EU Institutions so passive. However, it illustrates the potential power of the European Council vis-à-vis the other EU Institutions. There have, thus, been attempts to subject the European Council to supranational and wider democratic controls. It can be subject to review by the Court of Justice[221] and the President must submit reports after each meeting to the European Parliament.[222] However, the circumstances in which a court would strike down a decision by twenty-seven Heads of Government will be rare, and how seriously the latter take critical views of the Parliament is also open to question.[223] Accountability has, thus, principally been through domestic controls, notably by national parliaments. A 2013 study found strong involvement in eighteen of the Member States. In most cases, this went to holding the Head of Government to account for what took place in the meeting, with Germany and Denmark going further and formulating a position for him or her to take into the European Council.[224]

Secondly, the growth in the power of the European Council has led to a shift in the balance of power between the Member States. We have seen how national representation is carefully calibrated in each of the EU Institutions to mitigate the disparities in economic and political

---

[218] P. Alexandrova, A. Rasmussen and D. Toshkov, 'Agenda Responsiveness in the European Council: Public Priorities, Policy Problems and Political Attention' (2016) 39 *WEP* 205.

[219] M. Carammia, S. Princen and A. Timmermans, 'From Summitry to EU Government: An Agenda Formation Perspective on the European Council' (2016) 54 *JCMS* 809.

[220] Regulation 1175/2011 amending Council Regulation (EC) No. 1466/97 on the strengthening of the surveillance of budgetary positions and the surveillance and coordination of economic policies, OJ 2011, L 306/12, Article 2A.

[221] Articles 263 and 265 TFEU.   [222] Article 15(6)(d) TEU.

[223] Cf. B. Crum, 'Accountability and Personalisation of the European Council Presidency' (2009) 31 *JEI* 685.

[224] These were the Czech Republic, Estonia, Italy, Latvia, Poland and Slovakia.

size between the Member States. By contrast, influence is determined much more strongly within the European Council by a State's size, capabilities and wealth.[225]

J. Tallberg, 'Bargaining Power in the European Council' (2008) 46 *Journal of Common Market Studies* **685, 690–1**

[A]symmetries in aggregate structural power matter indirectly, by affecting a state's range of alternatives, the resources it can commit to an issue and the legitimacy of its claims to influence. A large home market makes a state more influential in economic negotiations, military capabilities enable a state to exercise leadership in the EU's foreign and security policy and population size grants voice in an EU conceiving of itself as a democratic community.

According to the interviewees, national executives representing structurally advantaged states are allowed greater latitude in the negotiations. Jean-Claude Juncker explains: 'If you are representing a medium-sized country, you can never say "Denmark thinks . . . ". You can only say "I would submit to your considerations, if not . . . " Those who are speaking for greater Member States, by opening their mouth and by referring to their national flag, they are immediately indicating that, behind their words, you have to accept size and demography. "La France pense que . . . " and "Deutschland denkt . . . " that is something different'. Göran Persson, former Prime Minister of Sweden, points to a parallel dynamic: 'If you are the Prime Minister of a country with five to ten million people, you simply cannot monopolize 20 per cent of the time devoted to the conclusions.' Furthermore, differences in structural power are perceived to affect the legitimacy of wielding the veto. According to one Prime Minister, it is a simple reality of politics that 'Luxemburg can issue a veto once in a decade and Britain once per week'. By the same token, the veto of large Member States is perceived to carry more weight than that of the small or medium-sized states, according to David O'Sullivan, former secretary general of the Commission: 'The veto of Cyprus is not the same as the veto of Germany'. Interviewees also testify that large Member States may get away with tactics that otherwise are considered inappropriate, such as exploiting the inadequate preparation of an issue to push through their own proposal, or launching entirely new initiatives at the negotiation table.

As a result, the interests of the larger Member States tend to set the framework for European Council negotiations. Where the interests of France, Germany and the UK conflict, they nevertheless set the terms within which agreements must be sought. Where these states see eye-to-eye on an issue, or even have arrived at pre-agreements, it is extremely difficult to achieve outcomes that diverge from this position. Frequently cited examples in recent years of France, Germany and the UK dominating negotiations and outcomes in the European Council include the provisions on a semi-permanent president of the European Council in the 2004 Constitutional Treaty, the deal in December 2005 on the new financial perspective for 2007–13 and the political agreement in July 2007 on the subsequent Lisbon Treaty.

Thirdly, its rise is associated with a new style of integration which developed in EU policy fields that emerged after Maastricht: employment, economic governance, foreign policy. This style focuses less on the creation of common laws through supranational institutions. Coined as 'new intergovernmentalism' by its advocates, its hallmarks are that Member States do not wish to roll back the European Union.[226] They prefer to do new things, but there is both scepticism about giving power to supranational institutions and awareness that if they opened up many of these

---

[225] On this first two see J. Tallberg, 'Bargaining Power in the European Council' (2008) 46 *JCMS* 685, 692–4 and 698–9.
[226] C. Bickerton, D. Hodson and U. Puetter, 'The New Intergovernmentalism: European Integration in the Post-Maastricht Era' (2015) 53 *JCMS* 703.

policy fields to wider political contestation and debate it may not be possible to work together. Integration, thus, centres on policy coordination. It involves national governments coming together to agree on common approaches with individual Member States orienting their policies around this consensus. The European Council is central to setting up these new fields of integration. It establishes the presence of a consensus around which further measures can be elaborated, and checks up on how the policy coordination is working. Its work has proliferated as these new policy fields have developed.[227]

6 THE EUROPEAN PARLIAMENT

(i) The Composition and Authority of the European Parliament

Since 1979, the European Parliament has been elected by direct universal suffrage at five-year intervals.[228] Representation is on the basis of degressive proportionality, whereby the principle of per head representation is combined with the principle that the larger the population of a Member State, the lower the weighting per head.[229] This means that smaller States are represented by more MEPs than a system which corresponded to population size alone would justify. A Maltese vote, therefore, counts more than a German vote. This weighting is buttressed by a further requirement that no State should either receive less than six MEPs or more than ninety-six MEPs.[230] The Parliament will comprise 705 members after the 2019 elections.[231]

All MEPs are elected by proportional representation. However, States can decide on the system of proportional representation to be used. They also have discretion on matters such as the size and boundaries of voting constituencies; the minimum age for voting and the voting entitlements of non-EU nationals; whether voting is compulsory; and whether parties need to achieve up to 5 per cent of the national vote before being allocated seats.[232] Furthermore, the European Parliament cannot challenge the administration of these elections even where it believes that Member States have not followed their own electoral procedures or some dubious practice has taken place.[233]

Finally, there are no European political parties. MEPs are elected as representatives of national political parties. However, most national political parties form part of European party groups. These bring together parties with common political affinities, seek agreement on common positions for votes and secure their members positions on European Parliament committees.[234] They have also been found to be cohesive with MEPs overwhelmingly following the instructions

---

[227] U. Puetter, 'The European Council' in C. Bickerton, D. Hodson and U. Puetter (eds.), *The New Intergovernmentalism: States and Supranational Actors in the Post-Maastricht Era* (Oxford University Press, 2015).

[228] Article 14(3) TEU.   [229] Article 14(2) TEU.   [230] Article 14(2) TEU.

[231] On the application of the degressive proportionality principle to the 2019 elections, Decision 2018/937 establishing the composition of the European Parliament, OJ 2018, L 165l/1. The apportionment of MEPs will be Belgium 21; Bulgaria 17; Czech Republic 21; Denmark 14; Germany 96; Estonia 7; Ireland 13; Greece 21; Spain 59; France 79; Croatia 12; Italy 76; Cyprus 6; Latvia 8; Lithuania 11; Luxembourg 6; Hungary 21; Malta 6; Netherlands 29; Austria 19; Poland 52; Portugal 21; Romania 33; Slovenia 8; Slovakia 14; Finland 14; Sweden 21.

[232] Decision 2002/772/EURATOM/EC, concerning the election of the members of the European Parliament by direct universal suffrage, OJ 2002, L 283/1 as amended by Decision 2018/994, OJ 2018, L 178/1.

[233] *Italy* v. *Parliament*, C-393/07, EU:C: 2009:275; *Donnici* v. *Parliament*, C-9/08, EU:C:2009:44.

[234] E. Bressanelli, 'National Parties and Group Membership in the European Parliament: Ideology or Pragmatism' (2012) 19 *JEPP* 737.

of the group.[235] The European Parliament elected in 2014 comprised eight groupings covering a wide political spectrum, of which the two largest were the European Peoples Party (right-of-centre parties) and the Progressive Alliance of Socialists and Democrats (left-of-centre parties).[236]

These traits have generated concerns about the representative qualities of the European Parliament, as they all go against the idea of the vote of each citizen having equal weight.[237] These concerns are exacerbated by a number of other features. Turn-out for European Parliament elections has steadily declined from 62 per cent in 1979 to where less than half of EU citizens, 43 per cent, voted in 2014, with only 18.2 per cent and 13.1 per cent casting votes in the Czech Republic and Slovakia respectively.[238] Furthermore, there is little evidence that votes are cast in anticipation of what the European Parliament will do or not on the basis of its past performance. Instead, the strongest determinants of voting preferences appear to be domestic political issues or satisfaction or dissatisfaction with how the European Union is performing more generally.[239] These features evidence a public engagement and public debate at a pan-Union level, and, for some, this would limit what the European Parliament can authoritatively do even if its representative limitations could be overcome.

D. Grimm, 'Does Europe Need a Constitution?' (1995) 1 *European Law Journal* 282, 293–4, 296–7

The democratic nature of a political system is attested not so much by the existence of elected parliaments ... as by the pluralism, internal representativity, freedom and capacity for compromise of the intermediate area of parties, associations, citizens movements and communication media. Where a parliament does not rest on such a structure, which guarantees constant interaction between people and State, democratic substance is lacking even if democratic forms are present.

... At European level, though, even the prerequisites are largely lacking. Mediatory structures have hardly been even formed here yet. There is no Europeanised party system, just European groups in the Strasbourg parliament, and apart from that, loose cooperation among programmatically related parties. This does not bring any integration of the European population, even at the moment of European elections. Nor have European associations or citizens' movements arisen, even though cooperation among national associations is further advanced than with parties. A search for European media, whether in print or broadcast, would be

---

[235] S. Bowler and G. McElroy, 'Political Group Cohesion and "Hurrah" Voting in The European Parliament' (2015) 22 *JEPP* 1355; C. Koop, C. Reh and E. Bressanelli, 'When Politics Prevails: Parties, Elections and Loyalty in the European Parliament' (2018) 57 *EJPR* 563.

[236] The groupings are European Peoples Party (217 MEPs); Progressive Alliance of Socialists and Democrats (190 MEPs); European Conservatives and Reformists (74 MEPs); Alliance of Liberals and Democrats for Europe (70 MEPs); European United Left and Nordic Green Left (52 MEPs); European Greens and European Free Alliance (50 MEPs); Europe of Freedom and Direct Democracy (45 MEPs); Europe of Nations and Freedom (39 MEPs). There are fourteen non-attached MEPs.

[237] They led to the German Constitutional Court stating that, in its current form, the EU cannot be considered to be a representative democracy, 2 BvE 2/08 *Treaty of Lisbon*, Judgment of 30 June 2009 (German Constitutional Court, paras. 280–9). For discussion of this see C. Lord and J. Pollak, 'Unequal but Democratic? Equality According to Karlsruhe' (2013) 20 *JEPP* 190.

[238] www.europarl.europa.eu/elections2014-results/en/turnout.html.

[239] O. Treib, 'The Voter Says No, but Nobody Listens: Causes and Consequences of the Eurosceptic Vote in the 2014 European Elections' (2014) 21 *JEPP* 1541; S. Hobolt and C. de Vries, 'Turning against the Union? The Impact of the Crisis on the Eurosceptic Vote in the 2014 European Parliament Elections' (2016) 44 *Electoral Studies* 504.

completely fruitless. This makes the European Union fall far short not just of ideal conceptions of a model democracy but even of the already deficient situation in Member States . . .

The absence of a European communication system, due chiefly, to language diversity, has the consequence that for the foreseeable future there will be neither a European public nor a European political discourse. Public discourse instead remains for the time bound by national frontiers, while the European sphere will remain dominated by professional and interest discourses conducted remotely from the public. European decisional processes are accordingly not under public observation in the same way as national ones. The European level of politics lacks a matching public. The feedback to European officials and representatives is therefore only weakly developed, while national politicians orient themselves even in the case of Council decisions to their national publics, because effective sanctions can come only from them. These circumstances give professional and technical viewpoints, particularly of an economic nature, excessive weight in European politics, while the social consequences and side-effects remain in the dark. This shortcoming cannot be made up for even by growing national attention to European policy themes, since the European dimension is just what is lacking there.

If this is true, the conclusion may be drawn that the full parliamentarisation of the European Union on the model of the national constitutional State will rather aggravate than solve the problem. On the one hand it would loosen the Union's ties back to the Member States, since the European Parliament is by its construction not a federal organ but a central one. Strengthening it would be at the expense of the Council and therefore inevitably have centralising effects. On the other hand, the weakened ties back to the Member States would not be compensated by any increased ties back to the Union population. The European Parliament does not meet with any European mediatory structure in being: still less does it constitute a European popular representative body, since there is yet no European people. This is not an argument against any expansion of Parliament's powers. That might even enhance participation opportunities in the Union, provide greater transparency and create a counterweight to the dominance of technical and economic viewpoints. Its objective ought not, however, to be full parliamentarisation on the national model, since political decisions would otherwise move away to where they can be only democratically accountable.

Others have observed, however, that this is a chicken-and-egg situation. The very purpose of the European Union is to stimulate pan-European public debate as, without it, there can be no democratic resolution of problems that transcend the State. The European Parliament is central to this process of democratisation. It opens up debate about EU lawmaking in a way that would not happen otherwise. The EU laws produced by this lawmaking in turn generate a sense that events in other States might affect politics in one's own more directly, with a corresponding increased concern and debate about what is taking place there.[240]

If stimulating public debate and interest in the European Union is the benchmark by which the European Parliament is to be judged, then the results are mixed. Certainly prior to 2010, news about the European Union, in the words of one of the largest studies on the subject, 'has not been a high priority beyond a small selection of elite newspapers'.[241] National media outlets focused on key events such as summits rather than on policies and the position of their respective

---

[240] J. Habermas, 'Democracy in Europe: Why the Development of the EU into a Transnational Democracy Is Necessary and How It Is Possible' (2015) 21 *ELJ* 546, 553–4.

[241] H. Boomgarden *et al.*, 'Across Time and Space: Explaining Variation in News Coverage of the European Union' (2013) 52 *EJPR* 608, 609.

national governments,[242] and were more likely to report EU news where it involved strong disagreements between powerful domestic political players.[243] In like vein, political reporting of the European Parliament concentrated on events, typically controversies rather than policy debates, believed to be of interest to national markets.[244] There is some evidence that both the sovereign debt and migration crises moved coverage of the European Union up the news agenda, both within typical media and social media. However, it transformed how the European Union was reported, with debate increasingly about whether it was a good or bad thing in itself rather than about the range of policy positions available to it or debates held within it.[245]

(ii) The Powers of the European Parliament

Three forms of power are traditionally associated with parliaments: lawmaking, powers over the executive and budgetary powers. These are all mentioned in Article 14 TEU.

> **Article 14 TEU**
>
> (1) The European Parliament shall, jointly with the Council, exercise legislative and budgetary functions. It shall exercise functions of political control and consultation as laid down in the Treaties. It shall elect the President of the Commission.

However, the powers enjoyed by parliaments over lawmaking, the executive and budgets range. To gauge the European Parliament's power, it is worth reflecting on this spectrum. Stronger parliaments are seen as controlling lawmaking whereas weaker parliaments are seen as only ratifying or influencing legislation.[246] In stronger parliamentary systems, executive power is derived from the legislature. The legislature appoints the executive and sets the conditions for the exercise of its powers.[247] In weaker systems, parliaments exercise powers of scrutiny over the executive and it is accountable to them. Finally, stronger parliaments have control over both revenue and expenditure. Weaker parliaments have no effective power to amend or reject budgets proposed to them by the executive.[248]

Gauging the European Parliament's powers requires, furthermore, looking beyond its formal powers to see how these are exercised. In this regard, a helpful distinction has been made by

---

[242] P. Statham, 'What Kind of Europeanized Public Politics' in R. Koopmans and P. Statham (eds.), *The Making of a European Public Sphere: Media Discourse and Political Contention* (Cambridge University Press, 2010).

[243] A. Schuck *et al.*, 'Party Contestation and Europe on the News Agenda: The 2009 European Parliamentary Elections' (2011) 30 *Electoral Studies* 41.

[244] K. Gattermann and S. Vasilopoulou, 'Absent Yet Popular? Explaining News Visibility of Members of the European Parliament' (2015) 54 *EJPR* 121; O. Eisele, 'Complementing, Competing, or Co-Operating? Exploring Newspapers' Portrayals of the European Parliament and National Parliaments in EU Affairs' (2017) 39 *JEI* 435.

[245] P. Nulty *et al.*, 'Social Media and Political Communication in the 2014 Elections to the European Parliament' (2016) 44 *Electoral Studies* 429; G. Bobba and A. Seddone, 'How Do Eurosceptic Parties and Economic Crisis Affect News Coverage of the European Union? Evidence from the 2014 European Elections in Italy' (2018) 19 *European Politics and Society* 147.

[246] P. Norton, *Legislatures* (Oxford University Press, 1990) 179.

[247] P. Raworth, 'A Timid Step Forwards: Maastricht and the Democratisation of the European Community' (1994) 19 *ELRev* 16–17.

[248] A. Schick, 'Can National Legislatures Regain an Effective Voice in Budget Policy?' (2002) 1(3) *OECD Journal on Budgeting* 15; P. Posner and C.-K. Park, 'Role of the Legislature in the Budget Process: Recent Trends and Innovations' (2007) 7(3) *OECD Journal on Budgeting* 1.

Dann between debating and working parliaments. Debating parliaments, of which the British House of Commons is a prime example, debate government policy and translate it into law. On paper these are formally supreme; governments have to do what they say. However, as the government usually has a majority within these parliaments, they can be less independent than they appear as they can be controlled by it. In a working parliament, of which the US Congress is an example, the legislature is separate from the executive. The US President, representing the government, may propose legislation to the Congress, which may often be of a different political hue, and he can veto legislation adopted by Congress. Working parliaments often have less formal power to adopt legislation than debating parliaments but more autonomy from the executive. Dann observes, furthermore, that working parliaments focus on reviewing the work of the executive, by reviewing and amending legislative proposals or looking at the work of the administrative. This is usually done by strong committees, which, free from the executive, can be powerful. The European Parliament is very much a working parliament. The extract below sets out the structure and work of the Committees.

P. Dann, 'European Parliament and Executive Federalism: Approaching a Parliament in a Semi-Parliamentary Democracy' (2003) 9 *European Law Journal* 549, 564–5

First, their role in acquiring information, discussing and analysing it, and finally formulating the political position of the European Parliament is absolutely central. The committees have the right to interrogate the Commission and to hold hearings with special experts. Building on these instruments, the committees can (and do) acquire specific expertise in their fields. On this basis, it is their task to file reports for the plenary, thereby formulating and pre-determining most of the final outcomes. These powers are a sword with two sharp sides: they not only facilitate the European Parliament's role in legislative procedures, but also contribute to the European Parliament's ability to competently scrutinise the executive, especially when it comes to implementation.

There is a second aspect which allows the committees to play such a pivotal part in the institution: their internal structure. They are not only small, but also specialised and oriented in their scope towards the division of subject matters in the Commission. Of salient importance is their special leadership structure. This consists of a chairman and a *rapporteur*. The latter is responsible for presenting a matter to the committee, drafting the report for the committee and arguing it in plenary and with other institutions. Therefore, a highly influential figure, he is chosen in a complicated and hotly contested procedure. Besides, this position creates clear responsibilities, giving the committee a distinct voice to communicate to the inside (between different committees and party groups) as well as to the outside (to other institutions). It renders the committee especially suited to negotiate with other institutions through an expert representative. It also contributes to the European Parliament's chances to fit into the consensus system of the EU, where different institutions have to constantly negotiate.

There is one more parameter to qualify a parliament as working or debating type and that is the size and organisation of its staff: whereas the *working parliament* can acquire its expertise and level of scrupulous scrutiny of the executive only because of the support of an extensive staff, the *debating parliament* traditionally has very little of it. Its approach is based more on the rhetorical skill of the single parliamentarian to surprise the government and disclose its weakness in debate than on counter-weighing governmental bureaucracies.

Looking at the European Parliament, the staff is yet another factor which underlines its basic nature as a working parliament. Compared to the US Congress of course, it looks petty. But compared to all national parliaments in Europe, it has one of the largest staffs. The EP staff is organised on different levels: on an individual level, every MEP has at least one full time assistant which she can freely employ. On a party level, every party group in the EP is ascribed a number of assistants according to their size and the number of languages spoken. Finally, there is the General Secretariat of the European Parliament in Luxembourg which provides further assistance for the parliamentarians.

The importance of the Committees is reflected in the influence that the dominant party groups seek to exert over them. Although Committee membership is intended to reflect the ideological and territorial composition of the full Parliament,[249] the Chairs of the Committees are determined by negotiation between the groups. Thus, for the 2014 Parliament, there are twenty-two Committees. In 2017, eighteen of these were chaired by an MEP belonging to the European Peoples Party, Alliance of Liberals and Democrats for Europe, or the Progressive Alliance of Socialists and Democrats.[250]

(a) The Legislative Powers of the European Parliament

On their face, the legislative powers of the Parliament seem weaker than national parliaments. The Parliament has neither a monopoly of adoption over any legislative proposal nor power of legislative initiative in any significant field of lawmaking. Instead, its legislative powers vary according to the legislative procedure adopted, with different procedures adopted for different EU competencies. There are three dominant procedures: the consultation, consent and ordinary legislative procedures. Under the first, the Parliament is consulted on a proposal. Under the second, it must actively agree to a proposal before it can become law. The most common is the third, the ordinary legislative procedure. The European Parliament's central powers here are a power of veto over any proposal and the power to negotiate joint texts with the Council.[251]

Irrespective of the procedure used, the Parliament also has the power to request the Commission to submit a proposal.[252] The Commission is not obliged to follow that request, though it must provide reasons if it does not submit a proposal. Equally, if it does make a proposal, it has complete freedom over the content of that proposal. The European Parliament can also, under all three legislative procedures, propose amendments to Commission proposals for legislation. As we shall see, significant numbers of these amendments are accepted.[253]

(b) Powers over the Executive

Parliament has a variety of tools to hold the other EU Institutions to account, including unlimited powers to challenge the acts and failures to act of the other EU Institutions before the Court.[254] However, its central powers over the executive are its powers of appointment and dismissal, on the one hand, and its powers of enquiry, on the other.

Powers of appointment and dismissal: The Parliament is exclusively responsible for appointing the European Ombudsman[255] and can apply for her to be dismissed by the Court of Justice if she no longer fulfils the conditions required for the performance of her duties or is guilty of

---

[249] G. Mcelroy, 'Committee Representation in the European Parliament' (2006) 7 *EUP* 5.
[250] www.europarl.europa.eu/meps/en/search.html?bodyType=OTH&bodyValue=PRCO.
[251] The significance of its input in each of these procedures is addressed in more detail in Ch. 3.   [252] Article 225 TFEU.
[253] See pp. 123–4.   [254] Articles 263 and 265 TFEU.   [255] Article 228(1) TFEU.

serious misconduct.[256] Of greater political significance are the Parliament's powers over the appointment of the Commission. The Parliament has a double power of approval. It must approve the President of the Commission, who has been nominated by the Heads of Government. If the nomination is accepted, it must also approve the College of Commissioners nominated by the President of the Commission and the Heads of Government.[257] Since 1999, the term of the Commission has been synchronised with that of the Parliament. This has allowed the Parliament to use its powers of assent extremely effectively. All prospective Commissioners are subject to questioning by Parliamentary Committees before assent is given to their appointment. They must answer questions about their professional past, their views on European integration and their legislative agenda for their term in office.

Parliament has regularly used its power of assent when dissatisfied with individual nominees. In 2004, it disapproved of the Italian, Rocco Buttiglione, because of his views on women and homosexuality; the Latvian, Ingride Udre, because of allegations surrounding corruption in her party; and the Hungarian, László Kovács, who was deemed to have insufficient knowledge about the Energy portfolio allocated to him. When it became clear that there was not a majority for the Commission because of these nominations, Barroso, the Commission President, had to arrange for the Italian and Latvian nominations to be replaced, and Kovács was reallocated the Taxation and Customs Union portfolio. In 2009, the Bulgarian, Rumiana Jeleva, had to be replaced, because of allegations over her financial interests. Finally, in 2014, the Slovenian, Alenka Bratušek, withdrew after it became clear that there was no support for her appointment after she performed poorly before the Parliamentary Committee considering her appointment.

The Parliament also has important powers to dismiss the Commission. If a motion of censure is passed by a two-thirds majority of the votes cast representing a majority of the total members of the Parliament, the Commission is obliged to resign as a body.[258] This is an 'all or nothing' power. It does not allow the Parliament to criticise or dismiss individual Commissioners. Nevertheless, it was threatened against the Santer Commission in 1998 following allegations of corruption and maladministration against some of its members.[259] The Commission resigned the day before a vote would have been taken sacking the entire College. Following this, a Framework Agreement was made between the Commission and Parliament which allows the Parliament to hold individual Commissioners more to censure. Under this, if the Parliament expresses no confidence in an individual Commissioner, the President must either sack the individual or justify not doing so to the Parliament.[260]

Powers of enquiry: EU citizens and residents of the Union are entitled to petition the Parliament.[261] In 1987, the Parliament set up a Committee of Petitions, consisting of MEPs, to consider the petitions. These petitions either express views on an issue, such as ecological degradation, which may have been caused by an EU Institution, national authority or private body. The process serves a number of functions. In cases where a political issue is raised, it allows the possibility for a hearing to be organised by the Parliament, thereby securing a voice for parties who might otherwise be disenfranchised. In cases where maladministration by an EU

---

[256] Article 228(2) TFEU.   [257] Article 17(7) TEU.   [258] Article 17(8) TEU, Article 234 TFEU.

[259] D. Judge and D. Earnshaw, 'The European Parliament and the Commission Crisis: A New Assertiveness?' (2002) 15 *Governance* 345.

[260] Framework Agreement on relations between the European Parliament and the European Commission, OJ 2010, L 304/ 47, para. 5.

[261] Articles 20(2)(d), 24 and 227 TFEU.

Institution is alleged, the Parliament may take the matter up itself. In cases where a failure of a Member State is alleged, it will ask the Commission to take the matter up with the Member State concerned. However, take-up of this procedure has been limited. In 2015, the Committee received 1,431 petitions of which 943 were admissible, a figure that the European Parliament admitted was small relative to the size of population of the Union.[262]

In addition, Parliament has the power to ask questions of or receive reports from most of the EU Institutions. The European Commission, ECB and Ombudsman must all submit Annual Reports to the Parliament.[263] In addition, the President of the European Council must report to the Parliament after each of its meetings.[264] Whilst there is no formal obligation to do so, it is customary for the State holding the Presidency of the Council to present the proposed work of the Council during its Presidency before the Parliament. Commissioners are also required to reply to questions put by parliamentary members.[265] A convention has also grown whereby the Council will answer questions put to it by members of the Parliament.[266] A corollary of this is that the Council and the European Council have a right to be heard by the Parliament.[267] Finally, the President of the ECB and members of the Executive Council may, at the request of the Parliament, or on their own initiative, be heard by the competent Committees of the Parliament.[268]

(c) The Power of Parliamentary Government?

Since 2014, Parliament has arguably acquired a power of parliamentary government: a power to be involved with setting out the policy agenda of the Commission and to be heavily involved with its execution. This is not a formal power but emerged out of the *Spitzenkandidat* system. For those elections, it will be remembered that the main European Parliament groups stated that they would only accept for President the person who had been nominated by the party group which won the most votes; in that instance the nominee of the European Peoples Party, Jean-Claude Juncker. Prior to the elections, each of the nominees consulted with the groups on the platforms on which they would run and the programmes that they would promote during their term. After the appointment of Juncker, delivery of this programme led to a very close relationship between the Commission and the European Parliament.[269]

> **M. Shackleton, 'Transforming Representative Democracy in the EU? The Role of the European Parliament' (2017) 39 *Journal of European Integration* 191, 198–9**
>
> The tightness of this bond can be seen in the way the policy programme of the Commission was developed. Already before the elections Juncker had campaigned on a set of five points (the promotion of jobs and growth, an energy union, a balanced trade agreement with the United States, reform of the monetary union

---

[262] European Parliament, *Report on the activities of the Committee on Petitions 2015*, A8–0366/2016.
[263] Articles 249, 284(3) and 228 TFEU.   [264] Article 15(6)(d) TEU.   [265] Article 230 TFEU.
[266] It is formally obliged to answer questions in the field of CFSP, Article 36 TEU.   [267] Article 230 TFEU.
[268] Article 284(3) TFEU.
[269] It has been argued that day-to-day interaction between staff has also fed a strong Parliamentary engagement in Commission work, M. Egeberg, Å. Gornitzka and J. Trondal, 'A Not So Technocratic Executive? Everyday Interaction between the European Parliament and the Commission' (2014) 37 *WEP* 1.

and a fair solution to the British problem). After the elections, these five points were expanded into ten priorities that bore the marks of his discussions with the political groups in the Parliament. The ability to compare the evolution of a document before and after the elections was a quite different process from what had taken place five years earlier when Barroso came to the Parliament after the elections with his own programme for the Commission.

The ten priorities effectively established a joint framework for the EU over the next five years. It contained detailed commitments, including a 300 million euro infrastructure fund (later known as the European Fund for Strategic Investment (EFSI), a shifting of resources to jobs and growth following the review of the multiannual financial framework in 2016 and a firm promise that a trade agreement with the United States would not be drawn up at the expense of European standards. The plan was highly political in nature, designed to win the support of as many of the political groups as possible, and constituted a significant challenge to the European Council, which adopted a much less detailed roadmap at the meeting when it confirmed Juncker as its candidate.

The Parliament for its part has started to see itself playing a different political game from the one it played before. It has been willing to change its behaviour significantly as a result of having accepted the Juncker framework for the five year term . . .

At the level of the plenary the EPP and S&D groups worked more closely together than they had done in the past. Voting cohesion increased markedly, with the two groups voting together around 80% of the time in the first six months of the legislature. In fact, cooperation extended to the Liberals so that the three groups constituted what Votewatch has called a 'super grand coalition', with the three groups on the winning side substantially more often than any other group in the Parliament. In substantive terms, this majority backed rapidly and massively the Juncker plan to boost the European economy through the European Fund for Strategic Investment and the Commission proposals to relocate 120,000 asylum seekers by the use of compulsory quotas, the latter within a week of receiving the proposal. The executive was winning the backing of the legislature that had helped to get its President elected; the legislature was developing a programme for government with the executive that it had chosen.

It is unclear whether the Member States will allow this close relationship to continue after 2019. It creates, in effect, a cabal between the Commission and the European Parliament at the expense of policy priorities sought by national governments, which will now be pushed down the legislative timetable. There may also be mixed feelings about this development. On the hand, it might be seen as democratising the Commission. It delivers programmes set out by European party groups and voted upon by EU citizens at European Parliament elections. Citizen awareness of these programmes is low, however, and likely to continue to remain low. More problematic is the relationship between the Parliament and the Commission after the elections. It is not an arms' length one in which an elected assembly holds the executive to account in (hopefully) a dispassionate manner. The European Parliament is now so engaged in Commission activities that it must be wondered whether it will be sufficiently committed to checking when these go wrong or whether they could be done better.

(d) The Financial Powers of the Parliament

Parliament has significant powers over the EU Budget and is the central player within the Council. A five-year multi-annual framework for expenditure sets out the limits on total expenditure and ceilings for each heading of expenditure to be set by the Council after obtaining the consent of the Parliament.[270] Annual budgets are then set each year. These have to be in balance, comply with the multi-annual framework and be based on individual institutions' estimates of expenditure. Within these constraints, the Commission sets a draft Budget, which may then be adopted by the Council. The Parliament then has the right to veto the Budget should it wish.[271]

7 THE PRINCIPLE OF TRANSPARENCY

The institutional settlement is required to operate transparently. The transparency principle is set out in Article 15(3) TFEU.[272]

Article 15 TFEU

(3) Any citizen of the Union, and any natural or legal person residing or having its registered office in a Member State, shall have a right of access to documents of the Union institutions, bodies, offices and agencies, whatever their medium, subject to the principles and the conditions to be defined in accordance with this paragraph.

General principles and limits on grounds of public or private interest governing this right of access to documents shall be determined . . . in accordance with the ordinary legislative procedure.

Article 15(3) TFEU has been implemented by a Regulation, Regulation 1049/2001, which sets out the scope of the right to access to documents as well as the limits on this right.[273]

(i) The Scope of the Right of Access to Documents

Access to documents is provided, in part, through all Union Institutions being required to keep electronic up-to-date registers to which the public should have access.[274] Parties can also request access to particular information. The scope of this entitlement is set out in Article 2 of the Regulation.

Regulation 1049/2001/EU, Article 2

(1) Any citizen of the Union, and any natural or legal person residing or having its registered office in a Member State, has a right of access to documents of the institutions, subject to the principles, conditions and limits defined in this Regulation.

(2) The institutions may, subject to the same principles, conditions and limits, grant access to documents to any natural or legal person not residing or not having its registered office in a Member State.

(3) This Regulation shall apply to all documents held by an institution, that is to say, documents drawn up or received by it and in its possession, in all areas of activity of the European Union.

---

[270] Article 312(1)–(2) TFEU.
[271] Article 314 TFEU. A process of conciliation takes place similar to that in the ordinary legislative procedure.
[272] The right is also contained in Article 42 EUCFR.
[273] Regulation 1049/2001 regarding public access to European Parliament, Council and Commission documents, OJ 2001, L 145/43.
[274] *Ibid.* Article 11.

The right is to documents held not just by EU Institutions but also by EU bodies, offices and agencies.[275] It covers not only documents drawn up by the institutions but also documents which fall into their possession (Article 2(3)). The latter is particularly significant insofar as the Commission, in particular, receives considerable documentation from private parties, other institutions and national governments. However, applicants may not ask EU Institutions to draw up new documents but only to grant access to existing ones.[276] This distinction has proved challenging in relation to databases where the information is continually changing. The Court has therefore stated that databases are not documents but, because of their technical specificities, information which can be extracted from them using pre-programmed search tools should be seen as a document.[277] Individuals, therefore, have a right to ask for these searches to be carried out on Union databases.

Access may be refused if providing the documents involves a manifestly unreasonable amount of work. Prior to refusing access the EU Institution must confer with the applicant to find a fair solution[278] and see whether the request could be tailored in a less exacting way that still secures the applicant's interests.[279] In the event of failure to agree, refusal will only be allowed in the most exceptional circumstances and, even then, the EU Institution must still choose the avenue which is most favourable to the applicant whilst not exceeding the limits of what may be reasonably required.[280]

The number of requests per annum floats at around 6,000.[281] These numbers are small for a polity of close to half a billion people. A wide range of interests seek access, however. In 2017, individual citizens accounted for 37.4 per cent of applications; academics and think tanks, 21.6 per cent of applicants; companies, 13.6 per cent; and lawyers, 13.2 per cent.[282] The territorial breakdown indicates that those most strongly engaged with the Brussels policy-making sphere are most likely to seek access with the highest number of requests coming from Belgium (25.7 per cent).[283]

(ii) The Exceptions to the Right of Access to Documents

Most litigation has focused on the public interests which require or allow access to information to be denied. Set out in Article 4 of Regulation 1049/2011, these demarcate which political and legal activity is to be kept be secret and which activities citizens and residents are allowed to know about, and can therefore hold institutions to account. Both Union Courts have repeatedly stated that these restrictions on access to documents should be interpreted and applied strictly as the Regulation seeks to give the public the widest possible right of access to documents.[284]

---

[275] *COSEPURI* v. *EFSA*, T-339/10 and T-532/10, EU:T:2013:38.
[276] *Strack* v. *Commission*, C-127/13 P, EU:C:2014:2250. [277] *Typke* v. *Commission*, C-491/15 P, EU:C:2017:5.
[278] Regulation 1049/2001, Article 6(3).
[279] *Verein für Konsumenteninformation* v. *Commission*, T-2/03, EU:T:2005:125; *Williams* v. *Commission*, T-42/05, EU:T:2008:325.
[280] *Evropaïki Dynamiki* v. *Parliament*, T-136/15, EU:T:2017:915.
[281] There were 6,255 applications in 2017 and 6,077 in 2016. European Commission, 'Report on the Application in 2017 of Regulation 1049/2001', COM(2018)633, 5.
[282] *Ibid.* 7.   [283] *Ibid.* 8.
[284] *Sweden and MyTravel Group* v. *Commission*, C-506/08 P, EU:C:2011:496; *ClientEarth* v. *Commission*, C-57/16 P, EU:C:2018:660; *Malta* v. *Commission*, EU:T:2018:241; *Deza* v. *ECHA*, T-189/14, EU:T:2017:4.

This disposition towards openness appears reinforced by the duty to provide partial access to the document where possible.

Regulation 1049/2001/EU, Article 4

(6) If only parts of the requested document are covered by any of the exceptions, the remaining parts of the document shall be released.

This possibility of partial access imposes a duty on the EU Institutions to consider whether it is possible to grant partial access to the documents. A failure to do this will make any refusal illegal. Furthermore, if documents can be redacted so that sensitive passages can be blanked out, this should also take place.[285]

That said, large amounts of institutional activity are screened off from public view. In 2017, full access to documents was granted in just under 62 per cent of applications with partial access in just over half of the remainder, and no access in 18 per cent of cases.[286] These figures also suggest a culture of secrecy in which EU Institutions are over-eager to categorise information as falling within one of the public interests which justify restricting dissemination. Thus, it will not be placed on the public registers and individual attempts to seek it will be opposed. Critics have, therefore claimed that the central problem with the EU transparency regime lies not in the case law but with the institutional practices of classification of information. The public interests justifying restriction are interpreted broadly and this is difficult to roll-back by case law.

Each EU Institution establishes how documents are to be classified through its own internal Rules of Procedure. In the extract below, Curtin examined the operation of the Council's practice.

D. Curtin, 'Overseeing Secrets in the EU: A Democratic Perspective' (2014) 52 *Journal of Common Market Studies* 684, 690

[T]he Council itself only acts as original classifier in a small fraction of the documents in the classified categories held by it. For example, it has never itself classified any document to date as 'Top Secret' and only very few of its documents have been classified as 'Secret' (33 in 2012). A somewhat larger category is the 'Confidential' documents category (353 such documents were classified or held by the Council in 2012). It is clear that these numbers are very small in relative terms. By far the largest category of classified documents is at the very lowest level of Restricted. 'Restricted' is defined in the Council's security rules in very open terms as where the disclosure of a document would be 'disadvantageous' to the interests of the EU or a Member State. Elastic substantive classification criteria are a source of largely unfettered executive discretion, and this is not taken away by the Council's own internal classification guidance. In the EU context, there is little control in practice over the substance of unnecessary classification, and there are virtually no internal controls. Until very recently there was no formal procedure for declassification of EUCI

---

[285] On both the procedural requirement and the duty to redact see *In't Veld* v. *Commission*, T-529/09, EU: T:2012:215.
[286] European Commission, n. 281 above, p. 9.

documents – only an *ad hoc* one. The fact that there now is an overall declassification framework is designed to facilitate declassification in the future.

Other originators will have originally classified a significant number of the documents in the four classification levels held by the Council, but no precise figures are available on the breakdown. Documents classified by other originators, including internal EU agencies and offices such as Europol and the European External Action Service (EEAS), need to give specific permission for documents before declassification can take place by the Council.

This bias seems to be propelled by two particular dynamics.[287] One is institutional advantage and culture. Documents should not be disclosed if they are disadvantageous to the EU Institution. The other goes to handling documents that originate from other parties. There is a concern to respect the classification made by the originator of the document.

It is now time to turn to the headings which justify restricting access to information. There are three headings.[288] The first requires access to be refused simply by the dint of the document falling within that heading. The second requires an EU Institution to refuse access to a document unless there is an overriding public interest. The third relates to documents provided by parties other than the EU Institutions. Institutions must consult with these parties and, subject to the constraints discussed below, Member States may request that documents not be disclosed without their prior agreement.

The first heading is set out in Article 4(1).

Regulation 1049/2011, Article 4

(1) The institutions shall refuse access to a document where disclosure would undermine the protection of:
  (a) the public interest as regards:
    - public security,
    - defence and military matters,
    - international relations,
    - the financial, monetary or economic policy of the Community or a Member State;
  (b) privacy and the integrity of the individual, in particular in accordance with Community legislation regarding the protection of personal data.

If a document falls under any of these grounds, no countervailing reason can be provided justifying disclosure. It should not be released.[289] Furthermore, Union Courts will confine themselves to seeing whether reasons have been given for the refusal, the facts are accurately stated, and whether there was a manifest error of assessment.[290] This test requires, in the first

---

[287] See also D. Galloway, 'Classifying Secrets in the EU' (2014) 52 *JCMS* 668; V. Abazi, *Secrecy and Oversight in the European Union: The Law and Practice of Classified Information* (Amsterdam, ACELG, 2015); D. Curtin, 'Second order secrecy and Europe's legality mosaics' (2018) 41 *WEP* 846.

[288] There has been extensive case law, and only the more salient issues are addressed here.

[289] *WWF European Policy Programme* v. *Council*, T-264/04, EU:T:2007:114; *Access Info Europe* v. *Commission*, T-852/16, EU:T:2018:71.

[290] *Sison* v. *Council*, C-266/05 P, EU:C:2007:75.

place, that EU Institutions consider each document. Blanket refusals to give access to a range of documents are, thus, illegal. In *Kuijer*, a Council decision to refuse access to human rights reports on third countries, as some were quite damning and this would damage relations, was declared illegal.[291] The General Court held that refusal had to be made by reference to the specific content and context of each human rights report. Some could be released as they contained general information on the protection of human rights which had already been made public and did not involve any politically sensitive appraisal of the State. The test requires, in the second place, that the risk of the protected interest being undermined must be reasonably foreseeable and not hypothetical. Plausible explanations must, therefore, be provided of how release could specifically and actually undermine the interest involved. A refusal to provide access to a document on whether a Greek appeals process complied with EU asylum law was illegal, therefore, because it could not (as the Commission argued) plausibly damage relations with Turkey.[292]

The second heading requires access to documents to be given unless there is an overriding public interest in disclosure.

Regulation 1049/2001, Article 4

(2) The institutions shall refuse access to a document where disclosure would undermine the protection of:
- commercial interests of a natural or legal person, including intellectual property,
- court proceedings and legal advice,
- the purpose of inspections, investigations and audits,
unless there is an overriding public interest in disclosure.

(3) Access to a document, drawn up by an institution for internal use or received by an institution, which relates to a matter where the decision has not been taken by the institution, shall be refused if disclosure of the document would seriously undermine the institution's decision-making process, unless there is an overriding public interest in disclosure.

Access to a document containing opinions for internal use as part of deliberations and preliminary consultations within the institution concerned shall be refused even after the decision has been taken if disclosure of the document would seriously undermine the institution's decision-making process, unless there is an overriding public interest in disclosure.

A powerful example of the interpretation of this heading is *EnBW*. The applicant was a German energy distribution company which applied for documents concerning competition law proceedings concluded by the Commission which resulted in a €750 million fine for its competitors. The Commission refused on the grounds that disclosure would undermine the protection of both the commercial interests of these competitors and the purpose of these investigations (Article 4(2) above). In addition, the documents were part of its own internal deliberations and disclosure would therefore undermine its own decision-making process (Article 4(3) above).

---

[291] *Kuijer* v. *Council*, T-211/00, EU:T:2002:30. [292] *Access Info Europe* v. *Commission*, T-852/16, EU:T:2018:71.

Commission v. EnBW, C–365/12 P, EU:C:2014:112

63 . . . the system of exceptions laid down in Article 4 of that regulation is based on a balancing of the opposing interests in a given situation, that is to say, first, the interests which would be favoured by the disclosure of the documents in question and, secondly, those which would be jeopardised by such disclosure. The decision taken on a request for access to documents depends on which interest must prevail in the particular case . . .

64 In accordance with well-established case-law, in order to justify refusal of access to a document the disclosure of which has been requested, it is not sufficient, in principle, for that document to be covered by an activity mentioned in Article 4(2) and (3) of Regulation No 1049/2001. The institution concerned must also provide explanations as to how access to that document could specifically and actually undermine the interest protected by an exception laid down in that article . . .

65 However, the Court has acknowledged that it is open to the EU institution concerned to base its decisions in that regard on general presumptions which apply to certain categories of documents, as considerations of a generally similar kind are likely to apply to requests for disclosure relating to documents of the same nature . . .

66 Accordingly, the Court has already acknowledged the existence of such presumptions in four particular cases, namely with regard to the documents in the administrative file relating to a procedure for reviewing State aid . . . , the documents exchanged between the Commission and notifying parties or third parties in the course of merger control proceedings . . . , the pleading lodged by one of the institutions in court proceedings . . . and the documents concerning an infringement procedure during its pre-litigation stage . . .

67 All those cases are characterised by the fact that the request for access in question covered not just one document but a set of documents . . .

68 In that type of situation, the recognition that there is a general presumption that the disclosure of documents of a certain nature will, in principle, undermine the protection of one of the interests listed in Article 4 of Regulation No 1049/2001 enables the institution concerned to deal with a global application and to reply thereto accordingly . . .

The test for the heading differs from that for the first heading in two notable regards.

First, the EU Institution must show that disclosure *specifically and actually undermines* the protected interest. By contrast, there must only be a risk that this is the case for the first heading. As it would be challenging for the EU Institution to examine every document individually to see if this is so, it may rely on a presumption that if access to that category of document or documents of a similar nature is generally denied then it can be denied for the document in hand.[293] The Court has indicated that this presumption is something which can be rebutted. However, it has not established how this may be done. The presumption means that the EU Institution does not have to look at the individual document,[294] and, as the applicant does not have the access to the document, it will not be able to provide evidence countering the presumption. The presumptions have, thus, become blankets which protect the EU Institutions from scrutiny.

---

[293] *LPN and Finland* v. *Commission*, C-514/11 P and C-605/11 P, EU:C:2013:528; *Pari Pharma* v. *EMA*, T-235/15, EU:T:2018:65.

[294] *LPN and Finland* v. *Commission*, C-514/11 P and C-605/11 P, EU:C:2013:528; *Sweden and Spirlea* v. *Commission*, C-562/14 P, EU:C:2017:356.

Secondly, if a document falls under this heading, access is not necessarily restricted. The EU Institution must weigh the interests jeopardised by disclosure against those advanced by it. The difficulty with this test is its vague and unprincipled nature. It is unclear what weight is to be given to particular interests or how they are to be evaluated against very different interests. The consequence is a test which is both very uncertain and grants considerable EU Institution discretion.

The third and final heading concerns documents which originate from third parties or the Member States.

> **Regulation 1049/2001, Article 4**
>
> (4) As regards third-party documents, the institution shall consult the third party with a view to assessing whether an exception in paragraph 1 or 2 is applicable, unless it is clear that the document shall or shall not be disclosed.
>
> (5) A Member State may request the institution not to disclose a document originating from that Member State without its prior agreement.

Litigation has focused here on when States can veto disclosure. In *Sweden* v. *Commission*,[295] the Court held that they do not have an unqualified veto as this would be incompatible with the Regulation's commitment to grant the widest possible access to documents and would also introduce arbitrary distinctions between documents of a similar kind held by the EU Institutions. If an EU Institution received a request for a document originating from a Member State it was required to open a dialogue with the Member State. The latter could only refuse disclosure if the document fell within one of the headings set out in Article 4(1)–(3) of the Regulation. The EU Institution is obliged to review the State's reasons but must merely check whether the reasons provide prima facie justify non-disclosure rather than substitute its own judgment for that of the Member State.[296]

FURTHER READING

C. Bergström and D. Ritleng (eds.), *Law-Making by the EU Commission: The New System* (Oxford University Press, 2016).

C. Bickerton, D. Hodson and U. Puetter (eds.), *The New Intergovernmentalism: States and Supranational Actors in the Post-Maastricht Era* (Oxford University Press, 2015).

R. Corbett, F. Jacobs and M. Shackleton, *The European Parliament,* 9th edn (London, John Harper, 2016).

D. Curtin, 'Challenging Executive Dominance in European Democracy' (2014) 77 *Modern Law Review* 1.

D. Curtin, 'Second Order Secrecy and Europe's Legality Mosaics' (2018) 41 *West European Politics* 846.

F. Häge, *Bureaucrats as Law-Makers: Committee Decision-Making in the EU Council of Ministers* (Abingdon, Routledge, 2013).

---

[295] *Sweden* v. *Commission*, C-64/05 P, EU:C:2007:802.
[296] *Germany* v. *Commission*, T-59/09, EU:T:2012:75; *France and Czech Republic* v. *Commission*, T-344/15, EU:T:2017:250.

M. Hartlapp, J. Metz and C. Rauh, *Which Policy for Europe? Power and Conflict inside the European Commission* (Oxford University Press, 2014).

C. Ossege, *European Regulatory Agencies in EU Decision-Making: Between Expertise and Influence* (Basingstoke, Palgrave Macmillan, 2016).

U. Puetter, *The European Council and the Council: New Intergovernmentalism and Institutional Change* (Oxford University Press, 2014).

A. Wille, *The Normalization of the European Commission: Politics and Bureaucracy in the EU Executive* (Oxford University Press, 2013).

3

Lawmaking

CONTENTS

1 INTRODUCTION

This chapter considers the different forms of EU law, the legislative and regulatory procedures deployed to enact them, the possibilities for groups of Member States to enact laws between themselves to further European integration, and the democratic legitimacy of EU lawmaking. It is organised as follows:

Section 2 discusses the different types of legal instrument in EU law. There are four types of binding instrument: Regulations, Directives, Decisions and International Agreements. In addition, the European Union relies heavily on soft law: non-binding instruments which come in a multiplicity of forms. In some instances, binding law and soft law will be used quite discretely from each other. There are others, most notably where soft law is used to provide interpretations of binding law or set out how EU Institutions will exercise powers, where binding law and soft law come together to create hybrid regimes where parties are governed by a mix of hard and soft law.

Section 3 looks at the allocation of legislative procedures. The Treaties make a distinction between legislation, laws adopted under the legislative procedures in the Treaties, and laws adopted according to other processes. The Treaties provide a series of legal bases which both grant the Union authority to legislate in a particular field and determine the legislative procedures and instruments to be used. Reference will be had to the predominant aim and content of the measure to determine the appropriate base. If the measure is so inextricably and equally associated with more than one base that the predominant one cannot be ascertained, the Court operates a formal hierarchy between legal bases.

Section 4 considers the central legislative procedures. The ordinary legislative procedure grants Parliament the power of veto and Council, acting by Qualified Majority Voting (QMV), the power of assent over any Commission proposal. In the consultation procedure, Parliament is merely consulted on a Commission proposal with the Council taking the final decision. The consent procedure requires the Parliament to behave actively and approve a proposal before it becomes law. The common procedure is the ordinary legislative procedure. Its formal features are blurred, however, by the predominance of trilogues. These are informal meetings between representatives of the Commission, Council and Parliament which seek to reach agreement on the legislative proposal. They usually occur early in the legislative procedure after the Parliament has first considered the proposal, and are controversial because of their lack of transparency and because they foreclose process.

Section 5 considers the role of national parliaments in EU lawmaking. Their central roles are threefold. There is, first, the political dialogue between them and the Commission. This is an informal process where they can give their views on draft Commission proposals or policy papers. Secondly, national parliaments can exercise influence over how their national governments vote in the Council. There is the mandate system in which an instruction is given to the national government and the scrutiny system in which the government cannot vote in the Council until the parliament has looked at it. Thirdly, there is the Early Warning Mechanism under which national parliaments can check legislative proposals for compliance with the subsidiarity principle: the principle which requires the Union only to legislate when it can show added value.

Section 6 discusses differentiated lawmaking in which a group of Member States enact laws or other binding instruments between themselves which cover the whole Union. The headline Treaty procedure is Enhanced Cooperation. This provides for the Council to authorise as few as nine Member States to adopt laws between themselves, but these laws must meet a number of constraints to protect Union and other Member State interests. They are, thus, rarely, used. In addition, there are a number of policies – the euro, the area of freedom, security and justice, and security and defence – where it is expected that participation by some Member States will be limited or non-existent. These have particular procedures allowing other States to proceed. The practice of differentiation has become widespread. In some instances, it is done through EU laws setting out differentiated obligations. In others, it occurs through the conclusion of international agreements outside the structures of the Treaties. Some are subsequently incorporated into EU law whereas others, more problematically, are used as a substitute for EU law.

Section 7 considers comitology, the procedures which govern the adoption of implementing measures by the Commission. There are two dominant procedures: the advisory procedure and the examination procedure. Both involve consideration of a draft Commission measure by a committee of national government representatives. Under the advisory procedure, this committee advises. Under the examination procedure, it can veto, or, in some instances, must positively approve the draft. Some accounts see these committees as exercising a form of national government control over the Commission whilst others see them as working in tandem with the Commission to engage in common problem-solving.

Section 8 discusses the democratic qualities of EU lawmaking. Some accounts see supranational lawmaking as inherently undemocratic as it does not have a political community with the necessary qualities of trust and mutual commitment to sustain democratic decision-making. By contrast, others argue that the absence of these qualities makes the case for supranational democracy in a world that has to deal with an increasing number of transnational phenomena – be it trade, international crime, migration, pollution or the Internet. Another perspective argues that EU lawmaking can be justified because States think that coming together to decide certain laws in common, whilst deciding others apart, might make decision-making more generally democratic. This is because EU democracy might have qualities not possessed by national democracies, and there are times when these qualities are more imperative. These qualities might include greater openness to underrepresented interests, more engagement with securing the justice of international markets, and a refusal to territorialise arguments so that they are simply the position of State A and that of State B. There are questions, however, about whether EU legislative practice has these qualities, and, even if it does, how the normative weight of these qualities are to be assessed when they come into conflict with the demands of national democracies.

2 TYPES OF EU LAW

(i) Binding Laws

EU law comprises a bewildering array of legal acts. There are the EU Treaties, which constitute primary EU law. The EU Treaties include a number of provisions, which set out rights and obligations for different actors. However, they are also framework Treaties. Much of them is given over to establishing procedures empowering EU Institutions to make EU secondary law, which will regulate activity in greater detail. The central provision setting out the different types of secondary law is Article 288 TFEU.

Article 288 TFEU

To exercise the Union's competences, the institutions shall adopt regulations, directives, decisions, recommendations and opinions.

A regulation shall have general application. It shall be binding in its entirety and directly applicable in all Member States.

A directive shall be binding, as to the result to be achieved, upon each Member State to which it is addressed, but shall leave to the national authorities the choice of form and methods.

A decision shall be binding in its entirety. A decision which specifies those to whom it is addressed shall be binding only on them.

Recommendations and opinions shall have no binding force.

The provision is unsatisfying. It sets out a list of binding instruments but, then, includes two instruments, recommendations and opinions, which are not binding. It also omits an important form of binding law, international agreements with non-EU States, which bind both the Union and the Member States.[1] A few words are necessary about each of the binding forms of secondary law: Regulations, Directives, Decisions and International Agreements.

Regulations are the most centralising of all of the instruments. They are used wherever there is a need for uniformity. One characteristic is that they have general application. Thus, they do not apply to individual sets of circumstances, but to an 'objectively determined situation and produce(s) legal effects with regard to categories of persons described in a generalised and abstract manner'.[2] The other hallmark of Regulations is direct applicability. They enter into force on the date specified in them or, failing that, on the twentieth day following publication in the Official Journal of the European Union.[3] From that date, they automatically form part of the domestic legal order of each Member State and require no further transposition. Indeed, unless permitted by the Regulation, it is illegal for a Member State to adopt national laws implementing the Regulation.[4] The reasons are that national measures might contain changes which affect the uniform application of the Regulation or obscure from citizens that the Regulation is the direct source of their rights and obligations.[5] However, there is a caveat. Regulations may require national authorities to adopt implementing measures. In such instances, a failure to implement the Regulation breaches EU law.[6]

Directives are binding as to the result to be achieved. They leave the choice as to form and methods used to implement it to the discretion of Member States. They are often adopted for more politically sensitive matters where States want some leeway over the exact content and phrasing of the law. Although, as with Regulations, Directives come into force on the date stipulated therein or on the twentieth following publication, this is usually not the most important date. All Directives provide a deadline, typically eighteen or twenty-four months after publication, by which Member States must transpose their obligations into national law. Between the dates of publication and transposition, Member States must refrain from measures which seriously compromise the attainment of the results sought by the Directive, notably by adopting measures which prevent them from transposing the Directive on time.[7] Otherwise, they have complete freedom as Directives do not have full binding effect until this date of transposition.

---

[1] Article 216(2) TFEU. [2] *AJD Tuna* v. *Direttur tal-Agrikoltura u s-Sajd*, C-221/09, EU:C:2011:153, para. 51.
[3] Article 297(1)–(2) TFEU. [4] *M.S.* v. *P.S.*, C-283/16, EU:C:2017:104.
[5] *Stichting Al-Aqsa* v. *Council*, C-539/10 P and C-550/10 P, EU:C:2012:711, para. 87.
[6] *Commission* v. *United Kingdom*, 128/78, EU:C:1979:32.
[7] *Inter-Environnement Wallonie* v. *Région Wallonne*, C-129/96, EU:C:1997:628; *Jetair* v. *FOD Financiën*, C-599/12, EU:C:2014:144.

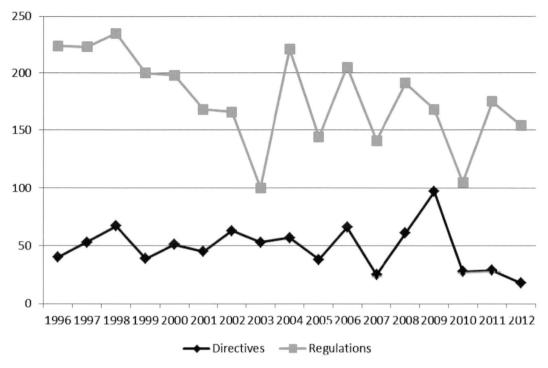

Figure 3.1 Union annual output of Regulations and Directives

EU law provides, first, for decisions addressed to particular parties. The majority of such decisions are addressed to Member States, with a small number addressed to private parties, mostly in the field of EU competition law, where the Commission can impose fines on parties or require them to desist from certain practices. These are binding only upon their addressees, and, for that reason, the addressee must be notified of the decision, which can only take effect from notification.[8] There are, secondly, decisions which have no addressee. These impose general obligations that bind the European Union as an organisational entity and, therefore, EU Institution and Member States, as part of that entity. However, as they are not addressed to private parties, they are thought not to impose obligations on them.[9]

The European Union can conclude international agreements with non-EU States where it and these States are the only parties to the agreement. Often, the scope of the international agreement also covers matters that do not fall within the European Union's competence. In such circumstances, the international agreement is concluded by both the European Union and the Member States. International agreements only generate legal effects within EU law where they are either exclusively concluded by the European Union or, where concluded by both the European Union

---

[8] Article 297(2) TFEU.
[9] A. v. Bogdandy, F. Arndt and J. Bast, 'Legal Instruments in European Union Law and Their Reform: A Systematic Approach on an Empirical Basis' (2004) 23 *YBEL* 91, 103–6.

and the Member States, for that part of the agreement that falls within EU competence. The EU legislature has discretion as to the internal legal effects of international agreements, and these will, therefore, depend upon the phrasing of the agreement.[10] If it imposes unconditional and precise obligations, these will not require implementation by further EU law but will form part of the EU legal order in just the same way as Regulations.[11] More vaguely phrased provisions or provisions requiring action by EU Institutions will necessitate implementation by EU law. In such circumstances, it has been held that the EU legislature did not intend the international agreement to generate effects in the internal legal order of the European Union, and it can, thus, neither be invoked directly in its own right nor as a measure against which the legality of other EU law can be reviewed.[12]

The most common measures are decisions. In 2016 and 2017, some 1,764 decisions were adopted. However, most are not general in nature. The most common general acts are Regulations with there being 954 Regulations during this period, whilst only 22 Directives were adopted.[13] The justification for these different instruments is to allow EU law different legal bite in different policy fields and, in other cases, to grant the legislature some discretion over what legal bite EU laws ought to have. This has somewhat been undermined by these instruments being used interchangeably. One finds Regulations that substitute for decisions as they apply to individual sets of circumstances rather than generally;[14] and Directives which look like Regulations because they are so detailed that they vitiate the discretion granted to Member States and must be transposed into national law verbatim.[15] Finally, decisions without addressees act as a substitute for Directives in that they require Member States to realise certain results without specifying the means of which to do so. In no instance has any of this been declared illegal.

(ii) Soft Law

Matters are further complicated by any account of EU law having to include not just the binding instruments set out in the previous section, but also soft law. Soft law includes any 'rules of conduct which … have no legally binding force but which nevertheless may have practical effects'.[16] Thus, it includes not only recommendations and opinions but also a panoply of other measures, which go under a variety of titles: resolutions and declarations, action programmes and plans, communications, guidelines and inter-institutional arrangements. Soft law is used for a variety of purposes:[17]

---

[10] *FIAMM* v. *Commission and Council*, C-120–1/06 P, EU:C:2007:212.

[11] E.g. *Camar* v. *Presidenza del Consiglio dei Ministri*, C-102/09, EU:C:2010:236.

[12] *C & J Clark International* v. *Commissioners for Her Majesty's Revenue & Customs*; *Puma* v. *Hauptzollamt Nürnberg*, C-659/13 and C-34/14, EU:C:2016:74.

[13] These figures can be found in the statistics section of Eur-Lex, the online repository of EU law, https://eur-lex.europa .eu/statistics/2017/legislative-acts-statistics.html.

[14] E.g. *International Fruit Company* v. *Commission*, C-41–44/70, EU:C:1971:53.

[15] *ENKA* v. *Inspecteur der Invoerrechten*, 38/77, EU:C:1977:190.

[16] F. Snyder, 'The Effectiveness of European Community Law: Institutions, Processes, Tools and Techniques' (1993) 56 *MLR* 19, 32. For an exhaustive discussion, L. Senden, *Soft Law in European Community Law* (Oxford-Portland, Hart, 2004) ch. 5.

[17] On how soft law is coming to supersede hard law in many fields see S. Smismans, 'From Harmonisation to Coordination? EU Law in the Lisbon Governance Architecture' (2011) 18 *JEPP* 504.

Lawmaking: Often soft law is used in the same way as binding law to set out substantive norms. In some fields of EU law this is because binding measures are excluded from these fields.[18] In fields where this is not the case it is still frequently preferred to binding measures for a number of reasons. The measure might be on a matter of particular national sensitivity. Binding measures might be over prescriptive by dint of the field of the diversity and complexity of the matters which have to be regulated. Or, finally, Member States might wish to take common action but not in a form which ties their hands so firmly.[19]

The Organisation of Cooperation between EU Institutions: Soft law is central to how the EU Institutions organise cooperation between themselves as it will set out a basis for cooperation where there was none or where it was poorly specified.[20] A good example is the *2016 Inter-institutional Agreement on Better Law-Making*. This addressed the lack of provision for cooperation between the EU Institutions across the whole of the legislative cycle. It, thus, set out how they would cooperate not just during the process of adopting EU laws, but also in the planning of legislative programmes and evaluation of existing EU law.[21]

Commitments as to how a single EU Institution will exercise its power: The Commission has used soft law to set out, for example, how it will enforce EU competition law and which infractions it will pursue.[22] Soft law can often be used here in far-reaching ways to establish new policies in which the EU Institution's values and *modus operandi* over a sweep of activity are set out. An example is the Commission Communication on strengthening the framework for the rule of law.[23] This exploited the Commission's power to propose to the Council that the latter find a clear risk of a serious breach of the values in Article 2 TEU (e.g. respect for human rights, democracy, and the rule of law) by a Member State. The Commission Communication stated that it would only make such a proposal after a 'structured exchange' with the Member State. This exchange would occur where the Commission perceived a systemic threat to the rule of law, and would involve assessments, recommendations and monitoring of the Member State by the Commission. The Commission would only make a proposal if there was no resolution of the matter after this exchange. Soft law thereby transformed the focus of the process from being on the Council's adjudicating on a Member State to its now being about the negotiation between the Commission and the Member State.

Programming legislation: The instrument, *par excellence*, for this is the Action Plan. Action Plans set out objectives and timetables for particular EU policies, alongside the measures to be taken to realise these policies. Thus, they are used both to justify specific legislation and to provide a backdrop which relates this legislation to the problems to be addressed and to the

---

[18] The fields include common foreign and security policy (Article 24(1) TEU) economic policy (Article 121(2) TFEU), employment (Article 148(2) TFEU), education, vocational training, youth and sport (Article 165(4) TFEU), culture (Article 166(5) TFEU, most areas of public health (Article 168(4)–(5) TFEU), industry (Article 173(3) TFEU), space (Article 189(2) TFEU), tourism (Article 195(2) TFEU), civil protection (Article 196(2) TFEU), administrative cooperation (Article 197(2) TFEU).

[19] European Convention, *Coordination of National Policies: the open method of coordination*, WG VI WD015, Brussels, 26 September 2002.

[20] H. Hofmann, G. Rowe and A. Türk, *Administrative Law and Policy of the European Union* (Oxford University Press, 2011) 536–66.

[21] Interinstitutional Agreement between the European Parliament, the Council of the European Union and the European Commission on Better Law-Making, OJ 2016, L 123/1.

[22] E.g. Commission Notice on agreements of minor importance which do not appreciably restrict competition under Article 101(1) TFEU (De Minimis Notice), OJ 2014, C 291/1.

[23] European Commission, 'A Framework to Strengthen the Rule of Law', COM(2014)158 final/2.

measures which are being taken by other actors in this regard. The range of Actions Plans are extremely diverse. In the years up to the new edition of this book, for example, there were, *inter alia*, Action Plans on integration of non-EU nationals, drugs, combating wildlife trafficking, sustainable finance and FinTech.[24]

Soft law has some advantages over binding law. It allows for greater diversity between Member States insofar as it only sets out an expectation as to how they are to behave rather than a requirement. In so doing, it creates more space for experimentation and adjustment, which is particularly valuable in situations where laws have to deal with uncertain environments.[25] In many fields, moreover, it sits alongside binding laws allowing a spectrum of commitments to coexist, with some seen as axiomatic, and therefore binding, and others seeking looser coordination, and therefore using soft law. It allows, therefore, for a wider range of EU policy styles and approaches to issues.[26]

Notwithstanding these possible virtues, soft law is criticised on a number of counts. It can generate legal uncertainty. This is not simply because parties may choose not to observe it, but also because its legal effects are less clear. As would be expected, soft law does not bind EU courts, national courts,[27] or national authorities.[28] However, it does bind the EU Institution(s) which made it.[29] Furthermore, national authorities can use it, if they want, to interpret the content of other binding laws, even if the soft law is not published in the language of that authority.[30] It is therefore often difficult to tell where soft law stops and binding law starts.[31] This has raised concerns about the controls over soft law.[32] Judicial review is only possible, therefore, when soft law is seen as doing more than fleshing out binding obligations, typically by using imperative language or defining the position of the EU Institution.[33]

The other concern with soft law is the lack of constraints it places on those in power. It has thus been suggested that there are also risks that it is more likely to be observed (and also breached) when it suits powerful vested interests.[34] This remains a question of speculation.

---

[24] European Commission, 'Action Plan on the Integration of Third Country Nationals', COM(2016)377; EU Action Plan on Drugs, OJ 2017, C 215/2; European Commission, 'EU Action Plan against Wildlife Trafficking', COM(2016)87; European Commission, 'Action Plan: Financing Sustainable Growth', COM(2018)97; European Commission, 'FinTech Action Plan: For a More Competitive and Innovative European Financial Sector', COM(2018)109.

[25] D. Trubek *et al.*, 'Hard and Soft Law in European Integration' in J. Scott and G. de Búrca (eds.), *New Governance and Constitutionalism* (Oxford-Portland, Hart, 2005).

[26] On this, S. Bekker, 'EU Coordination of Welfare States after the Crisis: Further Interconnecting Soft and Hard Law' (2014) 19 *International Review of Public Administration* 296; S. Vaughan, *EU Chemicals Regulation: New Governance, Hybridity and REACH* (Cheltenham, Edward Elgar, 2015) esp. Introduction.

[27] *Pfleiderer* v. *Bundeskartellamt*, C-369/09, EU:C:2011:389.

[28] *DHL Express (Italy) and Others* v. *Autorità Garante della Concorrenza e del Mercato*, C-428/14, EU:C:2016:27.

[29] *Dansk Rørindustri and Others* v. *Commission*, C-189/02 P, C-202/02 P, C-205–8/02 P and C-213/02 P, EU:C:2005:408; *Estado Português* v. *Banco Privado Português*, C-667/13, EU:C:2015:151.

[30] *Polska Telefonia Cyfrowa* v. *Prezes Urzędu Komunikacji Elektronicznej*, C-410/09, EU:C:2011:294.

[31] O. Stefan, 'Hybridity before the Court: A Hard Look at Soft Law in the EU Competition and State Aid Case Law' (2012) 37 *ELRev* 49; Z. Georgieva, 'Soft Law in EU Competition Law and its Judicial Reception in Member States: A Theoretical Perspective' (2015) 16 *German LJ* 223.

[32] S. Lefevre, 'Interpretative Communications and the Implementation of Community Law at National Level' (2004) 29 *ELRev* 808; J. Scott, 'In Legal Limbo: Post-Legislative Guidance as a Challenge for European Administrative Law' (2011) 48 *CMLRev* 329; L. Senden, 'Soft Post-Legislative Rulemaking: A Time for More Stringent Control' (2013) 19 *ELJ* 57.

[33] *France* v. *Commission*, C-325/91, EU:C:1993:245; *United Kingdom* v. *ECB*, T-496/11, EU:T:2015:133, para. 52.

[34] Senden, n. 16 above, 477–98; M. Dawson, 'New Governance in the EU after the Euro Crisis – Retired or Reborn?' in M. Cremona and C. Kilpatrick (eds.), *EU Legal Acts: Challenges and Transformations* (Oxford University Press, 2018) 106, 122–6.

However, EU Institutions have used soft law to expand the range of EU activities.[35] Soft law measures have been taken in almost all fields of economic and social policy on the grounds that EU law either allows coordination of Member State action in these fields or requires oversight of how euro area States are meeting their commitments to budgetary and economic performance. This may well be so, but the limits on EU action in these fields are very poorly specified, and the use of soft law raises a dilemma. If it is effective, it is an administrative process which is being used at the expense of more democratic and domestic processes. If it is not effective, there is the question of why it is being generated at all.

3 THE ALLOCATION OF LEGISLATIVE PROCEDURES

There is no single way to make laws in EU law. Instead, a distinction is made between legislative acts and other laws. Legislative acts are those binding legal acts which are adopted through processes identified as legislative procedures by the Treaties.[36] Other legal acts are those adopted by all other processes. EU law, then, makes a further distinction between the main legislative procedure, called (imaginatively) the ordinary legislative procedure, and 'special legislative procedures'.[37] The two special legislative procedures most frequently used are the consultation and consent procedures.

The Treaties set out a series of legal bases (e.g. Article 114 TFEU on the internal market) which entitle the Union to legislate in a particular field, and identify the legislative procedure to be used and determine which types of EU legal acts may be adopted.[38] Often, the legal base will not be self-evident as a proposed law may contain a number of elements or dimensions which seem to fall within many different legal bases. A law criminalising the dumping of waste, for example, has a criminal dimension insofar as it applies penalties; an ecological dimension insofar as it seeks to protect the environment; and an internal market dimension insofar as it will govern what sort of services may be offered by waste management service providers across the European Union.[39]

As both the TEU and TFEU have 'the same legal value',[40] a unitary approach operates across the two Treaties to determine the appropriate legal base for a measure.

The starting point is to look at the predominant aim and content of the measure, and then to ascertain the legal base with which this is identified. To do this, the Court will look at the principles informing the EU law rather than at the effect of the law. In *Exchange of Data on Road Safety Offences*,[41] the Commission challenged the adoption of a Directive on the basis of Article 87 TFEU, the legal base for police cooperation, arguing that it should have been based on Article 91(1) TFEU, the legal base for transport. The Directive provided that the Member State where the

---

[35] M. Dawson, 'Integration through Soft Law: No Competence Needed? Juridical and Bio-Power in the Realm of Soft Law' in S. Garben and I. Govaere (eds.), *The Division of Competences between the EU and the Member States Reflections on the Past, the Present and the Future* (Oxford, Bloomsbury, 2017); S. Garben, 'Competence Creep Revisited' (2017) *JCMS* (forthcoming).

[36] Article 289(3) TFEU. This provision does not refer to binding legal acts but the legislative procedures identified in Article 289(1)–(2) TFEU do refer to such acts.

[37] Article 289(1)–(2) TFEU.

[38] R. Barents, 'The Internal Market Unlimited: Some Observations on the Legal Basis of Community Legislation' (1993) 30 *CMLRev* 85, 92.

[39] Directive 2008/98/EC on waste and repealing certain Directives, OJ 2008, L 312/3, Article 36(2). The measure is based on Article 192(1) TFEU, the environmental base.

[40] Article 1 TEU and 1(2) TFEU.

[41] *Commission* v. *Parliament and Council* ('Exchange of Data on Road Safety Offences'), C-43/12, EU:C:2014:298.

alleged offence was committed could have access to the vehicle registration data of the Member State in which the vehicle was registered for eight road safety offences. These included drink driving, speeding, not using a helmet and not stopping at a red light. The Directive was, thus, about exchange of data for prosecuting criminal offences (policing). It also went to transport policy as it was concerned to protect road safety. The Court found that both the predominant aim of the measure and its central content were concerned with the latter, road safety. It noted that the Preamble to the Directive stated that its aim was road safety and that, according to the Preamble, this was compromised by sanctions not being enforced because the vehicle was registered in another Member State, particularly as this reduced deterrence in relation to road safety offences. The Court also found that the content of the Directive was concerned with establishing a system of exchange of information to improve road safety. Therefore, it held that as improving road safety was a central component of EU transport policy, the Directive should have been adopted under Article 91(1) TFEU, the transport legal base.

There are cases where the aim and content of the EU law is so inextricably and equally associated with two legal bases that the Court cannot identify one as predominant. In such circumstances, where the two legal bases involve different legislative procedures, it moves to a different test. It will decide the issue on the basis of there being a formal hierarchy between the different legal bases, looking to the relationship specified in the Treaties between each. Thus, Article 114 TFEU, the internal market provision enjoys a precedence over Article 192(2) TFEU, the provision governing Union environmental action on, *inter alia*, measures primarily of a fiscal nature, because the latter indicates that it is 'without prejudice to Article 114'. At the bottom of the pecking order of legal bases sits Article 352 TFEU, the flexibility provision, which allows the Union to take measures to meet its objectives where no other legal base provides the requisite power.[42]

The circumstances in which this happens are rare. In *Linguistic Diversity in the Information Society*, the Court had to consider a decision, which set up a programme to promote linguistic diversity in the information society. It had been adopted under Article 173(3) TFEU, the legal base for industrial policy. The Commission argued that this was because the principal object of the programme was not to enable companies to offer multilingual services. The Parliament challenged this, arguing that it should have also been based on Article 166(5) TFEU, the legal base for culture. It argued, and this was not contested, that linguistic wealth was central to the Union's cultural heritage. The Court stated that the presence of twin objectives was insufficient to bring the measure outside the 'predominant purpose' rule. Each component had to be equally essential to the measure and each had to be indissociable for the 'inextricably associated' rule to apply. This was not the case here as the predominant purpose was industrial. The beneficiaries of the programme were, almost exclusively, small and medium-sized enterprises, who might lose competitiveness because of the costs associated with linguistic diversity.[43]

Neither rule is easy to apply to particular sets of circumstances.[44] The 'predominant aim and content' rule assumes each legal base is characterised by a distinctive set of principles which can be identified in all legislation founded on it. This is rarely the case and the Court has to engage in highly

---

[42] *Parliament* v. *Council* ('Students Residence Directive'), C-295/90, EU:C:1992:294.

[43] *Parliament* v. *Council* ('Linguistic Diversity in the Information Society'), C-42/97, EU:C:1999:81.

[44] P. Leino, 'The Institutional Politics of Objective Choice: Competence as a Framework for Argumentation' in S. Garben and I. Govaere (eds.), *The Division of Competences between the EU and the Member States: Reflections on the Past, the Present and the Future* (Oxford, Bloomsbury, 2017).

selective analysis to justify a particular legal base. The 'inextricably associated' rule, if applied literally, is so narrow to be almost redundant as it requires two purposes to have equal weight and be completely entwined. Its occasional use suggests that sometimes, for ulterior motives, the Court simply wishes to discard the 'predominant purpose' rule. The consequence is that it is invariably quite easy for EU Institutions or Member States to litigate a measure simply by arguing that it was adopted on the wrong legal base. This is, to be sure, a source of legal uncertainty. However, it also allows the legal base of a measure to become (unhappily) the subject of legislative politics. EU Institutions can raise the threat of litigation during negotiations as leverage over the contents of the measure.[45]

4 THE LEGISLATIVE PROCEDURES

(i) The Ordinary Legislative Procedure

(a) The Central Features of the Ordinary Legislative Procedure

The legislative procedure used for about 90 per cent of legislation since the Lisbon Treaty is the ordinary legislative procedure.[46] It is set out in Article 294 TFEU.

Article 294 TFEU

(1) Where reference is made in the Treaties to the ordinary legislative procedure for the adoption of an act, the following procedure shall apply.

(2) The Commission shall submit a proposal to the European Parliament and the Council.

First reading

(3) The European Parliament shall adopt its position at first reading and communicate it to the Council.

(4) If the Council approves the European Parliament's position, the act concerned shall be adopted in the wording which corresponds to the position of the European Parliament.

(5) If the Council does not approve the European Parliament's position, it shall adopt its position at first reading and communicate it to the European Parliament.

(6) The Council shall inform the European Parliament fully of the reasons which led it to adopt its position at first reading. The Commission shall inform the European Parliament fully of its position.

Second reading

(7) If, within three months of such communication, the European Parliament:

(a) approves the Council's position at first reading or has not taken a decision, the act concerned shall be deemed to have been adopted in the wording which corresponds to the position of the Council;

(b) rejects, by a majority of its component members, the Council's position at first reading, the proposed act shall be deemed not to have been adopted;

(c) proposes, by a majority of its component members, amendments to the Council's position at first reading, the text thus amended shall be forwarded to the Council and to the Commission, which shall deliver an opinion on those amendments.

---

[45] H. Cullen and H. Charlesworth, 'Diplomacy by Other Means: The Use of Legal Basis Litigation as a Political Strategy by the European Parliament and Member States' (1999) 36 *CMLRev* 1243.

[46] European Parliament, *Handbook on the Ordinary Legislative Procedure* (Brussels, Directorate General for Internal Policies, 2017) 50.

(8) If, within three months of receiving the European Parliament's amendments, the Council, acting by a qualified majority:

(a) approves all those amendments, the act in question shall be deemed to have been adopted;

(b) does not approve all the amendments, the President of the Council, in agreement with the President of the European Parliament, shall within six weeks convene a meeting of the Conciliation Committee.

(9) The Council shall act unanimously on the amendments on which the Commission has delivered a negative opinion.

Conciliation

(10) The Conciliation Committee, which shall be composed of the members of the Council or their representatives and an equal number of members representing the European Parliament, shall have the task of reaching agreement on a joint text, by a qualified majority of the members of the Council or their representatives and by a majority of the members representing the European Parliament within six weeks of its being convened, on the basis of the positions of the European Parliament and the Council at second reading.

(11) The Commission shall take part in the Conciliation Committee's proceedings and shall take all necessary initiatives with a view to reconciling the positions of the European Parliament and the Council.

(12) If, within six weeks of its being convened, the Conciliation Committee does not approve the joint text, the proposed act shall be deemed not to have been adopted.

Third reading

(13) If, within that period, the Conciliation Committee approves a joint text, the European Parliament, acting by a majority of the votes cast, and the Council, acting by a qualified majority, shall each have a period of six weeks from that approval in which to adopt the act in question in accordance with the joint text. If they fail to do so, the proposed act shall be deemed not to have been adopted.

(14) The periods of three months and six weeks referred to in this Article shall be extended by a maximum of one month and two weeks respectively at the initiative of the European Parliament or the Council.

If the procedure looks intimidating, it is best to think of it as having four key features.

Joint agreement: Joint adoption of legislation by the Council and Parliament can happen at three junctures during the procedure.

- *First reading by the Parliament*: The Commission makes a proposal. The Parliament issues an opinion on it (the first reading). The Council can adopt the act by QMV if either the Parliament has made no amendments or it agrees with its amendments.

- *Second reading by the Parliament*: If there is no agreement after the first reading the Council can adopt a 'common position'. If it is adopting the Commission proposal, it does this by QMV. If it makes amendments of its own, it does this by unanimity. This common position is referred back to the Parliament for a second reading. If the Parliament does nothing for three months or agrees with the common position, the measure is adopted. Alternately, it may propose amendments. If the amendments have been approved by the Commission, they may be adopted by the Council by QMV. If, however, the Commission expresses a negative view of the Parliament's amendments, these have to be adopted by unanimity in the Council.

- *Third reading*: If there is no agreement following the second reading, a Conciliation Committee is established. It has six weeks to approve a joint text. This text must be adopted within six weeks, by both the Council, by QMV, and the Parliament to become law.

The double veto of the Parliament: The ordinary legislative procedure grants the Parliament a veto over legislation. The veto can be exercised at the second reading if the Parliament decides to reject the common position of the Council. The other possibility is at the third reading after the Conciliation Committee has provided a joint text. Technically speaking, it is not a veto being exercised here, but parliamentary assent. It must positively agree to it at this point for it to become law.

The Assent of the Council: A measure will only become law if the Council agrees to it. The number of votes required will either be QMV or unanimity. If the measure has been approved by the Commission or by the Conciliation Committee, it will be QMV. If the Council is proposing on its own amendments, it must act by unanimity to adopt these amendments.

The Conciliation Committee: This meets following the Parliament's second reading if the Council is unable to accept the amendments proposed by the Parliament. Modelled on the German Mediations Committee,[47] it comprises twenty-seven members from the Council and twenty-seven MEPs. Its job is to prepare a joint text with the Council members voting by QMV and the MEPs by simple majority. If it does not, the measure fails. If it does, the text must be agreed by both the Parliament and the Council (by QMV).

(b) The European Parliament as a Rival Agenda-Setter to the Commission

On paper, the ordinary legislative procedure seems to have the Commission as the agenda-setter. It proposes the legislation with it then being left to the Council and the Parliament to work it out. Alongside this, the Parliament is cast as the 'nay sayer'. Its most dramatic power is the power of veto.

In reality, the practice is more complicated. The Commission's influence does not stop after it has made the proposal for, as mentioned earlier, it has the power to withdraw the proposal at any time prior to the Council acting (i.e. adopting a common position).[48] The Commission must provide reasons and is committed to consult with the other EU Institutions about next steps when it does withdraw a proposal.[49] However, the fact remains that it has a power of *de facto* veto prior to the Council adopting a common position which can exercised by its withdrawing a proposal if it is unhappy with any development put forward by the other EU Institutions prior to then. Furthermore, it regularly withdraws proposals, with, for example, 19 of the 129 proposals before the other EU Institutions at the beginning of July 2014 withdrawn by the end of 2016.[50]

Conversely, the European Parliament rarely exercises its veto. Between 1 May 1999 and 1 January 2018, it was used only four times in 1,620 procedures.[51] In some instances, this is because a veto will bring the worst outcome from the Parliament's perspective, namely no EU law. Regular exercise of the veto would also be bad politics. Other parties will not communicate with the Parliament if, in the end, its position is inflexible as there is nothing to talk about. For the Parliament, it is rather the shadow of the veto which is important. By threatening to thwart other parties' objectives, it can secure influence to realise outcomes it desires.

---

[47] N. Foster, 'The New Conciliation Committee under Article 189b' (1994) 19 *ELRev* 185.

[48] *Council* v. *Commission* ('Macrofinancial Assistance to third countries'), C-409/13, EU:C:2015:217.

[49] Interinstitutional Agreement between the European Parliament, the Council of the European Union and the European Commission on Better Law-Making, OJ 2016, L 123/1, para. 9.

[50] European Parliament, Activity Report on the Ordinary Legislative Procedure, 4 July 2014–31 December 2016 (Brussels, European Parliament, PE 595.931, 2017) 6–7.

[51] Council of the European Union, Ordinary Legislative Procedure: Files concluded since the entry into force of the Treaty of Amsterdam (Brussels, Council General Secretariat, 2018) 6.

The enduring influence of the Commission within the process and the capacity of the Parliament to thwart the Commission has resulted in the European Parliament's power of amendment becoming very significant. For it is easier for the Council, if the Commission agrees with the Parliament, to accept parliamentary amendments than to produce its own.

Article 293 TFEU

(1) Where, pursuant to the Treaties, the Council acts on a proposal from the Commission, it may amend that proposal only by acting unanimously, except in the cases referred to in paragraphs 10 and 13 of Articles 294, in Articles 310, 312 and 314 and in the second paragraph of Article 315.[52]

To be sure, the Parliament is still dependent on the Commission as unanimity is required in the Council to adopt an amendment with which the Commission does not agree.[53] However, equally, the Commission is dependent on the Parliament, as it cannot make amendments of its own without reissuing the proposal, and even that is not possible after the Council's first reading. Furthermore, there is a danger that if it does not accept the Parliament amendments, Parliament may veto the proposal.

All this allows the European Parliament to be a rival agenda-setter to the Commission. Of the EU Institutions, it has the best opportunities to 'improve' any legislative proposal. Parties marginalised by a Commission proposal will thus often go to the Parliament to try and get counter-proposals included as amendments. In many cases, therefore, the Parliament puts forward something suggested by an interest group, national government or one of the other EU Institutions.[54] There is also scope for proposing quite significant amendments. A study of 470 proposals between 1999 and 2007, for example, found that 1,567 issues were raised by the Parliament which did not involve mere tidying but discrete substantive reforms. The Parliament was successful in 65.2 per cent of these cases – a high rate.[55]

(c) The Trilogue

The ordinary legislative procedure has been transformed by two developments.

The first is a commitment to reach early agreement.

Joint Declaration on Practical Arrangements for the [Ordinary Legislative] Procedure, OJ 2007, C145/2

11 The institutions shall cooperate in good faith with a view to reconciling their positions as far as possible so that, wherever possible, acts can be adopted at first reading.

---

[52] These last four provisions are budgetary provisions.

[53] A relatively old study found that the Council accepted 83% of amendments which had the Commission's agreement but only 12% of amendments to which it had not agreed, G. Tsebelis *et al.*, 'Legislative Procedures in the European Union: An Empirical Analysis' (2001) 31 *BJPS* 573.

[54] S. Hix and B. Høyland, 'Empowerment of the European Parliament' (2013) 16 *Annual Review of Political Science* 171, 176.

[55] R. Kardasheva, 'Legislative Package Deals in EU Decision-Making 1999–2007', PhD thesis, London School of Economics and Political Science (2009) 242–4.

In recent years, this commitment has been highly successful. Eighty-five per cent of all legislative files were agreed at first reading between 2009 and the end of 2016.[56] In this instance, the EU Institutions will come to a common agreement on the text after the European Parliament has had its first reading and usually before the Council has taken a formal common position. If anything, this figure of 85 per cent may understate the extent of early agreement. Since 2014, another form of early agreement has proliferated: agreement at early second reading.[57] Consequently, between 2009 and the end of 2016, 94 per cent of files have been agreed at first reading or early second reading.[58]

Early agreements telescope the procedure and foreclose spaces for public debate. Parties seeking legislative influence have to seek it as early as possible. The first reading is not an opportunity for initial consideration. It is usually the moment of final decision. The shortened time scale also forecloses input from national parliaments. Whilst most will see the original Commission proposal, a study found that only about a quarter get to see the text of agreement and provide input to their national government on that text before the agreement is itself concluded. Early agreements mean, therefore that most parliaments are consulted on a text which may be far removed from the final legislative text, whilst not being consulted on the latter.[59]

The second development is the trilogue.[60] The trilogue comprises representatives from the three EU Institutions. It is for each one to nominate its representatives.[61] The Council will be represented by two to three civil servants from the State holding the Presidency, one of these holding at least the level of Deputy Permanent Representative. The Commission will be represented by eight to ten people from the relevant Directorate General. The largest delegation will be from the European Parliament. It can have easily up to twenty or thirty persons. These will include MEPs from the relevant European Parliament Committee which considered the Commission proposal. These MEPs will usually include the Chair of that Committee, the Rapporteur who drafted that Committee's report on the proposal as well as representatives from the different political groups.[62]

The trilogue's job is to seek informal agreement between the EU Institutions on a legal text. In practice, they are more than that. They are where the action takes place. Although not legally required, all EU Institutions faithfully implement what is agreed within the trilogue. The negotiation and deliberation that takes place within the trilogue, thus, determines the content of the legislation, and there is considerable latitude for any institution to make proposals. The texts agreed often deviate significantly from the original Commission proposals or even what

---

[56] European Parliament, *Activity Report for 5th Parliamentary Term*, PE 287.644, 12–13.

[57] Early second reading is where the European Parliament Committee responsible is happy with the Council common position but wishes this to be endorsed by the European Parliament, typically because there have been amendments which depart from the Parliament's original position. Agreement at early second reading will happen where it adopts the Council common position without amendment, and this is then ratified by the full European Parliament without further discussion, European Parliament, *Rules of Procedure* (Brussels, European Parliament, Eighth Parliamentary Term, 2017) rule 69d.

[58] European Parliament, n. 46 above, 51.

[59] M. Jensen and D. Martinsen, 'Out of Time? National Parliaments and Early Decision-Making in the European Union' (2015) 50 *Government and Opposition* 240.

[60] On the emergence of the trilogue, see M. Shackleton, 'The Politics of Codecision' (2000) 38 *JCMS* 325, 334–6.

[61] Joint Declaration on Practical Arrangements for the [Ordinary Legislative] Procedure, OJ 2007, C 145/2, para. 8.

[62] For more details see C. Roederer-Rynning and J. Greenwood, 'The Culture of Trilogues' (2015) 22 *JEPP* 1148.

representatives were mandated to agree by their respective EU Institutions.[63] Trilogues are, thus, the epicentre of EU lawmaking under the ordinary legislative procedure.

Since the Lisbon Treaty, trilogues have also become endemic with Murphy finding that 97 per cent of legislative procedures in the 2009–14 period were subject to trilogues.[64] Trilogues are also used repeatedly during the same legislative process so that if an initial trilogue does not reach agreement, a subsequent one will usually be held. In recent times, the European Parliament has found that the average legislative file involves four trilogues.[65] To that end, the European Parliament has built a large administrative infrastructure just to deal with trilogues.[66]

Trilogues have raised concerns on a number of fronts. They undermine the legislative balance set out in the Treaties; they led to a culture of managerialism; and they foster a lack of transparency.

First, they subvert the checks and balances of the ordinary legislative procedure. Institutions, therefore, have powers within them that they do not formally have under the Treaty. The Commission can, for example, submit amendments to the proposal or Council representatives can decide matters without a QMV within the trilogue when these are not formally possible under the processes, as set out above in Article 294(1) TFEU. There are also issues of representativeness insofar as the trilogue excludes actors who can vote in the ordinary legislative procedure. The European Parliament has tried to mitigate these risks by sending relatively large groups to the trilogue. Equally, Council Presidencies go out of their way to represent the interests of all member States rather than their own.[67] For all this, as already mentioned, the autonomy of the trilogues entails that they often agree on texts which are quite far away from what non-present actors want.[68]

Secondly, the trilogue has led to a bureaucratisation of the legislative process. Civil servants, thus, represent the Council in the trilogue with a corresponding decline in ministerial involvement and accountability as the Council meeting itself, where the Ministers sit, just becomes a place to rubberstamp the work of the trilogue.[69] The trilogue has also transformed the European Parliament into a 'negotiating Parliament'.[70] The central work is done in the Committees which precede the trilogue and by the MEPs who negotiate with the Council. This reduces the amount of public debate that takes place within the European Parliament as, by the time something reaches the floor of the Parliament, the central matters have been decided. There is also less appetite for political contestation in which the implications of legislative proposals are exposed and

---

[63] T. Laloux and T. Delreux, 'How Much Do Agents in Trilogues Deviate from their Principals' Instructions? Introducing a Deviation Index' (2018) 25 *JEPP* 1049.

[64] K. Murphy, 'Why Trilogues? Determinants of the Use of Informal Negotiations in EU Codecision Making Processes 1999–2016', PhD thesis, Dublin City University (2017) 126.

[65] European Parliament, Activity Report on the Ordinary Legislative Procedure, 4 July 2014–31 December 2016 (Brussels, European Parliament, PE 595.931, 2017) 19–20.

[66] C. Roederer-Rynning and J. Greenwood, 'The European Parliament as a Developing Legislature: Coming of Age in Trilogues?' (2017) 24 *JEPP* 735.

[67] A. Rasmussen and C. Reh, 'The Consequences of Concluding Codecision Early: Trilogues and Intra-Institutional Bargaining Success' (2013) 20 *JEPP* 1006.

[68] Laloux and Delreux, n. 63 above.

[69] F. Häge and D. Naurin, 'The Effect of Codecision on Council Decision-Making: Informalization, Politicization and Power' (2013) 20 *JEPP* 953.

[70] K. Huber and M. Shackleton, 'Codecision: A Practitioner's View from Inside the Parliament' (2013) 20 *JEPP* 1040, 1044–7.

challenged. For the central thing of importance with the trilogue is influence with the Council,[71] and such influence is not secured by public argument.

The third, and loudest, criticism of trilogues concerns their lack of transparency. Historically, no information has been made publicly available about trilogues prior to their taking place. There are no joint minutes of the meetings and only the European Parliament provided for any subsequent general disclosure of documents.[72] The European Ombudsman was sufficiently concerned by this to open an enquiry in 2016. It noted that lack of transparency prevented input by national parliaments and interested private parties into the legislative process; reduced the accountability and visibility of the process; and generated fears about capture of the process by those interests who were in the know.[73]

This lack of transparency will have to be revised in the light of the *De Capitani* judgment. De Capitani sought access from the European Parliament to seven four-column tables under Regulation 1049/2001, the Regulation which set out the circumstances when private parties can have access to EU Institution documents. These tables set out the initial positions of the three EU Institutions in three columns with the compromise text in the fourth. The Parliament provided these tables in five cases, but refused to do so in the other two cases, which related to police cooperation and data management. Amongst the defences issued by the European Parliament were, first, that there should be a presumption against disclosing information about trilogues in which discussions were still taking place; secondly, information should not be disclosed where it might lead to external pressure on the EU Institutions; and, thirdly, information should not be provided where it undermined trust between the EU Institutions.

De Capitani v. *European Parliament*, T–540/15, EU:T:2018:167

80 Although, in general, giving the public the widest possible right of access ... entails that the public must have a right to full disclosure of the requested documents, the only means of limiting that right being the strict application of the exceptions provided for in Regulation No 1049/2001, those considerations are clearly of particular relevance where those documents are part of the European Union's legislative activity, a fact reflected in recital 6 of Regulation No 1049/2001, which states that even wider access must be granted to documents in precisely such cases. Openness in that respect contributes to strengthening democracy by allowing citizens to scrutinize all the information which has formed the basis of a legislative act. The possibility for citizens to find out the considerations underpinning legislative action is a precondition for the effective exercise of their democratic rights ...

81 The principles of publicity and transparency are therefore inherent to the EU legislative process ...

98 ... as regards the assertion that access, during a trilogue, to the fourth column of the documents at issue would increase public pressure on the rapporteur, shadow rapporteurs and political groups, that, in a system based on the principle of democratic legitimacy, co-legislators must be held accountable for their actions to the public ... the expression of public opinion in relation to a particular provisional legislative

---

[71] G. Brandsma, 'Co-Decision after Lisbon: The Politics of Informal Trilogues in European Union Lawmaking' (2015) 16 *EUP* 300; T. Delreux and T. Laloux, 'Concluding Early Agreements in the EU: A Double Principal–Agent Analysis of Trilogue Negotiations' (2018) 56 *JCMS* 300.

[72] On this, D. Curtin and P. Leino, 'In Search of Transparency for EU Law-Making: Trilogues on the Cusp of Dawn' (2017) 54 *CMLRev* 1673, 1689–93.

[73] Decision of the European Ombudsman setting out proposals following her strategic inquiry OI/8/2015/JAS concerning the transparency of Trilogues, Decision of 12 July 2016, paras. 16–27.

proposal or agreement agreed in the course of a trilogue and reflected in the fourth column of a trilogue table forms an integral part of the exercise of EU citizens' democratic rights, particularly since . . . such agreements are generally subsequently adopted without substantial amendment by the co-legislators.

99 Although . . . the risk of external pressure can constitute a legitimate ground for restricting access to documents related to the decision-making process, the reality of such external pressure must, however, be established with certainty, and evidence must be adduced to show that there is a reasonably foreseeable risk that the decision to be taken would be substantially affected owing to that external pressure . . . There is no tangible evidence in the case file establishing, in the event of disclosure of the fourth column of the documents at issue, the reality of such external pressure. Therefore, nothing in the case file before the Court suggests that, as regards the legislative procedure in question, the Parliament could reasonably expect there to be a reaction beyond what could be expected from the public by any member of a legislative body who proposes an amendment to draft legislation . . .

103 . . . as regards the ground relating to a potential loss of trust between the institutions of the European Union and the likely deterioration of cooperation between them . . . where the responsibility for conducting an EU legislative procedure is conferred on several institutions, they are required, in accordance with the duty of sincere cooperation also set out in the first subparagraph of Article 4(3) TEU, to act and cooperate so that the procedure can be conducted effectively, which implies that any deterioration in the confidence incumbent on the institutions would constitute a failure to fulfil that duty.

104 . . . the Parliament has not produced any tangible evidence, which implies that the alleged risk is hypothetical in the absence of any specific evidence capable of demonstrating that, as regards the legislative procedure in question, access to the fourth column of the documents at issue would have undermined the loyal cooperation incumbent on the institutions concerned. Moreover, since in the course of trilogues the institutions express their respective positions on a given legislative proposal, and accept that their position could thus evolve, the fact that those elements are then disclosed, on request, is not per se capable of undermining the mutual loyal cooperation which the institutions are required to practice pursuant to Article 13 TEU.

The judgment is a damning indictment of the trilogue culture. That said, care must be taken with its interpretation. It applies, first, only to documents. Insofar as records may not be kept of what is discussed, or it may differ from what was on the agenda of the trilogue, the public will still not know what has taken place. Secondly, the judgment establishes only a presumption of access to any document relating to the trilogue. This may be rebutted where there is tangible and specific evidence that disclosure would either lead to a reasonably foreseeable risk that decision-making would be substantially affected or to a breakdown in mutual trust between the EU Institutions. However, these will be difficult to prove. There is more likelihood of external pressure being applied to EU Institutions when decision-making is done in secret than when the world can see it. Equally, the Court has ensured that EU Institutions cannot be thin-skinned about disclosure of documents. They are under a duty to do so, and, therefore, cannot refuse to cooperate simply because an embarrassing document is released by another EU Institution.

(ii) The Consultation Procedure

The consultation procedure follows three stages:

(a) The Commission submits a proposal to the Council.
(b) The Council consults the Parliament.

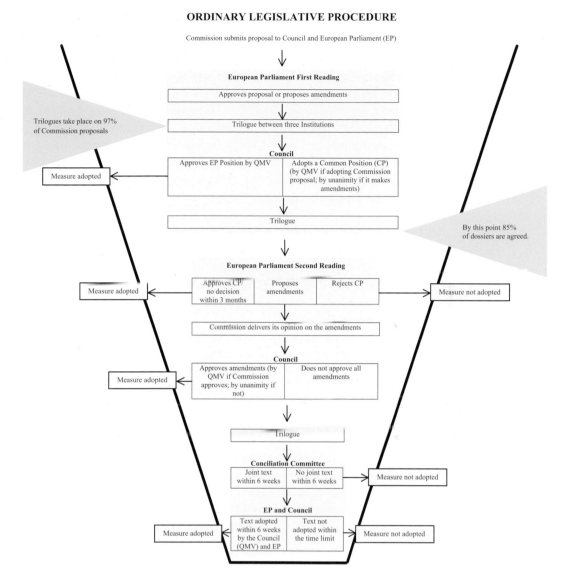

ORDINARY LEGISLATIVE PROCEDURE

Commission submits proposal to Council and European Parliament (EP)

European Parliament First Reading

Approves proposal or proposes amendments

Trilogue between three Institutions

Trilogues take place on 97% of Commission proposals

Council

| Approves EP Position by QMV | Adopts a Common Position (CP) (by QMV if adopting Commission proposal; by unanimity if it makes amendments) |

Measure adopted

Trilogue

By this point 85% of dossiers are agreed.

European Parliament Second Reading

| Approves CP/ no decision within 3 months | Proposes amendments | Rejects CP |

Measure adopted

Measure not adopted

Commission delivers its opinion on the amendments

Council

| Approves amendments (by QMV if Commission approves; by unanimity if not) | Does not approve all amendments |

Measure adopted

Trilogue

Conciliation Committee

| Joint text within 6 weeks | No joint text within 6 weeks |

Measure not adopted

EP and Council

| Text adopted within 6 weeks by the Council (QMV) and EP | Text not adopted within the time limit |

Measure adopted

Measure not adopted

Table 3.1 The Ordinary Legislative Procedure

(c) The Council adopts the measure, either by qualified majority or by unanimity, depending upon the field in question.

The most salient feature of the consultation procedure is the duty to consult the Parliament. In *Roquette Frères*, the Court stated that consultation

allows the Parliament to play an actual part in the legislative process of the [Union], such power represents an essential factor in the institutional balance intended by the Treaty. Although limited, it reflects at [Union] level the fundamental democratic principle that the peoples should take part in the exercise of power through the intermediary of a representative assembly. Due consultation of the Parliament in the cases provided for by the Treaty therefore constitutes an essential formality disregard of which means that the measure concerned is void.[74]

From this, the Court has crafted a number of mutual obligations. On the one hand, the Council is obliged to re-consult Parliament if the text is significantly amended, and cannot adopt the legislation otherwise.[75] However, this allows the Council considerable leeway as amendments will only be sufficiently significant to require re-consultation if the legislative text as a whole differs in essence from the previous one.[76] By contrast, Parliament must not abuse its right to consultation. In *General Tariff Preferences*,[77] the Council sought to consult Parliament on a proposal to extend preferential tax treatment to imports from States which had emerged from the collapse of the Soviet Union. The request was made in October 1992 and marked 'urgent' by the Council. Parliament postponed its decision until after a debate in January 1993 as its Committee on Development was not happy about granting this treatment to these States. The Council adopted the Regulation in December 1992 without further consultation on the grounds that the matter was urgent. The Court noted that the duty to consult the Parliament was matched by duties of mutual cooperation between the EU Institutions. The Council could go ahead as the Parliament had failed to discharge these duties by refusing to take heed of the urgency of the file and having regard to what the Court considered to be extraneous factors.

Parliament's powers under the consultation procedure are clearly more limited than under the ordinary legislative procedure. The Council is not required to take account of its views and its lack of leverage over the Council limits its influence with the Commission. As Parliament's views count for little, there are no incentives for the Commission to coordinate with it. This marginalisation is further increased by the fact that the Council is not required to wait until Parliament has been consulted before it considers a proposal, but can consider the matter pending consultation of the Parliament.[78]

The consultation procedure revolves, therefore, around the executive-dominated Commission–Council axis. The balance of power between these hinges on the vote required in the Council. If a unanimity vote is required, any government can veto the measure. Power is, therefore, concentrated in the government that is most resistant to the measure, as it holds the decision on whether or not to go forward. Power moves towards the Commission where QMV is required in the Council. Member States are aware that they can be outvoted, and so will seek to have interests included in the original proposal. Furthermore, as the Council can only amend the Commission's proposals by unanimity,[79] and there will be the consensus to come up with this, Member States rely heavily on the Commission's cooperation for any subsequent adjustment of the original proposal.

The Parliament still has influence. The one study on this, in 2008, found that about 19 per cent of its amendments are accepted: not an insignificant proportion.[80] The leverage for this has been

[74] *Roquette Frères* v. *Council*, 138/79, EU:C:1980:249.
[75] *Parliament* v. *Council* ('Cabotage II'), C-65/90, EU:C:1992:325.   [76] *RPO*, C-397/15, EU:C:2017:174.
[77] *Parliament* v. *Council* ('General Tariff Preferences'), C-65/93, EU:C:1995:91.
[78] *Parliament* v. *Council* ('TACIS'), C-417/93, EU:C:1995:127.   [79] Article 293(1) TFEU.
[80] R. Kardasheva, 'The Power to Delay: The European Parliament's Influence in the Consultation Procedure' (2009) 47 *JCMS* 385, 392–4.

made possible by two strategies: delaying giving an opinion and bundling laws which use the consultation procedure together with those that require the ordinary legislative procedure.

The first is, notwithstanding the *General Tariff Preferences* judgment, the deployment of delay. The Parliament invites the Commission to withdraw a proposal or to accept amendments. When the latter refuses, the Parliament refers it back to a Parliamentary Committee to consider its response.

> **R. Kardasheva, 'The Power to Delay: The European Parliament's Influence in the Consultation Procedure' (2009) 47 *Journal of Common Market Studies* 385, 404–5**
>
> The power to delay allows the EP [European Parliament] to enjoy important benefits in the legislative system. First, through delay the Parliament manages to force concessions from the Council and the Commission. Delay allows the Parliament to see many of its preferences incorporated in the final legislative texts. Second, delay opens the door for informal negotiations between the Council and Parliament. While informal negotiations have become a typical element of Council–Parliament legislative work under co-decision, there are few incentives for Member States to seek informal contacts in consultation. However, when the EP delays its opinion and Member States need an urgent decision, the Council has an incentive to speed up the procedure through informal contacts. Third, delay gives the consultation procedure two readings. Formally, the consultation procedure consists of only one reading. However, by delaying its final vote, the EP gains an additional reading. The EP makes its position on the Commission proposal known, but the plenary refrains from issuing an opinion. Once aware of the EP's preferences, the Council and Commission negotiate with MEPs and adjust their positions in order to speed up the decision-making process. Thus, through delay, the EP transforms the simple consultation procedure into a decision-making procedure with two readings.

The second is the widespread use of multi-proposal package deals.[81] These package deals involve the EU Institutions considering a number of legislative proposals together with a view to securing simultaneous political agreement about the central features of all of them. They will often include measures which require, respectively, the ordinary legislative procedure or the consultation procedure. To secure its preferences in relation to activities covered by the ordinary legislative procedure, the Council will have to make concessions in the field covered by the consultation procedure.

(iii) The Consent Procedure

The consent procedure is the procedure in which Parliament enjoys greatest formal powers. It governs a number of significant fields, which include EU anti-discrimination policy,[82] substantial parts of EU criminal justice,[83] the budget,[84] many international agreements[85] and, perhaps most prominently, the flexibility principle, which allows measures to be taken to realise Union objectives where there is no other legal base.[86] The consent procedure is an umbrella term which brings together a number of heterogeneous procedures:

- The Commission does not enjoy a monopoly of initiative in these. Depending on the field, a proposal can also be made by the Parliament, Member States or the European Council.

---

[81] R. Kardasheva, 'Package Deals in EU Legislative Politics' (2013) 57 *AJPS* 858.   [82] Article 19(1) TFEU.
[83] Articles 82(2)(d), 83(1) and 86(1) and (4) TFEU.   [84] Articles 311 and 312 TFEU.   [85] Article 218(6)(a) TFEU.
[86] Article 352 TFEU.

- The proposal may come direct to the Parliament. Alternatively, there may be other EU Institutions that have either to be consulted or to give their consent to the proposal first. The procedures depend on the legal base in question.
- The Parliament will then have to consent to the measure.
- In some instances, the Council or the European Council then has to consent to the measure before it can become law.

The common features of all these procedures are, first, that Parliament has to affirm a legislative proposal before it can be adopted. This is different from the ordinary legislative procedure in that, with consent, Parliament must actively say 'yes' to a proposal whereas the latter merely gives it a veto. Secondly, it has an indefinite time in which to do this. In all these fields the consent of the Council or European Council is also needed.[87] As a consequence, although the powers of the European Parliament are greater than in the ordinary legislative procedure, the process is not so different. The two institutions invariably negotiate to agree a common text.

5 NATIONAL PARLIAMENTS

The Treaty sets out representative democracy as the central model of democracy for the European Union.

Article 10 TEU

(1) The functioning of the Union shall be founded on representative democracy.

The article has, however, a particular view of representative democracy. Two parties are to be represented at EU level: EU citizens in the European Parliament and Member States in the European Council and the Council.[88] This is an odd choice as one would expect national parliaments, the epitome of representative democracy within Europe, to occupy pride of place here. This is not to be. A separate provision outlines their contribution to EU lawmaking, suggesting that they are to be secondary players within it.

Article 12 TEU

National Parliaments contribute actively to the good functioning of the Union:
(a) through being informed by the institutions of the Union and having draft legislative acts of the Union forwarded to them in accordance with the Protocol on the role of national Parliaments in the European Union;
(b) by seeing to it that the principle of subsidiarity is respected in accordance with the procedures provided for in the Protocol on the application of the principles of subsidiarity and proportionality ...

The first of these Protocols, the Protocol on National Parliaments, provides for general input by national parliaments into the EU lawmaking and policy-making processes. This input is

---

[87] The circumstances where the European Council are involved are rare. These include extension of the European Prosecutor Office's powers (Article 86(4) TFEU), use of the *passarelles* (Article 48(7) TEU), or convening an IGC without holding a convention (Article 47(3) TEU).
[88] Article 10(2) TEU.

secured through two main routes. The *political dialogue* provides for direct relations between the Commission and national parliaments prior to any legislative proposal. The information provided also allows national parliaments to influence their governments actions within the Council of Ministers. The second Protocol, the Protocol on the Application of the Principles of Subsidiarity and Proportionality, has them policing the EU lawmaker's compliance with the subsidiarity principle: the principle whereby the Union is only to legislate if the objects of a measure cannot be realised by Member States acting unilaterally and could be better realised by Union action.[89] This policing is known as the Early Warning Mechanism.

(i) National Parliaments Inputting into EU Lawmaking

The central aim of the Protocol on the Role of National Parliaments is to provide national parliaments with all EU policy documents and legislative proposals in sufficient time that they can consider these and influence the EU legislative process if they so wish. To that end, it requires that:

- Commission consultation documents, the annual legislative programme, as well as any other policy or legislative planning instrument shall be forwarded directly by the Commission to national parliaments upon publication.[90]
- All draft legislative acts will be sent directly to national parliaments, rather than to national governments to pass onto national parliaments.[91]
- All agendas and minutes of Council meetings will be sent to national parliaments.[92]
- An eight-week period will elapse between a draft legislative act being sent to national parliaments and its being placed on the agenda of the Council.[93]

These requirements have led to two forms of national parliamentary involvement in EU lawmaking: political dialogue and influencing how the national Minister votes in the Council.

At its broadest, *political dialogue* is a commitment by the Commission to ongoing engagement with national parliaments through visits and meetings and through providing evidence to national Parliamentary Committees. Its most tangible expression is, however, an open invitation to national parliaments to comment on any proposals made by the Commission with a corresponding commitment to aim to reply within three months.[94] This opportunity has been taken up quite extensively by some national parliaments. In 2016, 620 opinions were issued by national parliaments. However, 73 per cent of these came from ten parliamentary Chambers with one Chamber alone, the Italian Senate, responsible for eighty-one opinions.[95] There is, thus, a problem of asymmetry of representation.

The position is further complicated by the type of opinion offered by national parliaments. In some instances, the national parliament is seeking to exert influence over its own government. The opinion will, therefore, ask for its government to seek a number of amendments or clarifications. In others, the national parliament is seeking to influence the Commission directly. Its opinion will, thus, make detailed critiques of the proposal. In other cases, the opinion seems to be doing no more

---

[89] On this see pp. 383–5.   [90] Protocol on the Role of National Parliaments in the European Union, Article 1.
[91] *Ibid.* Article 2.   [92] *Ibid.* Article 5.   [93] *Ibid.* Article 4.
[94] The process is an informal one with details set out at https://ec.europa.eu/info/law/law-making-process/adopting-eu-law/relations-national-parliaments_en#politicaldialogue. On its origins see D. Jančić, 'The Barroso Initiative: Window Dressing or Democracy Boost?' (2012) 8 *Utrecht L Rev* 78.
[95] European Commission, 'Annual Report 2016 on Relations between the European Commission and National Parliaments', COM(2017)601, 2–3.

than indicating that the parliament is a player. Such opinions will describe the Commission proposal but not engage further. Analysis suggests that the most common form of proposal was one which sought to exercise influence directly over the Commission, but that the individual parliaments issuing the highest number of opinions were doing no more than branding, setting out little more than generic statements.[96] This suggests that national parliamentary engagement with the Commission is much lower than the figures suggest, with very few parliamentary chambers systemically attempting to influence the Commission.[97] Furthermore, many of these report strong dissatisfaction with Commission responses. There is little engagement, with justifications often being set out in very general terms or the original justification for the proposal just being repeated.[98]

The political dialogue is seen as insufficient by many national parliaments who believe that national parliaments should be able to invite the Commission to make legislative proposals. In 2015, the Dutch Tweede Kamer published a document, which had been prepared by the Chair of the United Kingdom House of Lords' European Union Committee at a meeting with representatives from fourteen national parliaments and the European Parliament, which proposed a 'green card' procedure. This envisaged that a proposal could be made to the Commission if it was supported by one-quarter of the national parliamentary chambers in the European Union and this support had been garnered within six months of the proposal first being circulated.[99] To date, the 'green card' is little more than an idea with the balance of opinion within national parliaments and the EU Institutions favourable to the idea but only if it does not involve Treaty amendment and, like the political dialogue, operates at an informal level.[100]

The other form of national parliamentary influence is exercising influence over how national Ministers vote in the Council. Two types of procedure are used for the expression of this influence.

The *document-based* procedure does not instruct the national Minister to take a position in the Council. Instead, on important proposals, it requires the Minister not to agree to any proposal until a Parliamentary Committee has scrutinised it and published its findings. The *mandate* procedure involves national parliaments authorising the government to take a position. The national government cannot deviate from that, or must provide reasons if it intends to do so.[101]

Both procedures allow national governments considerable latitude. The document-based procedure does not limit what concessions can be made by a national government in the Council. The Parliamentary Committee merely tweaks out issues and interests. The mandate procedure allows parliaments to constrain governments but its weakness is its lack of flexibility. Awareness that it can disempower

---

[96] On this see M. Rasmussen and M. Donigi, 'National Parliaments' Use of the Political Dialogue: Institutional Lobbyists, Traditionalists or Communicators?' (2018) 56 *JCMS* 1108.

[97] The research by Rasmussen and Dorigi looked at thirty legislative proposals and three policy proposals in 2013 and 2014. It found that only eight parliamentary chambers sought to influence the Commission on three or more instances. *Ibid.* 1117.

[98] D. Jančić, 'The Game of Cards: National Parliaments in the EU and the Future of the Early Warning Mechanism and the Political Dialogue' (2015) 52 *CMLRev* 939, 948.

[99] www.tweedekamer.nl/kamerstukken/detail?id=2015D00583&did=2015D00583.

[100] COSAC, *Twenty-Fifth Bi-Annual Report: Developments in European Union Procedures and Practices Relevant to Parliamentary Scrutiny* (Brussels, COSAC, 2016) 12–14. On the debate see K. Borońska-Hryniewiecka, 'From the Early Warning System to a "Green Card" for National Parliaments: Hindering or Accelerating EU Policy-making?' in D. Jančić (ed.), *National Parliaments after the Lisbon Treaty and the Euro Crisis: Resilience or Resignation?* (Oxford University Press, 2017).

[101] Austria, Belgium, Bulgaria, Cyprus, France, Germany, Ireland, Italy, Luxembourg, Netherlands, Portugal, Slovakia, Spain and the United Kingdom all adopt document-based systems. Croatia, Denmark, Estonia, Finland, Latvia, Lithuania, Poland, Romania, Slovakia, Slovenia and Sweden use mandate-based systems. Other Member States use a mix of the two, www.cosac.eu/eu-scrutiny-models/.

governments in negotiations often leads the parliament to soften the mandate so it is very vague or to use it selectively for only the most salient issues, with the government given a free hand elsewhere.

Furthermore, in many cases, legislative proposals are waved through without scrutiny or mandate because of lack of interest or time.[102] In that regard, the largest study on the subject found that levels of parliamentary scrutiny were informed most centrally by the institutional capabilities of the Committee carrying out that scrutiny. Committees with greater capabilities were more active.[103] These capabilities include the amount of information provided to them about the dossier before the Council; their infrastructure in terms of their support staff and the size of the Committee; and their formal powers with Committees with the power to mandate governments more likely to be actively engaged than those using document-based systems.

(ii) Policing the Subsidiarity Principle

National parliaments are the institutions whose powers are most encroached upon by EU legislation, and are also the institutions best-placed to pick up local concerns about its intrusiveness.[104] The Protocol on the Application of the Principles of Subsidiarity and Proportionality establishes an Early Warning Mechanism which allows any national parliament or parliament chamber to issue a reasoned opinion within eight weeks of transmission of a draft legislative act stating why the proposal does not comply with the subsidiarity principle.[105] This principle requires that the European Union is only to act if the objects of a measure cannot be realised by Member States acting unilaterally and, by reason of the scale or effects of the proposed action, could be better realised by Union action.[106] National parliaments are given two votes, which are shared between parliamentary chambers in bicameral systems.[107]

The Early Warning Mechanism involves two different procedures: the yellow card and the orange card.

The 'yellow card' procedure applies to all legislative procedures. Under it, one-third of national parliamentary chambers (or one-quarter in the area of freedom, security and justice) can ask for the proposal to be reconsidered.

Article 7 of the Protocol on the Application of the Principles of Subsidiarity and Proportionality

(2) Where reasoned opinions on a draft legislative act's non-compliance with the principle of subsidiarity represent at least one third of all the votes allocated to the national Parliaments . . . , the draft must be reviewed. This threshold shall be a quarter in the case of a draft legislative act submitted on the basis of Article 76 TFEU on the area of freedom, security and justice.

---

[102] K. Auel, 'Democratic Accountability and National Parliaments – Re-Defining the Impact of Parliamentary Scrutiny in EU Affairs' (2007) 13 *ELJ* 87.

[103] K. Auel, O. Rozenberg and A. Tacea, 'To Scrutinise or Not to Scrutinise? Explaining Variation in EU-Related Activities in National Parliaments' (2015) 38 *WEP* 282.

[104] I. Cooper, 'Bicameral or Tricameral? National Parliaments and Representative Democracy in the European Union' (2013) 35 *JEI* 531, 536–9.

[105] Protocol on the Application of the Principles of Subsidiarity and Proportionality, Article 6.

[106] Article 5(3) TFEU. See pp. 383–5.

[107] On the practice of national parliaments, A. Jonsson Cornell and M. Goldoni (eds.), *National and Regional Parliaments in the EU-Legislative Procedure Post-Lisbon The Impact of the Early Warning Mechanism* (Oxford, Bloomsbury, 2017).

> After such review, the Commission or, where appropriate, the group of Member States, the European Parliament, the Court of Justice, the European Central Bank or the European Investment Bank, if the draft legislative act originates from them, may decide to maintain, amend or withdraw the draft. Reasons must be given for this decision.

The 'orange card' procedure applies where a measure is to be adopted under the ordinary legislative procedure and a majority of national parliaments issue reasoned opinions that it violates the subsidiary principle.

> (3) ... under the ordinary legislative procedure, where reasoned opinions on the non-compliance of a proposal for a legislative act with the principle of subsidiarity represent at least a simple majority of the votes allocated to the national Parliaments ... , the proposal must be reviewed. After such review, the Commission may decide to maintain, amend or withdraw the proposal.
>
> If it chooses to maintain the proposal, the Commission will have, in a reasoned opinion, to justify why it considers that the proposal complies with the principle of subsidiarity. This reasoned opinion, as well as the reasoned opinions of the national Parliaments, will have to be submitted to the Union's legislator, for consideration in the procedure:
>
> (a) before concluding the first reading, the legislator (the European Parliament and the Council) shall consider whether the legislative proposal is compatible with the principle of subsidiarity, taking particular account of the reasons expressed and shared by the majority of national Parliaments as well as the reasoned opinion of the Commission;
>
> (b) if, by a majority of 55% of the members of the Council or a majority of the votes cast in the European Parliament, the legislator is of the opinion that the proposal is not compatible with the principle of subsidiarity, the legislative proposal shall not be given further consideration.

There are a couple of oddities.

The first are the features of the orange card procedure. It was introduced to appease Dutch and Czech concerns at the time of the Lisbon Treaty that the Commission could still go through with a measure even though national parliaments had issued a yellow card. However, there is no good reason for it only applying to the ordinary legislative procedure, particularly when more politically sensitive measures tend to involve other procedures. The other concern is its high thresholds. It will be rare indeed that a majority of national parliaments believe a measure violates the subsidiarity principle, and, if they do, there will be no majority in the Council for the measure unless national governments are willing to defy their own parliaments. It has, unsurprisingly, never been used.

The second is that there is no 'red card' procedure, namely that the national parliaments cannot veto the measure. This question formed part of the settlement with the United Kingdom that led to the Brexit referendum. It was agreed that if more than 55 per cent of national parliaments voted against a measure, it would not go forward unless, after discussion within the Council, the draft accommodated the concerns in the reasoned opinions.[108] Once the United Kingdom voted to leave, this commitment was withdrawn, however. To date, national

---

[108] A New Settlement for the United Kingdom within the European Union, OJ 2016, C 691/1, Section C.3.

parliaments have issued three yellow cards. The Commission withdrew one of its proposals.[109] It kept the other two on the book.[110] Both have now been adopted as EU law, with advocates and opponents of the red card system each likely to use this to support their respective cases.[111]

(iii) National Parliaments: A Third Legislative Chamber?

Reasoned opinions have often gone beyond verifying whether a proposal complies with the subsidiarity principle and gone more generally to the merits of the proposal's content.[112] The distinction between the political dialogue and the Early Warning Mechanism has blurred so that a continuum has emerged whereby national parliaments put forward their views at an early stage, and, insofar as these are not taken into account, they exert political muscle at a later stage by threatening a yellow or orange card. It has therefore been suggested that national parliaments form an informal virtual third legislative chamber through which EU laws have to be passed, with the Council and the European Parliament being the other two.[113] There is some evidence that parliaments look at what is taking place in other national parliaments,[114] but, even if we were to characterise national parliamentary engagement in this way, there are questions about the quality of this third legislative chamber.[115]

The thresholds for showing any card are high, requiring, usually, at least eighteen votes. Typically, EU laws will not violate some bright red line drawn by all national parliaments. Traditions cherished or values deeply felt in one State often arise precisely because of their idiosyncrasy. It will be difficult, in such circumstances, for the national parliament of that State to mobilise other parliaments. In 2016, for example, there were six proposals, which triggered reasoned opinions from parliaments from four or more Member States that it violated the subsidiarity principle. However, only one of these proposals, that on posted workers, triggered

---

[109] European Commission, 'Decision to Withdraw the Proposal for a Council Regulation on the Exercise of the Right to Take Collective Action within the Context of the Freedom of Establishment and the Freedom to Provide Services', COM(2012)130.

[110] European Commission, 'On the Review of the Proposal for a Council Regulation on the Establishment of the European Public Prosecutor's Office with Regard to the Principle of Subsidiarity', COM(2013)851; European Commission, 'On the Proposal for a Directive Amending the Posting of Workers Directive, with Regard to the Principle of Subsidiarity', COM(2016)505. D. Fromage, 'The Second Yellow Card on the EPPO Proposal: An Encouraging Development for Member State Parliaments?' (2016) 35 *YBEL* 5; D. Jančić, 'EU Law's Grand Scheme on National Parliaments: The Third Yellow Card on Posted Workers and the Way Forward' in D. Jančić (ed.), *National Parliaments after the Lisbon Treaty and the Euro Crisis: Resilience or Resignation?* (Oxford University Press, 2017).

[111] Regulation 2017/1939 implementing enhanced cooperation on the establishment of the European Public Prosecutor's Office, OJ 2017, L 283/1; Directive 2018/957 amending Directive 96/71/EC concerning the posting of workers in the framework of the provision of services, OJ 2018, L 173/16.

[112] Reasoned opinions are most common therefore from States where political contestation is strong, K. Gattermann and C. Hefftler, 'Beyond Institutional Capacity: Political Motivation and Parliamentary Behaviour in the Early Warning System' (2015) 38 *WEP* 305. Practice has evolved over the years with opinions likely now to include a veneer of language about subsidiarity before ranging wider, K. Granat, *The Principle of Subsidiarity and its Enforcement in the EU Legal Order: The Role of National Parliaments in the Early Warning System* (Oxford, Bloomsbury, 2018) ch. 3.

[113] I. Cooper, 'A "Virtual Third Chamber" for the European Union? National Parliaments after the Treaty of Lisbon' (2012) 35 *WEP* 441.

[114] T. Malang, L. Brandenberger and P. Leifeld, 'Networks and Social Influence in European Legislative Politics' (2017) *BJPS* (forthcoming).

[115] There is a burgeoning literature on the nature of this engagement, C. Neuhold *et al.* (eds.), *The Palgrave Handbook of National Parliaments and the European Union* (Basingstoke, Palgrave Macmillan, 2015); F. Wendler, *Debating Europe in National Parliaments: Public Justification and Political Polarization* (Basingstoke, Palgrave, 2016); C. Winzen, *Constitutional Preferences and Parliamentary Reform: Explaining National Parliaments' Adaptation to European Integration* (Oxford University Press, 2017).

a yellow card.[116] Furthermore, national parliaments are granted an unusual role in the Early Warning Mechanism, namely, to monitor the proposals of others. However, a traditional feature of parliamentary democracies is that parliaments have to assent actively to the proposal. This assent, it has been argued, generates the political contestation and debate, which sustains parliamentary democracy as it requires representatives to commit to and argue for particular policies before they can be adopted.[117] By contrast, monitoring involves a more managerial role in which a Parliamentary Committee first has to look at whether the proposal meets certain criteria even if, as we have seen, many then try to look beyond these criteria to enable more substantive engagement with the proposal.

6 DIFFERENTIATED LAWMAKING

(i) Differentiated Integration and the EU Treaties

Differentiated integration has to navigate a particular tension. On the one hand, it seems intuitively unfair for some Member States to prevent others from developing common laws between themselves, should they so wish. On the other, differentiated integration allows for the possibility of a core of Member States developing laws, which both exclude other Member States and impose costs onto these. If this core grew, furthermore, so that the centre of political energy and legal commitments revolved it, there is the further danger that the European Union would become a legal and political rump.[118]

To mediate this tension within most EU policies, procedures going under the unappealing title of Enhanced Cooperation put in place a number of safeguards. These are scattered across a number of Treaty articles.

Article 20 TEU

(1) Member States which wish to establish enhanced cooperation between themselves within the framework of the Union's non-exclusive competences may make use of its institutions and exercise those competences by applying the relevant provisions of the Treaties, subject to the limits and in accordance with the detailed arrangements laid down in this Article and in Articles 326 to 334 TFEU.

Enhanced cooperation shall aim to further the objectives of the Union, protect its interests and reinforce its integration process. Such cooperation shall be open at any time to all Member States, in accordance with Article 328 TFEU.[[119]]

(2) The decision authorising enhanced cooperation shall be adopted by the Council as a last resort, when it has established that the objectives of such cooperation cannot be attained within a reasonable period by the Union as a whole, and provided that at least nine Member States participate in it . . .

---

[116] European Commission, 'Annual Report 2016 on Relations between the European Commission and National Parliaments', COM(2017)600, Annex.

[117] T. Christiansen, A. Högenauer and C. Neuhold, 'National Parliaments in the Post-Lisbon European Union: Bureaucratization Rather than Democratization?' (2014) 12 *Comparative European Politics* 121.

[118] On this debate at the time of the Treaty of Amsterdam see A. Stubb, 'The 1996 Intergovernmental Conference and the Management of Flexible Integration' (1997) 4 *JEPP* 37.

[119] This Article requires that such States comply (like all others) with any conditions set out by the initial Decision authorising Enhanced Cooperation. On the latter, see Article 329(1) TFEU.

> ### Article 326 TFEU
>
> Any enhanced cooperation shall comply with the Treaties and Union law. Such cooperation shall not undermine the internal market or economic, social and territorial cohesion. It shall not constitute a barrier to or discrimination in trade between Member States, nor shall it distort competition between them.

> ### Article 327 TFEU
>
> Any enhanced cooperation shall respect the competences, rights and obligations of those Member States which do not participate in it. Those Member States shall not impede its implementation by the participating Member States.

These provisions suggest six substantive constraints on an Enhanced Cooperation procedure:

- There must be nine States.
- It must not be in a field where the Union has exclusive competence.[120]
- The measure must only be adopted as a matter of last resort.
- It must comply with other EU laws.
- It must not undermine the internal market or economic or social cohesion. In particular, it shall not constitute a barrier to or discrimination in trade between Member States or distort competition between them.
- It shall respect the rights, competences and obligations of other Member States.

The most loaded of these conditions is that the measure only be adopted as a last resort. Interpreted broadly, it could subject those States wishing to proceed to endless prevarication by States who do not wish to participate. Interpreted narrowly, it could allow aggressive States to threaten to go ahead without a State unless it caved into their demands in negotiations on the content of a legislative text. In *Unitary Patent*, twenty-five States proceeded without Spain and Italy to set up a unitary patent enjoying protection across the Union. Whilst the initial Commission proposal was in 2000, an accompanying proposal on translation arrangements for the patent was only made in 2010. There was only six months between this latter proposal and the decision authorising enhanced cooperation. Italy and Spain argued that this was insufficient time to secure agreement.

> ### *Spain and Italy* v. *Council (Unitary Patent)*, C-274/11 and C-295/11, EU:C:2013:240
>
> 47 In accordance with Article 20(2) TEU, the Council may not authorise enhanced cooperation except 'as a last resort, when it has established that the objectives of such cooperation cannot be attained within a reasonable period by the Union as a whole.'
> 48 This condition is particularly important and must be read in the light of the second paragraph of Article 20(1) TEU, which provides that enhanced cooperation is to 'aim to further the objectives of the Union, protect its interests and reinforce its integration process'.

---

[120] On the scope of this see p. 33.

49 The Union's interests and the process of integration would, quite clearly, not be protected if all fruitless negotiations could lead to one or more instances of enhanced cooperation, to the detriment of the search for a compromise enabling the adoption of legislation for the Union as a whole.

50 In consequence ... the expression 'as a last resort' highlights the fact that only those situations in which it is impossible to adopt such legislation in the foreseeable future may give rise to the adoption of a decision authorising enhanced cooperation ...

53 The Council ... is best placed to determine whether the Member States have demonstrated any willingness to compromise and are in a position to put forward proposals capable of leading to the adoption of legislation for the Union as a whole in the foreseeable future.

54 The Court, in exercising its review of whether the condition that a decision authorising enhanced cooperation must be adopted only as a last resort has been satisfied, should therefore ascertain whether the Council has carefully and impartially examined those aspects that are relevant to this point and whether adequate reasons have been given for the conclusion reached by the Council.

55 In this instance, the Council correctly took into account the fact that the legislative process undertaken with a view to the establishing of a unitary patent at Union level was begun during the year 2000 and covered several stages ...

56 It is apparent too that a considerable number of different language arrangements for the unitary patent were discussed among all the Member States within the Council and that none of those arrangements, with or without the addition of elements of compromise, found support capable of leading to the adoption at Union level of a full 'legislative package' relating to that patent.

57 Furthermore, the applicants have adduced no specific evidence that could disprove the Council's assertion that when the requests for enhanced cooperation were made, and when the proposal for authorisation was sent by the Commission to the Council, and at the date on which the contested decision was adopted, there was still insufficient support for any of the language arrangements proposed or possible to contemplate.

58 With regard, lastly, to the reasons for the contested decision, it is to be borne in mind that, when the measure at issue was adopted in a context with which the persons concerned were familiar, summary reasons may be given ... Having regard to the applicants' participation in the negotiations and to the detailed description of the fruitless stages before the contested decision set out in the proposal that was to lead to that decision, it cannot be concluded that that decision was vitiated by any failure to state reasons capable of resulting in its annulment.

The Council is granted a margin of discretion, therefore, in that the central question is not whether it was right but whether it looked at all the relevant issues and its reasoning was adequate. Furthermore, the Court will take a broad-brush approach in determining whether this is the case. It did not look, therefore, at the short period between the proposal on translation arrangements and the Enhanced Cooperation Decision or at the limited reasoning provided by the Council. Instead, it looked at the length of time for the whole negotiations and the degree of stalemate. This suggests that whilst the threat of Enhanced Cooperation cannot be used as leverage in negotiations, there need be only be a relatively short period of stalemate before Enhanced Cooperation can be used.

In addition to these substantive constraints, Enhanced Cooperation requires the consent of the three EU Institutions.[121]

---

[121] In CFSP, the proposal is notified to the Council, who consults the Commission and High Representative and notifies the Parliament. The Council can then grant authorisation, but only by unanimity, Article 329(2) TFEU.

Article 329 TFEU

(1) Member States which wish to establish enhanced cooperation between themselves in one of the areas covered by the Treaties, with the exception of fields of exclusive competence and the common foreign and security policy, shall address a request to the Commission, specifying the scope and objectives of the enhanced cooperation proposed. The Commission may submit a proposal to the Council to that effect. In the event of the Commission not submitting a proposal, it shall inform the Member States concerned of the reasons for not doing so. Authorisation to proceed with the enhanced cooperation ... shall be granted by a decision of the Council,[122] on a proposal from the Commission and after obtaining the consent of the European Parliament.

Not only is the procedure cumbersome, but participating Member States do not even have the freedom to negotiate between themselves as they must allow non-participating States to participate in the deliberations leading up to the adoption of legislation even if they cannot vote on it.[123] Finally, non-participating States can free-ride by waiting to see the effects of the measure and then joining later, subject to verification that they meet the conditions for participation.[124]

There are three policies which apply other rules to differentiated rule-making: the area of freedom, security and justice, security and defence, and the euro. The complicated features of Enhanced Cooperation entail that it is used for individual EU laws which some Member States wish to adopt. By contrast, there are doubts about whether a number of Member States wish to participate in these policies significantly, or even at all. Hence, they operate under particular regimes.

The area of freedom, security and justice is the most straightforward. Ireland does not have to take part in or be bound by any EU legislation adopted in the field of the area of freedom, security and justice.[125] It can, however, participate if, within three months of any proposal, it indicates that it wishes to do so.[126] It may also accede to existing laws in this field. It does this by making a request, and the Commission and Council verifying that it meets the 'conditions for participation', namely that it has the necessary domestic legislation and administration in place.[127]

The matter is complicated by the Protocol on Integrating the Schengen Acquis. Initially concluded between five States (BENELUX, France and Germany), the Schengen Conventions provided for an absence of controls on movement between States, police cooperation and facilitated extradition, a common external frontier as well as a common visa and asylum policy.[128] A large number of measures were adopted by an Executive Committee, comprising of national civil servants, to realise these aims. When the area of freedom, security and justice

---

[122] This is by QMV, Article 16(3) TEU.   [123] Articles 20(3) TEU and 330 TFEU.

[124] This is be done by Commission authorisation in all fields other than CFSP, Article 331(1) TFEU. In CFSP it is done by the Council in consultation with the High Representative, Article 331(2) TFEU.

[125] Protocol on the Position of the United Kingdom and Ireland in Respect of the Area of Freedom, Security and Justice, Articles 1 and 2.

[126] *Ibid.* Article 3(1). If negotiations stall, after a 'reasonable period of time' the measures may be adopted without their participation, Article 3(2).

[127] *Ibid.* Article 4.

[128] Agreement on the gradual abolition of checks at their common borders, OJ 2000, L 239/13; Convention implementing the Schengen Agreement the gradual abolition of checks at their common borders, OJ 2000, L 239/19. It now includes all Member States (except Ireland), Norway, Iceland and Switzerland. See pp. 530–1.

was established, these Conventions and their implementing measures (the 'Schengen acquis') were replaced by the Protocol on Integrating the Schengen Acquis. This Protocol allows Ireland to participate in EU laws that develop the *Schengen acquis*, but this is conditional on all EU Schengen States consenting to this.[129] Its possibilities for participation are, thus, much more limited. The Court has stated that if an EU law builds on the *Schengen acquis*, this Protocol governs Ireland's possibilities to participation.[130] To date, the Court has stated that visa policy and measures concerning procedures and policing at the external frontiers build on the Protocol are governed by the Protocol (so other States can veto Ireland's participation).[131] The rest of the area of freedom, security and justice falls outside it.

On security and defence, the Treaties provide for permanent and structured cooperation ('PESCO') between Member States 'whose military capabilities fulfil higher criteria and have made more binding commitments to one another in this area with a view to the most demanding missions'.[132] Participating States must commit to more active participation in multinational forces, greater mission capacity, cooperation on investment in defence expenditure, and alignment of defence apparatus and interoperability.[133] Authorisation for PESCO is granted by the Council acting by QMV.[134] This took place in 2017 for the first time, with all States bar Denmark and Malta participating.[135]

With regard to the euro, eight States do not participate in the third stage of Economic and Monetary Union (i.e. have the euro as their currency) either because they do not wish to or they do not meet the criteria for participation.[136] There is no detailed Treaty regime mediating the different interests of euro area and non-euro area States.[137] This posed few concerns prior to the sovereign debt crisis as the regime did not involve significant lawmaking but rather a series of disciplines applied to euro area States.

However, the crisis led a more integrated system of financial supervision within the euro area.

As part of this, the European Central Bank (ECB) acquired significant supervisory powers with spill-over effects for non-euro area States.[138] It was, therefore, granted powers over the authorisation and de-authorisation of significant banks in the euro area, their governance arrangements, their levels of exposure and their acquisition and disposal of holdings.[139] Banks with a

---

[129] Protocol on Integrating the Schengen Acquis, Article 4. This was inserted at the request of Spain who was concerned that, otherwise, measures on the common external frontier might be taken affecting the status of Gibraltar which overrode its views. With Brexit, this is less of an issue now.

[130] *United Kingdom* v. *Council*, C-77/05, EU:C:2007:803.

[131] Ibid.; *United Kingdom* v. *Council*, C-137/05, EU:C:2007:805; *United Kingdom* v. *Council*, C-482/08, EU:C:2010:631.

[132] Article 42(6) TEU.

[133] Protocol on Permanent and Structured Cooperation established by Article 42 TEU, Articles 1 and 2.

[134] Article 46(2) TEU.

[135] Decision 2017/2315 establishing permanent structured cooperation (PESCO) and determining the list of participating Member States, OJ 2017, L 331/57.

[136] On this see 662. The seven are Bulgaria, Croatia, Czech Republic, Denmark, Hungary, Poland, Romania and Sweden.

[137] The ECB is required to strengthen cooperation with their national central banks, Article 141(2) TFEU

[138] The British also successfully challenged an attempt by the ECB to get all euro central counterparty clearing systems (activities relating to and taking the risk for a transaction between when it is made and when it is settled) to be done in the euro area, as this would have closed down a lot of business in the City of London, *United Kingdom* v. *ECB*, T-496/11, EU:T:2015:133.

[139] Regulation 1024/2013 conferring specific tasks on the European Central Bank concerning policies relating to the prudential supervision of credit institutions, OJ 2013, L 287/63, Article 4. On this debate see A. Spendzharova and I. Bayram, 'Banking Union through the Back Door? How European Banking Union Affects Sweden and the Baltic States' (2016) 39 *WEP* 565.

head office in a non-euro State but a large number of branches or subsidiaries in the euro area found, therefore, much of their activities governed by the ECB. The only allowance is that non-euro area States can join the system of supervision, the Single Supervisory Mechanism, under which the ECB exercises these powers. Under this mechanism, their national regulatory authorities will follow ECB decisions,[140] but these States have very limited rights of participation in the ECB's decision-making process. They can participate in the body, the Supervisory Board, which prepares decisions, albeit their vote will count only as one of a minimum of twenty-six votes,[141] but not in the body, the Governing Council, which adopts the decisions.[142] They can ask it to reconsider its position but nothing more.[143]

The other connected concern is that euro area States will form a voting bloc within the Council to secure financial services legislation which benefits the euro area at the expense of non-euro area States. These States have enough votes to form a QMV and meet regularly with the Commission and ECB to discuss euro area State responsibilities relating to the single currency.[144] To that end, the settlement leading to the Brexit referendum put in place safeguards to address this concern. It stated that in any vote on EU legislation a non-euro area State could raise objections to the measure, of which the main ones were that the measure failed to respect the internal market or the rights of non-euro area States. In such circumstances, there would be further discussion within the Council to reach a mutually satisfactory solution.[145] It was emphasised that this possibility did not give non-euro area States a veto. The possibility to raise objections was rather to emphasise a sensitivity on the part of the euro area States to the interests of non-euro area States. The settlement was, of course, withdrawn following the United Kingdom referendum, and it remains to be seen whether there will be a commitment to sensitivity, particularly as the size of the non-euro area economy, following Brexit, is now much smaller.

(ii) The Practice of Differentiated Rule-Making beyond Enhanced Cooperation

The complexity of the Enhanced Cooperation procedures had led to only six measures being adopted under them in twenty years.[146] Instead, resort had been made to other forms of differentiated integration.

The first response has been for EU laws simply to set out differentiated rights and obligations. States unhappy about EU legislation get the benefit still of being able to vote on and influence it.

---

[140] *Ibid.* Article 7(2).
[141] *Ibid.* Article 26(1) and (6). The Board votes by simple majority. It comprises representatives from all the euro area States and participating non-euro area States as well as six ECB members.
[142] *Ibid.* Article 26(8).   [143] *Ibid.* Article 7(7).   [144] Article 137 TFEU. Protocol on the Euro Group, Article 1.
[145] A New Settlement for the United Kingdom within the European Union, OJ 2016, C 691/1, Section A and Annex II.
[146] Regulation 1259/2010 implementing enhanced cooperation in the area of the law applicable to divorce and legal separation, OJ 2010, L 343/10; Regulation 1257/2012 implementing enhanced cooperation in the area of the creation of unitary patent protection, OJ 2012, L 361/1; Regulation 1260/2012 implementing enhanced cooperation in the area of the creation of unitary patent protection with regard to the applicable translation arrangements, OJ 2012, L 361/89; Regulation 2016/1103 implementing enhanced cooperation in the area of jurisdiction, applicable law and the recognition and enforcement of decisions in matters of matrimonial property regimes OJ 2016, L 183/1; Regulation 2016/1104 implementing enhanced cooperation in the area of jurisdiction, applicable law and the recognition and enforcement of decisions in matters of the property consequences of registered partnerships, OJ 2016, L 183/30; Regulation 2017/1939 implementing enhanced cooperation on the establishment of the European Public Prosecutor's Office, OJ 2017, L 283/1. On this see S. Peers, 'Enhanced Cooperation: The Cinderella of Differentiated Integration' in B. de Witte, A. Ott and E. Vos (eds.), *Between Flexibility and Disintegration: The Trajectory of Differentiation in EU Law* (Cheltenham, Edward Elgar, 2017).

As a quid pro quo, enthusiastic States get some level of commitment from these other States. This is very common. One in six pieces of EU legislation provides for Member States to have different entitlements and obligations.[147] Such an approach, in many ways, secures a suitable accommodation between Member States in which they agree on an appropriate balance of interests and needs. It is not without challenges, however. It freezes in place an agreement that neither finds satisfying. Enthusiastic States have to ensure a certain amount of free-riding from other States for the sake of having them involved. Non-enthusiastic States are participating in laws that they (and possibly their electorates) wish were not there.

A second (and more problematic) form of differentiation is that a number of Member States make an international agreement between themselves rather than adopting an EU law.[148] In *Pringle*, it was provided such that an agreement is lawful if it does not fall within a field where EU law has established a specific task which requires the Union to act, and it does not breach any other EU law.[149] Member States may make agreements, therefore, in the field of general economic policy because the Treaties provide only for coordination of national policies rather than requiring the Union to act. By contrast, they could not make such agreements on anything that falls within the aegis of the internal market as the Treaties require the EU lawmaker to act here by requiring it to establish this market.[150]

The most famous examples of these agreements are the Schengen Agreements.[151] In addition to these, in 2005, the Prüm Convention was signed between Austria, Belgium, France, Germany, Luxembourg, Netherlands and Spain. This provided for greater exchange of DNA, fingerprint and vehicle data between security agencies than was previously possible.[152] The use of international agreements has increased since then. In 2012, the European Stability Mechanism was established between the euro area States to guarantee the public finances of those euro area States without access to the currency markets and to set out programmes of reform for these States in return for these guarantees.[153] The Treaty on Stability, Coordination and Governance (TSCG) was also signed in that year between twenty-five EU States committing these States to securing balanced budgets.[154] In 2013, twenty-five Member States agreed to establish a court, the Unified Patent Court, to hear actions concerning patents granted under the Unified Patent Regulation that was the subject of the Spanish and Italian action described earlier.[155] In 2014, twenty-six States agreed to establish a Single Resolution Fund to provide the financial support in cases where a failing euro area credit institution has to be wound up under the Single Resolution Mechanism procedures.[156]

The range of activities governed by these agreements is significant and extensive. Contrary to the stipulations in *Pringle*, they have been adopted in fields where the EU is required to carry out

---

[147] T. Duttle, 'Opting Out from European Union Legislation: The Differentiation of Secondary Law' (2017) 24 *JEPP* 406, 419–20.

[148] B. de Witte and T. Martinelli, 'Treaties between EU Member States as Quasi-Instruments of EU Law' in M. Cremona and C. Kilpatrick (eds.), *EU Legal Acts: Challenges and Transformations* (Oxford University Press, 2018) 157, 167–87.

[149] *Pringle* v. *Government of Ireland*, C-370/12, EU:C:2012:756.   [150] Article 114(1) TFEU.   [151] See pp 530–1.

[152] EU Council, *Prüm Convention*, EU Council Doc. 10900/05.   [153] www.esm.europa.eu/legal-documents/esm-treaty.

[154] www.consilium.europa.eu/media/20399/st00tscg26_en12.pdf. Croatia signed it on accession. Only the Czech Republic has not signed it.

[155] www.unified-patent-court.org/sites/default/files/upc-agreement.pdf. Croatia, Poland and Spain have not signed. The United Kingdom signed the agreement and ratified it in April 2018, indicating that it wishes to continue to participate in it after Brexit.

[156] www.ris.bka.gv.at/Dokumente/RegV/REGV_COO_2026_100_2_1105493/COO_2026_100_2_1106424.pdf. Only Sweden did not sign this agreement.

specific tasks. The Schengen Agreements and the decisions implementing them were therefore integrated into EU law by the Protocol Integrating the Schengen Acquis.[157] The Prüm Convention was made part of EU law in 2008.[158] There is a commitment in the TSCG to integrate it into the EU Treaty framework within five years of its entry into force.[159] States experiencing difficulties in their public finances are now subject to monitoring under EU law similar to that provided under the European Stability Mechanism (ESM).[160] The Unified Patent Court and Single Resolution Fund Agreements both provide infrastructure to allow the operation of particular EU Regulations.[161]

These measures almost invariably act as a substitute for EU law, and this gives rise to a number of concerns.

First, these measures are not subject to the same controls in their inception as EU laws. There is less transparency and parliamentary oversight than within the EU lawmaking process. The Prüm Convention was, thus, an agreement conceived by the intelligence agencies of seven States which dominated its negotiation. These focused on establishing a common pool of intelligence at the expense of other issues. At the time, there were no common rules on collection of the data and the collective rules on its protection were arguably insufficient.[162] When these International agreements are incorporated into EU law, the process is, however, just one of translation. There is no attempt to amend them, so defects which arose from the weaknesses of the initial process are incorporated into EU law. Secondly, these agreements imbalance relations between Member States. In some instances, these instances have generated significant exclusionary costs for non-participants. The Prüm and Schengen Conventions, thus, excluded non-participating States from shared intelligence. These costs provide strong reasons for others to join subsequently. The difficulty with such a process is a sense that publics are being bounced into something for which there might not be much support. Thirdly, there is the possibility of these arrangements excluding other EU States, with all the consequences of marginalisation and disintegration entailed by this. There is one instance of this. The Protocol Integrating the Schengen Acquis incorporated the *Schengen acquis*. Non-participating States may request to take part in measures building on this acquis but all Schengen States must consent to this.[163]

---

[157] The Schengen Agreements are an exception here as it can be argued that, at the time of their conclusion, the EU did not have competence in these fields. This is not true of the other instruments.

[158] Decision 2008/615/JHA on the stepping up of cross-border cooperation, particularly in combating terrorism and cross-border crime, OJ 2008, L 209/1; Decision 2008/616/JHA on the implementation of Decision 2008/615/JHA on the stepping up of cross-border cooperation, particularly in combating terrorism and cross-border crime, OJ 2008, L 210/12.

[159] TSCG, Article 16. This was no more than a tightening up of existing EU law requirements, Regulation 1466/97 on the strengthening of the surveillance of budgetary positions and the surveillance and coordination of economic policies. OJ 1997, L 209/1, as amended by Regulation 1175/2011, OJ 2011, L 306/12, Article 2A.

[160] Regulation 472/2013 on the strengthening of economic and budgetary surveillance of Member States in the euro area experiencing or threatened with serious difficulties with respect to their financial stability, OJ 2013, L 140/1, Article 2. On the ESM Treaty, see p. 665.

[161] Regulation 1257/2012 implementing enhanced cooperation in the area of the creation of unitary patent protection, OJ 2012, L 361/1; Regulation 806/2014 establishing uniform rules and a uniform procedure for the resolution of credit institutions and certain investment firms in the framework of a Single Resolution Mechanism and a Single Resolution Fund, OJ 2014, L 225/1.

[162] House of Lords European Union Committee, *Prüm: An Effective Weapon against Terrorism and Crime?*, 18th Report, Session 2006–7.

[163] Protocol Integrating the Schengen Acquis, Article 4. This was inserted at the request of Spain, which was concerned that otherwise measures on the common external frontier might be taken affecting the status of Gibraltar which overrode its views. With Brexit, this is less of an issue now.

7 COMITOLOGY

(i) The Committee Procedures

We saw in Chapter 2 that the Commission can be granted powers to adopt implementing and delegated measures.[164] A significant number of implementing measures are adopted by the Commission every year. In 2017, the Commission adopted 508 new measures, and amended 395 existing measures.[165] These are adopted under a set of procedures, known as comitology, in which the Commission works in tandem with a committee of representatives of national governments whose role is to oversee it.[166] At the end of 2016, there were 277 committees in operation.[167]

There are three procedures: the advisory procedure, the examination procedure and the regulatory procedure with scrutiny. However, we will only focus on the first two as there are proposals to phase out the last procedure.[168]

The advisory and examination committee procedures were established by Regulation 182/2011.[169] Article 2 of the Regulation sets out the criteria for when each is to be used.

Article 2 Regulation 182/2011

(1) A basic act may provide for the application of the advisory procedure or the examination procedure, taking into account the nature or the impact of the implementing act required.

(2) The examination procedure applies, in particular, for the adoption of:
   (a) implementing acts of general scope;
   (b) other implementing acts relating to:
      (i) programmes with substantial implications;
      (ii) the common agricultural and common fisheries policies;
      (iii) the environment, security and safety, or protection of the health or safety, of humans, animals or plants;
      (iv) the common commercial policy;
      (v) taxation.

---

[164] See pp. 68–72. [165] https://eur-lex.europa.eu/statistics/2017/legislative-acts-statistics.html.

[166] On the history see C. Bergström, *Comitology: Delegation of Powers in the European Union System* (Oxford University Press, 2005).

[167] European Commission, 'Report from the Commission on the Working of the Committees during 2016', COM(2017) 594, 5.

[168] European Commission, 'Proposal for a Regulation Adapting a Number of Legal Acts Providing for the Use of the Regulatory Procedure with Scrutiny to Articles 290 and 291 TFEU', COM(2016)799. In the regulatory procedure with scrutiny, the committee of national representatives gives an opinion by QMV on a Commission draft implementing measures. If the opinion is positive, the European Parliament and the Council each have three months to veto the measure but only on the grounds that the Commission is exceeding its powers or breaching the subsidiarity or proportionality principles. If there is no positive vote by the Commission, the draft fails, Decision 1999/468/EC laying down the procedures for the exercise of implementing powers conferred on the Commission, OJ 1999, L 184/23 as amended by Decision 2006/512, OJ 2006, L 200/11, Article 5a.

[169] Regulation 182/2011 laying down the rules and general principles concerning mechanisms for control by Member States of the Commission's exercise of implementing powers, OJ 2011, L 55/13. On the negotiation see G. Brandsma and J. Blom-Hansen, 'Negotiating the Post-Lisbon Comitology System: Institutional Battles over Delegated Decision-Making' (2012) 50 *JCMS* 939, 948–52.

(3) The advisory procedure applies, as a general rule, for the adoption of implementing acts not falling within the ambit of paragraph 2. However, the advisory procedure may apply for the adoption of the implementing acts referred to in paragraph 2 in duly justified cases.

In principle, therefore, the more significant and contentious measures are to be adopted under the examination procedure.

The procedures begin by the Commission submitting a draft of the implementing measure to a committee of representatives of national governments, which is convened and chaired by it.[170]

In the advisory procedure, the committee gives an opinion on the draft. Its opinion may be adopted without a vote, but, if a vote is necessary, it is taken by simple majority.[171] The Commission then decides on the act, 'taking the utmost account of the conclusions drawn from the discussions within the committee and of the opinion delivered'.[172] In principle, the Committee exists, therefore, only to advise the Commission. The latter can ignore its views and does not even have to justify itself to the Committee. However, the duty to take utmost account of the deliberations and opinion of the Committee is a significant constraint. As we shall see, there is some evidence that it does this, and any measure adopted by it is subject to appeal within the Appeal Committee. A failure to give due regard to the views expressed within and by the Committee may count against it there.

In the examination procedure, the Committee can approve the draft by QMV (positive opinion), vote against it by QMV (negative opinion) or, if there are not sufficient votes for either of these, give no opinion. The choice has a number of implications.

Article 5 Regulation 182/2011

(2) Where the committee delivers a positive opinion, the Commission shall adopt the draft implementing act.

(3) Without prejudice to Article 7,[[173]] if the committee delivers a negative opinion, the Commission shall not adopt the draft implementing act. Where an implementing act is deemed to be necessary, the chair may either submit an amended version of the draft implementing act to the same committee within 2 months of delivery of the negative opinion, or submit the draft implementing act within 1 month of such delivery to the appeal committee for further deliberation.

(4) Where no opinion is delivered, the Commission may adopt the draft implementing act, except in the cases provided for in the second subparagraph. Where the Commission does not adopt the draft implementing act, the chair may submit to the committee an amended version thereof.

Without prejudice to Article 7, the Commission shall not adopt the draft implementing act where:

(a) that act concerns taxation, financial services, the protection of the health or safety of humans, animals or plants, or definitive multilateral safeguard measures;

(b) the basic act provides that the draft implementing act may not be adopted where no opinion is delivered; or

(c) a simple majority of the component members of the committee opposes it.

---

[170] Regulation 182/2011, Article 3(2).   [171] *Ibid.* Article 4(1).   [172] *Ibid.* Article 4(2).
[173] This provision allows acts to be adopted immediately if delay would entail significant disruption to agricultural markets or the Union's financial interests. In such circumstances, the measure is passed to the Appeal Committee. A negative opinion by it requires the immediate repeal of the measure.

The position is clear enough where there is a consensus within the Committee. The draft is approved if the Committee approves it by QMV and falls if it votes against by QMV. The challenge is where the Committee is split. There is no qualified majority either way. In some fields – those in Article 5(4)(a), such as taxation or financial services, or where the parent legislation so specifies – the measure will not be adopted. The default, however, is that the measure will be adopted unless a majority opposes it (Article 5(4)(c)). This seems reasonable. A majority of States can stop the Commission proceeding. However, there is a problem if States abstain as a measure will get through, notwithstanding little Member State support for it. One can have a situation, for example, where five States vote for a measure, five against and the rest abstain. This led to 'no' opinion, so the Commission draft will prevail.

The procedures are subject to two forms of control.

The first is the Appeal Committee. The parent legislation determines whether there shall be such a Committee and the terms under which a party – be it the Commission or national government(s) – may refer a measure to it.[174] If it gives a positive or no opinion, the Commission may adopt the measure. It is only if it gives a negative opinion that the Commission is blocked from adopting the measure.[175] Thus, the procedure is stacked, as a qualified majority of States must vote against the Commission for the appeal to be successful.[176] Practice suggests that it, indeed, acts as a weak control. Up to the end of 2016, fifty-one measures had been referred to the Committee.[177] Of these, the appeal succeeded in blocking the implementing measure in only four instances.[178]

The second control is that the Parliament and Council may ask the Commission to check whether the measure is not *ultra vires*.

Article 11 Regulation 182/2011

Where a basic act is adopted under the ordinary legislative procedure, either the European Parliament or the Council may at any time indicate to the Commission that, in its view, a draft implementing act exceeds the implementing powers provided for in the basic act. In such a case, the Commission shall review the draft implementing act, taking account of the positions expressed, and shall inform the European Parliament and the Council whether it intends to maintain, amend or withdraw the draft implementing act.

It might seem odd that this check only applies to measures where the parent act is adopted under the ordinary legislative procedure. After all, the problem of *ultra vires* is a general one. The logic is that, in other fields, the EU Institution excluded by excessive implementing powers is the Council. This is protected by the national representatives in the Committees. This assumption may be, of course, false. National representatives may like resolving the issue themselves rather

---

[174] Regulation 182/2011, Article 3(7).

[175] *Ibid.* Article 6(3). There is one exception to this. Definitive safeguard measures against imports from non-EU States can only be adopted if there is a positive opinion from the Committee, *ibid.* Article 6(4).

[176] *Ibid.* Article 6(1).

[177] The Commission thinks that this is because matters are only referred if there has been a positive opinion by the Committee. It is proposing that this be changed so that they can be referred where there is no opinion. To incentivise Committee representatives to vote, however, Member States will only get a vote on the Appeal Committee if they voted in the initial Committee vote. European Commission, 'Proposal for a Regulation Amending Regulation182/2011 Laying Down the Rules and General Principles Concerning Mechanisms for Control by Member States of the Commission's Exercise of Implementing Powers', COM(2017)85.

[178] *Ibid.*; European Commission, 'Report from the Commission on the Working of the Committees during 2016', COM (2017)594, 7.

than passing it back to their respective Ministers. It also rests on the idea that the central problem with *ultra vires* acts is simply that they touch on another institution's prerogatives. This is, of course, not the case. The Commission is granted only defined powers as it is agreed that wider powers would pose a problem for democracy. There are insufficient checks and balances or possibilities for popular input for it to be deciding these broader issues.

(ii) The Practice of Comitology

Comitology can be seen as simply a series of controls to constrain the Commission's executive discretion: the committees, the Appeal Committee, and the Council and the Parliament police the limits of the process. Viewing comitology in this manner explains its design and why implementing measures are chosen at the expense of delegated measures. An exhaustive study by Brandsma and Blom-Hansen, therefore, found that the examination procedure is chosen in situations where the Council has most sway over the parent instrument as it grants national governments the most control. Thus, it is most likely to be chosen for measures which are politically sensitive and where the parent legislation is the consultation procedure. By contrast, delegated measures – which grant the Parliament more control over the Commission – tend to be chosen where the parent legislation is adopted under the ordinary legislative procedure.[179]

However, this vision does not explain the daily operation of these procedures well. To control the Commission on behalf of their governments, national representatives would need both to receive strong instructions from their governments beforehand, and to report back regularly to their government superiors directly afterwards. This does not happen. A study found 43 per cent of participants believe that their superiors were not interested in their work, and 84 per cent believed that their Minister and government were not interested.[180] The committees escape below the radar of national interest. Equally, we have seen that the Appeals Committee has once prevented a Commission measure becoming law.

Comitology can, alternately, be seen as a collective problem-solving exercise. National actors and the Commission do not monitor each other, on such a view, but rather collaborate to develop solutions which tap into a wider pool of resources than would otherwise have been possible. This vision is reflected in the Regulation which requires the Committee to seek consensus and allow alternatives to be proposed right up until the moment of the adoption.

Article 3 Regulation 182/2011

(4) Until the committee delivers an opinion, any committee member may suggest amendments and the chair may present amended versions of the draft implementing act. The chair shall endeavour to find solutions which command the widest possible support within the committee. The chair shall inform the committee of the manner in which the discussions and suggestions for amendments have been taken into account, in particular as regards those suggestions which have been largely supported within the committee.

This provision reflects much of the practice of comitology. In pioneering work, Joerges and Neyer studied the interaction between the Commission and two such committees, the Standing

---

[179] G. Brandsma and J. Blom-Hansen, *Controlling the EU Executive? The Politics of Delegation in the European Union* (Oxford University Press, 2017) 132–43.

[180] G. Brandsma, 'Backstage Europe: Comitology, accountability and democracy in the European Union' (Utrecht, PhD dissertation, 2010) 197.

Committee on Food Stuffs (StCF) and the Scientific Committee for Food (SCF).[181] They found it characterised by deliberative problem-solving in which actors took on board the suggestions and interests of each other, and concern focused on finding the optimal solution rather than representing fixed national standpoints.[182]

C. Joerges and J. Neyer, 'Transforming Strategic Interaction into Deliberative Problem-Solving: European Comitology in the Foodstuffs Sector' (1997) 4 *Journal of European Public Policy* **609, 619–20**

The importance of the SCF in supporting certain arguments does not derive from any formal power to decide issues of conflict (it has only an advisory status) but from the legal fiction of its scientific expertise and neutrality . . . Why do member state delegates nevertheless adhere to the fiction of objective science? To understand this, one needs to consider the functions of legal fictions: scientific findings are supposed to be accepted by all the parties concerned; science-based discourses have the power to discipline arguments; and they allow a clear distinction between legitimate and illegitimate arguments in cases of conflict over competing proposals. Therefore, the fact that the opinions of the SCF have never been seriously challenged by the StCF may be grounded less in the objectivity of its opinions than in the function of scientific discourses as a mechanism that is helpful in overcoming politically constituted preferences by relying on the fiction of objective science.

. . .

. . . in negotiations in the StCF – and even more so in the SCF – the particular economic costs of policies cannot be explicitly discussed, and information is primarily provided on nondistributional issues. *Ceteris paribus*, therefore, the knowledge of delegates about adequate problem-solving strategies will increase with the duration of negotiations, whereas their *relative* knowledge about economic effects will decline. This change in the perceptions and preferences of delegates becomes increasingly important for shaping national preferences as their informational advantage over their national administration increases over time. It is also important to note that negotiations sometimes last for years among nearly the same set of delegates. Moreover, delegates have frequent contacts outside the sessions of the Standing Committee, and have often previously met working on the preparation of a legislative proposal in negotiations about its adoption in Council working groups. During the course of this collaboration, delegates not only learn to reduce differences between national legal provisions but also to develop converging definitions of problems and philosophies for their solution. They slowly proceed from being representatives of national interests to being representatives of a Europeanized inter-administrative discourse characterized by mutual learning and an understanding of each other's difficulties in the implementation of specific solutions.

This characterisation has been challenged by a 2014 study identifying significant conflict in over a quarter of cases.[183] However, even if the levels of consensus and conflict will vary from case to case, taken together they revolve comitology as a significant arena of political interaction between supranational actors, experts and national interests. This raises two central concerns. One is that the technocratic language of scientific risks often masks the

---

[181] The former was the national committee of representatives whereas the latter was a separate committee of experts appointed by the Commission. It has now been replaced by the European Food Safety Authority.

[182] For similar findings see J. Trondal, 'Beyond the EU Membership-Non Membership Dichotomy? Supranational Identities among National EU Decision-Makers' (2002) 9 *JEPP* 468; J. Blom-Hansen and G. Brandsma, 'The EU Comitology System Intergovernmental Bargaining and Deliberative Supranationalism?' (2009) 47 *JCMS* 719.

[183] R. Dehousse, A. Fernández Pasarín and J. Plaza, 'How Consensual Is Comitology' (2014) 21 *JEPP* 842.

delicate political and social issues at stake.[184] The other is that its make-up is insufficiently pluralistic. Administrators may 'up their game' by responding to other administrators' arguments but, as Gerstenberg and Sabel artfully put it, this may only 'improve government performance and renovate the role of the bureaucrat without much changing the role of the citizen'.[185] The levels of European Parliament interest in the work of the Committees are often fairly weak.[186] Notwithstanding that, the relationship between this process and lobbying groups is a murky one. There is extensive lobbying,[187] but no rules regulate either conditions of access or even knowing who has been in touch with either the Commission or members of these committees.

8 EU LAWMAKING: THE MEASURE OF ITS DEMOCRACY

For some, the supranational elements in EU lawmaking are enough to render it undemocratic. Such critiques take two forms.

First, there is the 'not yet' critique. This critique accepts that a pan-Union democracy is possible but it states that the supporting infrastructure for this is simply not in place. It argues that EU democracy is impossible without fully fledged European political parties presenting alternative programmes for citizens to choose from; a pan-Union media framing debate; or some system where the votes of EU citizens have equal value.[188] These could be established but this would require significant further centralisation. Some argue that even this would be insufficient. A pan-Union requires citizen engagement and this would only happen when the Union took significant decisions on taxation and welfare, and it was the dominant actor which did this in the Union. Only such a monopoly of decisions over such issues would induce citizens to mobilise around its lawmaking structures to contest particular policies.[189]

The second critique goes further and is sceptical about democracy at pan-Union level ever being possible. In particular, it argues that a political domain must have certain features before democracy can be established, and these cannot be recreated at a pan-Union level.

D. Miller, 'Democracy's Domain' (2009) 37 *Philosophy & Public Affairs* 201, 205–6

[T]he idea of collective self-determination stands at the heart of democratic theory. Democracy is a system in which people come together to decide matters of common concern on the basis of equality, and the aim is to reach decisions that everyone can identify with, that is, can see as in some sense their decision. This cannot mean, obviously, that the decision reached represents everyone's first choice; if that degree

---

[184] J. Weiler, 'Epilogue – "Comitology" as Revolution – Infranationalism, Constitutionalism and Democracy' in C. Joerges and E. Vos (eds.), *EU Committees: Social Regulation, Law and Politics* (Oxford-Portland, Hart, 1999) 339, 345–6.

[185] O. Gerstenberg and C. Sabel, 'Directly-Deliberative Polyarchy: An Institutional Ideal for Europe' in C. Joerges and R. Dehousse (eds.), *Good Governance in Europe's Integrated Market* (Oxford University Press, 2002) 289, 320.

[186] M. Kaeding and K. Stack, 'Legislative Scrutiny? The Political Economy and Practice of Legislative Vetoes in the European Union' (2015) 53 *JCMS* 1268.

[187] R. Nørgaard, P. Nedergaard and J. Blom-Hansen, 'Lobbying in the EU Comitology System' (2014) 36 *JEI* 491.

[188] On this view see pp. 95–6.

[189] S. Bartolini, *Restructuring Europe: Centre Formation, System Building and Political Structuring between the Nation-State and the European Union* (Oxford University Press, 2005) 334–50.

of consensus existed, a political procedure for making decisions would hardly be needed. But the process by which the decision is reached – process here encompassing not only formal voting procedures and the like, but also the manner in which the debate between alternatives is conducted – is such that each person feels that he or she has had a chance to influence the outcome, and that the outcome itself is at least a fair compromise between competing interests or rival convictions . . .

We want . . . members to be engaged in collective self-determination in such a way that when decisions are taken, each of them is able to see the outcome as legitimate. Although formal procedures will matter here, procedures alone cannot ensure this result. It depends also on the personal qualities of the members, and the way that they relate to one another when deciding political issues: how far do they trust each other to argue sincerely, for example, and to appeal to principles consistently even when this works to their personal disadvantage? So questions of domain will be approached by asking, in the first place, whether any proposed political unit brings together a group of people whose qualities and relationships are of the right kind to form a *demos*.

Miller sees three qualities as central, qualities he does not believe are possessed at the Union level. First, individuals must not see others as obstacles to getting what they want but as peers with legitimate interests which must be accommodated. There must, secondly, be agreement on which underlying ethical principles matter in political debate. There need not be agreement on the content or weight of these but there must be agreement on which principles are valid. Finally, individuals have to have sufficient trust that others will abide by decisions and be sincere in the arguments that they make to each other.[190] It can, of course, be questioned how present these qualities are at the national level.[191] Furthermore, others have observed that this lack of sympathetic identification with other EU citizens and lack of trust in each other may, paradoxically, be a reason why there should be a pan-Union democracy.

J. Habermas, 'Democracy in Europe: Why the Development of the EU into a Transnational Democracy Is Necessary and How It Is Possible' (2015) 21 *European Law Journal* 546, 553–4

The lack of trust that we observe at present between European nations is not primarily an expression of xenophobic self-isolation against foreign nations, but instead reflects in the first place the insistence of self-conscious citizens on the normative achievements of their respective nation-states. In Europe's welfare-state democracies, there is a widespread conviction among self-conscious citizens that they owe the fragile resource of free and relatively equitable and socially secure living conditions to the institutions of their states. They have a well-founded interest in 'their' nation-states remaining guarantors of these achievements and in not being exposed to the risk of intrusions and encroachments by an unfamiliar supranational polity.

---

[190] D. Miller, 'Democracy's Domain' (2009) 37 *Philosophy and Public Affairs* 201, 208–9; D. Miller, 'Republicanism, National Identity and Europe' in C. Laborde and J. Maynor (eds.), *Republicanism and Political Theory* (Oxford, Blackwell, 2008).

[191] A. Føllesdal, 'The Future Soul of Europe: Nationalism or Just Patriotism? A Critique of David Miller's Defence of Nationality' (2000) 37 *Journal of Peace Research* 503; L. Valentini, 'No Global Demos, No Global Democracy? A Systematization and Critique' (2014) 12 *Perspectives on Politics* 789.

This is why I think that the lack of a 'European people' is not an insurmountable obstacle to joint political decision making in Europe. Indeed, translingual citizenship uniting such a wide variety of different language communities is a novelty. For this, we need a European public sphere; however, that does not mean a new one. Rather, the already existing infrastructure of the existing national public spheres is sufficient for Europe-wide communication. National arenas only have to be opened up to each other. And the existing national media are sufficient, too, provided that they perform a complex task of translation: they must learn to report also on the discussions being conducted in each other's countries about the issues of common concern to all citizens of the Union. Then the trust among citizens that currently exists in the form of a nationally limited civic solidarity can develop into the even more abstract form of trust that reaches across national borders. The 'no demos' thesis obscures a factor that we must take seriously – namely the conviction that the normative achievements of the democratic state are worth preserving. This self-assertion of a democratic civil society is something different from the reactive clinging to naturalised characteristics of ethnonational origin that lend support to right-wing populism.

Interestingly, democratic self-assertion is not only an empirical motive, but also a justifying reason that, under the given conditions, speaks for the attempt to realise a supranational democracy. It is not as if democracies confined within nation-states could preserve their democratic substance, as though they were unaffected by involvement in the systemic dynamics of a global society – at any rate not in Europe.

The gist of Habermas's argument is that one cannot close one's eyes to problems and issues which transcend the nation State. No amount of unilateral national legislation can resolve these and unilateral action may generate costs for other States that their citizens do not want. The Union, therefore, presents a more democratic option for regulation of these issues than national action as, on the one hand, it establishes a collective problem-solving capacity with calibrated democratic input, and, on the other, sensitivises national citizens to the concerns and needs of citizens elsewhere in the Union. The strength of this argument lies, in part, in its observation that nationalist accounts do not address sufficiently either limits of national State capacities or the intolerance of some nationalist discourse. It lies, also, in its emphasis that Union democracy has different foundations from those of nation States. For it is a political order which is different from that of the nation State and it is part of a democratic order which is composite, in which it seeks to supplement rather than supplant national democracies.

However, Habermas's argument does not deal with the specificities of the European Union as it can be applied to any issue anywhere with transnational dimensions.[192] Thus, it is an argument for involving Chinese or US citizens in EU decision-making insofar as its decisions affect them and for involving EU citizens, conversely, in the decision-making of these States. It can also not account for the many EU laws which do not address obvious transnational effects but seem to enjoy authority. EU equal opportunities legislation is a case in point.

Thus, there must be something more specific to the Union to justify its claim to democracy. Other authors have located this in a *choice* to be mutually dependent. This choice might be motivated in some circumstances by the scale of the problem to be addressed, whereas, in others, it will not. In all cases, the choice is made because it is believed that treating certain things as in common will result in

---

[192] It has been argued that the Union's greater interdependence might justify stronger reciprocal arrangements than elsewhere, D. Innerarity, 'Transnational Self-Determination: Resetting Self-Government in the Age of Interdependence' (2015) 53 *JCMS* 1061.

them being governed more democratically. That is to say that the treatment of a particular issue as a Union issue will lead to it being handled more democratically than if it was addressed nationally. This has been taken furthest by the *demoi-cracy* literature, which argues that the Union should be seen as a union of peoples (*demoi*) whereby democracy involves certain activities being decided in common by these peoples and certain things being left to unilateral action.[193]

F. Cheneval and K. Nicolaidis, 'The Social Construction of Demoicracy in the European Union' (2017) 16 *European Journal of Political Theory* 235, 245–6

Sovereign people in the international community are constituted both by internal recognition of its members' status and external recognition by other peoples. In circumstances of multiple demoi coexisting within one political order, the nature of this double-faced recognition of status changes. The very fact of democratic interdependence of the multiple peoples creates a new kind of deeper mutual recognition, while internal recognition is increasingly about distributing the costs/benefits of internalising the circumstances of such external recognition. While state sovereignty is by definition constituted by mutual recognition in the international system, in this story, it is popular sovereigns who ultimately constitute each other; from a political and legal point of view, they are only possible in a group.

It is only against this backdrop that constitutive rules take on their full import. In the EU context, they hold that the peoples are the *pouvoirs constituants* of the larger political unit, whose competences must be delegated case by case and unanimously by the peoples. The sovereignty of the peoples is respected and its pooling codified in an evolving mutual dependency. Firstly, this means that entry, exit and basic rules are in the competence of each people participating in the larger political unit. What exactly this entails procedurally can be debated, but at its core it means that their existence as sovereign peoples cannot be undone in the name of political incorporation into a larger unit – not against their own choice. Secondly, this means that the individual sovereign peoples hold the right to sit at the table of the sovereigns and to participate in common rule making. 'To sit at the table of the sovereign peoples' is a metaphor for common demoicratic rule-making in the areas delegated to the higher level by representative and direct democratic instruments. The term 'sovereignty of the peoples' (plural) expresses a procedural link of sovereigns constituting a common political unit. Other units, such as corporations, no matter how powerful in economic terms, are not possible members and co-deciders at the table of the sovereigns.

The key to such a construct is to sustain the tension between two concurrent requirements: legitimacy of separate, self-determined demoi on the one hand, and openness and interconnectedness implied in the notion of liberal democratic demoi, on the other hand. Demoicracy, in short, stands for the idea that separate sovereign peoples can freely affirm common political institutions and exercise political authority together within the institutional arrangement they have set up. In such a construct, citizens will vary widely in the manner in which they identify with what is in common but such identification needs to be analysed as horizontal – with other peoples – rather than purely vertical – with the EU.

Notwithstanding its many attractions, demoi-cracy leaves open the question of when an issue is to be treated as something in common (and decided at Union level) and when not.[194] This is

---

[193] K. Nicolaidis, 'European Demoicracy and Its Crisis' (2013) 51 *JCMS* 351; F. Cheneval and F. Schimmelfennig, 'The Case for Demoicracy in the European Union' (2013) 51 *JCMS* 334. For a related argument see R. Bellamy, 'A European Republic of Sovereign States: Sovereignty, Republicanism and the European Union' (2017) 16 *European Journal of Political Theory* 188.

[194] M. Ronzoni, 'The European Union as a Demoicracy: Really a Third Way' (2017) 16 *European Journal of Political Theory* 210; T. Hüller, 'Out of Time? The Democratic Limits of EU Demoicracy' (2016) 23 *JEPP* 1407.

because it acknowledges the issue is contested, but this may be too unspecified. We need some idea of when it may be more democratic for the Union to do something than for Member States, if only to allow us to recognise which arguments about Union action are plausible and which are not. This question of 'when it may be more democratic' cannot be ascertained simply by looking at the scale of the issue and seeing whether this has transnational effects, as this cannot explain and justify the particularity of EU action.[195] It must, instead, be that the Union pursues a certain ethos which, in certain circumstances, is democratically preferable to what is offered to nationals.

A number of authors have sought to identify this ethos.

The first and most established account is that the Union institutionalises an ethos of 'constitutional tolerance'.[196] This involves nationals acknowledging, on the one hand, the difference of foreigners, and, on the other, the value of this difference. This ethos extends beyond foreigners to acknowledging the difference and value of any traditionally underrepresented group within a Member States, be it ethnic, religious or racial minorities, LGBTQ communities, those with disabilities, women or the interests of future generations. A citizen is required not merely to recognise and respect interests, identity, needs and aspirations of these, but also to acknowledge that these are very different from her own, and that this diversity is valuable. However, this ethos extends beyond mutual recognition of one another. It insists that this difference is so valuable in how it enlarges our horizons that it is worth committing to common arrangements. The French citizen, thus, agrees to the Polish citizen having a say in the running of her life (and vice versa) because she recognises that the Polish citizens' difference so greatly enhances her own world view.

Secondly, it has been argued, that the Union secures a particular ethos of justice. In particular, only the European Union can secure, via democratic means, a market which is just. Van Parijs has argued that the European Union recognises that welfare cannot be secured by reliance on national markets alone. It has, therefore, established an EU market, the single market, and integrated it into wider international markets. It can secure the justice of this market order in ways that cannot easily be done by actors. It establishes the rules which allow goods to be transnationally traded. It can ensure, through competition and other laws, that the prices are transparent and reflect the social costs of production. And it can deal with the redistributive issues that accompany any market.[197]

Thirdly, it has been argued that the Union institutionalises a particular ethos of self-determination. Dawson and de Witte have argued that collective self-determination includes a right to challenge and contest the decisions that affect one's life.[198] To be sure, the value of this contestation lies in the influence that might be secured by it. It also lies, however, in the process of contestation. Contestation can generate support for the political structures enabling it, thereby preventing more dangerous social conflicts. It can lead to respect and understanding for other protagonists. And it can also be useful as a way of making the disempowered valued. For self-

---

[195] A. Somek, 'Europe: Political, not Cosmopolitan' (2014) 20 *ELJ* 142.

[196] J. Weiler, *The Constitution of Europe* (Cambridge University Press, 1999) esp. 332–48; M. Poiares Maduro, *We, the Court: The European Court of Justice and the European Economic Constitution* (Oxford, Hart, 1998) 166–74.

[197] P. van Parijs, 'Epilogue: Justifying Europe' in L. van Middelaar and P. Van Parijs (eds.), *After the Storm: How to Save Democracy in Europe* (Tielt, Lannoo, 2015). On what this ethos of justice might comprise see A. Sangiovanni, 'Solidarity in the European Union' (2013) 33 *OJLS* 213; F. de Witte, *Justice in the EU: The Emergence of Transnational Solidarity* (Oxford University Press, 2015).

[198] M. Dawson and F. de Witte, 'From Balance to Conflict: A New Constitution for the EU' (2016) 22 *ELJ* 204.

determination to happen, however, the terms of contestation must be transparent and mutually respectful. Traditional international relations prevents this, however. It allows the strong to bully the weak, and, even when this does not happen, arguments are framed in national terms, as a German, Czech or Greek position. This territorialisation of positions obscures the multiplicity of views held by Member State citizens and distorts the terms of contestation, thereby preventing collective self-determination. By contrast, the Union provides for the possibility of substantive contestation as it allows individuals and groups to align along more transparent axes: be it left versus right, socially conservative versus socially liberal, public ownership versus private etc.

These three ethoi justify EU lawmaking as they identify the democratic possibilities offered by a system of mutual dependence. However, they are also ideals against which the practice of EU lawmaking can be assessed. On that, it may well be that the Union does not perform very well. As we shall see, there are many EU laws which pursue neither constitutional tolerance nor justice. Equally, the Union's potential as a site for democratic deliberation and contestation is curbed by the dominance of executive actors within its legislative and quasi-legislative processes, notably the Commission and COREPER, and by the managerial and non-transparent approach that is taken to legislation in the trilogue.

A further challenge is the weight to be given to these ideals. This needs explaining with an example. Few, if any, would argue that it is ever democratically acceptable to adopt xenophobic or racist laws. Some restrictions on local choice imposed by the ethos of constitutional tolerance seem, therefore, unproblematic and desirable. However, how far do these restrictions on local choice extend? Would it require votes to be given in national elections to foreigners or any parliamentary legislation to be reconsidered if it failed to take account of a significant foreign interest? Many would baulk at this. If the exigencies of constitutional tolerance probably lie somewhere between these examples, it is still not clear where. As we shall see later, there is widespread debate about the circumstances when social benefits should be granted to citizens from other EU States.[199] These issues of weighting can be applied equally to the other justifications provided for mutual dependence. If a national parliament votes to default on debts to creditors in other EU States, whose investments in that parliament's State go to providing the pensions for citizens in other EU States, market justice would require this to be democratically worked out at the EU level. However, the defaulting State might say that, in the light of national parliamentary legislation, national democracy requires it not to recognise the interests of these creditors. Equally important, it is unclear who has the authority to do the weighing. The increasing contestation of the European Union and the growth of populist movement opposing the Union suggest that there are many who trust neither EU nor national institutions to do this well.[200]

One last challenge is that of democratic accountability. It is very difficult to change the EU lawmaker if one is unhappy with how it is doing its job.[201] To be sure, one can vote out one's MEP or the government that represents one in the Council of Ministers, but these are a small part of a much larger legislative apparatus. This is not simply a question of scale so one's vote counts for less. It is also to do with the EU legislative process being spread out across three different EU

---

[199] See pp. 484–95. On this A. Sangiovanni, 'Non-Discrimination, Free Movement, and In-Work Benefits in the European Union' (2017) 16 *European Journal of Political Theory* 143.

[200] P. de Wilde and M. Zürn, 'Can the Politicization of European Integration Be Reversed?' (2012) 50(S1) *JCMS* 137.

[201] S. Hix, *What's Wrong with the European Union and How to Fix It* (Oxford, Polity, 2008) ch. 5.

Institutions, of which one is unelected. It is, thus, never possible to talk of a moment when the EU legislature moved from the political right to the left (or vice versa). To compound matters, it is harder to change EU laws if one is unhappy with them. Within Member States, a simple majority of lawmakers is sufficient. Not in Brussels. A higher threshold is required in the Council, namely a QMV or unanimity vote, and one also needs to get the agreement of the Commission. The consequence has been that many voters transmit their dissatisfaction with an EU policy into a more general dissatisfaction with the EU itself. For, as they cannot change its personnel, the alternative is to change the organisation.[202]

FURTHER READING

G. Brandsma and J. Blom-Hansen, *Controlling the EU Executive? The Politics of Delegation in the European Union* (Oxford University Press, 2017).

F. Cheneval and F. Schimmelfennig, 'The Case for Demoicracy in the European Union' (2013) 51 *Journal of Common Market Studies* 334.

M. Cremona and C. Kilpatrick (eds.), *EU Legal Acts: Challenges and Transformations* (Oxford University Press, 2018).

M. Dawson and F. de Witte, 'From Balance to Conflict: A New Constitution for the EU' (2016) 22 *European Law Journal* 204.

D. Innerarity, *Democracy in Europe: A Political Philosophy of the EU* (Basingstoke, Palgrave Macmillan, 2018).

D. Jančić (ed.), *National Parliaments after the Lisbon Treaty and the Euro Crisis: Resilience or Resignation?* (Oxford University Press, 2017).

L. van Middelaar and P. Van Parijs (eds.), *After the Storm: How to Save Democracy in Europe* (Tielt, Lannoo, 2015).

C. Roederer-Rynning and J. Greenwood, 'The Culture of Trilogues' (2015) 22 *Journal of European Public Policy* 1148.

L. Senden, *Soft Law in European Community Law* (Oxford-Portland, Hart, 2004).

B. de Witte, A. Ott and E. Vos (eds.), *Between Flexibility and Disintegration: The Trajectory of Differentiation in EU Law* (Cheltenham, Edward Elgar, 2017).

---

[202] S. Hobolt and J. Tilley, *Blaming Europe? Responsibility without Accountability in the European Union* (Oxford University Press, 2014) 124–36.

4

The EU Judicial Order

CONTENTS

1   INTRODUCTION

This chapter looks at the judicial order of the Union: the Court of Justice and the relations between it and national courts and tribunals.

Section 2 considers the Court of Justice of the European Union, which comprises of two courts: the Court of Justice and the General Court. The Court of Justice gives single judgments usually in Chambers of three or five judges. Cases may come before in it a variety of ways. The procedure described at most length in this chapter is the preliminary reference procedure, which allows national courts to seek references from the Court of Justice on points of EU law. However, other central headings of jurisdiction include hearing enforcement actions brought against Member States for breach of EU law; adjudicating on disputes between the EU Institutions; giving opinions on the legality of international opinions and hearing appeals from the General Court. The General Court's caseload comes from three main sources: individuals seeking judicial review of the EU Institutions, appeals from the European Union Intellectual Property Office and disputes between EU Institutions and their employees.

Section 3 examines the architecture of the Union judicial order. At its heart is the preliminary reference procedure in Article 267 TFEU. This does not allow litigants direct access nor rights of appeal to the Court of Justice, rather it is for national courts – which continue to retain a monopoly over questions of fact and national law – to refer points of EU law to it. The Court has stated that the purpose of the procedure is to secure EU law as an autonomous legal order, and, in the light of this, has crafted a Union judicial order around this procedure. The autonomy of this procedure means that points of EU law can only be referred to the Court and all national courts have an unfettered and immediate right of reference. It also defines its own terms of membership such that the notion of 'court' includes not just courts, but a whole host of regulatory, professional and administrative bodies who also have the right to refer.

Section 4 considers the functions played by this judicial order. It contributes, first, to the development of EU law through national courts raising questions about the limits, contradictions and possibilities of EU law in the light of the litigation before them. Secondly, it is a central vehicle for judicial review of EU measures. Actors challenge implementation of an EU measure before a national court, which then questions the legality of the EU measure in a reference. Thirdly, it is central in preserving the uniformity of EU law. The Court of Justice claims an exclusive responsibility to declare EU measures invalid and to provide authoritative interpretations of EU law which bind courts and other administrative actors across the Union. Fourthly, it helps national courts resolve disputes involving EU law. Indeed the Court will not give a reference unless it is necessary to resolve a dispute.

Section 5 looks at how relations between the courts are managed within this judicial order. This is done, first, through setting out the circumstances when national courts must refer. This will be the case where national courts are a court against whose decision there is no judicial remedy in national law unless a materially identical question has already been decided by the Court (*acte éclairé*) or there is no reasonable doubt as to the interpretation of the provision of EU law (*acte clair*). It will also be the case if the national court thinks the EU measure is illegal. Secondly, it is done through legal effects being ascribed to judgments of the Court so that they bind all authorities in the Union, and not just the referring court.

Section 6 considers the status of the preliminary reference procedure and binding force of Court of Justice judgments after Brexit. During the transition period, the period between the day of Brexit and 31 December 2020, there will be little change from when the United Kingdom was a member of the European Union. Judgments of the Court will continue to bind UK courts and the preliminary reference procedure will continue to apply, albeit no UK court will be obliged to refer questions of EU law to the Court of Justice. The preliminary reference procedure will apply after the end of the transition period in respect of disputes whose facts occurred before the end of that period and, for eight years, in respect of the rights granted by the Withdrawal Agreement to Union citizens and their families resident in the United Kingdom at the moment of Brexit.

Judgments of the Court of Justice will, thereafter, continue to bind all UK courts other than the Supreme Court and the Scottish High Court of Justiciary on matters of retained EU law, the EU law and domestic law implementing or referring to it brought into or recognised as UK law by the European Union (Withdrawal Act). The Court's judgments do not bind them otherwise, although they may have regard to them insofar as they are relevant to any matter before them.

2 THE COURT OF JUSTICE OF THE EUROPEAN UNION

The Court of Justice currently comprises two courts: the Court of Justice and the General Court.

Article 19 TEU

(1) The Court of Justice of the European Union shall include the Court of Justice, the General Court and specialised courts. It shall ensure that in the interpretation and application of the Treaties the law is observed.

Member States shall provide remedies sufficient to ensure effective legal protection in the fields covered by Union law.

2 The Court of Justice shall consist of one judge from each Member State. It shall be assisted by the Advocates-General.

The General Court shall include at least one judge per Member State.

The Judges and the Advocates-General of the Court of Justice and the Judges of the General Court shall be chosen from persons whose independence is beyond doubt and who satisfy the conditions set out in Articles 253 and 254 TFEU. They shall be appointed by common accord of the governments of the Member States for six years. Retiring Judges and Advocates-General may be reappointed.

3 The Court of Justice of the European Union shall, in accordance with the Treaties:
  (a) rule on actions brought by a Member State, an institution or a natural or legal person;
  (b) give preliminary rulings, at the request of courts or tribunals of the Member States, on the interpretation of Union law or the validity of acts adopted by the institutions;
  (c) rule in other cases provided for in the Treaties.

Article 19 TEU merely provides a barebones description of these courts and the scope of their powers. As such, we will first consider who they are before examining what they do.

(i) The Court of Justice

The Court of Justice is made up of twenty-seven judges, one from each Member State. These are appointed for a renewable period of six years and are required to be persons whose independence is beyond doubt and who are either suitable for the highest judicial office in their respective countries or 'jurisconsults of recognised competence'.[1] Judges come from a variety of backgrounds with only a few having senior judicial experience before taking up their posts. The most detailed study of this found that 27 per cent had previously been civil servants, 19 per cent academics and 7 per cent were in private practice before being appointed. Surprisingly, only

---

[1] See also Article 253 TFEU. This is done on a three-yearly cycle, so that every three years half the Court is replaced.

28 per cent had been national judges.[2] There have, historically, been few women judges – in 2018, only seven, out of the thirty-nine judges and Advocates General of the Court of Justice are female.[3] Moreover, there has been no representation of racial or ethnic minorities.

Both the new judges and those seeking renewal of their term are nominated by individual governments and then appointed by the 'common accord' of the national governments.[4] To prevent a perception of over-politicisation of the process and to ensure that any candidate has the requisite expertise, a Panel comprising members of the Court of Justice and members of national supreme courts is consulted beforehand.[5] The Panel has indicated that it will look, *inter alia*, at the legal expertise of any candidate, their language skills and their ability to make an effective contribution quickly. More controversial is the requirement of professional experience because candidates with less than twenty years under their belt are unlikely to be favourably viewed for a judicial position at the Court of Justice.[6] The authority of the members of this Panel means that a negative opinion given by it acts as a *de facto* veto.[7] The Panel is no stranger to exercising this veto power: of the eighty opinions given between 2014 and 2018, seven were unfavourable.[8] Although reasons are given for its opinions, Panel deliberations are confidential. It is not clear why the Panel believes that it should be the one determining the criteria to be a judge, as opposed to national parliaments and governments or EU Institutions. That said, Article 255 TFEU has led to a welcome formalisation of the appointment procedures. In this regard, national governments, keen not to be embarrassed by a subsequent negative Panel opinion, engage far more in open and formal selection procedures before making a nomination.[9]

The Court works under the principle of collegiality, in which a single judgment is given. This has been criticised on the grounds that the compromises required for a single judgment affect the quality of legal reasoning, with the result that the Court often seems neither to counter a point nor consider a question and providing reasoning of 'a lowest common denominator' quality.[10] On the other hand, the principle of collegiality prevents Member States from undermining the authority of a judgment by pointing to sympathetic dissenting opinions of their national judge. Members of the Court also argue that there is value in consensus and that it allows for differing national legal traditions to filter through to the judgment.[11] However, Zhang's pioneering work suggests this is highly questionable. The basis for judicial deliberation is a draft which is written by one judge, the

---

[2] A. Zhang, 'The Faceless Court' (2016–17) 38 *University of Pennsylvania Journal of International Law* 71, 87.

[3] https://curia.europa.eu/jcms/jcms/Jo2_7026/en/.   [4] Article 19(2) TEU.

[5] Article 255 TFEU. The procedures are explored in depth in M. Bobek (ed.), *Selecting Europe's Judges: A Critical Review of the Appointment Procedures* (Oxford University Press, 2015), in particular the chapters by de Waele, Sauvé, Alemanno and Petkova.

[6] *Fifth Activity Report of the panel provided for by Article 255 TFEU* (Luxembourg, Court of Justice, 2018) 25–31.

[7] Opinions have always been followed by national governments, *ibid.* 14.

[8] *Ibid.* All were on first appointments rather than renewals with five relating to the General Court and two to the Court of Justice

[9] T. Dumbrovsky, B. Petkova and M. Van Der Sluis, 'Judicial Appointments: The Article 255 TFEU Advisory Panel and Selection Procedures in the Member States' (2014) 51 *CMLRev* 455, 466–81.

[10] J. Weiler, 'Je Suis Achbita!' (2018) 28 *EJIL* 989, 1002. See also H. Rasmussen and L. Rasmussen, 'Comment on Katalin Kelemen – Activist EU Court "Feeds" on the Existing Ban on Dissenting Opinions: Lifting the Ban is Likely to Improve the Quality of EU Judgments' (2013) 14 *German LJ* 1373.

[11] E.g. F. Jacobs, 'Advocates General and Judges in the European Court of Justice: Some Personal Reflections' in D. O'Keeffe and A. Bavasso (eds.), *Judicial Review in European Union Law: Liber Amicorum Lord Slynn* (The Hague, Boston and London, Kluwer Law International, 2000) vol. I; K. Lenaerts, 'The Court's Outer and Inner Selves: Exploring the External and Internal Legitimacy of the European Court of Justice' in M. Adams *et al.* (eds.), *Judging Europe's Judges: The Legitimacy of the Case Law of the European Court of Justice* (Oxford, Bloomsbury, 2013).

juge rapporteur. Zhang finds a number of judges admit that work levels mean that they focus on the judgments in which they are *juges rapporteur*, inputting little into other judgments.[12]

The Court is assisted by eleven Advocates General.[13] The same procedures for and conditions of appointment apply to them as to judges of the Court of Justice. The Advocate General is to make, in open court, impartial and independent submissions on any case brought before the Court.[14] She acts not as a legal representative of one of the parties, but as a legal representative of the public interest. These opinions are adopted in advance of the judgment to allow the Court sufficient time to consider them. They often provide a more detailed analysis of the context and the argument than is found in the judgment of the Court itself. However, they are not binding on the Court, although they are often referred to by the Court of Justice in its judgments. Furthermore, even when the conclusions reached are similar, it is difficult to know whether the same reasoning is adopted, given that the opinion is often discursive in nature whilst the judgment itself is very terse.

Cases are rarely decided by the full Court. It only sits in cases of 'exceptional importance' or where it is to rule on a senior EU official being deprived of office for not meeting the requisite conditions.[15] Between 2012 and 2017, only two judgments were given by the full Court.[16] Instead, most cases are heard by Chambers of judges. The judges elect the President from amongst themselves.[17] His central responsibility is to determine the case list and allocate cases between the Chambers.[18] The largest Chamber is the Grand Chamber, which will comprise fifteen judges. This will sit when a Member State or EU Institution party to the proceedings requests it.[19] This is still rare, accounting for just 7.32 per cent of completed cases between 2013 and 2017.[20] Instead, the vast majority of cases (over 90 per cent) are heard by Chambers of either three or five judges.[21]

Article 19(1) TEU states that the Court 'shall ensure that in the interpretation and application of the Treaties the law is observed'. Whilst this may suggest a general jurisdiction for the Court of Justice over both Treaties, in practice, it is subject to three forms of exclusion:

- It shall not have jurisdiction in the field of the common foreign and security policy.[22]
- In judicial cooperation in criminal matters and police cooperation, it shall have no jurisdiction to review the validity or proportionality of operations carried out by the police or other

---

[12] A. Zhang, 'The Faceless Court', mimeo, September 2015, 24–5; A. Zhang, J. Liu and N. Garoupa, 'Judging in Europe: Do Legal Traditions Matter?' (2018) 14 *Journal of Competition Law and Economics* 144.

[13] Article 252 TFEU and Decision 2013/336/EU increasing the number of Advocates-General of the Court of Justice of the European Union, OJ 2013, L 179/92. See also I. Solanke, 'The Advocate General: Assisting the CJEU of Article 13 TEU to Secure Trust and Democracy' (2012) 14 *CYEL* 697; J. Frankenreiter, 'Are Advocates General Political? An Empirical Analysis of the Voting Behavior of the Advocates General at the European Court of Justice' (2018) 14 *Review of Law and Economics* 1.

[14] Article 252 TFEU.

[15] The rules on the full Court and the Grand Chamber are set out in Article 251 TFEU and the Statute of the Court of Justice of the European Union, Article 16.

[16] *Annual Report of Judicial Activity 2017* (Luxembourg, Publications Office of the European Union, 2018) 107.

[17] Article 253(3) TFEU. The Presidency is for a three-year term and the President in 2018 was a Belgian, Judge Lenaerts.

[18] The President also chairs the Grand Chamber, determines the *juge rapporteur* for individual cases, and is responsible for interim measures.

[19] Statute of the Court of Justice, Article 16.   [20] *Annual Report*, n. 16 above, 107.

[21] *Ibid.* For evidence that these Chambers behave in very different ways see M. Malecki, 'Do ECJ judges All Speak with the Same Voice? Evidence of Divergent Preferences from the Judgments of Chambers' (2012) 19 *JEPP* 59.

[22] Articles 24(1) TEU and 275 TFEU. It can, however, rule on the limits of CFSP relative to other parts of the Treaties and refer back to the CFSP to determine the legality of EU sanctions as the latter rely on a decision being first taken under the former before sanctions can be adopted under the TFEU, *R* v. *HM Treasury, ex parte Rosneft*, C-72/15, EU: C:2017:236.

law-enforcement services of a Member State or the exercise of the responsibilities incumbent upon Member States with regard to the maintenance of law and order and the safeguarding of internal security.[23]

- If measures are taken to expel a Member State, the Court of Justice can rule on the procedure but not the substance of the grounds for expulsion.[24]

The Court's jurisdiction is further restricted by the rules on *locus standi* which determine when parties can bring actions before it. Matters can come before it in a variety of ways:

- *Preliminary references from national courts*: National courts may, or in some cases must, refer a point of EU law to the Court of Justice if it is necessary to decide the dispute. The Court of Justice will give judgment on the point of EU law, which the national judge will apply to the dispute in hand.[25]
- *Enforcement actions against Member States*: The Commission, or in rare cases another Member State, can bring a Member State before the Court of Justice for a declaration that the latter is in breach of EU law.[26] If a Member State fails to comply with a Court of Justice judgment, the Commission can bring it back before the Court in order to have it fined for its behaviour.[27]
- *Judicial review of EU Institutions by other EU Institutions and judicial review of the Parliament or Council by Member States.*[28]
- *Opinions on the conclusion of international agreements*: The Council, Parliament, Commission or any Member State can ask for an opinion of the Court as to whether the Union has lawfully concluded a draft treaty. If the Court rules that the international agreement is illegal, it can only enter into force if the treaty is first amended.[29]
- *Appeals from the General Court on points of law.*[30]

These procedures are discussed in more detail in subsequent chapters. For present purposes, it is sufficient to note that when combined, they make a substantial docket. In 2017 alone, the Court of Justice disposed of 654 cases and gave 466 judgments.[31]

(ii) The General Court

Unlike the Court of Justice, the General Court is not confined to a single judge from each Member State.[32] From 1 September 2019, it will comprise two judges per Member State.[33] The General Court does not sit as a full Court. It can sit as a Grand Chamber, composed of fifteen judges,[34] in cases where the issue is legally difficult, important, or 'special circumstances so justify'.[35] Usually, the General Court hears cases in Chambers of three or five judges.[36] In principle, the full Court decides which of these will hear the case,[37] but a Member State or EU Institution party to proceedings can insist that a case be heard by a Chamber of five judges.[38] The overwhelming

---

[23] Article 276 TFEU.   [24] Article 269 TFEU.   [25] Article 267 TFEU.   [26] Articles 258 and 259 TFEU.
[27] Article 260 TFEU.
[28] There are limited exceptions for national actions against Council exercise of delegated powers, Council measures authorising State aids, and Council measures defining the common commercial policy. These go to the General Court. Statute of the Court of Justice of the European Union, Article 51.
[29] Article 218(11) TFEU.   [30] Article 256(1) TFEU.   [31] *Annual Report*, n. 16 above, 106.   [32] Article 19(2) TEU.
[33] Protocol 3 of the Statute of the Court of Justice, as amended by Regulation 2015/2422, OJ 2015, L 341/14, Article 48.
[34] Rules of Procedure of the General Court, OJ 2015, L 105/1, Article 15(1) as amended by OJ 2016, L 217/71.
[35] *Ibid*. Article 28(1).   [36] *Ibid*. Article 13(1).   [37] *Ibid*. Article 28(3)–(4).   [38] *Ibid*. Article 28(5).

proportion of cases are heard by Chambers of three judges.[39] A single judge can give judgments in actions brought by private parties, where the Court has jurisdiction by virtue of an arbitration agreement, or where it is hearing an appeal from the Board of Appeals of the EU Intellectual Property Office. However, the case must be of limited importance, not raise difficult questions of law and fact and not concern measures of either a general nature or implementing measures in certain fields.[40] These restrictions mean that it is rare for single judges to give judgments.[41]

The General Court's jurisdiction covers the following:

- appeals from decisions of the European Union Intellectual Property Office[42] (This agency is responsible for the grant of two types of intellectual property right, Union trademarks and Community designs. There is an internal system of appeal to the Board of Appeals within this agency. Its decisions can be challenged before the General Court who can annul them.[43] These now can constitute the bulk of the General Court's work, amounting to 376 out of its 654 cases in 2017.[44])
- judicial review by individuals of actions or illegal action by EU Institutions and agencies or action for non-contractual damages against the EU Institutions[45]
- actions by Member States against the Commission, the European Central Bank (ECB) and the European Council[46]
- matters referred to the Court of Justice under an arbitration clause[47]
- disputes between EU Institutions, agencies and bodies and their employees.[48]

Jurisdiction over these matters results in the General Court being the key actor in the development of administrative principles of due process. Given that much of competition, intellectual property and external trade law is developed through challenges by private parties adversely affected by EU measures, the General Court is also the central judicial institution in these fields. The General Court's previous struggle to keep up with its docket led to reforms in 2015 which doubled the size of the Court.[49] It is also required to report on how it will use these effectively and establish specialised chambers.[50] The intention, therefore, is that the General Court will decide more cases and become more specialised, with particular Chambers dedicated to issues such as intellectual property or staff cases. It has also been suggested that the reforms might allow more cases to be decided by five-judge Chambers with a corresponding increase in the quality of judgment.[51] The jury is still out on these reforms. On the one hand, the rationales make

---

[39] 83.91% of cases in 2017 were heard by these. *Annual Report*, n. 16 above, 214.

[40] Rules of Procedure of the General Court, n. 34 above, Article 29. The excluded fields are State aids, mergers, agriculture and trade with non-EU States.

[41] No judgments were given in 2017 and 5 in 2016. *Annual Report*, n. 16 above, 214.

[42] Regulation 40/94/EC on the Community trade mark, OJ 2004, L 70/1, Article 63.

[43] Regulation 6/2002 on Community designs, OJ 2002, L 3/1; Regulation 2017/1001 on the European Union trade mark, OJ 2017, L 154/1, Article 72.

[44] *Annual Report*, n. 16 above, 213.   [45] Articles 263(4), 265(3), 268 and 340(2) TFEU.

[46] Articles 263 and 265 TFEU. Protocol on the Statute of the Court of Justice, Article 51. There is a limited exception for challenges against Commission authorisation of enhanced cooperation. These go to the Court of Justice.

[47] Article 272 TFEU.

[48] Protocol 3 to the Statute of the Court of Justice, Article 50a as amended by Regulation 2016/1192 on the transfer to the General Court of jurisdiction at first instance in disputes between the European Union and its servants, OJ 2016, L 200/137.

[49] Regulation 2015/2422. On the context and debate see A. Alemanno and L. Pech, 'Thinking Justice Outside the Docket: A Critical Assessment of The Reform of the EU's Court System' (2017) 54 *CMLRev* 129, 133–41.

[50] Regulation 2015/2422, Article 3(1).   [51] On this point see Alemanno and Pech, n. 49 above, 157–8.

a lot of sense but, on the other hand, there is the risk that specialisation could lead to fragmentation of the case law and coordination issues within the General Court. There will also be issues about recruiting good-quality judges. Finally, it is not clear that churning out case law is conducive to good law.

There is a right to appeal on points of law from the General Court to the Court of Justice within two months of notification of the decision.[52] This right exists both for parties to the dispute and Member States and EU Institutions where these intervened and the decision directly affects them.[53] An appeal will only be upheld if the mistake of law relates to the operative part of the judgment which cannot be justified on other legal grounds.[54] Between 2013 and 2017, 22 per cent of General Court judgments – which is a rather high number – were appealed; only about one in six of these successful.[55] These statistics tell only part of the story, as differences on significant and controversial areas of law have emerged between the two courts.[56]

If the Court of Justice finds the appeal to be well-founded, it will quash the decision of the General Court. It can then give final judgment or refer the matter back to the General Court. If it does the latter, the General Court is bound by the Court of Justice's decision on the point of law.[57] The General Court takes the view that it is formally only bound by the judgments of the Court where this happens and the matter is referred back, or the principle of *res judicata* operates: namely a dispute involving the same parties, subject matter and cause of action as one already decided by the Court of Justice comes back before it.[58]

Nevertheless, the circumstances in which the General Court will not follow judgments of the Court of Justice are rare since it sees judgments of the latter as highly authoritative. In *Kadi*, the General Court acknowledged criticisms of an earlier Court of Justice judgment,[59] which allowed EU law to ignore international law on sanctions. Nevertheless, it noted that this judgment was made by the Grand Chamber and had established general principles for EU law. In such circumstances, the General Court opined that any change in EU law had to be made by the Court of Justice amending its earlier judgment.[60] This suggests that the General Court feels that it has more room for action where the reasoning of any judgment of the Court of Justice is more confined or the judgment was made by a Chamber of three or five judges. In other circumstances, it will do no more than agitate for change. This might both act as a curb on Court of Justice power and a vehicle for greater debate. However, it could also be seen as undermining the authority of the Court of Justice.

---

[52] Article 256(1) TFEU. [53] Statute of the Court of Justice, Article 56.

[54] *Artegodan* v. *Commission*, C-221/10 P, EU:C:2012:216; *Commission* v. *United Kingdom*, C-584/10 P, C-593/10 P and C-595/10 P, EU:C:2013:518.

[55] *Annual Report*, n. 16 above, 223–5. The number of successful or partially successful appeals was thus 130 out of 839 appeals.

[56] There have been strong differences, for example, over the rules on *locus standi* of private parties to challenge EU acts and the information which should be made available to those wishing to defend themselves against EU sanctions, *Jégo-Quéré* v. *Commission*, T-177/01, EU:T:2002:112; *Commission* v. *Jégo-Quéré*, C-263/02 P, EU:C:2004:210; *Kadi* v. *Commission*, T-85/09, EU:T:2010:418; *Commission and United Kingdom* v. *Kadi*, C-584/10 P, C-593/10 P and C-595/10 P, EU:C:2013:518.

[57] Statute of the Court of Justice, Article 61. [58] *Sekula Aćimović* v. *Republic of Slovenia*, T-88/14, EU:T:2014:156.

[59] *Kadi and Al Barakaat International Foundation* v. *Council and Commission*, C-402/05 P and C-415/05 P.

[60] *Kadi* v. *Commission*, T-85/09, EU:T:2010:418, para. 121.

3 THE ARCHITECTURE OF THE EU JUDICIAL ORDER

(i) Article 267 TFEU and its Progenies

Litigation of EU law occurs not just before these two Union courts but, as we will see in more detail later,[61] before national courts also. The latter are more numerous, have greater resources and are more accessible to individual litigants. The EU judicial order must thus be seen as a system of administration of justice which comprises both Union and domestic courts. Indeed, Article 19(1) TEU alludes to this by stating that Member States must provide remedies sufficient to ensure effective legal protection.

The institutional relations between the Court of Justice and domestic courts are set out in Article 267 TFEU.

Article 267 TFEU

The Court of Justice of the European Union shall have jurisdiction to give preliminary rulings concerning:
(a) the interpretation of the Treaties;
(b) the validity and interpretation of acts of the institutions, bodies, offices or agencies of the Union;
Where such a question is raised before any court or tribunal of a Member State, that court or tribunal may, if it considers that a decision on the question is necessary to enable it to give judgment, request the Court to give a ruling thereon.

Where any such question is raised in a case pending before a court or tribunal of a Member State against whose decisions there is no judicial remedy under national law, that court or tribunal shall bring the matter before the Court.

If such a question is raised in a case pending before a court or tribunal of a Member State with regard to a person in custody, the Court of Justice of the European Union shall act with the minimum of delay.

The provision seems technical, doing no more than setting out terms of engagement between the Court of Justice and national courts. It is, however, one of the most central provisions in the Treaties, and has been developed by the Court of Justice to develop a pan-Union system of administration of justice with its own rules of jurisdiction, allocation of responsibilities, judicial hierarchies, and collective goals.

This pan-Union judicial order can be seen as simply comprising the Court of Justice and all those bodies recognised as national courts or tribunals under Article 267 TFEU. In recent years, however, it has become more permeable with a number of wider arrangements subject to the jurisdiction of the Court of Justice.

Three Association Agreements – those between the Union and Georgia, Moldova and Ukraine – provide for disagreements between these States and the Union over the interpretation and application of their respective agreements to be resolved by arbitration. In a number of fields,

---

[61] See Ch. 7.

the Arbitration Panel must refer the matter to the Court of Justice and is bound by its ruling. The relevant provision from the EU–Moldova agreement is set out below.[62]

Article 403

(1) The procedures set out in this Article shall apply to disputes concerning the interpretation and application of a provision of this Agreement relating to gradual approximation contained in Chapter 3 (Technical Barriers to Trade), Chapter 4 (Sanitary and Phytosanitary Measures), Chapter 5 (Customs and Trade Facilitation), Chapter 6 (Establishment, Trade in Services and Electronic Commerce), Chapter 8 (Public Procurement) or Chapter 10 (Competition) of Title v. (Trade and Trade-related Matters) of this Agreement, or which otherwise imposes upon a Party an obligation defined by reference to a provision of Union law.

(2) Where a dispute raises a question of interpretation of a provision of Union law referred to in paragraph 1, the arbitration panel shall not decide the question, but request the Court of Justice of the European Union to give a ruling on the question. In such cases, the deadlines applying to the rulings of the arbitration panel shall be suspended until the Court of Justice of the European Union has given its ruling. The ruling of the Court of Justice of the European Union shall be binding on the arbitration panel.

Whilst this arbitration panel does not form part of the EU judicial order, these agreements undoubtedly set up a judicial order which is governed by EU law and the Court of Justice. The procedure is distinct from that in Article 267 TFEU not simply because it involves an Arbitration Panel but because the Court of Justice decides all aspects of the dispute, and not simply points of EU law as is the case with Article 267 TFEU. The Arbitration Panel acts as no more than a transmission belt for the Court of Justice. It passes the matter on, and, after that, the matter is the exclusive responsibility of the Court of Justice.

There is also the case of the Unified Patent Court. The background to this court is that the European Patent Convention, a 1973 international agreement currently ratified by thirty-eight States, allows for the grant and registration of European patents at the European Patent Office, in Munich.[63] These patents are protected by the national patent laws of each Member State with consequence that the scope of protection varies according to the national law in question. In 2012, all EU States, except Croatia, Poland and Spain, agreed to rectify this by providing that these patents will have uniform protection and equal effect in all of them, and two EU Regulations were adopted to that effect by enhanced cooperation.[64] To oversee this regime, these States signed an international agreement establishing the Unified Patent Court.[65] This court is

---

[62] Association Agreement between the European Union and the European Atomic Energy Community and their Member States, of the one part, and the Republic of Moldova, of the other part, OJ 2014, L 260/4. See also Association Agreement between the European Union and its Member States, of the one part, and Ukraine, of the other part, Article 322, OJ 2014, L 161/3; Associate Agreement between the European Union and the European Atomic Energy Community and their Member States, of the one part, and Georgia, of the other part, Article 267, OJ 2014, L 261/4. The subject matter is a little different in the last case as the Agreement provides for Georgia to approximate its law to EU law in many fields. Failure to do so (or dispute about this) leads to a reference by the Panel.

[63] http://documents.epo.org/projects/babylon/eponet.nsf/0/029F2DA107DD667FC125825F005311DA/$File/EPC_16th_edition_2016_en.pdf.

[64] Regulation 1257/2012 of the European Parliament and of the Council implementing enhanced cooperation in the area of the creation of unitary patent protection, OJ 2012, L 361/1; Regulation 1260/2012 implementing enhanced cooperation in the area of the creation of unitary patent protection with regard to the applicable translation arrangements, OJ 2012, L 361/89.

[65] Agreement on a Unified Patent Court ('UPC'), OJ 2013, C 175/01.

not yet established,[66] but it will be bound by Court of Justice judgments and can seek rulings from it.[67] It establishes a judicial order which involves one non-EU State (the United Kingdom) and does not include all EU States, but will be heavily governed by EU law.

Finally, as we shall see, after Brexit, the United Kingdom will be a non-EU State but its courts will still be subject to the jurisdiction of the Court of Justice for a considerable period.[68] During the transitional period lasting until 31 December 2020, Article 267 TFEU shall continue to apply within the United Kingdom so that its courts can or must request a ruling on points of EU law from the Court of Justice if that point is necessary to decide a dispute before them,[69] and its judgments will be binding on them.[70] This possibility to refer is extended for eight years after the end of the transition period in respect of cases concerning the rights granted to Union citizens who were resident in the United Kingdom at the time of Brexit.[71]

(ii) The Structuring of Interaction between the Court of Justice and National Courts by Article 267 TFEU

Although Article 267 TFEU sets out when national courts are to refer EU law to the Court of Justice and the consequences of its judgments for them, it is still for the national court to decide the merits of the dispute. As such, not only will they decide pertinent points of national law but, even more centrally, the facts of the dispute and thus they decide how to apply EU law to the dispute.[72] It is clear that the Court of Justice will not look behind the facts presented to it by them. In *WWF*, a challenge was made to the transformation of the military airport in Bolzano, Italy into a commercial airport because there had been a failure to carry out an environmental impact assessment. The airport authorities argued that the facts presented by the national court were inaccurate and that, under Italian law, it had exceeded its jurisdiction by considering these questions of fact. The Court dismissed these arguments. It noted that it was for the national court to ascertain the facts and that it was not the Court of Justice's role to examine whether the reference had been made in accordance with national laws on court jurisdiction and procedure.[73]

Alongside this, Article 267 TFEU is a court-to-court procedure in which national courts act as gatekeepers to the Court. Private parties have no direct access to the Court of Justice, nor can they appeal against decisions of the national courts to the Court of Justice. However, when the reference has been made and is being heard by the Court, alongside Member States and EU Institutions, parties to the dispute can present arguments to it. The Court has thus characterised the procedure as:

> a non-contentious procedure excluding any initiative of the parties who are merely invited to be heard in the course of this procedure.[74]

---

[66] The international agreement has not entered into effect as one of the conditions is that the three States in which the highest number of European patents have effect, Article 89 UPC. On 1 August 2018, sixteen States had ratified it but Germany has not yet done so, and it is one of those three States.

[67] Articles 20 and 21 UPC.   [68] For more detail see pp. 197–200.   [69] Withdrawal Agreement, Article 86(2).

[70] *Ibid*. Article 89(1).   [71] *Ibid*. Article 158(1).

[72] *Foglia* v. *Novello*, 104/79, EU:C:1980:73. The national court is even free to change its mind and take a different view of the facts subsequent to making the reference if it so chooses, *Ogyanov*, C-614/14, EU:C:2016:514.

[73] *WWF* v. *Autonome Provinz Bozen*, C-435/97, EU:C:1999:418. See also *Mahdi*, C-146/14 PPU, EU:C:2014:1320.

[74] *Montis Design* v. *Goossens Meubelen*, C-169/15, EU:C:2016:383, Opinion of Advocate General Campos Sánchez-Bordona, para. 45.

The role of individual parties is confined to generating the dispute before the national court which may potentially lead to the reference and to submitting observations to the Court of Justice when a reference is indeed made.[75] However, it is for the national court to decide whether or not to refer in the first place. It can do this of its own motion, and irrespective of the wishes of the parties[76] or even without hearing the parties.[77] Furthermore, these cannot change the tenor of the question referred by the national court as the latter has exclusive responsibility for this.[78]

The reference takes the form of a question or a number of questions about EU law. The national court has a freedom as to how to do this, but the Court of Justice has tried to discipline this by providing detailed suggestions as to how this is best done.

Recommendations to national courts and tribunals in relation to the initiation of preliminary ruling proceedings[79]

14 The request for a preliminary ruling may be in any form allowed by national law in respect of procedural issues, but it should be borne in mind that that request serves as the basis of the proceedings before the Court and is served on all the interested persons referred to in [the Statute of the Court] ... Owing to the consequential need to translate it into all the official languages of the European Union, the request for a preliminary ruling should therefore be drafted simply, clearly and precisely by the referring court or tribunal, avoiding superfluous detail. As experience has shown, about 10 pages are often sufficient to set out adequately the legal and factual context of a request for a preliminary ruling.

15 The content of any request for a preliminary ruling is prescribed by Article 94 of the Rules of Procedure of the Court and is summarised in the annex hereto. In addition to the text of the questions referred to the Court for a preliminary ruling, the request for a preliminary ruling must contain:
    – a summary of the subject matter of the dispute and the relevant findings of fact as determined by the referring court or tribunal, or, at the very least, an account of the facts on which the questions referred are based,
    – the tenor of any national provisions applicable in the case and, where appropriate, the relevant national case-law, and
    – a statement of the reasons which prompted the referring court or tribunal to inquire about the interpretation or validity of certain provisions of EU law, and the relationship between those provisions and the national legislation applicable to the main proceedings.[80]
    In the absence of one or more of the above, the Court may have to decline jurisdiction to give a preliminary ruling on the questions referred or dismiss the request for a preliminary ruling as inadmissible.

16 In its request for a preliminary ruling, the referring court or tribunal must provide precise references for the national provisions applicable to the facts of the dispute in the main proceedings, and accurately identify the provisions of EU law whose interpretation is sought or whose validity is challenged. The request should

---

[75] Rules of Procedure of the Court of Justice, OJ 2012, L 265/1, as amended by OJ 2013, L 173/65 and OJ 2016, L 217/69, Article 96. Parties who did not participate in the proceedings before the national court cannot intervene before the Court of Justice, *Football Association Premier League and Others* v. *QC Leisure and Others*, C-403/08, EU:C:2009:789.

[76] *Huet* v. *Université de Bretagne occidentale*, C-251/11, EU:C:2012:133.

[77] *Secretary of State for Work and Pensions* v. *Tolley*, C-430/15, EU:C:2017:74.

[78] *Vlaamse Dierenartsenvereniging and Janssens*, C-42/10, C-45/10 and C-57/10, EU:C:2010:107. The Court of Justice will not, thus, look behind the statement provided by the national court, irrespective of how well or poorly the latter is conducting proceedings. For criticism see G. Butler and U. Šadl, 'The Preliminaries of a Reference' (2018) 43 *ELRev* 120.

[79] OJ 2018, C 257/1.   [80] These three indents repeat the requirements in Article 94 of the Rules of Procedure.

include, if need be, a brief summary of the relevant arguments of the parties to the main proceedings. It is helpful to bear in mind in that context that it is only the request for a preliminary ruling that will be translated, not any annexes to that request.

17   The referring court or tribunal may also briefly state its view on the answer to be given to the questions referred for a preliminary ruling. That information may be useful to the Court, particularly where it is called upon to give a preliminary ruling in an expedited or urgent procedure.

This statement frames the dispute. The Court of Justice cannot look behind it and will, indeed, sometimes look to it, rather than the explicit questions set out by the national court in providing its judgment.[81] Furthermore, the quality of the statement is increasingly becoming a precondition for the Court of Justice accepting a reference. The Court has stated that national courts must scrupulously observe the requirements to provide a summary of the subject matter of the dispute; the tenor of the applicable national law; and the reasons for the reference.[82] If there is no substantial attempt to provide all of these, the reference will be refused.[83] That said, this is largely still something of a paper requirement.

(iii)   The Autonomy of the EU Judicial Order

To many litigants, the national judge appears as the central figure in Article 267 TFEU, with whom they have direct relations as she is the one resolving their dispute. The Court of Justice's role appears analogous to that of the expert witness: it is called in to supply expertise on the EU law relevant to the dispute, but is something of a third party since the national court still has to apply this expertise to the dispute. Such a perspective only tells part of the story.

The other perspective is a systemic one in which the Court of Justice has used Article 267 TFEU to fashion a pan-Union court system, with its own judicial hierarchies, procedures and courts, and the Court of Justice sitting at the apex of this court system. Within this systemic perspective, the Court of Justice is a very significant player. It sets out national courts' relations with itself, with each other and, as we shall see in future chapters, with their litigants and other arms of government. The Court of Justice has achieved this by stating that EU law is an autonomous legal order which must be secured by Article 267 TFEU. This mission is then used to interpret the scope of Article 267 TFEU, with that provision rapidly becoming all about establishing an autonomous Union judicial order.

There are a number of dimensions to this.

The first is that the Court of Justice sits at the apex of this judicial order. This entails that it is subject to only limited controls by another court or dispute settlement body. *Opinion 2/13* arose out of a 2013 international agreement for European Union accession to the European Convention on Human Rights (ECHR).[84] This agreement provided, *inter alia*, that actions against the Union could be brought before the European Court of Human Rights (ECtHR) for breach of the

---

[81]   *Lindfors*, C-365/02, EU:C:2004:449.   [82]   *Talasca*, C-19/14, EU:C:2014:2049.

[83]   *Vivium*, C-250/15, EU:C:2015:569. On this see N. Wahl and L. Prete, 'The Gatekeepers of Article 267 TFEU: On Jurisdiction and Admissibility of References for Preliminary Rulings' (2018) 55 *CMLRev* 511, 537–9.

[84]   There is a requirement in EU law, as yet unmet, that the Union accede, Article 6(2) TEU.

ECHR and for that court's judgments to be executed within the Union. In this respect, the rights recognised in the ECHR form general principles of EU law and many are also identically worded to those in the EU Charter.[85]

European Convention for the Protection of Human Rights and Fundamental Freedoms, Opinion 2/13, EU:C:2014:2454[86]

176 The judicial system as thus conceived has as its keystone the preliminary ruling procedure provided for in Article 267 TFEU, which, by setting up a dialogue between one court and another, specifically between the Court of Justice and the courts and tribunals of the Member States, has the object of securing uniform interpretation of EU law . . . thereby serving to ensure its consistency, its full effect and its autonomy as well as, ultimately, the particular nature of the law established by the Treaties . . .

182 an international agreement providing for the creation of a court responsible for the interpretation of its provisions and whose decisions are binding on the institutions, including the Court of Justice, is not, in principle, incompatible with EU law; that is particularly the case where, as in this instance, the conclusion of such an agreement is provided for by the Treaties themselves. The competence of the EU in the field of international relations and its capacity to conclude international agreements necessarily entail the power to submit to the decisions of a court which is created or designated by such agreements as regards the interpretation and application of their provisions . . .

183 Nevertheless, the Court of Justice has also declared that an international agreement may affect its own powers only if the indispensable conditions for safeguarding the essential character of those powers are satisfied and, consequently, there is no adverse effect on the autonomy of the EU legal order.

184 In particular, any action by the bodies given decision-making powers by the ECHR, as provided for in the agreement envisaged, must not have the effect of binding the EU and its institutions, in the exercise of their internal powers, to a particular interpretation of the rules of EU law . . .

188 The Court of Justice has [stated] . . . that the application of national standards of protection of fundamental rights must not compromise the level of protection provided for by the Charter or the primacy, unity and effectiveness of EU law . . .

189 In so far as Article 53 of the ECHR essentially reserves the power of the Contracting Parties to lay down higher standards of protection of fundamental rights than those guaranteed by the ECHR, that provision should be coordinated . . . to ensure that the level of protection provided for by the Charter and the primacy, unity and effectiveness of EU law are not compromised.

190 However, there is no provision in the agreement envisaged to ensure such coordination.

196 Protocol No 16 permits the highest courts and tribunals of the Member States to request the ECtHR to give advisory opinions on questions of principle relating to the interpretation or application of the rights and freedoms guaranteed by the ECHR or the protocols thereto, even though EU law requires those same courts or tribunals to submit a request to that end to the Court of Justice for a preliminary ruling under Article 267 TFEU.

197 Since the ECHR would form an integral part of EU law, the mechanism established by that protocol could – notably where the issue concerns rights guaranteed by the Charter corresponding to those secured by the

---

[85] Article 6(3) TEU. See pp. 255–61.

[86] The ruling is an opinion because international agreements concluded by the Union can be brought before the Court by a Member State or one of the three EU legislative institutions to verify they are compatible with EU law. The Court gives an opinion in such circumstances, which is, in practice, invariably followed, Article 218(11) TFEU.

198 ECHR – affect the autonomy and effectiveness of the preliminary ruling procedure provided for in Article 267 TFEU.

198 In particular, it cannot be ruled out that a request for an advisory opinion made pursuant to Protocol No 16 by a court or tribunal of a Member State that has acceded to that protocol could trigger the procedure for the prior involvement of the Court of Justice, thus creating a risk that the preliminary ruling procedure provided for in Article 267 TFEU might be circumvented, a procedure which, as has been noted in paragraph 176 of this Opinion, is the keystone of the judicial system established by the Treaties.

199 By failing to make any provision in respect of the relationship between the mechanism established by Protocol No 16 and the preliminary ruling procedure provided for in Article 267 TFEU, the agreement envisaged is liable adversely to affect the autonomy and effectiveness of the latter procedure.

Decisions of an external body must not, therefore, threaten 'the essential character' of the Court of Justice's powers or affect the autonomy of the EU legal order. This is a little cryptic. However, the judgment suggests that the essential character of EU law is compromised if a decision by this external body has implications not just for the meaning of the agreement but also for how other EU law is understood. Interpretations of the ECHR were thus seen as problematic as they would affect how EU Charter rights were understood and the doctrine of primacy of EU law. The Court is more direct about the autonomy of the EU legal order. It is illegal for national courts to seek rulings, binding or advisory, on matters that go to the content of EU law from any court or body outside their jurisdiction other than the Court of Justice.

The result of *Opinion 2/13* is to restrict the external constraints which can be placed on the Court of Justice. It must be seen alongside *Achmea* which considered the Court of Justice's authority over dispute settlement processes within the Union. *Achmea* concerned a 1991 Bilateral Investment Treaty ('BIT') agreement between the Netherlands and Czechoslovakia which allowed, *inter alia*, investors to take Slovakia to an arbitral tribunal for failure to accord them fair and equitable treatment. The tribunal was a private body whose findings were not subject to judicial review. Achmea, a Dutch sickness insurance company, successfully sought compensation from Slovakia as a result of a 2007 law and 2011 judgment which prohibited distribution of profits from the sickness insurance sector. Slovakia argued that this system of arbitration violated EU law, and challenged the matter before a German court who referred it to the Court of Justice.

Slovak Republic v. *Achmea*, C–284/16, EU:C:2018:158

35 In order to ensure that the specific characteristics and the autonomy of the EU legal order are preserved, the Treaties have established a judicial system intended to ensure consistency and uniformity in the interpretation of EU law . . .

36 In that context, in accordance with Article 19 TEU, it is for the national courts and tribunals and the Court of Justice to ensure the full application of EU law in all Member States and to ensure judicial protection of the rights of individuals under that law . . .

37 In particular, the judicial system as thus conceived has as its keystone the preliminary ruling procedure provided for in Article 267 TFEU, which, by setting up a dialogue between one court and another, specifically between the Court of Justice and the courts and tribunals of the Member States, has the object of securing

uniform interpretation of EU law, thereby serving to ensure its consistency, its full effect and its autonomy as well as, ultimately, the particular nature of the law established by the Treaties . . .

43   It must therefore be ascertained . . . whether an arbitral tribunal such as that referred to in Article 8 of the BIT is situated within the judicial system of the EU, and in particular whether it can be regarded as a court or tribunal of a Member State within the meaning of Article 267 TFEU. The consequence of a tribunal set up by Member States being situated within the EU judicial system is that its decisions are subject to mechanisms capable of ensuring the full effectiveness of the rules of the EU . . .

45   The arbitral tribunal is not part of the judicial system of the Netherlands or Slovakia. Indeed, it is precisely the exceptional nature of the tribunal's jurisdiction compared with that of the courts of those two Member States that is one of the principal reasons for the existence of Article 8 of the BIT.

46   That characteristic of the arbitral tribunal at issue in the main proceedings means that it cannot in any event be classified as a court or tribunal 'of a Member State' within the meaning of Article 267 TFEU.

56   Consequently, having regard to all the characteristics of the arbitral tribunal mentioned in Article 8 of the BIT . . . it must be considered that, by concluding the BIT, the Member States parties to it established a mechanism for settling disputes between an investor and a Member State which could prevent those disputes from being resolved in a manner that ensures the full effectiveness of EU law, even though they might concern the interpretation or application of that law.

57   It is true that . . . an international agreement providing for the establishment of a court responsible for the interpretation of its provisions and whose decisions are binding on the institutions, including the Court of Justice, is not in principle incompatible with EU law. The competence of the EU in the field of international relations and its capacity to conclude international agreements necessarily entail the power to submit to the decisions of a court which is created or designated by such agreements as regards the interpretation and application of their provisions, provided that the autonomy of the EU and its legal order is respected . . .

58   In the present case, however, apart from the fact that the disputes falling within the jurisdiction of the arbitral tribunal referred to in Article 8 of the BIT may relate to the interpretation both of that agreement and of EU law, the possibility of submitting those disputes to a body which is not part of the judicial system of the EU is provided for by an agreement which was concluded not by the EU but by Member States. Article 8 of the BIT is such as to call into question not only the principle of mutual trust between the Member States but also the preservation of the particular nature of the law established by the Treaties, ensured by the preliminary ruling procedure provided for in Article 267 TFEU . . .

59   In those circumstances, Article 8 of the BIT has an adverse effect on the autonomy of EU law.

Essentially, the combined effect of *Opinion 2/13* and *Achmea* is to place the Court of Justice at the apex of an autonomous judicial order. It has a monopoly over the provision of rulings to national courts on the interpretation and application of EU law, and Member States are prohibited from establishing any dispute settlement bodies which are not subject to the Article 267 TFEU procedure and the authority of the Court of Justice.

This is controversial. At its strongest, the accusation is that, in *Opinion 2/13*, the Court of Justice placed the protection of its own prerogatives above the protection of fundamental rights.[87] After all, all EU States accede to the ECHR and regard the ECtHR as one of the most

---

[87]   E. Spaventa, 'A Very Fearful Court? The Protection of Fundamental Rights in the European Union after Opinion 2/13' (2015) 22 *MJECL* 35; S. Peers, 'The CJEU and the EU's Accession to the ECHR: A Clear and Present Danger to Human Rights Protection' (2014) *EU Law Analysis*, http://eulawanalysis.blogspot.com/2014/12/the-cjeu-and-eus-accession-to-echr.html.

respected authorities on human rights. It is troubling that the Union cannot make the same commitment. Even if one were more sceptical about the pedigree of the ECtHR and its ability to make top-notch human rights judgments, the Court of Justice's position still appears dogmatic.[88] Since no European State has refused accession to the ECHR and the authority of the ECtHR simply because of its effects on the autonomy of their constitutional orders, this begs questions as to why EU law should be different.[89] This dogmatism carries over into *Achmea*. To be sure, questions can be raised about the quality of justice provided by such arbitration tribunals and why foreign investors are given this privileged access to them. However, the European Union is guilty of double standards. It has historically insisted that non-EU States make these tribunals available to EU companies who invest there. This raises the question why something that may not be good enough for the EU legal order is being foisted on non-EU States.

This autonomous judicial order has a number of features. First, the relationship between the Court of Justice and the national courts is to be a direct one. National law should not impede the possibility for the national court to make a reference. Secondly, it must have priority over domestic processes. It can, therefore, be used prior to domestic appeals or references. Thirdly, the court structure is flat in that all domestic courts are to have equal possibilities to make a reference.

First, the Court of Justice enjoys direct relations with every court and tribunal within it. The requirement that all of these are free to refer questions of EU law to it poses a problem for national systems of precedent. A higher court judgment binding lower courts might appear to conflict with EU law. However, a reference to the Court of Justice challenges the higher court's judgment as it is a first step to disapplying it. In *Križan*, the Slovakian Supreme Court (Najvyšší súd Slovenskej republiky) suspended a permit for the construction of a landfill site in the Slovakian town of Pezinok on the grounds that a proper environmental impact assessment had not been carried out as required by (in its view) EU law. The matter went to the Slovakian Constitutional Court (Ústavný súd Slovenskej republiky) which held that the Supreme Court's decision was wrong and violated the Slovakian Constitution insofar as it breached the operator's constitutional right to enjoyment of his property. It set the decision aside and sent it back to the Supreme Court to give a new ruling. The latter, instead referred the matter to the Court on the point of EU law.

Križan v. *Slovenská inšpekcia životného prostredia*, C–416/10, EU:C:2013:8

66 A reference for a preliminary ruling is based on a dialogue between one court and another, the initiation of which depends entirely on the national court's assessment as to whether that reference is appropriate and necessary . . .

67 Moreover, the existence of a national procedural rule cannot call into question the discretion of national courts to make a reference to the Court of Justice for a preliminary ruling where they have doubts, as in the case in the main proceedings, as to the interpretation of European Union law . . .

---

[88] For a nuanced account of the challenges of EU accession to the ECHR see D. Halberstam, '"It's the Autonomy, Stupid!" A Modest Defence of *Opinion 2/13* on EU Accession to the ECHR, and the Way Forward' (2015) 16 *German LJ* 105.

[89] C. Krenn, 'Autonomy and Effectiveness as Common Concerns: A Path to ECHR Accession after *Opinion 2/13*' (2015) 16 *German LJ* 147.

68 A rule of national law, pursuant to which legal rulings of a higher court bind another national court, cannot take away from the latter court the discretion to refer to the Court of Justice questions of interpretation of the points of European Union law concerned by such legal rulings. That court must be free, if it considers that a higher court's legal ruling could lead it to deliver a judgment contrary to European Union law, to refer to the Court of Justice questions which concern it . . .

69 At this stage, it must be noted that the national court, having exercised the discretion conferred on it by Article 267 TFEU, is bound, for the purposes of the decision to be given in the main proceedings, by the interpretation of the provisions at issue given by the Court of Justice and must, if necessary, disregard the rulings of the higher court if it considers, in the light of that interpretation, that they are not consistent with European Union law . . .

70 The principles set out in the previous paragraphs apply in the same way to the referring court with regard to the legal position expressed, in the present case in the main proceedings, by the constitutional court of the Member State concerned in so far as it follows from well-established case-law that rules of national law, even of a constitutional order, cannot be allowed to undermine the unity and effectiveness of European Union law . . . Moreover, the Court of Justice has already established that those principles apply to relations between a constitutional court and all other national courts . . .

71 The national rule which obliges the Najvyšší súd Slovenskej republiky to follow the legal position of the Ústavný súd Slovenskej republiky cannot therefore prevent the referring court from submitting a request for a preliminary ruling to the Court of Justice at any point in the proceedings which it judges appropriate, and to set aside, if necessary, the assessments made by the Ústavný súd Slovenskej republiky which might prove to be contrary to European Union law.

72 Finally, as a supreme court, the Najvyšší súd Slovenskej republiky is even required to submit a request for a preliminary ruling to the Court of Justice when it finds that the substance of the dispute concerns a question to be resolved which comes within the scope of the first paragraph of Article 267 TFEU. The possibility of bringing, before the constitutional court of the Member State concerned, an action against the decisions of a national court, limited to an examination of a potential infringement of the rights and freedoms guaranteed by the national constitution or by an international agreement, cannot allow the view to be taken that that national court cannot be classified as a court against whose decisions there is no judicial remedy under national law within the meaning of the third paragraph of Article 267 TFEU.

Secondly, direct relations between national courts and the Court of Justice require national courts to be free to use the preliminary reference procedure at the expense of domestic systems of appeal or reference. In *Melki*, two Algerians, irregularly present in France, were detained and issued with a deportation order.[90] They argued, unsuccessfully, that the initial check was illegal under EU law. Under French law, the constitutionality of any French statute had to be referred, in the first place, to the French Conseil Constitutionnel. This implied that the matter should be heard by the French Conseil Constitutionnel prior to the Court of Justice, since a violation of EU law was treated in France as a violation of the constitution. The Court of Justice disagreed. It noted that national courts always had an unfettered freedom to refer if this was necessary to decide the

---

[90] *Melki and Abdeli*, C-188–9/10, EU:C:2010:363.

dispute before them. They should be free to exercise this discretion even if it meant breaching national legal requirements that the matter be referred to a higher domestic court.[91]

The details of these judgments appear technical, discussing when lower courts can use the Article 267 TFEU procedure to decide a dispute. However, their consequences are momentous, for they allow lower courts to break free from national judicial hierarchies. Lower courts are now part of the new Union judicial order, to which they can, if they so choose, grant precedence over the domestic one. In fields covered by EU law, they can ignore the judgments of higher courts and the domestic judicial hierarchies which allow them to be appealed (or referred) to higher courts in favour of a ruling from the Court of Justice. In other words, lower courts are empowered to flit between judicial bosses.

Thirdly, the court structure of the EU judicial order is a flat one. All national courts are granted equal possibilities to make a reference to the Court and no national court can disenfranchise another national court. Above them all, sits the Court of Justice which is empowered to make binding judgments. This judicial order offers new opportunities and relationships for lower courts, and those who litigate before them.

S. Schmidt, *The European Court of Justice & The Policy Process* (Oxford University Press, 2018) 37

But why do member-state courts address the ECJ and help to overturn the domestic legal system with European law? In fact, it took a few years until the courts began to take up this opportunity, with the first case reaching the ECJ in 1961 ... For lower courts, the preliminary procedure is quite attractive, as it strengthens their independence from the domestic court hierarchy to which they belong. Basing their decision on supreme European law shields them from the risk of being overturned by the next higher court ... And lower courts are said to be less concerned with the coherence of the national legal system ...

Domestic courts often frame the questions raised in the preliminary procedure in a way that gives clear indications of the sort of answer they would like to receive ... The ECJ has every incentive to follow this lead, which gives assurance that its verdict will be taken up rather than ignored by the lower court. Were lower courts not to follow its rulings, this would undermine the authority of the ECJ. The cooperation with lower national courts is particularly important for the ECJ, as they provide it with a case load and integrate European law into the judicial systems of the member states ... Acknowledging the important role of lower courts in actively asking for certain rulings, Gareth Davies has argued that the ECJ should not be blamed for its activism.[92] The contentious Case C-144/04 Mangold ruling on age discrimination shows how litigators may strategically address courts so as to derail domestic policies with the help of European law, thereby relying on the explicit framing of the issue by the lower court judge.[93] In this case, the litigator had first attempted to influence the policy in the German Parliament. After this had failed, he reverted to fabricating a case and litigating.

---

[91] They retain this freedom even if the domestic requirements are of a constitutional nature, *Kernkraftwerke Lippe-Ems* v. *Hauptzollamt Osnabrück*, C-5/14, EU:C:2015:354; *SEGRO* v. *Vas Megyei Kormányhivatal Sárvári Járási Földhivatala*, C-52/16 and C-113/16, EU:C:2018:157.

[92] G. Davies, 'Activism Relocated: The Self-Restraint of the European Court of Justice in Its National Context' (2012) 19 *JEPP* 76.

[93] *Mangold* v. *Helm*, C-144/04, EU:C:2005:709.

The reasons for references appear complex and multiple. In some instances, as Schmidt observes, lower courts may use the preliminary reference procedure to undermine perceived over-constraining domestic hierarchies.[94] In others, references may actually be made in the belief that it reinforces the national judicial system; in particular that anchoring it around a strong judicial authority and a large corpus of EU law will give it additional solidarity.[95] The level of Europeanisation of the judiciary also appears relevant with judges more likely to refer if they are familiar with EU law and their peers also refer.[96]

Schmidt also observes that litigants are fairly central to this process. The reference from the national court will often be at their request. In this respect, a large-scale study by Chalmers and Chaves found two styles of preliminary reference.[97] There were, first, patrolling references. These usually concerned detailed legislation in fields like the single market, tax or the environment, and went to narrowly confined entitlements that were narrow in the sense they were available only to a limited number of parties over a confined range of activities. The litigants were transnational industries or national administrations. These actors had also been heavily involved in the negotiation of the original EU legislation. Often, they just wanted to tilt the legislation a little in their favour or have it interpreted in the light of more recent developments. The judgments were financially significant but rarely high profile. There were, secondly, thickly evaluative references which asked the Court to reflect significantly on the values underpinning a particular EU law. These involved EU law provisions, typically in Treaties or Directives, which set out open-ended statements of principle because Member States could not agree in greater detail beyond that: be this in equal opportunities law, EU citizenship, free movement or fundamental rights. There was, thus, more scope for ambitious interpretations by the Court. Litigation frequently involved actors who had less influence in EU lawmaking, such as non-governmental organisations (NGOs) or domestic industries, and therefore more interest in aggressive judgments. These references tended to lead to the judgments which were more controversial.[98]

(iv) The Subjects of the EU Judicial Order

The establishment of a Union judicial order by the Court of Justice requires it to identify the members of that judicial order, namely the courts and tribunals which can seek references from it. This question is a charged one because Article 267 TFEU confers a prominent role on national courts and tribunals. In this regard, not only are they the gatekeepers for those seeking access to the Court of Justice, they are also independent actors in their own right with powers to ask questions of the Court of Justice and influence EU law. As such, recognition of a body as a court or tribunal grants that body significant power. The question is made more complicated by a variety of professional, regulatory and arbitral bodies adjudicating upon EU law, even though

---

[94] K. Alter, 'The European Court's Political Power' (1996) 19 *WEP* 458. Cf. T. Pavone, 'Revisiting Judicial Empowerment in the European Union: Limits of Empowerment, Logics of Resistance' (2018) *Journal of Courts* (forthcoming).

[95] J. Mayoral, 'In the CJEU Judges Trust: A New Approach in the Judicial Construction of Europe' (2017) 55 *JCMS* 551.

[96] J. Mayoral, U. Jaremba and T. Nowak, 'Creating EU Law Judges: The Role of Generational Differences, Legal Education and Judicial Career Paths in National Judges' Assessment Regarding EU Law Knowledge' (2014) 21 *JEPP* 1120.

[97] D. Chalmers and M. Chaves, 'The Reference Points of EU Judicial Politics' (2012) 19 *JEPP* 25.

[98] See also S. Jacquot and T. Vitale, 'Law as Weapon of the Weak? A Comparative Analysis of Legal Mobilization by Roma and Women's Groups at the European Level' (2014) 21 *JEPP* 587; L. Conant et al., 'Mobilizing European Law' (2018) 25 *JEPP* 1376.

these are not formally designated as courts under national law. Furthermore, the designation of bodies as courts varies between Member States.

The Court of Justice has insisted that the question of whether a body is a court or tribunal is a matter for EU law rather than national law.[99] The body's status does not depend, therefore, on its national designation but on whether it possesses a number of qualities. A clear summary of these is provided in *Ascendi*, a case that involved a dispute between a Portuguese company and the tax authorities over the amount of stamp duty to be reimbursed by the latter. Under Portuguese law, this went to arbitration with the award binding on both parties. The question arose whether the arbitrator was a court under Article 267 TFEU:

> [I]in order to determine whether a body making a reference is a 'court or tribunal' within the meaning of Article 267 TFEU, a question governed by EU law alone, the Court takes account of a number of factors, such as whether the body is established by law, whether it is permanent, whether its jurisdiction is compulsory, whether its procedure is *inter partes*, whether it applies rules of law and whether it is independent ... In addition, a national court may refer a question to the Court only if there is a case pending before it and if it is called upon to give judgment in proceedings intended to lead to a decision of a judicial nature.[100]

A number of public bodies have been found to be courts, notwithstanding that they are not part of the formal judiciaries of their Member States. They include immigration adjudicators,[101] professional disciplinary bodies,[102] arbitrators,[103] administrative bodies which review public contracts[104] and planning decisions,[105] and tax adjudicators.[106]

Whilst the Court will look at each of the criteria – legal establishment, permanence, compulsory jurisdiction, inter partes procedure, application of rules of law, and independence – to determine whether a body is a court or tribunal, the case law has coalesced around three debates.

The first goes to the official qualities of the body. In *Achmea*, the Court stated that, whatever its formal designation, a body would be a court if it was part of the system of judicial settlement provided for by the constitution.[107] This question has arisen most acutely with regard to private bodies, such as arbitration panels. Historically, arbitration panels have not been considered to fall within Article 267 TFEU as they are seen as private arrangements based on party consent which did not involve the State.[108] However, where these features are less present, the arbitration panel will be considered to be exercising judicial functions, as part of the general system of administration of justice. Therefore, private bodies such as arbitration panels can refer to the Court of Justice if they have been established by law, their decisions are binding and their jurisdiction does not depend on the consent of the parties.[109]

The second debate goes to the independence of the body. It must both be impartial and independent. Impartiality requires that it must neither have taken the contested decision nor

---

[99] *Broekmeulen* v. *Huisarts Registratie Commissie*, 246/80, EU:C:1981:218.
[100] *Ascendi* v. *Autoridade Tributária e Aduaneira*, C-377/13, EU:C:2014:1754, para. 23.
[101] *El Yassini* v. *Secretary of State for the Home Department*, C-416/96, EU:C:1999:107.
[102] *Koller*, C-118/09, EU:C:2011:388. [103] *Merck Canada* v. *Accord Healthcare*, C-555/13, EU:C:2014:92.
[104] *Consorci Sanitari del Maresme* v. *Corporació de Salut del Maresme i la Selva*, C-203/14, EU:C:2015:664.
[105] *Umweltanwalt von Kärnten* v. *Kärntner Landesregierung*, C-205/08, EU:C:2009:767.
[106] *De Coster*, C-17/00, EU:C:2001:651. [107] *Slovak Republic* v. *Achmea*, C-284/16, EU:C:2018:158.
[108] *Denuit* v. *Transorient – Mosaïque Voyages et Culture*, C-125/04, EU:C:2005:69.
[109] *Merck Canada* v. *Accord Healthcare*, C-555/13, EU:C:2014:92; *Ascendi* v. *Autoridade Tributária e Aduaneira*, C-377/13, EU:C:2014:1754.

been the subject of that decision.[110] It must also have no organisational links with the parties appearing before it and have no interest in the outcome of the proceedings before it.[111] Independence requires, on the one hand, that the body is not subject to any external constraint or instruction that would impair its decision-making, and, on the other, that it is sufficiently protected from undue influence being brought to bear on it.[112] Regard will be had to how members are appointed, the grounds on which they are rejected, and the composition of the body.[113] Members should also be paid an amount which is commensurate to the importance of the task.[114] Of particular importance is the length of term of office and that the reasons for dismissal are very circumscribed. In *Syfait* the Greek competition authority was not therefore considered to be a court – even though it was formally independent, there were insufficient guarantees against dismissal of its members by the government.[115] By contrast, in *Häupl*, an Austrian patent body which heard appeals against decisions of the Austrian patent office was held to be a court because the independence of its members was protected by a five-year term of office which could only be terminated for 'exceptional and well-defined reasons'.[116]

The third debate goes to the context in which the reference is made. A number of bodies perform a wide range of activities. They are only allowed to refer if the decision for which EU law is being used is of a judicial nature. They cannot refer if the decision is an administrative one. A decision is likely to be administrative if it does not prevent a judicial action being brought or, if it is final, it does not have the force of *res judicata*.[117] Beyond that, the distinction is not always clear. Allocating a surname to a child[118] or registering a company[119] are administrative activities which cannot give rise to a reference.

The breadth of the definition – wider than national definitions but with limits of its own – has drawn fire both from those who wish for a wider definition and those who believe it has already become too extended. The former criticism observes that much commercial arbitration falls outside Article 267 TFEU by dint of its private and consensual nature, and that this is a problem as it allows many rights under EU law to be decided without the possibility of reference to the Court of Justice. This is true, but it is something to which parties, commercial actors, have consented. Arguably a stronger criticism is that the definition is too wide. This was made forcefully by Advocate General Colomer, a Spanish Advocate General at the Court for nearly fifteen years.[120] He argued that it undermined the fundamental tenet of Article 267 TFEU, which was to provide a framework for judicial dialogue. The wide definition allowed professional, administrative and regulatory agencies to participate and shape this conversation. This had a number of consequences. The most problematic was that bodies with no legal training were shaping the law which also allowed these actors to disrupt domestic judicial hierarchies and systems of judicial precedent by making a reference if they did not agree with such. These criticisms are forceful, but the persistence of the Court with such a wide definition suggests that

---

[110] *Wilson* v. *Ordre des avocats du barreau de Luxembourg*, C-506/04, EU:C:2006:587; *Secretaria Regional de Saúde dos Açores*, C-102/17, EU:C:2018:294.

[111] *Corbiau*, C-24/92, EU:C:1993:118.   [112] *Panicello* v. *Martínez*, C-503/15, EU:C:2017:126.

[113] *MF 7* v. *MAFRA*, C-49/13, EU:C:2013:767.

[114] *Associação Sindical dos Juízes Portugueses* v. *Tribunal de Contas*, C-64/16, EU:C:2018:117.

[115] *Syfait* v. *Glaxo Smith Kline*, C-53/03, EU:C:2005: 333.   [116] *Häupl* v. *Lidl*, C-246/05, EU:C:2007:340.

[117] *Panicello* v. *Martínez*, C-503/15, EU:C:2017:126.   [118] *Standesamt Stadt Niebüll*, C-96/04, EU:C:2006:254.

[119] *Lutz*, C-182/00, EU:C:2002:19.

[120] See *De Coster*, C-17/00, EU:C:2001:366; *Umweltanwalt von Kärnten* v. *Kärntner Landesregierung*, C-205/08, EU:C:2009:397.

it values the range of references that come to it from these bodies. And this suggests something further, namely that it is not fully comfortable with judges being the only supply line through which domestic litigation can reach it.

4 THE FUNCTIONS OF THE UNION JUDICIAL ORDER

(i) The Development of EU Law

The reference procedure is significant both quantitatively and qualitatively. Between 2013 and 2017, they accounted for over 72 per cent of all proceedings before the Court of Justice.[121] In most fields, its significant rulings have come via the preliminary reference procedure. This is no surprise. National courts and tribunals are both more accessible to private parties than international bodies and they provide numerous decentralised laboratories for the testing and exploration of EU law. EU law's possibilities are tried out before them, and experiences of EU law, both good and bad, are exposed before them. Faced with this, many national courts may seek a reference as they see the Court of Justice as best equipped to develop EU law. Indeed, in its early years, the Court justified the preliminary reference procedure in these terms, stating that it made 'available to the national judge a means of eliminating difficulties which may be occasioned by the requirement of giving [Union] law its full effect'.[122]

This role as the authoritative interlocutor of EU law places the Court of Justice in an extremely powerful position. Nevertheless, over the years, a number of concerns have emerged as a result of this prominence.

The central charge of judicial activism, when unpacked, seems to contain a number of different elements.

The first is that of judicial legislation. The Court is not engaging in *bona fide* interpretation of an EU legal text, but is going beyond that by deciding matters which should be left either to the EU legislature or the Treaty framers. This is most forcefully expressed by the claim that a judgment is *contra legem* – it goes against the wording of the text. This concern is occasionally expressed by judiciaries. In recent years, Dutch judges[123] and senior courts in the Czech Republic, Denmark and the United Kingdom have all raised doubts about judgments which they believe push the limits of interpretation.[124] In 2013, the Dutch Government was sufficiently concerned to set out a policy paper which stated that the Court should not interpret EU laws in a manner unanticipated by the lawmaker and proactive behaviour should be taken by the latter to correct such judgments.[125] It is difficult to know how far these concerns extend beyond the odd judgment. If the Court of Justice was supplanting the EU legislature, one would expect the latter to step in frequently to correct its judgments. Studies have shown, however, that when a

---

[121] *Annual Report*, n. 16 above, 102.

[122] *Rheinmühlen-Düsseldorf* v. *Einfuhr- und Vorratstelle für Getreide*, 166/73, EU:C:1974:3, para. 2.

[123] On this, S. Garben, 'Sky-High Controversy and High-Flying Claims? The Sturgeon Case Law in Light of Judicial Activism, Euroscepticism and Eurolegalism' (2013) 50 *CMLRev* 15.

[124] Pl. ÚS 5/12: *Slovak Pensions*, Judgment of 31 January 2012 (Czech Constitutional Court); Case 15/2014, *DI acting for Ajos A/S vs Estate of A*, Judgment of 6 December 2016 (Danish Supreme Court); *Pham* v. *Secretary of State for the Home Department* [2015] UKSC 19, paras. 76–91, *pace* Lord Mance.

[125] www.government.nl/documents-and-publications/notes/2013/06/21/testing-european-legislation-for-subsidiarity-and-proportionality-dutch-list-of-points-for-action.html.

judgment triggers EU legislation, that legislation rarely overrides it. Instead, more frequently, it builds on the judgment either by elaborating and codifying it further[126] or by following it broadly whilst still making modifications to it.[127] This picture has the Court of Justice as an important player, one which can set the agenda for the EU lawmaker, but not one which is developing laws at the expense of the latter's wishes.

The second element in the charge of judicial activism is that Court of Justice judgments push too often towards greater integration.[128] The charge is, thus, one of bias. It has been facilitated by a Euro-law industry, comprising EU law academics, legal officials of the EU Institutions and EU law practitioners who have an interest in the growth of EU law. This industry uses Article 267 TFEU to bring test cases and develop new legal doctrines, which invariably extend the ambits of EU law.[129] There are thus far more references arguing for EU laws to cover new activities or situations than there are arguing for these laws to be curtailed. Insofar as the Court accedes to this, it can lead to a tilt. A number of authors have observed, however, that even if this narrative had force back in the 1980s and 1990s, there is little evidence for it in the last decade which has witnessed a much more cautious court.[130] Repeated studies have also shown that where two or more national governments make observations on a point of EU law before the Court, it is likely to follow the same path.[131]

The third element goes to the style of reasoning deployed by the Court. It focuses, particularly, on the use of teleological reasoning by the Court of Justice. This reasoning involves the legal provision being interpreted in the light of some *telos*, a broader objective (i.e. free movement of goods, effective protection of individual rights or equal treatment) or overall scheme to which the provision is claimed to give effect.[132]

G. Conway, *The Limits of Legal Reasoning and the European Court of Justice* (Cambridge University Press, 2012) 274–5

Teleological interpretation writ large presents several fundamental problems. First, the telos or ends can be understood in varying ways. Without some further control or definition, uncertainty and unpredictability become prominent. The level of generality of ends or teloi, especially, can be altered freely within the

---

[126] G. Davies, 'The European Union Legislature as an Agent of the European Court of Justice' (2016) 54 *JCMS* 846.

[127] D. Martinsen, *An Ever More Powerful Court? The Political Constraints of Legal Integration in the European Union* (Oxford University Press, 2015) chs. 4, 5 and 6; S. Schmidt, *The European Court of Justice and the Policy Process* (Oxford University Press, 2018) chs. 4 and 5.

[128] T. Hartley, 'The European Court, Judicial Objectivity, and the Constitution of the European Union' (1996) 112 *LQR* 95; G. Beck, 'Judicial Activism in the Court of Justice of the EU' (2017) 36 *U Queensland LJ* 333.

[129] H. Schepel and R. Wesseling, 'The Legal Community: Judges, Lawyers, Officials and Clerks in the Writing of Europe' (1997) 3 *ELJ* 165; S. Lee Mudge and A. Vauchez, 'Building Europe on a Weak Field: Law, Economics and Scholarly Avatars in Transnational Politics' (2012) 118 *American Journal of Sociology* 449.

[130] S. Saurugger and F. Terpan, *The Court of Justice of the European Union and the Politics of Law* (London, Palgrave, 2017) 34–42; M. Blauberger *et al.*, 'ECJ Judges Read the Morning Papers: Explaining the Turnaround of European Citizenship Jurisprudence' (2018) 25 *JEPP* 1422.

[131] See the ground-breaking work by M. P. Granger, 'When Governments Go to Luxembourg ... : The Influence of Governments on the European Court of Justice' (2004) 29 *ELRev* 1. This has since been confirmed in C. Carubba *et al.*, 'Judicial Behavior under Political Constraints: Evidence from the European Court of Justice' (2008) 102 *APSR* 435; O. Larsson and D. Naurin, 'Judicial Independence and Political Uncertainty: How the Risk of Override Affects the Court of Justice of the EU' (2016) 70 *IO* 377.

[132] For an example of such reasoning see *Valcheva v. Babanarakis*, C-335/17, EU:C:2018:359.

method of the ECJ. This is problematic because not every level of generality is equally valid or legitimate. The approach of the ECJ to identify the highest level of generality, ever-increasing integration, ignores the contestability of the extent of legal integration. This approach conceives of legitimacy on the basis of a simple linear narrative of integration. . . The extent to which integration should proceed is fundamentally a matter for the constituent power in the EU, which is the Member States, rather than for EU institutional practice to determine autonomously of the Member States. This understanding of the authority of the Member States is inherent in the principle of conferral.

Teleological interpretation as practised by the ECJ results in a strange epistemological asymmetry in how law is interpreted, by opening up a sharp cleavage between the interpretation of participants in the legal system and the judiciary. . . Ordinary citizens do not engage in meta-teleological interpretation in adhering to the law to the law on an everyday basis; they look to the most specific, relevant legal provisions, i.e. they adhere to lex specialis. This is inevitable, since in the absence of lex specialis as a controlling factor, every time a citizen was confronted with a choice of whether to obey the law or not, he or she would have to engage in an overall assessment of the legal system.

Whilst this style of reasoning has its critics, it also has its supporters. Support comes from two fronts. On the one hand, it is argued that interpretation is not a valueless process but must necessarily have reference to common values. Interpretation of EU laws must have reference to pan-Union values if this interpretation is to be autonomous, not partisan. Teleological reasoning both secures this and makes this process of interpretation more transparent.[133] The other support for teleological reasoning derives from the Court's institutional role. Securing a functioning legal order, it is claimed, necessarily requires elaboration of individual legal provisions to relate them to other parts of EU law, give some sense of coherence to EU law and enable it to be practically operable.[134] In this, there is a feeling that the two sides of the debate run past each other. Even if these reasons justify teleological reasoning, they do not address its slipperiness and unpredictability as a form of reasoning.

(ii) Judicial Review of EU Institutions

Article 267 TFEU allows the Court of Justice to rule on the validity of EU legislation and administrative acts of EU Institutions.[135] Typically, a national measure implementing the EU act will be challenged before a national court. In turn, it will ask the Court of Justice whether the EU measure, which provides the legal basis for the national measure, is lawful or not. This generates complications, however, about Article 267 TFEU's relationship to those EU law procedures which allow individuals to go directly to the Court of Justice to seek judicial review of EU measures.[136]

The Court must navigate a course between two positions here. There is, on the one hand, a danger of forum shopping. The preliminary reference procedure is used by litigants to

---

[133] J. Bengoetxea *et al.*, 'Integration and Integrity in the Legal Reasoning of the European Court of Justice' in G. de Búrca and J. Weiler (eds.), *The European Court of Justice* (Oxford University Press, 2001); A. Arnull, 'Judicial Activism and the European Court of Justice: How Should Academics Respond?' in M. Dawson *et al.* (eds.), *Judicial Activism at the Court of Justice* (Cheltenham, Edward Elgar, 2013).

[134] T. Horsley, 'Reflections on the Role of the Court of Justice as the "Motor" of European Integration: Legal Limits to Judicial Lawmaking' (2013) 50 *CMLRev* 931.

[135] *Rau* v. *Bundesanstalt für Landwirtschaftliche Marktordnung*, 133–6/85, EU:C:1987:244.

[136] On these procedures see pp. 388–405.

circumvent the restrictions that are placed on them going directly before the Court. This leads to the atrophy of these latter procedures, and the reasons for these restrictions – be they securing legal certainty or preventing continual second-guessing of the EU legislature by the EU courts – being undermined. The other sees Article 267 TFEU as correcting flaws in these procedures by allowing parties, wrongly deprived of the possibility of seeking review, the possibility of their day in court.

The matter was first addressed in *Jégo-Quéré*, in which the Court established that the preliminary reference procedure could be used to challenge an EU measure where the parties had no standing to challenge the measure directly before the EU courts.[137] In that instance, a French company fishing for whitebait (a very small fish), wished to challenge a Commission Regulation which set minimum mesh sizes for nets. It did not meet the standing requirements to challenge the Regulation directly before the Court under Article 263(4) TFEU (the provision allowing individuals to seek direct judicial review of acts of the EU Institutions).[138] The Court held that as individuals had both a right to effective judicial protection and the Treaties had established a complete set of legal remedies and procedures, a French court could refer to it the question of whether the Commission measure was lawful.

The preliminary reference procedure is, consequently, a central vehicle for individuals to seek judicial review of EU measures, for, as we shall, the standing requirements for direct access to the Court of Justice are highly restrictive.[139] This restrictiveness means that many must take the more time-consuming and expensive route of seeking a reference on the validity of the EU measure from a national court. However, it cannot be used if a party has *locus standi* to challenge a measure directly before the Court of Justice but failed to bring the action within the necessary time limits. In *TWD*, a German textile company sought to challenge a Commission Decision declaring a German subsidy granted to be an illegal State aid. It asked for a preliminary reference from a German court seven years later.[140] The company had standing to bring a direct action before the Court of Justice but this had to be done within two months of the decision becoming known to it.[141] The Court refused the reference on the grounds that once the time limit had expired legal certainty required that the national court be bound by the Commission Decision and not be able to challenge its validity.[142]

In some cases, it might not be clear whether parties have *locus standi*. The Court has, therefore, stated that references will only be barred where the direct action would 'unquestionably' have been admissible.[143] This will only be the case where it is 'obvious'[144] or 'beyond reasonable doubt'[145] that the parties had standing. This will be rare, with a reference likely to be denied only where a measure was addressed to them or they were one of a determinate number of parties identified in the EU measure.[146]

---

[137] *Jégo-Quéré* v. *Commission*, C-263/02 P, EU:C:2004:210.   [138] On these requirements see pp. 389–95.

[139] See pp. 395–7.

[140] *TWD Textilwerke Deggendorf* v. *Germany*, C-188/92, EU:C:1994:90. See also *R* v. *HM Treasury, ex parte Rosneft*, C-72/15, EU:C:2017:236.

[141] Article 263(5) TFEU.

[142] D. Wyatt, 'The Relationship between Actions for Annulment and References on Validity after TWD Deggendorf' in J. Lonbay and A. Biondi (eds.), *Remedies for Breach of EC Law* (Chichester, John Wiley, 1997).

[143] *A and Others*, C-158/14, EU:C:2017:202.   [144] Ibid.

[145] *Valimar* v. *Nachalnik na Mitnitsa Varna*, C-374/12, EU:C:2014:2231.

[146] *Georgsmarienhütte* v. *Germany*, C-135/16, EU:C:2018:582.

(iii) Preserving the Unity of EU Law

The unity of EU law requires that it 'normally be given an autonomous and uniform interpretation throughout the European Union'.[147] The Court has drawn out two sets of implications for the Article 267 TFEU procedure from this.

The first set of implications go to which legal instruments may be subject to a reference. Article 267 TFEU refers only to the Treaties and acts of the EU Institutions. However, the need for uniform interpretation of EU law has allowed the Court to give preliminary rulings on any other law which forms part of the wider EU legal order. This includes international agreements to which the Union has succeeded the Member States,[148] and general principles of law and fundamental rights.[149] The Court will also rule on international agreements which apply mainly to situations covered by domestic law if they could potentially fall within the scope of EU law on the grounds that the interests of EU law justifies the need for uniform interpretation of the agreement.[150]

The need for unity of interpretation of EU law also means that the Court will rule on national laws which reproduce the wording of EU provisions,[151] and contracts that incorporate terms of EU law.[152] This is justified by the necessity that every EU provision be given a uniform interpretation so as to forestall future differences in interpretation, irrespective of the circumstances in which it is to be applied.[153] This raises the question of how explicit the reference to EU law must be to generate jurisdiction for the Court. There need not be explicit reference to EU law in the national provision or contractual term as long as there is a clear intention to transpose EU law into these.[154] However, if the EU law only acts as a model for the national law, and there are significant differences between the two, the fact that certain national provisions replicate EU legal provisions is insufficient to permit a reference.[155]

The second set of implications goes to whether national courts can declare EU measures invalid. This is seen as particularly problematic for the unity of EU law as it may lead to a situation where an EU law is invalid in the State of that court, but not in other Member States. The Court of Justice has declared, therefore, that it has a monopoly over declaring EU measures invalid. In *Foto-Frost*, a Commission Decision requiring import duties to be paid on binoculars imported from the eastern part of Germany was challenged before a Hamburg court on the grounds that it conflicted with the 1957 Protocol on German Internal Trade, which allowed free trade between the two divided parts of Germany. The Hamburg court asked the Court of Justice whether it could declare the Commission Decision invalid.

---

[147] *Commission* v. *Spain*, C-281/09, EU:C:2011:767, para. 42.

[148] *Amministrazione delle Finanze dello Stato* v. *SPI*, 267–9/81, EU:C:1983:78.

[149] *Internationale Handelsgesellschaft* v. *Einfuhr und Vorratsstelle Getreide*, 11/70, EU:C:1970:114.

[150] *Hermès International* v. *FHT*, C-53/96, EU:C:1998:292; *Lesoochranárske zoskupenie*, C-240/09, EU:C:2011:125.

[151] *Dzodzi* v. *Belgium*, C-297/88 and C-197/89, EU:C:1990:360; *Allianz Hungária Biztosító* v. *Gazdasági Versenyhivatal*, C-32/11, EU:C:2013:160.

[152] *Federconsorzi* v. *AIMA*, C-88/91, EU:C:1992:276.

[153] For discussion, see S. Lefevre, 'The Interpretation of Community Law by the Court of Justice in Areas of National Competence' (2004) 29 *ELRev* 501.

[154] *Les Vergers du Vieux Tauves*, C-48/07, EU:C:2008:758.

[155] *Kleinwort Benson* v. *City of Glasgow District Council*, C-346/93, EU:C:1995:85.

Firma Foto-Frost v. *Hauptzollamt Lübeck-Ost*, 314/85, EU:C:1987:452

13 In enabling national courts, against those decisions where there is a judicial remedy under national law, to refer to the Court for a preliminary ruling questions on interpretation or validity, [Article 267 TFEU] did not settle the question whether those courts themselves may declare that acts of Community institutions are invalid.

14 Those courts may consider the validity of a Community act and, if they consider that the grounds put forward before them by the parties in support of invalidity are unfounded, they may reject them, concluding that the measure is completely valid. By taking that action they are not calling into question the existence of the Community measure.

15 On the other hand, those courts do not have the power to declare acts of the Community institutions invalid. As the Court emphasized . . . in Case 66/80 *International Chemical Corporation* v. *Amministrazione delle Finanze* (1981) ECR 1191, the main purpose of the powers accorded to the Court by Article [267 TFEU] is to ensure that Community law is applied uniformly by national courts. That requirement of uniformity is particularly imperative when the validity of a Community act is in question. Divergences between courts in the Member States as to the validity of Community acts would be liable to place in jeopardy the very unity of the Community legal order and detract from the fundamental requirement of legal certainty.

16 The same conclusion is dictated by consideration of the necessary coherence of the system of judicial protection established by the Treaty. In that regard it must be observed that requests for preliminary rulings, like actions for annulment, constitute means for reviewing the legality of acts of the community institutions. As the Court pointed out . . . in Case 294/83 *Parti Ecologiste 'Les Verts'* v. *European Parliament* [1986] ECR 1339, 'in Articles [263 and 268], on the one hand, and in Article [267 TFEU], on the other, the Treaty established a complete system of legal remedies and procedures designed to permit the Court of Justice to review the legality of measures adopted by the institutions'.

17 Since Article [263 TFEU] gives the Court exclusive jurisdiction to declare void an act of a Community institution, the coherence of the system requires that where the validity of a Community act is challenged before a national court the power to declare the act invalid must also be reserved to the Court of Justice.

18 It must also be emphasized that the Court of Justice is in the best position to decide on the validity of Community acts. Under Article 20 of the Protocol on the Statute of the Court of Justice of the EEC, Community Institutions whose acts are challenged are entitled to participate in the proceedings in order to defend the validity of the acts in question. Furthermore, under the second paragraph of Article 21 of that Protocol the Court may require the Member States and institutions which are not participating in the proceedings to supply all information which it considers necessary for the purposes of the case before it.

19 It should be added that the rule that national courts may not themselves declare Community acts invalid may have to be qualified in certain circumstances in the case of proceedings relating to an application for interim measures; however, that case is not referred to in the national court's question.

The view that only the Court of Justice can declare EU measures illegal has, as we shall see, been contested by national courts.[156] Nevertheless, the Court has been unwavering on it.[157] In *Schul*, a Dutch court asked whether it could strike down an EU instrument when an analogous instrument based on identical principles had already been struck down.[158] The Court of Justice

---

[156] See pp. 224–43.

[157] *Schrems* v. *Data Protection Commissioner*, C-362/14, EU:C:2015:650; *R* v. *HM Treasury, ex parte Rosneft*, C-72/15, EU:C:2017:236.

[158] *Schul* v. *Minister van Landbouw, Natuur en Voedselkwaliteit*, C-461/03, EU:C:2005:742.

stated that the uniformity of EU law and its procedural rules, in which all Member States and EU Institutions have the right to make observations, entailed that only it could declare EU acts invalid. This was the case even where an analogous measure had already been struck down. Analogies could be misleading in that the factual and legal context surrounding each measure would necessarily be different.

However, a simple challenge to the validity of an EU measure is not sufficient to require a reference. In *IATA*, IATA, the central association representing airlines, challenged Regulation 261/2004, which provided for compensation and assistance to passengers in the event of being denied boarding and of cancellation or long delay to long-haul flights.[159] The English court was sceptical of the challenge and, indeed, the challenge was eventually unsuccessful. It therefore asked for the threshold at which it must refer to the Court of Justice. The latter stated it was not required to refer simply because one party challenged the validity of a measure. It should only refer if it considers an argument as to the invalidity of a measure, brought up by either itself or by one of the parties, to be well-founded.

(iv) Dispute Resolution

This chapter has already set out how, under Article 267 TFEU, national courts rule on questions of facts, national law and who wins the case, whilst the Court of Justice rules on points of EU law. However, Article 267(2) TFEU stipulates that the national court may refer 'if it considers that a decision on the question is necessary to enable it to give judgment'. This creates a tension as it has been interpreted to mean that a reference should only take place when, and if, EU law meaningfully contributes to the resolution of the dispute. This would require the Court of Justice to look at the facts of the dispute despite being something reserved for the national court.

In *Foglia*, Foglia had contracted to sell Italian liqueur wine to Novello in France on condition that Novello reimburse any taxes incurred by Foglia as a consequence of the transaction, unless these were levied contrary to EU law. Novello subsequently refused to reimburse a small amount of French tax levied on Foglia, equivalent to about €70, on the grounds that it was contrary to EU law. The compatibility of these French taxes with EU law was then brought before an Italian court. The case had all the hallmarks of a test case. Both parties argued that the taxes were illegal, the amount of tax paid was derisory and Foglia indicated that he was litigating on behalf of Italian traders of this wine. The Court of Justice refused to give judgment to the initial reference on the grounds that there was no genuine dispute.[160] The Italian court re-referred the matter, asking about the respective roles of the national court and Court of Justice under Article 267 TFEU.

Foglia v. Novello (No. 2), 244/80, EU:C:1981:302

14 [Article 267 TFEU] is based on cooperation which entails a division of duties between the national courts and the Court of Justice in the interest of the proper application and uniform interpretation of Community law throughout all the Member States.

---

[159] *R, ex parte IATA* v. *Department for Transport*, C-344/04, EU:C:2006:10.
[160] *Foglia* v. *Novello*, 104/79, EU:C:1980:73.

15   With this in view it is for the national court – by reason of the fact that it is seized of the substance of the dispute and that it must bear the responsibility for the decision to be taken – to assess, having regard to the facts of the case, the need to obtain a preliminary ruling to enable it to give judgment.

16   In exercising that power of appraisal the national court, in collaboration with the Court of Justice, fulfils a duty entrusted to them both of ensuring that in the interpretation and application of the Treaty the law is observed. Accordingly the problems which may be entailed in the exercise of its power of appraisal by the national court and the relations which it maintains within the framework of [Article 267 TFEU] with the Court of Justice are governed exclusively by the provisions of Community law.

17   In order that the Court of Justice may perform its task in accordance with the Treaty it is essential for national courts to explain, when the reasons do not emerge beyond any doubt from the file, why they consider that a reply to their questions is necessary to enable them to give judgment.

18   It must in fact be emphasized that the duty assigned to the Court by [Article 267 TFEU] is not that of delivering advisory opinions on general or hypothetical questions but of assisting in the administration of justice in the Member States. It accordingly does not have jurisdiction to reply to questions of interpretation which are submitted to it within the framework of procedural devices arranged by the parties in order to induce the Court to give its views on certain problems of Community law which do not correspond to an objective requirement inherent in the resolution of a dispute. A declaration by the Court that it has no jurisdiction in such circumstances does not in any way trespass upon the prerogatives of the national court but makes it possible to prevent the application of the procedure under [Article 267 TFEU] for purposes other than those appropriate for it.

19   Furthermore, it should be pointed out that, whilst the Court of Justice must be able to place as much reliance as possible upon the assessment by the national court of the extent to which the questions submitted are essential, it must be in a position to make any assessment inherent in the performance of its own duties in particular order to check, as all courts must, whether it has jurisdiction. Thus the Court, taking into account the repercussions of its decisions in this matter, must have regard, in exercising the jurisdiction conferred upon it by [Article 267 TFEU], not only to the interests of the parties to the proceedings but also to those of the Community and of the Member States. Accordingly it cannot, without disregarding the duties assigned to it, remain indifferent to the assessments made by the courts of the Member States in the exceptional cases in which such assessments may affect the proper working of the procedure laid down by [Article 267 TFEU].

Foglia was contentious. The power to refuse a reference established a hierarchical element between the Court of Justice and national courts, as it allowed the Court of Justice to review decisions to refer and to examine the factual background to the dispute. There was consequently debate about whether this violated the cooperative spirit of Article 267 TFEU or transgressed unduly on the national court's monopoly over fact-finding.[161] There are also severe practical difficulties in applying *Foglia*.[162] Without its own fact-finding powers, however, the Court has little capacity to second-guess national courts.

[161] A. Barav, 'Preliminary Censorship? The Judgment of the European Court in Foglia v. Novello' (1980) 5 *ELRev* 443, 451–4; H. Rasmussen, *On Law and Policy in the European Court of Justice* (Dordrecht, Martijnus Nijhoff, 1986) 465–97; D. Wyatt, 'Foglia (No. 2): The Court Denies It Has Jurisdiction to Give Advisory Opinions' (1982) 7 *ELRev* 186.

[162] G. Bebr, 'The Existence of a Genuine Dispute: An Indispensable Precondition for the Jurisdiction of the Court under Article 177 EC?' (1980) 17 *CMLRev* 525, 532.

Within this context, the Court has accepted test cases. In *Leclerc Siplec*, Leclerc Siplec challenged a refusal by TF1, one of the major French television broadcasters, to televise an advertisement for petrol in its chain of supermarkets because of a law prohibiting television advertising of the distribution sector.[163] Both parties to the dispute were in agreement about the domestic legal situation and the need for a reference which the Court accepted. It noted that what was being sought was a declaration from the national court that the French law did not comply with EU law. The parties' agreement did not make the need for that declaration any less pressing or the dispute any less real. Whilst resolution of test cases is an important part of the judicial function, it is very difficult to distinguish them from hypothetical cases. In both instances, there is little conflict between the immediate parties to the dispute.

The *Foglia* line of reasoning survives, but in an attenuated form. In *Stichting Zuid-Hollandse Milieufederatie* the Court stated that it will only refuse to give a reference where it is 'quite obvious' that the alleged dispute is hypothetical, or the point of law referred bears no relationship to the dispute in question.[164] However, this 'quite obvious' requirement is interpreted loosely. In that instance, the Court accepted a reference from a Dutch court about the Directive on Biocides, notwithstanding that the litigation concerned legislation on another Directive – that on Plant Protection – on the grounds that the two Directives were closely related and governed by similar principles. By contrast, in *Stoilov*, it refused to answer a reference concerning the legality of a decision by Bulgarian customs officials to impose tariffs on materials for window blinds. The reasoning was that the annulment of the decision under Belgian law meant that there was no longer any decision to challenge.[165]

5 THE MANAGEMENT OF THE EU JUDICIAL ORDER

If the preliminary reference procedure establishes an EU judicial order to realise a series of functions, this order must still be managed. Two processes are particularly central to this management: identifying the circumstances under which a reference is made and determining the binding qualities of judgments of the Court of Justice.

(i) Managing the Circumstances in which National Courts Refer

In principle, all national courts enjoy a *discretion* whether to make a reference if they believe EU law is necessary to enable them to give a judgment.[166] However, this is subject to two exceptions. A national court must make a reference to the Court of Justice, first, if it considers an EU measure to be invalid,[167] or, secondly, if it is a court which falls within Article 267(3) TFEU and is not covered by the *CILFIT* exceptions.[168] This provision requires courts, against whose decision there is no judicial remedy in national law, to refer, where the point of EU law is necessary to decide the dispute at hand. It covers not just the highest courts in the land, but any court where a party has been denied the possibility to take the matter further because they have been denied leave to appeal to a higher court. In *Lyckeskog*, Lyckeskog was prosecuted for importing 500 kg

---

[163] *Leclerc Siplec* v. *TF1 Publicité*, C-412/93, EU:C:1995:26.
[164] *Stichting Zuid-Hollandse Milieufederatie* v. *Minister van Landbouw*, C-138/05, EU:C:2006:577.
[165] *Stoilov i Ko EOOD* v. *Nachalnik na Mitnitsa Stolichna*, C-180/12, EU:C:2013:693.   [166] Article 267(2) TFEU.
[167] *Firma Foto-Frost* v. *Hauptzollamt Lübeck Ost*, 314/85, EU:C:1987:452.   [168] See pp. 191–4.

of rice into Sweden without paying customs duties. He appealed to the Swedish Court of Appeal (Hovrätt för Västra Sverige), arguing that the relevant Regulation allowed duties not to be paid where the rice was for personal use. The Swedish Court of Appeal, whose decisions could be appealed to the Swedish Supreme Court (Högsta domstol), asked if it fell within Article 267(3) TFEU if it refused Lyckeskog leave to appeal.

Lyckeskog C-99/00, EU:C:2002:329

14 The obligation on national courts against whose decisions there is no judicial remedy to refer a question to the Court for a preliminary ruling has its basis in the cooperation established, in order to ensure the proper application and uniform interpretation of Community law in all the Member States, between national courts, as courts responsible for applying Community law, and the Court. That obligation is in particular designed to prevent a body of national case-law that is not in accordance with the rules of Community law from coming into existence in any Member State.

15 That objective is secured when, subject to the limits accepted by the Court of Justice . . . supreme courts are bound by this obligation to refer . . . as is any other national court or tribunal against whose decisions there is no judicial remedy under national law . . .

16 Decisions of a national appellate court which can be challenged by the parties before a supreme court are not decisions of a 'court or tribunal of a Member State against whose decisions there is no judicial remedy under national law' within the meaning of Article [267 TFEU]. The fact that examination of the merits of such appeals is subject to a prior declaration of admissibility by the supreme court does not have the effect of depriving the parties of a judicial remedy.

17 That is so under the Swedish system. The parties always have the right to appeal to the Högsta domstol against the judgment of a hovrätt, which cannot therefore be classified as a court delivering a decision against which there is no judicial remedy. Under Paragraph 10 of Chapter 54 of the Rättegångsbalk, [the Swedish Code of procedure] the Högsta domstol may issue a declaration of admissibility if it is important for guidance as to the application of the law that the appeal be examined by that court. Thus, uncertainty as to the interpretation of the law applicable, including Community law, may give rise to review, at last instance, by the supreme court.

18 If a question arises as to the interpretation or validity of a rule of Community law, the supreme court will be under an obligation, pursuant to the third paragraph of Article [267 TFEU], to refer a question to the Court of Justice for a preliminary ruling either at the stage of the examination of admissibility or at a later stage.

Lyckeskog secures the universal jurisdiction of the Court of Justice, albeit in a roundabout way. Paragraph 15 indicates that it is not merely the highest courts in the land who are covered by Article 267(3) TFEU, but also any other court against whom there is no judicial remedy. However, the absence of a judicial remedy will often not be decided by the court which made the substantive decision, but by a decision of a higher court which refuses the reference. It is the latter court which is bound to refer. In principle, in every case, there should be a point at which individuals are able to demand a reference, be it when leave to appeal is refused or the case is decided by the highest court in the land.

The duty to refer was reinforced by *Köbler*.[169] Köbler was an Austrian professor who lost bonuses, to which he would otherwise have been entitled for his length of service, because he had

---

[169] *Köbler* v. *Austria*, C-224/01, EU:C:2003:513.

spent some years working outside Austria at a German university.[170] The Austrian Administrative Court – a court of last resort – wrongly ruled that this did not breach EU law and that it was not, therefore, obliged to refer. The Court ruled that the action for damages, which is available against States for breaches of EU law, can also be applied where national courts breached EU law since they were also authorities of the State. The Court of Justice ruled that a failure to refer where a court was required to do so by Article 267(3) TFEU could, therefore, lead to an action for damages; though only where it was manifest that the national court was required to refer. In this instance, the Court held this was not the case as the Austrian court had mistakenly, but in good faith, thought that the matter was covered by a previous ruling of the Court which had held that the treatment was lawful.

This action for damages against a failure to refer is difficult to enforce. The redress is against the State, not the court. The incentives do not, therefore, fall directly on the court in question. Furthermore, it is for the national legal system to design the court which hears such an action.[171] This may well involve a lower court having to rule negatively on the actions of a more senior court. There are relatively few instances of the State being successfully sued under *Köbler* because of a failure to refer.[172] However, domestic constitutional developments in a number of States have provided an alternative remedy. In these States, a failure to refer is seen as an unlawful (usually unconstitutional) denial of access to justice or of a right to a fair trial on the grounds that access to the Court of Justice is something which must be provided to litigants by those States' legal systems.[173] However, this exists in only six States, and in only two – Austria and Germany – does there appear to have been successful litigation.[174]

Furthermore, none of the litigation has targeted constitutional court judgments. Indeed, a 2015 study found that only nine of the eighteen constitutional courts in the European Union had made a reference to the Court of Justice.[175] Equally, there are many courts of last resort who refer only irregularly. A study found that between 1978 and 2001, the French Conseil d'État, the French administrative court of last resort, considered EU law 191 times but made only eighteen references, whilst the Austrian Constitutional Court referred about half the cases in which EU law was invoked before it.[176]

The duty to refer is honoured, therefore, as much in breach as in observance.[177] The reason in large part is that the Court's case law has conveyed an impression of national judicial

---

[170] This case is dealt with in more detail in Ch. 7. On the principles of State liability see pp. 316–20.

[171] *ZPT* v. *Narodno sabranie na Republika Bulgaria*, C-518/16, EU:C:2018:126.

[172] On this see the excellent study by Z. Varga, 'National Remedies in the Case of Violation of EU Law by Member State Courts' (2017) 54 *CMLRev* 51, 56–8.

[173] R. Valutytė, 'Legal Consequences for the Infringement of the Obligation to Make a Reference for a Preliminary Ruling under Constitutional Law' (2012) 19 *Jurisprudence* 1171; C. Lacchi, 'Multilevel Judicial Protection in the EU and Preliminary References' (2016) 53 *CMLRev* 679.

[174] Varga, n. 172 above, 64–6. The six States are Austria, Czech Republic, Germany, Slovakia, Slovenia and Spain. Most recently in Germany, see 2 BvR 424/17 *D*, Order of 19 December 2017 (German Constitutional Court).

[175] The study did not categorise all supreme courts as constitutional courts (the United Kingdom Supreme Court was not included). Nevertheless, the level of disengagement demonstrated was significant. There had never been references, therefore, from the Bulgarian, Croatian, Czech, Latvian, Lithuanian, Luxembourg, Portuguese, Romanian or Slovakian courts. M. Dicosola, C. Fasone and I. Spigno, 'Foreword: Constitutional Courts in the European Legal System: After the Treaty of Lisbon and the Euro-Crisis' (2015) 16 *German LJ* 1317, 1318.

[176] N. Fenger and M. Broberg, 'Finding Light in the Darkness: On the Actual Application of the acte clair Doctrine' (2011) 30 *YBEL* 180, 188.

[177] It has been suggested, therefore, that only systemic rather than individual breaches of the duty to refer be punished, A. Kornezov, 'The New Format of the Acte Clair Doctrine and its Consequences' (2016) 53 *CMLRev* 1317, 1338–9.

contributions to the development and application of EU law which has been described by Davies in the following terms:

> Thus national court interpretations of Community law, while sometimes creative and purposive, take place in a grey area of semi-legitimacy, a sort of tolerated but not approved practice, where the assumption seems to be that ultimately any points of law will in fact make its way to the Court of Justice. Moreover, national final courts will have no interpretive competence at all.[178]

The refusal is, to some extent, a push-back against this perception. Characterisations of this push-back vary. Some see it as judicial jealousy with senior national courts simply protecting their turf,[179] whilst others perceive the issue as being Article 267 TFEU's emasculation of national judiciaries.[180]

These characterisations reflect wider tensions about the role of senior national judges within the EU judicial order – in particular, how much they should contribute to the development of EU law doctrines at the possible expense of the Court of Justice. This is because a new interpretation of EU law by a court of last resort will almost certainly preclude its making a reference. These tensions have crystallised around the exceptions to when national courts caught by Article 267(3) TFEU must refer: the doctrines of *acte éclairé* and *acte clair*.

Acte éclairé is where a materially identical matter has already been decided by the Court of Justice.[181] *Acte clair* is where the EU law provision in question is so clear that there is no scope for any reasonable doubt about its interpretation. This was, first, raised in *CILFIT*, a case before the Italian Court of Cassation, the highest civil court in Italy. The question was whether wool was an animal product, as the relevant Regulation prohibited levies on these.[182] The Court was exacting about the level of clarity required before a court caught by Article 267(3) TFEU did not have to refer. It stated that regard must be had to all the different language versions of EU law to make sure that it was clear in all of them, and also to the context and objectives of the provision which might cast some doubt on the meaning of the provision. Read literally, these constraints would make *CILFIT* so narrow as to be meaningless.[183] No court is, for example, going to hire twenty-three legal translators to check that the provision is equally clear in all the Union's official languages.

The question as to how *CILFIT* was to be interpreted came to a head in *X and Van Dijk*. The case concerned two Dutch boatmen who worked on boats going up and down the river Rhine and had obtained health insurance in Luxembourg. The Dutch tax authorities argued that they were still liable for compulsory contributions for the Dutch health insurance scheme. The relevant Regulation provided for mutual recognition for health insurance which would have meant that the boatmen were covered by the Luxembourg insurance in the Netherlands and did not need to contribute. However, it expressly stated that it was subject to the Rhine Agreement, an international agreement which provided for no mutual recognition in this case, and this was upheld

---

[178] G. Davies, 'The Division of Powers between the European Court of Justice and National Courts' (2004) 3 *ConWeb* 19.

[179] M. Claes, 'Luxembourg, Here We Come? Constitutional Courts and the Preliminary Reference Procedure' (2015) 16 *German LJ* 1331, 1332.

[180] P. Allott, 'Preliminary Rulings: Another Infant Disease' (2000) *ELRev* 538, 542; H. Rasmussen, 'Remedying the Crumbling EC Judicial System' (2000) 37 *CMLRev* 1071, 1092.

[181] *Da Costa* v. *Nederlandse Belastingadministratie*, 28–30/62, EU:C:1963:6.

[182] *CILFIT and Others* v. *Ministry of Health*, 283/81, EU:C:1982:335.

[183] H. Rasmussen, 'The European Court's Acte Clair Strategy in CILFIT' (1984) 9 *ELRev* 242; F. Mancini and D. Keeling, 'From CILFIT to ERT: The Constitutional Challenge Facing the European Court' (1991) 11 *YBEL* 1, 4.

by The Court and Advocate General in this. Nevertheless, the Dutch court of last resort asked if it could invoke *CILFIT* (and not refer), even though a lower Dutch court had already sought a reference on this question, therefore suggesting some doubt about the interpretation of EU law. The matter was addressed in some detail, first by the Advocate General.

Opinion of Advocate General Wahl in *X and Van Dijk*, C-72/14 and C-197/14, EU: C:2015:319

62 First, structurally speaking, times have changed radically since *Cilfit and Others* was handed down. In 1982, the European Economic Communities consisted of 10 Member States with 7 official working languages. In the year 2015, however, the EU is a more sophisticated union, with over 28 legal systems, 24 official working languages, much wider fields of competence and, as a clear innovation brought about by the Treaty of Lisbon, a greater emphasis on the role of national (supreme) courts under Article 19(2) TEU. If one were to adhere to a rigid reading of the case-law, coming across a 'true' *acte clair* situation would, at best, seem just as likely as encountering a unicorn.

63 Second, the system of checks and balances relating to Article 267(3) TFEU has also evolved. The Commission acknowledges a duty to oversee the way in which national courts of last instance make use of the *acte clair* doctrine. (50) Moreover, *Cilfit and Others* was handed down almost a decade before the judgment in *Francovich and Others*. (51)*Köbler* was a good 20 years away. Nowadays, the Court – and the European Court of Human Rights ('the ECtHR') – are regularly seised of proceedings relating to an alleged failure to refer under Article 267(3) TFEU.

64 Third, the simple truth is that national courts of last instance do not, in practice, exclude having recourse to the *acte clair* doctrine (explicitly or implicitly), even when the decisions appealed against – or a minority of the adjudicating formation – express differences of opinion. In the light of this, I would think it unwise for the Court to police the narrowest of interpretations of the scope of the conditions attaching to that doctrine. To do so would seem in contradiction both with reality and with the spirit of cooperation which characterises the relationship between the Court of Justice and the national (supreme) courts . . .

67 The expression 'the national court or tribunal must be convinced that the matter is equally obvious to the courts of the other Member States and to the Court of Justice', as I understand it, ought to be seen in the same light as the other qualifying factors listed by the Court in *Cilfit and Others* . . . Hence, that requirement cannot be understood in absolute terms. Rather, it should be understood as meaning that the judges of final appeal ruling upon the matter must be convinced, in their minds, that other judges would agree with them. As I see it, the circumstances mentioned in paragraphs 16 to 20 of the judgment in *Cilfit and Others* constitute a 'tool kit' for determining whether or not there might be any reasonable doubt. They are to be seen as warning signs rather than strict criteria and, read fairly, amount to no more than common sense. So, unlike certain commentators, I find myself unable to read *Cilfit and Others* as stating that reasonable doubt can be measured objectively merely by pointing to differences of interpretative opinion among members of the judiciary. Indeed, *Cilfit and Others* concerned a situation where a national court of last instance asked the Court whether it was at all conceivable for there not to be an obligation to refer an unresolved question of EU law to the Court of Justice. Having answered that question in the affirmative on the point of principle, the Court then attempted to draft the conditions attaching thereto in such a manner as to prevent judicial disagreement from arising. On the other hand, *Cilfit and Others* is silent as to the inferences to be drawn if judicial disagreement actually arises, as in the cases under consideration.

68 In this sense, it seems less important to me whether potential disagreement might come from a judge from another Member State or a judge from the same Member State. After all, the Court has highlighted 'the risk of divergences in judicial decisions within the Community', (60) which – given the particular aim of Article

267(3) TFEU to prevent a body of national case-law not in accord with the rules of EU law from coming into existence in any Member State – would, a priori, include the intra-State scenario. A different view would, in fact, make little sense in respect of Member States with different legal systems applicable in their constituent parts, such as the United Kingdom. In addition, although they are admittedly not treated alike in the context of Article 267 TFEU, it seems desirable to adopt a coherent approach in the relationship between national courts of a lower rank and courts of last instance: if a lower court is not bound by the ruling of a national court of last instance which the former deems to be incompatible with EU law, why ought the latter then to be bound by a difference of opinion expressed by a lower court?

69 So in essence, my view boils down to this: if a national court of last instance is sure enough of its own interpretation to take upon itself the responsibility (and possibly the blame) for resolving a point of EU law without the aid of the Court of Justice, it ought to be legally entitled to do so. But, in such a situation, there is a fly in the ointment: the prospect that legal action might be taken against the Member State of the court of last instance for failure to refer and/or incorrect application of EU law. That is a risk which that court must assume alone.

The Court's judgment was cryptic. Whilst it does not endorse the Advocate General's opinion, neither does the Court refute it.

X and Van Dijk, C-72/14 and C-197/14, EU:C:2015:564

54 It should be remembered, in particular, that the obligation on national courts and tribunals against whose decision there is no judicial remedy to refer a matter to the Court of Justice under the third paragraph of Article 267 TFEU is based on cooperation, established with a view to ensuring the proper application and uniform interpretation of EU law in all the Member States, between national courts, in their capacity as courts responsible for the application of EU law, and the Court . . .

55 The Court has held that a court or tribunal against whose decisions there is no judicial remedy under national law is required, where a question of EU law is raised before it, to comply with its obligation to bring the matter before the Court of Justice, unless it has established that the question raised is irrelevant or that the EU law provision in question has already been interpreted by the Court or that the correct application of EU law is so obvious as to leave no scope for any reasonable doubt. The Court has further held that the existence of such a possibility must be assessed in the light of the specific characteristics of EU law, the particular to which its interpretation gives rise and the risk of divergences in judicial decisions within the EU (judgment in *Cilfit and Others*, 283/81, EU:C:1982:335, paragraph 21) . . .

57 It must be borne in mind that it is solely for the national court before which the dispute has been brought, and which must assume responsibility for the subsequent judicial decision, to determine in the light of the particular circumstances of the case both the need for a preliminary ruling in order to enable it to deliver judgment and the relevance of the questions which it submits to the Court . . .

58 Moreover, the case-law as stated in *Cilfit and Others* . . . gives the national court sole responsibility for determining whether the correct application of EU law is so obvious as to leave no scope for any reasonable doubt and for deciding, as a result, to refrain from referring to the Court of Justice a question concerning the interpretation of EU law which has been raised before it . . .

59 It follows therefrom that it is for the national courts alone against whose decisions there is no judicial remedy under national law, to take upon themselves independently the responsibility for determining whether the case before them involves an 'acte clair'.

> 60 Thus, although in a situation such as that at issue in the main proceedings a supreme court of a Member State must bear in mind in its assessment that a case is pending in which a lower court has referred a question to the Court of Justice for a preliminary ruling, that fact alone does not preclude the supreme court of a Member State from concluding, from its examination of the case and in keeping with the criteria laid down in the judgment in *Cilfit and Others* . . . that the case before it involves an 'acte clair'.

The judgment is a curious mix. It can be read narrowly as simply stating that a reference by a lower court does not preclude use of *acte clair* by a more senior court. However, it can also be read more broadly as it references the language of the Advocate General, referring to the preliminary reference procedure as being based on cooperation and to national judges having responsibility for deciding whether the case before them is one of *acte clair*.

X and Van Dyck hints, therefore, at a divided Court in which the broad pattern of direction is to liberalise *CILFIT*,[184] but there is uncertainty and disagreement as to the extent of this liberalisation. This has carried over into the subsequent case law.

In *Ferreira da Silva e Brito*, the Court stated that the fact that other national courts may have given contradictory decisions did not stop a provision being *acte clair*.[185] It allowed, therefore, for some scope for disagreement about the interpretation of a provision before it had to be referred. However, this scope appears limited. In particular, the Court stated that a provision had to be referred if either national decisions revealed difficulties in interpretation or there was a risk of divergent judicial decisions in the different Member States. This suggested that the Court will allow considerable latitude for national courts not to refer, provided, that it does not lead to a distinctive national body of case law arising on interpretation of an EU law.

However, a more restrictive position was taken in *Association France Nature Environnement*.[186] The Court quoted none of the recent case law. It insisted that the national court in that instance had to refer for two reasons. First, the Court of Justice had not given a judgment on the provision in question in the prior four years and, secondly, the French court was invoking a provision which provided for a derogation from EU law. If the first ground was suggestive of a provision that was reasonably clear, no judgment had been given as there was little contestation about its meaning, the second suggests that attention is paid to the factual context of the dispute. If there is a suspicion that non-referral might lead to a departure from EU law, a reference is required. Otherwise, the situation is more relaxed.

The consequence is that there is considerable uncertainty as to when a national court is obliged to refer. It is not even clear how much this duty influences the number of references which come before the Court. Broberg and Fenger found that structural elements, such as population size, a society's litigiousness or a national government propensity to obey EU law

---

[184] The opinion of Advocate General Wahl is therefore very much at odds with that of Advocate General Bot in *Ferreira da Silva e Brito and Others* v. *Portugal*, C-160/14, EU:C:2015:390. See also A. Kornezov, 'The New Format of the Acte Clair Doctrine and its Consequences' (2016) 53 *CMLRev* 1317, 1323–9.

[185] *Ferreira da Silva e Brito and Others* v. *Portugal*, C-160/14, EU:C:2015:565. A. Limante, 'Recent Developments in the Acte Clair Case Law of the EU Court of Justice: Towards a More Flexible Approach' (2016) 54 *JCMS* 1384.

[186] *Association France Nature Environnement* v. *Premier ministre*, C-379/15, EU:C:2016:603.

were the most powerful dynamics behind references from different Member States.[187] Broberg has thus argued that the relationship between senior courts and the Court of Justice should be recast.

M. Broberg, 'Acte Clair Revisited: Adapting the Acte Clair Criteria to the Demands of the Times' (2008) 45 *Common Market Law Review* 1383, 1397

[T]he question is not simply whether or not to refer. Rather, the need is to have all the important matters referred to the Court of Justice whereas the less important ones should not be referred. Therefore, to better achieve the purpose underlying [Article 267(3)], an adjustment of the *CILFIT* criteria is required so that national courts of last instance will only be obliged to refer questions where there is a genuine need for a uniform interpretation and where the questions go beyond the main action . . .

The *CILFIT* criteria thus adjusted do not make it possible for the national courts of last instance to attribute any weight to the wishes of the parties in the main action when deciding whether or not to refer a question to the European Court of Justice. Likewise the adjusted criteria only lay down when a national court of last instance must refer a question for a preliminary ruling; they do not affect when such a court may refer. In order to ensure an effective and uniform application of the adjusted *CILFIT* criteria it is suggested that the adjustment is accompanied by two further initiatives. Thus, it is proposed that national courts of last instance shall be required to give reasons whenever they invoke the adjusted *CILFIT* criteria in support of not referring a question to the European Court of Justice. Moreover, it is proposed that the national courts of last instance shall be given access to sophisticated advice when they have to determine whether or not a question of Community law meets the adjusted *CILFIT* criteria.

Broberg's observation is that if the Court's concern is with the uniformity and development of EU law, it should only deal with cases which go significantly to these questions. There is some evidence that the Court is moving in this direction in *X and Van Dyck* and *Ferreira da Silva e Brito*, but any such movement is tentative and the reasons behind it less clearly formulated than they are by him. It has been argued that even this is insufficient as it still results in domestic judicial resources being largely under-utilised and too much faith being placed in a single court, the Court of Justice.

D. Chalmers, 'The European Court of Justice Is Now Little More than a Rubber Stamp for the EU. It Should Be Replaced with Better Alternative Arrangements for Central Judicial Guidance' LSE EUROPP, 8 March 2012

The referral procedure is . . . skewed by a long backlog, which biases the docket. Parties wishing to enlarge EU law through a Court ruling win not only the case in hand but they secure a more general change of the law within their jurisdiction, because domestic law has to be adapted to the new settlement. As a result many parties to cases are happy to accept the delay. By contrast, there are no such incentives for parties who wish to secure a retrenchment of EU law. It is rare that the Court will reverse its previous rulings, so a better path is to seek domestic legal resistance by asking for interpretations of domestic law that only just

---

[187] M. Broberg and N. Fenger, 'Variations in Member States' Preliminary References to the Court of Justice – Are Structural Factors (Part of) the Explanation?' (2013) 19 *ELJ* 488.

comply with EU law. The consequence of this asymmetry is that almost all the legal questions referred to the European Court of Justice ask for it to extend rather than to retract EU legal obligations. There is no pluralist process before the Court, but simply a relentless one-way traffic.

The final sin of the current system is that it supplants and thereby neglects Europe's rich legal resources. By investing the final word in a single isolated institution, it overlooks the twenty seven legal jurisdictions out there with years of diverse experimentation, creativity and experience behind them. In this linked up world, judges struggling with a thorny dispute or wishing to build a common European legal heritage should turn their eyes in the direction of Europe's accumulated wealth of legal ideas, which lies there ready to help.

So here's a thought. Replace the current 'preliminary reference procedure' for going to the ECJ for a ruling with a database. All the appellate courts within the European Union interpreting a point of EU law in each of the 27 member states would be required to submit their judgments to that database. Translators would then make the judgments available in the different languages of the European Union. Courts from states outside the European Union interpreting EU law (it happens more than you think!) would also be invited to submit their judgments to the database, if they so wish. Judges in the EU countries interpreting EU law would then be required to consider rulings in the database on the provision in question – but they could also give reasons why it would not be suitable for their jurisdiction, bearing in mind the obligations of EU membership.

This database would provide quicker justice than a reference to the European Court of Justice. It would almost certainly generate more legal certainty and uniformity, simply by dint of more judgments being available to the local judge to guide her. It would cultivate Europe's legal riches rather than seek to replace them with an inauthentic legal currency of its own. Lastly, it would possibly be cheaper because it would allow the Court's size to be reduced considerably.

(ii) The Binding Effects of Court of Justice Judgments

A judgment given by the Court of Justice binds the referring national court.[188] However, it is free to refer the question back to the Court of Justice if it is either dissatisfied with or unclear about the meaning of the ruling. In such circumstances, in a form of judicial ping-pong, the Court has tended to simply reiterate or extrapolate on its prior judgment.[189] National compliance is high. A study found implementation of the Court's rulings in 96.3 per cent of the cases studied.[190] However, the context for such high levels of compliance is that the Court of Justice will often seek to defuse conflict by giving judgments which are sufficiently vague to allow the national court considerable discretion as to how to resolve the dispute.[191]

There remains the question of the effects of the Court's judgments on the wider judicial community. The doctrines of *stare decisis* and precedent do not formally exist in EU law.

---

[188] *Benedetti* v. *Munari*, 52/76, EU:C:1977:16.

[189] *Da Costa* v. *Nederlandse Belastingadministratie*, 28–30/62, EU:C:1963:6; *Foglia* v. *Novello (No. 2)*, 244/80, EU:C:1981:302.

[190] This study is dated but there are few reasons to assume that circumstances have changed. S. Nyikos, 'The Preliminary Reference Process: National Court Implementation, Changing Opportunity Structures and Litigant Desistment' (2003) 4 *EUP* 397, 410.

[191] T. Tridimas, 'Constitutional Review of Member State Action: The Virtues and Vices of an Incomplete Jurisdiction' (2011) 9 *I-CON* 737; Davies, n. 92 above.

Judgments of the Court only clarify and define the pre-existing state of the law.[192] However, if judgments only bound the parties to the action in which the Court declared an EU measure invalid, it would lead to the instrument being invalid for the parties but binding for everybody else, albeit that anybody could challenge its legality. In *ICC*, therefore, the Court ruled that a judgment declaring an EU measure invalid binds all courts and authorities in the Union.[193]

In *Kühne*, the Court stated that other interpretations of EU law given by the Court of Justice bind national authorities in the Union, but on a slightly different basis – because they clarify and define how EU law should be understood.[194] Although *Kühne* concerned the binding effects of Court judgments for administrative authorities, subsequent case law has made clear that national judges are also bound by Court judgments and they must set aside national laws which conflict with these judgments.[195]

The question of whether national courts should reopen cases because they conflict with subsequent Court of Justice judgments is more complicated. The Court has acknowledged that the principles of legal certainty and finality of judicial decision militate against reopening these cases.[196] However, it is also unhappy about letting their effects frustrate the wider effective application of EU law.[197] The Court has balanced these tensions by looking at whether reopening would compromise the rights of defence, legal certainty or the proper conduct of proceedings. In circumstances where this does not appear to be the case, it will limit the effect of the national decision. It is particularly wary of allowing open-ended decisions to stand.[198] In *Fallimento Olimpiclub*, the Court of Justice stated, therefore, that a decision of an Italian tax court, which conflicted with EU law, had *res judicata* effects and so did not need to be reopened for that tax year. However, it stated that it could not have open-ended effects so that the taxpayer could avoid paying tax in breach of EU law for all future years. The Court held, therefore, the judgment did not apply to subsequent tax years.[199]

6 THE AUTHORITY OF THE EUROPEAN UNION COURTS IN THE UNITED KINGDOM AFTER BREXIT

(i) The Authority of the Court of Justice during the Transition Period

During the transition period – which is the period from the date of exit of the United Kingdom from the European Union until 31 December 2020 – there is little change regarding the jurisdiction of the Court of Justice and the authority of its judgments. The jurisdiction of the Court of Justice shall be the same as in the EU Treaties.[200] EU law continues to be applicable within the United Kingdom[201] and is to produce the same legal effects there as it does within the Union.[202]

---

[192] E.g. *Hochtief* v. *Budapest Főváros Önkormányzata*, C-300/17, EU:C:2018:635. For analysis, M. Jacobs, *Precedents and Case-Based Reasoning in the European Court of Justice* (Cambridge University Press, 2016) 243–53.

[193] *International Chemical Corporation* v. *Amministrazione Finanze*, 66/80, EU:C:1981:102.

[194] *Kühne and Heitz* v. *Productschap voor Pluimvee en Eieren*, C-453/00, EU:C:2004:17.

[195] *NPO* v. *Jonkman*, C-231–3/06, EU:C:2007:373.

[196] *Kapferer* v. *Schlank & Schlick*, C-234/04, EU:C:2006:178; *Impresa Pizzarotti*, C-213/13, EU:C:2014:206.

[197] *Târşia* v. *Statul român*, C-69/14, EU:C:2015:662.

[198] See in this regard, also, *Klausner Holz Niedersachsen* v. *Land Nordrhein-Westfalen*, C-505/14, EU:C:2015:742.

[199] *Fallimento Olimpiclub*, C-2/08, EU:C:2009:506.   [200] Withdrawal Agreement, Article 131.

[201] *Ibid.* Article 127(1).   [202] *Ibid.* Article 4(1).

Judgments of the Court of Justice are, in particular, to have the same binding effect within the United Kingdom as they do within the Union.[203]

(ii) The Endurance of the Preliminary Reference Procedure after the Transition Period

The European Union (Withdrawal) Act provides that no UK court can make a reference to the Court of Justice on or after exit day.[204] This will almost certainly have to be revisited in the light of the Withdrawal Agreement because that agreement provides for the possibility of references during the transition period. The jurisdiction of the Court will, in fact, extend significantly beyond that.

First, according to Article 86(2) of the Withdrawal Agreement, the Court of Justice shall continue to have jurisdiction to provide a ruling as long as the reference made by the UK court was prior to the end of the transition period. The Court of Justice may well, thus, be hearing cases from UK cases well into 2022.

Secondly, there is one field where the Court of Justice will have a longer-lasting jurisdiction over the United Kingdom. This concerns the rights of those Union citizens and their families granted the right to reside within the United Kingdom as a result of the Withdrawal Agreement. There was agreement that the rights of both Union citizens and their families resident in the United Kingdom and United Kingdom citizens and their families resident in the European Union at the end of the transitional period should be 'protected' and 'consistent'.[205] The Union believed that this was only possible if Court of Justice judgments on these rights applied both in the Union and the United Kingdom. The United Kingdom opposed this, arguing that its own courts could be trusted to protect Union citizens' rights. A compromise was reached where references will be able to be made from UK courts to the Court of Justice for a period of eight years after the end of the transition period.

Article 158 Withdrawal agreement

(1) Where, in a case which has commenced at first instance within 8 years from the end of the transition period before a court or tribunal in the United Kingdom, a question is raised concerning the interpretation of Part Two of this Agreement, and where that court or tribunal considers that a decision on that question is necessary to enable it to give judgment in that case, it may request the Court of Justice of the European Union to give a preliminary ruling on that question.

(2) The Court of Justice of the European Union shall have jurisdiction to give preliminary rulings on requests pursuant to paragraph 1. The legal effects in the United Kingdom of such preliminary rulings shall be the same as the legal effects of preliminary rulings given pursuant to Article 267 TFEU in the Union and its Member States.[206]

---

[203] *Ibid.* Articles 4(4) and 89(1).   [204] European Union (Withdrawal) Act 2018, s. 6(1)(b).

[205] European Commission, 'Press statement by Michel Barnier following the fifth round of Article 50 negotiations with the United Kingdom', 12 October 2017.

[206] There is one slight exception to this. The clock for cases concerning applications for residence documents runs from when the decision on the application was made, Withdrawal Agreement, Article 158(1).

On its face, this seems an odd compromise. It subjects the United Kingdom to the jurisdiction of the Court of Justice for a considerable period after Brexit, thereby going against a core goal of Brexit's advocates. Conversely, from the Union perspective, there remains the question of whether consistency will be secured in the interpretation of the rights of EU and UK citizens at the end of this eight-year period. The hope is, of course, that a body of case law will have developed during this period which will bind these courts and ensure little scope for deviation.

(iii) The Enduring Effects of Court of Justice Judgments after Brexit

Independently of the Withdrawal Agreement, UK law makes provision for (some of) the case law of the Court of Justice to continue to have binding effects within the United Kingdom after Brexit. Most centrally, existing case law on retained EU law,[207] that body of EU law that is transposed into UK law at the moment of Brexit, will continue to bind UK courts.

European Union (Withdrawal) Act 2018, s. 6

(3) Any question as to the validity, meaning or effect of any retained EU law is to be decided, so far as that law is unmodified on or after exit day and so far as they are relevant to it –

(a) in accordance with any retained case law and any retained general principles of EU law, and

(b) having regard (among other things) to the limits, immediately before exit day, of EU competences.

Insofar as retained EU law covers almost all EU law, this means that the overwhelming majority of existing Court of Justice cases will continue to bind UK courts for the indefinite future. This is subject to two caveats.

First, UK courts can have regard to the limits of EU competences in deciding whether to be bound by a Court of Justice judgment (s. 6(3)(b) above). The implication is that if a UK court believes that a Court of Justice judgment went too far and was too activist, it can declare that the latter was acting *ultra vires* or providing an interpretation of EU law that went beyond what the Union was actually competent to do. This caveat opens a route for UK courts to disregard judgments that they do not like since such accusations are relatively easy to make. If widely invoked, it is likely to generate confusion about the binding qualities of Court of Justice judgments.

Secondly, neither the United Kingdom Supreme Court nor the Scottish High Court of Justiciary is bound by this body of case law.[208] However, in deciding whether to depart from it, each 'must apply the same test as it would apply in deciding whether to depart from its own case law'.[209] This means that the United Kingdom Supreme Court can therefore decide to depart from that case law where it seems right to do so.[210] The position of the High Court of Justiciary is more confusing as it is not bound by previous decisions only where more judges are sitting in the case than were sitting in the decision to be overturned.[211] This would imply that

---

[207] On retained EU law see pp. 244–5.   [208] European Union (Withdrawal) Act 2018, s. 6(4).   [209] *Ibid.* s. 6(5).
[210] Practice Statement [1966] 3 All ER 77.   [211] *McCutcheon* v. *HMA* [2002] SLT 27.

departure from most case law of the Court of Justice would require a bench of at least seven judges, as most Court of Justice judgments were given by Chambers of five judges.

The position is different for judgments given by the Court of Justice after Brexit. These do not bind UK courts, and it does not matter whether they are on EU law that was adopted prior to Brexit, or whether it is EU law adopted subsequently.[212] However UK courts 'may have regard' to these judgments insofar as it is relevant to any matter before them.[213] This discretion is tempered by regard having to be had to the limits of Union competences.[214] UK courts must not reference or follow judgments, therefore, which go beyond what the Court of Justice is empowered to give or which grant the Union powers that it does not have. Furthermore, when Court judgments are on modifications to existing EU law that were made after Brexit, regard can only be had to the judgment if it is giving effect to the intention of the modification. If a judgment provides an interpretation that goes beyond this, it should be ignored.[215]

The breadth of discretion granted to the UK judiciary has caused concern. The President of the United Kingdom Supreme Court had, in particular, asked Parliament to give guidance on how much weight was to be given to future judgments of the Court of Justice, and to give as much clarity as possible.[216] This did not happen. It is a matter for speculation how UK courts will exercise their discretion here. It may be that they see interpretive alignment as defeating the point of Brexit and thus pay little regard to subsequent case law of the Court. Alternatively, they may view interpretive alignment as desirable because it generates synergies between the United Kingdom and the rest of the European Union and that the practice of the Union, insofar as it is the practice of twenty-seven States, is a good indicator of what others think as a reasonable interpretation of the law.

FURTHER READING

A. Alemanno and L. Pech, 'Thinking Justice Outside the Docket: A Critical Assessment of The Reform of the EU's Court System' (2017) 54 *Common Market Law Review* 129.

M. Broberg and N. Fenger, 'Variations in Member States' Preliminary References to the Court of Justice: Are Structural Factors (Part of) the Explanation?' (2013) 19 *European Law Journal* 488.

G. Conway, *The Limits of Legal Reasoning and the European Court of Justice* (Cambridge University Press, 2012).

Court of Justice of the European Union (ed.), *The Court of Justice and the Construction of Europe: Analyses and Perspectives on Sixty Years of Case-law* (The Hague, Asser, 2013).

M. Dawson *et al.*, *Judicial Activism at the Court of Justice* (Cheltenham, Edward Elgar, 2013).

A. Kornezov, 'The New Format of the Acte Clair Doctrine and its Consequences' (2016) 53 *Common Market Law Review* 1317.

D. Martinsen, *An Ever More Powerful Court? The Political Constraints of Legal Integration in the European Union* (Oxford University Press, 2015).

J. Mayoral, 'In the CJEU Judges Trust: A New Approach in the Judicial Construction of Europe' (2017) 55 *Journal of Common Market Studies* 551.

---

[212] European Union (Withdrawal) Act 2018, s. 6(1). [213] *Ibid.* s. 6(2). [214] *Ibid.* s. 6(3). [215] *Ibid.* s. 6(6).
[216] O. Bowcott, 'UK's New Supreme Court Chief Calls for Clarity on ECJ after Brexit', *The Guardian*, 5 October 2017.

S. Saurugger and F. Terpan, *The Court of Justice of the European Union and the Politics of Law* (Basingstoke, Palgrave, 2017).

S. Schmidt, *The European Court of Justice and the Policy Press* (Oxford University Press, 2018).

A. Vauchez, *Brokering Europe: Euro-Lawyers and the Making of a Transnational Polity* (Cambridge University Press, 2015).

N. Wahl and L. Prete, 'The Gatekeepers of Article 267 TFEU: On Jurisdiction and Admissibility of References for Preliminary Rulings' (2018) 55 *Common Market Law Review* 511.

5

The Authority of EU Law

CONTENTS

1   INTRODUCTION

This chapter considers the authority of EU law. It is organised as follows.

Section 2 considers the implications of *Van Gend en Loos* (*VGL*) and *Costa* v. *ENEL* holding EU law to be an autonomous legal order which limits national sovereignty. According to these judgments, EU law gives rise to rights that can be directly invoked in national courts and are to take precedence over all national law, even national constitutions. National judiciaries have generally accepted these propositions, albeit subject to some qualifications. Consequently, in the overwhelming majority of cases, EU law is invoked unproblematically in national courts, and often at the expense of national law.

Section 3 examines the doctrines which secure EU legal authority. The autonomy of EU law requires that EU law alone decides which activities it regulates and that EU law's central principles and institutional features cannot be compromised by other legal orders. The primacy of EU law stipulates that in cases of conflict between EU law and national law, precedence should be given to EU law. The doctrine of pre-emption determines that EU law, not national law, decides when there is a conflict between EU law and national law and the consequences of that conflict. The fidelity principle imposes duties on both EU and national authorities to ensure that the EU legal system functions effectively and its authority sustained.

Section 4 considers the foundations underpinning the authority of EU law. These foundations rely, first, on the pedigree of those recognising it. Historically, this was largely national courts. A Declaration to the Lisbon Treaty recognising the primacy of EU law provided government support for its authority, albeit that the use of a Declaration suggested such support to be less than enthusiastic. They comprise, secondly, the reasons for granting EU law authority. The best reasons are that EU law can grant rights not provided by national law, generate new types of relationship and awareness, and can civilise State power. However, there is no guarantee that it will do this, and anything provided by EU law must be set off against whatever is provided by national law. Thus the third part of this section notes that the case for one law having *a priori* authority over the other is not compelling. It then looks at the central schools which address how to mediate the competing claims of EU and national law. The constitutional pluralist school argues that this should be done by reference to shared constitutional principles and values. The pluralist school argues, by contrast, against any overarching principles. It seeks, instead, an incremental process where each legal system commits itself merely to be open to the claims of the other.

Section 5 considers how national constitutional courts have addressed the authority of EU law. Four types of condition on EU law's authority are prevalent in the case law. First, EU law must respect fundamental rights set out in national constitutions. For some legal systems, EU law does this by having mechanisms of its own to prevent and rectify abuses. For others, there is a straightforward duty on EU law not to violate these rights. The second source of review is *ultra vires* review. The Union must not exceed its competences. For some jurisdictions, EU measures will only be invalid if the Union exceeded its competences in a manifest and structurally significant way, and the Court of Justice had an opportunity to rectify this and failed to do so. For others, a simple *ultra vires* act is sufficient. The third form of review is *identity review*. This occurs in fields considered so central to a State's constitutional identity that it is believed the Union does not have the democratic credentials to act in them. Such fields include citizenship; foreign and defence policy; budgetary policy; fundamental rights; social policy; and cultural, family and education policy. Fourthly, the German Constitutional Court has intimated that an EU law may still have authority in these fields and in so-called 'dynamic' fields – fields where EU law's power is quite open-ended – if the national parliament also agrees to that law, and can monitor the operation of that law.

Section 6 looks at the status of EU law in the United Kingdom after it leaves the European Union. During any transition period, EU law, including new EU laws, will enjoy the same status as during the United Kingdom's period of membership. In the event of no transition period or after that period, a new category of 'retained EU law' is created. This comprises directly effective EU law; directly applicable EU law other than the EU Treaties and international agreements within non-EU States; and EU derived domestic legislation, which includes UK laws transposing or referring to EU law. This law will be retained EU law if adopted prior to the date of exit. It will continue to have legal effect within the United Kingdom and take precedence over all UK laws adopted prior to that date. New EU laws will have no direct legal effects within the United Kingdom unless they are modifications to existing EU law.

2 THE GENESIS OF EU LEGAL AUTHORITY

In the 1950s, it was widely assumed that the traditional model of international law, marked by State sovereignty, would apply to the European Union. Under this model, States are masters of the Treaties. Collectively, they can change the Union's powers and interpret the meaning of the Treaties.[1] Furthermore, as the EU Treaties are international treaties, it is for the States, as sovereigns, to determine the domestic legal effects of EU law and, in particular, whether it can be invoked in national courts and the relationship between it and national law.

However, the horrors of the Second World War had led to a belief in a much stronger role for international law and international organisations. Thus, in the negotiations surrounding the Council of Europe at the 1948 Hague Congress, there had been discussion about how the building of a European order might require some limitation of sovereignty.[2] This belief carried into a number of constitutional amendments. The German Basic Law, adopted in 1949, provided for sovereignty to be transferred to international organisations and the precedence of the Treaties over German legislation.[3] Amendments to the French Constitution (in 1946)[4] and the Italian (in 1947),[5] Dutch (in 1953)[6] and Luxembourg Constitutions (in 1956)[7] all either granted precedence for Treaties over national legislation or powers of government for international organisations.

Against this context, the Court of Justice adopted two judgments in the early 1960s which shape how we conceive the authority of EU law. First, the Court ruled in *Van Gend en Loos* that the Treaty did not merely regulate mutual obligations between Member States, but established a 'new legal order of international law for the benefit of which the states have limited their sovereign rights'. This meant that EU laws could be invoked in national courts if they met certain criteria.[8] This was taken further in *Costa* v. *ENEL*. An Italian law sought to nationalise the electricity production and distribution industries. Costa, a shareholder of Edison Volta, a company affected by the nationalisation, claimed that the law breached EU law. The Italian Government claimed that the matter was governed by Italian law as the Italian legislation post-dated the EC Treaty and, for that reason, should be held to be the applicable law.

---

[1] J. Weiler and U. Haltern, 'The Autonomy of the Community Legal Order: Through the Looking Glass' (1996) 37 *Harvard Int LJ* 411, 417–19.

[2] A. Simpson, *Human Rights and the End of Empire: Britain and the Genesis of the European Convention* (Oxford University Press, 2004) 603–27.

[3] Articles 24 and 25 Basic Law.

[4] Article 28, 1946 French Constitution. G. Neuman, 'The Brakes that Failed: Constitutional Restriction of International Agreements in France' (2012) 45 *Cornell Int'l LJ* 257, 263–7.

[5] Article 11 Italian Constitution 1947.

[6] Articles 63 and 65–67 Netherlands Constitution 1953, K. v. Leuwen, 'On Democratic Concerns and Legal Traditions: The Dutch 1953 and 1956 Constitutional Reforms "Towards" Europe' (2012) 21 *Contemporary European History* 357.

[7] An Article 49bis was added to the Luxembourg Constitution by a law of 25 October 1956.

[8] *Van Gend en Loos* v. *Nederlandse Administratie der Belastingen*, 26/62, EU:C:1963:1. On its historical context see M. Rasmussen, 'Revolutionizing European Law: A History of the *Van Gend en Loos* Judgment (2014) 12 *ICON* 136. This case is considered in detail in Chs. 1 and 7. See pp. 15–17 and 291–3.

Costa v. *ENEL*, 6/64, EU:C:1964:66

By contrast with ordinary international treaties, the EEC Treaty has created its own legal system which, on the entry into force of the Treaty, became an integral part of the legal systems of the Member States and which their courts are bound to apply.

By creating a Community of unlimited duration, having its own institutions, its own personality, its own legal capacity and capacity of representation on the international plane and, more particularly, real powers stemming from a limitation of sovereignty or a transfer of powers from the States to the Community, the Member States have limited their sovereign rights, albeit within limited fields, and have thus created a body of law which binds both their nationals and themselves.

The integration into the laws of each Member State of provisions which derive from the Community, and more generally the terms and the spirit of the Treaty, make it impossible for the States, as a corollary, to accord precedence to a unilateral and subsequent measure over a legal system accepted by them on a basis of reciprocity. Such a measure cannot therefore be inconsistent with that legal system. The executive force of Community law cannot vary from one State to another in deference to subsequent domestic laws, without jeopardizing the attainment of the objectives of the Treaty set out in Article [4(3) TEU] and giving rise to the discrimination prohibited by Article [18 TFEU].

The obligations undertaken under the Treaty establishing the Community would not be unconditional, but merely contingent, if they could be called in question by subsequent legislative acts of the signatories. Wherever the Treaty grants the States the right to act unilaterally, it does this by clear and precise provisions ... Applications, by Member States for authority to derogate from the Treaty are subject to a special authorization procedure ... which would lose their purpose if the Member States could renounce their obligations by means of an ordinary law.

The precedence of Community law is confirmed by Article [288 TFEU], whereby a regulation 'shall be binding' and 'directly applicable in all Member States'. This provision, which is subject to no reservation, would be quite meaningless if a state could unilaterally nullify its effects by means of a legislative measure which could prevail over Community law.

It follows from all these observations that the law stemming from the Treaty, an independent source of law, could not, because of its special and original nature, be overridden by domestic legal provisions, however framed, without being deprived of its character as Community law and without the legal basis of the Community itself being called into question.

The transfer by the States from their domestic legal system to the Community legal system of the rights and obligations arising under the Treaty carries with it a permanent limitation of their sovereign rights, against which a subsequent unilateral act incompatible with the concept of the Community cannot prevail.

Van Gend en Loos and *Costa* curb State power, and not in a small way. EU law is to limit its most absolute expression, national sovereignty. In the following years, these judgments met with a mixed response. Formally, all national legal systems committed themselves to accepting the primacy of EU law over national law.[9] However, many were unwilling to accept its authority

---

[9] B. de Witte, 'Direct Effect, Supremacy, and the Nature of the Legal Order' in P. Craig and G. de Búrca (eds.), *The Evolution of EU Law*, 1st edn (Oxford University Press, 1999) 196–8.

on issues of strong sensitivity. Issues of fundamental rights, national security and taxation provoked tensions.[10] Insofar as EU law rarely touched on these sensitive issues in the first years, however, conflicts were only occasional.[11]

As EU legal activities expanded, this tension between the formal commitment to primacy and concerns about the encroachment by EU law onto ever more sensitive activities became more intense.[12] In *Melloni*, an Italian was charged with fraud. He skipped bail, and, in his absence, was convicted in Italy to ten years' imprisonment. Eleven years later, he was arrested in Spain. He opposed his surrender back to Italy under a European Arrest Warrant on the grounds that he had been deprived the right to a fair trial by being convicted *in absentia*. The EU law regulating these warrants provided that trial *in absentia* was not a valid reason to refuse surrender. The matter went to the Tribunal Constitucional, the Spanish Constitutional Court, who thought the right to a fair trial, as protected by the Spanish Constitution, might be prejudiced. The matter concerned, therefore, a fundamental right, a constitutional text and the highest court in the land. Its import was shown by nine governments, the Council and the Commission intervening in the case. The Spanish court asked whether Article 53 of the European Union Charter of Fundamental Rights meant that EU law should allow national constitutions with a higher protection of fundamental rights to prevail. Article 53 states 'Nothing in this Charter shall be interpreted as restricting or adversely affecting human rights and fundamental freedoms as recognised, in their respective fields of application, by Union law and by the Member States' constitutions.'

Melloni v. *Ministerio Fiscal*, C–399/11, EU:C:2013:107

56 The interpretation envisaged by the national court at the outset is that Article 53 of the Charter gives general authorisation to a Member State to apply the standard of protection of fundamental rights guaranteed by its constitution when that standard is higher than that deriving from the Charter and, where necessary, to give it priority over the application of provisions of EU law. Such an interpretation would, in particular, allow a Member State to make the execution of a European arrest warrant issued for the purposes of executing a sentence rendered *in absentia* subject to conditions intended to avoid an interpretation which restricts or adversely affects fundamental rights recognised by its constitution, even though the application of such conditions is not allowed under Article 4a(1) of Framework Decision 2002/584.

57 Such an interpretation of Article 53 of the Charter cannot be accepted.

---

[10] *Frontini* v. *Ministero delle Finanze* [1974] 2 CMLR 372 (Italy, fundamental rights); *Internationale Handelsgesellschaft* v. *Einfuhr und Vorratsstelle für Getreide und Futtermittel* [1974] 2 CMLR 540 (fundamental rights, Germany); *Cohn-Bendit* [1980] 1 CMLR 543 (public security, France); *Re Value Added Tax Directives* [1982] 1 CMLR 427 (tax, Germany). On the reaction in Germany see B. Davies, *Resisting the European Court of Justice: West Germany's Confrontation with European Law, 1949–1979* (Cambridge University Press, 2012) 88 *et seq.*

[11] D. Chalmers, 'European Restatements of Sovereignty' in R. Rawlings *et al.* (eds.), *Sovereignty and the Law* (Oxford University Press, 2013).

[12] The primacy of EU law over national constitutions was established in *Internationale Handelsgesellschaft* v. *Einfuhr- und Vorratsstelle für Getreide und Futtermittel*, 11/70, EU:C:1970:114. The primacy of EU law over national constitutions has been reiterated by the Court in *M.A.S. and M.B.*, C-42/17, EU:C:2017:936.

58 That interpretation of Article 53 of the Charter would undermine the principle of the primacy of EU law inasmuch as it would allow a Member State to disapply EU legal rules which are fully in compliance with the Charter where they infringe the fundamental rights guaranteed by that State's constitution.

59 It is settled case-law that, by virtue of the principle of primacy of EU law, which is an essential feature of the EU legal order ... rules of national law, even of a constitutional order, cannot be allowed to undermine the effectiveness of EU law on the territory of that State ...

60 It is true that Article 53 of the Charter confirms that, where an EU legal act calls for national implementing measures, national authorities and courts remain free to apply national standards of protection of fundamental rights, provided that the level of protection provided for by the Charter, as interpreted by the Court, and the primacy, unity and effectiveness of EU law are not thereby compromised.

61 However ... [the European Arrest Warrant] does not allow Member States to refuse to execute a European arrest warrant when the person concerned is in one of the situations provided for therein.

In *Melloni*, the line of reasoning started by *VGL* and *Costa* now requires a constitutional court to disapply a constitutional provision if it conflicts with EU law. Such reasoning is audacious not simply in terms of its politics. It also requires significant legal innovation in the form of a mechanism within the national legal settlement to give effect to the authority of EU law.

B. de Witte, 'Direct Effect, Primacy, and the Nature of the Legal Order' in P. Craig and G. de Búrca (eds.), *The Evolution of EU Law*, 2nd edn (Oxford University Press, 2011) 323, 350–1

A benign interpretation is that national courts must necessarily find a way to recognise those principles and to achieve the result imposed by the European Court on them. A stronger interpretation would be that national courts have no choice and that they simply cannot resist the authority of EU law. The latter reading implies that national courts, when acting on the duties imposed on them by the European Court are exercising a jurisdiction attributed to them directly by Union law, and not a jurisdiction given to them by their own constitutions. This view was adopted by many European Community law scholars, particularly those of France and the BENELUX countries, but there is hardly any evidence of national courts adopting this radical approach. National courts see themselves as organs of their state, and try to fit their European mandate within the framework of the powers attributed to them by their national legal system. For them (and, indeed, for most constitutional law scholars throughout Europe) the idea that EU law can claim its primacy within the national legal system on the basis of its own authority seems as implausible as Baron von Munchhausen's claim that he had lifted himself from the sand by pulling on his bootstraps. The national courts (with the possible exception of those of the Netherlands) see EU law as rooted in their constitution, and seek a foundation for the primacy and direct effect of EU law in that constitution.

This is often not an easy task, as most national constitutions fail to deal explicitly with the internal effect of EU law (or international law in general). In the absence of such explicit provisions, recourse may be had to the constitutional clauses allowing for EU membership or, more generally, allowing for the attribution of state powers to organisations like the European Union. Such provisions *do* occur in all the written constitutions of the member States, except that of Finland; although their wording is different, they serve broadly the same purpose of enabling membership of advanced international organisations such as the European Union. In some countries they have been given an additional significance as the basis for the domestic effect of EU law.

3 THE CLAIMS OF EU LEGAL AUTHORITY

Costa and *VGL* are not sufficient, by themselves, to secure a system of EU legal authority. A number of further claims have to be made by EU law (and met). Over time, each has crystallised into a doctrine of EU law with its own features. The first is that it is for EU law alone to determine which activities are governed by it (*autonomy of EU law*). Secondly, EU law takes precedence over other law unless it expressly says otherwise (*primacy of EU law*). Thirdly, it determines when there is a conflict between it and national law, and the consequences of such a conflict (*pre-emption*). Finally, institutions, in particular national ones, are under a series of duties to secure the functioning of EU law (*fidelity principle*).

(i) The Autonomy of EU Law

The autonomy of EU law entails that it is for EU law to determine which activities are governed by it and how they are governed by it. *Costa*, in ruling that EU law had precedence over national law, addressed this question. As the nationalisation fell within the aegis of the Treaties, it was for EU law, according to *Costa*, to determine both whether it governed the nationalisation (i.e. whether there were specific EU rules that applied to it) and whether the nationalisation breached EU law.

International agreements pose particular challenges for this position. These form part of EU law where the Union has either concluded them or succeeded the Member States to them.[13] For the terms of the international agreement, rather than EU law, may determine which activities are governed by EU law, and how it does this. The European Economic Area Agreement, for example, provides that Norwegians, Icelanders and Liechtensteiners can work in the Union.[14] In this, it goes not only to how EU law is to protect these workers but also alters the remit of EU law as, otherwise, it would be for Member States to determine how many of these nationals could work in their territories.[15]

The Court has squared this circle by stating that international agreements can prevail over EU secondary legislation in determining what EU law governs and how, but the autonomy of EU law requires that these agreements cannot breach the constitutional principles of EU law.[16] Examples of the latter include the division of powers between the Union and Member States, or fundamental rights. In *Kadi*, the Court held that the EU was not bound by United Security Resolutions requiring it to impose sanctions on individuals for terror-related activities. For these Resolutions violated the fundamental rights of those subject to them, in particular their rights of defence, by not allowing them to see any inculpatory evidence or to make a case as to their innocence.[17]

---

[13] See, respectively, Article 216(2) TFEU and *International Fruit* v. *Produktschap voor Groenten en Fruit*, 21–4/72, EU: C:1972:115.

[14] Agreement on the European Economic Area, OJ 1994, L 1/3, Article 28(1).   [15] Article 79(5) TFEU.

[16] *Kadi and Al Barakaat International Foundation* v. *Council and Commission*, C-402/05 P and C-415/05 P, EU: C:2008:461. On a related manner, the Court of Justice cannot be bound by international dispute settlement bodies on matters which go to essential elements of EU law. See pp. 170–1.

[17] *Ibid.*

(ii) The Primacy of EU Law

The primacy of EU law is the most straightforward of all the doctrines. It states that when EU law has identified a conflict between it and national law, it should take precedence over national law, as in *Costa* and *Melloni*. The principle also has a jurisdictional dimension. It is not open to national law to determine which courts can hear conflicts. The primacy of EU law applies whenever a conflict appears before any court or body competent to take a legal decision. In *Simmenthal*, an Italian system of fees for veterinary inspections of beef imports had already been held by the Court of Justice to breach EU law. An Italian magistrate asked the Court whether he was required to disapply the relevant Italian law. This was a power which at that time was enjoyed only by the Italian Constitutional Court as only it had the power of legislative review.

Amministrazione delle Finanze dello Stato v. Simmenthal, 106/77, EU: C:1978:49

17 ... in accordance with the principle of the precedence of Community law, the relationship between provisions of the Treaty and directly applicable measures of the institutions on the one hand and the national law of the Member States on the other is such that those provisions and measures not only by their entry into force render automatically inapplicable any conflicting provision of current national law but – in so far as they are an integral part of, and take precedence in, the legal order applicable in the territory of each of the Member States – also preclude the valid adoption of new national legislative measures to the extent to which they would be incompatible with community provisions.

18 Indeed any recognition that national legislative measures which encroach upon the field within which the Community exercises its legislative power or which are otherwise incompatible with the provisions of Community law had any legal effect would amount to a corresponding denial of the effectiveness of obligations undertaken unconditionally and irrevocably by Member States pursuant to the Treaty and would thus imperil the very foundations of the Community.

...

21 ... every national court must, in a case within its jurisdiction, apply Community law in its entirety and protect rights which the latter confers on individuals and must accordingly set aside any provision of national law which may conflict with it, whether prior or subsequent to the Community rule.

22 Accordingly any provision of a national legal system and any legislative, administrative or judicial practice which might impair the effectiveness of Community law by withholding from the national court having jurisdiction to apply such law the power to do everything necessary at the moment of its application to set aside national legislative provisions which might prevent Community rules from having full force and effect are incompatible with those requirements which are the very essence of Community law.

The primacy of EU law expands, therefore, the scope of judicial review. If, in some jurisdictions, many courts do not have the power to disapply administrative acts or engage in legislative review, this is not the case when it comes to EU law. Any court can engage in administrative or legislative review if the measure breaches some EU law. Thus, primacy of EU law increases judicial power significantly. It also disperses power within the judiciary so that what in many jurisdictions was a very confined power is now shared across the judiciary.[18]

---

[18] E. Benvinisti and G. Downs, 'The Premises, Assumptions, and Implications of *Van Gend en Loos*: Viewed from the Perspectives of Democracy and Legitimacy of International Institutions' (2014) 25 *EJIL* 85, 91–4.

(iii) Pre-Emption

The doctrine of primacy deals with what happens in cases of conflict between EU and national law. However, it does not address *when* there is a conflict that must be resolved along these lines. Pre-emption goes to this question. It sets out when EU law will consider there to be a conflict.[19] Schütze has identified three forms of pre-emption in EU law.

- **Field pre-emption**: EU law has a jurisdictional monopoly over a field. National laws, irrespective of whether they conflict with EU measures, can only be enacted with the authorisation of EU law.
- **Rule pre-emption**: Where there is shared jurisdiction over a policy field, both EU laws and national laws can, in principle, be adopted. National measures will be set aside, however, if they conflict with an EU law.
- **Obstacle pre-emption**: Member States are free to adopt national measures but these measures must not obstruct the effectiveness of EU policies.[20]

The Treaties do not use this terminology. Instead, they make a distinction between areas of activity in which the Union has exclusive competence, and areas in which there are shared competences between the Union and the Member States.[21]

Article 2 TFEU

(1) When the Treaties confer on the Union exclusive competence in a specific area, only the Union may legislate and adopt legally binding acts, the Member States being able to do so themselves only if so empowered by the Union or for the implementation of acts of the Union.

(2) When the Treaties confer on the Union a competence shared with the Member States in a specific area, the Union and the Member States may legislate and adopt legally binding acts in that area. The Member States shall exercise their competence to the extent that the Union has not exercised its competence. The Member States shall exercise their competence again to the extent that the Union has decided to cease exercising its competence.

Exclusive competence corresponds to field pre-emption. It follows a model of integration which is that of dual federalism. The Union and Member States are co-equals. There is a division of power into mutually exclusive spheres with the Union governing some and Member States others.[22] In fields of exclusive competence, therefore, only the Union may legislate, with Member States able to legislate only if authorised by the Union or to implement EU measures. From a

---

[19] R. Schütze, 'Supremacy without Pre-Emption? The Very Slowly Emergent Doctrine of Pre-Emption' (2006) 43 *CMLRev* 1023, 1033. It has been argued, alternately, that these duties arise out of a different doctrine, loyalty to the Union interest, M. Klamert, *The Principle of Loyalty* (Oxford University Press, 2014) 106–23.

[20] This categorisation is taken from Schütze, n. 19 above, 1038. A. Arena, 'The Twin Doctrines of Primacy and Pre-Emption' in R. Schütze and T. Tridimas (eds.), *Oxford Principles of European Union Law* (Oxford University Press, 2018) vol. I, 300, 327.

[21] Article 2 TFEU mentions other form of Union competence: coordination of economic and employment policies; common foreign and security policy; and measures to support, coordinate or supplement national action. In these fields, however, a question of a conflict which will give rise to precedence of EU law, as EU law does not claim precedence in these fields.

[22] R. Schütze, 'Dual Federalism Constitutionalised: The Emergence of Exclusive Competences in the EC Legal Order' (2007) 32 *ELRev* 3.

national perspective, this is draconian as it involves a complete surrender of jurisdiction to the Union. For that reason, the fields of exclusive competence are rather limited.[23]

The model of integration in fields of shared competence is one of cooperative federalism. A shared responsibility is granted to the Union and the Member State to realise a common policy. There is no fixed division as they work together to realise this common goal with the balance of responsibilities determined by the terms, limits and presence of EU legislation.[24] This model of integration applies to: the internal market; social policy; cohesion policy; agriculture and fisheries, excluding the conservation of marine biological resources; environment; consumer protection; transport; trans-European networks; energy; freedom, security and justice; and common safety concerns in public health matters.[25]

As there is no fixed division in the sharing of responsibilities, one finds all three forms of pre-emption, described earlier, in areas of shared competences.

Field pre-emption occurs in certain areas, notably the single market and agriculture, where a piece of EU legislation has been adopted. This is deemed to occupy the field of activity and Member States are pre-empted from legislating on the activity in question. An example is *Commission* v. *United Kingdom*. The Commission brought an action against a British requirement that cars could only be driven on British roads if they were equipped with dim-dip lights.[26] The relevant Directive on motor vehicle lighting did not impose this requirement and, furthermore, provided that any car meeting its stipulations should be able to be driven on the roads. The Court of Justice found the British requirement to be illegal. It stated that the intention of the Directive was to regulate exhaustively the conditions for lighting devices on cars. As this was now exhaustively regulated by EU law, Member States were prohibited from imposing additional requirements on motor vehicle lighting.

This relationship makes sense where there is a need for uniformity. Within the context of the single market, the maintenance of differing national regimes can lead to distortions of competition and trade restrictions, with the consequence that the harmonisation process would be robbed of much of its effect. Even there, it creates a regime which is both monolithic and inflexible. It is impossible to maintain national provisions that impose higher standards, and the only way of adapting legislation to new risks and technologies is through amending the EU legislation in question.[27]

In spheres of activity where this need for uniformity is less pressing, field pre-emption is less common. Instead, in many areas of EU competence, the Treaties provide for a form of rule pre-emption known as minimum harmonisation.[28] Member States are free to take more protective laws, but EU law establishes a floor of protection below which national legislation must not go. The idea of legislation being more or less protective is, of course, a charged notion.

---

[23] They comprise the customs union; competition rules necessary for the functioning of the internal market; monetary policy for the euro area State; the conservation of marine biological resources under the common fisheries policy; and the common commercial policy, Article 3 TFEU.

[24] R. Schütze, 'Co-Operative Federalism Constitutionalised: The Emergence of Complementary Competences in the EC Legal Order' (2006) 31 *ELRev* 167, 168–9.

[25] Article 4(2) TFEU.   [26] *Commission* v. *United Kingdom*, 60/86, EU:C:1988:382.

[27] S. Weatherill, 'Beyond Preemption? Shared Competence and Constitutional Change in the European Community' in D. O'Keeffe and P. Twomey (eds.), *Legal Issues of the Maastricht Treaty* (London, Chancery, 1994) 13, 18–19.

[28] Notably criminal justice (Article 82(2) TFEU), social policy (Article 153(2)(b) TFEU); public health legislation on organs and blood (Article 168(4)(a) TFEU); consumer protection (Article 169 TFEU); environment (Article 193 TFEU).

In *Deponiezweckverband Eiterköpfe*, a landfill operator was refused permission to fill two sites with waste as it exceeded German limits on the proportion of organic waste that could be disposed of in landfill sites.[29] By contrast, the Directive (on which the German law was based) set limits only for biodegradable organic waste. The operator argued that the national legislation was, therefore, unlawful. The Court of Justice disagreed. It stated that the German legislation pursued the same objective as the Directive, namely the limitation of waste going into landfill. Insofar as it set limits for a wider range of waste, it was more stringent than the Directive and was, therefore, permissible. This is to be contrasted with *ŠKO-Energo*.[30] The EU climate change emissions Directive authorised States to allocate a fixed number of emission allowances for climate change gases to their industries. States were prohibited from levying charges on 95 per cent of these emission allowances. The Czech Government imposed a tax of 32 per cent on emission allowances where the electricity was produced by fuel combustion. It did not impose these taxes on other forms of electricity generation or steel production. The Czech Government argued that the tax was an environmental measure which was more protective than the Directive. The Court rejected this. It noted that the object of the Czech measure differed from that of the Directive, as the real object of the Czech measure was to secure more revenue for other electricity producers. It could not, therefore, be seen as more protective than the Directive.

Minimum harmonisation can also take place in fields where there is no provision for it in the Treaties but the relevant EU law so provides. Even where the EU law does not do this, in extreme circumstances, the Court will refuse to disapply the national legislation if it is pursuing a particularly overriding interest. *Commission* v. *Germany* is an example.[31] Member States were required by the Directive on conservation of wild birds to designate the most suitable habitats for certain species of wild birds. Designated habitats were to be preserved and the Directive envisaged no circumstances in which measures could be taken to reduce the size of these habitats. There was no provision for minimum harmonisation in the Directive and it was based on a Treaty provision which did not allow for it. Germany wished to build a dyke across one of its designated areas in the Leybucht region to prevent the coast being washed away. Despite there being no provision, the Court held that it could reduce the size of the designation area. This was because, the Court ruled, there was exceptionally in this case a general interest (protection of the coastline), which was superior to that represented in the Directive. The dyke could therefore be built but, the Court noted, must involve the smallest disruption possible to the protection area.

(iv) The Fidelity Principle

All legal systems confer responsibilities upon public bodies to ensure that the law is clear, generally applied and policed and that there are sufficient remedies for breach of the law. Known in the United States as the 'fidelity principle', the requirement is that 'each level and unit of government must act to ensure the proper functioning of the system of governance as a whole'.[32] In EU law, the principle is set out in Article 4(3) TEU.

---

[29] *Deponiezweckverband Eiterköpfe* v. *Land Rheinland-Pfalz*, C-6/03, EU:C:2005:222.
[30] *ŠKO-Energo* v. *Odvolací finanční ředitelství*, C-43/14, EU:C:2015:120.
[31] *Commission* v. *Germany*, C-57/89, EU:C:1991:89.
[32] D. Halberstam, 'The Political Morality of Federal Systems' (2004) 90 *Virginia L Rev* 101, 104.

Article 4 TEU

(3) Pursuant to the principle of sincere cooperation, the Union and the Member States shall, in full mutual respect, assist each other in carrying out tasks which flow from the Treaties.

The Member States shall take any appropriate measure, general or particular, to ensure fulfilment of the obligations arising out of the Treaties or resulting from the acts of the institutions of the Union.

The Member States shall facilitate the achievement of the Union's tasks and refrain from any measure which could jeopardise the attainment of the Union's objectives.

Article 4(3) TEU has been described as 'drawing all relevant institutions into the job of effectively sustaining [Union] policy'.[33] It applies both to the Member States and to the EU Institutions, which must cooperate with national bodies to secure the full effectiveness of EU law.[34]

The principle carries both negative and positive obligations for Member States.

The central negative obligation is that once EU Institutions have indicated a point of departure for common action, Member States are under a duty to abstain from any measure which could frustrate realisation of its objectives. In the field of external relations, if the Commission has been authorised to conclude an international agreement, therefore, Member States cannot enter independent bilateral agreements of their own or make unilateral proposals on the matter with the non-EU State concerned, unless this is done with the cooperation of the EU Institutions.[35] Internally, this duty applies with most force to Directives whose deadline for transposition has not yet expired. Prior to that date national authorities must abstain from any measure which would compromise the objectives of the Directive. The national legislature must not, therefore, pass legislation, which will make it impossible to meet the Directive's objectives by the transposition date,[36] and national courts must not interpret national law in such a way that might seriously compromise a State's meeting the Directive's requirements by that date.[37]

The positive obligations are multiple.

First, national institutions are required to secure legal certainty for EU law. Member States must, therefore, implement their obligations 'with unquestionable binding force and with the specificity, precision and clarity necessary to satisfy that principle'.[38] Mere administrative practice will not be enough to meet a State's obligations. Administrative or legal measures must be in place, which, whilst not necessarily legislation, are sufficiently binding that they cannot be changed at will. Such measures must be public so that citizens are able to identify the source of their rights.[39] This entails a duty to publish not only the national measure but also the EU measure which gave rise to it.[40]

---

[33] S. Weatherill, 'Beyond Preemption? Shared Competence and Constitutional Change in the European Community' in D. O'Keeffe and P. Twomey (eds.), *Legal Issues of the Maastricht Treaty* (Chichester, Chancery Law Publishing, 1994) 31.

[34] *Zwartveld*, C-2/88 IMM, EU:C:1990:315.

[35] *Commission* v. *Luxembourg*, C-266/03, EU:C:2005:341; *Commission* v. *Sweden*, C-246/07, EU:C:2010:203.

[36] *Stichting Natuur en Milieu* v. *College van Gedeputeerde Staten van Groningen*, C-165–7/09, EU:C:2009:393.

[37] *Adeneler and Others* v. *ELOG*, C-212/04, EU:C:2006:443.   [38] *Commission* v. *Italy*, C-159/99, EU:C:2001:278.

[39] *Mulgan and Others*, C-313/99, EU:C:2002:386. The principle of legal certainty also requires that if Member States amend a law to comply with EU law, the amendment must have the same legal force as the original measure, *Commission* v. *United Kingdom*, C-33/03, EU:C:2005:144.

[40] *Pimix*, C-146/11, EU:C:2012:450.

Secondly, Member States must actively police EU law. In *Commission* v. *France*, French farmers launched a violent campaign targeting the importation of Spanish strawberries.[41] Their action involved threatening shops, burning lorries carrying the goods and blockading roads. The French Government took almost no action either to stop these protests or to prosecute offences committed. While the acts stopping the imports were performed by *private* actors – the farmers – and while the relevant provision of EU law, Article 34 TFEU, imposed obligations only on States not to prevent the free movement of goods, the Court ruled that France had breached EU law. The State was required to adopt all appropriate measures to guarantee the full scope and effect of EU law. In taking measures that were manifestly inadequate, France had failed to do this. The requirement to police EU law, however, is not an absolute one. A Member State does not have to police EU law if this would result in public disorder, which it could not contain. Similarly, it must not police EU law in such a way that it violates fundamental rights and civil liberties.[42]

Thirdly, Member States are under a duty to notify the Commission if they have any problems applying or enforcing EU law. However, they cannot use Commission reservations, conditions or objections as a basis for derogating from EU law.[43]

Finally, there is a double stipulation on how Member States are to penalise infringements of EU law. In the first place, as a minimum, they must penalise breaches of EU law in an analogous way, both procedurally and substantively, to infringements of national law of a similar nature and importance.[44] Secondly, national courts must ensure that, irrespective of how breaches of national law are handled, penalties for breach of EU law are effective, proportionate and dissuasive.[45] In *Berlusconi*,[46] Advocate General Kokott set out what these criteria mean:

88 Rules laying down penalties are *effective* where they are framed in such a way that they do not make it practically impossible or excessively difficult to impose the penalty provided for and, therefore, to attain the objectives pursued by Community law.

89 A penalty is *dissuasive* where it prevents an individual from infringing the objectives pursued and rules laid down by Community law. What is decisive in this regard is not only the nature and level of the penalty but also the likelihood of its being imposed. Anyone who commits an infringement must fear that the penalty will in fact be imposed on him. There is an overlap here between the criterion of dissuasiveness and that of effectiveness.

90 A penalty is *proportionate* where it is appropriate (that is to say, in particular, *effective* and *dissuasive*) for attaining the legitimate objectives pursued by it, and also necessary. Where there is a choice between several (equally) appropriate penalties, recourse must be had to the least onerous. Moreover, the effects of the penalty on the person concerned must be proportionate to the aims pursued.

---

[41] *Commission* v. *France*, C-265/95, EU:C:1997:595.

[42] *Schmidberger* v. *Republic of Austria*, C-112/00, EU:C:2003:333.

[43] *Commission* v. *Germany*, C-105/02, EU:C:2006:637.

[44] *Draehmpaehl* v. *Urania Immobilienservice*, C-180/95, EU:C:1997:208. They must also penalise them in an equivalent manner to breaches of other EU law provisions of a similar importance, *Paquay* v. *Société d'architectes Hoet & Minne*, C-460/06, EU:C:2007:601.

[45] *LCL Le Crédit Lyonnais*, C-565/12, EU:C:2014:190; *Scialdone*, C-574/15, EU:C:2018:295.

[46] *Berlusconi and Others*, C-387/02, C-391/02 and C-403/02, EU:C:2004:624.

4 THE FOUNDATIONS OF EU LEGAL AUTHORITY

It is all very well for the Court of Justice to claim this authority for EU law, but at its crudest, this claim is a demand that there be acceptance that EU law should not only be obeyed but obeyed over national law. This does beg the question whether EU law warrants this acceptance, and this, in turn, raises two further questions.

The first is 'acceptance by whom?' The pedigree of the actors recognising EU law authority is central. If they are too insubstantial or unknown, EU law will not have authority either because the wider citizenry will not follow their lead or because this lead will not resonate strongly. The pedigree of these actors matters for a further reason. On the one hand, they become the interlocutors for EU law, committing their own institutional stature to establishing its authority, with the consequence that they become associated with the virtues and vices of EU law. On the other hand, EU law also becomes associated with its interlocutors' qualities, be it the manner in which they convey their authority (and thus EU law's authority) or the manner in which they assert their will.

The second is 'what good reasons are there for EU law's authority to be accepted?' After all, unlike the laws of early political communities, it is not being asserted as an escape from a world in which there is no law and only savagery. Its authority is being proclaimed over the authority of national laws. The threshold for its having authority would, therefore, seem to be higher as a consequence. Those proclaiming EU law's authority over national law would have to have a certain pedigree. The reasons for EU law having authority would also need to be particularly strong if there is already a law in place, national law, which has well-established credentials.

(i) The Pedigree of EU Legal Authority

EU law requires only the support of national judges to enjoy formal authority. This is, in part, because its authority takes the form of instructions to national judges. It requires them to grant parties standing to invoke EU law in their courtrooms and to apply it over national law. It is also because the commitment to the rule of law in the different Member States entails that other actors, both public and private, will observe EU law if judges state that is the prevailing law. As we shall see later in this chapter, this is what by and large happened, albeit that the initial *ad hoc* resistance on matters of particular sensitivity has crystallised into a series of doctrines which qualify EU legal authority as EU legal competence has expanded.[47] However, it resulted in the authority of the Union becoming tied to a form of legalese. EU law becomes a central vehicle for communicating both what the Union is about and the reason for its authority. Union activities are, thus, described often in legalistic terms as, for example, a series of Regulations and Directives whose authority and reach can only be understood through reading these legal texts. For lay people, this makes the Union less accessible, and also leads to its being something over which judges, lawyers and legal academy have a dominant, possibly undue, influence. All this qualifies EU law's legitimacy.[48]

---

[47] M. Claes, *The National Courts' Mandate in the European Constitution* (Oxford-Portland, Hart, 2005); A. Albi, *EU Enlargement and the Constitutions of Central and Eastern Europe* (Cambridge University Press, 2005).
[48] A. Vauchez, *Brokering Europe: Euro-Lawyers and the Making of a Transnational Polity* (Cambridge University Press, 2015) 194–7 and 230–1.

There was an attempt to secure wider assent for the authority of EU law in the Constitutional Treaty. This Treaty provided for EU law to have primacy over national law within the competences conferred upon the Union by it.[49] Following the failure of that Treaty, this provision was seen as too ambitious. At the Lisbon Treaty, a Declaration was attached to the EU Treaties.[50]

Declaration 17

The Conference recalls that, in accordance with well settled case law of the Court of Justice of the European Union, the Treaties and the law adopted by the Union on the basis of the Treaties have primacy over the law of Member States, under the conditions laid down by the said case law.

An opinion of the Council Legal Service was also attached, which provides sparse information.

Opinion of the Council Legal Service, EU Council Doc 11197/07, 22 June 2007

It results from the case-law of the Court of Justice that primacy of EC law is a cornerstone principle of Community law. According to the Court, this principle is inherent to the specific nature of the European Community. At the time of the first judgement of this established case-law (*Costa/ENEL*, 15 July 1964, Case 6/64) there was no mention of primacy in the treaty. It is still the case today. The fact that the principle of primacy will not be included in the future treaty shall not in any way change the existence of the principle and the existing case-law of the Court of Justice.

This Declaration enhances the authority of the *Costa* case law by stating that it has the support of all the national governments which negotiated the Lisbon Treaty and the parliaments which ratified it. However, a Declaration is not an instrument which bellows out EU law's authority. This is all the more so because the context is one in which this endorsement has been down-graded from a Treaty commitment. Furthermore, it raises questions about who can found this authority. If national governments can provide an interpretation alongside the Treaty, in this Declaration, as to the quality of EU law authority, this implies that they can also reinterpret the authority of EU law not merely through amendments to the Treaties but also through the practices which set out how they believe EU law should be interpreted.[51]

This Declaration also raises another troubling question. It was adopted by national executives. To be sure, as part of the Lisbon Treaty, it had to be ratified by national parliaments. However, these had no input into its negotiation and were offered a 'take it or leave it' position at the moment of ratification, with the added pressure that rejection would plunge the relations between their State and the Union into crisis. We have seen that national executives have strong sway over the making of EU laws.[52] From a national perspective, therefore, national executives have decided that those laws over which they have most influence should prevail over laws where national parliaments have most sway. It is not a good look. If, within a domestic context,

---

[49] Article I-13 Constitutional Treaty.
[50] L. Rossi, 'How Fundamental are Fundamental Principles? Primacy and Fundamental Rights after Lisbon' (2008) 28 *YBEL* 65, 74–7.
[51] This is indeed the usual practice in international law, Vienna Convention on the Law of Treaties 1969, Article 31(3)(b).
[52] See pp. 87–8.

the executive could make laws and then declare them supreme over parliamentary statutes, there would be talk of a dictatorship. The Union context is different from that, but not so different that the comparison can easily be dismissed.

(ii) Reasons for EU Legal Authority

In the last few years, the Court of Justice has sought to set out reasons for the authority of EU law. It has, therefore stated on a number of occasions:

> EU law is thus based on the fundamental premiss that each Member State shares with all the other Member States, and recognises that they share with it, a set of common values on which the EU is founded, as stated in Article 2 TEU. That premiss implies and justifies the existence of mutual trust between the Member States that those values will be recognised, and therefore that the law of the EU that implements them will be respected. It is precisely in that context that the Member States are obliged, by reason *inter alia* of the principle of sincere cooperation set out in the first subparagraph of Article 4(3) TEU, to ensure in their respective territories the application of and respect for EU law, and to take for those purposes any appropriate measure, whether general or particular, to ensure fulfilment of the obligations arising out of the Treaties or resulting from the acts of the institutions of the EU.[53]

The only problem with these reasons is that they are embarrassingly bad. The common values to which the passage refers are noble ones, including respect for human rights, the rule of law and democracy. However, the reasoning is profoundly flawed for two reasons. First, if the values are common to all Member States, as stated, EU law provides no added value. They are already protected by national law so it is not clear how disapplying national law in favour of EU law furthers these values. Secondly, even a quick glance through the EU Treaties shows that most of EU law is concerned with furthering policies which are neutral with regard to these values. The single market, euro, or EU environmental policy can be pursued in ways that respect human rights, the rule of law or democracy or in ways that do not. To argue that these policies further these values is simply not true, and some EU policies, particularly those on the area of freedom, security and justice, pose particular threats to these values.

Moving beyond this judicial propaganda, the advantages of EU legal authority are, broadly speaking, threefold.

The first is that individuals are granted rights, benefits and freedoms by EU law, which they are not granted in national law. At its most mundane, in *Van Gen den Loos*, it was the right to import goods tariff-free from other Member States. At its most ambitious, it has been argued that the European Union can allow individuals to do things which are otherwise not possible.[54] This might be individual liberties, such as the freedom to trade abroad, to move abroad, to meet foreigners at home, or it might be collective goods, such as better environmental protection or financial regulation, which might be more easily secured by pan-Union than national regulation.

---

[53] Opinion 2/13, *Accession of the EU to the ECHR*, EU:C:2014:2454; *Associação Sindical dos Juízes Portugueses* v. *Tribunal de Contas*, C-64/16, EU:C:2018:117; *Slovak Republic* v. *Achmea*, C-284/16, EU:C:2018:158.

[54] J. Kristeva, 'Europhilia, Europhoria' (1998) 3 *Constellations* 321.

Secondly, EU law can facilitate new types of relationships and awareness.[55] The supranational qualities of EU law require citizens to recognise the interests of citizens (foreigners) from other Member States, be it for reasons of interdependence[56] or interests and values which are more shared than historically admitted.[57] In *Melloni*, therefore, the Spanish authorities were asked to consider the interests of Italians defrauded by *Melloni*. This capacity to enlarge awareness and empathy with foreigners can be extended to stimulate awareness of any groups or individuals that are habitually marginalised within a domestic society. For one feature of EU law is that it asks us to reconsider and justify domestic traditions and *modi vivendi*, and another is that it provides a forum for those who have not been able to realise their wishes or interests domestically. EU law has been deployed to protect a series of groups and interests – women, people with disabilities, LGBTs, ethnic, religious and racial minorities, consumer and ecological interests – historically weakly protected within nation States.[58]

Thirdly, EU law can civilise State power. The phrase 'limitation of national sovereignty' implies the curbing of the raw power of the State.[59] In *Costa*, therefore, the applicant was pleading (unsuccessfully) for EU law to protect his property from what he perceived as an arbitrary nationalisation. Abuses may simply be abuse of administrative power. This civilisational capacity extends beyond protection from abuse. It sets out a disposition which, on the one hand, involves cooperating with an increasing circle of people to realise ever more possibilities together and, on the other, requires this cooperation to be done through the law. However, as this piece from Isiksel argues, EU law civilises not simply by acting as an external discipline on national administrations. It also requires them to acknowledge the continuum between how they act domestically and how they act externally.

T. Isiksel, *Europe's Functional Constitution: A Theory of Constitutionalism beyond the State* (Oxford University Press, 2016) 215

Whatever the causal factors explaining its development and resilience, the EU's legal system represents a signal triumph for law in the face of the unforgiving calculus of power politics. Much like constitutionalism in the domestic context, European integration embodies the logic of '*garantisme*,' a term Giovanni Sartori used to describe adherence to a fundamental law, or a fundamental set of principles, and a correlative institutional arrangement, which would restrict arbitrary power and ensure a 'limited government.' [60] Modern European history records an uneasy coexistence between the constitutional ideal and the nation-state as the political unit within which it has been instantiated. Although constitutionalism seeks to discipline sovereign power, it largely leaves the state's external relations and its treatment of foreigners unfettered. According to many observers, the EU complements domestic constitutionalism by constraining

---

[55] J. Weiler, 'In Defence of the Status Quo: Europe's Constitutional Sonderweg' in J. Weiler and M. Wind (eds.), *European Constitutionalism Beyond the State* (Cambridge University Press, 2003).

[56] E. Balibar, 'Europe: Vanishing Mediator' (2003) 10 *Constellations* 314; A. Sangiovanni, 'Solidarity in the European Union' (2013) 33 *OJLS* 213.

[57] J-P. Müller, 'A European Constitutional Patriotism? The Case Restated' (2008) 14 *ELJ* 542.

[58] J. Weiler, *The Constitution of Europe* (Cambridge University Press, 1999) esp. 332–48; M. Poiares Maduro, *We, the Court: The European Court of Justice and the European Economic Constitution* (Oxford, Hart, 1998) 166–74.

[59] J.-W. Müller, *Contesting Democracy: Political Ideas in Twentieth-Century Europe* (New Haven, Yale University Press, 2011) 147–9.

[60] G. Sartori, 'Constitutionalism: A Preliminary Discussion' (1962) 56 *APSR* 853, 855.

the arbitrary exercise of state power in the international sphere, expanding its scope of moral concern, and establishing a deliberative community among its member states. As Kant put it, 'The problem of establishing a perfect civil constitution is subordinate to the problem of a law-governed external relationship with other states, and cannot be solved unless the latter is also solved.'[61]

These might all be good reasons for obeying EU law. However, left like this, they present a one-sided picture. For there might also be good reasons for disobeying EU law. It is to these we now turn.

(iii) Mediating Challenges to EU Legal Authority

There are contrasting reasons why EU law should not have authority. First, it may simply not pursue these goals and do egregious things, instead; secondly, even where it does good things this may be at the expense of good things realised by national law; and thirdly, it may damage good realised by national law which EU law is not in a position to reproduce.

First, the practice of EU law may not live up to these ideals. Isiksel, for example, has noted, for example that the Union has established an 'epistocracy' where in many fields of EU law, citizens and decision-makers are required to surrender their own judgment in favour of expert pronouncements.[62] Equally, many EU laws can foreclose individual freedoms protected nationally whilst offering no new freedom in return. Indeed, it is quite possible for EU laws, as with any law, to pursue oppressive ends. In that regard, White has observed that there might be a case for principled disobedience.[63] He argues that, in practice, as it is very difficult for groups in particular national societies, particularly marginalised groups, to get EU law overturned, disobedience would be justified if it meets three conditions. (i) The disobedience must submit itself to public approval within the national territory, be this through e-democracy or a plebiscite. This is necessary to stop people breaching EU law for capricious or self-serving reasons. (ii) The disobedience must be justified as being in the public interest. It must not be for sectoral or private reasons. (iii) It must be committed to the values of constitutionalism. In other words, it must argue that the Union is breaching certain constitutional values (e.g. commitments to freedom or equality) and it is acting to protect these.

Secondly, whilst EU law may pursue worthwhile ends, it does so at the expense of equivalent interests and values protected by national laws. EU law might, therefore, generate new rights for certain individuals but, in so doing, it imposes new duties or external costs on others which had hitherto been averted by national law. Alternatively, EU law might pursue some collective values, such as the growth of international trade, at the expense of other values protected by national law, such as national solidarity. Such conflicts invite comparison of what is being offered respectively by EU and national law.[64]

---

[61] I. Kant, 'Idea for a Universal History with a Cosmopolitan Purpose' [1784] in *Political Writings*, ed. H. Reiss (Cambridge University Press, 1997) 47.

[62] T. Isiksel, *Europe's Functional Constitution: A Theory of Constitutionalism beyond the State* (Oxford University Press, 2016) 220–4. See also A. Vauchez, *Democratizing Europe* (New York, Palgrave, 2016) 29–47.

[63] J. White, 'Principled Disobedience in the EU' (2017) 24 *Constellations* 637.

[64] On the different types of conflict see F. de Witte, 'Interdependence and Contestation in European Integration' (2018) 3 *European Papers*, forthcoming.

There is a third reason for contesting EU legal authority. If EU law can offer certain things that national law cannot offer, national laws can offer certain goods, identified by Walker as common goods, which cannot be provided by EU law. The challenge with conflicts between EU and national law, in these circumstances, is one of commensurability. It is difficult to compare what is being gained by EU law against what is being lost by the disapplication of the national law.

N. Walker, 'The Place of European law' in G. de Búrca and J. Weiler (eds.), *The Worlds of European Constitutionalism* (Cambridge University Press, 2012) 57, 67

These common goods, in turn, can be both implicit and explicit. Implicit common goods refer to those benefits inherent in the very idea of living together in a stable community. These include the value of national (or other collective) solidarity – of an accomplished framework of mutual concern and support – and the sense of social, economic and spiritual or 'ontological security' such security brings to those who share in it. They also include a more general value associated with the development and preservation of a national (or other collective) culture, as well as the sense of belonging, of dignity, of posterity, and of distinctiveness or 'originality', such a culture brings to those who share it. Moreover, in addition to such implicit common goods, and indeed, building on the platform of capacities for common action provided by such implicit goods, communities may also determine and pursue certain other explicit common goods, such as economic egalitarianism (through redistribution), or an educated society, or a healthy society.

Acknowledgement of the value of these common goods is, indeed, provided by Article 4(2) TEU.[65]

Article 4 TEU

(2) The Union shall respect the equality of Member States before the Treaties as well as their national identities, inherent in their fundamental structures, political and constitutional, inclusive of regional and local self-government.

However, this provision has historically only been used to cover a restricted number of policies: promotion of that State's official languages,[66] a State's freedom to reorganise administrative power internally[67] and laws on abolishing the nobility.[68] Furthermore, any national measures adopted to further these policies have to be proportionate.[69]

The possibility for a more extensive interpretation came in *Coman*. Coman, a Romanian man, had worked in Brussels where he married Hamilton, an American man, as was provided for by

---

[65] B. Guastaferro, 'Beyond the Exceptionalism of Constitutional Conflicts: The Ordinary Functions of the Identity Clause' (2012) 31 *YBEL* 263; M. Claes, 'Negotiating Constitutional Identity or Whose Identity Is It Anyway?' in M. Claes *et al.* (eds.), *Constitutional Conversations in Europe. Actors, Topics and Procedures* (Antwerp, Intersentia, 2012); E. Cloots, *National Identity in EU Law* (Oxford University Press, 2015) chs. 7–10; E. Cloots, 'National Identity, Constitutional Identity, and Sovereignty in the EU' (2016) 45 *Netherlands Journal of Legal Philosophy* 82.

[66] *Las* v. *PSA Antwerp*, C-202/11, EU:C:2013:239.   [67] *Remondis* v. *Region Hannover*, C-51/15, EU:C:2016:985.

[68] *Sayn-Wittgenstein* v. *Landeshauptmann von Wien*, C-208/09, EU:C:2010:806.

[69] For an elaborate example see *von Wolffersdorff* v. *Standesamt der Stadt Karlsruhe*, C-438/14, EU:C:2016:401. On the proportionality principle see pp. 385–8.

Belgian law. They looked to return to Romania. However, the Romanian civil code prohibited marriages between people of the same sex, and Hamilton was told that as he was not a spouse of an EU citizen, he could only stay in Romania for three months. They argued that the relevant Directive provided that a non-EU spouse could join an EU citizen returning to his home State after having worked in another Member State, and that the status of the spouse was to be determined by the legislation of the latter State. They, therefore, claimed that Romania was bound to recognise the marriage under EU law. Romania responded that, even if this were so, the Directive violated article 4(2) TEU as marriage laws were central to a State's national identity.

Coman, Hamilton and Asociaţia Accept v. Inspectoratul General pentru Imigrări, C-673/16, EU:C:2018:385

37 Admittedly, a person's status, which is relevant to the rules on marriage, is a matter that falls within the competence of the Member States and EU law does not detract from that competence ... The Member States are thus free to decide whether or not to allow marriage for persons of the same sex ...

38 Nevertheless, it is well-established case-law that, in exercising that competence, Member States must comply with EU law, in particular the Treaty provisions on the freedom conferred on all Union citizens to move and reside in the territory of the Member States ...

42 ... a number of Governments that have submitted observations to the Court have referred in that regard to the fundamental nature of the institution of marriage and the intention of a number of Member States to maintain a conception of that institution as a union between a man and a woman, which is protected in some Member States by laws having constitutional status. The Latvian Government stated at the hearing that, even on the assumption that a refusal, in circumstances such as those of the main proceedings, to recognise marriages between persons of the same sex concluded in another Member State constitutes a restriction ... such a restriction is justified on grounds of public policy and national identity, as referred to in Article 4(2) TEU.

43 In that regard, it must be noted that the European Union is required, under Article 4(2) TEU, to respect the national identity of the Member States, inherent in their fundamental structures, both political and constitutional ...

44 Moreover, the Court has repeatedly held that the concept of public policy as justification for a derogation from a fundamental freedom must be interpreted strictly, with the result that its scope cannot be determined unilaterally by each Member State without any control by the EU institutions. It follows that public policy may be relied on only if there is a genuine and sufficiently serious threat to a fundamental interest of society ...

45 The Court finds, in that regard, that the obligation for a Member State to recognise a marriage between persons of the same sex concluded in another Member State in accordance with the law of that state, for the sole purpose of granting a derived right of residence to a third-country national, does not undermine the institution of marriage in the first Member State, which is defined by national law and, as indicated in paragraph 37 above, falls within the competence of the Member States. Such recognition does not require that Member State to provide, in its national law, for the institution of marriage between persons of the same sex. It is confined to the obligation to recognise such marriages, concluded in another Member State in accordance with the law of that state, for the sole purpose of enabling such persons to exercise the rights they enjoy under EU law.

46 Accordingly, an obligation to recognise such marriages for the sole purpose of granting a derived right of residence to a third-country national does not undermine the national identity or pose a threat to the public policy of the Member State concerned.

This judgment entitles same-sex married couples to the same rights of free movement, residence and non-discrimination as other married couples: a fine thing. Notwithstanding this, it has significant limits. It would have been more straightforward for the Court to state that, as the matter fell within the field of EU law, the fundamental rights of Coman and Hamilton had to be protected, in particular their right not to be discriminated on grounds of their sexual orientation.[70] This right would have had to be set against arguments about the religious and cultural significance of marriage as an institution involving both men and women. However, it would have forced the Romanian Government to explain what about its notion of marriage was so central to Romanian identity, and why it should be allowed to inflict human suffering. By setting out a right to prohibition of discrimination on grounds of sexual orientation in such a salient judgment, it would also have laid the ground for the elaboration of that principle in the struggle for LGBTQ rights.

Alongside this, the judgment makes it difficult for Article 4(2) TEU to be invoked in the future. Its central argument is that recognising the same-sex marriages of other EU citizens and Romanians returning to Romania in no way significantly challenges the Romanian conception of marriage as something between a man and a woman as these form a discrete category of their own. This is simply not true. The judgment allows a large number of Romanian and other EU citizens to have the same benefits as couples married according to Romanian law. There will be no practical legal difference between these married couples. Furthermore, the judgment was about more than securing justice for Coman and Hamilton, and people in their situation. *Asociaţia Accept*, the leading Romanian non-governmental organisations (NGOs) for LGBTQ rights, was joined to their case. It was part of a wider struggle for LGBTQ rights in Romania. As a consequence, any EU legal right, insofar it is discrete and does not overlap fully with the national institution, can always be said not to threaten national identity. For it creates a separate category of legal rights which still allows room for the national law.

This narrow interpretation of Article 4(2) TEU leaves us with a situation, therefore, where there are circumstances where EU law may provide a number of things that cannot be provided by national law. Conversely, there are circumstances where it may fail to provide these things; generate costs by disapplying countervailing national laws; or disrupt the supply of common goods by national law that it cannot provide itself. Very few in recent times argue, therefore, that EU law should prevail over national law all the time[71] or that national law should invariably prevail over EU law.[72]

The question is, therefore, rather *when* EU law should enjoy authority over national law. There are two dominant models: the constitutional pluralist model and the pluralist one.

The constitutional pluralist model argues that constitutionalism both provides a common vocabulary about the nature of public authority within Europe and sets demands for when laws

---

[70] This is, in fact, the position in EU law. See pp. 277–81.

[71] J. Baquero Cruz, 'The Legacy of the Maastricht-Urteil and the Pluralist Movement' (2008) 14 *ELJ* 389; F. Fabbrini, 'After the OMT Case: The Supremacy of EU Law as the Guarantee of the Equality of the Member States' (2015) 16 *German LJ* 1003.

[72] T. Schilling, 'The Autonomy of the Community Legal Order: An Analysis of Possible Foundations' (1996) 37 *Harvard Int'l LJ* 389; D. Phelan, *Revolt or Revolution: At the Constitutional Boundaries of the European Community* (Dublin, Round Hall Sweet & Maxwell, 1997); T. Hartley, 'The Constitutional Foundations of the European Union' (2001) 117 *LQR* 225.

should exert obedience over individuals. This allows it to provide a framework for when one law should prevail over another.[73] The central account of how this would work has been set out by Kumm.

> ## M. Kumm, 'The Jurisprudence of Constitutional Conflict: Constitutional Supremacy in Europe Before and After the Constitutional Treaty' (2005) 11 *European Law Journal* 262, 299–300
>
> The *first* principle is formal and is connected to the *idea of legality*. According to the principle of the effective and uniform enforcement of EU law, further strengthened by the recent explicit commitment by Member States to the primacy of EU law, national courts should start with a strong presumption that they are required to enforce EU law, national constitutional provisions notwithstanding. *The presumption for applying EU law can be rebutted, however, if, and to the extent that, countervailing principles have greater weight.* Here there are three principles to be considered. The first is *substantive*, and focuses on the effective *protection of fundamental rights of citizens.* If, and to the extent that, fundamental rights protection against acts of the EU is lacking in important respects, than that is a ground to insist on subjecting EU law to national constitutional rights review. If, however, the guarantees afforded by the EU amount to structurally equivalent protections, then there is no more space for national courts to substitute the EU's judgment on the rights issue with their own. Arguably the EU, and specifically the Court of Justice, has long developed substantially equivalent protections against violations of fundamental rights . . . The second of the counter-principles is *jurisdictional*. It protects national communities against unjustified usurpations of competencies by the European Union and undermines the legitimate scope of self government by national communities. Call this principle the principle of *subsidiarity*. Here the question is whether there are sufficient and effective guarantees against usurpation of power by EU institutions . . . Lastly, there is the *procedural* principle of *democratic legitimacy*, the third counter-principle. Given the persistence of the democratic deficit on the European level – the absence of directly representative institutions as the central agenda-setters of the European political process, the lack of a European public sphere, and a sufficiently thick European identity . . . – national courts continue to have good reasons to set aside EU Law *when it violates clear and specific constitutional norms that reflect essential commitments of the national community.*

The case for constitutional pluralism is that it sets out norms for evaluating conflicts which seem attractive and command significant assent. Furthermore, as we shall see later in this chapter, much of the national case law evaluating the authority of EU law has relied on these norms. The charges against this approach are twofold. The first is that it is too generic.[74] Values such as fundamental rights or democracy either do not help resolve disputes about which law is to be deployed[75] or, when they are used, are turned into overarching principles with a single meaning,

---

[73] D. Halberstam, 'Local, Global and Plural Constitutionalism: Europe Meets the World' in G. de Búrca and J. Weiler (eds.), *The Worlds of European Constitutionalism* (Cambridge University Press, 2012) 150, 170–5.

[74] Notable contributions to this literature include N. Walker, 'The Idea of Constitutional Pluralism' (2002) 65 *MLR* 317; D. Halberstam, 'Systems Pluralism and Institutional Pluralism in Constitutional Law: National, Supranational and Global Governance' in M. Avbelj and J. Komárek (eds.), *Constitutional Pluralism in the European Union and Beyond* (Oxford, Hart, 2012); K. Jaklic, *Constitutional Pluralism in the EU* (Oxford University Press, 2015) 316–26.

[75] J. Weiler, 'Dialogical Epilogue' in G. de Búrca and J. Weiler (eds.), *The Worlds of European Constitutionalism* (Cambridge University Press, 2012) 262, 291–7.

which invariably push for centralisation.[76] The second is that it relies on a template derived from national constitutions which pays little heed to the particular features of the Union.[77] On the one hand, it was established to deal with the consequences of State failure, namely that domestic constitutions failed to provide or could not provide certain goods to their citizens. Recreating a constitutional order using the same language as that of the nation State does not help supply these goods. On the other hand, this language of constitutionalism assumes all players are pulling in a similar direction. It might be that a value of the Union is the tension from EU policies and national policies having different dynamics. In short, unresolved conflict might sometimes be desirable.

The pluralist position, therefore, argues for few overarching principles. It argues that each legal system should takes its own position on questions of the primacy, central values and parameters of EU legal authority.[78] There is, however, a commitment to pluralism. Each legal order commits itself to considering the claims of others whilst holding on to its own beliefs and values. There is a disposition towards mutual accommodation and convergence, but it is no more than this. This will soften the possibilities for conflict but will not eradicate them.[79] The pluralist position is that the best one can hope for, in such circumstances, are fora where these conflicts can be worked out in a structured manner. However, as they are basically political conflicts, it is wrong to assume that there is a normative matrix which can decide who wins and who loses.

The advantages of pluralism lie in its modesty and respect for difference. However, therein may lie its greatest challenge. There may be certain commitments – human rights, the central provisions and instruments of EU law – which are seen as so fundamental that one cannot be agnostic about these. If a State cannot commit itself to these, then it has to be asked whether it is really committed to Union membership.[80] Pluralist approaches can also struggle to explain the stability and reach of EU law. If EU law is only what national legal systems concede, this would suggest a very unstable, limited legal order. The reality is that it prevails most of the time over a wide array of activities.

5 THE CONDITIONAL AUTHORITY OF EU LAW

(i) National Courts' Qualified Acceptance of the Authority of EU Law

The previous section indicates the types of issues which national legal orders had to address when confronted with the Court of Justice claims about the authority of EU law. It was possible for each to respond to these in different ways, but initial responses fell into three broad

---

[76] N. Krisch, 'The Case for Pluralism in Postnational Law' in G. de Búrca and J. Weiler (eds.), *The Worlds of European Constitutionalism* (Cambridge University Press, 2012) 203, 210–19.

[77] M. Dani, 'Constitutionalism and Dissonances: Has Europe Paid Off Its Debt to Functionalism?' (2009) 15 *ELJ* 324.

[78] For a range of pluralist writing see N. MacCormick, 'The Maastricht Urteil: Sovereignty Now' (1995) 1 *ELJ* 259; N. Barber, 'Legal Pluralism and the European Union' (2006) 12 *ELJ* 306.

[79] N. Kirsch, 'Who Is Afraid of Radical Pluralism? Legal Order and Political Stability in the Postnational Space' (2011) 24 *Ratio Juris* 386.

[80] Recently, there has been an attempt to address this through principled legal pluralism. This argues that certain normative commitments must be given by any legal system, notably to human dignity. It accepts, therefore, that many conflicts will be irreconcilable but argues that claims which violate this commitment to human dignity should carry no legal weight. M. Avbelj, *The European Union under Transnational Law: A Pluralist Approach* (Oxford and Portland, Bloomsbury, 2018) 32–40.

categories. At one end of the spectrum, some States, notably Austria and the BENELUX States,[81] accepted the authority of EU law pretty much on the terms set out by the Court of Justice. At the other end, one State, Poland, refused to accept the Treaties as different in nature from any other international treaty.[82] However, most States fell into an intermediate group which conditionally accepted the authority of EU law, albeit neither on the terms set out by the Court nor over their constitutions.[83] Over the years, a convergence has occurred, with most States from these two outlier groups moving to this position of granting conditional authority for EU law. States willing to grant full authority to EU law were not necessarily willing to grant full authority to Court of Justice judgments, granting these only conditional authority.[84] Conversely, Poland continued to see EU law as simply a form of international law in Poland, but granted international law (and therefore EU law) as much authority as other States accorded EU law.[85]

The case law of the German Constitutional Court has to come to epitomise the hegemonic national position on the quality of authority to be enjoyed by EU law. This position was expressed most elaborately in its judgment on the compatibility of the Lisbon Treaty with the German constitutional document, the Basic Law,[86] Article 23 of the Basic Law provides, *inter alia*, that the German Federation will consent to such limitations upon its sovereign powers as will bring about and secure a peaceful and lasting order in Europe.[87] It was argued that this consent was subject to other provisions in the Basic Law – in particular, those which provided that all State authority was derived from the people and that German citizens had a right to vote for members of the Bundestag, the German Parliament. These were violated, it was claimed, if excessive powers were transferred to the Union as its power was not derived from the people

---

[81] *Connect Austria*, VfSlg 15.427/1999 (Austria); *Orfinger* v. *Belgium* [2000] 1 CMLR 612 (Belgium); Articles 91–93 of the Constitution of the Kingdom of the Netherlands 2002. On Luxembourg case law see M. Claes, *The National Courts' Mandate in the European Constitution* (Oxford, Hart, 2006) 53–4.

[82] K 18/04, *Polish Membership of the European Union (Accession Treaty)*, Judgment of 11 May 2005 (Polish Constitutional Tribunal).

[83] *Crotty* v. *An Taoiseach* [1987] IR 713 (Ireland); *Carlsen* v. *Rasmussen* [1999] 3 CMLR 854 (Denmark); *Brunner* v. *The European Union* [1994] 1 CMLR 57 (Germany); *Re EU Constitutional Treaty and the Spanish Constitution* [2005] 1 CMLR 981; *Admenta and Others* v. *Federfarma* [2006] 2 CMLR 47 (Italy); *Re Ratification of the Lisbon Treaty* (France) [2010] 2 CMLR 26 (France); U-1–113/04, *Rules on the Quality Labelling and Packaging of Feeding Stuffs*, Judgment of 7 February 2007 (Slovenia); *Re Czech Sugar Quotas* [2006] 3 CMLR 15; *Ratification of the Lisbon Treaty* [2010] 1 CMLR 42 (Latvia); Case 3-4-1-6-12, *Request of the Chancellor of Justice to declare Article 4(4) of the Treaty establishing the European Stability Mechanism in conflict with the Constitution*, Judgment of 12 July 2012 (Estonia). On Lithuania see P. Ravluševičius, 'The Enforcement of the Primacy of European Union Law: Legal Doctrine and Practice' (2011) 18 *Jurisprudencija* 1369.

[84] On this within Belgium and the Netherlands see P. Popelier, 'Judicial Conversations in Multilevel Constitutionalism: The Belgian Case' in M. Claes *et al.* (eds.), *Constitutional Conversations in Europe: Actors, Topics and Procedures* (Cambridge, Intersentia, 2012) 73, 83–4; S. Garben, 'The *Sturgeon* Case Law in Light of Judicial Activism, Euroscepticism and Eurolegalism' (2013) 50 *CMLRev* 15. More recently, the Belgian Constitutional Court has indicated that EU law cannot take primacy over Belgian constitutional values or fundamental political and constitutional structures inherent to its national identity, Case 62/16, *Human Rights League*, Judgment of 28 April 2016 (Belgian Constitutional Court).

[85] K 32/09, *Treaty of Lisbon*, Judgment of 24 November 2010.

[86] The most well-known challenge to EU law on the basis of Article 23 was a challenge against the Maastricht Treaty in which the German court replied along similar lines, albeit less elaborately, to its *Lisbon Treaty* judgment, *Brunner* v. *The European Union* [1994] 1 CMLR 57.

[87] The literature on the judgment is enormous. C. Schonberger, 'Lisbon in Karlsruhe: Maastricht's Epigones at Sea' (2010) 10 *German LJ* 1201; D. Thym, 'In the Name of Sovereign Statehood: A Critical Introduction to the Lisbon judgment of the German Constitutional Court' (2009) 46 *CMLRev* 1795; D. Jančić, 'Caveats from Karlsruhe and Berlin: Whither Democracy after Lisbon' (2009) 16 *CJEL* 337; P. Kuiver, 'The Lisbon Judgment of the German Constitutional Court: A Court-Ordered Strengthening of the National Legislature in the EU' (2010) 16 *ELJ* 578.

and its powers came at the expense of the Bundestag, so that the latter became a Potemkin parliament with no significant legislative powers of its own and the German citizens' vote became worthless.

2 BvE 2/08 *Treaty of Lisbon*, Judgment of 30 June 2009

225 The constitutional mandate to realise a united Europe, which follows from Article 23.1 of the Basic Law and its Preamble . . . means in particular for the German constitutional bodies that it is not left to their political discretion whether or not they participate in European integration. The Basic Law wants European integration and an international peaceful order. Therefore not only the principle of openness towards international law, but also the principle of openness towards European law applies.

226 It is true that the Basic Law grants the legislature powers to engage in a far-reaching transfer of sovereign powers to the European Union. However, the powers are granted under the condition that the sovereign statehood of a constitutional state is maintained on the basis of an integration programme according to the principle of conferral and respecting the Member States' constitutional identity, and that at the same time the Member States do not lose their ability to politically and socially shape the living conditions on their own responsibility . . .

233 The Basic Law does not grant the German state bodies powers to transfer sovereign powers in such a way that their exercise can independently establish other competences for the European Union. It prohibits the transfer of competence to decide on its own competence (*Kompetenz-Kompetenz*) . . . Also a far-reaching process of independence of political rule for the European Union brought about by granting it steadily increased competences and by gradually overcoming existing unanimity requirements or rules of state equality that have been decisive so far can, from the perspective of German constitutional law, only take place as a result of the freedom of action of the self-determined people. According to the constitution, such steps of integration must be factually limited by the act of transfer and must, in principle, be revocable. For this reason, withdrawal from the European union of integration . . . may, regardless of a commitment for an unlimited period under an agreement, not be prevented by other Member States or the autonomous authority of the Union . . .

339 The primacy of application of European law remains, even with the entry into force of the Treaty of Lisbon, a concept conferred under an international treaty, i.e. a derived concept which will have legal effect in Germany only with the order to apply the law given by the Act Approving the Treaty of Lisbon. This derivative connection is not altered by the fact that the concept of primacy of application is not explicitly provided for in the treaties but was developed in the early phase of European integration in the case law of the Court of Justice by means of interpretation. It is a consequence of the continuing sovereignty of the Member States that in any case in the clear absence of a constitutive order to apply the law, the inapplicability of such a legal instrument to Germany is established by the Federal Constitutional Court. Such determination must also be made if, within or outside the sovereign powers conferred, these powers are exercised with the consequent effect on Germany of a violation of its constitutional identity, which is inviolable under Article 79.3 of the Basic Law and is also respected by European treaty law, namely Article 4(2) TEU.

340 The Basic Law strives to integrate Germany into the legal community of peaceful and free states, but does not waive the sovereignty contained in the last instance in the German constitution as a right of the people to take constitutive decisions concerning fundamental questions as its own identity. There is therefore no contradiction to the aim of openness to international law if the legislature, exceptionally, does not comply with international treaty law – accepting, however, corresponding consequences in international relations – provided this is the only way in which a violation of fundamental principles of the constitution

can be averted . . . The Court of Justice of the European Communities based its decision of 3 September 2008 in the *Kadi* case on a similar view according to which an objection to the claim of validity of a United Nations Security Council Resolution may be expressed citing fundamental legal principles of the Community . . . The Court of Justice has thus, in a borderline case, placed the assertion of its own identity as a legal community above the commitment that it otherwise respects. Such a legal construct is not only familiar in international legal relations as a reference to the *ordre public* as the boundary of a treaty commitment; it also corresponds, if used constructively, to the idea of contexts of political order which are not structured according to a strict hierarchy. It does not in any case factually contradict the objective of openness towards European law, i.e. to the participation of the Federal Republic of Germany in the building of a united Europe (Preamble, Article 23.1 first sentence of the Basic Law), if exceptionally, and under special and narrow conditions, the Federal Constitutional Court declares European Union law inapplicable in Germany.

There are three significant take-aways from this extract.

First, the power enjoyed by EU law is authorised power. That is, EU law cannot found its own authority. Sovereignty rests in the national constitutional settlements which provide for authority to be granted to the Union. It is, thus, for national constitutional courts, as guardians of these settlements, to determine the limits of EU legal authority and when EU measures transgress these limits.

Secondly, the authority granted to EU law is limited. To be sure, the judgment describes the powers granted to the European Union as 'far-reaching' (para. 226). However, it also states that EU law must operate according to the principle of conferred powers, which entails that the Union can neither have general nor excessively wide powers. In addition, limits are placed on EU law, irrespective of its breadth, intruding into certain fields which are seen as particularly sensitive. EU law must, therefore, respect Member States' constitutional identities, and not deprive Member States of their ability to 'politically and socially shape the living conditions' (para. 226) on their territories.

Thirdly, there is a constitutional commitment to European integration. The importance of this as a counterweight to the other two principles should not be understated. Thus, the judgment commits to an 'openness to EU law' which requires that EU law be granted precedence over German law other than in exceptional circumstances (para. 340).

These three principles are very generic, however. In the remainder of this section, we look at how they have evolved into discrete doctrines which have been deployed by national constitutional courts to place limits on the authority of EU law.

(ii) EU Law and Fundamental Rights

It is particularly problematic for EU law to have authority to do bad things. The clearest example is where an EU law violates fundamental rights. It would be odd, indeed, if the ideal of European integration was so treasured that it took precedence over these rights and freedoms which give expression to human dignity. This issue was addressed by both the Italian and German Constitutional Courts in the mid-1970s when challenges were made to EU laws on the grounds that these violated fundamental rights in their respective constitutions.[88] Both courts held that EU law could not prevail over fundamental rights protected in their national constitutions. There

---

[88] *Frontini* v. *Ministero delle Finanze* [1974] 2 CMLR 372 (Italy); *IHT* v. *Einfuhr ynd Vorratsstelle für Getreide aund Futtermittel* [1974] 2 CMLR 540.

was a tension in their reasoning which has pervaded national approaches since. On one view, the matter was simply that a substantive wrong had been done by the EU lawmaker and all that mattered was that the EU law was rectified. The mechanisms for doing this, be they in EU law or national, were unimportant. On the other view, there were also jurisdictional concerns. The issue was not simply that EU law should not violate fundamental rights, but that these were also something over which it should have no competence. For fundamental rights lay at the heart of national constitutional settlements. In *Frontini*, the Italian judgment referred to above, the Italian Constitutional Court stated, therefore, that EU law could 'have effect in civil, ethno-social or political relations through which [EU law's] provisions can conflict with the Constitution'.[89] On this latter view, the central responsibility for policing EU law's compliance with fundamental rights lay with national courts, as custodians of the national constitutional settlements.

This has led to a split in how national courts have treated potential clashes between EU law and fundamental rights. Some have taken the first view that EU law must not violate fundamental rights. However, it would be excessive if national courts could second-guess every Union decision that affected fundamental rights. It is, therefore, sufficient if EU law has checks in place to prevent and correct fundamental rights violations.[90] In 1986, the German Constitutional Court faced a challenge to a Regulation limiting imports of mushrooms into Germany from Taiwan on the ground that it violated the fundamental right to trade. It ruled that it would not strike down any EU law as long as (*so lange* in German) EU law in general had sufficient checks of its own to protect fundamental rights checks: something it was deemed to have.

Wünsche Handelsgesellschaft [Solange II] [1987] 3 CMLR 225

In so far as sovereign power is accorded to an international institution ... which is in a position within the sovereign sphere of the Federal Republic to encroach on the essential content of the fundamental rights recognized by the Basic Law, it is necessary, if that entails the removal of legal protection existing under the terms of the Basic Law, that instead, there should be a guarantee of the application of fundamental rights which in substance and effectiveness is essentially similar to the protection of fundamental rights required unconditionally by the Basic Law. As a general rule this will require a system of protection of individual rights by independent courts which are given adequate jurisdiction and, in particular, power to review and decide on factual and legal questions appropriate to the relevant claim to protection of rights, and by courts which reach their decisions on the basis of a proper procedure allowing the right to a legal hearing and providing for means of attack or defence appropriate to the subject matter of the dispute and for the availability of freely chosen expert assistance, and the decisions of which, if necessary, contain adequate and effective sanctions for the infringement of a fundamental right ...

In the judgment of this Chamber a measure of protection of fundamental rights has been established ... within the sovereign jurisdiction of the European Communities which in its conception, substance and manner of implementation is essentially comparable with the standards of fundamental rights provided for

---

[89] *Frontini* v. *Ministero delle Finanze* [1974] 2 CMLR 372 (Italy), para. 21.

[90] For other States which follow this line see Pl. ÚS 29/09, *Treaty of Lisbon II*, Judgment of 3 November 2009 (Czech Constitutional Court) para. 154; *Ratification of the Lisbon Treaty* [2010] 2 CMLR 26 (French Constitutional Council). The Austrian Constitutional Court has gone further by stating EU fundamental rights laws can be a standard for constitutional review within Austria, U 466/11-18 and U 1836/11-13, *EU Charter of Fundamental Rights*, Judgment of 14 March 2012 (Austrian Constitutional Court).

in the Basic Law. All the main institutions of the Community have since acknowledged in a legally significant manner that in the exercise of their powers and the pursuit of the objectives of the Community they will be guided as a legal duty by respect for fundamental rights, in particular as established by the constitutions of member states and by the European Convention on Human Rights. There are no decisive factors to lead one to conclude that the standard of fundamental rights which has been achieved under Community law is not adequately consolidated and is only of a transitory nature.

This standard of fundamental rights has . . . particularly through the decisions of the European Court, been formulated in content, consolidated and adequately guaranteed . . .

In view of those developments it must be held that, so long as the European Communities, in particular European Court case law, generally ensure effective protection of fundamental rights as against the sovereign powers of the Communities which is to be regarded as substantially similar to the protection of fundamental rights required un-conditionally by the Basic Law, and in so far as they generally safeguard the essential content of fundamental rights, the Federal Constitutional Court will no longer exercise its jurisdiction to decide on the applicability of secondary Community legislation cited as the legal basis for any acts of German courts or authorities within the sovereign jurisdiction of the Federal Republic of Germany, and it will no longer review such legislation by the standard of the fundamental rights contained in the Basic Law.

On a charitable view, the space granted to EU law to develop its own safeguards can lead to a productive dialogue between national courts and the Court of Justice on fundamental rights. It allows an EU fundamental rights law to develop which might be a little different from the fundamental rights laws in individual Member States. However, the need to ensure equivalent protection between EU law and national law entails that national courts and the Court of Justice will reflect on these differences with a view to improving their own law.[91] The preliminary reference provides a mechanism through which this process can take place with national constitutional courts asking questions of the Court of Justice where EU law appears to contradict rights in their constitutions. This has become more common since the Lisbon Treaty,[92] and it can go in different directions. In some cases, it can lead to the constitutional court revisiting its interpretations of the national constitution.[93] It has also led to the Court of Justice revisiting its case law on fundamental rights.[94]

A less benign view is that this approach grants excessive deference to EU law. It leads to insufficient verification by national courts of whether the fundamental rights of individuals have been protected. This view has been taken by national constitutional courts who have adopted the second approach outlined earlier, namely that fundamental rights are a matter above all for

---

[91] For an argument to this effect see A. Torres Pérez, *Conflicts of Rights in the European Union: A Theory of Supranational Adjudication* (Oxford University Press, 2009) ch. 5.

[92] M. Dicosola, C. Fasone and I. Spigno, 'Foreword: Constitutional Courts in the European Legal System After the Treaty of Lisbon and the Euro-Crisis' (2015) 16 *German LJ* 1317.

[93] The Spanish Constitutional Tribunal thus modified its position that it was always a breach of a fair trial for the accused to be tried *in absentia* in the light of the *Melloni* litigation, *Melloni* v. *Ministerio Fiscal*, C-399/11, EU:C:2013:107; STC 26/2014, *Melloni* v. *Ministerio Fiscal*, Judgment of 13 February 2014 (Spanish Constitutional Tribunal).

[94] In 2014, the Court of Justice agreed with national concerns that EU law requiring service providers to retain data and grant access to authorities without sufficient safeguards violated the right to respect for family life, *Digital Rights Ireland* v. *Minister for Communications, Marine and Natural Resources* and *Kärntner Landesregierung and Others*, C-293/12 and C-594/12, EU:C:2014:238. See also the concerns expressed in G 47/2012 *Data Retention Law*, Judgment of 27 June 2014 (Austrian Constitutional Court).

national constitutional law.[95] It is illustrated by the *Taricco* saga. In *Taricco*, the Court of Justice ruled on an Italian law which provided that where criminal proceedings were interrupted, the limitation period, beyond which the offence could not be prosecuted, could be extended but only up to a quarter of the length of the interruption. It found that this law breached an EU law requirement that Member States must impose effective and dissuasive penalties for commission of serious VAT fraud as it made it impossible to punish many offences which were time barred as a consequence of interruptions in the proceedings. The judgment conflicted with the principle of legality in Article 25 of the Italian Constitution. This requires that the rules for criminal offences must be reasonably foreseeable at the moment of commission of the alleged offence (in this case the limitation had been overturned by the Court of Justice judgment) and that they should be sufficiently precisely defined (the Court of Justice was vague as to the permissible length of limitation period). These matters were raised before the Italian Constitutional Court.

Order 24 of Year 2017, Order of 26 January 2017 (Italian Constitutional Court)

The recognition of the primacy of EU law is an established fact within the case law of this Court pursuant to Article 11 of the Constitution; moreover, according to such settled case law, compliance with the supreme principles of the Italian constitutional order and inalienable human rights is a prerequisite for the applicability of EU law in Italy. In the highly unlikely event that specific legislation were not so compliant, it would be necessary to rule unconstitutional the national law authorising the ratification and implementation of the Treaties, solely insofar as it permits such a legislative scenario to arise . . . Furthermore, there is no doubt that the principle of legality in criminal matters is an expression of a supreme principle of the legal order, which has been posited in order to safeguard the inviolable rights of the individual insofar as it requires that criminal rules must be precise and must not have retroactive effect . . .

The primacy of EU law does not express a mere technical configuration of the system of national and supranational sources of law. It rather reflects the conviction that the objective of unity, within the context of a legal order that ensures peace and justice between nations, justifies the renunciation of areas of sovereignty, even if defined through constitutional law. At the same time, the legitimation for (Article 11 of the Italian Constitution) and the very force of unity within a legal order characterised by pluralism (Article 2 TEU) result from its capacity to embrace the minimum level of diversity that is necessary in order to preserve the national identity inherent within the fundamental structure of the Member State (Article 4(2) TEU). Otherwise, the European Treaties would seek, in a contradictory fashion, to undermine the very constitutional foundation out of which they were born by the wishes of the Member States. These considerations have always underpinned the action both of this Court, when finding Article 11 of the Constitution to constitute the linchpin for the European legal order, and also of the Court of Justice when, anticipating Article 6(3) TEU, it incorporated into EU law the constitutional traditions common to the Member States. It follows as a matter of principle that EU law and the judgments of the Court of Justice that clarify its meaning for the purposes of its uniform application cannot be interpreted as requiring a Member State to give up the supreme principles of its constitutional order. Naturally, the Court of Justice is not exempt from the task of defining the scope of EU law and cannot be further encumbered by the

---

[95] See also SK 45/09, *Regulation 44/2001 on jurisdiction and the recognition and enforcement of judgments*, Judgment of 16 November 2011 (Polish Constitutional Tribunal).

> requirement of assessing in detail whether it is compatible with the constitutional identity of each Member State. It is therefore reasonable to expect that, in cases in which such an assessment is not immediately apparent, the European court will establish the meaning of EU law, whilst leaving to the national authorities the ultimate assessment concerning compliance with the supreme principles of the national order. It then falls to each of these legal systems to establish which body is charged with this task. The Constitution of the Republic of Italy vests this task exclusively in this Court . . .

The matter was referred back to the Court of Justice, who deferred to the Italian Constitutional Court by stating that no criminal rules could be retroactively imposed or be unclear.[96] Here, the national court was asserting a monopoly over the interpretation of fundamental rights, with the Court of Justice placed in a take it-or-leave it situation. This was made even clearer by a subsequent judgment by the Italian Constitutional Court, which concerned the constitutionality of taxes which were levied only on entrepreneurs with an annual revenue of more than €50 million on the grounds that these taxes discriminated. The Constitutional Court stated that often a matter would involve fundamental rights in a national constitution and in EU law that intersected. *Taricco* was such an example as it concerned the principle of legality, which was protected in both EU fundamental rights law and the Italian constitution. In such circumstances, it stated that it would make a single judgment, which dealt with all the fundamental rights issues, be they in EU law or national law. In short, whilst it may take guidance from the case law of the Court of Justice, the Italian court would exercise ultimate authority over the protection of fundamental rights from EU law.[97]

(iii) *Ultra Vires* Review

The second source of constraint is where national courts believe EU Institutions are acting outside the powers formally given to them by EU law. This *ultra vires* review poses practical challenges. It is easy for a national court, whenever it disagrees with a Court of Justice judgment, to argue that the EU Institutions exceeded their power. It will simply say that the Court was not interpreting an EU law but going beyond that and engaging in lawmaking, something it does not have the power to do. *Ultra vires* review can quickly be turned into an instrument for national courts to second-guess every EU law with all the possibility of chaos posed by that. However, the converse is also problematic. Awareness of the slipperiness of the *ultra vires* doctrine could paralyse national courts, with the consequence that they do not really patrol the limits of EU competences.

This has resulted in two approaches to *ultra vires* review. The first is to give considerable latitude to EU Institutions. It is not enough that they acted beyond their powers. The breach must be manifest and structurally significant. The second is to grant considerably less latitude to the EU Institutions, and hold that any *ultra vires* measure is illegal.

---

[96] *M.A.S. and M.B.*, C-42/17, EU:C:2017:936.

[97] *Judgment 269 of Year 2017*, Judgment of 18 December 2017, para. 5.2 (Italian Constitutional Court). On this saga see G. Vassallo, 'When Tradition Overrode Identity: The ECJ Decision on *Taricco II* as Two-Faced Judgment?', *Diritti comparati Working Paper 1/2018*; R. Di Marco, 'The "Path Towards European Integration" of the Italian Constitutional Court: The Primacy of EU Law in the Light of the Judgment No. 269/17', *European Papers, European Forum, Insight of 14 July 2018*, 1.

The first approach, in which EU laws can only be reviewed if the breach of power is manifest and structurally significant, was established in *Honeywell*. A challenge was made to a 2002 German law allowing fixed-term contracts only to be granted to employees older than 52 years of age.[98] Between February 2003 and March 2004, Honeywell, a supplier of cars, employed thirteen new employees over 52 years of age on such contracts. Such contracts were found in *Mangold* to be an illegal form of age discrimination under the Framework Directive, even though the deadline for transposition for that Directive was December 2006.[99] It was argued that the Court of Justice's judgment that a Directive could be invoked against a private company before the deadline for transposition was *ultra vires*. The German Constitutional Court found nothing awry with the judgment, but went on to set out its understanding of *ultra vires* review.

2 BvR 2661/06 *Honeywell*, Judgment of 6 July 2010

59 ... According to the legal system of the Federal Republic of Germany, the primacy of application of Union law is to be recognised and it is to be guaranteed that the control powers which are constitutionally reserved for the Federal Constitutional Court are only exercised in a manner that is reserved and open towards European law.

60 This means for the *ultra vires* review at hand that the Federal Constitutional Court must comply with the rulings of the Court of Justice in principle as a binding interpretation of Union law. Prior to the acceptance of an *ultra vires* act on the part of the European bodies and institutions, the Court of Justice is therefore to be afforded the opportunity to interpret the Treaties, as well as to rule on the validity and interpretation of the legal acts in question, in the context of preliminary ruling proceedings according to Article 267 TFEU. As long as the Court of Justice did not have an opportunity to rule on the questions of Union law which have arisen, the Federal Constitutional Court may not find any inapplicability of Union law for Germany ...

61 *Ultra vires* review by the Federal Constitutional Court can moreover only be considered if it is manifest that acts of the European bodies and institutions have taken place outside the transferred competences ... A breach of the principle of conferral is only manifest if the European bodies and institutions have transgressed the boundaries of their competences in a manner specifically violating the principle of conferral ... the breach of competences is in other words sufficiently qualified ... This means that the act of the authority of the European Union must be manifestly in violation of competences and that the impugned act is highly significant in the structure of competences between the Member States and the Union with regard to the principle of conferral and to the binding nature of the statute under the rule of law ...

66 If the supranational integration principle is not to be endangered, *ultra vires* review must be exercised reservedly by the Federal Constitutional Court. Since it also has to find on a legal view of the Court of Justice in each case of an *ultra vires* complaint, the task and status of the independent suprastate case-law must be safeguarded. This means, on the one hand, respect for the Union's own methods of justice to which the Court of Justice considers itself to be bound and which do justice to the 'uniqueness' of the Treaties and

---

[98] M. Payandeh, 'Constitutional Review of EU Law after Honeywell: Contextualizing the Relationship between the German Constitutional Court and the EU Court of Justice' (2011) 48 *CMLRev* 9; C. Möllers, 'German Federal Constitutional Court: Constitutional *Ultra Vires* Review of European Acts Only under Exceptional Circumstances' (2011) 7 *EUConst* 161.

[99] *Mangold* v. *Helm*, C-144/05, EU: C:2005:794.

goals that are inherent to them (see ECJ Opinion 1/91 *EEA Treaty* [1991] ECR I-6079 para. 51). Secondly, the Court of Justice has a right to tolerance of error. It is hence not a matter for the Federal Constitutional Court in questions of the interpretation of Union law which with a methodical interpretation of the statute can lead to different outcomes in the usual legal science discussion framework, to supplant the interpretation of the Court of Justice with an interpretation of its own. Interpretations of the bases of the Treaties are also to be tolerated which, without a considerable shift in the structure of competences, constitute a restriction to individual cases and either do not permit impacts on fundamental rights to arise which constitute a burden or do not oppose domestic compensation for such burdens.

There are two tests to be met, therefore, for an EU measure to be declared *ultra vires*. First, there is the substantive test that the breach must be manifest and structurally significant and, secondly, a procedural requirement that the Court of Justice must have had a prior opportunity to review the offending measure. In practice, the combination of these tests makes it unlikely that any EU measure will be declared *ultra vires* by the German court.

The test also creates a situation where EU measures can remain in place but with little credibility. This problem arose with the German Constitutional Court's *OMT* judgment. These concerned challenges to the Outright Monetary Transactions Decision of the European Central Bank (ECB), which committed the latter to purchase bonds on secondary markets (i.e. not directly from the governments themselves) of euro area States who were subject to financial assistance programmes. These governments were, otherwise, unable to secure finance to meet their countries' needs. The German Constitutional Court found that the decision was *ultra vires* because, first, it was an economic policy decision and the ECB only had powers in the field of monetary policy and, secondly, because it breached the EU law prohibition in Article 123 TFEU on the ECB financing public institutions.[100] It referred the questions to the Court of Justice, as required by *Honeywell*, who found the programme lawful but required purchases to be made in a proportionate manner, thereby heavily restricting the circumstances when they could be made.[101] When the matter returned to the German Constitutional Court, it continued to find the decision *ultra vires*, but stated that, because of the conditions imposed by the Court of Justice, it was not *manifestly* so.[102] This leaves the measures in a legal limbo. They are illegal but continue to enjoy validity, and, this being so, it begs the question why the German Constitutional Court thinks the measures should have any kind of authority.

The second approach, in which a national court only has to find a measure to be *ultra vires* for it to be declared invalid, was most prominently adopted by the Czech Constitutional Court in *Slovak Pensions*. Under the Agreement dissolving Czechoslovakia, pension entitlements were determined by the State of residence of the employer at the time of dissolution. Czechs working in Slovakia would thus receive Slovak entitlements and vice versa. However, the Slovak pension was very low relative to Czech living costs. All Czechs resident in the Czech Republic at the time of claiming their pension were, therefore, granted a supplement bringing their pension to the same level as if they had been working in the Czech Republic. This supplement was upheld by the

---

[100] 2 BvR 2728/13 *OMT/ESM*, Order of 14 January 2014 (German Constitutional Court).
[101] *Gauweiler and Others* v. *Deutscher Bundestag*, C-62/14, EU:C:2015:400.
[102] 2 BvR 2728/13, *OMT/ESM*, Judgment of 21 June 2016 (German Constitutional Court).

Czech Constitutional Court as a constitutional entitlement. It was not available to Slovaks and was declared illegal in the *Landtóva* case by the Court of Justice as it violated a Regulation which provided for equality of treatment in social security for EU migrant workers.[103] The matter was brought before the Czech Constitutional Court asking it to revisit the law. It refused.

Pl. ÚS 5/12: *Slovak Pensions*, Judgment of 31 January 2012 (Czech Constitutional Court)

[I]f European bodies interpreted or developed EU law in a manner that would jeopardize the foundations of materially understood constitutionality and the essential requirements of a democratic, law-based state that are, under the Constitution of the Czech Republic, seen as inviolable . . . such legal acts could not be binding in the Czech Republic . . .

This entire issue is not comparable to evaluating entitlements for social security in view of the inclusion of periods served in various countries; it is an issue of the consequences of the dissolution of Czechoslovakia and evaluating the entitlements of citizens of the Czech Republic with regard to the allocation of expenses for social security between the successor countries (as the secondary party also says in its statement). Insofar as, as previously stated, Art. 2 par. 1 of the Regulation states that it shall apply to persons (in particular employed persons or self-employed persons and students) who are or were subject to the legislation of one or more member states and who are nationals of one of the member states, then within the indicated case law of the Constitutional Court, in the case of citizens of the Czech Republic all the effects arising from their social security until 31 December 1992 must be considered to be subject to the legal regulation of the state of which they are citizens. Failure to distinguish the legal relationships arising from the dissolution of a state with a uniform social security system from the legal relationships arising for social security from the free movement of persons in the European Communities, or the European Union, is a failure to respect European history, it is comparing things that are not comparable.

. . . [W]e cannot do otherwise than state, in connection with the effects of [*Landtóva*] on analogous cases, that in that case there were excesses on the part of a European Union body, that a situation occurred in which an act by a European body exceeded the powers that the Czech Republic transferred to the European Union . . . this exceeded the scope of the transferred powers, and was ultra vires.

The judgment was criticised at the time on the ground that the Czech Constitutional Court's main concern was protecting its institutional prerogatives.[104] However, its central context was a highly sensitive one. It went to a constitutional right: the right for all Czechs to have a material security, particularly in their old age. To grant this entitlement to all Slovaks who chose to retire in the Czech Republic would have imposed – given the possible numbers – significant demands on its pension system with a possible reduction in the size of individual pensions.

This might suggest that this version of the *ultra vires* doctrine is only for highly sensitive matters. This interpretation would seem to be borne out by the judgment of the United Kingdom Supreme Court in *Pham*. This concerned a decision by the UK Government to strip a UK–Vietnamese dual national of his UK citizenship on the ground that he was a member of

---

[103] *Landtóva*, C-399/09, EU:C:2011:415.

[104] J. Komárek, 'Playing with Matches: The Czech Constitutional Court Declares a Judgment of the Court of Justice of the EU *Ultra Vires*' (2012) 8 *EUConst* 323; R. Zbíral, 'A Legal Revolution or Negligible Episode? Court of Justice Decision Proclaimed *Ultra Vires*' (2012) 49 *CMLRev* 1475.

Al Qaeda. The decision was challenged on the ground that, *inter alia*, it went against a Court of Justice judgment prohibiting a State from stripping a citizen of their national citizenship if it would lead to him losing his EU citizenship.[105] The United Kingdom court disagreed with this interpretation of the Court of Justice judgment, but stated that, if they were wrong, such a judgment would be *ultra vires* as EU law did not go to the conditions for acquiring or losing national citizenship, a matter of constitutional importance.[106]

This exceptionalism might, however, have to be revisited in the light of the *Ajos* judgment of the Danish Supreme Court.[107] The case concerned a refusal by a Danish company to pay a severance allowance to the estate of a former employee on his leaving the company. The allowance was not paid because, under Danish law, it did not have to be paid to anybody of pensionable age. The Court of Justice ruled that this was a violation of the principle prohibiting age discrimination, and this principle was a general principle of EU law which could be invoked against private parties.[108] The Danish Supreme Court refused to follow the Court of Justice's judgment. It stated that it could only give effect to those EU laws which were mentioned in the Act on Denmark's Accession to the European Union. The principle invoked here was a general principle of law, which had been developed purely by the Court of Justice. It was inferred from laws outside the EU Treaties and was not mentioned in the Act on Accession. It could not therefore be applied.

On its face, this judgment seems narrowly confined. It applies to a line of reasoning, general principles of law, on which there are only a few cases. It would seem, therefore, not to apply to any EU laws (as these are mentioned in the Act of Accession) or Court of Justice interpretations of these laws. However, academics have observed that the context to the judgment was both a sense that Danish courts were being micromanaged and that there was too much activism by the Court of Justice.[109] If that is so, *Ajos* might presage wide push-back against ambitious measures of EU Institutions or novel judgments of the Court of Justice.

(iv) EU Law and Identity Review

The requirements that EU laws neither violate fundamental rights nor be *ultra vires* do not address the question of what happens when EU laws encroach too far on things of domestic value. The German Constitutional Court turned to this in its *Lisbon Treaty* judgment, where it set out identity review as a further reason for refusing EU law authority. It found that the European Union did not meet the conditions for being a representative democracy, as EU citizens were not equally represented either through the allocation of seats in the European Parliament or votes within the Council. Consequently, it considered whether this limited the fields in which EU law could have authority.

---

[105] The judgment was *Rottmann* v. *Freistaat Bayern*, C-135/08, EU:C:2010:104.

[106] *Pham* v. *Secretary of State for the Home Department* [2015] UKSC 19, paras. 90–1, per Lord Mance.

[107] Case no. 15/2014, *Dansk Industri acting for Ajos vs. Estate of A*, Judgment of 6 December (Danish Supreme Court).

[108] *Dansk Industri* v. *Rasmussen*, C-441/14, EU: C:2016:278.

[109] M. Madsen, H. Olsen and U. Šadl 'Competing Supremacies and Clashing Institutional Rationalities: the Danish Supreme Court's Decision in the Ajos Case and the National Limits of Judicial Cooperation' (2017) 23 *ELJ* 140.

2 BvE 2/08, *Treaty of Lisbon*, Judgment of 30 June 2009

245 A permanent responsibility for integration is incumbent upon the German constitutional bodies. In the transfer of sovereign powers and the elaboration of the European decision-making procedures, it is aimed at ensuring that, seen overall, the political system of the Federal Republic of Germany as well as that of the European Union comply with democratic principles ...

247 Inward federalisation and outward supranationalisation can open up new possibilities of civic participation. An increased cohesion of smaller or larger units and better opportunities for a peaceful balancing of interests between regions and states grow from them. Federal or supranational intertwining creates possibilities of action which otherwise would encounter practical or territorial limits, and facilitates the peaceful balancing of interests. At the same time, it makes it more difficult to create a will of the majority that can be asserted and that directly derives from the people ... The assignment of decisions to specific responsible actors becomes less transparent, with the result that citizens have difficulty in having their vote guided by tangible contexts of responsibility. The principle of democracy therefore sets content-related limits to the transfer of sovereign powers, limits which do not already result from the inalienability of the constituent power and of state sovereignty.

248 The safeguarding of sovereignty, demanded by the principle of democracy in the valid constitutional system prescribed by the Basic Law in a manner that is open to integration and to international law, does not mean that a pre-determined number or certain types of sovereign rights should remain in the hands of the state. The participation of Germany in the development of the European Union ... also comprises a political union, in addition to the creation of an economic and monetary union. Political union means the joint exercise of public authority, including legislative authority, even reaching into the traditional core areas of the state's area of competence. This is rooted in the European idea of peace and unification especially when dealing with the coordination of cross-border aspects of life and when guaranteeing a single economic area and area of justice in which citizens of the Union can freely develop.

249 European unification on the basis of a treaty union of sovereign states may, however, not be achieved in such a way that not sufficient space is left to the Member States for the political formation of the economic, cultural and social living conditions. This applies in particular to areas which shape the citizens' living conditions, in particular the private sphere of their own responsibility and of political and social security, protected by fundamental rights, as well as to political decisions that rely especially on cultural, historical and linguistic perceptions and which develop in public discourse in the party political and parliamentary sphere of public politics. Essential areas of democratic formative action comprise, *inter alia*, citizenship, the civil and the military monopoly on the use of force, revenue and expenditure including external financing and all elements of encroachment that are decisive for the realisation of fundamental rights, above all in major encroachments on fundamental rights such as deprivation of liberty in the administration of criminal law or placement in an institution. These important areas also include cultural issues such as the disposition of language, the shaping of circumstances concerning the family and education, the ordering of the freedom of opinion, press and of association and the dealing with the profession of faith or ideology.

250 Democracy not only means respecting formal principles of organisation ... and not just a cooperative involvement of interest groups. Democracy first and foremost lives on, and in, a viable public opinion that concentrates on central acts of determination of political direction and the periodic allocation of highest-ranking political offices in the competition of government and opposition. Only this public opinion shows the alternatives for elections and other votes and continually calls them to mind also in decisions relating to individual issues in order that they may remain continuously present and effective in the political opinion-formation of the people via the parties, which are open to participation for all citizens, and in

the public information area. To this extent, Article 38 and Article 20.1 and 20.2 of the Basic Law also protect the connection between political decisions on facts and the will of the majority constituted by elections, and the resulting dualism between government and opposition in a system of a multiplicity of competing parties and of observing and controlling formation of public opinion.

251 Even if due to the great successes of European integration, a common European polity that engages in issue-related cooperation in the relevant areas of their respective states is visibly growing ... it cannot be overlooked, however, that the public perception of factual issues and of political leaders remains connected to a considerable extent to patterns of identification related to the nation-state, language, history and culture. The principle of democracy as well as the principle of subsidiarity ... therefore require factually to restrict the transfer and exercise of sovereign powers to the European Union in a predictable manner, particularly in central political areas of the space of personal development and the shaping of living conditions by social policy. In these areas, it is particularly necessary to draw the limit where the coordination of cross-border situations is factually required.

252 Particularly sensitive for the ability of a constitutional state to democratically shape itself are decisions on substantive and formal criminal law, on the disposition of the monopoly on the use of force by the police within the state and by the military towards the exterior, fundamental fiscal decisions on public revenue and public expenditure, the latter being particularly motivated, *inter alia*, by social policy considerations, decisions on the shaping of living conditions in a social state and decisions of particular cultural importance, for example on family law, the school and education system and on dealing with religious communities.

The limited democratic qualities of the Union mean, according to the German Constitutional Court, that it does not have authority to adopt laws which go to the constitutional identity of a Member State. These include the central features of criminal law, deployment of the use of force, central budgetary issues, the central issues of social policy and culturally important fields, in particular religion, education and family life (para. 252). Analogous identity-based approaches have been adopted by a number of other States.[110] This approach has been criticised for being too focused around the idea of 'identity', with its polarising associations of 'Them' (Europeans) and 'Us' (nationals).[111] It has been argued also that it gives Member States a free pass in these protected fields, and looks insufficiently at the quality of democracy there.[112]

These criticisms have to be viewed in light of the judgment of the Hungarian Constitutional Court concerning an EU Decision reallocating asylum seekers who had crossed the Mediterranean and arrived in Greece and Italy. The decision required Hungary to take 1,294 of these

---

[110] The German Constitutional Court has identified parallel reasoning in the Czech Republic, Denmark, Estonia, France, Ireland, Italy, Latvia, Poland, Spain and Sweden, 2 BvR 2728/13, *OMT/ESM*, Order of 14 January 2014 (German Constitutional Court), para. 30. Identity review has also been used in Belgium and Hungary, Case 62/16, *Human Rights League*, Judgment of 28 April 2016 (Belgian Constitutional Court); Decision 22/2016, *Interpretation of Article E(2) of the Fundamental Law*, Judgment of 30 November 2016 (Hungarian Constitutional Court).

[111] K. Nicolaidis, 'Germany as Europe: How the Constitutional Court Unwittingly Embraced EU Demoi-cracy' (2011) 9 *ICON* 786.

[112] F. Mayer, 'Rashomon in Karlsruhe: A Reflection on Democracy and Identity in the European Union' (2011) 9 *ICON* 757.

asylum seekers. The judgment did not seek to overturn the decision but merely to consider the question more abstractly. In this, it looked, in particular, at the limits on Article E(2) of Hungary's Fundamental Law, which provides for Hungarian accession to the European Union. The court found two limits, sovereignty control – EU laws should not violate Hungary's sovereignty – and identity control – EU law should not violate Hungary's constitutional identity.

Decision 22/2016 *Interpretation of Article E(2) of the Fundamental Law*, **Judgment of 30 November 2016 (Hungarian Constitutional Court)**

58 With regard to sovereignty control, the Constitutional Court notes the following.

59 According to Article B of the Fundamental Law, in Hungary, the source of public power shall be the people, and power shall be exercised by the people through elected representatives or, in exceptional cases, directly. The exercised state authority is not an unlimited power; the Parliament may only act in the framework of the Fundamental Law ... As long as Article B of the Fundamental Law contains the principle of independent and sovereign statehood and indicates the people as the source of public power, these provisions shall not be emptied out by the Union-clause in Article E.

60 Since by joining the European Union, Hungary has not surrendered its sovereignty, it rather allowed for the joint exercising of certain competences, the maintenance of Hungary's sovereignty should be presumed when judging upon the joint exercising of further competences additional to the rights and obligations provided in the Founding Treaties of the European Union (the principle of maintained sovereignty). Sovereignty has been laid down in the Fundamental Law as the ultimate source of competences and not as a competence. Therefore the joint exercising of competences shall not result in depriving the people of the possibility of possessing the ultimate chance to control the exercising of public power ...

61 ... With regard to identity control, the Constitutional Court notes the following.

62 According to Article 4(2) TEU, 'the Union shall respect the equality of Member States before the Treaties as well as their national identities, inherent in their fundamental structures, political and constitutional, inclusive of regional and local self-government.'

63 The protection of constitutional identity should be granted in the framework of an informal cooperation with [the EU] based on the principles of equality and collegiality, with mutual respect to each other, similarly to the present practice followed by several other Member States' constitutional courts and supreme judicial bodies performing similar functions.

64 The Constitutional Court of Hungary interprets the concept of constitutional identity as Hungary's self-identity and it unfolds the content of this concept from case to case, on the basis of the whole Fundamental Law and certain provisions thereof, in accordance with the National Avowal and the achievements of our historical constitution ...

65 The constitutional self-identity of Hungary is not a list of static and closed values, nevertheless many of its important components – identical with the constitutional values generally accepted today – can be highlighted as examples: freedoms, the division of powers, republic as the form of government, respect of autonomies under public law, the freedom of religion, exercising lawful authority, parliamentarism, the equality of rights, acknowledging judicial power, the protection of the nationalities living with us. These are, among others, the achievements of our historical constitution, the Fundamental Law and thus the whole Hungarian legal system are based upon.

66 The protection of constitutional self-identity may be raised in the cases having an influence on the living conditions of the individuals, in particular their privacy protected by fundamental rights, on their personal and social security, and on their decision-making responsibility, and when Hungary's linguistic, historical and cultural traditions are affected.

67 The Constitutional Court establishes that the constitutional self-identity of Hungary is a fundamental value not created by the Fundamental Law – it is merely acknowledged by the Fundamental Law. Consequently, constitutional identity cannot be waived by way of an international treaty – Hungary can only be deprived of its constitutional identity through the final termination of its sovereignty, its independent statehood. Therefore the protection of constitutional identity shall remain the duty of the Constitutional Court as long as Hungary is a sovereign State. Accordingly, sovereignty and constitutional identity have several common points, thus their control should be performed with due regard to each other in specific cases.

The context to the judgment was a referendum in October 2016 on the EU Decision. Despite 98 per cent of the ballots cast rejecting the allocation, the referendum failed as there was a turn-out of only 40.4 per cent and Hungarian law requires that the threshold be 50 per cent or above for the result to be binding. In addition, the government had tried unsuccessfully, at the beginning of November 2016, to have the Constitution amended so that it would be illegal for Hungarian public institutions to apply EU law where it threatened Hungary's constitutional identity. The Hungarian Constitutional Court was, therefore, seen as doing the government's work after more democratic routes had failed.[113]

Beyond that, the judgment is an unsettling and complex one.

In the first place, it introduces a new form of review of EU law: sovereignty control. This is related to identity review in that the court identifies the people as the ultimate source of public power in Hungary's constitutional settlement (para. 59). However, it is distinct from it in that, whereas other national constitutional courts have used identity review to shield certain fields of activity from EU law, sovereignty control has a more general sweep. It will allow plebiscites to be held on any EU law. If the turn-out is more than 50 per cent and the majority supports disapplication of the EU law, it will be disapplied. This raises an important question to which there is no clear answer, namely why EU laws should have authority in States where there is overwhelming rejection of it. Furthermore, as plebiscites are costly and time-consuming to arrange and a high threshold must be met, it is unlikely that sovereignty control will lead to swathes of EU law being disapplied. Yet plebiscites carry risks of being vehicles for intolerant populism. Populism often has a number of egregious features: disregard and even contempt for the arguments of others, scapegoating of minorities and foreigners, and indifference to the suffering caused by its decisions. Sovereignty control provides no reassurances about these risks.

The judgment is equally unsettling with regard to identity review. On the one hand, protection of constitutional identity is accepted across the EU as a reason for not applying EU law. The Hungarian court positions itself within this tradition (para. 63), and thus does not set out its judgment as at odds with the decisions of other national courts or as not recognising the authority of the Court of Justice. On the other hand, it has taken a particularly wide view of constitutional identity. The list of values and institutions to be protected is both open-ended and vague (paras. 65–6). Its view of constitutional identity is also not anchored in protecting the Hungarian Constitution. Constitutional identity is, instead, a notion which precedes the Constitution and is given effect by the constitution (para. 67).[114] This opens the way for a series

---

[113] G. Halmai, 'Abuse of Constitutional Identity: The Hungarian Constitutional Court on Interpretation of Article E) (2) of the Fundamental Law' (2017) 43 *Review of Central and East European Law* 23.

[114] On this, G. Halmai, 'The Hungarian Constitutional Court and Constitutional Identity', *VerfBlog*, 1 October 2017, https://verfassungsblog.de/the-hungarian-constitutional-court-and-constitutional-identity/.

of traditions to be included within it and to be invoked as a reason for not applying EU law. These traditions are not only vague, and therefore open to abuse, but can also be interpreted in highly illiberal ways.[115] This view of constitutional identity parallels that adopted by German fascists in the 1930s.[116] However, once again, there has to be some ambivalence about this. Others have observed that the formal provisions of national constitutions may offer only partial protection against the worse predations of EU law. There are, therefore, typically, no constitutional provisions which directly address what to do when EU Institution measures impose great suffering or injustice. Instead, constitutional provisions focus on violations of particular individual rights, which may fail to address the nature or scale of the wrong being perpetuated. In such circumstances, more wide-ranging protection against EU law may be warranted.[117]

(v) Dynamic EU Laws and Parliamentary Review

The controversies surrounding the difficulties of applying the *ultra vires* doctrine and the wider issues raised by identity review obscured the emergence of an intermediate approach, which was also adopted by the German Constitutional Court in its *Lisbon Treaty* judgment. This does not take a black-and-white view of fields of activity where the EU law has authority and fields where it does not. Instead, it sets out a number of fields where EU laws are only to have authority if they are also approved by the national parliament and subject to its oversight. This approach initially focused on fields of EU competence that were characterised by the German court as 'dynamic' in nature: they were so wide that it was difficult to be sure of their precise limits (i.e. at what point they stopped).[118]

---

2 BvE 2/08 *Treaty of Lisbon*, Judgment of 30 June 2009

238 Under the constitution, however, faith in the constructive force of the mechanism of integration cannot be unlimited. If in the process of European integration primary law is amended, or expansively interpreted by institutions, a constitutionally important tension will arise with the principle of conferral and with the individual Member State's constitutional responsibility for integration. If legislative or administrative competences are only transferred in an unspecified manner or with a view to further dynamic development, or if the institutions are permitted to re-define expansively, fill lacunae or factually extend competences,

---

[115] The National Avowal, which acts as the Preamble to the 2011 Hungarian Constitution, thus refers to a 'Christian Europe' and the 'intellectual and spiritual unity of our Nation', www.constituteproject.org/constitution/Hungary_2011.pdf.

[116] M. Polzin, 'Constitutional Identity, Unconstitutional Amendments and the Idea of Constituent Power: The Development of the Doctrine of Constitutional Identity in German Constitutional Law' (2016) 14 *ICON* 438.

[117] M. Wilkinson, 'Constitutional Pluralism: Chronicle of a Death Foretold?' (2017) 27 *ELJ* 213. It has been argued that reference should be had to the idea of a constitutional imagination in such circumstances. This may be less open to abuse than an identity-based constitutionalism, J. Komárek, 'Waiting for the Existential Revolution in Europe' (2014) 12 *ICON* 190.

[118] These are the passarelle provisions which allow measures decided by unanimity to be changed to decision by QMV (Articles 31(2) and 48(7) TEU, and Articles 81(3), 153(2), 192(2), 312(2) TFEU); the emergency brake provisions which allow measures touching on fundamental aspects of a State's social security or criminal justice system to be referred to the European Council (Articles 48(2), 82(3) and 83(3) TFEU); extension of the list of criminal offences which may be harmonised and the powers of the European public prosecutor (Articles 83(1)(3) and 86(4) TFEU); amendment of the statute of the European Investment Bank (Article 308 TFEU); and the flexibility provision which allows the Union to adopt laws to further its objectives where there is no other base (Article 352 TFEU).

they risk transgressing the predetermined integration programme and acting beyond the powers granted to them. They are moving on a road at the end of which there is the power of disposition of their foundations laid down in the treaties, i.e. the competence of freely disposing of their competences. There is a risk of transgression of the constitutive principle of conferral and of the conceptual responsibility for integration incumbent upon Member States if institutions of the European Union can decide without restriction, without any outside control, however restrained and exceptional, how treaty law is to be interpreted.

239 It is therefore constitutionally required not to agree dynamic treaty provisions with a blanket character or if they can still be interpreted in a manner that respects the national responsibility for integration, to establish, at any rate, suitable national safeguards for the effective exercise of such responsibility. Accordingly, the Act approving an international agreement and the national accompanying laws must therefore be capable of permitting European integration continuing to take place according to the principle of conferral without the possibility for the European Union of taking possession of *Kompetenz-Kompetenz* or to violate the Member States' constitutional identity, which is not open to integration, in this case, that of the Basic Law. For borderline cases of what is still constitutionally admissible, the German legislature must, where necessary, take precautions in its legislation accompanying approval to ensure that the responsibility for integration of the legislative bodies can sufficiently develop.

The thrust of the judgment is that because EU law is not operating according to the doctrine of conferred powers in these fields, the usual reasons for its having authority do not apply. It has, therefore, to rely on the democratic authority granted to it by national parliamentary assent.

The doctrine was elaborated in the German Constitutional Court's *ESM (Temporary Injunctions)* judgment. The judgment involved the European Stability Mechanism (ESM) Treaty, which consolidated the different forms of financial assistance granted to euro area States experiencing differences in their public finances into a single instrument, the ESM. This Treaty established a fund of €500 billion of which Germany was financially liable for just over €190 billion of it. A company in Luxembourg administered the fund, with its Board of Governors (comprising the Finance Ministers of the euro area States) being responsible for the central decisions. Two aspects of the challenge to the ESM were particularly significant. It concerned, first, a field, budgetary policy, which the *Lisbon Treaty* judgment had identified as one of the fields protected by identity review. It was not, therefore, about Union Institutions having powers that were too wide, but about intruding in politically sensitive fields of policy. The ESM, secondly, provided an institutional framework for providing financial assistance. The German parliament's approval of the treaty approved this framework. However, it would have no say in how that assistance was to be provided. There were concerns that parliamentary approval of the ESM Treaty was, therefore, something of a blank cheque.

2 BvR 1390/12, *ESM Treaty (Temporary Injunctions)*, Judgment of 12 September 2012 (German Constitutional Court)

210 There is a violation of Article 38 (1) of the Basic Law in particular if the German *Bundestag* relinquishes its parliamentary budget responsibility with the effect that it or a future *Bundestag* can no longer exercise the right to decide on the budget on its own responsibility . . . The decision on public revenue and public expenditure is a fundamental part of the ability of a constitutional state to democratically shape itself . . .

The German *Bundestag* must therefore make decisions on revenue and expenditure with responsibility to the people. In this connection, the right to decide on the budget is a central element of the democratic development of informed opinion ...

211 As representatives of the people, the elected Members of the German *Bundestag* must retain control of fundamental budgetary decisions even in a system of intergovernmental governing. In its openness to international cooperation, systems of collective security and European integration, the Federal Republic of Germany binds itself not only legally, but also with regard to fiscal policy. Even if such commitments assume a substantial size, parliament's right to decide on the budget is not necessarily infringed in a way that could be challenged with reference to Article 38 (1) of the Basic Law. Rather, the relevant factor for adherence to the principles of democracy is whether the German *Bundestag* remains the place in which autonomous decisions on revenue and expenditure are made, including those with regard to international and European liabilities ... If essential budget questions relating to revenue and expenditure were decided without the mandatory approval of the German *Bundestag*, or if supranational legal obligations were created without a corresponding decision by free will of the *Bundestag*, parliament would find itself in the role of mere subsequent enforcement and could no longer exercise its overall budgetary responsibility as part of its right to decide on the budget...

212 In its judgment of 7 September 2011 (BVerfGE 129, 124) the Senate stated in detail that the German *Bundestag* may not transfer its budgetary responsibility to other entities by means of imprecise budgetary authorisations. The larger the financial amount of the commitments to accept liability or of commitment appropriations is, the more effectively must the German *Bundestag*'s rights to approve and to refuse and its right of monitoring be elaborated. In particular, the German *Bundestag* may not deliver itself up to any mechanisms with financial effect which – whether by reason of their overall conception or by reason of an overall evaluation of the individual measures – may result in incalculable burdens with budget significance without prior mandatory consent, whether these are expenses or losses of revenue. This prohibition of the relinquishment of budgetary responsibility does not impermissibly restrict the budgetary competence of the legislature, but is specifically aimed at preserving it ...

...

215 The German *Bundestag* cannot exercise its overall budgetary responsibility without receiving sufficient information concerning the decisions with budgetary implications for which is accountable. The principle of democracy under Article 20 (1) and (2) of the Basic Law therefore requires that the German *Bundestag* is able to have access to the information which it needs to assess the fundamental bases and consequences of its decision ...

The *ESM (Temporary Injunctions)* judgment is, therefore, significant in two ways.

First, it joins the identity review and 'dynamic' treaty provision lines of reasoning together.[119] In any field where the Union has either vaguely defined powers or which goes to the constitutional identity of a Member State, an EU law will only have authority if it has also been approved by the national parliament. There is an additional democratic check.

Secondly, the level of national parliamentary involvement required to secure authority will often be significant. For it must be of a nature to allow the parliament to discharge its

[119] M. Wendel, 'Judicial Restraint and the Return to Openness: The Decision of the German Federal Constitutional Court on the ESM and the Fiscal Treaty of 12 September 2012' (2013) 14 *German LJ* 21.

responsibilities in the field in question. In *ESM (Temporary Injunctions)*, this involved the German parliament not just approving the ESM Treaty, but also agreeing to all significant revenue and expenditure decisions, and having sufficient information to review the activities of the ESM. In short, it was required to approve all significant ESM decisions and engage in active oversight.

A number of objections can be made to this involvement of national parliaments. If all Member States insist on it, it acts as a powerful brake on EU lawmaking. By contrast, there are problems if the consent of only some national parliaments is required. It allows these parliaments to intervene in the decision concerning another Member State with no countervailing position taken by that State's parliament. This seems unequal and there is no guarantee that these national parliaments will take the interests of the other State's citizens into account.[120] However, against this, this approach allows Union measures to be adopted where otherwise they might be precluded. It also addresses an arguably more pressing concern, namely parliamentary involvement in lawmaking. On identity review, the *Lisbon Treaty* judgment of the German Constitutional Court raised questions about the Union enjoying significant powers because of its lack of democratic credentials. However, it did not address the democratic credentials of domestic laws. This line of reasoning addresses this issue by stating that identity review cannot be used to preclude EU lawmaking but, instead, must be used to guarantee the involvement of the national parliament.

A dichotomy has, therefore, emerged. In most of its fields of activity, EU law has primacy subject to the *ultra vires* doctrine and its not violating fundamental rights. In fields where it is exercising more wide-ranging competences or intruding on more sensitive issues, a new test of relative democratic authority has emerged. An EU law will only enjoy authority if it has been approved by national parliaments, something which should only happen if these perceive that the overall gains provided by it exceed anything which could be secured through alternative measures and that these gains exceed any domestic costs. However, this begs a question: namely, why should national parliaments have this role in only some fields of EU law, as the issue of democratic authority touches on all its activities?[121]

6 THE AUTHORITY OF EU LAW IN THE UNITED KINGDOM AFTER BREXIT

(i) Existing EU Law after Brexit

The European Union (Withdrawal Act) 2018 creates a form of Year Zero. It repeals the European Communities Act 1972, the statute which gave EU law force within the United Kingdom during its period of membership.[122] It then puts in place a new regime to replace it.

Under this new regime, the authority of EU law in the United Kingdom during the transition period, which runs from exit day to 31 December 2020, is straightforward.[123] Subject to a few

---

[120] M. Dawson and F. de Witte, 'From Balance to Conflict: A New Constitution for the EU' (2016) 22 *ELJ* 204, 220.
[121] D. Chalmers, *Democratic Self-Government in Europe* (London: Policy Network, 2013).
[122] European Union (Withdrawal) Act 2018, s. 1. [123] Article 126 Withdrawal Agreement.

limited situations,[124] the authority of EU law within the United Kingdom remains the same as when the United Kingdom was an EU Member State.

Article 127 Withdrawal Agreement

(1) Unless otherwise provided in this Agreement, Union law shall be applicable to and in the United Kingdom during the transition period . . .

. . .

(3) During the transition period, the Union law applicable pursuant to paragraph 1 shall produce in respect of and in the United Kingdom the same legal effects as those which it produces within the Union and its Member States and shall be interpreted and applied in accordance with the same methods and general principles as those applicable within the Union.

In the event of no transition period or on the expiry of the transitional period, the European Union (Withdrawal) Act 2018 provides for a category of 'retained EU law'.[125] This law is to have legal effect in the United Kingdom. It falls into three main categories.

The first is directly effective EU law.

Section 4 European Union (Withdrawal) Act 2018

(1) Any rights, powers, liabilities, obligations, restrictions, remedies and procedures which, immediately before exit day –
   (a) are recognised and available in domestic law by virtue of section 2(1) of the European Communities Act 1972, and
   (b) are enforced, allowed and followed accordingly,
   continue on and after exit day to be recognised and available in domestic law (and to be enforced, allowed and followed accordingly).

Section 2(1) the European Communities Act 1972 simply gives legal effect in United Kingdom law to rights and procedures etc. established by EU law. Provision that the rights etc. recognised by it should continue to be recognised is, thus, enabling all law which could be invoked in United Kingdom courts as EU law prior to Brexit to continue to have legal force. We shall see in later chapters that there are certain exceptions. Notably, individuals will neither be able to invoke EU fundamental rights law directly in UK courts[126] nor sue the State for loss as a result of the latter's failure to comply with EU law.[127] There are also safeguards against activism by the Court of

---

[124] The central ones are that UK citizens will not be able to vote or stand for election in either European Parliament elections or municipal elections in other Member States, nor will they have the right to participate in the citizens' initiative or to petition the Ombudsman or Parliament. EU measures not binding on the United Kingdom before the Withdrawal Agreement enters into force will not apply. The United Kingdom cannot participate in any measures adopted within the areas of freedom, security and justice or permanent structured cooperation in the field of ESDP; and EU law may be superseded in the fields of CFSP and ESDP by any agreement made between the EU and the United Kingdom during the transition period, Article 127 Withdrawal Agreement.

[125] European Union (Withdrawal Act) 2018, s. 6(7).   [126] *Ibid.* s. 5(4) and Sch. I, para. 3(2).   [127] *Ibid.* Sch. I, para. 4.

Justice. Directives will only generate the types of right and obligation that they had on the exit date. If the Court subsequently decides to endow Directives with any new features as a legal instrument, these will not apply in the United Kingdom.[128]

The second category is direct EU legislation. This includes regulations, decisions and delegated or implementing measures which applied directly in the United Kingdom without the need for any UK law transposing them.[129]

Section 3 European Union Withdrawal Act 2018

(1) Direct EU legislation, so far as operative immediately before exit day, forms part of domestic law on and after exit day.

The third category are UK laws, be these statutes or statutory instruments, derived from EU law. This includes not only measures adopted under the European Communities Act 1972 to meet the United Kingdom's obligations to transpose EU law into UK law,[130] but also any UK law 'relating otherwise to the EU':[131] in other words, UK laws which simply reference EU law for no other reason than this was desirable. Such law is labelled EU-derived domestic legislation. It will continue to apply within the United Kingdom.

Section 2 European Union (Withdrawal Act) 2018

(1) EU-derived domestic legislation, as it has effect in domestic law immediately before exit day, continues to have effect in domestic law on and after exit day.

These three categories of retained EU law are given legal effect in the United Kingdom after the exit date, but the question is what legal effect, and, incredibly, the Act is silent on this.[132] According to the United Kingdom, this is because retained EU law will form a 'unique and new category of domestic law'.[133] If that is so, it would have been particularly helpful for the consequences of this unicity and novelty to be spelled out. This is all the more so because retained EU law should not be seen as a single class of EU law. The first two categories above – directly effective EU law and direct EU legislation – can be grouped together as these laws acquire legal force exclusively through the Act. However, this is not the case for EU-derived domestic legislation. This would continue to have legal force, be it as statutes or statutory instruments, independently of the Act, because these measures are already domestic legal acts. There is, thus, obscurity as to whether the Act changes the legal qualities of these measures (the implication of having a statutory provision on it) or whether it is simply stating that they will continue to have legal force as statutes or statutory instruments.

---

[128] *Ibid.* s. 4(2)(b).   [129] *Ibid.* s. 3(2).   [130] *Ibid.* s. 2(2)(a)–(b).   [131] *Ibid.* s. 2(2)(d).

[132] For criticism see House of Lords Constitution Committee, *European Union (Withdrawal) Bill*, 9th Report, Session 2017–19, HL Paper 69, paras. 44–5.

[133] Quoted in *ibid.* para. 42.

(ii) Retained EU Law and Other United Kingdom Law

The relationship between retained EU law and other UK law is addressed by the supremacy provision in the Act.

Section 5 European Union Withdrawal Act 2018

(1) The principle of the supremacy of EU law does not apply to any enactment or rule of law passed or made on or after exit day.

(2) Accordingly, the principle of the supremacy of EU law continues to apply on or after exit day so far as relevant to the interpretation, disapplication or quashing of any enactment or rule of law passed or made before exit day.

This provision suggests that retained EU law will have precedence over UK law passed before exit day. This duty of precedence requires, moreover, this UK law to be interpreted in the light of retained EU law or, where this is not possible, disapplied or quashed. However, retained EU law will not have precedence over UK law passed on or after that date. This might appear clear but it is not.

First, the relationship with the doctrine of parliamentary sovereignty is unclear. In particular, it is uncertain what happens when retained EU law conflicts with subsequent Acts of Parliament, and is expressly appealed or amended by these. Parliamentary sovereignty would suggest that the doctrine of implied repeal should kick in, and the subsequent Act of Parliament should prevail. However, the European Union (Withdrawal Act) sets out precise procedures for how retained EU law is to be amended, and implied repeal would undermine these.[134] Even if, notwithstanding this, the doctrine of implied repeal were to apply, matters are still nebulous. In particular, there is the question of how strongly the subsequent Act must contradict the retained EU law for the latter to be disapplied or whether the UK court should try to reconcile the two laws before declaring the retained EU law repealed or amended.

The second uncertainty goes to what is meant by 'EU law'. No EU law will apply in the United Kingdom after exit day as the Act transforms EU legal norms into UK law (retained EU law). Consequently, that law has force as UK law, not EU law.[135] This cannot simply be dismissed as a terminological slip. The UK Government's position is that the 'EU law' in section 5 is not synonymous with the 'retained EU law' described elsewhere in the Act. It does not include EU-derived domestic legislation, as there are domestic measures already in place, and so supremacy only applies to directly effective laws and direct EU legislation.[136] However, this begs the question why EU-derived domestic legislation is being addressed by the Act if its legal effects are already established. This obscurity has been described by the House of Lords Constitution Committee as 'constitutionally unacceptable'.[137]

---

[134] European Union (Withdrawal) Act 2018, s. 7(2)–(4).
[135] M. Elliott and S. Tierney, 'Political Pragmatism and Constitutional Principle: The European Union (Withdrawal) Act 2018' (2019) *PL* forthcoming.
[136] House of Lords Constitution Committee, *European Union (Withdrawal) Bill*, n. 132 above, para. 81.
[137] *Ibid.* para. 83.

(iii) The Status of EU Laws Adopted after Brexit

No general provision is made for EU laws adopted after exit day to have legal effects within the United Kingdom. That is unsurprising. A central mission of Brexit is not to be subject to future EU law and to be able to change existing EU law. This is, however, subject to two qualifications.

First, any EU laws coming into effect during the transition period form part of EU law and are therefore to be treated like all other EU law during that period. They are to apply in the United Kingdom by virtue of Article 127(1) of the Withdrawal Agreement. A curious anomaly is that such laws are not retained EU law as they were adopted after exit day, and, without subsequent action, they will lapse at the end of the transition period.

The second concerns amendments to existing EU laws which are made after exit day. Are these considered to be part of the earlier EU law, and thus have legal effect and even precedence over UK law, or are they to be considered as essentially new laws with no legal effects after exit day? An obscure answer is provided by section 5(3).

Section 5 European Union (Withdrawal) Act 2018

(3) Subsection (1) does not prevent the principle of the supremacy of EU law from applying to a modification made on or after exit day of any enactment or rule of law passed or made before exit day if the application of the principle is consistent with the intention of the modification.

It would seem, therefore, that modifications to existing EU law will be treated as part of that law, and have legal effect within the United Kingdom and precedence over UK law even passed many years after Brexit.[138] As with the other provisions, this provision raises a number of uncertainties.

The first goes to what counts as a modification. It is not clear whether EU implementing measures are modifications that will have legal effects after Brexit. It will be remembered that these are formally distinguished from delegated measures in that the latter can supplement and amend legislative acts whilst implementing measures cannot.[139] It would be odd, however, if automatic legal effect is given to delegated measures, particularly as these are likely to generate more sweeping change, whilst implementing measures, which are more limited in nature, have to be transposed into UK law every time that legal effect is to be given to them. There is also the question of when an EU measure ceases to be a modification and becomes a completely new act instead. For example, the Union often adopts consolidating Directives. These are tidying-up exercises, which make no substantive change to the law but integrate three or four Directives into a simple, clearer legal text whilst repealing the earlier Directives.[140] These Directives, however, formally repeal rather than amend the earlier Directives. If this might be insufficient to stop them from counting as modifications to the earlier law, the question is murkier if these consolidating Directives make any significant substantive changes to that law.

The second source of uncertainty goes to modifications only having supremacy when 'this is consistent with the intention of the modification'. The purpose of this phrase arises out of the

---

[138] To similar effect see European Union (Withdrawal) Act 2018, s. 6(6).

[139] Article 290(1) TFEU and 291(1) TFEU. See pp. 68–72.

[140] E.g. Directive 2006/54 on the implementation of the principle of equal opportunities and equal treatment of men and women in matters of employment and occupation, OJ 2006, L 204/23.

concern that a court, whether the Court of Justice or a British court, might interpret a modification to EU law in an expansive way to generate some new unanticipated and possibly undesirable state of legal affairs. It is, therefore, an instruction to UK courts to interpret modifications narrowly. They are to have regard to the intention of the legislature at the time of enactment rather than any wider object or purpose that might be subsequently read into it. The uncertainty arises because there is an incentive for parties to appeal any adverse interpretation, arguing that the UK court had not done its job properly and had looked at factors other than the intention of the modification. This test will, furthermore, be a difficult one for appeal courts to patrol as the sense of what a legislature intended is always somewhat nebulous.

FURTHER READING

M. Avbelj, *The European Union under Transnational Law: A Pluralist Approach* (Oxford and Portland, Bloomsbury, 2018).

M. Claes *et al.* (eds.), *Constitutional Conversations in Europe: Actors, Topics and Procedures* (Cambridge, Intersentia, 2012).

E. Cloots, *National Identity in EU Law* (Oxford University Press, 2015).

M. Elliot and S. Tierney, 'Political Pragmatism and Constitutional Principle: The European Union (Withdrawal) Act 2018' (2019) *Public Law*, forthcoming.

T. Isiksel, *Europe's Functional Constitution: A Theory of Constitutionalism beyond the State* (Oxford University Press, 2016).

K. Jaklic, *Constitutional Pluralism in the EU* (Oxford University Press, 2015).

M. Klamert, *The Principle of Loyalty* (Oxford University Press, 2014).

J. Komárek, 'Waiting for the Existential Revolution in Europe' (2014) 12 *ICON* 190.

R. Schütze, *From Dual to Cooperative Federalism: The Changing Structure of European Law* (Oxford University Press, 2009).

A. Vauchez, *Brokering Europe: Euro-Lawyers and the Making of a Transnational Polity* (Cambridge University Press, 2015).

M. Wilkinson, 'Constitutional Pluralism: Chronicle of a Death Foretold?' (2017) 27 *European Law Journal* 213.

6

Fundamental Rights

CONTENTS

1 INTRODUCTION

This chapter considers EU fundamental rights law. It is organised as follows.

Section 2 considers the three features of EU fundamental rights that are set out in the Treaties. First, the authority of the EU legal order is premised on respect for fundamental rights. This entails not merely that they be observed but that they must also be given pre-eminence in EU decision-making and be elaborated by EU law. Secondly, Article 6 TEU identifies the two sources of EU fundamental rights, namely the European Union Charter of Fundamental Rights and general principles of law. Thirdly, EU fundamental rights are also used to gauge and police breakdowns in constitutional democracy within the EU Member States. Therefore, Article 7 TEU allows the European Union to determine whether there is a clear risk of a serious breach of its founding values set out in Article 2 TEU, and to apply sanctions where a serious and persistent breach of these values exists.

Section 3 considers the European Charter of Fundamental Rights (EUCFR). It was established in 2000 but only given the same legal value as the EU Treaties by the Lisbon Treaty. One of the EUCFR's central goals was to set out in a single document the fundamental rights hitherto developed in EU law by the Court of Justice. It contains a wide array of civil, economic, ecological, political and social rights and freedoms. To sustain this wide array of rights, a distinction is made between rights (which can be used to strike down legislative and administrative measures) and principles (which are judicially cognisable only in relation to measures implementing them). It is unclear which provisions contain rights and which principles, but, in *AMS*, the Court indicated that provisions expressly reliant on either EU or national implementing measures will be principles.

Section 4 looks at general principles of law. Developed exclusively through the case law of the Court of Justice, these contain all the rights in the EUCFR. They also include a number of further principles, notably those on equal treatment, legitimate expectations, as well the proportionality and precautionary principles and general rights of defence. General principles have been seen as being inspired by the demands that must be met by EU law as a legal order if it is to command authority. Most significantly in recent years, the Court in *Egenberger* held that the right to equal treatment – a general principle of law – can be invoked in disputes between private parties. However, it is unclear whether this will be extended to other general principles of law.

Section 5 considers the standard of protection offered by EU fundamental rights law. This is determined, in part, by certain formal parameters of interpretation. Regard must be had to the Explanations of the Secretariat which drafted the EUCFR, the European Convention on Human Rights (ECHR) and national constitutional traditions. By themselves, these formal parameters are insufficient to guide interpretation. As such, interpretations will also have regard to the interests and objectives of the Union. This includes developing and protecting three forms of individual autonomy which, in turn, guide interpretation of EU fundamental rights: individual control, which is giving individuals sufficient presence; relational autonomy, which goes to ensuring their well-being and recognition within important relationships; and individual flourishing.

Section 6 considers the institutions bound by EU fundamental rights law. EU fundamental rights are used to review the administrative practices of EU Institutions quite extensively but are rarely used to strike down EU legislation. Rather, their significance goes to the interpretation of EU legislation, with fundamental rights used in some instances to provide a more liberal interpretation of the EU legislation and, in others, to justify laws which would be better off being struck down. Member States are only bound by EU fundamental rights law when they implement Union measures. This will be the case where a national measure intends to implement a Union law or has the same objectives, or where EU law authorises national action or that action is derogating from EU law.

Section 7 considers what impact Brexit will have on fundamental rights within the United Kingdom. After the implementation period, neither the EUCFR nor general principles of law will be available as independent bases for review of United Kingdom laws and administrative measures. They may be taken into account, however, when these are reviewed against other human rights standards. Furthermore, all British courts, other than the UK Supreme Court and the Scottish High Court of Justiciary, will be bound by existing interpretations of EU law (which have been interpreted in the light of EU fundamental rights) insofar as this law has been carried over into UK law.

Section 8 considers how EU fundamental rights are being used to police authoritarian regimes within the European Union. The procedure for censuring a Member State under Article 7 TEU has been proposed twice: once against Poland and once against Hungary. It is unlikely, however, the procedure will be used in the foreseeable future to impose sanctions on a Member State. Moreover, the likely effectiveness of such sanctions is unclear. In 2014, the Commission adopted a more tiered approach to enforcement with the Framework to Strengthen the Rule of Law. Under this, in cases of a systemic threat to the rule of the law, the Commission will first seek dialogue with the Member State, then make a public determination of a systemic threat, and would finally propose a determination under Article 7 TEU. However, in the one time it was used, this Framework failed to resolve differences between Poland and the Commission over Polish reforms to its constitutional court.

2 FUNDAMENTAL RIGHTS AND THE SCHEMA OF THE TREATIES

The place of fundamental rights within EU law is set out in three provisions near the beginning of the TEU.

(i) Fundamental Rights as the Premise for the EU Legal Order

First, as we saw in Chapter 1,[1] Article 2 TEU states that the Union is 'founded on the values of respect for human dignity, freedom, democracy, equality, the rule of law and respect for human rights, including the rights of persons belonging to minorities'. Until a few years ago, it was unclear whether this provision offered much beyond rhetoric. However, the Court, in its 2014 Opinion on whether the European Union could accede to the ECHR,[2] indicated that the EU legal order, along with its supranational qualities, was premised on respect for fundamental rights and the other values in Article 2 TEU.[3]

> **Opinion 2/13, Accession to the European Convention for the Protection of Human Rights and Fundamental Freedoms, EU:C:2014:2454**
>
> 167 These essential characteristics [primacy and direct effect] of EU law have given rise to a structured network of principles, rules and mutually interdependent legal relations linking the EU and its Member States, and its Member States with each other, which are now engaged, as is recalled in the second paragraph of Article 1 TEU, in a 'process of creating an ever closer union among the peoples of Europe'.

---

[1] See p. 35.

[2] Opinion 2/13, *Accession to the European Convention for the Protection of Human Rights and Fundamental Freedoms*, EU:C:2014:2454.

[3] See also *Associação Sindical dos Juízes Portugueses* v. *Tribunal de Contas*, C-64/16, EU:C:2018:117, paras. 31–2; *Slowakische Republik* v. *Achmea BV*, C-284/16, EU:C:2018:158, paras. 33–4.

168 This legal structure is based on the fundamental premiss that each Member State shares with all the other Member States, and recognises that they share with it, a set of common values on which the EU is founded, as stated in Article 2 TEU. That premiss implies and justifies the existence of mutual trust between the Member States that those values will be recognised and, therefore, that the law of the EU that implements them will be respected.

But what does it mean to say that the EU legal order is premised on respect for fundamental rights?

The Court has not developed this notion, but there are three possible dimensions. First, respect for fundamental rights becomes a precondition for the authority of EU law. For if the expressions of EU law's authority, its primacy and direct effect, are premised on fundamental rights, then it follows that if this respect is not present, there can be no authority. Secondly, *pre-eminence* is to be granted to fundamental rights in EU law. According foundational status to a fundamental right elevates it to a higher status than other values or goods pursued by EU law. Thirdly, if fundamental rights provide a *raison d'être* for EU legal authority, then it is insufficient for the Union simply to commit not to violate them; it must do what it can to develop them.

(ii) The Sources of EU Fundamental Rights

The second core provision is Article 6 TEU, which sets out, *inter alia*, the sources of EU fundamental rights.

Article 6 TEU

(1) The Union recognises the rights, freedoms and principles set out in the Charter of Fundamental Rights of the European Union ... which shall have the same legal value as the Treaties.

The provisions of the Charter shall not extend in any way the competences of the Union as defined in the Treaties.

The rights, freedoms and principles in the Charter shall be interpreted in accordance with the general provisions in Title VII of the Charter governing its interpretation and application and with due regard to the explanations referred to in the Charter, that set out the sources of those provisions.

(2) The Union shall accede to the European Convention for the Protection of Human Rights and Fundamental Freedoms. Such accession shall not affect the Union's competences as defined in the Treaties.[4]

(3) Fundamental rights, as guaranteed by the ECHR and as they result from the constitutional traditions common to the Member States, shall constitute general principles of the Union's law.

There is no single EU Bill of Rights. Instead, EU fundamental rights is constructed around:

- the EUCFR (Article 6(1) TEU)
- general principles of law (Article 6(3) TEU).

---

[4] After *Opinion 2/13* determined that the proposed EU accession to the ECHR was illegal (see pp. 170–2), accession was kicked into the long grass. The European Commission has stated that the opinion led to a reflection period because it raised issues of a 'certain complexity' but that it is still committed to accession. There is little strong evidence of this commitment, however, *Reply of the Commission to European Parliament Question E-001453–18*, 14 June 2018.

Matters are further complicated by both the EUCFR and general principles of law referring to the ECHR and national constitutional traditions as inspirations for their content.[5] To confuse matters a little more, EU fundamental rights law is seen as having an independent existence, with the EUCFR and general principles of law acting merely as authoritative indicators of its content. Thus, the EUFCR merely 'sets out' EU fundamental rights (Article 6(1) TEU) whilst EU fundamental rights 'constitute' general principles of law (Article 6(3) TEU). This leads to overlap so that the same EU fundamental right can be recognised both by the EUCFR and general principles of law.[6]

This multiplicity has been criticised for generating unnecessary complexity and obscurity about the content of EU fundamental rights.[7] By contrast, it is also seen as providing EU fundamental rights with a rich potential, since it allows an interplay between different instruments and doctrines with each acting to inform and interrogate each.[8] It also allows the development of EU fundamental rights to remain an open-ended process, such that a new ethical challenge does not present the problem of a rights deficit due to an outdated Bill of Rights. This is all the more so because general principles of law emerged not through interpretation of a single legal text but through the case law of the Court of Justice, and is sufficiently dynamic to generate new rights.[9] It is possible to agree with all these views. EU fundamental rights involves both a complexity and a possibility for dynamism that may not be possible if it were rooted in a single Bill of Rights. Whether this dynamism compensates for this complexity ultimately depends on whether a rich interplay has, indeed, been developed in the case law. We will look at this later in the chapter.

(iii) EU Fundamental Rights and Policing Domestic Constitutional Breakdown

The third core provision is Article 7 TEU which grants the Union the role of policing domestic constitutional breakdown.

Article 7 TEU

(1) On a reasoned proposal by one third of the Member States, by the European Parliament or by the European Commission, the Council, acting by a majority of four fifths of its members after obtaining the consent of the European Parliament, may determine that there is a clear risk of a serious breach by a Member State of the values referred to in Article 2. Before making such a determination, the Council shall hear the Member State in question and may address recommendations to it, acting in accordance with the same procedure.

   The Council shall regularly verify that the grounds on which such a determination was made continue to apply.

---

[5] See also Preamble, alinea 5, EUCFR.

[6] General principles of law has, thus, been held to include all rights in the EUCFR, *Liga van Moskeeën en Islamitische Organisaties Provincie Antwerpen* v. *Vlaams Gewest*, C-426/16, EU:C:2018:335.

[7] R. Schütze, 'Three "Bills of Rights" for the European Union' (2011) 30 *YBEL* 1.

[8] On how the Court of Justice influences the ECHR see T. Lock, 'The Influence of EU Law on Strasbourg Doctrines' (2017) 43 *ELRev* 804.

[9] S. Douglas Scott, 'A Tale of Two Courts: Luxembourg, Strasbourg and the Growing European Human Rights Acquis' (2006) 43 *CMLRev* 619; G. Harpaz, 'The European Court of Justice and Its Relations with the European Court of Human Rights: The Quest for Enhanced Reliance, Coherence and Legitimacy' (2009) 46 *CMLRev* 105.

(2) The European Council, acting by unanimity on a proposal by one third of the Member States or by the Commission and after obtaining the consent of the European Parliament, may determine the existence of a serious and persistent breach by a Member State of the values referred to in Article 2, after inviting the Member State in question to submit its observations.

(3) Where a determination under paragraph 2 has been made, the Council, acting by a qualified majority, may decide to suspend certain of the rights deriving from the application of the Treaties to the Member State in question, including the voting rights of the representative of the government of that Member State in the Council. In doing so, the Council shall take into account the possible consequences of such a suspension on the rights and obligations of natural and legal persons.

The obligations of the Member State in question under this Treaty shall in any case continue to be binding on that State.

Two procedures are contained in Article 7 TEU. The first amounts to a form of censure whereby a determination can be made that there is a 'clear risk of a serious breach' of the values in Article 2 TEU (Article 7(1) TEU). However, no further action can be taken. The second allows sanctions to be applied against a State (Article 7(2)–(3) TEU) where a 'serious and persistent breach' of the values in Article 2 TEU has been made. Sanctions can take various forms: financial in the form of not allowing EU funds to be spent in that State; political in the form of denial of voting rights in EU lawmaking; or legal in the form of legal entitlements which benefit that State and its citizens. The sanctions are also open-ended in that no cap is placed on them. Their potential gravity is reflected in the procedure required to activate them. It requires, *inter alia*, agreement by all the other Heads of Government voting in the European Council.

There is a paradox that such an undemocratic procedure is being deployed to police consti-tutional breakdown. The proposal for sanctions can only be made by executives – be it the Commission or the governments of one-third of the Member States – who, therefore, hold a veto over instigating the process. However, the real challenge is that the voting and substantive thresholds make it difficult for Article 7 TEU sanctions to be activated. A single Member State can veto sanctions by preventing the European Council from determining a breach under Article 7(2) TEU.[10] This veto can also be invoked for illiberal reasons, such as a belief in the violation of human rights.[11] The requirement that the breaches be both serious and persistent means the Union is, therefore, required to indulge breaches which are serious but not persistent (e.g. a quickly enacted genocide) and breaches which are persistent but not serious (e.g. States perman-ently violating fundamental rights in 'non-serious' ways).

Whilst the stringent requirements make it seem unlikely that we will ever see sanctions applied,[12] we shall see later in the chapter that Article 7 TEU is increasingly used as a backdrop for the development of other EU measures to police national constitutional democracies.

---

[10] The charged State does not vote, Article 354 TFEU.

[11] If this seems far-fetched, the Hungarian Prime Minister has talked of Hungary being an 'insurmountable roadblock' in the current Article 7(1) TEU proceedings against Poland, 'Hungary Will Block Punitive EU Action on Poland' *Deutsche Welle*, 22 December 2017.

[12] To date, therefore, there have been two proposals for a State to be censured under the first procedure. European Commission, 'Proposal for a Council Decision on the Determination of a Clear Risk of a Serious Breach by the Republic of Poland of the Rule of Law', COM(2017)835 final; European Parliament Resolution of 12 September 2018 on a proposal calling on the Council to determine, pursuant to Article 7(1) TEU the existence of a clear risk of a serious breach by Hungary of the values on which the Union is founded (2017/2131(INL)).

3 THE EUROPEAN CHARTER OF FUNDAMENTAL RIGHTS AND FREEDOMS

Understanding the EUCFR requires some knowledge about the history of EU fundamental rights. In this regard, the original Treaties contained no system of fundamental rights protection. Notwithstanding this, the Court of Justice held, towards the end of the 1960s, that where EU laws were capable of more than one interpretation, there was a requirement to choose the interpretation which did not prejudice fundamental rights protection.[13] However, the transformative moment in the history of EU fundamental rights law was *Internationale Handelsgesellschaft*.[14] The Court had to consider for the first time a potential conflict between an EU law and a fundamental right protected by a national constitution, which in that instance, was the right to trade protected by the German Basic Law. The Court pursued a dual track reasoning: stating on the one hand that EU law took precedence over all national law, even national constitutions; whilst on the other, to try and forestall clashes with national constitutional courts, it stated that fundamental rights form an integral part of EU law. EU Institutions were required to respect these fundamental rights, and therefore any EU law which violated fundamental rights would be illegal.

As a consequence of these origins, prior to the EUCFR, there was no document setting out EU fundamental rights. It was, instead, judge-made law. In *Internationale Handelsgesellschaft*, the Court stated that it would look to national constitutional traditions as inspiration for the content of EU fundamental rights law. From the mid-1970s onwards, it also began to look at international human rights treaties.[15] These included the International Covenant on Civil and Political Rights,[16] the UN Convention on the Rights of the Child,[17] the Community Charter of Fundamental Social Rights of Workers and the European Social Charter.[18] However, the most frequently referenced was the ECHR.[19]

The context to the adoption of the EUCFR was a push to raise the status of social rights and to prevent EU fundamental rights being hidden away in this case law.[20] In 1999, the Cologne European Council agreed, therefore, that a charter of fundamental rights should be established. The EUCFR was drafted by a Convention comprised of representatives from national governments, the Commission, the European Parliament and national parliaments. Other EU Institutions were given observer status. Human rights groups, regional bodies, trade unions and wider civil society were invited to make contributions.[21] The EUCFR was adopted by the Convention in October 2000. However, agreement on its legal status could not be reached at the Nice European Council in December 2000. Rather, the legal status of the EUCFR was only resolved with the adoption of the Lisbon Treaty. Notably, its provisions are not contained within

---

[13] *Stauder* v. *City of Ulm*, 29/69, EU:C:1969:57.
[14] *Internationale Handelsgesellschaft mbH* v. *Einfuhr- und Vorratsstelle für Getreide und Futtermittel*, 11/70, EU:C:1970:114.
[15] *Nold* v. *Commission*, 4/73, EU:C:1974:51.   [16] *Orkem* v. *Commission*, 374/87, EU:C:1989:387.
[17] *Parliament* v. *Council*, C-540/03, EU:C:2006:429.
[18] *Blaizot* v. *Belgium*, 24/86, EU:C:1988:43; *Defrenne* v. *Sabena*, 149/77, EU:C:1978:130.
[19] *Kremzow* v. *Austria*, C-299/95, EU:C:1997:58.
[20] Report of the Expert Group on Fundamental Rights, *Affirming Fundamental Rights in the European Union: Time to Act* (Brussels, EU Commission, 1999) ('Simitis' Report).
[21] G. de Búrca, 'The Drafting of the EU Charter of Fundamental Rights' (2001) 26 *ELRev* 126; O. de Schutter, 'Europe In Search of Its Civil Society' (2002) 8 *ELJ* 198, 206–12.

the EU Treaties;[22] instead, reference is made to it in Article 6 TEU, where it is granted the same legal value as these Treaties.[23]

EUCFR rights are taken from three sources: the EU Treaty, constitutions of the Member States, and international human rights treaties concluded by the Member States.[24] Its rights and principles are categorised under six headings, with the most prominent rights and freedoms set out below.[25]

Rights to Human Dignity: right to life; integrity of the person; prohibition of torture or inhuman and degrading treatment; prohibition of slavery or forced labour; prohibition on cloning or eugenics (Articles 1–5)

Freedoms: right to liberty and security; respect for private and family life; protection of personal data; right to marry and found a family; freedom of thought, conscience and religion; freedom of expression and information; freedom of assembly; freedom of the arts and sciences; right to education; freedom to choose an occupation and right to engage in work; freedom to conduct a business; right to asylum; right to property (Articles 6–19)

Equality: equality before the law; non-discrimination on sex, race, colour, ethnic or social origin, genetic features, language, religion or belief or political opinion, disability, sexual orientation, birth; cultural, religious and linguistic diversity; equality between men and women; rights of the elderly, integration of persons with disabilities (Articles 20–26)

Solidarity: workers' right to information and consultation; right of collective bargaining; protection in the event of unfair dismissal; right to placement services; fair and just working conditions; prohibition on child labour; right to social security; right to health care; protection of the family; high level of environmental and consumer protection; access to services of general economic interest (Articles 27–38)

Citizens' Rights: right to vote and stand in municipal and European Parliament elections; right to good administration; right of access to documents; right to refer matters to the European Parliament and to petition the Ombudsman; freedom of movement and residence; right to diplomatic protection (Articles 39–46)

Justice: right to an effective remedy and a fair trial; presumption of innocence; right not to be tried or punished twice for same offence; principle of legality and proportionality of criminal offences (Articles 47–50).

The EUCFR has a number of noteworthy features.

First, it incorporates a wider array of rights and freedoms than any other human rights treaties. It encompasses not just civil, political, economic and social rights, but protection of cultural and ecological interests as well. This can be seen as ambitious in what it sees humans as needing for a good life.[26] The counter-argument is that it devalues the language of rights. Treating everything as fundamental leads to nothing being special, with a dilution in the value of entitlements which were once held in the highest regard. For instance, the right of free access to a placement service

---

[22] Its full text can be found at OJ 2007, C 303/1.   [23] Article 6(1) TEU.   [24] CHARTE 4473/00, 11 October 2000.

[25] For detailed analysis of each right see S. Peers *et al.* (eds.), *The EU Charter of Fundamental Rights: A Commentary* (Oxford-Portland, Hart, 2014).

[26] Joint Committee of Houses of Parliament, *A Bill of Rights for the United Kingdom?*, 29th Report, Session 2007-8, vol. 1, para. 191.

is worthwhile (Article 29) but is hardly as central to human dignity as the prohibition on slavery (Article 5).

Secondly, notable rights are missing:[27] the right to nationality, the right to decent pay, the right to work and the right to housing are all not included.[28] Certain other rights (e.g. the right to marry, the right to collective bargaining, the right of workers to information and consultation, the right to protection against unfair dismissal, the right to social security and health care) are recognised only in accordance with the rules laid down by national or EU laws. National laws are to determine the content of these rights so that instead of acting as a basis for review of EU and national practices, EU fundamental rights are turned around to justify domestic practices, whatever these are.[29]

Thirdly, many rights are conditioned by limitations and exceptions. Article 52(1) EUCFR places a number of conditions on how these are to be deployed.

Article 52

(1) Any limitation on the exercise of the rights and freedoms recognised by this Charter must be provided for by law and respect the essence of those rights and freedoms. Subject to the principle of proportionality, limitations may be made only if they are necessary and genuinely meet objectives of general interest recognised by the Union or the need to protect the rights and freedoms of others.

This puts in play three requirements. Any limitation must be provided for by law.[30] A legal framework governing these limitations is not enough. It must also be accessible, and sufficiently clear and precise to enable subjects to foresee, to a reasonable degree, the legal consequences of their actions.[31] The essence of the rights must be protected. Any limitation or exception cannot be so extensive that exercise of the right is either impossible in practice or excessively difficult.[32] Limitations and exceptions must, therefore, apply only in limited and well-defined circumstances.[33] Protection of the essence of each right also requires that where fundamental rights clash, they must be reconciled in a way that draws a fair balance between each.[34] The most exigent requirement is that any limitation must be proportionate. Limitations can only be imposed if they are genuine and necessary to protect the rights of others or the general interest in question.

This was set out by the Court in *F*. F, a Nigerian fleeing persecution on grounds of his homosexuality, challenged Hungary's refusal to grant him protection on the grounds of an adverse psychologist's report. Hungarian legislation or rules required that anybody seeking international protection on the grounds of a well-founded fear of persecution in their country of origin due to their sexual orientation be subject to a pyschologist's examination to verify their

---

[27] J. Kenner, 'Economic and Social Rights in the EU Legal Order: The Mirage of Indivisibility' in T. Hervey and J. Kenner (eds.), *Economic and Social Rights under the EU Charter of Fundamental Rights* (Oxford, Hart, 2003) 1, 16–18.

[28] Albeit that the right to 'housing assistance' is provided for in Article 34(3) (II-94(3) CT).

[29] D. Ashiagbor, 'Economic and Social Rights in the European Charter of Fundamental Rights' (2004) 1 *European Human Rights L Rev* 62.

[30] *Knauf Gips* v. *Commission*, C-407/08 P, EU:C:2010:389, para. 91.

[31] Opinion of Advocate General Cruz Villalón, *Scarlet Extended* v. *SABAM*, C-70/10, EU:C:2011:255, paras. 95–6.

[32] Opinion of Advocate General Cruz Villalón, *Coty Germany* v. *Stadtsparkasse Magdeburg*, C-580/13, EU:C:2015:243, para. 39.

[33] *Florescu*, C-258/14, EU:C:2017:448.   [34] *Coty Germany* v. *Stadtsparkasse Magdeburg*, C-580/13, EU:C:2015:485.

orientation. The examination compromised Article 7 EUCFR – the right to respect for one's private life – but the Hungarian authorities argued that this was necessary to ensure the integrity of their international protection procedures. Their argument was rejected.

F v. Bevándorlási és Állampolgársági Hivatal, C-473/16, EU:C:2018:36

56 ... the principle of proportionality requires, according to the settled case-law of the Court, that the measures adopted do not exceed the limits of what is appropriate and necessary in order to attain the legitimate objectives pursued by the legislation in question, since the disadvantages caused by the legislation must not be disproportionate to the aims pursued ...

59 ... the impact of an expert's report such as that at issue in the main proceedings on the applicant's private life seems disproportionate to the aim pursued, since the seriousness of the interference with the right to privacy it constitutes cannot be regarded as proportionate to the benefit that it may possibly represent for the assessment of the facts and circumstances ...

60 In the first place, the interference with the private life of the applicant for international protection arising from the preparation and use of an expert's report, such as that at issue in the main proceedings, is, in view of its nature and subject matter, particularly serious.

61 Such an expert's report is based in particular on the fact that the person concerned undergoes a series of psychological tests intended to establish an essential element of his identity that concerns his personal sphere in that it relates to intimate aspects of his life ...

62 It is also necessary to take account, in order to assess the seriousness of the interference arising from the preparation and use of a psychologist's expert report, such as that at issue in the main proceedings, of Principle 18 of the Yogyakarta principles on the application of International Human Rights Law in relation to Sexual Orientation and Gender Identity, to which the French and Netherlands Governments have referred, which states, *inter alia*, that no person may be forced to undergo any form of psychological test on account of his sexual orientation or gender identity.

63 When those elements are looked at together, it is apparent that the seriousness of the interference with private life entailed by the preparation and use of an expert's report, such as that at issue in the main proceedings, exceeds that entailed by an assessment of the statements of the applicant for international protection relating to a fear of persecution on grounds of his sexual orientation or recourse to a psychologist's expert report having a purpose other than that of establishing the applicant's sexual orientation.

The proportionality principle still allows the imposition of onerous limitations on a person's fundamental rights. However, these must be the least onerous necessary to secure the interest sought. In some cases, this may justify significant curbs on an individual's rights. In *F*, therefore, the Court makes clear that authorities may question, possibly very intensively, a person's statements about their sexual orientation. Alternatively, they may insist on a general psychologist's report to see whether the person is a fantasist or manipulative. Both are highly intrusive (para. 63 above) but lawful. This is because they are not seen as unnecessarily so and are less intrusive than any alternative.

Fourthly, the EUCFR treats social, civil, political and environmental rights as fundamental rights. This is a vision which holds that a good life requires not only protection of civil liberties but the possibilities for political participation, a decent society and a good ecology. However, historically, individual rights have not been used to secure all these goals, and it is arguable whether courts are well-placed to determine choices for some of them (i.e. what constitutes an ecologically responsible climate change policy) at the expense of other institutions. Thus, the EUCFR makes a distinction between rights and principles.

Article 52

(5) The provisions of this Charter which contain principles may be implemented by legislative and executive acts taken by Institutions, bodies, offices and agencies of the Union and by acts of Member States when they are implementing Union law, in the exercise of their respective powers. They shall be judicially cognisable only in the interpretation of such acts and in the ruling on their legality.

Consequently, activity covered by some provisions will enjoy stronger judicial protection than that protected by others. If the provision protects a right, any institutional behaviour falling within its aegis can be judicially reviewed against it. By contrast, regard can only be had to principles where institutions are implementing these principles.

Two matters, in particular, were left unclear. First, the EUCFR is silent as to which of its provisions set out 'rights' and which set out 'principles'. Secondly, the bite of EUCFR principles in relation to implementing measures is unclear as Article 52(5) EUCFR simply states that these principles are judicially cognisable. Does this mean that they can be used to strike down implementing measures or simply that regard must be had to them in interpreting implementing measures?

These uncertainties were partially addressed in *AMS*. Directive 2002/14 provided for mandatory consultation of workers where firms had fifty employees or more. Article 27 EUCFR also provided that 'workers or their representatives must . . . be guaranteed information and consultation in good time in the cases and under the conditions provided for by Union law and national laws and practices'. In determining whether a firm met the threshold for consultation, French law excluded from the count, *inter alia*, apprentices and people on employment-initiative contracts. AMS was a firm concerned with reintegrating young people into the labour market who had social or professional difficulties. It believed that only nine employees did not fall into these excluded contracts, and there was, therefore, no obligation to consult. This was challenged by the trade union established within AMS, which argued that Article 27 EUCFR could be invoked to prevent this exclusion.

Association de Médiation Sociale v. *Union Locale des Syndicats CGT*, C-176/12, EU:C:2014:2

45 It is . . . clear from the wording of Article 27 of the Charter that, for this article to be fully effective, it must be given more specific expression in European Union or national law.

46 It is not possible to infer from the wording of Article 27 of the Charter or from the explanatory notes to that article that Article 3(1) of Directive 2002/14, as a directly applicable rule of law, lays down and addresses to the Member States a prohibition on excluding from the calculation of the staff numbers in an undertaking a specific category of employees initially included in the group of persons to be taken into account in that calculation. . . .

48 Accordingly, Article 27 of the Charter cannot, as such, be invoked in a dispute, such as that in the main proceedings, in order to conclude that the national provision which is not in conformity with Directive 2002/14 should not be applied.

49 That finding cannot be called into question by considering Article 27 of the Charter in conjunction with the provisions of Directive 2002/14, given that, since that article by itself does not suffice to confer on individuals a right which they may invoke as such, it could not be otherwise if it is considered in conjunction with that directive.

AMS suggests that provisions, whose content can only be realised through implementation by national or EU law, set out principles.[35] However, these might not be the only principles. In its Explanations to the EUCFR, the Secretariat responsible for drafting it stated that the provisions on rights of the elderly, integration of people with disabilities and protection of the environment are also examples of principles.[36] Those on equality between men and women, protection of the family, and the right to social security benefits and social services 'contain both elements of a right and of a principle'.[37] There are also provisions where the Union commits itself to respect certain values in its policies, such as a high level of environmental protection or consumer protection or respect for services of a general economic interest.[38] These seem too general to be anything other than principles.

More controversially, *AMS* suggests that principles have limited effect in the sense that they cannot be used to strike down EU laws. Nor can they be invoked directly by individuals, even when there is EU legislation implementing them. In *AMS*, the EU legislation was not even interpreted in the light of the principle in question.[39] This begs questions as to whether principles have anything more than rhetorical force. It also means that a lot is at stake in determining whether a EUCFR provision involves a right or a principle.[40]

4 GENERAL PRINCIPLES OF LAW

General principles of EU law have a longer history than the EUCFR. There is no list of them in the Treaties, and they have been developed exclusively through the case law of the Court of Justice. Furthermore, the EUCFR is seen as giving expression to these general principles of law, including all the rights within the EUCFR.[41] However, they extend beyond that to include a number of principles, which are either not mentioned in the EUCFR or are formulated in a different way. These include the right to equal treatment,[42] protection against arbitrary or disproportionate

---

[35] E.g. the right to marry (Article 9), the right to found educational establishments (Article 14(3)), workers' right to information and consultation within their undertaking (Article 27), the right to collective bargaining (Article 28), social and housing assistance (Article 34), the right to protection in the event of unjustified dismissal (Article 30), the right to health care (Article 35).

[36] Articles 25, 26 and 37 EUCFR.   [37] Explanations to the Charter of Fundamental Rights, OJ 2007, C 303/17, 35.

[38] Articles 37 and 38 EUCFR.

[39] This is to be contrasted with the earlier case of *Kamberaj* where EU legislation was interpreted in the light of a principle. *Kamberaj* v. *IPES*, C-571/10, EU:C:2012:233.

[40] It has, therefore, been suggested that it might be easier to abolish the distinction. The Court should, instead, interpret the provisions as articulating certain rights without ever striking down national measures, leaving this question to national discretion. D. Guðmundsdóttir, 'A Renewed Emphasis on the Charter's Distinction between Rights and Principles: Is a Doctrine of Judicial Restraint More Appropriate?' (2015) 52 *CMLRev* 685, 709–18.

[41] *Telefónica SA and Telefónica de España* v. *Commission*, C-295/12 P, EU: C:2014:2062; *Liga van Moskeeën en Islamitische Organisaties Provincie Antwerpen* v. *Vlaams Gewest*, C-426/16, EU:C:2018:335.

[42] *Chrysostomides* v. *Council*, T-680/13, EU:T:2018:486.

intervention,[43] the principle of legitimate expectations,[44] the proportionality[45] and precautionary[46] principles, the prohibition against measures having retroactive effects,[47] and general rights of defence.[48]

General principles of law are associated with two further significant questions.

First, it has been suggested that general principles set out the properties required for EU law to be a legal order. One argument is that principles of equal treatment, legitimate expectations and non-retroactivity can all be derived from a more general principle of legality, which requires that the law be clear, prospective, general and administered in a predictable manner.[49] Other principles, such as proportionality or precautionary, can be derived from a principle of coherence which requires that the different values come together in a mutually supportive way.[50] Whilst this conception justifies the need for general principles of law, it can neither explain the specific nature of many general principles of law nor their relationship to the EUCFR. Others have suggested, therefore, that this evolution of general principles of law beyond its initial inspiration by the needs for legality and coherence is not necessarily a bad thing; it allows them to go beyond mere legality and to generate arguments that the EU legal order should address and reset expectations about how it (the EU legal order) should operate.[51]

The second goes to the scope of general principles of law. We shall see later that EU fundamental rights only govern behaviour by EU Institutions and Member States when they are implementing EU law.[52] This has, however, been given a twist by *Egenberger*. Evangelisches Werk, a Protestant association, refused to offer Egenberger a two-year job preparing a country report on the United Nations International Convention on the Elimination of All Forms of Racial Discrimination. This was because she was not a Protestant and German law allowed Protestant associations to require that people were attached to a church for occupational work. She challenged this as an illegal form of religious discrimination. There was a Directive – Directive 2000/78 – which prohibited religious discrimination in the field of employment, but historically, it could not be invoked against private parties on this ground. Instead, Egenberger argued that she could invoke Article 21 EUCFR which prohibited, *inter alia*, religious discrimination. This was invoked with Article 47 EUCFR, which grants individuals a right to an effective judicial remedy.

---

[43] *Château du Grand Bois SC* v. *Etablissement national des produits de l'agriculture et de la mer*, C-59/17, EU:C:2018:641.

[44] *Di Lenardo and Dilexport* v. *Ministero del Commercio con l'Estero*, C-37–8/02, EU:C:2004:443.

[45] The proportionality principle is slightly different from that prohibiting arbitrary or disproportionate intervention. It requires that a measure does not exceed the limits of what is appropriate and necessary in order to attain the objectives legitimately pursued by it, recourse is had to the least onerous measure, and the disadvantages caused are not disproportionate to the aims pursued, *Estonia* v. *Parliament and Council*, C-508/13, EU:C:2015:403. It is dealt with in more detail at pp. 385–7.

[46] *Zoofachhandel Züpke and Others* v. *Commission*, T-817/14, EU:T:2016:157.   [47] *R* v. *Kirk*, 63/83, EU:C:1984:255.

[48] *Ispas* v. *Direcţia Generală*, C-298/16, EU:C:2017:843.

[49] For an argument that it has done so in a flawed manner, A. Somek, 'Is Legality a Principle of EU Law?' in S. Vogelaar and S. Weatherill (eds.), *General Principles of Law: European and Comparative Perspectives* (London, Hart, 2017).

[50] X. Groussot *et al.*, 'General Principles and the Many Faces of Coherence: Between Law and Ideology in the European Union' in S. Vogelaar and S. Weatherill (eds.), *General Principles of Law: European and Comparative Perspectives* (Oxford, Hart, 2017).

[51] U. Šadl and J. Bengoetxea, 'Theorising General Principles of EU Law in Perspective: High Expectations, Modest Means and the Court of Justice' in S. Vogelaar and S. Weatherill (eds.), *General Principles of Law: European and Comparative Perspectives* (Oxford, Hart, 2017).

[52] See pp. 277–81.

> ### *Egenberger* v. *Evangelisches Werk für Diakonie und Entwicklung*, C–414/16, EU:C:2018:257
>
> 76 The prohibition of all discrimination on grounds of religion or belief is mandatory as a general principle of EU law. That prohibition, which is laid down in Article 21(1) of the Charter, is sufficient in itself to confer on individuals a right which they may rely on as such in disputes between them in a field covered by EU law . . .
>
> 77 As regards its mandatory effect, Article 21 of the Charter is no different, in principle, from the various provisions of the founding Treaties prohibiting discrimination on various grounds, even where the discrimination derives from contracts between individuals . . .
>
> 78 Secondly, it must be pointed out that, like Article 21 of the Charter, Article 47 of the Charter on the right to effective judicial protection is sufficient in itself and does not need to be made more specific by provisions of EU or national law to confer on individuals a right which they may rely on as such.
>
> 79 Consequently, in the situation mentioned in paragraph 75 above, the national court would be required to ensure within its jurisdiction the judicial protection for individuals flowing from Articles 21 and 47 of the Charter, and to guarantee the full effectiveness of those articles by disapplying if need be any contrary provision of national law.
>
> 80 That conclusion is not called into question by the fact that a court may, in a dispute between individuals, be called on to balance competing fundamental rights which the parties to the dispute derive from the provisions of the FEU Treaty or the Charter, and may even be obliged, in the review that it must carry out, to make sure that the principle of proportionality is complied with. Such an obligation to strike a balance between the various interests involved has no effect on the possibility of relying on the rights in question in such a dispute.
>
> 81 Further, where the national court is called on to ensure that Articles 21 and 47 of the Charter are observed, while possibly balancing the various interests involved, such as respect for the status of churches as laid down in Article 17 TFEU, it will have to take into consideration the balance struck between those interests by the EU legislature in Directive 2000/78, in order to determine the obligations deriving from the Charter in circumstances such as those at issue in the main proceedings . . .

The judgment is notable for three things.

First, it established that the prohibition on discrimination can be invoked against private parties not because it is contained in the EUCFR, but because it is a general principle of law (para. 76). However, it is unclear whether all general principles of law can be invoked against private parties or only the principle of non-discrimination.

Secondly, one must be careful about the reach of the judgment. The activities were governed by a piece of EU legislation, Directive 2000/78/EC. On a conservative reading, the judgment only allows general principles of law to be applied where the activities are already governed by EU legislation, but, for whatever reason, the relevant EU legislation cannot be invoked in a court. Indeed, the Court has stated, subsequent to *Egenberger*, that EU fundamental rights may only be invoked in fields where Member States are implementing EU law (as was the case here).[53]

Thirdly, the judgment, in practice, involves a covert extension of the Directive. This is reflected in the Court's statement that the question of whether there was illegal religious discrimination (in breach of Article 21 EUCFR) had to be resolved by reference to the terms of the Directive (which allows religious organisations to impose a religious criterion for employment where this

---

[53] *'Spika' UAB*, C-540/16, EU:C:2018:565.

is necessary to meet a genuine, legitimate and justified occupational requirement). It was for the national court to determine whether this was so here.

5 THE STANDARD OF PROTECTION OF EU FUNDAMENTAL RIGHTS

(i) Interpretation and the European Union Context

The Union may develop a plethora of rights, but this means little if they are just paper rights. Article 53 EUCFR provides that the rights are not to be interpreted restrictively,[54] and it is not to undermine any right granted by EU law, international law or national constitutions. Beyond virtue signalling, however, the meaning of this provision is not clear. Adjudication on rights often involves choices between values. For example, laws about press reporting of politicians have to balance rights of freedom of expression against those on protection of privacy and family life. Equally, the values may be contested so that it is impossible to determine where the higher standard lies; as in the case of abortion where the rights of the unborn are asserted against the rights of the mother with proponents to the debate often denying the value of the opposing claim.

In *Melloni*, it will be remembered, an Italian challenged his surrender to Italy by the Spanish authorities on the grounds that, at that time, it violated the Spanish Constitution as the surrender was based on his having been tried *in absentia*.[55] The Spanish court asked whether Article 53 EUCFR required national constitutional rights to be applied over EU law as the provision stipulated that nothing could adversely affect them.[56] The Court rejected this, stating that no national law, not even a constitutional one, can undermine the primacy of EU law.[57] This begs the question as to how Article 53 EUCFR is to be interpreted. Advocate General Bot suggested a way forward in *Melloni*.

Melloni v. *Minsterio Fiscal*, C-391/11, EU:C:2012:600

107 . . . a principle that has long guided the interpretation of fundamental rights within the European Union, namely that the protection of fundamental rights within the European Union must be ensured within the framework of the structure and objectives of the European Union. In that regard, it is not irrelevant that the preamble to the Charter refers to the main objectives of the European Union, including the creation of an area of freedom, security and justice.

108 It is therefore not possible to reason only in terms of a higher or lower level of protection of human rights without taking into account the requirements linked to the action of the European Union and the specific nature of European Union law . . .

112 As regards the assessment of the level of protection for fundamental rights which must be guaranteed within the legal order of the European Union, the specific interests which motivate the action of the European Union must be taken into account. The same applies, *inter alia*, to the necessary uniformity of

---

[54] *Heimann* v. *Kaiser*, C-229–30/11, EU: C:2012:693.   [55] See pp. 206–7.

[56] On the early debates, J. Liisberg, 'Does the EU Charter of Fundamental Rights Threaten the Supremacy of Community Law' (2001) 38 *CMLRev* 1171.

[57] *Melloni* v. *Ministerio Fiscal*, C-391/11, EU:C:2013:107. For criticism see A. Pliakos and G. Anagnostaras, 'Fundamental Rights and the New Battle over Legal and Judicial Supremacy: Lessons from *Melloni*' (2015) 34 *YBEL* 97.

application of European Union law and to the requirements linked to the construction of an area of freedom, security and justice. Those specific interests cause the level of protection for fundamental rights to be adjusted depending on the different interests at stake.

The opinion suggests, therefore, that EU fundamental rights will be interpreted through bringing together two interpretative approaches. First, regard should be had to a series of formal constraints set out by the EUCFR: the Explanations provided by the Secretariat, international treaties, notably the ECHR, and national constitutional traditions. They act not only as indicators of what interpretation should be taken, but, in addition, no interpretation should seek to undermine the protection offered by them. A rationalisation – and no more – must be offered of how equivalent or better protection is secured. Secondly, regard should be had, therefore, to the specific interests and objectives of EU law: the vision of life it is trying to secure and the particular institutional challenges in realising this. This vision informs the Court's view of what counts as a better interpretation (and higher level of protection) of an EU fundamental right.

(ii) The Formal Parameters of Interpretation

There are three formal constraints on how EU fundamental rights are to be interpreted.

First, regard is to be had to the Explanations of the Secretariat to the Convention on the EUCFR.[58]

Article 52 EUCFR

(7) The explanations drawn up as way of providing guidance in the interpretation of the Charter of Fundamental Rights shall be given due regard by the courts of the Union and the Member States.

The purpose of Article 52(7) is to restrict unanticipated interpretations with far-reaching consequences by setting out a doctrine of original intent. One is to look at what meaning the drafters of the EUCFR intended its provisions to have. This is undercut by the Explanations being silent on the content of each right as they do no more than state its inspiration (e.g. a particular international human rights treaty). However, it encourages interpretations of EUCFR articles which see them as simply the culmination of prior case law or treaties. This backward-looking approach, in which the history of a provision is given prominence, can militate against interpretations that meet the demands of an evolving society. It may lead the Court to look simply at the law which gave rise to the EUCFR provision rather than giving that provision any autonomous meaning of its own.[59] These dangers are mitigated by the Court stating that it will merely take the Explanations into account.[60] As such, they will simply be one amongst a number of factors at which the Court will look. Typically, it uses the Explanations to confirm an interpretation rather than as a tie-breaker between interpretations.[61]

---

[58] These are found at OJ 2007, C 303/17.   [59] E.g. *Marques da Rosa* v. *Varzim Sol*, C-306/16, EU:C:2017:844.
[60] *Sky Österreich* v. *Österreichischer Rundfunk*, C-283/11, EU:C:2013:28; *Alemo-Herron* v. *Parkwood Leisure*, C-426/11, EU:C:2013:521.
[61] E.g. *R* v. *Secretary of State for the Home Department, ex parte MA*, C-648/11, EU: C:2013:367; *Gardella* v. *INPSS*, C-233/12, EU: C:2013:449.

Secondly interpretations are to be aligned with those of the ECHR where they concern rights which correspond to those in the ECHR.[62]

Article 52 EUCFR

(3) Insofar as this Charter contains rights which correspond to rights guaranteed by the Convention for the Protection of Human Rights and Fundamental Freedoms, the meaning and scope of those rights shall be the same as those laid down by the said Convention. This provision shall not prevent Union law providing more extensive protection.

Initially, there were concerns that this provision would lead to uncritical deference to the judgments of the European Court of Human Rights (ECtHR).[63] A considerable literature emerged making the case for a system of mutual justification whereby both the Court of Justice and ECtHR would continually re-evaluate their case law in the light of the other whilst critically engaging with this case law.[64]

Over time, neither this deference nor this interplay has happened. The formal position is that the Court of Justice will take account of the case law of that court.[65] In many instances, the Court will simply quote the case law of the ECtHR.[66] However, it will also distinguish that case law where it feels it does not offer sufficient individual protection. Therefore, in *MB*,[67] the Court refused to follow a judgment of the ECtHR, which, to protect the traditional concept of marriage, allowed authorities to make gender reassignment conditional on annulment of any marriage.[68] The case before it involved a refusal by British authorities to give the applicant a State pension when she reached 60, as was the case with other women, as she did not have the necessary gender reassignment certification. The certification was not given to those who were married, and the applicant had remained married for religious reasons. The Court of Justice argued that the ECtHR judgment went to civil status, namely when people could lawfully have gender reassignment surgery. It was different from the case in hand as the gender reassignment was both perfectly lawful, and entitlement to a British state pension at 60 was not dependent on being married (single women were entitled to that). It, therefore, decided that the judgment had no relevance and the British action constituted illegal discrimination against transgender women.

Thirdly, EU fundamental rights have to be interpreted to be in harmony with national constitutional traditions.

---

[62] J. Kokott and C. Subotta, 'Protection of Fundamental Rights in the European Union: On the Relationship between EU Fundamental Rights, the European Convention and National Standards of Protection' (2015) 34 *YBEL* 60.

[63] S. Greer and A. Williams, 'Human Rights in the Council of Europe and the EU: Towards "Individual", "Constitutional" or "Institutional" Justice?' (2009) 15 *ELJ* 462, 466–70.

[64] The most extensive theories are N. Krisch, 'The Open Architecture of European Human Rights Law' (2008) 71 *MLR* 183; A. Torres Pérez, *Conflicts of Rights in the European Union: A Theory of Supranational Adjudication* (Oxford University Press, 2009).

[65] *McB* v. *L.E.*, C-400/10 PPU, EU: C:2010:582; *C. K. and Others*, C-578/16 PPU, EU:C:2017:127.

[66] E.g. *Ardic*, C-571/17 PPU, EU:C:2017:1026; *Coman and Hamilton* v. *Inspectoratul General pentru Imigrări*, C-673/16, EU:C:2018:385; *MP* v. *Secretary of State for the Home Department*, C-353/16, EU:C:2018:276; *Sacko* v. *Commissione Territoriale per il riconoscimento della protezione internazionale di Milano*, C-348/16, EU:C:2017:591.

[67] *MB* v. *Secretary of State for Work and Pensions*, C-451/16, EU:C:2018:492.

[68] *Hämäläinen* v. *Finland*, CE:ECHR:2014:0716JUD003735909.

> **Article 52**
>
> (4) Insofar as this Charter recognizes fundamental rights as they result from the constitutional traditions common to the Member States, those rights shall be interpreted in harmony with those traditions.

As has already been discussed, EU law prevails over fundamental rights in individual national constitutions.[69] However, *common* constitutional traditions are to guide interpretation of the content of EU fundamental rights.[70] The interpretative power of these traditions is restricted by their not being codified into a single legal instrument, as well as their having different, and sometimes conflicting, value priorities.[71] This has made them less accessible than the ECHR as a tool of interpretation, thereby giving the Court more wiggle room. The Court, therefore, only occasionally engages in detailed comparative analysis of these constitutional traditions.[72] One does find some analysis in a few opinions of the Advocates General.[73] The number of such opinions is, however, disappointingly small and seems to have declined in recent years, possibly because Advocates General are under tight time constraints to deliver opinions and such analysis is highly time-consuming. This is a pity since national constitutional traditions offer a wider variety of expertise, experience and panoramas than any international court or tribunal can provide.

(iii) Fundamental Rights and a Union Vision of Individual Autonomy

Fundamental rights not only direct institutional action. They also inform citizens' ideas of right and wrong and provide powerful reasons for why we should obey a legal system. Legal systems, therefore, set out narratives and visions which detail what these fundamental rights are about: the lives, life styles, relationships, identities and collective goals that they value. These, in turn, inform the interpretation of these fundamental rights. The EU legal order is no different. This is reflected in the requirement in Advocate General Bot's opinion in *Melloni*, that EU fundamental rights be interpreted in light of the specific interests and objectives of EU law. Yet, what does this mean?

Early commentary suggested an idea of Europe should inform the interpretation of EU fundamental rights. This idea included greater insistence on social rights and more scepticism of 'market rights',[74] as well as particularly strong imperatives to rectify suffering and remedy injustices because of Europe's painful history – most notably the Holocaust.[75] Others, by contrast, bemoaned the lack of vision behind EU fundamental rights, arguing that they were

---

[69] See pp. 206–7 and 263–4.

[70] On the need for commonality, Opinion of Advocate General Tanchev, *Egenberger* v. *Evangelisches Werk für Diakonie und Entwicklung*, C-414/16, EU:C:2017:851.

[71] R. García, 'The General Provisions of the Charter of Fundamental Rights of the European Union' (2002) 8 *ELJ* 492, 508.

[72] E.g. *Trade Agency* v. *Seramico Investments*, C-619/10, EU:C:2012:531.

[73] Opinion of Advocate Mengozzi, *DEB*, C-279/09, EU:C:2010:489; Opinion of Advocate General Cruz Villalón, *European Air Transport* v. *Collège d'Environnement de la Région de Bruxelles-Capitale and Région de Bruxelles-Capitale*, C-120/10, EU:C:2011:94; Opinion of Advocate General Jääskinen, *Patriciello*, C-163/10, EU:C:2011:379; Opinion of Advocate General Trstenjak, *Dominguez* v. *Centre informatique du Centre Ouest Atlantique and Préfet de la Région Centre*, C-282/10, EU:C:2011:559.

[74] C. Leben, 'Is There a European Approach to Human Rights?' in P. Alston (ed.), *The EU and Human Rights* (Oxford University Press, 1999).

[75] K. Günther, 'The Legacies of Injustice and Fear: A European Approach to Human Rights and their Effects on Political Culture' in P. Alston (ed.), *The EU and Human Rights* (Oxford University Press, 1999).

simply deployed to protect the Union from more stinging criticism.[76] None of these are persuasive. They are remote from what most EU law does. It is difficult, therefore, for them to inform it. However, denials of any vision informing EU fundamental rights law can neither explain how the case law is made coherent nor why one interpretation of an EU fundamental right is preferred over another.

Chalmers and Trotter suggest this vision lies in value being accorded to a number of spheres of activity – the family, consumer transactions, the market, the workplace, the school, the Internet – as they are seen as elevating life beyond simply survival, and thereby giving it worth. EU fundamental rights value not only these spheres of activity but require that the individual be provided a presence within these spheres of activity and that the latter work to her benefit. This is achieved through three notions of individual autonomy being used to interpret EU fundamental rights.

D. Chalmers and S. Trotter, 'Fundamental Rights and Legal Wrongs: The Two Sides of the Same EU Coin' (2016) 22 *European Law Journal* 9, 17–18

Autonomy originated in Ancient Greece as meaning making one's own laws. It, therefore, comprises an individual presence which can *assert* itself and be asserted against others. Autonomy also involved a notion of the self and a quality of lawmaking which was derived from and could only be understood from the environment of which it formed part. The side of autonomy goes, therefore, to how the individual is *incorporated* within this wider order from which she is seen to come. The balance between assertion and incorporation is, as we shall see, a shifting one. Furthermore, the demands placed on it have led to different understandings of autonomy over time. EU fundamental rights law relies on three conceptions of individual autonomy: autonomy as *individual control, relational autonomy* and *individual flourishing*. Although one or other may attach more easily to particular fundamental rights provisions, any particular right can be interpreted in the light of any of them and different conceptions can be present within a single judgment. The reason is that these different conceptions of autonomy incorporate the individual into the other elements of the Union's socio-political order and assert a valued presence, agency and recognition within each of these. Autonomy as individual control is concerned to grant the individual sufficient presence and security within the wider European political economy. Relational autonomy is concerned to ensure that, in the ordering of the spheres of activity central to this political economy, those relationships central to individual well-being are protected and sufficient respect accorded to those within those relations. Individual flourishing is concerned to ensure that the ethos of self-betterment goes to a wider development of the self than simply realising Union collective goals.

They suggest that the foremost form of autonomy – autonomy as individual control – involves, first, a right to an identity.[77] This identity allows the individual the possibility to have rights protected by the law[78] and by the courts,[79] political recognition,[80] and requires her to be treated equally to others in the same position.[81] It involves, secondly, physical autonomy. The individual's body is neither to be subject to procedures without her prior informed

---

[76] I. Ward, 'Making Sense of Integration: A Philosophy of Law for the European Community' (1993) 17 *JEI* 101, 128–9 and 132–3; A. Williams, *EU Human Rights Policies: A Study in Irony* (Oxford University Press, 2004) 159–60.

[77] *U*, C-101/ 13, EU:C:2014:2249.   [78] *Volker und Markus Schecke and Eifert*, C-92–3/09, EU: C:2010:662.

[79] *UGT-Rioja and Others*, C-428–34/06, EU: C:2008:488.   [80] *Delvigne*, C-650/13, EU:C:2015:648.

[81] *Impresa Edilux and SICEF*, C-425/14, EU:C:2015:721; *Morcillo and García*, C-169/14, EU:C:2014:2099.

consent[82] nor to inhuman and degrading treatment.[83] Detention is only to take place where the conduct of the accused warrants it.[84] Thirdly, the individual is to be granted a secluded space to enable her personal development.[85] Individuals, thus, neither have to disclose information about themselves unnecessarily[86] nor may others do this in an unwarranted fashion.[87]

This vision has been used to justify striking down requirements that Internet service providers retain data identifying the source, location, destination and type of electronic communications for at least six months and to make this data available to public authorities.[88] Particularly egregious was the unspecified scope of the data to be retained, the lack of safeguards over its use, and the lack of clear criteria for why it had to be retained for so long. It has also been invoked to prevent a Member State transferring a person to another Member State where there is a serious risk she will suffer inhuman and degrading treatment either in that State or as a result of the transfer,[89] or to a non-EU State where there is a serious risk that she will commit suicide as a result of past torture.[90]

The most famous example is the establishment of the right to be forgotten in *Google Spain*. The case concerned an action by Costeja González to have Google Spain exclude from its search results two newspaper articles about auctions of his property as a result of bankruptcy proceedings. This came up whenever his name was searched via Google. He argued that the Data Protection Directive required that individuals could seek rectification of data where it no longer complied with the Directive, and that processors of data, such as search engines, should not keep it in a form which permits identification for longer than necessary. These requirements had to be read expansively in the light of the fundamental rights to protection of personal data and respect for privacy.

Google Spain v. *AEPD*, C-131/12, EU:C:2014:317

80 ... processing of personal data, such as that at issue in the main proceedings, carried out by the operator of a search engine is liable to affect significantly the fundamental rights to privacy and to the protection of personal data when the search by means of that engine is carried out on the basis of an individual's name, since that processing enables any internet user to obtain through the list of results a structured overview of the information relating to that individual that can be found on the internet – information which potentially concerns a vast number of aspects of his private life and which, without the search engine, could not have been interconnected or could have been only with great difficulty – and thereby to establish a more or less detailed profile of him. Furthermore, the effect of the interference with those

---

[82] *Netherlands* v. *Parliament and Council*, C-377/98, EU: C:2001:329.

[83] *N.S.*, C-411/10, EU: C:2011:865; *Abdida*, C-562/13, EU:C:2014:2453.   [84] *Lanigan*, C-237/15 PPU, EU: C:2015.

[85] *Ryneš*, C-212/13, EU:C:2014:2428; *Kušinová*, C-34/13, EU:C:2014:2189.   [86] *Stauder*, 29/69, EU:C:1969:57.

[87] C-465/00 and C-138–9/01 *Österreichischer Rundfunk and Others* [2003] ECR I-4989; *Google Spain*, C-131/12, EU: C:2014:317; *Schrems*, C-362/14, EU:C:2015:650.

[88] *Digital Rights Ireland* v. *Minister for Communications, Marine and Natural Resources*, C-293/12 and C-594/12, EU: C:2014:238. The Court has, subsequently, stated that any retention of data which is not related to a threat to public security or situations which may give rise to criminal proceedings is illegal. It must also be possible to challenge any retention before a court and there must be guarantees that the data will stay within the European Union, *Tele2 Sverige* v. *Post-och telestyrelsen; Secretary of State for the Home Department* v. *Watson and Others*, C-203/15 and C-698/15, EU:C:2016:970.

[89] *C. K. and Others*, C-578/16 PPU, EU:C:2017:127; *ML*, C-220/18 PPU, EU:C:2018:589.

[90] *MP* v. *Secretary of State for the Home Department*, C-353/16, EU:C:2018:276.

rights of the data subject is heightened on account of the important role played by the internet and search engines in modern society, which render the information contained in such a list of results ubiquitous . . .

81 In the light of the potential seriousness of that interference, it is clear that it cannot be justified by merely the economic interest which the operator of such an engine has in that processing. However, inasmuch as the removal of links from the list of results could, depending on the information at issue, have effects upon the legitimate interest of internet users potentially interested in having access to that information, in situations such as that at issue in the main proceedings a fair balance should be sought in particular between that interest and the data subject's fundamental rights under Articles 7 and 8 of the Charter. Whilst it is true that the data subject's rights protected by those articles also override, as a general rule, that interest of internet users, that balance may however depend, in specific cases, on the nature of the information in question and its sensitivity for the data subject's private life and on the interest of the public in having that information, an interest which may vary, in particular, according to the role played by the data subject in public life.

Whilst the formal reasoning locates the right to be forgotten in two EUCFR rights – the right to respect for one's private life and the right to protection of personal data – this alone cannot explain the judgment and the establishment of this right. It was perfectly possible to argue that González's privacy and data no longer needed protecting as they were out in the public domain. Further reasons need to be provided for this, and this was that the right to be forgotten was central to securing a secluded space for an individual's personal development. A wide interpretation had to be given this right to allow such space for development because, as the Court noted, the Internet can be so effective at eviscerating this space by allowing detailed profiles to be compiled.

The judgment also vividly illustrates the tensions associated with this vision of individual autonomy. Often, individual control is at odds with, and threatened by, the wider environment. Its protection can therefore be at the expense of the goods provided by this wider environment. In *Google Spain*, the right to be forgotten was established at the expense of a wider right to know information provided by search engines. How one is to be evaluated against the other is unclear as the two values are quite incommensurable, and the judgment reflects this uncertainty with its lack of clarity about when there is a right to know about people in the public eye.[91]

Relational autonomy, the second form of individual autonomy, goes to ensuring that the well-being of individuals is protected within relationships and they are afforded adequate recognition within these relations. These relationships can be family,[92] employment[93] or consumer ones.[94] They can involve social institutions such as the social partners,[95] the professions[96] or trade unions,[97] or relations between public authorities and the public.[98]

---

[91] O. Lynskey, *The Foundations of EU Data Protection Law* (Oxford University Press, 2015) 144–50 and 173–7; K. Ho Youm and A. Park, 'The "Right to Be Forgotten" in European Union Law: Data Protection Balanced with Free Speech?' (2016) 93 *Journalism and Mass Communication Quarterly* 273.

[92] *HR*, 512/77, EU:C:2018:513.

[93] *Defrenne* v. *Sabena*, 149/77, EU:C:1978:130; *Egenberger* v. *Evangelisches Werk für Diakonie und Entwicklung*, C-414/16, EU:C:2018:257.

[94] *Dynamic Medien*, C-244/06 EU:C:2008:85; *Deutsches Weintor*, C-544/10, EU:C:2012:526; *CHEZ Razpredelenie Bulgaria*, C-83/14, EU:C:2015:480.

[95] *Erny*, C-172/11, EU:C:2014:157.

[96] *Ordre des Barreaux francophones and germanophone and Others*, C-305/05, EU:C:2007:383.

[97] *Laval un Partneri*, C-341/05, EU:C:2007:809.

[98] *Edwards and Pallikaropoulos*, C-260/11, EU:C:2013:221; *East Sussex Council*, C-71/14, EU:C:2015:656.

A good example of this form of reasoning is *Detiček*. A Slovenian mother had absconded to Slovenia with her daughter the day after an Italian court awarded custody to the Italian father and required that she be placed in an Italian children's home. A Slovenian court placed the daughter in the custody of the mother on the grounds that the daughter was now settled in Slovenia, wished to stay with her mother, and it would be detrimental for her to be placed in a children's home. The relevant EU Regulation stated that it was for the court of the State of habitual residence, in this instance the Italian court, to award custody. However, it allowed other courts to make provisional awards. The Slovenian court therefore asked the Court of Justice if it could amend the order of the Italian court.

Detiček v. *Sgueglia*, C-403/09 PPU, EU:C:2009:810

54 One of [the] fundamental rights of the child is the right, set out in Article 24(3) of the Charter, to maintain on a regular basis a personal relationship and direct contact with both parents, respect for that right undeniably merging into the best interests of any child.

55 [The Regulation] cannot be interpreted in such a way that it disregards that fundamental right.

56 In this respect, it is clear that the wrongful removal of a child, following a decision taken unilaterally by one of the parents, more often than not deprives the child of the possibility of maintaining on a regular basis a personal relationship and direct contact with the other parent.

57 [The Regulation] cannot therefore be interpreted in such a way that it can be used by the parent who has wrongfully removed the child as an instrument for prolonging the factual situation caused by his or her wrongful conduct or for legitimating the consequences of that conduct.

58 It is true that, under Article 24(3) of the Charter, an exception may be made to the child's fundamental right to maintain on a regular basis a personal relationship and direct contact with both parents if that interest proves to be contrary to another interest of the child.

59 It follows that a measure which prevents the maintenance on a regular basis of a personal relationship and direct contact with both parents can be justified only by another interest of the child of such importance that it takes priority over the interest underlying that fundamental right.

60 However, a balanced and reasonable assessment of all the interests involved, which must be based on objective considerations relating to the actual person of the child and his or her social environment, must in principle be performed in proceedings before the court with jurisdiction as to the substance in accordance with the provisions of [the Regulation].

The reasoning is subtle and has three elements to it. In the first place, the presence of regular relations, in this case with both parents, is seen as central to generating well-being (paras. 54–6). However, in the second place, this is not completely synonymous with well-being. The child's interests, thus, have to be recognised as extending beyond this relationship so that other features can be brought into rebut the presumption that the relationships are beneficial (para. 60). Thirdly, this balancing has to be done in such a way that it does not disrupt the normal operation of EU law. It is for the Italian court, and not the Slovenian court, to make an assessment, possibly a reassessment as this is required by the Regulation.

The strengths of this style of reasoning lie in the importance it accords to relationships in making a good life. Its limits lie, on the one hand, in it being a highly stylised form of reasoning. It is assumed that the family relationships make the child happy rather than looking more simply at what makes her happy. Its limits lie, also, in regard being had to wider policy objectives of the EU legislation in interpreting the fundamental right. In this instance, the matter was returned to the Italian court even though it was unclear how much regard the Italian court would have to the child's happiness and relations with her parents, as it initially wanted to place her in a home. An alternative response would have been to state that the rights of the child required that the EU legislation be disapplied in this case, in favour of the matter being decided by the Slovenian court which was arguably best placed to give effect to the goals of the right, namely her welfare and family relations.

The third form of autonomy is that of individual flourishing. Individual flourishing goes to the possibility for individuals to be given the resources to develop their sense of self-worth and to be an active participant in the different spheres of activity mentioned earlier: be this the workplace, politics, the market etc. A good example is *Sobczyszyn*. This case concerned a Polish teacher who had accrued thirty-five days of annual leave. She was, however, ill and on convalescent leave for just over four months. Her employer refused to allow her to take or carry over her annual leave, arguing that the period for taking it had been when she had been on convalescent leave. The Directive on organisation of working time, Directive 2003/88, provides that all workers have the right to four weeks annual paid leave per year. In addition, Article 31(2) provides for a fundamental right to annual paid leave.

Sobczyszyn v. _Szkoła Podstawowa w Rzeplinie_, C-178/15, EU:C:2016:502

20 ... the right to paid annual leave is, as a principle of EU social law, not only particularly important, but is also expressly laid down in Article 31(2) EUCFR, which Article 6(1) TEU recognises as having the same legal value as the Treaties ...

21 ... the right to paid annual leave cannot be interpreted restrictively ...

22 In addition, the Court has already held that Article 7(1) of Directive 2003/88 does not preclude, as a rule, national legislation which lays down conditions for the exercise of the right to paid annual leave expressly conferred by the directive that include even the loss of that right at the end of a leave year, provided, however, that the worker whose right to paid annual leave is lost has actually had the opportunity to exercise that right ...

23 It is also clear from the Court's case-law that the purpose of the right to paid annual leave is to enable the worker to rest and to enjoy a period of relaxation and leisure ...

24 The Court has inferred therefrom that, in the event of periods of annual leave and sick leave overlapping, Article 7(1) of Directive 2003/88 must be interpreted as precluding national legislation or practices under which the right to paid annual leave is extinguished at the end of the leave year and/or of a carry-over period laid down by national law where the worker has been on sick leave, for the whole or part of the leave year, and therefore has not actually had the opportunity to exercise that right ...

25 Indeed, the Court has held that the purpose of the right to paid annual leave, which is to enable the worker to rest and to enjoy a period of relaxation and leisure, is different from that of the right to sick leave, which is to enable the worker to recover from an illness ...

26 In the light of those differing purposes of the two types of leave, the Court has concluded that a worker who is on sick leave during a period of previously scheduled annual leave has the right, at his request and in order that he may actually use his annual leave, to take that leave during a period which does not coincide with the period of sick leave ...

This judgment is worker-friendly since it ensures that workers who are ill have the same right to holidays as everybody else. Yet it is this characteristic which gives rise to two types of issue. The first goes to the level of benefit provided. In this instance, of course, the employer will argue that they get even less labour from the employee, and this is costly for them. Insofar as these types of benefit, which enable the individual to flourish, often incur costs for others, there is opposition to them, with the consequence that they may not be as generous as some may wish. There is no fundamental right, for example, to flexible working hours. The second concern is that such benefits are only granted to people who have acquired a certain status, in this case people in employment. Thus, they have a selective feel. This was addressed in *Fenoll* which considered whether a French facility offering occupational activities, medico-social support and educational assistance to those with mental disabilities was required to give attendees paid annual leave.[99] The Court stated that the national court had to look at whether these attendees – who were paid – did something of economic value and whether their activities formed part of the normal labour market. In such circumstances, it would seem that those with less severe disabilities would have a right to annual paid leave whereas others would not, particularly if they had to take medical leave. This sits very uncomfortably with *Sobczyszyn*.

6 FUNDAMENTAL RIGHTS AND THE INSTITUTIONAL SCHEME OF THE EUROPEAN UNION

(i) Fundamental Rights and the EU Institutions

Fundamental rights are most obviously used to review the behaviour of EU Institutions. Whilst the Union Courts are quite willing to strike down administrative acts by either the Commission or Council for breaching EU fundamental rights,[100] it is another matter when it comes to EU legislative acts. Here the Court of Justice is pusillanimous. There are, for example, only two instances of a Directive being struck down for failure to comply with fundamental rights.[101] The more central role for EU fundamental rights there is to orient and interpret EU legislation.

With regard to the orientation of EU legislation, the Commission has stated that the EUCFR should act as the 'compass for the Union's policies'.[102] This involves four stages. In initial consultation with stakeholders prior to any legislative proposal, the Commission should, first, highlight any potentially sensitive fundamental rights issues. Secondly, in carrying out impact assessments on any proposal, the Commission should also consider its impacts on fundamental rights. Thirdly, in drafting a proposal, the Commission should indicate how the legislation will comply with specific rights in the recitals in the Preamble, as well as expanding on this at more length in the Explanatory Memorandum accompanying the legislation. Fourthly, the Commission must verify that amendments by other EU Institutions comply with fundamental rights. These EU Institutions are committed to not proposing such amendments and the Commission is committed to opposing them if they are made.[103]

---

[99] *Fenoll* v. *Centre d'aide par le travail La Jouvene*, C-316/13, EU:C:2015:200.
[100] E.g. *FV* v. *Council*, T-639/16 P, EU:T:2018:22; *České dráhy* v. *Commission*, T-325/16, EU:T:2018:368; *NC* v. *Commission*, T-151/16, EU:T:2017:437; *EUIPO* v. *Puma*, C-564/16 P, EU:C:2018:509.
[101] *Association Belge des Consommateurs Test-Achats* v. *Conseil des ministers*, C-236/09, EU:C:2011:100; *Digital Rights Ireland* v. *Minister for Communications, Marine and Natural Resources*, C-293/12 and C-594/12, EU:C:2014:238.
[102] European Commission, 'Strategy for the Effective Implementation of the Charter of Fundamental Rights by the European Union', COM(2010)573, 4. See I. de Jesus Butler, 'Ensuring Compliance with the Charter of Fundamental Rights in Legislative Drafting: The Practice of the European Commission' (2012) 37 *ELRev* 397.
[103] European Commission, 'Strategy for the Effective Implementation of the Charter of Fundamental Rights by the European Union', n. 102 above, 4–10.

Commission practice has been subject to careful analysis by Mark Dawson. He found that this engagement with EU fundamental rights was double-edged. It could, positively, integrate and mainstream EU fundamental rights into policy-making. However, this process could also be used less positively as a defence against legal challenge through the Commission claiming that it did its best. Dawson therefore argues that much depends on the quality of Commission engagement, and particularly whether it does more than simply tick-box a number of fundamental rights. In this regard, he noted that when the quality of Commission Impact Assessments is reviewed by the Union's own procedures, there is little focus on fundamental rights (less than 5 per cent of opinions engaged with this in 2013 and 2014), suggesting that these are a low priority.[104]

With regard to interpretation, the Court frequently interprets EU legislation in the light of EU fundamental rights. This can have a significant impact on EU powers. A good example is *Jaeger*. The Directive on the organisation of working time required a minimum daily rest period of eleven consecutive hours per twenty-four-hour period. Jaeger was a doctor who worked in a hospital in the German town of Kiel. For about three-quarters of his working time, he was on call. This required him to be present in the hospital to be available when needed. It was agreed that he performed services about 49 per cent of the time he was on call. The hospital considered that the time on call counted as a rest period for the purposes of the Directive and limited his rest periods outside of this accordingly. Jaeger argued that what constituted working time should be interpreted broadly in light of the Community Charter of the Fundamental Social Rights of Workers 1989.[105] The Court agreed.

Landeshauptstadt Kiel v. *Jaeger*, C–151/02, EU:C:2003:437

47 In that context it is clear from the Community Charter of the Fundamental Social Rights of Workers 1989, and in particular points 8 and 19, first subparagraph, thereof, which are referred to in the fourth recital in the preamble to [the Directive], that every worker in the European Community must enjoy satisfactory health and safety conditions in his working environment and must have a right, *inter alia*, to a weekly rest period, the duration of which in the Member States must be progressively harmonised in accordance with national practices.

48 With regard more specifically to the concept of 'working time' for the purposes of [the Directive], it is important to point out that at paragraph 47 of the judgment in *Simap*,[106] the Court noted that the directive defines that concept as any period during which the worker is working, at the employer's disposal and carrying out his activity or duties, in accordance with national laws and/or practices, and that that concept is placed in opposition to rest periods, the two being mutually exclusive.

49 At paragraph 48 of the judgment in *Simap* the Court held that the characteristic features of working time are present in the case of time spent on call by doctors in primary care teams in Valencia (Spain) where their presence at the health centre is required. The Court found, in the case which resulted in that judgment, that it was not disputed that during periods of duty on call under those rules, the first two conditions set out in the definition of the concept of working time were fulfilled and, further, that, even if the activity actually performed varied according to the circumstances, the fact that such doctors were obliged to be present and available at the workplace with a view to providing their professional services had to be regarded as coming within the ambit of the performance of their duties.

---

[104] M. Dawson, *The Governance of EU Fundamental Rights* (Cambridge University Press, 2017) 90–4.
[105] The relevant paragraphs of this Charter have been largely replicated in Article 31(2) EUCFR.
[106] *Simap* v. *Conselleria de Sanidad y Consumo de la Generalidad Valenciana*, C–303/98, EU:C:2000:528.

The Charter was thus used to give a wide interpretation to what constitutes working time. This expanded Union powers by allowing the Union to determine what constitutes 'rest' in securing work–life balances. Moreover, the judgment, when taken together with the Directive which set a general limit of forty-eight hours works per week, had dramatic implications for the cost-base of many organisation as it changed what employers could ask of employees more broadly. This was particularly so in national health services, as evident in the extract below.

House of Lords European Union Committee, *The Working Time Directive: A Response to the European Commission's Review*, 9th Report, Session 2003–4, SO, London

327 The Royal College of Nursing also expressed concern about the potential impact of the *SiMAP* and *Jaeger* judgments. The College called for clarification of the definition of compensatory rest and how it should be applied. It drew attention to the particular difficulty in calculating working time where 24 hour nursing care was provided by agency nurses living in patients' homes.

331 The NHS Confederation agreed that 'sizeable numbers' of hospitals in the United Kingdom could not comply with the Directive by 1 August 2004 because of these judgments.

332 The BMA claimed that if the *Jaeger* ruling remained unchanged the effect would be tantamount to losing the equivalent of 3700 junior doctors by August 2004 and between 4300 and 9900 junior doctors by 2009 when the full 48 hour limit would come into effect. One BMA witness commented that the United Kingdom would be in 'real trouble'.

338 The Health Minister explained the implications of the *Jaeger* ruling for the NHS: 'To require compensatory rest to be taken immediately would potentially have a massively destructive effect across the NHS and might mean that doctors could not work the following shift on rota that they were required to do. This would have knock-on consequences right across the hospital. At the end of the day, the only people who would be negatively affected would be the patients and that is a ridiculous result'.

339 The NHS Confederation put it in equally strong terms: '*Jaeger* makes no sense at all in terms of how you run NHS organisations'. The BMA described how it might work in practice and commented 'This is nonsense'.

Reactions in Other Member States

340 The *Jaeger* judgment poses problems for other health sectors in the EU. In its Communication, the Commission cites Germany as saying that if both *SiMAP* and *Jaeger* were left unamended it would have to increase its doctors by 24% with costs running to €1.75 billion. It also reports that the Netherlands estimated the extra cost of both judgments to be €400 million to fund recruitment of 10,000 new staff.

As we saw in the cases above, the use of EU fundamental rights to interpret EU legislation can give that legislation a more liberal bent – fundamental rights were used in *Google Spain* to read the right to be forgotten into the Data Protection Directive and in *Sobczyszyn* to ensure that the Working Time Directive protected those with significant ill-health. However, the converse also happens. The Court of Justice has occasionally interpreted very illiberal EU legislation in the light of fundamental rights to try and make the former acceptable when it would have been better simply to declare the legislation illegal.

A notorious example is *Family Reunification Directive*. The Directive on family reunification set out the conditions under which family members of non-EU nationals resident in the Union could join them. For children over the age of 12, the Directive provided that they could be prevented from joining their family in the Union if they arrived independently from their family and did not meet integration requirements set by national law. In other words, these children could be required to take an integration test which might test their language skills, political beliefs or knowledge of the host society. If they failed, they could be barred from entry. The European Parliament believed that this violated the right to respect for family life in Article 7 EUCFR.

Parliament v. Council ('Family Reunification Directive'), C-540/03, EU:C:2006:429

62 [The provision] cannot be regarded as running counter to the right to respect for family life. In the context of a directive imposing precise positive obligations on the Member States, it preserves a limited margin of appreciation for those States which is no different from that accorded to them by the European Court of Human Rights, in its case-law relating to that right, for weighing, in each factual situation, the competing interests.

63 Furthermore, as required by Article 5(5) of the Directive, the Member States must when weighing those interests have due regard to the best interests of minor children.

64 Note should also be taken of Article 17 of the Directive which requires Member States to take due account of the nature and solidity of the person's family relationships and the duration of his residence in the Member State and of the existence of family, cultural and social ties with his country of origin ... such criteria correspond to those taken into consideration by the European Court of Human Rights when it reviews whether a State which has refused an application for family reunification has correctly weighed the competing interests.

65 Finally, a child's age and the fact that a child arrives independently from his or her family are also factors taken into consideration by the European Court of Human Rights, which has regard to the ties which a child has with family members in his or her country of origin, and also to the child's links with the cultural and linguistic environment of that country ...

68 The Community legislature thus considered that, beyond 12 years of age, the objective of integration cannot be achieved as easily and, consequently, provided that a Member State has the right to have regard to a minimum level of capacity for integration when deciding whether to authorise entry and residence under the Directive.

69 A condition for integration ... may therefore be taken into account when considering an application for family reunification and the Community legislature did not contradict itself by authorising Member States, in the specific circumstances envisaged by that provision, to consider applications in the light of such a condition in the context of a directive which, as is apparent from the fourth recital in its preamble, has the general objective of facilitating the integration of third country nationals in Member States by making family life possible through reunification.

70 The fact that the concept of integration is not defined cannot be interpreted as authorising the Member States to employ that concept in a manner contrary to general principles of Community law, in particular to fundamental rights. The Member States which wish to make use of the derogation cannot employ an unspecified concept of integration, but must apply the condition for integration provided for by their legislation existing on the date of implementation of the Directive in order to examine the specific situation of a child over 12 years of age arriving independently from the rest of his or her family.

The judgment is an exercise in sophistry. It states that separating a 12-year-old child from their family does not violate EU fundamental rights, provided that the national authorities consider a wide variety of factors: the child's ties with their country of origin, the solidity of their family ties, their length of residence in the Member States and, *inter alia*, their best interests. The risk for getting it right is thrown onto national administrations with little guidance as to how to weigh these conflicting and vague criteria. It is very difficult to conceive of any circumstances where it is in any way humane to separate a 12-year-old from their family because of features that go to the 12-year-old. Indeed, most people would see such separation as almost invariably barbaric. As such, a more honest approach would have been to declare the provision illegal. However, this would have required the Court of Justice to strike down EU legislation, which, as we have seen, it does only very rarely.

(ii) Fundamental Rights and the Member States

(a) Fundamental Rights and the Sensitivities of National Law

There are particular sensitivities over EU fundamental rights being used to review national laws. Traditionally, domestic institutions determine what is 'fundamental' in our societies, but under the Union, EU law is granted the authority to set out what is 'fundamental' in our societies and to do so at the expense of national institutions. The tensions generated as a result are described below by a distinguished academic who is now a judge on the Italian Constitutional Court.[107]

> ### M. Cartabia, 'Europe and Rights: Taking Dialogue Seriously' (2009) 5 *European Constitutional Law Review* 5, 20–1
>
> We must not, however, forget the ambivalent nature of fundamental rights. In the struggle for fundamental rights there is a longing for *universality* that justifies the need to go beyond the boundaries of the national legal systems; but there is also a *historical dimension* in which the traditions and deepest conscience of each people is reflected, of which the national constitutional charters are one of the salient expressions. Rooted in the value of human dignity, the idea of fundamental rights necessarily contains a *universal dimension.* Embedded in the historical, religious, moral, linguistic and political peculiarities of each people, such rights are fed by particularity and pluralism.
>
> The attraction to a European protection of human rights risks sacrificing the national historical and cultural traditions that characterise the pluralistic nature of Europe. Even more serious: what happens if one of the fundamental rights protected at the European and international level belongs only to one or some specific traditions or cultures and does not reflect any common shared value? Who will guarantee that the European and the international institutions will stick to the protection of the common fundamental rights and are not tempted to impose a particular interpretation of them as if it were universal?
>
> The position of the Court of Justice is crucial and extremely delicate. Its pronouncements on the subject of fundamental rights tend to establish *the* standard that must be respected throughout the 27 countries of the Union. Once a fundamental right enters the jurisdiction of the Court of Justice it becomes a European fundamental right. The decisions taken by the Court of Justice are binding in all the member states even if the case originated in a particular legal system.
>
> Herein lies the risk of 'judicial colonialism' in the field of fundamental rights. As history has shown us, colonialism often claims to promote progress and civilisation, but on more than one occasion pre-existing cultural and historical patrimonies have been sacrificed in the name of a specific culture, although more progressive. Fostering fundamental rights is indeed a clear sign of progress and civilization. But, what about the native cultures and traditions of the European peoples? And how can a society be able

---

[107] They are also well described in F. Fabbrini, *Fundamental Rights in Europe: Challenges and Transformations in Comparative Perspective* (Oxford University Press, 2014) 265–9.

to welcome and respect the cultures of immigrant peoples if it proves to be unable to take care of its own historical patrimony and diversity?

As has been highlighted, the very nature of the European Union is that of a pluralistic, tolerant, multiple, 'contra-punctual' legal order, where a plurality of voices tends to harmonisation. Should the European Union move towards a uniform standard in the field of fundamental rights, trampling on the plurality of national constitutional traditions, then it would betray its own ontological structure.

These tensions have been addressed in a number of ways.

First, some Member States have sought to exempt particularly sensitive laws from scrutiny by EU law. For instance, Malta secured protection of its abortion laws from EU law,[108] whereas Ireland obtained protection not only for these, but also for its family and education law.[109] Another example is Poland where, insofar as the EUCFR rights on solidarity create justiciable rights, they shall only be justiciable in Poland if so provided in Polish law.[110] Poland also secured a Declaration that the EUCFR does not affect in any way the right of Member States to legislate in the spheres of public morality, family law, protection of human dignity or respect for human physical and moral integrity.[111]

Another has been to place constraints on the interpretation of EU fundamental rights. The TEU states that the EUCFR does not extend in any way the competences of the Union,[112] and the EUCFR states that it neither establishes any new power or task for the Union nor does it modify existing ones.[113] However, this was insufficient for the United Kingdom and Poland who secured a Protocol stating that the EUCFR does not extend the ability of the Court of Justice to declare any of their laws or administrative practices incompatible with fundamental rights.[114]

(b) The Scope of Fundamental Rights Review over National Measures

The main way in which tensions are managed is that not all national measures are subject to review against EU fundamental rights. This will only be the case where they are implementing Union law.

Article 51 EUCFR

(1) The provisions of this Charter are addressed to the institutions, bodies, offices and agencies of the Union with due regard for the principle of subsidiarity and to the Member States only when they are implementing Union law.

---

[108] Protocol No. 7 Act of Accession 2003.

[109] Protocol on the Concerns of the Irish People on the Treaty of Lisbon, OJ 2013, L 60/131, Article 1.

[110] These are largely labour rights, but also include wider social rights such as the right to health care and social assistance as well as Union policies committing themselves to a high level of environmental and consumer protection, Protocol on the Application of the Charter to Poland and the United Kingdom, Article 1(2).

[111] Declaration 61 to the Treaty of Lisbon by the Republic of Poland on the Charter of Fundamental Rights of the European Union.

[112] Article 6(1) TEU.   [113] Article 51(2) EUCFR.

[114] Protocol on the Application of the Charter to Poland and the United Kingdom, Article 1(1). The effect of the Protocol is not evident, as it does not provide an opt-out and the EUCFR applies to Poland like any other Member State, *N.S.*, C-411/10, EU: C:2011:865.

This provision is quite obscure. Some language versions use the word 'apply' instead of 'implementing'.[115] The Explanations to Article 51 consider measures implementing Union law to be measures 'acting in the context' of EU law.[116] Furthermore, the previous law used the phrase 'acting within the scope of' to identify the measures caught by EU fundamental rights.[117] This is problematic because a wide interpretation of Article 51(1) EUCFR might be perceived as extending Union powers of review over national legislation.[118]

The matter was addressed in *Fransson*.[119] In this case, a Swede who had already been sanctioned for VAT fraud by the Swedish administrative courts was now subject to further sanctions by their criminal courts. He argued that this violated the principle of *ne bis in idem*, the right not to be tried twice for the same offence. The Court of Justice stated that the Swedish measures would be implementing Union law for the purposes of Article 51(1) EUCFR if they fell within the scope of Union law. This was found to be the case here, because of EU legislation requiring Member States to take all necessary measures to ensure the collection of VAT and prevent tax evasion. In addition, the Treaty – notably Article 325 TFEU – required Member States to take effective deterrent action against illegal measures which affected the Union's financial interests, as was the case here as VAT receipts contribute to the Union's budget.

The judgment above was vague as to when something fell within the scope of EU law, and the EU laws referenced in it were quite general. Neither those on ensuring the collection of VAT or taking measures to protect the Union's financial interests made any explicit mention of the need to establish criminal penalties for VAT fraud or the level of sanction that should be applied. As a result, the judgment drew a strong response from the German Constitutional Court. In *Counterterrorism Database*, two months after *Fransson*, the new German counterterrorism database was challenged as being incompatible with EU fundamental rights.[120] It was argued that it fell within the scope of EU law as two EU laws touched on it – the Directive on protection of personal data and a decision setting a framework for the exchange of information between national authorities about terrorist offences. Such an argument was rejected by the German Constitutional Court which stated that EU fundamental rights could not be used to extend EU competences and that any decision by the Court of Justice to the contrary would be *ultra vires*. It could not therefore be used to review national legislation which had domestic goals and was not pursuing EU goals, and therefore only indirectly affected EU law.

Since then, the Court of Justice has relied on a more specific test for when a Member State is implementing Union law. This is set out most clearly in *Hernández*.[121] Following the insolvency of their employer, Spanish workers brought an action for outstanding back pay. They received some compensation from a Spanish statutory fund, Fogasa, but this was capped. They thus sought the remainder of the outstanding back pay from the Spanish State, which was required under Spanish law to pay compensation if the dismissal was unfair and a court had not heard the case within sixty days of the dismissal. The compensation was refused on the grounds that there

---

[115] A. Rosas, 'When Is the EU Charter of Fundamental Rights Applicable at National Level?' (2012) 19 *Jurisprudencija* 1269, 1277.

[116] For a discussion see G. de Búrca, 'The Drafting of the EU Charter of Fundamental Rights' (2001) 26 *ELRev* 126, 136–7.

[117] *ERT* v. *DEP*, C-260/89, EU: C:1991:254.

[118] E.g. the Czech Government appended a Declaration to the Lisbon Treaty stating that the EUCFR only applied to States implementing EU law and not when they adopted measures independently from EU law, Declaration 53 of the Czech Republic on the Charter of the Fundamental Rights of the European Union.

[119] *Åklagaren* v. *Fransson*, C-617/10, EU:C:2013:105.

[120] 1 BvR 1215/07, *Counterterrorism Database*, Judgment of 24 April 2013, paras. 88–91.

[121] The test was first set out, albeit not as clearly in *Siragusa*, C-206/13, EU:C:2014:126.

had been no unfair dismissal. The employees argued that this violated Article 20 EUCFR, as it discriminated between them and those who were unfairly dismissed. They also argued that it fell within the scope of EU law as the Directive on the protection of employees in the event of the insolvency required Member States to set up funds to compensate workers, and EU law thus regulated compensation in situations of company insolvency. Spain had done this with Fogasa and was permitted by the Directive to limit the compensation offered by the latter.

Hernández, C-198/13, EU: C:2014:2055

33 As is apparent from the explanations relating to Article 51 of the Charter, which must be given due regard pursuant to Article 52(7) thereof, the concept of implementation provided for in Article 51 thereof confirms the case-law of the Court as to the applicability of the fundamental rights of the European Union as general principles of the EU law developed before the Charter entered into force . . . , according to which the requirement to respect fundamental rights guaranteed in the legal order of the European Union is binding on the Member States only when they are acting within the scope of EU law . . .

34 In this regard, it should be borne in mind that the concept of 'implementing Union law', as referred to in Article 51 of the Charter, presupposes a degree of connection between the measure of EU law and the national measure at issue which goes beyond the matters covered being closely related or one of those matters having an indirect impact on the other . . .

35 In particular, the Court has found that fundamental European-Union rights could not be applied in relation to national legislation because the provisions of EU law in the area concerned did not impose any specific obligation on Member States with regard to the situation at issue in the main proceedings . . .

36 In the same vein, the Court has already held that Article 13 EC (now Article 19 TFEU) could not, as such, bring within the scope of EU law, for the purposes of the application of fundamental rights as general principles of EU law, a national measure which does not come within the framework of the measures adopted on the basis of that article . . . Consequently, the mere fact that a national measure comes within an area in which the European Union has powers cannot bring it within the scope of EU law, and, therefore, cannot render the Charter applicable . . .

37 In accordance with the Court's settled case-law, in order to determine whether a national measure involves the implementation of EU law for the purposes of Article 51(1) of the Charter, it is necessary to determine, *inter alia*, whether that national legislation is intended to implement a provision of EU law; the nature of the legislation at issue and whether it pursues objectives other than those covered by EU law, even if it is capable of indirectly affecting EU law; and also whether there are specific rules of EU law on the matter or rules which are capable of affecting it . . .

The judgment sets out three circumstances when a Member State will be said to be implementing EU law (para. 37).

The first is where the national legislation is intended to implement EU law. This will most clearly be the case where a State is transposing a Directive.[122] Even when this is so, however, individuals will not be able to invoke EU fundamental rights if the EU law in question is not intended to benefit them.[123]

The second is where the national law is pursuing the same objectives as the EU law in question. Decisive to the Court finding that the Spanish law in *Hernández* fell outside the scope of EU law

---

[122] *Paoletti*, C-218/15, EU:C:2016:748.   [123] *Ymeraga and Others* v. *Ministre du Travail*, C-87/12, EU:C:2013:291.

was the fact that it pursued different objectives from the Directive. The purpose of the Spanish law was to compensate for failures in the Spanish judicial system. It thus did not cover the first sixty days after dismissal but allowed employees to pursue the State rather than the employer for subsequent days to punish the judiciary's slowness. By contrast, the Directive acted to insure the employees, to an extent, from the consequences of insolvency.

The third is where there are specific rules on the matter. National measures will fall within this category if they are authorised by EU law. In *'Spika' UAB*, fishermen challenged the allocation of herring and sprat catches to them by the Lithuanian fishing authorities, claiming that these violated the right to conduct a business and the principle of equal treatment.[124] Whilst the Court found no violation of EU fundamental law, it found that the measures were implementing EU law as States were exercising a competence granted by EU law.

National measures also fall within this category of specific EU rules on the matter if they breach an EU legal norm, such as one on free movement, but invoke a derogation in EU law to justify the breach. In *AGET Iraklis*, a Greek law required consultation with workforce representatives prior to any collective redundancies.[125] If agreement could not be reached about the way forward, the Greek authorities could block the redundancies after taking into account the conditions on the labour market, the situation of the undertaking and the interests of the national economy. This happened in the case of a French cement company who argued that the Greek law violated its freedom of establishment under the Treaty by making it tougher for it to do business in Greece. The Greek Government sought to justify the restriction on grounds of employee protection. The Court of Justice stated that it could invoke this derogation, a justifiable public interest, but it must comply with EU fundamental rights, notably Article 16 EUCFR on the freedom to conduct a business. In this instance, the Court found that this right had been violated as the criteria on which the Greek authorities could block the redundancies were so general and imprecise that it was impossible for the business to know how they would be applied.

There is no clear reason why national measures in these three sets of circumstances are caught by EU fundamental rights whereas other national measures are not.[126] The notion of 'implementation' of EU law is stretched in an unconvincing manner. Moreover, no other rationale is put in place which would allow these national measures to be distinguished from other national measures. This results in an arbitrariness whereby analogous situations have different EU fundamental rights protection, on the one hand, and where parties can engineer situations, on the other, so that that they can secure this protection.

The most celebrated example is *SPUC* v. *Grogan*. In 1986, the Irish Supreme Court ruled that it was against the Irish Constitution to help Irish women to have abortions by informing them about abortion clinics abroad. A number of Irish student unions continued to provide information about these for free. The Society for the Protection of the Unborn Child (SPUC) sought an undertaking that the student unions cease. The students invoked EU law arguing their right to freedom of expression had been violated. SPUC countered, arguing that the measure fell outside the field of EU law; in particular it did not constitute a restriction on the freedom to provide services so as to fall within Article 56 TFEU.

---

[124] *'Spika' UAB*, C-540/16, EU:C:2018:565.   [125] *AGET Iraklis* v. *Ypourgos Ergasias*, C-201/15, EU:C:2016:972.
[126] M. Dougan, 'Judicial Review of Member State Action under the General Principles and the Charter: Defining the "Scope of Union Law"' (2015) 52 *CMLRev* 1201, 1229–34.

Society for the Protection of the Unborn Child (SPUC) v. Grogan, C–159/90, EU:C:1991:378

24 As regards, first, the provisions of [Article 56 TFEU], which prohibit any restriction on the freedom to supply services, it is apparent from the facts of the case that the link between the activity of the students associations of which Mr Grogan and the other defendants are officers and medical terminations of pregnancies carried out in clinics in another Member State is too tenuous for the prohibition on the distribution of information to be capable of being regarded as a restriction within the meaning of [Article 56 TFEU] . . .

26 The information to which the national court's questions refer is not distributed on behalf of an economic operator established in another Member State. On the contrary, the information constitutes a manifestation of freedom of expression and of the freedom to impart and receive information which is independent of the economic activity carried on by clinics established in another Member State.

27 It follows that, in any event, a prohibition on the distribution of information in circumstances such as those which are the subject of the main proceedings cannot be regarded as a restriction within the meaning of [Article 56 TFEU].

The irony of *Grogan* was, therefore, that if it looked like SPUC had won the battle, Grogan had won the war. Whilst the students clearly lost the case in hand, all they needed to do to be protected by EU fundamental rights was to advertise, for a nominal fee, on behalf of the British abortion clinics.[127]

7 BREXIT AND EU FUNDAMENTAL RIGHTS

The use of EU fundamental rights to review national measures has long been controversial in the United Kingdom. Prior to signing the Treaty of Lisbon, the Prime Minister at the time, Tony Blair, stated that he would 'not accept a treaty that allows the Charter of Fundamental Rights to change UK law in any way'.[128] The government argued that it had secured this as it believed that the EUCFR did no more than codify pre-existing fundamental rights and, as mentioned above, they had secured a Protocol which stated that the EUCFR did not 'extend' the ability of the Court of Justice to declare any UK practice or law invalid.[129] However, such a view did not give much weight to the fact that the Court of Justice would necessarily interpret EU fundamental rights in an autonomous fashion, so that the law moved on, and it would never characterise even the most activist judgment as judicial lawmaking but simply as an exercise of its existing powers to interpret EU law.[130]

Notwithstanding this, the approach of the United Kingdom to EU fundamental rights since the referendum on Brexit has been more subdued. It has committed itself to applying EU

---

[127] Ireland managed to avoid this scenario by ring-fencing the relevant constitution from EU law at Maastricht, which was fortuitously being negotiated at that time, Protocol on Article 40.3.3 of the Irish Constitution.

[128] 'Blair's EU Safeguards "May Not Be Watertight"', *Daily Telegraph*, 26 June 2007.

[129] Protocol on the Application of the Charter to Poland and the United Kingdom, Article 1(1).

[130] On this position see Lord Goldsmith, 'A Charter of Rights, Freedoms and Principles' (2001) 38 *CMLRev* 1201. This was insufficient for the Conservatives who demanded a complete opt-out from the Charter, 'Cameron Speech on EU', 4 November 2009, http://news.bbc.co.uk/2/hi/8343145.stm. For a good description of this debate see House of Commons European Scrutiny Committee, *The Application of the EU Charter of Fundamental Rights in the UK: A State of Confusion*, 43rd Report, Session 2013–14, HC 979, 13–21.

fundamental rights during the transition period following Brexit going up to 31 December 2020.[131] The only exception to this is that UK citizens will lose their right to vote for MEPs and stand for the European Parliament, and EU citizens living in the United Kingdom will not be able to vote for or stand for election as British MEPs.[132]

After that period, EU fundamental rights will cease to have an independent existence in UK law. Given the prior political commotion surrounding the EUCFR, it is perhaps a little surprising that the UK Government thinks that this will not have much effect.

> ### *Legislating for the United Kingdom's Withdrawal from the European Union*, Cm. 9446 (Department for Exiting the European Union, 2017)
>
> 223 ... It cannot be right that the Charter could be used to bring challenges against the Government, or for UK legislation after our withdrawal to be struck down on the basis of the Charter. On that basis the Charter will not be converted into UK law by the Great Repeal Bill.
>
> 224 However, the Charter was not designed to create any new rights or alter the circumstances in which individuals could rely on fundamental rights to challenge the actions of the EU institutions or member states in relation to EU law. Instead the Charter was intended to make the rights that already existed in EU law more visible by bringing them together in a single document.
>
> 225 The Government's intention is that the removal of the Charter from UK law will not affect the substantive rights that individuals already benefit from in the UK. Many of these underlying rights exist elsewhere in the body of EU law which we will be converting into UK law.

This is put into effect by the European Union (Withdrawal) Act 2018. Section 5(4) sets out the legal status of the EUCFR.

> ### Section 5 European Union (Withdrawal) Act 2018
>
> (4) The Charter of Fundamental Rights is not part of domestic law on or after exit day.
>
> (5) Subsection (4) does not affect the retention in domestic law on or after exit day in accordance with this Act of any fundamental rights or principles which exist irrespective of the Charter (and references to the Charter in any case law are, so far as necessary for this purpose, to be read as if they were references to any corresponding retained fundamental rights or principles).

The legal status of general principles of law is addressed later in the Act.

> ### Schedule I, para. 3.1
>
> There is no right of action in domestic law on or after exit day based on a failure to comply with any of the general principles of EU law.

As a result, individuals will not be able to invoke the EUCFR or general principles of EU law as an independent basis for review of UK legislation or administration. They are still likely to be

---

[131] Article 127(1) Withdrawal Agreement.   [132] Article 127(1)(b) Draft Withdrawal Agreement.

influential, however. Eighteen EUCFR rights overlap with ECHR rights,[133] and the latter can be invoked before British courts. Moreover, the ECtHR has regularly referenced the EUCFR.[134] Furthermore, as we have seen,[135] UK courts may still have regard to decisions of the Court of Justice, even when these do not bind them.[136] There will also be pressure on UK courts to follow the latter's judgments. If they adopt a more illiberal interpretation than the Court of Justice, it will be positioning the United Kingdom as one of the most illiberal States in Europe, certainly more illiberal than the twenty-seven EU Member States. And this is not a good look.

The bigger challenge is likely to be where the EUCFR provides for rights that are more extensive than those in the ECHR. In such circumstances, there is likely to be less protection after the end of the transition period.[137] One example is *Benkharbouche*, which concerned two cleaners who were prevented from suing the Libyan and Sudanese Embassies in the United Kingdom for the minimum wage on the ground that the latter were protected by State immunity. The British courts, including the Supreme Court, held that the plaintiff's human rights were violated: both Article 6 ECHR (the right to a fair and public hearing of one's civil rights and obligations) and Article 47 EUCFR (the right to an effective remedy before a tribunal). However, the Supreme Court unanimously noted that the rights were identical, implying, therefore, that Article 47 EUCFR may offer certain protections not offered by Article 6 ECHR (and possibly vice versa).[138]

We have also seen that EU fundamental rights are used, more frequently, to inform interpretation of EU legislation. This legislation shall continue to have effect as 'retained EU law' until either amended or repealed.[139] All courts, other than the United Kingdom Supreme Court and the Scottish High Court of the Justiciary, are, furthermore, to interpret it 'in accordance with any retained case law and any retained general principles of EU law'.[140] In other words, all case law of the Court of Justice on fundamental rights adopted prior to Brexit will continue to have legal effect within the United Kingdom insofar as it shapes the meaning of other EU law.

If the central contribution of EU fundamental rights lies in how it shapes EU legislation, then the consequences of Brexit for fundamental rights may not be that great. Most EU fundamental rights will continue to be applied within the United Kingdom. On such a scenario, the central danger is not some bonfire of rights but drift.[141] This might involve, on the one hand, United Kingdom courts lazily applying dated Court of Justice judgments without reflection on whether thinking on fundamental rights has moved on. It might involve, on the other, gradual

---

[133] Department for Exiting the European Union, *Charter of Fundamental Rights of the EU Right by Right Analysis*, 5 December 2017, 4–5, https://assets.publishing.service.gov.uk/government/uploads/system/uploads/attachment_data/file/664891/05122017_Charter_Analysis_FINAL_VERSION.pdf.

[134] B. Dickson, 'The EU Charter of Fundamental Rights in the Case Law of the European Court of Human Rights' (2015) *European Human Rights L Rev* 27.

[135] See p. 200.   [136] European Union (Withdrawal) Act 2018, s. 6(2).

[137] A central concern is data protection where the EUCFR grants specific rights, notably the right to protection of personal data, Article 8 EUCFR. UK, Joint Committee on Human Rights, *The Human Rights Implications of Brexit*, 5th Report, Session 2016–17, HL Paper 88/HC 695, paras. 67–71.

[138] *Benkharbouche* v. *Secretary of State for Foreign and Commonwealth Affairs; Secretary of State for Foreign and Commonwealth Affairs and Libya* v. *Janah* [2017] UKSC 62, para. 78.

[139] The definition of retained EU law is European Union (Withdrawal) Act 2018, s. 6(7). Provision for its continuation is set out in ss. 2–5 of the Act. For more detail see pp. 244–5.

[140] European Union (Withdrawal) Act 2018, s. 6(3)(a). The Supreme Court and High Court of Justiciary must use the same test for departing from this case law as they do for departing from their own case law, s. 6(4)(5). See p. 199.

[141] T. Lock, 'Human Rights Law in the UK after Brexit' (2017) *PL* (Brexit Special Issue) 117.

amendment or repeal of this retained EU law with subsequent laws not being subject to the guarantees of EU fundamental rights. Whether this will happen is, of course, a matter of speculation.

8 EU FUNDAMENTAL RIGHTS AND DOMESTIC AUTHORITARIANISM

The European Union has a long history of dealing with authoritarian governments in its neighbourhood. In the 1990s, the Mečiar government in Slovakia, the Tudjman government in Croatia and the Milosevic government in Serbia all had difficulties in their relationship with the European Union because of the Union's concern about the quality (or lack thereof) of constitutional democracy in those States. In the 2000s, concerns have been raised about FYROM, Turkey and Ukraine, in particular. However, it believed, somewhat smugly, that there were no analogous issues concerning EU Member States. The presence of Article 7 TEU reinforced this sense that illiberal government was an issue that lay beyond the borders of the Union for, as was discussed at the beginning of this chapter, it offered the possibility of open-ended sanctions against any State which either violates fundamental rights or undermines the rule of law or democracy in a serious and persistent manner.[142] However, we also saw that the constraints on the Article 7 TEU make it unlikely that it will ever be used.

This question ceased to be a hypothetical one with the election of the Orbán government in Hungary in 2010. It passed a series of laws that were seen by its critics as weakening the independence of its constitutional court, central bank, media regulator and the data protection authority. Alongside this, was the concern regarding increasingly ineffective policing of hate-crimes in Hungary and new laws that made it harder for many religious organisations to be recognised.[143] Problems also occurred in 2012 in Romania, where the government illegally tried to impeach the President, who was from the main opposition party.[144] The difficulties facing any response was not simply the limits of Article 7 TEU but the unpredictable consequences of sanctions.

U. Sedelmeier, 'Political Safeguards against Democratic Backsliding in the EU: The Limits of Material Sanctions and the Scope of Social Pressure' (2017) 24 *Journal of European Public Policy* 337, 341–2

Although the EU has never used sanctions internally, there is a body of literature that can provide clues about the conditions under which material sanctions are effective. Studies of EU conditionality towards candidate countries suggest that the EU's material incentives – the prospect of EU membership, and conversely, the threat of withholding membership and its associated benefits – can be highly effective in

---

[142] See pp. 253–4. The literature on EU law responses to authoritarian governments is voluminous: C. Closa and D. Kochenov (eds.), *Reinforcing Rule of Law Oversight in the European Union* (Cambridge University Press, 2016); M. Blauberger and D. Kelemen, 'Special Issue: Democratic Backsliding' (2017) 24(3) *JEPP*; L. Pech and K. Scheppele, 'Illiberalism Within: Rule of Law Backsliding in the EU' (2017) 19 *CYELS* 3.

[143] *European Parliament Report on the Situation of Fundamental Rights: Standards and Practices in Hungary* (2012/2130 (INI)) ('Tavares Report').

[144] A. v. Bogdandy and P. Sonneveld, *Constitutional Crisis in the European Constitutional Area: Theory, Law and Politics in Hungary and Romania* (London, Bloomsbury, 2015).

bringing about domestic changes. Yet this literature also suggests that material incentives are insufficient when used towards illiberal governments. In cases like Slovakia under Vladimír Mečiar or Croatia under Franjo Tuđman, EU incentives were unable to bring about democratic domestic changes. These governments precisely relied on illiberal practices in order to maintain power and renouncing such practices would have threatened to undermine their ability to retain office. Even when faced with the threat of remaining outside the EU, illiberal leaders chose to maintain undemocratic practices. EU conditionality might have helped to lock in democratic change in fragile democracies when voter dissatisfaction led to the defeat of illiberal parties in 'watershed elections'. But EU interventions did not determine the outcome of such elections. At best, the EU played an indirect role through providing a focal point for opposition parties to unite and to moderate their platforms ...

These findings of the literature on pre-accession conditionality imply that the capacity of material sanctions to reverse democratic backsliding is limited. If illiberal governments are prepared to forego the possibility of joining the EU, would the threat of expulsion from the EU or withholding EU funds (let alone weaker material sanctions) make them change the practices that keep them in power?

In 2014, frustrated by the limits of Article 7 TEU, the Commission adopted the *Framework to Strengthen the Rule of Law*.[145]

European Commission, 'A Framework to Strengthen the Rule of Law', COM(2014)158 final, 2, 7–8

The main purpose of the Framework is to address threats to the rule of law ... which are of a systemic nature. The political, institutional and/or legal order of a Member State as such, its constitutional structure, separation of powers, the independence or impartiality of the judiciary, or its system of judicial review including constitutional justice where it exists, must be threatened – for example as a result of the adoption of new measures or of widespread practices of public authorities and the lack of domestic redress. The Framework will be activated when national 'rule of law safeguards' do not seem capable of effectively addressing those threats.

The process is composed, as a rule, of three stages: a Commission assessment, a Commission recommendation and a follow-up to the recommendation.

The Commission's Assessment

The Commission will collect and examine all the relevant information and assess whether there are clear indications of a systemic threat to the rule of law as described above ... If, as a result of this preliminary assessment, the Commission is of the opinion that there is indeed a situation of systemic threat to the rule of law, it will initiate a dialogue with the Member State concerned, by sending a 'rule of law opinion' and substantiating its concerns, giving the Member State concerned the possibility to respond ... The Commission expects that the Member State concerned cooperates throughout the process and refrains from adopting any irreversible measure ...

---

[145] D. Kochenov and L. Pech, 'Monitoring and Enforcement of the Rule of Law in the EU: Rhetoric and Reality' (2015) 11 *EUConst* 512; E. Crabit and N. Bel, 'The EU Rule of Law Framework' in W. Schroeder (ed.), *Strengthening the Rule of Law in Europe: From a Common Concept to Mechanisms of Implementation* (London, Bloomsbury, 2016).

The Commission's Recommendation

In a second stage, unless the matter has already been satisfactorily resolved in the meantime, the Commission will issue a 'rule of law recommendation' addressed to the Member State concerned, if it finds that there is objective evidence of a systemic threat and that the authorities of that Member State are not taking appropriate action to redress it. In its recommendation the Commission will clearly indicate the reasons for its concerns and recommend that the Member State solves the problems identified within a fixed time limit and informs the Commission of the steps taken to that effect . . . The sending of its recommendation and its main content will be made public by the Commission.

Follow-Up to the Commission's Recommendation

In a third stage, the Commission will monitor the follow-up given by the Member State concerned to the recommendation addressed to it . . . If there is no satisfactory follow-up to the recommendation by the Member State concerned within the time limit set, the Commission will assess the possibility of activating one of the mechanisms set out in Article 7 TEU.

The *Framework* offers a more tiered response to government measures posing a significant threat to the rule of law and fundamental rights. Thus the Commission initially begins with confidential discussions with the national government in question. It then escalates the matter by 'naming and shaming' the State. And, if this does not work, it further escalates things by proposing that the State be subject to condemnation or sanction by all other EU States. Underpinning this approach was the response of the Romanian Government to Commission intervention in 2012, where informal discussions led to a series of reforms to secure the rule of law.[146]

There remain, however, a number of issues with the *Framework*.

First, there is a question of institutional overreach. The Commission believes that it has the power to adopt the *Framework* as it is simply setting out how it will exercise its discretion on whether to propose action under Article 7 TEU. Others see it as doing more than this: establishing a new policing mechanism over Member States for which it has no basis in the Treaty.[147]

Secondly, possibly because of these concerns about its authority, the Commission has used the *Framework* to raise the threshold for Union action. A systemic threat to the rule of law is not necessarily enough to amount to a clear risk of a serious breach of the values in Article 2 TEU – the threshold for the weakest action under Article 7 TEU. If it were, there would be no need for the Commission to enter discussions with the Member State. A systemic threat to the rule of law is, thus, merely something – and this includes phenomena such as the ending of separation of powers or judicial independence – which, in the words of the Commission, 'could develop' into such a risk.[148]

Thirdly, the procedure has been used by the Commission to prevaricate.[149] The *Framework* was used for the first time in relation to Polish reforms to the constitutional court which were seen by

---

[146] U. Sedelmeier, 'Political Safeguards against Democratic Backsliding in the EU: The Limits of Material Ssanctions and the Scope of Social Pressure' (2017) 24 *JEPP* 337, 343–6.

[147] On this debate see P. Oliver and J. Stefanelli, 'Strengthening the Rule of Law in the EU: The Council's Inaction' (2016) 54 *JCMS* 1075.

[148] European Commission, 'A Framework to Strengthen the Rule of Law', COM(2014)158 final 2, 6.

[149] D. Kochenov and L. Pech, 'Better Late than Never? On the European Commission's Rule of Law Framework and its First Activation' (2016) 54 *JCMS* 1062.

the Commission as weakening that court's independence and to a refusal by the Polish Government to publish judgments of that court, meaning that under Polish law these had no force. The Polish measures occurred in December 2015 and March 2016. However, it was only on 20 December 2017, two years after the first breach, that the Commission proposed action under Article 7 TEU.[150] It is really not clear what took it so long, and the effect of the *Framework* seems simply have been to allow the Commission to avoid hard decisions.

EU Institutions are beginning to look at other routes to put pressure on authoritarian governments.[151] In 2015, Jan-Werner Müller suggested that if an independent commission adopted a recommendation that a Member State was systematically undermining the rule of law and democracy, the Commission should deny EU funding to that State.[152] In May 2018, the Commission proposed a variation on this.

European Commission, 'Proposal for a Regulation on the Protection of the Union's Budget in Case of Generalised Deficiencies as Regards the Rule of Law in the Member States', COM(2018)324

Article 3

(1) Appropriate measures shall be taken where a generalised deficiency as regards the rule of law in a Member State affects or risks affecting the principles of sound financial management or the protection of the financial interests of the Union

(2) The following may, in particular, be considered generalised deficiencies as regards the rule of law,
  (a) endangering the independence of judiciary;
  (b) failing to prevent, correct and sanction arbitrary or unlawful decisions by public authorities, including by law enforcement authorities, withholding financial and human resources affecting their proper functioning or failing to ensure the absence of conflicts of interests;
  (c) limiting the availability and effectiveness of legal remedies, including through restrictive procedural rules, lack of implementation of judgments, or limiting the effective investigation, prosecution or sanctioning of breaches of law

Article 4

(3) The measures taken shall be proportionate to the nature, gravity and scope of the generalised deficiency as regards the rule of law. They shall, insofar as possible, target the Union actions affected or potentially affected by that deficiency.

If adopted, this Regulation would facilitate sanctions against authoritarian States as these would now be dependent solely on Commission judgment. However, therein lies the rub. The Commission would not have general powers to sanction a breakdown in the rule of the law but only to sanction breakdown where this affects Union financial interests, namely programmes involving Union money. The most significant consequences of a breakdown in the rule of law will often

---

[150] European Commission, 'Proposal for a Council Decision on the Determination of a Clear Risk of a Serious Breach by the Republic of Poland of the Rule of Law', COM(2017)835 final.

[151] Another proposal is that the Commission bring infringement proceedings before the Court of Justice for systemic violations of the Article 2 TEU values, K. Scheppele, 'Enforcing the Rule of Law through Systemic Infringement Proceedings' in C. Closa and D. Kochenov (eds.), *Reinforcing Rule of Law Oversight in the European Union* (Cambridge University Press, 2016).

[152] J.-W. Müller, 'Should the EU Protect Democracy and the Rule of Law inside Member States?' (2015) 21 *ELJ* 141.

not involve these, and it appears as if the Commission is illicitly using the grant of an audit function – namely checking whether the money is well spent – to try to bring about wider constitutional change. There is also something very concerning about an unelected executive body such as the Commission having such sweeping powers to police the rule of law. It thus raises real questions over how it will exercise (or not exercise) such powers.

FURTHER READING

D. Chalmers and S. Trotter, 'Fundamental Rights and Legal Wrongs: The Two Sides of the Same EU Coin' (2016) 22 *European Law Journal* 9.

M. Dawson, *The Governance of EU Fundamental Rights* (Cambridge University Press, 2017).

M. Dougan, 'Judicial Review of Member State Action under the General Principles and the Charter: Defining the "Scope of Union Law"' (2015) 52 *Common Market Law Review* 1201.

F. Fabbrini, *Fundamental Rights in Europe: Challenges and Transformations in Comparative Perspective* (Oxford University Press, 2014).

S. Greer and A. Williams, 'Human Rights in the Council of Europe and the EU: Towards "Individual", "Constitutional" or "Institutional" Justice?' (2009) 15 *European Law Journal* 462.

A. Jakab and D. Kochenov (eds.), *The Enforcement of EU Law and Values: Ensuring Member States' Compliance* (Oxford University Press, 2017).

S. Peers *et al.* (eds.), *The EU Charter of Fundamental Rights: A Commentary* (Oxford-Portland, Hart, 2014).

R. Schütze, 'Three "Bills of Rights" for the European Union' (2011) 30 *Yearbook of European Law* 1.

A. Torres Pérez, *Conflicts of Rights in the European Union: A Theory of Supranational Adjudication* (Oxford University Press, 2009).

S. Vogelaar and S. Weatherill (eds.), *General Principles of Law: European and Comparative Perspectives* (London, Hart, 2017).

7

Rights and Remedies in Domestic Courts

1 INTRODUCTION

This chapter considers the rights and remedies that EU law provides for in national courts. It is organised as follows.

Section 2 looks at the emergence of direct effect. Initially confined to a narrow range of provisions, direct effect allows any EU Treaty provision to be invoked in a domestic court if it is sufficiently precise and unconditional. Provisions can be invoked against both the State (vertical direct effect) and against private parties (horizontal direct effect).

Section 3 considers the remedies and procedures available where an EU provision is invoked in a domestic court. The law is increasingly oriented around a right to effective judicial protection, recognised in both Article 19 TEU and Article 47 of the European Union Charter for Fundamental Rights and Freedoms (EUCFR). This right grants parties the right to challenge the legality of any act which affects EU law rights before a court and for due process to be observed. However, it is for domestic law to designate remedies and procedures provided that these are no less favourable than those for similar domestic claims and do not make it practically impossible or excessively difficult to exercise EU rights. EU law will step in, however, if it is apparent that no domestic legal remedy exists to protect the individual's rights. In this regard, EU law has intervened in four circumstances, independently of the national legal position. There is a right to restitution for illegally levied taxes; a right to interim relief pending a preliminary reference to the Court of Justice; a right to claim damages or force repayment of illegal subsidies in the field of EU competition law; and, finally, a right to sue the State for damages where the State commits a serious breach of EU law that leads to loss for the individual.

Section 4 looks at the direct effect of EU secondary laws. Vertical and horizontal direct effect is granted to Treaty provisions, Regulations and international agreements. Directives and decisions are only capable of vertical direct effect. The reason is that Directives are only addressed to the State who is thereby estopped by its illegal failure to comply with them from arguing that the Directive should not be invoked against it. This is not true for private parties, and therefore obligations cannot be placed directly on them. Additionally, during the transposition period, national courts are required to disapply any measure which is liable to seriously compromise the realisation of a Directive's objectives. Incidental direct effect can occur where the individual invokes a directly effective provision of a Directive against the State and this imposes burdens on private parties. More controversially, it may also occur where a Directive grants a private actor the right for certain activities to be protected from State interference. This, in turn, may allow that actor to use the Directive to protect it from other private actors who invoke national laws to prevent or impede those activities.

Section 5 considers indirect effect. This requires national courts to interpret all national law, insofar as this is possible, in light of all EU law. The extent of this duty is considerable as it requires national courts to give effect to EU law if this is, in any way, interpretively possible. It does not require, however, *contra legem* interpretations and is not to be used to aggravate possible criminal liabilities.

Section 6 examines State liability. This requires States to compensate individuals where a serious breach of EU law by the State caused loss for the individual and the EU law in question was intended to create rights for the individual. There are four circumstances where the breach of EU law is considered sufficiently serious to generate liability: a failure to transpose a Directive; breach of a clear provision of EU law; a failure to comply with settled case law; and failure to comply with an order of the Court of Justice. State liability also covers illegal conduct by domestic courts against whose decisions there is no judicial remedy but only where the decision manifestly disregards EU law.

Section 7 considers the duty on domestic courts to disapply domestic law where it conflicts with an EU law which gives expression to an EU fundamental right. This duty has been used to allow Directives to govern relations between private parties in instances where a Directive gives effect to a fundamental right. The Directive must give specific expression to that right, however, by detailing how that right applies in EU law. The remit of this principle is uncertain as, to date, it has only been used in respect of cases governed by the Framework Directive, Directive 2000/78, which prohibits discrimination in the field of employment on grounds of age, religious belief, sexual orientation or disability.

Section 8 examines when EU law provisions may be invoked in UK courts after Brexit. Formally, the doctrines of direct effect and indirect effect will not apply as EU law, qua EU law, will cease to apply in the United Kingdom. Retained EU law will be invoked in UK courts, however, if it was previously directly effective. As far as possible, UK courts are also to interpret UK law adopted prior to Brexit in a manner that complies with retained EU law. The doctrine of State liability will no longer apply. It is uncertain whether there will be a duty to disapply UK law where it conflicts with a retained EU law which gives effect to an EU fundamental right. The case law of the Court of Justice is ambiguous on the source of this obligation. If UK courts see it as stemming from the retained EU law, they will disapply the other UK law. Otherwise, they will not do so as the Act prohibits them from disapplying a UK measure on the grounds that it conflicts with an EU fundamental right.

2 DIRECT EFFECT AND THE DEVELOPMENT OF INDIVIDUAL RIGHTS

(i) *Van Gend En Loos* and the Early Hesitant Conceptions of an EU Right

We already considered *Van Gend en Loos* in Chapters 1 and 5. There are two central elements to that judgment.

The first concerns claims made about the quality of EU law, namely that EU law was a new legal order with its own powerful authority. These were addressed in Chapter 5. The second is the establishment of a system of individual rights through the doctrine of direct effect. It calls for us to rethink EU law in terms of the benefits it grants individuals. Less attention is paid to systemic questions such the relationship between EU law and national law and more focus is placed on whether the individual is being allowed to enjoy the right, what the right entails and whether its exercise is adequately protected. If these elements have different dynamics, in *Van Gend en Loos*, these dynamics nevertheless inform one another. If the justification for the establishment of these rights is the presence of a new legal order, the vehicle for the expression of this order is the development of a system of judicially protected rights.

The facts of *Van Gend en Loos* were discussed earlier.[1] The central bone of contention was whether the Treaty provision, now Article 28 TFEU, prohibiting the imposition of customs duties or charges having equivalent effect on imports from other Member States, could be invoked as a matter of EU law in the Dutch court where it had been asserted.

Van Gend en Loos v. *Nederlandse Administratie der Belastingen*, 26/62, EU:C:1963:1

The first question . . . is whether Article [28 TFEU] has direct application in national law in the sense that nationals of member states may on the basis of this article lay claim to rights which the national court must protect.

---

[1] See pp. 15–16.

To ascertain whether the provisions of an international treaty extend so far in their effects it is necessary to consider the spirit, the general scheme and the wording of those provisions . . .

. . . The Community constitutes a new legal order of international law for the benefit of which the States have limited their sovereign rights, albeit within limited fields, and the subjects of which comprise not only Member States but also their nationals. Independently of the legislation of Member States, Community law therefore not only imposes obligations on individuals but is also intended to confer upon them rights which become part of their legal heritage. These rights arise not only where they are expressly granted by the Treaty, but also by reason of obligations which the Treaty imposes in a clearly defined way upon individuals as well as upon the Member States and the Institutions of the Community.

With regard to the general scheme of the Treaty as it relates to customs duties and charges having equivalent effect it must be emphasized that . . . [basing] the Community upon a customs union, includes as an essential provision the prohibition of these customs duties and charges. This provision is found at the beginning of the part of the Treaty which defines the 'foundations of the Community'. It is applied and explained by Article [28 TFEU].

The wording of Article [28 TFEU] contains a clear and unconditional prohibition which is not a positive but a negative obligation. This obligation, moreover, is not qualified by any reservation on the part of states which would make its implementation conditional upon a positive legislative measure enacted under national law. The very nature of this prohibition makes it ideally adapted to produce direct effects in the legal relationship between member states and their subjects.

The implementation of Article [28 TFEU] does not require any legislative intervention on the part of the states. The fact that under this article it is the member states who are made the subject of the negative obligation does not imply that their nationals cannot benefit from this obligation.

It follows from the foregoing considerations that according to the spirit, the general scheme and the wording of the Treaty, Article [28 TFEU] must be interpreted as producing direct effects and creating individual rights which national courts must protect.

If ground-breaking in its development of the EU legal order, the judgment is narrow in terms of its elaboration of an EU system of rights.

First, only provisions meeting certain criteria – namely that they are clear, unconditional, negatively phrased and require no legislative intervention – can be invoked. Moreover, the judgment only indicated with certainty that one provision met this: the arcane Article 28 TFEU prohibiting customs duties and charges having equivalent effect.

Secondly, the judgment is narrow in its understanding of a right.[2] It is vague about the extent and nature of the obligations owed to the right-holder by others. At its narrowest EU law may only grant certain rights vis-à-vis the State: a requirement that the latter not violate certain interests. Such rights are little more than immunity from national law in which the holder can do things that others cannot (e.g. withhold taxes). A broader conception allows the holder to call on all parties to respect, protect and make good the interests that lie at the heart of the right. Such a right can be asserted against anybody and calls for full redress of the interests infringed. The wording of *Van Gend en Loos* suggests that it was concerned with the narrower type of protection.[3] The stipulation that provisions be negatively phrased meant that national administrations can only be called upon

---

[2] For a useful discussion see T. Downes and C. Hilsom, 'Making Sense of Rights: Community Rights in E.C. Law' (1999) 24 *ELRev* 121.

[3] On this early period see T. Eilmansberger, 'The Relationship between Rights and Remedies in EC Law: In Search of the Missing Link' (2004) 41 *CMLRev* 1199, 1202–6.

to refrain from doing things but not be called upon to take positive action to protect individuals. Equally, the proviso that provisions be unconditional suggested that courts could not be called upon to weigh individual entitlements against other public interests recognised by EU law.

(ii) Relaxing the Criteria: Towards a Test of Justiciability

In the 1960s the Court applied the doctrine of direct effect only to a limited number of provisions.[4] This was largely because most Treaty provisions only entered fully into force with the end of the transitional period in 1970. In the 1970s the Court relaxed the criteria for when a Treaty provision may be directly effective.[5] The issue came up most acutely in *Defrenne (No. 2)*. Under Belgian law female air stewards were required to retire at the age of 40, unlike their male counterparts. Defrenne, forced to retire on this ground, brought an action claiming that the lower pension payments generated by this breached Article 157(1) TFEU. This required that 'each Member State shall ensure and maintain the principle that men and women should receive equal pay for work of equal value'. It was argued that the provision was not directly effective because it set out only general principles and was programmatic in nature, requiring further measures for its implementation.

Defrenne v. *Sabena (No. 2)*, 43/75, EU:C:1976:56

18 . . . a distinction must be drawn within the whole area of application of Article [157 TFEU] between, first, direct and overt discrimination which may be identified solely with the aid of the criteria based on equal work and equal pay referred to by the Article in question and, secondly, indirect and disguised discrimination which can only be identified by reference to more explicit implementing provisions of a Community or national character.

19 It is impossible not to recognise that the complete implementation of the aim pursued by Article [157 TFEU], by means of the elimination of all discrimination, direct or indirect, between men and women workers, not only as regards individual undertakings but also entire branches of industry and even of the economic system as a whole, may in certain cases involve the elaboration of criteria whose implementation necessitates the taking of appropriate measures at Community and national level . . .

21 Among the forms of direct discrimination which may be identified solely by reference to the criteria laid down by Article [157 TFEU] must be included in particular those which have their origin in legislative provisions or in collective labour agreements and which may be detected on the basis of a purely legal analysis of the situation.

22 This applies even more in cases where men and women receive unequal pay for equal work carried out in the same establishment or service, whether public or private.

23 As is shown by the very findings of the judgment making the reference, in such a situation the court is in a position to establish all the facts which enable it to decide whether a woman worker is receiving lower pay than a male worker performing the same tasks.

24 In such situation, at least, Article [157 TFEU] is directly [effective] and may thus give rise to individual rights which the courts must protect.

---

[4] *Lütticke* v. *HZA Sarrelouis*, 57/65, EU: C:1966:34; *Firma Fink-Frucht GmbH* v. *Hauptzollamt München-Landsbergerstrasse*, C-27/67, EU:C:1968:22; *Salgoil* v. *Italian Foreign Trade Ministry*, 13/68, EU:C:1968:54.

[5] On the early developments see A. Dashwood, 'The Principle of Direct Effect in European Community Law' (1978) 16 *JCMS* 229; P. Craig, 'Once Upon a Time in the West: Direct Effect and the Federalization of EEC Law' (1992) 12 *OJLS* 453, 460–70.

The Court gave the provision a double meaning to enable a finding of direct effect. On the one hand, the provision had a programmatic, wide-ranging purpose, namely to secure equality between men and women within the economic system as a whole. On the other hand, a particular form of discrimination – overt pay discrimination between men and women in individual workplaces – was hived off from the other activities covered by the provision. This was considered sufficiently concrete and precise to be invoked in national courts. This relaxed the requirement for legal clarity as, whilst the Court did not find the provision as a whole clear, it was able to identify a prohibition in relation to some of the activities covered by it which was sufficiently clear for the provision to be invoked in a court.

Since *Defrenne (No. 2)*, the criteria set out in *Van Gend en Loos* are not deployed. Instead, the test is whether the content of a provision is sufficiently precise and unconditional.[6] The Court will not look at whether the provision is qualified by other provisions or constraints, but simply at whether the provision is 'unequivocal'.[7] This suggests that a provision must set out some entitlements which are clearly for the benefit of individuals and impose direct duties on national administrations to protect these entitlements. That these administrations may have some discretion about how to protect the entitlements is not important.

(iii) The Emergence of Horizontal Direct Effect

Defrenne (No. 2) is important for a second reason. It was the first case to address the institutional implications of holding a positively phrased obligation to be directly effective.[8] The Belgian Government argued that it could not be held liable because the discrimination was perpetrated by Sabena, a commercial operator. Furthermore, it argued that Sabena could not be liable for obligations under Article 157 TFEU as the latter explicitly addressed these to the Member States, and only the administration was bound.

Defrenne v. Sabena (No. 2), 43/75, EU:C:1976:56

31 . . . as the Court has already found in other contexts, the fact that certain provisions of the Treaty are formally addressed to the Member States does not prevent rights from being conferred at the same time on any individual who has an interest in the performance of the duties thus laid down.

32 The very wording of Article [157 TFEU] shows that it imposes on States a duty to bring about a specific result to be mandatorily achieved within a fixed period.

33 The effectiveness of this provision cannot be affected by the fact that the duty imposed by the Treaty has not been discharged by certain Member States and that the joint institutions have not reacted sufficiently energetically against this failure to act.

34 To accept the contrary view would be to risk raising the violation of the right to the status of a principle of interpretation, a position the adoption of which would not be consistent with the task assigned to the Court by Article [19(1) TEU].

---

[6] More recently, *Lombard Ingatlan Lízing v. Nemzeti Adó- és Vámhivatal Fellebbviteli Igazgatóság*, C-404/16, EU:C:2017:759; *Cristal Union v. Ministre de l'Économie et des Finances*, C-31/17, EU:C:2018:168.

[7] *Belgische Staat v. Cobelfret*, C-138/07, EU:C:2009:82.

[8] This had been done earlier in *Reyners v. Belgium*, 2/74, EU:C:1974:68.

35 Finally, in its reference to 'Member States', Article [157 TFEU] is alluding to those States in the exercise of all those of their functions which may usefully contribute to the implementation of the principle of equal pay.

36 Thus, contrary to the statements made in the course of the proceedings this provision is far from merely referring the matter to the powers of the national legislative authorities.

37 Therefore, the reference to 'Member States' in Article [157 TFEU] cannot be interpreted as excluding the intervention of the courts in direct application of the Treaty.

38 Furthermore it is not possible to sustain any objection that the application by national courts of the principle of equal pay would amount to modifying independent agreements concluded privately or in the sphere of industrial relations such as individual contracts and collective labour agreements.

39 In fact, since Article [157 TFEU] is mandatory in nature, the prohibition on discrimination between men and women applies not only to the action of public authorities, but also extends to all agreements which are intended to regulate paid labour collectively, as well as to contracts between individuals.

Direct effect is not therefore just about protecting individuals from States violating their duties. It also imposes duties upon the State to secure the protection of these individual rights. In this regard, *Defrenne (No. 2)* makes two particularly important findings. First, it reminds national courts that that they are part of the State and that this duty to protect falls particularly strongly on them. Secondly, as a consequence of this institutional duty, Treaty provisions can be invoked against private parties, who, correspondingly, have a duty to respect EU law. It therefore established two forms of direct effect which have been referred to in the academic literature in the following manner:

– **Vertical direct effect:** a party invokes a provision of EU law in a national court against a Member State.
– **Horizontal direct effect:** a party invokes a provision of EU law in a national court against a private party. A corollary of this right is that private parties have responsibilities in EU law for which they can be held liable in national courts if they fail to discharge them.

In terms of developing individual EU rights, this judgment can be viewed very positively. In a market economy, most violations of legal actors' rights are committed not by the State but by other private parties. Discrimination on grounds of gender is a case in point. It is an egregious and long-standing problem in workplaces, and the majority of discrimination cases take place in the private sector. At the beginning of this chapter, however, we noted that the story of direct effect was not just about rights but also about the reorganisation of legal power. Private litigation allows EU law to be deployed in a much wider array of disputes, and, in turn, this provides more opportunities for private parties to challenge national law as they can now do this not only by formally seeking judicial review but by saying it does not govern the legal dispute between them and another private party.

This was all too much for the British and Irish Governments. They argued, shamefully, that to allow the principle of equal pay for men and women for work of equal value to be invoked in national courts would lead to an unmanageable disruption of economic life. The Irish Government argued that the costs of compliance would exceed Irish receipts from the European Regional Development Fund for the period 1975–7 and the British Government argued that it would add 3.5 per cent to labour costs – a considerable admission!

Defrenne v. *Sabena (No. 2)*, 43/75, EU:C:1976:56

69 The Governments of Ireland and the United Kingdom have drawn the Court's attention to the possible economic consequences of attributing direct effect to the provisions of Article [157 TFEU], on the ground that such a decision might, in many branches of economic life, result in the introduction of claims dating back to the time at which such effect same into existence.

70 In view of the large number of people concerned such claims, which undertakings could not have foreseen, might seriously affect the financial situation of such undertakings and even drive some of them to bankruptcy.

71 Although the practical consequences of any judicial decision must be carefully taken into account, it would be impossible to go so far as to diminish the objectivity of the law and compromise its future application on the ground of the possible repercussions which might result, as regards the past, from such a judicial decision.

72 However, in the light of the conduct of several of the Member States . . . it is appropriate to take exceptionally into account the fact that, over a prolonged period, the parties concerned have been led to continue with practices which were contrary to Article [157 TFEU], although not yet prohibited under their national law . . .

74 In these circumstances, it is appropriate to determine that, as the general level at which pay would have been fixed cannot be known, important considerations of legal certainty affecting all the interests involved, both public and private, make it impossible in principle to reopen the question as regards the past.

75 Therefore, the direct effect of Article [157 TFEU] cannot be relied on in order to support claims concerning pay periods prior to the date of this judgment, except as regards those workers who have already brought legal proceedings or made an equivalent claim.

To manage the consequences of departing so far from Member State expectations, the Court therefore had to grant Article 157 TFEU two meanings. For discrimination occurring prior to the date of the judgment, the provision is interpreted as not being directly effective. The opposite is true for discrimination which occurs after the date of the judgment. As Rasmussen has observed, these two interpretations destroy the illusion that the Court is merely giving effect to the text. It is impossible 'to maintain this myth while ruling that Article [157] was deprived of direct effects until the day of pronouncement of the Court's decision; only to produce such effects from that day onwards'.[9]

3 REMEDIES AND PROCEDURES IN DOMESTIC COURTS

(i) The Right to Effective Judicial Protection

Although direct effect mentions only the right to invoke a provision in a national court, this would be less meaningful if remedies did not follow from its successful invocation. Whilst the EU law on remedies and procedures was developed for many years through the case law of the Court of Justice, more recently it has been reoriented around two provisions which set out this link. The first is Article 19(1) TEU.

---

[9] H. Rasmussen, *On Law and Policy in the European Court of Justice* (Dordrecht, Martinus Nijhoff, 1986) 441.

Article 19 TEU

(1) Member States shall provide remedies sufficient to ensure effective legal protection in the fields covered by Union law.

This must be seen alongside Article 47 EUCFR.

Article 47 EUCFR

Everyone whose rights and freedoms guaranteed by the law of the Union are violated has the right to an effective remedy before a tribunal in compliance with the conditions laid down in this Article.

Everyone is entitled to a fair and public hearing within a reasonable time by an independent and impartial tribunal previously established by law. Everyone shall have the possibility of being advised, defended and represented.

Legal aid shall be made available to those who lack sufficient resources in so far as such aid is necessary to ensure effective access to justice.

The architecture established by these provisions was set out most clearly in *Associação Sindical dos Juízes Portugueses*. In this case, the Portuguese trade union for judges challenged salary cuts for judges, introduced by the Portuguese legislature as part of a package of austerity measures, on the grounds that it violated Article 19(1) TEU as it threatened judicial independence. The Court found that it did not, but elaborated on the consequences of Article 19(1) TEU.

Associação Sindical dos Juízes Portugueses v. *Tribunal de Contas*, C-64/16, EU:C:2018:117

31 The European Union is a union based on the rule of law in which individual parties have the right to challenge before the courts the legality of any decision or other national measure relating to the application to them of an EU act . . .

32 Article 19 TEU, which gives concrete expression to the value of the rule of law stated in Article 2 TEU, entrusts the responsibility for ensuring judicial review in the EU legal order not only to the Court of Justice but also to national courts and tribunals . . .

33 Consequently, national courts and tribunals, in collaboration with the Court of Justice, fulfil a duty entrusted to them jointly of ensuring that in the interpretation and application of the Treaties the law is observed . . .

34 The Member States are therefore obliged, by reason, *inter alia*, of the principle of sincere cooperation, set out in the first subparagraph of Article 4(3) TEU, to ensure, in their respective territories, the application of and respect for EU law . . . In that regard, as provided for by the second subparagraph of Article 19(1) TEU, Member States are to provide remedies sufficient to ensure effective judicial protection for individual parties in the fields covered by EU law. It is, therefore, for the Member States to establish a system of legal remedies and procedures ensuring effective judicial review in those fields . . .

35 The principle of the effective judicial protection of individuals' rights under EU law, referred to in the second subparagraph of Article 19(1) TEU, is a general principle of EU law stemming from the constitutional traditions common to the Member States, which has been enshrined in Articles 6 and 13 ECHR, and which is now reaffirmed by Article 47 of the Charter . . .

36   The very existence of effective judicial review designed to ensure compliance with EU law is of the essence of the rule of law . . .

37   It follows that every Member State must ensure that the bodies which, as 'courts or tribunals' within the meaning of EU law, come within its judicial system in the fields covered by that law, meet the requirements of effective judicial protection . . .

41   In order for that protection to be ensured, maintaining such a court or tribunal's independence is essential, as confirmed by the second subparagraph of Article 47 of the Charter, which refers to the access to an 'independent' tribunal as one of the requirements linked to the fundamental right to an effective remedy.

42   The guarantee of independence, which is inherent in the task of adjudication . . . is required not only at EU level as regards the Judges of the Union and the Advocates-General of the Court of Justice, as provided for in the third subparagraph of Article 19(2) TEU, but also at the level of the Member States as regards national courts.

43   The independence of national courts and tribunals is, in particular, essential to the proper working of the judicial cooperation system embodied by the preliminary ruling mechanism under Article 267 TFEU, in that . . . that mechanism may be activated only by a body responsible for applying EU law which satisfies, *inter alia*, that criterion of independence.

44   The concept of independence presupposes, in particular, that the body concerned exercises its judicial functions wholly autonomously, without being subject to any hierarchical constraint or subordinated to any other body and without taking orders or instructions from any source whatsoever, and that it is thus protected against external interventions or pressure liable to impair the independent judgment of its members and to influence their decisions . . .

45   Like the protection against removal from office of the members of the body concerned . . . the receipt by those members of a level of remuneration commensurate with the importance of the functions they carry out constitutes a guarantee essential to judicial independence.

There is a right, therefore, to effective judicial protection. This right to effective judicial protection, *pace* the judgment, includes a right to challenge the legality of any act which affects EU law rights, a right to judicial review, before an independent court. This right to judicial review means that States cannot screen off certain sectors, such as the military, from judicial review if activities within this sector give rise to EU law rights.[10] Member States must also ensure that any professional, regulatory or administrative body which takes decisions that affect EU law rights is subject to judicial review.[11] Furthermore, to allow effective review, these bodies must provide sufficient reasons for their decisions for the individual to have both full knowledge of the facts and be in a position to defend themselves.[12]

The right to effective judicial protection, as Article 47(2) EUCFR makes clear, also imposes a number of due-process requirements. Right-holders should be able, in principle, to take the initiative before the court.[13] They must be able to bring their action before a single court for a single claim rather than to bring different elements of it before different courts.[14] Parties must be

[10]   *Johnston* v. *Chief Constable of the Royal Ulster Constabulary*, 222/84, EU:C:1986:206.
[11]   *Wilson* v. *Ordre des avocats du barreau de Luxembourg*, C-506/04, EU:C:2006:587.
[12]   *Peñarroja Fa*, C-372–3/09, EU:C:2011:156; *ZZ* v. *Secretary of State for the Home Department*, C-300/11, EU: C:2013:363.
[13]   *Hochtief* v. *Budapest Főváros Önkormányzata*, C-300/17, EU:C:2018:635.
[14]   *Impact* v. *MAFF*, C-268/06; EU:C:2008:223; *Martínez Andrés* v. *Vasco de Salud*; *López* v. *Ayuntamiento de Vitoria*, C-184/15 and C-197/15, EU:C:2016:680.

given a genuine opportunity to raise pleas based on EU law,[15] sufficient opportunity to enable them to comment effectively on any evidence[16] or any point raised by the court of its own motion,[17] sufficient time to prepare their defence and protection from abusive use of the litigation process by their adversaries.[18]

It also includes, as Article 47(3) EUCFR indicates, the right to legal aid. Member States may put conditions on the grant of legal aid. These conditions must have regard to the subject matter of the litigation, the applicant's prospect of success, the importance of the stakes for her, the legal complexity of the case and her capacity to represent herself effectively. Account must be taken as to whether the costs for which advance payment must be made represent an insurmountable obstacle to access to the courts.[19]

The big question, however, is whether the right to effective judicial protection gives parties the right to a remedy before a national court. Where an EU law right is violated, would EU law require, for example, a right to monetary compensation, and would it set out the principles used to determine the level of compensation? The general answer is that remedies and procedures are, in principle, a matter for domestic law provided these neither make the exercise of the EU law right impossible nor excessively difficult, or offer less protection than analogous breaches of domestic law.

In *Unibet*, Swedish authorities obtained injunctions and initiated criminal proceedings against parties providing advertising space to Unibet, a British Internet gambling company, whose activities contravened Swedish law. Unibet considered that all this violated its right under Article 56 TFEU, which provides for the right to provide services in another Member State. However, Unibet felt it was powerless as Swedish law did not allow a self-standing action seeking a declaration that a Swedish statute is illegal, and the Swedish authorities did not prosecute it. The Swedish court asked whether effective judicial protection required this self-standing action to be created.

Unibet v. *Justitiekanslern*, C–432/05, EU:C:2007:163

40 Although the EC Treaty has made it possible in a number of instances for private persons to bring a direct action, where appropriate, before the Community Court, it was not intended to create new remedies in the national courts to ensure the observance of Community law other than those already laid down by national law . . .

41 It would be otherwise only if it were apparent from the overall scheme of the national legal system in question that no legal remedy existed which made it possible to ensure, even indirectly, respect for an individual's rights under Community law . . .

42 Thus, while it is, in principle, for national law to determine an individual's standing and legal interest in bringing proceedings, Community law nevertheless requires that the national legislation does not undermine the right to effective judicial protection . . .

Unibet indicates a dual-track approach to remedies and procedures. On the one hand, it is for national law to provide remedies and procedures to protect individual EU legal rights. As we shall

---

[15] *Van der Weerd* v. *Minister van Landbouw; Natuur en Voedselkwaliteit*, C–222–5/05, EU:C:2007:318.
[16] *Steffenson*, C–276/01, EU:C:2003:228.   [17] *Banif Plus Bank* v. *Csipai*, C–472/11, EU: C:2013:88.
[18] *Leffler* v. *Berlin Chemie*, C–443/03, EU:C:2005:665.
[19] *DEB*, C–279/09, EU:C:2010:811; *R* v. *Environment Agency, ex parte Edwards and Pallikaropoulos*, C–260/11, EU: C:2013:221.

see, these are overseen by EU law and must meet certain EU law safeguards. In *Unibet*, therefore, the Court held that the Swedish judicial system provided remedies for the protection of Unibet's EU law rights. Unibet could sue the Swedish State in damages and seek an administrative authorisation from the Swedish authorities to provide gambling services, which it could then challenge before a court. On the other hand, EU law will step in and provide a remedy if it is apparent that no domestic legal remedy exists to protect the individual's rights. In this regard, EU law has intervened in a limited number of circumstances to provide remedies of its own which do not rely on the domestic law.

(ii) Union Oversight of Domestic Remedies and Procedures

The *locus classicus* for EU law oversight of domestic remedies and procedures is *Rewe*, which grants national legal discretion over the remedies and procedures to be deployed to secure EU rights. However, these must not make it practically impossible to exercise the right, or be less favourable than those provided for analogous breaches of domestic law. Rewe, a trader, claimed a refund for charges unlawfully levied by the German authorities for health inspections on fruit and vegetables. The German authorities argued that the limitation period had passed and Rewe would not have been able to claim a refund if the measure had breached an equivalent domestic law.

Rewe–Zentralfinanz and Others v. *Landwirtschaftskammer für das Saarland*, 33/76, EU: C:1976:188

5   Applying the principle of cooperation laid down in Article [4(3) TEU], it is the national courts which are entrusted with ensuring the legal protection which citizens derive from the direct effect of the provisions of Community law.

Accordingly, in the absence of Community rules on this subject, it is for the domestic legal system of each member state to designate the courts having jurisdiction and to determine the procedural conditions governing actions at law intended to ensure the protection of the rights which citizens have from the direct effect of Community law, it being understood that such conditions cannot be less favourable than those relating to similar actions of a domestic nature.

Where necessary . . . the Treaty enable[s] appropriate measures to be taken to remedy differences between the provisions laid down by law, regulation or administrative action in member states if they are likely to distort or harm the functioning of the common market.

In the absence of such measures of harmonization the right conferred by Community law must be exercised before the national courts in accordance with the conditions laid down by national rules.

The position would be different only if the conditions and time-limits made it impossible in practice to exercise the rights which the national courts are obliged to protect. This is not the case where reasonable periods of limitation of actions are fixed. The laying down of such time-limits with regard to actions of a fiscal nature is an application of the fundamental principle of legal certainty protecting both the tax-payer and the administration concerned.

The default position for remedies and procedures has evolved so that these should 'not be less favourable than those governing similar domestic situations (principle of equivalence) and . . . not render impossible in practice or excessively difficult the exercise of rights.'[20]

---

[20] *Euro Park Service* v. *Ministre des Finances et des Comptes publics*, C-14/16, EU:C:2017:177.

The equivalence principle is the less contentious of these two principles. The question of whether a domestic measure is equivalent to an EU measure is gauged by looking at the purpose and essential characteristics of each law to see if this is the case.[21] If the measures are equivalent, the remedies or procedures available for the domestic law must also be available for the EU law.

The question of when domestic processes or remedies render the exercise of EU rights impossible or excessively difficult is more intricate.

On remedies, the Court has said that compensation must be adequate.[22] National caps limiting compensation to very low levels are illegal,[23] as are those which provide for only nominal compensation with no regard to the damage sustained.[24] Similarly, Member States must allow compensation for certain types of damage, notably economic loss.[25] However, national laws can require claimants to mitigate or exercise due diligence to avoid the loss.[26] This requires them to use all legal remedies available to them before claiming for loss unless it would be excessively difficult or unreasonable to ask this of them.[27]

There is more detailed case law on procedures. The Court has stated that regard must be had to a number of elements in determining whether a procedure makes the exercise of a right impossible or excessively difficult. These include its impact on the rights of the defence, the principle of legal certainty and the proper conduct of the proceedings.[28] The greatest challenges have been posed by limitation periods, namely those provisions which set a time limit on any action being brought. These must give the applicant sufficient practical time to prepare and bring an effective action.[29] This can be very short, however. Sixty days to bring civil proceedings before a court has been held to be sufficient.[30] A thirty-day period to claim a tax advantage from the Slovenian tax authorities was considered fine, albeit that the limitation applied to bringing the matter before the administration rather than the judiciary.[31] The most draconian example, however, is *Samba Diouf* in which a period of only fifteen days for asylum seekers to appeal to the court against an administrative decision refusing asylum was held to be sufficient.[32] Although it seems as if all limitation periods are permitted, this is not the case. Limitation periods with unclear starting dates are likely to be declared illegal. Thus, a limitation period restricting litigation against anti-competitive practices, which starts on the first day of the practice, is illegal, as individuals are often unable to ascertain the nature and impact of the anti-competitive practice until too late.[33] Similarly, in the case of people employed on a series of short-term contracts, the limitation period must begin from the end of the relationship and not from the end of each of these contracts.[34] Related to this, the Court will also look at whether

---

[21] *Santana* v. *Consejería de Justicia y Administración Pública de la Junta de Andalucía*, C-177/10, EU:C:2011:557.

[22] *Irimie* v. *Administratia Finantelor Publice Sibiu*, C-565/11, EU:C:2013:250. See K. Havu, 'Full, Adequate and Commensurate Compensation for Damages under EU Law: A Challenge for National Courts?' (2018) 43 *ELRev* 23.

[23] *Marshall* v. *Southampton and South West Hampshire AHA (No. 2)*, C-271/91, EU:C:2004:40.

[24] *Von Colson and Kamann* v. *Land Nordrhein-Westfalen*, 14/83, EU:C:1984:153.

[25] *Brasserie du Pêcheur* v. *Germany* and *R* v. *Secretary of State for Transport, ex parte Factortame (No. 3)*, C-46/93 and C-48/93, EU:C:1996:79.

[26] *Ecotrade* v. *Agenzia delle Entrate – Ufficio di Genova 3*, C-95–6/07, EU:C:2008:267.

[27] *Fuß* v. *Stadt Halle*, C-429/09, EU:C:2010:717.   [28] *TDC* v. *Teleklagenævnet*, C-327/15, EU:C:2016:974.

[29] *Palmisani* v. *INPS*, C-261/95, EU:C:1997:351.

[30] *Asturcom Telecomunicaciones* v. *Rodríguez Nogueira*, C 40/08, EU:C:2009:615.

[31] *Pelati*, C-603/10, EU:C:2012:639.

[32] *Samba Diouf* v. *Ministre du Travail, de l'Emploi et de l'Immigration*, C-69/10, EU:C:2011:524.

[33] *Manfredi* v. *Lloyd Adriatico Assicurazioni*, C-295–8/04, EU:C:2006:461.

[34] *Preston* v. *Wolverhampton Health Care Trust*, C-78/98, EU:C:2000:247.

individuals did not bring a claim within the required time because of unconscionable behaviour by the defendant,[35] or the State,[36] which induced them to defer their action.

(iii) EU Law Remedies and Procedures in Domestic Courts

Unibet hinted that where the national system provides no remedies, there may be a case for an EU remedy to be imposed. There are, however, four limited circumstances where EU law requires particular remedies to be provided in national courts.

First, the principle of State liability allows individuals to sue a Member State for loss suffered as a result of the latter's breach of EU law. It is a self-standing procedure, which is dealt with later in the chapter.[37]

Secondly, parties who had to pay taxes or State charges in breach of directly effective EU law have a right to demand repayment of these before a national court.[38] This right applies also to taxes and charges levied by public bodies,[39] illegal requirements to pay tax in advance[40] and levying of guarantees in breach of EU law.[41] The Court has also touched on the level of compensation to be provided. Complainants are entitled not only to repayment of the tax, but also to compensation for any losses accrued as a result of not having this revenue available to them.[42] States are also obliged to pay interest on these losses.[43] However, States may refuse to pay compensation where this would lead to unjust enrichment. If the illegally levied sum has been passed on to other persons (e.g. by a trader increasing the prices to be paid by consumers on the taxed good), the national authority does not have to pay that amount which has been passed on.[44] To determine this, national courts must engage in some economic analysis as they must have regard not only to the increase in price but also to possible declines in volumes of sales as a result of that increase.[45]

Thirdly, in the field of competition, individuals can sue for damages arising from breaches of Article 101 TFEU, the provision prohibiting anti-competitive conduct by two or more parties, where they can show that there is a direct causal link between the harm suffered and the illegal act.[46] Similar reasoning operates in the field of State aids. If a national court finds that unlawful aid has been paid to an undertaking by a national authority, it must order repayment of that aid by that undertaking.[47]

The fourth category concerns interim relief pending a judgment on EU law. In instances going simply to interpretation of an EU law, this relief must be provided where a failure to do so would imperil the full effectiveness of the final decision, whether given by the Court of Justice[48] or a

---

[35] *Levez* v. *Jennings*, C-326/96, EU:C:1998:577.   [36] *Lämmerzahl*, C-241/06, EU:C:2007:597.   [37] See pp. 314–22.
[38] *Amministrazione delle Finanze dello Stato* v. *San Giorgio*, 199/82, EU:C:1983:318. P. Wattel, 'National Procedural Autonomy and the Effectiveness of EC Law: Challenge the Charge, File for Restitution, Sue for Damages?' (2008) 35(2) *LIEI* 109.
[39] *GT-Link* v. *DSB*, C-242/95, EU:C:1997:376.
[40] *Test Claimants in the FII Group Litigation* v. *IRC*, C-446/04, EU:C:2006:774.
[41] *N* v. *Inspecteur van de Belastingdienst Oost/kantoor Almelo*, C-470/04, EU:C:2006:525.
[42] *Metallgesellschaft* v. *IRC*, 397/87 and C-410/98, EU:C:2001:370.
[43] *Irimie* v. *Administraţia Finanţelor Publice Sibiu*, C-565/11, EU:C:2013:250.
[44] *Comateb and Others*, C-192–218/95, EU:C:1997:12; *Petrotel-Lukoil* v. *Ministerul Economie*, C-76/17, EU:C:2018:139.
[45] *Marks & Spencer* v. *CCE*, C-309/06, EU:C:2008:211.   [46] *Courage* v. *Crehan*, C-453/99, EU:C:2001:465.
[47] *SFEI*, C-39/94, EU:C:1996:285; *Xunta de Galicia*, C-71/04, EU:C:2005:493.
[48] *R* v. *Secretary of State for Transport, ex parte Factortame Ltd*, C-213/89, EU:C:1990:257.

national court.[49] Different principles apply when the relief is sought against a national law implementing an EU measure.[50] In such circumstances, the challenge is seen as being, in reality, against the EU measure. There is greater Union interest, therefore, in relief not being granted. There was also concern that national courts would use the grant of interim relief in these circumstances as a back route for rendering EU legislation inapplicable: something over which the Court of Justice claims a monopoly.[51] Relief should, therefore, only be given if there is serious and irreparable damage to the applicant and this must be weighed against other considerations such as the damage to the EU legal order and its financial interests.

4 DIRECT EFFECT AND EU SECONDARY LAWS

(i) Regulations and International Agreements

Most EU law is secondary legislation.[52] After the transitional period, the question quickly arose as to whether this legislation was capable of direct effect. The most straightforward case was that of Regulations. Regulations are the closest thing the Union has to domestic statutes because they have general application and are binding and directly applicable in all Member States.[53] They were therefore held to be capable of direct effect in the same way as Treaty provisions.[54] Some international agreements with non-EU States are also capable of direct effect. If the overall agreement is considered to depend on the reciprocal meeting of obligations by all parties to it, no provision in that agreement will be directly effective. Otherwise, according to the Court, the Union would be at a disadvantage vis-à-vis other parties that do not provide for direct effect in their territories.[55] If there is no issue here, the specific provision invoked will be considered. It will only be directly effective if, interpreted in the light of the nature and purpose of the agreement, it is unconditional, sufficiently precise and not dependent for implementation on any subsequent measure.[56]

(ii) The Vertical Direct Effect of Directives

Directives are the legislative instrument used most often for politically significant and controversial issues. These sensitivities are reflected in their only being binding upon Member States as to the result to be achieved, whilst leaving them discretion as to the forms and methods to realise this result. This has given rise to two objections, in particular, about why Directives should not be capable of direct effect:

- The discretion granted to Member States to implement Directives should result in individuals being able to derive rights only from the acts of national authorities themselves, and not from the Directives themselves.

---

[49] *Aziz* v. *Catalunyacaixa*, C-415/11, EU:C:2013:164.
[50] *Zuckerfabrik Süderdithmarschen and Zuckerfabrik Soest*, C-143/88 and C-92/89, EU:C:1991:65.
[51] *Foto-Frost* v. *Hauptzollamt Lübeck-Ost*, 314/85, EU:C:1987:452. See pp. 184–6.
[52] The different types of secondary law have been considered at pp. 113–16.
[53] J. Winter, 'Direct Effect and Direct Applicability: Two Distinct and Different Concepts in Community law' (1972) 9 *CMLRev* 425.
[54] *Leonesio* v. *Italian Ministry of Agriculture*, 93/71, EU:C:1972:39.
[55] *Portugal* v. *Council*, C-149/96, EU:C:1999:574.
[56] *Air Transport Association of America* v. *Secretary of State for Energy and Climate Change*, C-366/10, EU:C:2011:864.

- It would blur the distinction between Directives and Regulations, a distinction clearly spelt out in Article 288 TFEU, as both would have similar legal effects.[57]

Notwithstanding these arguments, the Court of Justice ruled in *Van Duyn* that Directives could be capable of direct effect.[58] Van Duyn was refused leave to enter the United Kingdom to take up a job at the Church of Scientology, as the UK Government had imposed a ban on foreign scientologists entering the United Kingdom. She challenged the ban on the grounds, *inter alia*, that it breached a Directive which required that any ban be based upon the personal conduct of the individual. She noted that she personally had done nothing wrong. The Court considered that her association with the Church of Scientology met the requirements of the Directive. However, prior to that, it considered whether the Directive was capable of direct effect.

Van Duyn v. *Home Office*, 41/74, EU: C:1974:133

12 ... It would be incompatible with the binding effect attributed to a Directive by Article [288 TFEU] to exclude, in principle, the possibility that the obligation which it imposes may be invoked by those concerned. In particular, where the Community authorities have, by Directive, imposed on Member States the obligation to pursue a particular course of conduct, the useful effect of such an act would be weakened if individuals were prevented from relying on it before their national courts and if the latter were prevented from taking it into consideration as an element of Community law. Article [267 TFEU], which empowers national courts to refer to the Court questions concerning the validity and interpretation of all acts of the Community institutions, without distinction, implies furthermore that these acts may be invoked by individuals in the national courts. It is necessary to examine, in every case, whether the nature, general scheme and wording of the provisions in question are capable of having direct effects on the relations between Member States and individuals.

The Court asks whether there is any good reason why Directives should not have direct effect. However, one would normally argue the opposite, namely that good reasons would have to be presented why a law should have certain powers. The arguments that the binding nature and effectiveness of Directives require that they be invoked in national courts are equally weak. Put simply, these qualities could mean a range of things. Neither prescribes the types of effect a Directive should have in a domestic legal system. Indeed, no less a figure than Federico Mancini, a former judge at the Court, has admitted that 'this judgment goes beyond the letter of Article [288 TFEU]', the provision that sets out the central characteristics of Regulations and Directives.[59] More significantly, the ruling provoked a strong counter-reaction from national courts. The Dutch Council of State, the French *Conseil d'État*, the highest administrative law court in France, and the Bundesfinanzhof, the highest tax court in Germany, all refused to accord Directives direct effect.[60]

---

[57] On this debate see S. Prechal, *Directives in European Community Law: A Study of Directives and their Enforcement in National Courts*, 2nd edn (Oxford University Press, 2005) 216–20.

[58] Decisions have also been held, on similar grounds, to be capable of bearing direct effect: see *Grad* v. *Finanzamt Traustein*, C-9/70, EU:C:1970:78.

[59] G. Mancini and D. Keeling, 'Language, Culture and Politics in the Life of the European Court of Justice' (1995) 1 *CJE L* 397, 401.

[60] *Minister of the Interior* v. *Cohn-Bendit* [1980] 1 CMLR 543; *Re Value Added Tax Directives* [1982] 1 CMLR 527. On the Dutch Council of State see M. Claes and B. de Witte, 'Report on the Netherlands' in A.-M. Slaughter *et al.* (eds.), *The European Courts and National Courts: Doctrine and Jurisprudence* (Oxford-Portland, Hart, 1998).

The Court resorted, therefore, to a new justification for Directives: the estoppel argument. Under this line of reasoning, as Member States have a duty to secure the legal result required by the Directive by a certain date, it would be wrong for them to gain an advantage through failing to carry this out.[61] This would be the case if they fail to transpose a Directive which requires legal rights to be established that can be invoked against them. By dint of their failure to transpose the Directive, there are no domestic law rights against them, and they would have legal impunity if the Directive could also not be invoked against them directly. As a consequence, parties may invoke Directives against the State. It does not follow, according to this logic, that parties may invoke Directives against other private parties. Private parties have no duties to transpose the Directive into national law, and, thus, are not at 'fault' if this does not take place. In other words, the estoppel argument may be used to justify the vertical direct effect of Directives, but not their horizontal direct effect. In *Marshall*, a dietician employed by a British health authority was dismissed at the age of 62 on the ground that she had passed the pensionable age, which was, at that time, 60 years for women. Men would not have been dismissed at that age as they did not receive their pension until 65. Marshall had no redress as British law excluded contractual conditions relating to retirement from equal opportunities law. She claimed a breach of the Equal Treatment Directive, which provides for equal treatment for men and women concerning *all* terms and conditions of dismissal, including when this occurred because an employee had reached pensionable age.

Marshall v. *Southampton and SW Hampshire Area Health Authority*, 152/84, EU:C:1986:84

48 With regard to the argument that a Directive may not be relied upon against an individual, it must be emphasised that according to Article [288 TFEU], the binding nature of a Directive, which constitutes the basis for the possibility of relying on the Directive before a national court, exists only in relation to 'each Member State to which it is addressed'. It follows that a Directive may not of itself impose obligations on an individual and that a provision of a Directive may not be relied upon as such against such a person.

49 In that respect it must be pointed out that where a person involved in legal proceedings is able to rely on a Directive as against the State he may do so regardless of the capacity in which the latter is acting, whether employer or public authority. In either case it is necessary to prevent the State from taking advantage of its own failure to comply with Community law...

51 The argument submitted by the United Kingdom that the possibility of relying on provisions of the Directive against the respondent *qua* organ of the State would give rise to an arbitrary and unfair distinction between the rights of State employees and those of private employees does not justify any other conclusion. Such a distinction may easily be avoided if the Member State concerned has correctly implemented the Directive in national law.

Marshall distinguished between Regulations and Directives by holding that only Regulations were capable of horizontal direct effect. As Directives could now only be invoked against the State, this raised the immediate question of which bodies formed part of the State. Defining the State is, to be sure, a challenge. The State's multiple legal structures are frequently a

---

[61] Early cases using the estoppel argument are *Ratti*, 148/78, EU:C:1979:110; *Becker* v. *Finanzamt Münster-Innenstadt*, 8/81, EU:C:1982:7.

consequence of historical happenstance, on the one hand, and the recurring revisiting of the role of public intervention, on the other.[62]

This question was addressed in *Foster* v. *British Gas*.[63] This concerned similar facts to *Marshall* except the dismissed employee was suing British Gas, the main gas supplier in the United Kingdom. The company had been privatised but its board members were appointed by a British Minister who could also issue them various directions and instruments and, alongside this, it could propose legislation to the United Kingdom Parliament. The Court established a dual test for whether a body was part of the State.[64] First, the courts will apply a functional test. Even if the organisation was a private body, a Directive could be invoked against it if it was performing a public service pursuant to a State measure and had, for that reason, special powers. The body, in such circumstances, can be sued because it is performing a *State function*. Its legal form and the presence of State control is not determinative. In *Vassallo*, therefore, a Directive could be invoked against an Italian hospital which received public funding, but was not run by the Italian State and was an autonomous establishment with its own directors, as it was seen as performing a public service.[65] Secondly, a Directive can be invoked against a body when it is subject to State control. This will be where it forms part of the State itself, is an entity controlled by the State or is empowered by the State to act on its behalf.[66] In such circumstances, the element of State control is central. In *Rohrbach*, for example, two Austrian companies carrying out laundrette and gardening activities were held to be part of the State purely by virtue of their local authority ownership, albeit that their mission was to employ people with disabilities.[67]

Unfortunately, the problematic style of analysis in Marshall raised profound issues that went beyond the complexities of defining State bodies It sits uncomfortably with *Defrenne* v. *Sabena*,[68] which held that it was the binding qualities of EU law, addressed to Member States, which led to horizontal direct effect. Courts, as part of the State, were required to apply EU law in cases before them. In *Marshall* the opposite is stated. The binding qualities of Directives upon the State is held as a reason why courts should not apply Directives in disputes between private parties. The judgment also rests on a false assumption. Almost all the public bodies against whom Directives can be invoked have no more responsibilities for transposing Directives into national law than any private body. It is the legislature or Ministers and Ministries, through executive orders and statutory instruments, who have this responsibility, and not health authorities or gardeners. It is difficult to see how the latter are at fault if a Directive is not transposed into national law, and, therefore, why the estoppel argument can used against them.

Most significantly, *Marshall* creates incongruous outcomes. Marshall could rely on the Directive because she was employed by a public authority, which is considered a part of the State. Had she been employed by a private hospital, she would not have been able to rely on

---

[62] D. Curtin, 'The Province of Government: Delimiting the Direct Effect of Directives in the Common Law Context (1990) 15 *ELRev* 195, 198–9.

[63] *Foster* v. *British Gas*, C-188/89, EU:C:1990:313.

[64] There was doubt for many years as to whether a single test was required, an entity performing a public service also had to be under the control of the State. This is not the case. There are now two separate tests, one going to State functions and the other to State control, *Farrell* v. *Whitty*, C-413/15, EU:C:2017:745.

[65] *Vassallo* v. *Azienda Ospedaliera Ospedale San Martino di Genova e Cliniche Universitarie Convenzionate*, C-180/04, EU:C:2006:518.

[66] *Fish Legal and Shirley* v. *Information Commissioner*, C-279/12, EU:C:2013:853.

[67] *Sozialhilfeverband Rohrbach* v. *Arbeiterkammer Oberösterreich*, C-297/03, EU:C:2005:315.

[68] *Defrenne* v. *Sabena (No. 2)*, 43/75, EU:C:1976:56.

the Directive. The practical effect of *Marshall* is that a two-tier legal system is created, in which parties have greater protection against public bodies than against private ones, notwithstanding that their activities are otherwise identical.

(iii) Directives and the Burdens and Rights of Third Parties

Marshall raises the question of whether a Directive can ever be invoked if it imposes burdens on individuals. *Marshall* indicated that Directives cannot impose obligations on private parties, which can be the basis for a law suit against them in a domestic court. However, there is still the issue of triangular situations. These concern a dispute between two parties which affects the legal rights or imposes a financial burden on a third party. The dilemma arises where the defendant is the State, so a Directive can be invoked against it in a domestic court, but the third party is a private actor. The successful litigation may then impose burdens on or affect the legal rights of that private actor.

Notwithstanding these consequences, Directives can still be invoked in national courts. In this context, it is worth distinguishing three sets of circumstances.[69]

The first is when a Directive entitles an individual to require the Member State to do something which places a burden on another party. This is uncontroversial. It happens when individuals invoke Directives requiring local authorities to set things out properly for public tender. Such tenders require significant information from other companies and are costly.

The second is where Directives require States to impose a burden on private parties. Another party cannot require that they impose these burdens. Nevertheless, it can invoke the Directive where a decision is taken which affects it rights, and the review might impose burdens.[70] In *Arcor*,[71] three telephone service providers challenged a decision by the German regulatory authority to allow Deutsche Telekom, the owner of the telephone network in Germany, to charge for use of that network, charges which they had to pay. Two Directives precluded this charge where the network was run by a business which had a dominant position on the market and the fee was unrelated to the costs of connection. Whilst the case was brought against the German regulators, its central target was, of course, Deutsche Telekom, a private company. Nevertheless, the Court held that the providers could sue the German authorities, and were not prevented from doing so even though a successful action would have significant repercussions for Deutsche Telekom as it would no longer be able to charge for use of the network.

The third is the most controversial. This is where a Directive grants a party a legal right to engage in certain activities. However, in violation of the Directive, the Member State permits third parties to stop these activities, typically through litigation. The doctrine of incidental direct effect allows the party a right to protect itself from claims made by these third parties.[72] In this

---

[69] This categorisation was set out in H. Nyssens and K. Lackhoff, 'Direct Effect of Directives in Triangular Situations' (1998) 23 *ELRev* 397, 401–2.

[70] For an earlier example of this second situation see *R* v. *Secretary of State for Transport, Local Government and the Regions, ex parte Wells*, C-201/02, EU:C:2004:12.

[71] *Arcor* v. *Germany*, C-152–4/07, EU:C:2008:426.

[72] See D. Colgan, 'Triangular Situations: The Coup de Grâce for the Denial of Horizontal Direct Effect of Community Directives' (2002) 8 *EPL* 545; F. Becker and A. Campbell, 'The Direct Effect of European Directives: Towards the Final Act? (2007) 13 *CJEL* 401.

instance, the Directive is invoked in litigation between private parties, but it is invoked as a shield, a defence by one private party against the action of another. The most famous example is *CIA*. Signalson and Securitel sought to restrain CIA Security from marketing an alarm system on the grounds that it had not received authorisation as required by Belgian law. They argued that by marketing an illegal good, CIA was engaging in unfair competition. However, this requirement of prior authorisation breached EU law as it had not been notified to the Commission as required by Directive 83/189. CIA argued that this breach of the Directive meant that the national law could not be invoked against it.

CIA Security International v. Signalson & Securitel, C-194/94, EU:C:1996:172

44 ... Articles 8 and 9 of Directive 83/189 lay down a precise obligation on Member States to notify draft technical regulations to the Commission before they are adopted. Being, accordingly, unconditional and sufficiently precise in terms of their content, those articles may be relied on by individuals before national courts. ...

46 The German and Netherlands Governments and the United Kingdom consider that Directive 83/189 is solely concerned with relations between the Member States and the Commission, that it merely creates procedural obligations which the Member States must observe when adopting technical regulations, their competence to adopt the regulations in question after expiry of the suspension period being, however, unaffected, and, finally, that it contains no express provision relating to any effects attaching to non-compliance with those procedural obligations.

47 ... none of those factors prevents non-compliance with Directive 83/189 from rendering the technical regulations in question inapplicable.

48 ... As pointed out above, it is undisputed that the aim of the directive is to protect freedom of movement for goods by means of preventive control and that the obligation to notify is essential for achieving such Community control. The effectiveness of Community control will be that much greater if the directive is interpreted as meaning that breach of the obligation to notify constitutes a substantial procedural defect such as to render the technical regulations in question inapplicable to individuals.

The case needs to be read carefully. CIA had an underlying right to free movement of goods, in this case importing burglar alarms from other Member States. The Directive does not give rise to this right but protects it by requiring Belgium to notify potential obstacles to the free movement of goods. Insofar as CIA's competitors were seeking to remove that protection through the back-door by enforcing Belgian law through a private action, CIA was entitled to protection from them. Consequently, incidental direct effect can only be used as a shield from litigation by other parties.[73] It does not grant parties the right to use Directives as a cause of action, but this distinction is not a happy one. It still allows individuals to impose burdens on a wide array of other parties. In *CIA*, therefore, the consequence was that the regulations governing burglar alarms did not apply. Insofar as this might allow cheap, unreliable burglars alarms with no noise level restrictions to flood the market, it could have implications for competitors, consumers and neighbours.[74]

---

[73] J. Jans, 'The Effect in National Legal Systems of the Prohibition of Discrimination on Grounds of Age as a General Principle of Community Law' (2007) 34 *LIEI* 53, 61–2.

[74] S. Weatherill, 'Breach of Directives and Breach of Contract' (2001) 26 *ELRev* 177, 182–3.

Consequently, incidental direct effect has been applied very rarely.[75] Indeed, it may be that it applies only in the case of that particular Directive. In *Smith*,[76] an insurer refused to pay out to a passenger for injuries suffered as a result of a motor vehicle accident in which he was in the back of a van, as Irish insurance law only required cover for those in the back if they were sitting in fixed seats. This breached a Directive which required cover to be extended to these passengers. The Court rejected the argument that Irish law was inapplicable and the passenger should be able to claim from the insurance company. It stated that *CIA* did not apply where the Directive in question determined the substantive legal content of the national legal rule governing the action. In this instance, the Directive did do that as both it and the national law went to the provision of motor vehicle insurance.

(iv) The Duty to Refrain from Compromising the Result Prescribed by the Directive

Direct effect only bites from the date of transposition set out in the Directive.[77] This date will usually be several years after the Directive's adoption. There is the issue of whether Member States are free to do as they wish during this period. In this regard, Member States must refrain from taking any measures during this period which are liable seriously to compromise the realisation of the results prescribed by the Directive.[78] In other words, Member States may not take new measures during this time which breach the Directive. These measures may be new laws[79] or new interpretations of the law by judges.[80]

The position with regard to administrative measures is more complicated. The national court must make an overall assessment, looking at whether the measures and policies combined will lead to the Member State not complying with its obligations by the transposition date. In *Stichting Natuur en Milieu*, a 2001 Directive required States to establish national emission ceilings for sulphur dioxide and nitrogen dioxide. For the Netherlands these had to be met by 2010. In 2007 and 2008, the Dutch authorities authorised the construction of three new power stations. These only came on line in 2012 and it was estimated that these would increase emissions of sulphur dioxide by just under 6 per cent and nitrogen dioxide by just under 1 per cent. The Court of Justice ruled that the Dutch were free to construct them as it noted that a single measure (or here, three measures!) could not by itself seriously compromise annual Dutch targets.

> ### *Stichting Natuur en Milieu and Others* v. *College van Gedeputeerde Staten van Groningen*, C-165–7/09, EU: C:2011:348
>
> 78 ... it is settled case-law that, during the period prescribed for transposition of a directive, the Member States to which it is addressed must refrain from taking any measures liable seriously to compromise the attainment of the result prescribed by that directive ... must be understood as referring to the adoption of any measure, general or specific, liable to produce such a compromising effect.

---

[75] It was applied with regard to the same Directive in *Unilever Italia* v. *Central Food*, C-443/98, EU:C:2000:496.
[76] *Smith* v. *Meade*, C-122/17, EU:C:2018:631.
[77] Indirect effect also kicks in at that date, *VG Wort* v. *Kyocera*, C-457–60/11, EU:C:2013:426.
[78] *Inter-Environnement Wallonie* v. *Région wallonne*, C-129/96, EU:C:1997:628; *Stichting Zuid-Hollandse Milieufederatie* v. *Minister van Landbouw*, C-138/05, EU:C:2006:577.
[79] *Mangold* v. *Helm*, C-144/04, EU:C:2005:709.   [80] *Adeneler and Others* v. *ELOG*, C-212/04, EU:C:2006:443.

79 This obligation to refrain from taking measures is also owed by the Member States, by virtue of the application of Article 4(3) TEU in conjunction with the third paragraph of Article 288 TFEU, during a transitional period in which they are authorised to continue to apply their national systems, even though those systems do not comply with the directive in question . . .

80 It therefore follows that such an obligation is also to be complied with in the transitional period provided for . . . during which the Member States are authorised not to comply for the time being with the annual national emission quantities laid down in Annex I to that directive. It is for the national court to review whether this obligation has been complied with in the light of the provisions and measures whose legality it is called upon to examine . . .

81 Nevertheless, such a review must necessarily be conducted on the basis of an overall assessment, taking account of all the policies and measures adopted in the national territory concerned.

82 Having regard to the system established by the NEC Directive and, in particular, to the programmatic approach . . . for which it provides, attainment of the result prescribed by that directive can be seriously impeded by the Member States only by the adoption and implementation of a body of policies and measures which, given, in particular, their effects in practice and their duration in time, allow or give rise to a critical situation in light of the total quantity of emissions discharged into the atmosphere by all sources of pollution, such as necessarily to compromise compliance, at the end of 2010, with the ceilings laid down in Annex I to the directive

83 It follows that a simple specific measure relating to a single source of SO_2 and NO_x, consisting in the decision to grant an environmental permit for the construction and operation of an industrial installation, does not appear liable, in itself, seriously to compromise the result prescribed by the [Directive], namely limiting emissions from those sources of pollution into the atmosphere to annual total amounts not exceeding the national ceilings in 2010 at the latest. This conclusion applies all the more where, in circumstances such as those in the main actions, the installation in question is not to be brought into operation until 2012 at the earliest.

The judgment does not say that the adoption of a single administrative measure may never be illegal during the transposition period. It all depends on how much that measure contributes to that State's realisation, or not, of its obligations. In this instance, these power stations contributed only slightly to the Netherlands' overall emissions. That said, there is a danger that EU law may be blind to a State's direction of travel. These power stations were indicative of a government that was not taking its commitments seriously, as evidenced by a Dutch Environment Agency report that noted it was already going to miss its 2010 targets. In other words, the power stations made a bad situation worse and increased the likelihood that the Netherlands would take longer to meet its commitments.

5 INDIRECT EFFECT

Because of the partial and, in the view of many, arbitrary effects it accorded to Directives, *Marshall* came under withering attack from academic commentators.[81] Yet, notwithstanding

---

[81] D. Curtin, 'The Effectiveness of Judicial Protection of Individual Rights' (1990) 27 *CMLRev* 709; S. Prechal, 'Remedies after Marshall' (1990) 27 *CMLRev* 451; J. Coppell, 'Rights, Duties and the End of Marshall' (1994) 57 *MLR* 859; T. Tridimas, 'Horizontal Effect of Directives: A Missed Opportunity?' (1994) 19 *ELRev* 621.

this, the Court has resolutely stated that Directives are not capable of horizontal direct effect because they cannot impose obligations on individuals.[82] This has provided the context for the development of a number of doctrines which attempt to soften the consequences of this. The first and possibly most significant of these is indirect effect.

The doctrine of indirect effect is a duty to interpret national law in the light of EU law. While national law formally governs the dispute, the substance of the decision will be shaped or even determined by EU law insofar as national laws are interpreted in light of it. Hence, EU law has indirect effects.

Indirect effect has evolved in three stages.

The first stage, prior to 1990, required national law only to be interpreted in the light of an EU law where the national law in question was giving effect to that EU law. Furthermore, EU law was to have a relatively light interpretive effect. It was only to bite where the national law was genuinely ambiguous and the reference to EU law would not lead to a contrived interpretation of the national law.[83]

The second stage emerged in *Marleasing*. The case concerned whether the Spanish Civil Code could be interpreted in the light of a subsequent EU Company Law Directive. The Court of Justice indicated that it should and that national courts must interpret the Code 'as far as possible, in the light of the wording and the purpose of the Directive in order to achieve the result pursued by the latter'.[84] *Marleasing* thereby expanded indirect effect in two ways. First, it expanded its scope as it required *all* national legislation to be interpreted in the light of EU law, irrespective of whether it is implementing legislation or not and irrespective of whether it was enacted prior or subsequent to the provision of EU law in question. Secondly, it strengthened the national courts' interpretive duty. As Docksey and Fitzpatrick observed, 'it is no longer sufficient for a national court to turn to Community law only if the national provision is "ambiguous". Its priority must be to establish the meaning of the Union obligation and only then to conclude whether it is possible to achieve the necessary reconciliation with the national law.'[85]

The third stage occurred in *Pfeiffer*. The national legal system as a whole, and not just individual national laws, had to be interpreted in the light of EU law.[86] This included procedural rules going to which national law should apply to a particular dispute. The Court ruled that national courts should consider, within the discretion allowed to them by national law, whether it is possible to apply the particular law that is compliant with EU law by interpreting the other as not applying to the dispute. Thus, indirect effect set out a hierarchy of laws in which national laws compliant with EU law will take precedence over other national laws insofar as the latter are presumed not to apply to disputes where this would involve a breach of EU law.

The current situation on indirect effect is most elaborately set out in *Dansk Industri*. After working for Ajos, a Danish company, for twenty-five years, Rasmussen was dismissed. He left at the age of 60 to take a job at another Danish company. Under Danish law, his length of service

---

[82] E.g. *DI*, C-441/14, EU:C:2016:278; *Farrell* v. *Whitty*, C-413/15, EU:C:2017:745. For reasons why the Court sticks with no horizontal direct effect see J. Dickson, 'Directives in European Union Legal Systems: Whose Norms Are They Anyway?' (2011) 17 *ELJ* 190.

[83] *Von Colson and Kamann* v. *Land Nordrhein-Westfalen*, 14/83, EU:C:1984:153.

[84] *Marleasing SA* v. *La Comercial Internacionale de Alimentacion*, C-106/89, EU:C:1990:395.

[85] C. Docksey and B. Fitzpatrick, 'The Duty of National Courts to Interpret Provisions Of National Law in Accordance with Community Law' (1991) 20 *ILJ* 113, 119.

[86] *Pfeiffer and Others* v. *Deutsches Rotes Kreuz*, C-397–403/01, EU:C:2004:584.

entitled him to a severance allowance of three months' pay from Ajos. This was denied because it was not available under that law if a person has reached an age where he was entitled to a pension paid by the employer. Rasmussen began a claim, subsequently taken up by his estate, that this violated the Directive on Age Discrimination. On its face, the Danish law seemed to conflict with the requirements of the Directive.

***Dansk Industri (DI) acting on behalf of Ajos* v. *Estate of Rasmussen*, C–441/14, EU: C:2016:278**

30 While it is true that, in relation to disputes between individuals, the Court has consistently held that a directive cannot of itself impose obligations on an individual and cannot therefore be relied upon as such against an individual . . . the fact nonetheless remains that the Court has also consistently held that the Member States' obligation arising from a directive to achieve the result envisaged by that directive and their duty to take all appropriate measures, whether general or particular, to ensure the fulfilment of that obligation are binding on all the authorities of the Member States, including, for matters within their jurisdiction, the courts . . .

31 It follows that, in applying national law, national courts called upon to interpret that law are required to consider the whole body of rules of law and to apply methods of interpretation that are recognised by those rules in order to interpret it, so far as possible, in the light of the wording and the purpose of the directive concerned in order to achieve the result sought by the directive and consequently comply with the third paragraph of Article 288 TFEU . . .

32 It is true that the Court has stated that this principle of interpreting national law in conformity with EU law has certain limits. Thus, the obligation for a national court to refer to EU law when interpreting and applying the relevant rules of domestic law is limited by general principles of law and cannot serve as the basis for an interpretation of national law *contra legem* . . .

33 It should be noted in that connection that the requirement to interpret national law in conformity with EU law entails the obligation for national courts to change its established case-law, where necessary, if it is based on an interpretation of national law that is incompatible with the objectives of a directive . . .

34 Accordingly, the national court cannot validly claim in the main proceedings that it is impossible for it to interpret the national provision at issue in a manner that is consistent with EU law by mere reason of the fact that it has consistently interpreted that provision in a manner that is incompatible with EU law.

The expansion of indirect effect in this manner has closed to a considerable degree the lacunae created by *Marshall*. Directives will regulate disputes between private parties by requiring that national law be interpreted in the light of them in all but three circumstances. The first is where there is no national law to interpret, such as where a Directive establishes a new field of law and there are no national laws transposing it. The second is where the national legislation is *contra legem*. The language of the national legislation is so at odds with the Directive that it cannot be interpreted to comply with it. The third is that indirect effect cannot be used to determine or aggravate the criminal liability of private actors.[87]

Despite the greater academic attention given to direct effect, it has therefore been argued persuasively that indirect effect 'is currently the main form of ensuring [the] effect of Directives'.[88]

---

[87] *Arcaro*, C–168/95, EU:C:1996:363; *Ognyanov*, C–554/14, EU:C:2016:835. See P. Craig, 'The Legal Effects of Directives: Policy, Rules and Exceptions' (2009) 34 *ELRev* 349, 360–4.

[88] G. Betlem, 'The Doctrine of Consistent Interpretation: Managing Legal Uncertainty' (2002) 22 *OJLS* 397, 399.

Indeed, an empirical study back in 1998 found that indirect effect was deployed more widely in UK courts than direct effect.[89]

It has been suggested that this has established a form of 'inter-legality', in which a mix of national and EU law regulates a dispute. The EU element opens up adjudication to wider norms and concerns, whilst the national law element ensures that the local traditions and contexts surrounding the dispute are not overlooked.

> **M. Amstutz, 'In–Between Worlds:** *Marleasing* **and the Emergence of Interlegality In Legal Reasoning' (2005) 11** *European Law Journal* **766, 781–2**
>
> The internal culture-specific 'constraints' on national adjudication remain unaffected by the requirement for interpretation in conformity with Directives; local specificities of the various legal discourses are not pushed aside, say, by rational arguments that in the end are always weaker than the constraints of organically grown legal cultures. For ultimately it is the legal policies present in the private law of the individual Member States that act as 'regulators' in the process of incorporating Community private-law positions into the national legal discourses. They are ensuring that two separate sets of norms do not emerge in Member States' civil legal systems – one deriving from the historical trajectory of the State concerned, the other dictated by the Community. They alone can offer guarantees for a Community private law integrated into the national legal culture, and this fact immediately makes it clear how they ensure the evolutionary capacity of national law in the biotope of the European Community: by on the one hand – as artful combinations of 'flexible' and 'fixed' control parameters – blocking the propagation of the 'perturbations' from European law throughout the national private law, without on the other losing the national law's responsiveness to EC law.

If this hybridity shows some sensitivity to both national and EU concerns, it also generates issues of its own. The pre-eminent one is legal uncertainty.[90] There is the difficulty of deciding how an interpretation of national law can be contrived to comply with EU law before it becomes *contra legem*. In addition, indirect effect asks parties to look at two laws, EU and national, but it is unclear which is the governing norm. Finally, although indirect effect was developed in the context of Directives, it can also be used with other binding legal instruments (i.e. regulations, decisions and international agreements). However, there is uncertainty as to how far it can be used with soft law. In *Grimaldi*,[91] the Court stated that national courts should take into account recommendations in interpreting national law which implemented these recommendations. In that instance, it concerned ambiguous national law implementing the recommendation. This duty has since been extended to other forms of soft law,[92] albeit that it only applies when the national law is implementing the soft law. It is not clear, however, whether there is the same demanding duty to strain the interpretation of national law as there is when it is being interpreted in the light of EU hard law.

---

[89] D. Chalmers, 'The Positioning of EU Judicial Politics within the United Kingdom' (2000) 23 *WEP* 169, 190.
[90] G. de Búrca, 'Giving Effect to European Community Directives' (1992) 55 *MLR* 215.
[91] *Grimaldi* v. *Fonds des Maladies Professionelles*, C-322/88, EU:C:1989:646.
[92] *'Baltlanta'* v. *Lietuvos valstybė*, C-410/13, EU:C:2014:2134.

6 STATE LIABILITY

(i) The Establishment of State Liability

The limits of indirect effect and direct effect in the case of Directives were apparent by the early 1990s. Neither protected against flagrant violations of EU law by Member States where these either passed no legislation to transpose a Directive or had legislation in place which explicitly contradicted it. In *Francovich*, Italy had persistently failed to implement Directive 80/987, which granted employees privileged claims vis-à-vis other creditors in the event of the insolvency of their employer for unpaid wages. In 1987 the Commission brought a successful enforcement action against the Italian Government.[93] Even after the judgment, there was still no transposition. *Francovich* concerned an action by thirty-four employees, owed back pay by bankrupt employers, against the Italian State for the losses suffered as a consequence of its failure to transpose the Directive.

Francovich and Bonifaci v. *Italy*, C–6/90 and C–9/90, EU:C:1991:428

33 The full effectiveness of Community rules would be impaired and the protection of the rights which they grant would be weakened if individuals were unable to obtain redress when their rights are infringed by a breach of Community law for which a Member State can be held responsible.

34 The possibility of obtaining redress from the Member State is particularly indispensable where, as in this case, the full effectiveness of Community rules is subject to prior action on the part of the State and where, consequently, in the absence of such action, individuals cannot enforce before the national courts the rights conferred upon them by Community law.

35 It follows that the principle whereby a State must be liable for loss and damage caused to individuals as a result of breaches of Community law for which the State can be held responsible is inherent in the system of the Treaty.

36 A further basis for the obligation of Member States to make good such loss and damage is to be found in Article [4(3) TEU], under which the Member States are required to take all appropriate measures, whether general or particular, to ensure fulfilment of their obligations under Community law. Among these is the obligation to nullify the unlawful consequences of a breach of Community law ...

37 It follows from all the foregoing that it is a principle of Community law that the Member States are obliged to make good loss and damage caused to individuals by breaches of Community law for which they can be held responsible.

38 Although State liability is thus required by Community law, the conditions under which that liability gives rise to a right to reparation depend on the nature of the breach of Community law giving rise to the loss and damage.

39 Where, as in this case, a Member State fails to fulfil its obligation under the third paragraph of Article [288 TFEU] to take all the measures necessary to achieve the result prescribed by a Directive, the full effectiveness of that rule of Community law requires that there should be a right to reparation provided that three conditions are fulfilled.

40 The first of those conditions is that the result prescribed by the Directive should entail the grant of rights to individuals. The second condition is that it should be possible to identify the content of those

---

[93] *Commission* v. *Italy*, 22/87, EU:C:1989:45.

rights on the basis of the provisions of the Directive. Finally, the third condition is the existence of a causal link between the breach of the State's obligation and the loss and damage suffered by the injured parties.

41 Those conditions are sufficient to give rise to a right on the part of individuals to obtain reparation, a right founded directly on Community law.

42 Subject to that reservation, it is on the basis of the rules of national law on liability that the State must make reparation for the consequences of the loss and damage caused. In the absence of Community legislation, it is for the internal legal order of each Member State to designate the competent courts and lay down the detailed procedural rules for legal proceedings intended fully to safeguard the rights which individuals derive from Community law ...

43 Further, the substantive and procedural conditions for reparation of loss and damage laid down by the national law of the Member States must not be less favourable than those relating to similar domestic claims and must not be so framed as to make it virtually impossible or excessively difficult to obtain reparation ...

Francovich was a seminal judgment.[94] At that time, most States did not provide a system of governmental liability for equivalent breaches of national law.[95] Most academic commentators welcomed the decision on the grounds that it would lead to better enforcement of EU law[96] and greater citizen empowerment.[97] A wise, cautionary voice was offered by Harlow who observed that little thought had been given to who paid for and who benefited from State liability.

C. Harlow, '*Francovich* and the Problem of the Disobedient State' (1996) 2 *European Law Journal* 199, 204

At the outset we should dismiss the vision of a squad of citizen policemen engaged in law enforcement. There are, of course, actions fought by individuals or groups of individuals. *Marshall* falls into this category; *Francovich* . . . In the field of environmental law, we find a developing pattern derived from human rights law, where a number of specialist organisations (NGOs) dedicated to the enforcement of human rights through courts operate; in Article [288] cases, their place has largely been assumed by State-funded agencies. Whether or not these groups and agencies can be said to represent 'citizens' is a moot point but they do embody the private enforcement machinery to which the ECJ apparently aspires. This is not to imply, however, that the model of 'politics through law' espoused by the ECJ is best pursued through the medium of the action for damages; . . . there is much to be said in favour of judicial review as the standard procedure, with annulment or declaratory orders as the standard remedy, in this type of citizen enforcement. In other areas, citizen enforcement is in any event a fantasy . . . [A]n overwhelming majority of actions against the Community are brought by corporations . . . [in litigation that] typically involves licences and other economic interests.

---

94 The academic literature is voluminous, e.g. P. Craig, '*Francovich*, Remedies and the Scope of Damages Liability' (1993) 109 *LQR* 595; R. Caranta, 'Governmental Liability after *Francovich*' [1993] *CLJ* 272; M. Ross, 'Beyond *Francovich*' (1993) 56 *MLR* 55; R. Caranta, 'Judicial Protection against Member States: A New *Jus Commune* Takes Shape' (1995) 32 *CMLRev* 703.

95 J. Tallberg, 'Supranational Influence in EU Enforcement: The ECJ and the Principle of State Liability' (2000) 7 *JEPP* 104, 114–16.

96 Caranta, 'Judicial Protection', n. 94 above, 710.

97 E.g. E. Szyszczak, 'Making Europe More Relevant to its Citizens' (1996) 21 *ELRev* 35; J. Steiner, 'From Direct Effects to Francovich: More Effective Means of Enforcement of Community Law' (1993) 18 *ELRev* 3.

This was particularly apposite, she argued, because systems of government liability locked courts into tragic choices. Compensation was not made from some limitless budget. Instead, as States never increased taxes to pay for liability claims, compensation was provided at the expense of other public goods, typically – as welfare spending is the highest proportion of national budgets – money intended for the old, the sick and the poor. She wondered whether such a distributive exercise was best done through the happenstance of individual litigation.[98]

It may also be, however, that *Francovich*'s effects, be they positive or negative, have been overstated. A series of case studies of litigation in relation to nature protection Directives in the Netherlands, France and Germany found that litigation was conditioned by a series of features, which were rarely all in place at the same time.[99] These included the organisational capacity of groups to litigate; effective access of parties to courts, unimpeded by standing rules or financial restrictions; the willingness by courts to give full interpretations; and the propensity of the administration to implement court rulings fully and quickly. Thus, analysis of patterns of State liability and litigation in Germany and the United Kingdom, found both very low levels of litigation and low levels of success. A total of sixty-two cases had been brought in these two large States in twenty years, of which seventeen had been successful: less than one per year for Germany and the United Kingdom combined.[100]

(ii) The Conditions of Liability

Francovich left open the question of when a Member State would be liable for breaching Union law. This was addressed in *Brasserie du Pêcheur* and *Factortame III*. Brasserie du Pêcheur, a French firm, had been forced to discontinue exports of beer to Germany in 1981 by virtue of a prohibition on the marketing of beers in Germany if they contained additives. In 1987, this law was found to restrict free movement of goods illegally.[101] Brasserie du Pêcheur sought compensation for the loss of sales between 1981 and 1987. In *Factortame*, a British law requiring, *inter alia*, other EU citizens to have a base and be resident in the United Kingdom to fish in United Kingdom waters had been declared illegal on the grounds that it restricted freedom of establishment.[102] A number of Spanish fishermen subsequently claimed for loss suffered as a result of their illegal exclusion from British waters.

Brasserie du Pêcheur v. Germany and R v. Secretary of State for Transport, ex parte Factortame, C–46/93 and 48/93, EU:C:1996:79

40   . . . it is pertinent to refer to the Court's case law on non-contractual liability on the part of the Community.

41   First, . . . Article [340 TFEU] refers as regards the non-contractual liability of the Community, to the general principles common to the laws of the Member States, from which, in the absence of written rules, the Court also draws inspiration in other areas of Community law.

---

[98] C. Harlow, 'Francovich and the Problem of the Disobedient State' (1996) 2 *ELJ* 199, 210–12.

[99] R. Slepcevic, 'The Judicial Enforcement of EU Law through National Courts: Possibilities and Limits' (2009) 16 *JEPP* 378.

[100] T. Lock, 'Is Private Enforcement of EU Law through State Liability a Myth? An Assessment 20 Years after Francovich' (2012) 49 *CMLRev* 1675, 1685.

[101] *Commission* v. *Germany*, 178/84, EU:C:1987:126.

[102] *R* v. *Secretary of State for Transport, ex parte Factortame*, C-221/89, EU:C:1991:320.

42 Second, the conditions under which the State may incur liability for damage caused to individuals by a breach of Community law cannot, in the absence of particular justification, differ from those governing the liability of the Community in like circumstances. The protection of the rights which individuals derive from Community law cannot vary depending on whether a national authority or a Community authority is responsible for the damage.

43 The system of rules which the Court has worked out with regard to Article [340 TFEU], particularly in relation to liability for legislative measures, takes into account, *inter alia*, the complexity of the situations to be regulated, difficulties in the application or interpretation of the texts and, more particularly, the margin of discretion available to the author of the act in question.

44 Thus, in developing its case law on the non-contractual liability of the Community, in particular as regards legislative measures involving choices of economic policy, the Court has had regard to the wide discretion available to the institutions in implementing Community policies.

45 The strict approach taken towards the liability of the Community in the exercise of its legislative activities is due to two considerations. First, even where the legality of measures is subject to judicial review, exercise of the legislative function must not be hindered by the prospect of actions for damages whenever the general interest of the Community requires legislative measures to be adopted which may adversely affect individual interests. Second, in a legislative context characterised by the exercise of a wide discretion, which is essential for implementing a Community policy, the Community cannot incur liability unless the institution concerned has manifestly and gravely disregarded the limits on the exercise of its powers . . .

46 That said, the national legislature – like the Community institutions – does not systematically have a wide discretion when it acts in a field governed by Community law. Community law may impose upon it obligations to achieve a particular result or obligations to act or refrain from acting which reduce its margin of discretion, sometimes to a considerable degree. This is so, for instance, where, as in the circumstances to which the judgment in *Francovich* relates, Article [288 TFEU] places the Member State under an obligation to take, within a given period, all the measures needed in order to achieve the result required by a directive. In such a case, the fact that it is for the national legislature to take the necessary measures has no bearing on the member State's liability for failing to transpose the directive.

47 In contrast, where a Member State acts in a field where there it has a wide discretion, comparable to that of the Community institutions in implementing Community policies, the conditions under which it may incur liability must, in principle, be the same as those under which the Community institutions incur liability in a comparable situation . . .

50 . . . in each case the German and United Kingdom legislatures were faced with situations involving choices comparable to those made by the Community institutions when they adopt legislative measures pursuant to a Community policy.

51 In such circumstances, Community law confers a right to reparation where three conditions are met: the rule of law infringed must be intended to confer rights on individuals; the breach must be sufficiently serious; and there must be a direct causal link between the breach of the obligation resting on the State and the damage sustained by the injured parties . . .

54 The first condition is manifestly satisfied in the case of Article [34 TFEU], the relevant provision in Case C-46/93, and in the case of Article [49 TFEU], the relevant provision in Case C-48/93 . . .

55 As to the second condition, as regards both Community liability under Article [340 TFEU] and Member State liability for breaches of Community law, the decisive test for finding that a breach of Community law is sufficiently serious is whether the Member State or the Community institution concerned manifestly and gravely disregarded the limits of its discretion.

56 The factors which the competent court may take into consideration include the clarity and precision of the rule breached, the measure of discretion left by that rule to the national or Community authorities, whether the infringement and the damage caused was intentional or involuntary, whether any error of law was excusable or inexcusable, the fact that the position taken by a Community institution may have contributed towards the omission, and the adoption or retention of national measures or practices contrary to Community law.

57 On any view, a breach of Community law will clearly be sufficiently serious if it has persisted despite a judgment finding the infringement in question to be established, or a preliminary ruling or settled case-law of the Court on the matter from which it is clear that the conduct in question constituted an infringement . . .

65 As for the third condition, it is for the national courts to determine whether there is a direct causal link between the breach of the obligation borne by the State and the damage sustained by the injured parties . . .

82 Reparation for loss or damage caused to individuals as a result of breaches of Community law must be commensurate with the loss or damage sustained so as to ensure the effective protection for their rights.

83 In the absence of relevant Community provisions, it is for the domestic legal system of each Member State to set the criteria for determining the extent of reparation. However, those criteria must not be less favourable than those applying to similar claims based on domestic law and must not be such as in practice to make it impossible or excessively difficult to obtain reparation.

Following *Brasserie du Pêcheur*, the Court moved to a threefold test for establishing liability:

- The rule of EU law infringed must be intended to confer rights on the individual litigants.
- The breach of that rule must be sufficiently serious.
- There must be a direct causal link between the breach and the loss or damage sustained by the individuals.

With regard to the first requirement that the EU law must be intended to confer rights on the individual litigants, the EU law in question must clearly state the identity of both the right-holder and the party owing legal duties to her. In addition, the obligations set out by it must be clear and precise.[103] If this seems reasonably clear on paper, it has proved less so in practice. For questions as to whether beneficiaries' or incumbents' identities can be sufficiently identified leaves much scope to judicial discretion. *Muñoz* is a case in point.[104] This case concerned the quality standards demanded of table grapes within the Union. The relevant Regulation stated that 'the holder of products covered by the quality standards . . . may not offer them for sale, or deliver or market them in any other manner than in conformity with those standards'. A competitor sought to sue a product-holder in a domestic court for failing to do this. The Court held that he could sue as this would strengthen the effectiveness of these standards. This would imply that a State failure to police these standards would generate *Francovich* liability. However, the Regulation is silent on the rights of competitors which are not identified in any way at all by it.

The second requirement has proved to be more complex. *Brasserie du Pêcheur* distinguishes between situations where EU law accords Member States no discretion over how to implement it, and simple breach is sufficient to incur liability, and situations where they enjoy some margin

---

[103] *Grenville Hampshire* v. *The Board of the Pension Protection Fund*, C-17/17, EU:C:2018:674.

[104] *Muñoz* v. *Frumar*, C-253/00, EU:C:2002:497. On the challenges with this requirement see M. Dougan, 'Addressing Issues of Protective Scope within the Francovich Right to Reparation' (2017) 13 *EUConst* 124.

for discretion, and must manifestly and gravely disregard the limits of this discretion to incur liability. In reality, this dichotomy is somewhat false as, in the latter case, the Court has stated that Member States enjoy no discretion to do certain things. If they do these, they will incur liability. As a consequence, breaches of EU law are sufficiently serious to incur liability in four circumstances:

- a failure to transpose a Directive[105] or a clearly incorrect transposition of a Directive[106]
- breach of an order of the Court of Justice[107]
- breach of settled case law[108]
- breach of a provision of EU law whose interpretation leaves no room for reasonable doubt.[109]

Otherwise, liability will not be incurred. If provisions are reasonably capable of bearing the meaning understood by the Member State[110] or the case law is unsettled or extremely recent, then no liability will be found.[111] State liability is thus a backstop measure. It focuses on sanctioning egregious or highly neglectful behaviour rather than securing redress for litigants. It has proved to be the highest hurdle for litigants to surmount when claiming loss from illegal State behaviour,[112] and leaves them exposed when the provision is neither clear nor can be interpreted to comply with EU law. This, in turn, raises an important further question: namely, whether the Court should be imposing punitive measures not to secure individual protection but rather to enforce national compliance with EU law.

The third condition, that of causation, has also proved challenging. In principle, it is for the national court to establish that the illegal behaviour has led to loss. However, two circumstances have been identified in EU law where it will not be possible to establish loss. First, the loss suffered must be as a consequence of the State's illegal behaviour. A failure to observe a particular procedural requirement is therefore unlikely to lead to liability. In *Leth*, a claimant was unable to claim for the loss of value in her home which occurred as a result of the extension of an airport in Vienna.[113] This extension had been done illegally as no environmental impact assessment had been carried out. However, the Court noted that this procedural failure did not of itself generate liability, as the requirement to carry out an assessment involved no substantive requirements to balance ecological versus other needs which would necessarily have led to the extension not taking place. Secondly, there must usually be a *direct* causal link between the illegality and the loss. In *Danfoss*, the cost of an excise duty on oil illegally levied on oil companies by Denmark was passed on by them to Danfoss when it bought the oil from them.[114] Danfoss sued the Danish State who claimed that it should have sued the oil companies for the loss, and not it, as these were the parties who imposed the financial burden. The Court agreed. It

---

[105] *Dillenkofer and Others*, C-178–9/94 and C-188–90/94, EU:C:1996:375.

[106] E.g. *Fenoll* v. *Centre d'aide par le travail 'La Jouvene'*, C-316/33, EU:C:2015:200; *Ambisig* v. *AICP*, C-46/15, EU:C:2016:530.

[107] There was an allegation that the British Government had done this in *Brasserie du Pêcheur* v. *Germany* and *R* v. *Secretary of State for Transport, ex parte Factortame*, C-46/93 and C-48/93, EU:C:1996:79.

[108] *Fuß* v. *Stadt Halle*, C-429/09, EU:C:2010:717.

[109] *Stockholm Lindöpark*, C-150/99, EU:C:2001:34; *R* v. *Licensing Authority of the Department of Health, ex parte Synthon*, C-452/06, EU:C:2008:565; *Ogieriakhi* v. *Minister for Justice and Equality*, C-244/13, EU:C:2014:2068.

[110] *R* v. *HM Treasury, ex parte British Telecommunications*, C-392/93, EU:C:1996:131.

[111] *N* v. *Inspecteur van de Belastingdienst Oost/kantoor Almelo*, C-470/04, EU:C:2006:525; *Specht and Others* v. *Land Berlin*, C-501–6/12 and C-540–1/12, EU:C:2014:2005.

[112] Lock, n. 100 above, 1688–97.   [113] *Leth* v. *Republik Österreich*, C-420/11, EU:C:2013:166.

[114] *Danfoss and Sauer-Danfoss* v. *Skatteministeriet*, C-94/10, EU:C:2011:674.

stated that there was no direct causal link between the excise duty and Danfoss's loss. This was caused by the independent decisions of the oil companies to raise prices. However, it stated that Danfoss could sue the Danish State if it was virtually impossible or excessively difficult under national law to secure compensation from these companies.

(iii) Liability for Acts of Judicial Institutions

A particularly challenging dimension to State liability concerns liability for rulings by national courts. This arose in *Köbler*.[115] An Austrian university professor had part of his salary calculated on his length of university service but periods of employment in universities in other Member States did not contribute to this calculation. The Austrian Administrative Court, a court of last resort required to refer questions of EU law to the Court of Justice unless these had already been decided by the latter, withdrew a reference on the mistaken grounds that the Court of Justice had ruled such a practice to be lawful.[116] Köbler argued that the State was liable for both this failure to refer and the misinterpretation of the case law. The Court of Justice agreed that a misinterpretation had taken place, and then considered whether this gave grounds for liability.

Köbler v. *Austria*, C–224/01, EU:C:2003:513

33 In the light of the essential role played by the judiciary in the protection of the rights derived by individuals from Community rules, the full effectiveness of those rules would be called in question and the protection of those rights would be weakened if individuals were precluded from being able, under certain conditions, to obtain reparation when their rights are affected by an infringement of Community law attributable to a decision of a court of a Member State adjudicating at last instance.

34 It must be stressed, in that context, that a court adjudicating at last instance is by definition the last judicial body before which individuals may assert the rights conferred on them by Community law. Since an infringement of those rights by a final decision of such a court cannot thereafter normally be corrected, individuals cannot be deprived of the possibility of rendering the State liable in order in that way to obtain legal protection of their rights.

35 Moreover, it is, in particular, in order to prevent rights conferred on individuals by Community law from being infringed that under the third paragraph of Article [267 TFEU] a court against whose decisions there is no judicial remedy under national law is required to make a reference to the Court of Justice.

36 Consequently, it follows from the requirements inherent in the protection of the rights of individuals relying on Community law that they must have the possibility of obtaining redress in the national courts for the damage caused by the infringement of those rights owing to a decision of a court adjudicating at last instance . . .

51 As to the conditions to be satisfied for a Member State to be required to make reparation for loss and damage caused to individuals as a result of breaches of Community law for which the State is responsible, the Court has held that these are threefold: the rule of law infringed must be intended to confer rights on individuals; the breach must be sufficiently serious; and there must be a direct causal link between the breach of the obligation incumbent on the State and the loss or damage sustained by the injured parties. . .

---

[115] P. Wattel, 'Köbler, *CILFIT* and *Welthgrove*: We Can't Go on Meeting Like This' (2004) 41 *CMLRev* 177.
[116] The Austrian court sought to rely on *Schöning-Kougebetopoulou* v. *Freie und Hansestadt Hamburg*, C-15/96, EU: C:1998:3.

52 State liability for loss or damage caused by a decision of a national court adjudicating at last instance which infringes a rule of Community law is governed by the same conditions.

53 With regard more particularly to the second of those conditions and its application with a view to establishing possible State liability owing to a decision of a national court adjudicating at last instance, regard must be had to the specific nature of the judicial function and to the legitimate requirements of legal certainty, as the Member States which submitted observations in this case have also contended. State liability for an infringement of Community law by a decision of a national court adjudicating at last instance can be incurred only in the exceptional case where the court has manifestly infringed the applicable law.

54 In order to determine whether that condition is satisfied, the national court hearing a claim for reparation must take account of all the factors which characterise the situation put before it.

55 Those factors include, in particular, the degree of clarity and precision of the rule infringed, whether the infringement was intentional, whether the error of law was excusable or inexcusable, the position taken, where applicable, by a Community institution and non-compliance by the court in question with its obligation to make a reference for a preliminary ruling under [Article 267(3) TFEU].

56 In any event, an infringement of Community law will be sufficiently serious where the decision concerned was made in manifest breach of the case-law of the Court in the matter . . .

At the time, only Spain and Austria had systems of liability for judicial decisions. The judgment, therefore, raised questions about legal certainty and traditional judicial hierarchies.

H. Scott and N. Barber, 'State Liability under *Francovich* for Decisions of National Courts' (2004) 120 *Law Quarterly Review* 403, 404–5

The extension of *Francovich* liability to courts of final decision has profound implications for the domestic legal hierarchy. After *Köbler* the English High Court could find itself compelled to pass judgment on a decision of the English House of Lords. A litigant disappointed by the House of Lords' decision could start a fresh action against the United Kingdom. The High Court, a few months later, would then be called on to assess whether the House of Lords had made an error of law that was sufficiently serious to warrant damages. The High Court would, almost certainly, refer the question to the ECJ under Article [267 TFEU] if it thought there was any doubt as to the correctness of the Lords' ruling. In response to such a reference the ECJ would give a ruling on the content of European law . . .

This prospect raises a number of problems for domestic legal systems. First, and most superficially, it reduces legal certainty. This is not, as some in *Köbler* tried to argue, because it allows the reopening of concluded cases. Once the State's highest court has ruled, the judgment is definitive between the parties and cannot be challenged; the principle of *res judicata* is not affected. The *Francovich* action is a separate legal right and is directed against the State; a body which, ordinarily, would not have been a party to the original action. However, *Köbler* does have the effect of allowing litigants a second chance to raise the legal question apparently resolved in the primary action: frustrated in the House of Lords, the litigant could re-start the process through *Francovich* in the High Court. Secondly, the decision upsets the domestic legal hierarchy. The High Court would be obliged to question the correctness of a decision of the House of Lords made a few months earlier: it would have to decide whether there was a sufficient chance of error to warrant a reference to the ECJ, and, when this ruling was returned, how severe the error had been. Further problems might arise as this secondary action progressed up the legal order, perhaps ending with one group of Law Lords ruling on the judgment of their colleagues. Thirdly, the decision has the potential to create serious constitutional conflict within the domestic legal order. The German Constitutional Court has ruled that in exceptional cases it might refuse to accept rulings of the ECJ (see *Brunner* [1994] 1 CMLR 57). If such a decision was then challenged under *Francovich*, a first instance judge might be forced to choose between loyalty to the final court of appeal and to the ECJ.

Liability will be found in only the most exceptional circumstances. States are not liable for breaches by most courts as there is the possibility of appeal within the domestic judicial system where these breach EU law. Liability is only, therefore, for judgments given by courts of last resort against whose decisions there can be no appeal.[117] Decisions by these courts must also manifestly infringe EU law.[118] This is likely to be the case only where a clear EU law is breached; there is an intentional or inexcusable breach; the position of an EU Institution on the law is ignored; or there is failure to refer to the Court of Justice when required to do so by virtue of Article 267(3) TFEU (see para. 55 of the *Köbler* judgment above).[119] A 2017 study, therefore, found a very limited response. Only about twelve States had implemented *Köbler* into national law, and even in these States successful invocations of the principle numbered no more than a handful.[120]

It is uncertain, therefore, when the Court of Justice would insist on judicial liability, particularly as the Union judicial order relies on cooperation between senior national courts and the Court of Justice. Even occasional invocation of national judicial liability would destroy the ethos behind this cooperation.[121] Liability being imposed when a senior court fails to make a reference possibly gives the game away. It is there to make national senior courts engage with the Court of Justice. Yet a failure to refer is likely to occur where the national court is deeply unhappy with the development of a line of reasoning by the Court of Justice or believes the latter has overstepped its authority. As we have seen in Chapter 5,[122] this dissatisfaction is widespread. Furthermore, it is no bad thing as it checks the Court of Justice and provides alternate sources of legal ideas. Judicial liability gets the lower courts in a national jurisdiction to do the Court of Justice's dirty work for it. If a senior court challenges the Court of Justice, there is now the possibility that litigants can take the matter before a junior court which must not only consider whether to award compensation but also how to arbitrate between the Court of Justice and the senior national court. This cannot be a good thing.

7 THE DUTY TO DISAPPLY EU LAW AND FUNDAMENTAL RIGHTS

State liability seemed insufficient where private parties were carrying out the most egregious violations of EU law. In such circumstances, there seems a stronger case for going directly

---

[117] *Tomášová*, C-168/15, EU:C:2016:602.

[118] B. Beutler, 'State Liability for Breaches of Community Law by National Courts: Is the Requirement of a Manifest Infringement of the Applicable Law an Insurmountable Obstacle?' (2009) 46 *CMLRev* 773.

[119] *Traghetti del Mediterraneo* v. *Italian Republic*, C-173/03, EU:C:2006:391.

[120] Z. Varga, 'National Remedies in the Case of Violation of EU Law by Member State Courts' (2017) 54 *CMLRev* 51, 56–7.

[121] A. Davies, 'State Liability for Judicial Decisions in European Union and International Law' (2012) 61 *ICLQ* 585, 604–7.

[122] See pp. 224–43.

had been illegal discrimination in that instance. Instead, the general principle is seen as a self-standing right which can be invoked in disputes between individuals provided that these fall within the scope of EU law.

However, *Egenberger* must be contrasted with *Grupo Norte Facility*.[128] This concerned the legality of a Spanish law that provided less compensation for those who were unfairly dismissed when they were on fixed-term contracts than for those on contracts of an indefinite duration. This was governed by the Directive on Fixed Term Contracts which requires no less favourable terms for fixed-term workers than those on permanent contracts. The Spanish court asked whether this Directive gives effect to the general principles on prohibiting discrimination and providing for equal treatment. If this were the case, then, following *Egenberger*, these principles could be invoked directly in the dispute. Notwithstanding that it was asked, the Court of Justice was silent, referring only to the provisions of the Directive. There can only be speculation over the reasons, but it is possible that the rights at stake were not seen to be as pressing as those in *Egenberger*, and therefore they could not be invoked directly before a court in a private dispute.

8 EU LAW IN UNITED KINGDOM COURTS AFTER BREXIT

Finally, there is the question of how far, after Brexit, EU law rights will be able to be invoked in UK courts. There are two answers to this. In formal terms, the doctrines, as central features of EU law, will cease to apply in the United Kingdom because EU law, qua EU law, will cease to apply. This is, furthermore, not a moot point. If a central point of Brexit is for the United Kingdom to cease to be subject to the jurisdiction of the Court of Justice,[129] then it is important that the key doctrines through which the Court has established a supranational legal order do not apply there. However, the position is very different in substantive terms. Counterpart doctrines have been established which will allow EU law rights, in all but name, to continue to be invoked more than one might think.

It pays, therefore, to go through each of the doctrines outlined in this chapter to see what counterpart, if any, they will have in the United Kingdom after Brexit.

Turning first to direct effect, we saw in Chapter 5 that directly effective EU law will become 'retained EU law' after Brexit. As such, it will have both legal effects within the United Kingdom and will take precedence over all UK law that was adopted before the day of Brexit.[130] Thus, individuals will be able to invoke this law in UK courts. Furthermore, the procedures and remedies accompanying these rights must be the same as those for analogous breaches of other domestic rights and must not make the exercise of these rights impossible or excessively difficult.[131]

The situation with indirect effect is a little more complex. It would seem that there is a duty to interpret all UK law adopted prior to Brexit in the light of all retained EU law, and that duty is to interpret it, wherever possible, to comply with retained EU law unless it aggravates a criminal liability.[132] The basis for this view is that section 4(1) of the European Union (Withdrawal) Act

---

[128] *Grupo Norte Facility* v. *Gómez*, C-574/16, EU:C:2018:390.

[129] HM Government, *The United Kingdom's Exit from and New Partnership with the European Union*, Cm. 9417 (London, SO, 2017) para. 2.3.

[130] European Union (Withdrawal) Act 2018, ss. 4(1) and 5(2).

[131] *Euro Park Service* v. *Ministre des Finances et des Comptes publics*, C-14/16, EU:C:2017:177.

[132] *Ognyanov*, C-554/14, EU:C:2016:835.

states that all EU legal 'obligations' in force immediately before exit day shall continue to have legal effect post-Brexit. Indirect effect is such an obligation, as it is an obligation on the national court to interpret national law in the light of EU law, pursuant to Article 4(3) TEU. The UK Government has also suggested another basis for this view: the supremacy provision.[133] It claims that this provision includes a duty to interpret domestic law in the light of retained EU law. Furthermore, this duty applies not just to directly effective EU law. Therefore, the government states that domestic law must be interpreted 'in light of the wording and purpose of relevant directives' even though there will be circumstances where Directives do not generate directly effective rights, notably in actions against private parties.[134]

There is also the question of whether UK courts are to interpret domestic law adopted after Brexit in the light of retained EU law or to interpret domestic law in the light of EU laws adopted after Brexit. There is clearly no obligation to do either of these things, but nor are UK courts precluded from doing either of these things. It is a matter of discretion for them, and, in this regard, the Act makes clear that courts can have regard to judgments by the Court of Justice adopted after Brexit.[135] However even if a choice is made for interpretative alignment, the duty is likely to be less strong than set out by *Marleasing.* It is unlikely that a UK court will stretch the meaning of a UK law to align it with EU law. Reference to EU law is more likely where there is genuine ambiguity and a choice has to be made between two equally plausible interpretations.

The situation with regard to State liability, by contrast, is straightforward. Recourse to it is excluded by the European Union (Withdrawal) Act.[136] Individuals will not be able to sue the British Government for loss suffered as a result of its failure to comply with retained EU law.

The future of this duty to disapply domestic law is uncertain. The European Union (Withdrawal) Act is clear that neither the EUCFR nor general principles of law can be invoked as a basis for either legislative or administrative review in domestic courts.[137] However, the basis for this doctrine in EU law is unclear. Put simply, it is ambiguous whether it is a combination of the Directive and the fundamental right which gives rise to the doctrine to disapply, or just the fundamental right. If it is the former, UK courts might find that, insofar as the obligation is generated partly by the Directive, they are obliged to apply it in cases involving retained EU law. However, the most recent judgment, *Egenberger*, suggests that this is not the case and that the EU fundamental right gives rise to the duty to disapply the domestic law, independently of any other EU law.[138] If that is so, it is likely that this doctrine will not apply in the United Kingdom after Brexit.

FURTHER READING

G. Betlem, 'The Doctrine of Consistent Interpretation: Managing Legal Uncertainty' (2002) 22 *Oxford Journal of Legal Studies* 397.

P. Craig, 'The Legal Effects of Directives: Policy Rules and Exceptions' (2009) 34 *European Law Review* 349.

---

[133] European Union (Withdrawal) Act 2018, s. 5(2).
[134] *European Union (Withdrawal) Act 2018: Explanatory Notes Chapter 16* (Norwich, TSO, 2018) para. 104.
[135] European Union (Withdrawal) Act 2018, s. 6(2).   [136] *Ibid.* Sch. 1, para. 4.
[137] *Ibid.* s. 5(4) and Sch. 1, para. 3 respectively.
[138] *Egenberger* v. *Evangelisches Werk für Diakonie und Entwicklung*, C-414/16, EU:C:2018:257.

A. Dashwood, 'From *Van Duyn* to *Mangold* via *Marshall*: Reducing Direct Effect to Absurdity?' (2006–7) 9 *Cambridge Yearbook of European Legal Studies* 81.

M. Dougan, 'When Worlds Collide: Competing Visions of the Relationship Between Direct Effect and Supremacy' (2007) 44 *Common Market Law Review* 931.

T. Eilmansberger, 'The Relationship between Rights and Remedies in EC Law: In Search of the Missing Link' (2004) 41 *Common Market Law Review* 1199.

M.-P. Granger, '*Francovich* and the Construction of a European Administrative *Ius Commune*' (2007) 32 *European Law Review* 157.

K. Havu, 'Full, Adequate and Commensurate Compensation for Damages under EU Law: A Challenge for National Courts?' (2018) 43 *European Law Review* 23.

T. Lock, 'Is Private Enforcement of EU Law through State Liability a Myth? An Assessment 20 Years after Francovich' (2012) 49 *Common Market Law Review* 1675.

E. Muir, 'Of Ages in – and Edges of – EU Law' (2011) 48 *Common Market Law Review* 39.

L. Pech, 'Between Judicial Minimalism and Avoidance: The Court of Justice's Sidestepping of Fundamental Constitutional Issues in *Römer* and *Dominguez*' (2012) 49 *Common Market Law Review* 1841.

Z. Varga, 'National Remedies in the Case of Violation of EU Law by Member State Courts' (2017) 54 *Common Market Law Review* 51.

8

The Infringement Proceedings

CONTENTS

1 INTRODUCTION

This chapter considers the infringement and sanctions proceedings that the Commission may bring before the Court of Justice against Member States for failure to comply with EU law. It is organised as follows.

Section 2 considers the central dimensions to the infringement proceedings. The main provision, Article 258 TFEU, allows the Commission to take a Member State to the Court of Justice and to obtain a ruling for failing to comply with EU law. The proceedings serve three purposes. They are, first, an instrument for policing Member State compliance with EU law. In this, they seek to promote the authority of the EU legal order. Secondly, they contribute to the effective functioning of EU policies by ensuring sufficient compliance for these to function effectively. On this view, the proceedings are a public policy tool, less concerned with protecting the authority of EU law and more with ensuring that EU policies work. Thirdly, the proceedings provide an arena where domestic concerns about an EU law that were not articulated at the moment of its adoption can be expressed and thought be given to how, if at all, they can be accommodated. On this view, the proceedings serve to structure interaction between the demands of EU law and the constellations of interests that will have to apply it.

Section 3 considers the scope of Member State responsibilities under Article 258 TFEU. Actions can only be brought against the State though this may include a State agency, even one which is constitutionally independent of the central government. The State is also responsible not just for legal instruments that conflict with EU law but also administrative practices that conflict with EU law. These usually have to be general and consistent in nature to attract liability. Finally, since the State is under a duty to secure the effective functioning of EU law, it will be held liable for a failure to do so.

Section 4 considers the three stages of the Article 258 TFEU proceedings prior to the matter being referred to the Court of Justice. Proceedings will either by triggered by the Commission of its own initiative or following a complaint by a third party. In either case, the first stage involves an initial screening to check if there is a case to answer, and, if there is, an initial attempt to resolve the matter with the Member States. In instances where it is useful, the Commission will use EU Pilot, an online procedure whereby it set outs a file on the case. Member States have, in principle, seventy days to set out their position on the file; the Commission has the same amount of time to consider their response. If there is no resolution, the Commission moves to the second stage – the formal pre-litigation procedure – in which it sends a letter of formal notice to the Member States setting out the complaint and then gives the Member State the opportunity to submit observations. If there is still no resolution, the third stage requires the Commission to adopt a reasoned opinion setting out the details of the complaint and a deadline for compliance. If compliance is not secured by the deadline, the matter is referred by the Commission to the Court of Justice.

Section 5 considers the management of the process by the Commission. It has complete freedom to decide whether to start the proceedings or to cease them. This has raised concerns about the transparency of the process and the accountability of the Commission for what takes place. Complainants, in particular, are granted only modest procedural guarantees. Centrally, there is a commitment to keep the complainant informed about the process and to reach a decision about whether to close a file or to instigate proceedings within twelve months. The secrecy of the process has come under increasing criticism from both the European Ombudsman and the European Parliament with the former stating that there are no good general reasons for it and the latter pushing for a Regulation to structure the process and make it more transparent.

Section 6 considers what sanctions may be imposed by the Court of Justice on a Member State. There are two procedures. First, where the proceedings concern a failure by the Member State to notify of its transposition of a Directive, Article 260(3) TFEU allows the Court to impose a fine at the time of giving judgment for non-compliance with EU law. The second, set out in Article 260(2) TEU, allows it to impose a fine where a Member State has failed to comply with a judgment finding that it has breached EU law. This procedure involves no reasoned opinion. The Commission adopts a letter of formal notice which gives the Member State a deadline for compliance and an opportunity to submit observations. There are two types of sanction. The lump sum penalises the State for its failure to comply with EU law whereas the penalty payment acts to deter the Member State from continuing non-compliance. The central principles governing the size of the sanction are the seriousness of the breach, the duration of the breach and the ability of the Member State to pay the sanction, calculated by reference to its GDP and voting weight within the Council.

2 THE DIFFERENT DIMENSIONS TO THE INFRINGEMENT PROCEEDINGS

The enforcement of EU law through the invocation of individual rights before national courts is an important and distinctive feature of EU law. However, it requires the EU law in question to actually confer rights on the individual, though there are many circumstances where it does not do so.[1] Furthermore, even when individual rights are conferred, questions of EU law compliance are tailored to secure individual redress. As such, the judgment might address only some features of the illegal behaviour that is taking place and fail to extend to other activities that fall outside the scope of the litigation.

The centralised procedures for the enforcement of EU law against the Member States are, thus, particularly important. They cover the full range of EU law for which the Court of Justice has jurisdiction. They can also be framed so they cover all the behaviour which breaches a particular EU law, and, finally, they go against the bodies with the most extensive responsibilities for the administration of EU law in the Union: the Member States. The central procedure is Article 258 TFEU.

> ### Article 258 TFEU
>
> If the Commission considers that a Member State has failed to fulfil an obligation under the Treaties, it shall deliver a reasoned opinion on the matter after giving the State concerned the opportunity to submit its observations.
>
> If the State concerned does not comply with the opinion within the period laid down by the Commission, the latter may bring the matter before the Court of Justice of the European Union.

Member States can also take other Member States before the Court of Justice for failure to comply with EU law.[2] This is rare, however.[3] Member States prefer the Commission to take action rather than to institute legal proceedings themselves. Article 108(2) TFEU allows legal proceedings to be brought against Member States for breach of the EU law provisions on State aids. Article 258 TFEU, therefore, plays the central role in enforcement and is used extensively.[4]

---

[1] On when EU law generates individual rights see Chapter 7 and pp. 291–6 in particular. [2] Article 259 TFEU.
[3] E.g. *France* v. *United Kingdom*, 141/78, EU:C:1979:225; *Belgium* v. *Spain*, C-388/95, EU:C:2000:244; *Spain* v. *United Kingdom*, C-145/04, EU:C:2006:543; *Hungary* v. *Slovakia*, C-364/10, EU:C:2012:630.
[4] There also are a number of specialised procedures. In the field of State aids, Member States or the Commission can take a Member State to Court for failure to comply with the Commission's Decisions in this field, Article 108(2) TFEU. In the fields of budgetary and macroeconomic policy, States can be taken to the Court to be fined for running variously an excessive budgetary deficit, a budget which is not in balance or having excessive macroeconomic imbalances. On these see pp. 674–7.

A total of 1,559 infringement proceedings were open at the end of 2017.[5] Proceedings were open against all Member States: Denmark was subject to the lowest number of proceedings, with twenty-eight, and Spain the highest, at ninety-three. The proceedings stretched, furthermore, across all the significant fields of EU law, with the highest number (308) being in the field of the environment.[6]

Infringement proceedings will still be able to be instigated against the United Kingdom during the transition period which runs until 31 December 2020.

Article 87 Withdrawal Agreement

(1) If the European Commission considers that the United Kingdom has failed to fulfil an obligation under the Treaties or under Part Four of this Agreement before the end of the transition period, the European Commission may, within 4 years after the end of the transition period, bring the matter before the Court of Justice of the European Union in accordance with the requirements laid down in Article 258 TFEU . . .

The United Kingdom appears to be subject to wider obligations than EU Member States insofar as it can be brought before the Court not merely for breaching EU law but also for breaching Part Four of the Withdrawal Agreement.[7] However, this does not amount to much, as the central additional obligation set out by Part Four is for almost all EU law to apply within the United Kingdom during the transitional period.[8] It is important to note that Article 87(1) allows infringement proceedings to be brought against the United Kingdom for four years after the end of the transition period if the breach occurred during that period. There will, therefore, be a long period of Commission oversight after this period. Finally, the United Kingdom retains the right to bring other Member States to Court, and they a converse right to start infringement proceedings against it, during the transition period.[9]

If the use of Article 258 TFEU is wide-ranging, it is less easy to sum up its mission. The procedure can be characterised in different ways in terms of what it does and which elements of it are most significant. Each of these, correspondingly, provides a different prism through which to evaluate its success and limits.

(i) Policing Compliance with EU Law

The first view of Article 258 TFEU is that it is a policing procedure to secure EU law's place within the Union. This is the view expressed in much legal scholarship[10] and the case law of the Court.[11] In *Commission* v. *Germany*, the government of Lower Saxony concluded a contract for the collection of waste water, and this contravened EU law on public procurement. The

---

[5] European Commission, *Monitoring the Application of Union Law, 2017 Annual Report: General Statistical Overview Part 1*, SWD (2018) 377, 12.

[6] *Ibid.* 13.   [7] This comprises Articles 126–32 Withdrawal Agreement.

[8] Article 127(1) Withdrawal Agreement. Certain EU laws will not apply. Most notably, UK citizens will not be able to vote or stand for election in either European Parliament elections or municipal elections in other Member States, nor will they have the right to participate in the citizens' initiative or to petition the Ombudsman or Parliament, Article 127 (1)(b) Withdrawal Agreement.

[9] Article 86(1) Withdrawal Agreement.

[10] A. Gil Ibañez, *The Administrative Supervision and Enforcement of EC Law, Powers, Procedures and Limits* (Oxford-Portland, Hart, 1999) esp. 26–35; L. Prete and B. Smulders, 'The Coming of Age of Infringement Proceedings' (2010) 47 CMLRev 9.

[11] In like vein, *Commission* v. *Malta*, C-76/08, EU:C:2009:535; *Commission* v. *Ireland*, C-456/08, EU:C:2010:46.

German Government admitted it violated EU law but stated that the contract could not be terminated without payment of substantial compensation to the contractor. It, therefore, argued that the Commission proceedings were inadmissible as there was no good reason for the Commission's action.

Commission v. Germany, C–20/01 and C–28/01, EU:C:2003:220

29 ... in exercising its powers under Article [258 TFEU] the Commission does not have to show that there is a specific interest in bringing an action. The provision is not intended to protect the Commission's own rights. The Commission's function, in the general interest of the Community, is to ensure that the Member States give effect to the Treaty and the provisions adopted by the institutions thereunder and to obtain a declaration of any failure to fulfil the obligations deriving there from with a view to bringing it to an end.

30 Given its role as guardian of the Treaty, the Commission alone is therefore competent to decide whether it is appropriate to bring proceedings against a Member State for failure to fulfil its obligations and to determine the conduct or omission attributable to the Member State concerned on the basis of which those proceedings should be brought. It may therefore ask the Court to find that, in not having achieved, in a specific case, the result intended by the directive, a Member State has failed to fulfil its obligations ...

41 The Court has already held that it is responsible for determining whether or not the alleged breach of obligations exists, even if the State concerned no longer denies the breach and recognises that any individuals who have suffered damage because of it have a right to compensation ...

42 Since the finding of failure by a Member State to fulfil its obligations is not bound up with a finding as to the damage flowing therefrom ... the Federal Republic of Germany may not rely on the fact that no third party has suffered damage ...

44 In the light of the foregoing, the actions brought by the Commission must be held to be admissible.

Policing compliance with EU law is a central mission of Article 258 TFEU. The procedure cannot, however, been seen exclusively in these terms.

First, such a view can be excessively doctrinaire in individual cases. In *Commission v. Germany*, therefore, the German Government argued that complying with EU law and rescinding the contracts would violate individual property rights, disrupt construction of the waste water system as everything would have to be restarted, and lead to the public authorities having to pay large amounts of compensation. It had admitted its guilt and the payment of compensation was disproportionately large when put next to the benefits of securing the EU law in question. The German Government's upset was, thus, marked by its only rescinding the contract after it was subsequently fined.[12] The problems remained, however.

Secondly, compliance with EU law is often not the only value at stake, and these other values are taken into account. Thus, as *Commission v. Germany* indicates, the Commission has discretion whether or not to prosecute. In exercising that discretion, it has to decide the best thing to do, which may not always be the same thing as policing EU law in the most rigorous way possible. As such, the Commission has stated that it will pursue infringement proceedings where there is an 'added value' in so doing.[13] There is a threshold issue here, namely whether the illegal action is sufficiently serious to warrant action. Börzel has, thus, noted that the

---

[12] *Commission* v. *Germany*, C–503/04, EU:C:2007:432.

[13] European Commission, *EU Law: Better Results through Better Application*, OJ 2017, C 18/10, 15.

mission of Article 258 TFEU is to consider whether 'the observed level of non-compliance is considered as a serious problem for a community'.[14] However, as we shall see later on in this section, decisions on whether to pursue States also involves the setting of priorities in which certain interests, values and institutions are to be protected more aggressively than others.[15]

Thirdly, the Commission does not have the powers to seek full compliance with all EU law. The procedure can only be used against certain types of illegal behaviour. Cases can always be brought where a domestic law violates EU law but the position is more complex in respect of administrative practices. Usually in this regard actions may only be brought if there is a general and consistent administrative practice breaching EU law. In *Commission* v. *Greece*, the Commission brought an action against Greece on the grounds that its hospitals' tendering procedures were excluding medical devices that met EU legal standards. The Greek Government claimed that it had transposed the relevant Directives into Greek law and had sent a circular to hospitals reminding them of their obligations under EU law. The Court nevertheless found a breach of EU law.[16]

Commission v. *Greece*, C–489/06, EU: C:2009:165

46 ... even if the applicable national legislation itself complies with Community law, a failure to fulfil obligations may arise due to the existence of an administrative practice which infringes that law ...

48 In order for a failure to fulfil obligations to be found on the basis of the administrative practice followed in a Member State, the Court has held that the failure to fulfil obligations can be established only by means of sufficiently documented and detailed proof of the alleged practice; that administrative practice must be, to some degree, of a consistent and general nature; and, in order to find that there has been a general and consistent practice, the Commission may not rely on any presumption ...

49 It must be pointed out that, according to the information in the file before the Court, the products in question are products fulfilling the requirements of the European Pharmacopoeia technical standard and must, by their very nature, be purchased repeatedly and regularly by hospitals and, consequently, with an established degree of regularity.

50 None the less, at least 16 hospital contracting authorities rejected the medical devices in question, during tendering procedures ...

51 The list of the hospitals mentioned by the Commission shows a variety in the size of the establishments, since some of the largest Greek hospitals such as Agios Savvas, Kyriakou and Asklipiio Voula are referred to, as well as medium-sized hospitals such as Argos, Agios Nikolaos of Crete or Sparta.

52 Moreover, that list refers to establishments with a geographical coverage encompassing the entire country with, in particular, hospitals in Athens, in the Peloponnese and on Crete, but concerns also a wide field of competence, including general hospitals, a children's hospital, a hospital treating cancer-related illnesses and a maternity hospital.

53 Therefore, it can be deduced that the administrative practice of the contracting authorities in question, ... demonstrates a certain degree of consistency and generality.

---

[14] T. Börzel, 'Non Compliance in the European Union: Pathology or Statistical Artefact' (2001) 8 *JEPP* 803, 818.

[15] The Commission is indeed explicit about this need for prioritisation, European Commission, n. 13 above, 14.

[16] In like vein, *Commission* v. *Czech Republic*, C-525/14, EU:C:2016:714; *Commission* v. *Luxembourg*, C-274/15, EU:C:2017:333.

In most fields, there must be a consistent and general practice of illegality. To determine whether this is present, regard is had to the duration, geographical spread and number of illegal acts.[17] However, the nature of the sector is important as this will determine the interests at stake. There have been instances, therefore, where a single isolated act has been sufficient to justify infringement proceedings. These have been cases involving civil liberties concerns[18] or significant public purchases in the field of public procurement where the particularity of each tender would make it difficult to identify a general practice.[19]

Therefore, Article 258 TFEU is about giving the Commission discretion to police certain breaches of EU law. In exercising this discretion, it will look at the significance and nature of the breach, as well as the wider values and interests at stake. Consequently, the central question becomes which breaches of EU law the Commission is particularly keen to police. In 2017, the Commission set out a 'more strategic approach to enforcement'[20] in which it set out the priorities guiding its enforcement action. The highest priority will be given to taking action against breaches which threaten either the Union's legal or financial autonomy.

European Commission, *EU law: Better results through better application*[21]

As a matter of priority, the Commission will investigate cases where Member States have failed to communicate transposition measures or where those measures have incorrectly transposed directives; where Member States have failed to comply with a judgment of the Court of Justice as referred to in Article 260(2) TFEU; or where they have caused serious damage to EU financial interests or violated EU exclusive powers.

The obligation to take the necessary measures to comply with a judgment of the Court of Justice has the widest effect where the action required concerns systemic weaknesses in a Member State's legal system. The Commission will therefore give high priority to infringements that reveal systemic weaknesses which undermine the functioning of the EU's institutional framework. This applies in particular to infringements which affect the capacity of national judicial systems to contribute to the effective enforcement of EU law. The Commission will therefore pursue rigorously all cases of national rules or general practices which impede the procedure for preliminary rulings by the Court of Justice, or where national law prevents the national courts from acknowledging the primacy of EU law. It will also pursue cases in which national law provides no effective redress procedures for a breach of EU law or otherwise prevents national judicial systems from ensuring that EU law is applied effectively in accordance with the requirements of the rule of law and Article 47 of the European Union Charter of Fundamental Rights (EUCFR).

These cases are no doubt prioritised because the infringement is seen as a threat to the Union rather than to particular interests or parties within it. However, therein lies the rub because it means the Commission will focus its infringement actions on protecting the existing politico-legal order: chasing down States which do not transpose Directives or comply with judgments, courts who do not refer or accept the primacy of EU law, or States acting in fields where only the

---

[17] P. Wennerås, 'A New Dawn for Commission Enforcement under Articles 226 and 228: General and Persistent (GAP) Infringements, Lump Sums and Penalty Payments' (2006) 43 *CMLRev* 31, 38.

[18] *Commission v. Germany*, C-441/02, EU:C:2006:253; *Commission v. Spain*, C-157/03, EU:C:2005:225; *Commission v. Spain*, C-503/03, EU:C:2006:74.

[19] *Commission v. Germany*, C-20/01 and C-28/01, EU: C:2003:220; *Commission v. Ireland*, C-456/08, EU:C:2010:46.

[20] European Commission, n. 13 above, 14.   [21] OJ 2017, C 18/10, 15.

Union should act. In all this, however, there is no reference to individual rights or interests. The prioritisation of litigation to protect the Union politico-legal order, necessarily, means that less attention will be focused on illegal domestic practices which affect private parties' rights, often in large numbers. The following example illustrates the problem.

The Commission indicated in the extract above that it targets non-transposition of Directives. It has been true to its word: in 2017, of the 1,559 cases taken forward by it, over half, 808, focused on these non-transposed Directives.[22] Yet, it is not clear that non-transposition of Directives is a crucial problem. For instance, transposition rates with respect to the single market averaged out at 99.1 per cent at the end of 2017. Though this is the only field in which the Commission records transposition rate, if one assumes that the transposition rate is similar in other areas, it appears that the Commission would be focusing over half its enforcement efforts on less than 1 per cent of all Directives. Many would argue that this is strange if the central concern is to ensure that EU law, in general, is observed.

(ii) Securing Effective Performance of Union Policies

The second vision of Article 258 TFEU has it as a public policy tool whose dominant role is to secure the effective functioning of EU policies. On such a view, it is unnecessary that there be full compliance with all EU law all the time. Rather, it is sufficient if there is sufficient compliance to ensure that the policy, of which the EU laws form part, can function effectively. The necessary levels of compliance may well vary from policy to policy.[23] Furthermore, priority may be given to the implementation of particular policies so that infringement proceedings are focused there.[24] This casts Article 258 TFEU as a less even-handed instrument than one which is simply concerned with securing the operation of the law. It is used to realise certain political preferences at the expense of others, and this may well disadvantage certain Member States and social groups relative to others.[25] In its 2017 communication, the Commission made clear that the infringement proceedings will also be used in this way:

> It is important that the Commission use its discretionary power in a strategic way to focus and prioritise its enforcement efforts on the most important breaches of EU law affecting the interests of its citizens and business. In this context, the Commission will act firmly on infringements which obstruct the implementation of important EU policy objectives, or which risk undermining the four fundamental freedoms.[26]

Such an approach sees enforcement as merely one dimension to policy delivery more generally.[27] In its 2017 communication, the Commission emphasised that dialogue should be seen as part of the compliance process, with dialogues to take place with Member States in different specialised fora about how to comply with particular EU laws.[28] In the field of the single market, there are, therefore, annual compliance dialogues with each Member State in which the

---

[22] European Commission, n. 5 above, 12 and 15.
[23] M. Mendrinou, 'Non-Compliance and the Commission's Role in Integration' (1996) 3 *JEPP* 1; M. Smith, *Centralised Enforcement, Legitimacy and Good Governance in the EU* (Abingdon, Routledge, 2009) 10–15 and 114–17.
[24] On how the logic of this would apply across the policy cycle, see M. Smith, 'Evaluation and the Salience of Infringement Data' (2015) 6 *European Journal of Risk Regulation* 90.
[25] S. Andersen, *The Enforcement of EU Law: The Role of the European Commission* (Oxford University Press, 2012) 24–7.
[26] European Commission, n. 13 above, 14.   [27] Andersen, n. 25 above, 83–9.   [28] *Ibid.* at 12.

Commission raises particular enforcement issues that it has noticed in that Member State, whilst the Member States raises difficulties encountered with the legislation and where it is not working well.[29]

The Commission has also stated that it has to be mindful of domestic capacities and what these realistically can achieve.[30] It may not be possible for any Member State to realise perfect application of EU law on the ground on a day-to-day basis as this relies on many things, not least administrative resources and the general law-abidingness of the society.[31] Public policy specialists have therefore noted that the capacity of States to implement EU law falls into a number of categories.[32]

G. Falkner and O. Treib, 'Three Worlds of Compliance or Four? The EU–15 Compared to New Member States' (2008) 46 *Journal of Common Market Studies* 293, 296–7 and 308–9

In the *world of law observance*, the compliance goal typically overrides domestic concerns. Even if there are conflicting national policy styles, interests or ideologies, transposition of EU Directives is usually both in time and correct. This is supported by a 'compliance culture' in the sense of an issue-specific 'shared interpretive scheme' . . . , a 'set of cognitive rules and recipes' . . . Application and enforcement of the national implementation laws is also characteristically successful, as the transposition laws tend to be well considered and well adapted to the specific circumstances and enforcement agencies as well as court systems are generally well-organized and equipped with sufficient resources to fulfil their tasks. Non-compliance, by contrast, typically occurs only rarely and not without fundamental domestic traditions or basic regulatory philosophies being at stake. In addition, instances of non-compliance tend to be remedied rather quickly . . .

Obeying EU rules is at best one goal among many in the *world of domestic politics*. Domestic concerns frequently prevail if there is a conflict of interests, and each single act of transposing an EU Directive tends to happen on the basis of a fresh cost-benefit analysis. Transposition is likely to be timely and correct where no domestic concerns dominate over the fragile aspiration to comply. In cases of a manifest clash between EU requirements and domestic interest politics, non-compliance is the likely outcome. While in the countries belonging to the world of law observance breaking EU law would not be a socially acceptable state of affairs, it is much less of a problem in one of the countries in this second category. At times, their politicians or major interest groups even openly call for disobedience with European duties – an appeal that is not met with much serious condemnation in these countries. Since administrations and judiciaries generally work effectively, application and enforcement of transposition laws are not a major problem in this world – the main obstacle to compliance is political resistance at the transposition stage . . .

In the countries forming the *world of transposition neglect*, compliance with EU law is not a goal in itself. Those domestic actors who call for more obedience thus have even less of a sound cultural basis for doing so than in the world of domestic politics. At least as long as there is no powerful action by supranational actors, transposition obligations are often not recognized at all in these 'neglecting' countries. A posture of

---

[29] European Commission, 'Upgrading the Single Market: More Opportunities for People and Business', COM(2015) 550, 16.

[30] European Commission, n. 13 above, 12.

[31] For a case study of British, German, Spanish and Dutch application of the Safety Data Sheets Directive, see E. Versluis, 'Even Rules, Uneven Practices: Opening the 'Black Box' of EU Law in Action' (2007) 30 *WEP* 50.

[32] Most extensively see G. Falkner *et al.*, *Complying with Europe: EU Harmonisation and Soft Law in the Member States* (Cambridge University Press, 2005).

'national arrogance' (in the sense that indigenous standards are typically expected to be superior) may support this, as may administrative inefficiency. In these cases, the typical reaction to an EU-related implementation duty is inactivity. After an intervention by the European Commission, the transposition process may finally be initiated and may even proceed rather swiftly. The result, however, is often correct only on the surface. Where literal translation of EU Directives takes place at the expense of careful adaptation to domestic conditions, for example, shortcomings in enforcement and application are a frequent phenomenon. Potential deficiencies of this type, however, do not belong to the defining characteristics of the world of transposition neglect . . .

. . . we suggest a fourth category: the 'world of dead letters'. Countries belonging to this cluster of our typology may transpose EU Directives in a compliant manner, depending on the prevalent political constellation among domestic actors, but then there is non-compliance at the later stage of monitoring and enforcement. In this group of countries, what is written on the statute books simply does not become effective in practice. Shortcomings in the court systems, the labour inspections and finally also in civil society systems are among the detrimental factors accounting for this.

Such analyses would have the Commission be mindful that infringement proceedings can only stimulate limited change and that their use in the wrong circumstances could be counter-productive.[33] Alongside this, there is the question of anticipating how States will respond to infringement proceedings: a drastically different question from their capacities. Börzel, Hofmann and Panke found in a large study that two features guided Member State responses. *Enforcement responses* are where State behaviour is guided by the likelihood and size of any sanction. In this regard, sanctions are likely to have less effect on wealthier, more powerful States as they can bear these costs more easily. *Managerial responses* are informed by government capacities to implement EU law. These will be more restricted where many actors can veto government action (i.e. coalition partners, powerful local governments) or where the State has limited administrative resources to impose its will on its subjects.

T. Börzel, T. Hofmann and D. Panke, 'Caving In or Sitting Out? Longitudinal Patterns of Non-Compliance in the European Union' (2012) 19 *Journal of European Public Policy* 454, 467

[W]e find strong empirical support for the effect of bureaucratic efficiency and a low number of domestic veto players on the ability to overcome violations of EU law. At the same time, the power of recalcitrance allows member states to sit out long and escalating infringement proceedings. The power of deterrence, in contrast, cannot explain why countries such as Portugal, Denmark and the UK tend to settle cases early, while Italy, France, Greece and Belgium wait until the later stages. Finally, legitimacy does not seem to influence the persistence of noncompliance at all.

. . . Power and veto players keep infringement cases alive, while capacities increase the likelihood of early settlement. The findings show that states combining high capacities with low power, such as Denmark, tend

---

[33] A study of environmental and social policy case studies in Germany found that enforcement proceedings could stimulate compliance by shaming the national administration and mobilising social groups in favour of change. It was not always effective and could stimulate a backlash, however. See D. Panke, 'The European Court of Justice as an Agent of Europeanization? Restoring Compliance with EU Law' (2007) 14 *JEPP* 847.

to be the better compliers, whereas countries that lack government capacity and autonomy, but have political influence (e.g. Italy), are the biggest compliance laggards. However, our findings also hint at what the Commission and the ECJ can do to foster compliance and keep infringement proceedings from escalating. While changing member states' political system and influence might be out of reach, capacity building through the transfer of financial resources and managerial know-how has long been a priority of the European Commission. Our findings suggest that this might actually be a feasible way to substantially reduce the persistence of non-compliance the stages of the infringement proceedings.

This piece illustrates the limits and possibilities of infringement proceedings. As we shall see, these proceedings are long, drawn-out affairs. There are incentives for States to tough it out, particularly where the domestic politics of compliance is complicated, as sanctions will only be imposed many years after the infringement was brought to the Commission's notice. This creates a dynamic for negotiation. There is a Commission interest in a speedy resolution and Member States can exploit this to try and negotiate a generous settlement. However, as the piece above illustrates, the negotiating power of different States varies and there is also little guarantee that States will take the interests of the different stakeholders into account in a transparent or equitable way.

(iii) A Framework for Structuring Domestic Accommodation of EU Law's Demands

The third vision of the infringement proceedings notes that only certain domestic interests are likely to be represented in the EU legislative process. The time of domestic application or transposition of EU law is when these unrepresented interests have an opportunity to exercise a voice in fora more receptive to their views. Often these views will not be as positive about the EU law as those interests which pushed for it in Brussels. It is therefore unsurprising that rates of non-compliance are higher when States voted against a measure.[34] Within this context, the infringement proceedings form part of a wider process of administering EU law in which the Commission has to respond to domestic politics and any push-back. On this view, Article 258 TFEU should be characterised not 'simply as single-faceted legal provision, but also a unique space of interaction for a multitude of actors'.[35]

> **E. Chiti, 'The Governance of Compliance' in M. Cremona (ed.), *Compliance and the Enforcement of EU Law* (Oxford University Press, 2012) 35–6**
>
> The key point, obviously, is not that EU measures need to be implemented also through administrative activities. This has always been true, and national public administrations have been since the very beginning called to implement EU legislation. The key point is rather that the effective implementation of EU law by national administrations – and therefore their compliance with EU law – is not only controlled 'externally' by the Commission or by litigants before a court. The effective implementation of EU law by national

---

[34] T. König and B. Luetgert, 'Troubles with Transposition? Explaining Trends in Member State Notification and the Delayed Transposition of EU Directives' (2009) 39 *BJPS* 163; B. Steunenberg and D. Toshkov, 'Comparing Transposition in the 27 Member States of the EU: The Impact of Discretion and Legal Fit' (2009) 16 *JEPP* 951.

[35] M. Smith, *Centralised Enforcement, Legitimacy and Good Governance in the EU* (Abingdon, Routledge, 2009) 17.

authorities and private actors is rather driven and structured 'within' a European administrative system. Such a European administrative system obviously aims at carrying out the various public functions exercised by the EU, from the management of the internal market to social regulation and to the emerging core of welfare and security activities. What is relevant for our purposes, however, is that the European administrative system also operates as a set of governance instruments aimed at enhancing compliance by the addressees of EU policies through the facilitation and institutionalization of negotiation, cooperation, and mutual learning among the national public powers and private actors to which EU law and policies are addressed. Compliance is 'internalized' in the European administrative system, which works, among other things, also as a machine for a gradual development of obedience by national public powers and the relevant private actors.

This vision sees the infringement proceeding as a central element of a wider European administrative politics in which a variety of political interests interact. This requires a public law framework to structure and regulate it.

This framework is necessary, first, to structure the to-ing and fro-ing between the Commission and national administration that is necessary for successful policy implementation. It would also, secondly, focus on issues of participation, representation and accountability. It would look at whether different interests can participate sufficiently and whether they are sufficiently represented. It would also look at how accountable the Commission is to these different interests during the infringement proceedings.[36] It might, also, constrain the expansion of EU power. In the United States, 'anti-commandeering' (whereby Congress, the federal legislature, cannot require States to enact or enforce federal programmes)[37] and 'uncooperative federalism' (whereby State administration of federal programmes is used by States to subvert programmes seen as unconstitutional or undemocratic)[38] are not seen as evidence of a collapse of the legal system there. They are rather seen as healthy constraints which not only curb central power but also foster local innovation and debate. If the United States can allow this level of local challenge to central rule-making, similarly, it might be thought that the European Union should be able to. There is a further reason. In the United States, a key ingredient in curbing central power is the extreme difficulty in passing federal law. In contrast, this difficulty is not present in the Union whereby the most effective check on excessive lawmaking may well lie in the fact that the vast bulk of European law is administered by domestic authorities.[39]

On such a view, infringement proceedings allow domestic democracy to interact with Union democracy – namely that German or Slovenian citizens can talk about how an EU measure affects Germany or Slovenia respectively. Its other notable feature is that it is an *ex post facto* debate. It does not occur at the time of enactment of an EU law where many of the consequences

---

[36] R. Rawlings, 'Engaged Elites: Citizen Action and Institutional Attitudes in Commission Enforcement' (2000) 6 *ELJ* 4.

[37] D. Halberstam, 'Comparative Federalism and the Issue of Commandeering' in K. Nicolaidis and R. Howse (eds.), *The Federal Vision: Legitimacy and Levels of Government in the United States of America and the European Union* (Oxford University Press, 2001).

[38] J. Bulman-Pozen and H. Gerken, 'Uncooperative Federalism' (2009) 118 *Yale LJ* 1256.

[39] E. Young, 'Protecting Member State Autonomy in the European Union: Some Cautionary Tales from American Federalism' (2002) 77 *NYULRev* 1612; G. Bermann, 'Taking Subsidiarity Seriously: Federalism in the European Community and the United States' (1994) 94 *Colum L Rev* 331, 399.

of this law may be speculative, but at that moment when the implications of an EU law on the ground are either imminent or evident and local concerns might be more focused.

All this might provide reasons for the rigour of EU law to be tempered. Concerns or problems emerge in the transposition or implementation of EU law in a Member State which suggest that the benefits of full compliance with EU law might be outweighed by the costs. This was addressed in *Commission* v. *Poland*. The Commission brought an action against a Polish law – the Law on Seeds – which prohibited the marketing of genetically modified seeds in Poland. This violated Directive 2001/18 which concerned the deliberate release of genetically modified organisms into the environment and which allowed the marketing of these where they had been authorised by EU authorities. The Polish Government justified its non-compliance by arguing that genetically modified food was both unpopular in Poland and violated important tenets of Catholic thought.

Commission v. Poland, C–165/08, EU:C:2009:473

49 In its defence and its rejoinder, the Republic of Poland concentrated its arguments wholly on the ethical or religious considerations on which the contested national provisions are based . . .

56 However, a Member State cannot rely in that manner on the views of a section of public opinion in order unilaterally to challenge a harmonising measure adopted by the Community institutions . . . As the Court observed in a case specifically concerning Directive 2001/18, a Member State may not plead difficulties of implementation which emerge at the stage when a Community measure is put into effect, such as difficulties relating to opposition on the part of certain individuals, to justify a failure to comply with obligations and time-limits laid down by Community law . . .

57 Secondly, and as regards the more specifically religious or ethical arguments put forward by the Republic of Poland for the first time in the defence and rejoinder submitted to the Court, it must be held that that Member State has failed to establish that the contested national provisions were in fact adopted on the basis of such considerations.

58 The Republic of Poland essentially referred to a sort of general presumption according to which it can come as no surprise that such provisions were adopted in the present case. First, the Republic of Poland relies on the fact that it is well known that Polish society attaches great importance to Christian and Roman Catholic values. Secondly, it states that the political parties with a majority in the Polish Parliament at the time when the contested national provisions were adopted specifically called for adherence to such values. In those circumstances, according to that Member State, it is reasonable to take the view that the Members of Parliament, who do not, as a general rule, have scientific training, are more likely to be influenced by the religious or ethical ideas which inspire their political actions, rather than by other considerations, in particular, those linked to the complex scientific assessments relating to the protection of the environment or of human health.

59 However, such considerations are not sufficient to establish that the adoption of the contested national provisions was in fact inspired by the ethical and religious considerations described in the defence and the rejoinder, especially since the Republic of Poland had, in the pre-litigation procedure, based its defence mainly on the shortcomings allegedly affecting Directive 2001/18, regard being had to the precautionary principle and to the risks posed by that directive to both the environment and human health.

Whilst a State cannot defy EU law for populist reasons, the Court leaves open the question of whether it can do so for ethical or religious reasons. Any such defence must be argued from the outset and justified on these ethical or religious grounds. Such a defence would transform the infringement proceedings into procedures that incentivise domestic politics to engage with, deliberate and contest the application of EU laws in Member States. At the moment, however, the state of the law is too uncertain to say whether that is the case.

3 THE SCOPE OF MEMBER STATE RESPONSIBILITIES

Infringement proceedings may only be instigated against Member States for actions or omissions by them. This begs questions as to what counts as the State and what responsibilities it is expected to discharge for these purposes.

(i) The Acts and Omissions of All State Agencies

Two implications have been drawn from the notion that, under Article 258 TFEU, it is the Member State which is responsible for any illegality. The first is that only acts and omissions of State agencies attract liability. The second is that the State is responsible for the acts and omissions of all these agencies even if they are constitutionally independent.[40]

A State agency is any institution from any tier of government, be it national, regional or local.[41] It also comprises private bodies which are subject to particular public controls.[42] In *CMA*, a public body financed by a levy on the German food and agriculture sector, the Fund, was set up to promote German agriculture. A private company, the CMA, was further established to realise the objectives of the Fund. It had to observe the latter's guidelines and was financed by it. The CMA adopted a quality label certifying the qualities of produce from Germany. The Commission argued this label violated the EU provisions on free movement, as it was only available to German produce. The German Government argued, to no avail, that the CMA was a private body and therefore it was not responsible.

Commission v. Germany ('CMA'), C–325/00, EU:C:2002:633

17 . . . it must be recalled that the CMA, although set up as a private company is
  – established on the basis of a law . . . is characterised by that law as a central economic body and has, among the objects assigned to it by that law, the promotion, at central level, of the marketing and exploitation of German agricultural and food products;
  – is bound, according to its Articles of Association, originally approved by the competent federal minister, to observe the rules of the Fund, itself a public body, and additionally to be guided, in particular in relation to the commitment of its financial resources, by the general interest of the German agricultural and food sector;
  – is financed, according to the rules laid down by the AFG, by a compulsory contribution by all the undertakings in the sectors concerned.
18 Such a body, which is set up by a national law of a Member State and which is financed by a contribution imposed on producers, cannot, under Community law, enjoy the same freedom as regards the promotion of national production as that enjoyed by producers themselves or producers' associations of a voluntary character . . . Thus it is obliged to respect the basic rules of the Treaty on the free movement of goods when

---

[40] *Commission* v. *Belgium*, 77/69, EU:C:1970:34.   [41] *Commission* v. *Italy*, 199/85, EU:C:1987:115.
[42] *Commission* v. *Ireland*, 249/81, EU:C:1982:402.

it sets up a scheme, open to all undertakings of the sectors concerned, which can have effects on intra-Community trade similar to those arising under the scheme adopted by the public authorities.

19 Furthermore, it must be observed that:
  – the Fund is a public law body;
  – the CMA is required to respect the Fund's guidelines;
  – the financing of the CMA's activities, under legislation, comes from resources which are granted to it through the Fund, and
  – the Fund supervises the CMA's activities and the proper management of the finances which are granted to it by the Fund.

20 In those circumstances, it must be held that the Commission could rightly take the view that the contested scheme is ascribable to the State.

It is unclear whether the definition of what constitutes a State body is, for the purpose of infringement proceedings, the same as that taken for the direct effect of Directives.[43] In the latter instance, a body would also be part of the State if, whilst not subject to public controls, it performs a public service and, for that reason, has special powers.[44] Adoption of this definition would not only lead to more coherence but also prevent States escaping responsibility for infringements of EU law by simply contracting out their responsibilities.

The second dimension – holding States responsible for the actions of constitutionally independent units – is more controversial. It has led to governments being accountable when they were unable, despite their best intentions, to get legislation through parliament.[45] It has also led to central governments being responsible for the actions of regional authorities even when they have no power under their constitutions to compel action by the latter.[46] Most controversially, States are held accountable for the actions of national courts. In *Commission* v. *Italy*, infringement proceedings were brought against a series of decisions by the Italian Court of Cassation, the highest Italian civil court, which consistently interpreted Italian law on customs duties in a way that conflicted with EU law.

Commission v. *Italy*, C–129/00, EU:C:2003:656

29 A Member State's failure to fulfil obligations may, in principle, be established under Article [258 TFEU] whatever the agency of that State whose action or inaction is the cause of the failure to fulfil its obligations, even in the case of a constitutionally independent institution . . .

30 The scope of national laws, regulations or administrative provisions must be assessed in the light of the interpretation given to them by national courts . . .

31 In this case what is at issue is Article 29(2) of Law No 428/1990 which provides that duties and charges levied under national provisions incompatible with Community legislation are to be repaid, unless the amount thereof has been passed on to others. Such a provision is in itself neutral in respect of Community law in relation both to the burden of proof that the charge has been passed on to other persons and to the

---

[43] It will be remembered that Directives can only be invoked directly against the State in domestic courts. See pp. 305–7.
[44] *Farrell* v. *Whitty*, C–413/15, EU:C:2017:745.   [45] *Commission* v. *Belgium*, 77/69, EU:C:1970:34.
[46] *Commission* v. *Belgium*, 1/86, EU:C:1987:297.

evidence which is admissible to prove it. Its effect must be determined in the light of the construction which the national courts give it.

32 In that regard, isolated or numerically insignificant judicial decisions in the context of case-law taking a different direction, or still more a construction disowned by the national supreme court, cannot be taken into account. That is not true of a widely-held judicial construction which has not been disowned by the supreme court, but rather confirmed by it.

33 Where national legislation has been the subject of different relevant judicial constructions, some leading to the application of that legislation in compliance with Community law, others leading to the opposite application, it must be held that, at the very least, such legislation is not sufficiently clear to ensure its application in compliance with Community law.

Whilst the issue was framed as one of poor Italian legislation, in reality, it was the Italian Court of Cassation's interpretation of this legislation which generated the problem. This slightly evasive reasoning by the Court of Justice was probably used to minimise the risk of directly confronting national courts. Holding national courts in breach of EU law can pose difficulties for judicial independence and the *res judicata* principle as it can require the national government to suspend the effects of judgments and cast doubt on their binding effects.[47] Notwithstanding this, the Court and Advocates General have repeatedly asserted that the judiciary, including the highest courts in the land, is just like any other State agency. The State is liable for its actions, including judgments which breach EU law.[48] These issues came back to haunt the Court in *Commission* v. *Slovak Republic*. A Slovak court approved an arrangement between a bankrupt Slovak company, Frucona, and its creditors, where the latter would receive only 35 per cent of the money owed to them. As compensation, they would receive a tax write-off for the money received. The Commission subsequently found that this tax write-off was an illegal State aid, and issued a decision requiring Slovakia to recover the tax. The Slovak authorities claimed this was impossible because they were bound by the initial Slovak judgment authorising the deal, which acquired the force of *res judicata*. The Commission then took Slovakia before the Court of Justice.[49]

Commission v. Slovak Republic, C-507/08, EU:C:2010:802

57 In the present case, the court judgment possessed of the force of *res judicata* relied on by the Slovak Republic precedes the decision whereby the Commission requires the recovery of the aid at issue . . .

59 . . . attention should be drawn to the importance, both in the European Union legal order and in the national legal orders, of the principle of *res judicata*. In order to ensure stability of the law and legal relations, as well as the sound administration of justice, it is important that judicial decisions which have become definitive after all rights of appeal have been exhausted or after expiry of the time-limits provided to exercise those rights can no longer be called into question . . .

---

[47] Cf. *Köbler* v. *Austria*, C-224/01, EU:C:2003:513. This is discussed in more detail at pp. 320–2.

[48] E.g. *Commission* v. *Spain*, C-154/08, EU:C:2009:695; Advocate General Mazák in *Commission* v. *Greece*, C-489/06, EU:C:2008:638; Advocate General Bot in *Liga Portuguesa de Futebol Profissional* v. *Departamento de Jogos da Santa Casa da Misericórdia de Lisboa*, C-42/07, EU:C:2009:519; Advocate General Mengozzi in *Commission* v. *Spain*, C-423/07, EU:C:2009:639; Advocate General Sharpston in *Commission* v. *Italy*, C-433/15, EU:C:2017:552.

[49] The action was brought under the special procedures for State aids in Article 108(2) TFEU rather than under Article 258 TFEU. The issues are the same, however.

60 Accordingly, European Union law does not in all circumstances require a national court to disapply domestic rules of procedure conferring the force of *res judicata* on a judgment, even if to do so would make it possible to remedy an infringement of European Union law by the judgment in question . . .

61 As stated by the Advocate General in his Opinion, it is clear both from the documents before the Court and from the observations made at the hearing by the Slovak Republic that under national law there were available to the national authorities resources which, if diligently used, could have ensured that the Slovak Republic was able to recover the aid at issue.

62 Nonetheless, the Slovak Government has not provided any precise information on the circumstances in which it used the resources which were available to it.

63 In particular, the Slovak Republic has not clearly explained what action was taken in response to the request by the tax office that an extraordinary appeal be brought against the contested judgment.

64 The Court can therefore do no other than hold that, standing the Commission's specific criticism, the information provided by the Slovak Republic is insufficient to allow the conclusion that it took, within the prescribed period, all the measures which it could have employed in order to obtain the repayment of the aid at issue.

65 In the light of the foregoing, it must be held that, by failing to take within the prescribed period all the measures necessary to recover from the beneficiary the aid . . . the Slovak Republic has failed to fulfil its obligations . . .

Based on the case above, if the judgment precedes the Commission action, Member States will not be required to compromise the principle of *res judicata*.[50] As such, any judgment will continue to stand. However, within the limits of this principle, a State must do everything necessary to secure compliance with EU law. This includes, if the court is not a court of last resort, exhausting the appeal process.[51]

If the challenge is most intense for breaches by the judiciary, the problem of central authorities by-passing established checks and balances to secure compliance with EU law arises whenever actions by any constitutionally independent actor are alleged to breach EU law. It is a consequence of Article 258 TFEU seeing the State in unitary terms. By contrast, in domestic law, individuals rarely sue the State but rather the agency harming their interests. This unitary vision of the State poses challenges for the domestic rule of law as it encourages central actors to violate domestic constitutional arrangements in the name of securing compliance with EU law. It also establishes a system of perverse incentives. As other governmental actors will not be litigated against, there is no reason for them to take measures to comply with EU law, as they know that the central government (with whom they are often in competition) will take the rap.[52]

(ii) The Accountability of State Actors

The State is responsible for any measure that formally conflicts with EU law, be it a law, statutory instrument or judgment. It is for the Commission to prove that the national law

---

[50] Namely that once a matter has been resolved by a court it cannot be pursued further by the parties.

[51] M. Taboroski, 'Infringement Proceedings and Non-Compliant National Courts' (2012) 49 *CMLRev* 1881.

[52] E.g. in Belgium administrative coordination was so difficult and there was so much mistrust the Wallonian regional government actually took the Flemish regional government to the Court of Justice through the preliminary reference procedure for its failure to observe the free movement provisions, *Government of the French Community and Walloon Government* v. *Flemish Government*, C-212/06, EU:C:2008:178.

conflicts with EU law.[53] However, the meaning given to these measures is that provided by national case law.[54] If there is none, they are to be given their literal meaning.[55] The State is also responsible for administrative practices conflicting with EU law. As we have seen, in some cases, a specific act must be sufficient whilst in others the Court will look for a generalised practice.[56] Finally, the State is responsible for failures to meet its positive duties to secure the effective functioning of EU law, as required by the fidelity principle in Article 4(3) TEU.[57] States can be subject to infringement proceedings for:

- a failure to secure legal certainty for EU law[58]
- a failure to police EU law actively[59]
- a failure to penalise infringements of EU law in a similar manner to infringements of national law of an analogous nature and importance and to ensure that penalties for breach of EU law are effective, proportionate and dissuasive[60]
- a failure to notify the Commission of any problems applying or enforcing EU law.[61]

There is, also, one further duty specific to the infringement proceedings. If the Commission provides sufficient evidence to a Member State of a possible breach of EU law, the State has a duty to investigate if it wishes to prove otherwise. In *Commission* v. *Ireland*, the Commission received twelve complaints of dumping of waste or operating unlicensed waste dumps across Ireland in breach of EU environmental law. It wrote to the Irish Government but received only limited replies. The Irish Government argued that the Commission had failed to provide sufficient proof of any infringement.

Commission v. Ireland, C–494/01, EU:C:2005:250

41 ... in proceedings under Article [258 TFEU] for failure to fulfil obligations it is incumbent upon the Commission to prove the allegation that the obligation has not been fulfilled. It is the Commission's responsibility to place before the Court the information needed to enable the Court to establish that the obligation has not been fulfilled, and in so doing the Commission may not rely on any presumption ...

42 However, the Member States are required, under Article [4(3) TEU], to facilitate the achievement of the Commission's tasks, which consist in particular, pursuant to Article [17(1) TEU], in ensuring that the provisions of the Treaty and the measures taken by the institutions pursuant thereto are applied ...

43 In this context, account should be taken of the fact that, where it is a question of checking that the national provisions intended to ensure effective implementation of the directive are applied correctly in practice, the Commission which ... does not have investigative powers of its own in the matter, is largely reliant on the information provided by any complainants and by the Member State concerned ...

---

[53] E.g. *Commission* v. *Italy*, C–369/11, EU:C:2013:636.
[54] *Commission* v. *United Kingdom*, C–300/95, EU:C:1997:255; *Commission* v. *Germany*, C–490/04, EU:C:2007:430.
[55] Advocate General Sharpston, *Commission* v. *Malta*, C–557/15, EU:C:2017:613.   [56] See pp. 333–4.
[57] On the principle see pp. 212–14.
[58] *Commission* v. *Italy*, C–159/99, EU:C:2001:278; *Commission* v. *Germany*, C–441/02, EU:C:2006:253.
[59] *Commission* v. *France*, C–265/95, EU:C:1997:595.
[60] *Commission* v. *Greece*, C–68/88, EU:C:1989:339; *Commission* v. *United Kingdom*, C–383/92, EU:C:1994:234.
[61] *Commission* v. *Germany*, C–105/02, EU:C:2006:637.

44 It follows in particular that, where the Commission has adduced sufficient evidence of certain matters in the territory of the defendant Member State, it is incumbent on the latter to challenge in substance and in detail the information produced and the consequences flowing therefrom . . .

45 In such circumstances, it is indeed primarily for the national authorities to conduct the necessary on-the-spot investigations, in a spirit of genuine cooperation and mindful of each Member State's duty, recalled in paragraph 42 of the present judgment, to facilitate the general task of the Commission . . .

46 Thus, where the Commission relies on detailed complaints revealing repeated failures to comply with the provisions of the directive, it is incumbent on the Member State to contest specifically the facts alleged in those complaints . . .

47 Likewise, where the Commission has adduced sufficient evidence to show that a Member State's authorities have developed a repeated and persistent practice which is contrary to the provisions of a directive, it is incumbent on that Member State to challenge in substance and in detail the information produced and the consequences flowing therefrom.

If allegations of specific breaches are brought to their attention, States are required to find out what has gone on. The premise is that only they have the resources and authority to investigate, and they must know what is going on in their backyard. Failure to do this is, by itself, a breach of EU law.[62] It also makes it more likely that they will be found liable for the alleged conduct as they have failed to provide plausible alternate explanations.

4 THE THREE STAGES OF THE ARTICLE 258 TFEU PROCEEDINGS

The description of the infringement proceedings set out in the text of Article 258 TFEU is brief. It has been elaborated on over the years by case law, and the proceedings are best seen as a series of stages:

- an initial screening by the Commission
- the launch of EU Pilot where it is useful
- a letter of formal notice by the Commission to the Member State that it is in breach of EU law
- the submission of observations by the Member State
- the issuing of a reasoned opinion by the Commission setting out the breach of EU law
- a period for the Member State to comply with the reasoned opinion and submit observations
- lodging of the case with the Court by the Commission
- judgment by the Court.

The process is time-consuming. However, there are three central points. There is, first, an informal pre-litigation process in which potential infringements are screened and resolution attempted prior to the starting of formal proceedings; secondly, a formal pre-litigation stage in which the Commission sends out the letter of formal notice setting out the breach and receives the Member State's observations; and thirdly, there is a litigation stage in which the Commission issues a reasoned opinion that there has been a breach of EU law with referral to the Court if the Member State does not comply with that opinion.

---

[62] See also *Commission* v. *United Kingdom*, C-301/10, EU:C:2012:633.

(i) The Informal Pre-Litigation Stage: The Initial Screening and Resolution of Potential Infringements

The proceedings can be triggered in two ways. The first is that the Commission starts proceedings on its own initiative based on information acquired that the Member State is not complying with EU law ('own initiative cases'). The second is that it initiates proceedings on the basis of a complaint or petition from private parties ('complaints'). Either route involves an initial screening of whether, on the facts, the Member State appears to have breached EU law. There is no data available on how often a Commission checks, of its own initiative, whether a State has complied with EU law and decides that there is no case to answer. However, in 2017, the Commission handled 3,611 complaints. It has taken only 146 of these forward, arguing that in the vast majority (over 3,200), there was no finding of a breach of EU law or that the correspondence did not reveal a complaint.[63]

If, after the screening, the Commission believes that a State has a case to answer it can either issue a letter of formal notice, and move to the formal pre-litigation proceedings, or deploy EU Pilot. EU Pilot will be used where it is 'useful in a given case'.[64] In 2017, the Commission used EU Pilot 178 times, with 139 of these involving own initiative cases and the other 39 complaints.[65] By contrast, the Commission issued 716 letters of formal notice in 2017.[66] EU Pilot is, therefore, used in about 20 per cent of cases.[67] This is significant, but, in the nine years prior to 2017, it was used in almost all cases prior to the Commission issuing a letter of formal notice.

EU Pilot is an online database, located in Brussels, which acts as a vehicle through which the Commission and the Member States are to try and resolve matters so as to forestall further action by the Commission. The Commission uploads individual files onto it which raise issues about a particular Member State's failure to comply with EU law. These files will set out the relevant facts and the legal issues. National authorities are given ten weeks to respond to the questions and propose a solution, albeit they can ask for an extension. The Commission is then given a further ten weeks to make an assessment of the Member State's response. It can ask for further information and also seek solutions with the Member State during that period. If there is no resolution at the end of this, the Commission is to issue a letter of formal notice.[68] About three-quarters of all files are resolved with EU Pilot and go no further.[69]

The concerns with EU Pilot are twofold. First, the Commission was of the view that it significantly added to the amount of time before a matter would arrive before the Court of Justice, and should therefore only be used for matters which are easily resolvable.[70] The difficulty with this view is that it is at odds with the high resolution rate of EU Pilot. Insofar as matters are resolved there and go no further, EU Pilot saves time. And that is what happens three-quarters of the time. A second, more substantial, set of concerns were raised in a 2016 decision of the Ombudsman which found more generalised problems with the Commission's administration of EU Pilot. There were instances of excessive delays in opening files after

---

[63] European Commission, n. 5 above, 7.   [64] European Commission, n. 13 above, 12.

[65] European Commission, n. 5 above, 8.   [66] *Ibid.* 10.

[67] Of the 716 letters of formal notice, 60 were issued because of a lack of resolution within EU Pilot. There were thus 656 instances in 2017 where the Commission decided not to use EU Pilot and 178 times where it did.

[68] EU Pilot was established in European Commission, 'A Europe of Results – Applying Community Law', COM(2007)502, 7–8. M. Smith, 'Enforcement, Monitoring, Verification, Outsourcing: The Decline and Decline of the Infringement Process' (2008) 33 *ELRev* 777.

[69] The figure was 77% in 2017, European Commission, n. 5 above, 9.   [70] European Commission, n. 13 above, 12.

individual complaints; the Commission struggled to meet its own deadlines for responding to Member State statements; complainants were not informed of the progress of their file; and the public were not even allowed to know that the Commission had opened a file for a Member State.[71] These problems are acute if EU Pilot is the place where the majority of infringement proceedings are resolved. Resolution occurs at a moment when the Commission is overstretched and in a secret manner, so there are no guarantees that resolution secures either compliance with EU law or addresses complainants' concerns. A third concern goes to the legal status of EU Pilot, and associated questions of legal uncertainty. Resolution of a matter within EU Pilot does not prevent the Commission from subsequently reinstigating infringement proceedings over the issue if it so chooses. Nor does it prevent the compatibility of the domestic law with EU law being raised in a domestic court and referred to the Court of Justice.[72] Resolution leaves the domestic law in an unsatisfactory state of suspended administration. Its legal status is unclear but the Commission is not going to do anything about it for the time being.

Less frequent use of EU Pilot does not make these problems go away. It just means that they apply to a smaller, albeit still sizeable, number of cases. There is also a further worry. The reason for the instigation of EU Pilot was that prior to it, informal negotiations took place between the Commission and the national authorities after the former had sent the latter an administrative letter. These proceedings were as opaque as EU Pilot and lengthier.[73] It is to be hoped that there will not be a return to these practices as a means of informal resolution now that there is less resort to EU Pilot.

(ii) The Formal Pre-Litigation Stage

The pre-litigation stage of proceedings pursues three objectives: to allow the Member State to put an end to any infringement, to enable it to exercise its rights of defence and to define the subject matter of the dispute with a view to bringing an action before the Court.[74] As a consequence, the formal pre-litigation begins with the Commission issuing a letter of formal notice. This letter is not mentioned in Article 258 TFEU but is required because that article only allows the Commission to issue a reasoned opinion once the Member State concerned has had the opportunity to submit observations. The letter of formal notice makes this submission of observations possible by setting out the case against the Member State. It is thus central for the purposes of safeguarding the rights of defence of the Member State and to frame the dispute. The Commission can only take a Member State to Court for complaints specifically set out in the letter of formal notice.[75] However, this letter does not have to provide considerable detail; a brief summary of the complaints is sufficient.[76] A sense of its role is set out in *Commission* v. *Denmark* below. The Commission brought an action against the Danish Government for failing to transpose Directive 76/891/EC on electrical energy meters into Danish law. The Danish

---

[71] *Decision of the European Ombudsman setting out suggestions following her strategic inquiry OI/5/2016/AB on timeliness and transparency in the European Commission's handling of infringement complaints*, 14 September 2017.

[72] On both these points see *SC Paper Consult* v. *Direcția Regională a Finanțelor Publice Cluj-Napoca*, C-101/16, EU:C:2017:775.

[73] Between 1999 and 2006, the average time between when the Commission first opened a file and it referring the matter to the Court of Justice was twenty-three months, European Commission, '25th Annual Report on Monitoring the Application of Community Law', COM(2008)777, 2.

[74] *Commission* v. *Slovakia*, C-433/13, EU:C:2015:602.   [75] *Commission* v. *Romania*, C-522/09, EU:C:2011:251.

[76] *Commission* v. *Bulgaria*, C-97/17, EU:C:2018:285.

Government claimed that the letter of formal notice was insufficient as it had merely noted Denmark's failure to act and not set out what positive steps the Danish Government needed to take to remedy the breach.

> ### *Commission* v. *Denmark*, 211/81, EU:C:1982:437
>
> 8 It follows from the purpose assigned to the pre contentious stage of the proceedings for failure of a state to fulfil its obligations that a letter giving formal notice is intended to delimit the subject matter of the dispute and to indicate to the Member State which is invited to submit its observations the factors enabling it to prepare its defence.
>
> 9 ... the opportunity for the Member State concerned to submit its observations constitutes an essential guarantee required by the Treaty and, even if the Member State does not consider it necessary to avail itself thereof, observance of that guarantee is an essential formal requirement of the procedure under Article [258 TFEU].
>
> 10 It appears from the documents before the Court that by a letter dated 23 May 1979 giving formal notice the Commission merely asserted that in its view the Danish Government had not put into force the measures necessary to transpose Directive 76/891 into national law but refrained from specifying the obligations which, in its view, were imposed on that State by virtue of the directive and which had been disregarded.
>
> 11 In the present case, however, that fact did not have the effect of depriving the Danish government of the opportunity of submitting its observations to good effect. On 7 June 1978 the Commission had addressed to the Danish Government a letter setting out the precise reasons which led it to conclude that the Kingdom of Denmark had failed to fulfil one of the obligations imposed on it by Directive 76/891. It was by reference to the position adopted by the Commission in that letter of 7 June 1978 that the Danish Government submitted its observations on 22 August 1979.

Any complaint not mentioned in the letter of formal notice will, therefore, be inadmissible.[77] However, the Commission can subsequently bring in new evidence to clarify the grounds on which it is making the complaint, provided that this evidence does not alter the subject matter of the dispute.[78]

(iii) The Reasoned Opinion and the Period for National Compliance

If, after the Member State has submitted its observations on the letter of formal notice, agreement is still not reached, the Commission will issue a reasoned opinion. As the subject matter of the dispute is delimited by the formal letter of notice, the reasoned opinion cannot introduce new claims.[79] However, account can be taken of changes in circumstances. In *Commission* v. *Belgium*, the Commission challenged, in its letter of formal notice, a 1987 broadcasting law set up by the Flemish Communities.[80] The 1987 law was then replaced by a 1994 law. This latter law was challenged in the reasoned opinion. The Court rejected Belgium's claim that this amendment compromised its rights of defence, noting instead that the national provisions mentioned need not be identical if the change in legislation resulted in the subject matter of the proceeding being altered or extended.[81] Moreover, Commission arguments before the Court can

---

[77] *Commission* v. *Italy*, C-371/04, EU:C:2006:668.   [78] *Commission* v. *Ireland*, C-494/01, EU:C:2005:250.

[79] *Commission* v. *Denmark*, 278/85, EU:C:1987:439; *Commission* v. *Poland*, C-569/10, EU:C:2013:425.

[80] *Commission* v. *Belgium*, C-11/95, EU:C:1996:316.   [81] See also *Commission* v. *Germany*, C-490/04, EU:C:2007:430.

include events that took place after the reasoned opinion, provided that they are of the same kind as those described in the opinion.[82]

The content of the reasoned opinion must be much more elaborate than that of the letter of formal notice. It must provide a coherent and detailed statement of the reasons that led the Commission to believe that the Member State has breached EU law, and must be sufficiently precise to enable the Court to determine whether a breach has taken place as alleged.[83] This should include a detailed statement of the legal and factual context to the dispute and respond to any arguments made by the Member State.[84]

The Commission must afford Member States sufficient time to respond to its views and to comply with the opinion. This will depend upon a number of factors, including the urgency of the matter and when it was first brought to the attention of the Member State by the Commission.[85] An example of what circumstances might be taken into account is *Commission v. Belgium*. Under a 1985 Belgian law, universities were authorised to charge a supplementary fee (a 'minerval') on nationals from other Member States who enrolled with them. The Commission considered such action to be illegal following the *Gravier* judgment, given on 13 February 1985.[86] It had an informal meeting with Belgian officials on 25 June 1985, where it expressed that view but also stated that it was still considering the effects of the judgment. On 17 July 1985 it issued a letter of formal notice stating that, in view of the onset of the new academic year, the Belgian Government should submit its observations within eight days. The Belgian authorities asked for more time. On 23 August 1985, the Commission issued a reasoned opinion with the Belgian Government being given fifteen days to comply. The Belgians claimed that the action was inadmissible given the limited period offered for compliance.

Commission v. Belgium, 293/85, EU:C:1988:40

13 It should be pointed out first that the purpose of the pre litigation procedure is to give the Member State concerned an opportunity, on the one hand, to comply with its obligations under Community law and, on the other, to avail itself of its right to defend itself against the complaints made by the Commission.

14 In view of that dual purpose the Commission must allow Member States a reasonable period to reply to the letter of formal notice and to comply with a reasoned opinion, or, where appropriate, to prepare their defence. In order to determine whether the period allowed is reasonable, account must be taken of all the circumstances of the case. Thus, very short periods may be justified in particular circumstances, especially where there is an urgent need to remedy a breach or where the Member State concerned is fully aware of the Commission's views long before the procedure starts.

15 It is therefore necessary to examine whether the shortness of the periods set by the Commission was justified in view of the particular circumstances of this case . . .

---

[82] *Commission v. Cyprus*, C-340/10, EU:C:2012:143; *Commission v. Bulgaria*, C-488/15, EU:C:2017:267.

[83] *Commission v. Slovenia*, C-365/10, EU: C: 2011:183; *Commission v. Portugal*, C-34/11, EU:C:2012:712.

[84] *Commission v. Spain*, C-266/94, EU:C:1995:235; *Commission v. Slovakia*, C-433/13, EU:C:2015:602.

[85] In determining the latter, the Court will not look to when the letter of formal notice was sent but when informal contacts were first made, *Commission v. United Kingdom*, C-56/90, EU:C:1993:307; *Commission v. Luxembourg*, C-473/93, EU:C:1996:263.

[86] *Gravier* v. *City of Liège*, 293/83, EU:C:1985:69.

16 ... the imminent start of the 1985 academic year may indeed be regarded as a special circumstance justifying a short time limit. However, the Commission could have taken action long before the start of the academic year because the major part of the Belgian provisions were already part of its legislation before the law of 21 June 1985. They were therefore known to the Commission at the latest when the judgment of 13 February 1985 was delivered, which was six months before the start of the 1985 academic year. Furthermore, it should be noted that at the time the Commission had not made any criticism of the minerval and had even given the impression, prior to the entry into force of the law in question, that it accepted that the minerval was compatible with Community law. In those circumstances the Commission cannot rely on urgency which it itself created by failing to take action earlier.

17 As for the Commission's alternative argument that the time limits laid down were not absolute and that consequently replies given after their expiry would have been accepted, it should be remarked that that factor is not relevant. A Member State to which a measure subject to a time limit is addressed cannot know in advance whether, and to what extent, the Commission will if necessary grant it an extension of that time limit. In this case, moreover, the Commission did not reply to the Kingdom of Belgium's request for an extension of time.

18 As regards the question whether the Kingdom of Belgium was aware sufficiently in advance of the Commission's views, it is common ground that although the commission had expressed its views to the competent officials of the Belgian ministries of national education on 25 June 1985, at a meeting of the education committee of 27 and 28 June 1985 it stated that it was still considering the effects of the judgments of the Court in the field of university education. It follows that the Kingdom of Belgium was not fully informed of the definitive views of the Commission before these proceedings were brought against it.

If there is no compliance within the period set out in the reasoned opinion, a Member State cannot prevent the matter being heard by the Court. The Court will consider the position at the end of the period laid down in the reasoned opinion, and will not take account of subsequent changes.[87] Compliance before judgment will not, therefore prevent the Court from declaring that the Member State has acted illegally.[88] The reasons are that the unwieldy nature of the procedure would otherwise be unable to capture breaches of a relatively short duration,[89] and Member States could also manipulate the process by bringing their conduct to an end shortly before judgment is given.[90]

The reasoned opinion binds how the Commission presents its case before the Court in a similar manner to the way in which the letter of formal notice constrains the reasoned opinion. The Commission's actions must be based on the same grounds and pleas as those set out in the opinion. However, these do not have to be worded in a formally identical way as long as the subject matter has not been altered or extended. They may also rely on events that happened after the reasoned opinion was issued, provided that these are of the same kind as those described in the opinion and constitute the same conduct.[91]

[87] *Commission* v. *Greece*, C-200/88, EU:C:1990:422; *Commission* v. *Poland*, C-336/16, EU:C:2018:94.
[88] E.g. *Commission* v. *Spain*, C-446/01, EU:C:2003:347.
[89] Advocate General Lenz, *Commission* v. *Greece*, 240/86, EU:C:1988:4.
[90] Advocate General Lagrange, *Commission* v. *Italy*, 7/61, EU:C:1961:25.
[91] On all this see *Commission* v. *Poland*, C-441/17, EU:C:2018:255.

5 THE ADMINISTRATION OF THE INFRINGEMENT PROCEEDINGS

(i) The Commission's Discretion over the Management of the Proceedings

There are a number of striking features about the Article 258 TFEU process. First, only a few proceedings result in judgments against the State. In 2017, the Court gave only twenty judgments under this procedure.[92] The vast majority of cases are, consequently, settled. The heart of the infringement procedure is thus an administrative process, with judicial proceedings predominantly acting as a backdrop to structure negotiations between the Commission and the Member States. Secondly, the Commission wins the overwhelming majority of cases that reach the Court. In 2017, for example, it won all its cases, and in 2016 it won twenty-seven out of thirty-one.[93] Thirdly, the instigation and cessation of proceedings is entirely a matter of Commission discretion.[94] Neither its motives nor delays in instigating proceedings can be challenged unless these are so extreme that they infringe the Member State's rights of defence, notably by making it more difficult for it to refute the Commission's arguments.[95]

All this raises a number of concerns. First, there is a concern about Commission leniency. Its settlement and win rates suggest that it may cease proceedings when national compliance is far from perfect. In 2018, the European Parliament noted, indeed, that some cases had been closed for 'political reasons'.[96] Whilst this has not been raised recently, the Parliament has also noted in the not so distant past that it has been petitioned repeatedly by citizens who believed settlements did not fully protect their legal rights.[97] There has also been occasional abuse of the process – one striking instance was where a Greek Commission official, publicly involved with the governing Greek political party, chose not to take action against the Greek Government.[98]

Secondly, there is a concern about whether the Commission acts in a coherent and systematic manner in this field. As we have seen, the Commission set out certain priorities for which breaches it will act against.[99] However, as the piece below by Smith observes, the practice of enforcement may be more haphazard, owing as much to the organisational structures and politics of the organisation as anything else.

M. Smith, *Centralised Enforcement, Legitimacy and Good Governance in the EU* (Abingdon, Routledge, 2009) 136–7

When assessing the statistical information produced by the Commission, it must be acknowledged that there does seem to be a coherent output of the enforcement policy, although not one that necessarily matches the stated policy criteria. Whatever the stated approach to the enforcement policy, the result appears to guarantee that the environment sector always produces the greatest number of investigation and referrals to the ECJ. This sector is followed by cases on the internal market and/or energy and transport,

---

[92] Court of Justice, *Annual Report 2017: Judicial Activity* (Luxembourg, Court of Justice, 2018) 113.   [93] *Ibid.*

[94] *Lütticke* v. *Commission*, 48/65, EU:C:1966:8. More recently see *Commission* v. *Austria*, C-205/98, EU:C:2000:493.

[95] *Commission* v. *Lithuania*, C-350/08, EU:C:2010:642.

[96] European Parliament Resolution of 14 June 2018 on monitoring the application of EU law 2016 (A8–0197/2018) para. 10.

[97] *European Parliament Report on the 28th Annual Report from the Commission on Monitoring the Application of EU Law (2012)*, A7–0330/2012, para. 14.

[98] For analysis see Smith, n. 35 above, 175–83.   [99] See pp. 334–5.

although neither of these sectors are mentioned in the priority criteria at all. This of course may not be a result of the policy on enforcement, but rather the particular organisation of the Commission and the way in each DG mobilises its resources to combat infringements. For instance, DG Environment is one of the few DGs that contain a unit specifically responsible for dealing with infringements, as opposed to (say) DG Justice, Freedom and Security, which has no such department and generates very few infringement cases. It may be that the type of legislation produced by DG Environment (predominantly directives) is particularly prone to generating infractions (which appears to be confirmed by the Commission's Annual Reports), or it may be that the subject matter is particularly unpopular with Member States. It could be that DG Environment is particularly focused upon enforcement more than other DGs.

Finally, the process is unconstrained by the usual public law disciplines of participation, accountability and transparency. Scant data is provided. Currently, the Commission publishes that it has started proceedings against a Member State, the incident or EU law at the heart of the proceedings, and the stage of the proceedings.[100] However, no detail whatsoever is provided, nor are the contents of the letters of formal notice and reasoned opinions publicly available. Neither is any correspondence during the proceedings between the Commission and the Member State or between the Commission and third parties made public. This is justified on the grounds that the EU Access to Information Regulation requires EU Institutions to refuse access to documents where disclosure would undermine the 'protection of . . . the purpose of investigations' unless there is an overriding public interest in disclosure.[101]

The implications of this were considered in *ClientEarth*. The Commission refused to give a United Kingdom non-governmental organisation (NGO), ClientEarth, access to the legal analysis contained in forty-one studies prepared by a consultancy for it on whether Member State legislation complied with EU law. In one instance ('the first category'), it had not yet decided whether the measure was lawful or not. In the other forty instances (the 'second category') it had decided, in some cases, to initiate the pre-litigation stage of the infringement proceedings but was still pondering what to do in others. The General Court refused access to all the legal analyses, so ClientEarth appealed to the Court of Justice.

ClientEarth v. *Commission*, C–612/13 P, EU:C:2015:486

72 . . . the Commission was entitled to consider that the full disclosure of the contested studies which, when the express decision was adopted, had already led it to send a letter of formal notice to a Member State, under the first paragraph of Article 258 TFEU, and had, consequently, been placed in a file relating to the pre-litigation stage of infringement proceedings, would have been likely to disturb the nature and progress of that stage of proceedings, by making more difficult both the process of negotiation between the Commission and the Member State and the pursuit of an amicable agreement whereby the alleged infringement could be brought to an end, without it being necessary to resort to the judicial stage of those proceedings. The Commission was, consequently, justified in considering that such full disclosure would

---

[100] http://ec.europa.eu/atwork/applying-eu-law/infringements-proceedings/infringement_decisions/?lang_code=en.

[101] Regulation 1049/2001 laying down the principles, conditions and limits of the right of access to documents, OJ 2001, L 145/43, Article 4(2).

have undermined the protection of the purpose of investigations, within the meaning of the third indent of Article 4(2) of Regulation No 1049/2001 ...

75 ... in the light of the legal analysis and the conclusions contained in the contested studies the pre-litigation stage of infringement proceedings was opened by the Commission against some Member States. That analysis and those conclusions therefore constituted the basis for negotiations commenced by the Commission with each of the Member States concerned in order to arrive at an amicable solution to the alleged infringements of EU law. That being the case, full disclosure of those studies would have been likely, in particular, to create external pressures which might have placed in jeopardy the possibility of those negotiations being conducted in a climate of mutual trust and, consequently, to undermine the protection of the purpose pursued by the Commission's investigations.

76 It follows that the General Court was correct to hold that the Commission was entitled to consider, in general terms, that full disclosure of the contested studies which, when the express decision was adopted, had already been placed in a file relating to the pre-litigation stage of infringement proceedings opened with the sending of a letter of formal notice to the Member State concerned, under the first paragraph of Article 258 TFEU, would have undermined the protection of that purpose.

77 As regards, on the other hand, the contested studies other than those referred to in paragraphs 71 to 76 of this judgment, it must, first, be observed that, as the law stands, the Court has recognised five types of documents which enjoy a general presumption of confidentiality: the documents in an administrative file relating to a procedure for reviewing State aid; the pleadings lodged by an institution in court proceedings; the documents exchanged between the Commission and notifying parties or third parties in the course of merger control proceedings; the documents concerning an infringement procedure during its pre-litigation stage; and the documents relating to a proceeding under Article 101 TFEU ...

78 In all the cases which gave rise to the judgments cited in the preceding paragraph, the refusal of access in question related to a set of documents which were clearly defined by the fact that they all belonged to a file relating to ongoing administrative or judicial proceedings ... That cannot however be said of the contested studies other than those referred to in paragraphs 71 to 76 of this judgment.

79 Second, while ... the Commission could justifiably take the view, in general terms, that the disclosure of documents relating to the pre-litigation stage of infringement proceedings would have jeopardised the proper progress of that stage and the pursuit, in a climate of mutual trust, of an amicable resolution to the dispute between the Commission and the Member State under investigation, such a general presumption could not, on the other hand, prevail with respect to those of the contested studies which, when the express decision was adopted, had not led to the sending by the Commission of a letter of formal notice to the Member State concerned, under the first paragraph of Article 258 TFEU, and where, consequently, it remained uncertain, at that time, that the outcome of those studies would be the opening of the pre-litigation stage of infringement proceedings against that Member State. It must, in that regard, be recalled that the Commission, when it considers that a Member State has failed to fulfil its obligations, remains free to assess whether it is appropriate to bring legal proceedings for infringement and to decide when it will initiate infringement proceedings against that Member State ...

80 That being the case, by accepting, in the judgment under appeal, that the Commission could lawfully extend the scope of the presumption of confidentiality to the contested studies referred to in the preceding paragraph of this judgment, the General Court erred in law.

81 Such reasoning is incompatible with the requirement that such a presumption must be interpreted and applied strictly, since that presumption is an exception to the rule that the institution concerned is obliged to make a specific and individual examination of every document which is the subject of an application for access ... and, more generally, to the principle that the public should have the widest possible access to the documents held by the institutions of the European Union ...

A strict division is therefore made between the pre-litigation stage, namely the opening of a file by the Commission, and the period prior to that. Once a file has been opened, the Commission can refuse to disclose any document which forms part of that file, even if the document was produced prior to any Commission decision to initiate proceedings and even if it was produced by a third party.[102] There is a blanket exclusion on access to information about the detail of the infringement proceedings. The situation is different if the Commission has not yet opened a file. It does not have to give the public access to documents while it is still mulling over what to do. Rather, it must consider each document individually and come to a view on whether disclosure will prejudice future infringement proceedings or not. Invariably, the likelihood of such proceedings will be a factor to be considered in deciding whether to grant access to the document or not.

This blanket exclusion on information about the detail of the proceedings has been subject to criticism. In 2013, the European Ombudsman caustically noted:

> The Commission is convinced that public disclosure of documents exchanged with the member states during infringement procedures will necessarily harm the purpose of that procedure, which is to ensure the correct application of EU law. The Ombudsman considers, however, that this position is not immediately evident or self explanatory. Indeed, it is not reasonably foreseeable that a confidential exchange of arguments between the Commission and the Member State will always promote a solution to an infringement more than would a transparent discussion of the various legal viewpoints and interests at stake. On the contrary, one can imagine infringement procedures where public disclosure of the different opinions and arguments exchanged, exactly because of the robust involvement of public opinion and civil society, both national and European, could actually favour or facilitate an end to the infringement. One can even reasonably suppose that public disclosure of documents in infringement procedures where environmental issues are at stake would likely be one of those situations. It is indeed plausible that, with an eye to bringing the member state legislation in line with EU law, involvement of civil society and public opinion would be highly favourable. The general and blanket assertion that public disclosure of documents exchanged in infringement procedures will always harm the purpose of that procedure . . . appears to be too general in nature and can therefore be understood as merely hypothetical.[103]

The Commission has rejected this view, arguing that a lack of confidentiality would damage negotiations between itself and the Member State, and there is a public interest in these negotiations being concluded successfully.[104] As can be seen, the Ombudsman is sceptical about how often negotiations would actually be damaged. However, even if the Commission is right about this, it raises an interesting point about how it believes the infringement proceedings should be perceived. For the Commission, the central point is to get a deal with the Member State. The quality of the deal, and how it affects certain interests, seems less central. Alas, without disclosure, it is difficult to know how these are affected.

---

[102] There is a presumption, therefore, that files in EU Pilot are not to be disclosed, *Sweden* v. *Commission*, C-562/14 P, EU:C:2017:356.

[103] *Decision of the European Ombudsman closing his inquiry into complaint 1947/2010/PB against the European Commission*, 26 September 2013, para. 63.

[104] These views are cited *ibid.* para. 60.

(ii) Complainants and Article 258 TFEU

Notwithstanding their key role in prompting many infringement proceedings and their consequent stake in the outcomes of these, complainants are frozen out of the proceedings. They have no right to require the Commission to commence proceedings or to be otherwise involved. In *Star Fruit*, a Belgian banana trader alleged that it had been prejudiced by the organisation of the French banana market in a manner that was contrary to EU law. It complained to the Commission, but the latter did not commence proceedings against France. Star Fruit sought to take the Commission before the Court for failure to act. The Court of Justice ruled that the action was inadmissible.

Star Fruit v. Commission, 247/87, EU:C:1989:58

11 ... it is clear from the scheme of Article [258 TFEU] that the Commission is not bound to commence the proceedings provided for in that provision but in this regard has a discretion which excludes the right for individuals to require that institution to adopt a specific position.

12 It is only if it considers that the Member State in question has failed to fulfil one of its obligations that the Commission delivers a reasoned opinion. Furthermore, in the event that the State does not comply with the opinion within the period allowed, the institution has in any event the right, but not the duty, to apply to the Court of Justice for a declaration that the alleged breach of obligations has occurred.

13 It must also be observed that in requesting the Commission to commence proceedings pursuant to Article [258 TFEU] the applicant is in fact seeking the adoption of acts which are not of direct and individual concern to it within the meaning of the second paragraph of Article [263(4) TFEU] and which it could not therefore challenge by means of an action for annulment in any event.[105]

14 Consequently, the applicant cannot be entitled to raise the objection that the Commission failed to commence proceedings against the French republic pursuant to Article [258 TFEU].

This exclusion led, in the 1990s, to a large number of parties turning to the European Ombudsman to complain about the Commission's handling of their complaints.[106] Matters reached a nadir in 2001 with the *Macedonian Metro* decision. This concerned a complaint that the Greek authorities had violated EU public procurement law in a tender for the construction of a metro in Thessaloniki. The Ombudsman found that the Commission had lied to the complainant by telling him that it was closing the file because there was no breach of EU law when in fact the file was closed as an act of political discretion.[107] Secondly, the Commission had violated the complainant's right to be heard as it had sent its provisional views to the complainant eight days before closing the file and at the beginning of the summer holidays. This clearly gave the complainant insufficient time to comment on these views.[108] As a consequence, in 2002, the Commission set out certain procedural entitlements for complainants.[109] These have been updated and now involve the following principles:

---

[105] There are the *locus standi* requirements for judicial review of EU acts. They are discussed at pp. 390–7.

[106] On these see Rawlings, n. 36 above, 27.

[107] *Decision of the European Ombudsman on complaint 995/98/OV against the European Commission*, 31 January 2001, paras. 3.1–3.7.

[108] *Ibid.* paras. 4.1–4.6.

[109] European Commission, 'On Relations with the Complainant in Respect of Infringements of Community Law', COM (2002)141.

- Anybody may bring a complaint free of charge without having to prove an interest.
- All correspondence shall be recorded. The Commission shall acknowledge receipt within fifteen days. It shall not be investigable if the complaint is anonymous; fails to refer to a Member State; denounces private parties unless public authorities are involved or fail to act; fails to set out a grievance or sets out one on which the Commission has adopted a clear, public, consistent position; or concerns something which falls outside EU law. In such circumstances, the Commission shall inform the complainant and also inform them of other possible avenues, such as national courts or the Ombudsman.
- The Commission will inform the complainant if it examines the complaint. If proceedings are launched, the Commission will also inform complainants in writing of each procedural step taken.
- The Commission will endeavour to close the case or issue a formal notice within one year from registering the complaint.
- If the Commission closes the case, unless there are exceptional circumstances justifying urgent measures, the Commission shall give the complainant four weeks to submit comments having set out the reasons for its decision.[110]

Whilst bringing some structure to the processes, this leaves several procedural matters unaddressed. For the most part, the complainant is only notified of what takes place after the event. More active involvement is left until late in the day – four weeks before the closing of the file – and this rarely allows for effective input. Furthermore, there are few overarching norms governing the handling of the process.[111] This has been picked up by the European Parliament which has stated that there should be a series of norms which, *inter alia*, allow the Commission only to delay or stop proceedings if there is a clear public interest; impose a duty on it to carry out careful and impartial investigations; and require it to give complainants a hearing.[112]

6 SANCTIONS AND ARTICLE 260 TFEU

(i) Article 260 TFEU and the Two Routes to Sanctions

Article 258 TFEU alone does not provide for the imposition of sanctions where the Court of Justice finds that the State has breached EU law. It merely allows for a State to be declared in breach. This does no more, therefore, than name and shame Member States. This carries little stigma, however, when all Member States are found to breach EU law regularly. Research found that, in 2002, for example, Member States failed to comply with 37.33 per cent of the judgments within twelve months.[113] Article 260 TFEU, therefore, establishes two procedures for sanctioning Member States.[114]

---

[110] European Commission, n. 13 above, Annex.   [111] Smith, n. 35 above, 191–4.
[112] Most recently, Resolution of 9 June 2016 for an open, efficient and independent European Union administration, B8–0685/2016.
[113] D. Chalmers, 'Judicial Authority and the Constitutional Treaty' (2005) 4 *ICON* 448, 453.
[114] S. Peers, 'Sanctions for Infringement of EU Law after the Treaty of Lisbon' (2012) 18 *EPL* 33.

Article 260 TFEU

(1) If the Court of Justice of the European Union finds that a Member State has failed to fulfil an obligation under the Treaties, the State shall be required to take the necessary measures to comply with the judgment of the Court.

(2) If the Commission considers that the Member State concerned has not taken the necessary measures to comply with the judgment of the Court, it may bring the case before the Court after giving that State the opportunity to submit its observations. It shall specify the amount of the lump sum or penalty payment to be paid by the Member State concerned which it considers appropriate in the circumstances.

   If the Court finds that the Member State concerned has not complied with its judgment it may impose a lump sum or penalty payment on it.

   This procedure shall be without prejudice to Article 259.

(3) When the Commission brings a case before the Court pursuant to Article 258 on the grounds that the Member State concerned has failed to fulfil its obligation to notify measures transposing a directive adopted under a legislative procedure, it may, when it deems appropriate, specify the amount of the lump sum or penalty payment to be paid by the Member State concerned which it considers appropriate in the circumstances.

   If the Court finds that there is an infringement it may impose a lump sum or penalty payment on the Member State concerned not exceeding the amount specified by the Commission. The payment obligation shall take effect on the date set by the Court in its judgment.[115]

The first procedure, set out in Articles 260(2) TFEU, provides for where a Member State has failed to comply with a judgment of the Court given under Article 258 TFEU (or 259 TFEU) that it is in breach of EU law. The second procedure, laid out in Article 260(3) TFEU, provides that sanctions can be imposed where a State has failed to transpose a Directive. In this instance, sanctions do not rely on a prior judgment but can be given at the moment that the Court finds that a Member State is in breach of EU law.

(ii) The Procedure for Failure to Transpose a Directive

Since the sanctions procedure for failure to transpose a Directive under Article 260(3) TFEU is more straightforward, it makes sense to address it first. The rationale for this fast-track procedure is because the transposition of Directives is seen as a priority, and there is the perception of widespread illegality here. In 2017, for example, of the 1,008 domestic transpositions required, the Commission commenced late-transposition proceedings in 558 cases.[116] The procedure is used both where the Member State has not notified the Commission of any measures taken to transpose the Directive but also where the transposition has only been partial. In the latter instance, the measures taken either do not cover the whole of the national territory or are in some other way, incomplete. It will not be used, however, where the State believes that it has met its duties under the Directive but the Commission believes the measures are insufficient. In such circumstances, the Commission will bring an infringement proceeding merely for a declaration to comply with EU law (under Article 258 TFEU) and nothing more.[117]

---

[115] Article 260 TFEU shall continue to apply to the United Kingdom with regard to judgments given during the transition period, Article 131 Withdrawal Agreement.

[116] European Commission, n. 5 above, 15. The figures give only a sense of the problem as some of these proceedings will have been started for Directives which were due to be transposed in 2016.

[117] European Commission, *Implementation of Article 260(3) of the Treaty*, OJ 2011, C 12/1, para. 19.

There is one final thing to note about the procedure for sanctions for non-transposition of a Directive. It relies on the Commission asking the Court for a sanction to be applied. In this regard, the Commission has indicated that sanctions 'should be used as a matter of principle in all cases of failure to fulfil an obligation covered by this provision'.[118] It has also stated that once a case has been referred to the Court under Article 258 TFEU, transposition by the State prior to judgment given by the Court of Justice will not necessarily stop it pressing for sanctions.[119] The reason is to stop Member States gaming the system. There would, otherwise, be no reason for them to transpose the Directive until right before judgment.

(iii) The Procedure for Failure to Comply with a Court Judgment

Other breaches of EU law are governed by the procedure in Article 260(2) TFEU. Actions can only be brought, therefore, in relation to infringements which have already been established by the Court, be it under Article 258 or 259 TFEU.[120] Following this, the Commission may issue a letter of formal notice in respect of which the Member State can submit its observations. If there is no resolution at this point, the Commission can refer the case to the Court of Justice for the State to be sanctioned. There is no need for the Commission to issue a reasoned opinion.

This raises the question as to whether the letter of formal notice is subject to the same legal constraints as the reasoned opinion in Article 258 TFEU. In *Commission* v. *Portugal* the Court stated that the opportunity for Member States to submit observations is an essential guarantee of both procedures.[121] The Commission cannot subsequently include complaints not in the original letter of formal notice and is under a duty both to consider national observations submitted in response to it and to give Member States a date for compliance. The letter of formal notice must also set out a date for compliance, giving the State a reasonable period to comply. The date for determining whether a State has failed in its obligations to comply with the judgment of the Court of Justice is that set out in the letter of formal notice.[122] Compliance after that date does not prevent the Court from being referred to the Court or absolve it from penalty.[123]

The greatest challenge with the Article 260(2) TFEU procedure has not been the process itself but its limited use. As of October 2018, there have been only fifteen instances of the Court of Justice giving judgment under it since the adoption of the Lisbon Treaty. Thus, there is a strong suspicion that the Commission is indulgent of national non-compliance with Court of Justice judgments.

B. Jack, 'Article 260(2) TFEU: An Effective Judicial Procedure for the Enforcement of Judgments?' (2013) 19 *European Law Journal* 404, 406–7

In the first three enforcement actions that come before the Court, the Commission waited between 2 and 3 years from the Court's initial judgment before serving a formal notice under Article 260(2). In more recent cases, it has, generally, acted more quickly. In two of the last three cases before the Court, the formal notice was issued within 8 months of the Court's initial judgment, while in three earlier

---

[118] *Ibid.* para. 17.   [119] European Commission, n. 13 above, 16.
[120] *Commission* v. *Germany*, C-95/12, EU:C:2013:676; *Commission* v. *Italy*, C-196/13, EU:C:2014:2407.
[121] *Commission* v. *Portugal*, C-457/07, EU:C:2009:531.
[122] E.g. *Commission* v. *Italy*, C-196/13, EU:C:2014:2407; *Commission* v. *Greece*, C-328/16, EU:C:2018:98.
[123] *Commission* v. *Greece*, C-407/09, EU:C:2011:196.

cases it was issued within 3 months of that judgment. However, more than 3 years elapsed in its most recent case. Once the formal notice has been served, the Commission has, since 2007, set an objective of referring cases back to the Court within 12–24 months. Following the abolition of the use of the reasoned opinion, it has revised this objective to between 8 and 18 months. Overall, however, the period between the Court's initial judgment and its judgment under Article 260(2) was still more than 3 years in two of the last three cases that it considered, and over 7 years in the third. The abolition of the use of the reasoned opinion will reduce this period. But, in practice, a period of at least 2–3 years is still likely to remain between the Court's judgments.

There is one other issue to consider before we look at the sanctions applied. This is the assumption that a financial penalty is sufficient to secure compliance and provide restoration for damage. There seems to be some evidence to support this. Jack looked at the responses where financial sanctions were applied. There were eight at the time of the article. In two instances, it was too early to tell but in the other instances compliance was relatively fast.

B. Jack, 'Article 260(2) TFEU: An Effective Judicial Procedure for the Enforcement of Judgments?' (2013) 19 *European Law Journal* 404, 412–13

The remaining six cases, with one important exception, suggest that penalty payments have, ultimately, been effective in achieving Member State compliance with Court judgments. Greece initially ignored the Court's first penalty payment order, neither addressing the requirement to close the illegal waste site involved nor making the required penalty payments. The European Parliament's Environment Committee, by making the issue a standing item on its agenda, pressurised the Commission and, indirectly, Greece to secure compliance. Greece eventually complied with the Court's judgment and discharged the penalty payments due. Their delay transformed the daily €20 000 penalty payment into a total penalty of €4.7 million. This is equivalent to a delay of 235 days. Subsequently, Portugal took 189 days to comply with the Court's judgment, confirming that its national laws infringed EU public procurement law, turning a daily payment of €19 392 into a total penalty of almost €3.7 million. In the remaining cases, however, Member States complied more quickly. In one, a penalty payment was suspended for 1 month to enable Greece to produce evidence establishing the recovery of illegal state aid payments. Greece complied, and consequently no penalty payment fell due. Equally, France was ordered to pay €57 761 250 for each 6-month period in which it continued not to adequately enforce fishery conservation laws. Only one such payment was made before the Commission adjudged compliance had been fully achieved. Finally, France took just 24 days to comply with the Court's judgment, confirming that its national laws failed to fully comply with Directive 85/374 on producer responsibility for defective products. This, therefore, turned a daily penalty payment of €31 650 into a total payment of €759 000. Ultimately, however, compliance was achieved in each case, and the penalty payments levied paid to the Commission.

The relative success of these cases, however, obscures an ongoing failure. In October 2006, the Court held that Greek legislation making the installation and operation of electrical, electromechanical and electronic games illegal contravened the free movement of goods and services and the freedom of establishment. In June 2009, the Court ordered Greece to pay a penalty payment of €31 536 per day until it complied with its initial judgment. Greece has so far paid a total of €23 841 216 in penalty payments to the Commission, but its failure to comply with the Court's initial judgment continues. The Court's financial penalty clearly has not had the intended coercive effect. This highlights the danger that penalty payments may prove ineffective where Member States consider that broader national interests outweigh the economic pressure that they apply.

(iv) The Sanctions Levied under Article 260 TFEU

Article 260 TFEU provides for two types of financial sanction: the lump sum and the penalty payment. The relationship between these was established in *Commission* v. *France*. In 1991 the Court found that France had failed to comply with EU fisheries law between 1984 and 1987 by insufficiently monitoring the mesh size of fishing nets, thereby allowing undersized fish to be caught and sold.[124] Little was done to implement this judgment, and the Commission therefore started Article 260 TFEU proceedings. It asked for a lump sum sanction to be imposed to punish France for its current and past behaviour and a penalty payment to induce it to comply as quickly as possible.

Commission v. *France*, C–304/02, EU:C:2005:444

80 The procedure laid down in Article [260 TFEU] has the objective of inducing a defaulting Member State to comply with a judgment establishing a breach of obligations and thereby of ensuring that Community law is in fact applied. The measures provided for by that provision, namely a lump sum and a penalty payment, are both intended to achieve this objective.

81 Application of each of those measures depends on their respective ability to meet the objective pursued according to the circumstances of the case. While the imposition of a penalty payment seems particularly suited to inducing a Member State to put an end as soon as possible to a breach of obligations which, in the absence of such a measure, would tend to persist, the imposition of a lump sum is based more on assessment of the effects on public and private interests of the failure of the Member State concerned to comply with its obligations, in particular where the breach has persisted for a long period since the judgment which initially established it.

82 That being so, recourse to both types of penalty provided for in Article [260(2) TFEU] is not precluded, in particular where the breach of obligations both has continued for a long period and is inclined to persist . . .

91 . . . The procedure provided for in Article [260(2) TFEU] is a special judicial procedure, peculiar to Community law, which cannot be equated with a civil procedure. The order imposing a penalty payment and/or a lump sum is not intended to compensate for damage caused by the Member State concerned, but to place it under economic pressure which induces it to put an end to the breach established. The financial penalties imposed must therefore be decided upon according to the degree of persuasion needed in order for the Member State in question to alter its conduct . . .

103 As to those submissions, while it is clear that a penalty payment is likely to encourage the defaulting Member State to put an end as soon as possible to the breach that has been established . . . it should be remembered that the Commission's suggestions cannot bind the Court and are only a useful point of reference. . . In exercising its discretion, it is for the Court to set the penalty payment so that it is appropriate to the circumstances and proportionate both to the breach that has been established and to the ability to pay of the Member State concerned . . .

104 In that light . . . the basic criteria which must be taken into account in order to ensure that penalty payments have coercive force and Community law is applied uniformly and effectively are, in principle, the duration of the infringement, its degree of seriousness and the ability of the Member State to pay. In applying those criteria, regard should be had in particular to the effects of failure to comply on private and public interests and to the urgency of getting the Member State concerned to fulfil its obligations . . .

[124] *Commission* v. *France*, C-64/88, EU:C:1991:240.

113 ... the French Republic should be ordered to pay to the Commission, into the account 'European Community own resources', a penalty payment of 182.5 x EUR 316 500, that is to say of EUR 57 761 250, for each period of six months from delivery of the present judgment at the end of which the judgment in Case C-64/88 Commission v. France has not yet been fully complied with.

114 In a situation such as that which is the subject of the present judgment, in light of the fact that the breach of obligations has persisted for a long period since the judgment which initially established it and of the public and private interests at issue, it is essential to order payment of a lump sum (see paragraph 81 of the present judgment).

115 The specific circumstances of the case are fairly assessed by setting the amount of the lump sum which the French Republic will have to pay at EUR 20 000 000.

The lump sum is punitive in nature. It is to sanction the State for the damage caused. By contrast, the periodic penalty has a deterrent objective, namely to provide incentives for the State to comply with EU law by imposing financial penalties until it does. The judgment indicates that – possibly contrary to the explicit wording of Article 260(3) TFEU – both a lump sum sanction and penalty payment can be imposed for the same breach. In general, the Commission will press for both.[125] However, by dint of their different functions, there are certain instances where this cannot be done. As it is to deter future conduct, a penalty payment may not be imposed if the State has complied with the EU law by the time of judgment.[126] By contrast, a lump sum can still be imposed. The deadline to avoid its sanction is the period set out in the letter of formal notice.[127]

The judgment also sets out the general principles governing the level of sanctions to be applied: the duration of the infringement, its seriousness and the ability of the Member State to pay. In a 2005 Communication, updated annually to take account of inflation and changes in Member State GDP, the Commission elaborated on these criteria and set out coefficients to determine the levels of sanctions it will seek.[128] The amounts are significant. The minimum lump sum in 2018 ranges from €217,000 (Malta) to €11.8 million (Germany). The daily penalty payment, which runs from the date of the judgment given under Article 258 TFEU until compliance with EU law, is €690. A coefficient is applied to take account of the State's GDP and voting rights in the Council, which varies from 0.38 (Malta) to 20.74 (Germany).[129] A further multiplier (1–20) is applied to take account of the seriousness of the infringement and another to take account of its duration (1–3).[130] For serious breaches of a long duration, Germany is, therefore, potentially subject to a penalty of several hundred thousand euros per year.

This communication acts as the starting point for determining the sanctions to be paid. Whilst the Court has indicated that it will do no more than take account of it,[131] it also cannot impose more than that requested by the Commission.[132] In fact, the Court will often impose less than

---

[125] European Commission, 'Application of Article 228 of the EC Treaty', SEC(2005)1658, paras. 10.3 and 10.4.

[126] *Commission* v. *Italy*, C-496/09, EU:C:2011:740; *Commission* v. *Ireland*, C-374/11, EU:C:2012:827.

[127] *Commission* v. *Spain*, C-610/10, EU:C:2012:781.

[128] European Commission, 'Application of Article 228 of the EC Treaty', SEC(2005)1658.

[129] European Commission, *Updating of Data Used to Calculate Lump Sum and Penalty Payments to be Proposed by the Commission to the Court of Justice in Infringement Proceedings*, C(2018)5851 final.

[130] European Commission, n. 128 above, paras. 16.6 and 17.

[131] *Commission* v. *Czech Republic*, C-241/11, EU:C:2013:423.   [132] Article 260(3) TFEU.

that requested by the Commission. This is in large part because the sanction must be appropriate to the circumstances and proportionate to the infringement. This constraint overlaps with the principles above but has been used to introduce certain additional factors (e.g. if it is the first time the State is being sanctioned[133] or if a State has made progress towards implementation[134]) which may push the sanction down.

FURTHER READING

S. Andersen, *The Enforcement of EU Law: The Role of the European Commission* (Oxford University Press, 2012).

T. Börzel, T. Hofmann and D. Panke, 'Caving In or Sitting Out? Longitudinal Patterns of Non-Compliance in the European Union' (2012) 19 *Journal of European Public Policy* 454.

M. Cremona (ed.), *Compliance and the Enforcement of EU Law* (Oxford University Press, 2012).

S. Drake and M. Smith (eds.), *New Directions in the Effective Enforcement of EU Law and Policy* (Cheltenham, Edward Elgar, 2016).

B. Jack, 'Article 260(2) TFEU: An Effective Judicial Procedure for the Enforcement of Judgments?' (2013) 19 *European Law Journal* 404.

L. Prete and B. Smulders, 'The Coming of Age of Infringement Proceedings' (2010) 47 *Common Market Law Review* 9.

M. Smith, *Centralised Enforcement, Legitimacy and Good Governance in the EU* (Abingdon, Routledge, 2009).

B. Steunenberg and D. Toshkov, 'Comparing Transposition in the 27 Member States of the EU: The Impact of Discretion and Legal Fit' (2009) 16 *Journal of European Public Policy* 951.

M. Taboroski, 'Infringement Proceedings and Non-Compliant National Courts' (2012) 49 *Common Market Law Review* 1881.

P. Wennerås, 'Sanctions against Member States under Article 260 TFEU: Alive but Not Kicking?' (2012) 49 *Common Market Law Review* 145.

---

[133] *Commission* v. *Sweden*, C-270/11, EU:C:2013:339.   [134] *Commission* v. *Italy*, C-196/13, EU:C:2014:2407.

9

Judicial Review

CONTENTS

1 INTRODUCTION

This chapter considers judicial review by the Court of Justice. It is organised as follows.

Section 2 considers the scope of Article 263 TFEU, the central provision governing direct actions for judicial review of Union acts. It can be invoked against all EU Institutions, agencies, offices and bodies. Moreover, any act intended to produce legal effects is susceptible to review. As for the United Kingdom and persons resident or established in the United Kingdom, they shall only be entitled to challenge acts during the transition period after the United Kingdom leaves the Union and the challenges will have to be made during that period.

Section 3 considers the grounds for review. An act will be annulled, first, if the EU Institution does not have the formal competence to adopt it. It will occur secondly, if the EU Institution misuses its discretion. This may be where there is an abuse of power and a power is used for purposes other than that for which it was granted. It may also be where there is a manifest error of assessment, avoidance of which requires Union acts to be substantiated by accurate, reliable, consistent and sufficiently complete evidence. The third heading of review comprises rights of process. These include rights to defence where EU acts will lead to sanction; the right to a hearing where one's interests are adversely restricted by a Union measure; and finally, the right to administration of one's affairs with due care by the EU Institutions. The final heading of review is infringement of the Treaties or any rule of law relating to its application. This includes breach of any substantive provision of EU law, fundamental rights, and general principles of law. The latter includes the principles of non-discrimination, legal certainty, protection of legitimate expectations, subsidiarity and proportionality.

Section 4 considers the standing requirements under Article 263 TFEU. Privileged applicants – the Member States, Parliament, the Commission and Council – have unlimited standing to challenge a measure. Semi-privileged applicants – the Court of Auditors, European Central Bank (ECB) and Committee of the Regions – may bring an action to protect their institutional prerogatives. All other parties may bring an action against acts addressed to them, be it a regulatory act which is of direct concern to them and entails no implementing measures or against other acts of direct and individual concern to them. Regulatory acts are non-legislative measures which are general in nature. Direct concern will be established where the Union act directly affects a legal entitlement of the applicant without any significant intermediation by another party. For regulatory acts, the measure must also entail no implementing measure, be it by an EU Institution or Member State. Individual concern is governed by the *Plaumann* formula. This requires the interest affected to be part of a fixed, ascertainable and limited group of interests which is not capable, even hypothetically, of being added to.

Section 5 examines Article 265 TFEU which allows parties to challenge omissions by Union Institutions where these are under a duty to act. The standing requirements are similar to Article 263 TFEU as it complements this provision. However, an action under Article 265 TFEU can only be commenced against an EU Institution if it is under a duty to perform a task. The Union Institution must also have been called upon to act by the applicant and failed to do so within two months before any action can be begun.

Section 6 considers the plea of illegality set out in Article 277 TFEU. This is not an independent action but, in an action against a measure brought under another provision (e.g. Article 263 TFEU), it allows challenge of a parent measure. It is subject to two constraints. It cannot be brought where the measure is being challenged before a court elsewhere by the parties. Also it cannot be brought by parties who have already had the opportunity to challenge the measure but did not take that opportunity up.

Section 7 considers the action for non-contractual liability under Article 340(2) TFEU. Parties can sue EU Institutions for damages where three conditions are met. First, the EU Institution has infringed a rule of law intended to confer rights on individuals; secondly, the breach is sufficiently serious; and finally, that there is a direct causal link between the breach and the loss sustained. In fields where EU Institutions enjoy little or no discretion, a simple breach of EU law or failure to exercise reasonable care may be sufficient to establish liability. In other fields, liability will only exist if they manifestly and gravely disregard the limits of their discretion.

Section 8 considers the consequences of a finding of annulment. Such a ruling is binding on all institutional actors within the Union. In only the most grave cases of illegality will measures be declared void and found to have produced no legal effect. Usually, a measure produces legal effects until it is annulled. At the moment of annulment, the Court has a wide discretion over the legal effects a measure will have after it is annulled. Part of the measure may continue in force or temporal limitations may be established allowing it to continue in force for a period.

2 THE SCOPE OF JUDICIAL REVIEW AND ARTICLE 263 TFEU

The starting point for considering when EU Institutions can be judicially reviewed is Article 263 TFEU.

Article 263 TFEU

The Court of Justice of the European Union shall review the legality of legislative acts, of acts of the Council, of the Commission and of the European Central Bank, other than recommendations and opinions, and of acts of the European Parliament and of the European Council intended to produce legal effects vis-à-vis third parties. It shall also review the legality of acts of bodies, offices or agencies of the Union intended to produce legal effects vis-à-vis third parties.

It shall for this purpose have jurisdiction in actions brought by a Member State, the European Parliament, the Council or the Commission on grounds of lack of competence, infringement of an essential procedural requirement, infringement of the Treaties or of any rule of law relating to their application, or misuse of powers.

The Court shall have jurisdiction under the same conditions in actions brought by the Court of Auditors, by the European Central Bank and by the Committee of the Regions for the purpose of protecting their prerogatives.

Any natural or legal person may, under the conditions referred to in the first and second subparagraphs, institute proceedings against an act addressed to that person or which is of direct and individual concern to them, and against a regulatory act which is of direct concern to them and does not entail implementing measures.

Acts setting up bodies, offices and agencies of the Union may lay down specific conditions and arrangements concerning actions brought by natural or legal persons against acts of these bodies, offices or agencies intended to produce legal effects in relation to them.

The provision can be invoked against a wide range of actors which includes not just all EU Institutions, but also EU agencies, offices and other bodies. The inclusion of the European Council is particularly intriguing, as subjecting the decisions of twenty-seven Heads of

Government to judicial challenge is unprecedented in human history and illustrates the symbolic importance attached to the rule of law in the European Union.

The United Kingdom and natural and legal persons established or residing in the United Kingdom shall not be able to challenge Union acts after the United Kingdom leaves the Union. They shall be entitled to challenge any acts addressed to the United Kingdom during the transition period, albeit under the standing rules set out in Article 263 TFEU.[1]

Equally important are the acts which may be reviewed. If a narrow view is taken of which acts are reviewable, this would allow many activities to escape judicial scrutiny whilst the reverse is true if a wide view is taken. In this regard, something is an act when it is intended to produce legal effects.[2] The designation of the measure is unimportant, but some gauge of what is sought can be seen from *Mallis*. The context was the restructuring of the Cypriot banking system as a condition for a programme of financial assistance subsequent to the financial crisis that hit Cyprus in 2012. The programme was provided by the European Stability Mechanism (ESM), a company set up by the euro area States. Shortly before the programme was formally agreed, the Eurogroup – the body of euro area Finance Ministers established by the EU Treaties, at which the Commission and ECB participated – put out a statement welcoming the programme and the financial restructuring. The applicants argued that this statement was, in reality, a decision of the ECB and the Commission which produced legal effects as it led to the restructuring of the Cypriot banking sector.

Mallis and Others v. *Commission and ECB*, C-105–109/15 P, EU:C:2016:702

51 ... it should be recalled that an action for annulment is available against all measures adopted by the EU institutions, whatever their nature or form, which are intended to have binding legal effects capable of affecting the interests of the applicant by bringing about a distinct change in his legal position ...

53 ... it must be pointed out that the role of the Commission and the ECB as defined by Article 1 of Protocol No 14 on the Eurogroup cannot be wider than the role accorded to those institutions by the ESM Treaty ... whilst the ESM Treaty entrusts to the Commission and the ECB certain tasks relating to the attainment of the objectives of that Treaty, first, the duties conferred on the Commission and ECB within the ESM Treaty do not entail the exercise of any power to make decisions of their own and, secondly, the activities pursued by those two institutions within the ESM Treaty commit the ESM alone ...

57 In the light of those points, the fact that the Commission and the ECB participate in the meetings of the Eurogroup does not alter the nature of the latter's statements and cannot result in the statement at issue being considered to be the expression of a decision-making power of those two EU institutions.

58 Nor is there anything in the statement at issue reflecting a decision of the Commission and the ECB to create a legal obligation on the Member State concerned to implement the measures which it contains.

59 ... that statement, of a purely informative nature, was intended to inform the general public of the existence of a political agreement between the Eurogroup and the Cypriot authorities reflecting a common intention to pursue the negotiations in accordance with the statement's terms.

60 Accordingly, the adoption by the Republic of Cyprus of the Law of 22 March 2013, which created the legal framework necessary for the restructuring of the banks concerned ... cannot be regarded as having been imposed by a supposed joint decision of the Commission and the ECB that was given concrete expression in the statement at issue.

---

[1] EU–United Kingdom Withdrawal Act, Article 91(2).   [2] *Commission* v. *Council ('ERTA')*, C-22/70, EU:C:1971:32.

The measure was, therefore, found not to be a decision because it was only informative in nature, describing a political will to put a programme in place, and because it did not bring a change in Cypriot legal obligations.

To be characterised as 'intended to have legal effects' and therefore reviewable, a measure must have two features. First, it must bring about a change in another party's legal position and, secondly, it must be definitive. Arguably, neither was present in *Mallis*.

In respect of the first requirement – a change in a party's legal position – regard is had to the content of the measure, the legal context, and the powers of the EU Institution, to ascertain whether it brought about a change in the party's legal position.[3]

In interpreting the content of the measure, the Court will look at its wording, whether it is mandatory or not[4] and the intention of the EU Institution.[5] A restatement of an existing position is not reviewable.[6] Neither is indicating an intention to follow a particular line of conduct[7] or giving a legal opinion.[8] There must be a stronger statement about a change in a party's legal status. Identifying it as exposed to additional requirements under EU law is, thus, reviewable.[9] So is refusing to instigate, terminating or suspending competition or State aids proceedings as all these indicate that the party will not be legally sanctioned when there was, otherwise, a possibility that it might be.[10]

The context is used to identify the purpose of the measure, and whether this purpose was intended to change a party's legal position. In *Belgium* v. *Commission*, the General Court, therefore, found that a Commission Recommendation recommending a high level of consumer protection for online gambling was not a reviewable act.[11] One of the reasons was that the Commission had published a communication two years earlier setting out an overall framework for online gambling in which it indicated that it did not wish to propose any sector-specific legislation. There was, therefore, no intent to change the legal situation.

Finally, if the EU Institution does not have the power to adopt a legal binding act, the EU Courts are less likely to find a reviewable act as it is presumed that the EU Institution knows that it cannot adopt binding acts on the matter in question.[12]

The second requirement for a measure to be reviewable is that the EU Institution has set out a definitive position. In *IBM*, the Court found that a Commission decision to initiate competition proceedings was not reviewable as it was a preparatory measure instigating a process which would conclude in a reviewable decision. A measure will only be reviewable, therefore, if it is the culmination of a process.[13] There is one qualification to this. A measure is reviewable if it forms part of a discrete process that does not go to the substance of the main process at hand. In *Österreichische Postsparkasse*, the Freedom Party, an Austrian political party, asked the Commission to investigate an alleged Austrian banking cartel.[14] The Commission obtained

---

[3] *Hungary* v. *Commission*, C-31/13 P, EU:C:2014:70.   [4] *Belgium* v. *Commission*, C-16/16 P, EU:C:2018:79.

[5] *Esso Raffinage* v. *ECHA*, T-283/15, EU:T:2018:263.   [6] *Deutsche Bahn* v. *Commission*, T-351/02, EU:T:2006:104.

[7] *Italy* v. *Commission*, T-185/05, EU:T:2008:519.   [8] *Slovak Republic* v. *Commission*, C-593-4/15 P, EU:C:2017:800.

[9] *Commission* v. *Council*, C-27/04, EU:C:2004:436; *Rütgers Germany* v. *ECHA*, T-96/10, EU:T:2013:109.

[10] *SFEI* v. *Commission*, C-39/93 P, EU:C:1994:253. See R. Greaves, 'The Nature and Binding Effect of Decisions under Article 189 EC' (1996) 21 *ELRev* 3, 9–10.

[11] *Belgium* v. *Commission*, T-721/14, EU:T:2015:829.

[12] *Slovak Republic* v. *Commission*, C-593/15 P, EU:C:2017:800.

[13] *IBM* v. *Commission*, 60/81, EU:C:1981:264. See also *NDSHT* v. *Commission*, C-322/09 P, EU:C:2010:701.

[14] *Österreichische Postsparkasse and Bank für Arbeit und Wirtschaft* v. *Commission*, T-213–14/01, EU:T:2006:151. See also *Nexans France* v. *Commission*, T-135/09, EU:T:2012:596.

information from the banks which, it indicated to the banks, it intended to disclose to the Freedom Party. The General Court held that the banks could challenge this disclosure as the question of whether to disclose or not was quite separate from whether they had engaged in anti-competitive conduct.

The law here relies on fine-grained distinctions. For example, it will often not be evident whether the measure has produced changes in the applicant's legal position; or whether it is an intermediate measure leading to a final act (non-reviewable); or part of a process discrete from that (non-reviewable). It leads to some uneasy distinctions: a decision to start competition proceedings is not reviewable whilst a decision not to start them is reviewable. In actual fact, these are identical processes which just lead to different conclusions. Not only does the possibility for many cases to be argued either way lead to some legal uncertainty, it also raises a suspicion that the Court is often guided by the policy background in deciding whether the measure *ought* to be reviewed. In the case of competition proceedings, the Court showed an unwillingness to allow every undertaking against which proceedings were instigated to bully the Commission by threatening litigation from the onset. Decisions to start competition proceedings were, therefore, not reviewable. By contrast, if no proceedings were started, the only remedy for competitors or consumers groups, if there was evidence of illegal behaviour, was often to challenge the failure to proceed.

3 GROUNDS OF REVIEW

Four grounds of review are listed in Article 263 TFEU: lack of competence, infringement of an essential procedural requirement, infringement of the Treaty or of any rule of law relating to its application and misuse of power. These can be re-categorised in the following way. First, the EU Institution in question must not exceed the power granted to it. Secondly, it must not abuse its discretion by committing a manifest error of assessment or an abuse of power. Thirdly, there must be no breach of process. Finally, the EU Institution must comply with the substantive obligations imposed by EU law: explicit provisions of EU law, fundamental rights and general principles of law.

(i) Lack of Competence

The Union has very broad powers. As such, there has only been one instance of an adopted measure being found to fall beyond the Union's competences.[15] It is more common for a specific EU Institution to have adopted a measure which it does not have the particular power to adopt. Two doctrines camouflage this: (i) legal base and (ii) the grant of excessively wide implementing or delegated powers to an EU Institution by an EU law or the breach of the conditions imposed by this law. Both doctrines have been addressed earlier in the book.[16] In either case, the EU Institution does not have the competence to do what it did.[17] However, these doctrines are not treated as being about questions of lack of competence. Instead, they also raise questions about institutional balance. The illegal exercise of power is invariably at the expense of another Union

---

[15] *Opinion 2/94* (Accession of the Community to the ECHR), EU:C:1996:140.

[16] See pp. 119–21 and 68–72 respectively.

[17] See, respectively, *Parliament v. Council ('Safe Countries of Origin')*, C-355/10, EU:C:2012:516; *Dyson v. Commission*, C-44/16 P, EU:C:2017:357.

Institution and the interests represented by it. In addition, if left unchecked, it weakens the system of checks and balances established by the Treaties.

Occasionally, there is a straightforward example of an EU Institution exceeding its competence. In 2011, the ECB adopted a Policy Framework which required, *inter alia*, central counterparty clearing houses ('CCP') for euro transactions to be located in the euro area. These are financial institutions which assume the risk for any transaction in case one party does not pay. In addition, they provide clearing and settlement services (i.e. ensure payments are made and delivery of title deeds). The ECB believed that, unregulated, these posed a systemic risk to the euro area. A considerable amount of clearing in euro-denominated securities takes place in London, and the United Kingdom, supported by Sweden, argued that the ECB had no general power to regulate clearing. In this regard, Article 127(2) TFEU requires the ECB to promote the 'smooth operation of payment systems'. To this end, Article 22 of the Statute of the ECB grants it the power to adopt regulations 'to ensure efficient and sound clearing and payment systems'.

United Kingdom v. *ECB*, T–496/11, EU:T:2015:133

89 . . . The power to adopt regulations pursuant to Article 22 of the Statute is one of the means available to the ECB for performing the task, entrusted to the Eurosystem by Article 127(2) TFEU, of promoting the smooth operation of payment systems. That task itself serves the primary objective set out in Article 127(1) TFEU.

90 It necessarily follows that the term 'clearing systems' in Article 22 of the Statute must be read in conjunction with the 'payment systems' to which reference is made in the same article and the smooth operation of which constitutes one of the Eurosystem's tasks.

91 It must accordingly be determined whether the task of promoting the smooth operation of payment systems which has been assigned to the Eurosystem, and for which the ECB has competence to adopt regulations, may be regarded as including securities clearing systems and, therefore, the activity of CCPs when they act in that context.

92 Therefore, it is necessary, in the first place, to interpret the terms 'payment systems' and 'clearing and payment systems', used in the fourth indent of Article 127(2) TFEU and Article 22 of the Statute respectively, in order to determine whether they may include the activity of clearing securities . . .

94 First, it may be observed that the term 'payment system' has been defined by the legislature in Article 4(6) of Directive 2007/64/EC . . . as designating 'a funds transfer system with formal and standardised arrangements and common rules for the processing, clearing and/or settlement of payment transactions' . . .

96 Second, it must also be noted that the Court of Justice has had occasion to interpret the concept of 'payments', when it is used in the context of Article 63(2) TFEU, as designating transfers of funds intended to provide consideration for a transaction . . .

97 It follows from the foregoing that a 'payment system' within the meaning of Article 127(2) TFEU falls within the field of the transfer of funds. Therefore, whilst such a definition may include the 'cash' leg of clearing operations, that is not true of the 'securities' leg of the clearing operations of a CCP, since while such securities may be regarded as being the subject-matter of a transaction giving rise to the transfer of funds, they do not, however, in themselves constitute payments.

98 A similar conclusion is also required in respect of the term 'clearing and payment systems' that is used in Article 22 of the Statute.

99 For the reasons set out in paragraph 89 above, this term must be interpreted in the light of the task, conferred on the Eurosystem by the fourth indent of Article 127(2) TFEU, of promoting the 'smooth operation of payment systems'. It necessarily follows that the ability which the ECB is granted by

Article 22 of the Statute to adopt regulations 'to ensure efficient and sound clearing and payment systems' cannot be understood as according it such a power in respect of all clearing systems, including those relating to transactions in securities.

103 It is necessary, in the second place, to reject the ECB's line of argument to the effect, in essence, that the carrying out of the task consisting in promotion of the sound operation of payment systems pursuant to the fourth indent of Article 127(2) TFEU means that it necessarily has the power to regulate the activity of securities clearing infrastructures, in the light of the effect that their default could have on payment systems.

104 It is true that the Court of Justice has acknowledged that powers not expressly provided for by the provisions of the Treaties may be used if they are necessary to achieve the objectives set by the Treaties ... Thus, when an article of the Treaty confers a specific task on an institution, it must be accepted, if that provision is not to be rendered wholly ineffective, that it confers on that institution necessarily and per se the powers which are indispensable in order to carry out that task ...

105 Nevertheless, the existence of an implicit regulatory power, which constitutes a derogation from the principle of conferral laid down by Article 13(2) TEU, must be appraised strictly. It is only exceptionally that such implicit powers are recognised by case-law and, in order to be so recognised, they must be necessary to ensure the practical effect of the provisions of the Treaty or the basic regulation at issue ...

106 In the present case, the existence of very close links between payment systems and securities clearing systems cannot be denied, nor can the possibility that disturbances affecting securities clearing infrastructures will have repercussions for payment systems and be injurious to their smooth operation.

107 Nevertheless, the existence of those links cannot be sufficient to justify accepting that the ECB has implicit powers to regulate securities clearing systems, since the FEU Treaty envisages the possibility of such powers being conferred explicitly upon the ECB.

Although the General Court ruled against the ECB in this instance, the reasoning illustrates why it will be rare that a Union Institution will be found to exceed its powers. Teleological reasoning, interpreting EU provisions in the light of their aim and purpose, will often be used to determine the extent of the powers conferred. The wording of the provision conferring the power will be finessed to secure these wider aims. The doctrine of implied powers will then be applied to confer further powers if these are deemed necessary for the EU Institution to perform these tasks. Thus, the judgment spent no time examining the wording of the two provisions, Article 127(2) TFEU and Article 22 of the Statute. Instead, it looked at what they were established to do, namely regulate the flow of payments. As payments included only the transfer of funds, the ECB does not have an express power to regulate the clearing of securities. The Court then went on, notwithstanding this, to consider whether there was implied power to do this, namely whether it would obstruct regulation of the clearing of payments if the ECB could not regulate the clearing of securities. Whilst it acknowledged some disruption, this was held to be insufficient to confer such a power.

(ii) Manifest Error of Assessment and Abuse of Power

There is only a scattering of cases where a lack of competence is found. More common is the finding of an abuse of institutional discretion. This will happen in two circumstances: (i) a manifest error of assessment and (ii) an abuse of power.

The central judgment on manifest error of assessment is *Tetra Laval*. It concerned a merger ('concentration') between Tetra Laval, the world-leader for carton packaging, and Sidel, a company specialising in PET packaging, a packaging comprised of a resin through which oxygen and light can pass. The Commission disallowed the merger on the grounds that Tetra Laval would leverage its dominant position on the market for cartons to persuade its customers to use Sidel's PET packaging, thereby eliminating competition in that market. The General Court found that the Commission had committed a manifest error of assessment in that it had used reports which overestimated the possibility for leveraging and the possibility for growth in the PET market. The Commission appealed to the Court of Justice.

Commission v. *Tetra Laval*, C-12/03 P, EU:C:2005:87

39 Whilst the Court recognises that the Commission has a margin of discretion with regard to economic matters, that does not mean that the Community Courts must refrain from reviewing the Commission's interpretation of information of an economic nature. Not only must the Community Courts, *inter alia*, establish whether the evidence relied on is factually accurate, reliable and consistent but also whether that evidence contains all the information which must be taken into account in order to assess a complex situation and whether it is capable of substantiating the conclusions drawn from it . . .

41 Although the [General Court] stated . . . that proof of anti-competitive conglomerate effects of a merger of the kind notified calls for a precise examination, supported by convincing evidence, of the circumstances which allegedly produce those effects, it by no means added a condition relating to the requisite standard of proof but merely drew attention to the essential function of evidence, which is to establish convincingly the merits of an argument or, as in the present case, of a decision on a merger.

42 A prospective analysis of the kind necessary in merger control must be carried out with great care since it does not entail the examination of past events – for which often many items of evidence are available which make it possible to understand the causes – or of current events, but rather a prediction of events which are more or less likely to occur in future if a decision prohibiting the planned concentration or laying down the conditions for it is not adopted.

43 Thus, the prospective analysis consists of an examination of how a concentration might alter the factors determining the state of competition on a given market in order to establish whether it would give rise to a serious impediment to effective competition. Such an analysis makes it necessary to envisage various chains of cause and effect with a view to ascertaining which of them are the most likely.

44 The analysis of a 'conglomerate-type' concentration is a prospective analysis in which, first, the consideration of a lengthy period of time in the future and, secondly, the leveraging necessary to give rise to a significant impediment to effective competition mean that the chains of cause and effect are dimly discernible, uncertain and difficult to establish. That being so, the quality of the evidence produced by the Commission in order to establish that it is necessary to adopt a decision declaring the concentration incompatible with the common market is particularly important, since that evidence must support the Commission's conclusion that, if such a decision were not adopted, the economic development envisaged by it would be plausible.

The Court states that it will not provide a substantive assessment of its own but will simply check that any measure is sufficiently substantiated by evidence that is accurate, reliable, consistent and sufficiently complete. However, the excerpt below illustrates that the distinction is a slippery one, particularly where the EU Institution is basing its decision on the possible consequences of an activity. Since the EU Institution's decision is forward-looking, it cannot provide evidence about what has already happened. In such circumstances, the Court will assess the plausibility of its reasoning.

A. Fritzsche, 'Discretion, Scope of Judicial Balance and Institutional Review in European Law' (2010) 47 *Common Market Law Review* 361, 399–400 and 401–2

Bo Vesterdorf (the former President of the Court of First Instance) speaking extra-judicially has suggested his understanding of the appropriate standard of review, that it should be 'intense and effective'.[18] It is for the General Court to check whether the Commission has 'clearly overlooked, underestimated, or exaggerated the relevant economic data, drawn unconvincing, in the sense of implausible, direct inferences from primary material facts or adopted an erroneous approach to assessing the material facts'.[19] In the absence of such errors, the Court should uphold the decision, 'even if it would not itself have subscribed to the Commission's economic assessment'.[20] However, this standard is far-reaching. There is no discretion if the General Court double-checked the inferences drawn from primary facts, as any deviating evaluation may be attributed to overlooking, underestimating, or exaggerating primary data. The same is true if the Court substitutes judgment on the approach adopted to assess material facts. Economic assessments require many methodological choices and a preselection and weighing of material to be taken into account. According to this standard, the court could intervene at any stage and it seems hardly conceivable that an economic assessment not shared by the court could be upheld. Under these circumstances, to invoke the Commission's discretion in economic matters is close to paying lip-service, as has occasionally been done in the *Tetra Laval* case.

More latitude in assessing economic facts and circumstances would follow from the proposal of former Judge Hubert Legal.[21] For him, the discretion lies within the freedom of choice of the economic methodology to be applied and in the global determination reached on the basis of this methodology; the latter applies as long as it is not contradicted by facts and not obviously contrary to accepted methods of economic reasoning. Yet, Legal wants inferences drawn from primary facts to be subjected to full control. These inferences are made on the basis of the methodological choice for which, according to Legal, the Commission is to enjoy some latitude . . .

In *Tetra Laval*, the ECJ held that for prospective analyses (but this also true for retrospective assessments) it is necessary to 'envisage various chains of cause and effect with a view to ascertaining which of them are the most likely'. It has to be added that the choice of the most likely chain of cause and effect is within the Commission's power. The General Court only checks whether various likely chains of cause were addressed and excluded for logical and consistent reasons and whether state of the art forensic social science methods were applied.

As Fritzsche observes, a premium is placed on scientific methodology. If the EU Institution can show it has deployed a robust methodology, it is less likely to be successfully reviewed. However, the quality of this robustness is often in the eye of the beholder. Uncertainty about the quality of reasoning to be provided has, thus, been a fertile source of litigation. A study of challenges to Commission Decisions punishing cartels between 1995 and 2004 found that they were only fully successful in getting it overturned in 6 per cent of cases. However, they were successful in 61 per cent of cases in securing a reduction of the fine imposed with the predominant reason being that the Commission had committed a manifest error of assessment.[22]

---

[18] B. Vesterdorf, (2005) 1 *Eur Comp Journal* 3, 32. [19] *Ibid.* [20] *Ibid.*

[21] H. Legal, 'Standards of Proof and Standards of Judicial Review in EU Competition Law' in B. Hawk (ed.), *Annual Proceedings of the Fordham Corporate Law Institute, International Antitrust Law and Policy 1999* (New York, Juris Publishing, 2000).

[22] C. Harding and A. Gibbs, 'Why Go to Court in Europe? An Analysis of Cartel Appeals 1995–2004' (2005) 30 *ELRev* 349, 365–7.

In contrast to the doctrine of manifest error of assessment, the doctrine of misuse of powers can be mentioned almost as a postscript. It arises if a measure appears:

> on the basis of objective, relevant and consistent indications to have been adopted to achieve purposes other than those for which it was intended.[23]

It requires applicants not merely to prove bad faith, namely that the EU Institution intentionally used a power for a purpose for which it should not be used. They must also show that the measure was guided exclusively or predominantly by this motivation.[24] This is difficult to prove and the principle has not been successfully invoked in recent times.

(iii) Rights of Process

Procedural guarantees are scattered throughout the Treaties and EU secondary legislation in relation to specific activities. There are also general rights of process which exist, in the absence of these, across all fields of EU law. These can be categorised into three: (i) rights of defence, (ii) the right to a hearing and (iii) the right to good administration of one's affairs.

(a) Rights of Defence

Parties have rights of defence before EU Institutions wherever the latter may impose some penalty on them. The rights of defence are available in penalty-imposing proceedings as well as in preparatory proceedings – such as inspections or investigations – leading to the former. Parties are entitled to such rights in these preparatory proceedings as they have to be in a position where they can understand the scope of their duty to cooperate with the EU Institutions whilst preserving their rights of defence.[25]

These rights of defence include, first, the right to a hearing. This was explored at greatest length in *Kadi*. EU Regulations restricted the money and other assets available to Kadi as he was on a UN list of people suspected of associating with Al Qaeda. This list was compiled by a Sanctions Committee set up by the United Nations. A statement of reasons was provided by the Committee which the Commission communicated to Kadi. This stated that he had, *inter alia*, set up a foundation operating under the umbrella of Al Qaeda. This foundation had hired people who worked with Bin Laden and funded terrorist activities in Bosnia Herzegovina. Kadi disputed this. After hearing him, the Commission, nevertheless, adopted a new Regulation continuing the restrictions. The Court found for Kadi, as insufficient evidence had been provided to substantiate these claims.

***Commission and Others* v. *Kadi*, C-584/10 P, C-593/10 P and C-595/10 P, EU:C:2013:518**

99 The [rights of defence], which is affirmed in Article 41(2) EUCFR includes the right to be heard and the right to have access to the file, subject to legitimate interests in maintaining confidentiality.

100 The second of those fundamental rights, which is affirmed in Article 47 of the Charter, requires that the person concerned must be able to ascertain the reasons upon which the decision taken in relation to him is based, either by reading the decision itself or by requesting and obtaining disclosure of those reasons,

---

[23] *Sermes* v. *Directeur de Service des Douanes de Strasbourg*, C-323/88, EU:C:1990:299.
[24] *Dalmine* v. *Commission*, C-407/04 P, EU:C:2007:53.
[25] *Hoechst* v. *Commission*, 46/87 and C-227/88, EU:C:1989:337; *Nexan* v. *Commission*, C-37/13 P, EU:C:2014:2030.

without prejudice to the power of the court having jurisdiction to require the authority concerned to disclose that information, so as to make it possible for him to defend his rights in the best possible conditions and to decide, with full knowledge of the relevant facts, whether there is any point in his applying to the court having jurisdiction, and in order to put the latter fully in a position to review the lawfulness of the decision in question.

101 Article 52(1) of the Charter nevertheless allows limitations on the exercise of the rights enshrined in the Charter, subject to the conditions that the limitation concerned respects the essence of the fundamental right in question and, subject to the principle of proportionality, that it is necessary and genuinely meets objectives of general interest recognised by the European Union.

102 Further, the question whether there is an infringement of the rights of the defence and of the right to effective judicial protection must be examined in relation to the specific circumstances of each particular case . . . including, the nature of the act at issue, the context of its adoption and the legal rules governing the matter in question .

112 When that disclosure takes place, the competent Union authority must ensure that that individual is placed in a position in which he may effectively make known his views on the grounds advanced against him . . .

114 When comments are made by the individual concerned on the summary of reasons, the competent European Union authority is under an obligation to examine, carefully and impartially, whether the alleged reasons are well founded, in the light of those comments and any exculpatory evidence provided with those comments . . .

116 Lastly, without going so far as to require a detailed response to the comments made by the individual concerned . . . the obligation to state reasons laid down in Article 296 TFEU entails in all circumstances, not least when the reasons stated for the European Union measure represent reasons stated by an international body, that that statement of reasons identifies the individual, specific and concrete reasons why the competent authorities consider that the individual concerned must be subject to restrictive measures.

The right to be heard, thus, includes a number of further rights. The authority must disclose sufficient evidence and reasons for the penalty so that the accused can defend his case in the best conditions possible, with access to his file unless reasons of confidentiality or security prevent this.[26] The accused must have an opportunity to comment on this evidence and the reasons, following which there must be a careful re-examination of the case by the authority, with reasons furnished to explain why the penalties are being imposed. That said, this right to be heard only goes to those matters which form the basis for the measure and not to the final position adopted.[27] The EU Institution is thus not obliged to provide a hearing on the final factual assessment which forms part of its decision.[28]

Moreover, the rights of defence comprise a number of further rights beyond the right to be heard. These include prosecution only for clearly and unambiguously defined criminal or administrative penalties;[29] the presumption of innocence;[30] the right not to be tried twice on

---

[26] This will usually involve access to the file setting out the obligation. This is subject to restrictions for reasons of security and confidentiality, *ZZ* v. *Secretary of State for the Home Department*, C-300/11, EU:C:2013:363. Failure to disclose inculpatory information will render a measure automatically illegal. Failure to disclose exculpatory information will only render a measure illegal if it effectively hinders the applicant's rights of defence, *Heineken Nederland and Heineken* v. *Commission*, T-240/07, EU:T:2011:284.

[27] *Safariland* v. *OHIM*, T-262/09, EU:T:2011:171.   [28] *Stella Kunststofftechnik* v. *OHIM*, T-27/09, EU:T:2009:492.

[29] *Advocaten voor de Wereld* v. *Leden van de Ministerraad*, C-303/05, EU:C:2007:261; *R* v. *HM Treasury, ex parte Rosneft*, C-72/15, EU:C:2017:236.

[30] *Rubach*, C-344/08, EU:C:2009:482.

the same facts;[31] the right to legal assistance and for lawyer–client communications prepared for the purposes of defence to be privileged;[32] and protection from self-incrimination.[33]

Finally, the rights of defence include the right to effective judicial protection which derives from the right to be heard by an independent and impartial tribunal. In cases where there is no provision for this, there is a right to judicial review of the penalty imposed by it.[34] This right continues even where the measure no longer exists as judicial review may be necessary to restore the applicant to her original position and to induce suitable behaviour from the EU Institution in the future.[35] The right to effective judicial protection includes the adversarial principle. This requires that the applicant must have the right to examine all the documents or observations submitted to the court for the purpose of influencing its decision and be able to comment on them.[36] The right to effective judicial protection also requires that the court be in a position where it can sufficiently scrutinise the measure. It must be able to verify whether the reasons supporting a decision are substantiated by the evidence. The Court must, therefore, be able to ask the relevant EU authority to supply the information or evidence that supports these reasons, and is to base its judgment only on that evidence provided.[37]

The rights of defence might be restricted where there is an overriding public interest, notably State security, though such interests do not provide a *carte blanche* for them to be ignored. In *ZZ*, the Court stated that, in such circumstances, a balance must be struck between legitimate security considerations and the applicant's procedural rights, notably their right to a hearing and the adversarial principle. This entails that the Court must first verify that the security considerations justify non-disclosure of evidence or information to the applicant. If this is so, it must, secondly, still enable a contest on the grounds of the decision to the greatest extent possible with the applicant being provided the essence of the reasons on which the decision was based.[38]

The rights of defence are extensive but are subject to caveats. Parties may only claim a right to judicial review if it procures them an advantage. That advantage must persist until delivery of the final judgment. The Court will refuse to give judgment, therefore, if it sees no benefit accruing to the applicant from it.[39] Alongside this, any violation of the rights of defence will only result in annulment of the measure, if, but for the violation, the result might have been different. There are circumstances, therefore, where a finding of a violation has little more than declaratory value.[40]

(b) The Right to a Hearing

Whilst parties will only have rights of defence in proceedings which expose them to possible penalties, they may still have a right to a hearing (without these wider rights of defence)

---

[31] *Miraglia*, C-469/03, EU:C:2005:156; *Kossowski*, C-486/14, EU:C:2016:483.
[32] *AM & S Europe* v. *Commission*, 155/79, EU:C:1982:157; *Schenker* v. *Commission*, T-265/12, EU:T:2016:111.
[33] *ORKEM* v. *Commission*, 374/87, EU:C:1989:387; *Buzzi Unicem* v. *Commission*, T-297/11, EU:T:2014:122.
[34] *Berlioz Investment Fund* v. *Directeur de l'administration des contributions directes*, C-682/15, EU:C:2017:373.
[35] *Abdulrahim* v. *Council and Commission*, C-239/12 P, EU:C:2013:331.
[36] *ZZ* v. *Secretary of State for the Home Department*, C-300/11, EU:C:2013:363.
[37] *Commission and Others* v. *Kadi*, C-584/10 P, C-593/10 P and C-595/10 P, EU:C:2013:518.
[38] *ZZ* v. *Secretary of State for the Home Department*, C-300/11, EU:C:2013:363.
[39] *Abdulrahim* v. *Council and Commission*, C-239/12 P, EU:C:2013:331; *HX* v. *Council*, C-423/16 P, EU:C:2017:848.
[40] *M.G. and N.R.* v. *Staatssecretaris van Veiligheid en Justitie*, C-383/13 PPU, EU:C:2013:533; *Storck* v. *OHIM*, C-96/11 P, EU:C:2012:537.

wherever proceedings culminate in a measure adversely affecting them.[41] In such cases, the party has a right to be heard prior to adoption of any decision. The authority must pay due attention to its observations, examine carefully and impartially all the relevant aspects of the case, and give a statement which is sufficiently specific and concrete to allow the party to understand why it was treated the way it was.[42] The reason for this right is that it allows the authority to take account of all relevant information whilst ensuring that the party can correct any error or submit information relevant to its circumstances which may inform the decision.[43]

A measure adversely affects a party's interest where it simply denies them a benefit rather than actively penalising them.[44] They will not have a right to a hearing, however, if the measure affecting them is a general measure.[45] They will only acquire it if they are named or addressed in the Union measure and their interests are significantly affected,[46] or the measure is one which they have *locus standi* to challenge before Union Courts.[47]

(c) The Right to Good Administration

The right to good administration is set out in Article 41 of the European Union Charter for Fundamental Rights and Freedoms (EUCFR).[48]

Article 41 EUCFR

(1) Every person has the right to have his or her affairs handled impartially, fairly and within a reasonable time by the institutions and bodies of the Union.

(2) This right includes:

- the right of every person to be heard, before any individual measure which would affect him or her adversely is taken;
- the right of every person to have access to his or her file, while respecting the legitimate interests of confidentiality and of professional and business secrecy;
- the obligation of the administration to give reasons for its decisions.

In addition to the rights set out in Article 41(2) EUCFR, which have already been addressed, the right to good administration imposes a number of duties on EU Institutions.

---

[41] *Kamino International Logistics and Datema Hellmann Worldwide Logistics*, C-129–30/13, EU:C:2014:2041.

[42] *M.M* v. *Minister for Justice, Equality and Law Reform*, C-277/11, EU:C:2012:744.

[43] *Prequ' Italia* v. *Agenzia delle Dogane e dei Monopoli*, C-276/16, EU:C:2017:1010.

[44] *M.M.* v. *Minister for Justice, Equality and Law Reform*, C-277/11, EU:C:2012:744; *Boudjlida* v. *Préfet des Pyrénées-Atlantiques*, C-249/13, EU:C:2014:2431.

[45] *BEUC & NCC* v. *Commission*, T-37/92, EU:T:1994:54.

[46] *Commission* v. *Lisrestal and Others*, C-32/95 P, EU:C:1996:402; *Foshan Shunde Yongjian Housewares & Hardware Co.* v. *Commission*, C-141/08 P, EU:C:2009:598.

[47] *Al-Jubail Fertilizer* v. *Council*, C-49/88, EU:C:1991:276; *CHEMK* v. *Council*, T-169/12, EU:T:2015:231. On when this is so, see pp. 388–404. There is one exception. There will be no right to a hearing where a party has acquired standing merely by making a complaint to the EU Institution, as the Court has ruled that it is only providing information, and this is insufficient to justify a hearing, *Technische Glaswerke Ilmenau* v. *Commission*, T-198/01, EU:T:2004:222.

[48] On the evolution of this right see H.-P. Nehl, *Principles of Administrative Procedure in EC Law* (Oxford-Portland, Hart, 1999) 127–49; J. Wakefield, *The Right to Good Administration* (The Hague, Kluwer, 2007).

First, it imposes a duty to act diligently.[49] The EU Institutions must give due consideration and attention to all the arguments presented[50] and to the task at hand.[51] This duty of consideration requires them to provide coherent reasons for the measure, which take account of the evidence provided.[52] They must also be proactive in gathering information, seeking it from parties who have a right to a hearing where there are gaps.[53]

Secondly, there is a requirement of impartiality. No member of the EU Institution concerned may show bias or personal prejudice. Moreover, there must be sufficient guarantees to exclude any legitimate doubt as to bias on its part.[54]

Thirdly, EU Institutions cannot impose unreasonable demands on parties subject to proceedings in the form of unreasonable requests for information.[55]

Fourthly, EU Institutions must exercise their powers within a reasonable period of time.[56] This duty applies even to the Court of Justice which can be sued for failure to give a judgment within a reasonable period of time.[57] The reasonableness of the time taken will be assessed in relation to the particular circumstances of each case.[58] The complexity of a case alone may justify a lengthy investigation.[59] If it is uncomplicated, twenty-six months has been ruled excessive.[60] However, if the applicant has contributed to the delay or the matter has had to go through the domestic courts, periods of up to twelve years have not been found to be unduly long.[61]

The only parties who have a right to seek good administration are those who are already in a position to enjoy other rights of process: be it rights of defence, a right to a hearing or a right to complain granted by specific legislation. Others do not enjoy it.[62] Mendes has argued that the narrow range of parties granted these rights of process prevents a more wide-ranging participatory democracy in which anybody whose interests are affected by EU measures would have the possibility to have that interest considered by the EU Institutions.

J. Mendes, *Participation in EU Rule-Making: A Rights-Based Approach* (Oxford University Press, 2011) 463

[I]t is possible to distinguish two categories of persons concerned: holders of subjective rights and holders of legally protected interests affected by the final decision. The former are persons who, in the light of the applicable norms, may aim to acquire a certain good or advantage through the decision that is being adopted or prevent an effect that this decision is intended to produce in their legal sphere. The latter, while being sufficiently connected to the material situation under examination, voice 'objectivized interests' the

---

[49] *European Ombudsman* v. *Staelen*, C-337/15 P, EU:C:2017:256.

[50] *Demo-Studio Schmidt* v. *Commission*, 210/81, EU:C:1983:277; *EasyJet Airline* v. *Commission*, T-355/13, EU:T:2015:36.

[51] *Nölle* v. *Hauptzollamt Bremen-Freihafen*, C-16/90, EU:C:1991:402.

[52] *Commission* v. *Estonia*, C-505/09 P, EU:C:2012:179.   [53] *Vischim* v. *Commission*, T-420/05, EU:T:2009:391.

[54] *Ziegler* v. *Commission*, C-439/11 P, EU:C:2013:513; *Spain* v. *Council*, C-521/15, EU:C:2017:982.

[55] *Godrej Industries* v. *Council*, T-6/12, EU:T:2013:408.

[56] *Falck and Acciaierie di Bolzano* v. *Commission*, C-74-5/00, EU:C:2002:524.

[57] *ASPLA and Armando Álvarez* v. *European Union*, T-40/15, EU:T:2017:105.

[58] *Oliveira* v. *Commission*, T-73/95, EU:T:1997:3; *Regione autonoma della Sardegna* v. *Commission*, T-394/08, EU:T:2011:493.

[59] *Papierfabrik August Koehler* v. *Commission*, C-322/07 P, C-327/07 P and C-338/07 P, EU:C:2009:500.

[60] *RSV* v. *Commission*, 223/85, EU:C:1987:502.   [61] *Branco* v. *Commission*, T-347/03, EU:T:2005:265.

[62] *Commission* v. *Sytraval and Brink's France*, C-367/95 P, EU:C:1998:154.

fulfilment of which is, at the same time, one of the goals of the legal system and should therefore be considered in the exercise of the decisional function. Holders of legally protected interests cannot aspire to having their personal situation considered as such by the decision-maker, since their intervention is legally valued on the basis of their contribution to the procedure. Provided that they have a substantive link to the material situation, their capacity as persons concerned ... derives from the fact that they defend legally protected interests which may be adversely affected by the decision and which ought to be considered by the decision-maker as part of the overall assessment that forms the basis of the decision. On the contrary, holders of subjective rights who might be adversely affected by the decision have a qualified subjective entitlement vis-à-vis the decision-maker. The latter needs to consider their subjective position as such while assessing the material situation that is being regulated.

Mendes, therefore, suggests a dual system. Parties currently granted a right to a hearing would continue to enjoy the right to present their arguments before the EU Institution. Whilst other parties affected by the measure would not have such a right, the EU Institution would nevertheless have a duty to show that it had taken these interests into account even though the former had not had a right to a hearing.

(iv) Infringement of the Treaties or of any Rule of Law Relating to their Application

The final grounds of review relate to infringement of the Treaties or any rule of law relating to their application. This 'rule of law' can be a Treaty provision, binding EU law,[63] fundamental rights or general principles of law. As fundamental rights have been addressed in detail elsewhere,[64] we will focus on the central general principles of law: non-discrimination, legal certainty, legitimate expectations, proportionality and subsidiarity.

(a) Non-Discrimination

EU law protects parties against discrimination by virtue of their gender, ethnicity, race, age, disability, religion, belief or sexual orientation. Particular protection is granted by EU legislation and the Charter, and this is discussed elsewhere.[65] However, there is a more general principle that like cases be treated alike.

Article 20 EUCFR

Everyone is equal before the law.

The seminal case is *Ruckdeschel*. Identical subsidies were historically granted to starch and quellmehl (a form of flour) producers by the EU Institutions as the two products were seen as

---

[63] There is one exception. No judicial review is available for non-compliance with an international treaty which is not one which generates rights for individuals, *Van Parys* v. *BIRB*, C-377/02, EU:C:2005:121; *Blaas* v. *Agenzia delle Dogane e dei Monopoli*, C-207/17, EU:C:2018:840.

[64] See Chapter 6.

[65] See Directive 2000/78 establishing a general framework for equal treatment in employment and occupation, OJ 2000, L 303/16 and Article 21 EUCFR respectively. On their interaction see *Egenberger* v. *Evangelisches Werk für Diakonie und Entwicklung*, C-414/16, EU:C:2018:257.

economically substitutable. The quellmehl subsidy was withdrawn whereas that for starch was maintained. Ruckdeschel, a quellmehl producer, challenged this arguing that this discriminated between it and starch producers. The Court agreed.

Ruckdeschel v. Council, 117/76 and 16/77, EU:C:1977:160

7   ... the prohibition of discrimination laid down in [Article 40(2) TFEU] is merely a specific enunciation of the general principle of equality which is one of the fundamental principles of Community law.

   This principle requires that similar situations shall not be treated differently unless differentiation is objectively justified.

8   It must therefore be ascertained whether quellmehl and starch are in a comparable situation, in particular in the sense that starch can be substituted for quellmehl in the specific use to which the latter product is traditionally put.

   In this connexion it must first be noted that the Community Regulations were, until 1974, based on the assertion that such substitution was possible ...

   While the Council and the Commission have given detailed information on the manufacture and sale of the products in question, they have produced no new technical or economic data which appreciably change the previous assessment of the position.

   It has not therefore been established that, so far as the Community system of production refunds is concerned, quellmehl and starch are no longer in comparable situations.

   Consequently, these products must be treated in the same manner unless differentiation is objectively justified.

There is a prohibition not just with like cases being treated differently but also with different cases being treated in like manner.[66] In practice, it is rare that there will be a finding of discrimination. Often, the Court will simply state that the cases are not alike, and this will be invariably argued where a reason can be provided for the differential treatment.[67] In *Melli Bank*, for example, an Iranian bank pleaded that EU sanctions targeting it and not other British subsidiaries of Iranian banks was discriminatory.[68] The General Court had little difficulty in finding that there was no discrimination. It noted that the Regulation in question implemented a UN Security Council Resolution which targeted financial institutions engaged in assisting nuclear proliferation. This rationale provided a basis for the differential treatment of Iranian-owned banks. The identification of a reason for differentiation suggests that the Court is largely looking at the reasonableness of the Union measure in such cases. In instances where the EU Institution has little discretion, the Court will simply look at whether there is a good reason for the distinction. However, where the Union exercises a broad discretion, more leeway is granted. If the measure is based on 'objective criteria' appropriate to the aim pursued by the EU legislature no discrimination be found.[69]

---

[66] *Martinez and Others* v. *Parliament*, T-222/99, T-327/99 and T-329/99, EU:T:2001:242.

[67] For an example see *bpost* v. *IBTT*, C-340/13, EU:C:2015:77. On this see J. Croon, 'Comparative Institutional Analysis, the European Court of Justice and the General Principle of Non-Discrimination – or – Alternative Tales on Equality Reasoning' (2013) 19 *ELJ* 153.

[68] *Melli Bank* v. *Council*, T-246/08 and T-332/08, EU:T:2009:266. This was upheld in *Council* v. *Melli Bank*, C-380/09 P, EU:C:2012:137.

[69] *Arcelor* v. *Premier Ministre*, C-127/07, EU:C:2008:728. This reasoning is very similar to that used for proportionality, and it will be rare that a measure will be found to be discriminatory and not be found to be disproportionate. M. Herdegen, 'The Equation between the Principles of Equality and Proportionality' (1985) 22 *CMLRev* 683.

(b) Legal Certainty

The principle of legal certainty requires that:

> [Union] rules enable those concerned to know precisely the extent of the obligations which are imposed on them. Individuals must be able to ascertain unequivocally what their rights and obligations are and take steps accordingly.[70]

The principle has two expressions: a ban on retroactivity and a requirement that an EU law is sufficiently clear to allow subjects to identify their rights and obligations.

The first, the prohibition on retroactivity, requires that a measure should not take effect prior to its publication.[71] It will not be retroactive if it regulates the future effects of situations which arose prior to publication but will be if it applies to events which have already been concluded.[72] The principle is absolute in relation to penal measures[73] and where the measure is liable to have financial consequences.[74] Other measures may exceptionally take effect before publication where the purpose to be achieved so demands and the legitimate concerns of those concerned are respected. In *Fedesa*, following the annulment of a Directive outlawing the use of certain hormones, the subsequent Directive, which was published on 7 March 1988, stipulated that it was to take effect from the beginning of 1988.[75] The reason was to prevent the market being unregulated for that earlier period as a consequence of the annulment of the earlier Directive. The Court considered there to be no breach of the legal certainty principle in light of the short time-span between the annulment of the first Directive and the publication of the second. It did not accept that traders had, in such a short time, been led to believe that the EU Institutions had changed their stance on regulation of the matter.

The second requirement of legal certainty is that EU law is sufficiently clear that it enables EU law's subjects to know their rights and obligations. At the very least, this means that the EU law in question must be published. In *Heinrich*, an unpublished Annex to a Regulation which prohibited tennis rackets from being taken on civil aircraft was found to be void because it had not been published.[76] Alongside this, the Court has repeatedly stated that EU legislation must be clear and its application foreseeable by those subject to it.[77] This would suggest that if an EU measure is too obscure it could be struck down though this has yet to happen.

(c) Legitimate Expectations

The roots of the principle of legitimate expectations lie in the concept of good faith; requiring that if an authority induces an operator to take a course of action, it should not renege so that the individual suffers loss.[78] The principle of legitimate expectation is breached if three conditions are met:

---

[70] *Heinrich*, C-345/06, EU:C:2009:140, para. 44.
[71] *Ognyanov*, C-554/14, EU:C:2016:835; *Jinan Meide Casting* v. *Council*, T-424/13, EU:T:2016:378.
[72] *Kirk*, 63/83, EU:C:1984:255; *Italy* v. *Commission*, T-358/11, EU:T:2015:394.
[73] *R* v. *MAFF, ex parte FEDESA*, C-331/88, EU:C:1990:391.
[74] *Emsland-Stärke* v. *Landwirtschaftskammer Hannover*, C-94/05, EU:C:2006:185.
[75] *R* v. *MAFF, ex parte FEDESA*, C-331/88, EU:C:1990:391.   [76] *Heinrich*, C-345/06, EU:C:2009:140.
[77] *Ireland* v. *Commission*, 325/85, EU:C:1987:546; *Spain* v. *Commission*, T-548/14, EU:T:2016:739.
[78] S. Schonberg, *Legitimate Expectations in Administrative Law* (Oxford University Press, 2000).

First, precise, unconditional and consistent assurances originating from authorised and reliable sources must have been given to the person concerned by the Community authorities. Second, those assurances must be such as to give rise to a legitimate expectation on the part of the person to whom they are addressed. Third, the assurances given must comply with the applicable rules . . . [79]

If we turn to the first of these – the nature of the assurance – it must be 'precise, unconditional and consistent' and originate 'from authorised, reliable sources, have been given to the person concerned by the competent authorities of the European Union'.[80] Ambiguous or general statements about future conduct are insufficient. The assurance must set out a specific course of action[81] but it does not have to be addressed to the application. The adoption by an EU Institution of a Code of Conduct will, therefore, generate legitimate expectations if it sets out the practices that the EU Institution will follow.[82] However, the assurance can take any form. In *Mulder*, payments to farmers to take land out of milk production to reduce milk surpluses was held to generate a legitimate expectation that if a farmer subsequently resumed milk production, he would not be penalised for not producing milk during the period when he received payments.[83]

The second requirement is that the assurance must both create an expectation, on the part of the applicant, and that expectation must be well-founded.[84] In looking at whether this is so, the Court will consider whether a prudent and alert operator would have relied on the assurance.[85] A simple reversal of policy will, thus, rarely generate a legitimate expectation as the Court considers that such operators ought usually be able to anticipate this possibility.[86] However, in exceptional circumstances, a reversal in policy can give rise to a successful claim. In *CNTA* the Commission suddenly stopped granting subsidies in the colza and rape seed sectors to protect traders against losses from currency fluctuations.[87] This reversal of policy was unusual in that it was a sudden withdrawal of a subsidy. The financial effects were immediate and unexpected. The Court found that whilst the subsidies could not be considered a guarantee against risks on the exchange rate, nevertheless, they meant, in practice, that a prudent trader might not insure himself against the risk. In the absence of an overriding public interest, the Court considered that the immediate withdrawal of the subsidies with no provision for transitional measures breached the principle of legitimate expectations.

Finally, the assurance must not breach an EU law which is unambiguous.[88]

The principle of legitimate expectations is not an absolute one: an EU Institution can justify breaching it to protect an overriding public interest.[89] This interest will invariably require the EU Institution to take immediate action in breach of the assurance, in which case it will normally be required to adopt transitional measures to protect those who have acquired a legitimate

---

[79] *Branco v. Commission*, T-347/03, EU:T:2005:265, para. 102.
[80] *Kotnik*, C-526/14, EU:C:2016:570; *Chrysostomides & Co. v. Council*, T-680/13, EU:T:2018:486.
[81] *Applied Microengineering v. Commission*, T-387/09, EU:T:2012:501.
[82] *Stichting Corporate Europe Observatory v. Commission*, T-93/11, EU:T:2013:308.
[83] *Plantanol*, C-201/08, EU:C:2009:539; *Valsts ieņēmumu dienests v. 'Veloserviss' SIA*, C-427/14, EU:C:2015:803.
[84] *HGA and Others v. Commission*, C-630–33/11 P, EU:T:2013:387; *Kotnik*, C-526/14, EU:C:2016:570.
[85] *Van den Bergh en Jurgens v. Commission*, 265/85, EU:C:1987:121. See E. Sharpston, 'Legitimate Expectations and Economic Reality' (1990) 15 *ELRev* 103, 108–15.
[86] *Faust v. Commission*, 52/81, EU:C:1982:369.   [87] *CNTA v. Commission*, 74/74, EU:C:1976:84.
[88] *Erzeugerorganisation Tiefkühlgemüse v. Agrarmarkt Austria*, C-516/16, EU:C:2017:101; *Administratīvā rajona tiesa v. Ministru kabinets*, C-120/17, EU:C:2018:638.
[89] *Kotnik*, C-526/14, EU:C:2016:570.

expectation.[90] However, in some instances, protection of the overriding public interest will not allow this. In *Affish*, an EU legal regime provided for import of fresh fish from Japan.[91] Following health concerns, the Commission placed an immediate ban on imports of these fish. The Court rejected an argument by Affish, a Dutch trader, that its consignments of fish en route from Japan could be traded under a legitimate expectation established by the prior EU legal regime. It noted, in this case, that public health was an overriding public interest which justified the lack of transitional measures for such consignments.

(d) Subsidiarity

The subsidiarity principle has been touched on in Chapter 3 when we considered the role of national parliaments in EU lawmaking given that one of their duties is to police the observance of this principle in EU lawmaking.[92] The content of the principle is set out in Article 5(3) TEU.

Article 5 TEU

(3) Under the principle of subsidiarity, in areas which do not fall within its exclusive competence, the Union shall act only if and insofar as the objectives of the proposed action cannot be sufficiently achieved by the Member States, either at central level or at regional and local level, but can rather, by reason of the scale or effects of the proposed action, be better achieved at Union level.

The subsidiarity principle institutionalises two logics: self-government and comparative effectiveness.

The philosophy of self-government is expressed in the phrase in Article 5(3) TEU that the Union should act only if the objectives of the proposed action cannot be sufficiently achieved by the Member States. Its ethos is that local decisions are, in principle, better than more central ones.[93] This ethos is not fully followed through as the article does not express a preference for local or regional laws over national laws. However, the preference for national law over EU law seems to be for two reasons. The first reason is ownership over the laws. As Member States are smaller than the Union, there is a sense of individual citizens having the possibility of proportionately more voice and these laws being more proximate to them. The second reason is a cultural one. National laws express traditions and beliefs which are seen as valuable insofar as they give meaning to citizens' lives, symbolise belonging and allow these citizens to orient themselves in the world. The British decision to drive on the left-hand side of the road is thus idiosyncratic but is valued because it is seen as an expression of distinctiveness and, for British people, a reminder of home.[94]

The other logic, that of comparative effectiveness, is expressed in the Article 5(3) TEU requirement that the objectives of the proposed action, by reason its scale or effect, can be better achieved at Union level. The test is whether one central measure would be more effective

---

[90] *Belgium and Forum 187* v. *Commission*, C-182/03 and C-217/03, EU:C:2006:416.

[91] *Affish* v. *Rijksdienst voor de Keuring van Vee en Vlees*, C-183/95, EU:C:1997:373.

[92] Protocol on the Application of the Principles of Subsidiarity and Proportionality, Articles 6 and 7. See pp. 135–7.

[93] A. Føllesdal, 'Subsidiarity' (1998) 6 *Journal of Political Philosophy* 190; Y. Soudan, 'Subsidiarity and Community in Europe' (1998) 5 *Ethical Perspectives* 177; N. Barber, 'The Limited Modesty of Subsidiarity' (2005) 11 *ELJ* 308.

[94] On scepticism about these see T. Latimer, 'Against Subsidiarity' (2018) 26 *Journal of Political Philosophy* 282.

at realising a policy than twenty-seven different ones. A case can usually be made that this is so. In this regard, a single policy will bring about economies of scale so that operators can have one standard rather than twenty-seven; escape the difficulties of having to coordinate twenty-seven different laws; prevent barriers to trade that might arise as a result of differences in laws; and ensure more consistent interpretation and application of central Union values. This test is, thus, very much a centralising test.

The two logics slide past each other as they not only value different things but also apply different criteria for determining what they value.[95] The subsidiarity principle is, thus, a challenging one for Union courts to apply. Its application has been weakened in two ways, however. First, there is the constraint in Article 5(3) itself that it does not apply in fields where the Union has exclusive competence.[96] Secondly, and more significantly, the Court has never been guided by the first of these two logics, that of self-government. It looks only at the question of comparative effectiveness. An example is the challenge by Estonia to the Directive on the annual financial statements and financial reporting that have to be made by companies. Estonia argued that a provision exempting small and medium-size enterprises from these requirements if they complied with domestic tax law violated the subsidiarity principle. It could not see why the Union was better equipped to regulate the reporting requirement of these enterprises who tended to trade locally; moreover, compliance with national tax law was, above all, a matter of domestic concern. The Court rejected Estonia's arguments.

Estonia v. *Parliament and Council*, C-508/13, EU:C:2015:403

45 As regards an area, in this case the improvement of the conditions of freedom of establishment, which is not among those for which the European Union has exclusive competence, it must be considered whether the objective of the proposed action could be better achieved at EU level ...

46 In that regard ... the objectives of the Directive are twofold, consisting not only of harmonising financial information of EU undertakings so that addressees of the financial information have comparable data, but also of doing so by taking into account, through a special scheme, itself also largely harmonised, of the particular situation of small undertakings on which the application of accounting requirements laid down for medium and large undertakings would impose an excessive administrative burden.

47 Even if, as claimed by the Republic of Estonia, the second of those two objectives were better achieved by action at Member State level, the fact remains that the pursuit of that objective at such a level is likely to consolidate, if not create, situations in which some Member States would reduce the administrative burden on small undertakings to a greater extent than or in a different way from other Member States, thus clearly running counter to the first objective of the Directive, which is to establish minimum equivalent legal requirements as regards the accounts of undertakings that are in competition with one another.

48 The interdependence of the two objectives pursued by the Directive means that the EU legislature could legitimately take the view that it had to include a special scheme for small undertakings, and that, because of that interdependence, that twofold objective could best be achieved at EU level ...

49 The Directive has consequently not been adopted in breach of the subsidiarity principle.

---

[95] F. Scharpf, 'Community and Autonomy: Multi-Level Policy Making in the European Union' (1994) 1 *JEPP* 219, 225–6.
[96] These competences are set out in Article 3 TFEU. See p. 33.

50 The line of argument put forward by the Republic of Estonia on the allegedly defective way the EU legislature ensured compliance with the subsidiarity principle prior to taking action is not such as to invalidate that conclusion.

51 In that regard, the Republic of Estonia cannot successfully argue that the determination of compliance with the subsidiarity principle should have been made not for the Directive as a whole, but for each of its provisions individually . . .

52 Finally, whereas the Republic of Estonia claims that the EU legislature has not sufficiently taken into account the situation of each Member State and, therefore, its own situation, that argument cannot succeed.

53 The subsidiarity principle is not intended to limit the EU's competence on the basis of the situation of any particular Member State taken individually, but requires only that the proposed action can, by reason of its scale or effects, be better achieved at EU level, given its objectives listed in Article 3 TEU and provisions specific to various areas, including to the various freedoms, such as the freedom of establishment, laid down in the Treaties.

54 It follows that the principle of subsidiarity cannot have the effect of rendering an EU measure invalid because of the particular situation of a Member State, even if it is more advanced than others in terms of an objective pursued by the EU legislature, where, as in the present case, the legislature has concluded on the basis of detailed evidence and without committing any error of assessment that the general interests of the European Union could be better served by action at that level.

There is not a single instance, therefore, of the Court striking down a measure because it violates the subsidiarity principle. The reason is that the Court's reasoning does not balance between Member State and Union interests but takes the Union's objectives as a given, and then asks whether the measure helps to realise them.[97] There is a circularity about this as the EU decision-maker determines the objectives. It is being assessed against criteria it has set. In the judgment above, the Court, therefore, simply stated that the purpose of the law was to harmonise financial information for EU undertakings and to exempt small enterprises from the burdens associated with this. It looked at whether the measure did this, and that was sufficient. There is no real analysis of whether the Union could do this more effectively than Member States and certainly nothing on its implications for self-government.[98] Subsidiarity's central effects, as a control on decision-making, rest, therefore, with its use by national parliaments to restrain EU lawmaking rather than as a principle of judicial review.

(e) Proportionality

The proportionality principle is concerned with the coherence and intrusiveness of EU law. Its philosophy is a presumption in favour of private autonomy and that State intrusion on that should always be justified.[99] It is set out in Article 5(4) TEU.

---

[97] G. Davies, 'Subsidiarity: The Wrong Idea, in the Wrong Place, at the Wrong Time' (2006) 43 *CMLRev* 63, 67–8; M. Bartl, 'The Way We Do Europe: Subsidiarity and the Substantive Democratic Deficit' (2015) 21 *ELJ* 23, 25–9.

[98] See, to similar effect, *United Kingdom* v. *Council*, C-84/94, EU:C:1996:431; *Netherlands* v. *European Parliament and Council*, C-377/98, EU:C:2001:523; *British American Tobacco*, C-491/01, EU:C:2002:741; *R* v. *Secretary of State for Health, ex parte Alliance for Natural Health*, C-154–5/04, EU:C:2005:449.

[99] J. Schwarze, *European Administrative Law* (London, Sweet & Maxwell, 1992) 685.

> **Article 5 TEU**
>
> (4) Under the principle of proportionality, the content and form of Union action shall not exceed what is necessary to achieve the objectives of the Treaties.

The provision is cryptic. The principle was established in a long line of case law,[100] and a more detailed formulation is set out in *Fedesa*. This concerned a challenge to a Directive which prohibited the use of five hormonal substances in livestock farming on the grounds that, *inter alia*, that the prohibition was disproportionate.

> **R v. *Minister of Agriculture, Fisheries and Food, ex parte Fedesa* C-331/88, EU:C:1990:39**
>
> 13 ... the principle of proportionality is one of the general principles of Community law. By virtue of that principle, the lawfulness of the prohibition of an economic activity is subject to the condition that the prohibitory measures are appropriate and necessary in order to achieve the objectives legitimately pursued by the legislation in question; when there is a choice between several appropriate measures recourse must be had to the least onerous, and the disadvantages caused must not be disproportionate to the aims pursued.

Proportionality involves two balancing processes. The first goes to whether there is an appropriate balance between the ends and means, namely whether the measure is *appropriate* for realising the aims sought. This is often a question of degree as it goes to how well the law realises its goals. The other form of balancing goes to the *onerousness* of the measure, in particular whether its effect on other interests and values are excessive.[101] This balancing is seen by some as securing both value pluralism and coherence between conflicting legal values.[102] Others have pointed to a rule of thumb feel to it, as it allows relatively unconstrained choices to be made.[103]

Whatever view is taken, the principle grants judges considerable discretion as it is very easy to argue that an EU act is either inappropriate or too onerous. In some instances, this has led the Union courts to be very much on the other EU Institutions' shoulder. The Court has, for example, regularly invoked the proportionality principle to reduce the fines sought by the Commission for Member States.[104]

Consequently, the principle is not applied in this manner in any field where the EU Institution enjoys a margin of discretion. A different formulation is used. In such circumstances, a measure

---

[100] The principle was first stated to be a general principle of law in *Internationale Handelsgesellschaft* v. *Einfuhr- und Vorratsstelle Getreide*, C-11/70, EU:C:1970:114.

[101] On the history and evolution of the principle see M. Cohen-Eliya and I. Porat, *Proportionality and Constitutional Culture* (Cambridge University Press, 2013) 10–24 and 32–43. Within EU law see T. Tridimas, *The General Principles of EU Law*, 2nd edn (Oxford University Press, 2006) 139–40; A. Portuese, 'Principle of Proportionality as a Principle of Economic Efficiency' (2013) 19 *ELJ* 612.

[102] R. Alexy, 'On Balancing and Subsumption: A Structural Comparison' (2003) 16 *Ratio Juris* 433; M. Klatt and M. Meister, *The Constitutional Structure of Proportionality* (Oxford University Press, 2012) esp. chs. 4 and 5.

[103] J. Habermas, *Between Facts and Norms* (Polity, Cambridge, 1997) 244 *et seq.*; G. Webber, 'Proportionality, Balancing, and the Cult of Constitutional Rights Scholarship' (2010) 23 *Canadian Journal of Law and Jurisprudence* 179.

[104] *Commission* v. *Greece*, C-378/13, EU:C:2014:2405; *Commission* v. *Portugal*, C-557/14, EU:C:2016:471; *Commission* v. *Greece*, C-328/16, EU: C:2018:98.

will only be illegal under the principle if it is manifestly inappropriate to the objective pursued. In *Slovakia and Hungary* v. *Council*, these States, supported by Poland, challenged a Council Decision which provided for relocation of 120,000 people who had crossed the Mediterranean and entered Greece and Italy. The decision required them to be relocated in other Schengen States with each State allocated a certain number of people. It was argued that the measure was disproportionate. Over 320,000 people had arrived in those States since the beginning of that year, and the real problem was the lack of reception capacity and ability to process arrival in Greece and Italy.

Slovakia and Hungary v. *Council*, C–643/15, EU:C:2017:631

207 With regard to judicial review of compliance with [the proportionality] principle, it should also be borne in mind . . . that the EU institutions must be allowed broad discretion when they adopt measures in areas which entail choices on their part, including of a political nature, and in which they are called upon to undertake complex assessments. Consequently, the legality of a measure adopted in one of those areas can be affected only if the measure is manifestly inappropriate having regard to the objective which those institutions are seeking to pursue.

212 The objective of the relocation mechanism provided for in the contested decision, in the light of which the proportionality of that mechanism must be considered, is, according to Article 1(1) of the decision, read in conjunction with recital 26 thereof, to help the Hellenic Republic and the Italian Republic cope with an emergency situation characterised by a sudden inflow, in their respective territories, of third country nationals in clear need of international protection, by relieving the significant pressure on the Greek and Italian asylum systems.

213 The mechanism for relocating a significant number of applicants in clear need of international protection for which the contested decision provides cannot be considered a measure that is manifestly inappropriate for working towards that objective.

214 It is equally hard to deny that any asylum system, even one without structural weaknesses in terms of reception capacity and capacity to process applications for international protection, would have been seriously disrupted by the unprecedented influx of migrants that occurred in Greece and Italy in 2015.

215 In addition, the relocation mechanism provided for in the contested decision forms part of a set of measures intended to relieve the pressure on Greece and Italy. The specific purpose of a number of those measures is to improve the functioning of their respective asylum systems. Consequently, the appropriateness of the relocation mechanism for attaining its objectives cannot be assessed in isolation but must be viewed within the framework of the set of measures of which it forms part.

216 Thus, Article 8 of the contested decision provides for complementary measures, in particular to enhance the capacity, quality and efficiency of the asylum systems, which must be taken by the Hellenic Republic and the Italian Republic . . .

219 Moreover . . . the Hellenic Republic and the Italian Republic have received substantial operational and financial support from the European Union in the framework of the migration and asylum policy.

220 Lastly, it cannot be concluded, a posteriori, from the small number of relocations so far carried out pursuant to the contested decision that the latter was, from the outset, inappropriate for attaining the objective pursued, as is argued by the Slovak Republic and by Hungary . . .

221 In fact, the Court has consistently held that the legality of an EU act cannot depend on retrospective assessments of its efficacy. Where the EU legislature is obliged to assess the future effects of rules to be adopted and those effects cannot be accurately foreseen, its assessment is open to criticism only if it

appears manifestly incorrect in the light of the information available to it at the time of the adoption of the rules in question . . .

222 In the present case . . . when the Council adopted the mechanism for the relocation of a large number of applicants for international protection, it carried out, on the basis of a detailed examination of the statistical data available at the time, a prospective analysis of the effects of the measure on the emergency situation in question. In the light of those data, that analysis does not appear manifestly incorrect.

This test as to whether a measure is manifestly inappropriate is a weak one which grants EU Institutions considerable latitude.[105] One reason suggested is that the Court of Justice places a premium on European integration. It will thus intervene only exceptionally where other EU Institutions have established common EU laws.[106] However, simply realising a system is not so valuable as to justify this level of unaccountability. Another possible reason is that the Court does not have the authority to second-guess the legislature on issues which are either politically salient or have significant distributive consequences. It has, therefore, been suggested that in such cases the 'manifestly inappropriate' test is being used as a form of process-review.[107] The Court will look to see what steps have been taken by the legislature to ensure considered lawmaking. In *Slovakia and Hungary* v. *Council*, the Court, therefore, looked at how the decision related to other measures and the use of statistical evidence to support decision-making. This may well be the case but it is still unclear how awry a process would have to be for a measure to be found to be manifestly inappropriate.

4 STANDING UNDER ARTICLE 263 TFEU

(i) Privileged and Semi-Privileged Applicants

Privileged applicants are the Member States, the Commission, the Council and the European Parliament. Article 263(2) TFEU grants these a general power to seek judicial review of acts of the EU Institutions. Each represents an important public interest. The Member States represent individual national interests; the Council, collective national interests; the European Parliament, a pan-Union democratic voice; and the Commission, the pan-Union public interest. The actors named in Article 263(3) TFEU – the European Central Bank, the Court of Auditors and the Committee of the Regions – are semi-privileged applicants. They can only seek judicial review of other EU Institutions' acts to protect their institutional prerogatives. This is only likely to occur where either another EU Institution failed to observe a procedural requirement at their expense – such as, most notably, failing to consult them – or legislation is adopted in fields where the ECB is empowered to act, thereby displacing it.[108]

---

[105] For a rare example of where an EU measure was found illegal under this test see *Spain* v. *Council*, C-310/04, EU:C:2006:521.

[106] T.-I. Harbo, 'The Function of the Proportionality Principle in EU Law' (2010) 16 *ELJ* 158, 172–3.

[107] D. Harvey, 'Towards Process-Oriented Proportionality Review in the European Union' (2017) 23 *EPL* 93.

[108] For an example of where the ECB was accused of doing that see *United Kingdom* v. *ECB*, T-496/11, EU:T:2015:133.

(ii) Non-Privileged Applicants

(a) The Distinction between Regulatory Acts and Other Acts

Most debate has centred around when other parties, non-privileged applicants, can seek judicial review of acts of EU Institutions. Article 263(4) TFEU provides that such a party will have standing, first, if the act is addressed to her; secondly if the act is a regulatory act which does not entail implementing measures and is of direct concern to her; and, thirdly, if the act is of direct and individual concern to her. In all instances where the act is not addressed to the party, the test for standing depends, therefore, upon whether the act is a regulatory act or not.

The Treaty provides no definition of regulatory acts. The matter was addressed at some length in *Inuit Tapiriit Kanatami*.[109] A Canadian Inuit organisation challenged a Regulation adopted under the ordinary legislative procedure which banned the marketing of seal products within the European Union, subject to a number of limited exceptions.

***Inuit Tapiriit Kanatami* v. *Council*, C-583/11 P, EU:C:2013:625**

58 As regards the concept of 'regulatory act', it is apparent from the third limb of the fourth paragraph of Article 263 TFEU that its scope is more restricted than that of the concept of 'acts' used in the first and second limbs of the fourth paragraph of Article 263 TFEU, in respect of the characterisation of the other types of measures which natural and legal persons may seek to have annulled. The former concept cannot ... refer to all acts of general application but relates to a more restricted category of such acts. To adopt an interpretation to the contrary would amount to nullifying the distinction made between the term 'acts' and 'regulatory acts' by the second and third limbs of the fourth paragraph of Article 263 TFEU.

59 Further, it must be observed that the fourth paragraph of Article 263 TFEU reproduced in identical terms the content of Article III-365(4) of the proposed treaty establishing a Constitution for Europe. It is clear from the *travaux préparatoires* relating to that provision that while the alteration of the fourth paragraph of Article 230 EC was intended to extend the conditions of admissibility of actions for annulment in respect of natural and legal persons, the conditions of admissibility laid down in the fourth paragraph of Article 230 EC relating to legislative acts were not however to be altered. Accordingly, the use of the term 'regulatory act' in the draft amendment of that provision made it possible to identify the category of acts which might thereafter be the subject of an action for annulment under conditions less stringent than previously, while maintaining 'a restrictive approach in relation to actions by individuals against legislative acts ...

60 In those circumstances, it must be held that that the purpose of the alteration to the right of natural and legal persons to institute legal proceedings, laid down in the fourth paragraph of Article 230 EC, was to enable those persons to bring, under less stringent conditions, actions for annulment of acts of general application other than legislative acts.

The General Court refused them standing on the grounds that regulatory acts were general acts, which were not legislative acts, and they could not meet the test for individual concern which was required for other acts. On appeal, the Court of Justice upheld the reasoning of the General Court.

---

[109] P. van Malleghem and N. Baeten, 'Before the Law Stands A Gatekeeper – Or, What Is a "Regulatory Act" in Article 263(4) TFEU? *Inuit Tapiriit Kanatami* ' (2014) 51 *CMLRev* 1187.

A regulatory act is, thus, a general act which is not a legislative act.[110] Ascertaining legislative acts is easy as these are acts adopted by the legislative procedures identified in the Treaty.[111] In *Microban*, the General Court considered the other relevant issue, namely when a measure will be sufficiently general to be a regulatory act. The Commission had exercised implementing powers to adopt a decision banning a single additive, triclosan. A manufacturer challenged this ban even though it was not individually concerned as it argued the measure was a regulatory act. The General Court agreed. It held that any non-legislative measure is a regulatory act, notwithstanding its formal designation, if it:

> applies to objectively determined situations and it produces legal effects with respect to categories of persons envisaged in general and in the abstract.[112]

The decision was, thus, held to be a regulatory act despite being designated as a decision and banning only one product. This was because the good could be produced by anybody and the decision failed to identify particular parties. As such, it applied to an abstract, open-ended group of producers and, consequently, fell within the definition. Therefore, the scope of regulatory acts is wide: they include measures which do not identify, or, are not addressed to, particular actors.

These judgments have been criticised as subjecting legislative acts to more restrictive standing conditions than other acts, resulting in less legislative accountability.[113] The counter-argument is that legislative acts involve representative institutions and allow for public participation. As such, overly relaxed standing rules would allow policy-making by litigation. Historic reasons for restricting judicial review of legislation are that the judiciary is unelected and litigation distorts public participation by prioritising the position of litigants over other members of the public.[114] However, these considerations do not apply with the same force to administrative rule-making as the democratic credentials of these administrative processes are weaker. Therefore, this supports a case for regulatory acts being subject to stronger judicial control than legislative ones.

(b) Direct Concern

Direct concern has two elements. The first is causal, requiring the applicant's legal situation to be affected directly by the Union rather than by the act of some other body. The second goes to the nature of the interest affected, whereby the Union act must affect a legal entitlement of the applicant.

On the first of these, the Court has stated:

> The contested measure must directly produce effects on the legal situation of the person concerned and its implementation must be purely automatic and follow solely from the [Union] rules, without the application of other intermediate measures.[115]

---

[110] *Bayer CropScience and Syngenta Crop Protection* v. *Commission*, T-429/13 and T-451/13, EU:T:2018:280.
[111] Article 289(3) TFEU. *Ferracci* v. *Commission*, T-219/13, EU:T:2016:485.
[112] *Microban* v. *Commission*, T-262/10, EU:T:2011:623, para. 23. See also *Plantavis* v. *Commission*, T-334/12, EU:T:2015:376.
[113] S. Peers and M. Costa, 'Judicial Review of EU Acts after the Treaty of Lisbon' (2012) 8 *EUConst* 82; A. Albors Llorens, 'Remedies against the EU Institutions after Lisbon: An Era of Opportunity?' (2012) 71 *CLJ* 507, 526–7.
[114] A. Türk, 'Oversight of Administrative Rulemaking: Judicial Review' (2013) 19 *ELJ* 126, 141.
[115] *Commission* v. *Ente per le Ville Vesuviane*, C-445/07 P and C-455/07 P, EU:C:2009:529, para. 45.

The central question is whether the Union measure allows domestic authorities discretion as to whether to implement it or not. If it does, the chain of causation is broken as the domestic measure will be deemed responsible for the change in the applicant's legal situation by virtue of the choice available to the domestic authorities.

In determining whether there is discretion, the Court will look not merely at the formal leeway granted to national authorities but also at whether they will actually exercise that discretion. In *Piraiki-Pitraiki*, Greek cotton exporters challenged a restriction on exports applied during the transitional period for Greek membership of the Union.[116] The background to this restriction was that the French Government applied a pre-existing regime and came to the Commission to ask for authorisation to continue it. The Commission argued that, as the authorisation did not compel the French authorities to do anything, the applicants were not directly concerned by it. The Court of Justice rejected this argument. It noted the pre-existing French regime, and stated that there was no more than a theoretical possibility that the French would not continue it. The Commission authorisation, therefore, directly concerned the applicants by legalising a national regime.[117]

The establishment of direct concern is only where domestic authorities have no choice as to implementation. This is arguably an unfair allocation of liabilities. In many instances, where these authorities have some discretion, there is, arguably, a shared responsibility as they would not have taken the action but for the Union measure. In such circumstances, it would seem more appropriate, as both parties are responsible, that action should lie against both of them.

Secondly, the measure must directly affect the applicant's legal situation. This requires the presence of some pre-existing legal claim to have been affected by the act. In *Front National*, the French Front National challenged a decision by the European Parliament which prevented its establishing a political grouping within the European Parliament on the grounds that it did not meet the Parliament's criteria.[118] The Court of Justice held the Front National was not directly concerned. It stated that the Parliament's decision did affect individual MEPs directly as it set out the criteria for when they could form a grouping. However, unlike MEPs, national political parties were not granted rights to establish political groupings if they met certain criteria. As such a party, the Front National was not directly concerned as the decision in no way affected its legal situation.[119]

(c) The Absence of Implementing Measures for Regulatory Acts

To establish *locus standi* for regulatory acts, the act must also not entail domestic implementing measures. This will, in practice, prevent many regulatory acts from being challenged and can lead to injustice. In *T & L Sugars*, two sugar refiners challenged a series of Commission Regulations increasing the amount of sugar that could be produced within the European Union and opening up the Union market (to a point) to non-EU producers. These Regulations were

[116] *Piriaiki-Pitraiki* v. *Commission*, 11/82, EU:C:1985:18.

[117] See also *Green Source Poland* v. *Commission*, T-512/14, EU:T:2017:299. *Piraiki-Pitraiki* was unusual because of the complicity between the Commission and French authorities. The Court will usually assume that if domestic authority has been granted a discretion, they will exercise it and there will be no direct concern. *Commission* v. *Ente per le Ville Vesuviane*, C-445/07 P and C-455/07 P, EU:C:2009:529.

[118] *Front National* v. *European Parliament*, C-486/01 P, EU:C:2004:394.

[119] See also *Commission* v. *Ente per le Ville Vesuviane*, C-445/07 P and C-455/07 P, EU:C:2009:529.

implemented in Portugal through the authorities granting a series of licences to importers and producers of sugar. The refiners argued that the authorities had no real discretion as to whether to implement the Regulation as, in practice, they had little room for manoeuvre in granting the licences. The refiners were, for a number of reasons, unable to challenge these in Portuguese courts. Thus, they would be deprived of any judicial remedy if they were also unable to seek review before the Union courts.

T&L Sugars and Sidul Açúcares v. Commission, C-456/13 P, EU:C:2015:284

29 The concept of 'regulatory act which . . . does not entail implementing measures' within the meaning of the final limb of the fourth paragraph of Article 263 TFEU must be interpreted in the light of the objective of that provision, which is, as is apparent from its drafting history, to ensure that individuals do not have to break the law in order to have access to a court. Where a regulatory act directly affects the legal situation of a natural or legal person without requiring implementing measures, that person could be denied effective judicial protection if he did not have a direct legal remedy before the European Union judicature for the purpose of challenging the legality of the regulatory act. In the absence of implementing measures, natural or legal persons, although directly concerned by the act in question, would be able to obtain a judicial review of that act only after having infringed its provisions, by pleading that those provisions are unlawful in proceedings initiated against them before the national courts . . .

30 However, where a regulatory act entails implementing measures, judicial review of compliance with the European Union legal order is ensured irrespective of whether those measures were adopted by the European Union or the Member States. Natural or legal persons who are unable, because of the conditions governing admissibility laid down in the fourth paragraph of Article 263 TFEU, to challenge a regulatory act of the European Union directly before the European Union judicature are protected against the application to them of such an act by the ability to challenge the implementing measures which the act entails . . .

31 Where responsibility for the implementation of such acts lies with the institutions, bodies, offices or agencies of the European Union, natural or legal persons are entitled to bring a direct action before the European Union judicature against the implementing acts under the conditions stated in the fourth paragraph of Article 263 TFEU, and to plead in support of that action, pursuant to Article 277 TFEU, the illegality of the basic act at issue. Where that implementation is a matter for the Member States, those persons may plead the invalidity of the basic act at issue before the national courts and tribunals and cause the latter to request a preliminary ruling from the Court of Justice, pursuant to Article 267 TFEU . . .

32 As the Court has already held, whether a regulatory act entails implementing measures should be assessed by reference to the position of the person pleading the right to bring proceedings under the final limb of the fourth paragraph of Article 263 TFEU. It is therefore irrelevant whether the act in question entails implementing measures with regard to other persons . . .

49 As regards persons who do not fulfil the requirements of the fourth paragraph of Article 263 TFEU for bringing an action before the Courts of the European Union, it is for the Member States to establish a system of legal remedies and procedures which ensure respect for the fundamental right to effective judicial protection . . .

50 That obligation on the Member States was reaffirmed by the second subparagraph of Article 19(1) TEU, which states that Member States 'shall provide remedies sufficient to ensure effective judicial protection in the fields covered by EU law' . . . That obligation also follows from Article 47 of the Charter as regards measures taken by the Member States to implement Union law within the meaning of Article 51(1) of the Charter.

T & L introduces a paradox. The concept of regulatory act was introduced by the Lisbon Treaty to allow such acts to be more easily challenged than other acts. However, there will be circumstances where it will be possible to challenge other acts but not regulatory acts. This is because the notion of direct concern allows for acts to be challenged where domestic authorities are implementing them (albeit with no choice as whether to do so or not) but applicants will be barred from challenging regulatory acts in such circumstances by dint of the presence of implementing measures. Of even more concern is the insouciance with which the question of the absence of judicial remedies is addressed. The Court of Justice simply states that the domestic system should do something about this. This suggests that where the domestic system provides for no recourse, precious little can be done.

(d) Individual Concern

Applicants can only challenge non-regulatory acts which are not addressed to them if they are individually concerned by the act. The seminal ruling is *Plaumann*. The German authorities wished to suspend customs duty on importation of clementines. They needed authorisation from the Commission, which was refused. The applicant, an importer of clementines, sought judicial review of this refusal. He had to show individual concern as the Commission Decision had been addressed to the German authorities and not to him. The Court of Justice ruled that he lacked standing.

> ### *Plaumann & Co.* v. *Commission*, 25/62, EU:C:1963:17
>
> Persons other than those to whom a decision is addressed may only claim to be individually concerned if that decision affects them by reason of certain attributes which are peculiar to them or by reason of circumstances in which they are differentiated from all other persons and by virtue of these factors distinguishes them individually just as in the case of the person addressed. In the present case the applicant is affected by the disputed Decision as an importer of clementines, that is to say, by reason of a commercial activity which may at any time be practised by any person and is not therefore such as to distinguish the applicant in relation to the contested Decision as in the case of the addressee.

The test needs dissecting. *Plaumann* states that private parties are only individually concerned if they can distinguish themselves by virtue of certain attributes or circumstances from all other persons. These attributes or circumstances must be fixed and determinate and distinguish those identified from the rest of the world. The test, furthermore, is not whether the group is fixed and determinate at a particular date, such as the date of the decision or commencement of litigation, but rather whether it is irrevocably fixed and determinate. It has, in the jargon, to be a closed category which can never be added to.

An example is *Koninklijke Friesland Campina (KFC)*. A Dutch law created a scheme to give tax benefits to Dutch companies providing international financing activities (the GFA scheme). In 2000, KFC applied for authorisation to join the scheme. In 2001 the Commission announced it was investigating the scheme to see if it was illegal State aid. Following this, the Dutch Government announced it would not admit any more undertakings to the scheme, and would not, therefore, admit KFC to the scheme. In 2003, the Commission declared the scheme illegal but stated that all undertakings who were currently members of the scheme could continue to enjoy its benefits. KFC successfully challenged the Commission Decision.

Commission v. Koninklijke Friesland Campina, C–519/07 P, EU:C:2009:556

52 . . . natural or legal persons may claim that a contested provision is of individual concern to them only if it affects them by reason of certain attributes which are peculiar to them or by reason of circumstances in which they are differentiated from all other persons . . .

53 An undertaking cannot, in principle, contest a Commission decision prohibiting a sectoral aid scheme if it is concerned by that decision solely by virtue of belonging to the sector in question and being a potential beneficiary of the scheme. Such a decision is, vis-à-vis that undertaking, a measure of general application covering situations which are determined objectively and entails legal effects for a class of persons envisaged in a general and abstract manner . . .

54 By contrast, the Court has held that, where a contested measure affects a group of persons who were identified or identifiable when that measure was adopted by reason of criteria specific to the members of the group, those persons might be individually concerned by that measure inasmuch as they form part of a limited class of traders . . .

55 It is not in dispute, first, that the contested decision had the effect that requests for first GFA authorisation, which were pending on the date of notification of the contested decision, were rejected without being examined and, second, that the undertakings concerned were easily identifiable, owing to the very existence of such a request, at the time when that decision was adopted. In that regard, it should be recalled that KFC was part of a group of, at most, 14 applicants for first GFA authorisation, whose requests were pending at the time of the 11 July 2001 decision, that those requests were suspended following that decision, and that the Netherlands authorities announced on 5 December 2002 that they would be ceasing, with immediate effect, to consider any new requests for the application of the GFA scheme.

56 Thus, . . . KFC formed part of a closed group of undertakings – and not of an indefinite number of undertakings belonging to the sector concerned – specifically affected by the contested decision.

57 It should be borne in mind that, in order to benefit from the GFA scheme, an undertaking which had made a request for first GFA authorisation must have had already taken the necessary measures in order to fulfil the criteria required for that scheme. Furthermore, as the Netherlands authorities did not have any discretion in that regard, they were obliged to grant such an authorisation if those criteria were fulfilled. Thus, the undertakings whose requests for first GFA authorisation were pending must be regarded as being concerned by the contested decision, by reason of attributes which are peculiar to them and by reason of circumstances in which they are differentiated from every other undertaking in that sector which had not lodged a request for first GFA authorisation.

58 It follows that those undertakings have standing to bring an individual action against the contested decision.

A distinction was thus made between open and closed groups of undertakings. There were companies engaging in international financial activities who were eligible to join the GFA scheme. These formed an open category as, theoretically, anybody could start engaging in such activities. They were not individually concerned. KFC, by contrast, belonged to a group of undertakings who had already made an application to join the GFA scheme at the time of the Commission Decision and were identifiable. This was a closed category as nobody could join it, even theoretically, after the Commission Decision was taken. Because KFC formed part of this closed category, it was individually concerned.

There are a couple of twists to the rule.

The first is where EU law requires the EU decision-maker to take account of a closed group of actors who would otherwise form part of a larger open group. In *Sofrimport*, a Regulation required the Commission, when it imposed restrictions of imports of fruit and vegetables from outside the Union, to take account of the position of goods in transit.[120] The Commission took a decision banning the import of dessert apples from Chile. Sofrimport had a shipment in transit which was refused entry into the Union. On the one hand, it formed part of an open category, namely all apple importers. However, the Court ruled that it had standing as the Regulation required the Commission to take account of a closed group – importers with goods in transit on the date of the decision – and it had failed to do this.

The second is where EU legislation grants parties procedural rights and an identifiable number of parties, who would otherwise be part of an open category, exercise these procedural rights by a certain date.[121] These are also considered to be individually concerned. In *Vischim*, EU legislation phased out certain plant protection products.[122] During a transitional period, manufacturers were invited by the legislation to present dossiers setting out the qualities of these products. Vischim did this in relation to a product which was duly prohibited by a subsequent Directive. The General Court held that Vischim was individually concerned as it was involved in the procedure leading up to the act banning the product, it had been provided procedural safeguards and it was one of only two parties who submitted dossiers on the product in question.

Two justifications are provided for *Plaumann*. The first is set out below.[123]

A. Arnull 'Private Applicants and the Action for Annulment under Article 173 of the EC Treaty' (1995) 32 *Common Market Law Review* 7, 46

One other consideration seems worth mentioning. This is that a proliferation of direct challenges to Community acts by natural and legal persons, perhaps accompanied by applications for interim measures, could have seriously disrupted the proper functioning of the Community system . . . The most progressive of the Court's decisions have been concerned principally with making the Community work. Where, as in cases on direct effect, this has meant protecting the rights of the individual under Community law against encroachment by national authorities, the Court has not hesitated to uphold the rights of the individual. Where the conflict was between the rights of the individual and those of the Community's still immature institutions, however, the Court initially tended to give precedence to the latter . . .

This may be an argument for restrictive rules of standing but it does not explain the arbitrariness of the current test. The Court has ruled that a party is not individually concerned by an act even where it is the only party affected on the grounds that it belongs to an open category.[124] If the measure was concerned solely with restricting applicants, it would look at whether those actually affected could be identified, and their number.[125] It would not speculate on who might theoretically be affected in the most contrived of circumstances.

---

[120] *Sofrimport* v. *Commission*, C-152/88, EU:C:1990:259.

[121] The legislation must provide for specific procedural rights. Mere participation in the procedures is insufficient to grant standing, *Rica Foods* v. *Commission*, T-47/00, EU:T:2002:7.

[122] *Vischim* v. *Commission*, T-420/05, EU:T:2009:391; *BASF Agro* v. *Commission*, T-584/13, EU:T:2018:279.

[123] See also C. Harding, 'The Private Interest in Challenging Community Action' (1980) 5 *ELRev* 354. It should be noted that Arnull is critical of this argument. A. Arnull, *The European Union and Its Court of Justice*, 2nd edn (Oxford University Press, 2006) 91–4.

[124] *Spijker* v. *Commission*, 231/82, EU:C:1983:220.

[125] This argument has been rejected, *Stichting Woonpunt* v. *Commission*, C-132/12 P, EU:C:2014:100.

The second justification is that applicants should, in principle, commence actions for judicial review before domestic courts which can act as a filter by referring questions about the validity of EU acts to the Court of Justice under Article 267 TFEU.[126] This justification relies on parties having *locus standi* before domestic courts, and this may well vary between jurisdiction. Moreover, if a party has standing, the domestic court cannot act as an effective filter: domestic courts are not allowed to declare EU acts invalid, thus it will be required to refer any EU act carrying a whiff of illegality to the Court.[127] Finally, it begs questions about the relationship between the General Court and the Court of Justice as an action under Article 263(4) TFEU is brought before the former whilst a reference goes to the latter.[128] It would be absurd if the Treaty preference for individual administrative challenges to be a central concern of the General Court was undermined in this way.

Plaumann is also seen as partisan as the test is more easily met by those who can point to some individual financial or material interest that has been prejudiced. It thus benefits trading interests over groups representing public interests such as the environment, the regions or the consumer.[129] In *Greenpeace*, three environmental campaigning groups and several individuals resident on the Canary Islands challenged the legality of a series of Commission decisions granting aid to assist the construction of two power stations, one on Gran Canaria and the other on Tenerife. The General Court ruled that neither the associations nor the individuals had standing.[130]

Greenpeace and Others v. *Commission*, T–585/93, EU:T:1995:147

32 The applicants ask the Court to adopt a liberal approach on this issue and recognize that, in the present case, their *locus standi* can depend not on a purely economic interest but on their interest in the protection of the environment ...

39 In the alternative, the applicants submit that the representative environmental organizations should be considered to be individually concerned by reason of the particularly important role they have to play in the process of legal control by representing the general interests shared by a number of individuals in a focused and coordinated manner ...

60 The three applicant associations ... claim that they represent the general interest, in the matter of environmental protection, of people residing on Gran Canaria and Tenerife and that their members are affected by the contested decision; they do not, however, adduce any special circumstances to demonstrate the individual interest of their members as opposed to any other person residing in those areas. The possible effect on the legal position of the members of the applicant associations cannot, therefore, be any different from that alleged here by the applicants who are private individuals. Consequently, in so far as the applicants in the present case who are private individuals cannot, as the Court has held, be considered to be individually concerned by the contested decision, nor can the members of the applicant associations, as local residents of Gran Canaria and Tenerife ...

---

[126] See, critically, H. Rasmussen, 'Why Is Article 173 Interpreted against Private Plaintiffs?' (1980) 5 *ELRev* 112. For a defence see J. Usher, 'Direct and Individual Concern: An Effective Remedy or a Conventional Solution?' (2003) 28 *ELRev* 575.

[127] *Foto-Frost* v. *Hauptzollamt Lübeck-Ost*, 314/85, EU:C:1987:452.   [128] Article 256(1) TFEU.

[129] M. Führ *et al.*, 'Access to Justice: Legal Standing for Environmental Associations in the European Union' in D. Robinson and J. Dunkley (eds.), *Public Interest Perspectives in Environmental Law* (Chichester, Chancery, 1995); L. Krämer, 'Public Interest Litigation in Environmental Matters before European Courts' (1996) 8 *JEL* 1.

[130] The judgment was affirmed on appeal. *Greenpeace and Others* v. *Commission*, C-321/95 P, EU:C:1998:153.

Since *Greenpeace*, the Court has consistently refused to relax standing requirements for public interest litigation.[131] The argument that EU law should do more to allow public interest groups to seek judicial review, whilst apparently attractive, must be treated cautiously. There are dangers with substituting judicial review for political accountability. In *Greenpeace*, for example, it is not evident why the decision to allow funds for the construction of a new power station should be characterised as a *legal* concern rather than one for the political process. To accept this might lead to a 'dilution of the objectivity and neutrality of the law'.[132] Harlow suggests, therefore, that a better way might be to give public interest groups wider rights of intervention in proceedings – something that has not yet happened.

C. Harlow, 'Towards a Theory of Access for the European Court of Justice' (1992) 12 *Yearbook of European Law* 213, 247–8

The most economical way to increase interest representation without overloading the Court is, however, undoubtedly through Intervention procedure. Many modern courts feel able to allow intervention freely and interventions by interest groups are particularly a feature of constitutional courts. In the Court of Justice, in sharp contrast, group interventions are rare and Articles 37 and 20[133] of the Statute are largely the preserve of the privileged applicants.

The Court's distinctive inquisitorial procedures could be used to design an appropriate intervention procedure without adding to burdens on applicants in the shape of greater expense or delay. Strict time-limits can already be imposed for interventions with limited rights of contradiction and oral observations already require the Court's permission. Submissions could be limited as to length. Increased use could be made of the *juge rapporteur* if orality were thought necessary; alternatively, they could be collected and evaluated by the Advocate General, forming part of his Opinion.

---

5 ARTICLE 265 TFEU AND THE FAILURE TO ACT

In particular situations, positive duties are placed upon the EU Institutions to act by both the Treaties[134] and secondary legislation.[135] If they fail to act, Article 265 TFEU sets out the conditions for bringing an action against them.

Article 265 TFEU

Should the European Parliament, the European Council, the Council, the Commission or the European Central Bank, in infringement of the Treaties, fail to act, the Member States and the other institutions of the

---

[131] The Court of Justice upheld the judgment, albeit with very terse reasoning, in *Greenpeace and Others* v. *Commission*, C-3231/95 P, EU:C:1998:153.

[132] C. Harlow, 'Public Law and Popular Justice' (2002) 65 *MLR* 1, 13.

[133] The right to intervene is set out in Article 40 of the Statute of the Court of Justice. Private actors may intervene if they can show an interest and the dispute is not between Member States, EU Institutions or between a Member State and an EU Institution.

[134] E.g. on the common transport policy, see *Parliament* v. *Council*, 13/83, EU:C:1985:220.

[135] E.g. the Commission must examine the particulars of any complaint about a breach of EU competition law which is made by a person with a legitimate interest, *Automec* v. *Commission*, T-24/90, EU:T:1992:97.

Union may bring an action before the Court of Justice to have the infringement established. This Article shall apply, under the same conditions, to bodies, offices and agencies of the Union which fail to act.

The action shall be admissible only if the institution, body, office or agency concerned has first been called upon to act. If, within two months of being so called upon, the institution, body, office or agency concerned has not defined its position, the action may be brought within a further period of two months.

Any natural or legal person may, under the conditions laid down in the preceding paragraphs, complain to the Court that an institution, body, office or agency of the Union has failed to address to that person any act other than a recommendation or an opinion.

Privileged applicants comprise a wider group than under Article 263 TFEU as all EU Institutions and Member States are granted that status. Beyond this, Articles 263 and 265 TFEU were described in an early judgment as prescribing 'one and the same method of recourse'.[136] The reason is that:

the system of remedies ... would be incomplete if [Union] institutions were subject to judicial control only in respect of their positive actions while they could evade the obligations imposed upon them by simply failing to act.[137]

The provisions are, therefore, interpreted in a parallel manner. Non-privileged applicants can only invoke Article 265 TFEU if they are directly concerned by the regulatory act or directly and individually concerned by the non-regulatory act which should have been adopted.[138]

However, there are some distinctive features to Article 265 TFEU.

First, an action under Article 265 TFEU can only be commenced against an EU Institution if it is under a duty to perform a task rather than if it simply enjoys a discretion as to whether to perform it.[139] We saw earlier how the discretion enjoyed by the Commission over the launch of infringement proceedings against a Member State led to private parties being largely excluded from this important process.[140] Secondly, an action may be brought not only against failures to adopt binding measures but also against failures to adopt preparatory acts that are a necessary part of a procedure leading to a binding act.[141] Thirdly, the EU Institution must have been called upon to act and failed to define its position within two months of that call.[142] Defining its position can take the form of acting in the way called for; acting in a different way from that called for;[143] or refusing to act at all.[144] This definition of position is an act which is reviewable under Article 263 TFEU.[145] Finally, the EU Institution must be called upon to act by the applicant.[146] The call to act need not take any form but must be sufficiently clear and precise

[136] *Chevalley* v. *Commission*, C-15/70, EU:C:1970:95.

[137] A. Toth, 'The Law as It Stands on the Appeal for Failure to Act' (1975/2) *LIEI* 65, 65.

[138] *Air One* v. *Commission* T-395/04, EU:T:2006:123; *Asklepios Kliniken* v. *Commission*, T-167/04, EU:T:2007:215.

[139] *Ryan Air* v. *Commission*, T-423/07, EU:T:2011:226.

[140] *Star Fruit* v. *Commission*, 247/87, EU:C:1989:58. See p. 356.

[141] *Bionorica and Diapharm* v. *Commission*, C-596-7/15 P, EU:C:2017:886.

[142] *Diputación Foral de Álava* v. *Commission*, T-30-2/01 and T-86-8/02, EU:T:2009:314.

[143] *Pesqueras Echebastar* v. *Commission*, C-25/91, EU:C:1993:131; *Vischim* v. *Commission*, T-420/05, EU:T:2009:391.

[144] *Laboratoires CTRS* v. *Commission*, T-12/12, EU:T:2012:343.

[145] *Schlüsselverlag JS Moser* v. *Commission*, T-3/02, EU:T:2002:64. If, however, this definition of a position leads to a subsequent act which is reviewable, only the latter is reviewable, *Makhteshim-Agan Holding BV and Others* v. *Commission*, T-34/05 R, EU:T:2005:147.

[146] *Diputación Foral de Álava* v. *Commission*, T-30-2/01 and T-86-8/02, EU:T:2009:314.

to enable the EU Institution to ascertain the specific content of the measure it is being asked to adopt, and it must make clear that its purpose is to compel the EU Institution to state its position.[147]

6 THE PLEA OF ILLEGALITY

Particularly in the field of delegated or implementing powers, parties face a problem if they want to challenge a measure on the basis that the parent measure is illegal. The time limits for challenging the parent instrument may have passed, or they may not satisfy the *locus standi* requirements for challenging it. The plea of illegality addresses this by allowing a party, in proceedings against a measure, to plead the illegality of its parent measure.

Article 277 TFEU

Notwithstanding the expiry of the period laid down in Article 263, fifth paragraph, any party may, in proceedings in which an act of general application adopted by an institution, body, office or agency of the Union is at issue, plead the grounds specified in Article 263, second paragraph, in order to invoke before the Court of Justice of the European Union the inapplicability of that act.

The plea of illegality is thus a parasitic procedure. It can only be invoked in the context of proceedings brought under some other procedure, whose *locus standi* requirements and time limits have been observed.[148] Moreover, for it to succeed, the parent legislation must apply to the issue that is the subject of the litigation and there must be a direct link between the parent legislation and the implementing measure.[149] A final consequence of these parasitic qualities is that a finding of illegality will not lead to the parent measure being illegal, but would only lead to its inapplicability in the dispute at hand.[150]

That said, the concern with the plea of illegality – that it should not be used to subvert other procedures – has led to three refinements.

First, it may not be invoked where a matter is pending before another court or in another action before the same court (*lis pendens*). This only occurs if the action is between the same parties, seeks the same object and does so on the basis of the same submissions.[151] This will very rarely be the case. Even if the substance of the dispute is similar, the litigation before the courts may look at different dimensions, and parties will, in any case, often use different arguments.

Secondly, a party who failed to exercise an earlier opportunity to challenge the parent measure cannot subsequently raise the plea of illegality. The most obvious example is privileged parties under Article 263 TFEU who have standing to challenge the parent measure at the time of adoption. Allowing them to subsequently raise a plea of illegality would enable them to evade the time limits in that procedure and generate uncertainty.[152] The principle, however, also applies to non-privileged parties. In *TWD (No. 2)*, the applicant, a textile company, failed to

---

[147] *Usinor* v. *Commission*, 81/85 and 119/85, EU:C:1986:234; *Laboratoires CTRS* v. *Commission*, T-12/12, EU:T:2012:343.
[148] *Antrax It* v. *EUIPO*, T-828–9/14, EU:T:2017:87.   [149] *KF* v. *European Union Centre*, T-286/15, EU:T:2018:718.
[150] *ECB* v. *Cerafogli*, T-787/14 P, EU:T:2016:633.   [151] *Melli Bank* v. *Council*, T-246/08 and T-332/08, EU:T:2009:266.
[152] *Spain* v. *Commission*, C-135/93, EU:C:1995:201.

challenge a 1986 Commission Decision that a subsidy granted to it was illegal.[153] A new subsidy was authorised by a second Commission decision on the condition that the initial subsidy was repaid to the authorities. The applicant challenged the 1986 decision, under a plea of illegality, claiming that its economic effects only became apparent following the second decision. The General Court deemed this inadmissible, stating that the applicant was debarred from bringing a challenge because it could have challenged the first decision using Article 263 TFEU.

Thirdly, if it is possible still to challenge the parent measure using other procedures, these should be used. The plea of illegality may not be used if the party still has standing to challenge a measure directly before the Union courts.[154]

7 NON-CONTRACTUAL LIABILITY

The final head of action under which Union measures can be reviewed is that of non-contractual liability. In such circumstances, the applicant will not merely be seeking annulment of the measure but also damages from the EU Institution. This is governed by Article 340(2) TFEU.

Article 340 TFEU

(2) In the case of non-contractual liability, the Union shall, in accordance with the general principles common to the laws of the Member States, make good any damage caused by its institutions or by its servants in the performance of their duties.

The law on the non-contractual liability of EU Institutions was reshaped by the *Brasserie du Pêcheur* judgment, which detailed when Member States were liable for individual loss as a result of their breaching EU law. Aware of possible inconsistencies, the Court stated that the same criteria should govern both State liability and the liability of EU Institutions under Article 340(2) TFEU.[155] To be sure, it has proved difficult for the Court to apply these parallels too formulaically but it has tried to reason from similar principles for both.

(i) The Conditions for Liability

As with State liability, mere illegal behaviour is insufficient to incur the liability of the EU Institutions. The illegality must have a certain gravity. In *Bergaderm*, a Commission Decision banned the use of a chemical, bergapten, in sun oil on the ground that it was carcinogenic. Bergaderm was the only company that produced sun oil using this chemical. Following the decision, it went into liquidation. It sued the Commission, claiming that the latter had misinterpreted the scientific evidence. It failed but the Court set out parameters for Article 340(2) TFEU.

---

[153] *TWD Textilwerke Deggendorf* v. *Commission*, T-244/93 and T-486/93, EU:T:1995:160.
[154] *Sina Bank* v. *Council*, T-15/11, EU:T:2012:661.
[155] *Brasserie du Pêcheur* v. *Germany*, C-46/93 and C-48/93, EU:C:1996:79, paras. 42–5. See pp. 316–19. See also T. Tridimas, 'Liability for Breach of Community Law: Growing Up and Mellowing Down?' (2001) 38 *CMLRev* 301.

> ### *Laboratoires Pharmaceutiques Bergaderm* v. *Commission*, C–352/98 P, EU:C:2000:361
>
> 40 The system of rules which the Court has worked out with regard to [Article 340(2) TFEU] takes into account, *inter alia*, the complexity of the situations to be regulated, difficulties in the application or interpretation of the texts and, more particularly, the margin of discretion available to the author of the act in question . . .
>
> 41 The Court has stated that the conditions under which the State may incur liability for damage caused to individuals by a breach of Community law cannot, in the absence of particular justification, differ from those governing the liability of the Community in like circumstances. The protection of the rights which individuals derive from Community law cannot vary depending on whether a national authority or a Community authority is responsible for the damage . . .
>
> 42 As regards Member State liability for damage caused to individuals, the Court has held that Community law confers a right to reparation where three conditions are met: the rule of law infringed must be intended to confer rights on individuals; the breach must be sufficiently serious; and there must be a direct causal link between the breach of the obligation resting on the State and the damage sustained by the injured parties . . .
>
> 43 As to the second condition, as regards both Community liability under Article [340(2) TFEU] and Member State liability for breaches of Community law, the decisive test for finding that a breach of Community law is sufficiently serious is whether the Member State or the Community institution concerned manifestly and gravely disregarded the limits on its discretion . . .
>
> 44 Where the Member State or the institution in question has only considerably reduced, or even no, discretion, the mere infringement of Community law may be sufficient to establish the existence of a sufficiently serious breach . . .

Three conditions must thus be met for an EU Institution to incur liability:

- There must be an infringement of a rule of law intended to confer rights on individuals.
- The infringement must be sufficiently serious.
- There must be a direct causal link between the breach and the loss sustained by the applicant.

It is time to look at each in turn.

(ii) Breach of a Rule of Law Intended to Confer Rights on Individuals

The first requirement is that the EU Institution must breach a rule of law intended to confer rights on individuals.

The illegality can involve either an illegal act or an omission to act where legally required.[156] A legal act will not lead to liability no matter how much harm it generates for particular individuals.[157] Liability is centred, therefore, on the fault of the EU Institution. A risk-based test has been eschewed since it would have involved deciding, in conditions of uncertainty, when EU Institutions or private parties are better equipped to bear responsibility for things going wrong. Illegality by EU Institutions would have been irrelevant in such circumstances.

Furthermore, regard is had not to whether the applicant is individually concerned by the EU law breached but to whether that law is intended to create rights.[158] General principles of EU law,

---

[156] *Šumelj* v. *Commission*, T-546/13, EU:T:2016:107.   [157] *Bueno* v. *Commission*, C-12–13/13 P, EU:C:2014:2284.
[158] *Camós Grau* v. *Commission*, T-309/03, EU:T:2006:110.

fundamental rights and the doctrine of misuse of powers have been held to be norms that will lead to liability.[159] By contrast, a failure to state reasons will not generate liability unless this compromises the applicant's rights of defence.[160] If the EU Institution breaches a substantive norm of EU law, the Court will look at whether the relevant instrument is capable of generating individual rights and then at whether the provision breached is intended to create individual rights. International agreements not intended to confer individual rights will, thus, not lead to liability.[161]

(iii) The Breach Must Be Sufficiently Serious

The second condition is that the breach of EU law must be sufficiently serious.

In situations where EU Institutions have considerably reduced discretion or no discretion at all, simple illegality may be enough for the breach to be considered sufficiently serious to incur liability.[162] However, this will not automatically lead to liability. The complexity of the situations being regulated and the difficulties in applying or interpreting the relevant EU law are also relevant.[163] Consequently, it is only if there is, in addition to the illegality, a lack of due diligence on the part of the EU Institution that the behaviour will be sufficient to incur liability.[164]

In situations where the EU Institution enjoys a discretion, a higher threshold is applied. *Bergaderm* indicates that the EU Institution must have manifestly and gravely exceeded the limits of its discretion (para. 43 above). Even here, it is difficult to ascertain a single standard. Instead, there is a spectrum.

At one end are situations where the Court believes that the Union Institutions are pursuing important objectives. It is particularly loathe to impose liability where this is the case. For instance, it has, in the field of international sanctions, stated that the Union is pursuing the wider objective of international peace and security, thereby justifying even significant negative consequences for operators. Union Institutions will only be liable where they violate their obligations in not merely a flagrant but inexcusable way.[165]

Next are situations which involve substantial assessments by the EU Institutions but whose objective are not attributed the same importance. A slightly less draconian test applies here. In *Schneider*, the Court considered erroneous analysis of a merger by the Commission.[166] It stated that such assessments would only lead to liability if there was both a manifest breach of law and this breach could not be justified by the constraints under which the Commission was operating. The test was not that it had to be manifestly illegal and then inexcusable as a further layer of egregiousness. Rather, the test was whether it was a manifest breach of law that could not be explained away by the pressures under which the Commission worked.

---

[159] *Vereniging van Exporteurs in Levende Varkens* v. *Commission*, T-481/93 and T-484/93, EU:T:1995:209.

[160] *Eurocoton* v. *Council*, C-76/01 P, EU:C:2003:511; *HTTS Hanseatic Trade Trust & Shipping* v. *Council*, T-692/15, EU:T:2017:890.

[161] *FIAMM* v. *Council*, C-120–1/06 P, EU:C:2008:476.

[162] *Commission* v. *Camar and Tico*, C-312/00 P, EU:C:2002:736; *Chart* v. *EEAS*, T-138/14, EU:T:2015:981.

[163] *ATC* v. *Commission*, T-333/10, EU:T:2013:451.

[164] *Sison* v. *Council*, T-341/07, EU:T:2011:687; *Safa Nicu Sepahan* v. *Council*, T-384/11, EU:T:2014:986.

[165] *HTTS Hanseatic Trade Trust & Shipping* v. *Council*, T-692/15, EU:T:2017:890. In the field of public health, see also *Zoofachhandel Züpke* v. *Commission*, T-817/14, EU:T:2016:157.

[166] *Schneider* v. *Commission*, T-351/03, EU:T:2007:212.

There are, finally, situations where the central issue is a failure of process. Here, the Court looks simply to see if there was illegality. In *Guardian Europe*, the General Court found that the Court of Justice had taken twenty-six months longer than it should have done to hear an appeal.[167] It held that this violated the fundamental right to be heard by a tribunal within a reasonable period of time. In the General Court's view, the simple violation of this fundamental right was sufficiently serious to justify liability. There was, thus, no examination of whether it was manifestly illegal or inexcusable.

(iv) The Loss Must Be Caused by the Illegal Act

The third condition is the presence of a direct causal link between the breach and the loss. The burden of proof is upon applicants to show causation.[168]

The loss must be directly caused by the breach, namely it would not have happened but for the breach.[169] Thus, the chain of causation can be severed by acts of third parties, such as those of a Member State.[170] There must also be sufficient proximity between the loss and the illegal act.[171] The EU Institutions are not liable for consequences of their illegality which are remote.[172] The loss must finally be actual and certain.[173] There is no liability for hypothetical or indeterminate loss.[174]

The principles governing recovery of loss were most clearly set out by Advocate General Capotorti in *Ireks-Arkady*:

> [T]he legal concept of 'damage' covers both a material loss stricto senso, that is to say, a reduction in the person's assets and also the loss of an increase in those assets which would have occurred if the harmful act had not taken place (these two alternatives are known respectively as damnum emergens and lucrum cessans) . . . The object of compensation is to restore the assets of the victim to the condition in which they would have been apart from the unlawful act, or at least to the condition closest to that which would have been produced if the unlawful act had not taken place: the hypothetical nature of that restoration often entails a certain degree of approximation.[175]

Recoverable losses can include incidental loss, such as penalties the applicant had to pay as a result of having to repudiate a contract[176] or bank interest as a result of loans taken out to pay money wrongfully levied.[177] Compensation will also be awarded for non-pecuniary loss such as anxiety, hurt feelings[178] and slurs on professional reputation.[179] The 'expectation interest' is also protected as loss of profits are recoverable.[180]

Whilst the range of recoverable losses is considerable, two hurdles often prevent or limit reparation.

---

[167] *Guardian Europe* v. *European Union*, T-673/15, EU:T:2017:377.
[168] *Safa Nicu Sepahan* v. *Council*, C-45/15 P, EU:C:2017:402.
[169] *Galileo International Technology and Others* v. *Commission*, T-279/03, EU:T:2006:121.
[170] *Société pur l'Exportation des Sucres* v. *Commission*, 132/77, EU:C:1978:99.
[171] *Safa Nicu Sepahan* v. *Council*, C-45/15 P, EU:C:2017:402.
[172] *Dumortier and Others* v. *Council*, 64/76, 113/76, 167/78, 239/78, 27–8/79 and 45/79, EU:C:1979:223; *Klein* v. *Commission*, T-309/10, EU:T:2014:19.
[173] *Ombudsman* v. *Staelens*, C-337/15 P, EU:C:2017:256.   [174] *Dufour* v. *ECB*, T-436/09, EU:T:2011:634.
[175] *Ireks-Arkady* v. *Council and Commission*, 238/78, EU:C:1979:203.
[176] *CNTA* v. *Commission*, 74/74, EU:C:1976:84.   [177] *Nölle* v. *Commission and Council*, T-167/94, EU:T:1997:195.
[178] *Willame* v. *Commission*, 110/63, EU:C:1966:40.   [179] *Franchet & Byk* v. *Commission* T-485/05, EU:T:2008:257.
[180] *Kampffmeyer* v. *Commission and Council*, 56–60/74, EU:C:1976:78.

The first is the issue of joint or concurrent liability: situations where both an EU Institution and a Member State may be liable.[181] This may arise where a domestic authority implements or administers an unlawful Union measure. It may also arise where a decision is taken jointly by a Member State and a Union Institution, such as in the field of external trade where Member States are permitted to restrict imports of third country goods with the permission of the Commission.[182] The most equitable solution in such cases would be to establish a system of joint and several liability. The applicant could choose whom to sue, with unsuccessful defendants recovering contributions from each other afterwards. However, this is not the case in EU law. Instead, the Court presumes that parties should first exhaust remedies in domestic courts,[183] but that presumption is rebuttable where these remedies would be ineffective and be incapable of leading to compensation.[184] The applicant does not have to go through the domestic process to show this is so. It can simply be argued before the Court that there is no point pursuing domestic avenues because of the lack of effective redress. Inevitably, there is scope for argument here, and this is unsatisfactory as it encourages applicants to commence litigation in domestic courts and the Court of Justice simultaneously.[185]

The second are a number of doctrines which may limit the compensation received. Compensation will be reduced if there is: contributory negligence and the applicant is considered to have contributed to the damage as a result of a failure to take due care;[186] a failure by the applicant to mitigate the loss;[187] or there is evidence that the applicant has, or could have, passed the loss on to somebody else.[188]

8 THE CONSEQUENCES OF ANNULMENT

The consequences of a finding of illegality are set out in Article 264 TFEU.

Article 264 TFEU

If the action is well founded, the Court of Justice shall declare the act concerned to be void.

In the case of a regulation, however, the Court of Justice shall, if it considers this necessary, state which of the effects of the regulation which it has declared void shall be considered as definitive.

A finding of invalidity can be made as a consequence of any of the direct actions against Union acts discussed in this chapter: judicial review, the plea of illegality or the action for damages.[189] This finding has *erga omnes* effects and is binding on all domestic courts in the European Union.[190] In *BASF*, the Court ruled that Union acts are presumed to be lawful and thus continue to produce legal effects until annulled by the Court. It then added the following rider:

[181] For detailed critique see A. Ward, *Judicial Review and the Rights of Private Parties in EU Law*, 2nd edn (Oxford University Press, 2007) 375–90.

[182] W. Wils, 'Concurrent Liability of the Community and a Member State' (1992) 17 *ELRev* 191, 194–8.

[183] *Haegeman* v. *Commission*, 96/71, EU:C:1972:88.

[184] *Schroeder* v. *Council and Commission*, T-205/14, EU:T:2015:673.

[185] *Nölle* v. *Council and Commission*, T-167/94, EU:T:1997:195.   [186] *Adams* v. *Commission*, 145/83, EU:C:1985:323.

[187] *Mulder* v. *Council and Commission*, C-104/89 and C-37/90, EU:C:1992:217.

[188] *Ireks-Arkady* v. *Council and Commission*, 238/78, EU:C:1979:203.

[189] *Kampfmeyer* v. *Commission*, 5, 7, 13–24/66, EU:C:1967:8.

[190] *International Chemical Corporation* v. *Amministrazione delle Finanze*, 66/80, EU:C:1981:102.

by way of exception to that principle, acts tainted by an irregularity whose gravity is so obvious that it cannot be tolerated by the [Union] legal order must be treated as having no legal effect, even provisional, that is to say that they must be regarded as legally non-existent. The purpose of this exception is to maintain a balance between two fundamental, but sometimes conflicting, requirements with which a legal order must comply, namely stability of legal relations and respect for legality.[191]

In principle, therefore, in the absence of such irregularities, parties are bound by Union measures until a finding of invalidity. Whilst a ruling under Article 264(1) TFEU has the effect of releasing all parties from any obligation to which they might otherwise have been subject under the measure, considerable discretion is given to the Court by Article 264(2) TFEU to determine the effects of a ruling. Accordingly, the Court may declare that only part of a measure invalid, maintaining in place other aspects. Temporal limitations may also be placed upon an annulment, meaning that the law will remain in force until a new law is passed to replace it.[192]

FURTHER READING

A. Albors Llorens, 'Remedies against the EU Institutions after Lisbon: An Era of Opportunity?' (2012) 71 *Cambridge Law Journal* 507.

M. Bartl, 'The Way We Do Europe: Subsidiarity and the Substantive Democratic Deficit' (2015) 21 *European Law Journal* 23.

P. Craig, *EU Administrative Law*, 3rd edn (Oxford University Press, 2018) Part II.

A. Fritzsche, 'Discretion, Scope of Judicial Balance and Institutional Review in European Law' (2010) 47 *Common Market Law Review* 361.

D. Harvey, 'Towards Process-Oriented Proportionality Review in the European Union' (2017) 23 *European Public Law* 93.

K. Gutmann, 'The Evolution of the Action for Damages against the European Union and its Place in the System of Judicial Protection' (2011) 48 *Common Market Law Review* 695.

H. Hoffmann, G. Rowe and A. Türk, *Administrative Law and Policy of the European Union* (Oxford University Press, 2011) chs. 7, 18 and 25.

J. Mendes, *Participation in EU Rule-Making: A Rights-Based Approach* (Oxford University Press, 2011).

T. Tridimas, *The General Principles of EU Law*, 2nd edn (Oxford University Press, 2006).

A. Türk, 'Oversight of Administrative Rulemaking: Judicial Review' (2013) 19 *European Law Journal* 126.

---

[191] *Commission* v. *BASF*, C-137/92 P, EU:C:1994:247, para. 49.
[192] E.g. *Parliament* v. *Council ('Visas')*, C-392/95, EU:C:1997:289.

10

Brexit

CONTENTS

1 INTRODUCTION

This chapter looks at Brexit and future relations between the European Union and the United Kingdom.

Section 2 considers the uncertainty surrounding Brexit in December 2018. In November 2018, negotiators reached agreement on a Withdrawal Agreement providing for the orderly withdrawal of the United Kingdom. Agreement was also reached on a Political Declaration setting out a Framework for the Future Relationship between the European Union and the United Kingdom. This is to structure treaty negotiations on this relationship that are to start once the United Kingdom has withdrawn from the Union. Both the Agreement and the Political Declaration have, *inter alia*, to be approved by a Resolution of the House of Commons. The United Kingdom government withdrew the Resolution in December 2018 because of lack of parliamentary support for it. This opens four possibilities: the Withdrawal Agreement will be eventually concluded with little or no amendment; the Agreement is not concluded but the Political Declaration provides a template for a future relations; relations break down so badly that the trade relations of the United Kingdom and the European Union are governed exclusively by World Trade Organisation (WTO) law; or the United Kingdom has a new referendum which leads to it remaining in or re-joining the Union.

Section 3 considers three aspects of the Withdrawal Agreement. A transition period is agreed, first, to run until 31 December 2020 to facilitate an orderly transition from Brexit to the anticipated new treaty relationship. The United Kingdom is to apply almost all EU law and be bound by the principles of the EU legal order (direct effect, primacy etc.) during this period. It and its citizens shall have, however, no significant rights to participate or be represented in Union decision-making or lawmaking. Secondly, we look at the Agreement's governance arrangements. The most powerful body is a Joint Committee comprised of EU and UK representatives. It has significant decision-making powers but there is no formal possibility for parliamentary input or judicial accountability. Thirdly, the Protocol on Ireland and Northern Ireland provides the conditions for no hard border in the island of Ireland. To this end, it requires the United Kingdom as a whole to align its laws with EU laws on the common customs tariff, competition and State aids, and not to lower the level of protection offered by central labour and environmental laws. Northern Ireland must, in addition, align its law with a further seventy-five-page list of those EU laws that establish the single market in goods. In principle, the Protocol is intended to be temporary and to be superseded by the new treaty. As no other alternatives have been found for avoiding a hard border, the regime for Northern Ireland might end up shaping future trade relations more generally.

Section 4 examines the Political Declaration on the Future Relationship between the European Union and the United Kingdom. It focuses on three aspects. The first, the so-called Basis for Cooperation, contains one particularly important commitment. The United Kingdom will not leave the European Convention on Human Rights (ECHR). The second, the Economic Partnership, leaves open the possibility for significant free movement of goods and a customs union between the European Union and the United Kingdom, whilst also allowing for less economic integration. It provides for much more limited liberalisation in the fields of freedom of establishment and services with no requirement that non-discriminatory restrictions on market access be removed, and there is no significant commitment to free movement of persons. The Security Partnership, thirdly, provides for institutional arrangements to secure Europe's security both internally and externally, with the possibility that the protection of Europe's security claimed by it will be used to justify significant powers for interior ministries and intelligence agencies.

Section 5 looks at other possible models for future EU–UK relations. The European Economic Area (EEA) creates a single market and requires parties to adopt EU law in a number of fields, including environment, energy, competition, transport and equal pay for work of equal value. EEA law also has considerable bite as it has indirect effect and generates State liability. Finally, a significant institutional settlement governs it. The Joint Committee, comprising representatives from the Commission and the non-EU EEA States, ensures EEA law is aligned with EU law. The European Free Trade Association (EFTA) Court of Justice can not only hear infringement proceedings, but also has jurisdiction to hear preliminary references from national courts. The Ukraine model, based on the Association Agreement between the Union and Ukraine, establishes a Deep and Comprehensive Free Trade Area. Ukraine must align its laws with EU law in the single market for goods; most of the single market for services, environment and labour law; and competition and State aids. In return, it is granted significant access to the Union market for its goods and increasing access to Union service markets as it incorporates and complies with EU law. Finally, there is the Canadian model, a free trade agreement modelled on the Comprehensive Economic and Trade Agreement between Canada and the Union. This provides some liberalisation in goods markets by abolishing tariffs and requiring the parties to justify failures to recognise the regulatory standards of the other party. It also grants significant protection to investors who can take the host State to an Investment Tribunal for compensation, if, in particular, it discriminates against them or fails to accord them fair and equitable treatment. Finally, it offers significant protection to each party's environment and labour laws so should not be seen as offering deregulatory opportunities. None of these models, unmodified, would prevent a hard border on the island of Ireland.

Section 6 considers trade relations in the event of no deal between the Union and the United Kingdom. WTO law would require the same tariffs to be imposed on trade in goods by each as are imposed on other WTO members who have no trade agreement with them. The costs of these tariffs are significant. It would also be difficult for traders to challenge regulatory requirements that barred market access for their goods. There would, furthermore, be very few guarantees for cross-border trade in services or cross-border establishments. The United Kingdom might still, however, be exposed to the influence of EU law because of two phenomena. The Brussels effect involves companies applying EU law over and above their law because it is easier for them to conform to a single standard than two differing standards, and the value of the single market entails that they often choose the EU legal standard. Territorial extension is where EU law conditions access to its market or territory on the person's activities in their home State complying with EU law or international law.

2 THE IMMEDIATE UNCERTAINTIES OF BREXIT

On 29 March 2017, as required by Article 50 TEU, the UK Government formally notified the European Union of its intention to leave the Union. That article, it will be remembered, states that the 'Union shall negotiate and conclude an agreement with [the United Kingdom], setting out the arrangements for its withdrawal, taking account of the framework for its future relationship with the Union.' This was interpreted as requiring two things to be kept discrete.[1] A Withdrawal Agreement was necessary, first, to allow the United Kingdom to transition from being a member State to non-EU State in an orderly manner that protected a number of important interests. Beyond these matters, this Agreement was not to govern future relations between the United Kingdom and the European Union more broadly. A framework was, secondly, to be set out for these other matters. It would provide a non-binding roadmap for future negotiations on these. These negotiations would take place subsequent to withdrawal in just the same manner as those between the Union and other non-EU States.

The European Council set out the interests to be protected in Guidelines a month after the United Kingdom notification. They were:

- protecting the rights of EU citizens resident in the United Kingdom and UK citizens resident in the rest of the European Union
- a single financial settlement covering obligations arising out of UK membership of the Union
- the avoidance of a hard border within the island of Ireland so that the integrity of the EU legal order would be respected
- dispute settlement and enforcement mechanisms regarding the application and interpretation of the withdrawal agreement that would protect the autonomy of the EU legal order
- preventing a legal vacuum which might disrupt existing contacts or business arrangements within both the United Kingdom and the European Union
- safeguarding the rights and interests of EU citizens working and resident in the UK Sovereign Base Areas in Cyprus
- as the United Kingdom would no longer be covered by international agreements, a dialogue on possible common approaches to non-EU States and international organisations
- potential issues arising from withdrawal, most notably in judicial cooperation, law enforcement and security
- securing the legal position for cases pending before the Court of Justice and other EU Institutions and agencies that involve the United Kingdom or persons in the United Kingdom.

This list sets out the remit of the Withdrawal Agreement. Everything else was to be deferred until after withdrawal. Although the list looks long, the first four items were the centre of most political controversy.[2]

On 14 November 2018, after over one and a half years of tortuous negotiations, negotiators agreed a draft Withdrawal Agreement to be ratified by both the European Union and the United Kingdom. Eight days later, they agreed a draft Political Declaration on the Future Relationship between the European Union and the United Kingdom ('Political Declaration'). On 25 November

---

[1] On the debates surrounding the requirement of Article 50 TEU see A. Lazowski, 'Exercises in Legal Acrobatics: The Brexit Transitional Arrangements' (2017) 2 *European Papers* 845, 847–53; C. Hillion, 'Withdrawal under Article 50 TEU: An Integration-Friendly Process' (2018) 55 *CMLRev* 29.

[2] On this period see P. Craig, 'Brexit – An Interregnum' (2017) 36 *YBEL* 3.

2018, the European Council endorsed both the Withdrawal Agreement and the Political Declaration.[3] However, that was very much only the beginning of the endgame. To enter into effect, the agreement still had to be concluded by the Union and the United Kingdom. For the Union, *pace* Article 50 TEU, this was to be done by the Council, acting by qualified majority voting (QMV), after obtaining the consent of the European Parliament. The situation was more complicated in the United Kingdom. The European Union Withdrawal Act 2018 provided that the United Kingdom could only conclude the Withdrawal Agreement if:

- the draft Agreement and Political Declaration has been approved by a Resolution of the House of Commons and a motion taking note of them had been debated by the House of Lords[4] and
- an Act of Parliament had been passed providing for implementation of the Withdrawal Agreement.[5]

This two-stage process might seem repetitive but was significant because the Act provided that if the House of Commons does not approve the Resolution, the government had to set out within twenty-one days how it will proceed.[6] When the government set the Resolution for debate before the House of Commons at the beginning of December 2018, the opposition was such that it withdrew the Resolution even before the vote, and went back to the Union to ask for more concessions, notably withdrawal or significant amendment of the Protocol on Ireland and Northern Ireland in the Withdrawal Agreement. To date, the Union has refused to do that, offering only a possible clarification of it.

This has led to considerable uncertainty about the future of United Kingdom–European Union relations. This chapter assumes four possible scenarios:

- The Withdrawal Agreement is eventually concluded by the United Kingdom with little or no amendment.
- The United Kingdom is unable to conclude the Withdrawal Agreement. Whilst there is a period of uncertainty, relations between the United Kingdom and the European Union remain sufficiently civil that the Political Declaration provides a realistic template for a future relationship between the two.
- The United Kingdom is unable to conclude the Withdrawal Agreement and relations break down between the United Kingdom and the European Union. In such circumstances, relations would be governed by the WTO, as both the European Union and the United Kingdom are party to it. However, EU laws may still to continue to have significant impact in the United Kingdom.[7]
- The United Kingdom decides to have another referendum. The European Union extends the Article 50 TEU period to allow that referendum to take place, and the United Kingdom votes to remain in the European Union.

This chapter does not deal with the last scenario as that if that happened, there would be no Brexit. It considers the other three scenarios. This is, in part because of this uncertainty about what will happen. However, there is a value beyond that. These scenarios offer different visions

---

[3] Conclusions of the European Council of 25 November 2018, EUCO XT 20015/18.

[4] European Union Withdrawal Act 2018, s. 13(1)(a)–(c). The House of Lords does not need to have finished debating the motion if it has debated it for five sitting days.

[5] *Ibid.* s. 13(1)(d).   [6] *Ibid.* s. 13(3) and (4).   [7] See pp. 244–5 and 460–2.

for future relations between the European Union and the United Kingdom. Comparison of these visions exposes particularly vividly the benefits, challenges and choices contained within each of them.

3 THE WITHDRAWAL AGREEMENT

The Withdrawal Agreement is detailed and long. It contains some very specific points of interest to only a narrow range of parties. Of the most salient debates, the financial settlement involves a lot of money but raises few wider legal issues.[8] The chapter on Citizenship looks at how the Withdrawal Agreement addresses the rights of EU and UK citizens residing in the United Kingdom and European Union respectively.[9] This section, therefore, focuses on three aspects of the Agreement: the central legal features of the transition period; the governance of the Withdrawal Agreement; and, finally, the provisions on the avoidance of a hard border in the island of Ireland and how this may structure future trade relations between the European Union and the United Kingdom.

(i) The Transition Period

As no agreement establishing trade relations between the United Kingdom and the European Union can be negotiated until the United Kingdom has left the European Union, Brexit does something unusual. It allows, within the space of an eye blink, the United Kingdom and the European Union to go from having one of the closest of legal relationships for trade, namely the single market, to having one of the weakest, namely operating under the general regime provided by the WTO. Many transactions permissible under the former are not allowed under the latter. Furthermore, a whole operational infrastructure has to be established to govern things which, post Brexit, may now require authorisation: regulatory checks, customs posts and formalities, or migration controls for EU and UK citizens. Both parties realised, therefore, that it was in their mutual interest to establish a transition period which would allow the new legal relationship for trade to be established and the necessary operational infrastructure for it constructed.

> **Withdrawal Agreement, Preamble, para. 8**
>
> . . . it is in the interest of both the Union and the United Kingdom to determine a transition or implementation period during which – notwithstanding all consequences of the United Kingdom's withdrawal from the Union as regards the United Kingdom's participation in the institutions, bodies, offices and agencies of the Union . . . – Union law, including international agreements, should be applicable to and in the United Kingdom, and, as a general rule, with the same effect as regards the Member States, in order to avoid disruption in the period during which the agreement(s) on the future relationship will be negotiated.

The transition period is, in principle, to be short. It is due to finish on 31 December 2020 (twenty-one months after Brexit)[10] although the Joint Committee set up to monitor the agreement can extend this prior to 1 July 2020.[11] The central requirement of the transition period is the following:

---

[8] The estimates of United Kingdom liabilities are been £35 billion and £39 billion, National Audit Office, *Exiting the EU: The Financial Settlement*, HC 946, Session 2017–19.
[9] See Ch.11.   [10] Withdrawal Agreement, Article 126.   [11] *Ibid.* Article 132.

> **Withdrawal Agreement, Article 127**
>
> (1) Unless otherwise provided in this Agreement, Union law shall be applicable to and in the United Kingdom during the transition period.

The United Kingdom continues to be bound by EU law during the transition period in just the same way as during its period of membership. Although different aspects of this have been explained throughout the book, it is worth summarising the extent of this obligation. The principles of the Union legal order (direct effect, primacy etc.) continue to apply within the United Kingdom, and its institutions are to interpret and apply EU law in the same manner as they are applied in the Union.[12] The EU Institutions, agencies and bodies will also continue to exercise powers in respect of the United Kingdom during the transition period.[13] The Court of Justice will, thus, continue to give preliminary rulings on references provided by UK courts.[14] The Commission will be able to launch infringement proceedings against the United Kingdom[15] or take enforcement action under its competition law powers against undertakings based in the United Kingdom.[16] Decisions of EU Institutions, agencies and bodies will have the same binding effects on and in the United Kingdom as they do in the member States.[17] This is equally true of Court judgments.[18]

However, there is a twist. The short length of the transition period could allow the United Kingdom not to comply with many decisions as there would be little time for Union Institutions to prosecute illegal acts and, by the time the matter reached the Court of Justice, the United Kingdom would have left. Provision is, therefore, made for the Commission to take the United Kingdom before the Court of Justice for up to four years after the United Kingdom failed to comply with EU law or give it proper effect.[19] As the United Kingdom might commit illegal acts right up until the end of the transition period, there is, therefore, the possibility for infringement proceedings to be launched against it four years after the end of that period.[20]

There is one significant exception to this obligation to obey all EU law. In fields of EU exclusive competence, the United Kingdom may enter into international agreements with non-EU States during the transition period provided that these do not enter into force during the transition period unless so authorised by the Union.[21] The important fields here are commercial policy (trade agreements with non-EU States) and fisheries.[22] However, this derogation may be of less use than imagined. First, the United Kingdom must conclude these in a way which is 'not prejudicial to the Union interests'.[23] Aggressive undercutting of the Union trade relations with non-EU States would, therefore, probably be seen as illegal. Secondly, and less legalistically, very few non-EU States will be willing to conclude an agreement with the United Kingdom until its long-term trade relations with the Union are settled. This is because the Union will remain for the foreseeable period the United Kingdom's largest trading partner. Non-EU States will, therefore, want to see if the EU–UK trading relationship offers competitive advantages to Union traders that are not offered to their own businesses. The United Kingdom's relationship with the

---

[12] *Ibid.* Article 127(3).   [13] *Ibid.* Article 131.   [14] *Ibid.* Article 86(2).   [15] *Ibid.* Article 87(1).
[16] *Ibid.* Article 95(2).   [17] *Ibid.* Article 95(1).   [18] *Ibid.* Article 89.
[19] *Ibid.* Article 87(2). There is also provision for the Commission to start administrative proceedings for breach of State aid rules for four years after the transition period, *ibid.* Article 93(1).
[20] *Ibid.* Article 87(1).   [21] *Ibid.* Article 129(4).   [22] Article 3(1) TFEU.   [23] Withdrawal Agreement, Article 129(3).

Union will also affect its value as a place of investment for non-EU businesses. If trade is easy between the European Union and the United Kingdom, the latter becomes more attractive as a place for investment for non-EU businesses as investments in the United Kingdom can then sell easily to the Union.

If United Kingdom obligations are extensive, the political rights of the UK authorities and citizens are highly limited during the transitional period. The general rule is that the United Kingdom is not to have representatives or participate in the decision-making of the EU Institutions, agencies or bodies.[24] The UK Parliament shall not be able to participate in the yellow or orange card procedures policing EU legislative proposals for their compliance with the subsidiarity principle[25] and the Bank of England will not be participate in the European System of Central Banks (ESCB).[26] The UK Government will not be able to submit initiatives, proposals or requests to the EU Institutions.[27] UK citizens will not be able to participate in the European Citizens Initiative, or stand or vote in European Parliament elections or municipal elections in EU States.[28]

There are some limited exceptions to this policy of exclusion. UK representatives or experts can participate, but not vote, in comitology committees if either the measures involved are individual acts addressed to the United Kingdom or persons residing or established there, or United Kingdom presence is necessary and in the interest of the Union, particularly for effective implementation of EU law during the transition period.[29] The UK Government shall also be consulted on draft Union acts which refer specifically to the United Kingdom with a view to its proper application and implementation of these.[30] It shall also be able to intervene in cases before the Court of Justice.[31] Finally, Commission consultation papers and annual legislative programmes shall be forwarded to the UK Parliament.[32]

Two central concerns have been expressed about the transition period.

The first is that the United Kingdom is a rule-taker during the period with little political voice. The transitional period was, thus, described polemically as making the United Kingdom a 'vassal State'.[33] However, few EU laws will have both been agreed after Brexit and have had to be transposed by the end of 2020. The central EU laws in which the United Kingdom will not have a voice are likely, therefore, to be some Regulations and some comitology measures. Moreover, it can always repeal these at the end of the transition period.

The second concern goes to the length of the transition period. It is predicated on there being a trade agreement by the end of it. In 2012, the average trade agreement around the world was found to take twenty-eight months to conclude. However, this time increases significantly if either the economies involved are complex, there are many States involved or the agreement seeks to be ambitious (all true here).[34] The European Commission claims, for example, that there are over thirty stages to concluding a deal because of the wide array of interests that must be accommodated.[35] Its recent practice gives few grounds to be optimistic. Its agreement with

---

[24] *Ibid.* Articles 7(1) and 128(1).   [25] *Ibid.* Article 128(2).   [26] *Ibid.* Article 128(4).   [27] *Ibid.* Article 128(3).
[28] *Ibid.* Article 127(1)(b).   [29] *Ibid.* Article 128(5).   [30] *Ibid.* Article 128(7).   [31] *Ibid.* Article 90.
[32] *Ibid.* Article 128(2).
[33] 'David Davis Rejects "Vassal State" Claim over Brexit Transition', *The Guardian*, 24 January 2018.
[34] C. Moser and A. Rose, 'Why Do Trade Negotiations Take So Long?' (2012) 27 *JEI* 280. See also L. Lechner and S. Wüthrich, 'Seal the Deal: Bargaining Positions, Institutional Design, and the Duration of Preferential Trade Negotiations' (2018) 44 *International Interactions* 833.
[35] http://trade.ec.europa.eu/doclib/docs/2012/june/tradoc_149616.pdf.

Canada took eight years of negotiations before it entered into force; that with Japan was approved by the Council after six years but is still not in force; that with Singapore took eleven years and has been agreed but part of it has still to be implemented by every national parliament. Negotiations have been going on with India and Indonesia since 2007 without success.[36]

Possible extension of the transition period makes concerns about its undemocratic qualities more acute. One starts to run into situations where large numbers of Directives have been agreed during the transition period without British voice now have to be implemented by the United Kingdom. It raises further challenges. As extension of the period has to be agreed by both parties, there is always the danger that one party loses patience with the consequence that it terminates the transition period before the new trading relationship has been established, in which case one is in the worst of all worlds. The United Kingdom will have had to incur the democratic costs of the transition period without securing the benefits for both parties of an orderly readjustment to a new trading relationship. Finally, there is the danger that extension becomes a bargaining chip. One side, probably the European Union because of its relative strength, threatens to refuse extension unless concessions are made by the other because it knows that premature termination of the transition period would generate such acute dislocation.[37]

(ii) The Governance of the Withdrawal Agreement

Following the end of the transition period, arguably the most significant part of the Withdrawal Agreement for individual rights, the part on the rights of EU citizens resident in the United Kingdom is subject to a special regime. UK courts may refer questions on interpretation of that part of the Agreement for eight years after the end of the transition period[38] and an independent authority will be established to police (and take before UK courts) administrative authorities who are breaching EU citizens' rights under the Agreement.[39] This regime is addressed in more detail in the chapter on EU Citizenship.[40]

There are three central bodies or processes governing the rest of the Agreement. First, a Joint Committee is responsible for the implementation and application of the Agreement. Secondly, a judicial dialogue is to facilitate consistent interpretation of the Agreement. Thirdly, a system of arbitration is to settle disputes between the European Union and the United Kingdom.

(a) The Joint Committee

On paper, the Joint Committee seems the most powerful body established by the Withdrawal Agreement. It comprises representatives of the Union and the United Kingdom,[41] and each may refer to it any 'any issue relating to the implementation, application and interpretation of this Agreement.'[42]

---

[36] http://trade.ec.europa.eu/doclib/docs/2006/december/tradoc_118238.pdf.

[37] For an interesting critique that it would have been better to have a 'transition and implementation facility' in which the transition period simply ends when a new trade relationship is established, see K. Armstrong, 'Transition Time: 3 Options for Extending the Transition Period', 24 October 2018, www.cam.ac.uk/sites/www.cam.ac.uk/files/transition_time_-_3_options_for_a_new_transitional_periodths.pdf.

[38] Withdrawal Agreement, Article 158.   [39] *Ibid*. Article 159(1).   [40] See Ch. 11.

[41] Withdrawal Agreement, Article 164(1).   [42] *Ibid*. Article 164(3).

However, the Agreement envisages that the Joint Committee will not be a hands-on body. It is only to supervise and facilitate implementation and application of the Agreement,[43] and there is only provision for it to meet a minimum of once per year.[44] To that end, its central roles seem to be twofold.

It is, first, to establish and supervise specialised committees, comprising representatives of both parties, covering particular aspects of the Agreement.[45] These are to consider points of mutual interest that fall within their remit, seek to prevent problems arising and resolve disputes.[46] The Agreement itself provides for such committees over citizens' rights, Ireland/Northern Ireland, the Sovereign Bases on Cyprus, the financial settlement, and Gibraltar.[47] The Agreement anticipates that most of the daily work surrounding the Agreement will be done by these specialised committees.

The Joint Committee is, secondly, to take Decisions regarding the Agreement where the latter so provides.

Withdrawal Agreement, Article 108

(1) The Joint Committee shall, for the purposes of this Agreement, have the power to adopt decisions in respect of all matters for which this Agreement so provides and to make appropriate recommendations to the Union and the United Kingdom.

(2) The decisions adopted by the Joint Committee shall be binding on the Union and the United Kingdom, and the Union and the United Kingdom shall implement those decisions. They shall have the same legal effect as this Agreement.

(3) The Joint Committee shall adopt its decisions and make its recommendations by mutual consent.

The Agreement provides for the Joint Committee to take many significant decisions. It decides, *inter alia*, when citizens from the EEA States (Norway, Iceland and Liechtenstein) and Switzerland resident in the United Kingdom shall be granted the same rights as EU citizens;[48] whether to extend the transition agreement;[49] how much the United Kingdom will contribute to the EU Budget during any extension of the transition period;[50] whether the authority policing the safeguard of EU citizens' rights in the United Kingdom[51] or the Protocol ensuring no hard border in the island of Ireland needs to be retained;[52] and whether the United Kingdom has to adopt further laws to ensure a level playing field between it and the European Union.[53]

The extent of these decision-taking powers makes the governance arrangements surrounding this Joint Committee concerning. There is to be no oversight by either the United Kingdom, European (or in the case of the Protocol on Ireland/Northern Ireland) or Irish parliaments. There is no requirement for it to engage with civil society or other stakeholders. It does not appear that it can be judicially reviewed. Most concerning, its work can be done in secrecy.

---

[43] *Ibid.* Article 164(4)(a). [44] *Ibid.* Article 164(1). [45] *Ibid.* Article 164(4)(b). [46] *Ibid.* Article 164(5).
[47] *Ibid.* Article 165. [48] *Ibid.* Article 33(2). [49] *Ibid.* Article 132(1). [50] *Ibid.* Article 132(3)(a).
[51] *Ibid.* Article 159(3). [52] *Ibid.* Protocol on Ireland/Northern Ireland, Article 20.
[53] *Ibid.* Protocol on Ireland/Northern Ireland, Article 6.

> **Withdrawal Agreement, Annex VIII, Rule 10**
>
> (1) Unless otherwise decided by the co-chairs, the meetings of the Joint Committee shall be confidential.
> (2) Where the Union or the United Kingdom submits information considered as confidential or protected from disclosure under its laws and regulations to the Joint Committee or any specialised committee, the other party shall treat that information received as confidential.
> (3) Without prejudice to paragraph 2, the Union and the United Kingdom may each decide individually on whether to publish the decisions and recommendations adopted by the Joint Committee in their respective official publication journals.

Although the Agreement provides that the parties have the option of transparency, there are grounds for being pessimistic. EU law prohibits access to documents where this would undermine the Union's international relations.[54] As the United Kingdom is now a non-EU State, the Union Institutions will now simply be able to refuse access to information on the grounds that it will affect relations with the United Kingdom. This seems a weak reason to give on matters of such import as the state of peace in the island of Ireland or the rights of EU citizens, some of whom will have lived their whole lives in the United Kingdom.

(b) The Regular Dialogue

The second central process in the Withdrawal Agreement is the regular dialogue.

> **Withdrawal Agreement, Article 163**
>
> In order to facilitate the consistent interpretation of this Agreement and in full deference to the independence of courts, the Court of Justice of the European Union and the United Kingdom's highest courts shall engage in regular dialogue, analogous to the dialogue in which the Court of Justice of the European Union engages with the highest courts of the Member States.

It will be curious to see how this dialogue unfolds. It may be quite limited. Whilst there may well be significant litigation on the rights of EU and UK citizens resident in the United Kingdom and European Union respectively, it is not clear how much of the rest of Withdrawal Agreement will be litigated. However, its significance may lie in its being the only institutional forum where senior UK courts and the Court of Justice can meet. It provides an opportunity, possibly informally, for them to discuss the more general interaction of EU and UK law. As discussed earlier,[55] this interaction will be extensive. Judgments of the Court of Justice given prior to Brexit will continue to have strong binding effects after Brexit,[56] with only the UK Supreme Court and the High Court of Justiciary in Scotland able to depart from it.[57] Furthermore, whilst UK courts are not bound by the case law of the Court of Justice delivered after Brexit,

---

[54] Regulation 1049/2001/EC regarding public access to European Parliament, Council and Commission documents, OJ 2001, L 145/43, Article 4(1)(a). See pp. 103–9.

[55] See pp. 197–200.   [56] European Union Withdrawal Act 2018, s. 6(3)(a).

[57] *Ibid.* s. 6(4). Even these courts only depart from the case law of the Court of Justice under the same test as they would depart from their own case law. *Ibid.* s. 6(5).

they can have due regard to it, and it may continue to have significant authoritative effects.[58] There is likely to be much to discuss. The dialogue might be a place where senior UK courts can set out to their Court of Justice counterparts how established EU law doctrines, if left untempered, cause problems for UK law. Conversely, it might be a place where the Court of Justice seeks to persuade UK courts of the merits of a new doctrine of EU law. In short, the regular dialogue could become a place of mutual influence.

(c) Dispute Settlement

The Agreement commits the European Union and the United Kingdom to attempt to settle disputes informally and in good faith, in the first resort. If one party has a grievance with the interpretation or application of the Agreement by the other, it must commence any dispute settlement proceedings, therefore, by proving a written notice to the Joint Committee.[59] The parties must then try to find mutual agreement within three months.[60]

It is only at the expiry of this three-month period that a party may require the establishment of an arbitration panel,[61] which shall be comprised of five members.[62] Two will be nominated by each of the parties, and the fifth will be nominated by mutual agreement.[63] The arbitrators shall be chosen from a list of twenty-five persons, of whom the Union and the United Kingdom each propose ten and jointly propose five persons to be possible chairs.[64] These persons must be independent, act in their personal capacity, and not take instruction from any organisation or government.[65]

The panel should, in principle, be established within fifteen days of the request for its establishment.[66] It must seek to work by consensus. If this is not possible, it can provide a majority ruling but dissents should not be published.[67] It should, in principle, notify the parties of its ruling within twelve months of its establishment or provide reasons for the delay and when it intends to conclude its work.[68] Within ten days of its establishment, either party may make a reasoned request that the case is urgent. The panel must decide on whether this is the case within fifteen days, and, if this is the case, it must notify the parties of its ruling within six months.[69]

This arbitration panel process has two particularly distinctive features.

First, there is its relationship to the Court of Justice. The rulings of the arbitration panel are binding on both the European Union and the United Kingdom.[70] In principle, the Court of Justice is, therefore, bound by its rulings as authoritative interpretations of an international agreement concluded by the Union. However, the Court of Justice regards any international agreement by the Union which does not respect the autonomy of the EU legal order as illegal.[71] In *Achmea*, it will be remembered, the Court held that an international agreement between

---

[58] *Ibid.* s. 6(2).   [59] Article 169(1) Withdrawal Agreement.   [60] *Ibid.* Article 170(1).

[61] *Ibid.* It may be established earlier by mutual agreement. *Ibid.* Article 170(2).

[62] Failing that, the parties may request the Secretary General of the Permanent Court of Arbitration to nominate somebody. *Ibid.* Article 171(3).

[63] *Ibid.* Article 171(5).   [64] *Ibid.* Article 171(1).   [65] *Ibid.* Article 181(1).

[66] *Ibid.* Article 171(4). If this is not procedures to allow the Secretary General of the Permanent Court of Arbitration to impose a panel at the request of either party. *Ibid.* Article 171(8) and (9).

[67] *Ibid.* Article 180(1).   [68] *Ibid.* Article 173(1).   [69] *Ibid.* Article 173(2).   [70] *Ibid.* Article 175.

[71] Opinion 2/13, *Accession of the EU to the ECHR*, EU:C:2014:2454.

Netherlands and Slovakia which allowed investors to take the host State to an arbitration panel violated this principle.[72] The arbitration panel could make rulings on EU law which displaced those of the national courts, and, as it was not a court and could not therefore, refer questions of EU law to the Court of Justice, there was a consequent undermining of the effectiveness of EU law. This judgment has been taken into account in the Withdrawal Agreement.

Withdrawal Agreement, Article 174

(1) Where a dispute submitted to arbitration in accordance with this Title raises a question of interpretation of a concept of Union law, a question of interpretation of a provision of Union law referred to in this Agreement or a question of whether the United Kingdom has complied with its obligations under Article 89 (2),[73] the arbitration panel shall not decide on any such question. In such case, it shall request the Court of Justice of the European Union to give a ruling on the question. The Court of Justice of the European Union shall have jurisdiction to give such a ruling which shall be binding on the arbitration panel.

The arbitration panel shall make the request referred to in the first subparagraph after having heard the parties.

If this article is an attempt to protect the system of arbitration against legal challenge by requiring it to defer to the Court of Justice on points of EU law, it raises further uncertainty, namely what is caught by a 'concept of Union law' or 'a provision of Union law'. On one view, every concept and provision of the Withdrawal Agreement is a concept and provision of EU law as, being an international agreement concluded by the European Union, it forms an integral part of the EU legal order.[74] On this view, the arbitration panels would have to refer interpretation of any Withdrawal Agreement provision to the Court of Justice. Such an interpretation would result in their being little more than a post box for the Court of Justice, who would, in practice, be the body that settles all disputes. This would be an unusual situation in which the court of one party settles disputes between it and another party. On another view, references to the Court of Justice should only be made when the panel is called to interpret a provision which either explicitly references another EU law or involves a core principle of EU law, such as free movement of persons or equal treatment.

The second noteworthy feature concerns non-compliance with an arbitration panel ruling. A party (the respondent) has a reasonable period of time to comply with any ruling. It shall set out the time it requires. If there is disagreement about that, the complainant can go back to the panel to ask it to set a time. The respondent is to notify the complainant of the measures it has taken to comply with the ruling. However, if the complainant feels that compliance has not taken place within the reasonable period of time, it can request the original arbitration panel to rule on the matter.[75]

A ruling of non-compliance generates sanctions.

---

[72] *Slovak Republic* v. *Achmea*, C-284/16, EU:C:2018:158.

[73] This provision concerns judgments by the Court of Justice which have found the United Kingdom in breach of the Agreement. It requires the United Kingdom to take the necessary measures to comply with the judgment.

[74] *R* v. *HM Commissioners for Her Majesty's Revenue and Customs, ex parte Western Sahara Campaign UK*, C-266/16, EU:C:2018:118.

[75] *Ibid.* Article 177(2).

> ### Withdrawal Agreement, Article 178
>
> (1) If the arbitration panel rules in accordance with Article 177(2) that the respondent has failed to comply with the arbitration panel ruling referred to in Article 173, at the request of the complainant it may impose a lump sum or penalty payment to be paid to the complainant. In determining the lump sum or penalty payment, the arbitration panel shall take into account the seriousness of the non-compliance and underlying breach of obligation, the duration of the non-compliance and underlying breach of obligation.

In allowing the arbitration panel to impose either a lump sum or a penalty, Article 178(1) mirrors the text of Article 260(2) TFEU, which allows the Court of Justice to impose these when a Member State has failed to comply with an earlier judgment. It also largely follows the case law of the Court of Justice and Commission practice on Article 260 TFEU with regard to the principles which will guide the size of the fine, namely the duration of the infringement and its seriousness.[76] One would expect this practice, therefore, to guide panels in the sanctions that they impose.

The Withdrawal Agreement allows for further sanctions to be imposed where either these fines are not paid within one month or the respondent has not complied with the arbitration panel ruling within six months. In such circumstances, the complainant can suspend any part of the Withdrawal Agreement other than that on EU and UK citizens' rights and parts of any other agreement between the two which set that out. Any suspension must be proportionate, taking into account the gravity of the breach and the rights in question, and whether, if the respondent is not complying with an earlier ruling, it has paid or is paying any fine imposed.[77]

This suspension is likely to be calibrated to hurt the respondent's (who is the party in breach) interests. The latter, furthermore, cannot resort to countermeasures as a response. Furthermore, they are not allowed to walk away from the Agreement. However, suspension is intended to be temporary and must be stopped if either the respondent withdraws the measure and starts to comply with the Agreement or the parties settle the dispute.[78] Dispute about whether compliance has taken place or the countermeasures are proportionate can be referred back to the original arbitration panel to rule on these.[79]

The use of arbitration here has been criticised on the grounds that it will take time to establish and is likely to generate less legal certainty than a court system.[80] However, the centrality of the arbitration procedure can, therefore, be overstated. The system of arbitration must be seen alongside other institutional procedures. The use of the preliminary reference procedure and the independent authority for citizens' rights for eight years after the end of the transition period has already been mentioned.[81] In addition, the United Kingdom can be brought before the Court of Justice after the end of the transitional period if it breaches its obligations with regard to the financial settlement and its liabilities thereunder.[82]

---

[76] *Commission* v. *France*, C-304/02, EU:C:2005:444; European Commission, 'Application of Article 228 of the EC Treaty', SEC(2005)1658. One principle is omitted, namely the ability of a Member State to pay, possibly because this is difficult to apply to the Union as a whole. On the principles more broadly, see pp. 361–3.

[77] Withdrawal Agreement, Article 178(2).

[78] *Ibid.* Article 179(5). The respondent must notify the complainant of the measures taken and request an end to the penalty payment or suspension of obligations. *Ibid.* Article 179(1).

[79] *Ibid.* Article 179(2) and (3) respectively.

[80] C. Baudenbacher, '"Britzerland": The Problem of Dispute Resolution Post-Brexit', *LSE Brexit Blog*, 29 October 2018.

[81] Withdrawal Agreement, Articles 158 and 159(1).   [82] *Ibid.* Article 160.

(iii) The Protocol on Ireland/Northern Ireland

(a) The Dilemma of the Border: The Need for External Borders to Have Customs Checks versus the Imperative of No Hard Border on the Island of Ireland

The most politically contentious and technically difficult challenge for the Withdrawal Agreement was ensuring the absence of a hard border within the island of Ireland. This was addressed in a Protocol to the Withdrawal Agreement, the Protocol on Ireland/Northern Ireland.

> **Withdrawal Agreement, Protocol on Ireland/Northern Ireland, Article 1**
>
> (3) This Protocol sets out arrangements necessary to address the unique circumstances on the island of Ireland, maintain the necessary conditions for continued North-South cooperation, avoid a hard border and protect the 1998 Agreement in all its dimensions.

The border question raises two issues which pull in opposite directions: the role of border controls in relation to trade in goods, on the one hand, and the significance of no hard border in the island of Ireland for both the peace process and inter-communal relations, on the other.

Border controls regulate the movement of people through the use of immigration controls. The absence of these between Ireland and Northern Ireland does not pose an issue here. A Common Travel Area exists between Ireland and the United Kingdom which harks back to 1922 and provides for no border controls between the two.[83] This does not operate as a backdoor for non-EU nationals whereby they could enter the rest of the Union from the United Kingdom without EU controls, or vice versa for the United Kingdom. This is because Ireland is not part of the Schengen area, and controls on movement of persons are placed between it and the rest of the European Union.[84]

The Withdrawal Agreement provides that Ireland and the United Kingdom shall continue to make arrangements for the Common Travel Area, and that the United Kingdom shall ensure that the Common Travel Area shall continue to apply without affecting Ireland's obligations under EU law with regard to free movement of EU citizens.[85] If free movement of persons within the island of Ireland is relatively unproblematic for EU–UK relations, it may raise other concerns. As the only land frontier between the United Kingdom and the rest of the world, it might lead to Northern Ireland being treated by UK authorities the same way as some other EU States treat such areas, namely as a border zone particularly vulnerable to irregular migration and criminality, with this leading, in turn, to increased checks and controls within its territory.[86]

The position on free movement of goods is more fraught. Borders control the movement of goods by establishing customs checks. These checks do a multiplicity of things:

- *Regulatory compliance and conformity assessment*: They check that the good entering the territory was made under a legal regime that allows it to be lawfully marketed in the territory

---

[83] On its history and institutional basis see B. Ryan, 'The Common Travel Area between Britain and Ireland' (2001) 64 *MLR* 855; I. Maher, *The Common Travel Area: More Than Just Travel* (Dublin–London, RIA & British Academy, 2017).

[84] Protocol on the Application of Certain Aspects of Article 26 TFEU to the United Kingdom and Ireland, Article 3.

[85] Protocol on Ireland/Northern Ireland, Article 5. The last requirement was added to prevent the United Kingdom ever insisting on Ireland putting controls between it and other Member States that would violate EU law as a condition for continuation of the Common Travel Area.

[86] House of Commons Northern Ireland Affairs Committee, *The Land Border between Northern Ireland and Ireland*, 2nd Report, Session 2017–19, 31. On this elsewhere within the Union see pp. 536–9.

(i.e. that the Chinese law which regulates a good coming from China is one that is recognised as allowing it to be lawfully marketed within the European Union). They also check for conformity assessment, namely that the good, in question, actually does comply with the conditions required (i.e. it followed the requirements of the law in question).

- *Tariffs and Trade Measures*: Unless a free trade area is established, tariffs must be applied on all goods which cross the border. In addition, checks will have to be made that the goods are ones for which liberalised trade is allowed (i.e. not subject to quotas) and that they are not subject to trade sanctions.
- *Collection of Excise Duties and VAT*: Tariffs are taxes where the taxable event is the foreign good crossing the border. This is not true of excise duties and VAT which are taxes on the sale and consumption of goods within a territory. However, to avoid tax fraud, most States collect such taxes at customs controls with traders able to reclaim the tax subsequently if the taxable event (i.e. sale or consumption) does not occur within the State's territory.
- *Border Inspection Post Controls*: Livestock, animal feed and food pose particular risks to human (and animal) health. Checks are made at the border to protect against these threats. In the case of the Union, these have to be done at identified Border Inspection Posts with the necessary expertise to identify these threats.
- *Transport Service Checks*: Checks may be made to ensure that the vehicle is safe and complies with the necessary legislation and that the driver (or pilot) is qualified to drive it, and meets other regulatory requirements such as not having driven for excessive numbers of hours.

As the Irish border will be a border with a non-EU State after Brexit, Ireland would, in principle, be expected to carry out all these checks at the Irish/Northern Irish border on behalf of the Union as a whole. The Common Travel Area does not help here because single-market legislation prohibits the imposition of such checks between Member States – so between Ireland and France – irrespective of the huge and unwanted cost that such checks would impose on Ireland.

A number of further things have to be noted about these checks.

First, technology and administrative cooperation can allow much of the work to be done away from the border, particularly with regard to collection of taxes. However, any one of the grounds above will necessitate border controls. Furthermore, technology does not erase the need for some border checks for any of the above. If it did, this technology would be used around the world as customs checks are administratively expensive and impose significant costs for business. There would, thus, be every reason to use it.

Secondly, the requirement of customs checks applies equally to the United Kingdom. The most-favoured-nation principle of the General Agreement on Tariffs and Trade, the central agreement governing international trade in goods, requires that import and export rules and formalities applied to goods from one State must also be equally applied to goods originating from or destined for other States from around the world.[87] If the United Kingdom applies no customs checks to goods coming directly from the European Union (as would be the case here) it must, therefore, also do so for all goods that arrive directly, be it by ship or plane, from China or the United States. The European Union would have to do likewise if it allows goods from the United Kingdom to enter its market without import checks.

The only exception from this requirement of customs checks is if the European Union and the United Kingdom establish a free trade agreement, customs union or single market between

---

[87] General Agreement on Tariffs and Trade (1994), 1867 UNTS 187, Article I(1).

themselves.[88] If they do this, there is the possibility for them to apply fewer border formalities to trade crossing the island of Ireland than to trade coming from other parts of the world. However, this means that there can be unilateral relaxation of border controls. The relaxation of customs checks by each depends on reciprocal action by the other.

Thirdly, the abolition of customs checks is possible if there is harmonisation of laws in those areas of activity which require these checks. Common rules on animal health or product standards can remove the need for health checks and regulatory compliance, for example, as they allow the importing State to be confident that identical standards to its own were applied in the exporting State. In addition, there must also be common standards for inspections, authorisation and certification of particular activities. There must, finally, be administrative trust and cooperation so that authorities picking up an issue within one territory can liaise with authorities in another if the issue arises because of activities in the latter's territory. This is, indeed, what has taken place within the single market, and why there is no need for customs controls. However, it requires a lot of common rules and extensive administrative cooperation.

However, as was mentioned, in opposition to all this, the absence of a hard border between Northern Ireland and the Republic of Ireland is seen as underpinning the Belfast Agreement 1998 ('Good Friday Agreement') which has secured peace in Northern Ireland. The Agreement contains three elements of particular importance for this debate. First it established significant self-government for Northern Ireland with a number of important issues requiring agreement of both communities within its Assembly and its executive requiring cross-community representation. Secondly, it provided for many policy fields to be coordinated for the whole of the island of Ireland through institutional arrangements comprising both Northern Irish and Irish authorities. Thirdly, it allowed Northern Irish citizens to have Irish or UK passports, or both. This allowed Northern Irish citizens to give expression to their different identities. An Irish nationalist could hold an Irish passport, feel that she was governed by local and pan Irish arrangements and, as there was no visible frontier, travel within the country of Ireland, as she saw it, without being aware of when she moved from one part to another. Equally, a Unionist could hold a UK passport, know she was governed by local and UK arrangements, and travel freely as within the United Kingdom as somebody living in the Isle of Wight or the Scottish islands.[89]

The absence of visible borders between Northern Ireland and either the Republic or the rest of the United Kingdom is central to all this. It has huge political and cultural value for both communities within Northern Ireland.[90]

K. Hayward, 'The Pivotal Position of the Irish Border in the UK's Withdrawal from the European Union' (2018) 22 *Space and Polity* 238, 239

The acute difficulty facing the negotiators was that it was common UK and Irish EU membership that had created the very conditions through which the border has been transformed from a sharp

---

[88] *Ibid.* Article XXIV(5).

[89] W. Hazleton, 'Devolution and the Diffusion of Power: The Internal and Transnational Dimensions of the Belfast Agreement' (2000) 15 *Irish Political Studies* 25.

[90] For other accounts of how Brexit challenges this balance see E. Tannam, 'Intergovernmental and Cross-Border Civil Service Cooperation: The Good Friday Agreement and Brexit' (2018) 17 *Ethnopolitics* 243; C. Macall, 'Brexit, Bordering and Bodies on the Island of Ireland' (2018) 17 *Ethnopolitics* 292.

dividing line between states into a meeting point between 'friendly neighbours and partners in the European Union'.[91] The peace process embodied in the 1998 Good Friday (Belfast) Agreement was facilitated by EU membership. In its most simple terms, European integration enabled national sovereignties and identities to be viewed as complementary rather than oppositional. Such partnership is built into the cross-border institutions established by the 1998 Agreement that function specifically to ensure direct input from the Irish government into matters of common concern. The North/South Ministerial Council, its Joint Secretariat and 'implementation bodies' working on an all-island of Ireland basis, demonstrate the integral role played by cross-border cooperation in the governance of Northern Ireland. And at a wider level, the British–Irish Council facilitates closer cooperation between regions and nations across Ireland, the United Kingdom and the Crown Dependencies.

The innovation of the 1998 Agreement centred on a careful compromise: to accept the validity of both Irish nationalism and British unionism, each of which have competing views about the legitimacy of the Irish border, but to weaken the violent potential of these competing ideologies by reducing the actual significance of the Irish border in day-to-day terms. If it is less important as an economic, social and cultural barrier, it is less powerful as a tool for political and ideological mobilization. As a consequence, any significant shift in the status of the border has consequences not just for Northern Ireland but for the peace process more broadly.

This embedding of the border question within support for the peace process and the maintenance of the Good Friday Agreement was evident in other commitments in the Protocol.

Withdrawal Agreement. Protocol on Ireland/Northern Ireland, Article 4

(1) The United Kingdom shall ensure that no diminution of rights, safeguards and equality of opportunity as set out in that part of the 1998 Agreement entitled Rights, Safeguards and Equality of Opportunity results from its withdrawal from the Union, including in the area of protection against discrimination as enshrined in the provisions of Union law listed in Annex 1 to this Protocol,[92] and shall implement this paragraph through dedicated mechanisms.

(2) The United Kingdom shall continue to facilitate the related work of the institutions and bodies set up pursuant to the 1998 Agreement, including the Northern Ireland Human Rights Commission, the Equality Commission for Northern Ireland and the Joint Committee of representatives of the Human Rights Commissions of Northern Ireland and Ireland, in upholding human rights and equality standards.

This provision is significant as the United Kingdom commitments about the status of Northern Ireland, the rights of citizens there, and its institutional arrangements are now longer made just to the Republic of Ireland. They are also now made to the European Union and its Member States as breach of these commitments will also involve breaches of the Withdrawal Agreement, which will justify intervention by the European Union. Undoubtedly, this changes the terms of trade surrounding the Agreement. The United Kingdom's counterpart is no longer a State with a smaller GDP and population but a polity with a much larger GDP and population, and correspondingly greater leverage over the United Kingdom.

Within this context, the EU, Irish and UK authorities all recognised the importance of no hard border on the island of Ireland. In December 2017, in a Joint Report on the progress of

---

91 Phrase taken from the Preamble to the British–Irish Agreement (1998).
92 Annex 1 contains all EU equal opportunities legislation.

negotiations, the United Kingdom set out a definition of what it was committed to avoiding. A hard border would include 'any physical infrastructure or related checks or controls'.[93] There had, in other words, to be nothing at the border, not even a camera or a sign. There also had to be no controls or checks that were related to movement between the north and the south, be these checks in Belfast of food or animals destined for Dublin or schemes allowing traders not to pay customs duties on goods destined for Cork if they registered with authorities in Larne and paid their customs there.

(b) The Single Customs Territory

If customs checks could not be imposed on the island of Ireland, this begged the question where the external customs controls of the United Kingdom and the European Union would be. The Joint Report set out the answer:

> 49. The United Kingdom remains committed to protecting North-South cooperation and to its guarantee of avoiding a hard border. Any future arrangements must be compatible with these overarching requirements. . . . In the absence of agreed solutions, the United Kingdom will maintain full alignment with those rules of the Internal Market and the Customs Union which, now or in the future, support North-South cooperation, the all island economy and the protection of the 1998 Agreement.[94]

These principles were largely incorporated into the Withdrawal Agreement.

Withdrawal Agreement, Protocol on Ireland/Northern Ireland, Article 6

(1) Until the future relationship becomes applicable, a single customs territory between the Union and the United Kingdom shall be established ('the single customs territory'). Accordingly, Northern Ireland is in the same customs territory as Great Britain.

The single customs territory shall comprise:

(a) the customs territory of the Union . . . ; and

(b) the customs territory of the United Kingdom.

The rules set out in Annex 2 to this Protocol shall apply in respect of all trade in goods between the territories referred to in the second subparagraph, as well as, where so provided, between the single customs territory and third countries. With a view to ensuring the maintenance of the level playing field conditions required for the proper functioning of this paragraph, the provisions set out in Annex 4 to this Protocol shall apply. Where appropriate, the Joint Committee may modify Annex 4 in order to lay down higher standards for these level playing field conditions.

The Joint Committee shall adopt before 1 July 2020 the detailed rules relating to trade in goods between the two parts of the single customs territory for the implementation of this paragraph. In the absence of such a decision adopted before 1 July 2020, Annex 3 shall apply.

---

[93] European Commission, *Joint Report from the Negotiators of the European Union and the United Kingdom Government on Progress during Phase 1 of Negotiations under Article 50 TEU on the United Kingdom's Orderly Withdrawal from the European Union*, TF50 (2017) 19, para. 43.

[94] This definition has been replicated in the European Union Withdrawal Act 2018, s. 10(2)(b) which states nothing in that Act shall authorise border arrangements which 'feature physical infrastructure, including border posts, or checks and controls'.

> **(2)** ... The provisions of Union law listed in Annex 5 to this Protocol shall also apply, under the conditions set out therein, to and in the United Kingdom in respect of Northern Ireland.
>
> Articles 30 and 110 TFEU shall apply to and in the United Kingdom in respect of Northern Ireland. Quantitative restrictions on exports and imports shall be prohibited between the Union and Northern Ireland.

The provision is long and complex. The key sentence for the avoidance of a hard border is the last one in Article 6(2), which prohibits quantitative restrictions on exports and imports between the Union and Northern Ireland. In principle, this obviates the need for customs checks. Crucially, it does not do this between the European Union and the rest of the United Kingdom. However, it is the legislative apparatus necessary to secure this last sentence that makes the Protocol contentious. There are three types of legislative alignment that must take place:

- There are EU laws which must be applied across the whole of the United Kingdom to allow the establishment of a single customs territory. These are contained in the Annexes 2 and 3 referred to in Article 6(1) above.
- There are EU laws that only Northern Ireland must apply to allow free movement of goods to takes place between it and the Union. These are contained in the Annex 5 referred to in Article 6(2).
- There are, finally, requirements that must be applied by the whole of the United Kingdom to 'ensure the maintenance of level playing conditions' (Article 6(1) above). The Union was concerned that the absence of customs checks would be exploited. The United Kingdom might either not apply costly EU legislation or grant subsidies to its industries. United Kingdom industries, benefiting from this competitive advantage over Union industries, would then export to the Union surreptitiously via Ireland. These are set out in the Annex 4 referred to in Article 6(1).

It is now necessary to explore in more detail what each of these includes.

The common rules of the Single Customs Territory: The Single Customs Territory prohibits customs duties or charges having equivalent effect being placed on imports or exports between the European Union and all of the United Kingdom.[95] Any charge levied, no matter how small, because a good crossed from one into the other is prohibited unless it is part of a general internal system of taxation (e.g. VAT) or paid for services rendered (e.g. fees for veterinary inspections).[96] The United Kingdom must, in addition, align its laws with EU laws on the common customs tariff, rules of origin and the value of goods for customs purposes.[97] It is also to follow the Union Customs Code which sets out the procedures to be observed in applying EU customs legislation.[98]

Rules specific to Northern Ireland to ensure no hard border: Northern Ireland must apply EU legislation, by contrast, across a much wider swathe of activities. This includes all EU laws governing the single market in goods (e.g. laws on motor vehicles, textiles, pharmaceuticals and

---

[95] Protocol on Ireland/Northern Ireland, Annex II, Article 2(1).

[96] *Lubrizol France* v. *Caisse nationale du Régime social des indépendants participations extérieures*, C-39/17, EU: C:2018:438.

[97] Protocol on Ireland/Northern Ireland, Annex II, Article 3(1). This may be replaced by other rules if the Joint Committee so decides by 1 July 2020. *Ibid.*, Article 6(1).

[98] *Ibid.* Annex 3, Article 1.

medicinal products, cosmetics, toys, construction products and machinery, chemicals, food and animal feed, pesticides and biocides, GMOs, and intellectual property); animal health and veterinary checks; common commercial policy with non-EU States; administrative cooperation over collection of customs duties; waste; environmental law insofar as it relates to energy or product standards;[99] VAT and excise;[100] and electricity.[101] The extent of this alignment should not be understated. It runs to seventy-five pages in the draft Agreement.

Pan-UK rules to maintain a level playing field: There are few other EU laws that the United Kingdom as a whole must apply. It commits itself to certain thresholds in the fields of taxation, protection of the environment, and labour and social law, and to a series of robust institutional checks and balances. It will align UK law to EU law, however, only in the fields of competition and State aids.

In taxation, the parties agree to follow international standards on the governance and transparency of taxation and non-erosion of the fiscal base. The United Kingdom is also to apply three EU laws on tax avoidance, administration cooperation, and credit institutions' disclosure of profits/losses and taxes paid on these.[102] In both protection of the environment and labour and social law, the parties commit to non-regression. They shall not reduce the level of protection below that offered at the end of the transition period in the central fields of environmental, labour and social law.[103] Such commitments parallel those found in recent free trade agreements made between the European Union and other States, notably those with Canada and Singapore.[104] Trade agreements involving other States around the world contain weaker but similar commitments.[105] Such requirements are, thus, not uncommon and would almost certainly be contained in free trade agreements that the United Kingdom might sign in the future with either the European Union or many other States.

The United Kingdom does agree, however, to align its laws with EU laws on State aids.[106] Furthermore, the Withdrawal Agreement commits the European Union and United Kingdom to adopt competition laws on cartels, abuses of a dominant position, concentrations and public undertakings whose wording mirrors the wording of EU law in this field.[107] Insofar as these provisions reflect EU law, both parties are to interpret them in the light of the EU law criteria that have developed over time in this field.[108] The practical consequence is that the United Kingdom will be aligning its laws with EU law in these fields.

The most striking commitments concern the UK governance arrangements. An independent authority is, therefore, to be established to police UK environmental laws with the powers to receive complaints, launch its own enquiries and take UK authorities to court.[109] Another independent authority is to enjoy the same powers in respect of State aids as the Commission currently enjoys, namely to be notified of any State aid, to declare it illegal and to order

---

[99] These are all set out *ibid*. Annex 5.   [100] *Ibid*. Article 9 and Annex 6.   [101] *Ibid*. Article 11 and Annex 7.

[102] *Ibid*. Annex 4, Article 1(1) and (2).   [103] *Ibid*. Annex 4, Articles 2(1) and 4(1).

[104] Comprehensive Economic and Trade Agreement (CETA) between Canada, of the one part, and the European Union and its Member States, of the other part, OJ 2017, L 11/23, Articles 23.4 and 24.5; Free Trade Agreement between the European Union and Singapore (2018), Article 12.2, http://trade.ec.europa.eu/doclib/press/index.cfm?id=961.

[105] Comprehensive and Progressive Agreement for Trans-Pacific Partnership (2018), Articles 20.3.3 and 19.4, respectively; United States–Mexico–Canada Agreement (2018) Article 24.3.2, https://ustr.gov/trade-agreements/free-trade-agreements/united-states-mexico-canada-agreement/agreement-between.

[106] Protocol on Ireland/Northern Ireland, Annex 4, Article 7(1) and Annex 8. There is a limited exception for agriculture up to a certain level of subsidy to be determined by the Joint Committee. *Ibid*. Annex 4, Article 7(2).

[107] *Ibid*. Annex 4, Articles 17–20 respectively.   [108] *Ibid*. Annex 4, Article 21.   [109] *Ibid*. Annex 4, Article 3(2).

repayment.[110] This authority is be subject judicial oversight for its both actions and inaction with interested parties, including the European Commission, to have standing to challenge State aids before these courts.[111] The United Kingdom must also ensure an effective system of inspections, available administrative and judicial procedures, and effective remedies in the field of labour and social law.[112] There must, finally, be an effective system of enforcement of competition law within the United Kingdom, which must include available administrative and judicial proceedings that both permit effective and timely action against violations, and provide effective remedies.[113] However, as a quid pro quo, these provisions on competition law cannot be subject to arbitration proceedings between the United Kingdom and the European Union in the same way as most other fields of the Withdrawal Agreement.[114]

There are three possible concerns about the arrangements surrounding the Single Customs Territory from the United Kingdom perspective.

First, the restrictions on the United Kingdom as a whole are excessive. These will prevent the United Kingdom deregulating in the fields of environmental and labour law. The United Kingdom will also be a rule-taker in the fields of competition law and State aids, having to adapt its laws to what the Union legislates. However, the biggest anxiety expressed by opponents of the Withdrawal Agreement is that it be very difficult for the United Kingdom to have its own trade policy, and to conclude trade and investment agreements with non-EU States. The United Kingdom will not be able to negotiate on tariffs, offering tariff-free access in exchange for quid pro quos from the other State. Whilst it would be able to negotiate on services, intellectual property, public procurement, data and regulatory barriers to trade, tariffs are a central part of any trade agreement. Being unable to negotiate these both weakens UK leverage and might skew any deal.[115] It will also be very difficult for the United Kingdom to negotiate as a single territory as Northern Ireland has to observe other EU trade disciplines, most notably its trade defence rules. The United Kingdom might only be able to open part of its market to other States.

Secondly, if the United Kingdom, in general, is a rule-taker, this is even more so for Northern Ireland, which must follow a much wider number of EU laws concerning significant matters with no possibility for voice in the amendment or repeal of these laws. There is, indeed, an irony about a territory whether the question of democratic self-government has been so hotly contested and engaged with being robbed of that possibility for large swathes of its laws.

The third concern goes to what the Protocol might do to the relationship between Northern Ireland and the rest of the United Kingdom. The former is subject to considerable EU legislation, whereas the latter is not. It allows that goods marketed in the rest of the United Kingdom cannot be marketed in Northern Ireland, with the corresponding needs for checks at Northern Irish points of entry. To this end, the Protocol seeks to protect the internal market of the United Kingdom.

---

[110] *Ibid.* Annex 4, Article 9. On Commission powers here see pp. 989–91.   [111] *Ibid.* Annex 4, Article 11.
[112] *Ibid.* Annex 4, Article 6.   [113] *Ibid.* Annex 4, Article 24(1).   [114] *Ibid.* Annex 4, Article 24(2).
[115] For an interesting counterargument see S. Lowe, *An Effective UK Trade Policy and a Customs Union are Compatible* (London, Centre for European Reform, 2018).

Withdrawal Agreement, Protocol on Ireland/Northern Ireland, Article 7

(1) Nothing in this Protocol shall prevent the United Kingdom from ensuring unfettered market access for goods moving from Northern Ireland to the rest of the United Kingdom's internal market . . .

(2) Having regard to Northern Ireland's integral place in the United Kingdom's internal market, the Union and the United Kingdom shall use their best endeavours to facilitate, in accordance with applicable legislation and taking into account their respective regulatory regimes as well as their implementation, the trade between [Norther Ireland] and other parts of the territory of the United Kingdom. The Joint Committee shall keep under constant review the application of this paragraph and adopt appropriate recommendations with a view to avoiding, to the extent possible, controls at the ports and airports of Northern Ireland.

There is an asymmetry between this provision and the commitments concerning the island of Ireland. There is no commitment to the absence of a hard border but only to allow the United Kingdom to 'ensure unfettered market access'. This is a weaker commitment. To be sure, such checks are not inconsistent with being part of the same State. India, for example, has a tradition of internal regulatory and fiscal checkpoints and controls because of legislative differences between its States on sale taxes, product standards, and what can be sold.[116] However, even if this so, different things are being offered to the two communities. Irish nationalists are being offered an absence of a hard border on the island of Ireland whilst Unionists are not being guaranteed the same lack of checks within the United Kingdom. The commitment by the Union and the United Kingdom to use their 'best endeavours' to facilitate trade between Northern Ireland and the rest of the United Kingdom is telling, in this regard. It is not a particularly strong obligation and facilitating trade suggests a situation where trade is not unimpeded.

The problem of checks between Northern Ireland and the rest of the United Kingdom only arises if the latter adopts legislation which allows goods to be marketed which cannot be marketed under EU law (in which case checks have to be established in Northern Ireland) or prohibits the marketing of goods allowed under EU law (in which case checks have to be made in the rest of the United Kingdom). The UK authorities have made no legal commitment to refrain from doing either, and as the range of activities over which Northern Ireland must align with EU law is extensive, one would ordinarily expect this to become an issue over time.

Concerns led to a legislative amendment which prohibits customs duties or charges having equivalent effect being imposed on goods moving between Northern Ireland and the rest of the United Kingdom.

Taxation (Cross–border Trade) Act 2018, s. 55

(1) It shall be unlawful for Her Majesty's Government to enter into arrangements under which Northern Ireland forms part of a separate customs territory to Great Britain.

---

[116] On these traditions see *Towards an Indian Common Market: Removal of Restrictions on Internal Trade in Agriculture Commodities* (Rome, Food and Agriculture Organisation, 2005); A. Das-Gupta, 'Internal Trade Barriers in India: Fiscal Check-Posts' (2006) 7 *South Asia Economic Journal* 231.

In some ways, this amendment rather missed the point.[117] The bulk of customs checks have nothing to do with the collection of tariffs. There would still be a need for these other checks. Furthermore, insofar as the whole of the United Kingdom forms a Single Customs Territory with the European Union, the one thing which will not need checks between Northern Ireland and the United Kingdom are customs duties. However, such a criticism misses the broader motivation behind section 55, which is simply that there should be no checks between Northern Ireland and the United Kingdom. The only way to avoid this is for the rest of the United Kingdom to align its legislation with those EU laws with which Northern Ireland must align. This raised the vista for many that the Protocol on Ireland/Northern Ireland is setting out the template for future EU–UK trade relations more generally.

(c) The Indeterminate Length of the Protocol and the 'Jersey' Option

The Withdrawal Act agreement seeks to contain the tensions generated by it about the relationship between Northern Ireland and the rest of the United Kingdom by identifying the Protocol on Ireland/Northern Ireland as temporary.[118] The parties are, therefore, to use their 'best endeavours' to conclude by 31 December 2020 an agreement which supersedes it. This has led to the Protocol being characterised as a backstop.[119] It will not need to apply prior to 31 December 2020 as the whole of the United Kingdom will be applying pretty much all of EU law during that time, as this will be the transition period. A new arrangement will then come into play resolving the tensions between the need for customs checks at external borders and the imperative of no hard border in the island of Ireland. The Protocol will only be triggered if this does not happen.

To emphasise the temporary nature of the Protocol, the Parties agreed an interpretive instrument on this in March 2019.

Instrument relating to the agreement on the withdrawal of the United Kingdom of Great Britain and Northern Ireland from the European Union and the European Atomic Energy Community

3 Article 2(1) of the Protocol contains the obligation for the Union and the United Kingdom to 'use their best endeavours to conclude, by 31 December 2020, an agreement which supersedes this Protocol in whole or in part'.

4 The Union and the United Kingdom consider that, for example, a systematic refusal to take into consideration adverse proposals or interests, would be incompatible with their obligations under Article 2(1) of the Protocol ...

5 In light of their obligation under Article 2(1) of the Protocol, the Union and the United Kingdom will start negotiations on a subsequent agreement as soon as possible after the United Kingdom's withdrawal from the Union. Those negotiations should be conducted as a matter of priority, and efforts redoubled should the negotiations not be concluded within 1 year from the date of the United Kingdom's withdrawal ...

12 The Union and the United Kingdom agree that it would be inconsistent with their obligations under ... Article 2(1) of the Protocol for either party to act with the objective of applying the Protocol indefinitely.

---

[117] The imposition of any such duties is, in any case, prohibited by the Protocol on Ireland/Northern Ireland, Article 6(2).
[118] Protocol on Ireland/Northern Ireland, Article 1(4).   [119] *Ibid.* Article 2(1).

Should the Union or the United Kingdom consider the other party was acting in this way after the Protocol became applicable, it could make use of the dispute settlement mechanism enshrined in Articles 167 to 181 of the Withdrawal Agreement.

There is, however, a fantastical element to all this. If there were a way of resolving this tension – be it legally, administratively or technologically – the Protocol would not have been agreed in the first place. The conditions leading to the need for the Protocol in 2018 are likely still to be there in 2020, and possibly for many years beyond that. Furthermore, the European Union will only agree to a solution if it can trust the UK authorities to apply it in a sufficiently robust and reliable manner so that the public interests otherwise protected by customs checks are not undermined.

If the Protocol is, therefore, to apply until any new agreement comes into force,[120] such an agreement must address the issues met by the Protocol in a way that is to the satisfaction of both the European Union and the United Kingdom. If there is no agreement during the transitional period, the Protocol can only be subsequently terminated if one party notifies the other that it is no longer necessary to realise these objectives, presumably because there are other means to secure these. Both parties need, then, to decide jointly that this is indeed the case for the Protocol to cease to apply.[121] This lock raised consternation within large parts of the British Conservative Party as it gives the European Union a veto over the United Kingdom's exit from the process, and, therefore, raised the prospect that its arrangements are not really temporary. Furthermore, the grounds justifying the Union veto, set out in the objectives of the Protocol in Article 1(3) earlier, are wide-ranging. The alternative arrangements must involve no hard border, and must also not imperil the peace process in Northern Ireland. The European Union would, of course, observe that the importance of the issues at stake, namely the peace process in Northern Ireland and the integrity of the single market, require such a veto.

The prospect of the Protocol on Ireland/Northern Ireland being enduring and the political divisiveness of the imposition of regulatory checks between Northern Ireland and the rest of the United Kingdom generates a dynamic whereby it sets a template for future EU–UK trade relations. Under this template, the whole of the United Kingdom accepts the obligations currently imposed on Northern Ireland with the consequence that it agrees to align its legislation with much wider swathes of EU law. In return, there would be no need for customs checks between anywhere in the United Kingdom and anywhere in the European Union. Nor would there be any need for checks on goods between the Northern Ireland the rest of the United Kingdom.

This model is called the 'Jersey option' because it follows the arrangement governing relations, pre-Brexit, between the European Union and the Channel Islands and Isle of Man.[122] This model requires the following things:

- *The establishment of a Customs Union between the United Kingdom and the European Union* in which the United Kingdom applies the common external tariff and there are no customs duties or charges having equivalent effect between the two.

---

[120] *Ibid.* Article 1(4).

[121] *Ibid.* Article 20. The parties can decide either that the Protocol ceases to apply in full or that certain parts of it cease to apply.

[122] These are set out in Article 355(5)(c) TFEU and Protocol 3 to the Treaty of Accession of the United Kingdom to the EEC, OJ 1972, L 73/5.

- *Free movement of goods between the European Union and the United Kingdom.* This will involve the United Kingdom applying those EU laws which Northern Ireland is committed to applying (e.g. notably motor vehicles, textiles, pharmaceuticals and medicinal products, cosmetics, toys, construction products and machinery, chemicals, food and animal feed, pesticides and biocides, GMOs, intellectual property, VAT and electricity).

- *Alignment of United Kingdom laws with some of the laws of the common agricultural policy.* The Jersey option provides this, in part to secure the necessary health checks on animals and in part because agricultural markets rely on government subsidies to farmers. Alignment of UK laws on subsidies secures a level playing field.

- *UK application of EU trade defence laws.* These are laws preventing non-EU goods entering the Union market either because their producers are accused of engaging in illicit trade practices or it is felt necessary to protect Union interests. Whilst such alignment is not included in the European Union's arrangements with the Channel Islands and Isle of Man, they were included in the Protocol on Ireland/Northern Ireland. The risk is that, otherwise, such non-EU goods will enter the Union market via the United Kingdom.

The attractiveness of the Jersey option is that it resolves the tension within the United Kingdom caused by the Protocol and secures free movement of goods between the United Kingdom and the European Union. Furthermore, insofar as it builds upon the Protocol, it is not too complex to negotiate within the limited time frame provided by the transition period.[123] However, it runs into a number of challenges.

First, for many, it involves the United Kingdom rule-taking from the European Union in too many fields of law, and this simply seems undemocratic. It also makes it very difficult for the United Kingdom to make trade agreements with non-EU States, as it ties its hands on an important element of these, namely tariffs.

Secondly, it weakens the United Kingdom's negotiating position vis-à-vis the European Union on other aspects of international trade. Put simply, the European Union exports more goods to the United Kingdom than the United Kingdom exports to the European Union. However, the opposite is true for services.[124] If the United Kingdom has already opened its market to EU goods, the things in which the Union generally holds a competitive advantage, it has lost considerable leverage over the Union to persuade it to open its services markets.

Thirdly, there is the problem of the United Kingdom being 'Turkeyed'.[125] The customs union between the European Union and Turkey, which covers fewer goods than the Jersey option as it does not include agriculture, coal or steel.[126] By aligning its tariffs with those of the European Union, Turkey has impeded its ability to make trade agreements with other States. It also has no voice in the Union's agreements with other States but must let any goods onto its market that the Union lets onto its market as a result of such agreements as it cannot impose restrictions on goods entering its market from the Union. However, and this is the real bite of the trap, as the

---

[123] Its advocates include S. Lowe, *Inching our Way towards Jersey* (London, CER, 2018); P. Legrain, 'Britain's Best Brexit Bet Is the Jersey Option', *LSE EUROPP Blog*, 13 February 2018.

[124] In 2017, the United Kingdom had a £95 billion trade deficit in goods with the European Union and a £28 billion surplus in services, M. Ward, 'Statistics on UK–EU Trade', House of Commons Briefing Paper 7831 (2018) 4–8.

[125] On this debate see S. Lowe, *Is Labour Selling the UK a Turkey?* (London, CER, 2018).

[126] Its elements are set out in Decision No 1/95 of the EC–Turkey Association Council on implementing the final phase of the Customs Union, OJ 1996, L 35/1.

other State has only made a deal with the European Union, it is under no obligation to open its markets to Turkish goods in the same way as for EU goods.[127]

Such an arrangement is also not unproblematic from an EU perspective. The central concerns go to whether the United Kingdom would commit to a level playing field. To be sure, the Protocol on Ireland/Northern Ireland commits the United Kingdom not to deregulate in the fields of environmental, social or labour law. It is also not to engage in fiscal competition or grant illegal State aids. However, there remains an anxiety that such a competing neighbouring economy will impede the Union from adopting further environmental or labour legislation, if it so wishes, or raising taxes. For under the Protocol, if the Union raises levels of protection, the United Kingdom does not have to increase the level of protection offered by its law in parallel fashion.

4 THE FRAMEWORK FOR THE FUTURE RELATIONSHIP BETWEEN THE EUROPEAN UNION AND THE UNITED KINGDOM

The Political Declaration agreed alongside the Withdrawal Agreement to provide the framework for the future relationship between the European Union and the United Kingdom ('Political Declaration') does not establish any legal obligation. Instead, it contains thirty-one substantive pages of detail, which are to structure the treaty negotiations between the United Kingdom and the European Union that will begin immediately after Brexit.

Political Declaration

138 In setting out the framework of the future relationship between the Union and the United Kingdom, this declaration confirms, as set out in the Withdrawal Agreement, that it is the clear intent of both Parties to develop in good faith agreements giving effect to this relationship and to begin the formal process of negotiations as soon as possible after the United Kingdom's withdrawal from the Union, such that they can come into force by the end of 2020.

The Declaration is divided into four parts: the Basis for Cooperation, the Economic Partnership, the Security Partnership and Governance.

(i) The Basis for Cooperation

The Basis for Cooperation commits the Union and the United Kingdom to put arrangements in place to secure free movement of data[128] and to cooperate in areas of shared interest.[129] However, its central commitment is to shared core values and principles.

Political Declaration

6 The Parties agree that the future relationship should be underpinned by shared values such as the respect for and safeguarding of human rights and fundamental freedoms, democratic principles, the rule of law and support for non-proliferation. The Parties agree that these values are an essential prerequisite for the

---

[127] S. Booth, 'Turkey Is No Model for Britain's Post-Brexit Trade Policy', *Open Europe*, 12 September 2016.
[128] Political Declaration, paras. 8–10.   [129] *Ibid.* paras. 11–15.

cooperation envisaged in this framework. The Parties also reaffirm their commitment to promoting effective multilateralism.

7 The future relationship should incorporate the United Kingdom's continued commitment to respect the framework of the European Convention on Human Rights (ECHR) . . .

The significance of this commitment is not just symbolic: a relationship based on values and shared understandings of what is good and right rather than a transactional one geared merely to self-interest. If implemented, it would tie the United Kingdom much more firmly to the ECHR. The Political Declaration raises the possibility that such a departure might violate the future economic and security treaty with the European Union, thereby raising the possibility of countermeasures by EU States within these fields and the costs of any such departure.

(ii) The Economic Partnership

The most extensive part of the Political Declaration is that on the Economic Partnership, which is to be 'ambitious, wide-ranging and balanced'.[130] The vacuity of this phrase captures much of the ambiguity in this section, notwithstanding that it goes on for sixty-three paragraphs. This gives negotiators wiggle room to conclude a wide array of different trade relationships.

This ambiguity is most apparent with regard to free movement of goods, where the provisions are both most elaborate and most contradictory. The Framework has, therefore, the ambition to create:

> a free trade area, combining deep regulatory and customs cooperation, underpinned by provisions ensuring a level playing field for open and fair competition.[131]

A free trade area requires merely that no tariffs be imposed on movement of goods between the parties and substantial liberalisation of other measures that restrict trade in goods. However, it does not require complete free movement of goods nor does it require a common customs tariff. In line with this, the Political Declaration only talks about a 'trading relationship on goods that is as close as possible, with a view to facilitating the ease of legitimate trade'[132] and that the United Kingdom should have an 'independent trade policy'.[133] However, there are also paragraphs which suggest a more integrated vision.

Political Declaration

23 The economic partnership should ensure no tariffs, fees, charges or quantitative restrictions across all sectors, with ambitious customs arrangements that, in line with the Parties' objectives and principles above, build and improve on the single customs territory provided for in the Withdrawal Agreement which obviates the need for checks on rules of origin.

The reference to the abolition of quantitative restrictions is a commitment to abolish all restrictions on free movement of goods. Equally, the suggestion that the future relationship should build on the Single Customs Territory suggests that there might be a common external

---

[130] *Ibid.* para. 17.   [131] *Ibid.* para. 22.   [132] *Ibid.* para. 20.   [133] *Ibid.* para. 17.

tariff. Finally, there is considerable space for regulatory and legislative harmonisation. Whilst preserving regulatory autonomy, parties are to promote regulatory approaches that 'are compatible to the extent possible',[134] and the United Kingdom is to consider 'aligning with Union rules in relevant areas'.[135]

There is, finally, a commitment to developing significant level playing arrangements which build on those in the Protocol.

Political Declaration

79 The future relationship must ensure open and fair competition. Provisions to ensure this should cover state aid, competition, social and employment standards, environmental standards, climate change, and relevant tax matters, building on the level playing field arrangements provided for in the Withdrawal Agreement and commensurate with the overall economic relationship. The Parties should consider the precise nature of commitments in relevant areas, having regard to the scope and depth of the future relationship. These commitments should combine appropriate and relevant Union and international standards, adequate mechanisms to ensure effective implementation domestically, enforcement and dispute settlement as part of the future relationship.

Whilst there are similarly ambitious aims for free movement of capital,[136] the extensive aims for free movement of goods contrast with those on freedom of establishment and free movement of services.

Political Declaration

31 The arrangements should include provisions on market access and national treatment under host state rules for the Parties' service providers and investors, as well as address performance requirements imposed on investors. This would ensure that the Parties' services providers and investors are treated in a non-discriminatory manner, including with regard to establishment.

The parties aim to give companies the right to establish in each other's territories and to be treated there on the same terms as the host State's own companies. However, there is no aim to emulate the more extensive obligations set out in the EU law on freedom of establishment and free movement of services, which require States to remove and justify many non-discriminatory restrictions.[137] In practice, this will provide incentives for UK companies to relocate or to set up subsidiaries within the European Union. Once established there, these benefit from EU laws on freedom of establishment and freedom to provide services. If a British company establishes, for example, a subsidiary in France, that subsidiary will be able to offer services to customers in Germany relying on EU freedom of services law.

The aims on free movement of persons are even less ambitious. They are to provide visa-free travel for short-term visits;[138] to discuss conditions for entry and stay for research, study, training and youth exchanges;[139] and to consider addressing social security coordination issues concerning future migrants.[140] This is very small beer, indeed. It is consistent with the

---

[134] *Ibid.* para. 24.   [135] *Ibid.* para. 25.   [136] *Ibid.* para. 43.   [137] On these see Chapters 17 and 18.
[138] Political Declaration, para. 52.   [139] *Ibid.* para. 53.
[140] *Ibid.* para. 54. This is to ensure that persons accruing rights in one State (e.g. pensions) can take them with them to another State.

development of regimes which impose significant restrictions on free movement with migrant citizens having to adapt to more hostile legal environments in their host States.

(iii) The Security Partnership

The goals for the Security Partnership can be summarised more briefly. The broad ones are the following:

Political Declaration

80 With a view to Europe's security and the safety of their respective citizens, the Parties should establish a broad, comprehensive and balanced security partnership. This partnership will take into account geographic proximity and evolving threats, including serious international crime, terrorism, cyber-attacks, disinformation campaigns, hybrid-threats, the erosion of the rules based international order and the resurgence of state-based threats. The partnership will respect the sovereignty of the United Kingdom and the autonomy of the Union.

To these ends, the Political Declaration suggests four themes. The first is *Law Enforcement and Judicial Cooperation in Criminal Matters*. This would involve common action on data exchange and money laundering, as well as operation cooperation in law enforcement and policing. The second is *Foreign Policy, Security and Defence*. This would include common action on foreign affairs and crises, as they come up in the world, but also in the field of defence capability development, intelligence, sanctions and development. The third is an assortment of activities going under the heading of *Thematic Cooperation*. It includes cyber security, civil protection, health security, illegal migration, counterterrorism and countering violent extremism. The fourth heading is a commitment to conclude a *Security of Information Agreement*, which will provide the guarantees that will allow exchange of classified information.

The overarching structure linking all these activities is that of security. A notion of Europe's security is established in paragraph 80 which includes and transcends domestic security (i.e. policing) and external security (i.e. defence). This security is not just about protecting the safety of citizens but a further opaque set of interests. It thus, includes phenomena such as overseas development and irregular migration which do not touch directly on the physical safety of Europe's citizens. Loader and Walker have talked of a notion of European public order with its own social relations, values and sense of community underpinning this vision of security which justifies administration cooperation and intervention in this field.

I. Loader and N. Walker, *Civilizing Security* (Cambridge University Press, 2007) 260–1

[F]irst . . . the fact that states have a strong self-interest in security means that they are, and will always remain, willing participants in collaborative strategies, notwithstanding the difficulties in stabilizing these strategies in institutional terms. Indeed, the problems of stabilization do not arise from a lack of awareness of their interdependence, but, rather, from an *acute and constant* awareness of interdependence coupled with a sometimes unbridled determination to assert one's own national interest in the light of the factors of interdependence. Secondly, as the content of the internal security imperative of states is in all cases strikingly similar, states may be encouraged nevertheless to think of the global public good as something more than the optimal convergence of presumptively diverse individual state interests . . . perhaps more so than in any other policy domain all states adhere to the same broad conception of general order – the same appreciation of (and appreciation of their need to respond to) their populations' desire to live in a state of tranquility and in a context of predictable social relations. Thirdly, and relatedly, states may find common cause in their very understanding of the social quality of the public good of security . . . For all that their particular interests may differ, states also have a common understanding of the social and public quality of that which they seek to defend, which in turn allows, however unevenly and intermittently, for a greater imaginative openness to the possibility of *other* sites and levels of social and public 'added value' in the accomplishment of security.

Developed by foreign office and internal ministry officials, the Partnership will be concerned to protect well-established interests and power relations. This justification may also be used to enhance the powers of officials. This is, in itself, likely to be controversial. However, the idea of security implies that we should protect anything we value. It opens the possibility for suggestions, as the excerpt points out, that the Partnership should embrace and protect other interests, values and relations: be these human security, ecological security, social security or economic security.

(iv) Governance of the Future Relationship

The provisions on the governance of the Future Relation are very general and send out conflicting signals. The relationship should include dialogue between not just executives, but also parliaments and civil society.

Political Declaration

125 The future relationship should include dialogue between the Parties at summit, ministerial and technical level, as well as at parliamentary level. The Parties should encourage civil society dialogue.

This dialogue suggests that governance of the future relationship will involve a broad-based engagement which provides for inclusion of a wide array of interests and democratically elected representatives and encourages recognition of each other's views, interests and identities. However, the reasons for being less than fully optimistic about this are that the terms of any engagement will be framed by the EU and UK executives. They will set the agenda, the limits of cooperation and monitor the dialogue.

Political Declaration

126 In this context, the summit and ministerial level should oversee the future relationship, provide strategic direction and discuss opportunities for cooperation in areas of mutual interest, including on regional and global issues.

Furthermore, implementation and operation of the Future Relationship through a Joint Committee, which will be analogous to the Joint Committee in the Withdrawal Agreement (and indeed, it might even be the same Committee).[141] This Committee will comprise ministers and officials, and, if it follows the one in the Withdrawal Agreement, its operation will be secret. It will, therefore, be difficult for parliamentarians or civil society either to have input into it or to hold it to account.

The proposals for dispute settlement are similar to the central ones in the Withdrawal Agreement,[142] with all their attendant legal uncertainties. The Joint Committee will seek resolution through mutual agreement, initially.[143] If agreement is not reached, the matter is taken to arbitration.[144] However, if the dispute raises a question of EU law, the matter must be referred to the Court of Justice, whose judgment will be binding on the panel.[145]

There is, however, one interesting tweak in the Political Declaration. This concerns the interpretation and application of any future agreement. Whilst respecting the autonomy of each other's legal orders, the parties will seek to ensure that it is consistent.[146] The Framework is silent on how this is done, whether it will be done through a commitment for courts to follow the decisions of the arbitration panels or, possibly more creatively, through allowing courts in their legal orders to interpret and apply the Future Agreement and to have regard to each other's judgments in so doing.

5 MODELS FOR FUTURE EU–UK RELATIONS

The proposed Economic Partnership is vague about the details of any future trade relationship between the European Union and the United Kingdom. The Framework for Future Relations is, moreover, only a political document. There is nothing to stop the parties agreeing something that does not fit within its suggested terms. If the parties wish to establish a trade relationship regulated by a bilateral treaty,[147] there are four broad models to choose from. There is, first, a single-market model. This is the so-called 'Norway' option because the EEA Agreement between the European Union, Iceland, Liechtenstein and Norway provides for this.[148] There, is, secondly, a customs union model, known as the 'Jersey' model. This has already been described.[149] There is, thirdly, the Association Agreement model. Known as the 'Ukraine' model after the Association Agreement between the European Union and the Ukraine.[150] This provides for a free trade area plus significant regulatory convergence and institutional cooperation. Finally, there is the possibility of simply a free trade agreement, usually referred to as the 'Canada' model after the EU–Canada Comprehensive Economic and Trade Agreement.[151]

It is time to explore each of the three models not so far detailed.

---

[141] *Ibid.* paras. 129–30.   [142] See pp. 417–20.   [143] Political Declaration, para. 132.   [144] *Ibid.* para. 133.
[145] *Ibid.* para. 134.   [146] *Ibid.* para. 131.
[147] The implications of no bilateral treaty are explored in the next section of this chapter.
[148] The Agreement was signed on 2 May 1992 and entered into force on 1 January 1994. Decision 94/1/EC, ECSC on the conclusion of the Agreement on the European Economic Area, OJ 1994, L 1/1.
[149] See pp. 429–32.
[150] Association Agreement between the European Union and its Member States, of the one part, and Ukraine, of the other part, OJ 2014, L 161/3. This entered into force on 1 September 2017.
[151] Decision 2017/37 on the signing on behalf of the European Union of the Comprehensive Economic and Trade Agreement (CETA) between Canada, of the one part, and the European Union and its Member States, of the other part, OJ 2017, L 11/1. It entered provisionally into force on 21 September 2017.

(i) The European Economic Area (EEA)

The EEA provides for free movement of goods, persons, services and capital within the EEA as well as for freedom of establishment.[152] Alongside this, it provides for EEA competition,[153] transport,[154] and State aids policies[155] as well as a number of horizontal policies: social policy, including the requirement that men and women receive equal pay for work of equal value;[156] consumer protection;[157] environment protection;[158] statistics;[159] and company law.[160] Twenty-two annexes to the agreement provide lists of EU laws which must be adopted by the non-EU EEA States in these policy fields.[161] The number of measures in these annexes is considerable. In 2018, it was estimated that there were over 5,500 EU acts which non-EU States were required to adopt.[162] In addition, the EEA provides for cooperation in a number of further flanking policies. These are research and technological development education, training and youth, employment, tourism, culture, civil protection, enterprise, entrepreneurship, and small and medium-sized enterprises.[163] In addition, non-EU States must contribute sums, albeit lesser amounts, to the EU Budget.[164]

It is, thus, perhaps, easier to set out the major policies in which non-EU States do not participate. These are the common agricultural policy, cohesion policy, the customs union and common commercial policy, the area of freedom, security and justice, the common foreign and security policy, direct and indirect taxation, and economic and monetary union. However, if the United Kingdom were to adopt this model, because of the requirements surrounding the Irish/ Northern Irish border, it would have to participate in the customs union, indirect taxation, much of the common commercial policy and significant parts of the agricultural policy. There would, thus, be very little EU law which would cease to apply in the United Kingdom. It has been suggested, however, that the EEA might be attractive for the United Kingdom because Liechtenstein, a non-EU EEA State, has been granted a derogation from free movement of persons:

> **Agreement Establishing the European Economic Area 1994, Annex 8**
>
> The following shall apply to Liechtenstein. Duly taking into account the specific geographic situation of Liechtenstein, this arrangement shall be reviewed every five years, for the first time before May 2009.
>
> Nationals of Iceland, Norway and the EU Member States may take up residence in Liechtenstein only after having received a permit from the Liechtenstein authorities. They have the right to obtain this permit, subject only to the restrictions specified below. No such residence permit shall be necessary for a period less than three months per year, provided no employment or other permanent economic activity is taken up, nor for persons providing cross-border services in Liechtenstein.
>
> The conditions concerning nationals of Iceland, Norway and the EU Member States cannot be more restrictive than those which apply to third country nationals.

---

[152] Articles 8–45 EEA.   [153] Articles 53–60 EEA.   [154] Articles 47–52 EEA.   [155] Articles 61 and 62 EEA.
[156] Articles 66–71 EEA.   [157] Article 72 EEA.   [158] Articles 73–75 EEA.   [159] Article 76 EEA.
[160] Article 77 EEA.
[161] These can be found at www.efta.int/legal-texts/eea. On this see H. Fredriksen, 'EEA Main Agreement and Secondary EU Law Incorporated into the Annexes and Protocols' in C. Baudenbacher, *Handbook of EEA Law* (Springer, Dordrecht, 2016).
[162] www.efta.int/Legal-Text/EEA-Agreement-1327.   [163] Article 78 EEA.
[164] On these amounts see Z. Darvas, 'Single Market Access from Outside the EU: Three Key Prerequisites', *Bruegel Blog*, 19 July 2016, http://bruegel.org/2016/07/single-market-access-from-outside-the-eu-three-key-prerequisites/.

The derogation applies, however, largely because of Liechtenstein's 'specific geographic situation', namely its small size and population. It is also temporary and it is not at all clear that the United Kingdom can make a persuasive case on the same grounds as Liechtenstein.[165]

(a) The Qualities of EEA law

The EEA legal order is dominated by four principles: the internalisation of EEA law, the prevalence of EEA law, fidelity to EEA law and the homogeneity of EEA law. The internalisation principle requires EEA law to be made part of the 'internal legal order' of the non-EU EEA States.

Article 7 EEA

Acts referred to or contained in the Annexes to this Agreement or in decisions of the EEA Joint Committee shall be binding upon the Contracting Parties and be, or be made, part of their internal legal order as follows: (a) an act corresponding to an EEC regulation shall as such be made part of the internal legal order of the Contracting Parties; (b) an act corresponding to an EEC directive shall leave to the authorities of the Contracting Parties the choice of form and method of implementation.

However, this, in turn, raises the questions about the legal status of these internalised laws, in particular their relationship to other domestic laws. This relationship is governed by the second principle, the prevalence principle, which is contained in the oddly placed Protocol 35.

Protocol 35 on the Implementation of EEA Rules

Sole Article For cases of possible conflicts between implemented EEA rules and other statutory provisions, the EFTA States undertake to introduce, if necessary, a statutory provision to the effect that EEA rules prevail in these cases.

Beyond the requirement that non-EU States ensure that EEA laws prevail over national statutes, but not over national constitutions, Protocol 35 is silent on the authority of EEA law and the implications of such authority. This has been set out by the EFTA Court, the EEA court for the non-EU States, relying upon the other two principles of EEA law.

The third principle, the fidelity principle, is worded in a similar manner to Article 4(3) TEU. It requires authorities to ensure that they fulfil their obligations under the EEA and abstain from any measure which could jeopardise the attainment of the objectives of this agreement.[166]

The fourth principle is the homogeneity principle. This requires both that EEA law be interpreted in an analogous manner to identical EU legal provisions[167] and that it be given a uniform interpretation across the EEA. In *Sveinbjörnsdóttir*, the plaintiff brought a claim against

---

[165] On the debate see M. Pérez Crespo, 'After Brexit . . . The Best of Both Worlds? Rebutting the Norwegian and Swiss Models as Long-Term Options for the UK' (2017) 36 *YBEL* 94, 102–3.

[166] Article 3 EEA.

[167] On the EFTA Court following the case of the Court of Justice see T. Burri and B. Pirker, 'Constitutionalization by Association? The Doubtful Case of the European Economic Area' (2013) 32 *YBEL* 207, 213–20.

the Icelandic government for unpaid back pay owed to her when her employer went bankrupt. The reason for non-payment was that Icelandic law precluded back pay to be privileged vis-à-vis other claims when the person was 'close' to the insolvent entity and Sveinbjörnsdóttir was the sister of somebody who owned 40 per cent of the shares of the bankrupt company. This breached EU law. Sveinbjörnsdóttir, therefore, argued that the Icelandic State was liable for her back pay under the EU principle of State liability[168]

Case E-9/97, *Sveinbjörnsdóttir* v. *Government of Iceland* [1998] EFTA Ct Rep 95

47 ... The general aim of the EEA Agreement, as laid down in Article 1(1) EEA, is to promote a continuous and balanced strengthening of trade and economic relations between the Contracting Parties with equal conditions of competition and the respect of the same rules, with a view to creating a homogeneous European Economic Area.

48 The scope of the EEA Agreement is laid down in Article 1(2) EEA, which states that, in order to attain those objectives, the association envisaged therein shall entail, in accordance with the provisions of the EEA Agreement, six elements specified in that Article: the free movement of goods, persons, services, and capital, the setting-up of a system ensuring that competition is not distorted, and closer cooperation in certain other fields.

49 As stated in Article 1(1) EEA, one of the main objectives of the Agreement is to create a homogeneous EEA. This homogeneity objective is also expressed in the fourth and fifteenth recitals of the Preamble to the EEA Agreement.

50 The fourth recital of the Preamble reads: 'CONSIDERING the objective of establishing a dynamic and homogeneous European Economic Area, based on common rules and equal conditions of competition and providing for the adequate means of enforcement including at the judicial level, and achieved on the basis of equality and reciprocity and of an overall balance of benefits, rights and obligations for the Contracting Parties;'

51 The fifteenth recital of the Preamble reads: 'WHEREAS, in full deference to the independence of the courts, the objective of the Contracting Parties is to arrive at, and maintain, a uniform interpretation and application of this Agreement and those provisions of Community legislation which are substantially reproduced in this Agreement and to arrive at an equal treatment of individuals and economic operators as regards the four freedoms and the conditions of competition;'

52 The achievement of the homogeneity objective rests, in particular, on two main foundations.

53 First, the material provisions of the EEA Agreement shall, within the agreed scope of co-operation, be largely identical to corresponding provisions of the EC Treaty and the ECSC Treaty. Such material provisions shall be made applicable in the EFTA States by means of incorporation into their respective national laws.

54 Secondly, the EEA Agreement establishes elaborate mechanisms with a view to ensuring homogeneous interpretation and application of the incorporated material provisions ...

57 Another important objective of the EEA Agreement is to ensure individuals and economic operators equal treatment and equal conditions of competition, as well as adequate means of enforcement. Again, reference can be made to the fourth and fifteenth recitals of the Preamble ... and, in particular, to the eighth recital in the Preamble to the EEA Agreement, which states: 'CONVINCED of the important role that individuals will play in the European Economic Area through the exercise of the rights conferred on them by this Agreement and through the judicial defence of these rights;'

58 The Court notes that the provisions of the EEA Agreement are, to a great extent, intended for the benefit of individuals and economic operators throughout the European Economic Area. Therefore, the proper

---

[168] On this principle see pp. 314–22.

59 functioning of the EEA Agreement is dependent on those individuals and economic operators being able to rely on the rights thus intended for their benefit.

59 The Court concludes from the foregoing considerations that the EEA Agreement is an international treaty sui generis which contains a distinct legal order of its own. The EEA Agreement does not establish a customs union but an enhanced free trade area ... The depth of integration of the EEA Agreement is less far-reaching than under the EC Treaty, but the scope and the objective of the EEA Agreement goes beyond what is usual for an agreement under public international law.

60 The Court finds that the homogeneity objective and the objective of establishing the right of individuals and economic operators to equal treatment and equal opportunities are so strongly expressed in the EEA Agreement that the EFTA States must be obliged to provide for compensation for loss and damage caused to an individual by incorrect implementation of a directive.

61 A further basis for the obligation of the Contracting Parties to provide for compensation is to be found in Article 3 EEA, under which the Contracting Parties are required to take all appropriate measures, whether general or particular, to ensure fulfilment of their obligations under the Agreement ... With regard to the implementation of directives integrated into the EEA Agreement, this means that the Contracting Parties have a duty to make good loss or damage resulting from incorrect implementation of those directives.

62 It follows from all the forgoing that it is a principle of the EEA Agreement that the Contracting Parties are obliged to provide for compensation for loss and damage cause to individuals by breaches of the obligations under the EEA Agreement for which the EFTA States can be held responsible.

Sveinbjörnsdóttir characterises the EEA legal order as less far-reaching than the Union one but more ambitious than other public international law treaties. This characterisation was used to establish the doctrine of indirect effect in EEA law in the case of *A*. Liechtenstein prohibited lawyers from other EEA States from representing clients in Liechtenstein in criminal cases unless they did so in conjunction with a Liechtenstein lawyer. This would only have been lawful under Directive 77/249/EEC, the relevant EU Directive, if it related to activities which required a lawyer to do the work. However, as for many activities use of a lawyer was not mandatory in Liechtenstein and people could represent themselves, the EFTA Court held that the requirement was in violation of the Directive. The question was asked whether the Directive could be invoked in the Liechtenstein court and take precedence over national law.

Case E-1/07, *A* [2007] EFTA Ct Rep 246

37 The EEA Agreement is based on the objectives of establishing a dynamic and homogeneous European Economic Area and of ensuring individuals and economic operators equal treatment and equal conditions of competition, as well as adequate means of enforcement ... The EEA Agreement is an international treaty sui generis that contains a distinct legal order of its own. The depth of integration of the EEA Agreement is less far-reaching than under the EC Treaty, but the scope and objective of the EEA Agreement goes beyond what is usual for an agreement under public international law ...

38 The EEA Agreement establishes a particular system of means and mechanisms in order to achieve the abovementioned objectives. Article 7 EEA and Protocol 35 EEA are part of this system. Article 7 EEA stipulates that Acts referred to or contained in Annexes to the EEA Agreement or in decisions of the EEA Joint Committee shall be binding upon the Contracting Parties and be, or be made, part of their internal legal order. Protocol 35 EEA obliges the EFTA States to introduce, if necessary, a statutory provision to the

39 Moreover, it is inherent in the objectives of the EEA Agreement referred to in paragraph 37 above, as well as in Article 3 EEA, that national courts are bound to interpret national law, and in particular legislative provisions specifically adopted to transpose EEA rules into national law, as far as possible in conformity with EEA law. Consequently, they must apply the interpretative methods recognised by national law as far as possible in order to achieve the result sought by the relevant EEA rule.

40 It follows from Article 7 EEA and Protocol 35 EEA that the EEA Agreement does not entail transfer of legislative powers. In *Karlsson*, the Court held this to mean that EEA law does not require that individuals and economic operators can rely directly on non-implemented EEA rules before national courts[169] . . . This applies to all EEA law, including provisions of a directive such as the one at issue. Furthermore, this entails that EEA law does not require that non-implemented EEA rules take precedence over conflicting national rules, including national rules which fail to transpose the relevant EEA rules correctly into national law.

41 It follows from the above that, in cases of conflict between national law and non-implemented EEA law, the Contracting Parties may decide whether, under their national legal order, national administrative and judicial organs can apply the relevant EEA rule directly, and thereby avoid violation of EEA law in a particular case. It also follows that the Contracting Parties may decide on which administrative and judicial organs they confer such a power. However, even Contracting Parties which have introduced principles of direct effect and primacy of EEA law in their internal legal order remain under an obligation to correctly transpose directives into national law.

42 Furthermore, the Court notes that in cases of violation of EEA law by a Contracting Party, the Contracting Party is obliged to provide compensation for loss and damage caused to individuals and economic operators, in accordance with the principle of State liability which is an integral part of the EEA Agreement, if the conditions laid down in *Sveinbjörnsdóttir* . . . are fulfilled.

EEA law has, thus, a curious status within the non-EU EEA States. It is not directly effective, and cannot be invoked independently over national law. However, it does have indirect effect and State liability. This gives individuals fairly complete legal protection. If a national law cannot be interpreted to comply with EU law, a State can be sued for non-compliance. In this regard, it seems it has much of the practical effectiveness of EU law without some of the latter's more grandiose rhetoric.[170]

(b) The Institutional Settlement of the EEA

The central institutions within the EEA are the Joint Committee, the EFTA Supervisory Authority and the EFTA Court of Justice.[171]

---

[169] Case E-4/01, *Karlsson* [2002] EFTA Ct Rep 240.

[170] H. Fredriksen and C. Franklin, 'Of Pragmatism and Principles: The EEA Agreement 20 Years On' (2015) 52 *CMLRev* 629, 664–8.

[171] In addition to the EEA Institutions considered in this chapter, there is the EEA Council and the Joint Parliamentary Committee. The EEA Council comprises members from the Council, the Commission and one from each non-EU government, Article 90(1) EEA. It meets biannually and is to generate political impetus by setting down guidelines for the Joint Committee, Article 89(1) EEA. The Joint Parliamentary Committee comprises MEPs and parliamentarians from the non-EU States, Article 95(1) EEA, and it is to feed parliamentary opinion into the process through reports and resolutions, Article 95(4) EEA.

The Joint Committee: The Joint Committee comprises 'representatives of the Contracting Parties',[172] usually the Commission and the permanent representatives of the non-EU States. It is to 'secure the effective operation and implementation of the Agreement'[173] through bringing EEA law into line with EU law.

Article 102 EEA

In order to guarantee the legal security and the homogeneity of the EEA, the EEA Joint Committee shall take a decision concerning an amendment of an Annex to this Agreement as closely as possible to the adoption by the [Union] of the corresponding new [Union] legislation with a view to permitting a simultaneous application of the latter as well as of the amendments of the Annexes to the Agreement. To this end, the [Union] shall, whenever adopting a legislative act on an issue which is governed by this Agreement, as soon as possible inform the other Contracting Parties in the EEA Joint Committee.[[174]]

The procedure in Article 102 EEA is curious. Formally, it is not a legislative procedure but merely about bringing EEA law into line with EU law. It is, thus, done by civil servants and parliamentary input is weak. However, the reality is that the procedure makes EU Directives or Regulations apply in the non-EU States in a parallel fashion to the way EU lawmaking procedures do for the Union States.

There are some limited safeguards for non-EU States.

First, Joint Committee decisions require agreement by both the Union and the non-EU States 'speaking with one voice'.[175] If a single non-EU State can veto adoption of a decision, there are strong pressures not to do this. This is, in part, because all parties have a duty to make every effort to find a mutually acceptable solution where a problem arises.[176] It is also because of the consequences of no agreement. The Joint Committee has six months to reach an alternate agreement.[177] If not, the affected part of the Annex is suspended.[178] Whilst the individual rights already acquired cannot be touched (e.g. existing contracts),[179] the threat is clear. Without agreement, the Union can suspend market access in the activity in question.[180]

Secondly, if a decision can only be binding in a State after meeting 'constitutional requirements', that State shall be given some time to meet these requirements.[181] If the State is unable to implement the decision within six months, the decision enters into force for the other parties, with the possibility of suspension of the Agreement between that State and the other parties.[182] The practical consequence of the 'constitutional requirements' provision is that it allows matters to be taken back to national parliaments. As of 1 December 2018, this has happened 645 times since 1 January 2004.[183]

---

[172] Article 93(1) EEA.   [173] Article 92(1) EEA.

[174] Similar downloading responsibilities apply to new judgments of the Court of Justice, Article 105 EEA.

[175] Article 93(2) EEA.   [176] Article 102(3) EEA.   [177] Article 102(4) EEA.   [178] Article 102(5) EEA.

[179] Article 102(6) EEA.

[180] In 2011, Norway, for example, refused to agree to implement Directive 2008/6/EC, which liberalised services in the delivery of mail. In 2013, after pressure from the European Union, it backed down and implemented it. EEA Joint Committee, 'Annual Report of the EEA Joint Committee 2013: The Functioning of the EEA Agreement', 26 June 2014, Annex I, para. 22.

[181] Article 103(1) EEA.   [182] Article 103(2) EEA.

[183] www.efta.int/sites/default/files/documents/legal-texts/eea/other-legal-documents/list-of-constitutional-requirements/list-of-constitutional-requirements.pdf.

Thirdly, States can derogate from EEA law in very exceptional circumstances.

> ### Article 112 EEA
>
> (1) If serious economic, societal or environmental difficulties of a sectorial or regional nature liable to persist are arising, a Contracting Party may unilaterally take appropriate measures under the conditions and procedures laid down in Article 113.
> (2) Such safeguard measures shall be restricted with regard to their scope and duration to what is strictly necessary in order to remedy the situation. Priority shall be given to such measures as will least disturb the functioning of this Agreement.
> (3) The safeguard measures shall apply with regard to all Contracting Parties.

Prior to adopting any measure, the State must consult for at least one month with the other parties to see if a mutually acceptable solution can be found.[184] Any adopted measures are then subject to consultations every three months by the Joint Committee to see if they can be abolished.[185] Furthermore, if these measures create 'an imbalance between the rights and obligations under this Agreement', any other party can adopt 'such proportionate rebalancing measures as are strictly necessary to remedy the imbalance'.[186] This limits incentives to derogate. However, a 2011 Norwegian report found that in the first eighteen years of the EEA, Norway secured 55 such derogations, Iceland 349 and Liechtenstein 1,056. The majority of Iceland derogations were because its geographic circumstances made some EU law inappropriate for it whilst Liechtenstein's went to possible disruption of its relations with Switzerland.[187] It is likely that Liechtenstein's small size makes other parties more indulgent of these derogations as the cost for them is correspondingly lower.

The EFTA Surveillance Authority: The EFTA Surveillance Authority comprises a college (like the Commission) of three individuals from each of the non-EU States.[188] They are to act independently and hold their post for four years.[189] It holds analogous policing powers to the Commission, except that it is for the non-EU EEA States. It regulates competition and merger law, and can issue fines to undertakings.[190] It also holds similar powers to the Commission in the fields of public undertakings and State aids.[191] However, its central power is the power to bring infringement proceedings before the EFTA Court of Justice for breach of EEA law in parallel fashion to the Commission's powers in EU law.[192]

The EFTA Court of Justice: Based in Luxembourg, this comprises three judges appointed for six years each.[193] The EFTA Court has some of the powers of the Court of Justice of the European Union, but there are important ones missing. First, as already mentioned, the EFTA Surveillance

---

[184] Article 113(1)–(3) EEA.   [185] Article 113(5) EEA.   [186] Article 114(1) EEA.

[187] Norwegian Ministry of Foreign Affairs, *The EEA Agreement and Norway's Other Agreements with the EU* (Oslo, 2013) 17.

[188] Its composition and powers as well as those of the EFTA Court of Justice are contained in the Agreement between the EFTA States on the establishment of a Surveillance Authority and Court of Justice, OJ 1994, L 344/3. The relevant provision is Article 7.

[189] Agreement between the EFTA states, Articles 8 and 9.

[190] Articles 56, 57 and 110 EEA. Agreement between the EFTA states, Articles 19 and 25.

[191] Articles 59(3) and 62 EEA. Agreement between the EFTA States, Article 24.

[192] Agreement between the EFTA States, Article 31.   [193] *Ibid.* Articles 28 and 30.

Authority or non-EU EEA States can bring infringement proceedings before it for non-compliance with EEA law by other non-EU EEA States.[194] The EFTA Court has, however, no power to fine States for non-compliance with EEA law. Secondly, there is provision for judicial review of the EFTA Surveillance Authority.[195] Non-EU EEA States have unlimited standing to challenge the Surveillance Authority's Decisions if this is done within two months of adoption of the decision. Natural and legal persons may bring actions against decisions addressed or of direct and individual concern to them. Judicial review is more confined than in EU law. Notably, there is no possibility to seek judicial review of the Joint Committee, which operates in a space of complete legal unaccountability. Thirdly, national courts in non-EU EEA States may seek preliminary references on points of EEA law from the EFTA Court.[196] The decisions of the latter are, however, only advisory opinions and not formally binding on the court seeking the reference.[197] The procedure is restricted in two further ways. First, EFTA States may limit the power to refer to those national courts against whose decision there is no judicial remedy under national law. Secondly, references can only be made on interpretations of EEA law. They cannot be made to challenge the validity of acts of EEA institutions. The procedure is not therefore a source of judicial review of central institutional behaviour.

(ii) The 'Ukraine' Model: 'Close and Privileged Links' between the European Union and the United Kingdom

Shortly after the referendum in 2016, the commentator and former MEP, Andrew Duff, made an innovative suggestion.[198] The future relationship between the European Union and the United Kingdom should be based on an association agreement, provision for which is made in Article 8 TEU.

> ### Article 8 TEU
>
> (1) The Union shall develop a special relationship with neighbouring countries, aiming to establish an area of prosperity and good neighbourliness, founded on the values of the Union and characterised by close and peaceful relations based on cooperation.

Support for this model is provided in the Political Declaration which states that the 'overarching institutional framework could take the form of an Association Agreement'.[199] Duff had in mind the Association Agreements concluded in 2014 between the European Union and Ukraine, Georgia and Moldova.[200] These agreements are not characterised as a first step to membership of the European Union. However, neither are they just trade and investments agreements as they also have a political dimension. The Ukrainian agreement, used as the model in the rest of this

---

[194] *Ibid.* Articles 31 and 32.   [195] *Ibid.* Article 36.   [196] *Ibid.* Article 34.

[197] They are, however, usually followed by the national courts. Burri and Pirker, n. 167 above, 222–5.

[198] A. Duff, 'After Brexit: Learning to Be Good Neighbours', European Policy Centre, 18 November 2018, www.epc.eu/documents/uploads/pub_7194_afterbrexit.pdf?doc_id=1799.

[199] Political Declaration, para. 122.

[200] Association Agreement between the European Union and its Member States, of the one part, and Ukraine, of the other part, OJ 2014, L 161/3 ('EU–Ukraine Agreement'); Association Agreement between the European Union and the European Atomic Energy Community and their Member States, of the one part, and Georgia, of the other part, OJ 2014, L 261/4; Association Agreement between the European Union and the European Atomic Energy Community and their Member States, of the one part, and the Republic of Moldova, of the other part, OJ 2014, L 260/4.

section, refers therefore to 'close and privileged links'.[201] The Agreement provides for three things in particular a 'Deep and Comprehensive Free Trade Area';[202] Political Dialogue; and close cooperation in fields of mutual interest.

(a) The Deep and Comprehensive Free Trade Area (DCFTA)

The DCFTA is based on two principles. The first is significant but differentiated access to each other's markets for goods, services and companies. The second is very extensive alignment of Ukrainian law with EU law.

Market access under the DCFTA: Market access is most extensive for goods. The parties commit to the abolition of customs duties and charges equivalent effect on movement of goods between them,[203] no quantitative restrictions being placed on imports and exports,[204] and imports being given the same treatment as national goods on the domestic market.[205] Technical regulations cannot restrict trade if the reasons that led to the adoption of the regulation no longer exist or their objectives can be realised in a less trade-restrictive manner.[206]

This allows significant restrictions and checks to be maintained on the movement of goods. As there is no common customs tariff, rules of origin can be demanded to check that the good is not from a third State which is not entitled to free movement,[207] and can be subject to customs duties at the EU–Ukraine border. Safeguard measures can be taken to restrict imports from either party if it is part of a package directed at all imports threatening the domestic industry, wherever their source.[208] Restrictions can also be imposed to protect a variety of public interests (e.g. public morals, public health, intellectual property rights, the environment, archaeological heritage) or for security reasons.[209] Furthermore, no principle of mutual recognition operates so if a standard protecting public health of one party is different from that of the other party, it is easy for the latter to argue that it does not offer equivalent health protection. As a consequence, unless goods conform to the importing party's standards, they may often be refused market access.[210]

Market access is more limited for companies. First, there is not liberalisation in all sectors. The agreement sets out a series of sectors where either both or one of the parties has closed off the market, and where there is to be no liberalisation.[211] The sectors subject to liberalisation are, moreover, subject to only limited liberalisation. There must simply be no discrimination. Companies of have to be able to establish subsidiaries, branches and offices and operate on the terms which are no less favourable than those provided to companies of the host party.[212] However, unlike the case for companies trading within the European Union, they cannot challenge any non-discriminatory restriction on their establishing themselves within a State or, once they are there, on how they operate within that State.[213]

---

[201] EU–Ukraine Agreement, Article 1(2)(a). On the EU–Ukraine agreement see G. van der Loo, *The EU–Ukraine Association Agreement and Deep and Comprehensive Free Trade Area: A New Legal Instrument for Integration without Membership* (Leiden, Brill, 2016).

[202] EU–Ukraine Agreement, Article 2(2)(d).   [203] *Ibid.* Articles 29, 31 and 78.   [204] *Ibid.* Article 35.

[205] *Ibid.* Article 34.

[206] *Ibid.* Article 54. WTO Agreement on Technical Barriers to Trade (1994) 1868 UNTS 120, Article 2(3).

[207] EU–Ukraine Agreement, Article 26(2).   [208] *Ibid.* Article 40(1).   [209] *Ibid.* Article 36.

[210] For admission of this see European Commission, 'Second Biannual Report on the Application of Mutual Recognition', COM(2002)419, 18–25.

[211] EU–Ukraine Agreement, Articles 87 and 88(1) and (2).   [212] *Ibid.* Article 88.

[213] *Ibid.* Article 91. On EU law see pp. 791–6 and 806–10.

Market access is even more limited for services. The parties adopt a positive-list approach. Liberalisation only takes place in those sectors in which each party commits to liberalisation in the agreement.[214] The default position, therefore, is no liberalisation unless the sector has been identified as one that should be opened up. Even in liberalised sectors, the commitment is weak. Each party must not discriminate against services offered from the other party vis-à-vis services offered on its own territory.[215] However, there is only a ban on formal discrimination (i.e. explicitly offering worse treatment to services from Ukraine because they are Ukrainian).[216] Covert or indirect discrimination is permitted where apparently neutral criteria are applied which act to the substantial disadvantage of services from abroad.[217]

There is, finally, little free movement of persons under this model beyond a loose commitment to endeavour to enhance the mobility of citizens.[218] Ukrainians lawfully working in the Union must also not be subject to discrimination.[219] This all allows significant restrictions to be kept in place. There is some liberalisation of movement for persons associated with direct investment in each other's territories. The key personnel of a company establishing in the territory of the other can be employed there for up to three years,[220] and graduate trainees can work there for up to one year[221] There is also provision for limited stays for sellers of business services,[222] and those offering contractual services in a limited number of fields.[223]

Ukrainian legislative alignment with EU law: There is, by contrast, extensive alignment of Ukrainian law with EU law, with Ukraine having to adopt far more EU laws than Northern Ireland under the Protocol on Ireland/Norther Ireland. The fields in which Ukraine must align its laws with EU law are technical regulations for goods,[224] sanitary and phytosanitary and animal welfare laws,[225] customs law (albeit not the common customs tariff),[226] e-commerce,[227] financial services, telecommunications, postal services, maritime transport,[228] public procurement,[229] competition,[230] State aids,[231] environmental and labour law,[232] taxation,[233] statistics,[234] consumer protection[235] and public health.[236]

The attraction for UK autonomy is that the association agreement imposes no obligation to follow the common external tariff so the United Kingdom would be free to conclude its own trade agreements under this arrangement. It might also be that any association agreement would require itself to align with far less EU law than is required of Ukraine, Georgia and Moldova. However, the model provides for extensive alignment. The market established is one based on positive integration, common rules, rather than negative integration, the abolition of national restrictions on trade. It is a market where one party sets all the rules. The rules extend, moreover, beyond merely securing a single market in goods and services to include many flanking policies, such as consumer protection, public health, environmental and labour law.

These Association Agreements are exercises in building up institutions and capacities in Ukraine, Georgia and Moldova. They have been constructed in these terms, and, therefore, might not be well suited for the United Kingdom, which has exercised capacities in these fields for

---

[214] *Ibid.* Article 95.   [215] *Ibid.* Articles 93 and 94.   [216] *Ibid.* Article 94(3).
[217] Restrictions can only also be imposed on establishment and service movement for the same public interest and security reasons as for goods. *Ibid.* Articles 141 and 143.
[218] *Ibid.* Article 19(2).   [219] *Ibid.* Article 17(1).   [220] *Ibid.* Article 98(1).   [221] *Ibid.* Article 99.
[222] *Ibid.* Article 100.   [223] *Ibid.* Article 101(1).   [224] *Ibid.* Article 56.   [225] *Ibid.* Article 64(1).
[226] *Ibid.* Article 84.   [227] *Ibid.* Article 124(2).   [228] These are all *ibid.* Annex XVII, Article 1(1).
[229] *Ibid.* Article 153.   [230] *Ibid.* Article 256.   [231] *Ibid.* Article 264.   [232] *Ibid.* Article 290.
[233] *Ibid.* Article 353.   [234] *Ibid.* Article 358.   [235] *Ibid.* Article 417.   [236] *Ibid.* Article 428.

years. The other great challenge for the Ukrainian model is that it does not resolve the issue of no hard border within the island of Ireland unless the United Kingdom aligns itself with the common external tariff and EU trade defence law. It might well be, therefore, that it is easier for the United Kingdom just to follow the model set out in the Protocol on Ireland and NorthernIreland.

(b) Political Dialogue and Close Cooperation

The EU–Ukrainian Agreement provides for close cooperation across a wide variety of sectors that include amongst others, migration, asylum and borders,[237] taxation,[238] education[239] and civil society.[240] However, a distinctive feature of this agreement, and those with Georgia and Moldova, is the Political Dialogue.

> ### EU–Ukraine Agreement 2014, Article 4
>
> (1) Political dialogue in all areas of mutual interest shall be further developed and strengthened between the Parties. This will promote gradual convergence on foreign and security matters with the aim of Ukraine's ever-deeper involvement in the European security area.

The mention of a 'European security area' parallels the language of the Security Partnership in the Political Declaration. When the latter was discussed, it was argued that ministries might use the language of security to seek both greater powers for themselves and to protect vested interests and wider imbalances of power. The Political Dialogue offers an alternative vision in this regard. It has a broader vision of the human condition than simply seeing security about protecting human safety. It is to strengthen respect for democratic principles, the rule of law, good governance, human rights, and diversity,[241] and look at whether the parties' domestic policies observe these principles.[242] There is also more institutional pluralism. To be sure, the Dialogue involves dialogue between all levels of government: Heads, ministers and officials.[243] However, it is also to involve a parliamentary dialogue between the Ukrainian parliament and the European Parliament.[244] Elected representatives will have some input into the content of this security arrangement, therefore.[245]

(c) The EU–Ukraine Agreement Institutional Settlement

The EU–Ukraine Association Agreement comprises four bodies: the Summit, the Association Council, the Association Committee, and a Parliamentary Association Committee.

The Summit takes place once a year, and provides overall guidance for the implementation of the agreement.[246] The Association Council comprises ministers of both parties and members of the European Commission, and is to meet regularly.[247] It supervises and monitors the application and implementation of the agreement as well as examining any major issues arising out of it.[248] An Association Committee, comprised of civil servants, assists the Council with the performance of the latter's duties.[249] Finally, there is a Parliamentary Association Committee which provides a

---

[237] *Ibid.* Article 16.   [238] *Ibid.* Article 349.   [239] *Ibid.* Article 430.   [240] *Ibid.* Article 443.
[241] *Ibid.* Article 4(2)(e).   [242] *Ibid.* Articles 6 and 14.   [243] *Ibid.* Article 5(3).   [244] *Ibid.* Article 5(5).
[245] Although not formally part of the Political Dialogue, further democratisation is to be provided by a civil society platform which shall comprise members of the European Economic and Social Committee and Ukrainian civil society. It shall provide input into implementation of the Agreement. *Ibid.* Article 469.
[246] *Ibid.* Article 460.   [247] *Ibid.* Articles 461(2) and 462(1).   [248] *Ibid.* Article 461(1) and (3).
[249] *Ibid.* Article 464.

forum for the European and Ukrainian Parliament to meet and exchange views.[250] Arguably, more importantly, it can hold the Association Council to account by asking for information from the latter about the implementation of the agreement and making recommendations to it.[251]

Both the Association Council and the Committee have, where provided in the agreement, decision-making power.[252] In this, the central decision-making power granted goes to monitoring Ukraine's compliance with the agreement.

EU Ukraine Agreement 2014, Article 475

(1) Monitoring shall mean the continuous appraisal of progress in implementing and enforcing measures covered by this Agreement.

(2) Monitoring shall include assessments of approximation of Ukrainian law to EU law as defined in this Agreement, including aspects of implementation and enforcement. These assessments may be conducted individually, or, by agreement, jointly by the Parties ...

(3) Monitoring may include on-the-spot missions, with the participation of EU institutions, bodies and agencies, nongovernmental bodies, supervisory authorities, independent experts and others as needed.

(4) The results of monitoring activities, including the assessments of approximation as set out in paragraph 2 of this Article, shall be discussed in all relevant bodies established under this Agreement. Such bodies may adopt joint recommendations, agreed unanimously, which shall be submitted to the Association Council.

(5) If the Parties agree that necessary measures covered by Title IV (Trade and Trade-related Matters)[253] of this Agreement have been implemented and are being enforced, the Association Council, under the powers conferred on it by Article 463 of this Agreement, shall agree on further market opening ...

The central purpose of the institutional settlement is, thus, to police Ukrainian compliance with EU law. Strong compliance is rewarded with increasing market access, most notably in services and establishment. The institutional settlement, consequently, acts as a ratchet ensuring that ever more EU law is transposed. This procedure also provides, as Article 475(2) indicates, for very intrusive policing of this compliance through missions on Ukraine's territory. It is doubtful how politically acceptable this would be.

There is, finally, provision for dispute settlement.

The system for disputes concerning the DCFTA is almost identical to that in the Withdrawal Agreement. There is provision for consultation with a view to resolution, and, if this fails, the matter can be taken to arbitration with the same sanctions being applied against the party that does not comply with a decision as were agreed in the Withdrawal Agreement.[254] One significant difference is that the EU–Ukraine Agreement allows for mediation. The parties can appoint a third party as mediator who is to offer advice and propose solutions with a view to resolving the dispute.[255]

To protect the autonomy of the EU law,[256] if a dispute involving interpretation of EU law arises in fields where Ukraine must align its laws with EU law, the arbitration panel shall refer the matter to the Court of Justice who shall give a ruling on the point of EU law which will bind the arbitration panel.[257]

---

[250] *Ibid.* Article 467(1).   [251] *Ibid.* Article 468.   [252] *Ibid.* Articles 463(1) and 466(4) respectively.
[253] These are the provisions that concern the DCFTA.   [254] EU–Ukraine Agreement, Articles 303–21.
[255] *Ibid.* Articles 327–6.   [256] See pp. 170–7.
[257] EU–Ukraine Agreement, Article 322. It should be noted that points of EU law will only come up in this context.

Finally, for disputes concerning parts of the Agreement other than the DCFTA, the parties agree to seek to resolve these within the Association Council.[258] If there is no agreement within three months, the aggrieved party may take 'appropriate measures'.[259] These should 'least disturb the functioning of the Agreement' and not involve suspension of obligations under the DCFTA.[260]

(iii) A Free Trade Agreement: The Canada Model

The EU–Canada Comprehensive Economic and Trade Agreement (CETA) was concluded in 2017, and is advanced by those who wish the United Kingdom to have a trade relationship with the European Union which is not too institutionally constraining.

CETA provides for a free trade area characterised by three things. First, there is significant liberalisation of goods markets, protection of foreign investors and limited liberalisation of services markets. Secondly, it provides for commitments about the terms of competition on the parties' markets by establishing common principles on competition policy; providing for the enforcement of intellectual property rights; requiring competition to be allowed between public enterprises and private companies; and regulating the terms under which government procurement takes place.[261] Thirdly, it seeks to provide some safeguards for labour and environmental law.

It has only a limited institutional settlement governing it. However, its machinery for dispute settlement is more extensive as it provides not only for dispute settlement between the parties but also Investor–State Dispute Settlement (ISDS), procedures where investors can seek compensation from host States before an Investment Tribunal.

(a) Market Access and Liberalisation under CETA

Under CETA, the parties formally establish a free trade area.[262] It is characterised by three (qualified) freedoms: freedom of movement of goods, freedom of direct investment and liberalisation of services.

With regard to trade in goods, parties commit to abolishing customs duties and charges having equivalent effect on goods originating from or going to each other.[263] There can also be no discrimination against imports on the domestic market vis-à-vis domestic goods,[264] nor, in principle, restrictions on imports or exports to or from each other.[265] As with the EU–Ukraine Agreement, technical regulations are not allowed to restrict trade if the reasons that led to the adoption of the regulation no longer exist or the regulation's objectives can be realised in a less trade-restrictive manner.[266]

This might imply substantial liberalisation but that is not the case. There is no common customs tariff. Rules of origin are, therefore, imposed to verify that goods are not from third States.[267] Parties can restrict imports from each other if producers are engaging in unfair trade practices, such as dumping,[268] or as part of general safeguard measures to protect their

---

[258] *Ibid.* Article 477.   [259] *Ibid.* Article 478(1).   [260] *Ibid.* Article 478(2).
[261] As only a brief summary of CETA is being provided, these policies will not be discussed further here.
[262] CETA 2017, Article 1.4.   [263] *Ibid.* Articles 2.4, 2.6 and 2.9.   [264] *Ibid.* Article 2.3.   [265] *Ibid.* Article 2.11.
[266] *Ibid.* Article 4.2. WTO Agreement on Technical Barriers to Trade, n. 206 above, Article 2(3).
[267] CETA 2017, Article 4.2.1.   [268] *Ibid.* Article 3.1.1.

industry from a rise in imports that is causing or threatening serious injury to that industry.[269] Finally, parties can restrict marketing of goods if this threatens a public interest (e.g. public health, the environment).[270] As noted earlier, it is common for authorities to argue that because an import has been made according to a different standard, this difference means that the public interest is not protected as well as by the local regulation. *All these limitations mean a free trade area is incompatible with the commitment to no hard border on the island of Ireland.*

CETA tries to facilitate mutual recognition of technical regulations. If one party is developing a technical regulation, it should ask for the studies and information upon which the other relied in preparing its own regulation in the field.[271] More broadly, the principle of mutual recognition applies unless a party can provide reasons why not.[272]

CETA 2017, Article 4.4

2   A Party that has prepared a technical regulation that it considers to be equivalent to a technical regulation of the other Party having compatible objective and product scope may request that the other Party recognise the technical regulation as equivalent. The Party shall make the request in writing and set out detailed reasons why the technical regulation should be considered equivalent, including reasons with respect to product scope. The Party that does not agree that the technical regulation is equivalent shall provide to the other Party, upon request, the reasons for its decision.

The liberalising force of this principle is, however, limited. There are no requirements on the quality of the reasons given, and there is little redress if the party fails to give reasons. The force of the provision may, therefore, lie in it providing a mood music which is receptive to rather than sceptical of equivalence in these regulations.

CETA, secondly, provides significant protection for direct investment in each other's territories. The Agreement does not give a person or company in one territory the right to invest in another. It forbids a number of restrictions, however, that place quantitative limits on foreign investment (i.e. how many enterprises may carry out an activity, or limits on the total numbers of transactions or operations that may be carried out, or the amount of foreign shares in a company) or require that investments be carried through a particular legal form such as a joint venture. It, thus, allows many restrictions on investments (e.g. planning laws, authorisation requirements, merger laws). The central protections are national treatment, most-favoured-nation treatment, and fair and equitable treatment. National treatment requires that investors be given treatment that is no less favourable than treatment given to domestic investors,[273] whilst most-favoured-nation treatment imposes the same protection vis-à-vis investors from third States.[274] The United Kingdom could not, under this arrangement, give sweetheart deals to investors from the Far East, for example, if these are not also offered to Union investors. Fair and equitable treatment is the most controversial standard as

---

[269] *Ibid.* Article 3.4.1.   [270] *Ibid.* Article 28.3.   [271] *Ibid.* Article 4.1.
[272] The position is different for phytosanitary standards, which govern food safety. The good shall be admitted if the exporter can prove that the standard 'objectively' achieves the appropriate level of protection. *Ibid.* Article 5.6.1.
[273] *Ibid.* Article 8.6.1.   [274] *Ibid.* Article 8.7.1.

it affords a privileged protection to foreign investors which is not granted to a party's own undertakings.

CETA 2017, Article 8.10

2 A Party breaches the obligation of fair and equitable treatment ... if a measure or series of measures constitutes:

(a) denial of justice in criminal, civil or administrative proceedings;

(b) fundamental breach of due process, including a fundamental breach of transparency, in judicial and administrative proceedings;

(c) manifest arbitrariness;

(d) targeted discrimination on manifestly wrongful grounds, such as gender, race or religious belief;

(e) abusive treatment of investors, such as coercion, duress and harassment ...

The central demands of the standard are those of good governance, namely that due process is observed, and it is rare, but not unheard of, that regulatory standards are successfully challenged under it.[275] This has still led to significant concerns about foreign investors using the standard to challenge local environment, labour, or public health laws. An interpretative statement was, therefore, added to protect these.

Joint Interpretative Instrument on the Comprehensive Economic and Trade Agreement (CETA) between Canada and the European Union and its Member States[276]

2 CETA preserves the ability of the European Union and its Member States and Canada to adopt and apply their own laws and regulations that regulate economic activity in the public interest, to achieve legitimate public policy objectives such as the protection and promotion of public health, social services, public education, safety, the environment, public morals, social or consumer protection, privacy and data protection and the promotion and protection of cultural diversity.

The final field in which there is any significant liberalisation is services. Liberalisation is provided in all sectors unless these are excluded by CETA.[277] However, the degree of liberalisation provided is limited. No quantitative limits may be placed on the number of services or providers from the other party (e.g. requirements as to the number of service suppliers or services or ceilings on the value of transactions).[278] Equally, services and suppliers must be offered no less favourable treatment than either than domestic or third State counterparts are offered in the territory.[279] However, this all provides for limited market access because of the following qualification.

---

[275] B. Kingsbury and S. Schill, 'Investor-State Arbitration as Governance: Fair and Equitable Treatment, Proportionality and the Emerging Global Administrative Law', NYU Public Law Research Paper 09-46 (2009); F. Ortino, 'The Obligation of Regulatory Stability in the Fair and Equitable Treatment Standard: How Far Have We Come?' (2018) *JIEL*, forthcoming; M. Sattorova, *The Impact of Investment Treaty Law on Host States: Enabling Good Governance?* (Oxford: Hart, 2018) ch. 2.

[276] EU Council, Joint Interpretative Instrument on the Comprehensive Economic and Trade Agreement (CETA) between Canada and the European Union and its Member States, 13541/16, 27 October 2016.

[277] CETA 2017, Articles 9.2 and 9.7.   [278] *Ibid.*, Article 9.6.   [279] *Ibid.* Articles 9.3 and 9.5.

CETA 2017, Article 9.4

Article 9.3 [national treatment] does not prevent a Party from adopting or maintaining a measure that prescribes formal requirements in connection with the supply of a service, provided that such requirements are not applied in a manner which would constitute a means of arbitrary or unjustifiable discrimination.

Many requirements for a service provider to secure an authorisation in the host State before she can provide services there are, thus, lawful even though they take no account of her authorisation to provide services in her home State. This is also the case with requirements which go to the content of the service or the requirements surrounding its supply, be it safety requirements for construction or restaurants or rules on how estate agents are to market houses.

(b) Regulatory Cooperation and Regulatory Protection in the Free Trade Area

There is nothing in CETA that provides for the adoption of common rules. The nearest is its provision for regulatory cooperation.[280] This regulatory cooperation is concerned first with building the stock of regulatory knowledge.[281] Thus, it provides for exchanges of information and of experiences with different regulatory instruments between the parties. It is, secondly, concerned with regulatory improvement through mutual discussion of reforms and alternative forms of regulation.[282] Thirdly, it provides a tilt towards regulatory convergence. Parties are to consider the regulatory initiatives of the other party with a view to enhancing compatibility, albeit they are under no obligation to follow each other's standards,[283] and they are also to explore mutual recognition and the use of international standards.[284]

The effects of any future regulatory cooperation between the Union and the United Kingdom are speculative. The Political Declaration does provide, however, for possible UK cooperation with a number of EU agencies.[285] This possibility and the legacy of significant regulatory cooperation and interdependence from UK membership of the Union suggest that regulatory interactions might be extensive and significant. As the piece below indicates, the purpose of such interactions is not to bring about common rules. The process itself and the lessons drawn from it provide its value to policy-makers.

J. Wiener and A. Alemanno, 'The Future of International Regulatory Cooperation: TTIP as a Learning Process Toward a Global Policy Laboratory' (2015) 78 *Law and Contemporary Problems* 103, 130–1

Even if [international regulatory convergence] IRC is pursuing convergence via harmonized standards, the process of IRC itself can be used as an experiment: the change in regulatory impacts can be studied during the transition from variation toward convergence. Such transitions toward convergence may be desirable –

---

[280] On the growth of such cooperation across the world see J. Dunoff, 'Mapping a Hidden World of International Regulatory Cooperation' (2015) 78 *Law and Contemporary Problems* 267.

[281] CETA 2017, Article 21.4(c)–(e).   [282] *Ibid.* Article 21.4(a).   [283] *Ibid.* Article 21.5.   [284] *Ibid.* Article 21.4(r).

[285] Political Declaration, para. 24.

they may already be justified based on accumulated learning from past variation – but they too can be studied as they proceed through time to identify changing impacts associated with changing regulations. This evaluation may, in turn, be useful to other jurisdictions. Or the study of changing regulatory impacts during the transition from variation to convergence might reveal that the convergence was undesirable, perhaps because the initial variation was preferable or because the convergence should have moved to a different regulatory approach. In such a case, the evaluation should be taken into account in the next round of IRC to revise the policies again with continued study and evaluation. And even if regulatory convergence is desirable, the range of different IRC mechanisms to pursue convergence offers yet another dimension of variation deserving study to inform future selection of approaches to IRC.

Nevertheless, the absence of common rules and the technocratic qualities of regulatory cooperation lead to concerns that such free trade areas still have too strong a deregulatory bias. CETA tries to address this through a commitment that its trade should promote sustainable development.[286] To that end, it affirms the parties' right to regulate in the fields of labour and environmental law in a manner that is consistent with international commitments and seeks to secure a high level of protection.[287] Moreover, the parties go further by putting in place a non-regression commitment not to weaken existing levels of protection.[288]

CETA 2017, Article 24.5

1 The Parties recognise that it is inappropriate to encourage trade or investment reducing the levels of protection afforded in their environmental law.
2 A Party shall not waive or otherwise derogate from, or offer to waive or otherwise derogate from, its environmental law, to encourage trade or the establishment, acquisition, expansion or retention of an investment in its territory.
3 A Party shall not, through a sustained or recurring course of action or inaction, fail to effectively enforce its environmental law to encourage trade or investment.

Free trade arrangements, thus, do not offer the possibility for deregulation sought by some of their advocates. These provisions suggest not only that CETA's market liberalising provisions cannot be used to weaken or undermine environmental and labour protections but, independently of that, CETA also involves a mutual commitment to a certain quality of labour and environmental law. Existing levels are a base line from which parties should seek to improve protection, with a view to innovating and with an eye to garnering ideas from what the other party does.

These commitments are overseen by a Committee of Sustainable Development,[289] and are given further institutional force in a number of ways. In the field of labour law, each party must have a system of labour inspections[290] and ensure that plaintiffs have timely access to justice where costs are not prohibitive and there are effective remedies.[291] In the environmental field, there is a similar commitment to access to justice for parties granted individual rights or with a

---

[286] CETA 2017, Article 22.3.2.   [287] *Ibid.* Articles 23.2 and 24.3.
[288] For protection of labour laws see *ibid.* Article 23.4.   [289] *Ibid.* Articles 23.8.3 and 24.13.3.
[290] *Ibid.* Article 23.5.1(a).   [291] *Ibid.* Article 23.5.1(b) and 2.

legally recognised interest in a matter.[292] In addition, there must be authorities competent to enforce environmental law within the jurisdictions of each party who will give due consideration to violations of environmental law brought to their attention.[293] Finally, there is a commitment to participatory democracy. Domestic processes have to be in place which allow civil society and stakeholders to be able to submit opinions and recommendations on issues arising in these fields.[294] Both parties are also to give 'due consideration' to submissions from the public, particularly on implementation of CETA's labour commitments.[295]

(c) CETA's Institutional Settlement

CETA's institutional settlement is sparse. Only one body of note is established, a Joint Committee comprising representatives of both Canada and the European Union.[296] The Joint Committee decides matters by mutual agreement and has the power to take decisions binding on the parties where CETA grants it competences to do so.[297] However, there are few cases where this is so as its central missions are to supervise implementation and application of CETA and to seek ways of preventing problems and resolving disputes.[298] CETA is, thus, not a framework agreement which provides a forum for further legal norms to be developed but one which is self-contained.

These qualities make the free trade model attractive to sovereigntists compared to the other models. However, it allows development of the agreement to take place mainly through dispute settlement. To that end, arguably the Joint Committee's most significant power might be the power to give interpretations of CETA, which bind others, including tribunals.[299] This, of course, rests on both parties being able to agree an alternate interpretation.

CETA provides for three forms of dispute settlement, depending upon the matter in dispute.

The first, and central, one for disputes between the parties is the same as that in the EU–Ukraine Agreement. The parties are to try and resolve any dispute about the interpretation or application of the agreement through consultations with each other.[300] If these do not work, they may have recourse to mediation if the measure in question adversely affects trade and investment.[301] Alternately, if agreement has not been reached within forty-five days after the initial request for consultations has been received, the complainant may take the measure to arbitration.[302] The procedures for arbitration are the same as for the agreements described in this chapter.[303] The decision of the arbitration panel is binding upon the parties with a finding of non-compliance justifying countermeasures or compensation.[304]

The second procedure applies to disputes about commitments to protect environment and labour laws. Parties shall try to resolve any disagreements about the implementation of their commitments through consultations.[305] If agreement has not been reached within ninety days, a Panel of Experts (comprising labour or environmental lawyers respectively) shall provide a report on the dispute.[306] The parties are to endeavour within three months to agree a mutually

---

[292] *Ibid.* Article 24.6.1(b) and 2.   [293] *Ibid.* Article 24.6.1(a).   [294] *Ibid.* Articles 23.8.4 and 24.13.5.
[295] *Ibid.* Article 23.8.5.   [296] *Ibid.* Article 26.1.   [297] *Ibid.* Article 26.3.   [298] *Ibid.* Article 26.1.4(a) and (c).
[299] *Ibid.* Article 26.1.5(e).   [300] *Ibid.* Article 29.4.   [301] *Ibid.* Article 29.5.
[302] *Ibid.* Article 29.6.1(a). It can be twenty-five days if the dispute concerns seasonal or perishable goods. *Ibid.* Article 29.6.1(b).
[303] See pp. 417–20.   [304] The arbitration process is contained in CETA 2017, Articles 29.6–29.17.
[305] *Ibid.* Articles 23.9.1 and 24.14.1.   [306] *Ibid.* Articles 23.10 and 24.15.

satisfactory action plan, taking into account this report.[307] Whilst there are no sanctions if there is a failure to reach agreement, in many instances it is likely that the Panel of Expert's report will inform resolution. It will be made public,[308] and a party refusing to follow it will have to address the accusation that not only the other party but also a panel of experts agreed by it thinks it is breaching its obligations.

The most controversial form of dispute settlement, however, is the third, which allows foreign investors from either party (so Canadians investing in the Union and vice versa) to submit a claim for compensation against their host State to an Investment Tribunal on the grounds that it has violated a number of obligations.[309] The central ones are failing to grant treatment no less advantageous than that granted to its own nationals (national treatment) or to investors from other States (most-favoured-nation treatment); and that it failed to accord the investor fair and equitable treatment and she suffered loss as a result. The investor must seek consultations with the host State with a view to resolving the dispute[310] and must also withdraw or discontinue any existing proceeding before a domestic court.[311] If agreement is not reached within 180 days,[312] the investor can bring the claim before the Tribunal,[313] which shall have three members (a Union citizen, a Canadian, and a third State citizen) drawn from a corpus of fifteen persons appointed for a five-year renewable term.[314] The Investment Tribunal's decision may, in turn, be appealed to an Appellate Tribunal, also comprised of three members, who can overrule the initial decision, most centrally, on grounds of errors of law or manifest errors of fact.[315]

The central criticisms of this system are twofold. First, it grants foreign investors a privileged position vis-à-vis other parties. They can use a system of dispute settlement that is unavailable to others who must use the domestic courts. Foreign investors can also pick and choose. If they believe the domestic judicial process will grant greater remedies, they can use that. Alternatively, they can use the Investment Tribunal if it offers greater prospects. Secondly, Investment Tribunals replace a system of arbitration but do not 'eliminate the fundamental risk that now drives critics of the investment regime: namely the risk that sovereign decisions in the public interest will be second-guessed and chilled by the bringing of investor claims'.[316] To be sure, CETA and other EU free trade agreements install safeguards to protect the right to regulate and ensure that investor claims cannot lower levels of worker or environment protection. However, many claims are not against the laws themselves but against particular administrative applications of them. Investors can still challenge these, and this may lead to administrations soft-pedalling vis-à-vis such investors.[317]

---

[307] *Ibid.* Articles 23.10.12 and 24.15.11.   [308] *Ibid.* Articles 23.10.11 and 24.15.10.   [309] *Ibid.* Article 8.18.1.

[310] *Ibid.* Article 8.19.   [311] *Ibid.* Article 8.22(g).   [312] *Ibid.* Article 8.22(b).   [313] *Ibid.* Article 8.23.1.

[314] *Ibid.* Article 8.27.6. The division within the fifteen is five EU citizens, five Canadians and five third State nationals. *Ibid.* Article 8.27.2.

[315] *Ibid.* Article 8.28.2(a) and (b).

[316] J. Alvarez, 'Is the Trans-Pacific Partnership's Investment Chapter the New "Gold Standard"?', NYU IILJ Working Paper 2016/3 (2016) 38.

[317] On the debate surrounding the move to a multilateral investment court as an alternative see R. Howse, 'Designing a Multilateral Investment Court: Issues and Options' (2017) 36 *YBEL* 209.

6 'NO DEAL' BREXIT

(i) A World of World Trade Organisation (WTO) Rules

If no deal is made between the European United and the United Kingdom, trade relations will be governed by WTO rules. This is a detailed subject in its own right, and therefore, only its broadest principles are outlined here.[318]

Two WTO agreements are central to the government of trade in goods: the General Agreement on Tariffs and Trade (GATT)[319] and the Agreement on Technical Barriers to Trade.[320] They combine to impose a number of requirements.

Parties cannot, in principle, restrict trade in goods, be it exports or imports.[321] Restrictions can be imposed, however, for security-related reasons,[322] or where this is necessary to protect a wide range of public interests.[323] In determining when this is so, regard will had here to whether the restriction makes a material contribution to the public interest in question, the importance of that interest and the trade restrictiveness of the measure.[324] In addition, any such measure must not be a form of disguised discrimination or restriction on trade.[325] Parties can also restrict imports to protect their industry if these are entering in such increased quantities and under such conditions as to cause or threaten serious injury to their domestic industry. However, any such restriction must apply to all imports of that good rather than imports from simply one party.[326]

Imports not compliant with local technical regulations can be refused market access unless the reasons that led to the adoption of the regulation no longer exist or its objectives can be realised in a less trade-restrictive manner.[327] A regulation will only be unlawful under this test if there is a less trade restrictive alternative that is reasonably available and that will make an equivalent contribution to fulfilment of these objectives, taking account of the risks that non-fulfilment would create.[328] If this test sounds restrictive, in recent years there are no instances of measures being struck down for failing to meet it.

In principle, all these restrictions can be imposed on goods traded within a free trade area. However, the central difference is that under WTO rules, parties can impose tariffs on imports (and exports). A tax must be paid on these by virtue of their entering the territory. The WTO requires that these tariffs be subject to the most favoured nation principle.

---

[318] For a useful comparison between it and other options see F. Baetens, '"No Deal Is Better than a Bad Deal"? The Fallacy of the WTO Fall-Back Option as a Post-Brexit Safety Net' (2018) 55 *CMLRev* 133 (Brexit issue).

[319] General Agreement on Tariffs and Trade (1994), n. 87 above.

[320] WTO Agreement on Technical Barriers to Trade (1994), n. 206 above.   [321] GATT, Article XI(1).

[322] GATT, Article XXI.   [323] GATT, Article XX.

[324] *China – Measures Affecting Trading Rights and Distribution Services for Certain Publications and Audiovisual Entertainment Products*, WT/DS363/AB/R, 21 December 2009, para. 310.

[325] *United States – Import Prohibition of Certain Shrimp and Shrimp Products*, WT/DS58/AB/R, 12 October 1998, para. 184.

[326] GATT, Article XIX(1). The duty to apply the restriction to all imports is because the most favoured nation principle applies to safeguard measures.

[327] WTO Agreement on Technical Barriers to Trade, n. 206 above, Article 2(3).

[328] *United States – Measures Concerning the Importation, Marketing and Sale of Tuna and Tuna Products*, WT/DS381/AB/R, 16 May 2012, para. 322.

The General Agreement on Tariffs and Trade, Article I

(1) With respect to customs duties and charges of any kind imposed on or in connection with importation or exportation . . . and with respect to all rules and formalities in connection with importation and exportation . . . any advantage, favour, privilege or immunity granted by any contracting party to any product originating in or destined for any other country shall be accorded immediately and unconditionally to the like product originating in or destined for the territories of all other contracting parties.

Whilst there are some exceptions to this, most notably for parties within a free trade area or customs union,[329] the most-favoured-nation principle requires that if a party imposes a tariff on a good imported from one State, it must impose the same tariff on like goods coming from all other WTO parties. If the European Union imposes a 10 per cent tariff on cars imported from the United States, for example, it must also impose a 10 per cent tariff on cars imported from the United Kingdom, if the two are trading just on WTO terms. The challenges imposed by tariffs are not merely the added financial cost, but as this report indicates, the administrative hassle that surrounds them.[330] Some of the central ones are detailed below.

House of Lords European Union Committee, *Brexit: The Customs Challenge*, 20th Report, Session 2017–19, HL Paper 187

24 . . . While current EU tariffs are, on average, relatively low, certain sectors, such as agriculture and the automotive sector, could be particularly affected by higher tariffs that could result from trading on WTO terms. John Foster of the CBI, in evidence to the European Union Select Committee for its Brexit: deal or no deal inquiry, stated that in a 'no deal' scenario, 'The UK would face tariffs on 90% of our EU goods exports by value', and estimated that trading on WTO most-favoured nation terms would equate to 'an average tariff of 4%, which is about £4.5 billion to £6 billion-worth of increased costs per year on our exports'.

25 In addition to any tariff costs, from a business perspective, trade on WTO rules means that administrative and customs procedures previously reserved for the UK's rest-of-the-world trade (for example, with the US or China) would apply to trade with the EU27.

26 While some businesses are already trading with non-EU countries and may be familiar with the processes involved, others – including many small and medium-sized businesses and newly established businesses generally – may struggle, particularly if lead-in times are short . . .

27 HMRC estimates that, currently, there are 145,000 VAT-registered businesses and, potentially, a further 100,000 under the VAT threshold that export only to the EU. They are therefore unfamiliar with rest-of-the-world customs arrangements. From a survey of their members, the Federation of Small Businesses have found that 20% of members are exporting firms and nine out of ten of those businesses trade with the EU, with 20% doing so exclusively. However, they cautioned that these figures may underestimate the number of firms that deal with goods for export. This is because some smaller firms may not actually be aware that

---

[329] GATT, Article XXIV(5).

[330] The British tax authorities gave evidence that these administrative costs could amount to between £17 billion and £20 billion per year, House of Lords European Union Committee, *Brexit: The Customs Challenge*, 20th Report, Session 2017–19, HL Paper 187, para. 65.

their products are part of an export supply chain. Current UK customs procedures when trading with non-EU countries.

28 On 23 August 2018 the Government provided some clarity for businesses by confirming that, in the case of 'no deal', the requirements for 'rest-of-the-world' trade would apply to trade with the EU27. This information was not included in either of the UK Government's two White Papers on customs. It is possible that, in the longer term, some of the administrative processes could be simplified, including through bilateral agreements with the EU, but in the short and medium term at least, the existing 'rest-of-the-world' trade processes would apply.

29 HMRC has based its planning on the fact that, in a 'no deal' scenario, 'customs controls would operate both ways on goods moving between the UK and the EU, meaning customs declarations and the potential for checks on goods'. It has accordingly estimated that there would be a five-fold increase in customs declarations that would need to be submitted, from currently 55 million to 250 million a year. Before non-EU goods arrive at the border.

30 Exporters – be they UK businesses exporting to non-EU countries or non-EU businesses exporting to the UK – must, as a first step, register for an Economic Operator Registration Identification (EORI) number with HMRC. This is a one-time process that involves completing a short application form. An EORI number is then usually allocated within three working days. The EORI number will subsequently be needed to make any customs declarations.

31 Before a consignment of goods arrives at the border, a customs entry for that consignment needs to be built and other forms need to be completed, so that the goods can be cleared following their arrival.

32 The main customs form used to fulfil customs and duty obligations to HMRC is the Single Administrative Document (SAD) for import or export. It contains 54 data fields and comes in eight parts for use at different stages of the trading process, depending whether the goods are being exported, imported or are in transit. Information about the goods, their arrival and value is required. Typically, this information must be sourced from a variety of documents, such as invoices and shipping documents. While both exports and imports need to be declared, it is the administration of import processes that is usually more onerous as, when exporting, there is no revenue collection involved . . .

Movement of services is even more restricted under WTO terms. Under the WTO, there is no general right to provide services in or to the territory of another WTO State. Instead, under the General Agreement in Trade in Services (GATS), States set out schedules of services that they are to be liberalised and the modes of supply that will be liberalised for each of these.[331] The latter involves the schedule identifying whether liberalisation allows the service to be supplied from one territory to another; consumers to receive the service in the territory of the other party; suppliers to set up a commercial presence there; or a service supplier to have people who are not nationals of the host State helping with the supply of the service there.[332]

The schedule provided by the European Union is extensive,[333] and the GATS imposes a most-favoured-nation requirement so a service liberalised for suppliers from one party must be liberalised for services supplied from all other parties.[334] However, the liberalisation provided for the services liberalised is still very limited. There is a market access requirement. Like the EU–Canada Agreement, this prohibits quantitative limits on the number of service suppliers, the total number

---

[331] General Agreement on Trade in Services (1994) 1869 UNTS 183, Articles XVI(1) and XXVII(1).
[332] GATS, Articles XVI(1) and I(2).   [333] http://trade.ec.europa.eu/doclib/docs/2012/november/tradoc_150087.pdf.
[334] GATS, Article II. Exemptions can be secured from this obligation, however, GATS, Article II(2) and Annex II.

or value of transactions and foreign capital participation or persons employed in a service sector.[335] It also prohibits requirements that services be provided through a particular legal form such as a joint venture.[336] There is also a national treatment requirement. Foreign service providers and services must be offered no less favourable treatment than domestic suppliers or services.[337] This will be the case if they are given formally identical treatment.[338]

These requirements, together, secure only restricted market access. Parties can impose authorisation or licence requirements before a service can be offered or imposes conditions that must be met by the service supplied. As with the EU–Canada Agreement, the only way that a foreign service provider can be sure of benefiting from the liberalisation provided by the GATS is establishing a commercial presence in the European Union (if this is permitted under the schedule) and then trading under the rights given by EU law.

(ii) The Influence of EU Law in the United Kingdom in a No Deal Brexit

The attractions of a No Deal Brexit are that it will secure legislative and regulatory autonomy. Even if there may be immediate costs as a result of No Deal, these may be a price worth paying for some if it secures democratic self-government within the United Kingdom. Parliament can legislate unconstrained. However, the huge EU law *acquis* will continue to apply in the United Kingdom as retained EU law.[339] To be sure, this retained EU law can be amended or repealed, but there is a lot of it, so this will take considerable time, and there will be a status quo effect. Many parties within the United Kingdom have aligned their behaviour and relationships to comply with EU law. This *modus vivendi* is comfortable and beneficial for many, has shaped expectations and will necessarily involve adjustment costs. All these militate against change.

Furthermore, new EU laws may continue to exert pull on the United Kingdom. We will examine two forms of pull: the 'Brussels effect' where private parties continue to apply EU law over and above requirements of their domestic law and 'territorial extension' where EU law requires certain activities within the non-EU State to be done in accordance with EU law or international law if parties want access to its territory.

(a) The 'Brussels Effect'

Bradford identified the Brussels effect when she noted a paradox. The United States is both economically and politically powerful and is not part of any free trade area with the European Union. However, many EU laws are, nevertheless, applied within the United States.

> ### A. Bradford, 'The Brussels Effect' (2012) 107 *Northwestern University Law Review* 1, 2–3
>
> It is common to hear Europe described today as the power of the past. Europe is perceived to be weak militarily. Its relative economic power is declining as Asia's is rising. Its common currency may be on the verge of disintegrating. On the world stage, the European Union is thought to be waning into

---

[335] GATS, Article XVI(2)(a)–(d) and (f). A prohibition on the offering a service has been found to fall within this, however, as it amounts to a zero quota, *United States – Measures Affecting the Cross-Border Supply of Gambling and Betting Services*, WT/DS285/AB/R, 7 April 2005, para. 238.

[336] GATS, Article XVI(2)(e).   [337] GATS, Article XVII(1).   [338] GATS, Article XXVII(2).

[339] European Union Withdrawal Act 2018, ss. 2–5. See pp. 244–6.

irrelevance due to its inability to speak with one voice. Given its seemingly declining power status and inability to get its way alone, the EU is perceived as needing to retreat to weak multilateralism and international institutions. Contrary to this prevalent perception, this Article highlights a deeply underestimated aspect of European power that the discussion on globalization and power politics overlooks: Europe's unilateral power to regulate global markets. The European Union sets the global rules across a range of areas, such as food, chemicals, competition, and the protection of privacy. EU regulations have a tangible impact on the everyday lives of citizens around the world. Few Americans are aware that EU regulations determine the makeup they apply in the morning, the cereal they eat for breakfast, the software they use on their computer, and the privacy settings they adjust on their Facebook page. And that's just before 8:30 AM. The EU also sets the rules governing the interoffice phone directory they use to call a coworker. EU regulations dictate what kind of air conditioners Americans use to cool their homes and why their children no longer find soft plastic toys in their McDonald's Happy Meals.

Bradford argues that this occurs because the single market is the largest market in the global economy. It is central to the success of export-oriented industries around the world who must be able to sell their goods or services on it. She also noted that the single market tends to have higher regulatory standards than many other markets.[340] As a consequence, industries from these other markets cannot seamlessly sell goods intended for their domestic market onto the Union market. This is particularly problematic for the non-EU industry where the Union market is highly valuable to it and the standard in question is non-divisible.

A. Bradford, 'The Brussels Effect' (2012) 107 *Northwestern University Law Review* 1, 17–18

The exporter has an incentive to adopt a global standard whenever its production or conduct is nondivisible across different markets or when the benefits of a uniform standard due to scale economies exceed the costs of forgoing lower production costs in less regulated markets. Complying with just one regulatory standard allows a corporation to maintain a single production process, which is less costly than tailoring its production to meet divergent regulatory standards. A single standard also facilitates the preservation of a uniform global brand. Thus, unilateral regulatory globalization follows from the nondivisibility of a corporation's production or conduct. Non-divisibility of a corporation's production or conduct occurs in three primary types: legal nondivisibility, technical non-divisibility, and economic non-divisibility. 'Legal non-divisibility' can be seen in global mergers, which cannot be consummated on a jurisdiction-by-jurisdiction basis – the most stringent antitrust jurisdiction gets to determine the fate of the transaction worldwide. The principle of 'technical non-divisibility' often applies for the regulation of privacy. For example, the EU forces companies like Google to amend their data storage and other business practices to conform to European privacy standards. Unable to isolate its data collection for the EU for technical reasons, Google is forced to adjust its global operations to the most demanding EU standard. 'Economic non-divisibility' is exemplified in market participants' responses to the EU's health, environmental, and other product standards. An illustrative example is European chemical regulation, which applies to all companies seeking to enter the EU market. Numerous U.S. manufacturers, who would find it too costly to develop

---

[340] For further development of this argument see A. Bradford, 'Exporting Standards: The Externalization of the EU's Regulatory Power via Markets' (2015) 42 *International Review of Law and Economics* 158.

different products for different consumer markets, choose to conform their entire global chemical production to the EU standard. The scale economies associated with a single global production process therefore often allow the EU to effectively dictate the global product standards.

Bradford's examples suggest there are many standards which are non-divisible and, where this is the case, there are strong incentives for non-EU industries to apply EU law within their home markets. Furthermore, this has an escalating effect. Insofar as it leads non-EU States to adopt EU laws,[341] incentives to adopt EU laws grow, for compliance secures access not only to the Union market but these other markets as well.[342]

This raises some profound questions. The presence of such a phenomenon within the United States suggests that a State, such as the United Kingdom, whose laws are already aligned with EU law and whose industry is more dependent on the Union market is likely to be more exposed to these pressures. It also generates democratic concerns. Laws are being decided by industrial actors and not political processes without fanfare and with little accountability. If a Union standard transpires subsequently to be dangerous, this might, of course, lead to a political scandal within the Union but would lead only in the non-EU State to private law damages against the industry. Furthermore, having adapted their standard to EU law, export industries may then lobby their home legislature for that standard to become the relevant national law. However, such a law may be completely unsuitable for other actors on the domestic market.

Other observers have also pointed to other actors who might pressure for EU law to be applied in the United Kingdom. Opponents of central administration or legislation elsewhere have used EU law as a template to mobilise opposition. It is particularly suited to this, because, as EU law is applied by so many States, advocates can point to wide acceptance of its values and authority. In such circumstances, these advocates often seek to have it applied in institutional fora which are not controlled by the central administration, asking for local courts to interpret domestic law in the light of EU law or for local or regional administrations to enact EU law within their fields of competence. Scott has, therefore, found examples of states within the United States adopting EU environmental law[343] and, in similar vein, Resnik observed the adoption of CEDAW, the international treaty prohibiting discrimination against women, by many US states.[344] However, Resnik also observed that a foreign law's pedigree could generate the opposite reaction with some US states refusing to consider laws with a foreign origin independently of their content.[345]

---

[341] On the adoption of EU chemicals laws in China, South Korea and the United States see M. Morpurgo, 'The European Union as a Global Producer of Transnational Law of Risk Regulation: A Case Study on Chemical Regulation' (2013) 19 *ELJ* 779.

[342] D. Bach and A. Newman, 'Governing Lipitor and Lipstick: Capacity, Sequencing and Power in International Pharmaceuticals and Cosmetics Regulation' (2010) 17 *Review of International Political Economy* 665; C. Damro, 'Market Power Europe: Exploring a Dynamic Conceptual Framework' (2015) 22 *JEPP* 1336; A. Newman and E. Posner, 'Putting the EU in its Place: Policy Strategies and the Global Regulatory Context' (2015) 22 *JEPP* 1316.

[343] J. Scott, 'From Brussels with Love: The Transatlantic Travels of European Law and the Chemistry of Regulatory Attraction' (2009) 57 *AJCL* 897.

[344] J. Resnik, 'Comparative (In)Equalities: CEDAW, the Jurisdiction of Gender, and the Heterogeneity of Transnational Law Production' (2012) 10 *I-CON* 531.

[345] *Ibid.* 540.

The wider political authority generated by this application of EU law across Europe might also stop the United Kingdom from changing its laws precisely because EU law is seen as a civilisational marker. A useful thought experiment is to think which EU labour laws a UK government would repeal if it leaves without a deal. These laws are unpopular with right-of-centre politicians,[346] but is it conceivable that the United Kingdom might abolish or restrict the rights granted to parents under, for example, the Parental Leave Directive, and thus be seen as treating working parents worse than any other State in Europe?

This is not without its complications. EU law is invoked here opportunistically by actors disenchanted by the position of the legislative majority within that State. It relies, therefore, on nooks and crannies within the settlement to filter its way into the territory and activism of political entrepreneurs. This can be attractive if it appears that the legislative majority seem to have neglected an important interest, but it is an unstructured process, vulnerable both to abuse and to hostile counter-reaction.

(b) The Territorial Extension of EU Law

Territorial extension occurs where the Union takes account of activities or conduct that occurred in non-EU States in order to determine whether somebody in the Union is complying with EU law. A good example is Directive 2011/11/EU, which goes to the circumstances when Alternative Investment Fund Managers (AIFMs) – more commonly known as hedge funds or private equity funds, who often handle quite risky financial products – may operate within the Union. It allows fund managers operating outside the Union to raise capital with a view to investing it (AIFs) within the Union and to manage this capital within the Union. However, they need authorisation to do this, which will only be granted if they either comply with EU law or with a local law which offers equivalent protection.

> ### Directive 2011/61/EU on Alternative Investment Fund Managers, Article 37[347]
>
> (2) A non-EU AIFM intending to obtain prior authorisation . . . shall comply with this Directive . . . If and to the extent that compliance with a provision of this Directive is incompatible with compliance with the law to which the non-EU AIFM and/or the non-EU AIF marketed in the Union is subject, there shall be no obligation on the AIFM to comply with that provision of this Directive if it can demonstrate that:
> (a) it is impossible to combine such compliance with compliance with a mandatory provision in the law to which the non-EU AIFM and/or the non-EU AIF marketed in the Union is subject;
> (b) the law to which the non-EU AIFM and/or the non-EU AIF is subject provides for an equivalent rule having the same regulatory purpose and offering the same level of protection to the investors of the relevant AIF; and
> (c) the non-EU AIFM and/or the non-EU AIF complies with the equivalent rule referred to in point (b).

Territorial extension is particularly present in environmental and financial law. Its *modus operandi* can also vary as the excerpt below illustrates.

---

[346] EU Fresh Start Group, *Options for Change: Renegotiating the UK's Relationship with the EU* (London, Fresh Start Project, 2012) 119–37.

[347] Directive 2011/61/EU on Alternative Investment Fund Managers, OJ 2011, L 174/1.

J. Scott, 'Extraterritoriality and Territorial Extension in EU Law' (2014) 62 *American Journal of Comparative Law* **87, 105–6**

EU legislation that gives rise to territorial extension serves to construct a number of concentric spheres of regulatory intervention which are delimited by the boundaries of an individual transaction, a firm, a country or the globe. Depending upon which sphere(s) of regulatory intervention are constructed by the EU measure in question, the regulatory perimeter demarcated by this measure will be differently, and more or less broadly, drawn. Where the sphere of regulatory intervention constituted by a measure is defined by the boundaries of an individual transaction, the EU regulator will be required to take into account conduct or circumstances outside of the EU that relate exclusively to that transaction. For example, in assessing whether a product originating in a third country may be imported into the EU, the EU regulator may be obligated to take into account the manner in which a specific EU-bound shipment of that product is harvested or produced. When EU measures construct a broader sphere of regulatory intervention, the EU regulator will be required to look beyond the confines of an individual transaction and to examine conduct or circumstances outside the EU that relate more broadly to a firm, a third country or the globe. As has already been noted, the EU's Aviation Directive constructs three different spheres of regulatory intervention. It constructs a transaction-specific sphere of regulatory intervention because the EU regulator is required to take into account the worldwide volume of emissions generated by a single EU-departing or landing flight. It constructs a countrywide sphere of regulatory intervention because the EU regulator is required to take into account whether a third country has adopted its own measures to reduce the climate change impact of flights. And it constructs a global sphere of regulatory intervention because the EU regulator must consider amending the Directive if a global agreement to regulate the climate impact of aviation emissions is reached.

Territorial extension has, of course, overbearing qualities for non-EU States and actors.[348] Scott argues that this may be tempered where the Union is either seeking to promote international law or it leads to negotiations between the Union and the non-EU State in which there is some mutual accommodation.[349]

(c) The Autonomous Adoption of EU Law

There are strong pressures on lawmakers to manage the pulls and tensions generated by EU law. The extent of these is best illustrated in Switzerland, a non-EU State. Since 1988, Swiss authorities have pursued a policy of autonomous adoption (*autonomer Nachvollzug*). All planned Swiss legislation has a so-called European Chapter attached to it which explains its relationship to existing or planned EU law. The Swiss Federal Office for Justice will look at the perceived intention behind the Swiss measure and see if it should be made compatible with EU law even though there is no treaty obligation to do.[350] The impact has been significant with swathes of EU law being incorporated in EU law. Sabine Jenni found that between 1990 and 2010 this autonomous adoption had influenced 24.04 per cent of all Swiss federal parliamentary measures.

---

[348] On the response of the United States to the application of EU climate change emission targets to the US aviation industry see E. Fahey, 'On the Use of Law in Transatlantic Relations: Legal Dialogues between the EU and US' (2014) 20 *ELJ* 368.

[349] J. Scott, 'Extraterritoriality and Territorial Extension in EU Law' (2014) 62 *AJCL* 87, 113–23.

[350] S. Kux, 'Zwischen Isolation und autonomer Anpassung: Die Schweiz im integrationpolitischen Abseits?', ZEI Discussion Paper C 3, Bonn (1998) 8–9.

Almost a quarter of its time was, thus, spent adapting Swiss law to EU law. The influence of EU law varied, however. In only about 20 per cent of the cases was EU law fully transposed into EU law. It was partially transposed in just over 25 per cent of cases, and checks were made to ensure that it did not conflict with EU law in the remainder of cases.[351]

   If engagement with the pull of EU law will be a central feature of any Brexit, but particularly of a No Deal Brexit, the structures for mediating the different tensions, values and interests created by this pull are pivotal. In this regard, a depressing outcome is that this is likely to be done by Whitehall in the field of agricultural standards, where there is most possibility for legislative reform simply because there are most EU laws to change. In that field, for agricultural product standards, the Secretary of State will simply adopt regulations which may or may not align with EU law.[352] This is unlikely to offer a revitalised independent British democracy or British political economy as a reward for Brexit. Civil servants will be dominating the process, and lawmaking is likely to be treated as something which must be done cautiously, not generate undue disruption and pay strong heed to experts and stakeholders. These are, of course, the interests who are likely to be most disposed to keeping UK law aligned with EU law.

FURTHER READING

F. Baetens, '"No Deal Is Better than a Bad Deal"? The Fallacy of the WTO Fall-Back Option as a Post-Brexit Safety Net' (2018) 55 *Common Market Law Review* 133 (Brexit issue).

A. Bradford, 'Exporting Standards: The Externalization of the EU's Regulatory Power via Markets' (2015) 42 *International Review of Law and Economics* 158.

T. Burri and B. Pirker, 'Constitutionalization by Association? The Doubtful Case of the European Economic Area' (2013) 32 *Yearbook of European Law* 207.

H. Fredriksen and C. Franklin, 'Of Pragmatism and Principles: The EEA Agreement 20 Years On' (2015) 52 *Common Market Law Review* 629.

A. Lazowski, 'Withdrawal from the European Union and Alternatives to Membership' (2012) 37 *European Law Review* 523.

M. Pérez Crespo, 'After Brexit...The Best of Both Worlds? Rebutting the Norwegian and Swiss Models as Long-Term Options for the UK' (2017) 36 *Yearbook of European Law* 94.

J. Scott, 'Extraterritoriality and Territorial Extension in EU Law' (2014) 62 *American Journal of Comparative Law* 87.

G. van der Loo, *The EU–Ukraine Association Agreement and Deep and Comprehensive Free Trade Area: A New Legal Instrument for Integration without Membership* (Leiden, Brill, 2016).

B. de Witte, 'An Undivided Union? Differentiated Integration in Post-Brexit Times' (2018) 55 *Common Market Law Review* 227 (Brexit Issue).

---

[351] S. Jenni, *Switzerland's Differentiated European Integration: The Last Gallic Village?* (Basingstoke, Palgrave, 2016) 68–80.

[352] Agriculture Bill 2018, s. 22(1).

11

Citizenship of the Union

CONTENTS

1 INTRODUCTION

This chapter considers the ideas and rights associated with European Union citizenship. This is granted by the Treaty to all those who are citizens of one of the Member States of the European Union. The chapter is organised as follows.

Sections 2 and 3 discuss ideas of citizenship.

(a) Modern citizenship evolved in the period of the industrial revolution, following the American and French Revolutions. Society became less feudal and more democratic and individuals acquired more rights and possibilities. The core elements of the resulting notion of citizenship were legally enforceable rights, loyalty, a sense of belonging to the national community and participation in political decision-making.

(b) One view of EU citizenship is that it follows this tradition. On this view, citizenship is a limited success. Rights are primarily for those who migrate and who are economically active or independent. The sense of a community of Europeans is but a pale shadow of that found in nation States and citizens do not have political rights to participate in some of the most important elections.

(c) Others would like to see Union citizenship break with nationality and include all those living within the European Union, even if they have the nationality of a non-EU State. This would make Union citizenship more open, accessible and a true challenge to nationalism, arguably in the original spirit of the Union.

(d) An alternative view of Union citizenship is that its value is not as a free-standing institution at all, but as a mechanism for changing what national citizenship means. It works to transform national societies, requiring them to redefine and reconstitute their own structures of membership, and it should be judged against this measure.

Section 4 considers the right of Union citizens to move and reside throughout the Union.

(a) This right is found in Articles 20 and 21 TFEU. It is complemented by Article 18 TFEU, the prohibition on nationality discrimination. The rights in these Articles are expressed in more detail in Directive 2004/38/EC (Citizenship Directive).

(b) The right to free movement and residence is subject to conditions: citizens must either be economically active, or they must be economically independent of the State in which they live. Those who are not economically active must also show that they have sickness insurance covering their costs in the host State, which may be difficult for some to obtain. This exclusion of the disadvantaged from migration rights inspires the criticism that Union citizenship is still a quasi-economic policy as opposed to a proper constitutional citizenship embodying solidarity, equality and universality.

(c) Lawfully present migrant citizens and their families enjoy a right to equal treatment with nationals in their host State. A particularly sensitive issue concerns equal access to public benefits and support. Member States sometimes make these conditional upon a period of prior residence, or some degree of integration into society. Such requirements can come close to nationality discrimination, but the Court of Justice finds that they are acceptable if they are justified and proportionate in the particular circumstances.

(d) As a corollary of their own free movement rights, Union citizens who migrate may bring their family to live with them, even if these family members are not Union citizens. The Court of Justice has extended this right to citizens returning home with family members from a period living in another Member State and, where the citizen is sufficiently dependent that their own residence in the European Union requires the presence of family members, even to citizens who have never migrated at all.[1]

---

[1] *Gerardo Ruiz Zambrano* v. *ONEm*, C-34/09, EU:C:2011:124.

(e) Union citizens and their family members can only be excluded from a Member State under very serious circumstances. Mere criminality is not enough. They must represent a current and serious threat to one of the fundamental interests of society. In general, if a migrant citizen misbehaves, the host State should punish or prosecute him just as they would their own citizens. Expulsion is the exception.

Section 5 concerns the political rights of citizens. The most important of these is that Union citizens may vote for the European Parliament in whichever State they live and may vote in local elections in the State where they live. However, if they are in a host State EU law gives them no right to vote in national elections.

Section 6 discusses the rights of Union citizens in the United Kingdom and British citizens in the European Union after Brexit, and considers briefly whether the loss of Union citizenship by an entire nation requires us to rethink what that citizenship is or means.

2 EVOLUTION OF MODERN CITIZENSHIP

Contemporary national citizenship is the product of modernity. Economic, social and political change in the eighteenth and nineteenth centuries transformed the State, the national community and the position of the individual in that community.[2]

R. Bellamy, 'Introduction: The Making of Modern Citizenship' in R. Bellamy *et al.* (eds.), *Lineages of European Citizenship: Rights, Belonging and Participation in Eleven Nation States* (Basingstoke, Palgrave Macmillan, 2004) 1, 6–7

[The American and French Revolutions] provided the basis for a distinctly modern conception of citizenship. First, it gave rise to the new political context of the nation-state. Rather than being the fiefdoms of monarchs, these new political units found legitimacy through being the territorial expression of a given culture and people. The political apparatus no longer referred simply to the administration of the monarch's domain and subjects, but likewise had a popular justification. Second, this development was linked in its turn to the emergence of commercial and increasingly industrial market economies. These required regular forms of government and justice that, in various ways facilitated the free movement and exchange of goods, capital, labour and services. Thus, states had to uphold the rule of law, particularly freedom of contract and the protection of property rights. Nation-building and a state education system that promoted a common language and guaranteed standards of numeracy and literacy helped create a mobile workforce capable of acquiring the generic skills needed for industry. Nation-states could also provide the infrastructural public goods required by market economies, such as a unified transport system, a single currency and a standardized system of weights and measures. Third, markets broke down traditional social hierarchies and systems of ascribed status, thereby fostering equality of opportunity. This feature was also associated with demands for equal political as well as legal rights by hitherto politically excluded sections of the nation. The national people gradually transformed into a demos, who sought to ensure that the state governed in their interest.

---

[2] On the broader evolution of the term 'citizenship', see R. Bendix, *Nation-Building and Citizenship* (New York, Wiley, 1964); W. Brubaker, *Citizenship and Nationhood in France and Germany* (Cambridge, MA, Harvard University Press, 1992); P. Riesenberg, *Citizenship in the Western Tradition: Plato to Rousseau* (Chapel Hill, NC, University of North Carolina Press, 1992).

These three interrelated developments associated with the rise of national industrial states promoted the three key components of modern citizenship. First, they fostered an emphasis on individual rights. Lack of ascribed status led individuals to being treated as equals possessing certain rights simply by virtue of their humanity – including the right to be treated equally before the law. Their involvement as actors in markets also gave them equal rights to pursue their interests by buying and selling goods, services and labour. Meanwhile, they looked to the state to provide social and economic rights, as part of its regulatory function and demanded political rights to secure equal access and recognition within its policies, decision-making and organizational structures. Second, citizenship became closely associated with belonging to the national community. National identity shaped a common civic consciousness and allegiance to the state and one's fellow citizens. It encouraged reciprocity and solidarity in both politics and economics. National systems of education created a public political language and inducted citizens into a certain civic culture and set of values. Third, as a mark of citizenship was the capacity and right to participate as a full and equal member within the economy and the polity, the right to vote was often obligatory and in any case tied to the payment of taxes, military service, and the undertaking of such public duties as sitting on juries. Similarly, social and economic rights were linked to the duty and ability to work and to contribute to national schemes of social insurance. Those deemed socially irresponsible, a label that at various times and places has been applied to lunatics, children, criminals, women, the propertyless and the indigent, either forfeited or were ineligible for most citizenship rights

As the State was transformed from a personal fiefdom into a rational and efficient socio-economic machine, the subject was transformed into a citizen. The marks of this citizenship were rights, a sense of belonging and political participation. All three enhanced the position of the individual, protecting them from arbitrariness and extending their influence over the society around them. Yet, they also served the national interest, helping to create a cohesive and loyal population, better able to work and live together and act responsibly. Citizenship was part of a pragmatic and multifaceted social contract.

The specific content of citizenship has varied from State to State and over time. The Cambridge historian T. H. Marshall observed that the growth of the Welfare State and its importance in contemporary understandings of justice following the Second World War led to a greater emphasis on social rights, as increasingly it was felt that equal membership of the political community entailed a right to participate in the wealth and welfare provided by that community.[3] More recently, the sociologist Bryn Turner has observed that politics has concerned itself with the protection of the individual against risk.[4] These risks might be environmental risks, such as that posed by floods or pollution, uncertainty generated by terrorism or risks associated with financial markets, such as losing one's savings or pension. In such a world, he has argued, equal membership within a political community entails equal protection against risk. He speaks of the emergence of a new citizenship right, a 'right to security', which would give all citizens minimum assurances against certain types of risks.

---

[3] This division was first made, most famously, in T. Marshall, *Citizenship and Social Class*, ed. T. Bottomore (London, Pluto, 1992). This model was first applied to the European Union in J. Shaw, 'The Interpretation of Union Citizenship' (1998) 61 *MLR* 293.

[4] B. Turner, 'The Erosion of Citizenship' (2001) 52 *British Journal of Sociology* 189.

Another event to transform understandings of citizenship was the migration into Western Europe since the Second World War. From being less than or around 1 per cent in most Western European States in 1960, the foreign population grew, by 1990 to between 3 and 9 per cent of the general population, and continues to grow.[5] An important feature of this foreign population is its permanence. Many migrants who came to Europe did not return to their home States, something for which the States hosting them were ill-prepared.

This non-native population challenged the existing notion of citizenship. Although Shaw has argued that the decoupling of rights and identity is an important post-war phenomenon, as long as citizenship remained a significant vehicle for rights its link to nationality was problematic.[6] This tie turned citizenship into an exclusionary device. When citizens are just a subset of those living and participating in the nation, then citizenship takes on a less universalistic and idealistic flavour and tribal and ethnic undertones emerge. Is it about recognition of the dignity and rights of the individual or about closure against the outsider?

Scholars have sought to resolve the resulting tensions in different ways, with many arguing that citizenship should become more open. This can either occur by making nationality more accessible (it has traditionally been very hard to acquire the nationality of some EU Member States, even after decades of residence), or by decoupling citizenship from nationality. Balibar has proposed a citizenship based on factual presence rather than the accident of birth, although he is more concerned to expose the contradictions of national citizenship – to deconstruct it – than to lobby for concrete change.[7] His view of citizenship seems less exclusionary, as it opens up membership of a community to anyone who chooses to participate and to all those who do participate. Yet concerns have been raised that mere practical participation may not suffice to generate commitment of citizens to each other and to society, without which shared projects may not be achievable.[8] Participation may also not provide a shared identity, without which the community may not be a satisfying or enriching context for individuals to live in. This commitment and identity may be more likely to materialise in communities of fate – those where membership is not a choice, but is ascribed on the basis of factors outside individual control such as family origin or place of birth.[9] Commitment to such communities is arguably more profound because the individual enjoys unconditional membership. This also gives the community a certain tolerance, as people of opposing political views can seek to impose their own interpretation of the community without calling membership as such into question. An identity is maintained despite such political diversity through the use of myths and symbols, such as those surrounding the nation State.

---

[5] Y. Soysal, *Limits of Citizenship: Migrants and Postnational Membership in Europe* (University of Chicago Press, 1994) 23. These figures do not include migrants who subsequently became naturalised and thereby citizens of the nation States in which they were resident.

[6] J. Shaw, 'Citizenship of the Union: Towards Post-National Membership?', Jean Monnet Working Paper No. 6/97 (1997), www.jeanmonnetprogram.org/archive/papers/97/97-06-.html.

[7] E. Balibar, *We the Peoples of Europe: Reflections on Transnational Citizenship* (Princeton University Press, 2004). See also D. Schnapper, 'The European Debate on Citizenship' (1997) 126 *Daedalus* 199; L. Bosniak, 'Citizenship Denationalised' (2000) 7 *Indiana Journal of Global Law Studies* 447; D. Kochenov, 'Ius Tractum of Many Faces: European Citizenship and the Difficult Relationship between Status and Rights' (2009) 15 *Columbia Journal of European Law* 169.

[8] D. Miller, *Citizenship and National Identity* (Oxford, Polity, 2000) ch. 2. See also R. Bellamy, 'Evaluating Union Citizenship: Belonging, Rights and Participation within the EU' (2008) 12 *Citizenship Studies* 597.

[9] Miller, n. 8 above.

Habermas is the best known of those who seek a middle way between these extremes. He has suggested that a commitment to the values of a community, such as democracy and human rights, should be a condition for citizenship. This requirement, combined with participatory political practices, would offer a foundation for a citizenship lying between the mystical and closed, but tough, community of fate and the possibly shallow and unstable community of participation.[10] His view of citizenship has been prominent in the debate on Union citizenship and he places his arguments in the context of Europe.

Like many other contemporary and recent scholars, Habermas is trying to reconcile closure with humanity. As Bosniak puts it, citizenship is inherently about membership and can never be fully open; a 'purely inclusionary inside' is a fantasy.[11] The task, in their view, is not to eliminate the bounded community, but to keep trying to make it more decent and fair. This is, rather like Kostakopoulou suggests in the next section, citizenship at least partly as process.

3 NATURE OF UNION CITIZENSHIP

There was no mention of citizenship in the initial EC Treaty. Indeed, there was no discussion of the term until the 1970s. First use of the term was made in the Tindemans Report in 1975, which contained a chapter entitled 'Towards a Europe for Citizens'. The thrust of this was a number of proposals aimed at integrating Member State nationals resident in other Member States more fully into their host States. It was, therefore, proposed that they should be given a bundle of civil, political and social rights which would place them on an equal footing with that State's own nationals. Throughout the 1970s and 1980s, the Commission and Parliament brought forward a series of proposals to try and flesh out and implement the ideas in this Report, but to little avail.[12] The breakthrough moment was the Intergovernmental Conference on Political Union that preceded the adoption of the Treaty on European Union at Maastricht. In September 1990, the Spanish Government submitted a proposal entitled 'The Road to European Citizenship'. The Spanish Government indicated in this paper that the move to political and economic union meant that it was no longer sufficient for EU nationals to be treated as 'privileged aliens' in other Member States. A European Union citizenship should be established. This was defined as:

> The personal and indivisible status of nationals of the Member States, whose membership of the Union means that they have special rights and duties that are specific to the nature of the Union and are exercised and safeguarded specifically within its boundaries.[13]

This proposal attracted support from both the Commission and the Parliament and from a number of Member States. The resulting citizenship provisions are now found in Part 2 of the TFEU. The rights of citizens are stated in full detail in Articles 21–24 of this Part. However,

---

[10] J. Habermas, 'Citizenship and National Identity: Some Reflections on the Future of Europe' (1992) 12 *Praxis International* 1. See also the thinking of Hannah Arendt on citizenship, presented in P. Hansen, *Hannah Arendt: Politics, History and Citizenship* (Stanford, CA, Stanford University Press, 1993).

[11] L. Bosniak, *The Citizen and the Alien* (Princeton University Press, 2006) 139.

[12] On the history of European Union citizenship, see A. Wiener, *European Citizenship Practice: Building Institutions of a Non-State* (Boulder, CO, Westview, 1998); S. O'Leary, *The Evolving Concept of Community Citizenship: From the Free Movement of Persons to Union Citizenship* (The Hague, Kluwer, 1996) 18–30.

[13] Council Document SN/3940/90, 24 September 1990, reproduced in F. Laursen and S. van Hoonacker (eds.), *The Intergovernmental Conference on Political Union: Institutional Reforms, New Policies and International Identity of the European Community* (Dordrecht, Martinus Nijhoff, 1992).

Article 20 is the central article. It establishes citizenship of the Union and summarises the associated rights.

Article 20 TFEU

(1) Citizenship of the Union is hereby established. Every person holding the nationality of a Member State shall be a citizen of the Union. Citizenship of the Union shall be additional to and not replace national citizenship.

(2) Citizens of the Union shall enjoy the rights and be subject to the duties provided for in the Treaties.[14] They shall have, *inter alia*:

    (a) the right to move and reside freely within the territory of the Member States;

    (b) the right to vote and to stand as candidates in elections to the European Parliament and in municipal election in their Member State of residence, under the same conditions as nationals of that State;

    (c) the right to enjoy, in the territory of a third country in which the Member State of which they are nationals is not represented, the protection of the diplomatic and consular authorities of any Member State on the same conditions as the nationals of that State;

    (d) the right to petition the European Parliament, to apply to the European Ombudsman, and to address the institutions and advisory bodies of the Union in any of the Treaty languages and to obtain a reply in the same language.

These rights shall be exercised in accordance with the conditions and limits defined by the Treaties and by the measures adopted hereunder.

Article 20(1) TFEU ties Union citizenship to national citizenship. A person is a citizen of the Union if and only if she is a citizen of a Member State. The idea of replacing national citizenship is explicitly rejected. This has conceptual and practical consequences. Martiniello has said of Union citizenship:

> It stimulates a European political identity which is largely linked to a prior communitarian belonging: one can be a European citizen only if one is previously a French, a Belgian or a German citizen, for example. In its present shape, the citizenship of the European Union is thus a complementary set of rights which confirms the existence of the cultural and political identities corresponding to the Member States.[15]

On the one hand, Article 20(1) gives Member States the power to control access to Union citizenship, since it is they who determine who is a national citizen.[16] However, as ever where national measures may influence EU rights, this link cuts both ways, and means that national citizenship laws may be subject to EU law constraints. Mr Rottmann was initially an Austrian citizen who gave up this citizenship to become a German. When the German authorities later discovered that he had fraudulently concealed information about an Austrian criminal prosecution on his application for German nationality they revoked his German citizenship retroactively.

---

[14] D. Kochenov, 'EU Citizenship without Duties' (2014) 20 *ELJ* 482–98; R. Bellamy, 'A Duty-Free Europe?' (2015) 21 *ELJ* 558–65.

[15] M. Martiniello, 'The Development of European Union Citizenship' in M. Roche and R. van Berkel (eds.), *European Citizenship and Social Exclusion* (Aldershot, Ashgate, 1998) 35, 37–8.

[16] D. Kochenov and J. Lindeboom, 'Pluralism through its Denial: The Success of EU Citizenship' in G. Davies and M. Avbelj (eds.), *Research Handbook on Legal Pluralism and EU Law* (Cheltenham, Edward Elgar, 2018) 179.

This meant that under German law Mr Rottmann would not be, nor ever have been, a German. However, this would leave him stateless, and also deprive him of Union citizenship, reason enough for the German court to refer a question to the Court of Justice.

Janko Rottmann v. *Freistaat Bayern*, C–135/08, EU:C:2010:104

39 It is to be borne in mind here that, according to established case-law, it is for each Member State, having due regard to Community law, to lay down the conditions for the acquisition and loss of nationality.

[The Court then refers to declaration 2, annexed to the TEU, which provides that 'the question whether an individual possesses the nationality of a Member State shall be settled solely by reference to the national law of the Member State concerned'.]

41 Nevertheless, the fact that a matter falls within the competence of the Member States does not alter the fact that, in situations covered by European Union law, the national rules concerned must have due regard to the latter.

42 It is clear that the situation of a citizen of the Union who, like the applicant in the main proceedings, is faced with a decision withdrawing his naturalisation, adopted by the authorities of one Member State, and placing him, after he has lost the nationality of another Member State that he originally possessed, in a position capable of causing him to lose the status conferred by Article [20 TFEU] and the rights attaching thereto falls, by reason of its nature and its consequences, within the ambit of European Union law.

43 As the Court has several times stated, citizenship of the Union is intended to be the fundamental status of nationals of the Member States ...

48 The proviso that due regard must be had to European Union law does not compromise the principle of international law previously recognised by the Court, and mentioned in paragraph 39 above, that the Member States have the power to lay down the conditions for the acquisition and loss of nationality, but rather enshrines the principle that, in respect of citizens of the Union, the exercise of that power, in so far as it affects the rights conferred and protected by the legal order of the Union, as is in particular the case of a decision withdrawing naturalisation such as that at issue in the main proceedings, is amenable to judicial review carried out in the light of European Union law.

49 Unlike the applicant in the case giving rise to the judgment in *Kaur* who, not meeting the definition of a national of the United Kingdom of Great Britain and Northern Ireland, could not be deprived of the rights deriving from the status of citizen of the Union, Dr Rottmann has unquestionably held Austrian and then German nationality and has, in consequence, enjoyed that status and the rights attaching thereto.

50 Nevertheless, as several of the governments having submitted observations to the Court have argued, if a decision withdrawing naturalisation such as that at issue in the main proceedings is based on the deception practised by the person concerned in connection with the procedure for acquisition of the nationality in question, such a decision could be compatible with European Union law.

51 A decision withdrawing naturalisation because of deception corresponds to a reason relating to the public interest. In this regard, it is legitimate for a Member State to wish to protect the special relationship of solidarity and good faith between it and its nationals and also the reciprocity of rights and duties, which form the bedrock of the bond of nationality ...

55 In such a case, it is, however, for the national court to ascertain whether the withdrawal decision at issue in the main proceedings observes the principle of proportionality so far as concerns the consequences it entails for the situation of the person concerned in the light of European Union law, in addition, where appropriate, to examination of the proportionality of the decision in the light of national law.

56 Having regard to the importance which primary law attaches to the status of citizen of the Union, when examining a decision withdrawing naturalisation it is necessary, therefore, to take into account the

consequences that the decision entails for the person concerned and, if relevant, for the members of his family with regard to the loss of the rights enjoyed by every citizen of the Union. In this respect it is necessary to establish, in particular, whether that loss is justified in relation to the gravity of the offence committed by that person, to the lapse of time between the naturalisation decision and the withdrawal decision and to whether it is possible for that person to recover his original nationality . . .

59   Having regard to the foregoing, the answer to the first question and to the first part of the second question must be that it is not contrary to European Union law, in particular to Article [20 TFEU], for a Member State to withdraw from a citizen of the Union the nationality of that State acquired by naturalisation when that nationality has been obtained by deception, on condition that the decision to withdraw observes the principle of proportionality.

The substantive rule, formulated in the later paragraphs, appears to be that any decision resulting in the loss of Union citizenship must be proportionate, in the sense of representing a fair balance of interests. By contrast, where a person has never been a Union citizen the Court suggests, by reference to *Kaur* (which concerned an application for British citizenship by someone who was not already a Union citizen), that EU law will not necessarily apply.

This distinction is more troublesome than may appear. If a third-country national acquires Union citizenship and then has it retroactively withdrawn is that more like *Rottmann* or *Kaur*? According to national law, such a person was never a Union citizen, but in practice they did enjoy the rights of one until the decision undoing their naturalisation. The reason why that decision should be subject to judicial review, as in *Rottmann*, is that otherwise it would create differences in the application of EU law between States who withdraw retroactively or prospectively, which is no more than an artefact of national administrative law.[17] It also reflects more appropriately that in substance the individual lived as a Union citizen, and was recognised as one, until the State changed its mind. This may be why *Rottmann* found that both acquisition and removal of nationality fall within the scope of EU law, thereby undercutting formal arguments based on retroactive removal.

Rottmann therefore opens the door to a reversal of the traditional relationship between nationality and Union citizenship. Prior to the case it was conventional to refer to Union citizenship as derivative or dependent, and to emphasise the gate-keeping role of Member States. Now it seems that tying Union citizenship to national citizenship was not just an act of legal dependency, but also one of legal colonialism, allowing the Court of Justice to engage and supervise yet another field of national law.[18]

Nevertheless, its hard-wiring to national citizenship has meant that Union citizenship sometimes seems to lack substance. It has not escaped the nation State to become a truly new, open and voluntary form of community, for example by including all residents of Europe, as Kochenov has argued it should.[19] Yet sticking close to nationality has not given it richness: by

---

[17]   *Micheletti* v. *Delegación del Gobierno Cantabria*, C-369/90, EU:C:1992:295.

[18]   See also *Tjebbes*, C-221/17 EU:C:2019:189; G. Davies and K. Rostek, 'The Impact of Union Citizenship on National Citizenship Policies' (2006) 10 *European Integration Online Papers* no. 5; D. Kochenov, *Rounding up the Circle: The Mutation of Member States' Nationalities under Pressure from EU Citizenship*, EUI RSCAS Working Paper 2010/23; *Lounes*, C-165/16, EU:C:2017:862.

[19]   D. Kochenov, 'Ius Tractum of Many Faces: European Citizenship and the Difficult Relationship between Status and Rights' (2009) 15(2) *Columbia Journal of European Law* 169.

the standards of traditional modern citizenship it offers a weak and shallow identity and it has inspired nothing close to the loyalty or sense of belonging that attach to nation States.[20]

Kostakopoulou has argued that this is an incomplete analysis of what Union citizenship is and what it does. It should not be judged solely on its contents, but also on its effects. She argues that the value of Union citizenship is partly that it transforms national communities. These are vulnerable to insularity, but the imposition of Union citizenship on top of its national counterparts inserts a globalising element into the nation. The fact that to be French is also to be a Union citizen changes what it means to be French. Thus, Union citizenship is not to be understood as a free-standing entity, but as something that penetrates national citizenship and changes it.[21]

> ### D. Kostakopoulou, 'European Union Citizenship: Writing the Future' (2007) 13(5) *European Law Journal* 623
>
> But the reduction of European citizenship to a transnational citizenship downplays both the resourcefulness of Union citizenship and the supranational character of EU law , , , Above all, it conceals the extent to which European citizenship penetrates and subverts national citizenship, thereby triggering off tensions, institutional displacement and the incremental transformation of domestic structures and practices in ways that had not been anticipated ...
>
> I would suggest that the novelty, and in many respects the challenge, of the European citizenship design does not lie simply in the emergence of 'nested' citizenships (supranational, national, sub-national citizenships) and institutional pluralism. More significant is the interaction between 'old' (national) and 'new' (European) citizenships and the ensuing process of incremental, transformative change. European legal and political dynamics subvert the fundamental premises of the nationality model of citizenship and change the organisational logic and practices of national citizenship.

This transformative view of Union citizenship resonates upon reading the case law. A recurring theme in this chapter is the way in which the institution of Union citizenship requires Member States to redefine and reconstitute their own structures of membership and identity.

4 RIGHT TO MOVE AND RESIDE WITHIN THE UNION

The most useful right for Union citizens, and the one demanding most adaptation from national authorities, is the right to move and reside throughout the Union. This right is conceptually very similar to the free movement rights relating to goods, economically active persons, services and capital, discussed in later chapters in this book.[22] Many of the abstract themes, such as the notions of discrimination, of the proportionality of national measures and of wholly internal situations, will recur in those chapters, which provide a useful complement to this one. However, the citizenship right also has its own nuances. The constitutional tone of citizenship, and the fact that citizens are not just factors of production, but human beings, with correspondingly broad needs and concerns, has generated a diverse and purposive body of law that is increasingly self-contained.

---

[20] See section 6 below, and n. 9 above.
[21] Bellamy, n. 8 above; P. Magnette, 'How Can One Be European? Reflections on the Pillars of European Civic Identity' (2007) 13(5) *ELJ* 664.
[22] See Chs. 14–19; also A. Tryfonidou, *The Impact of Union Citizenship on the EU's Market Freedoms* (Oxford, Hart, 2017).

This right to move and reside within the Union is first stated in Article 20(2)(a) TFEU and then repeated in Article 21.

Article 21 TFEU

(1) Every citizen of the Union shall have the right to move and reside freely within the territory of the Member States, subject to the limitations and conditions laid down in the Treaties and by the measures adopted to give them effect.

This is elaborated in the Citizenship Directive.[23] This Directive consolidates previous Directives applying to different categories of persons and now provides the framework for almost all legal issues concerning the free movement of persons. It sets out the rights of citizens to move and reside in other Member States, bring their families to live with them and participate in socio-economic life without experiencing discrimination.

Yet where the Citizenship Directive contains a loophole, or a situation involving the movement and equality of Europeans confronts the Court which is outside that Directive's scope, it does not hesitate to invoke Article 21 as a direct source of rights. Some of the most far-reaching Citizenship rights are either based on Article 21 alone, or on it and the Directive together. The two sources therefore need to be seen as a legal whole. Much of what follows in the sections below concerns the meaning and use of the Directive, but as will be seen, it is regularly complemented by Article 21 and also by general principles of EU law.

These sections address the right to live in other Member States and in the Union as a whole, to be treated without nationality discrimination and to move freely, as well as the extension of these rights to the family members of the Union citizens involved.

(i) Categories of Residence under the Directive

The provisions on movement and residence fall naturally into three categories.

(1) *Right to movement and short-term residence*: Articles 4 to 6 of the Directive provide that citizens may move throughout the territory of the Union and live in any State for up to three months, without any formalities other than the possession of a valid identity card or passport.

The only condition imposed is that the citizen not be an unreasonable burden on the social assistance system of the host State.[24] This is probably of limited impact, since the Directive provides later that migrants in this first period of residence have no right to social assistance anyway.[25] It is therefore unlikely that they will be an unreasonable burden. Citizens who are employed or self-employed, or looking for work and able to show that they have a genuine chance of finding it, may in any case not be expelled.[26] They are effectively exempted from the 'unreasonable burden' condition.[27]

(2) *Residence in another Member State for periods of more than three months*: For periods greater than three months, the conditions are more restrictive.

---

[23] Directive 2004/38/EC on the right of citizens of the Union and their family members to move and reside freely within the territory of the Member States [2004] OJ L158/77 ('Citizenship Directive').

[24] *Ibid.* Article 14(1).   [25] *Ibid.* Article 24(2).   [26] *Ibid.* Article 14(4).   [27] *Ibid.* Article 14(4).

Citizenship Directive, Article 7

(1) All Union citizens shall have the right of residence on the territory of another Member State for a period of longer than three months if they:

   (a) are workers or self-employed persons in the host Member State; or

   (b) have sufficient resources for themselves and their family members not to become a burden on the social assistance system of the host Member State during their period of residence and have comprehensive sickness insurance cover in the host Member State;

   (c) are enrolled at a private or public establishment, accredited or financed by the host Member State on the basis of its legislation or administrative practice, for the principal purpose of following a course of study, including vocational training; and have comprehensive sickness insurance cover in the host Member State and assure the relevant national authority, by means of a declaration or by such equivalent means as they may choose, that they have sufficient resources for themselves and their family members not to become a burden on the social assistance system of the host Member State during their period of residence.

To fall into the first category, the citizen must be employed or self-employed within the definitions in the Court of Justice's case law on Articles 45 and 49 TFEU, respectively.[28] They can retain this status and its associated residence rights if they subsequently cease to fulfil these definitions. The general position is that the person who loses their job or self-employment involuntarily, is temporarily unable to work because of ill-health or makes a choice to stop working in order to do further training, continues to enjoy the status of worker or self-employed person for the purposes of residence, for a certain period.[29]

(3) *Permanent residence*: Citizens who have resided legally in another Member State for five years acquire the right of permanent residence.[30] This brings certain benefits, notably exemption from conditions concerning sufficient resources.[31] Once acquired, the status is only lost after two consecutive years of absence.[32]

The requirement to reside 'legally' is satisfied when the residence complies with the substantive conditions of Article 7(1).[33] The possession of a residence document is entirely irrelevant,[34] as is even whether the person was a Union citizen for the entire period – some cases have involved citizens of the Eastern Member States who successfully argued that residence in another Member State prior to the accession of their own Member State should still count towards the five years.[35] Several Member States argued that the residence prior to accession had been outside the scope of EU law, and so to take account of it was giving a form of retroactive effect to the Citizenship Directive. The Court of Justice rejected this with the slightly cryptic statement that 'the Court has held that the provisions on citizenship of the European Union are applicable as soon as they enter into force and must therefore be applied to the present effects of situations

---

[28] See Ch. 18.

[29] Citizenship Directive, Article 7(3); *Gusa*, C-442/16, EU:C:2017:1004; *Saint Prix*, C-507/12, EU:C:2014:2007.

[30] Citizenship Directive, Article 16. There are shorter time limits for certain groups in Article 17.

[31] *Ibid.* Article 16(1).   [32] *Ibid.* Article 16(4).

[33] *Lassal*, C-162/09, EU:C:2010:592; *Czop and Punakova*, C-147–8/11, EU:C:2012:538.

[34] *Dias*, C-325/09, EU:C:2011:498.

[35] *Ziolkowski and Szeja v. Land Berlin*, C-424–5/10, EU:C:2011:866; *Czop and Punakova*, C-147–8/11, EU:C:2012:538. See also *Wieland*, C-465/14, EU:C:2016:820.

arising previously'.[36] Permanent resident status cannot be acquired prior to accession, but integration into the host society may occur, and can then be recognised as soon as the migrant becomes a Union citizen.

On the other hand, residence that was lawful under national law, but not in compliance with the Directive's conditions, will not count, and if occurring after permanent residence is acquired, for more than two years, could even undermine it.[37] Permanent residence is a reward for those whose integration into their host State is based on sustained economic activity or self-sufficiency.[38] In the view of the Court this approach reflects the status of permanent residence as 'a key element in promoting social cohesion' which works to 'strengthen the feeling of Union citizenship'.[39]

This idea that permanent residence is an earned status, which in rewarding integration and participation strengthens the fabric of society, also has its negative corollary: in *Onuekwere* the Court found that time spent in prison could not count towards permanent residence, as receiving a prison sentence 'is such as to show the non-compliance by the person concerned with the values expressed by the society of the host Member State in its criminal law'.[40]

(ii) Conditions of Residence

(a) The Requirement to Be Self-Sufficient

The fear of Member States has traditionally been that citizens would use their free movement rights to move to States with high levels of public assistance, where they would live as parasites, enjoying benefits without contributing to society. In order to ease this fear, EU law has always imposed conditions of self-sufficiency on free movement, requiring certain categories of migrants to have sickness insurance and sufficient resources to live from. On the one hand, these conditions make free movement viable: Member States do not yet feel enough mutual solidarity to accept a free movement regime which permits migration purely for the purposes of claiming benefits. More practically, national communities are the primary locus of taxation and spending. In the absence of mechanisms for redistribution between States (e.g. as exist in a federal State such as Germany or the United States), benefit tourism is easily portrayed as inequitable.

Yet the practical effect of these conditions is that 'expensive' members of society do not enjoy free movement rights. Those dependent upon State support or suffering medical conditions which are expensive to treat or difficult to insure are excluded from the Europe without borders. Union citizenship is a citizenship for all Europeans who are not poor or sick. This goes to the justice of citizenship, but also to the question of whether it deserves its name.[41] Are not equality

---

[36] *Ziolkowski and Szeja v. Land Berlin*, C-424–5/10, EU:C:2011:866, para. 58.

[37] *Ibid.*; *Dias*, C-325/09, EU:C:2011:498.

[38] E. Spaventa, 'Earned Citizenship: Understanding Union Citizenship through its Scope' in D. Kochenov (ed.), *EU Citizenship and Federalism: The Role of Rights* (Cambridge University Press, 2017) 204–25; D. Kramer, 'Earning Social Citizenship in the European Union: Free Movement and Access to Social Assistance Benefits Reconstructed' (2016) 18 *CYELS* 270–301.

[39] Citizenship Directive, recital 17; *Lassal*, C-162/09, EU:C:2010:592, para. 32; see M. Jesse, 'Annotation of *Ziolkowski*' (2012) 49 *CMLRev* 2003. See also *Onuekwere*, C-378/12, EU:C:2014:13.

[40] *Onuekwere*, C-378/12, EU:C:2014:13, para. 26; see also *M.G.*, C-400/12, EU:C:2014:9.

[41] Kochenov, n. 19 above; C. O'Brien, 'Civis Capitalist Sum: Class as the New Guiding Principle of EU Free Movement Rights' (2016) 53(4) *CMLRev* 937–77.

and solidarity a part of what citizenship entails? The cases below suggest that the Court of Justice's answer is 'to some extent'.

A caveat is that these conditions do not apply to economically active persons. It may be the case, therefore, that a worker or self-employed citizen earns little from their activity and so is entitled to social assistance, perhaps even significant social assistance. Yet, this has no consequences for their residence rights.[42] This softens the conditions a little in practice, since the threshold for economic activity is relatively low and may often be met by just a 'small number' of hours of work per week.[43] Yet, it also highlights the economic roots of free movement and suggests that despite its constitutional tone, citizenship has not fully transformed the law on free movement of persons from an economic policy tool to a dignified and socially cohesive institution.

For the non-economically active citizen, however, residence for more than three months in a host State is conditional upon possessing 'sufficient resources . . . not to become a burden on the social assistance system of the host Member State' as well as 'comprehensive sickness insurance'.[44]

By far the most difficult and controversial question this condition has raised is what happens when a migrant does in fact apply for social assistance. This is dealt with in section 4(iv)(b) below. However, some other general points may be made on how these conditions are interpreted.

(b) Proportionality

Despite the apparent strictness of the conditions, they must nevertheless be read and applied in a way respecting the principle of proportionality. Typically this means that minor technical breaches, particularly where no or little blame is to be attached and the consequences are not serious, will not lead to a loss of residence rights.

In *Baumbast*, the UK Government objected to the fact that a German citizen and his family had sickness insurance which did not cover all of the costs which they might incur (although had not incurred) in the United Kingdom.[45] This looked like a fairly straightforward breach of the Directive then in force, which was similarly worded to the Citizenship Directive. However, the family had been in the United Kingdom for some time, had never been a burden on the State in the past and it seemed harsh to deny them further residence for a breach which had not actually cost the United Kingdom any money and was, it seemed, fairly minor.

Baumbast v. *Secretary of State for the Home Department*, C–413/99, EU:C:2002:493

90 In any event, the limitations and conditions which are referred to in Article [21 TFEU] and laid down by Directive 90/364 are based on the idea that the exercise of the right of residence of citizens of the Union can be subordinated to the legitimate interests of the Member States. In that regard, according to the fourth

---

[42] Citizenship Directive, Article 7; see also *Kempf*, 139/85, EU:C: 1986:223.

[43] *LN* v. *Styrelsen for Videregående Uddannelser og Uddannelsesstøtte*, C–46/12, EU:C: 2013:97, para. 41; *Levin* v. *Staatssecretaris van Justitie*, 53/81, EU:C:1982:105. Cf. O'Brien, n. 41 above.

[44] Citizenship Directive, Article 7(1)(b); see p. 477.

[45] *Baumbast* v. *Secretary of State for the Home Department*, C–413/99, EU:C:2002:493.

recital in the preamble to Directive 90/364 beneficiaries of the right of residence must not become an 'unreasonable' burden on the public finances of the host Member State.

91 However, those limitations and conditions must be applied in compliance with the limits imposed by Community law and in accordance with the general principles of that law, in particular the principle of proportionality. That means that national measures adopted on that subject must be necessary and appropriate to attain the objective pursued . . .

93 Under those circumstances, to refuse to allow Mr Baumbast to exercise the right of residence which is conferred on him by Article [21(1) TFEU] by virtue of the application of the provisions of Directive 90/364 on the ground that his sickness insurance does not cover the emergency treatment given in the host Member State would amount to a disproportionate interference with the exercise of that right.

It was probably relevant in *Baumbast* that the comprehensive sickness insurance referred to in the Directive is particularly problematic in the United Kingdom: it does not have an insurance-based health-care system, making the clause hard to understand. Probably, lawful residence, entitling use of the national health service, is enough. Alternatively, the clause could be read to mean that migrants to the United Kingdom must purchase private health insurance, but apart from this being extremely expensive, fully comprehensive private insurance does not in fact exist in the United Kingdom.

The UK Government took the view that migrants should purchase nearly comprehensive private insurance, but did not enforce this until people claimed permanent residence status, at which point it would be suggested retrospectively that their previous residence had not been lawful. This is what happened to the Baumbasts. Disproportionate is probably an unreasonably polite word for what the UK Government attempted in this case.[46]

By contrast, in *Alimanovic* the Court allowed precise rules to be applied precisely.[47] Ms Alimanovic, following a period of work, retained worker status for six months according to the Directive, after which she became a work-seeker again, with the consequence that she lost access to social assistance. She argued that this cliff-edge was disproportionate – implicitly, that she should get an extension. The Court found that proportionality was built into the rules, because the period for which worker status was retained was linked to how long one had worked before. There was thus nothing disproportionate about applying them as written. Proportionality does not make rules as such unacceptable, even strict ones. It becomes relevant where something about the use or consequences of those rules is distinctively problematic, often where the rule is not working as intended. In *Alimanovic*, although the consequences were harsh for the family involved, they were precisely what legislature intended. In *Baumbast*, by contrast, had the United Kingdom won it would have made lawful non-economic movement to the United Kingdom more or less impossible and deprived the Directive of much useful effect.

[46] G. Davies, 'The UK and Sickness Insurance for Mobile Citizens: An Inequitable Mess for Brexit Negotiators to Address', European Law Blog, 17 March 2017, https://europeanlawblog.eu/2017/03/17/the-uk-and-sickness-insurance-for-mobile-citizens-an-inequitable-mess-for-brexit-negotiators-to-address/.

[47] *Alimanovic*, C-67/14, EU:C:2015:597; see also Anastasia Iliopoulou-Penot, 'Deconstructing the Former Edifice of Union Citizenship? The Alimanovic Judgment' (2016) 53(4) *CMLRev* 1007–35.

(c) Level of Resources Required

The determination of a sufficient level of resources is to be decided with reference to the particular circumstances of the individual. A State may use rules of thumb, but inflexible rules are prohibited.

Citizenship Directive, Article 8

(4) Member States may not lay down a fixed amount which they regard as 'sufficient resources' but they must take into account the personal situation of the person concerned. In all cases this amount shall not be higher than the threshold below which nationals of the host Member State become eligible for social assistance, or where this criterion is not applicable, higher than the minimum social security pension paid by the host Member State.

This citizen-centred approach to resources makes it difficult to know exactly what a Member State may demand. In *Commission* v. *Netherlands*, the Court of Justice found that a State could not require demonstrable resources sufficient for a year of residence before recognising the residence right.[48] This was, again, disproportionate.

(d) Source of Resources

The citizen does not need to personally possess any resources at all provided there is someone covering their costs. In *Chen*, a baby was able to establish residence because her non-EU mother had sufficient resources to care for her,[49] and in *Kuldip Singh* the Court found that the source could be the citizen's third-country spouse. On the other hand, in *Commission* v. *Belgium*, the Court found that there was no need for the provider of resources to be either a family member or someone with a legal relationship with the citizen.[50]

(e) Time of Assessment

The sufficient resources condition will be, for most citizens, a one-time test. Once they have received their residence document they should not generally be subject to continuing checks on their resources, as long as they do not in fact behave in a way raising a legitimate doubt about their self-sufficiency. If they get by without public assistance there is no reason why the State should revisit the issue.

Citizenship Directive, Article 14

(2) Union citizens and their family members shall have the right of residence provided for in Articles 7, 12 and 13, as long as they meet the conditions set out therein. In specific cases where there is a reasonable doubt as to whether a Union citizen or his/her family member satisfies the conditions set out in Articles 7, 12 and 13, Member States may verify if these conditions are fulfilled. This verification shall not be carried out systematically.

---

[48] *Commission* v. *Netherlands*, C-398/06, EU:C:2008:461.   [49] *Zhu and Chen*, C-200/02, EU:C:2004:639.
[50] *Kuldip Singh*, C-218/14, EU:C:2015:476; *Commission* v. *Belgium*, C-408/03, EU:C:2006:192.

On the other hand, in *Commission* v. *UK* the Court confirmed that a Member State may have a policy of re-checking the lawful residence of all those applying for social assistance.[51] Such an application clearly does raise the question whether their resources are still sufficient, albeit that this question is more complex and messy than one would expect – see section 4(iv)(b) below.

(iii) Administrative Formalities

Member States are entitled to ask EU migrants and their families to comply with a number of administrative formalities. For entry to a State, a valid passport or identity card may be demanded from Union citizens, whereas non-EU family members may also have to have a visa under certain circumstances, at least until they have obtained a residence card, whereupon this and their passport are sufficient for travel.[52]

For short-term residence, up to three months, no conditions or formalities may be imposed other than the requirement that the citizen and family members report their presence to the police within a reasonable and non-discriminatory time.[53]

For longer residence, Member States may require that citizens and their families register with the authorities.[54] To do so they may be required to present valid identity documents and evidence that they comply with the substantive conditions for residence. Thus, citizens may be required to show that they are economically active, or that they have resources and sickness insurance. Students do not have to show evidence of resources, but can simply sign a declaration that they have them.[55] Family members have to show evidence of their relationship with the migrant citizen. Those falling within the 'extra' family members whose entry is to be facilitated under Article 3 of the Citizenship Directive are required to produce evidence that they are indeed dependents or family members.[56] However, no other documents may be required than those necessary for the Directive.[57]

Despite the sometimes forbidding sound of all these requirements, a number of factors mitigate them so that they should (in principle) rarely be a cause of problems for migrants. Most important, it has long been established that the residence documents issued by States upon registration are merely evidentiary and not constitutive of the rights of the citizen, and in *Petrea* the Court confirmed comprehensively that this remains the case.[58]

Petrea, C-184/16, EU:C:2017:684

32 . . . it has been held by the Court that the right of nationals of a Member State to enter the territory of another Member State and to reside there for the purposes intended by the EC Treaty is a right conferred directly by the Treaty, or, as the case may be, by the provisions adopted for its implementation. Therefore, the grant of a residence permit to a national of a Member State is to be regarded, not as a measure giving rise to rights, but as a measure by a Member State serving to prove the individual position of a national of another Member State with regard to provisions of European Union law.

---

[51] *Commission* v. *UK*, C-308/14, EU:C:2016:436.   [52] Citizenship Directive, Article 5(2).   [53] *Ibid.* Article 5(5).
[54] *Ibid.* Article 8(1).   [55] *Ibid.* Article 8(3); C-424/98 *Commission* v. *Italy* [2000] ECR I-4001.   [56] *Ibid.* Article 8(5).
[57] *Sean McCarthy*, C-202/13, EU:C:2014:2450.
[58] See also *Dias*, C-325/09, EU:C:2011:498, para. 54. Cf. *Trojani*, C-456/02, EU:C:2004:488, para. 46; *Oulane* v. *Minister voor Vreemdelingenzaken en Integratie*, C-215/03, EU:C:2005:638.

33 Consequently, just as such a declaratory character means that a citizen's residence may not be regarded as illegal, within the meaning of European Union law, solely on the ground that he does not hold a residence permit, it precludes a Union citizen's residence from being regarded as legal, within the meaning of European Union law, solely on the ground that such a permit was validly issued to him.

The citizen or family member who fails to obtain documents is therefore not in any sense illegally present in the host State and cannot be expelled. In fact, the Directive goes further than this.

Citizenship Directive, Article 25

(1) Possession of a residence certificate as referred to in Article 8, of a document certifying permanent residence, of a certificate attesting submission of an application for a family member residence card, of a residence card or of a permanent residence card, may under no circumstances be made a precondition for the exercise of a right or the completion of an administrative formality, as entitlement to rights may be attested by any other means of proof.

A failure to register should therefore have no consequences for functioning in the host State. Work, education, access to benefits and other aspects of life should be unaffected. The registration procedure and documents are not conditions for access to host State life, but merely a mechanism for States to gather information and establish those present on their territory. In practice, obtaining the registration documents tends to make life in the host State much easier, as they comprise evidence that the State has recognised the right of residence. Despite Article 25, it is common for public authorities to want to see these documents before granting access to other rights and benefits.

Since Article 25 prohibits registration being a condition for the exercise of other rights, States who wish to enforce the registration requirement have to hunt for and punish non-registered migrants and their families. However, the Directive limits any sanctions to those that are proportionate and non-discriminatory.[59] Sanctions of such a severity that they seriously impair the very right of residence are disproportionate.[60] A proper approach to determining appropriate sanctions is to consider how comparable infringements by nationals are punished; for example, violations of an obligation to inform the authorities of a new address when moving house.

The importance of formalities and documentary requirements is further diminished by the Court of Justice's approach to evidence, which is highly pragmatic and non-formalistic. In *Oulane*, it went so far as to find that possession of a valid passport or identity card is not a condition for lawful residence, since nationality may be proved in other ways:

> If the person concerned is able to provide unequivocal proof of his nationality by means other than a valid identity card or passport, the host Member State may not refuse to recognise his right of residence on the sole ground that he has not presented one of those documents.[61]

---

[59] See also *Awoyemi*, C-230/97, EU:C:2004:59.   [60] *Watson and Belmann*, 118/75, EU:C:1976:106.
[61] *Oulane* v. *Minister voor Vreemdelingenzaken en Integratie*, C-215/03, EU:C:2005:638.

This approach was continued in *MRAX*, where the Court of Justice considered Belgian practice on third-country partners of Union citizens.[62] The Belgian State took the view that if these were not in possession of a valid identity document and visa, as the Directives in force required, they were not entitled to a residence card and could be deported. In a long but important judgment, the Court affirmed that just as with Union citizens, the right of the third-country partner stems directly from the Treaty and a failure to comply with formalities does not remove it. If they have no documents, they may have difficulty proving their identity and family relationship, but if they can somehow do this (the Court noted that an expired passport may still be evidence of identity), then the responsibility of the State is to assist them in obtaining the necessary documents in the host State, as quickly as possible, while any sanctions imposed must be no more than are proportionate.

(iv) Equality in the Host State

(a) The General Principle

For the migrant who has gained entry to a host State, the most useful additional legal tool is usually the prohibition on nationality discrimination. This enables her to participate in work and society on equal terms with nationals. The primary rule is found in Article 18 TFEU.

> ### Article 18 TFEU
>
> Within the scope of application of the Treaties, and without prejudice to any special provisions contained therein, any discrimination on grounds of nationality shall be prohibited.

Article 24(1) of the Citizenship Directive extends and refines this slightly.

> ### Citizenship Directive, Article 24
>
> (1) Subject to such specific provisions as are expressly provided for in the Treaty and secondary law, all Union citizens residing on the basis of this Directive in the territory of the host Member State shall enjoy equal treatment with the nationals of that Member State within the scope of the Treaty. The benefit of this right shall be extended to family members who are not nationals of a Member State and who have the right of residence or permanent residence.

The Directive chooses to speak of equal treatment rather than discrimination, and extends the right to non-EU family members. This extension is important and not yet fully reflected in the practices of national institutions and national laws. One still sees job vacancies, for example, that are 'open to Union citizens', which should, correctly, be 'open to Union citizens and their family members'.

Discrimination is often defined by the Court of Justice in these classical words: 'the principle of non-discrimination requires that comparable situations must not be treated differently and that different situations must not be treated in the same way'.[63] This elegant formulation is not

---

[62] *MRAX*, C-459/99, EU:C:2002:461.   [63] *Garcia Avello*, C-148/02, EU:C:2003:539, para. 31.

always the most transparent or practical. It does not reveal how to determine what is comparable and what is different, which is really the essence of the matter. A less compressed approach, which amounts to the same in substance and is also reflected in case law, is to ask two questions. First, does a measure tend to advantage or disadvantage one group or another? Secondly, if so, is it sufficiently justified: does it serve a legitimate goal, is it based on objective and legitimate criteria and is it proportionate? This approach originated in older cases on free movement of workers, *Sotgiu* and *O'Flynn*, but is still relied on by the Court of Justice.[64] It reflects the understanding of discrimination that is also used in other areas of EU law, such as employment regulation.[65] The more explicit the distinction between nationalities – the greater the discriminatory effect – the harder it will usually be to justify it. A rule providing free museum entry only to national citizens would have to have truly exceptional justifications to survive, but a municipal rule providing free entry to local school children, while it might tend to relatively disadvantage foreign tourists, would probably be easier to justify.[66]

The prohibition applies 'within the scope of the Treaty'. In the context of citizenship, the Court of Justice has repeatedly found that where a national measure affects a migrant citizen exercising her Treaty rights to move and reside, this is in itself enough to bring the measure within the Treaty. As a result, the non-discrimination rule may affect all areas of national law. Even if these are primarily national and not EU competences, if they discriminate against migrants the rule will bite. Thus, Article 18 has been applied to compensation for victims of crime in France and criminal procedure in Italy, motorway toll reductions for disabled people, extradition to third countries, as well as to national laws implementing the European Arrest Warrant, among other matters.[67] Some of the cases involve discrimination against mere movers, those transiting a State or on holiday there.[68] However, the majority involve discrimination against migrant residents.

In *Garcia Avello*, it was the Belgian law on surnames that was in issue.[69] A Spanish citizen resident in Belgium was unable to persuade the Belgian authorities to register his children with a Spanish-style surname, consisting of the father's surname followed by the mother's surname. The children were Spanish–Belgian dual nationals.

Garcia Avello, C-148/02, EU:C:2003:539

20 It is first of all necessary to examine whether, contrary to the view expressed by the Belgian State and by the Danish and Netherlands Governments, the situation in issue in the main proceedings comes within the scope of Community law and, in particular, of the Treaty provisions on citizenship of the Union.

---

[64] *Sotgiu v. Deutsche Bundespost*, 152/73, EU:C:1974:13; *O'Flynn v. Adjudication Officer*, C-237/94, EU:C:1996:206; see G. Davies, *Nationality Discrimination in the European Internal Market* (The Hague, Kluwer Law International, 2003).

[65] See generally C. Costello and E. Barry (eds.), *Equality in Diversity: The New Equality Directives* (Dublin, Irish Centre for European Law, 2003).

[66] See *Commission v. Italy*, C-388/01, EU:C:2003:30; *Commission v. Spain*, C-45/93, EU:C:1994:101.

[67] *Wood*, C-164/07, EU:C:2008:321; *Bickel and Franz*, C-274/96, EU:C:1998:563; see also *Cowan v. Trésor Public*, 186/87, EU:C:1989:47; *Gottwald v. Bezirkshauptmannschaft Bregenz*, C-103/08, EU:C:2009:597; *Petruhnin*, C-182/15, EU:C:2016:630; *Pisciotti*, C-191/16, EU:C:2018:222; *Wolzenburg v. London Borough of Ealing and Secretary of State for Education and Skills*, C-123/08, EU:C:2009:616.

[68] See e.g. *Gottwald v. Bezirkshauptmannschaft Bregenz*, C-103/08, EU:C:2009:597; *Commission v. Italy*, C-388/01, EU:C:2003:30.

[69] See also *Standesamt Stadt Niebüll*, C-96/04, EU:C:2006:254.

21 Article [20 TFEU] confers the status of citizen of the Union on every person holding the nationality of a Member State. Since Mr Garcia Avello's children possess the nationality of two Member States, they also enjoy that status.

22 As the Court has ruled on several occasions, citizenship of the Union is destined to be the fundamental status of nationals of the Member States.

23 That status enables nationals of the Member States who find themselves in the same situation to enjoy within the scope *ratione materiae* of the EC Treaty the same treatment in law irrespective of their nationality, subject to such exceptions as are expressly provided for.

24 The situations falling within the scope *ratione materiae* of Community law include those involving the exercise of the fundamental freedoms guaranteed by the Treaty, in particular those involving the freedom to move and reside within the territory of the Member States, as conferred by Article [21 TFEU].

25 Although, as Community law stands at present, the rules governing a person's surname are matters coming within the competence of the Member States, the latter must none the less, when exercising that competence, comply with Community law, in particular the Treaty provisions on the freedom of every citizen of the Union to move and reside in the territory of the Member States.

This is the reply to national authorities who claim that a certain matter is 'a Member State competence outside EU law'.[70] Belgium went on to lose the case, since it could not show an adequate justification for its refusal to take account of the Garcia Avello family's particular situation and the problems that the law caused for them.[71]

A. Iliopoulou Penot, 'The Transnational Character of Union Citizenship' in M. Dougan, N. Nic Shuibhne and E. Spaventa (eds.), *Empowerment and Disempowerment of the European Citizen* (Oxford, Hart, 2012) 19–20

Interestingly, in *Garcia Avello*, the Belgian Government argued that its practice could be justified by the objective of promoting *integration* (and equality) into Belgian society of nationals from other Member States. The Court rejects this argument in view of the fact that migration within the Union has already led to the co-existence in Member States of different systems for the attribution of surnames applicable to residents. As a result of this migration, the situation of the children in the *Garcia Avello* case, as well as in the *Grunkin Paul* case, cannot be assessed by reference to the framework of only one society. Instead, it has to be repositioned within a wider social context, recomposed at the European level. The legal bond of EU citizenship reflects a certain social reality resulting from migration and membership in European society conceived as a 'society of societies'. This status protects against the risk, somehow inherent to migration, that original identity will be changed or even erased against the will of the individual. Therefore, new identity elements can only be chosen by the migrant (as in *Grunkin Paul*); they cannot be imposed on him or her. It is certain that integration into the host society is desirable. But integration does not mean assimilation. Instead, it can sometimes be achieved by recognition of the migrant's difference. In other words, when in Rome, you do not (necessarily) have to do as the Romans do.

---

[70] See also *Huber* v. *Bundesrepublik Deutschland*, C-524/06, EU:C:2008:724.

[71] See also on naming *Grunkin and Paul*, C-353/06, EU:C:2008:559; *Freitag*, C-541/15, EU:C:2017:432; *Bogendorff von Wolfersdorff*, C-438/14, EU:C:2016:401.

The case law under examination also illustrates the changing conception of the State. Member States can no longer be represented as bounded worlds which correspond to closed and isolated entities. Instead, they belong to a wider area where movement is continuous and where diversity is accepted, preserved, and even encouraged as a source of richness. As parts of a larger organism, Member States have to consider the potential impact of their choices on transnational situations. Interests beyond the confines of the national polity have to be taken into account within the policy- and decision-making system. Judicial review on grounds of Union citizenship seeks to ensure precisely this. Therefore, Union citizenship enhances a phenomenon already taking place because of the internal market where Member States are 'forced to confront and internalize the externalities that they cause for one another'.[72] This phenomenon is now extended as a result of Union citizenship to new areas such as personal and family status.

Garcia Avello also raises a challenge to equality, in a different way: the family were dual Belgian–Spanish nationals, and by allowing them to use their Spanish nationality to claim rights in Belgium it effectively creates different classes of Belgians, with different rights against the State. The recognition of the difference of foreigners is one thing, but legally recognising different sorts of one's own citizens is constitutionally problematic for many States, particularly those of a republican bent.[73]

(b) Citizenship, Equality and Social Assistance

It is long established that if a migrant citizen is lawfully resident in a host State, they are entitled to equal treatment, including in social assistance.[74] In principle they can claim benefits on equal terms with nationals.

However, there is a sting in the tail: if they are economically inactive, then a condition of their lawful residence is that they have sufficient resources not to be a burden on the social assistance system.[75] That leads to a feedback between benefits and residence rights: if they do apply for social assistance, this suggests they no longer have sufficient resources, and therefore no longer fulfil the conditions for lawful residence. In turn, if they are not lawfully resident, then they no longer have the basis for claiming equal treatment, and thus social assistance.[76]

In reality this would then seem to exclude social assistance, if the mere fact of claiming it leads to a loss of lawful residence. However, the Citizenship Directive also contains hints of a softening of this rule, as did the Directives preceding it. In its preamble it maintains that Member States should not take expulsion measures against economically inactive citizens unless they are an *unreasonable* burden on the social assistance system.[77]

The difference between being a burden (Article 7) and being an 'unreasonable burden' (recitals 10 and 16) is enormous, not just because one implies that a degree of social assistance is in fact

---

[72] A. Somek, 'The Argument from Transnational Effects: Representing Outsiders through Freedom of Movement' (2010) 16 *ELJ* 315.

[73] See now *Lounes*, C-165/16, EU:C:2017:862.

[74] *Martinez-Sala*, C-85/96, EU:C:1998:217; Article 24(1) Citizenship Directive.

[75] Article 7(1)b and 7(1)c Citizenship Directive.

[76] G. Davies, 'Migrant Union Citizens and Social Assistance: Trying to Be Reasonable about Self-Sufficiency' (2016) College of Europe Research Papers in Law, No. 2/2016.

[77] Recitals 10 and 16.

acceptable but because a fairly clear rule is changed into an open norm, inviting consideration of a wide range of circumstances and factors. So which rule applies?

Grzelczyk was the first case in which the Court attempted to reconcile these conflicting aspects of the legislation.[78] It was also the first case in which it used Union citizenship to create new substantive rights for citizens, and perhaps for that reason the Court began its reasoning with a remarkable assertion, often repeated since: 'Union citizenship is destined to be the fundamental status of nationals of the Member States.'

Although the judgment is brief, and not particularly tightly reasoned, the essence of the Court's approach is that it allows the more generous preamble to trump the strict wording of the provision. Despite the wording of what has now become Article 7(1)(b), migrant citizens will only lose their status as lawful residents if they become an *unreasonable burden* on the social assistance system.

That means that some degree of social assistance, in some circumstances, is in fact compatible with lawful residence. The Court justified this by reference to the preambles, which it said showed that the free movement legislation 'accepts a certain degree of financial solidarity between nationals of a host Member State and nationals of other Member States, particularly if the difficulties which a beneficiary of the right of residence encounters are temporary'.[79]

While this softens the rule, its effect must be kept in perspective. Not all requests for social assistance will be reasonable, and if they are not then, as the Court emphasised in *Grzelczyk*, the Member State is free to take steps to deny the lawful status of the citizen and to expel them.[80] However, unless the Member State can successfully deny that lawfulness, it is obliged to treat them as equals – subject to the very specific exceptions discussed below.

In order to make this law functional, and assess its consequences, three terms remain to be defined: 'social assistance', 'unreasonable' and 'lawfully resident'. It is the way that these are filled in which determines how much impact *Grzelczyk* actually has.

(1) Social Assistance

This was defined in *Brey* as 'all assistance introduced by the public authorities, whether at national, regional or local level, that can be claimed by an individual who does not have resources sufficient to meet his own basic needs and the needs of his family'.[81]

This ambiguous phrase seems to suggest that the same service or benefit might be social assistance or not depending on the degree of need of the claimant, which would create odd situations – the rich migrant may use subsidised transport but not the poor one.[82] More plausibly, it means that social assistance encompasses those benefits specifically provided on a basis of need to those who are not able to support themselves, rather than universal and subsidised public services. Nevertheless, matters such as social housing, which are on the basis of need, but often cover large parts of the population, could be argued to fall somewhere in between these extremes.

The purpose of the benefit or payment is also relevant: the Court has ruled that if it is primarily aimed at getting people into employment, rather than helping them live, a benefit is not social

---

[78] *Grzelczyk*, C-184/99, EU:C:2001:458.   [79] *Ibid.* para. 44.   [80] *Trojani*, C-456/02, EU:C:2004:488.
[81] *Brey*, C-140/12, EU:C:2013:565, para. 61.
[82] Daniel Thym, 'The Elusive Limits of Solidarity: Residence Rights of and Social Benefits for Economically Inactive Union Citizens' (2015) 52 *CMLRev* 17.

assistance.[83] That logic should be transferrable to subsidies for non-essential matters such as sports or home improvements, even if they involve an element of means-testing.

(2) Unreasonable

The Court outlined factors which would make a request for assistance reasonable in *Grzelczyk*, after which they were copied into recital 16 of the Citizenship Directive. Their use was explained in *Brey*.

Brey, C–140/12, EU:C:2013:565

69 Furthermore, it is clear from recital 16 in the preamble to Directive 2004/38 that, in order to determine whether a person receiving social assistance has become an unreasonable burden on its social assistance system, the host Member State should, before adopting an expulsion measure, examine whether the person concerned is experiencing temporary difficulties and take into account the duration of residence of the person concerned, his personal circumstances, and the amount of aid which has been granted to him.

70 Lastly, it should be borne in mind that, since the right to freedom of movement is – as a fundamental principle of EU law – the general rule, the conditions laid down in Article 7(1)(b) of Directive 2004/38 must be construed narrowly and in compliance with the limits imposed by EU law and the principle of proportionality.

71 In addition, the margin for manoeuvre which the Member States are recognised as having must not be used by them in a manner which would compromise attainment of the objective of Directive 2004/38, which is, *inter alia*, to facilitate and strengthen the exercise of Union citizens' primary right to move and reside freely within the territory of the Member States, and the practical effectiveness of that directive.

72 By making the right of residence for a period of longer than three months conditional upon the person concerned not becoming an 'unreasonable' burden on the social assistance 'system' of the host Member State, Article 7(1)(b) of Directive 2004/38, interpreted in the light of recital 10 to that directive, means that the competent national authorities have the power to assess, taking into account a range of factors in the light of the principle of proportionality, whether the grant of a social security benefit could place a burden on that Member State's social assistance system as a whole. Directive 2004/38 thus recognises a certain degree of financial solidarity between nationals of a host Member State and nationals of other Member States, particularly if the difficulties which a beneficiary of the right of residence encounters are temporary.

One aspect of this judgment which caused confusion was the suggestion that a single applicant could place a measurable burden on a State as a whole. However, any decision on benefits has a precedential value and creates entitlements for people in similar circumstances. In *Alimanovic* the Court confirmed that it is the total resulting burden which is relevant here.

The other factors mentioned are to do with the individual. There has to be an assessment of their individual circumstances, taking account of factors relevant to the merits and proportionality of their claim. How long have they lived in the State self-sufficiently? How much help do they need? How long will they need it for? Implicit in proportionality is also the question of what the consequences might be of granting or refusing the aid.

---

[83] *Vatsouras* v. *Arbeitsgemeinschaft Nürnberg*, C–22/08, EU:C:2009:344; *Alimanovic*, C–67/14, EU:C:2015:597.

Mr Grzelczyk was thus a claimant with a fairly strong case: after living self-sufficiently in Belgium for several years while studying, he was advised by his supervisor that he should give up his part-time work to concentrate on his graduation thesis. His Belgian co-students all did this and claimed the minimax, a Belgian basic income benefit, while finishing their studies, and he followed their example. He thus did not need assistance for very long, he had not come to Belgium for the purposes of claiming it – something the Court showed a particular aversion to in the later *Dano* – and the difference between granting it or not was potentially the difference between him not graduating, or being able to enter the labour market and become a productive member of society.[84] On the other hand, it should also be considered how many foreign students there are in Belgium, and what the consequences for the public purse should be and the Court explicitly left it to the national court to come to a final conclusion on reasonableness.

By contrast, Mr Brey appears to have had a very weak case. He went to live in Austria on a small, but sufficient, German pension. Under a generous Austrian law, those with low pensions were entitled to top-ups, and it was these he applied for. While one can hardly blame him for this, the Court's criteria fitted him ill: he had no history of self-sufficient residence in Austria, and he was asking for significant social assistance for the long-term – essentially until he dies, since he had no prospect of an increase in pension or other income. Moreover, while there was no accusation that he had moved for the purposes of the benefits, allowing them to him would make it possible for any EU pensioner with a just-adequate pension to go to Austria and have it transformed into a significant one, perhaps for several decades.[85]

(3) Lawful Residence

In *Dano* the Court said 'so far as concerns access to social benefits, such as those at issue in the main proceedings, a Union citizen can claim equal treatment with nationals of the host Member State only if his residence in the territory of the host Member State complies with the conditions of Directive 2004/38'.[86]

With respect to the Court, the statement is probably more general than it intended. The substantive question at issue in that case was whether persons who had no right of residence in Germany could nevertheless rely on Article 24 of the Directive or Article 18 TFEU to claim social assistance. The answer must clearly be negative: it would simply undo the conditions of residence in Article 7.

However, what about persons who are lawfully resident, but based on other provisions of EU law, notably Regulation 492/2011, and perhaps also Article 21 TFEU?[87] As a matter of logic, such persons are within the scope of EU law and thus Article 18 TFEU. As a matter of policy, it is relevant that these residence rights are intended to protect the residence of children and their carers. It would seem inconsistent with that goal to exclude them from equal treatment or social assistance entirely. These residence rights were not at issue in *Dano*, and it seems unlikely that the Court intended to exclude such persons from equal treatment. It is suggested that all persons lawfully resident on the basis of EU law should enjoy this right.

---

[84] *Dano*, C-333/13, EU:C:2014:2358; generally, G. Davies, 'Has the Court Changed or Have the Cases? The Deservingness of Litigants as an Element in Court of Justice Citizenship Adjudication' (2018) 25 *JEPP* 1442.
[85] Davies, n. 84 above.   [86] *Dano*, C-333/13, EU:C:2014:2358, para. 69.   [87] See pp. 507–11.

The more difficult question is whether persons can claim equal treatment if they are resident in a host State purely on the basis of national law. In *Martinez-Sala* the Court suggested that they could,[88] but after *Dano* the issue is seen as uncertain again.[89] On the one hand, the idea that Member States could 'voluntarily' admit citizens who do not comply with the Directive conditions but then subject them to a discriminatory rights regime seems at odds with the 'fundamental status' claims of *Grzelczyk*. It would provide an incentive for Member States to read the Directive very strictly, denying EU residence wherever they possibly can, but then granting migrants residence rights nominally on the basis of national law. That would avoid the costs and practicalities of expulsion, while quarantining the Welfare State.[90] On the other hand, there seems a plausible formal argument that if an individual is not in fact exercising EU rights of movement or residence then they do not fall within the scope of the Treaty and so have no basis for engaging Article 18. The question remains uncertain.

(4) Specific Exceptions to Equal Treatment

Article 24(2) provides a specific derogation from equal treatment, concerning certain kinds of benefits:

Article 24 Citizenship Directive

(2) By way of derogation from paragraph 1, the host Member State shall not be obliged to confer entitlement to social assistance during the first three months of residence or, where appropriate, the longer period provided for in Article 14(4)(b), nor shall it be obliged, prior to acquisition of the right of permanent residence, to grant maintenance aid for studies, including vocational training, consisting in student grants or student loans to persons other than workers, self-employed persons, persons who retain such status and members of their families.

There are two kinds of exclusions here. First, students are not entitled to study grants unless they are permanent residents, or also economically active, or family members of economic migrants.[91] The significant differences in study financing raised the fear of migration just in order to live off generous grants and, whether or not this risk was ever real, it is here addressed. However, the mere fact that a student takes a part-time job in order to get worker status and qualify for a grant or subsidised loan does not make this abusive or illegitimate: as in similar situations, the Court finds the reason why one works irrelevant.[92]

Secondly, those who have been in a State for less than three months, or who are there in order to find work, are not entitled to social assistance. Regarding work-seekers (those in Article 14(4)(b)) the situation is essentially unchanged since the Court first found a right to seek work to be inherent

---

[88] *Martinez-Sala*, C-85/96, EU:C:1998:217; see annotation by S. O'Leary, 'Flesh on the Bones of European Citizenship' (1999) 24 *ELRev* 68.

[89] H. Verschueren, 'Preventing "Benefit Tourism" in the EU: A Narrow or Broad Interpretation of the Possibilities Offered by the ECJ in Dano?' (2015) 52 *CMLRev* 363; D. Thym, 'The Elusive Limits of Solidarity: Residence Rights of and Social Benefits for Economically Inactive Union Citizens' (2015) 52 *CMLRev* 17.

[90] See on this idea, D. Kramer, J. Sampson Thierry and F. Van Hooren, 'Responding to Free Movement: Quarantining Mobile Union Citizens in European Welfare States' (2018) 25 *JEPP* 1501.

[91] *C v. Netherlands*, C-233/14, EU:C:2016:396.

[92] *L.N.*, C-46/12, EU:C:2013:97; see also *Levin*, 53/81, EU:C:1982:105.

in Article 45, long before the Directive, or even Union Citizenship. In *Antonissen* several Member States argued that such a right would lead to excessive unemployment benefit claims for foreign work-seekers.

Antonissen, C-292/89, EU:C:1991:80.

20 That argument cannot be upheld. As the Advocate General has rightly observed, there is no necessary link between the right to employment benefit in the Member State of origin and the right to stay in the host State.

21 In the absence of a Community provision prescribing the period during which Community nationals seeking employment in a Member State may stay there, a period of six months, such as that as laid down in the national legislation at issue in the main proceedings, does not appear in principle to be insufficient to enable the persons concerned to apprise themselves, in the host Member State, of offers of employment corresponding to their occupational qualifications and to take, where appropriate, the necessary steps in order to be engaged and, therefore, does not jeopardize the effectiveness of the principle of free movement. However, if after the expiry of that period the person concerned provides evidence that he is continuing to seek employment and that he has genuine chances of being engaged, he cannot be required to leave the territory of the host Member State.

In a typical example of the Commission's cut-and-paste approach to codifying case law, this is exactly the approach in the Citizenship Directive, including all its ambiguities. Thus the Directive, quite strangely, nowhere says that work-seekers have any right to reside in a host State. However, it does say that Member States cannot expel them as long as they are genuinely and plausibly looking for work – arguably bringing them within the scope of the Directive and its equal treatment principle. To mitigate the effects of this, it excludes, as the Court suggested above, any right to social assistance.

This exclusion makes the distinction between social assistance and other benefits particularly important, as these latter are not excluded. In *Vatsouras* the Court stated that benefits 'intended to facilitate access to the employment market' are not social assistance. They are rather employment activation benefits. The distinction is not precise, but if a benefit's main function is to keep someone in their basic needs it is likely to be social assistance, whereas if it is, for instance, specifically for transport to interviews or application coaching then it will not be.

(c) Real Links and Integration

Even if a work-seeker, or other migrant, has a right to equal treatment in social benefits, the defence mechanisms of the State are not exhausted. A trend of recent years is to make all kinds of social assistance and benefits only available to those who are to some extent integrated in that State's society.[93] Typical clauses make benefits only available to those who have been resident for a certain period, or who have been schooled in that State, or who have family or other links with the State which demonstrate a genuine bond. Such rules are not directly discriminatory, but of course do tend to favour nationals over migrants, and must therefore be justified by some

---

[93] See C. O'Brien, 'Real Links, Abstract Rights and False Alarms: The Relationship Between the ECJ's "Real Link" Case Law and National Solidarity' (2008) 33 *ELRev* 643.

policy need and proportionate. Older case law tended to find residence clauses unlawful, the Court of Justice clearly seeing them as unmeritorious and smacking of nationalism.[94] However, there appears to be an increasing recognition in the Court, as among policy-makers, that a restriction of some benefits to those who are in some sense 'members' of society is not only legitimate but perhaps even necessary to ensure the stability and sustainability of benefit systems.[95]

Ioannidis concerned a Belgian allowance available to those seeking their first job, but only if they had completed their secondary schooling in Belgium – the same allowance as in *D'Hoop*. Mr Ioannidis, a Greek citizen, had been to school in Greece, but was now seeking work in Belgium.

Ioannidis, C-258/04, EU:C:2005:559

30 As the Court has already held, it is legitimate for the national legislature to wish to ensure that there is a real link between the applicant for that allowance and the geographic employment market concerned.

31 However, a single condition concerning the place where the diploma of completion of secondary education was obtained is too general and exclusive in nature. It unduly favours an element which is not necessarily representative of the real and effective degree of connection between the applicant for the tideover allowance and the geographic employment market, to the exclusion of all other representative elements. It therefore goes beyond what is necessary to attain the objective pursued.

If a requirement to have completed school in Belgium is too strict, this begs the question of what kind of requirements can legitimately be imposed. In *Prete*, with almost identical facts, the Court of Justice suggested that marrying a national of the host State, moving there and then having sought work in the State for a 'reasonable time' might all be factors providing evidence of a 'real link'.[96] In *Bidar*, concerning a student applying for a subsidised loan in their host State, the Court suggested that integration might be demonstrated by having 'resided in the host Member State for a certain length of time'.[97] Yet that is not to say that prior residence is always a legitimate requirement. Where a citizen works in the host Member State this is usually enough evidence that the citizen is integrated, and a further residence requirement will generally be disproportionate.[98]

However, if the benefit is destined for family members living abroad, then the situation may be more nuanced. If the children of a frontier worker or migrant worker still live in their home State they may feel little connection to the country where their parent works. If they then claim study finance from the State of parental employment, intending to use this in their home State, the paying State tends to feel that it is not getting much from the deal. Allowing students to take their study finance abroad is premised on the idea that they will probably return, and bring international experience to the labour market. If that finance goes to students with no real connection with the paying State this goal is undermined. Hence in *Martens* the Netherlands

---

[94] *Sotgiu* v. *Deutsche Bundespost*, 152/73, EU:C:1974:13.   [95] See O'Brien, n. 93 above.

[96] *Prete*, C-367/11, EU:C:2012:668.

[97] *Bidar*, C-209/03, EU:C:2005:169; this was prior to the implementation of the Citizenship Directive, which addresses financial aid for studies in Article 24.

[98] *Caves Krier*, C-379/11, EU:C:2012:798; *Giersch*, C-20/12 EU:C:2013:411. See also *Verruga*, C-238/15, EU:C:2016:949.

only allowed its study finance to be used for study outside the Netherlands if the recipient had lived for the previous three years in the Netherlands.[99]

The Court found the policy goal, and the idea of an integration requirement, legitimate, but as in many cases the Dutch lost because of their focus on a single factor:

> 41 The legislation at issue in the main proceedings, inasmuch as it constitutes a restriction on the freedom of movement and residence of a citizen of the Union, such as the appellant in the main proceedings, is also too exclusive because it does not make it possible to take account of other factors which may connect such a student to the Member State providing the benefit, such as the nationality of the student, his schooling, family, employment, language skills or the existence of other social and economic factors. Likewise, as the Advocate General stated at point 103 of her Opinion, the employment of the family members on whom the student depends in the Member State providing the benefit may also be one of the factors to be taken into account in assessing those links.

Striking here is the breadth and open-endedness of the integrating factors, and the inclusion of nationality. This idea that nationality as such may be a reason to grant or refuse benefits is usually taboo, although not entirely unprecedented, and blurs the distinction between direct and indirect discrimination.[100] Yet it is also realistic, at least to some extent.

It is clear that there are no simple rules, rather a general principle of proportionality which may lead to different conclusions in different cases. In *Commission* v. *Austria*, a case on discounted transport for certain students (which was, on the particular facts, neither a grant, which would be excluded by Article 24(2), nor social assistance which might threaten compliance with Article 7(1)),[101] the Court of Justice remarked that:

> the genuine link required between the student claiming a benefit and the host Member State need not be fixed in a uniform manner for all benefits, but should be established according to the constitutive elements of the benefit in question, including to its nature and purpose or purposes. The objective of the benefit must be analysed according to its results and not according to its formal structure.[102]

This suggests that the particular nature of each benefit must be taken account of in determining appropriate conditions. *Gottwald* applies a similar particularist philosophy to the recipient, suggesting that it is legally desirable for national rules to have flexibility, so that they can take account of the various forms of connection with a society that applicants may have.[103] In that case, an Austrian rule exempting disabled drivers from motorway tolls was only available to the ordinarily resident, but the Court noted, in finding the Austrian rule to be justified, that the 'conditions are interpreted widely, so that other connecting factors allow a sufficiently close connection to Austrian society to be established for the purposes of grant of the free toll disc'.[104]

---

[99] *Martens*, C-359/13, EU:C:2015:118; *Commission* v. *Netherlands*, C-542/09, EU:C:2012:346; *Prinz and Seeberger*, C-523/11, EU:C:2013:524; *Thiele Meneses*, C-220/12, EU:C:2013:683; *Elrick*, EU:C:2013:684.

[100] *Förster* v. *Hoofddirectie van de Informatie Beheer Groep*, C-158/07, EU:C:2008:630; O'Brien, n. 93 above.

[101] See also *Commission* v. *Netherlands*, C-233/14, EU:C:2016:396.

[102] *Commission* v. *Austria*, C-75/11, EU:C:2012:605, para. 59.

[103] See on this flexibility O'Brien, n. 93 above; E. Spaventa, 'Seeing the Wood Despite the Trees? On the Scope of Union Citizenship and its Constitutional Effects' (2008) 45(1) *CMLRev* 13.

[104] *Gottwald* v. *Bezirkshauptmannschaft Bregenz*, C-103/08, EU:C:2009:597; see also *Commission* v. *Netherlands*, C-233/14, EU:C:2016:396; *Stewart*, C-503/09, EU:C:2011:500; *Morgan* v. *Bezirksregierung Köln*, C-11/06, EU:C:2007:626; *Thiele Meneses*, C-220/12, EU:C:2013:683.

This concern not to apply over-rigid exclusionary rules to migrants is consistent with other free movement case law, but nevertheless fits a little uncomfortably with the assertion, also in the judgment in *Gottwald*, that:

> with regard to the degree of connection of the recipient of a benefit with the society of the Member State concerned ... Member States enjoy a wide margin of appreciation in deciding which criteria are to be used when assessing the degree of connection to society.

(v) Restrictions on Movement and U-Turns

As well as the right to equal treatment, or non-discrimination, the Treaty also provides a directly effective right to free movement.[105] This enables citizens to rely on the right to move and reside against their own State, in circumstances where an analysis in terms of nationality discrimination would often be artificial or even impossible.[106] Typically this is the case where a citizen returns home from residence abroad, but it can also be relevant where the home State restricts exit, and can even sometimes be used against a host State, where a rule obstructs movement but is not discriminatory.

(a) The Returnee

D'Hoop concerned a Belgian allowance, available to job-seeking school-leavers if they had been to school in Belgium. Ms D'Hoop had been to school in France and was therefore refused the benefit. However, she was a Belgian citizen, making it impossible for her to argue nationality discrimination. She therefore simply claimed that the rule deterred interstate movement.

D'Hoop, C-224/98, EU:C:2002:432

30 In that a citizen of the Union must be granted in all Member States the same treatment in law as that accorded to the nationals of those Member States who find themselves in the same situation, it would be incompatible with the right of freedom of movement were a citizen, in the Member State of which he is a national, to receive treatment less favourable than he would enjoy if he had not availed himself of the opportunities offered by the Treaty in relation to freedom of movement.

31 Those opportunities could not be fully effective if a national of a Member State could be deterred from availing himself of them by obstacles raised on his return to his country of origin by legislation penalising the fact that he has used them ...

Another example of this type of reasoning is found in *Grunkin and Paul*, where German parents gave their child, born in Denmark, the surname Grunkin-Paul.[107] Although this was on the Danish birth certificate, the German authorities refused to recognise it, because Germany did not allow such composite surnames. The Court of Justice found this to violate Article 21 because it

---

[105] *D'Hoop*, C-224/98, EU:C:2002:432; *Pusa*, C-224/02, EU:C:2004:273; *Schwarz and Gootjes-Schwarz* v. *Finanzamt Bergisch Gladbach*, C-76/05, EU:C:2007:492; *Tas-Hagen and Tas* v. *Raadskamer WUBO van de Pensioen- en Uitkeringsraad*, C-192/05; EU:C:2006:676; *Morgan* v. *Bezirksregierung Köln*, C-11/06, EU:C:2007:626; *Zablocka*, C-221/07, EU:C:2008:681; *Nerkowska*, C-499/06, EU:C:2008:300; *Schempp*, C-403/03, EU:C:2005:446.

[106] M. Cousins, 'Citizenship, Residence and Social Security' (2007) 32 *ELRev* 386.

[107] *Grunkin and Paul*, C-353/06, EU:C:2008:559.

disadvantaged migration. The interest of the case lies in the fact that the parents were not obliged to choose a hyphenated surname in Denmark, but freely chose to. Clearly, if a migrant makes use of wider rights and opportunities available in a host State, their home State must respect and take account of these choices when the migrant returns.

This raises the prospect that citizens might deliberately go abroad in order to exercise rights not available in their home State, and then bring these home. That is particularly important where family rights are concerned, and discussed below.[108] However, it has also been relevant to the stream of naming cases. In *Freitag* a German–Romanian dual national who lived and had grown up in Germany travelled to Romania in order to change his Romanian name to Pavel, his mother's maiden name.[109] When he returned to Germany he insisted that the German authorities recognise his name-change also for his German identity, in order to avoid him having different names in different documents. The Court agreed that this was a 'compelling reason' for them to do so.

Yet the most colourful case to date is that of the German Nabiel Bagdadi, who, while living in the United Kingdom, acquired British as a second nationality and changed his British name to Peter Mark Emanuel Graf von Wolffersdorff Freiherr von Bogendorff.[110] One objection raised to recognising his name when he returned to Germany was that he had done it entirely voluntarily, and unlike litigants in the other naming cases it had no family or other connection with him. He just decided he'd like a new name, and was using his British name to try and leverage a German one.

The Court rejected the relevance of this. It did not provide a justification for refusing to recognise his new name. On the other hand, they suggested that if he had just gone to Britain briefly, changed his British name, and come home, for no purpose other than forcing the Germans to change his German one, then that would be different (at para. 57):

> [T]he Court has held that a Member State is entitled to take measures designed to prevent certain of its nationals from attempting, under cover of the rights created by the Treaty, improperly to circumvent their national legislation or to prevent individuals from improperly or fraudulently taking advantage of provisions of EU law.

Mr von Bogendorff was not caught by this because he lived in the United Kingdom for several years, making it hard to see his as a case of merely avoiding German law. Mr Freitag was not caught, because he had genuine family reasons for wanting to change his Romanian name, and then a legitimate interest in having the same name in both nationalities. Who would be caught? The distinction between a genuine exercise of rights and an abusive one remains somewhat obscure.

In any case, Mr von Bogendorff probably lost. Although neither the voluntary nature of his name-change, nor the length of his new name, provided good reasons not to recognise it, the latter being a matter of 'mere administrative convenience', the fact that it contained elements implying aristocracy quite possibly did. These elements offended the German ban on aristocratic titles, which the Court found to reflect the principle of equality and to be legitimate. It was for the national judge to weigh the extent to which the name really did imply aristocracy, the fact that

---

[108] See pp. 511–15.   [109] *Freitag*, C-541/15, EU:C:2017:432.
[110] *Bogendorff von Wolfersdorff*, C-438/14, EU:C:2016:401.

he had no reason other than choice to include these elements, and the risk of leaving him with a name different from his daughter, and come to a conclusion on proportionality.

(b) Free Movement Restrictions by Other Member States

Mr Rüffler, a German citizen, lived in Poland but received a pension from Germany, where he had worked.[111] Polish tax calculations did not take account of insurance premiums deducted from that pension in Germany before it was paid to Mr Rüffler, but they would have taken account of equivalent deductions made in Poland. The rule mainly disadvantaged Poles who had worked in Germany, so Mr Rüffler could not claim nationality discrimination. Still, he had a problem. The judgment is similarly reasoned to *D'Hoop*, but by contrast to paragraph 31 quoted above, the Court of Justice in *Rüffler* said:

> it would be incompatible with the right to freedom of movement were a citizen to receive, *in the host Member State*, treatment less favourable than that which he would enjoy if he had not availed himself of the opportunities offered by the Treaty in relation to freedom of movement. [Emphasis added.]

(c) Exit Restrictions

Mr Radziejewski, a Swedish citizen, was penalised for leaving Sweden by Swedish rules which granted him post-bankruptcy debt relief but only on the condition that he continued to live in Sweden.[112] Exit would therefore lead to Swedish debtors rushing to claim money from him. The Court found the rule to be an unjustified deterrent to emigration.

Another case in which a home State hindered exit is *Sayn-Wittgenstein*. In this case, Ilonka Kerekes, an Austrian, was adopted by Lothar, Prince of Sayn-Wittgenstein, a German.[113] Her new name was entered on both German and Austrian official documents as Ilonka, Princess (Fürstin) of Sayn-Wittgenstein. However, after a period of some fifteen years, the Austrian authorities realised that this was contrary to an Austrian law which prohibited the use of aristocratic titles, and they took steps to amend her name in the Austrian register, and ultimately in her passport, to Ilonka Sayn-Wittgenstein. She challenged this decision on the grounds that it would lead to practical problems in Germany, where people might doubt her identity or the authenticity of her title as her Austrian and German documents showed different names. It might also hinder her in her business, which was selling castles. The Court of Justice accepted that such discrepancies could cause problems which might be seen as a hindrance to free movement, but found that in this case the Austrian rule could be justified, as the rejection of aristocratic titles reflected genuine and fundamental Austrian constitutional values, notably equality.

What these cases create is a new kind of non-discrimination rule, not between citizens of different nationalities, but between citizens who exercise their EU rights and those who do not.[114] Where cross-border activities are treated less advantageously than domestic ones, or

---

[111] *Rüffler*, C-544/07, EU:C:2009:258.   [112] *Radziejewski*, C-461/11, EU:C:2012:704.
[113] *Ilonka Sayn-Wittgenstein* v. *Landeshauptmann von Wien*, C-208/08, EU:C:2009:80.
[114] N. Bernard, 'Discrimination and Free Movement' (1996) 45 *ICLQ* 82, 85–6; see e.g. *Morgan* v. *Bezirksregierung Köln*, C-11/06, EU:C:2007:626.

where national rules discourage migration or create specific problems for those who move, Article 21 TFEU applies.

There are however limits to this right. *Runevič-Vardyn and Wardyn* was yet another name case, but this time it was a question of whether the Lithuanian authorities were compelled to write Mrs Runevič-Vardyn's name as Runiewicz-Wardyn, the Polish way, because she had married a Pole: his name was Wardyn. The case is politically sensitive, as Ms Runevič-Vardyn was a member of the Polish minority in Lithuania, and her request was symbolic of wider disputes about identities, languages and minorities in the Baltic States. Perhaps for this reason, or perhaps because they were fed up with the increasingly obscure stream of naming cases, or perhaps simply because they did not believe that there would really be any problems, the Court of Justice left it to the national judge, but not before stating that

> according to the Court's case-law, in order to constitute a restriction on the freedoms recognised by Article 21 TFEU, the refusal to amend the joint surname of the applicants in the main proceedings under the national rules at issue must be liable to cause 'serious inconvenience' to those concerned at administrative, professional and private levels.

If the genuineness of their marriage or documents was really likely to be challenged, this could be the case. Otherwise, it would not. Thus while even minor instances of nationality discrimination are prohibited,[115] non-discriminatory measures will not comprise restriction on free movement if their practical consequences for movement are minimal, and the inconvenience they cause is less than 'serious'.

(vi) Family Rights

(a) The Right to Be with One's Family

People are less likely to move between States if they cannot take their families with them, and if their families cannot live a decent life in the host State. For this reason the Citizenship Directive provides that family members enjoy a series of parallel rights to the Union citizen herself. Family members thus have the same rights to movement, temporary and permanent residence, equal treatment, and to engage in study and work in the host State.[116] These rights apply whatever the nationality of the family members, provided they are 'accompanying or joining' a Union citizen who resides on the basis of the Directive in a host State.[117]

These last provisions have been important, as they allow a migrant citizen not just to take their family from one Member State to another, but also to bring their non-European family members from outside the Union, directly to their host State. This was confirmed in *Metock*, a case concerning asylum seekers in Ireland, who had seen their applications rejected and were unlawfully present.[118] However, they had married UK citizens resident in Ireland and thereby become the spouses of migrant citizens. The question was whether they were then transformed

---

[115] *Huber* v. *Bundesrepublik Deutschland*, C-524/06, EU:C:2008:724.
[116] Articles 4, 5, 7, 16, 23 and 24 Citizenship Directive.   [117] Article 7(2) Citizenship Directive.
[118] *Metock*, C-127/08, EU:C:2008:449; see C. Costello, '*Metock*: Free Movement and "Normal Family Life" in the Union' (2009) 46 *CMLRev* 587; S. Currie, 'Accelerated Justice or a Step Too Far? Residence Rights of Non-EU Family Members and the Court's Ruling in *Metock*' (2009) 34 *ELRev* 310.

into lawfully resident family members. In a complex judgment, partly overturning more restrict-ive earlier cases, the Court set out a number of important points:[119]

- The right of a family member to live with the Union citizen is simply dependent upon compliance with the definitions and conditions in the Directive. A State may impose no other conditions (such as previous lawful residence in another Member State). Their previous location or legal status is irrelevant.
- Specifically, it does not matter that the citizen met and married their partner in the host State, as in *Metock*. This still counts as family 'joining' the citizen.[120]
- It also does not matter if the partner previously entered the country illegally, or prior to the marriage was illegally present.
- Becoming a family member in the Directive sense has the effect of wiping the slate almost clean. The slate is only wiped 'almost' clean because the State may still impose proportionate sanctions upon the family member for any previous violations of immigration law, but these must not go so far as to deter free movement – one should think of a fine, but not of a denial of residence.[121]

The policy reasons for the *Metock* decision are diverse. One is that it could be difficult to police a requirement that family members were previously lawfully resident in a Member State, and lead to complex constructions to give this appearance. Another reason, given by the Court, was to align the law on migrant Union citizens with that concerning third-country nationals who are long-term residents in the European Union. This group does have the right to bring their family into the European Union.[122] It would perhaps be odd if migrant Union citizens then had lesser rights.

In any case, *Metock* has huge implications. In a time where many Member States make it difficult for their own nationals to bring family members in from outside the Union, EU migrants have a significant legal advantage. The Danish citizen struggling to bring his Angolan wife to Denmark because of Danish immigration law may move to Sweden, whereupon both he and she can rely on the Directive rights. A small but growing number of Union citizens now engage in such migration for the purposes of family reunification, to the concern of some national authorities. Moreover, as will be discussed below, if they return home the Court has said they must be able to take their family with them, making the avoidance of national law complete.[123]

That picture shows that the person who moves between States enjoys a relatively generous legal regime, by comparison with the strictness of much national immigration law. This has raised the claim of 'reverse discrimination'; that national citizens who stay put in their home State are actually worse off than migrants, and indeed, legally, this is largely true. The Belgian in the Netherlands has more and better family rights than her Dutch neighbour. That might seem to conflict with the very idea of citizenship, which surely is linked to the equality of citizens.[124] However, the Court avoids this issue on jurisdictional grounds, claiming consistently that free movement law simply does not apply to 'wholly internal' situations, where all the elements are

---

[119] *Akrich*, C-109/01, EU:C:2003:491. [120] See also *Sahin*, C-551/07, EU:C:2008:755. [121] See p. 483.
[122] *Metock*, C-127/08, EU:C:2008:449, para. 69; see Directive 2003/86/EC. [123] See pp. 511–15.
[124] A. Tryfonidou, 'Reverse Discrimination in Purely Internal Situations: An Incongruity in a Citizens' Europe' (2008) 35 *LIEI* 43.

confined to a single Member State.[125] Having said that, as will be seen below, the presence of some cross-border element which engages the Treaty has been surprisingly easily found.[126]

(b) The EU Idea of the Family

The family members who have a right to reside with the Union citizen are set out in Article 2(2):[127]

(a) the spouse

(b) the partner with whom the Union citizen has contracted a registered partnership, on the basis of the legislation of a Member State, if the legislation of the host Member State treats registered partnerships as equivalent to marriage and in accordance with the conditions laid down in the relevant legislation of the host Member State

(c) the direct descendants who are under the age of 21 or are dependants and those of the spouse or partner as defined in point (b)

(d) the dependent direct relatives in the ascending line and those of the spouse or partner as defined in point (b).

In *Coman*, the Court ruled that spouse, being a sex-neutral term, included a same-sex spouse. The consequence is that a Union citizen can bring their same-sex spouse to live with them even in a Member State that does not itself marry those of the same sex, and which may even have constitutional objections to the idea. Same-sex marriage is thus introduced into States that have not chosen for it, which will be intensely controversial.

Coman, C-673/16, EU:C:2018:385

34 The term 'spouse' used in that provision refers to a person joined to another person by the bonds of marriage.

35 As to whether that term includes a third-country national of the same sex as the Union citizen whose marriage to that citizen was concluded in a Member State in accordance with the law of that state, it should be pointed out, first of all, that the term 'spouse' within the meaning of Directive 2004/38 is gender-neutral and may therefore cover the same-sex spouse of the Union citizen concerned.

36 Next, it should be noted that, whereas, for the purpose of determining whether a partner with whom a Union citizen has contracted a registered partnership on the basis of the legislation of a Member State enjoys the status of 'family member', Article 2(2)(b) of Directive 2004/38 refers to the conditions laid down in the relevant legislation of the Member State to which that citizen intends to move or in which he intends to reside, Article 2(2)(a) of that directive, applicable by analogy in the present case, does not contain any such reference with regard to the concept of 'spouse' within the meaning of the directive. It follows that a Member State cannot rely on its national law as justification for refusing to recognise in its territory, for the sole purpose of granting a derived right of residence to a third-country national, a marriage concluded by that national with a Union citizen of the same sex in another Member State in accordance with the law of that state.

37 Admittedly, a person's status, which is relevant to the rules on marriage, is a matter that falls within the competence of the Member States and EU law does not detract from that competence. The Member States are thus free to decide whether or not to allow marriage for persons of the same sex.

---

[125] *Uecker and Jacquet*, C-64–5/96, EU:C:1997:285; *Morson and Jhanjan* v. *Netherlands*, 35–6/82, EU:C:1982:368; *Garcia Avello*, C-148/02, EU:C:2003:539; *Government of the French Community and Walloon Government* v. *Flemish Government* (Flemish Insurance Case), C-212/06, EU:C:2008:178.

[126] See pp. 511–15.

[127] See on when a child is a family member, *SM*, C-129/18, EU:C:2019:248. See also *Netherlands* v. *Ann Florence Reed*, 59/85, EU:C:1986:157.

38 Nevertheless, it is well established case-law that, in exercising that competence, Member States must comply with EU law, in particular the Treaty provisions on the freedom conferred on all Union citizens to move and reside in the territory of the Member States.

39 To allow Member States the freedom to grant or refuse entry into and residence in their territory by a third-country national whose marriage to a Union citizen was concluded in a Member State in accordance with the law of that state, according to whether or not national law allows marriage by persons of the same sex, would have the effect that the freedom of movement of Union citizens who have already made use of that freedom would vary from one Member State to another, depending on whether such provisions of national law exist. Such a situation would be at odds with the Court's case-law, cited by the Advocate General in point 73 of his Opinion, to the effect that, in the light of its context and objectives, the provisions of Directive 2004/38, applicable by analogy to the present case, may not be interpreted restrictively and, at all events, must not be deprived of their effectiveness.

40 It follows that the refusal by the authorities of a Member State to recognise, for the sole purpose of granting a derived right of residence to a third country national, the marriage of that national to a Union citizen of the same sex, concluded, during the period of their genuine residence in another Member State, in accordance with the law of that State, may interfere with the exercise of the right conferred on that citizen by Article 21(1) TFEU to move and reside freely in the territory of the Member States. Indeed, the effect of such a refusal is that such a Union citizen may be denied the possibility of returning to the Member State of which he is a national together with his spouse.

41 That said, it is established case-law that a restriction on the right to freedom of movement for persons, which, as in the main proceedings, is independent of the nationality of the persons concerned, may be justified if it is based on objective public-interest considerations and if it is proportionate to a legitimate objective pursued by national law. It is also apparent from the Court's case-law that a measure is proportionate if, while appropriate for securing the attainment of the objective pursued, it does not go beyond what is necessary in order to attain that objective.

42 As regards public-interest considerations, a number of Governments that have submitted observations to the Court have referred in that regard to the fundamental nature of the institution of marriage and the intention of a number of Member States to maintain a conception of that institution as a union between a man and a woman, which is protected in some Member States by laws having constitutional status. The Latvian Government stated at the hearing that, even on the assumption that a refusal, in circumstances such as those of the main proceedings, to recognise marriages between persons of the same sex concluded in another Member State constitutes a restriction of Article 21 TFEU, such a restriction is justified on grounds of public policy and national identity, as referred to in Article 4(2) TEU.

43 In that regard, it must be noted that the European Union is required, under Article 4(2) TEU, to respect the national identity of the Member States, inherent in their fundamental structures, both political and constitutional.

44 Moreover, the Court has repeatedly held that the concept of public policy as justification for a derogation from a fundamental freedom must be interpreted strictly, with the result that its scope cannot be determined unilaterally by each Member State without any control by the EU institutions. It follows that public policy may be relied on only if there is a genuine and sufficiently serious threat to a fundamental interest of society.

45 The Court finds, in that regard, that the obligation for a Member State to recognise a marriage between persons of the same sex concluded in another Member State in accordance with the law of that state, for the sole purpose of granting a derived right of residence to a third-country national, does not undermine the institution of marriage in the first Member State, which is defined by national law and, as indicated in

paragraph 37 above, falls within the competence of the Member States. Such recognition does not require that Member State to provide, in its national law, for the institution of marriage between persons of the same sex. It is confined to the obligation to recognise such marriages, concluded in another Member State in accordance with the law of that state, for the sole purpose of enabling such persons to exercise the rights they enjoy under EU law.

The Court finds that there is no basis for a restriction based on public policy or constitutional identity because Member States are not forced to marry same-sex couples themselves, merely to recognise marriages performed by other Member States. What is particularly important here is the emphasis in the last paragraph above that such recognition is for the 'sole purpose' of residence rights. This implies that while the same-sex spouse must be admitted and allowed to reside, they need not be treated as married for all purposes – for example tax or parental rights purposes. If that is correct, it will create a certain tension with equality, and will undoubtedly be the subject of further litigation.

In addition, a second group of family members enjoy more conditional rights.

Citizenship Directive, Article 3

(2) Without prejudice to any right to free movement and residence the persons concerned may have in their own right, the host Member State shall, in accordance with its national legislation, facilitate entry and residence for the following persons:

(a) any other family members, irrespective of their nationality, not falling under the definition in point 2 of Article 2 who, in the country from which they have come, are dependants or members of the household of the Union citizen having the primary right of residence, or where serious health grounds strictly require the personal care of the family member by the Union citizen;

(b) the partner with whom the Union citizen has a durable relationship, duly attested. The host Member State shall undertake an extensive examination of the personal circumstances and shall justify any denial of entry or residence to these people.

The notion of a 'dependant' was defined in *Jia*, a case in which the mother-in-law of a German resident in Sweden sought entry to Sweden from China on the basis of the legislation then in force that was equivalent to Article 2(2)(d). A family member qualifies as a dependant, the Court of Justice found, when 'having regard to their financial and social conditions they are not in a position to support themselves. The need for material support must exist in the State of origin of those relatives or the state whence they came at the time when they apply to join the Community national.'[128] The Court went on to consider how dependency could be proved and rejected the Swedish Government's claim that only an official document from the Chinese authorities could suffice. The Court found that 'evidence could be adduced by any appropriate means'.

An important element of this definition is that a dependant is a relative who depends upon the Union citizen in the country where she (the dependant) is coming from. Dependency must exist prior to reunification: it is a reason for reunification, not a result of it. This is particularly

---

[128] *Jia* v. *Migrationsverket*, C-1/05, EU:C:2007:1; see also *Reyes*, C-432/12, EU:C:2013:719.

important for parents from relatively poor countries, who may be able to support themselves in their home State, but would become dependent if living in an expensive EU country where they do not speak the language. They would not, following *Jia*, be dependants within the sense of the Directive. On the other hand, if the family member is dependent in their home State then their rights are not affected by the fact that they plan to work – and so cease to be dependent – when they arrive in the European Union.[129]

In *Rahman* the Court of Justice explained what it means to 'facilitate entry'.[130]

Secretary of State for the Home Department v. Rahman, C–83/11, EU:C:2012:519

21 Whilst it is therefore apparent that Article 3(2) of Directive 2004/38 does not oblige the Member States to accord a right of entry and residence to persons who are family members, in the broad sense, dependent on a Union citizen, the fact remains, as is clear from the use of the words 'shall facilitate' in Article 3(2), that that provision imposes an obligation on the Member States to confer a certain advantage, compared with applications for entry and residence of other nationals of third States, on applications submitted by persons who have a relationship of particular dependence with a Union citizen.

22 In order to meet that obligation, the Member States must, in accordance with the second subparagraph of Article 3(2) of Directive 2004/38, make it possible for persons envisaged in the first subparagraph of Article 3(2) to obtain a decision on their application that is founded on an extensive examination of their personal circumstances and, in the event of refusal, is justified by reasons.

23 As is clear from recital 6 in the preamble to Directive 2004/38, it is incumbent upon the competent authority, when undertaking that examination of the applicant's personal circumstances, to take account of the various factors that may be relevant in the particular case, such as the extent of economic or physical dependence and the degree of relationship between the family member and the Union citizen whom he wishes to accompany or join.

Although their right of entry may be weaker, if Article 3 family members are in fact admitted then it seems probable that they fall within the scope of 'family members' as used elsewhere in the Directive and as such enjoy the same rights to employment and equality as Article 2 family members.

(c) Separation, Death and Divorce

If family members lose their link with the migrant citizen, either through his or her death or the break-up of the relationship, their own rights of residence may become threatened. The Directive provides a degree of protection.

For EU family members, their right of residence continues after divorce or the death of the partner.[131] For non-EU family members, it continues under a number of conditions: that they had lived together in the State for at least a year before the death or divorce, and in the case of divorce had also been married for at least three years.[132] The stricter approach partly reflects a fear of marriages of convenience, and partly a view that non-EU family members who have only been present for a short period have less right to remain. Non-EU family members also maintain their right of residence after a divorce if they have custody of the Union citizen's children or a

---

[129] *Reyes*, C–432/12, EU:C:2013:719; see also *Depesme*, C–401/15, EU:C:2016:955.
[130] See also *Banger*, C–89/17 EU:C:2018:570, applying this to unmarried partners.
[131] Citizenship Directive, Articles 12–13.   [132] *Ibid.*

right of access to them, or if particular circumstances such as domestic violence warrant more generosity.[133] A problem with this law is that the divorce must be started while both partners are resident in the host State. If the citizen simply abandons his partner and returns home, then she ceases to be the family of a lawfully resident Union citizen, and her residence right lapses immediately. If a divorce is later started this does not revive her residence rights. In substance, the special protection for family members is only triggered by the legal ending of a marriage, whereas the loss of their rights can be triggered by its *de facto* end, with the space in between representing a significant gap in the law.[134]

For both EU and non-EU partners, the post-relationship right of residence is subject to conditions. EU family members are subject to the same Article 7 conditions as any other citizen, while non-EU family members must be either economically active or have resources and sickness insurance.[135] However, these conditions do not apply to the children of the dead or departed Union citizen if they are in school in the host State, nor to the parent who has custody of them.[136] Irrespective of nationality or resources, these retain their right of residence at least until school-leaving age has been reached.

If children have come to a host State to join a migrant worker, who has subsequently departed the family for whatever reason, or lost the status of worker, those children and their carer enjoy an additional right of residence on the basis of Article 10 of Regulation 492/211. This right is not dependent on resources, and extends until education is completed and care is no longer necessary, even potentially well into adulthood.[137]

In reality, family life may encompass more options than married cohabitation and divorce. For various reasons, partners may live apart while still having a legal bond to each other. In *Diatta* and *Baumbast*, the Court maintained that (i) until a marriage was finally dissolved, it was to be considered as existing,[138] and so a divorce in progress did not affect residence rights; and (ii) cohabitation was not as such a condition for residence rights for a family member.[139]

(d) The Rights of Children and Carers

Children who are Union citizens also enjoy an independent right of free movement and residence; they are citizens just as much as adults are.[140] However, it may be hard for them to genuinely exercise this right without someone to look after them.

Baby Catherine Zhu had Irish nationality and to the dismay of the Irish and UK Governments, her mother, Mrs Chen, who was Chinese, asserted a right for them both to live in the United Kingdom. They had sufficient resources and sickness insurance.[141]

---

[133] *Ibid.* Article 13(2).
[134] *Kuldip Singh*, C-218/14, EU:C:2015:476; see Francesca Strumia, 'Divorce Immediately, or Leave. Rights of Third Country Nationals and Family Protection in the Context of EU Citizens' Free Movement: *Kuldip Singh and Others*' (2016) 53(5) *CMLRev* 1373–93.
[135] *Kuldip Singh*, C-218/14, EU:C:2015:476; Citizenship Directive, Articles 12 and 13.
[136] Citizenship Directive, Article 12(3).
[137] *Ibrahim*, C-310/08, EU:C:2010:80; *Teixeira*, C-480/08, EU:C:2010:83; *Alarape*, C-529/11, EU:C:2013:290, applying Article 12 of Regulation 1612/68, which has now been replaced by the identically worded Article 10 of Regulation 492/211; *NA*, C-115/15, EU:C:2016:487; *Depesme*, C-401/15, EU:C:2016:955.
[138] See *Diatta* v. *Land Berlin*, 267/83, EU:C:1985:67; *Baumbast* v. *Secretary of State for the Home Department*, C-413/99, EU:C:2002:493; *Iida*, C-40/11, EU:C:2012:691.
[139] *Ogierakhi*, C-244/13, EU:C:2014:2068.
[140] See H. Stalford and E. Drywood, 'Coming of Age: Children's Rights in the EU' (2009) 46 *CMLRev* 143.
[141] See *Alokpa*, C-86/12, EU:C:2013:645.

Zhu and Chen, C–200/02, EU:C:2004:639

20 Moreover, contrary to the Irish Government's contention, a young child can take advantage of the rights of free movement and residence guaranteed by Community law. The capacity of a national of a Member State to be the holder of rights guaranteed by the Treaty and by secondary law on the free movement of persons cannot be made conditional upon the attainment by the person concerned of the age prescribed for the acquisition of legal capacity to exercise those rights personally . . .

45 On the other hand, a refusal to allow the parent, whether a national of a Member State or a national of a non-member country, who is the carer of a child to whom Article [21 TFEU] and Directive 90/364 grant a right of residence, to reside with that child in the host Member State would deprive the child's right of residence of any useful effect. It is clear that enjoyment by a young child of a right of residence necessarily implies that the child is entitled to be accompanied by the person who is his or her primary carer and accordingly that the carer must be in a position to reside with the child in the host Member State for the duration of such residence.

46 For that reason alone, where, as in the main proceedings, Article [21 TFEU] and Directive 90/364 grant a right to reside for an indefinite period in the host Member State to a young minor who is a national of another Member State, those same provisions allow a parent who is that minor's primary carer to reside with the child in the host Member State.

The Court of Justice here adds a new category of family member to those in the Directive. Where EU children exercise their EU movement and residence rights, the person primarily responsible for their care is granted parallel rights of movement and residence, irrespective of the carer's nationality. It does not even appear from the judgment that the carer must necessarily be a parent or even a family member, simply 'the person who is his or her primary carer'. Following the cases on carers in other contexts, one may expect this dependent right to continue until education is completed.[142] Since, in most cases, by this time the family will have been present in the State for a number of years, it is then less likely that it will be possible to remove the carer, for reasons of human rights. It is also arguable that as family members assimilated to those covered by the Directive, carers should have a parallel right to acquire permanent resident status after five years.[143] Helen Stalford has commented that the child is in a sense an 'anchor' for her carer in their host State, a phenomenon which she traces through the different lines of case law about children, not just *Chen*, but also the situations of family break-up discussed above, and *Ruiz Zambrano*, discussed below.[144]

H. Stalford, *Children and the European Union: Rights, Welfare and Accountability* (Oxford University Press, 2012) 48–9

Historically, children's status as EU citizens has been regarded as rather vacuous and incidental: given that children do not, for the most part, migrate independently, they only benefit from the rights associated with free movement as a consequence of their parents' decision to live and work in another Member State. More recent case law, however, has seen the Court of Justice heightening the currency of children's status as EU citizens in their own right. Indeed, this has occurred to such a degree that the

---

[142] Cf. *SM*, C-129/18, EU:C:2019:248. See pp. 503–4.   [143] See *Alarape*, C-529/11, EU:C:2013:290.
[144] See pp. 511–15.

tables have turned: while children have traditionally derived their citizenship entitlement from their parents it is becoming increasingly common for parents to derive valuable entry and residence rights within the EU from their children. This is particularly decisive, for instance, for adults of third country nationality who, having lived and perhaps even worked for a period in the host state with their family, no longer qualify for ongoing residence under national immigration law. In such cases, the Court of Justice has willingly extended the residence rights of third country national parents who have children of EU nationality. This is in acknowledgment of the fact that the entitlement accruing to their children by virtue of their EU citizenship status – notably their right to pursue education in the host state – can only be exercised if their primary carers (usually the parents) are allowed to remain with them.

This development in the case law is significant in that it establishes, first and foremost, that EU citizenship yields tangible and direct entitlement for individuals regardless of their age or level of dependency. Furthermore, it explicitly acknowledges the important social, emotional and material interdependence between family members. On the one hand, the application of EU citizenship is a key illustration of how children's rights are operable largely by virtue of the support and assistance of their parents. The very existence of that dependency, on the other hand, can 'anchor' their parents to the host state too. The conceptualization provides a useful illustration of the distinction between child autonomy and self-sufficiency that pervades children's rights and citizenship literature more broadly: children have an autonomous right to reside in a Member State founded on their status as EU citizens but are not expected to exercise that right without appropriate parental support, even if recognition of this might serve to undermine domestic immigration law, and even, it seems, if it implies an additional burden on the host state's welfare system.

It is not only children who benefit from the presence of their carer; so may another parent, who is thereby freed to go to work. If that work is cross-border, then this argument may find support in EU law. Mr Carpenter regularly travelled to provide services in other EU States, and argued that the expulsion of his non-EU wife would effectively prevent this, since she looked after his children while he was gone.[145] The case was controversial, as some considered it a stretch to use the free movement of services to restrain national immigration law. Yet the reasoning is clear and plausible, and he won in principle. Having acknowledged the importance to States of enforcing their immigration rules, which were claimed to be vital to public order, the Court continued:

43 A decision to deport Mrs Carpenter, taken in circumstances such as those in the main proceedings, does not strike a fair balance between the competing interests, that is, on the one hand, the right of Mr Carpenter to respect for his family life, and, on the other hand, the maintenance of public order and public safety . . .

45 In those circumstances, the decision to deport Mrs Carpenter constitutes an infringement which is not proportionate to the objective pursued.

This was then applied in *S and G* to the free movement of workers, where a grandmother was faced with expulsion.[146] However, she looked after her grandson while her son-in-law worked. Since the family lived in the Netherlands, but he worked several days a week in Belgium, the

---

[145] *Carpenter*, C-60/00, EU:C:2002:434.   [146] *S and G*, C-457/12, EU:C:2014:136.

question arose whether her expulsion would obstruct his free movement. The Court found that a family member who has a role as carer derives a right of residence from this if denying them that right 'discourages the worker from effectively exercising his rights under Article 45 TFEU'. They added:

> However, it must be noted that, although in the judgment in *Carpenter* the fact that the child in question was being taken care of by the third-country national who is a family member of a Union citizen was considered to be decisive, that child was, in that case, taken care of by the Union citizen's spouse. The mere fact that it might appear desirable that the child be cared for by the third-country national who is the direct relative in the ascending line of the Union citizen's spouse is not therefore sufficient in itself to constitute such a dissuasive effect.

Grandmothers, it implies, are substitutable, although the last word on that is for the national judge.

(e) The Right to Remain in the Union

In *Ruiz Zambrano* the Court applied *Chen*-style reasoning to Union citizens living in their home State.[147] Two Colombians living in Belgium had children with Belgian passports, and when the parents were threatened with expulsion to South America they claimed that then they would take their children, of course, and this would violate their children's rights as Union citizens.

The Court agreed. It found that in substance Union citizens have a right to live in the Union. However, if they are minor children then expelling their parents would in fact cause the children to have to leave, and so violate this right. Thus it followed that the parents had a derivative residence right.

Ruiz Zambrano v. *Office national de l'emploi (ONEm)*, C-34/09, EU:C:2011:124

41 As the Court has stated several times, citizenship of the Union is intended to be the fundamental status of nationals of the Member States.

42 In those circumstances, Article 20 TFEU precludes national measures which have the effect of depriving citizens of the Union of the genuine enjoyment of the substance of the rights conferred by virtue of their status as citizens of the Union.

43 A refusal to grant a right of residence to a third country national with dependent minor children in the Member State where those children are nationals and reside, and also a refusal to grant such a person a work permit, has such an effect.

44 It must be assumed that such a refusal would lead to a situation where those children, citizens of the Union, would have to leave the territory of the Union in order to accompany their parents. Similarly, if a work permit were not granted to such a person, he would risk not having sufficient resources to provide for

---

[147] See e.g. L. Azoulai, '"Euro-Bonds": The Ruiz Zambrano Judgment or the Real Invention of EU Citizenship' (2011) 3(2) *Perspectives on Federalism* 31; D. Kochenov, 'The Essence of EU Citizenship Emerging from the Last Ten Years of Academic Debate: Beyond the Cherry Blossoms and the Moon?' (2013) 62(1) *ICLQ* 97; N. Nic Shuibhne, '(Some of) the Kids Are All Right: Comment on McCarthy and Dereci' (2012) 49(1) *CMLRev* 349; A. Wiesbrock, 'Union Citizenship and the Redefinition of the "Internal Situations" Rule: The Implications of Zambrano' (2012) 12 *German LJ* 2077; G. Davies, 'The Family Rights of European Children: Expulsion of Non-European Parents', EUI Working Paper RSCAS 2012/04; C. O'Brien, 'I Trade Therefore I Am: Legal Personhood in the European Union' (2014) 50 *CMLRev* 1643.

> himself and his family, which would also result in the children, citizens of the Union, having to leave the territory of the Union. In those circumstances, those citizens of the Union would, in fact, be unable to exercise the substance of the rights conferred on them by virtue of their status as citizens of the Union.

It is conventional that citizens have a right to live in the territory of which they are a citizen, and the Court's judgment is also supported by the text of Article 20(1)(a) and Article 21 TFEU which both state the right of citizens to 'move and reside freely within the territory of the Member States'. It is hardly strange to claim that they are deprived of the genuine enjoyment of this right if they are forced to leave the Union.[148] It should be noted that it is only expulsion from the Union as a whole which engages this doctrine: if the family has the option of going to another Member State, then *Ruiz Zambrano* is no longer relevant.[149]

Ruiz Zambrano was not, however, a typical fact set. It is more common that a Union citizen child has one parent who is also a Union citizen, and one who is not. In *Chavez-Vilchez*, the Court was asked whether such a child could anchor their non-Union parent. It involved a number of mothers facing expulsion from the Netherlands, all of whom were primary carers of their Dutch children. The role of the Dutch fathers in the child's life varied from entirely absent to marginal.

The Netherlands argued that the existence of the fathers meant the mothers could be expelled: as long as there was a single parent staying in the Union, there was no question of forcing a child to leave, since the remaining parent could take over the care. They were however prepared to make exceptions to this rule if the remaining parent was dead, insane, in prison or banned from parental authority by a court order. The real aim of the Netherlands in these cases, it may be noted, was not actually to expel the mothers but to keep them in a state of unlawfulness, so that they could be excluded from social housing and benefits. Many of the children and their mothers had been in homeless shelters for quite some time.

Chavez-Vilchez, C–133/15, EU:C:2017:354

68   In that regard, it must be recalled that, in the judgment of 6 December 2012, *O and Others*, the Court held that factors of relevance, for the purposes of determining whether a refusal to grant a right of residence to a third-country national parent of a child who is a Union citizen means that that child is deprived of the genuine enjoyment of the substance of the rights conferred on him by that status, include the question of who has custody of the child and whether that child is legally, financially or emotionally dependent on the third-country national parent.

69   As regards the second factor, the Court has stated that it is the relationship of dependency between the Union citizen who is a minor and the third country national who is refused a right of residence that is liable to jeopardise the effectiveness of Union citizenship, since it is that dependency that would lead to the Union

---

[148] Although the Court's apparent view that it is free movement more than residence which is hindered is a little odd, even if it does not seem to matter; see *Iida*, C-40/11, EU:C:2012:691; S. Reynolds, 'Exploring the "Intrinsic Connection" between Free Movement and the Genuine Enjoyment Test: Reflections on EU Citizenship after Iida' (2013) 38 *ELRev* 376–92.

[149] *Rendon Marin*, C-165/14, EU:C:2016:675; see also *Alokpa*, C-86/12, EU:C:2013:645.

70   In this case, in order to assess the risk that a particular child, who is a Union citizen, might be compelled to leave the territory of the European Union and thereby be deprived of the genuine enjoyment of the substance of the rights conferred on him by Article 20 TFEU if the child's third-country national parent were to be refused a right of residence in the Member State concerned, it is important to determine, in each case at issue in the main proceedings, which parent is the primary carer of the child and whether there is in fact a relationship of dependency between the child and the third-country national parent. As part of that assessment, the competent authorities must take account of the right to respect for family life, as stated in Article 7 of the Charter of Fundamental Rights of the European Union, that article requiring to be read in conjunction with the obligation to take into consideration the best interests of the child, recognised in Article 24(2) of that charter.

71   For the purposes of such an assessment, the fact that the other parent, a Union citizen, is actually able and willing to assume sole responsibility for the primary day-to-day care of the child is a relevant factor, but it is not in itself a sufficient ground for a conclusion that there is not, between the third-country national parent and the child, such a relationship of dependency that the child would be compelled to leave the territory of the European Union if a right of residence were refused to that third-country national. In reaching such a conclusion, account must be taken, in the best interests of the child concerned, of all the specific circumstances, including the age of the child, the child's physical and emotional development, the extent of his emotional ties both to the Union citizen parent and to the third-country national parent, and the risks which separation from the latter might entail for that child's equilibrium.

Whether a parent can be expelled thus depends on the degree to which their child is legally, financially and emotionally dependent upon them. This dependency is the central concept in the law, because it is dependency which forces one family member to follow another.

Implicit in the judgment is the idea that sometimes it may be possible for the child to stay with the remaining parent, and other cases have confirmed that a parent does not acquire a derived right of residence automatically, but only when their presence is necessary.[150] However, merely because the remaining parent is prepared to take the child does not make the non-European one superfluous. On the contrary, the consideration proposed by the Court is more human and holistic: the child's relationship with the parent facing expulsion is the central factor to be considered, with an assessment made of the degree of their dependency and emotional bonds, and the consequences for the child's wellbeing of their separation.

Thus although the Court still speaks of whether the child would be compelled to leave the Union, in substance it is now asking a different question: whether separating parent and child is compatible with the interests of the child, and with human rights, and implicitly with Union values. These factors form the test for whether the parent derives a right of residence.

That is far from a precise test, but the judgment suggests that expulsion of the parent of a minor child will be the exception rather than the rule, and will only be possible where their relationship is already distant enough that separation would not harm the child's 'equilibrium'. Indeed, in *O and Others* the Court emphasised that even where the child and non-Union parent

---

[150] *Iida*, C-40/11, EU:C:2012:691; *K.A.*, C-82/16, EU:C:2018:308; see also *O and S* v. *Maahanmuuttovirasto; Maahanmuuttovirasto* v. *L*, C-356–7/11, EU:C:2012:776.

do not live together, it may still be the case that their relationship involves sufficient dependency to prevent expulsion.[151] It also confirmed in that case that a blood relationship, contrary to the arguments of the German and Italian Governments, is not essential for such dependency.

At a minimum, it seems to follow from *Chavez-Vilchez* that a parent cannot be expelled if the forced separation of that parent from their child would be a violation of the right to family life. However, reading the judgment above, it seems to go beyond this, requiring a more global approach, more accurately captured by the idea that expulsion is only possible when it is not seriously contrary to the best interests of the child. That would, in the context of modern family law, and the values of the Union, not be an inappropriate rule.[152]

K.A. then dealt with some of the procedural aspects of this.[153] Belgium required parents with an entry ban to leave the Union and prove their relationship with the Belgian child from outside, before then being allowed to return. The Court pointed out that if a sufficient relationship did in fact exist, then this policy was obviously a systematic violation of the law. On the contrary, dependency must be assessed before any steps towards expulsion may be taken, as otherwise the effectiveness of the primary *Zambrano* rule would be undermined.

Does a similar logic apply to entry? A question which *Ruiz Zambrano* raises is when a carer's rights begin. It seems clear following these cases that a parent arriving from outside the Union with a baby in their arms which they can demonstrate to be a Union citizen will consequently have a right to remain. However, suppose that they cannot prove that the baby is a Union citizen, but they have a plausible claim that he has a right to such citizenship – perhaps it is the fruit of a holiday romance with an EU tourist? Arguably, the Member State where they are present should grant them a period, for example, to make contact with the father and take legal steps to establish paternity.[154] This may seem far-fetched but the alternative is that a Member State risks deporting a Union citizen from the Union, possibly to deeply disadvantageous socio-economic circumstances, which is at odds with the perspective the cases seem to express. One might even extrapolate to the position of a pregnant woman arriving at Frankfurt airport from a non-EU State and claiming she carries a baby which will be entitled to citizenship of a Member State upon its birth, say a few months away. Would it be in the spirit of the law, in the light of *K.A.*, to turn her away and let the little proto-European be born in possibly dangerous conditions outside the European Union?

Where adults are concerned, the situation is different. In *K.A.* the Court stated:

> [I]t must, at the outset, be emphasised that, unlike minors and a fortiori minors who are young children, such as the Union citizens concerned in the case that gave rise to the judgment of 8 March 2011, *Ruiz Zambrano*, an adult is, as a general rule, capable of living an independent existence apart from the members of his family. It follows that the identification of a relationship between two adult members of the same family as a relationship of dependency, capable of giving rise to a derived right of residence under Article 20 TFEU, is conceivable only in exceptional cases, where, having regard to all the relevant circumstances, there could be no form of separation of the individual concerned from the member of his family on whom he is dependent.

---

[151] *O and S* v. *Maahanmuuttoverasto; Maahanmuuttoverasto* v. *L*, C-356–7/11, EU:C:2012:776.
[152] See here Article 2 TEU; *Carpenter*, C-60/00, EU:C:2002:434.   [153] *K.A.*, C-82/16, EU:C:2018:308.
[154] See *Janko Rottmann* v. *Freistaat Bayern*, C-135/08, EU:C:2010:104, para. 58.

There is thus a distinction to be made, between situations where the presence of a family member is truly necessary, and when it is simply desirable.[155] The former founds a residence right, the latter does not. Facts may however get in the way of this tidy rule. For one thing, even parents are not necessary in the strictest sense: it is imaginable, however sad, that in some situations parents might leave their children with family or friends rather than take them back to countries where they had few prospects and might not be safe. In rich Western Welfare States those children, with their Union citizenship, would not be left homeless or without care. The need for their parents is thus, as the cases recognise, primarily emotional. However, for some people it would be as emotionally inconceivable to abandon their elderly and dependent parent, or their disabled adult brother, or even their spouse – whom they have sworn to accompany and care for, a promise demanded in marriage by the same State now claiming they can reasonably separate – as it would be to abandon their child. The Court leaves it open for national judges to decide whether these situations entail sufficient dependency – are sufficiently exceptional – a decision which may often be difficult, and perhaps culturally variable too.

(f) U-Turns and Family Rights

When Union citizens live in a host State, they often enjoy better family rights than they would in their home State: the Directive is relatively generous, and Member States are not allowed to impose any restrictions other than the ones it mentions. However, when those migrant citizens return home, the Directive no longer applies, as they are no longer in a Member State 'other than their own'.[156] They would appear to be exposed to the full shock of national immigration law.

In *Singh* the Court made sure this was not the case. A British woman had been living and working in Germany, her Indian husband accompanying her on the basis of EU law.[157] After a few years she wanted to return to the United Kingdom, but was told that her husband would not be granted a right of residence – which he had enjoyed before they left. The United Kingdom considered that if she was in the United Kingdom, then as a British citizen she would be in an internal situation, outside the scope of EU law and so only national immigration rules would apply, to the disadvantage of Mr Singh.

The Court of Justice took a different view. It argued that to take away Ms Singh's EU rights upon her return would be a deterrent to movement: had she known this would happen it would have made it less attractive for her to go to Germany in the first place. This remark must be understood in the context of Ms Singh's family situation – her husband would not want to lose his UK residence status, as would happen if he moved to Germany, unless he could be sure of getting it back when he returned. However, the principle is broader: when an individual returns to their home State after exercising EU rights, they do not return to an internal situation. On the contrary, the status of migrant 'sticks' and they can rely on EU rights against their home State to challenge any measures making their return more difficult, or 'punishing' them for having been away.[158] Movement to the home State is still, it might be commented, cross-border movement.

---

[155] *Dereci*, C-526/11, EU:C:2013:543.   [156] *McCarthy*, C-434/09, EU:C:2011:277; *Lounes*, C-165/16, EU:C:2017:862.
[157] *Singh*, C-370/90, EU:C:1992:296; see also *Government of the French Community and Walloon Government* v. *Flemish Government* (Flemish Insurance Case), C-212/06, EU:C:2008:178; see C. Dautricourt and S. Thomas, 'Reverse Discrimination and the Free Movement of Persons under Community Law: All for Ulysses, Nothing for Penelope?' (2009) 34 *ELRev* 433.
[158] *D'Hoop*, C-224/98, EU:C:2002:432; see also *O and B*, C-456/12, EU:C:2014:135.

This decision acquires a new dimension when it is read alongside *Metock*, discussed above, in which the Court confirmed that the Directive allows a citizen to bring their family members from outside the Union to their host State.[159] Combining these two cases means that a citizen can go abroad, bring their family member to the European Union – or bring them out of illegality by marrying them – and then take them home.

This has since been clarified and confirmed in *Eind*.[160] In this case, a Dutch citizen working in the United Kingdom brought his daughter to live with him in Britain from outside the Union. When he returned to the Netherlands, the Dutch authorities claimed that the situation was internal and governed by Dutch immigration law, which did not permit the daughter's residence. Mr Eind, by contrast, claimed that he could continue to rely on EU rights as a returning migrant. The Court of Justice agreed with him.

Minister voor Vreemdelingenzaken en Integratie v. Eind, C–291/05, EU:C:2007:771

35 A national of a Member State could be deterred from leaving that Member State in order to pursue gainful employment in the territory of another Member State if he does not have the certainty of being able to return to his Member State of origin, irrespective of whether he is going to engage in economic activity in the latter State.

36 That deterrent effect would also derive simply from the prospect, for that same national, of not being able, on returning to his Member State of origin, to continue living together with close relatives, a way of life which may have come into being in the host Member State as a result of marriage or family reunification.

37 Barriers to family reunification are therefore liable to undermine the right to free movement which the nationals of the Member States have under Community law, as the right of a Community worker to return to the Member State of which he is a national cannot be considered to be a purely internal matter.

38 It follows that, in circumstances such as those in the case before the referring court, Miss Eind has the right to install herself with her father, Mr Eind, in the Netherlands, even if the latter is not economically active.

Returning migrants therefore continue to enjoy the family rights that they have exercised for the first time while abroad. The Dane who has brought his Angolan wife to Sweden and lived there for a while may then return to Denmark and rely on EU law against his own State to enforce her right to live with him. The U-turn thus allows national immigration law to be completely avoided, and is both controversial and popular for this reason.

Nevertheless there are limits. In *O and B*, the Court found that U-turn rights exist to protect family life which was created or strengthened abroad. Thus they do not arise after very brief residence, or where a citizen merely brings a family member over for weekends. On the other hand, the Court found that when the family resides on the basis of Article 7 of the Directive, evidencing an intention to stay for at least three months, this should normally suffice. That is, it may be noted, a low hurdle.[161]

Nevertheless, attempts to bring family rights home when there was no substantive exercise of family life and rights abroad will amount to abuse, the Court found. Yet this is a less formidable

---

[159] *Metock*, C–127/08, EU:C:2008:449; see pp. 499–500 above; see also A. Tryfonidou, 'Family Reunification Right of (Migrant) Union Citizens: Towards a More Liberal Approach' (2009) 15 *ELJ* 634.

[160] *Minister voor Vreemdelingenzaken en Integratie* v. *Eind*, C–291/05, EU:C:2007:771.

[161] See *O and B*, C–456/12, EU:C:2014:135. See also *Banger*, C–89/17 EU:C:2018:570.

exclusion than it seems, for the mere fact that the migration was for the purpose of acquiring family rights will not make it abusive, as long as those rights were genuinely exercised in the host State to a sufficient degree.[162] The deliberate U-turn, as long as it is done properly, is legitimate.

The legal basis for the U-turn rights is not the Directive, since that does not apply in a home State, but Article 21(1). However, the scope of the rights is the same as those in the Directive, and Member States may not impose any new or extra conditions.[163] It is almost as if one continues to fall within the Directive's scope. Almost, but better, because the residence conditions in the Directive do not apply – in *Eind* the Netherlands argued that since the Directive only gave family rights to those who were self-sufficient or economically active, that should also be the case for returnees. The Court rejected this, since the right to live in one's home State is not subject to conditions.

All this has acquired a new dimension as a result of *Coman*, in which the Court ruled that same-sex spouses were included in the Directive.[164] It is no longer just immigration law which can be avoided, but also restrictions on who is able to marry. That case involved a Romanian man who married his American husband while living in Belgium, and successfully insisted that Romania recognise his husband as a spouse, and grant him residence rights analogous to those in the Directive, on the basis of the case law above. The power and challenges of mutual recognition are displayed here vividly: while Member States still choose who they marry, they no longer choose who in their State must be seen as married. If the *Coman* route is widely used, Member States' formal sovereignty over marriage may come to seem rather hollow. As in other areas of law, mutual recognition can make it hard to sustain regulatory choices which deviate from the European norm.[165]

What the U-turn cases show powerfully is that the most important difference in EU law is not between citizens of different Member States, but between those who stay at home, and those who move. The latter enter a specialised legal regime, with the Court of Justice as their ultimate legal guardian, and maintain their status within this regime wherever they move – even if it is back home. They have in a sense become transnationals, privileged clients of the Union, and so are no longer comparable with compatriots do who do not cross borders, and are not agents of integration.

Lounes takes this to new limits. It involves a citizen who returned home without ever having left. Ms Ormazabal is a Spanish citizen who moved to the United Kingdom, and after many years of lawful residence naturalised to become a dual national. A few years later, she met and married Mr Lounes, who is Tunisian, and was not lawfully present in the United Kingdom. After their marriage, she attempted to regularise his position, as the spouse of a Spanish worker in the United Kingdom. The problem was that the Directive did not apply, because she was also British.

However, Article 21 is broader, covering all those who move, and there is no longer any novelty in enforcing this against one's own State if its measures obstruct movement or discriminate. It was not obvious that the United Kingdom was doing this though. It was treating Ms Lounes as a normal British citizen. As a long-term naturalised resident, perhaps that was what she was. What rights does Article 21 grant someone in her position?

---

[162] *Ibid.* para. 58; *Akrich*, C-109/01, EU:C:2003:491; *Levin*, 53/81, EU:C:2003:491.
[163] *O and B*, C-456/12, EU:C:2014:135; *Coman*, C-673/16, EU:C:2018:385.   [164] *Coman*, C-673/16, EU:C:2018:385.
[165] See pp. 716–19.

Lounes, C–165/16, EU:C:2017:862

52 The rights which nationals of Member States enjoy under that provision include the right to lead a normal family life together with their family members, in the host Member State.

53 A national of one Member State who has moved to and resides in another Member State cannot be denied that right merely because he subsequently acquires the nationality of the second Member State in addition to his nationality of origin, otherwise the effectiveness of Article 21(1) TFEU would be undermined.

54 In the first place, denying him that right would amount to treating him in the same way as a citizen of the host Member State who has never left that State, disregarding the fact that the national concerned has exercised his freedom of movement by settling in the host Member State and that he has retained his nationality of origin.

55 A Member State cannot restrict the effects that follow from holding the nationality of another Member State, in particular the rights which are attendant thereon under EU law and which are triggered by a citizen exercising his freedom of movement.

56 In the second place, the rights conferred on a Union citizen by Article 21(1) TFEU, including the derived rights enjoyed by his family members, are intended, amongst other things, to promote the gradual integration of the Union citizen concerned in the society of the host Member State.

57 Union citizens, such as Ms Ormazabal, who, after moving, in the exercise of their freedom of movement, to the host Member State and residing there for a number of years pursuant to and in accordance with Article 7(1) or Article 16(1) of Directive 2004/38, acquire the nationality of that Member State, intend to become permanently integrated in that State.

58 As is stated, in essence, by the Advocate General in point 86 of his Opinion, it would be contrary to the underlying logic of gradual integration that informs Article 21(1) TFEU to hold that such citizens, who have acquired rights under that provision as a result of having exercised their freedom of movement, must forego those rights – in particular the right to family life in the host Member State – because they have sought, by becoming naturalised in that Member State, to become more deeply integrated in the society of that State.

59 It would also follow that Union citizens who have exercised their freedom of movement and acquired the nationality of the host Member State in addition to their nationality of origin would, so far as their family life is concerned, be treated less favourably than Union citizens who have also exercised that freedom but who hold only their nationality of origin. The rights conferred on Union citizens in the host Member State, particularly the right to a family life with a third-country national, would thus be reduced in line with their increasing degree of integration in the society of that Member State and according to the number of nationalities that they hold.

60 It follows from the foregoing that, if the rights conferred on Union citizens by Article 21(1) TFEU are to be effective, citizens in a situation such as Ms Ormazabal's must be able to continue to enjoy, in the host Member State, the rights arising under that provision, after they have acquired the nationality of that Member State in addition to their nationality of origin and, in particular, must be able to build a family life with their third-country-national spouse, by means of the grant of a derived right of residence to that spouse.

The Court reasons that if migrants lost their Article 21 rights when they naturalised, this would essentially punish them for integration, which would be paradoxical, and would also deter that integration. One can respond that the special status and rights awarded to migrants are precisely because they are outsiders in a host State, and when they naturalise that shows that they have integrated fully, and no longer need such special protection.

However, the Court's view was that having exercised free movement rights a Union citizen can no longer be compared to someone who has not, even many years after that movement. The status and rights of migrant stick, for life, even after naturalisation. Not all national citizens are equal: their background and past govern their future rights.[166]

Thus if Ms Ormazabal stays in Britain, and starts a new relationship thirty years in the future, and forty years after she became British, *Lounes* suggests that the rights of her partner will not be governed by British immigration law, but by Article 21 – or at least that would be the case if it had not been Britain involved, but any other Member State. For *Lounes* is above all a Brexit case. As negotiations attempt to secure the rights of Union citizens in Britain, and British citizens in the Union, the question for many of those migrants is whether they will lose the benefits of any agreement if they naturalise in their host State. Will they then cease to be the free movers for whom arrangements are being made? The view of the Court – a nudge to the Union negotiators – is that they should not.

(vii) Expulsion and Exclusion

In tandem with other provisions on movement of EU nationals, the Citizenship Directive sets out certain circumstances in which Union citizens or their family members can be expelled from or refused entry to another Member State, even though they would otherwise meet the requirements for entry or residence.[167] The Court has also effectively extended these provisions to cover family members outside the Directive, but with a derived right of residence based on Article 21.[168]

The rules in Article 27 also apply to national measures restricting a migrant to a particular part of the national territory, or excluding him from one part of it.[169]

Citizenship Directive, Article 27

(1) Subject to the provisions of this Chapter, Member States may restrict the freedom of movement and residence of Union citizens and their family members, irrespective of nationality, on grounds of public policy, public security or public health. These grounds shall not be invoked to serve economic ends.

(2) Measures taken on grounds of public policy or public security shall comply with the principle of proportionality and shall be based exclusively on the personal conduct of the individual concerned. Previous criminal convictions shall not in themselves constitute grounds for taking such measures. The personal conduct of the individual concerned must represent a genuine, present and sufficiently serious threat affecting one of the fundamental interests of society. Justifications that are isolated from the particulars of the case or that rely on considerations of general prevention shall not be accepted.

---

[166] Cf. *Metock*, C-127/08, EU:C:2008:449.

[167] See generally N. Nic Shuibhne, 'Derogating from the Free Movement of Persons: When Can Union Citizens be Deported?' (2006) 8 *CYELS* 187; D. Kostakopoulou and N. Ferreira, 'Testing Liberal Norms: The Public Policy and Public Security Derogations and the Cracks in European Citizenship' (2014) 20(3) *Columbia Journal of European Law* 167; D. Kochenov and B. Pirker, 'Deporting EU Citizens: A Counter-Intuitive Trend' (2013) 19 *Columbia Journal of European Law* 369.

[168] *CS*, C-304/14, EU:C:2016:674.   [169] *Ministre de l'Intérieur* v. *Olazabal*, C-100/01, EU:C:2002:712.

In any case where a decision is made to deport an individual, the person must be notified in writing of the decision. They must be told the reasons for exclusion, precisely and in full, unless this is contrary to the interests of State security.[170] All persons must have access to judicial and administrative redress procedures to appeal against or seek review of any decision taken against them.[171] These procedures will consider the legality and proportionality of the decision, as well as the facts and circumstances on which the decision was based.[172] Individuals must be told in the initial decision by the relevant court or administrative authority where they may lodge an appeal, the time limits for the appeal and the time allowed to leave the territory.[173]

These procedural guarantees apply to all migrant citizens, not just those lawfully present in the Member State.[174] To impose a condition of lawfulness on the procedural protections would be to some extent to pre-empt precisely the issue that the procedures in question are to determine.

The most commonly used grounds for exclusion are public policy and public security. Although these are two separate criteria, Article 27(2) provides that they both turn on the question whether the individual's conduct poses a genuine, present and sufficiently serious threat to the fundamental interests of society. States have some discretion in determining the threshold here, since norms may vary. However, the derogations are EU law concepts, subject to the jurisdiction of the Court of Justice, which interprets them restrictively, since they are derogations from the fundamental freedom to move. The Court is particularly vigilant in asking whether a consistent approach is being taken to nationals and foreigners.[175] In *Adoui*,[176] Belgium wished to deport some French women who were 'waitresses in a bar which was suspect from the point of view of morals'.[177]

Adoui and Cornuaille v. *Belgian State and City of Liège; Dominique Cornuaille* v. *Belgian State*, 115–16/81, EU:C:1982:183

8 Although Community law does not impose upon the Member States a uniform scale of values as regards the assessment of conduct which may be considered as contrary to public policy, it should nevertheless be stated that conduct may not be considered as being of a sufficiently serious nature to justify restrictions on the admission to or residence within the territory of a Member State of a national of another Member State in a case where the former Member State does not adopt, with respect to the same conduct on the part of its own nationals, repressive measures or other genuine and effective measures intended to combat such conduct.

The deportation of foreign prostitutes was conditional upon adequately harsh repression of national ones.

The threat to society which the individual represents must, moreover, be a present one. However bad their behaviour has been in the past, if there is no reason to believe that they will

---

[170] Citizenship Directive, Article 30(1)–(2); see now *ZZ*, C-300/11, EU:C:2013:363.
[171] Citizenship Directive, Article 31(1).   [172] *Ibid.* Article 31(3).   [173] *Ibid.* Article 30(3).
[174] *MRAX*, C-459/99, EU:C:2002:461; C-50/06 *Commission* v. *Netherlands*, C-233/14, EU:C:2016:396; *Dörr and Ünal*, C-136/03, EU:C:2005:340; cf. *Hungary* v. *Slovak Republic*, C-364/10, EU:C:2012:630.
[175] *Van Duyn* v. *Home Office*, 41/74, EU:C:1974:133; *R* v. *Secretary of State for the Home Department, ex parte Shingara and ex parte Radiom*, C-65/95 and C-111/95, EU:C:1997:300; *Conegate* v. *Customs and Excise Commissioners*, 121/85, EU:C:1986:114; *R* v. *Henn and Darby*, 34/79, EU:C:1979:295; cf. *Hungary* v. *Slovak Republic*, C-364/10, EU:C:2012:630.
[176] *Adoui and Cornuaille* v. *Belgian State and City of Liège; Dominique Cornuaille* v. *Belgian State*, 115–16/81, EU:C:1982:183.
[177] *Ibid.* para. 2; they were accused of prostitution.

reoffend, then there are no grounds for deportation. This demands that each case be looked at on its facts and rules which provide for automatic deportation after committal of certain offences will inevitably contravene the Directive. In *Orfanopoulos*, a Greek and an Italian drug addict had each been convicted of multiple drugs-related offences, as well as for violent offences and for theft. Germany had a law that any foreigner sentenced to a custodial sentence of two years or more for drugs-related offences would be automatically deported. The German court asked whether the automatic nature of the deportation was disproportionate.

Orfanopoulos and Oliveri v. *Land Baden-Württemberg*, C–482/01 and C–493/01, EU: C:2004:262

65 ... a particularly restrictive interpretation of the derogations from that freedom is required by virtue of a person's status as a citizen of the Union ...

67 While it is true that a Member State may consider that the use of drugs constitutes a danger for society such as to justify special measures against foreign nationals who contravene its laws on drugs, the public policy exception must, however, be interpreted restrictively, with the result that the existence of a previous criminal conviction can justify an expulsion only insofar as the circumstances which gave rise to that conviction are evidence of personal conduct constituting a present threat to the requirements of public policy.

68 ... Community law precludes the deportation of a national of a Member State based on reasons of a general preventive nature, that is one which has been ordered for the purpose of deterring other aliens, in particular where such measure automatically follows a criminal conviction, without any account being taken of the personal conduct of the offender or of the danger which that person represents for the requirements of public policy.

69 The question asked by the national court refers to national legislation which requires the expulsion of nationals of other Member States who have received certain sentences for specific offences.

70 It must be held that, in such circumstances, the expulsion automatically follows a criminal conviction, without any account being taken of the personal conduct of the offender or of the danger which that person represents for the requirements of public policy.

71 In the light of the foregoing, the answer to the first question must be that [EU law] preclude[s] national legislation which requires national authorities to expel nationals of other Member States who have been finally sentenced to a term of youth custody of at least two years or to a custodial sentence for an intentional offence against the Law on narcotics, where the sentence has not been suspended.

A similar automatism was present in *Commission* v. *Spain*, which addressed a Spanish practice of denying entry to those against whose name an alert had been entered in the Schengen Information System.[178] Although the System is part of EU law, and exists precisely to prevent the free movement of dangerous persons within the European Union, nevertheless the Court of Justice found that Spain had an obligation to make its own independent assessment of the degree of threat, and could only give the alert 'due consideration'.

The requirement that the threat must be present has further consequences. If an expulsion order is enforced more than two years after it was issued (as will often be the case where the citizen has to serve a lengthy prison sentence before deportation), the Member State must

---

[178] *Commission* v. *Spain*, C–503/03, EU:C:2006:74; see also *Calfa*, C–348/96, EU:C:1999:6; *K*, C–331/16, EU:C:2018:296.

consider whether, at the moment of enforcement, the individual is still a current and genuine threat to public policy or security.[179] A propensity to commit the same kinds of offences in the future could support this conclusion, although the decision must be based on proper assessment.[180] In any case, if a citizen has been deported, she can submit an application for a lifting of the exclusion order after a reasonable period and, in any event, after three years, on the basis that there has been a material change to circumstances.[181]

There is also a scale of seriousness which determines whether exclusion can take place. Residents, or those applying for residency, can be excluded for conduct which would not justify exclusion if they were permanent residents, for the latter may only be expelled on 'serious grounds' of public policy or security.[182] Moreover, if a citizen has been resident in another State for the previous ten years or is a minor, she may not be expelled except for 'imperative' grounds of public security, (public policy is not a sufficient reason to expel these groups), or, in the case of the minor, if it is in the best interests of the child.[183] In *Tsakouridis*, the Court of Justice found that being part of an organised drugs gang could be sufficient to engage 'imperative grounds' of public security, while in *PI* it found that sexual crimes against children might meet this standard too, if the crimes had 'particularly serious characteristics'. Controversially, the Court took account not just of the consequences for victims, but also of the possible impact on the 'calm and physical security of the population'.[184] Kostakopoulou and Ferreira have commented that the Court does not seem to be really assessing the degree of threat to the State, more the general seriousness of the crime, the behaviour of the individual and its circumstances, moving from what they call the 'security threat' to the 'security constellation'.

> **D. Kostakopoulou and N. Ferreira, 'Testing Liberal Norms: The Public Policy and Public Security Derogations and the Cracks in European Citizenship' (2014) 20(3) *Columbia Journal of European Law* 167**
>
> While the 'everydayness' or 'normalization' of the public security derogation will please Member States which remain free to categorise conduct as contrary to public security 'according to the particular values of their legal order', it is deeply problematic and worrying from the point of view of EU law. The phrase 'threat to the calm and physical security of the population' constitutes an interpretational innovation (*Tsakouridis* referred to the economic and social danger for society) which undermines the rationale of the Citizenship Directive and its objectives of promoting security of residence for long-term resident EU citizens and enhancing their citizenship status. Similarly, the reference to the referring court's assessment of conduct leading to expulsion in the light of 'the particular values of the legal order of the Member State' (paragraph 29) is so ambiguous that it is bound to lead to legal uncertainty and the unequal treatment of Union citizens throughout the European Union. The Grand Chamber's deference to the Member States' 'interpretational freedom' may be attuned to the present rise in Euro-scepticism in several countries, but it is certainly at odds with its traditional attestation of the strict interpretation of the derogations.

---

[179] Citizenship Directive, Article 33(2); see also *Orfanopoulos and Oliveri* v. *Land Baden-Württemberg*, C-482/01 and C-493/01, EU:C:2004:262.

[180] *E*, C-193/16, EU:C:2017:542.   [181] Citizenship Directive, Article 32(1).

[182] *Ibid.* Article 28(2); see also *B*, C-316/16, EU:C:2018:256.

[183] Citizenship Directive, Article 28(3); see also *M.G.*, C-400/12, EU:C:2014:9.

[184] *Tsakouridis*, C-145/09, EU:C:2010:708; *PI*, C-348/09, EU:C:2012:300; see Kostakopoulou and Ferreira, n. 167 above.

The exceptions also apply to restrictions on exit. In *Jipa*, the Romanian Government imposed an order on one of its own citizens that he not travel to Belgium for three years.[185] This was because he had earlier been expelled from Belgium. The order had as its background a cooperation agreement between these States relating to 'illegal' Romanians in Belgium. The Court of Justice accepted that such an order could, in principle, be legitimate. It seems reasonable that if one State legitimately expels a Union citizen, there should be little objection to other States helping to make this expulsion effective. However, the judgment shows suspicion of whether the measure was actually disproportionate, with the Court emphasising that such measures, given their fundamental conflict with free movement, should not go beyond what was strictly necessary. A part of the doubt was whether the Belgian order had in fact been legitimate. This was something the national judge should examine.

Even if the citizen's conduct poses a sufficient threat to public policy or public security, it will still not automatically follow that she can be excluded. Article 28(1) of the Citizenship Directive lists a whole host of factors which must be taken into account before making an exclusion order. To these may be added fundamental rights, as reflected in the European Union Charter of Fundamental Rights (EUCFR) and the European Convention on Human Rights (ECHR).

Citizenship Directive, Article 28

(1) Before taking an expulsion decision on grounds of public policy or public security, the host Member State shall take account of considerations such as how long the individual concerned has resided on its territory, his/her age, state of health, family and economic situation, social and cultural integration into the host Member State and the extent of his/her links with the country of origin.

Public policy and public security are not trump cards, but rather factors to be weighed in the balance against the interests and circumstances of the individual in question and those close to them.

5 POLITICAL RIGHTS OF UNION CITIZENS

At the heart of modern citizenship is the right to engage fully and equally in the common affairs of the political community. This is usually translated into a series of political rights: the right to vote, to hold office and to hold office-holders accountable.[186] For Union citizens residing in a Member State not their own, Article 22 TFEU (and Article 20(2)(b) TFEU) grant them the right to vote and stand in municipal and European elections on the same conditions as nationals of that State.[187] The procedure is regulated by two Directives, which also provide for limited exceptions and conditions in municipalities where there are particularly high levels of non-national Union citizens. Only Luxembourg and Belgium have made use of these.[188] However, the most important

---

[185] *Jipa*, C-33/07, EU:C:2008:396; see also *Aladzhov*, C-434/10, EU:C:2011:750.

[186] See J. Shaw, *The Transformation of Citizenship in the European Union* (Cambridge University Press, 2007); H. Lardy, 'The Political Rights of Union Citizenship' (1997) 3 *EPL* 611; D. Kostakopoulou, 'Ideas, Norms and European Citizenship: Explaining Institutional Change' (2005) 68 *MLR* 233, 239–40.

[187] *Delvigne*, C-650/13, EU:C:2015:648.

[188] Directive 94/80/EC, Article 12 [1994] OJ L 368/38; Directive 93/109/EC, Article 14 [1993] OJ L 329/34; European Commission, 'Report on the Right to Vote and to Stand as a Candidate in Elections to the European Parliament', COM(2007)846 final; European Commission, 'Report on the Right to Vote and Stand as a Candidate in Municipal Elections', COM(2005)382 final.

cases to date have concerned issues which are less to do with migrating citizens, and more to do with the very nature of the European political community.

Spain v. *United Kingdom* raised the question whether only Union citizens can vote for the European Parliament.[189] Spain challenged the United Kingdom's grant of voting rights to some Commonwealth citizens resident in Gibraltar.

The Court was in principle prepared to defer to different constitutional traditions, and noted that '[n]o clear conclusion can be drawn in that regard from Article [14 TFEU] relating to the European Parliament, which state[s] that it is to consist of representatives of the peoples of the Member States, since the term "peoples", which is not defined, may have different meanings in the Member States and languages of the Union'. The Court also made repeated references to the ways in which EU law grants and acknowledges rights for non-Union citizens within the Union. The judgment is symbolically important for setting out a vision in which non-Union citizens are still part of the community of Europe.[190] However, Article 14(2) TEU now provides that 'The European Parliament shall be comprised of representatives of the Union's citizens', so the Court's small step may have been into a dead end.

The Court of Justice intervened in national electoral procedure for the European Parliament in a more critical way in *Eman and Sevinger*, a judgment delivered on the same day as *Spain* v. *United Kingdom*.[191] These two Dutch citizens complained that they were not allowed to vote in European elections because they lived in Aruba, an overseas territory of the Netherlands to which EU law, in general, does not apply. Moreover, to rub salt in the wound, Dutch citizens resident in a third country (the United States, or Australia, for example) could vote for the European Parliament. It was only those in the overseas territories that were excluded.

The Court did not object to States having territorial requirements for voting 'best adapted to their constitutional structure'. However, it found that any such rules had to comply with the principle of equality, which is a general principle of EU law and therefore applied to European Parliament elections. This prevented arbitrary distinctions of any kind and the Court was not convinced that the distinction between Dutch citizens in Aruba and those in third countries had any coherent reasoning behind it. In fact it does, but that reasoning is of a highly political and historical nature and reflects the complex ex-colonial relationship between the Netherlands and Aruba. The Dutch Government was, however, unable to explain the distinction in a way that made it seem constitutionally rational.[192]

More recently, in *Delvigne*, the Court allowed those convicted of serious crimes to be excluded from voting, even though the exclusion was indefinite.[193] It remarked that Article 20 was confined to a right to vote under the same conditions as nationals, and so did not help Mr Delvigne, while the Charter right to vote in Article 39(2) was applicable, but allowed for proportionate restrictions, which this was, given that it was confined to serious offences and Mr Delvigne had the right to apply for the ban to be lifted. The primary significance of the judgment may be establishing jurisdiction over voting restrictions, something which the United Kingdom at the time was concerned about, but will be less so now.

---

[189] *Spain* v. *United Kingdom*, C-145/04, EU:C:2006:543.

[190] Cf. M. Bell, 'Civic Citizenship and Migrant Integration' (2007) 13 *EPL* 311; Kochenov, n. 19 above.

[191] *Eman and Sevinger*, C-300/04, EU:C:2006:545.

[192] See annotations of *Spain* v. *United Kingdom* and *Eman and Sevinger* by J. Shaw in (2008) 4 *ELRev* 162; L. Besselink in (2008) 45 *CMLRev* 787.

[193] *Delvigne*, C-650/13, EU:C:2015:648; S. Coutts, 'Delvigne: A Multi-Levelled Political Citizenship' (2017) 42 *ELRev* 867–81.

Despite this fairly high-powered litigation, Union citizenship has not been a great success as a political citizenship. Turn-out in European Parliament elections is generally low, presenting a challenge to the idea of a European political community and to the idea that by stimulating public participation in the political process, Union citizenship can add to Union legitimacy.[194] Similarly, the rate of participation by migrant citizens in local elections in their host States has also been low.[195] Clearly, many non-national citizens do not feel sufficient attachment to their place of residence to wish to participate in the management of its affairs. This may be because their political horizons hark back to their State of origin, because there are no transnational political parties reflecting their interests, or because they conceive of themselves only as temporary residents of their host State.[196]

A factor limiting the impact of EU political rights is that they do not extend to participation in core national political decision-making processes. First, migrant citizens do not acquire a right to participate in national elections, either as voters or candidates.[197] Even in federal States such as Spain, Belgium and Germany, these remain the most high-profile and most significant elections in every State in the European Union. Secondly, Union citizenship also does not give citizens any right to hold high office or exercise any duties intimately connected with essential public power or interests. These exclusions are set out in Articles 45(4) and 51 TFEU, discussed in Chapter 19 below. While they have been interpreted narrowly, they show that there is an inner core of national membership to which the migrant is not admitted. Fundamentally, she cannot be trusted, because she is foreign.

6 UNION CITIZENSHIP AND BREXIT

At some point in 2019 the UK currently intends to leave the EU. If this occurs, it will mean that the 60 million UK nationals will cease to be citizens of the Union, and the UK will no longer be a Member State. As a result, the rights to live, work and study which are outlined in this chapter and in Chapters 18 and 19, will cease to be available to UK nationals wishing to move to the European Union or EU citizens wishing to move to the United Kingdom.

In order to prevent a cliff-edge situation, in which the loss of individual rights is sudden and immediate, the United Kingdom and the Union have negotiated a withdrawal agreement which contains provisions making the loss of rights more gradual and partial. This may be complemented in due course by a treaty between the United Kingdom and the Union concerning their future relationship so that the changes in individual rights are ultimately less dramatic than the loss of citizenship status would imply.

However, at time of writing the withdrawal agreement has not been signed, due to resistance by the British Parliament. That resistance is not to do with the Citizenship provisions, but the so-called Northern Irish backstop, discussed in Chapter 10.

---

[194] Bellamy, n. 8 above.

[195] European Commission, 'Report to the European Parliament and Council on the Application of Directive 94/80/EC on the Right to Vote and Stand as a Candidate in Municipal Elections', COM(2002)260 final; see also Bellamy, n. 8 above.

[196] H. Schmitt, 'The European Parliament Elections of June 2004: Still Second-Order?' (2005) 28 *WEP* 650; S. Hix and M. Marsh, 'Punishment or Protest? Understanding European Parliament Elections' (2007) 69 *Journal of Politics* 495.

[197] See R. Bauböck, P. Cayla and C. Seth (eds.), 'Should EU Citizens Living in Other Member States Vote There in National Elections?', EUI Working Paper RSCAS 2012/32.

If the Withdrawal Agreement does finally get British approval, the text below describes how it regulates the transition in status for Britains and Union Citizens. If the Withdrawal Agreement is not adopted, than at some point it will nevertheless be necessary to address the issue of 'stranded citizens' and the approach it takes, since it is not controversial, may well be the basis for a future accord, or for unilateral measures taken by the UK or EU Member States.

Finally, in the event of a chaotic and unregulated Brexit, or indeed of a reversal of the decision to leave and no Brexit at all, the Withdrawal Agreement will have a historical value as a picture of what might have been – and in particular, of the problems that arise when Union Citizenship rights are taken away.[198]

(i) The Withdrawal Agreement

The withdrawal agreement takes two particularly important steps, from the perspective of Union citizens. First, it creates a transitional period, lasting at least until the end of 2020, during which Union law applies to the United Kingdom and its people as if it was still a Member.[199] During this period free movement between the United Kingdom and the Union continues as described in this book.[200]

Secondly, where UK nationals are already lawfully living or working in an EU State or Union citizens are living or working in the United Kingdom at the end of the transitional period the withdrawal agreement essentially freezes their legal situation, so that they continue to enjoy residence and other rights identical in most respects to those of a migrant citizen.[201]

In order to benefit from this a Union citizen must have lived in the United Kingdom on the basis of Union law before the cut-off date, and must be still residing there – and vice versa for the UK citizen in the Union.[202] If that is the case then they maintain a right of residence for the rest of their life provided that they continue to comply with the conditions and limitations found in the Treaty and the Citizenship Directive.[203] Alongside this they have the right to equal treatment, and the same rights as a student, self-employed person or worker that they would have if Union law applied directly.[204] After five years, they acquire permanent residence status under the same terms as in the Directive.[205]

Importantly, their family rights are also continued, at least for two groups: those who are already family members – as defined in EU law, including those not mentioned in the Directive but considered necessary following the *Chen* and *Zambrano* case law[206] – before the end of the transition period, whether or not they have already joined the migrant citizen, and also the children of that migrant citizen, even if those children are born later.[207] As in Union law, these family members have the right to equal treatment, work, and study.[208]

As well as this, the agreement addresses more technical, but practically important matters: those covered continue to enjoy recognition of their qualifications – provided that recognition was completed or underway before the end of the transition period – and coordination of their social security payments.[209]

Thus the Polish citizen studying in the United Kingdom in December 2020 can continue to finish her study, and seek work, and bring her husband to live with her, just as if the United

---

[198] Draft Agreement on the withdrawal of the United Kingdom of Great Britain and Northern Ireland from the European Union and the European Atomic Energy Community, TF50 (2018) 55, 14 November 2018. See Chapter 10 for further discussion.
[199] Articles 127–132 Withdrawal Agreement.   [200] *Ibid.*
[201] See Part Two of the Withdrawal Agreement on Citizens' Rights.   [202] Article 10 Withdrawal Agreement.
[203] *Ibid.* Article 13.   [204] *Ibid.* Articles 1, 17 and 23–25.   [205] *Ibid.* Article 15.   [206] *Ibid.* Article 9(c).
[207] *Ibid.* Article 10(1)(e)(iii).   [208] *Ibid.* Articles 22–23.   [209] *Ibid.* Articles 27–32.

Kingdom was still a Member State and so the Treaty and Directive still applied to her – as long as she complies with the relevant conditions, just as she would have to do in any host Member State. If the couple have a child, that child will be able to grow up in the United Kingdom under conditions of equality with nationals. The same applies, *mutatis mutandis*, to the British national lawfully living or working in Portugal, whose rights continue just as if he was still a citizen of the Union. It is almost as if those who vest their rights in time get a personal exemption from Brexit.

This arrangement was, perhaps surprisingly, fairly uncontroversial. It was quite quickly agreed that despite the United Kingdom's concerns about free movement of persons, those who had already moved would not be made to pay the price of Brexit. The door is closed to newcomers in 2021, but those already inside can stay.

Nevertheless, there are some provisos to this generally comforting picture.

First, the migrant must be able to prove that they were lawfully residing at the cut-off date, which may be a challenge for those who have not registered with the authorities, and particularly for those in the United Kingdom, where there is no population register. The withdrawal agreement requires the United Kingdom to make the procedure for establishing status easy and accessible, which it has not been in the past.[210] Documentary and evidential problems could potentially still undermine the position of people who in substance should be protected.

Secondly, the withdrawal agreement does not extend to relationships formed after the transition period.[211] If a migrant forms a new relationship at a later date, then there are no residence or other rights explicitly extended to that family member. This does not seem illogical, given that the aim is to protect vested rights. However, it needs to be read alongside *Lounes*, where the Court found that Article 21 TFEU encompasses a life-long right to be accompanied or joined by one's spouse, independently of the provisions in the Citizenship Directive. Formally, the persons covered by the withdrawal agreement are not beneficiaries of Article 21, suggesting that the *Lounes* rule will not apply. Having said that, it would not be impossible for the Court to interpret their right to reside as being analogous to that in Article 21, so that it did encompass such a *Lounes* right.[212]

Thirdly, and probably most important, the agreement protects rights of residence, but not of free movement. The British national in France can stay living in France, but their right to move to other Member States ceases after the transition period. For some this may not be such a big deal, but for others it leaves them perhaps trapped in a small State with career or family options seriously curtailed. The reason for this absence is that the European Union took the view that agreement on post-Brexit movement of citizens did not belong in the withdrawal agreement – which should only address existing situations – but instead in the subsequent agreement on a new EU–UK relationship. If this is successfully negotiated, it is thus still possible that this gap will be filled, but it is something of great concern to British expats.

Finally, the terms of expulsion are changed. For behaviour before the cut-off date, the usual Union law rules apply, but for crimes or delinquency after that period the situation is much different. Article 20(2) provides:

> The conduct of Union citizens or United Kingdom nationals, their family members, and other persons, who exercise rights under this Title, where that conduct occurred after the end of the

---

[210] Article 18(1)(e), (f), (n)–(o). See Elspeth Guild, 'Brexit and the Treatment of EU Citizens by the UK Home Office', CEPS Policy Insights, No. 2017–33/September 2017.

[211] Article 10(1)(e) Withdrawal Agreement. Although see Article 10(1)(e)(iii) on children born or adopted after the transition date, who are included.

[212] See Article 13 Withdrawal Agreement. Also Polly Polak, 'A Commentary on the Lounes Case and the Protection of EU Citizens' Rights Post-Brexit' (2018) 44 *Revista General de Derecho Europeo* 190.

transition period, may constitute grounds for restricting the right of residence by the host State or the right of entry in the State of work in accordance with national legislation.

This would appear to suggest that expulsion is purely a matter of national law, unless some proportionality concept is to be read into this.

Many of the gaps in the withdrawal agreement, and other post-Brexit problems, can be avoided by naturalisation, and for the long-term resident this will often be a logical step. However, a significant number of Member States do not allow dual nationality or impose strict restrictions, compelling the migrant to live permanently as a foreigner or give up full access to their State of origin.

For those who do naturalise, the application of the withdrawal agreement to their situation is ambiguous. This could be important, as Union rights are often more generous than national ones. So the Pole who acquires a British passport might still want to rely on the withdrawal agreement to bring in their non-European spouse, or perhaps to ensure the continued recognition of their Polish qualifications.

For those who give up their original nationality, it would appear that they cease to be within the scope of the agreement, which speaks of Union citizens residing in the United Kingdom and vice versa.[213] *Lounes* gives some pause for thought, reminding us that one can never be quite sure what the Court will do, but the wording is prima facie clear.

The larger group is likely to be those who become dual nationals. In order to be within the scope of the agreement they must have exercised their Union right to reside in the United Kingdom/another Member State and 'continue to reside there'.[214] The notable aspect of this phrasing is that the continued residence does not have to be based on Union law, provided the initial migration was.

This precisely covers, for instance, the Polish situation above. That person came to the United Kingdom on the basis of Union law, and continues to reside there, even though they now do so on the basis of their UK nationality. The wording of the agreement covers them.

However, the rights which the agreement then grants are essentially a cut-and-paste of Union law regarding persons, suggesting that if the relevant Union law does not grant rights to persons living in their own State, neither will the agreement. So when the agreement grants Union citizens in the United Kingdom the right to reside 'under the limitations and conditions' in the Citizenship Directive, that gives nothing to the Pole who is also a UK citizen, since as a person in their home State they are outside the Directive's scope. On the other hand, the right not to experience discrimination because of one's other nationality would still be enjoyed.[215]

There is much space for doubt and development here, and a major factor in resolving that will be the role of the Court of Justice and its (future) case law in interpreting the agreement. For the first eight years after the transition period ends, it will continue to accept references from UK courts regarding the citizens' rights aspects of the withdrawal agreement, allowing it in principle to harmonise the agreement fully with its existing case law, and even to continue to develop it, although the different context of the withdrawal agreement provisions, no longer being part of a Treaty dedicated to ever closer union, might plausibly justify a more restrained approach.[216]

After those eight years, it will be essentially up to the UK courts to interpret the Agreement within the United Kingdom, but they will be obliged to do so 'in conformity with' case law before the end of the transition period – giving the Court two years to shape new rules – and 'with due

---

[213] Article 10(1)(a)–(b).   [214] *Ibid.*   [215] *Garcia Avello*, C-148/02, EU:C:2003:539.   [216] Article 158.

regard' to case law coming later.[217] There is no reference to the situation regarding courts of other Member States, who may need to consider the legal position of British citizens, but they will be free under the normal preliminary reference procedure to refer questions to the Court on the concepts of EU law which are incorporated into the Agreement.

In the period after the Brexit referendum, there was some academic exploration of whether Union citizenship could be withdrawn from UK citizens, and what legal limits there might be to the resulting loss of rights.[218] Was the loss of Union citizenship by individuals as a result of a national decision not contrary to the Court's claim that it was a 'fundamental status'? Did the Union not have an obligation to protect the fundamental rights of Union citizens, including their free movement rights, even from their home States?[219] While thought-provoking, these ideas ran into the brick wall of Article 50: the Treaty allows States to leave, and part of leaving is giving up Union citizenship. A certain rethinking of some of the claims of Union citizenship seemed inevitable; however deep the bonds of membership it entails, they remain politically contingent, and can be broken.[220] The challenge of the next few years will be to see whether those bonds can be rebuilt in some reasonably functional form, or perhaps to see whether the bonds of identity which may, or may not, have been formed over the decades survive the fracturing of their formal legal frame.

FURTHER READING

N. Barber, 'Citizenship, Nationalism and the European Union' (2002) 27 *European Law Review* 241.

L. Bosniak, *The Citizen and the Alien* (Princeton University Press, 2006).

S. Coutts, 'Citizens of Elsewhere, Everywhere and . . . Nowhere? Rethinking Union Citizenship in Light of Brexit' (2018) 69 *Northern Ireland Legal Quarterly* 231.

M. Dougan, N. Nic Shuibhne and E. Spaventa (eds.), *Empowerment and Disempowerment of the European Citizen* (Oxford, Hart Publishing, 2012).

E. Guild, *Brexit and its Consequences for UK and EU Citizenship: Or Monstrous Citizenship* (Leiden, Brill & Nijhoff, 2016).

D. Kochenov, 'Ius Tractum of Many Faces: European Citizenship and the Difficult Relationship between Status and Rights' (2009) 15 *Columbia Journal of European Law* 169.

D. Kochenov 'Neo-Mediaeval Permutations of Personhood in the European Union' in L. Azoulai, S. Barbou des Places and E. Pataut (eds.), *Constructing the Person: Rights, Roles, Identities in EU Law* (Hart Publishing, Oxford, 2016) 133–58.

D. Kochenov (ed.), *EU Citizenship and Federalism: The Role of Rights* (Cambridge University Press, 2017).

D. Kostakopoulou, 'European Union Citizenship: Writing the Future' (2007) 13(5) *European Law Journal* 623.

D. Kostakopoulou and N. Ferreira, 'Testing Liberal Norms: The Public Policy and Public Security Derogations and the Cracks in European Citizenship' (2014) 20(3) *Columbia Journal of European Law* 167.

---

[217] Article 4(4)–(5).

[218] William Worster, 'International Law Limitations on the Loss of EU Citizenship After Brexit' (20 February 2017), https://ssrn.com/abstract=2920611; O. Garner, 'After Brexit: Protecting European Citizens and Citizenship from Fragmentation', EUI Department of Law Working Paper No. 2016/22 (2016).

[219] Francesca Strumia, 'From Alternative Triggers to Shifting Links: Social Integration and Protection of Supranational Citizenship in the Context of Brexit and Beyond' (2018) 3(2) *European Papers* 733; D. Kostakopoulou, 'Scala Civium: Citizenship Templates Post-Brexit and the European Union's Duty to Protect EU Citizens' (2018) 56 *JCMS* 854.

[220] See Jo Shaw, *EU Citizenship: Still a Fundamental Status?*, Robert Schuman Centre for Advanced Studies Research Paper No. RSCAS 2018/14 (March 2018); S. Coutts, 'Citizens of Elsewhere, Everywhere and . . . Nowhere? Rethinking Union Citizenship in Light of Brexit' (2018) 69 *Northern Ireland Legal Quarterly* 231.

P. Magnette, 'How Can One Be European? Reflections on the Pillars of European Civic Identity' (2007) 13(5) *European Law Journal* 664.

N. Nic Shuibhne, 'Limits Rising, Duties Ascending: The Changing Legal Shape of Union Citizenship' (2015) 52(4) *Common Market Law Review* 889–937.

C. O'Brien, 'I Trade Therefore I Am: Legal Personhood in the European Union' (2014) 50 *Common Market Law Review* 1643.

C. O'Brien, 'Civis Capitalist Sum: Class as the New Guiding Principle of EU Free Movement Rights' (2016) 53(4) *Common Market Law Review* 937–77.

S. Sankari and S. Frerichs, 'From Resource to Burden: Rescaling Solidarity with Strangers in the Single Market' (2016) 22 *European Law Journal* 806–21.

J. Shaw, *The Transformation of Citizenship in the European Union* (Cambridge University Press, 2007).

A. Somek, 'Solidarity Decomposed: Being and Time in European Citizenship' (2007) 32(6) *European Law Review* 818.

E. Spaventa, 'Seeing the Wood Despite the Trees? On the Scope of Union Citizenship and its Constitutional Effects' (2008) 45(1) *Common Market Law Review* 13.

12

Non-EU Nationals

CONTENTS

1 INTRODUCTION

This chapter considers the treatment of non-EU nationals by EU law.[1] It is organised as follows.

Section 2 looks at the central Union competences on non-EU nationals. These provide for common policies on borders, international protection and immigration. They were established against the backdrop of the Schengen Conventions. Agreed in 1985 and 1990 between all

---

[1] It does not consider where non-EU nationals acquire rights by virtue of a relationship with an EU citizen. This is addressed in Chapter 11. See pp. 499–515.

Member States, other than Ireland and the United Kingdom, these provided for the adoption of collective measures (the 'Schengen acquis') to establish common external frontiers and visa, immigration and asylum policies. The Conventions have paved the way for considerable differentiation in this field. Non-Schengen States (Bulgaria, Croatia, Cyprus, Ireland and Romania) can only participate in those EU laws considered to be constituting elements of the Schengen acquis if all the Union Schengen States agree. Beyond this, Ireland has a right to choose whether to participate or not in other EU laws in this field. Meanwhile, Denmark is a Schengen State but is unwilling to be subject to EU law in this field. It is, thus, only bound by those EU laws which build on the Schengen acquis, and then only as a matter of international law.

Section 3 considers the central themes governing this field. This field is influenced, first, by EU law on non-EU nationals forming part of the Union Area of Freedom, Security and Justice. This Area requires the fundamental rights of non-EU nationals to be respected but also conceives EU policy on non-EU nationals as something which must contribute to, and not threaten, a wider European way of life. EU law is also guided by policy-makers' experiences of the impact of migration as a powerful force of social change within the European Union. Three narratives have been particularly central in their making sense of this. The first, economic mercantilism, treats non-EU nationals as a human resource who are to be assessed in terms of their impact on labour markets, welfare systems and EU competitiveness. The second is the protection of national security. Non-EU nationals are considered in terms of their perceived cultural, political and social risks. This has led to a strong emphasis on policing non-EU nationals and territorial control with visa policy used to enable the latter. Thirdly, humanitarianism has formed the basis for Union international protection policy and the idea that the Union should shelter those in danger, as well for a number of laws on the treatment of non-EU nationals resident in the Union, most notably in the fields of non-discrimination and family rights.

Section 4 considers how the Union treats non-EU nationals that it does not want. The Returns Directive, Directive 2008/115/EC, requires Member States to return non-EU nationals who have irregularly entered or remained on their territory unless there are strong compassionate reasons. Return should not be forced unless the non-EU national does not leave within the time set or, inter alia, there is a risk of her absconding. There is also provision for a ban on her re-entering the Union and for the possibility of detention, notably where she has not complied with an order to leave the Union or has tried to re-enter.

Section 5 considers the non-EU nationals that the Union seeks to attract, notably those granted worker resident and long-term resident status. The right to work within the Union (worker resident status) is largely governed by national law although a system of Union preference requires any vacancy to be offered to a non-EU national only if there is no European Economic Area (EEA) citizen or permanent resident non-EU national suitable for it. Long-term resident status is acquired by lawful residence in a Member State for five years and proof of sufficient resources to support oneself and one's family. Worker residents are entitled to freedom from discrimination in the marketplace and a limited number of social entitlements, notably in education and housing. Long-term residents are entitled to the same socio-economic entitlements as a State's own nationals, albeit that States can limit these to those core social benefits. There is also a right to family reunification where a non-EU national has been lawfully resident in a Member State for more than one year and has reasonable prospects of permanent residence.

Section 6 considers the Union international protection regime. International protection is where the non-EU national is granted either refugee status or subsidiary protection, or has applied for these and is awaiting a decision (asylum). The Dublin Regulation, Regulation 604/2013/EU, provides that only one application can be made in the Union, and, in practice, the application should usually be made in the State where the applicant first entered the Union. This system of allocation has placed disproportionate burdens on States at the geographical periphery of the Union. The applicant has an entitlement to remain on the territory of the Member State pending consideration of her case unless there is a safe first country of asylum which has already offered her haven or a safe third country to which it would reasonable for her to go. Member States must provide material reception conditions for applicants. These include housing, food, health care and education for minors. All these benefits are contingent on, *inter alia*, applicants complying with the reporting and accommodation requirements set by Member States.

2 THE UNION COMPETENCES ON BORDER CHECKS, ASYLUM AND IMMIGRATION

The Union competencies on non-EU nationals form a key part of the Union's area of freedom, security and justice.

Article 67 TFEU

(1) The Union shall constitute an area of freedom, security and justice with respect for fundamental rights and the different legal systems and traditions of the Member States.

(2) It shall ensure the absence of internal border controls for persons and shall frame a common policy on asylum, immigration and external border control, based on solidarity between Member States, which is fair towards third-country nationals. For the purpose of this Title, stateless persons shall be treated as third-country nationals.

In addition to a commitment to respect the fundamental rights of non-EU nationals, the area of freedom, security and justice establishes three distinct policies to govern them.[2]

The first is a common borders policy. It covers not merely the abolition of internal controls within the Union and the establishment of a common external frontier, but also a common visa policy, for this goes to who can present themselves at the external frontier for lawful admission into the Union.

Article 77 TFEU

(1) The Union shall develop a policy with a view to:
  (a) ensuring the absence of any controls on persons, whatever their nationality, when crossing internal borders;
  (b) carrying out checks on persons and efficient monitoring of the crossing of external borders;
  (c) the gradual introduction of an integrated management system for external borders.

---

[2] They all use the ordinary legislative procedure with two exceptions. The rights of non-EU national family members of EU citizens residing in another Member State and emergency measures to deal with a sudden inflow of non-EU nationals into one Member State require the consultation procedure, Articles 77(3) and 78(3) TFEU respectively.

The second is a common policy on international protection. International protection covers a range of policies which allow the Union to be a haven for non-EU nationals for humanitarian reasons.

Article 78 TFEU

(1) The Union shall develop a common policy on asylum, subsidiary protection and temporary protection with a view to offering appropriate status to any third-country national requiring international protection and ensuring compliance with the principle of *non-refoulement*. This policy must be in accordance with the Geneva Convention of 28 July 1951 and the Protocol of 31 January 1967 relating to the status of refugees, and other relevant treaties.

The third is a common immigration policy for non-EU nationals. This is a sweeper policy as it does not deal with the issues addressed by Articles 77 and 78 TFEU but a host of other issues concerning non-EU nationals: conditions for their admission to the Union, their family rights, conditions of treatment within the Union, expulsion and trafficking.

Article 79 TFEU

(1) The Union shall develop a common immigration policy aimed at ensuring, at all stages, the efficient management of migration flows, fair treatment of third-country nationals residing legally in Member States, and the prevention of, and enhanced measures to combat, illegal immigration and trafficking in human beings.

There was significant intergovernmental integration prior to the Union acquiring competencies in this field. Two international agreements, the Schengen Conventions, were concluded in 1985 and 1990 between all of the then fifteen Member States other than Ireland and the United Kingdom, Norway and Iceland.[3] These require the abolition of internal frontier checks,[4] a common external frontier[5] and common visa,[6] asylum[7] and immigration policies.[8] These policies were to be realised through the adoption of implementing measures by an Executive Committee comprised of national governmental representatives.

In the Treaty of Amsterdam, it was agreed to incorporate these measures, known as the *Schengen acquis*, into the TEU framework.[9] A Protocol was also agreed, the Protocol on Integrating the Schengen Acquis, which allows those EU Member States who are also parties to the Schengen Conventions to continue to take measures to build on the *Schengen acquis*, albeit that these have to use the relevant TFEU procedures and any measures adopted will be adopted as EU laws.[10] The *Schengen acquis* matters because it is central to a system of differentiation within this field.

There are, first, EU States who are not party to the Schengen Conventions because they do not want to be. Ireland and (prior to Brexit) the United Kingdom are in this category. These States do

---

[3] Liechtenstein and Switzerland are also parties. The central Convention is the Implementing Convention (CISA) agreed in 1990. The text is at OJ 2000, L 239/19.

[4] *Ibid*. Article 2. [5] *Ibid*. Articles 3–8. [6] *Ibid*. Articles 9–18. [7] *Ibid*. Articles 28–39.

[8] *Ibid*. Articles 19–27.

[9] This was done by a 1999 Decision which granted EU legal status to every measure in the *acquis*, Decision 1999/436/EC determining the legal basis for each of the provisions or decisions which constitute the Schengen *acquis*, OJ 1999, L 176/19.

[10] Protocol on the Schengen Acquis Integrated into the Framework of the European Union, Articles 1 and 5(1).

not have a right to participate in measures which build upon the *Schengen acquis*. They have to request to participate and all other Member States have to agree to it unanimously.[11] Measures build upon the *acquis* if they are 'constituting elements' of the Schengen Conventions (para. 60). The Court has found this to include measures on external frontiers and visa policies.[12] Beyond that, institutional practice is uncertain. The Directive on the return of irregular migrants, part of immigration policy, is seen as developing the *Schengen acquis*.[13] By contrast, EU legislation on States responsible for processing asylum application makes no reference to the *acquis*,[14] notwithstanding that the Schengen Conventions provide common rules on this.[15]

With measures which do not build upon the *acquis*, Ireland has a right to 'opt in', irrespective of other State wishes, within three months of the Commission's publication of a proposal. However, it cannot try to block the measure as it can be adopted without its participation after a reasonable period.[16] It may also subsequently opt-in to a measure which has already been adopted by notifying the Council and Commission of its intention to do so.[17] If it does not opt-in, the measure will not bind it.[18]

There are, secondly, States who have not demonstrated to the other Schengen States that they can meet the commitments required by the *acquis*. These are currently Bulgaria, Cyprus, Croatia and Romania. In Cyprus, the dispute within the island means that no common external frontier can be established for the island. In the cases of Bulgaria and Romania, issues have been raised with regard to corruption and organised crime. Croatia will likely form part of the Schengen area at the end of 2018 as there is agreement that has met what is required of it. These States do not participate in measures which build upon this *acquis*,[19] albeit that they participate fully in all other measures adopted in the field of freedom, security and justice.

Thirdly, Denmark is party to the Schengen Conventions but did not want to be bound by the supranational commitments of EU law in these fields. It neither participates in nor is bound by any measure in this field,[20] unless it builds upon the *Schengen acquis*, in which case it has six months to decide whether it will implement the decision.[21] If it does, the measure is binding only in international law and not in EU law. If Denmark decides against implementation, it will consult with the other Member States to consider what appropriate measures should be taken.[22]

---

[11] *Ibid.* Article 4. *United Kingdom* v. *Council*, C-77/05, EU:C:2007:803.

[12] *Spain* v. *Parliament and Council*, C-44/14, EU:C:2015:554; *United Kingdom* v. *Council*, C-482/08, EU:C:2010:631.

[13] Directive 2008/115/EC on common standards and procedures in Member States for returning illegally staying third-country nationals, OJ 2008, L 348/98.

[14] Regulation 604/2013/EU establishing the criteria and mechanisms for determining the Member State responsible for examining an application for international protection lodged in one of the Member States by a third-country national or a stateless person, OJ 2013, L 180/31.

[15] CISA 1990, Articles 28–38.

[16] Protocol on the Position of the United Kingdom and Ireland in respect of the Area of Freedom, Security and Justice, Article 3(1). The United Kingdom will lose the right to opt-in to measures during the transition period other than measures which amend existing EU law, Withdrawal Agreement, Article 127(5).

[17] *Ibid.* Article 4.   [18] *Ibid.* Article 2.

[19] Act concerning the conditions of accession of [*inter alia*], the Republic of Cyprus, OJ 2003, L 236/33, Article 3(2); Treaty between the Member States of the European Union and the Republic of Bulgaria and Romania, concerning the accession of the Republic of Bulgaria and Romania to the European Union, OJ 2005, L 157/11, Article 4(2); Treaty between the Member States of the European Union and the Republic of Croatia concerning the accession of the Republic of Croatia to the European Union, OJ 2012, L 112/10, Article 4(2).

[20] Protocol on Position of Denmark, Articles 1 and 2.   [21] *Ibid.* Article 4(1).   [22] *Ibid.* Article 4(2).

3 CENTRAL THEMES SHAPING EU GOVERNMENT OF NON-EU NATIONALS

One misses out if one simply discusses the law here without regard to the surrounding context. This context acts as a driver for much of the law, informing its adoption and interpretation. It also governs its authority. A failure by EU law to respond to particular concerns frequently leads to sharp criticisms. It also conditions the application of that law as parties seek ways to stymie it or evade it. Finally, regard to the wider context is necessary to understand many of the contradictions in this field. For this context pulls the law in different directions and puts particularly acute pressures on it to go in these different directions.

In this regard, it pays to look at three things. The first is what the Area of Freedom, Security and Justice (AFSJ) is conceived as being about. For, insofar as EU laws serve to realise the AFSJ, they are likely to pursue this vision. There is, secondly, the practice of migration and international protection. Officials have to engage with it on a daily basis, be it in Ministries, border posts, patrols or through immigration raids. Politicians have to listen regularly to citizens' accounts of how it is touching their lives. These experiences, inevitably, shape the development of EU law and policy. Thirdly, institutional narratives have developed over time on the meaning and consequences of migration, borders and international protection. These, for better or worse, are powerful because they allow citizens and policy-makers to make sense of the complexity of this field.

If one turns, first, to what the AFSJ is seen as being about. To be sure, it is about realising common border, immigration and international protection policies. Yet what are these for? There seem to be two official refrains.

On the one hand, there is a human rights dimension. Article 67(1) TFEU talks of the AFSJ being an area which respects fundamental rights. The competence on international protection, Article 78(1) TFEU, provides for the principle of *non-refoulement*, namely that asylum seekers cannot be returned to a State where they would be in likely danger of persecution on account of their religion, nationality, membership of a social group or political opinion. It also provides for EU refugee policy to observe the 1951 Geneva Convention on Refugees and its subsequent instruments, the central international instrument offering refugees protection.

On the other, the AFSJ is conceived as contributing towards and protecting a European way of life. Thus the Commission has talked of the AFSJ as 'an integral part of the European model of society'.[23] The Working Group on Freedom, Security and Justice at the *Future of Europe* Convention argued that the AFSJ should lead to citizens feeling a 'proper sense of "European public order" has taken shape and is actually visible in their daily lives'.[24] This is a more charged and potentially ethno-centric vision.

If one looks at the practice, migration is a significant force of social change within the European Union. Some 2.4 million non-EU nationals migrated to an EU State in 2016 whilst only 1.8 EU citizens migrated to another EU State in that year. In that year, 994,800 non-EU nationals became EU citizens. In 2017, 36.9 million citizens born outside EU and 21.6 million non-EU citizens lived in the Union. After Brexit, these populations would be, respectively, equivalent to the sixth- and seventh-largest EU States. In 2017, foreigners (including EU citizens) comprised over 10 per cent of the population in ten member States: Cyprus, Germany, Latvia,

---

[23] European Commission, 'An Area of Freedom, Security and Justice Serving the Citizen', COM(2009)262, 2.
[24] European Convention, 'Final Report of Working Group X "Freedom, Security and Justice"', CONV 426/02, 2.

Luxembourg, Estonia, Austria, Ireland, Belgium, Malta and Spain.[25] Alongside this, albeit not as much as some other States around the world, the Union is a significant haven for international protection. In 2017, about 650,000 people applied for asylum for the first time within the European Union. Forty-six per cent of applications were successful with 36 per cent of those appealing these decisions successful.[26] These figures present a more complex picture than the insulting and false caricatures of racist immigration officials and mendacious asylum claimants.

However, the policing of the Union's external frontier has come with a high human cost. With most land and air crossings effectively closed to those seeking international protection from Africa and the Middle East, these have had to make hazardous boat crossings across the Mediterranean. The number has declined from 856,735 entering the Union this way in 2015 to 80,602 arrivals for the first ten months of 2018. The toll in human life is still considerable. As of 8 November 2018, 2,019 had died crossing the Mediterranean in 2018. If this is lower than the 4,303 deaths in 2016, the crossings have become more dangerous with 1.4 deaths for every one hundred attempted crossings.[27] Migration has also resulted in extensive domestic policing. In 2015, over 2 million non-EU nationals were found be illegally present in the European Union. This had declined to 618,780 by 2017 of whom over 516,000 were ordered to leave.[28]

Finally, three narratives have been particularly central in shaping EU law on non-EU nationals. The first, *economic mercantilism*, is concerned to manage migration in a way that advantages national economies and does not impose burdens on Welfare States. The second perceives non-EU nationals, often in quite racist terms, as posing particular risks for *national security*. The third, *humanitarianism*, embodies a view that European values require hospitality to be offered to the stranger, particularly those in most need. These narratives pull in different ways with the influence of each on different EU laws quite intense. It is now time to explore each in a little more detail.

(i) Economic Mercantilism

Policy towards non-EU nationals has been strongly framed by the economic benefits and costs these are perceived to bring. Attitudes depend as much on the circumstances of the time as the skills of the individual. The 1950s were a period of labour market shortages with workers actively recruited from outside Europe to fill posts. This was reflected in the Treaty of Rome. It was initially envisaged that the right to move freely to work within the Union was available to all.[29] By the end of the 1960s, the European Union was facing increasing unemployment. Thus, EU legislation confining the right to work within the Union to EU nationals was enacted.[30] As this period of unemployment continued, non-EU nationals were, increasingly, seen as threats to national labour markets and Member States developed restrictive immigration laws throughout

---

[25] All these statistics are available at https://ec.europa.eu/eurostat/statistics-explained/index.php/Migration_and_migrant_population_statistics.

[26] https://ec.europa.eu/eurostat/statistics-explained/index.php/Asylum_statistics#Final_decisions_taken_in_appeal.

[27] https://missingmigrants.iom.int/region/mediterranean. To put this in perspective, the Berlin wall was in place for twenty-eight years. Some 140 were killed or died attempting to cross it during that whole period.

[28] https://ec.europa.eu/eurostat/statistics-explained/index.php/Statistics_on_enforcement_of_immigration_legislation.

[29] See Articles 52 and 48 EEC Treaty respectively.

[30] Directive 68/360/EEC, [1968] OJ Special Edn, L 257/13, Article 1. See the debates in W. Böhning, *The Migration of Workers in Britain and the EC* (Oxford University Press/Institute for Race Relations, 1972); P. Oliver, 'Non-Community Nationals and the Treaty of Rome' (1985) 5 *YBEL* 57.

the 1980s and 1990s to foreclose economic migration by non-EU nationals.[31] By the beginning of the millennium, the pendulum began swinging back towards liberalisation. In 2000, a Commission Communication suggested that economic migration could address falling populations within the Union, skills shortages and the lack of a sufficient workforce to pay for the increased cost of pensions.[32]

The consequence has been a shift away from *restricting* economic migration towards *managing* it. Treatment of non-EU nationals has become a human resource strategy with the Union trying to cherry-pick those non-EU nationals who will benefit its economy, whilst preventing others from entering its markets.[33]

This resource strategy has two dimensions.

Levels of economic migration are treated as domestic political economy matters rather than Union ones. That is to say, Member States are to exploit levels of migration to do what they perceive as best for their labour markets, economies and welfare costs, whether this be pursuing a liberal policy or a restrictive one. Overall levels of migration are, thus, a matter of exclusive domestic concern.

Article 79 TFEU

(5) This Article shall not affect the right of Member States to determine volumes of admission of third-country nationals coming from third countries to their territory in order to seek work, whether employed or self-employed.

By contrast, the skills-set of the migrant labour force is seen as an EU matter. There is concern that Member States do not secure cheap labour in a way that undercuts other States. Thus, a 1996 Council Resolution set out the 'Union preference' principle:

> Member States will consider requests for admission to their territories for the purpose of employment only where vacancies in a Member State cannot be filled by national and Community manpower or by non-Community manpower lawfully resident on a permanent basis in that Member State and already forming part of the Member State's regular labour market.[34]

This approach is elaborated in the Directive on Seasonal Workers.[35] This Directive does not require Member States to take seasonal workers. However, it sets out the circumstances when they can take these workers, the procedures for admission to the territory and the treatment of these workers once there.[36] Much of this was borne from a concern that, without a supply of

---

[31] C. Joppke, *The Challenge to the Nation State: Immigration in Western Europe and the United States* (Oxford University Press, 1998); A. Messina, *The Logics and Politics of Post-WW II Migration to Western Europe* (Cambridge University Press, 2007).

[32] European Commission, 'On a Community Immigration Policy', COM(2000)757.

[33] European Commission, 'Communication on Migration', COM(2011)248, 12. See also European Commission, 'Towards a Job-Rich Recovery', COM(2012)173, 18; European Commission, 'Entrepreneurship 2020 Action Plan', COM(2012)795, 24–5.

[34] Council Resolution on limitation on admission of third-country nationals to the territory of the Member States for employment, OJ 1996, C 274/3.

[35] Directive 2014/36/EU on the conditions of entry and stay of third-country nationals for the purpose of employment as seasonal workers, OJ 2014, L 98/375. Ireland does not participate in this Directive.

[36] *Ibid.* Articles 5, 6, 8 and 23.

regulated cheap labour, there would either be resort to irregular labour or an unending quest for ever cheaper seasonal labour amongst employers. These alternatives impose not only social costs but also destabilise conditions of competition within the Union. States are, thus, required not only to sanction employers who do not comply with the Directive but also prohibit them for taking seasonal labour subsequently.[37]

By contrast, States are freer to compete with each other for high-skills migrants.[38] The Union has, therefore, a 'Blue Card' scheme which allows States to grant access to the Union labour market for non-EU nationals who hold higher-education qualifications or at least five years of equivalent professional experience, and have been offered a contract of employment of at least one year's length by an EU employer where the salary is at least one and a half times the national average.[39] There is no requirement to apply Union preference[40] and the State may give the non-EU national general access to the labour market after two years.[41] In like vein, the Students Directive makes provision for Member States to admit, *inter alia*, non-EU students and researchers. Those admitted have a right to stay for employment or self-employment for nine months after completion of their studies.[42]

(ii) National Security

The second narrative identifies non-EU nationals as a source of insecurity. At its bleakest and most problematic, it identifies non-EU nationals with criminality either because they are characterised as more likely to commit crimes or because various forms of migration are treated in similar manner to crime. However, this narrative of insecurity extends beyond that. Migration is identified as a threat to material security because it destabilises labour markets or puts pressure on public institutions' (such as schools or hospitals) particular ways of life. It is also often characterised as a source of cultural insecurity in the challenge it poses to established identities, notions of belonging or ways of life. Finally, migration is seen as threatening simply because the free flow of people is seen as making it difficult for governments to exercise control and, therefore, do their job.[43]

At its worst, this narrative lapses into racism or xenophobia and, even in its most innocuous form, it accentuates (and creates) differences between EU citizens and non-EU nationals.

---

[37] *Ibid.* Articles 8(2)(c), 9(2)(c) and 17.

[38] On how different States have exploited this see L. Cerna, 'The Crisis as an Opportunity for Change? High-Skilled Immigration Policies across Europe' (2016) 42 *Journal of Ethnic and Migration Studies* 1610.

[39] Directive 2009/50/EC on the conditions of entry and residence of third-country nationals for the purposes of highly qualified employment, OJ 2009, L 155/17, Article 5. Ireland does not participate in this Directive. See Y. Gümüs, 'EU Blue Card Scheme: The Right Step in the Right Direction?' (2010) 12 *EJML* 435; L. Cerna, 'The EU Blue Card: Preferences, Policies, and Negotiations between Member States' (2014) 2 *Migration Studies* 73.

[40] Directive 2009/50/EC on the conditions of entry and residence of third-country nationals for the purposes of highly qualified employment, OJ 2009, L 155/17, Article 8(2).

[41] *Ibid.* Article 12.

[42] Directive 2016/801/EU on the conditions of entry and residence of third-country nationals for the purposes of research, studies, training, voluntary service, pupil exchange schemes or educational projects and au pairing, OJ 2016, L 131/27, Article 25. Ireland does not participate in this Directive.

[43] J. Huysmans, 'The European Union and the Securitization of Migration' (2000) 38 *JCMS* 751; A. Triandafyllidou, *Immigrants and National Identity in Europe* (London, Routledge, 2001); R. v. Munster, *Securitizing Immigration: The Politics of Risk in the EU* (Basingstoke, Palgrave Macmillan, 2009).

However, for all that, it is a powerful dynamic within EU law. The security threatened is, invariably, cast as a national one rather than a Union one, be it national identities, labour markets or Welfare States. And this is reflected in the Treaties.

> ### Article 72 TFEU
>
> This Title shall not affect the exercise of the responsibilities incumbent upon Member States with regard to the maintenance of law and order and the safeguarding of internal security.

Whilst this provision requires EU law not to destabilise domestic internal security or law and order functions, it does not follow that the Union is not to act in this field. The contrary is true. The protection of national security becomes something which justifies the Union adopting a series of doctrines and measures of its own. It is most evident in the Union's borders and frontiers policies.

(a) Internal Union Borders as Policing Zones

Borders have, historically, been granted a cultural significance. They marked a point between an enclosed space, the national territory, characterised by civilisation and certain common features and a wilder less hospitable environment.[44] The commitment to an absence of internal border controls between Member States involves an abandonment of this view within the Union. It conveys the idea of the Union as a civilised space marked by certain commonalities. The commitment is set out in Article 67 TFEU and is reiterated in Regulation 2016/399, which is also known as the Schengen Borders Code.[45]

> ### Regulation 2016/399, Article 22
>
> Internal borders may be crossed at any point without a border check on persons, irrespective of their nationality, being carried out.

The commitment is a qualified one, however. Ireland is allowed to retain border controls between it and other EU States, as is the United Kingdom during the transition period.[46] Furthermore, border controls remain in place between those States who are not yet permitted to join Schengen and the other EU States.[47] Even for Schengen States, reintroduction of border controls exists as a last resort.[48]

---

[44] W. Brown, *Walled States, Waning Sovereignty* (Boston, MIT Press, 2014) 40–7. She gives the example of the pale used by the British in colonial Ireland to map the outer point of this 'civilised' enclosure, leading to the current expression of 'beyond the pale'.

[45] Regulation 2016/399 on a Union Code on the rules governing the movement of persons across borders (Schengen Borders Code), OJ 2016, L 77/1.

[46] Protocol on the Application of Certain Aspects of Article 26 TFEU, Articles 1 and 2; Withdrawal Agreement, Article 127(1).

[47] Schengen Borders, Code, Preamble, alinea 44.

[48] On the reintroduction being used only as a last resort see Schengen Borders Code, Article 25(2).

> **Regulation 2016/399, Article 25**
>
> (1) Where, in the area without internal border control, there is a serious threat to public policy or internal security in a Member State, that Member State may exceptionally reintroduce border control at all or specific parts of its internal borders for a limited period of up to 30 days or for the foreseeable duration of the serious threat if its duration exceeds 30 days. The scope and duration of the temporary reintroduction of border control at internal borders shall not exceed what is strictly necessary to respond to the serious threat.

Prior to imposing such controls, the Member State must carry out an impact assessment, examining the extent of threat and the likely impact of the measures on free movement of persons.[49] It must all notify the other Member States and the Commission before the reintroduction of these controls, setting out the scope and duration of the controls and the reasons for their reintroduction.[50]

Significant controls were first introduced in 2011 by France at the Italian border in response to an increase in migration as a consequence of the Arab Spring. However, 2015 witnessed a step change in the use of this provision. This was as a consequence, on the one hand, of a series of terrorist attacks in France and, on the other, a dramatic increase in the number of non-EU nationals crossing the Eastern Mediterranean into Greece. Greek facilities were not only overwhelmed but large numbers of people began making their way across the Schengen area looking to settle in other Member States. Governments reacted differently. Some, notably Hungary, created a hostile environment. By contrast, the German Government declared that any Syrian asylum seeker could apply for asylum in Germany irrespective of whether they should have applied for asylum in another Member State. As a consequence of these events, ten EU States introduced border controls between June 2015 and June 2016: some to stop other States gaming the system, others to limit movements of people, others to stop the entry of asylum seekers, and others to combat terrorism.

The reasons provided for these controls are often terse.[51] Furthermore, States have repeatedly sought not only to impose controls for thirty days but to adopt the other option in Article 25, namely imposing controls for the foreseeable duration. The consequence is that three years after their imposition, five Member States plus Norway still have border controls in place.[52] Border controls have thus become something marked by uncertainty: uncertainty about when they may be reintroduced and uncertainty about their duration. The Schengen area is, thus, a curious mix of border-free movement and *ad hoc* control.

The reimposition of temporal controls indicates that border controls are not just civilisational markets but points at which policing is taking place. In instances where Member States have abolished internal border controls, they are keen to keep these powers of policing. Provision is made for this in the Schengen Borders Code.

---

[49] *Ibid.* Article 26.

[50] *Ibid.* Article 27(1). There is also provision for the Council in exceptional circumstances to authorise the imposition of controls where serious deficiencies in external frontier control is putting the operation of the area within internal border control at risk, *ibid.* Article 29(1).

[51] On the context to the imposition of these controls and the weak limits placed on them see E. Guild *et al.*, *Internal Border Controls in the Schengen Area: Is Schengen Crisis-Proof?* (Brussels, European Parliament, Policy Department C: Citizens' rights and Constitutional Affairs, PE 571 356, 2006).

[52] https://ec.europa.eu/home-affairs/what-we-do/policies/borders-and-visas/schengen/reintroduction-border-control_en.

Regulation 2016/399, Article 23

The absence of border control at internal borders shall not affect:

(a) the exercise of police powers by the competent authorities of the Member States under national law, insofar as the exercise of those powers does not have an effect equivalent to border checks; that shall also apply in border areas. Within the meaning of the first sentence, the exercise of police powers may not, in particular, be considered equivalent to the exercise of border checks when the police measures:

    (i)   do not have border control as an objective;

    (ii) are based on general police information and experience regarding possible threats to public security and aim, in particular, to combat cross-border crime;

    (iii) are devised and executed in a manner clearly distinct from systematic checks on persons at the external borders;

    (iv) are carried out on the basis of spot-checks . . .

Border policing is, thus, allowed provided it is not equivalent to border checks. This was addressed in most detail in *A*. A, a German, was asked for his ID in Germany, 500 metres after crossing the border from France. The German police officers were operating under powers which allowed them to check the ID of any person, irrespective of circumstances or behaviour, within 30 kilometres of the border to see whether they were an irregular migrant or had committed any criminal offences connected with migration. After a struggle, he was arrested for possession of narcotics and resisting arrest. It was argued that these powers were disguised border controls.

_A_, C-9/16, EU:C:2017:483

37 . . . compliance with EU law and, in particular, [Articles 22 and 23 of Regulation 2016/399] must be ensured by setting up and complying with a framework of rules guaranteeing that the practical exercise of that power, consisting in carrying out identity controls, cannot have an effect equivalent to border checks . . .

38 In particular, in the face of evidence of an effect equivalent to that of border checks, compliance by those controls with [Article 23(a)] must be ensured by the details and limitations contained in the framework for the practical exercise of the police powers enjoyed by the Member States, a framework which should be such as to avoid such an equivalent effect . . .

39 In that regard, national legislation granting a power to police authorities to carry out identity checks – a power which, first, is restricted to the border area of the Member State with other Member States and, second, does not depend upon the behaviour of the person checked or on specific circumstances giving rise to a risk of breach of public order – must, *inter alia*, guide the discretion which those authorities enjoy in the practical application of that power . . .

40 . . . the more extensive the evidence of the existence of a possible equivalent effect, within the meaning of [Article 23(a)], apparent from the objective pursued by the checks carried out in a border area, from the territorial scope of those checks and from the existence of a distinction between the basis of those checks and that of those carried out in the remainder of the territory of the Member State concerned, the greater the need for strict detailed rules and limitations laying down the conditions for the exercise by the Member States of their police powers in a border area and for strict application of those detailed rules and limitations, in order not to imperil the attainment of the objective of the abolition of internal border controls . . .

41 Last, the framework required must be sufficiently clear and precise to enable the need for the checks and the checks actually authorised themselves to be checked . . .

47　The fact that the checks ... aim to prevent or terminate illegal entry into the territory of the Federal Republic of Germany or to prevent criminal offences such as crimes which undermine border security or the carrying out of Federal Police tasks – whereas [Article 23(a)] does not refer specifically to that objective – does not mean that there is an objective of border control contrary to [Article 23(a)(i)] ...

52　... as regards the question of whether the exercise of control powers granted ... has an equivalent effect within the meaning of [Article 23(a)], it must be recalled that the fact that the territorial scope of those powers is limited to a border area does not suffice in itself to warrant the finding of such an effect. The first sentence of that provision refers expressly to the exercise of police powers by the competent authorities of the Member States under national law, also in border areas ...

53　However, the checks ... are subject, as far as their territorial scope is concerned, to specific rules ... a factor which might constitute evidence of the existence of such an equivalent effect ...

54　In that regard, it is not apparent from the order for reference that the checks governed are based on police knowledge of the situation or experience, as is provided for in [Article 23(a)(ii) of the Regulation].

55　Therefore, it seems that those checks are authorised irrespective of the behaviour of the person checked and of circumstances giving rise to a risk of breach of public order.

56　Moreover, it is not apparent from the documents before the Court that the checks provided for in ... are carried out, in conformity with [Article 23(a)(iii)] in a manner clearly distinct from systematic checks on persons at the external borders of the European Union.

58　Therefore, it appears that the checks ... may be carried out in a border area within a 30 kilometre radius, without any detailed rules or limitations being provided in that provision.

59　In those circumstances, it must be stated that the powers ... must be subject to a regulatory framework meeting the requirements set out in paragraphs 38 to 41 of the present judgment. In the absence of such detailed rules or limitations, themselves sufficiently precise and detailed, in national legislation for the purposes of defining the intensity, frequency and selectivity of checks, it cannot be ruled out that the practical exercise of the police powers granted under German law results [contrary to Article 23] in controls which have an effect equivalent to border checks.

The reasoning is a two-stage process and is complex. The first stage looks at whether the measures have 'equivalent effect' to border controls. In *A*, the Court indicated that they would look to whether the powers to ask for ID were special rules which were territorially confined (i.e. they only applied near the border) and could be used irrespective of behaviour or circumstances which gave rise to a public order. If the answer to both these questions is 'yes', the second test applies. The checks cannot be systematic, and they must not have too high an intensity or frequency. It is only if this is the case or there is no legal framework to regulate the checks that the measure will be illegal.

This replaces internal borders with an amorphous form of borderlands policing which can be much more intense and repressive than elsewhere in the territory.[53] It allows States to use irregular migration and border offences as a justification for more intense policing near the border (para. 47). The only requirement is that this policing should be subject to a regulatory framework and not systematic. These constraints are very general indeed.

[53] S. Colombeau, 'Policing the Internal Schengen Borders – Managing the Double Bind between Free Movement and Migration Control' (2017) 27 *Policing and Society* 480.

(b) The External Frontier

The relaxation of internal border controls is to be accompanied by the establishment of a common external Union frontier, at least for the Schengen States. The reason is vested in a particular notion of security. A Member State can only dispense with its border controls with other Member States if it can be sure that these will protect it against the threats posed by those from outside the Union at least as well as it could do by acting alone. This logic has led not merely to common controls at the external frontier but ever tougher measures to protect the external frontier from those attempting to breach it.

The duties of Member States at the external frontier are to let people enter their territories only through designated border points;[54] to carry out border checks at those points[55] except in unforeseen and exceptional circumstances where waiting times become excessive;[56] and to stamp systematically the entry and exit of non-EU nationals from their territories.[57] They are also under duties to carry out border surveillance and to put aside appropriate resources for this.[58] The central duty, however, is to consider whether non-EU nationals meet the conditions for entry to the Union. For most visitors, these are set out below.[59]

Regulation 2016/399, Article 6

(1) For intended stays on the territory of the Member States of a duration of no more than 90 days in any 180-day period, which entails considering the 180-day period preceding each day of stay, the entry conditions for third-country nationals shall be the following:

(a) they are in possession of a valid travel document entitling the holder to cross the border satisfying the following criteria:

(i) its validity shall extend at least three months after the intended date of departure from the territory of the Member States. In a justified case of emergency, this obligation may be waived;

(ii) it shall have been issued within the previous 10 years;

(b) they are in possession of a valid visa, if required . . . except where they hold a valid residence permit or a valid long-stay visa;

(c) they justify the purpose and conditions of the intended stay, and they have sufficient means of subsistence, both for the duration of the intended stay and for the return to their country of origin or transit to a third country into which they are certain to be admitted, or are in a position to acquire such means lawfully;

(d) they are not persons for whom an alert has been issued in the SIS for the purposes of refusing entry;

(e) they are not considered to be a threat to public policy, internal security, public health or the international relations of any of the Member States, in particular where no alert has been issued in Member States' national data bases for the purposes of refusing entry on the same grounds.

---

[54] Schengen Borders Code, Article 5(1). This is subject to a very limited number of exceptions, Article 5(2).
[55] *Ibid.* Article 8(1).   [56] *Ibid.* Article 9(1).
[57] *Ibid.* Article 11(1). Limited exception is provided for those for whom such a stamp may cause serious difficulties. A record must still be kept, *ibid.* Article 11(3).
[58] *Ibid.* Articles 13 and 15.
[59] In principle, any visitor not meeting these should not be admitted, *ibid.* Article 14(1). There are limited exceptions where visas may be issued at the frontier or for humanitarian reasons, *ibid.* Article 6(5)(b)–(c).

Non-EU nationals have a right of appeal against any refusal of entry.[60] However, this right is tempered by this appeal not having suspensive effect. The non-EU national cannot remain on the EU territory pending the appeal.

A great challenge for the Union is that non-EU nationals enter the Union without meeting the conditions in Article 6. This might be because they enter the Union by by-passing the designated border points. Alternately, they might arrive at the Union's external frontier and claim asylum. The Union is obliged to admit them in such circumstances to see whether they should be granted international protection,[61] irrespective of whether they would, otherwise, meet the conditions in Article 6.

The Union has taken a number of measures to prevent many non-EU nationals from reaching its territory.

The most central instrument is visa policy. The requirement in Article 6(1)(b) that a non-EU national have a visa if that is required by EU law might seem arcane and be irrelevant to whether a non-EU national can reach the Union territory or not. However, the possession of a visa will be central to whether the non-EU national can get transport to the Union or not. The Carriers Sanctions Directive imposes sanctions on carriers for bringing people to Union frontiers without proper travel documents. Penalties are a minimum of €3,000 for each case.[62] Furthermore, even when the migrant has the right travel documents, the carrier is responsible for the costs of return and for returning the migrant as soon as possible.[63] Thus carriers become a central form of pre-arrival migration control for those who need visas.[64] They will check that travellers have the necessary travel documents and visas and carry out their own assessment as to the risk of refusal of entry before letting the traveller board. Decisions are likely to be cautious because of, on the one hand, the risk of having to bear the costs of return and, on the other, contracts providing for the traveller having no legal comeback if denied entry to the vessel.[65] The policing role of the carrier is completed by its having to communicate information about passenger names, travel documents and dates of birth to the authorities in the State of destination before the end of check-in in the State of departure.[66]

The States whose nationals require short-term visas to enter the Union are considerable.[67] It includes States whose nationals are seen as a significant source of economic migration, irregular

---

[60] *Ibid.* Article 14(3).

[61] Directive 2013/32/EU on common procedures for granting and withdrawing international protection, OJ 2013, L 180/60, Article 9(1). Ireland does not participate in this Directive. This is, furthermore, not a legislative choice as Article 78(1) TFEU commits the Union to the principle of *non-refoulement*, which requires this.

[62] Directive 2001/51/EC supplementing the provisions of Article 26 of the Convention implementing the Schengen Agreement of 14 June 1985, OJ 2001, L 187/45, Article 4. Ireland does participate in this Directive and the United Kingdom will participate during the transition period.

[63] *Ibid.* Articles 2 and 3.

[64] T. Gammeltoft-Hansen, 'The Rise of the Private Border Guard: Accountability and Responsibility in the Migration Control Industry' in T. Gammeltoft-Hansen and N. Sorensen (eds.), *The Migration Industry and the Commercialization of International Migration* (Abingdon and New York, Routledge, 2013).

[65] In recent years, the amount of fines imposed on carriers has increased, thereby raising the incentives for them to be cautious about allowing migrants to board, T. Baird, 'Carrier Sanctions in Europe: A Comparison of Trends in 10 Countries' (2017) 19 *EJML* 307.

[66] Directive 2004/82 on the obligation of carriers to communicate passenger data, OJ 2004, L 261/24. Article 3. Ireland participates in the Directive and the United Kingdom will participate during the transition period.

[67] Regulation 539/2001 listing the third countries whose nationals must be in possession of visas when crossing the external borders and those whose nationals are exempt from that requirement, OJ 2001, L 81/1. This has been amended a number of times, most recently by Regulation 2017/850, OJ 2017, L 133/1.

migration, political radicalism and asylum seekers. Visa applicants must apply in their State of residence,[68] and must go there to the consular office of the Member State which is their main destination.[69] A visa can only refused for the reasons set out in Regulation 810/2009, the Community visa code.[70] The grounds for refusal are identical to those set out in Article 6 of the Schengen Borders Code (outlined above), with one addition, namely that the applicant will be refused a visa if they have already stayed in the Union on a visa for three months in the last six.[71] However, a further proviso indicates that the process of enquiry is more far-reaching than that at the border.

Regulation 810/2009, Article 32

(1)(b) Without prejudice to Article 25(1), a visa shall be refused ... if there are reasonable doubts as to the authenticity of the supporting documents submitted by the applicant or the veracity of their contents, the reliability of the statements made by the applicant or his intention to leave the territory of the Member States before the expiry of the visa applied for.

Applicants will normally have to submit extensive documentation which will often have to be verified or certified to secure a visa in many instances. This has led to an extensive visa processing industry with private companies have emerged as intermediaries. For a fee, these will advise applicants on how to prepare applications and submit the application on their behalf.[72]

Of possibly even more pressing concern is the question whether asylum seekers can apply for a visa in these consulates. The matter is governed by Article 25(1) of the Community Visa Code, which allows Member States to grant visas exceptionally where they consider it necessary on humanitarian grounds or because of international obligations. However, the question is one of national discretion.[73] If the consulate refuses, the applicant has no recourse in EU law. In practice, therefore, asylum to the Union is closed off to those who have to rely on regular air or marine transport.

The Union is also taking increasing numbers of measures, euphemistically known as European integrated border management, to police the external frontier.[74] The European Border and Coast Guard, often known as Frontex, is at the centre of this. Established in 2005, this Union agency's mission is to 'ensure European integrated border management at the external borders with a view to managing the crossing of the external borders efficiently'.[75] To this end, it has a number of tasks which have expanded over the years. The most high-profile are its operational activities. These involve coordinating joint operations between Member States to police the external frontier, most visibly in the Mediterranean; establishing European border- and coast-guard

---

[68] Regulation 810/2009/EC establishing a Community Code on Visas, OJ 2009, L 243/1, Article 6(1). Ireland does not participate in this. It can be in the State in which they are present if a justification is provided, Article 6(2). More broadly see A. Meloni, 'The Community Code on Visas: Harmonisation at Last?' (2009) 34 *ELRev* 671.

[69] Regulation 810/2009/EC, Article 5(1)–(2).   [70] *Koushkaki*, C-84/12, EU:C:2013:862.

[71] Regulation 810/2009, Article 32(1)(a).

[72] On this industry and the concerns it generates, see M. Sánchez-Barrueco, 'Business as Usual? Mapping Outsourcing Practices in Schengen Visa Processing' (2018) 44 *Journal of Ethnic and Migration Studies* 382.

[73] *X and Y*, C-638/16 PPU, EU:C:2017:173.

[74] Regulation 2016/1624 on the European Border and Coast Guard, OJ 2016, L 251/1.   [75] *Ibid.* Article 1.

teams from participating Member States, which are sent as rapid reaction forces to migration hot spots, assisting in search and rescue operations, most notably in the Mediterranean, and conducting joint operations with non-EU States.[76] As the crisis in the Mediterranean developed, its budget tripled between 2014 and 2017 to over €280 million,[77] and there are plans to expand its operational capacity still further with the Commission proposing a standing corps of 10,000 border guards with a budget of €2.2 billion over six years.[78]

The Agency has been controversial. Its joint operations have involved the interception and turning back of ships which might have on board those wishing to seek asylum. They have also resulted in drownings at sea.[79] Amendments to its powers have reflected this, with the Agency explicitly required to observe fundamental rights and the principle of *non-refoulement*.[80] Non-EU nationals intercepted in the EU territorial seas and contiguous seas have a right to claim asylum as they will be disembarked in the Union.[81] The position is more complicated on the high seas with interceptions only violating the principle of *non-refoulement* if those on board the ship are returned or forced to return to a place or authorities where there is a risk of serious harm or persecution.[82] However, it will often be very unclear when this is so and there are no procedural guarantees to ensure that appropriate weight is given to evaluating the risks during operations out at sea during operations.

In this world which is subject to EU laws but to few significant legal processes, how officials perceive their role, and its tension between protecting fundamental rights and securing the external frontier, becomes crucial. Aas and Gundhus carried out a study of attitudes amongst Frontex officials whose central findings are captured below.

K. Aas and H. Gundhus, 'Policing Humanitarian Borderlands: Frontex, Human Rights and the Precariousness of Life' (2015) 55 *British Journal of Criminology* 1, 5–6 and 8–9

Our interviews with Norwegian police officers, who have taken part in Frontex operations, reveal that they by and large see their presence at the border as a means of improving conditions for migrants. As one senior officer put it:

'Well. After we . . . I would say, without bragging, I would say that things have become much better. Because we pointed out, when we started coming to Greece, we pointed out that conditions were terrible for the migrants. It was like watching, it is terrible to say that, but it was like watching a war movie from 1943. Simply like that. Coming close to concentration camps. And we wrote a lot about it. What has happened now is that they have expanded the camps. They have gotten in, among other, Medicins sans Frontiers, nurses which are in the area, and the threshold for being sent to a hospital is quite low. So I have to say that

---

[76] *Ibid.* Article 14(2).

[77] On the expansion of these resources see P. Slominski and F. Trauner, 'How Do Member States Return Unwanted Migrants? The Strategic (Non-)Use of "Europe" during the Migration Crisis' (2018) 56 *JCMS* 101, 107–8.

[78] European Commission, 'Proposal for a Regulation on the European Border and Coast Guard', COM(2018)631.

[79] S. Léonard, "EU Border Security and Migration into the European Union: FRONTEX and Securitisation through Practices" (2010) 19 *European Security* 231; E. Papastavridis, "Fortress Europe" and Frontex: Within or Without International Law?' (2010) 79 *NJIL* 75.

[80] Regulation 2016/1624, Article 34.

[81] Regulation 656/2014 establishing rules for the surveillance of the external sea borders in the context of operational cooperation, OJ 2014, L 189/93, Article 10(2).

[82] *Ibid.* Article 4(1)–(2). On these issues see R. Mungeanu, *Frontex and Non Refoulement* (Cambridge University Press, 2016) 207–12.

if Frontex hadn't been there, this would never have happened. Never. So one can criticize as much as one wishes, but things have become better. I would say that.'

Although rarely explicitly referring to human rights, the informants see Frontex as contributing not only to better conditions in terms of detention, but also to higher levels of policing standards at the border, which is partly also what motivated them to participate in Frontex operations ...

While some our interviewees are quite vocal and engaged about humanitarian issues, for the majority, migrants' suffering nevertheless seems to be experienced as part of the job and is not considered particularly challenging. The officers participating in Frontex operations are generally quite experienced and see the tragedies at the border as part of a broader specter of hardship they have encountered throughout the years. This professional distance is also revealed in the fact that, when asked about the most challenging part of their mission, weather conditions were regularly mentioned, while suffering of the migrants was generally not. They seem to be quite clear that they are not a humanitarian but a police organization and see humanitarian concerns as something that can be outsourced to the Medecins sans Frontieres.

Moreover, the nature of the police officers' tasks also seems to direct their focus towards establishing the truthfulness of the migrants' stories rather than seeing their vulnerability. Migrants are being 'screened' and 'debriefed' about their identity, about facilitators of their journeys, travel routes, false documents, etc. In such a setup, migrants appear first and foremost as a source of information to reveal smugglers and other crime-related activities rather than subjects deserving of protection.

The article suggests that officials see themselves as on a humanitarian mission and justify their work accordingly. However, in pursuing that mission, they are relatively indifferent to suffering and are concerned to establish what they see as truth so that they can distinguish the deserving from the undeserving.[83] This mind-set is very black-and-white, with little time for the complexity and ambiguity of many non-EU nationals' circumstances. There is a danger that it generates not only mistakes but little room to admit those mistakes.

In addition to visas and policing, the third way in which the Union tries to keep non-EU nationals away from its external frontiers is through agreements with non-EU States. Under such agreements, these States will limit non-EU nationals transiting through them to the Union and/or will offer an alternate place of sanctuary to non-EU nationals seeking asylum. The most high-profile is the agreement between EU Member States and Turkey in March 2016. Under this agreement, Turkey is to police its land and sea borders with the Union to prevent irregular migration into the Union, and to cooperate with Union border authorities to prevent such migration. It must also take back any future irregular migrants that cross into Greece from Turkey. However, in exchange for every Syrian returned to Turkey, a Syrian refugee currently in Turkey would be resettled in the Union. Turkey received €3 billion, liberalisation of Union short-term visas for its citizens if it met certain benchmarks, and some progress in its accession talks with the Union.[84]

Such agreements raise significant human rights concerns. There are no guarantees about how individuals prevented from reaching the Union or returned to Turkey will be treated. Nor are

---

[83] See also P. Pallister-Wilkins, 'The Humanitarian Politics of European Border Policing: Frontex and Border Police in Evros' (2015) 9 *International Political Sociology* 53.

[84] European Council, 'EU–Turkey Statement', 18 March 2016, www.consilium.europa.eu/en/press/press-releases/2016/03/18/eu-turkey-statement/.

there any that Turkey will not send them back to the places where they were at risk of harm or persecution.[85] The agreement with Turkey was, thus, deliberately framed as an agreement between Turkey and the EU Member States to prevent its legality being successfully challenged in the Union courts.[86]

The matter was taken further in 2018 with the European Council calling on the Commission to 'explore the concept of regional disembarkation platforms, in close cooperation with relevant third countries as well as UNHCR and IOM[87]. Such platforms should operate distinguishing individual situations, in full respect of international law and without creating a pull factor.'[88] The Commission has indicated how these platforms would work:

> UNHCR and IOM have outlined in their proposal a number of steps that would need to be undertaken when disembarkation takes place. First, after determining the place of disembarkation, those rescued at sea would be disembarked promptly and transported to reception facilities providing adequate, safe and dignified reception conditions. There, they would be registered, screened and receive assistance based on their specific needs. Points of reception should be established as far away as possible from points of irregular departure, in particular from sections of the coast where smugglers operate in order to reduce possibilities for re-departures and thereby reducing risks of pull factors. Furthermore, swift further processing of disembarked and registered migrants is necessary for the well-functioning of such arrangements. In the case of third countries, UNHCR and IOM could, after disembarkation, provide support to quickly distinguish between irregular migrants and those in need of international protection, taking into account individual situations, and operating in full respect of international law.[89]

These proposals involve an outsourcing of international protection by intimating that cases should be considered by UN bodies in non-EU States before beneficiaries can come to the Union. They raise the same concern as the EU–Turkey agreement as the Union is turning a blind eye to any human rights issues which might be generated by these platforms, and these may be considerable if they are poorly resourced and have to house large numbers of people. At the time of writing, no non-EU State has agreed to house them.

(iii) Humanitarianism

The third narrative in this field is that of fundamental rights. This emphasises the universality of the human condition and the arbitrariness of distinguishing between individuals on grounds of nationality.[90] It presses for lenient immigration policies and more extensive rights for non-EU

---

[85] On UNHCR concerns see İ. Toygür and B. Benvenuti, *One Year On: An Assessment of the EU-Turkey Statement on Refugees* (Madrid, Elcano Royal Institute, ARI 21/2017, 2017).

[86] On the unsuccessful challenge see *NG v. European Council*, T-193/16, EU:T:2017:129.

[87] These are the UN High Commission for Refugees and the International Maritime Organisation.

[88] Conclusions of the European Council of 28 June 2018, EUCO 9/18, para. 5.

[89] European Commission, 'Non-Paper on Regional Disembarkation Arrangements', 24 June 2018, https://ec.europa.eu/home-affairs/sites/homeaffairs/files/what-we-do/policies/european-agenda-migration/20180724_non-paper-regional-disembarkation-arrangements_en.pdf.

[90] For a variety of arguments see V. Bader, 'The Ethics of Immigration' (2005) 12 *Constellations* 331; L. Ypi, 'Justice in Migration: A Closed Borders Utopia?' (2008) 16 *Journal of Political Philosophy* 391; A. Shachar, *The Birthright Lottery: Citizenship and Global Inequality* (Cambridge, MA, Harvard University Press, 2009), chs. 2 and 3; C. Offe, 'From Migration in Geographic Space to Migration in Biographic Time: Views from Europe' (2011) 19 *Journal of Political Philosophy* 333.

nationals. Despite enjoying a lower profile than the other two narratives, this narrative is a powerful one, possibly because its advocates – non-governmental organisations (NGOs) and big business – are usually capable of exercising significant clout within the political decision-making procedures and judicial processes,[91] but also because policy-makers are wary of the dangers of populism.[92]

This narrative informs three fields, in particular. First, it provides the basis for granting international protection to those suffering persecution and harm in their country of origin. To be sure, EU laws can be subject to much criticism here but its presence can only be explained by a concern about human need. Secondly, there is a concern with family rights: whether these be non-EU relatives of EU citizens residing in other States,[93] families of Turkish nationals exercising their rights under the EU–Turkey Association Agreement[94] or family members of non-EU nationals lawfully resident in the Union.[95] The third field concerns non-EU nationals lawfully resident in the Union. Union policy is to seek to integrate these into Union society as much as possible and, in the case of long-term residents, to approximate their rights to those of Union citizens.[96]

There are a number of fundamental rights which are particularly salient. In migration, the right to respect for family life is prominent (Article 7 of the European Union Charter for Fundamental Rights and Freedoms (EUCFR) and Article 8 of the European Convention on Human Rights (ECHR)), as are the rights of the child (Article 24 EUCFR). The fundamental right most identified with seeking international protection is that of *non-refoulement*. Persons covered by this principle may not be expelled or returned to frontiers of territories where their lives or freedom would be threatened.[97]

The principle of *non-refoulement* covers three categories of person.

The first is refugees. These are persons who have a 'well-founded fear of being persecuted for reasons of race, religion, nationality, political opinion or membership of a particular social group and is outside the country of nationality'.[98]

The second is subsidiary protection. Persons benefiting from subsidiary protection will persons who are not refugees but have shown substantial grounds for believing that, if returned, they would face a real risk of suffering serious harm.[99] Serious harm is understood here as comprising the death penalty or execution; torture or inhuman or degrading treatment or punishment; or, if

---

[91] G. Freeman, 'Modes of Immigration Politics in Liberal States' (1995) 29 *International Migration Review* 881; G. Sasse, 'Securitization or Securing Rights? Exploring the Conceptual Foundations of Policies towards Minorities and Migrants in Europe' (2005) 43 *JCMS* 673.

[92] C. Joppke, 'Why Liberal States Accept Unwanted Immigration' (1998) 50 *World Politics* 266.

[93] Directive 2004/38/EC, on the right of citizens of the Union and their family members to move and reside freely within the territory of the Member States, OJ 2004, L 158/77. This is discussed at pp. 499–515.

[94] Articles 7 and 9 of Decision 1/80 of the EC-Turkey Association Council. This can be found in EU Council, *EEC-Turkey Association Agreement and Protocols and Other Basic Texts* (Luxembourg, Office for Official Publications of the European Communities, 1992).

[95] See pp. 556–7.   [96] See pp. 551–6.

[97] The right is established by the Convention Relating to the Status of Refugees 1951, 189 UNTS 150, Article 33. It has also been accepted in EU law in *B & D*, C-57/09 and C-101/09, EU:C:2010:661.

[98] Directive 2011/95 on standards for the qualification of third-country nationals or stateless persons as beneficiaries of international protection, for a uniform status for refugees or for persons eligible for subsidiary protection, and for the content of the protection granted, OJ 2011, L 337/9, Article 2(d).

[99] Directive 2011/95, Article 2(f).

they are a civilian, serious and individual threat to their life or person by reason of indiscriminate violence in situations of international or internal armed conflict.[100]

The third group are asylum seekers, namely those applying for refugee or subsidiary protection status but for whom it has not yet been established that they meet the criteria. Insofar as they may do so, States are bound by the principle of *non-refoulement*, as otherwise there is a danger of returning people to harm or persecution who are entitled to sanctuary. Asylum seekers have a right to *non-refoulement* until a decision has been taken on their status.[101]

These humanitarian norms grant entitlements that both allow Union and national measures to be struck down and guide the interpretation of individual EU laws.[102] The judiciary are at the forefront of this, and much depends, therefore, on how the Court of Justice interprets these principles. An indication of the ebb and flow of the reasoning is provided by *X, Y and Z*. Three asylum seekers from Sierra Leone, Uganda and Senegal sought refugee status in the Netherlands as they were gay, and homosexuality was a criminal offence in these African States, with the possibility of prison terms up to life imprisonment in the first two, and five years in Senegal. It was argued by the men's lawyers that there was a violation of the right to respect for private life (Article 7 EUCFR) and the right to non-discrimination (Article 21 EUCFR). The Dutch authorities argued that possible criminalisation was insufficient to justify the well-founded fear of persecution necessary for such status. The relevant EU legislation indicated that such persecution must be sufficiently serious and this would only be the case with imprisonment if it was disproportionate or discriminatory.[103]

X, Y and Z, C–199–201/12, EU:C:2013:720

53   ... for a violation of fundamental rights to constitute persecution within the meaning ... of the Geneva Convention, it must be sufficiently serious. Therefore, not all violations of fundamental rights suffered by a homosexual asylum seeker will necessarily reach that level of seriousness.

54   In that connection, it must be stated at the outset that the fundamental rights specifically linked to the sexual orientation concerned in each of the cases in the main proceedings, such as the right to respect for private and family life, which is protected by Article 8 of the ECHR, to which Article 7 of the Charter corresponds, read together, where necessary, with Article 14 ECHR, on which Article 21(1) of the Charter is based, is not among the fundamental human rights from which no derogation is possible.

55   In those circumstances, the mere existence of legislation criminalising homosexual acts cannot be regarded as an act affecting the applicant in a manner so significant that it reaches the level of seriousness necessary for a finding that it constitutes persecution ...

56   However, the term of imprisonment which accompanies a legislative provision which, like those at issue in the main proceedings, punishes homosexual acts is capable, in itself of constituting an act of persecution ... provided that it is actually applied in the country of origin which adopted such legislation.

---

[100]   Directive 2011/95, Article 15.

[101]   It is thus set out as a right to asylum in Article 18 EUCFR. It is also acknowledged in Directive 2013/32/EU on common procedures for granting and withdrawing international protection, OJ 2013, L 180/60, Article 9(1).

[102]   On the scope of national and EU Institution fundamental rights responsibilities see pp. 272–81.

[103]   Directive 2011/95 on standards for the qualification of third-country nationals or stateless persons as beneficiaries of international protection, for a uniform status for refugees or for persons eligible for subsidiary protection, and for the content of the protection granted, OJ 2011, L 337/9, Article 9(2)(c).

57 Such a sanction infringes Article 8 ECHR, to which Article 7 of the Charter corresponds, and constitutes punishment which is disproportionate or discriminatory.

58 In those circumstances, where an applicant for asylum relies ... on the existence in his country of origin on legislation criminalising homosexual acts, it is for the national authorities to undertake, in the course of their assessments of the facts and circumstances ... an examination of all the relevant facts concerning that country of origin, including its laws and regulations and the manner in which they are applied ...

59 In undertaking that assessment it is, in particular, for those authorities to determine whether, in the applicant's country of origin, the term of imprisonment provided for by such legislation is applied in practice

There is wavering in the judgment. On the one hand, the Court finds the length of prison terms to be, in principle, disproportionate and discriminatory. On the other, it states that they will only actually be disproportionate and discriminatory if they are enforced, as if having the possibility of a life sentence on the books does not, by itself, cast a long shadow. This equivocation is possibly because liberal judgments can lead to powerful political reactions. In *Metock* the Court held that EU citizens residing in another Member State had a right to marry non-EU nationals granted asylum there.[104] The Danish Government responded by asking for an amendment to the EU legislation in question and by seeking to impose a new criterion before non-Danish EU citizens could marry non-EU nationals in Denmark: namely that the former had to show genuine and effective residence in Denmark.[105] These measures were intended not just to counter the judgment but also as a shot across the bows of the Court of Justice not to develop that case law further.

4 'UNWELCOME FOREIGNERS': THE RETURNS DIRECTIVE

Non-EU nationals can only be in the Union if they entered through a designated border point and comply with the conditions on which they have been admitted. The consequences of failure to do either of these are set out by the Returns Directive, Directive 2008/115/EC.[106] They are deemed to be staying illegally within the Union.

Returns Directive, Directive 2008/115/EC, Article 3

(2) 'illegal stay' means the presence on the territory of a Member State, of a third-country national who does not fulfil, or no longer fulfils the conditions of entry as set out in [Article 6] of the Schengen Borders Code or other conditions for entry, stay or residence in that Member State ...

In addition to breach of the conditions of entry, the central conditions which may result in the non-EU national staying illegally within the Union are no longer having a valid travel document

---

[104] *Metock* v. *Minister for Justice, Equality and Law Reform*, C-127/08, EU:C:2008:449.

[105] On this saga see M. Wind, 'When Parliament Comes First: The Danish Concept of Democracy Meets the European Union' (2009) 27 *Nordisk Tidsskrift For Menneskerettigheter* 272.

[106] Directive 2008/115/EC on common standards and procedures in Member States for returning illegally staying third-country nationals, OJ 2008, L 348/98. Ireland is not participating in this Directive. The Directive does not apply to non-EU nationals who enjoy more favourable status by virtue of rights given to them by other EU laws, Article 4(1)–(2).

or visa or sufficient means; or being a threat to public policy,[107] public health or public security. Thus, falling ill, being robbed or civil disobedience could all be reasons for return.[108]

A non-EU national staying illegally on Union territory must be returned to his State of origin or, failing that, to a State of transit with which the Union has an agreement or any other State to which he is willing to return and which will accept him.[109]

Returns Directive, Directive 2008/115/EC, Article 6

(1) Member States shall issue a return decision to any third country national staying illegally on their territory, without prejudice to the exceptions referred to in paragraphs 2 to 5.

The obligation on the Member States to issue a return decision is intended to stop large-scale amnesties to irregular migrants. There are a number of exceptions, of which the most significant is that Member States may authorise stays for 'compassionate, humanitarian or other reasons',[110] which grant Member States a discretion not to deport. States must also 'take due account' of the best interests of any children, family life or the state of health of the non-EU national.[111] Hearings must be given to potential returnees in such circumstances so that information on these questions can be provided. The State has a discretion whether to return after considering these.[112]

However, States must not return a non-EU national if this would violate the principle of *non-refoulement*. No return can be take place, therefore, once an individual has applied for international protection whilst their application is being considered or pending an appeal against that decision.[113] This has generated questions on whether ill irregular migrants should be deported. On this, the Court has stated that the principle of *non-refoulement* would be breached where return would expose the individual to a serious risk of grave and irreversible deterioration in his state of health and there are no appropriate facilities in the State to which he is being returned. However, return should take place if the non-EU State has facilities which are simply less good than those in the Union.[114]

---

[107] This must be done on a case-by-case basis. The individual must pose a genuine and present risk with criminal conviction by itself insufficient to warrant deportation, *Zh. and O.*, C-554/13, EU:C:2015:377.

[108] Member States may decide not to apply the Directive to those refused entry or subject to a criminal sanction, Directive 2008/115/EC on common standards and procedures in Member States for returning illegally staying third-country nationals, OJ 2008, L 348/98, Article 2(2). In addition family members of EU citizens or those covered by an agreement between the EU and a non EU State which grants them rights of free movement are excluded from the Directive, Article 2(3).

[109] *Ibid.* Article 3(3).

[110] *Ibid.* Article 6(4). Other exceptions include where the non-EU national has a right to reside in another Member State in which case she should go to the latter State unless there is a security risk, *ibid.* Article 6(2); or where she is the subject of a pending decision renewing her authorisation to stay in which case there is a discretion not to return, *ibid.* Article 6(5). She can be transferred to another Member State if there is a bilateral agreement on this which existed prior to the Directive. In such circumstances, the latter is responsible for returning the non-EU national, *ibid.* Article 6(3).

[111] *Ibid.* Article 5.   [112] *K.A. and Others*, C-82/16, EU:C:2018:308.

[113] *Gnandi*, C-181/16, EU:C:2018:465. This only applies in the case of the initial appeal and not to any subsequent events which may be made in national law, *X and Y*, C-180/17, EU:C:2018:775.

[114] *Centre public d'action sociale d'Ottignies-Louvain-la-Neuve* v. *Abdida*, C-562/13, EU:C:2014:2453; *MP* v. *Secretary of State for the Home Department*, C-353/16, EU:C:2018:276.

A return decision should usually provide for voluntary departure within between seven and thirty days.[115] This is to make the issue as consensual as possible. There are thus possibilities for extension because of schooling issues or family reasons.[116] There are also certain procedural guarantees. The non-EU national is granted the right of appeal and review against the decision before an independent judicial or administrative body.[117] She should also be provided with legal advice and linguistic help.[118]

Forced return will take place where the non-EU national does not voluntarily return within the period granted.[119] It can also happen as a matter of first resort where there is a risk of the non-EU national absconding; she poses a risk to public policy or national security; or her application to stay is manifestly fraudulent or unfounded.[120]

In the case of forced removal two sanctions kick in.

The first is an automatic ban on re-entry into the Union.[121] This can be up to five years and longer where there is a risk to public policy or public security.[122] This automatic ban is to incentivise voluntary return. However, Member States still have discretion to impose a re-entry ban even in cases of voluntary return.[123] More generally, this re-entry ban provides incentives for determined non-EU nationals to seek irregular entry, possibly through being trafficked or other hazardous means.[124]

The second sanction is detention.

Returns Directive, Directive 2008/115/EC, Article 15

(1) Unless other sufficient but less coercive measures can be applied effectively in a specific case, Member States may only keep in detention a third-country national who is the subject of return procedures in order to prepare the return and/or carry out the removal process, in particular when:
 (a) there is a risk of absconding or
 (b) the third-country national concerned avoids or hampers the preparation of return or the removal process.
 Any detention shall be for as short a period as possible and only maintained as long as removal arrangements are in progress and executed with due diligence.

Detention is a matter of last resort and one of discretion. Furthermore, it should only be used to prepare the return. This possibility of detention still raises the question of the criminalisation of the irregular migrant, whereby her stay is not just deemed illegal but she is also deemed to be a criminal by virtue of it.[125] This was addressed at most length in *Achughbabian*.[126] An Armenian was charged under a French law which provided for imprisonment solely by virtue of his irregular presence in France. The Court of Justice found such a law to violate the Returns Directive. It made such a finding not on civil liberties grounds but on the basis that any detention

---

[115] Directive 2008/115/EC on common standards and procedures in Member States for returning illegally staying third-country nationals, OJ 2008, L 348/98, Article 7(1).
[116] *Ibid.* Article 7(2).   [117] *Ibid.* Article 13(1).   [118] *Ibid.* Article 13(3).   [119] *Ibid.* Article 8(1).
[120] *Ibid.* Article 7(4).   [121] *Ibid.* Article 11(1).   [122] *Ibid.* Article 11(2).   [123] *Ibid.* Article 11(1).
[124] A. Baldaccini, 'The Return and Removal of Irregular Migrants under EU Law: An Analysis of the Returns Directive' (2009) 11 *EJML* 1, 9–10.
[125] R. Rafaelli, 'Criminalizing Irregular Immigration and the Returns Directive: An Analysis of the *El Dridi* Case' (2011) 13 *EJML* 467.
[126] *Achughbabian*, C-329/11, EU:C:2011:807; *El Dridi*, C-61/11 PPU, EU:C:2011:268.

must contribute to the removal of the non-EU national. Imprisonment did not do that and thwarted the objective of removal insofar as it could delay it. However, it did find that the Directive did not preclude imprisonment if the non-EU national stayed on illegally after a return decision had been issued (i.e. did not go back by the stipulated date). Member States can also imprison non-EU nationals who try to re-enter their territory illegally after already being subject to a return decision.[127]

Any detention must be reviewed regularly and should not be for an initial period of more than six months.[128] It can be extended by a further twelve months if the non-EU national is uncooperative or there are delays securing documentation from third countries.[129] Notwithstanding this, eighteen months is a long period of incarceration, and suggests the pseudo-criminalisation of the irregular migrant.[130]

5 'DESIRABLE FOREIGNERS': WORKER RESIDENTS AND LONG-TERM RESIDENTS

If irregular migrants sit at one end of the spectrum of Union responses to migration, non-EU nationals lawfully working or residing long-term in the Union occupy the other end. These enjoy favourable rights under two Directives: the Single Permit Directive, Directive 2011/98/EU, which, *inter alia*, grants a common set of rights to non-EU workers legally resident in a Member State,[131] and Directive 2003/109/EC which governs the rights of long-term resident non-EU nationals.[132]

Two philosophies underpin this regime. On the one hand, there is a concern to grant these individuals significant membership rights within the communities within which they live. At the Tampere European Council in 1999, the European Council committed itself to integrating long-term residents within host societies and granting rights analogous to those of Union citizenship. This was reaffirmed by the Stockholm Programme in 2010 and extended to all those legally resident within the Union.[133] On the other, there is a philosophy of 'managed migration'. This grants rights almost exclusively to those who bring skills to the Union in which there is a shortage of supply, and, even there, holds that there are certain thresholds to levels of migration, provision of welfare or tolerance of belief which must not be exceeded if national economies, Welfare States and cultural traditions are not to be endangered. These notional thresholds are sometimes used in invidious ways to deny these non-EU nationals key membership rights in the societies of their host Member States.

---

[127] *Celaj*, C-290/14, EU:C:2015:640.   [128] Directive 2008/115/EC, Article 15(3) and (5).   [129] *Ibid.* Article 15(6).

[130] On the wider civil liberties concerns see H. Askola, '"Illegal Migrants", Gender and Vulnerability: The Case of the EU's Returns Directive' (2010) 18 *Feminist Legal Studies* 159; S. Peers, 'Irregular Migrants: Can Humane Treatment Be Balanced against Efficient Removal?' (2015) 17 *EJML* 289.

[131] Directive 2011/98/EU on a single application procedure for a single permit for third-country nationals to reside and work in the territory of a Member State and on a common set of rights for third-country workers legally residing in a Member State, OJ 2011, L 343/1. Ireland does not participate in this Directive.

[132] Directive 2003/109/EC concerning the status of third-country nationals who are long-term residents, OJ 2003, L 16/44, as amended by Directive 2011/51/EU, OJ 2011, L 132/1. Ireland is not participating in the Directive. See E. Guild, *The Legal Elements of European Identity* (Dordrecht, Kluwer, 2004) ch. 12; L. Halleskov, 'The Long-Term Residents Directive: A Fulfilment of the Tampere Objective of Near Equality' (2005) 7 *EJML* 181; K. Groenendijk and E. Guild, 'Converging Criteria: Creating an Area of Security of Residence for Europe's Third Country Nationals' (2001) 3 *EJML* 37.

[133] The Stockholm Programme sets out the programme of Union action to be taken between 2010 and 2014 in the area of freedom, security and justice, OJ 2010, C 115/1. This point is at pt. 6.1.4.

(i) The Acquisition of Employment and Long-Term Residence Status

The Directives establish two types of status for non-EU nationals: the resident worker and the long-term resident. These grant comparable but different sets of rights and responsibilities.

Resident worker status is granted by Directive 2011/98 on the following basis:

Article 3

(b) third-country nationals who have been admitted to a Member State for purposes other than work in accordance with Union or national law, who are allowed to work and who hold a residence permit in accordance with Regulation 1030/2002[134]; and

(c) third-country nationals who have been admitted to a Member State for the purpose of work in accordance with Union or national law.

Non-EU nationals meeting these conditions will be issued with a 'single permit' setting out their permission to work.[135] Whilst certain Union requirements must be met, notably that of Union preference, before this permit can be granted, access to this status is largely governed by national law.

EU law governs more extensively the acquisition of long-term resident status. Individuals must apply to the competent national authority, providing documentary evidence showing that they satisfy three conditions.[136]

The first is that they have lawfully and continuously resided for a period of five years in the Member State in question.[137] The question of what constitutes lawful residence is a matter for national law.[138] However, many forms of lawful residence will be insufficient. These include residence as students, those who have applied for international protection, seasonal workers, au pairs and diplomats.[139]

The second is that they have stable and regular resources which are sufficient to maintain themselves and their families without recourse to the host State's social assistance system of the Member State concerned, and, alongside this, have sickness insurance for themselves and their families.[140] There is something pernicious about asking individuals to provide this after they have already lawfully resided five years in a society, and contributed to that society.

Thirdly they can be required to comply with national integration conditions: typically tests to show their knowledge of local culture, language or history.[141] Such tests are historically reserved for the granting of citizenship status where the individual is seeking full membership rights within a society. Kofman has observed, in this, a shift to a limited cultural tolerance of migrants where these have to show that they fit before they are granted important entitlements.

---

[134] This merely sets out the format for the resident permit these must possess. Regulation 1030/2002/EC laying down a uniform format for residence permits for third-country nationals, OJ 2002, L 157/1.

[135] *Ibid*. Article 6.   [136] Directive 2003/109/EC, Article 7(1).

[137] *Ibid*. Article 4(1). Being a family member of a long-term resident does not exempt a non-EU national from the five-year requirement to secure long-term status, *Tahir* v. *Ministero dell'Interno*, C-469/13, EU:C:2014:2094.

[138] *Iida* v. *Stadt Ulm*, C-40/11, EU:C:2012:691.   [139] Directive 2003/109/EC, Article 3(2).   [140] *Ibid*. Article 5(1).

[141] *Ibid*. Article 5(2). Status can also be refused if an individual poses a threat to public policy or public security, *ibid*. Article 6(1).

E. Kofman, 'Citizenship, Migration and the Reassertion of National Identity' (2005) 9 *Citizenship Studies* 453, 461–2

Though the values to which migrants are increasingly required to subscribe are in fact general liberal values such as human rights, the rule of law, tolerance for others, and so on, they are also presented with a certain view of national identity re-inscribing these liberal values within a national framework. Amongst these values, tolerance by the majority is seen to have been stretched to a breaking point, and . . . tolerance is clearly showing its limits. In critiquing the acceptance of tolerance as a quality of European societies, Essed suggests that the dominated is dependent on the goodwill of the dominant who have the power to be tolerant and what, in effect, is a form of cultural control[142]. The identity of the dominant group or 'us' is formulated around its tolerance and adherence to human rights compared to the intolerant other. In the latest Dutch integration measures, it is stipulated that people must integrate into and understand the norms and values of a broadly tolerant Dutch community.

In the United Kingdom, David Blunkett, the Home Secretary, was to announce on the eve of the publication of the Cantle Report on the disturbances, 'We have norms of acceptability and those who come into our home – for that is what it is – should accept these norms'. As he had already stated in the White Paper, newcomers would have to 'develop a sense of belonging, an identity and shared mutual understanding which can be passed from one generation to another'. The White Paper also noted problematic practices, such as arranged marriages, especially where these involved bringing in partners from countries of origin.

Demands for conformity to an unchanging and homogeneous cultural norm have advanced furthest in Denmark. We hear echoes of the earlier British rhetoric of the 1970s of the swamping of the settled population by newcomers. A conservative Danish politician expounded the view that: Denmark is a country that is built around one people . . . Danish Christianity, history, culture, view on democracy and our thoughts about freedom must continue to be the foundation that Denmark rests on . . . We don't want a Denmark where the Danish become a temporary ethnic minority and where our freedom is pulled away.

Long-term resident status may be lost if there is subsequent evidence it was fraudulently acquired or the non-EU national poses a threat to public policy and is expelled as a consequence.[143] Perhaps more draconian is the possibility for loss if she spends more than twelve consecutive months outside the Union.[144] Whilst this is a matter of discretion for the Member States, it is difficult to believe that such a short period indicates any kind of loss of attachment, particularly in light of the length of time required for a person to acquire the status of long-term resident.

(ii) Rights Acquired against the Host State

Worker resident and long-term resident status secure three sets of rights: rights of entry and residence, rights to equal treatment and the right to family reunion.

Worker resident status grants the non-EU national the right to enter and reside in the territory. These rights exist only for the period of the permit. Furthermore, national law may limit the territory to which there is access.[145] By contrast, long-term resident status grants the non-EU

---

[142] P. Essed, *Understanding Everyday Racism: An Interdisciplinary Theory* (London, Sage, 1991) 210.
[143] Directive 2003/109/EC, Article 9(1)(a)–(b).   [144] *Ibid.* Article 9(1)(c).
[145] Directive 2011/98/EU, Article 11(a)–(c).

national the right to reside permanently in the Member State in question.[146] She may be expelled only where she constitutes an actual and sufficiently serious threat to public policy or security.[147] However, before expulsion, Member States must have regard to the duration of her residence in the territory, her age, the consequences for her and her family, and the relative links she has with both her country of residence and country of origin.[148] She must also have the possibility to seek judicial review of any such decision.[149]

Secondly, both worker residents and long-term residents have the right to equal treatment with a State's own nationals with regard to a number of socio-economic entitlements. The differences granted to each reflect, maybe crudely, perceptions about their relative contributions to the host society.

For worker residents the entitlements include a number of economic benefits – most notably, working conditions, freedom of association and recognition of diplomas and other professional qualifications[150] – and tax advantages.[151] They also comprise some social advantages. These include education and vocational training, 'social security branches'[152] and access to goods and services including those made available to the public such as housing, and employment advice services.[153] Many of these social advantages are subject to qualifications, however. Equal access to education and vocational training can be limited to those in employment, can exclude non-EU nationals who entered as students and can exclude maintenance grants and loans.[154] Access to social security branches can be limited to those who have been in work for more than six months.[155] Finally, access to housing can be restricted if a State chooses.[156] The default is, however, that non-EU worker residents will receive these benefits. Access will only be denied if the Member State has expressly indicated that it is excluding non-EU workers from receiving them.[157]

Long-term residents secure equal access to a wider array of entitlements.[158]

Directive 2003/109/EC, Article 11

(1) Long-term residents shall enjoy equal treatment with nationals as regards:

(a) access to employment and self-employed activity, provided such activities do not entail even occasional involvement in the exercise of public authority, and conditions of employment and working conditions, including conditions regarding dismissal and remuneration;

(b) education and vocational training, including study grants in accordance with national law;

---

[146] Directive 2003/109/EC, Article 8.   [147] *Ibid.* Article 12(1).   [148] *Ibid.* Article 12(3).   [149] *Ibid.* Article 12(4).

[150] Directive 2011/98/EU, Article 12(1)(a), (b) and (d).

[151] *Ibid.* Article 12(1)(f). These can be denied to non-resident family members, *ibid.* Article 12(2)(c). Their accrued pension rights are also treated in the same way as that State's own nationals when these reside in a third country, *ibid.* Article 12(4).

[152] These comprise a number of benefits: invalidity, survivors', unemployment, pre-retirement, family, accidents at work and occupational diseases, as well as death grant. Regulation 883/2004 on the coordination of social security systems, OJ 2004, L 166/1, Article 3(1).

[153] Directive 2011/98/EU, Article 12(1)(c), (e), (g)–(h).   [154] *Ibid.* Article 12(2)(a).   [155] *Ibid.* Article 12(2)(b).

[156] *Ibid.* Article 12(2)(d).

[157] A failure to extend these benefits to non EU workers will, therefore, still allow them the benefit as this does not amount to an exclusion, *Martinez Silva* v. *INPS*, C-449/16, EU:C:2017:485.

[158] Member States can grant additional benefits beyond these if they wish, Directive 2003/109/EC, Article 11(5).

(c) recognition of professional diplomas, certificates and other qualifications, in accordance with the relevant national procedures;

(d) social security, social assistance and social protection as defined by national law;

(e) tax benefits;

(f) access to goods and services and the supply of goods and services made available to the public and to procedures for obtaining housing;

(g) freedom of association and affiliation and membership of an organisation representing workers or employers or of any organisation whose members are engaged in a specific occupation, including the benefits conferred by such organisations, without prejudice to the national provisions on public policy and public security;

(h) free access to the entire territory of the Member State concerned, within the limits provided for by the national legislation for reasons of security.

Notwithstanding this, the provision is less generous than it might appear due to a series of limitations.[159] The most significant exclusion is in Article 11(4):

Member States may limit equal treatment in respect of social assistance and social protection to core benefits.

The Preamble to the Directive states that the notion of 'core benefits' is one for national law, but must cover at least minimum income support, assistance in case of illness and pregnancy, parental assistance and long-term care.[160] The breadth of this exception was addressed in *Kamberaj*. An Albanian who enjoyed permanent resident status in Italy was refused social housing by the municipality of Bolzano as the fund allocating for housing for non-EU nationals had been exhausted. The authorities argued that Article 11(4) granted Member States a discretion to decide that housing was not a core benefit. The Court rejected this argument.

Kamberaj v. *IPES*, C–571/10, EU:C:2012:233

85 It must, first, be observed that the list set out in recital 13 which illustrates the concept of 'core benefits' stated in Article 11(4) of Directive 2003/109 is not exhaustive, as is clear from the use of the wording 'at least'. The fact that no express reference is made in that recital to housing benefits does not therefore mean that they do not constitute core benefits to which the principle of equal treatment must in any event be applied.

86 Second, it must be noted that, since the integration of third-country nationals who are long-term residents in the Member States and the right of those nationals to equal treatment in the sectors listed in Article 11(1) of Directive 2003/109 is the general rule, the derogation provided for in Article 11(4) thereof must be interpreted strictly . . .

89 Finally, it must be noted that the reference to national law in recital 13 in the preamble to Directive 2003/109 is limited to the modalities of the grant of the benefits in question, that is the laying down of the conditions of access and of the level of such benefits and of the procedures relating thereto.

---

[159] They can be excluded from public sector employment and activities like EU citizens, *ibid*. Article 11(2)–(3).

[160] *Ibid*. Preamble, para. 13.

90 The meaning and scope of the concept of 'core benefits' in Article 11(4) of Directive 2003/109 must therefore be sought taking into account the context of that article and the objective pursued by that directive, namely the integration of third-country nationals who have resided legally and continuously in the Member States.

91 Article 11(4) of Directive 2003/109 must be understood as allowing Member States to limit the equal treatment enjoyed by holders of the status conferred by Directive 2003/109, with the exception of social assistance or social protection benefits granted by the public authorities, at national, regional or local level, which enable individuals to meet their basic needs such as food, accommodation and health.

92 In that regard, it should be recalled that, according to Article 34 of the Charter, the Union recognises and respects the right to social and housing assistance so as to ensure a decent existence for all those who lack sufficient resources. It follows that, in so far as the benefit in question in the main proceedings fulfils the purpose set out in that article of the Charter, it cannot be considered, under European Union law, as not being part of core benefits within the meaning of Article 11(4) of Directive 2003/109 . . .

The core paragraph in the judgment is paragraph 91 which enlarges the notion of core benefits to comprise those benefits which 'enable individuals to meet their basic needs such as food, accommodation and health'. This is a generous interpretation of Article 11(4) but few would argue that States should not provide for the basic needs of those who have been at least five years resident in their societies.

The third right is that of family reunion. This is not granted by either of the two Directives described above but by Directive 2003/86/EC on the right to family reunification.[161] Its relationship with the other two Directives is an awkward one.

Directive 2003/86/EC, Article 3

(1) This Directive shall apply where the sponsor is holding a residence permit issued by a Member State for a period of validity of one year or more who has reasonable prospects of obtaining the right of permanent residence, if the members of his or her family are third country nationals of whatever status.[162]

The right is thus granted to many residents who are far away from having long-term resident status. On the other hand, not all worker residents secure this right as the permit must be for one year or more and there must be a reasonable prospect of permanent residence. If the exclusion of many worker residents from the right to family reunion is harsh, most notably where they have a long contract of employment but no prospect of permanent residence, the Directive also sets out a very narrow conception of the family. Member States are only required to admit the spouse of the sponsor and minor children (including those adopted) over whom the sponsor or spouse has exclusive custody.[163]

The right to family reunification is also a contingent one. Any family member may be refused entry for reasons of public policy, public health or public security.[164] Member States may also

---

[161] OJ 2003, L 251/12. Ireland is not participating in this Directive.

[162] The Directive also applies where national measures grant a right to permanent residence independently of the Directive. Refugees benefit from the Directive, *ibid.* Articles 9–12 but not those seeking international protection, *ibid.* Article 3(2).

[163] *Ibid.* Article 4(2).   [164] *Ibid.* Article 6.

require that the sponsor demonstrate sufficient resources to support herself and her family without recourse to social assistance; sickness insurance for all the family; and can provide family accommodation that is regarded as normal for the region and complies with health and safety requirements.[165] This assessment can be a prospective one so that authorities look not merely at whether the sponsor has sufficient resources on the date of their application but at whether they are likely to have it in the future.[166] If this introduces some uncertainty as to how far domestic authorities can look into the future, the amount of resources demanded cannot be excessive. In *Chakroun* a Dutch requirement that a sponsor earn 120 per cent of the minimum income was found to be illegal.[167] The Court found that the sponsor need only show stable and regular resources sufficient to maintain himself and the members of his family in the absence of specific needs, which would, in this instance, be the minimum wage. Recourse to the social assistance system for specific needs such as tax refunds or local authority schemes to supplement his income would not deny him the right to family reunification.

There are two more controversial requirements. First, Member States are permitted to require the sponsor to have lawfully resided for two years in the territory before her family can join her: a period of separation which seems draconian.[168] Secondly, Member States can require family members to comply with 'integration' measures, such as language assessments and tests on the culture, politics and history of the host State.[169] The Court has stated that these tests must not go beyond what is necessary 'to attain the objective of facilitating' the integration of the family members,[170] but there is obscurity as to what this means. Particularly contentiously, these tests can be applied to children as young as 12 years old where they arrive independently of the rest of the family.[171] In exercising that discretion, the Court has stated that Member States have to observe the right to respect for family life and the interests of the child.[172] There is an air of disingenuousness in this as it is impossible to conceive of circumstances where separating a 12-year-old child from their family because they fail an integration test has regard either to the interests of the child or respects family life.

Family members are granted a limited number of rights of equal access once they have entered the European Union: education, employment and self-employment, vocational guidance and training.[173] Member States may restrict access to employment and self-employment during family member's first twelve months of residence.[174] Significant entitlements are lacking, notably social assistance and social security.

6 'SUSPICIOUS FOREIGNERS': THE EU REGIME ON INTERNATIONAL PROTECTION

Until the mid-1980s, Member States regimes for asylum seekers were liberal and the number of asylum seekers entering the Union vis-à-vis other forms of migrants were quite limited. However asylum applications to the Union tripled from 200,000 p.a. in 1980 to 700,000 p.a. in 1990.[175]

---

[165] *Ibid.* Article 7(1).   [166] *Khachab v. Subdelegación del Gobierno en Álava*, C-558/14, EU:C:2016:285.
[167] *Chakroun v. Minister van Buitenlandse Zaken*, C-578/08, EU:C:2010:117.   [168] Directive 2003/86/EC, Article 8(1).
[169] *Ibid.* Article 7(2).   [170] *C and A*, C-257/17, EU:C:2018:876, para. 62.   [171] Directive 2003/86, Article 4(1).
[172] *Parliament v. Council*, C-540/03, EU:C:2006:429.   [173] Directive 2003/86/EC, Article 13(1).
[174] *Ibid.* Article 13(2).
[175] For trends see ECRE, *Asylum Trends in 35 Industrialised Countries 1982–2002* (Brussels, ECRE, 2004).

This led to increasingly draconian measures being taken to deny asylum seekers many welfare benefits.[176] In 1986, Denmark introduced a law whereby it would not hear an asylum seeker's claim if she could have applied for protection in a safe third country – that is, one she had passed through on route to its territory. This law marked the beginning of a swathe of restrictive national legislation being enacted across the Union, with the most high-profile being the German amendment to the unconditional right to asylum in its constitution in 1993.[177]

Tensions have materialised most acutely over two aspects of the regime, in particular. The first goes to which State is to consider the asylum seeker's application for international protection, as that State will have to incur the costs and responsibilities of managing the process. There are, thus, incentives for States to try and pass the buck to other States here. The system for preventing this and allocating responsibilities between Member States is known as the Dublin regime, after the 1990 Dublin Convention which put in place the central elements which remain in place today.[178] The second concerns the entitlements offered to those applying for international protection once they arrive in the Union. For, until an applicant's need for protection has been established as bona fide, there is institutional suspicion over whether she is merely engaged in economic migration or welfare tourism.

(i) The Dublin Regime and the Allocation of National Responsibilities for International Protection

The Dublin regime is now set out in Regulation 604/2013/EU.[179] The thrust of this Regulation is centred around two principles. The first is that the Union is a one-stop shop. Persons seeking international protection can make only a single application within the Union rather than going from one Member State to another until their application is successful.

Regulation 604/2013/EU, Article 3

(1) Member States shall examine any application for international protection by a third-country national or a stateless person who applies on the territory of any one of them, including at the border or in the transit zones. The application shall be examined by a single Member State, which shall be the one which the criteria set out in Chapter III indicate is responsible.

This principle has had limited success, with the Commission finding that in 2014, for example, 24 per cent of all applicants had made multiple claims for asylum.[180]

---

[176] See Regulation 604/2013/EU establishing the criteria and mechanisms for determining the Member State responsible for examining an application for international protection lodged in one of the Member States by a third-country national or a stateless person, OJ 2013, L 180/31.

[177] On asylum law in 1980s and 1990s Europe see I. Boccardi, *Europe & Refugees: Towards an EU Asylum Policy* (The Hague, Kluwer, 2002). On the wider ethical issues, see M. Gibney, *The Ethics and Politics of Asylum: Liberal Democracy and the Response to Refugees* (Cambridge University Press, 2004).

[178] Convention determining the State responsible for examining applications for asylum lodged in one of the Member States of the European Communities – Dublin Convention, OJ 1997, C 254/1.

[179] Regulation 604/2013/EU establishing the criteria and mechanisms for determining the Member State responsible for examining an application for international protection lodged in one of the Member States by a third-country national or a stateless person, OJ 2013, L 180/31. Ireland participates in this Regulation, as do all the non-EU Schengen States.

[180] European Commission, 'Proposal for a Regulation Establishing the Criteria and Mechanisms for Determining the Member State Responsible for Examining an Application For International Protection Lodged in one of the Member States by a Third-Country National or a Stateless Person (Recast)', COM(2016)270, 11–12.

The second principle goes to the establishment of criteria for determining which State will consider the application for international protection. As Article 3(1) indicates, Chapter III sets out the criteria. The hierarchy of criteria provided is bedevilled by exceptions but, broadly speaking, its (most important first) order of priority is:

- for unaccompanied minors, the State where a family member is present provided it is in the best interests of the child[181]
- the State of any family member who has received or is seeking international protection provided that the parties have expressed their desire for that in writing
- in the case of multiple applications by family members which are close enough in time to be considered together, the State in which the largest number are present or, failing that, the State where the oldest is present
- the State which issued a valid residence permit or visa for the applicant
- the State by which the applicant irregularly entered into the Union
- the State which allowed the applicant to enter the Union by waiving his visa requirement
- if the application was made in an international transit area, the State where the application was made.[182]

If the applicant does not fall within one of the categories above, the State where she first lodged her application for international protection is responsible for considering it.[183] The consequence is that the State where the applicant first entered the Union ('first entry') is usually the State is responsible for considering the application, be it because it issued the applicant a visa, waived that requirement or because the applicant irregularly entered the Union there or made her application for international protection there. A 2013 study found that this first entry is the most common reason given for State transferring an applicant back to another State, accounting for 53 per cent of cases.[184] More recently, a 2017 UNHCR study found that many States often ignored the family criteria and focused instead on whether the applicant first entered the Union there in determining whether they should hear the application.[185]

This working principle of first entry results in applicant burdens not being shared equitably between Member States. It puts greater burdens on States at the geographical periphery of the Union, particularly when applicants are arriving by land or by sea. In the second quarter of 2018, for example, Cyprus and Greece had both over 12 times as many applications per capita of population as Denmark, 70 times as many as Portugal and 180 times as many as Slovakia.[186]

This raises not simply a question of equity, of richer States piggybacking on poorer States, but also one of fundamental rights. The resources of the latter States may be overwhelmed with the consequence that they may provide unacceptable reception conditions for asylum seekers, fail to keep families together, offer inadequate support to trauma victims or do a negligent job of examining whether the applicant warrants international protection. In October 2017, for

---

[181] If there is more than one family member, the State where the application was made is to consider which was in the best interests of the child. Regulation 604/2013, Article 8(3).

[182] *Ibid*. Articles 7–15.   [183] *Ibid*. Article 3(2).

[184] ECRE, *Dublin II Regulation: Lives on Hold* (Brussels, ECRE, 2013) 131.

[185] UN High Commissioner for Refugees, *Left in Limbo: UNHCR Study on the Implementation of the Dublin III Regulation* (Geneva, UNHCR, 2017) 86–8.

[186] https://ec.europa.eu/eurostat/statistics-explained/images/a/a0/Table_2_Asylum_applicants%2C_Q2_2017_%E2% 80%93_Q2_2018.png.

example, nineteen human rights organisations wrote an open letter to the Greek Prime Minister about the reception conditions in the Aegean islands in Greece. They described the situation in Lesbos, one Greek island, in the following terms:

> On Lesbos, more than 5,400 people live in overcrowded tents and containers, with little access to proper shelter, food, water, sanitation, health care, or protection. Dozens of people, including very young children, are crammed into tents with only a canvas cloth separating one family from another. The living conditions are particularly harsh for pregnant women to endure, and place themselves and their babies' health at risk. Summer camping tents, designed to accommodate not more than two people, are now holding families of up to seven. Accessing water, sanitation and food is particularly difficult for the many people with physical disabilities – for example, people using wheelchairs simply cannot reach these basic services. Single women in the hotspots report harassment by some of the men. And some asylum seekers have gone through their asylum interview without having had the requisite vulnerability assessment critical for determining both the asylum pathway available to them and the care they may require to prevent further deterioration of their health. These conditions have a devastating impact on the long-term well-being of people trapped there.
>
> A number of human rights and humanitarian non-governmental organisations, including Médecins Sans Frontières (Doctors Without Borders) and Human Rights Watch, have documented the impact of these conditions on the mental health of asylum seekers and migrants – including incidents of self-injury, suicide attempts, anxiety, aggression, and depression. Professionals who have interacted with the asylum seekers note that in many cases, the psychological distress they experience has been factored and/or exacerbated by the policy of 'containing' them on islands, which also impedes their access to adequate support and mental health care.[187]

The criteria were thrown into doubt in 2015 with the huge increase in asylum seekers crossing from Turkey into Greece. This led to accusations that Greece was not only failing to provide these adequate care but failing to register them or process them through an external frontier control as required by the Schengen Borders Code. Most asylum seekers used Greece as a transit point before seeking international protection elsewhere in the European Union. Further doubts were generated by the German government's decision in August 2015 to suspend their application on humanitarian grounds for applicants from Afghanistan, Iraq and Syria, and not ask other States to take back asylum seekers because these States were responsible under these criteria for considering their applications.[188] By contrast, Hungary, in particular, took hostile measures to prevent applicants entering its territory so that it would have to consider their applications. These included the construction of border fences, criminalisation of irregular entry, immediate physical deportations to the Serbian border, beatings and dog attacks.[189]

Since then, three alternative forms of allocation of responsibilities have been proposed.

---

[187] *Joint Letter to Prime Minister Tsipras re Deteriorating Conditions for Asylum Seekers Trapped on the Aegean Islands*, 23 October 2017, www.hrw.org/news/2017/10/23/joint-letter-prime-minister-tsipras-re-deteriorating-conditions-asylum-seekers.

[188] There is provision for doing this in the Regulation on humanitarian grounds. Regulation 604/2013, Article 17(2).

[189] 'Hungary: UNHCR Concerned about New Restrictive Law, Increased Reports of Violence, and a Deterioration of the Situation at Border with Serbia', 16 July 2016, www.unhcr.org/news/briefing/2016/7/5788aae94/hungary-unhcr-concerned-new-restrictive-law-increased-reports-violence.html.

The first proposal is that where large numbers of asylum seekers arrive at the external frontier of an EU State, it should be possible for a State to admit them to the Union on humanitarian grounds without having to take full responsibility for considering all their applications, with this presumably worked out between member States subsequently. This argument was raised in *Jafari*. Three Afghan sisters entered the Union via Croatia. The authorities did not register them but put them on a bus to Slovenia. From there, they went on to Austria where they sought international protection. The Austrian authorities claimed that their case should be heard by Croatia as, under Article 13 of the Dublin Regulation, it was responsible as the State which had let them enter the Union irregularly. The Court of Justice agreed with them.

Jafari, C–646/16, EU:C:2017:586

87 The application of the various criteria . . . , should, as a general rule, enable the responsibility for examining an application for international protection that may be lodged by a third-country national to be allocated to the Member State which that national first entered or stayed in upon entering in the territory of the Member States . . .

89 In the light of the foregoing, the criteria . . . cannot, without calling into question the overall scheme of that regulation, be interpreted to the effect that a Member State is absolved of its responsibility where it has decided to authorise, on humanitarian grounds, the entry into its territory of a third-country national who does not have a visa and is not entitled to waiver of a visa.

90 Furthermore, the fact that, as in the present case, the third-country national in question entered the territory of the Member States under the watch of the competent authorities without in any way evading border control is not decisive . . .

91 The purpose of the responsibility criteria . . . is not to penalise unlawful conduct on the part of the third-country national in question but to determine the Member State responsible by taking into account the role played by that Member State when that national entered the territory of the Member States.

92 It follows that a third-country national admitted into the territory of one Member State, without fulfilling the entry conditions generally imposed in that Member State, for the purpose of transit to another Member State in order to lodge an application for international protection there, must be regarded as having 'irregularly crossed' the border of that first Member State within the meaning of Article 13(1) of the Dublin III Regulation, irrespective of whether that crossing was tolerated or authorised in breach of the applicable rules or whether it was authorised on humanitarian grounds by way of derogation from the entry conditions generally imposed on third-country nationals.

93 The fact that the border crossing occurred in a situation characterised by the arrival of an unusually large number of third-country nationals seeking international protection cannot affect the interpretation or application of Article 13(1) of the Dublin III Regulation.

94 It should be noted, in the first place, that the EU legislature has taken account of the risk that such a situation may occur and therefore provided the Member States with means intended to be capable of responding to that situation appropriately, without, however, providing for the application, in that case, of a specific body of rules for determining the Member State responsible.

95 Thus, Article 33 of the Dublin III Regulation establishes a mechanism for early warning, preparedness and crisis management designed to implement preventive Action Plans in order, *inter alia*, to prevent the application of that regulation being jeopardised due to a substantiated risk of particular pressure being placed on a Member State's asylum system.

96 In parallel, Article 3(1) of the Dublin III Regulation provides for the application of the procedure established by that regulation to any application for international protection by a third-country national or a stateless

person on the territory of any one of the Member States, without precluding applications which are lodged in a situation characterised by the arrival of an unusually large number of third-country nationals seeking international protection.

If, to date, the Court of Justice has been unwilling to countenance circumstances where the Dublin criteria will not apply, this is not true of the other EU Institutions. The second proposal has been to allocate responsibilities on the basis of a series of criteria, which include GDP per capita of host States, population size, current unemployment rates and current number of asylum seekers and refugees situated in the host territory. In 2015, the Council adopted two decisions providing for the relocation of asylum seekers from Italy and Greece. The first provided for the relocation of 40,000 asylum seekers with other States to volunteer to take these, facilitated by the payment of €6,000 for each asylum seeker.[190] The second was more controversial. It provided for the compulsory reallocation of 120,000 asylum seekers from Italy and Greece with each State allocated a number of asylum seekers it should take, which were calculated according to the criteria outlined above.[191] Slovakia and Hungary, supported by Poland, challenged this decision unsuccessfully before the Court.[192] The legal validity of the decision did not make it easy to operationalise. A European Parliament Report found that at the end of 2016, over twelve months after the decisions, just under 12,000 asylum seekers out of a possible total of 160,000 had been relocated. The reason was Member State resistance. Nine member States had relocated less than 5 per cent of the asylum seekers for whom they were responsible and three (Austria, Hungary and Poland) had not relocated a single one.[193] Whatever the equity and merits of this approach, it has buckled under national resistance.[194]

Faced with this intransigence, the third solution proposed by the European Council is that those rescued in the Mediterranean should be processed through 'controlled centres'.

6. On EU territory, those who are saved, according to international law, should be taken charge of, on the basis of a shared effort, through the transfer in controlled centres set up in Member States, only on a voluntary basis, where rapid and secure processing would allow, with full EU support, to distinguish between irregular migrants, who will be returned, and those in need of international protection, for whom the principle of solidarity would apply.[195]

Applicants would be detained in these centres whilst it is ascertained whether they warrant international protection. The features of these controlled centres are voluntary participation,

---

[190] Decision 2015/1523/EU establishing provisional measures in the area of international protection for the benefit of Italy and of Greece, OJ 2015, L 239/146.

[191] Decision 2015/1601/EU establishing provisional measures in the area of international protection for the benefit of Italy and Greece, OJ 2015, L 248/80.

[192] *Slovakia and Hungary* v. *Council*, C-643/15 and C-647/15, EU:C:2017:631.

[193] *Implementation of the 2015 Council Decisions establishing Provisional Measures in the area of International Protection for the Benefit of Italy and of Greece* (Brussels, Directorate General for Internal Policies Policy Department C: Citizens' Rights And Constitutional Affairs, PE 583 132, European Parliament, 2017) 27. A total of 33,846 asylum seekers had been relocated by 7 March 2018, European Commission, 'Progress Report on the Implementation of the European Agenda on Migration', COM(2018)250, Annex 4.

[194] On this see M. Scipioni, 'Failing Forward in EU Migration Policy? EU Integration after the 2015 Asylum and Migration Crisis' (2018) 25 *JEPP* 1357.

[195] Conclusions of the European Council, 28 June 2018.

dispersion and Union support. States can choose whether or not to operate one. These centres will be spread across the Union with applicants possibly sent to ones far away from the coastal waters where they were picked up. Union support will take the form of paying States €6,000 for each application considered and providing an average of 500 professionals to support each centre.[196]

Central challenges will be the quality of conditions offered by these centres and the quality of the decisions taken by them. Human rights organisations have criticised earlier 'hotspots' where large numbers of non-EU nationals were processed, arguing that facilities were simply inadequate for the sheer number of people who had to be received and considered.[197] The dispersion of these centres across the Union might, on the one hand, alleviate pressures as they may be sited in better-resourced States rather than many current reception centres on the periphery of the Union who currently face unpredictable numbers of asylum seekers. Against this, however, the Union is providing few incentives for States to resource these controlled centres well. States are paid a fixed amount which is unrelated to the costs involved or the quality of the job done. This may induce some to be indifferent to the quality of these centres.

(ii) The Dublin Regime and the Humanity of the Transfer

The other central issue of concern about the Dublin Regulation is the humanity of the transfer itself in which a Member State agrees to take back an applicant from another Member State in order to process her application.

One troubling aspect is negative mutual recognition. Whilst Member States are not bound to recognise positive decisions by other authorities granting international protection, the 'one-stop shop' principle in Article 3(1) requires them to recognise decisions by other national authorities denying that status. When they make transfers, they consequently recognise the capacity of other Member States to consider the claims of international protection in an equivalent manner.[198] However, there are huge variations in whether States find international protection to be warranted. In 2017, therefore, 68 per cent of first instance decisions in Slovakia were positive whilst it was only 12 per cent in its neighbour, the Czech Republic. Some 89 per cent of Irish first instance decisions were positive whilst this was the case in only 29 per cent of French decisions.[199] It matters, therefore, where an asylum seeker's case is heard, and the Dublin Regulation adds an element of chance to her prospects of safe haven.

There is also the question of the treatment of the applicant, be it during the transfer itself or in the State to which she is transferred. The early response of the Court of Justice was shameful. It stated that transfers should occur even where they resulted in violation of the fundamental rights of the applicant. The only circumstance in which they should not occur was where there were

---

[196] https://ec.europa.eu/home-affairs/sites/homeaffairs/files/what-we-do/policies/european-agenda-migration/20180724_factsheet-controlled-centres-eu-member-states_en.pdf.

[197] ECRE, *Wrong Counts and Closing Doors: The Reception of Refugees and Asylum Seekers in Europe* (Brussels, ECRE, 2016) 19–25.

[198] For long-standing criticism, see A. Hurwitz, 'The 1990 Dublin Convention: A Comprehensive Assessment' (1999) 11 *IJRL* 646; R. Marx, 'Adjusting the Dublin Convention: New Approaches to Member State Responsibility for Asylum Applications' (2001) 3 *EJML* 7; G. Noll, 'Formalism v. Empiricism: Some Reflections on the Dublin Convention on the Occasion of Recent European Case Law' (2001) 70 *NJIL* 161.

[199] https://ec.europa.eu/eurostat/documents/2995521/8817675/3-19042018-AP-EN.pdf/748e8fae-2cfb-4e75-a388-f06f6ce8ff58.

substantial grounds for believing that there were 'systemic flaws' which would result in the applicant being subject to inhuman and degrading treatment.[200] This case law was incorporated into the Dublin Regulation.

Regulation 604/2013, Article 3

(2) Where it is impossible to transfer an applicant to the Member State primarily designated as responsible because there are substantial grounds for believing that there are systemic flaws in the asylum procedure and in the reception conditions for applicants in that Member State, resulting in a risk of inhuman or degrading treatment within the meaning of Article 4 EUCFR, the determining Member State shall continue to examine the criteria set out in Chapter III in order to establish whether another Member State can be designated as responsible.

The law was revisited in *C.K.*[201] This concerned a Syrian woman who was suffering from post-natal depression from the birth of her child. Her psychological distress was such that there were concerns about her harming herself and others. In addition, she was carrying a high risk pregnancy. She had entered the Union with a visa for Croatia but had then gone to Slovenia where she sought international protection. The Slovenian authorities sought to transfer her back to Croatia. Nobody argued that medical facilities in Croatia were deficient. It was argued, however, that the removal from the centre in Slovenia might exacerbate her psychiatric condition and might also carry dangers given the nature of her pregnancy. This breached Article 4 EUCFR as it subjected her to inhuman and degrading treatment.

C.K., C–578/16 PPU, EU:C:2017:127

62 The Court has … already held that, with regard to the rights granted to asylum seekers, the Dublin III Regulation differs in essential respects from the Dublin II Regulation (see, to that effect, judgment of 7 June 2016, *Ghezelbash*, C–63/15, EU:C:2016:409, paragraph 34).

63 As regards the fundamental rights that are conferred on them, in addition to the codification, in Article 3(2) of the Dublin III Regulation, of the case-law arising from the judgment of 21 December 2011, *N. S. and Others* (C–411/10 and C–493/10, EU:C:2011:865) … the EU legislature stressed, in recitals 32 and 39 of that regulation, that the Member States are bound, in the application of that regulation, by the case-law of the European Court of Human Rights and by Article 4 of the Charter.

64 More specifically, as regards decisions to transfer, first, the EU legislature made their legality subject to the granting, *inter alia*, to the asylum seeker concerned, in Article 27 of the Dublin III Regulation, of the right to an effective remedy before a court against that decision, the scope of which covers both the factual and legal circumstances surrounding it. Secondly, it set out, in Article 29 of that regulation, the rules for those transfers in greater detail, something which it had not done in the Dublin II Regulation.

65 It follows from all of the preceding considerations that the transfer of an asylum seeker within the framework of the Dublin III Regulation can take place only in conditions which preclude that transfer from

---

[200] *NS* v. *Secretary of State for the Home Department; ME* v. *Refugee Applications Commissioner*, C–411/10 and C–493/10, EU:C:2011:865, para. 86; *Abdullahi*, C–394/12, EU:C:2013:813.

[201] On the intellectual gymnastics accompanying this see K. Lenaerts, 'La Vie après l'avis: Exploring the Principle of Mutual (Yet Not Blind) Trust' (2017) 54 *CMLRev* 805, 828–34.

resulting in a real risk of the person concerned suffering inhuman or degrading treatment, within the meaning of Article 4 of the Charter.

66   In that regard, it is not possible to exclude from the outset the possibility that, given the particularly serious state of health of an asylum seeker, his transfer pursuant to the Dublin III Regulation may result in such a risk for him . . .

71   In the present case, neither the decision to refer nor the material in the case file shows that there are substantial grounds for believing that there are systemic flaws in the asylum procedure and the conditions for the reception of asylum seekers in Croatia, with regard to access to health care in particular, which is, moreover, not alleged by the appellants in the main proceedings. On the contrary, it is apparent from that decision that the Republic of Croatia has, in, *inter alia*, the town of Kutina, a reception centre designed specifically for vulnerable persons, where they have access to medical care provided by a doctor and, in urgent cases, by the local hospital or even by the hospital in Zagreb. Furthermore, it appears that the Slovenian authorities have obtained from the Croatian authorities an assurance that the appellants in the main proceedings would receive any necessary medical treatment . . .

73   That said, it cannot be ruled out that the transfer of an asylum seeker whose state of health is particularly serious may, in itself, result, for the person concerned, in a real risk of inhuman or degrading treatment within the meaning of Article 4 of the Charter, irrespective of the quality of the reception and the care available in the Member State responsible for examining his application.

74   In that context, it must be held that, in circumstances in which the transfer of an asylum seeker with a particularly serious mental or physical illness would result in a real and proven risk of a significant and permanent deterioration in his state of health, that transfer would constitute inhuman and degrading treatment, within the meaning of that article.

C.K. can be read narrowly. It went only to whether the transfer itself violated fundamental rights rather than the conditions of reception within Croatia or how Croatian evaluations of applications for international protection. However, the tenor of the judgment is that the conditions and procedures in the States to which asylum seekers are being returned must also be subjected to much more rigorous vetting for compliance with fundamental rights. It occurred against a context in which a number of authorities were refusing to transfer applicants back to Greece, Bulgaria, Italy and Hungary because of civil liberties concerns about the situations there.[202] A more robust approach to safeguarding the fundamental rights of asylum seekers is, therefore, likely.

(iii)   The Right to Remain Pending Examination of the Application

The process for securing international protection begins with the applicant making an application for protection to competent national authorities, which will be registered by these.[203] Typically, this will involve the applicant simply saying to a border guard, immigration official or police officer that they are claiming asylum. There is, then, a responsibility on the applicant to

---

[202] European Commission, *Evaluation of the Implementation of the Dublin III Regulation: Final Report* (Brussels, DG Migration and Home Affairs, 2016) 21–2. Transfers have also been stopped by the German courts, most notably 2 BvR 157/17 *H*. Judgment of 8 May 2017 (German Constitutional Court).

[203] Directive 2013/32/EU on common procedures for granting and withdrawing international protection, OJ 2013, L 180/60, Article 6(1). Ireland does not participate in this Directive.

lodge the application as soon as possible,[204] and she must be given an effective opportunity to do so.[205] She will then usually have a right to individual examination of their application.

Directive 2013/32, Article 10

(1) Member States shall ensure that applications for international protection are neither rejected nor excluded from examination on the sole ground that they have not been made as soon as possible.

(2) When examining applications for international protection, the determining authority shall first determine whether the applicants qualify as refugees and, if not, determine whether the applicants are eligible for subsidiary protection.

(3) Member States shall ensure that decisions by the determining authority on applications for international protection are taken after an appropriate examination. To that end, Member States shall ensure that:
   (a) applications are examined and decisions are taken individually, objectively and impartially;
   (b) precise and up-to-date information is obtained from various sources, such as EASO and UNHCR and relevant international human rights organisations, as to the general situation prevailing in the countries of origin of applicants and, where necessary, in countries through which they have transited, and that such information is made available to the personnel responsible for examining applications and taking decisions;
   (c) the personnel examining applications and taking decisions know the relevant standards applicable in the field of asylum and refugee law;
   (d) the personnel examining applications and taking decisions have the possibility to seek advice, whenever necessary, from experts on particular issues, such as medical, cultural, religious, child-related or gender issues.

(4) The authorities referred to in Chapter v. shall, through the determining authority or the applicant or otherwise, have access to the general information referred to in paragraph 3(b), necessary for the fulfilment of their task.

(5) Member States shall provide for rules concerning the translation of documents relevant for the examination of applications.

Member States are in principle, required to come to a decision within six months, albeit that this can be extended.[206] Applicants are entitled to remain within the Member State whilst the application is being considered.

Directive 2013/32/EU, Article 9

(1) Applicants shall be allowed to remain in the Member State, for the sole purpose of the procedure, until the determining authority has made a decision in accordance with the procedures [set out] ... This right to remain shall not constitute an entitlement to a residence permit.

This examination must involve explaining the time frame and process to the applicant, providing interpreter services, and giving her an opportunity for a personal interview.[207] The applicant also

---

[204] Lodging the application will involve filling out a form setting out the case for international protection. The application is not to be penalised for late lodging, *ibid*. Article 10(1), but a failure to lodge will result in the application being seen as withdrawn, *ibid*. Article 28.

[205] *Ibid*. Article 6(2).   [206] *Ibid*. Article 31(3).   [207] *Ibid*. Article 12(a), 12(b) and 14(1).

has a right to legal services at her own cost.[208] The onus can be put on the applicant to furnish proof of all the elements necessary to substantiate her case.[209]

The applicant is entitled to a decision in writing setting out the reasons for the decision.[210] She is entitled to appeal this decision before a court or tribunal and to an effective remedy where this appeal is successful.[211] The applicant has a right to legal assistance for this appeal,[212] but not to a hearing if the court or tribunal considers that it is able to carry out an examination on the basis of the case file and the applicant's earlier interview.[213] The appeal can be on both questions of fact and question of law and can raise new facts that have come to light since the original decision.[214] However, these new facts must be sufficiently specific that they can be properly considered, and, to be considered as new evidence, they must be sufficiently distinct from evidence presented at the initial interview.[215]

There are, however, restrictions on the right to individual examination of the applicant's case. The application will not be examined if another State is responsible under the Dublin Regulation. There are a number of other circumstances where it will be declared inadmissible and not be considered.

Directive 2013/32/EU, Article 33

(2) Member States may consider an application for international protection as inadmissible only if:
   (a) another Member State has granted international protection;
   (b) a country which is not a Member State is considered as a first country of asylum for the applicant, pursuant to Article 35;
   (c) a country which is not a Member State is considered as a safe third country for the applicant, pursuant to Article 38;
   (d) the application is a subsequent application, where no new elements or findings relating to the examination of whether the applicant qualifies as a beneficiary of international protection . . . have arisen or have been presented by the applicant; or
   (e) a dependant of the applicant lodges an application, after he or she has . . . consented to have his or her case be part of an application lodged on his or her behalf, and there are no facts relating to the dependant's situation which justify a separate application.

Two concepts above require explanation: 'first country of asylum' and 'safe third country'.

The first country of asylum is a State to which the applicant will be readmitted and where she has already been given safe haven, be it because she has been admitted as a refugee or because she enjoys sufficient protection there, including benefiting from the principle of *non-refoulement*.[216]

---

[208] *Ibid.* Article 22(1).
[209] Directive 2011/95/EU on standards for the qualification of third-country nationals or stateless persons as beneficiaries of international protection, for a uniform status for refugees or for persons eligible for subsidiary protection, and for the content of the protection granted, OJ 2011, L 337/9, Article 4(1).
[210] Directive 2013/32/EU, Article 11(1).   [211] *Ibid.* Article 46.   [212] *Ibid.* Article 20(1).
[213] *Sacko* v. *Commissione Territoriale per il riconoscimento della protezione internazionale di Milano*, C-348/16, EU: C:2017:591.
[214] *Alheto* v. *Zamestnik-predsedatel na Darzhavna agentsia za bezhantsite*, C-585/16, EU:C:2018:584.
[215] *Ahmedbekova* v. *Zamestnik-predsedatel na Darzhavna agentsia za bezhantsite*, C-652/16, EU:C:2018:801.
[216] Directive 2013/32/EU, Article 35.

The 'safe third country' must be a State to which it would be 'reasonable' for the applicant to go.[217]

Directive 2013/32/EU, Article 38

(1) Member States may apply the safe third country concept only where the competent authorities are satisfied that a person seeking asylum will be treated in accordance with the following principles in the third country concerned:

    (a) life and liberty are not threatened on account of race, religion, nationality, membership of a particular social group or political opinion;

    (b) there is no risk of serious harm as defined in Directive 2011/95/EU;

    (c) the principle of *non-refoulement* in accordance with the Geneva Convention is respected;

    (d) the prohibition of removal, in violation of the right to freedom from torture and cruel, inhuman or degrading treatment as laid down in international law, is respected; and

    (e) the possibility exists to request refugee status and, if found to be a refugee, to receive protection in accordance with the Geneva Convention.

Each Member State draws up its own list of safe States, using a methodology set out in national law.[218] That said, the criteria above, on which these methodologies are to be based, are troublingly vague. The civil liberties organisation, Statewatch, noted that when the issue was initially discussed in the Council, there was substantial disagreement about whether at least nine States were safe third countries. The criteria also seemed to be applied in ways that gave misgivings. Senegal had, in 2001, about 10,000 refugees living in neighbouring States but was considered safe in thirteen out of seventeen responses.[219]

(iv) The Provision of Material Reception Conditions

Member States must provide material reception conditions adequate for the health and subsistence of those seeking international protection.[220]

Directive 2013/33/EU, Article 17

(1) Member States shall ensure that material reception conditions are available to applicants when they make their application for international protection.

(2) Member States shall ensure that material reception conditions provide an adequate standard of living for applicants, which guarantees their subsistence and protects their physical and mental health.

---

[217] *Ibid.* Article 38(2)(a). All EU States are considered safe States. This is governed by the Protocol on Asylum for Nationals of Member States of the European Union.

[218] *Ibid.* Article 38(2)(b). A failure to do this will lead to the Member State being unable to invoke the safe third country principle, *A* v. *Migrationsverke*, C-404/17, EU:C:2018:588.

[219] www.statewatch.org/analyses/no-38-safe-countries.pdf.

[220] These are contained in Directive 2013/33/EU laying down the standards for the reception of applicants for international protection, OJ 2013, L 180/96. Ireland is not participating in this Directive.

Material reception conditions include housing, food and clothing. However, these can be provided in a way that separates out the applicant. In the case of food and clothing, provision may take the form of vouchers or a daily expense allowance.[221] Housing 'in kind' can be housing used specifically for those applying for international protection (e.g. accommodation centres).[222] In such cases, Member States must ensure that the housing protects family life; applicants can communicate with relatives, legal advisers and UNHCR representatives; and that these and family members have access to the accommodation to assist applicants unless security grounds justify limits.[223] Alongside these material reception conditions, Member States shall ensure that applicants receive necessary health care which, at the least, shall include emergency care and essential treatment of illness.[224] However, Member States are allowed to apply means tests to require the applicant to cover the cost of material reception conditions and health care if she is deemed to have sufficient resources.[225]

In addition, a number of family and economic rights are granted.

Applicants do not have a right to respect for their family life. Member States must only take appropriate measures as far as possible to secure family unity.[226] The best interests of the child are also to be a primary consideration for Member States.[227] These are weak provisions which allow for families to be split up. Although this must be done with the applicant's agreement,[228] it will be difficult for an individual, aware that the decision to award her refugee status is a matter of discretion, to refuse to cooperate with the authorities. Member States should, finally, grant minors access to the education system to minor asylum seekers under *similar* conditions as for their own nationals. These are not the same conditions, however. Member States can therefore provide for the ghettoisation of these children by requiring them to be educated in accommodation centres.[229]

Applicants enjoy certain employment rights. They shall have access to the labour market no later than nine months from the date when their application was lodged if a decision on their application has not been taken and the delay cannot be attributed to the applicant.[230] The level of access is to be determined by national law but must allow effective access to the market. Preference on that market, for reasons of labour market policy, may, however, be granted to EU citizens, EEA nationals and non-EU nationals lawfully resident in the Union.[231]

(v) The Policing of Applicants through Welfare

The right to remain and the socio-economic entitlements granted to applicants for international protection differentiate them from other non-EU nationals in need, such as economic migrants or migrants fleeing from starvation, who have no access to these.[232] This is something of a mixed blessing for these applicants as the entitlements are used to police their behaviour, with applicants having to meet a series of conditions if almost all the benefits on offer are not to be subject to withdrawal.

---

[221] *Ibid.* Article 2(g). [222] *Ibid.* Article 18(1). [223] *Ibid.* Article 18(2). [224] *Ibid.* Article 19.
[225] *Ibid.* Article 17(3)–(4). [226] *Ibid.* Article 12. [227] *Ibid.* Article 23(1). [228] *Ibid.* Article 12.
[229] *Ibid.* Article 14(1). [230] *Ibid.* Article 15(1). [231] *Ibid.* Article 15(2).
[232] J. Hathaway, 'A Reconsideration of the Underlying Premises of Refugee Law' (1990) 31 *Harvard Int'l LJ* 129.

Directive 2013/33EU, Article 20

(1) Member States may reduce or, in exceptional and duly justified cases, withdraw material reception conditions where an applicant:

    (a) abandons the place of residence determined by the competent authority without informing it or, if requested, without permission; or

    (b) does not comply with reporting duties or with requests to provide information or to appear for personal interviews concerning the asylum procedure during a reasonable period laid down in national law; or

    (c) has lodged a subsequent application as defined in Article 2(q) of Directive 2013/32/EU.[233]

    In relation to cases (a) and (b), when the applicant is traced or voluntarily reports to the competent authority, a duly motivated decision, based on the reasons for the disappearance, shall be taken on the reinstallation of the grant of some or all of the material reception conditions withdrawn or reduced.

(2) Member States may also reduce material reception conditions when they can establish that the applicant, for no justifiable reason, has not lodged an application for international protection as soon as reasonably practicable after arrival in that Member State.

(3) Member States may reduce or withdraw material reception conditions where an applicant has concealed financial resources, and has therefore unduly benefited from material reception conditions.

(4) Member States may determine sanctions applicable to serious breaches of the rules of the accommodation centres as well as to seriously violent behaviour.

These sanctions seek to ensure that the applicant is traceable (the reporting and residence requirements), not disruptive (violent behaviour and breach of rules of the accommodation centre) and frank about her financial circumstances. The most draconian is the possibility for the withdrawal of material reception conditions if the application is not made as soon as reasonably practical after arrival. This condition was criticised in particular by the UNHCR when it was introduced in the 2003 Directive.[234]

E. Guild, 'Seeking Asylum: Storm Clouds between International Commitments and Legislative Measures' (2004) 29 *European Law Review* 198, 216–17

By the draft of April 2002, agreement had been reached in the Council that withdrawal of reception conditions would apply where: the asylum applicant abandons the place of residence allocated without permission; fails to comply with report duties; has already lodged an application in the same Member State; where the individual has sufficient resources of his or her own; or for serious breaches of the rules on places of accommodation or violent behaviour. The ground proposed by the Commission of withdrawal for war crimes and national security had been removed.[235] It was believed that political agreement on the Directive had been reached in April 2002, indeed UNHCR prepared a press release regarding the proposal, referring to the achievement of political agreement. However, this was not the case.

    By September 2002 new demands for changes to the text were put forward by the UK Government which had decided to introduce draconian national legislation to exclude asylum seekers who failed to apply for asylum at the port of entry from any benefits. Apparently the Council could not agree the new insertion at the

---

[233] This is where an applicant makes a further application for international protection after a final decision on the initial application has been made.

[234] *R* v. *Secretary of State for the Home Department, ex parte Adam* (2006) 1 AC 396.

[235] Council Document 8351/02 of 29 April 2002: Outcome of Proceedings of Council on 25 April 2002.

Justice and Home Affairs Council meeting of October 2002. It is believed that the Swedish delegation refused to accede to the UK demand. However, by the December 2002 JHA meeting the issue was resolved in favour of the United Kingdom. A change to the 'almost' agreed text was made to Article 16(2) that 'a Member State may refuse conditions in cases where an asylum seeker has failed to demonstrate that the asylum claim was made as soon as reasonably practicable after arrival in that Member State.' UNHCR reserved its strongest criticism of the Directive for this provision in general and Article 16(2) in particular. It considered that if Member States identify real abuse in their asylum systems these should be dealt with in the procedures themselves not be used as an excuse to starve asylum seekers or leave them homeless. It noted that 'the core content of human rights applies to everyone in all situations'. As regards Article 16(2) UNHCR stated 'this provision may constitute an obstacle for asylum-seekers to have access to fair asylum procedures. Asylum-seekers may lack basic information on the asylum procedure and be unable to state their claims formally or intelligibly without adequate guidance . . . These difficulties would be exacerbated where asylum-seekers arrive with insufficient means and are denied assistance through the rigid application of the "reasonably practicable" criteria.'

Equally concerning is the sense that Member States are using withdrawal of material reception to incentivise applicants either to leave or to seek protection in other Member States.

P. Slominski and F. Trauner, 'How Do Member States Return Unwanted Migrants? The Strategic (Non-)Use of "Europe" during the Migration Crisis' (2018) 56 *Journal of Common Market Studies* **101, 110–11**

The EU has few competences in areas such as social policy or migrants' integration policies, which provides considerable leeway for Member States seeking to discourage asylum seekers from staying in their country. A widely-reported case was the decision by the Danish government in autumn 2015 to confiscate cash from migrants seeking international protection in Denmark. Germany adopted three so-called 'asylum packages' in 2015 and 2016 that contributed to reduced social benefits for asylum seekers, more restrictive rules for family reunification, and higher hurdles for receiving international protection. Due to these reforms, the number of people who enjoy full refugee status (including those from the Syrian civil war has considerably reduced. Subsidiary forms of protection have become the new normal. Since most of these measures fall outside EU competences, Member States can adopt these measures as long as they are in compliance with national constitutional law or international human rights standards. Indeed, planned measures in Austria, such as capping social benefits for asylum seekers, were dropped due to suspicion of them being unconstitutional. Similar concerns exist with regard to German plans to restrict family reunification of beneficiaries of subsidiary protection or the return of sick migrants.

In most cases, the disincentives to stay have been coupled with incentives to go. Assisted voluntary returns are conducted by Member States (often in co-operation with the International Organisation for Migration). For instance, Germany is providing migrants willing to return with a plane ticket and up to EUR 6,000 to start a small business back home.

A further controversial feature is that applicants may be detained. This must only be done where there are no less coercive alternatives available and after an individual assessment of each case.[236] It must also only be done under one of the following grounds.

---

[236] Directive 2013/33/EU, Article 8(2).

Directive 2013/33/EU, Article 8

(3) An applicant may be detained only:

    (a) in order to determine or verify his or her identity or nationality;

    (b) in order to determine those elements on which the application for international protection is based which could not be obtained in the absence of detention, in particular when there is a risk of absconding of the applicant;

    (c) in order to decide, in the context of a procedure, on the applicant's right to enter the territory;

    (d) when he or she is detained subject to a return procedure under Directive 2008/115/EC . . . in order to prepare the return and/or carry out the removal process, and the Member State concerned can substantiate on the basis of objective criteria, including that he or she already had the opportunity to access the asylum procedure, that there are reasonable grounds to believe that he or she is making the application for international protection merely in order to delay or frustrate the enforcement of the return decision;

    (e) when protection of national security or public order so requires;

    (f) in accordance with Article 28 of Regulation 604/2013 . . .

    The grounds for detention shall be laid down in national law.

(4) Member States shall ensure that the rules concerning alternatives to detention, such as regular reporting to the authorities, the deposit of a financial guarantee, or an obligation to stay at an assigned place, are laid down in national law.

The grounds for detention are vague, and this has given rise to civil liberties concerns. In almost all instances, national authorities can make a case, for example, that there is a risk that the applicant will be abscond. To try and restrict this, the Court has stated that the matter cannot simply be one of administrative discretion. Provision for what constitutes such a risk must be made in a binding law and must set out the level of risk required for detention in a clear manner according to objective criteria.[237]

FURTHER READING

L. Cerna, 'The Crisis as an Opportunity for Change? High-Skilled Immigration Policies across Europe' (2016) 42 *Journal of Ethnic and Migration Studies* 1610.

S. Colombeau, 'Policing the Internal Schengen Borders: Managing the Double Bind between Free Movement and Migration Control' (2017) 27 *Policing and Society* 480.

M. Fullerton, 'Asylum Crisis Italian Style: The Dublin Regulation Collides With European Human Rights Law' (2016) 29 *Harvard Human Rights Law Journal* 57.

A. Meloni, 'The Community Code on Visas: Harmonisation at Last?' (2009) 34 *European Law Review* 671.

R. Mungeanu, *Frontex and Non Refoulement* (Cambridge University Press, 2016).

C. Offe, 'From Migration in Geographic Space to Migration in Biographic Time: Views from Europe' (2011) 19 *Journal of Political Philosophy* 333.

---

[237] *Al Chodor*, C-528/15, EU:C:2017:213. The judgment interpreted the issue of detention under the Dublin Regulation but would seem equally applicable to interpretation of Article 8 of Directive 2013/33/EU.

S. Peers, *EU Justice and Home Affairs Law, I: EU Immigration and Asylum Law*, 4th edn (Oxford University Press, 2016).

M. Scipioni, 'Failing Forward in EU Migration Policy? EU Integration after the 2015 Asylum and Migration Crisis' (2018) 25 *Journal of European Public Policy* 1357.

P. Slominski and F. Trauner, 'How Do Member States Return Unwanted Migrants? The Strategic (Non-)Use of "Europe" during the Migration Crisis' (2018) 56 *Journal of Common Market Studies* 101.

N. Zaun, *EU Asylum Policies: The Power of Strong Regulating States* (Basingstoke, Palgrave, 2017).

13

Equal Opportunities Law and Policy

CONTENTS

1 INTRODUCTION

EU law today regulates discrimination on grounds of sex, gender, race, ethnic origin, religion or belief, sexual orientation, age and disability. In this chapter we examine the key legislative provisions, the judgments of the European Court of Justice (ECJ) that have shaped the law and the evolution of the European Union's equal opportunities policy.

Section 2 explores four issues to place the law in a wider context. First we ask why the Union needs an equal opportunities policy. On the one hand, banning discrimination is a necessary complement to the economic project of creating an internal market: discrimination reduces economic welfare and so must be prohibited.[1] On the other hand, the tasks of the Union are wider: to enhance the rights of its citizens, irrespective of economic considerations. Secondly, and related, we look to the various sources of law that may be utilised to protect victims of discrimination. In addition to the Directives, we note that the Court also makes increasing reference to the EU Charter of Fundamental Rights (EUCFR), the European Convention of Human Rights (ECHR), the case law of the European Court of Human Rights (ECtHR) as well as international treaties as sources to aid the interpretation of the Directives. Thirdly, we consider what kind of anti-discrimination policy the European Union is developing. One model sees discrimination law as promoting equality of opportunities, at another extreme models suggest that discrimination laws can be successful only if they yield substantive equality.[2] Fourthly, we outline the common core of EU equal opportunities law, which is found in the field of labour law, where a rights-based model operates and has been utilised successfully in the past forty years by victims of sex discrimination.[3]

In Section 3 we examine the common core of EU equal opportunities law more fully by considering the three main grounds upon which an employee may assert her rights (direct discrimination, indirect discrimination and harassment); what justifications might be offered by employers to escape liability; and the remedies available to the employee.

Section 4 considers the grounds upon which discrimination is forbidden. It explores how the ECJ has begun to trace the boundaries of each ground of discrimination and the distinct features of these grounds.

In Section 5 we consider the limitations of the rights-based policy in section 3 and discuss four novel ways through which EU equal opportunities law is evolving. First, the policy is extended to areas beyond the workplace, for example protecting victims who experience discrimination in education or the provision of services; secondly, inviting Member States to experiment with affirmative action programmes; thirdly, promoting various forms of dialogue to entrench existing rights; finally, utilising 'mainstreaming' as a means of integrating equality rights within the framework of EU law.

2 DEVELOPMENT OF EU EQUAL OPPORTUNITIES LAW

(i) Economic versus Non-Economic Visions of EU Law

The beginnings of equal opportunities law were humble, limited to guaranteeing equal pay between men and women, and only a more limited version of the first two paragraphs of what is now Article 157 TFEU was in place.[4]

---

[1] E.g. Q. T. Wodon and B. de la Brière, *Unrealized Potential: The High Cost of Gender Inequality in Earnings. The Cost of Gender Inequality* (Washington, DC, World Bank, 2018), https://openknowledge.worldbank.org/handle/10986/29865.

[2] The model of substantive equality that we use here is that developed by S. Fredman, *Discrimination Law*, 2nd edn (Oxford, Clarendon Press, 2011).

[3] It is beyond the scope of this chapter to examine this field exhaustively. See C. Barnard, *EU Employment Law*, 4th edn (Oxford University Press, 2012).

[4] For a helpful account of the development of equality law, see M. Bell, 'The Principle of Equal Treatment: Widening and Deepening' in P. Craig and G. de Búrca (eds.), *The Evolution of EU Law*, 2nd edn (Oxford University Press, 2011); M. Bell, *Anti-Discrimination Law and the European Union* (Oxford University Press, 2002).

Article 157 TFEU

(1) Each Member State shall ensure that the principle of equal pay for male and female workers for equal work or work of equal value is applied.

(2) For the purpose of this Article, 'pay' means the ordinary basic or minimum wage or salary and any other consideration, whether in cash or in kind, which the worker receives directly or indirectly, in respect of his employment, from his employer.

Equal pay without discrimination based on sex means:

(a) that pay for the same work at piece rates shall be calculated on the basis of the same unit of measurement;

(b) that pay for work at time rates shall be the same for the same job.

(3) The European Parliament and the Council, acting in accordance with the ordinary legislative procedure, and after consulting the Economic and Social Committee, shall adopt measures to ensure the application of the principle of equal opportunities and equal treatment of men and women in matters of employment and occupation, including the principle of equal pay for equal work or work of equal value.

(4) With a view to ensuring full equality in practice between men and women in working life, the principle of equal treatment shall not prevent any Member State from maintaining or adopting measures providing for specific advantages in order to make it easier for the underrepresented sex to pursue a vocational activity or to prevent or compensate for disadvantages in professional careers.

The reason for including this provision was a concern of the French Government that it would be at a competitive disadvantage because its laws guaranteed equal pay for men and women while the laws of other States did not.[5] This suggests that one rationale for EU discrimination law is economic: it prevents Member States who do not safeguard equality at work from exploiting lower labour costs thereby gaining an advantage. Discrimination is also economically harmful because it means that human resources are not used to their full capacity: if an employer has a policy of not hiring women, he may lose out by not hiring the best candidate for the job. This can undermine the European Union's desire to develop a competitive single market.[6] From an economic perspective then, harmonised discrimination legislation complements the internal market rules and enhances competitiveness.[7]

An alternative justification for equal opportunities is that the Union is gradually recognising the political aspect to European integration.[8] Those who support this argument draw upon the underlying intentions of the Treaties; the development, especially since the late 1980s by the then President of the Commission, Jacques Delors, of a 'social' dimension to accompany economic integration, resulting in the Community Charter of Basic Social Rights for Workers;[9]

---

[5] B. Ohlin, 'Social Aspects of European Economic Co-operation: Report by a Group of Experts' (1956) 102 *International Labour Review* 99; C. Barnard, 'The Economic Objectives of Article 119' in T. Hervey and D. O'Keefe (eds.), *Sex Equality Law of the European Union* (Chichester, Wiley, 1996).

[6] See Recital 9 of Directive 2000/43/EC implementing the principle of equal treatment between persons irrespective of racial or ethnic origin [2000] OJ L 180/22 (Race Directive).

[7] 'Green Paper on Equality and Non-Discrimination in an Enlarged European Union', COM(2004)379 final, 15–16.

[8] For a helpful account, see D. Scheik, 'Broadening the Scope and the Norms of EU Gender Equality Law: Towards a Multidimensional Conception of Equality Law' (2005) 12 *MJECL* 427.

[9] 'Declaration by Council of the Community Charter of Basic Social Rights for Workers', COM(1989)568 final.

and the Court of Justice's recognition that the principle of equal treatment set out in Article 157 TFEU enshrines a fundamental right:[10]

> the economic aim pursued by Article [157 TFEU], namely the elimination of distortions of competition between undertakings established in different Member States, is secondary to the social aim pursued by the same provision, which constitutes the expression of a fundamental human right.[11]

This judicial pronouncement is reflected in the enlargement of the Union's competence in the field of social policy in the Amsterdam Treaty,[12] the evolution of the concept of citizenship (noted in Chapter 11), and the increased role of fundamental rights in the European Union (discussed in Chapter 6).[13]

Today, the Union's equal opportunities policy is largely based upon Article 19 TFEU, first included in the Treaty of Amsterdam.[14]

Article 19 TFEU

(1) Without prejudice to the other provisions of the Treaties and within the limits of the powers conferred by them upon the Union, the Council, acting unanimously in accordance with a special legislative procedure and after obtaining the consent of the European Parliament, may take appropriate action to combat discrimination based on sex, racial or ethnic origin, religion or belief, disability, age or sexual orientation.

(2) By way of derogation from paragraph 1, the European Parliament and the Council, acting in accordance with the ordinary legislative procedure, may adopt the basic principles of Union incentive measures, excluding any harmonisation of the laws and regulations of the Member States, to support action taken by the Member States in order to contribute to the achievement of the objectives referred to in paragraph 1.

Article 19(1) TFEU grants the EU legislative competence to safeguard the rights of a range of groups, and it is not confined to prohibiting discrimination in the workplace. This breadth was achieved with certain limitations: the article does not have direct effect, the European Parliament (the institution which had most assiduously pursued the cause of discrimination law) is given a relatively limited role in the lawmaking process[15] and the requirement for unanimity creates a risk that the legislation imposes only low standards, or results in texts that are so ambiguous that they can be watered down by national implementation measures. During the negotiations leading to the Treaty of Nice there were attempts to make it easier for the European Union to legislate. The result was Article 19(2) TFEU, but this only applies for measures designed to help Member States in giving effect to the legislation enacted in Article 19(1).[16]

---

[10] *Defrenne (No. 2)* v. *Sabena*, 43/75, ECLI:EU:C:1976:56; *P* v. *S and Cornwall County Council*, C-13/94, ECLI:EU:C:1995:444.

[11] *Deutsche Telekom AG* v. *Lilli Schröder*, C-50/96, ECLI:EU:C:2000:72, para. 57.

[12] Article 153 TFEU (ex Article 137 EC). See C. Barnard, 'The United Kingdom, the "Social Chapter" and the Amsterdam Treaty' (1997) 26 *ILJ* 275.

[13] See e.g. E. Spaventa, 'From Gebhard to Carpenter: Towards a (Non) Economic Constitution' (2004) 41 *CMLRev* 743.

[14] M. Bell and L. Waddington, 'The 1996 Intergovernmental Conference and the Prospects of a Non-Discrimination Treaty Article' (1996) 25 *ILJ* 320; L. Waddington, 'Article 13 EC: Mere Rhetoric or a Harbinger of Change?' (1998) 1 *CYELS* 175.

[15] But Article 19 TFEU enhances it. Under Article 13 EC it merely had the right to be consulted.

[16] An alternative (but more limited) legal basis would be Article 153 TFEU (ex Article 137 EC).

The Preambles to the discrimination Directives based on Article 19 TFEU lend support to the non-economic vision by their reference to the importance of creating an ever closer Union among the peoples of Europe; the principles of liberty, democracy, human rights and fundamental freedoms that underpin the Union; and the universality of the right to equality, recognised in several international instruments.[17] Nevertheless, it should be noted that when new equality measures are proposed, an attempt is made to emphasise the economic dimension so as to persuade recalcitrant Member States that the measure in question contributes to the traditional economic aims of the Treaties.[18] One's vision about anti-discrimination law may shape the way the rules are interpreted, for instance a focus on safeguarding individual rights would tolerate measures that may be economically harmful to businesses that bear the costs of adjusting their practices to accommodate the rights of workers. This is most notable in the duty employers have to make accommodations to facilitate that disabled employees can thrive in the workplace.

(ii) Sources of Equal Opportunities Law

Having sketched the economic and rights-based approaches to EU equal opportunities law, we turn to observe that there are four overlapping frameworks for EU discrimination law.[19]

First are the various equality Directives and the scope of protection varies depending on which ground of protection is at stake.[20] The Racial Equality Directive offers the widest range, addressing discrimination in the workplace and also prohibiting discrimination regarding access to welfare systems (e.g. heath and education), social security and goods and services. Sex discrimination is addressed in a set of instruments (e.g. a Directive that consolidates previous disparate Directives on equal pay and equal treatment,[21] a Directive relating to equal treatment in the access to and supply of goods and services[22] and a Directive extending non-discrimination in the field of social security).[23] But no instrument addresses sex discrimination regarding welfare systems. The other protected grounds (religion, belief, disability, age and sexual orientation discrimination) are regulated by a single Directive (the Framework Directive 2000/78/ EC) which only applies to discrimination in the workplace. This contradicts the Council's position that the 'different forms of discrimination cannot be ranked: all are equally intolerable'.[24] The lack of consolidated protection for discriminated groups is not a problem that besets EU law

---

[17] Race Directive, recitals 1–3; Directive 2000/78 establishing a general framework for equal treatment in employment and occupation, recitals 1, 3 and 4 [2000] OJ L 303/16 (Framework Directive); Directive 2006/54/EC on the implementation of the principle of equal opportunities and equal treatment of men and women in matters of employment and occupation (recast), recitals 2 and 4 [2006] OJ L 204/23 (Recast Equal Treatment Directive).

[18] M. A. Pollack and E. Hafner-Burton, 'Mainstreaming Gender in the European Union' (2000) 7 *JEPP* 432, 441–2.

[19] This draws on C. Kilpatrick, 'The Court of Justice and Labour Law in 2010: A New EU Discrimination Law Architecture' (2011) 40(3) *ILJ* 280, 300–1.

[20] L. Waddington and M. Bell, 'More Equal than Others: Distinguishing European Union Equality Directives' (2001) 38 *CMLRev* 587.

[21] Recast Equal Treatment Directive. N. Burrows and M. Robinson, 'An Assessment of the Recast of Community Equality Laws' (2006) 13 *ELJ* 186.

[22] Council Directive 2004/113/EC of 13 December 2004 implementing the principle of equal treatment between men and women in the access to and supply of goods and services.

[23] Council Directive 79/7/EC [1979] OJ L 6/24 (Social Security Directive).

[24] Council Decision 2000/750 establishing a Community Action Programme to combat discrimination, recital 5 [2000] OJ L 303/23.

exclusively: differentiated political willingness to address all forms of discrimination equally is deeply embedded in national politics.[25]

Secondly, the Court of Justice has discovered that the principle of non-discrimination is a general principle of EU law.[26] This is discussed in Chapter 7 for its significance with respect to EU constitutional law. For present purposes, what matters is the impact that this general principle has on supplementing the protection afforded by the equality Directives. In *Mangold* the claimant argued that his contract was in breach of the Framework Directive and constituted discrimination based on age. At that time the Directive had not yet been transposed into German law; it appears that the parties to the litigation had designed the employment contract as a means of launching a challenge to test the legality of the German legislation against the forthcoming EU standards. The Court of Justice found that the Directive applied even though it had not yet been transposed into German law. This was based on the Court discovering a general principle in EU law prohibiting age discrimination. This means that, provided the action complained of is linked to the implementation of EU law, Member States have a general obligation not to discriminate on grounds of age.[27] Professor Schiek thought the judgment constituted 'a first step in what will hopefully lead towards judicial development of a coherent framework for equal treatment of persons from a less than satisfactory legislative package'.[28] On the other hand, critics have noted that supplementing the equality Directives in this way is unwise because it shatters the delicate political balance that the Member States had reached in negotiating the secondary legislation.[29] As we will see below, anti-discrimination law can have a major impact on the design of national economic policy, and a general principle risks undermining this. Since *Mangold*, the Court of Justice's use of this general principle has been uneven; in a number of cases, the Court declined to apply it.[30] Moreover, while the general principle was used to find the source of the rights to be protected in *Mangold*, the Court then returned to the structure of the Directive to test how far the law in question complied with equality principles, so the Court did not see it as necessary to develop a parallel case law-based equality law: the principle discovered in *Mangold* only supplements the equality Directives. Indeed, in more recent cases it has been used as an aid to interpret the Directive against contrary readings offered by Member States.[31]

---

[25] At the time of writing this is best exemplified by controversies in some Member States with regard to laws recognising same-sex relationships.

[26] *Werner Mangold* v. *Rüdiger Helm*, C-144/04, ECLI:EU:C:2005:709; *Seda Kücükdeveci* v. *Swedex GmbH & Co. KG*, C-555/07, ECLI:EU:C:2010:21.

[27] For support, see Kilpatrick, n. 19 above, 285–7, but see also the critical reflections in E. Muir, 'Enhancing the Effects of Community Law on National Employment Policies: The *Mangold* Case' (2006) 31 *ELRev* 879.

[28] D. Schiek, 'The ECJ Decision in *Mangold*: A Further Twist on Effects of Directives and Constitutional Relevance of Community Equality Legislation' (2006) 35 *ILJ* 329.

[29] *Sonia Chacón Navas* v. *Eurest Colectividades SA*, C-13/05, ECLI:EU:C:2006:184, Opinion of Advocate General Geelhoed, paras. 50–5.

[30] E.g. in three cases on age discrimination. In *Birgit Bartsch* v. *Bosch und Siemens Hausgeräte*, C-427/06, ECLI:EU:C:2008:517, the Court found that the national rules did not fall within the scope of EU law; in *Félix Palacios de la Villa contro Cortefiel Servicios SA*, C-411/05, ECLI:EU:C:2007:604, the Court applied the relevant Directive; in *Maria-Luise Lindorfer* v. *Council*, C-227/04 P, ECLI:EU:C:2007:490 (a mixed age and sex discrimination case) the Court decided on grounds of sex discrimination. In *Valeri Hariev Belov* v. *CHEZ Elektro Balgaria AD and Others*, C-394/11, ECLI:EU:C:2012:585, Advocate General Kokott took the view that there was also a principle against race discrimination, but the case was dismissed for procedural reasons.

[31] *Dansk Industri (DI), acting on behalf of Ajos A/S* v. *Estate of Karsten Eigil Rasmussen*, C-441/14, ECLI:EU:C:2016:278 (requiring the court to disapply national law which did not transpose the Directive correctly); *Vera Egenberger* v. *Evangelisches Werk für Diakonie und Entwicklung eV*, C-414/16, ECLI:EU:C:2018:257 (requiring that aggrieved parties have a right to seek judicial review of a decision not to employ them reached by a religious organisation).

As such it offers an alternative means of policing the Member State's transposition of the equality Directives.

Thirdly, the EUCFR may serve as a basis for testing national and EU law. The most striking illustration is the Court of Justice's approach in *Test-Achats*. In 2004 the Union adopted a Directive to protect discrimination based on sex in the provision of goods and services.[32] The car insurance industry lobbied extensively for an exemption. Their argument was that insurance premiums are fixed having regard to actuarial data and this necessarily results in women paying lower premiums than men because they are less likely to cause accidents. The Directive accommodated this, building in a transitional period for the insurance sector to adjust.[33] This was challenged by a Belgian consumer association. The Court held (relying on Articles 21 and 23 EUCFR) that the Directive was contrary to EU law because it created a risk that insurers would be able to retain discrimination based on gender indefinitely.[34] As with *Mangold*, one must be careful not to read too much into this approach. The Court has not always found it necessary to rely on the EUCFR, even when asked to do so by the applicant, when the equality Directives appear to offer an appropriate answer instead.[35] It appears that, just as in the *Mangold* line of cases, the Court of Justice is probably not constructing a parallel set of discrimination rules, but is using the EUCFR to test EU legislation.[36] It remains to be noted that the EUCFR contains a wider range of equality grounds than Article 19 TFEU (e.g. ethnic or social origin, genetic features, language and political or any other opinion are covered by Article 21 and cultural, religious and linguistic diversity are covered by Article 22). In the implementation of EU law one will have to ensure that these rights are safeguarded, but it is not likely that a person would be able to make a claim simply on the basis that they suffered discrimination because of, say, their social origin.[37]

The fourth source that is relevant is the European Convention on Human Rights (ECHR). This has relevance for two reasons. First, the principles developed by the ECtHR may prove a source of law for interpreting EU equality law. Moreover, there have been some litigants who, dissatisfied with the degree of protection afforded by the EU Directives, have explored whether the ECHR offers more protection. An example of this is *Eweida* v. *United Kingdom*. There, the applicant challenged the employer's decision to ban the wearing of crucifixes at work. Her claim based on discrimination law was unsuccessful, but the ECtHR found that her right to manifest her religious belief (under Article 9 ECHR) had been infringed.[38] The ECHR thus provides an alternative basis for securing one's rights.

From this account, two lessons should be drawn. The first is that there are multiple sources that protect the same (or similar) rights, each of these having a different framework and impact. The

---

[32] Directive 2004/113 implementing the principle of equal treatment between men and women in the access to and supply of goods and services [2004] OJ L 373/37.

[33] *Ibid.* Article 5(2).

[34] *Association belge des Consommateurs Test-Achats ASBL and Others* v. *Conseil des ministres*, C-236/09, ECLI:EU:C:2011:100, para. 32.

[35] *Tyrolean Airways* v. *Betriebsrat Bord*, C-132/11, ECLI:EU:C:2012:329; *Odar* v. *Baxter*, C-152/11, ECLI:EU:C:2012:772.

[36] E.g. in *Wolfgang Glatzel* v. *Freistaat Bayern*, C-356/12, ECLI:EU:C:2014:350 the ECJ examined EU legislation that required a more demanding eyesight test for drivers of heavy goods vehicle against the standards of equality in the EUCFR.

[37] *Fag og Arbejde, acting on behalf of Karsten Kaltoft* v. *Kommunernes Landsforening*, C-354/13, ECLI:EU:C:2014:2463, paras. 31–40.

[38] *Eweida and Others* v. *United Kingdom* [2013] ECHR 37, paras. 89–95.

second lesson is that the Court has increasingly joined up the general principle it discovered in *Mangold* with the EUCFR. However these two sources do not yet create a general, overarching basis for equality laws, such that a claim by an aggrieved party may be brought on the basis that a private party is in breach of the general equality principle. However, there some support this more expansive approach, while the case law remains ambiguous.[39]

(iii) Equal Opportunities versus Substantive Equality

It is beyond the scope of this chapter to explore all the theories that have been deployed to justify discrimination legislation.[40] However, in order to be able to evaluate the efforts of the European Union, we need to have an idea of what discrimination law might be used to achieve. We therefore sketch two contrasting approaches: one focusing on equality of opportunity, the other on equality of results. The first view provides that when an employer hires someone, race, religion, sex, sexual orientation or age must not play a part in selecting the successful candidate. This approach guarantees formal equality among persons. The competing model favours the use of discrimination law to generate substantive equality. From this perspective, discrimination laws are successful if the result is that more underrepresented groups have access to employment, education and other opportunities; that underrepresented groups are able to participate in policy-making and that differences are accommodated.[41] This may entail discriminating in favour of an excluded group, for example by determining that a certain percentage of the workforce should consist of women or ethnic minorities.[42]

There are three main differences between the formal and the substantive approach to equality. First, formal equality does not guarantee equality of results and does not address the causes of inequality; it assumes that discrimination is a discrete wrong against a person and not an institutionalised practice against certain types of person. Secondly, the formal equality model is concerned with individual rights, while the substantive equality model is concerned to promote the rights of groups of persons who have been systemically discriminated against. The primary means of enforcement of the formal equality model is litigation by the person who is wronged and an individual remedy is obtained. Advocates of the substantive equality model prefer regulatory means of achieving equality (e.g. affirmative action or mainstreaming) and call for lawsuits which support group rights (i.e. bringing cases against indirect forms of discrimination). A third and wider difference between the two models is that the formal equality model requires everyone to act like the privileged group. From a feminist perspective, '[g]ender neutrality is thus simply the male standard'.[43] This does not recognise the legitimacy of differences between groups.[44] Substantive equality models entail the integration and celebration

[39] See Advocate General Kokott in *Association belge des Consommateurs Test-Achats ASBL and Others* v. *Conseil des ministres*, C-236/09, ECLI:EU:C:2011:100. Cf. *Elegktiko Sinedrio* v. *Ipourgeio Politismou kai Tourismou*, C-363/11, Judgment of 19 December 2012, Opinion of Advocate General Sharpston, para. 80. In *Egenberger* (n. 13 above, paras. 76–82) the Court first suggests that Article 21 creates a cause of action, but then appears to attach this right to the Directive.

[40] See e.g. Fredman, n. 2 above (on whose work the account in this section is based) and T. Khaitan, *A Theory of Discrimination Law* (Oxford University Press, 2015).

[41] Fredman, n. 2 above.

[42] For an attempted justification of reverse discrimination, see M. Rosenfeld, *Affirmative Action and Justice: A Philosophical and Constitutional Inquiry* (New Haven, CT, Yale University Press, 1991); L. Jacobs, *Pursuing Equal Opportunities* (Cambridge University Press, 2004) ch. 5.

[43] C. MacKinnon, *Feminism Unmodified* (Cambridge, MA, Harvard University Press, 1988) 34.

[44] For this critique, see S. Fredman, *Women and the Law* (Oxford University Press, 1997) chs. 1 and 4.

of differences within society. For example, dress codes should accommodate all faiths; working hours should be adapted for those who have child-care obligations in ways that do not affect their employment prospects adversely. In examining the Union's equal opportunities law and policy, we see traces of both formal and substantive equality.

3 COMMON CORE OF EU EQUAL OPPORTUNITIES LAW: THE LABOUR MARKET

All protected groups benefit from protection from discrimination in the labour market.

Framework Directive, Article 3

(1) Within the limits of the areas of competence conferred on the Community, this Directive shall apply to all persons, as regards both the public and private sectors, including public bodies, in relation to:
  (a) conditions for access to employment, to self-employment or to occupation, including selection criteria and recruitment conditions, whatever the branch of activity and at all levels of the professional hierarchy, including promotion;
  (b) access to all types and to all levels of vocational guidance, vocational training, advanced vocational training and retraining, including practical work experience;
  (c) employment and working conditions, including dismissals and pay;
  (d) membership of, and involvement in, an organisation of workers or employers, or any organisation whose members carry on a particular profession, including the benefits provided for by such organisations.

The rights listed above are also available for victims of discrimination on grounds of race and sex, but are based on different Directives.[45] The right is to be free from four forms of discrimination: direct discrimination (which is aimed at an individual because of, for example, her race or religion); indirect discrimination (when an apparently neutral job requirement is more easily satisfied by one sex or racial group than another – for example, if a job is only available to people who are clean-shaven this indirectly excludes Sikhs); harassment and victimisation (that is, adverse treatment directed at a person who has made a discrimination claim against an employer).

If we consider sex discrimination, which has been regulated since the 1970s the first key theme to emerge is the sustained effort to utilise the rules to secure improved working conditions for women. For example, in *Macarthys Ltd* v. *Smith*, a woman made a claim for equal pay based on the fact that her predecessor (a man) had been paid more for doing the same work as her. At that time it was not clear whether her claim was admissible under the British Equal Pay Act 1970, but the Court of Justice held that Article 157 TFEU did cover this dispute,[46] and therefore the national court was required to disapply national law in order to afford the plaintiff her EU law

---

[45] Race Directive, Article 3(1)(a)–(d); Article 157 TFEU, and Recast Equal Treatment Directive. In the main text in this chapter we only extract the provision from the Framework Directive unless specific differences arise.

[46] *Macarthys Ltd* v. *Smith*, 129/79, ECLI:EU:C:1980:103.

rights.[47] In the 1980s, the UK Equal Opportunities Commission devised a highly successful litigation strategy bringing test cases like this one to challenge national sex equality laws based on their infringement of EU equality law.[48]

Secondly, the case law of the ECJ has sought to read the rights of victims of discrimination broadly. For example, throughout the 1980s and early 1990s the Court of Justice expanded the concept of 'pay' to include a range of benefits, for example occupational pension schemes,[49] travel concessions,[50] redundancy pay,[51] maternity leave pay,[52] unfair dismissal compensation[53] and statutory sick pay.[54] The test set out by the Court is that any consideration that the worker receives directly or indirectly in respect of employment from her employer is to be considered pay.[55] On the one hand the Court's wish to widen the benefits of EU law can lead to tangible benefits for employees. On the other hand, this comes at a cost for employers who will likely find ways to circumvent these rulings, leading to further litigation. One person who came under this cross-fire is Ms Allonby. She was a part-time employee at a teaching college. In earlier cases, the Court of Justice had moved to protect part-time workers (who are predominantly female) using sex discrimination rules, thus guaranteeing that their remuneration was comparable to full-time workers.[56] As a result employers were compelled to grant equivalent rights to part-time workers.[57] Ms Allonby's employer thus decided to change his relationship with Ms Allonby by making her redundant and engaging a third company (ELS) who then supplied her as a teacher but with the status as self-employed and in this way it hoped to avoid having to give her the right to register for a pension scheme. However the ECJ held that she remained a worker for the purposes of EU law, irrespective of the way her contractual relationship had been designed, affording her an entitlement to pension rights.[58] The takeaway from this example is that widening the scope of protection does not always mean that the weaker party receives protection: one has to observe the ways in which employers respond to the new legal order. Generalising from this, one might suggest that simply giving rights for claimants does not suffice to eradicate gender inequalities.[59] We now turn to explore the key ways by which discrimination law may be applied and enforced.

---

[47] *Macarthys Ltd* v. *Smith* [1980] ICR 672, 693–4.

[48] K. J. Alter and J. Vargas, 'Explaining Variation in the Use of European Litigation Strategies: European Community Law and British Gender Equality Policy' (2000) 33 *Comparative Political Studies* 452; C. Kilpatrick, 'Gender Equality: A Fundamental Dialogue' in S. Sciarra (ed.), *Labour Law in the Courts* (Oxford, Hart Publishing, 2001).

[49] *Bilka-Kaufhaus GmbH* v. *Karin Weber von Hartz*, 170/84, ECLI:EU:C:1986:204.

[50] *Garland* v. *British Rail Engineering*, 12/81, ECLI:EU:C:1982:44.

[51] *Barber* v. *Guardian Royal Exchange Assurance Group*, 262/88, ECLI:EU:C:1990:209.

[52] *Gillespie* v. *Northern Health and Social Services Board*, C-342/93, CLI:EU:C:1996:46.

[53] *R* v. *Secretary of State for Employment, ex parte Seymour-Smith and Perez*, C-167/97, ECLI:EU:C:1999:60.

[54] *Rinner-Kühn* v. *FWW Spezial-Gebäudereinigung GmbH & Co. KG*, 171/88, ECLI:EU:C:1989:328.

[55] *R* v. *Secretary of State for Employment, ex parte Seymour-Smith and Perez*, C-167/97, ECLI:EU:C:1999:60.

[56] See Directive 97/81/EC on part-time work [1998] OJ L 14/9, which broadly codifies the case law.

[57] Employment Protection (Part-time Employees) Regulations 1995, SI 1995/31, which were the result of *R* v. *Secretary of State for Employment, ex parte EOC* [1994] 1 All ER 910, where the House of Lords held that inferior rights for part-time workers were contrary to EU law.

[58] *Allonby* v. *Accrington and Rossendale College*, C-256/01, ECLI:EU:C:2004:18.

[59] See e.g. C. L. Ridgeway, *Framed by Gender* (Oxford University Press, 2011) ch. 4, suggesting that the organisation of the workplace retains gendered assumptions.

(i) Direct Discrimination

The discrimination Directives use a common formula in defining direct discrimination:

> direct discrimination shall be taken to occur where one person is treated less favourably than another is, has been or would be treated in a comparable situation on grounds of [sex, race, ethnic origin, religion, belief, age, disability, sexual orientation].[60]

There is no need to show that the employer intended to discriminate, nor that he was negligent. Direct discrimination is found when 'but for' the relevant 'ground' (e.g. sex or race) the employer would not have discriminated against the claimant. To show the causal link between the relevant ground and the less favourable treatment, the plaintiff must compare her treatment with that of others. The 'others' must be persons working for the same employer. In the *Allonby* case (discussed above) one of her claims was that ELS paid her less than male lecturers who were employed by the college. However, the ECJ decided that she could not compare her salary with that of men employed by another employer. As a general matter this makes sense for one cannot expect employers to know the salaries of other firms, but on the specific facts of this case (where the claimant had been originally employed by the defendant, and her termination and re-hiring through ELS was a cost-cutting measure) the court might have been more helpful.[61]

Normally, claims of direct discrimination are brought by an individual who suffers a disadvantage, a wider approach is possible. The Centre for Equal Opportunities and Opposition to Racism, a body charged with the promotion of equal treatment in Belgium, took action against an employer who had stated publicly that he was not going to recruit persons of certain races, seeking a declaration that these statements breached the Belgian laws implementing the Race Directive. Significantly, there was no evidence that the employer had in fact rejected a job applicant on the basis of race or ethnicity, so the question arose whether on the facts the defendant had acted illegally.

Centrum voor gelijkheid van kansen en voor racismebestrijding v. Firma Feryn NV, C–54/07, ECLI:EU:C:2008:155

22 It is true that . . . Article 2(2) of Directive 2000/43 defines direct discrimination as a situation in which one person 'is treated' less favourably than another is, has been or would be treated in a comparable situation on grounds of racial or ethnic origin. Likewise, Article 7 of that directive requires Member States to ensure that judicial procedures are available to 'all persons who consider themselves wronged by failure to apply the principle of equal treatment to them' and to public interest bodies bringing judicial proceedings 'on behalf or in support of the complainant'.

23 Nevertheless, it cannot be inferred from this that the lack of an identifiable complainant leads to the conclusion that there is no direct discrimination within the meaning of Directive 2000/43. The aim of that directive, as stated in recital 8 of its preamble, is 'to foster conditions for a socially inclusive labour market'.

---

[60] Race Directive, Article 2(1); Framework Directive, Article 2(2)(a); Recast Equal Treatment Directive, Article 2(1)(a).
[61] See n. 58 above, para. 50. See S. Fredman, 'Marginalising Equal Pay Laws' (2004) 33 *ILJ* 281. The Commission was persuaded not to alter this approach when the Directive was recast, see J. Shaw, J. Hunt and C. Wallace, *Economic and Social Law of the European Union* (Basingstoke, Palgrave Macmillan, 2007) 372–3.

For that purpose, Article 3(1)(a) states that the directive covers, *inter alia*, selection criteria and recruitment conditions.

24 The objective of fostering conditions for a socially inclusive labour market would be hard to achieve if the scope of Directive 2000/43 were to be limited to only those cases in which an unsuccessful candidate for a post, considering himself to be the victim of direct discrimination, brought legal proceedings against the employer.

25 The fact that an employer declares publicly that it will not recruit employees of a certain ethnic or racial origin, something which is clearly likely to strongly dissuade certain candidates from submitting their candidature and, accordingly, to hinder their access to the labour market, constitutes direct discrimination in respect of recruitment within the meaning of Directive 2000/43. The existence of such direct discrimination is not dependent on the identification of a complainant who claims to have been the victim.

While the ruling might be criticised for not explaining that the rights of those discriminated against trump the defendant's freedom of expression, this ruling serves to emphasise the role both of national equality bodies in promoting the rights of victims of discrimination, and of strategic litigation.[62] In a subsequent ruling, the Court of Justice stretched this precedent a little further. The facts involved a shareholder of a football club in Romania, who presented himself as the club's patron. He made a statement suggesting he would not recruit gay players. Asociaţia Accept (a Romanian lesbian, gay, bisexual and transgender organisation) brought charges to the Romanian anti-discrimination council against the shareholder and the club. The club argued that since the person who made the statement had no role in recruitment (unlike the director in *Feryn*) then there should be no liability attaching to it. The Court disagreed. In its view, in such a situation the club should have publicly distanced itself from the statement. What counted was the perception of the public.[63]

Clearly, this line of cases facilitates strategic public interest litigation by activist organisations: there is no need to find a victim, and it is easy to infer discrimination.[64] Shifting the onus onto the employer forces that person to make visible changes to its policy to remove the perception that it has a discriminatory policy, and such change is beneficial to all.

(ii) Indirect Discrimination

(a) Concept of Indirect Discrimination

Indirect discrimination takes place where, even though the conditions for access to employment appear on their face to be non-discriminatory, they do in fact exclude a particular group. For example, a rule that employees must work all of Friday indirectly discriminates against Muslims who require time off for prayers. Note that by prohibiting indirect discrimination, the law safeguards the interests of an entire group, not just those of the individual plaintiff, because a

---

[62] According to some, encouraging this kind of litigation was precisely one of the factors behind the design of the Race Directive. See E. Evans Case and T. E. Givens, 'Re-Engineering Legal Opportunity Structures in the European Union? The Starting Line Group and the Politics of the Racial Equality Directive' (2010) 48(2) *JCMS* 221.

[63] *Asociaţia Accept* v. *Consiliul Naţional pentru Combaterea Discriminării*, C-81/12, ECLI:EU:C:2013:275, paras. 50–1.

[64] For an assessment of this in the context of the responsiveness of courts to LGBTI claims, see A. van der Vleuten, 'Transnational LGBTI Activism and the European Courts: Constructing the Idea of Europe' in P. M. Ayoub and D. Paternotte (eds.), *LGBT Activism and the Making of Europe* (Basingstoke, Palgrave Macmillan, 2014).

finding that one person is indirectly discriminated against requires that the employer change the unlawful working practice, which benefits everyone in the underrepresented group. The discrimination Directives provide a uniform definition:

> indirect discrimination shall be taken to occur where an apparently neutral provision, criterion or practice would put persons of [the protected group] at a particular disadvantage compared with other persons, unless that provision, criterion or practice is objectively justified by a legitimate aim and the means of achieving that aim are appropriate and necessary.[65]

Establishing a valid claim requires evidence of a neutral rule, which has a more significant effect on the protected group than on others. Often statistical evidence will be necessary to establish this. For example, when Ms Kalliri sought to join the police force she found a rule requiring that each recruit should be at least 1.70 m tall. This was indirectly discriminatory against women for 'a much larger number of women than men are of a height of less than 1.70m, such that, by the application of that law, women are very clearly at a disadvantage compared with men as regards admission to the competition for entry to the Greek Officers' School and School for Policemen'.[66] However statistical evidence is not always necessary to convince the Court that a measure has a disproportionately harmful impact on the claimant. In *Oder*, for example, persons aged above 54 received less redundancy pay than younger employees; while it was found that this did not constitute direct discrimination on the basis of age, the Court held that the claimant was indirectly discriminated because he was disabled, the court finding that while the calculation of pay was done by a standard formula, this was based on different retirement ages for employees with a disability (60) and those without (63). Accordingly the disabled employees would always suffer a disadvantage.[67]

The dividing line between direct and indirect discrimination is not always clear. A telling example is *Achbita*. The claimant began work with the defendant in 2003 and was aware of an unwritten policy that employees should not wear visible signs of their political, philosophical or religious beliefs in the workplace. In 2006 the claimant informed her employer that she would henceforth be wearing an Islamic headscarf. A month later the employer transformed the unwritten rule into a written one, and a month after that Ms Achbita's employment was terminated for infringing the company's dress policies. She claimed that the employer's conduct constituted discrimination.

Samira Achbita, Center for Equal Opportunities and Opposition to Racism v. G4S Secure Solutions NV, C–157/15, ECLI:EU:C:2017:203

28 In so far as the ECHR and, subsequently, the Charter use the term 'religion' in a broad sense, in that they include in it the freedom of persons to manifest their religion, the EU legislature must be considered to have intended to take the same approach when adopting Directive 2000/78, and therefore the concept of

---

[65] Recast Equal Treatment Directive, Article 2(1)(b); Race Directive, Article 2(1)(b); Framework Directive, Article 2(2)(b) (although note special provisos for disability discrimination, discussed further below).

[66] *Ypourgos Esoterikon e Ypourgos Ethnikis paideias kai Thriskevmaton* v. *Maria-Eleni Kalliri*, C-409/16, ECLI:EU:C:2017:767.

[67] *Johann Odar* v. *Baxter Deutschland GmbH*, C-152/11, ECLI:EU:C:2012:772, paras. 57–9.

'religion' in Article 1 of that directive should be interpreted as covering both the *forum internum*, that is the fact of having a belief, and the *forum externum*, that is the manifestation of religious faith in public.

30 In the present case, the internal rule at issue in the main proceedings refers to the wearing of visible signs of political, philosophical or religious beliefs and therefore covers any manifestation of such beliefs without distinction. The rule must, therefore, be regarded as treating all workers of the undertaking in the same way by requiring them, in a general and undifferentiated way, *inter alia*, to dress neutrally, which precludes the wearing of such signs.

31 It is not evident from the material in the file available to the Court that the internal rule at issue in the main proceedings was applied differently to Ms Achbita as compared to any other worker.

32 Accordingly, it must be concluded that an internal rule such as that at issue in the main proceedings does not introduce a difference of treatment that is directly based on religion or belief, for the purposes of Article 2(2)(a) of Directive 2000/78 . . .

34 In the present case, it is not inconceivable that the referring court might conclude that the internal rule at issue in the main proceedings introduces a difference of treatment that is indirectly based on religion or belief, for the purposes of Article 2(2)(b) of Directive 2000/78, if it is established – which it is for the referring court to ascertain – that the apparently neutral obligation it encompasses results, in fact, in persons adhering to a particular religion or belief being put at a particular disadvantage.

This approach has been criticised for comparing people who wear visible signs of a religious or political nature and those who do not, whereas a better comparison would have been between *religious people* who do not wear religious attire and *religious people* who do: this would be more consistent with the notion of religion the court embraced at paragraph 28, noting the existence of a belief and its manifestation as two separate aspects of the freedom of religion. Furthermore, some religions require the wearing of religious attire and others do not, so there is a class who is directly targeted by the employer's dress code. Finally, from a policy perspective, finding that a practice is directly discriminatory would be beneficial for it reduces the chances for the defendant to justify its practices (as discussed in section (b) below employers may justify indirect discrimination when this pursues a legitimate aim) and it also makes for a richer conception of equality by protecting two groups: those who choose to wear religious attire at work and those who believe they must do so.[68]

(b) Legitimate Aim Defence

A specific defence applies in indirect discrimination cases. The discrimination Directives codify the case law: first, there must be a legitimate aim; secondly, the means to achieve the aim must be appropriate; and thirdly, the means to achieve that end must be necessary.[69] This means that if there is a less discriminatory alternative practice that achieves the same goal, the defence is defeated.[70]

---

[68] For a richer discussion, see E. Cloots, 'Safe Harbour or Open Sea for Corporate Headscarf Bans? *Achbita* and *Bougnaoui*' (2018) 55 *CMLRev* 589.

[69] *Bilka-Kaufhaus GmbH* v. *Karin Weber von Hartz*, 170/84, ECLI:EU:C:1986:204.

[70] M. Connolly, 'Discrimination Law: Justification, Alternative Measures and Defences Based on Sex' (2001) 30 *ILJ* 311, 318.

Two questions remain: first, what reasons can be put forward to justify discrimination; and, secondly, how much discretion is afforded to the defendant? Many of the decisions where the Court of Justice has had to confront these questions concern provisions which give lesser benefits to part-time workers. These constitute indirect sex discrimination because women are more likely to be part-time workers. It seems that lesser benefits may be justified if they are an incentive for persons to take up full-time employment,[71] or if the employer wishes to ensure that there are staff working at all times and part-time workers tend not to want to work at weekends or evenings.[72] The Court has also insisted that there must be convincing evidence that indirect discrimination is necessary to obtain the results sought and that generalisations about certain types of worker are insufficient.[73] In the *Achbita* judgment (discussed above) the ECJ offered an interpretation of this defence which appears too accommodating for employers.

Samira Achbita, Center for Equal Opportunities and Opposition to Racism v. *G4S Secure Solutions NV*, C-157/15, ECLI:EU:C:2017:203

37 As regards, in the first place, the condition relating to the existence of a legitimate aim, it should be stated that the desire to display, in relations with both public and private sector customers, a policy of political, philosophical or religious neutrality must be considered legitimate.

38 An employer's wish to project an image of neutrality towards customers relates to the freedom to conduct a business that is recognised in Article 16 of the Charter and is, in principle, legitimate, notably where the employer involves in its pursuit of that aim only those workers who are required to come into contact with the employer's customers.

39 An interpretation to the effect that the pursuit of that aim allows, within certain limits, a restriction to be imposed on the freedom of religion is moreover, borne out by the case-law of the European Court of Human Rights in relation to Article 9 of the ECHR.

40 As regards, in the second place, the appropriateness of an internal rule such as that at issue in the main proceedings, it must be held that the fact that workers are prohibited from visibly wearing signs of political, philosophical or religious beliefs is appropriate for the purpose of ensuring that a policy of neutrality is properly applied, provided that that policy is genuinely pursued in a consistent and systematic manner.

41 In that respect, it is for the referring court to ascertain whether G4S had, prior to Ms Achbita's dismissal, established a general and undifferentiated policy of prohibiting the visible wearing of signs of political, philosophical or religious beliefs in respect of members of its staff who come into contact with its customers.

42 As regards, in the third place, the question whether the prohibition at issue in the main proceedings was necessary, it must be determined whether the prohibition is limited to what is strictly necessary. In the present case, what must be ascertained is whether the prohibition on the visible wearing of any sign or clothing capable of being associated with a religious faith or a political or philosophical belief covers only G4S workers who interact with customers. If that is the case, the prohibition must be considered strictly necessary for the purpose of achieving the aim pursued.

---

[71] *Jenkins* v. *Kingsgate (Clothing Productions) Ltd*, 96/80, ECLI:EU:C:1981:80.
[72] *Bilka-Kaufhaus GmbH* v. *Karin Weber von Hartz*, 170/84, ECLI:EU:C:1986:204.
[73] See e.g. *Rinner-Kühn* v. *FWW Spezial-Gebäudereinigung*, 171/88, ECLI:EU:C:1989:328 ECR 2743; *Nimz* v. *Freie und Hansestadt Hamburg*, C-184/89, ECLI:EU:C:1991:50; *Seymour-Smith and Perez*, C-167/97, ECLI:EU:C:1999:60.

43   In the present case, so far as concerns the refusal of a worker such as Ms Achbita to give up wearing an Islamic headscarf when carrying out her professional duties for G4S customers, it is for the referring court to ascertain whether, taking into account the inherent constraints to which the undertaking is subject, and without G4S being required to take on an additional burden, it would have been possible for G4S, faced with such a refusal, to offer her a post not involving any visual contact with those customers, instead of dismissing her. It is for the referring court, having regard to all the material in the file, to take into account the interests involved in the case and to limit the restrictions on the freedoms concerned to what is strictly necessary.

Critics pointout that the reference to the Charter is one-sided for it also recognises an employee's right to working conditions which respect their dignity;[74] moreover the notion of neutrality is one that some Member States have embraced (e.g. in Belgium where the case originates) but one would expect some justification as to why such a principle should extend to private corporations. Finally, the balancing of interests is said to place little weight on the right of the employee, and many commentators find the approach intimated by AG Sharpston to have been more appropriate.[75] She suggested that clashes of this sort require a conversation between employer and employee to 'explore the options together in order to arrive at a solution that accommodates both the employee's right to manifest his religious belief and the employer's right to conduct his business'.[76] In contrast the Court was more receptive to the views of AG Kokott who appears to take the view that unlike other protected grounds (e.g. gender or race) the employee may 'moderate' her religious commitment when in the workplace.[77]

(iii) Harassment

There is a broad consensus that harassment is a harmful workplace practice, which can range from unwanted, unpleasant remarks directed at a person to the creation of a work environment that is intimidating or humiliating for a group (e.g. displaying pornography in the workplace), to acts of physical violence.[78] In 2015 the Fundamental Rights Agency published a survey where it estimated that 45–55 per cent of women in the EU-28 had suffered from some form of sexual harassment since the age of 15 and that 13–21 per cent had this experience in the year preceding the survey. The survey also found that sexual harassment is more commonly experienced by women in the highest employment levels (i.e. management). However there is significant under-reporting of this phenomenon.[79]

---

[74] Article 31(1) EUCFR.
[75] E. Howard, 'Islamic Headscarves and the CJEU: Achbita and Bougnaoui' (2017) 24(3) *MJECL* 348.
[76] In a case with similar facts, *Asma Bougnaoui and Association de défense des droits de l'homme (ADDH)* v. *Micropole SA*, C-188/15, ECLI:EU:C:2016:553, Opinion of AG Sharpston, para. 128. She continues that as a last resort the employee's rights should prevail.
[77] *Samira Achbita, Center for Equal Opportunities and Opposition to Racism* v. *G4S Secure Solutions NV*, C-157/15, ECLI:EU:C:2016:382, Opinion of AG Kokott, para. 116.
[78] European Commission, *Sexual Harassment at the Workplace in the European Union* (1998).
[79] European Union Agency for Fundamental Rights, *Violence Against Women: An EU-Wide Survey. Main Results Report* (2015) ch. 6.

The Commission began by recommending that Member States promote awareness of sexual harassment and implement a code of practice.[80] Today, harassment is covered in the discrimination Directives. There are two ways to address harassment: first, in the context of American and UK law, the lack of a specific statute prohibiting discrimination led the courts to extend the meaning of discrimination to encompass sexual harassment;[81] secondly, in some Member States (e.g. Ireland, France, Germany and Sweden) harassment is a discrete wrong.[82] Today's Directives are a mix of the two approaches: harassment is discrimination, but there is no need to prove that the victim is discriminated against. The Framework Directive and Race Directive provide:

> Harassment shall be deemed to be a form of discrimination ... when unwanted conduct related [to any of the protected grounds] takes place with the purpose or effect of violating the dignity of a person and of creating an intimidating, hostile, degrading, humiliating or offensive environment. In this context, the concept of harassment may be defined in accordance with the national laws and practice of the Member States.[83]

H. Samuels, 'A Defining Moment: A Feminist Perspective on the Law of Sexual Harassment in the Workplace in the Light of the Equal Treatment Amendment Directive' (2004) 12 *Feminist Legal Studies* 181, 203–4

One of the most important changes that the [Recast Equal Treatment Directive] makes is to deem sexual harassment as discrimination, which eliminates the need for a comparator of the opposite sex ... It also resonates with the approach taken with regard to pregnancy by the European Court of Justice in *Webb* where dismissal of a woman on the grounds of pregnancy was deemed to be discrimination. This is an important development that denies a defence to the 'equal opportunity harasser' who is accused of harassing men and women equally ... Despite the fact that the comparator has been removed in sexual harassment cases, the male standard may still prevail if women have to establish that the conduct complained of was not reasonable. The complete elimination of the male comparator will also depend on the way in which the courts are likely to interpret concepts such as reasonableness and unwelcomeness. If men can argue that behaviour that is offensive to women is reasonable then the law on sexual harassment will be ineffective in tackling harassment. These imprecise concepts may well provide opportunities for courts and tribunals to reintroduce sexist ideas on acceptable behaviour in the workplace and women's response to such conduct.

---

[80] Commission Recommendation 92/131/EEC of 27 November 1991 on the protection of the dignity of women and men at work [1992] OJ L 49/1.

[81] *Porcelli* v. *Strathclyde Regional Council* [1986] ICR 564; *Meritor Savings Bank* v. *Vinston* 477 US 57 (1986). See generally, Fredman, n. 2 above, 320–30.

[82] Irish Employment Act 1998, s. 26; French Labour Code, Article L.122-46; German Act for the Protection of Employees against Sexual Harassment 1994. For comment, see A. C. Saguy, 'French and American Lawyers Define Sexual Harassment' in C. A. MacKinnon and R. B. Siegal (eds.), *Directions in Sexual Harassment Law* (New Haven, CT, Yale University Press, 2004); S. Baer, 'Dignity or Equality? Responses to Workplace Harassment in European, German, and U.S. Law' in C. A. MacKinnon and R. B. Siegal (eds.), *Directions in Sexual Harassment Law* (New Haven, CT, Yale University Press, 2004).

[83] Race Directive, Article 2(3); Framework Directive, Article 2(3). The recast Equality Diretcive does not include the final sentence, avoiding risks of uneven protection.

(iv) Defences

The discrimination Directives provide a further set of defences for direct and indirect discrimination. Here we consider those that are of general application. Specific defences applicable for discrimination on grounds of religion and age are discussed in **section 3**.

(a) Genuine Occupational Requirements

It has been argued that there should be no basis for the defendant to justify directly discriminatory practices.[84] However, outside of the equal-pay context, the discrimination Directives provide that differences in treatment may be justified:

> where, by reason of the nature of the particular occupational activities concerned or of the context in which they are carried out, such a characteristic constitutes a genuine and determining occupational requirement.[85]

Examples may include a rule that favours the recruitment of women gynaecologists over men, or banning men from the profession of midwifery, but past cases are not necessarily an indication of what might be justified today as societies evolve.[86] It must be shown that the objective sought is legitimate, and that the discrimination in proportionate to the objective being sought.[87] The defence applies in 'very limited circumstances'.[88] The Court has denied blanket bans on women working in the army, but it tolerated this for specific positions where the exclusion of women could be seen as necessary.[89] Oddly, when it comes to the army the Framework Directive does not apply to discrimination on the grounds of age and disability.[90]

In the context of a spate of cases on age discrimination in employment the court has held that a maximum recruitment age of 30 years for fire-fighters in *Wolf* and a maximum recruitment age of 35 for front-line policemen in *Salaberia Sorondo* could be tolerated.[91] While the view may be taken that the Court appeared to accept too easily the stereotype that older persons are unable to perform the roles this job entails,[92] it appears that the employers had evidence upon which certain tasks could only be done by younger people and the age limits were also with an eye to diversifying the force with a good mix of older and younger workers. At times a blunt rule is more easily applicable than testing each person's physical state irrespective of age.

The key to the ECJ's review is well summarised in *Bouganoui*: 'the concept of a "genuine and determining occupational requirement", within the meaning of that provision, refers to a

---

[84] E. Ellis and P. Watson, *EU Anti-Discrimination Law*, 2nd edn (Oxford University Press, 2012) 111–13.

[85] Article 14(2) Recast Equal Treatment Directive; Article 4 Race Directive; Article 4(1) Framework Directive.

[86] *Commission* v. *United Kingdom*, 165/82, ECLI:EU:C:1983:311.   [87] Recast Equal Treatment Directive, recital 19.

[88] Race Directive, recital 18; Framework Directive, recital 23.

[89] *Kreil* v. *Germany*, C-285/98, ECLI:EU:C:1999:525; *Sirdar* v. *Army Board and Secretary of State for Defence*, C-273/97, ECLI:EU:C:1999:523. P. Koutrakos, 'EC Law and Equal Treatment in the Armed Forces' (2000) 25 *ELRev* 433.

[90] Article 3(4) Framework Directive.

[91] *Wolf* v. *Stadt Frankfurt am Main*, C-229/08, ECLI:EU:C:2010:3; *Gorka Salaberria Sorondo* v. *Academia Vasca de Policía y Emergencias*, C-258/15, ECLI:EU:C:2016:873. But a maximum age for police work that was not physically taxing was rejected in *Mario Vital Pérez* v. *Ayuntamiento de Oviedo*, C-416/13, ECLI:EU:C:2014:2371.

[92] For comment, see D. Schiek, 'Age Discrimination before the ECJ: Conceptual and Theoretical Issues' (2011) 48 *CMLRev* 777, 791.

requirement that is objectively dictated by the nature of the occupational activities concerned or of the context in which they are carried out. It cannot, however, cover subjective considerations, such as the willingness of the employer to take account of the particular wishes of the customer.'[93] On the facts the Court held that the fact that a client was uncomfortable being served by a woman wearing an Islamic headscarf did not allow the employer to terminate her employment. However, recall that if a dress code is indirectly discriminatory the Court is more tolerant of the employer's stance against religious dress.[94]

(b) Public Security

The Framework Directive contains an additional defence:

Framework Directive, Article 2

(5) This Directive shall be without prejudice to measures laid down by national law which, in a democratic society, are necessary for public security, for the maintenance of public order and the prevention of criminal offences, for the protection of health and for the protection of the rights and freedoms of others.

Tolerance of others is the norm in liberal society but the rationale for this defence is that acts which undermine the moral and political values of the State must be suppressed.[95] Seen in this light, the defence is necessary and it may be surprising that a similar provision is not present in other Directives. The defence seems to have been inserted at the insistence of the United Kingdom, which wished to make it clear that measures to 'protect the public from the activities of religious cults or individuals with a disabling illness such as paranoid schizophrenia which could make them a danger to others would not be prohibited under the Directive'.[96] However, the defence might have a greater impact. In *Petersen*, for example, a maximum working age of 68 for dentists was challenged. The Court of Justice was willing to consider two justifications under Article 2(5): first, the risks to patient health if operated on by a dentist over the age of 68; and, secondly, the financial balance of the statutory health insurance scheme, which is maintained by forcibly retiring older dentists so that the costs of running dental services is lower than if they were able to remain on the payroll. On the facts, the Court of Justice was not convinced that the risk to patient health was maintained by the legislation, because of the exceptions to the mandatory retirement rule. It left it to the national court to consider the financial balance of the scheme.[97] For present purposes, what matters is that the Court appears to apply the exception beyond the narrow confines for which it had been designed. This is unhelpful because there is a specific exception for age discrimination, and to find an alternative angle from which this may be justified is not conducive to legal certainty.

---

[93] *Asma Bougnaoui and Association de défense des droits de l'homme (ADDH)* v. *Micropole SA*, C-188/15, ECLI:EU:C:2017:204, para. 40.

[94] Above p. 588.   [95] S. Mendus, *Toleration and the Limits of Liberalism* (London, Macmillan, 1989) 8–9.

[96] House of Lords Select Committee on the EU, 'The EU Framework Directive on Discrimination', 4th Report, Session 2000–1, HL Paper 13, para. 37.

[97] *Petersen* v. *Berufungsausschuss für Zahnärzte für den Bezirk Westfalen-Lippe*, C-341/08, ECLI:EU:C:2010:4.

(v) Remedies

(a) Procedures

Rights are meaningless without remedies, and the discrimination Directives seek to enhance the plaintiffs' prospects. Complainants are protected from victimisation,[98] and a minimum common procedure is prescribed in the Directives obliging Member States to afford administrative and/or judicial procedures for those who consider themselves to be victims of discrimination and that associations with a legitimate interest in anti-discrimination law may support complainants or act on their behalf.[99] However, these organisations have limited budgets and evidence from the United Kingdom suggests that little of it is spent on assisting claimants.[100] Moreover, the Directives do not require that these organisations should be empowered to bring a claim directly. Finally, Member States may determine which groups have a legitimate interest, which can lead to the exclusion of certain influential groups. The Commission has not so far considered proposing legislation to facilitate class actions in this field. This is problematic, for it is clear that the phenomenon of discrimination is often directed at groups (especially clearly in cases of indirect discrimination).[101]

A particularly problematic issue for claimants is proving discrimination. If a candidate's job application is rejected there is little they can do to allege their gender/race had something to do with it.[102] If pay scales are not visible alleging unequal pay is impossible. As a means of ameliorating this, the Directives propose a sharing of the burden of proof.[103]

Framework Directive, Article 10

(1) Member States shall take such measures as are necessary, in accordance with their national judicial systems, to ensure that, when persons who consider themselves wronged because the principle of equal treatment has not been applied to them establish, before a court or other competent authority, facts from which it may be presumed that there has been direct or indirect discrimination, it shall be for the respondent to prove that there has been no breach of the principle of equal treatment.

(2) Paragraph 1 shall not prevent Member States from introducing rules of evidence which are more favourable to plaintiffs.

The application of this provision was brought up by a Bulgarian court. Having decided that the statements of a football club's patron that the club would not recruit gay players could render the club liable, the court then asked whether this placed the club in an impossible position: how could they refute the claim? Surely they would not be able to point to evidence of having recruited gay players in the past as this would breach their privacy. Does the Directive then not put the defendant in a corner? The Court said that the club could have publicly distanced itself

---

[98] Article 11 Framework Directive; Article 9 Race Directive; Article 24 Recast Equal treatment Directive.

[99] Article 9 Framework Directive; Article 7 Race Directive; Article 17 Recast Equal Treatment Directive.

[100] H. Collins, K. Ewing and A. McColgan, *Labour Law: Text and Materials* (Oxford, Hart, 2005) 332.

[101] B. Lahuerta, 'Enforcing EU Equality Law through Collective Redress: Lagging Behind?' (2018) 55 *CMLR* 783.

[102] The best that EU Law can do is that if the rejected candidate is refused information on whether someone was recruited this could be one factor to take into account in presuming discrimination. *Galina Meister* v. *Speech Design Carrier Systems GmbH*, C-415/10, ECLI:EU:C:2012:217.

[103] Article 8(1) Race Directive; Article 19 Recast Equal Treatment Directive.

from the statement or by showing that it had in place a recruitment policy aimed at ensuring compliance with the principle of equal treatment.[104] One has to be naïve to believe that this is meaningful: well-advised companies now have the tools to draft a set of documents that will protect them against similar claims. In this light the views of some that this article would have a deterrent effect seem somewhat optimistic.[105]

(b) Compensation

The victim of sex discrimination normally has a right to damages. In its case law the Court of Justice has exercised some control over the quantum by indicating that no upper limit may be imposed, except in cases where even without sex discrimination the applicant would not have obtained employment because she is less well qualified than the successful applicant,[106] and that the award must be adequate in relation to the damage suffered.[107] These principles have now been codified in the context of sex discrimination claims.

Recast Equal Treatment Directive, Article 18

Member States shall introduce into their national legal systems such measures as are necessary to ensure real and effective compensation or reparation as the Member States so determine for the loss and damage sustained by a person injured as a result of discrimination on grounds of sex, in a way which is dissuasive and proportionate to the damage suffered. Such compensation or reparation may not be restricted by the fixing of a prior upper limit, except in cases where the employer can prove that the only damage suffered by an applicant as a result of discrimination within the meaning of this Directive is the refusal to take his/her job application into consideration.

In contrast, the Race Directive and Framework Directives are less prescriptive.[108] However, it may well be that, as in the case of sex discrimination, the Court of Justice will bolster the remedies available by removing national limits like caps on remedies. Looking at individual Member States reveals some with more progressive remedies. For instance, in Italy a finding of discrimination may lead to a bar on public tenders. In Italy, Spain and Hungary the findings are published in the press; and in some States like France criminal law applies.[109] Particularly weak regimes may be challenged for infringing EU law – for example, those that impose purely symbolic penalties (such as, a reprimand to the defendant) which are not adequate to ensure that the enforcement of the Directive has dissuasive effects.[110] Nevertheless a comprehensive review of national provisions concludes that there are weaknesses in nearly all Member States:

---

[104] *Asociaţia Accept* v. *Consiliul Naţional pentru Combaterea Discriminării*, C-81/12, ECLI:EU:C:2013:275, paras. 57–8.

[105] D. Chalmers, 'The Mistakes of the Good European?' in S. Fredman (ed.), *Discrimination and Human Rights: The Case of Racism* (Oxford University Press, 2001) 216–17.

[106] *Draehmpaehl* v. *Urania Immobilienservice*, C-180/95, ECLI:EU:C:1997:11.

[107] *Marshall* v. *Southampton and South-West Hampshire AHA*, C-271/91, ECLI:EU:C:1993:335.

[108] Race Directive, Article 15; Framework Directive, Article 17.

[109] V. Guiraudon, 'Equality in the Making: Implementing European Non-Discrimination Law' (2009) 13 *Citizenship Studies* 527, 536–7.

[110] See the Discussion in *Asociaţia Accept* v. *Consiliul Naţional pentru Combaterea Discriminării*, C-81/12, ECLI:EU:C:2013:275, paras. 60–73.

low levels of litigation are reported and there is concern that not all legal systems offer adequate remedies.[111] Comparing EU and US equality law what emerges is that, while the EU rules are more fine-grained and possibly more protective, the use of anti-discrimination law in the United States is much more developed. This may be because the US legal system offers more powerful discovery rules, class actions and punitive damages that stimulate litigation.[112] In this light the measures considered by the Commission in its Action Plan to address the gender pay gap (e.g. fixing minimum levels of compensation, making current recommendations on pay transparency binding and strengthening the enforcement powers of equality bodies) appear rather modest in light of persistent gender inequalities.[113]

4 EQUALITY GROUNDS

The EU legislature has identified certain personal attributes that make discrimination unlawful, but has excluded others. Furthermore, one important omission in the discrimination Directives is any definition of the protected group. This gives Member States discretion on setting out a definition, but it also means that the Court of Justice will have a determinative role in shaping the meaning of concepts like race, ethnicity and religion. The disadvantages of legal uncertainty and diversity among the Member States can be balanced by the potential for the definitions to evolve organically in response to changing social conditions.

A preliminary remark is important: the Directives protect a person who is a member of a protected group, but they also safeguard the rights of a person who does not belong to a protected group but suffers discrimination on the grounds of, for example, sex or race.[114] This means that if a person is discriminated against because he is caring for an elderly relative, or because he has homosexual friends, he is discriminated against on grounds of age or sexual orientation.[115] The Court of Justice confirmed this in *Coleman*, where the claimant was the primary carer of a disabled child and claimed she was harassed and discriminated against on the grounds of her child's disability when she sought flexible working arrangements to care for him.

S. Coleman v. Attridge Law and Steve Law, C–303/06, ECLI:EU:C:2008:415

38 ... the purpose of the directive, as regards employment and occupation, is to combat all forms of discrimination on grounds of disability. The principle of equal treatment enshrined in the directive in that area applies not to a particular category of person but by reference to the grounds mentioned in Article 1. That interpretation is supported by the wording of Article [19 TFEU], which constitutes the legal basis of Directive 2000/78, and which confers on the Community the competence to take appropriate action to combat discrimination based, *inter alia*, on disability ...

---

[111] European Network of Legal Experts in Gender Equality and Non-Discrimination, *Gender Equality Law in Europe: How Are EU Rules Transposed into National Law in 2017?* (European Union, 2018) ch. 10.

[112] J. Dammann, 'Place aux dames: The Ideological Divide Between U.S. and European Gender Discrimination Laws' (2012) 45 *Cornell Int'l LJ* 25.

[113] 'EU Action Plan 2017–2019: Tackling the Gender Pay Gap', COM(2017)678 final.

[114] Recast Equal Treatment Directive, Article 2(1); Race Directive, Article 1; Framework Directive, Article 2(1).

[115] R. Whittle, 'The Framework Directive for Equal Treatment in Employment and Occupation: An Analysis from a Disability Rights Perspective' (2002) 27 *ELRev* 303, 321–2.

50   Although, in a situation such as that in the present case, the person who is subject to direct discrimination on grounds of disability is not herself disabled, the fact remains that it is the disability which, according to Ms Coleman, is the ground for the less favourable treatment which she claims to have suffered. As is apparent from paragraph 38 of this judgment, Directive 2000/78, which seeks to combat all forms of discrimination on grounds of disability in the field of employment and occupation, applies not to a particular category of person but by reference to the grounds mentioned in Article 1.

51   Where it is established that an employee in a situation such as that in the present case suffers direct discrimination on grounds of disability, an interpretation of Directive 2000/78 limiting its application only to people who are themselves disabled is liable to deprive that directive of an important element of its effectiveness and to reduce the protection which it is intended to guarantee.

However, while a victim is entitled to damages, it is not clear how far the employer has a duty to accommodate the employee who cares for a disabled person, because the Court of Justice considered that the duties imposed in the Directive to make reasonable accommodation for the disabled were specifically designed to integrate the disabled person in the workplace and not for the protection of persons like the claimant in this case.[116]

In other circumstances, widening the number of persons entitled to protection may provide other advantages. In *CHEZ*, the defendant electricity company installed electricity meters high above the ground in areas of the country with a substantial Roma population, while in districts without a significant Roma population the meters were set at a lower height allowing a user to check electricity usage and make sure that the bill was accurate. The claimant was not of Roma origin and complained that CHEZ's policy made it difficult for her to check her meter. The ECJ held that she was entitled to bring a claim because the Roma origin of her neighbours led CHEZ to pursue a discriminatory policy against the Roma ethnic group that harmed her interests.[117] Moreover the remedy she sought (an injunction to place the meters at a lower height) would benefit all those in such districts.

(i) Sex and Gender

The active use of litigation to establish gender equality through the use of the EU courts has a long heritage.[118] In developing the coverage under this ground the ECJ's approach has been criticised for its inconsistency. In *Dekker* the Court was progressive in declaring that 'only women can be refused employment on grounds of pregnancy and such a refusal therefore constitutes direct discrimination on grounds of sex'.[119] However, the Court then refused to treat a reduction of pay on the grounds of pregnancy-related illness occurring after the period of maternity leave as sex discrimination.[120] This is hard to reconcile with the broad statement of principle in *Dekker*: applying the broad dictum cited above it is arguable that pregnancy-related

---

[116] *S. Coleman* v. *Attridge Law and Steve Law*, C-303/06, ECLI:EU:C:2008:415, para. 42.
[117] *CHEZ Razpredelenie Bulgaria AD* v. *Komisia za zashtita ot diskriminatsia*, C-83/14, ECLI:EU:C:2015:480, para. 59.
[118] C. Harlow and R. Rawlings, *Pressure Through Law* (London, Routledge, 1992) 282–4.
[119] *Dekker* v. *Stichting Vormingscentrum voor Jong Volwassenen (VJV-Centrum)*, C-177/88, ECLI:EU:C:1990:383.
[120] See e.g. *North Western Health Board* v. *Margaret McKenna*, C-191/03, ECLI:EU:C:2005:513.

illnesses may only be suffered by women and as such pay cuts constitute direct sex discrimination.[121] However, once a child is born the legislation sustains a gendered division of labour: fathers may only secure unpaid leave while mothers' maternity leave entitlements are more generous. It has been thus suggested that in this context fathers' parental leave entitlements should be 'levelled up' to those women enjoy.[122]

In *P* v. *S and Cornwall County Council*, P was dismissed by her employer after informing him of her decision to undergo male-to-female gender reassignment, a medical procedure designed to allow her to have a more integrated identity. The Court found that this constituted discrimination on the basis of sex in breach of the Equal Treatment Directive in force at that time (Directive 76/207/EEC [1976] OJ L39/40).

P v. S and Cornwall County Council, C–13/94, ECLI:EU:C:1996:170

20 . . . [t]he scope of the Directive cannot be confined simply to discrimination based on the fact that a person is of one or other sex. In view of its purpose and the nature of the rights which it seeks to safeguard, the scope of the Directive is also such as to apply to discrimination arising, as in this case, from the gender reassignment of the person concerned.

21 Such discrimination is based, essentially if not exclusively, on the sex of the person concerned. Where a person is dismissed on the ground that he or she intends to undergo, or has undergone, gender reassignment, he or she is treated unfavourably by comparison with persons of the sex to which he or she was deemed to belong before undergoing gender reassignment.

22 To tolerate such discrimination would be tantamount, as regards such a person, to a failure to respect the dignity and freedom to which he or she is entitled, and which the Court has a duty to safeguard.

This was welcomed because the Court moved away from a narrow emphasis on sex discrimination towards an appreciation of gender identities.[123] However in *Grant* v. *South-West Trains* where a lesbian employee was told that her partner was unable to obtain travel concessions, while opposite-sex partners would be entitled to such benefits, the ECJ declined to find that this constituted discrimination on the basis of gender.[124] While this gap of coverage is now (in part) addressed by the Framework Directive which protects sexual orientation,[125] it reveals the Court's difficulty in reaching consistent results: Grant's predecessor was a man who had obtained travel concessions for his female partner so it is arguable that the refusal to provide the same benefit to

---

[121] See J. Mulder, *EU Non-Discrimination Law in the Courts* (Oxford, Hart, 2017) 58–9.

[122] S. Fredman, 'Past and Futures: EU Equality Law' in A. Bogg, C. Costello and A. C. L. Davies, *Research Handbook on EU Labour Law* (Cheltenham, Edward Elgar, 2016) 401–6.

[123] It was applied to retirement pensions for transsexuals in *Richards* v. *Secretary of State for Work and Pensions*, C-423/04, ECLI:EU:C:2006:256. The court however, in requiring surgical treatment appears to avoid a wider notion of gender identity: 'each person's deeply felt internal and individual experience of gender, which may or may not correspond with the sex assigned at birth, including the personal sense of the body (which may involve, if freely chosen, modification of bodily appearance or function by medical, surgical or other means) and other expressions of gender, including dress, speech and mannerisms'. The Yogiyakarta Principles: Principles on the application of international human rights law, in relation to sexual orientation and gender identity (March 2007). M. O'Flaherty and J. Fisher, 'Sexual Orientation, Gender Identity and International Human Rights Law: Contextualising the Yogyakarta Principles' (2008) 8(2) *Human Rights L Rev* 207.

[124] *Grant* v. *South West Trains Ltd*, C-249/96, ECLI:EU:C:1998:63.

[125] It is partial, for the right to be free from sexual orientation discrimination applies only in the workplace while the right to be free from sex discrimination applies also when the claimant suffers discrimination in the provision of services etc. See p. 615.

Grant is based on sex.[126] More generally it has been argued that sex and sexual orientation are categories where discrimination occurs because of gender stereotypes and heteronormative ideals (e.g. that women are attracted to men), and as a result the ECJ will struggle to address discrimination against intersex persons, or even with such prosaic issues as dress codes in the workplace when faced with people who cross-dress.[127] Indeed, the Recast Equality Directive provides that it applies 'to discrimination arising from the gender reassignment of a person'[128] strengthening the physical aspect of sex discrimination against a wider conception of gender identity.

(ii) Racial or Ethnic Origin

As with gender, race and ethnic origin are addressed by a discrete legal instrument. The main reason was the election of a far-right government in Austria in 2000 and the wish of the European Union to assert a set of values to underscore its commitment to racial equality.[129] A second factor was the forthcoming enlargement of the Union. Incorporating non-discrimination in the Community *acquis* was not only a means of sending a strong message against racial intolerance to new Member States, but also of addressing concerns expressed about manifestations of racism in the older Member States, for example France and the United Kingdom.[130]

The Preamble to the Race Directive states that the European Union 'rejects theories which attempt to determine the existence of separate human races'.[131] This recognises that a person's race is a social construct based upon certain attributes – for example skin colour, language, culture or religion – which leads society to stigmatise those who have these attributes. One criticism of the Directive is its failure to suggest that 'observable characteristics' can be the basis for defining race, as this would have facilitated the implementation of effective protection.[132]

In two cases relating to discrimination against Roma communities the ECJ has held that 'the concept of ethnicity, which has its origin in the idea of societal groups marked in particular by common nationality, religious faith, language, cultural and traditional origins and backgrounds, applies to the Roma community'.[133] In these cases the Court intervened to identify discriminatory conduct based on stereotypes about a given ethnic group. In *Jyske Finans* the Court was given the opportunity of developing its approach. Mr Huskic (a Danish national born in Bosnia-Herzegovina) sought a loan to finance the purchase of a car, and the lender, upon learning that he was not born in the EU requested, in addition to the driver's licence, a copy of his passport as an additional proof of identity. Mr Huskic, supported by the Danish Equality Board, considered this was discriminatory based on race or ethnicity.

---

[126] For more detail on this point, see M. Bell, 'Shifting Conceptions of Sexual Discrimination at the Court of Justice: From *P v. S* to *Grant v. SWT* (1999) 5(1) *ELJ* 63.

[127] Mulder (n. 121 above) ch. 2.

[128] Recital 3 recast Equality Directive. Compare this with the Yogikarta Principles (n. 123 above).

[129] See G. de Búrca, 'The Drafting of the European Union Charter of Fundamental Rights' (2001) 26 *ELRev* 126, 136.

[130] For background, see C. Brown, 'The Race Directive: Towards Equality for All Peoples of Europe?' (2002) *YEL* 195, 196–204.

[131] Race Directive, recital 6.

[132] F. Brennan, 'The Race Directive: Recycling Racial Inequality' (2002–3) 5 *CYELS* 311, 320–1.

[133] *CHEZ Razpredelenie Bulgaria AD* v. *Komisia za zashtita ot diskriminatsia*, C-83/14, ECLI:EU:C:2015:480, para. 46.

Jyske Finans A/S v. *Ligebehandlingsnævnet (Danish Equality Board)*, C–668/15, ECLI:EU:C:2017:278

20 . . . [A] person's country of birth cannot, in itself, justify a general presumption that that person is a member of a given ethnic group such as to establish the existence of a direct or inextricable link between those two concepts.

21 Furthermore, it cannot be presumed that each sovereign State has one, and only one, ethnic origin.

23 It cannot therefore be concluded that, even if it were possible to classify it as 'unfavourable treatment', the requirement to provide the additional identification requested in the main proceedings is directly based on ethnic origin.

24 Moreover, as is apparent from recital 13 and Article 3(3) of Directive 2000/43, the directive does not cover different treatment on grounds of nationality.

26 With regard, in the second place, to whether such a practice constitutes indirect discrimination based on ethnic origin, it is necessary to determine whether, in the light of Article 2(2)(b) of Directive 2000/43, that practice, although on the face of it neutral, would put persons of a given racial or ethnic origin at a particular disadvantage compared with other persons.

27 The words 'particular disadvantage' used in that provision must be understood as meaning that it is particularly persons of a given ethnic origin who are at a disadvantage because of the measure at issue.

28 In that connection, it was argued before the Court that, whatever the 'less favourably' treated ethnic origin of Mr Huskic, persons of 'Danish ethnicity' will be treated more favourably as a result of the practice at issue in the main proceedings as they are not subject to the requirement in question.

29 However, it is sufficient to note that that requirement is applicable without distinction to all persons born outside the territory of a Member State of the European Union or the EFTA.

30 It should also be noted that indirect discrimination is liable to arise when a national measure, albeit formulated in neutral terms, works to the disadvantage of far more persons possessing the protected characteristic than persons not possessing it.

31 Nonetheless, as observed in paragraph 27 above, the concept of 'indirect discrimination' within the meaning of Article 2(2)(b) of Directive 2000/43 is applicable only if the allegedly discriminatory measure has the effect of placing a person of a particular ethnic origin at a disadvantage.

32 As the Advocate General observed in point 64 of his Opinion, for the purposes of ascertaining whether a person has been subject to unfavourable treatment, it is necessary to carry out, not a general abstract comparison, but a specific concrete comparison, in the light of the favourable treatment in question.

33 It follows that the argument that the use of the neutral criterion at issue in the main proceedings, namely a person's country of birth, is generally more likely to affect persons of a 'given ethnicity' than 'other persons' cannot be accepted.

Two aspects are worth noting in this judgment – first the absence of the notion of 'race'. The Advocate General considered that defining race had become increasingly unacceptable. While one might object to scientific definitions of race, it is quite another to reject trying to engage with identifying what counts as racist conduct in contemporary Europe.[134] As the preambles of the Race Directive show the legislature specifically intended to fight racism and xenophobia.[135] And as Shreya Atrey argues, convincingly, the policy at play in this case is precisely one that

---

[134] See e.g. the work of the Council of Europe's European Commission Against Racism and Intolerance, www.coe.int/t/dghl/monitoring/ecri/default_en.asp.

[135] Preamble, para. 7. Racism is mentioned five times in the preambles.

identifies those born outside of the EU/EFTA States as the 'other' who 'was taken to be a potential money launderer or terrorist financier and thus, had to provide additional proof of identity'.[136]

Secondly, the Court's reading of how to construe indirect discrimination betrays a literal interpretation of the Directive, requiring that discrimination is affecting a specific race or ethnic origin. However, this would seem to take the sting out of this provision in allowing discriminatory acts which impact more than one ethnic group. The Court might however have been concerned with not allowing the notion of discrimination on the ground of nationality to seep into the Directive when, as seen below, it was excluded deliberately.

(iii) Religion or Belief

Forbidding discrimination on grounds of religion is particularly significant because while some religious groups would be able to secure protection on the basis of the Race Directive, others might fall outside it. In the context of the United Kingdom, for example, Muslims found it difficult to make a claim for race discrimination.[137] The precise scope of the notion of belief will require elucidation and one can take the approach under the ECtHR as inspiration: it suggests the belief in question must be coherent and serious, and must be one which merits respect in a democratic society.[138] Atheism and humanism fall within this definition, but the support of a political party or a football team would probably not. Absence of belief is also protected, so a religious employer may not refuse a job to a non-believer.[139] As discussed above, the only two judgments of the ECJ in this field (*Achbita* and *Bougnaoui*) appear to forbid an employer from devising a dress code that indirectly discriminates against those of certain religions.[140] However, the employer may maintain this policy if he claims that he wishes to pursue a policy of neutrality vis-à-vis his clients and he can offer the employee 'a post not involving any visual contact with those customers.'[141] This position is objectionable to anyone wishing that anti-discrimination law can have the potential to foster integration, but it also shows that these two judgments are irreconcilable. In *Bougnaoui* the ECJ refused to consider that one may justify religious discrimination because of what clients think, but isn't the dictum in *Achbita* effectively admitting that her employer too was imposing a dress code out of concern with the potential opinion of its customers?

Recall, however, that religion is a highly sensitive field for many jurisdictions. Indeed a specific defence applies to shield religious organisations from the Directive and was inserted at the request of some Member States, in particular the Irish Government, concerned that the Directive may hamper the employment practices of religious institutions.[142]

---

[136] S. Atrey, 'Race Discrimination after *Jyske Finans*' (2018) 55 *CMLRev* 625, 636.

[137] B. Hepple and T. Choudhury, *Tackling Religious Discrimination: Practical Implications for Policy-Makers and Legislators*, Home Office Research Study 221 (London, Home Office, 2001) 12; S. Poulter, 'Muslim Headscarves in School: Contrasting Approaches in England and France' (1997) *OJLS* 43.

[138] *Campbell and Cosans* v. *United Kingdom* (1982) 4 EHRR 293, 304.

[139] *Kokkanikis* v. *Greece* (1994) 17 EHRR 397, 418.

[140] For discussion of these judgments, see J. H. H. Weiler 'Je Suis Achbita' (2017) 28(4) *EJIL* 989.

[141] *Achbita, Center for Equal Opportunities and Opposition to Racism* v. *G4S Secure Solutions NV*, C-157/15, ECLI:EU: C:2017:203, para. 43.

[142] Bell, n. 4 above, 154–5.

Framework Directive, Article 4

(2) Member States may maintain national legislation in force at the date of adoption of this Directive or provide for future legislation incorporating national practices existing at the date of adoption of this Directive pursuant to which, in the case of occupational activities within churches and other public or private organisations the ethos of which is based on religion or belief, a difference of treatment based on a person's religion or belief shall not constitute discrimination where, by reason of the nature of these activities or of the context in which they are carried out, a person's religion or belief constitute a genuine, legitimate and justified occupational requirement, having regard to the organisation's ethos. This difference of treatment shall be implemented taking account of Member States' constitutional provisions and principles, as well as the general principles of Community law, and should not justify discrimination on another ground.

Provided that its provisions are otherwise complied with, this Directive shall thus not prejudice the right of churches and other public or private organisations, the ethos of which is based on religion or belief, acting in conformity with national constitutions and laws, to require individuals working for them to act in good faith and with loyalty to the organisation's ethos.

The exception is in conformity with the autonomy that States tend to grant to religious organisations, although it may be argued that such organisations could be protected by the genuine occupational requirement defence. In *Egenberger* the Court was called upon to explore the scope of this exception. The claimant applied for a job as a researcher for an association affiliated with the Protestant Church in Germany. The task was to write a report on Germany's compliance with the United Nations International Convention on the Elimination of All Forms of Racial Discrimination and it stipulated that the would-be employee should be a member of a Protestant church or a church belonging to the Working Group of Christian Churches in Germany. The claimant had no such religious affiliation and considered that her application had been unsuccessful because of this, and challenged the association. The ECJ first held that the claimant had a right to challenge the decision of the defendant in front of an independent authority and ultimately a national court.[143] The Court then moved to explore how to interpret Article 4(2).[144]

Vera Egenberger v. Evangelisches Werk für Diakonie und Entwicklung e.V, ECLI:EU:C:2018:257

61 In this respect, it is true that in the balancing exercise provided for in Article 4(2) of Directive 2000/78 . . . , the Member States and their authorities, including judicial authorities, must, except in very exceptional cases, refrain from assessing whether the actual ethos of the church or organisation concerned is legitimate (see, to that effect, ECtHR, 12 June 2014, *Fernández Martínez* v. *Spain*, CE:ECHR:2014:0612JUD005603007, § 129). They must nonetheless ensure that there is no infringement of the right of workers not to be discriminated against on grounds *inter alia* of religion or belief. Thus, by virtue of Article 4(2), the purpose of the examination is to ascertain whether the occupational requirement imposed by the church or

---

[143] *Vera Egenberger* v. *Evangelisches Werk für Diakonie und Entwicklung e.V*, ECLI:EU:C:2018:257, para. 53.
[144] See also *IR* v. *JQ*, C-68/17, ECLI:EU:C:2018:696 embodying the same approach.

organisation, by reason of the nature of the activities concerned or the context in which they are carried out, is genuine, legitimate and justified, having regard to that ethos.

62 As regards the interpretation of the concept of 'genuine, legitimate and justified occupational requirement' in Article 4(2) of Directive 2000/78, it follows expressly from that provision that it is by reference to the 'nature' of the activities concerned or the 'context' in which they are carried out that religion or belief may constitute such an occupational requirement.

63 Thus the lawfulness from the point of view of that provision of a difference of treatment on grounds of religion or belief depends on the objectively verifiable existence of a direct link between the occupational requirement imposed by the employer and the activity concerned. Such a link may follow either from the nature of the activity, for example where it involves taking part in the determination of the ethos of the church or organisation in question or contributing to its mission of proclamation, or else from the circumstances in which the activity is to be carried out, such as the need to ensure a credible presentation of the church or organisation to the outside world.

64 Furthermore, the occupational requirement must, as required by Article 4(2) of Directive 2000/78, be 'genuine, legitimate and justified', having regard to the ethos of the church or organisation. Although in principle, as stated in paragraph 61 above, it is not for the national courts to rule on the ethos as such on which the purported occupational requirement is founded, they are nevertheless called on to decide on a case-by-case basis whether those three criteria are satisfied from the point of view of that ethos.

65 With respect to those criteria, it should be stated, first, as regards the 'genuine' nature of the requirement, that the use of that adjective means that, in the mind of the EU legislature, professing the religion or belief on which the ethos of the church or organisation is founded must appear necessary because of the importance of the occupational activity in question for the manifestation of that ethos or the exercise by the church or organisation of its right of autonomy.

66 Secondly, as regards the 'legitimate' nature of the requirement, the use of that term shows that the EU legislature wished to ensure that the requirement of professing the religion or belief on which the ethos of the church or organisation is founded is not used to pursue an aim that has no connection with that ethos or with the exercise by the church or organisation of its right of autonomy.

67 Thirdly, as regards the 'justified' nature of the requirement, that term implies not only that compliance with the criteria in Article 4(2) of Directive 2000/78 can be reviewed by a national court, but also that the church or organisation imposing the requirement is obliged to show, in the light of the factual circumstances of the case, that the supposed risk of causing harm to its ethos or to its right of autonomy is probable and substantial, so that imposing such a requirement is indeed necessary.

68 The requirement in Article 4(2) of Directive 2000/78 must comply with the principle of proportionality . . . As the principle of proportionality is one of the general principles of EU, . . . the national courts must ascertain whether the requirement in question is appropriate and does not go beyond what is necessary for attaining the objective pursued.

In light of this approach it is unlikely that a church can deny a non-religious applicant a researcher's job.[145] Furthermore, note how here, unlike in *Achbita*, the ECJ's examination was more probing.

---

[145] For a wide-ranging analysis of the difficulties in reconciling the demands of liberal society with religious doctrine, see B. Barry, *Culture and Equality* (London, Polity Press, 2001) ch. 5. Note possible divergences between EU law and the approach of the ECtHR, R. McCrea, 'Singing from the Same Hymn Sheet? What the Differences between the Strasbourg and Luxembourg Courts Tell Us about Religious Freedom, Non-Discrimination, and the Secular State' (2016) 5(2) *Oxford Journal of Law and Religion* 183.

(iv) Disability

The Framework Directive should be read together with the UN Convention on the Rights of Persons with Disabilities (UNCRPD) which forms part of EU law.[146] This Convention has proven helpful in aiding the Court of Justice in drawing a line between disability and illness.

The leading case was brought by a Danish trade union on behalf of two of its members. One suffered from constant lumbar pain which could not be treated, the other suffered the effects of a whiplash injury: both were unable to work full time but both remained capable of working reduced hours, and the trade union argued that the Directive imposed a duty on their employers to offer them this arrangement.

HK Danmark, acting on behalf of Jette Ring v. *Dansk almennyttigt Boligselskab and HK Danmark, acting on behalf of Lone Skouboe Werge* v. *Dansk Arbejdsgiverforening acting on behalf of Pro Display A/S*, C–335/11 and C–337/11, ECLI:EU:C:2013:222

37 The UN Convention, which was ratified by the European Union … acknowledges in recital (e) that 'disability is an evolving concept and that disability results from the interaction between persons with impairments and attitudinal and environmental barriers that hinder their full and effective participation in society on an equal basis with others'. Thus the second paragraph of Article 1 of the Convention states that persons with disabilities include 'those who have long-term physical, mental, intellectual or sensory impairments which in interaction with various barriers may hinder their full and effective participation in society on an equal basis with others'.

38 … the concept of 'disability' must be understood as referring to a limitation which results in particular from physical, mental or psychological impairments which in interaction with various barriers may hinder the full and effective participation of the person concerned in professional life on an equal basis with other workers.

39 In addition, it follows from the second paragraph of Article 1 of the UN Convention that the physical, mental or psychological impairments must be 'long-term'.

40 It may be added that, as the Advocate General observes in point 32 of her Opinion, it does not appear that Directive 2000/78 is intended to cover only disabilities that are congenital or result from accidents, to the exclusion of those caused by illness. It would run counter to the very aim of the directive, which is to implement equal treatment, to define its scope by reference to the origin of the disability.

41 It must therefore be concluded that if a curable or incurable illness entails a limitation which results in particular from physical, mental or psychological impairments which in interaction with various barriers may hinder the full and effective participation of the person concerned in professional life on an equal basis with other workers, and the limitation is a long-term one, such an illness can be covered by the concept of 'disability' within the meaning of Directive 2000/78.

42 On the other hand, an illness not entailing such a limitation is not covered by the concept of 'discrimination' within the meaning of Directive 2000/78. Illness as such cannot be regarded as a ground in addition to those in relation to which Directive 2000/78 prohibits discrimination.

43 The circumstance that the person concerned can work only to a limited extent is not an obstacle to that person's state of health being covered by the concept of 'disability'. Contrary to the submissions of DAB and Pro Display, a disability does not necessarily imply complete exclusion from work or professional life.

---

[146] Council Decision 2010/48/EC of 26 November 2009 [2010] OJ L 23/35.

This ruling qualifies the narrower position the Court of Justice had taken earlier.[147] It is to be welcomed insofar as it allows those who experience long-term illness to be brought within the scope of the Directive. Moreover, reliance on the UNCRPD also leads the courts away from a medical model to a social model of understanding disability.[148] The latter gives protection to a wider range of persons (e.g. those who have a facial disfigurement).[149] The Court's case law since then has been slightly erratic. In *Kaltoft* the court followed this judgment in ruling that an obese person could be classified as disabled if obesity 'hindered his full and effective participation in professional life on an equal basis with other workers on account of reduced mobility'.[150] However, the Court was less open-minded in *Z*. The claimant was a female who, unable to bear children entered into a surrogacy agreement; subsequently her employer denied her paid maternity leave. The Court denied the claim because the claimant's condition did not fall within the scope of the Directive: 'the inability to have a child by conventional means does not in itself, in principle, prevent the commissioning mother from having access to, participating in or advancing in employment'.[151] This would appear to fly in the face of the whole purpose of affording parents leave so that people may find an appropriate balance between work and family life.[152]

The Directive recognises that disability is the result of barriers in the workplace;[153] and that it is socially constructed.[154] Therefore special duties are imposed on the employer.

Framework Directive, Article 5

In order to guarantee compliance with the principle of equal treatment in relation to persons with disabilities, reasonable accommodation shall be provided. This means that employers shall take appropriate measures, where needed in a particular case, to enable a person with a disability to have access to, participate in, or advance in employment, or to undergo training, unless such measures would impose a disproportionate burden on the employer. This burden shall not be disproportionate when it is sufficiently remedied by measures existing within the framework of the disability policy of the Member State concerned.

The practical significance of this policy can be illustrated by returning to the judgment above. It will be recalled that the two claimants felt that they would have been able to continue work if their work hours were reduced. The employers claimed that this was not the sort of accommodation that Article 5 had in mind, but the Court of Justice disagreed.

---

[147] *Sonia Chacón Navas* v. *Eurest Colectividades SA*, C-13/05, ECLI:EU:C:2006:456, para. 43.

[148] M. Perlin, *International Human Rights and Mental Disability Law: When the Silenced are Heard* (Oxford University Press, 2011) ch. 7; G. Quinn, 'The United Nations Convention on the Rights of Persons with Disabilities: Towards a New International Politics of Disability' (2009) 15 *Texas Journal on Civil Liberties and Civil Rights* 33–50.

[149] D. L. Hosking, 'A High Bar for EU Disability Rights' (2007) 36 *ILJ* 228. See further M. Oliver and C. Barnes, *Disabled People and Social Policy: From Exclusion to Inclusion* (Harlow, Longman, 1998).

[150] *Fag og Arbejde (FOA), acting on behalf of Karsten Kaltoft* v. *Kommunernes Landsforening (KL)*, C-354/13, ECLI:EU:C:2014:2463, para. 60.

[151] *Z* v. *A Government Department*, C-363/12, ECLI:EU:C:2014:159, para. 81.

[152] Cf. the approach of the ECJ with that of AG Kokott in *C.D.* v. *S.T.*, C-167/12, ECLI:EU:C:2013:600. For discussion, see E. Caracciolo di Torella and P. Foubert, 'Surrogacy, Pregnancy and Maternity Rights: A Missed Opportunity for a More Coherent Regime of Parental Rights in the EU' (2015) 40(1) *ELR* 52.

[153] K. Wells, 'The Impact of the Framework Employment Directive on UK Disability Discrimination Law' (2003) 32 *ILJ* 253.

[154] See generally, C. Barnes, 'A Working Social Model? Disability, Work and Disability Politics in the 21st Century' (2000) 20 *Critical Social Policy* 441.

HK Danmark, acting on behalf of Jette Ring v. **Dansk almennyttigt Boligselskab and HK Danmark, acting on behalf of Lone Skouboe Werge** v. **Dansk Arbejdsgiverforening acting on behalf of Pro Display A/S**, C-335/11 and C-337/11, ECLI:EU:C:2013:222

53 In accordance with the second paragraph of Article 2 of the UN Convention, 'reasonable accommodation' is 'necessary and appropriate modification and adjustments not imposing a disproportionate or undue burden, where needed in a particular case, to ensure to persons with disabilities the enjoyment or exercise on an equal basis with others of all human rights and fundamental freedoms'. It follows that that provision prescribes a broad definition of the concept of 'reasonable accommodation'.

54 Thus, with respect to Directive 2000/78, that concept must be understood as referring to the elimination of the various barriers that hinder the full and effective participation of persons with disabilities in professional life on an equal basis with other workers.

55 As recital 20 in the preamble to Directive 2000/78 and the second paragraph of Article 2 of the UN Convention envisage not only material but also organisational measures, and the term 'pattern' of working time must be understood as the rhythm or speed at which the work is done, it cannot be ruled out that a reduction in working hours may constitute one of the accommodation measures referred to in Article 5 of that directive.

56 It should be observed, moreover, that the list of appropriate measures to adapt the workplace to the disability in recital 20 in the preamble to Directive 2000/78 is not exhaustive and, consequently, even if it were not covered by the concept of 'pattern of working time', a reduction in working hours could be regarded as an accommodation measure referred to in Article 5 of the directive, in a case in which reduced working hours make it possible for the worker to continue employment, in accordance with the objective of that article.

57 It must be recalled, however, that, as stated in recital 17 in the preamble, Directive 2000/78 does not require the recruitment, promotion or maintenance in employment of a person who is not competent, capable and available to perform the essential functions of the post concerned, without prejudice to the obligation to provide reasonable accommodation for people with disabilities, which includes a possible reduction in their hours of work.

58 Moreover, in accordance with Article 5 of that directive, the accommodation persons with disabilities are entitled to must be reasonable, in that it must not constitute a disproportionate burden on the employer.

59 In the disputes in the main proceedings, it is therefore for the national court to assess whether a reduction in working hours, as an accommodation measure, represents a disproportionate burden on the employers.

60 As follows from recital 21 in the preamble to Directive 2000/78, account must be taken in particular of the financial and other costs entailed by such a measure, the scale and financial resources of the undertaking, and the possibility of obtaining public funding or any other assistance . . .

62 It may be of relevance for the purposes of that assessment that, as noted by the referring court, immediately after the dismissal of Ms Ring, DAB advertised a position for an office worker to work part-time, 22 hours a week, in its regional office in Lyngby. There is nothing in the documents before the Court to show that Ms Ring was not capable of occupying that part-time post or to explain why it was not offered to her. Moreover, the referring court stated that soon after her dismissal Ms Ring started a new job as a receptionist with another company and her actual working time was 20 hours a week.

63 In addition, as the Danish Government pointed out at the hearing, Danish law makes it possible to grant public assistance to undertakings for accommodation measures whose purpose is to facilitate the access to the labour market of persons with disabilities, including initiatives aimed at encouraging employers to recruit and maintain in employment persons with disabilities.

The judgment has been welcomed by the European Disability Forum, and one may wonder whether the obligations found in Article 5 may not be worth considering for other grounds, because positive obligations to integrate previously excluded groups can be vital to develop a sound equality policy. Return to the controversial judgment in *Achbita*: would it not be preferable to require the employer to take greater steps to integrate those wearing religious clothing?

As a final consideration one might wonder whether the State's support for an employer making adjustments to the workplace should be relevant: it may make it too easy for employers to escape from having to modify their workplace when such funds are unavailable. Moreover, if the government makes such funds available, it may be more effective to create incentives for employers to take advantage of these funds than to use strategic litigation to force an allocation of these resources.

(v) Age

The Framework Directive is not limited to discrimination against the elderly. Discrimination against young employees is also forbidden.[155] This is in contrast to American law where comparable legislation is directed at persons aged 40 or over.[156] Given that workers of all ages require protection, it may be suggested that the aim of age discrimination law should be to promote age diversity among the working population. This aspiration is reflected in the Commission's *Green Paper on Demographic Change*, which suggests that EU policy should develop to ensure solidarity across generations by granting opportunities and benefits to all age groups.[157] However, there are two limits to what the Framework Directive can achieve in this context: first, discrimination is not the sole cause of the current social problems, and it must be seen as part of a wider range of social policy measures. Secondly, an empirical study of the American statute outlawing discrimination of older workers suggests that it has mainly benefited white men.[158] Taken together, these observations indicate the inherent limitations of a legal framework premised upon a formal equality model.

Litigation under this ground has largely focused on the special defence in cases of age discrimination, which allows direct age discrimination.

Framework Directive, Article 6

(1) Notwithstanding Article 2(2), Member States may provide that differences of treatment on grounds of age shall not constitute discrimination, if, within the context of national law, they are objectively and reasonably justified by a legitimate aim, including legitimate employment policy, labour market and vocational training objectives, and if the means of achieving that aim are appropriate and necessary.

Such differences of treatment may include, among others:

---

[155] Young workers are also protected by Directive 94/33/EC of 22 June 1994 on the protection of young people at work [1994] OJ L 216/12, establishing a minimum age for work and several protective measures for young workers.

[156] Age Discrimination in Employment Act 1967, 29 USC 621–34.

[157] 'Green Paper on Confronting Demographic Change: A New Solidarity Between the Generations', COM(2005) 94 final.

[158] G. Rutherglen, 'From Race to Age: The Expanding Scope of Employment Discrimination Law' (1995) 24 *Journal of Legal Studies* 491.

(a) the setting of special conditions on access to employment and vocational training, employment and occupation, including dismissal and remuneration conditions, for young people, older workers and persons with caring responsibilities in order to promote their vocational integration or ensure their protection;

(b) the fixing of minimum conditions of age, professional experience or seniority in service for access to employment or to certain advantages linked to employment;

(c) the fixing of a maximum age for recruitment which is based on the training requirements of the post in question or the need for a reasonable period of employment before retirement.

The significance of this defence has become increasingly prominent as Member States face significant youth unemployment as a result of the ongoing economic crisis. Member States pursue two kinds of policies that discriminate on the grounds of age: they try and retain older workers at the expense of younger ones, or they may impose compulsory retirement on older workers to facilitate the entry of younger workers (this is often referred to as inter-generational solidarity). At the time of writing the legality of these policies is the issue which has been referred to the Court of Justice most frequently. The case law is not wholly consistent.[159]

In *Mangold*, the Court found that legislation making the conclusion of fixed-term contracts with older workers easier was based on a legitimate objective: 'to promote the vocational integration of unemployed older workers, in so far as they encounter considerable difficulties in finding work'.[160] But the Court ruled that the law went beyond what was necessary to achieve that aim by taking into consideration only age and not the personal circumstances of the individual or the conditions in the labour market.[161] This suggested a strict standard of review. However, when the Court has been faced with schemes of compulsory employment termination for older workers, a less searching kind of scrutiny appears to have been applied. In *Rosenbladt*, for example, the Court of Justice considered a challenge to a scheme (established as a result of collective bargaining between employers and workers) which made retirement compulsory at the age of 65. The Court held that one must test whether the measure in question is appropriate and necessary to meet a legitimate aim.

Gisela Rosenbladt v. Oellerking Gebäudereinigungsges mbH, C–45/09, ECLI:EU:C:2010:601

62 The Court has held that clauses on automatic termination of employment contracts of employees who are eligible to receive a retirement pension may be justified in the context of a national policy seeking to promote better access to employment, by means of better distribution of work between the generations and aims of that kind must, in principle, be considered to justify 'objectively and reasonably', 'within the context of national law', as provided in the first subparagraph of Article 6(1) of Directive 2000/78, a difference in treatment on the ground of age prescribed by Member States. It follows that objectives such as those described by the referring court are 'legitimate' within the meaning of that provision . . .

67 In the light of the assessment made by the referring court, it must be observed that the clause on the automatic termination of employment contracts at issue in the main proceedings is the result of an

---

[159] In addition to the cases referred to in the text, see *Lindorfer* v. *Council*, C-227/04 P, ECLI:EU:C:2007:490; *Félix Palacios de la Villa* v. *Cortefiel Servicios SA*, C-411/05, ECLI:EU:C:2007:604.

[160] *Werner Mangold* v. *Rüdiger Helm*, C-144/04, ECLI:EU:C:2005:709, para. 59. P. Skidmore, 'The European Employment Strategy and Labour Law: a German Case Study' (2004) 29 *ELRev* 52.

[161] *Werner Mangold* v. *Rüdiger Helm*, C-144/04, ECLI:EU:C:2005:709, paras. 64–5.

agreement negotiated between employees' and employers' representatives exercising their right to bargain collectively which is recognised as a fundamental right. The fact that the task of striking a balance between their respective interests is entrusted to the social partners offers considerable flexibility, as each of the parties may, where appropriate, opt not to adopt the agreement.

68 By guaranteeing workers a certain stability of employment and, in the long term, the promise of foreseeable retirement, while offering employers a certain flexibility in the management of their staff, the clause on automatic termination of employment contracts is thus the reflection of a balance between diverging but legitimate interests, against a complex background of employment relationships closely linked to political choices in the area of retirement and employment.

69 Accordingly, in the light of the wide discretion granted to the social partners at national level in choosing not only to pursue a given aim in the area of social policy, but also in defining measures to implement it, it does not appear unreasonable for the social partners to take the view that a measure such as Paragraph 19 (8) of the RTV [framework collective agreement for commercial cleaning sector employees] may be appropriate for achieving the aims set out above . . .

The Court of Justice then considered the appropriateness of this policy. Finally, the Court of Justice considered whether the measure was necessary.

73 In order to examine whether the measure at issue in the main proceedings goes beyond what is necessary for achieving its objective and unduly prejudices the interests of workers who reach the age of 65, when they may obtain liquidation of their pension rights, that measure must be viewed against its legislative background and account must be taken both of the hardship it may cause to the persons concerned and of the benefits derived from it by society in general and the individuals who make up society.

74 . . . German employment law does not prevent a person who has reached the age at which he is eligible for payment of a pension from continuing to work. Furthermore, according to those explanations, a worker in that position continues to enjoy protection from discrimination on grounds of age under the AGG. The referring court made clear, in that connection, that the AGG [General Law on Equal Treatment] prevents a person in Mrs Rosenbladt's position, after termination of her employment contract on the ground that she has reached retirement age, from being refused employment, either by her former employer or by a third party, on a ground related to her age.

75 Viewed against that background, the termination by operation of law of an employment contract as a result of a measure such as Paragraph 19(8) of the RTV does not have the automatic effect of forcing the persons concerned to withdraw definitively from the labour market. It follows that that provision does not establish a mandatory scheme of automatic retirement . . . It does not prevent a worker who wishes to do so, for example, for financial reasons, from continuing to work beyond retirement age. It does not deprive employees who have reached retirement age of protection from discrimination on grounds of age where they wish to continue to work and seek a new job.

The Court of Justice is not wholly deferential to national policy; indeed, in some cases it has found that measures that discriminate against older workers may not be justified.[162] However,

---

[162] E.g. *Ingeniørforeningen i Danmark, acting on behalf of Ole Andersen* v. *Region Syddanma*, C-499/08, ECLI:EU: C:2010:600.

the approach is not without problems. First, it appears to defer to collective bargaining, which is different from the position taken in sex discrimination (where instead one sees the Court noting the risk that collective agreements may also be discriminatory). It thus substitutes a close look as to whether the measure in question is appropriate with a procedural question. On the facts, the national court had been sceptical as to whether the measure was indeed working to stimulate employment, but the Court deemed this irrelevant. Secondly, when applying the necessity test, the Court does not ask whether the measure is the least restrictive way to achieve the policy objectives at hand, but instead considers if the measure strikes a fair balance between the interests of employers and employees. Again, it is instructive to note that the referring court appeared to be more concerned about whether there were less onerous measures for the welfare of the employees. It is not clear that this approach really safeguards the interests of the claimant, who will not find it easy to secure employment after compulsory termination.[163]

Furthermore, with two different standards of review (a stricter one as in *Mangold*; a looser one as in *Rosenbladt*) there is a risk of inconsistency in how similar policies are assessed by national courts. More generally, it is not even clear how best to resolve the matter: the difficult balance between promoting youth employment and safeguarding an elderly workforce means that Member States are operating in a field where there is no right answer. However, it would be a step too far to conclude that the Court of Justice should just defer to national policies. A closer look as to whether the relevant retirement policy is well designed to achieve the ends it is said to achieve would be desirable.[164]

(vi) Sexual Orientation

Discrimination on grounds of sexual orientation operates at two levels: first, there is discrimination against those who are open about their sexuality, but secondly (and perhaps distinct from other grounds of discrimination) some choose to keep their sexual orientation a secret for fear of discrimination. The Framework Directive addresses the first type of discrimination, but the second requires a societal shift in attitudes. Nevertheless, a potentially helpful dimension for those who do not wish to disclose their sexuality is that discrimination arises if an *assumption* is made about their sexual orientation. This seems to be the position in the Directive, and according to some, this might help encourage litigation.[165]

While the Framework Directive might be seen to provide an effective means for guaranteeing the rights of the homosexual employee, it excludes any interference with the design of national law insofar as family rights are concerned. Recital 22 of the Framework Directive provides that '[t]his Directive is without prejudice to national laws on marital status and the benefits dependent thereon'. However, this recital was read narrowly by the Court of Justice in *Tadao Maruko*. The claimant was in a same-sex registered partnership (a 'life partnership' under German law) and was denied a widower's pension on his partner's death because the rules of the association managing that pension made no provision for same-sex partners. After finding that the pension constituted 'pay' so that the dispute fell within the Framework Directive, the Court noted that the

---

[163] Kilpatrick, n. 19 above, 290–8.

[164] See the valuable guidance offered by E. Dewhurst, 'Intergenerational Balance, Mandatory Retirement and Age Discrimination in Europe: How Can the ECJ Better Support National Courts in finding a Balance between the Generations?' (2013) 50 *CMLRev* 1333.

[165] H. Oliver, 'Sexual Orientation Discrimination: Perceptions, Definitions and Genuine Occupational Requirements' (2004) 33 *ILJ* 1. But some have expressed caution: Bell, n. 4 above, 115.

conditions for life partnerships were increasingly aligned with those of marriage. It followed that if the national court should decide that surviving spouses and surviving life partners are in a comparable situation, then the denial of a widower's pension to the latter would constitute direct discrimination.[166] This leaves national courts with the task of determining if married couples and registered partners are in a comparable situation having regard to the issue at stake. On the facts, the German law gave life partners increasingly similar rights to married couples, allowing a successful claim. However, in Member States where the rights of registered partners are not similar to those of married couples, claimants will have to rest their arguments on indirect discrimination, which may prove more arduous.

The approach of the Court of Justice in this and similar cases is problematic from two different perspectives.[167] First, it requires the same-sex couple to assimilate their relationship to that of marriage. In this view the law does not so much recognise homosexual partnerships as it forces them into the framework for heterosexual ones: if you get close enough, you can claim equality rights, if you don't then no rights accrue.[168] This is more oppressive than emancipatory. The second line of criticism starts from a different premise: the law requires a Member State that has designed a legal form whereby homosexuals can secure recognition of their union to extend a wide range of benefits to the couple. However, in so doing the Court ignores the reasons why benefits are paid to married couples. For example, the survivor's pension in *Maruko* was probably based on the assumption that there was a spouse bearing the child-care obligations who would receive help from the pension. It does not then follow that a childless couple should be entitled to similar levels of support.[169] However, this raises an even wider issue about how to design pension rights appropriately: limiting them to married couples is discriminatory, but extending them to registered partners is also invidious, for it leaves out those whose lifestyle choices do not conform to the registered partnership model designed by the State. But focusing on categories at all makes one lose sight of a wider issue: how best to design the Welfare State. Thus EU law, under the guise of equality, has a profound impact on national welfare policies where the European Union ostensibly lacks competence. It may be preferable to tackle these head on rather than through the lens of discrimination law, by reformulating the way benefits are paid out.

Finally, it is worth noting that in this round of litigation the Court of Justice preferred to base itself upon finding direct discrimination. However, it seems as if the problem raised is one of indirect discrimination: the national laws all use one seemingly neutral criterion (marriage) to determine entitlements to pay, which affects a wide range of persons who, by virtue of the legal framework, are unable to qualify. This approach would then have led the Member State to articulate reasons why this form of discrimination is justified and would thus have allowed for one to consider the appropriate design of widowers' pension entitlements by considering expressly the policy objectives pursued by such benefits.[170]

---

[166] *Tadao Maruko* v. *Versorgungsanstalt der deutschen Bühnen*, C-267/06, ECLI:EU:C:2008:179, para. 72.

[167] See also *Römer* v. *Freie und Hansestadt Hamburg*, C-147/08, ECLI:EU:C:2011:286.

[168] J. Mulder, 'Some More Equal than Others? Matrimonial Benefits and the CJEU's Case Law on Discrimination on the Grounds of Sexual Orientation' (2012) 19(4) *MJECL* 505.

[169] J. Cornides, 'Three Case Studies on "Anti-discrimination"' (2012) 32(2) *EJIL* 517, 523–6. Obviously homosexual couples may have children just as much as heterosexual couples could be childless.

[170] See Mulder, n. 168 above, for this approach.

(vii) Excluded Groups

In view of the universality of the right to equality, and the recognition that discrimination against foreigners was likely in the face of increased migration into the European Union, the Council's expert committee on racism (the Kahn Commission) recommended that Article 19 TFEU should prohibit discrimination against EU and non-EU citizens. However, there is no reference to citizenship in Article 19, and the Directives expressly exclude from their coverage discrimination on the basis of nationality.

Framework Directive and Race Directive, Article 3

(2) This Directive does not cover differences of treatment based on nationality and is without prejudice to provisions and conditions relating to the entry into and residence of third-country nationals and stateless persons in the territory of Member States, and to any treatment which arises from the legal status of the third-country nationals and stateless persons concerned.

While EU nationals have little to worry about, since they remain protected by Article 18 TFEU (which we discussed in Chapter 11), third-country nationals are open to discrimination on the basis of nationality. In some Member States, discrimination on the grounds of nationality is covered by race discrimination legislation, but in other Member States the exclusion of nationality can lead to the risk that nationality discrimination is used as a way of concealing race discrimination. Moreover, Article 3(2) of the Framework Directive and Race Directive means that discrimination against nationalities like the Welsh or the Catalans is not covered, thus a sign excluding Scots from a bar would not fall foul of the Directive. The major criticism to be levelled at this provision is that it threatens to undermine the Union's equality policy and in particular its race equality policy, by maintaining discrimination against immigrants.[171]

B. Hepple, 'Race and Law in Fortress Europe' (2004) 67 *Modern Law Review* 1, 7

The effects of this exclusion are felt disproportionately by ethnic minorities, who make up the majority of third country nationals (TCNs). Their inferior legal status has serious repercussions on the perception of ethnic minorities generally, and on their integration. Any policy that aims to promote integration needs to take account of the interrelationship between human rights, citizenship and the labour market. The recent history of European immigration shows that migrants are often seen simply as a means of filling temporary needs in the labour market. This means that little attention is paid to citizenship or human rights. It is an illusion to believe that the forces of the labour market, generated by globalisation, can be halted by limiting the rights of TCNs to those of temporary 'guest workers' or by withholding citizenship rights. The political rhetoric of 'Fortress Europe' and restrictions on migrant workers and other legal residents, undermines the civil and social rights which belong to all human beings. Inhumane restrictions on welfare benefits, harsh policies against family reunification, and marginalization in the labour market prevent the realisation of the principle of equality which must be the foundation of all integration policies.

---

[171] See also J. Weiler, 'Thou Shalt Not Oppress a Stranger: On the Judicial Protection of the Human Rights of Non-EC Nationals: A Critique' (1992) 3 *EJIL* 65; Lord Lester, 'New European Equality Measures' (2000) *PL* 562; Brown, n. 130 above, 212.

However, note that a third-country national living in the European Union has every right to claim on the basis of race, sex or other forms of discrimination.[172] In addition, there are other grounds of discrimination which have been omitted. Article 21 EUCFR, for example, has a wider list of discrimination grounds.

Article 21 EUCFR

(1) Any discrimination based on any ground *such as* sex, race, colour, ethnic or social origin, genetic features, language, religion or belief, political or any other opinion, membership of a national minority, property, birth, disability, age or sexual orientation shall be prohibited.

(2) Within the scope of application of the Treaty establishing the European Community and of the Treaty on European Union, and without prejudice to the special provisions of those Treaties, any discrimination on grounds of nationality shall be prohibited.

As the italicized words make clear this text opens the possibility for the recognition of new grounds for protection, for instance whether persons with tattoos merit protection.[173]

The Directives also fail to take into consideration the phenomenon of 'intersectional discrimination', first raised by American scholars.

K. Crenshaw, 'Demarginalizing the Intersection of Race and Sex: A Black Feminist Critique of Antidiscrimination Doctrine, Feminist Theory and Antiracist Politics' (1989) *University of Chicago Legal Forum* 139, 149–50

Black women can experience discrimination in ways that are both similar to and different from those experienced by white women and Black men. Black women sometimes experience discrimination in ways similar to white women's experiences; sometimes they share very similar experiences with Black men. Yet often they experience double-discrimination – the combined effects of practices which discriminate on the basis of race, and on the basis of sex. And sometimes, they experience discrimination as Black women – not the sum of race and sex discrimination, but as Black women. Black women's experiences are much broader than the general categories that discrimination discourse provides. Yet the continued insistence that Black women's demands and needs be filtered through categorical analyses that completely obscure their experiences guarantees that their needs will seldom be addressed.

For example, a black woman may be passed over for promotion but fail in a claim for sex discrimination if there is evidence that the employer promotes white women, and may fail on grounds of racial discrimination because the employer promotes black men. The employer discriminates against 'black women' but there is no such legal category.[174] The Framework Directive and Race Directive allude to this problem by exhorting Member States, when implementing the principle of equal treatment, to 'promote equality between men and women, especially since women are often victims of multiple discrimination' but provide no concrete

---

[172] Race Directive, recital 13; Framework Directive, recital 12.

[173] For discussion, see Y. Solanke, *Discrimination as Stigma: A Theory of Anti-Discrimination Law* (Oxford, Bloomsbury, 2016).

[174] For examples in the UK and US courts that show the salience of this issue, see S. Hannett, 'Equality at the Intersections: The Legislative and Judicial Failure to Tackle Multiple Discrimination' (2003) 23 *OJLS* 65.

means for addressing the issue.[175] The matter fell to be considered in *Parris*. The claimant was the beneficiary of a retirement package; his partner could secure a survivor's pension provided their relationship was legally recognised before he turned 60. This might be justified as avoiding the risk of a marriage of convenience where a younger person marries someone near death to secure pension benefits. Mr Parris was gay and he was only able to have the relationship with his partner recognised in Ireland in 2011, at which time he was 64. Therefore his partner would not be entitled to a survivor's pension. The Court held that there was no discrimination on the basis of age (because fixing the age of entitlement is allowed by the Directive), nor was there discrimination on the basis of sexual orientation (both homosexual and heterosexual couples had to have their relationship legally recognised before the age of 60). Moreover the Court declined to find a third category: it agreed that there may be discrimination based on 'several grounds' (i.e. a person might be discriminated because of her sexuality and her age) but there was no 'new category' for the Court to discover.[176] This judgment is disappointing for it is precisely the kind of case where a group of people (homosexuals born before a certain year) are unable to situate their legitimate claim anywhere other than by judicial recognition that they are discriminated against because of their age and sexuality.[177]

5 WIDENING THE SCOPE OF EU EQUAL OPPORTUNITIES POLICY

For most commentators, the common core of EU equality law reviewed above is disappointing because it rests on an antiquated approach to discrimination.[178] As Hepple put it in discussing the Race Directive, the Union's approach borrows from the UK Race Relations Act 1976 and reproduces a model for combating racism which is out of date with modern conceptions about how to address discrimination and integrate excluded groups more fully in society.[179] However, this criticism may be countered by noting that the discrimination Directives have to be implemented across a diverse range of jurisdictions, not all of which have engaged seriously with discrimination in the workplace in the past.[180] Thus, as the Commission notes, for some States the Directives 'involved the introduction of an entirely new rights-based approach to anti-discrimination legislation and policy'.[181] In this light, they constitute a necessary starting point, equalising the scope of protection across the European Union.

In this section we consider some of the more innovative means by which EU equality law moves beyond protecting rights in the labour market, and towards a model that might secure the fulfilment of the right to equality in a more effective manner.

(i) Beyond the Labour Market

In addition to safeguarding rights in the labour market, the Race Directive was the first to forbid discrimination in other fields as well. It has been suggested that this indicates a move to a

---

[175] Framework Directive, recital 3; Race Directive, recital 14. S. Fredman, 'Equality: A New Generation?' (2001) 30 *ILJ* 145, 159.

[176] *Parris* v. *Trinity College Dublin and Others*, C-443/15, ECLI:EU:C:2016:897, para. 80.

[177] S. Atrey, 'Illuminating the CJEU's Blind Spot of Intersectional Discrimination' (2018) 47(2) *ILJ* 278.

[178] A. Masselot, 'The New Equal Treatment Directive: Plus ça Change . . . ' (2004) 12 *Feminist Legal Studies* 93, 103.

[179] B. Hepple, 'Race and Law in Fortress Europe' (2004) 67 *MLR* 1.

[180] For a critique of French discrimination law, see K. Berthou, 'New Hopes for French Anti-Discrimination Law' (2003) 19 *International Journal of Comparative Labour Law and Industrial Relations* 109.

[181] Green Paper, 'Equality and Non-Discrimination in an Enlarged European Union', COM(2004) 379 final (May 2004) 11.

broader conception of European social law.[182] This seems necessary because otherwise the law disenfranchises many by assuming that the central form of citizenship is manifested by participation in the labour market.

Race Directive, Article 3

(1) Within the limits of the powers conferred upon the Community, this Directive shall apply to all persons, as regards both the public and private sectors, including public bodies, in relation to: . . .

(e) social protection, including social security and health care;

(f) social advantages;

(g) education;

(h) access to and supply of goods and services which are available to the public, including housing.

Thus, EU norms regulate matters like university fees, restrictions on the preparation of Halal meat, the allocation of housing by municipal authorities, employer bans on the playing of rap music because of its misogynistic content and bans on wearing the veil at school.[183] However, there is some uncertainty over the scope of these four categories. In Article 3(1)(e), it is not clear whether social security embraces the rules set out in the Social Security Directive 79/7/EC, which applies to sex discrimination. It is not clear to what 'social protection' extends, and how far non-discrimination in health care can be regulated given that the Treaty indicates that the delivery of health care is a matter for the Member States.[184] The reference to 'social advantages' in Article 3(1)(f) is drawn from the law on free movement of persons.[185] It includes subsidised public transport, free school meals, unemployment benefits and assistance with funeral costs. On the other hand, some have suggested that because the Race Directive is premised upon equality and not merely encouraging the free movement of workers, the phrase 'social advantages' might be read more widely.[186] In the context of education it is not clear whether the Directive is only about access to school for persons of a given race or whether it can also forbid the teaching of subjects that may be discriminatory (e.g. a law requiring schools to teach the virtues of colonisation). Services for the public may include the provision of housing, although it is unclear if this also applies to the provision of private services such as banking, hotels and shops. Moreover, it has been argued that the provision of general public services such as policing should also be included, especially in the light of evidence that the police may discriminate by providing less effective investigations in cases involving racial minorities,[187] as graphically illustrated by the findings of 'institutional racism' in the Stephen Lawrence Inquiry.[188] In sum, the potential for the Race Directive to integrate racial and ethnic minorities by preventing such a potentially wide range of discriminatory practices is undermined by the uncertainty as to the scope of the obligations imposed by the Directive and as to the 'constitutional validity' of the

---

[182] M. Bell, 'Beyond European Labour Law? Reflections on the EU Racial Equality Directive' (2002) 8 *ELJ* 384, 387.
[183] Chalmers, above n. 105, 215.   [184] Article 168(7) TFEU.
[185] Regulation 1612/68, [1968] OJ Special Edn, L 257/2, Article 7(2).
[186] E. Ellis, 'Social Advantages: a New Lease of Life?' (2003) 40 *CMLRev* 639.
[187] C. Brown, 'The Race Directive: Towards Equality for All the Peoples of Europe?' (2002) 21 *YEL* 195, 215.
[188] W. MacPherson, *Stephen Lawrence Inquiry Report*, Cm. 4262-I, 1999. Race Relations (Amendment) Act 2000, s. 1.

Directive when it comes to health care and housing, which seem to fall outside the Union's competences.[189]

The Race Directive pioneered these measures. In the context of sex discrimination, the Council later agreed a Directive establishing the right of equal treatment in the access to and supply of goods and services.[190]

Directive 2004/113/ EC implementing the principle of equal treatment between men and women in the access to and supply of goods and services, Article 3

(1) Within the limits of the powers conferred upon the Community, this Directive shall apply to all persons who provide goods and services, which are available to the public irrespective of the person concerned as regards both the public and private sectors, including public bodies, and which are offered outside the area of private and family life and the transactions carried out in this context.

(2) This Directive does not prejudice the individual's freedom to choose a contractual partner as long as an individual's choice of contractual partner is not based on that person's sex.

(3) This Directive shall not apply to the content of media and advertising nor to education.

The scope of this Directive is narrower than the Race Directive because it does not apply to education, but it is potentially wider because it applies to both public and private services, although the Commission insisted that in this respect the scope of the two Directives is the same.[191] Article 3 also shows how the European Union's thinking in this sphere has evolved: the Race Directive was criticised in some quarters for infringing freedom of contract, thus this Directive is careful to stipulate that the obligation not to discriminate in the provision of services affects freedom of contract only insofar as this is necessary to prevent discrimination.

One of the criticisms of the 2004 Directive was that the evidence base on which the legislation had been implemented was weak, and insufficient attention had been paid to the needs of certain industries.[192] In proposing a similar Directive for other protected groups, the Commission has consulted more broadly, but at the time of writing the proposal has not yet been enacted.[193]

---

[189] Brown, n. 187 above, 214–15; M. Bell, 'The New Article 13 EC Treaty: a Sound Basis for European Anti-Discrimination Law?' (1999) 6 *MJECL* 5.

[190] Directive 2004/113/ EC of 13 December 2004 implementing the principle of equal treatment between men and women in the access to and supply of goods and services, OJ 2004, L 373/37.

[191] COM(2003)657, 13.

[192] In particular there was criticism from the insurance market. See Paul MacDonnell, 'Equal Treatment Directive Misunderstands Risk and Threatens Insurance Markets' (2005) 25 *Economic Affairs* 48; House of Lords European Union Committee *Sexual Equality in Access to Goods and Services*, 27th Report, Session 2003–4, HL Paper 165-I, ch. 9. As noted earlier, the Court then nullified their lobbying efforts.

[193] 'Proposal for a Council Directive on Implementing the Principle of Equal Treatment between Persons Irrespective of Religion or Belief, Disability, Age or Sexual Orientation', COM(2008)426 final. See Joint NGO Statement on the 10th Anniversary of the Horizontal Directive: Ten years on and nothing to show for it (2 July 2018), www.edf-feph.org/newsroom/news/10-years-after-equal-treatment-directive-was-proposed-ngos-call-eu-council-finally.

(ii) Positive Action

Equality of opportunities does not guarantee equality of results because the problem of discrimination is more deeply rooted in society, which has historically denied rights to certain groups.[194] One solution to this gap are measures of positive discrimination that discriminate in favour of an underrepresented group, for instance by giving a job to a woman in favour of a man because women are underrepresented.[195] EU law does not compel Member States to deploy positive action; rather, the Commission has encouraged Member States to take positive action to promote women in employment as far back as 1984 on the one hand,[196] while the Court of Justice has limited the scope of such programmes when these are incompatible with EU law, on the other.

The new generation of discrimination legislation seeks to give Member States greater freedom to design positive action measures. The principle in Article 157(4) TFEU is replicated in the Race Directive and in the Framework Directive:[197]

> With a view to ensuring full equality in practice, the principle of equal treatment shall not prevent any Member State from maintaining or adopting specific measures to prevent or compensate for disadvantages linked to [race, ethnic origin, sexual orientation, age, religion, or disability].

In practice EU law forbids a measure providing that a percentage of jobs should go to women, and measures whereby if a man and a woman are equally well qualified, the job should go to the woman, also infringe the equality principle.[198]

In contrast, EU law allows a measure which introduces a presumption that the (equally qualified) female should be employed, which is in turn rebuttable by the man on grounds of certain characteristics that entitle him to the post (so-called 'secondary selection criteria'). For example, he could point out that his seniority made him a worthier candidate.[199] These schemes satisfy two conditions: they do not give automatic priority to women and allow for an objective evaluation that takes into account the personal situation of each candidate.[200] Several criticisms were levelled at the Court of Justice's approach.[201] First, the Court narrowed down considerably the ability of Member States to engage in positive discrimination and undermined the potential of such measures. Moreover, such positive discrimination policies are easy to evade. For instance, it has been said that it is easy for the employer to claim that the woman is not equally qualified, and the 'secondary selection criteria' cannot be subjected to strict judicial scrutiny, therefore

---

[194] S. Joseph, J. Schultz and M. Castan, *The International Covenant on Civil and Political Rights: Cases, Materials and Commentary* (Oxford University Press, 2000) 563–4 referring to this as systemic discrimination.

[195] See generally S. Fredman, 'Reversing Discrimination' (1997) 113 *LQR* 575.

[196] Council Recommendation 84/635/EEC of 13 December 1984 on the promotion of positive action for women, OJ 1984, L 331/34.

[197] Article 7 Directive 2000/78/EC and Article 5 Directive 2000/43/EC. Article 3 Recast Equality Directive simply makes reference to the TFEU provision.

[198] *Kalanke* v. *Freie Hansestadt Bremen*, C-450/93, ECLI:EU:C:1995:322.

[199] *Marschall* v. *Land Nordrhein-Westfalen*, C-409/95, ECLI:EU:C:1997:533.

[200] It is not clear if the ECJ, in view of the new legal framework in Article 157(4) would adopt a more expansive reading in C-407/98 *Abrahamsson and Anderson* v. *Fogelqvist* [2000] ECR I-5539. Paragraph 55 may be read to suggest that a scheme that favours the underrepresented candidate may be allowed if it is proportionate, but it is risky to base this conclusion on a single paragraph. In *Brihenche* v. *Ministre de l'Interieur*, C-319/03, ECLI:EU:C:2004:574 the Court also noted that Article 157 TFEU warrants a different interpretation from Article 2(4), but what this means in practice remains to be specified.

[201] See generally S. Fredman, 'After *Kalanke* and *Marschall*: Affirming Affirmative Action' (1998) 1 *CYELS* 199.

leaving the employer free to favour men instead of women.[202] The upshot is that Member States find it very difficult to implement meaningful positive discrimination measures.

The language of the Framework Directive and Race Directive can also be read as permitting discrimination as a way of promoting an underrepresented group, because all the texts begin with the same prefatory words: 'with a view to achieving full equality in practice'. This suggests that equality of results is now an EU objective, which may open the way for more aggressive positive discrimination schemes, perhaps even allowing for a quota system whereby a given proportion of persons from an underrepresented group must be employed provided this is the least restrictive way of achieving equal participation. Support for this may be drawn from the use of the language in Article 19 TFEU (combating discrimination, not merely preventing it),[203] and from the fact that the Framework Directive tolerates a fairly aggressive form of positive discrimination in one region of the European Union.

Framework Directive, Article 15

(1) In order to tackle the under-representation of one of the major religious communities in the police service of Northern Ireland, differences in treatment regarding recruitment into that service, including its support staff, shall not constitute discrimination insofar as those differences in treatment are expressly authorised by national legislation.

(2) In order to maintain a balance of opportunity in employment for teachers in Northern Ireland while furthering the reconciliation of historical divisions between the major religious communities there, the provisions on religion or belief in this Directive shall not apply to the recruitment of teachers in schools in Northern Ireland insofar as this is expressly authorised by national legislation.

While this provision was included to safeguard a policy of specific interest to a politically troubled region, it represents a sign of increased support for positive discrimination more generally. However, that EU law leaves positive discrimination measures to the Member States does not imply that these measures will be put in place. In contrast, the transposition of the Race Directive in the Netherlands led to a limited positive action measure being rescinded; and in Germany and Hungary, where the law was amended to take into account the Court of Justice's case law, there has been no use of positive action measures.[204] At the time of writing the Commission has tried to buck this trend by proposing legislation that would set large publicly listed companies in the Union a target of ensuring that 40 per cent of members of non-executive boards are women by 2020, but progress has stalled.[205]

Perhaps there is an alternative: to impose positive duties on those best placed to eliminate discrimination. This model has been advocated by Professor Sandra Fredman, making reference to legislation that places statutory duties on public bodies (and sometimes on private actors) to

---

[202] D. Caruso, 'Limits of the Classic Method: Positive Action in the European Union after the New Equality Directives' (2003) 44 *Harvard Int'l LJ* 331, 342.

[203] Z. Apostolopoulou, 'Equal Treatment of People with Disabilities in the EC: What Does "Equal" Mean?', Jean Monnet Working Paper No. 09/04 (2004) 10–11.

[204] Guiraudon, n. 109 above, 538.

[205] 'Proposal for a Directive on Improving the Gender Balance among Non-Executive Directors of Companies Listed on Stock Exchanges and Related Measures' COM(2012)614 (final). On this issue generally, see C. Fagan, M. González Menèndez and S. Gómez Ansón (eds.), *Women on Corporate Boards and in Top Management: European Trends and Policy* (Basingstoke, Palgrave Macmillan, 2012).

promote equality, which do not give rise to individual rights. In her view this kind of legislation has the following advantages: it spreads the obligation to remedy inequality to those who have the power and capacity to change it; reform is systematic and not dependent upon individual lawsuits; finally the causes of discrimination are addressed collectively, harnessing local actors who know where the barriers lie and are best placed to propose measures to resolve them. By increasing participation among stakeholders, the system gains more legitimacy and is also flexible to adjust as needs change.[206] An example of this is found in the United Kingdom's Equality Act which imposes a duty on public bodies to advance equality of opportunity and to foster good relations between the disadvantaged group and others. For example this may take into consideration the needs of the disabled when licensing taxis (thus ensuring taxies are accessible) or taking into account religious observance when designing a school uniform policy.[207]

(iii) Dialogue

To a limited extent, the discrimination Directives introduce some methods for promoting equality suggested by Fredman by establishing three types of dialogue. First, the Member State has an obligation to inform those concerned of their rights and obligations under the Directives.[208] This is a relatively inexpensive way of bringing employers and other potential defendants up to date on their obligations.

Secondly, Member States are to promote social dialogue between employers and employees. All three Directives impose the following obligations.[209]

Race Directive, Article 11

(1) Member States shall, in accordance with national traditions and practice, take adequate measures to promote the social dialogue between the two sides of industry with a view to fostering equal treatment, including through the monitoring of workplace practices, collective agreements, codes of conduct, research or exchange of experiences and good practices.

(2) Where consistent with national traditions and practice, Member States shall encourage the two sides of the industry without prejudice to their autonomy to conclude, at the appropriate level, agreements laying down anti-discrimination rules ... which fall within the scope of collective bargaining. These agreements shall respect the minimum requirements laid down by this Directive and the relevant national implementing measures.

Moreover, all the Directives call upon Member States to encourage dialogue with non-governmental organisations (NGOs) with a legitimate interest in discrimination.[210] These forms of dialogue encourage 'reflexive regulation' – that is, a kind of self-regulation which encourages

---

[206] Sandra Fredman, *Human Rights Transformed: Positive Rights and Positive Duties* (Oxford University Press, 2008) 190.

[207] S. Manfredi, L. Vickers and K. Clayton-Hathway, 'The Public Sector Equality Duty: Enforcing Equality Rights Through Second-Generation Regulation' (2018) *ILJ* 365.

[208] Article 10 Race Directive; Article 12 Framework Directive; Article 30 Recast Equal Treatment Directive.

[209] Article 21 Recast Equal Treatment Directive; Article 13 Framework Directive.

[210] Article 12 Race Directive; Article 14 Framework Directive; Article 22 Equal Treatment Directive.

the employer to be self-reflective and self-critical about his practices. One potential use of these forms of dialogue is to address the problem of 'intersectional discrimination', which as we noted earlier is not covered by the Directives. An employer employing several Asian women might use social dialogue as a means of understanding and remedying the specific concerns of this group which would remain invisible if he merely sought to avoid sex and race discrimination separately. Given that the Race Directive extends beyond the labour market, it is unfortunate that the provisions for dialogue are restricted to the labour market and are not extended to other points of authority (such as schools or hospitals).[211]

Thirdly, and perhaps most significantly, Member States must set up a regulatory body under the Race Directive and Equal Treatment Directives.[212]

Race Directive, Article 13

(1) Member States shall designate a body or bodies for the promotion of equal treatment of all persons without discrimination on the grounds of racial or ethnic origin. These bodies may form part of agencies charged at national level with the defence of human rights or the safeguard of individuals' rights.

(2) Member States shall ensure that the competences of these bodies include:

- without prejudice to the right of victims and of associations, organisations or other legal entities . . . providing independent assistance to victims of discrimination in pursuing their complaints about discrimination,
- conducting independent surveys concerning discrimination,
- publishing independent reports and making recommendations on any issue relating to such discrimination.

In addition the Recast Equality Directive requires that national bodies share information with the European Institute for Gender Equality which can stimulate the identification of best practices and sharing ideas about how to address certain issues.[213] The success of national bodies will depend on how much power and how many resources Member States commit, and some have appeared to do as little as necessary.[214] The UK agency, which in the past has been at the forefront of encouraging equality, has seen its funding cut substantially.[215] One inherent limitation is that none of these organisations have any independent powers to enforce the law. This has been criticised because many entrenched forms of discrimination cannot be easily resolved through individuals litigating to assert individual rights.[216] However, as suggested above, the litigation model should not be seen as the exclusive means to bring about equality.

---

[211] Chalmers, n. 105 above, 238.

[212] Article 20 Equal Treatment Directive; for discussion, see B. De Witte, 'New Institutions for Promoting Equality in Europe: Legal Transfers, National Bricolage and European Governance' (2012) 60 *AJCL* 49.

[213] http://eige.europa.eu/. See e.g. the toolkit and best practices on gender mainstreaming that the institute has published.

[214] Guiraudon, n. 109 above, singling out Italy and Spain as having weak agencies to address racial discrimination.

[215] B. Hepple, *Equality: The Legal Framework*, 2nd edn (Oxford, Hart, 2014) 190–1.   [216] Bell, n. 182 above, 397–8.

(iv) Mainstreaming

Perhaps the most significant commitment to promoting equality outside the framework of the rights-based model is found in the Lisbon Treaty's commitment to 'mainstreaming' equality.[217]

> **Article 10 TFEU**
>
> In defining and implementing its policies and activities, the Union shall aim to combat discrimination based on sex, racial or ethnic origin, religion or belief, disability, age or sexual orientation.

According to the Commission, mainstreaming means:

> The systematic integration of the respective situations, priorities and needs of women and men in all policies and with a view to promoting equality between women and men and mobilizing all general policies and measures specifically for the purpose of achieving equality by actively and openly taking into account, at the planning stage, their effects on the respective situation of women and men in implementation, monitoring and evaluation.[218]

Potentially, this is an imaginative way of addressing the systemic causes of inequality between men and women. Mainstreaming is not premised upon legislative measures that Member States must implement. Rather, it is designed to create incentives for the EU and Member States to embed gender consideration in their policies. For example, in deciding whether to increase funding to train workers one has to consider how such funding can be used to stimulate employment of those that have been traditionally excluded (e.g. certain ethnicities or persons with disability). To this end, the European Union's role is to facilitate increased action at national level. This role was enhanced by the Union's employment and social solidarity programme, PROGRESS, launched in 2007. It is designed to promote mainstreaming of the principle of non-discrimination and to promote gender equality by commissioning studies on the effect of current legislation, supporting the implementation of EU discrimination law and raising awareness of the key policy issues.[219] However, with the economic crisis mainstreaming has become a less relevant priority.[220]

Mainstreaming also occurs in the context of the European Employment Strategy.[221] In brief, the strategy provides for the Council to review national employment policies and make recommendations to Member States on, *inter alia*, the success of national policies in improving the work prospects of women.[222] However, the effectiveness of gender mainstreaming on national

---

[217] The separate provision for gender in Article 8 TFEU is probably the result of lobbying. See M. Bell, 'Equality and the European Constitution' (2004) 33 *ILJ* 242, 257–8.

[218] Communication from the Commission, 'Incorporating Equal Opportunities for Women and Men into All Community Policies and Activities', COM(96)67 final, 2.

[219] Articles 2, 7 and 8 Decision 1672/2006 establishing a Community Programme for Employment and Social Solidarity [2006] OJ L 315/1.

[220] R. Cavanagh and M. O'Dwyer, 'European Economic Governance in 2017: A Recovery for Whom?' (2018) *JCMS* 1.

[221] F. Beveridge and S. Velluti (eds.), *Gender and the Open Method of Coordination* (Farnham, Ashgate, 2008).

[222] See e.g. Council Recommendation on the implementation of Member States' employment policies, OJ 2004, L 326/47 where each Member State's employment policy towards women is assessed.

employment policies is uneven and one study concludes that, aside from Sweden, there is little sustained effort in mainstreaming in employment policy.[223]

C. Fagan and J. Rubery, 'Advancing Gender Equality through European Employment Policy: The Impact of the UK's EU Membership and the Risks of Brexit' (2018) 17(2) *Social Policy and Society*, 297, 303

The most enduring legacies of the gender mainstreaming of the European Employment Strategy (EES) are twofold. First increasing women's integration into employment has become a standard employment policy objective, recognised to bring economic benefits, particularly with an ageing population ... Second, the widening scope of employment policy to include care services also marked a major change from regarding labour markets as disconnected from the domestic and care sphere, and also promoted a drive towards more public provision of childcare across the EU member states.

That said, many policy areas of the EES remain either gender blind or provide examples where the gender equality goal has been instrumentally subordinated to other agendas. A gender blind approach persists in relation to wage setting: most recommendations to member states link wages to productivity or advocate moderate minimum wage level, with no analysis of contradictions with policies to reduce the gender pay gap. Likewise, policy debates and country-specific recommendations on skill shortages rarely include a systematic consideration of gender segregation. Thus gender mainstreaming has remained rather superficial and is often totally ignored at both member state and EU level.

The risk that gender equality objectives may be subverted into supporting policies harmful to gender equality in the longer term is particularly evident in the area of work life balance. The gender equality goal of more equal sharing of care work became a means of legitimising the promotion of flexible labour markets. A stereotyped and normative notion of women's preferred arrangements for caring for children and other family members was used to recommend more part-time work opportunities to further gender equality even in countries where women were already well integrated in full-time work and had shown little preference for part-time hours. The instrumental nature of some gender equality policies became more evident after the financial crisis: for example, the promotion of women's employment up to that juncture had had a generally positive impact on women's opportunities and was associated with increasing care services. Austerity brought to an end the prospect of convergence around the high level of care services found in Scandinavia but the pressure on women to engage in wage work remains even when support for that work is reduced.

The effect of mainstreaming on EU Institutions is mixed. On the one hand, the Commission undertook to increasing the participation of women (the number of women in committees and expert groups has increased somewhat as a result),[224] establishing a Commissioner's Group on Equal Opportunities chaired by the President, and training Commission staff on the impact of

---

[223] C. Fagan *et al.*, 'Gender Mainstreaming in the Enlarged European Union: Recent Developments in the European Employment Strategy and Social Inclusion Process' (2005) 36 *Industrial Relations Journal* 568, 587. See also L. Mósesdóttir and R. Gerlingsdóttir, 'Spreading the Word Across Europe: Gender Mainstreaming as a Political and Policy Project' (2005) 7 *International Feminist Journal of Politics* 513.

[224] E.g. Decision 2000/407/EC of 19 June 2000 relating to gender balance within the committees and expert groups established by it, OJ 2000, L 154/34. See European Commission, 'Work Programme for 2002 for the Implementation of the Framework Strategy on Gender Equality', SEC(2001)773 final, 5, noting an increase in women from 13% to 29% from 2000 to 2001.

Community policies on gender equality.[225] However, women remained underrepresented, and mainstreaming was also marginalised in the *White Paper on Governance*,[226] and has had less of an impact on the Council and the Court of Justice.

In terms of EU policies, a test case for implementing mainstreaming is in the field of the European Union's Structural Funds. In brief, the European Union has four funds (the Regional Fund, the Social Fund, the Fisheries, and the Guidance and Guarantee Fund) from which it provides financial support to reduce the gap in living standards across the Union and to promote economic and social cohesion. The Commission's efforts in this field were to insert gender equality as one criterion to allocate the relevant funds. Thus, in all Regulations setting out the operation of the structural funds we find reference to the promotion of gender equality as a condition for releasing funds.[227] In practical terms, the funds have financed a range of programmes designed to facilitate women's access to jobs that were traditionally reserved for men, or to facilitate working opportunities for women in poor European regions.[228] In addition to supporting programmes directly linked to improving the economic position of women, the release of funds for any other purpose is conditional on applicants indicating how their proposal promotes gender equality, which allows the Union to force Member States to embed gender equality as a condition for Community assistance. But the results are modest: between 2000 and 2006, only 6 per cent of the European Social Fund went to gender-specific actions.[229] A similar approach is presently attempted in the field of public procurement: that is, when Member States and local authorities purchase goods and services to discharge their functions.[230] However, this is also likely to prove difficult to realise in practice. Public procurement law is already quite complex so that to include a provision that favours the supply of goods from firms that, say, employ many disabled workers, is an approach that some purchasers will shy away from because of the legal risks should their tenders be challenged and quashed.[231]

The other concern is that in areas where the impact of policy on a protected group is more remote, mainstreaming has no bite. A provocative example is provided by Heather MacRae. She notes how airline liberalisation increased the number of cheap flights to Estonia and this is linked to an increase in sex tourism in the area, with a concomitant increase in prostitution and sex trade. But while the effects of airline liberalisation on the environment and on employment practices of airlines have been looked at, the impact of liberalisation on the sex trade has not been identified. Her conclusion is that gender mainstreaming has not influenced the core policies that the European Union implements, those pertaining to opening up markets.[232] One riposte to this claim may be to question whether we really expect gender issues to play a role even when they are so remotely linked to the main policy issue at hand: if the concern is the sexual

---

[225] European Commission, 'Work Programme for 2005 for the Implementation of the Framework Strategy on Gender Equality', SEC(2005)1044, 7.

[226] J. Shaw, 'The European Union and Gender Mainstreaming: Constitutionally Embedded or Comprehensively Marginalised?' (2002) 10 *Feminist Legal Studies* 213, 224–6.

[227] E.g. Regulation 1784/1999 on the European Social Fund OJ 1999, L 213/5, Article 2.

[228] See http://europa.eu.int/comm/employment_social/esf2000/index-en.htm for an overview.

[229] 'Assessment Document', SEC(2006)275. S. Mazey, 'Gender Mainstreaming Strategies in the E.U.: Delivering on an Agenda?' (2002) 10 *Feminist Legal Studies* 227.

[230] C. Tobler, 'Encore: Women's Clauses in Public Procurement under Community Law' (2000) 25 *ELRev* 618.

[231] T. Uyen Do, 'In the Face of Diversity: Public Procurement to Promote Social Objectives' (2013) 16 *European Anti-Discrimination L Rev* 10, identifying the options and the challenges for this strategy.

[232] H. MacRae, 'The EU as a Gender Equal Polity: Myths and Realities' (2010) 48(1) *JCMS* 155.

exploitation of women in Eastern Europe, then this is an issue that can be tackled more effectively through other means. The counter-argument is that unless all policies are integrated there is a risk that some nullify the effectiveness of others.

Mainstreaming also occurs beyond the sphere of gender.[233] For example, disability-related issues have affected a number of legislative initiatives: a Directive on special provisions for certain vehicles requires that they should be accessible to disabled persons,[234] and the Directive on Universal Services in the field of electronic communication, which is designed to ensure that all citizens have affordable access to telecommunication services, guarantees access to disabled persons by requiring Member States to ensure that disabled users have access 'equivalent to that enjoyed by other end-users'.[235] These measures are supported by the European Parliament's Disability Intergroup and, as their work programme makes clear, the effect of provisions like these is to remove barriers faced by disabled people.[236] This takes us very far away from the traditional vision of discrimination law, which is about granting individuals the right to sue. Rather, the political philosophy that motivates mainstreaming is that of ensuring social inclusion.[237] That said, mainstreaming has yet to achieve significant results.[238] This may be for the reasons suggested by MacRae (mainstreaming fails when it faces the more embedded discourses in EU law, like market opening) or perhaps because it remains limited in ambition: it identifies the harm suffered by a group rather than demanding a more wholesale transformation of society to accommodate the interests of all groups.[239] However, this more ambitious approach may take mainstreaming outside the competence of the European Union, or may even be too idealistic to achieve.

6 BREXIT

The Equality Act 2010 is the principal legal basis that implements the various equality Directives and in many respects it goes beyond the requirements of EU law.[240] However, leaving the Union may have consequences nevertheless.[241] First, EU law and the ECJ have been responsible for bolstering the rights of employees for decades.[242] It remains to be seen whether British courts will contribute to strengthening existing safeguards when they develop the Equality Act independently. For instance in *Walker* v. *Innospec* the UK Supreme Court disapplied provisions of the Equality Act 2010 which were contrary to EU law insofar as they limited the rights of a gay

---

[233] In the sphere of race, see M. Bell, *Racism and Equality in the European Union* (Oxford University Press, 2008) 123–7.

[234] Article 7, Regulation (EC) No. 661/2009 concerning type-approval requirements for the general safety of motor vehicles, their trailers and systems, components and separate technical units intended therefor [2009] OJ L 200/1.

[235] Article 7 Directive 2002/22/EC (Universal Service Directive), OJ 2002, L 108/51.   [236] http://www.edf-feph.org/.

[237] H. Collins, 'Discrimination, Equality and Social Inclusion' (2003) 66 *MLR* 16.

[238] F. Beveridge, 'Bulding Against the Past: The Impact of Mainstreaming on EU Gender Law and Policy' (2007) 32 *ELRev* 193.

[239] J. Rubery, 'Gender Mainstreaming and Gender Equality in the EU: The Impact of the EU Employment Strategy' (2002) 33 *Industrial Relations Journal*, 500, 503.

[240] See Hepple, n. 215 above.

[241] For a detailed discussion of the specific impact for Northern Ireland, see C. McCrudden, 'EU Equality Law in the Age of Brexit' (2018) 1 *European Equality Review* 30.

[242] E.g. *Marshall* v. *Southampton and South West Hampshire Area Health Authority*, C-271/91, ECLI:EU:C:1993:335, ensuring compensation levels were adequate. More generally on the dialogue between the courts, see C. Kilpatrick, 'Community or Communities of Courts in European Integration? Sex Equality Dialogues Between UK Courts and the ECJ' (1998) 4(2) *ELJ* 121.

married couple: the court held that the husband is entitled to a survivor's pension on the same terms as a spouse of the opposite sex. On the facts it meant that all the contributions made by Mr Walker since the commencement of his employment would be taken into account.[243] Without EU law, UK courts might simply defer to parliamentary sovereignty and accept that the legislature is entitled to limit the entitlement of survivors' pensions to gays and lesbians. Secondly, there is a risk of loss of EU funding sources which contribute to enhancing equality; for instance, Wales receives GBP370 million annually in structural funds, some of which is destined to schemes addressing the underlying causes of the gender pay gap in Wales.[244] Thirdly, the EU is unwavering in its support for equality, reinforced by the general principle of non-discrimination. Some take the view that there is a risk that, once the UK is no longer bound by EU law and by the EUCFR, this will lead conservative governments to water down anti-discrimination law under the guise of cutting costs for business.[245] Conversely, the United Kingdom's exit from the Union might serve to strengthen EU equal opportunities legislation as the United Kingdom staunchly preferred regulation that favoured the interests of employers rather than workers.[246] One should not assume that a trade agreement between the European Union and the United Kingdom will safeguard EU equality rules.[247] Conversely, trade agreements with other States may well place pressure on the United Kingdom to reduce equality norms that are seen as non-tariff barriers.

FURTHER READING

K. J. Alter and J. Vargas, 'Explaining Variation in the Use of European Litigation Strategies: European Community Law and British Gender Equality Policy' (2000) 33 *Comparative Political Studies* 452.

S. Atrey, 'Illuminating the CJEU's Blind Spot of Intersectional Discrimination' (2018) 47(2) *Industrial Law Journal* 278.

C. Barnard, 'The Changing Scope of the Fundamental Principle of Equality?' (2001) 46 *McGill Law Journal* 955.

M. Bell, *Anti-Discrimination Law and the European Union* (Oxford University Press, 2002).

C. Brown, 'The Race Directive: Towards Equality for *All* Peoples of Europe?' (2002) *Yearbook of European Law* 195.

D. Caruso, 'Limits of the Classic Method: Positive Action in the European Union after the New Equality Directives' (2003) 44 *Harvard International Law Journal* 331.

J. Cornides, 'Three Case Studies on "Anti-Discrimination"' (2012) 32(2) *European Journal of International Law* 517, 523–6.

---

[243] *Walker* v. *Innospec Ltd and Others* [2017] UKSC 47.

[244] Equality and Human Rights Commission, *Pressing for Progress: Women's Rights and Gender Equality in 2018* (2018) 14.

[245] R. Wintemute, 'Goodbye EU Anti-Discrimination Law? Hello Repeal of the Equality act 2010?' (2016) 27(3) *King's LJ* 387. Indeed this has already occurred; e.g. s. 2 of the Deregulation Act 2015 removes the power of employment tribunals to make wider recommendations than those affecting the complainant which had been introduced in s. 124 of the Equality Act 2010, employer's liablity for harassment by third parties (e.g. customers harassing an employee, covered by s. 40(2)–(4) of the Equality Act) and provisions concerning intersectional discrimination (s. 14 of the Equality Act) were repealed by s. 65 of the Enterprise and Regulatory Reform Act 2013.

[246] R. Guerrina and A. Masselot, 'Walking into the Footprint of EU Law: Unpacking the Gendered Consequences of Brexit' (2018) 18(2) *Social Policy and Society* 319.

[247] McCrudden, n. 241 above, 35, who compares Norway (significant market access and the requirement to conform to the rules on gender equality only) and Canada (less market access and no equality provision in the trade agreement).

E. Dewhurst, 'Intergenerational Balance, Mandatory Retirement and Age Discrimination in Europe: How Can the ECJ Better Support National Courts in Finding a Balance between the Generations?' (2013) 50 *Common Market Law Review* 1333.

E. Ellis and P. Watson, *EU Anti-Discrimination Law*, 2nd edn (Oxford University Press, 2012).

S. Fredman, *Discrimination Law*, 2nd edn (Oxford University Press, 2011).

V. Guiraudon, 'Equality in the Making: Implementing European Non-Discrimination Law' (2009) 13 *Citizenship Studies* 527.

C. Hoskins, *Integrating Gender: Women, Law and Politics in the European Union* (London, Verso, 1996).

E. Howard, 'The European Year of Equal Opportunities for All 2007: Is the EU Moving Away from a Formal Idea of Equality?' (2008) 14 *European Law Journal* 168.

H. MacRae, 'The EU as a Gender Equal Polity: Myths and Realities' (2010) 48(1) *Journal of Common Market Studies* 155.

J. Mulder, *EU Non-Discrimination Law in the Courts: Approaches to Sex and Sexualities Discrimination in EU Law* (Oxford, Bloomsbury, 2017).

H. Oliver, 'Sexual Orientation Discrimination: Perceptions, Definitions and Genuine Occupational Requirements' (2004) 33 *Industrial Law Journal* 1.

D. Schiek, 'Broadening the Scope and the Norms of EU Gender Equality Law: Towards a Multidimensional Conception of Equality Law' (2005) 12 *Maastricht Journal of European and Comparative Law* 427.

A. Somek, *Engineering Equality: An Essay in European Anti Discrimination Law* (Oxford University Press, 2011).

14

The Internal Market

CONTENTS

1 INTRODUCTION

This chapter provides an overview of what the internal market is, and the current debates about what it should be. It provides background and context to the chapters on free movement which follow. The chapter is organised as follows.

Section 2 sets out the purposes of the internal market. Primarily, the internal market aims to integrate the national markets of the Member States into a single European market. It does this by removing regulatory barriers to trade between States. The reasons for pursuing this project are partly economic, but also social and political: for some, the market entrenches a form of individualism (ordoliberalism) that has strong roots in Continental European philosophy, while for others, its main benefit is that it sucks Member States into deeper integration in other areas. More recently, it has come to be seen by many as a regulatory project, balancing social and economic interests.

Section 3 considers the kinds of laws which construct the internal market. Having explained the stages of economic integration, it then looks at the essential rules and concepts required to achieve this. The way that positive and negative integration, non-discrimination, mutual recognition and market access complement and relate to each other is explained. Together they are intended to provide the tools to create a market in which economic actors in all Member States can compete freely and fairly with each other throughout the European Union, without State or private distortions or limitations. However, this apparent economic Utopia is contingent on the requisite political will.

Section 4 discusses competence to harmonise. Harmonisation is the replacement of national laws by a common Union-wide law. The most important legal basis for internal market harmonisation is Article 114 TFEU, which is controversial because it appears to be very broad. In *Tobacco Advertising I*,[1] the Court of Justice set some limits: distortions of competition can only be harmonised away when they are 'appreciable' or likely to become so. However, this is not very precise. Moreover, other cases show that, under certain conditions, Article 114 can be used to set up new agencies and regulatory bodies.

Sections 5 and 6 consider techniques of harmonisation and the problems they bring. Harmonisation is a difficult political and technical process. In recent years, the Union has been using the 'new approach', in which legislation concentrates on laying down general safety and health standards, while European standardisation agencies work these out in detail. This has been fairly successful, but attracts some democratic criticism: are these agencies accountable and do they take into account interests that are not scientific or economic? This last question is particularly important where EU law touches on matters that are politically sensitive, such as genetically modified organisms (GMOs).

Others argue that this is precisely the point: Member States want the Union to be an objective regulator, beyond the reach of populist whims. Section 6 also discusses how a parallel critique has been made of the Court of Justice: that it is too quick to set aside national measures in order to promote free movement, and does not give full enough consideration to the national values, preferences and interests which those measures may protect. In particular, it neglects the way that free movement redistributes power and wealth within States, and the way it individualises society.

Section 7 discusses regulatory competition. Many internal market debates can be reduced to 'Should the Union regulate, or should the Member States?' Regulatory competition is an important part of this question. If States can choose their own rules, some fear that they will lower standards in order to attract business. Other States will be forced to follow and there will be a 'race to the bottom', in which social and environmental policies are sacrificed to business interests. This view supports widespread harmonisation. Others argue that the race to the bottom does not happen in practice: businesses do not just want low standards. There are reasons why they may even prefer States with high standards and well-functioning social welfare systems. Finding the right compromise means preventing destructive competition, while still allowing States enough autonomy to experiment, reflect local preferences and learn from each other.

2 PURPOSE OF THE INTERNAL MARKET

For most of the history of the Union, its central policy has been the creation of the internal market (or single market, or common market, as it has been called at various times).[2] The reasons

---

[1] *Germany* v. *Parliament and Council (Tobacco Advertising I)*, C-376/98, EU:C:2000:544.

[2] See K. Mortelmans, 'The Common Market, the Internal Market and the Single Market: What's in a Market?' (1998) 35 *CMLRev* 101; L. W. Gormley, 'Competition and Free Movement: Is the Internal Market the Same as a Common Market?' (2002) 13 *EBLRev* 522.

for this are diverse. The classical economic perception that because nations do not do everything equally well or efficiently, trade between nations can be beneficial for all, has of course always been important.[3] However, the internal market has ambitions beyond interstate trade. It aims to merge the markets of the Member States into one larger market, something which entails a greater degree of uniformity of structure and conditions. This is partly at odds with the simple trade-maximisation approach: instead of only capitalising on difference, the Union aims to reduce it. While such homogeneity may bring economic benefits, notably via economies of scale as firms become European rather than purely national operators, the integrative goals of the market reveal that it is not, and never has been, just an economic policy.

On the contrary, a number of normative agendas were prominent in defining and shaping the Treaty rules. First, economic integration was seen as an essential step towards social and political integration. The neofunctionalist analysis of European integration, associated with Haas, argued that because of the interconnection of policy areas, integration in one would lead inevitably to integration in another.[4] This theory is no longer dominant, or even widely accepted in its pure form, but it played a significant role in early support for the internal market. Even today it resonates. Many of the cases in the following chapters show how an apparently simple desire to facilitate interstate transactions has led to involvement of the Union in matters of broader social concern, be it with the families and working conditions of workers, or with the quality of foodstuffs.[5] Secondly, many of the most ardent early supporters of the internal market were believers in ordoliberalism. This political view, with origins in early twentieth-century Germany, regards the regulation of economic activity as essentially about the regulation of public and private power.[6] On the one hand, competition law is necessary to prevent private power becoming dominant enough to challenge the State. But on the other hand, individual economic rights are a normative good in themselves and an important bulwark against tyranny.

M. Maduro, 'Reforming the Market or the State? Article 30 and the European Constitution: [7] Economic Freedom and Political Rights' (1997) 3 *European Law Journal* 55, 61–2

Neo-liberal or '*laissez-faire*' interpretations of the free movement rules and of the European Economic Constitution owe much to traditional ordo-liberal theories and their contribution in both the initial debate on European integration and in the provision of a coherent theoretical framework for an understanding of integration. The ordo-liberal aim is the creation of a free-market, liberal economy, protected through constitutional principles ... The main concern is a political one: the protection of a free and equal society. 'Within society itself no power groups should be formed which would make it possible for others, individually or as groups, to be subjugated and exploited.' Ordo-liberals and other neo-liberals have been

---

[3] See D. Ricardo, *On the Principles of Political Economy and Taxation* (London, John Murray, 1821), www.econlib.org/library/Ricardo/ricP.html; and S. Suranovic, 'The Theory of Comparative Advantage' in *International Trade Theory and Policy* (Center for International Economic Policy, George Washington University, 2007) ch. 40, http://internationalecon.com/Trade/Tch40/Tch40.php.

[4] See J. Ruggie, P. Katzenstein, R. Keohane and P. Schmitter, 'Transformations in World Politics: The Intellectual Contributions of Ernst B. Haas' (2005) 8 *Annual Review of Political Science* 271.

[5] A. Stone Sweet and W. Sandholtz, 'European Integration and Supranational Governance' (1997) 4 *JEPP* 297.

[6] See D. Gerber, *Law and Competition in Twentieth Century Europe: Protecting Prometheus* (Oxford University Press, 1998).

[7] Article 30 is now Article 34 TFEU.

active participants in the project of European integration; they entrusted to Community law the process of constitutionalising a free market economy with undistorted competition.

... It should be recalled that these neo-liberal ideas developed as a reaction to recent German and European history. For Röpke, there was an inevitable connection between the aims of individual freedom and the avoidance of nationalism, on the one hand, and free trade and the prevention of state control of the economy, on the other. According to ordo-liberals and other neo-liberals, the failure of the initial device of separation of powers to achieve its aim of controlling power and government meant that a new device had to be created. That device was a federation of States with an international authority to limit governments' economic powers and assure international order without taking over the power of the States. The division of powers inherent in this form of federalism 'would inevitably act at the same time also as a limitation of the power of the whole as well as of the individual state'. Hence, a federation is seen more as a source of individual rights than as a source of common policies.

Trade facilitation, empowerment of individuals and the integration of Europe all continue to influence market-building decisions today.

At the same time, criticisms of all these perspectives have also been vigorous. Could not the internal market be less restrictive of national autonomy: more focused on practical matters and less on grand integrative ambitions? Or should it not be seen less as an exercise in applied economics and more as a project with social and political consequences, and therefore in need of deep social embedding and democratic legitimacy? Is it perhaps time to retreat from individualism and transnational market-making and to pay more attention to local and communitarian concerns? These criticisms are not all aligned with each other, but reflect a wider current scepticism towards transnational markets – towards globalisation and loss of local control. The European apotheosis of this is perhaps Brexit, and the interaction between this and the internal market is discussed at length in Chapter 10. However, the tensions between the economic and the non-economic, the local and the transnational, and between expertise and democracy are also considered in the sections below.

3 LEGAL FRAMEWORK OF THE INTERNAL MARKET

(i) Economic Integration

Economic integration between States is commonly considered to take place in stages, each one involving new constraints on national autonomy. The first stage is the free trade area, in which States agree not to impose customs duties or import quotas on each other's goods. They thereby give up their capacity to protect domestic industries by excluding foreign competition. Articles 34–36 on the free movement of goods, and Article 30, which prohibits internal customs duties, would create a basic free trade area for the EU.

A free trade area leaves each Member State free to determine its relations with third countries. In particular, they can decide on the customs duties they impose. However, this can create practical problems. If Member State A sets lower duties on third-country goods than Member State B, then third countries will have an incentive to export to A, and then transport their goods to B. B would then miss out on its duties, and not be happy. To avoid this, it would be necessary to have checks on goods entering B from A, to see whether they are a genuine production of A, or third-country goods in transit – and if third-country goods, they would then pay B's duties, and perhaps be entitled to reclaim what they paid to A. Thus a free trade area still requires some kind of border controls in order to check where goods actually come from.

A step towards removing borders is achieved by the second stage, the customs union.[8] Here, Member States merge their customs policies, so that there is a common customs tariff at the external borders and the duties collected go into a common fund. In the European Union a small percentage goes to the Member State, to cover costs of collection, while the rest goes to the EU budget. In a customs union, as long as the external border is well-policed, there is no need to be concerned about which Member State third-country goods enter first, and no need for internal customs controls.

Nevertheless, there can still be practical problems with cross-border trade – difficulties complying with strange foreign laws or having the quality of one's goods and services recognised as adequate. Addressing these kinds of problems is the goal of the third stage, the internal market, or single market. The idea of an internal market is that all the factors of production – goods, services, persons, businesses and capital – can move freely between Member States just as if they were moving within a Member State.[9] Cross-border transactions – sale of goods or services, establishment of companies, employment agreements or investment – should be just as simple as domestic ones, so that none of the actors in the single market enjoys any protection from competitors based outside their jurisdiction.

The final stage in economic integration is often described as economic and monetary union. Monetary union involves having a common currency. That reduces transaction costs and prevents competitive devaluation, which is always tempting for economically struggling States but would upset their neighbours. Economic union is not a very precise term, but involves at least a partially harmonised tax policy, in which Member States agree on certain tariffs and tax rules, preventing these from being used as competitive weapons. It typically also involves agreement on government spending limits and budget deficits, the idea being that financial instability in one Member State quickly becomes a problem for others when they are economically intertwined, and that use of excessive lending to pimp the economy, like devaluation, would be seen as politically unacceptable by neighbours. Economic integration may also involve redistribution – tax and spending rules constructed in a way that poorer States receive from richer ones, just as poorer regions within a State typically receive net benefits. The Union is currently engaged in a limited form of harmonisation of government spending rules. Tax harmonisation is much discussed, but harder to achieve politically.

A major question is whether limited economic integration is politically and economically stable.[10] An internal market may lead to benefits for poorer countries, as they attract investment because of their low costs, so that gradually levels of wealth equalise within the European Union. However, others suggest that free movement leads to the strongest and most efficient economies extending their advantage over others, as they can best exploit economic opportunities. They may effectively colonise other States economically, so that inequalities become entrenched, rather than removed. From this point of view, the internal market needs to be accompanied by

---

[8] Articles 30–32 TFEU.   [9] See AG Maduro in *Alfa Vita Vassilopoulos*, C-158–9/04, ECLI:EU:C:2006:562.

[10] See e.g. E. Jones, R. Daniel Kelemen and S. Meunier, 'Failing Forward? The Euro Crisis and the Incomplete Nature of European Integration' (2015) 49 *Comparative Political Studies* 1010; F. Nicoli, 'Democratic Legitimacy in the Era of Fiscal Integration' (2017) 39 *JEI* 389.

policies addressing intra-EU inequality. However, if such policies become extensive, particularly if they involve direct redistribution between States, they amount to deeper integration and the creation of a State-like community, which is politically controversial. The Union is thus in a difficult place: it has a fairly well-functioning market, but, from some points of view, lacks the tools or the political will to address all the problematic consequences of that market.

(ii) Achieving the Internal Market

The internal market is defined in Article 26 TFEU.

Article 26 TFEU

(1) The Union shall adopt measures with the aim of establishing or ensuring the functioning of the internal market, in accordance with the relevant provisions of the Treaties.

(2) The internal market shall comprise an area without internal frontiers in which the free movement of goods, persons, services and capital is ensured in accordance with the provisions of the Treaties . . .

The core idea is that of free movement, meaning movement as if frontiers between the Member States did not exist. In order to achieve this, there are a number of EU policies in place, each based on distinct Treaty articles.

(a) *Prohibiting measures which restrict movement*: The core articles here are those on the free movement of goods, services, persons and capital. The first three of these are addressed in Chapters 16–19, as well as Chapter 11 on Union citizenship. These Treaty articles require Member States to refrain from adopting, maintaining or enforcing any measures which restrict free movement, unless those measures are truly necessary for essential public interest objectives. The application of these Treaty articles by courts, resulting in the disapplication of conflicting national law, is called negative harmonisation or negative integration.

As well as this, there are Treaty articles which prohibit customs duties between Member States, and which prohibit discriminatory taxation, ensuring that imported goods are not disadvantaged by unequal tax burdens.[11]

(b) *Harmonisation*: Negative integration cannot solve all problems. Simply removing national rules which affect movement might lead to undesirable regulatory gaps, for example if those rules protect health or the environment. Yet if Member States maintain different rules on matters like this it can create practical problems for traders trying to comply with multiple laws. In such a situation it may be appropriate to harmonise – to adopt EU-wide rules agreeing on common (minimum) standards or rules, concerning goods or services or investment. This positive integration, or positive harmonisation, replaces diverse national laws with a common EU-wide one achieving the same or similar goals.

Another reason for harmonisation is to achieve fair competition.[12] If rules on, say, labour or the environment vary between States, this can create competitive advantages for businesses

---

[11] Articles 30–32 TFEU; Article 110 TFEU.

[12] S. Weatherill, 'Why Harmonise?' in T. Tridimas and P. Nebbia (eds.), *European Union Law for the Twenty-First Century* (Oxford-Portland, Hart, 2004) 11; R. Van der Laan and A. Nentjes, 'Competitive Distortions in EU Environmental Legislation: Inefficiency versus Inequity' (2001) 11 *EJL* 131.

located in States with light regulation. This is called a distortion of competition. In order to achieve a level playing field, the Union may adopt common standards on such matters.

Finally, harmonisation powers may be used to address the more institutional aspects of market-building, for example creating regulatory agencies, or rules concerning public procurement: the State is the biggest purchaser in many markets, and if it only purchases national goods or services that limits the possibilities for foreign firms to access the market of that State. Hence there are detailed rules policing procurement and enforcing non-discrimination.[13]

The scope of power to legislate for the internal market is addressed in the next section of this chapter.

(c) *Preventing State aid*: Once the market is open, there is a temptation for States to subsidise national industries to help them withstand competition, and perhaps to conquer foreign markets. This is usually perceived by others as unfair. A condition for allowing reciprocal access to markets is competition on the 'merits' without public interference. Hence there are strict rules limiting State aid. These are addressed in Chapter 22.

(d) *Ensuring fair competition between undertakings*: Finally, in order to ensure that the internal market remains competitive and does not succumb to cartels or monopolies which prevent the economic advantages of free trade from being realised, there are rules regulating the competitive behaviour of undertakings. These are addressed in Chapters 20 and 21.

(iii) Achieving Free Movement

Movement is rarely free. There may be train tickets to be bought, and a trip might become less attractive because of the monolingual natives, the national cuisine, or the notoriously bad local airports. The Court speaks in its case law of removing all measures which hinder free movement, or even make it less attractive, yet these are not at all transparent concepts.[14] Similarly, when in other cases it speaks of removing all measures which impede market access,[15] one may legitimately wonder whether, for example, a tax on vehicle fuel, or strictly enforced parking rules, or a refusal to allow high-rise flats to be built in an ancient city centre, or music to be played outside all night, could be seen as such impediments if a foreign entrepreneur explained why they create costs for his business. Surely the free movement articles are not intended to encompass all measures which somehow reduce the freedom or profits of anyone moving to another Member State?[16]

In practice this has not happened. The somewhat ambiguous headline concepts mentioned above can be broken down into a set of more precise and limited concepts which explain the cases in Chapters 16–19.

---

[13] See e.g. 'Communication from the Commission to the European Parliament, the Council, the European Economic and Social Committee and the Committee of the Regions: Making Public Procurement Work in and for Europe', COM(2017) 572 final. For background: C. Bovis, 'The Regulation of Public Procurement as a Key Element of European Economic Law' (1998) 4 *ELJ* 220; S. Arrowsmith and P. Kunzlik (eds.), *Social and Environmental Policies in EC Procurement Law* (Cambridge University Press, 2009); C. McCrudden, *Purchasing Social Justice* (Oxford University Press, 2007); C. Hilson, 'Going Local? EU Law, Localism and Climate Change' (2008) 33 *ELRev* 194.

[14] See pp. 703–4 and 744–7.   [15] Ibid.

[16] E. Spaventa, 'From Gebhard to Carpenter: Towards a (Non)Economic European Constitution' (2004) 41 *CMLRev* 743.

(a) Non-Discrimination

It is clear and uncontroversial that discrimination against foreign goods, services or persons is prohibited by the free movement articles. This includes direct discrimination, where the foreign is explicitly excluded or disadvantaged, but also indirect discrimination, where an apparently neutral rule works to the disadvantage of foreign actors, and cannot be sufficiently justified by some non-discriminatory reason.[17] For example, a rule prohibiting Internet gambling will actually tend to protect local casinos or lotteries from foreign competition. On the other hand, the rule might perhaps be genuinely necessary to prevent gambling addiction or crime. It would be for the national court to decide.[18]

As well as this, the Court has often found that rules which specifically impede cross-border movement are prohibited. For example, a rule which does not allow use of a foreign registered company car will discourage locals from taking jobs abroad, since they cannot use their car at home.[19] This rule is disadvantaging local workers, so it is not really nationality discrimination, but rather 'discrimination against cross-border movement'. Advocate General Maduro suggested that the whole of the internal market can in fact be understood as a ban on measures which make cross-border movement less advantageous than domestic movement, with nationality discrimination merely being a special instance of this:

> *Alfa Vita Vassilopoulos*, C-158–9/04, ECLI:EU:C:2006:562, Advocate General M. Poiares Maduro
>
> 41 In such circumstances it is obvious that the task of the Court is not to call into question as a matter of course Member States' economic policies. It is instead responsible for satisfying itself that those States do not adopt measures which, in actual fact, lead to *cross-border situations being treated less favourably than purely national situations*.

(b) Mutual Recognition

Since *Cassis de Dijon* the Court has insisted that Member States accept each other's goods and services onto their domestic markets, even if they do not comply with domestic standards.[20] The reason for this is that while such standards might be different from State to State, they should all be sufficient to protect the most essential interests – health and safety primarily – and while they might vary significantly concerning pure quality issues, decisions on quality should be left to the consumer. The underlying idea is that of functional equivalence – that even though Member States regulate goods and services differently, in the really important ways they achieve the same ends: the sausage is safe to eat and the washing machine is safe to use.[21]

Mutual recognition can be seen as a specific instance of non-discrimination: to reject foreign goods or services because they are the product of different regulation is clearly protectionist in

---

[17] See pp. 484–5.   [18] *Zeturf*, C-212/08, EU:C:2013:33.

[19] *Commission* v. *Denmark (Danish Company Cars)*, C-464/02, EU:C:2005:546.

[20] *Rewe-Zentral AG* v. *Bundesmonopolverwaltung für Branntwein (Cassis de Dijon)*, 120/78, EU:C:1979:42. See pp. 716–19.

[21] J. H. H. Weiler, 'Mutual Recognition, Functional Equivalence and Harmonization in the Evolution of the European Common Market and the WTO' in F. K. Padoa Schioppa (ed.), *The Principle of Mutual Recognition in the European Integration Process* (London, Palgrave, 2005) 25.

effect, and, if one believes in functional equivalence, it is not justified. However, mutual recognition is now an autonomous concept, which takes a central place in the internal market. It serves as the basis of much EU product regulation – as is discussed later in this chapter – and is applied in fields as diverse as financial services and the European Arrest Warrant. Its great merit is that it allows different Member State laws to continue to exist side by side, and coordinates their relationship, rather than requiring them to be replaced by harmonised rules.[22]

(c) Market Access

The Court repeatedly states that the free movement articles prohibit measures hindering market access. What does this mean?

In general, if a State regulates in a way that imposes costs on market actors – which might be the case with labour law, environmental rules, transport costs, and all kinds of other measures – those costs will be passed on to the consumer. A producer will only be seriously worried in two situations:

(i)   if the costs affect them more than their competitors for some reason, for example because they are an artisanal producer who uses more labour, or because they rely on a particular sales method

(ii) if the costs are so significant that consumers turn away from the market as a whole, spending their money somewhere else, for example if the costs of car ownership made owning a car unattractive.

In these situations they might claim that it has become less attractive to enter the market, and so their market access is restricted. However, in both situations the measure is effectively diverting consumers from their products to competing ones: either to similar ones, or to alternatives that fulfil the same need.

It is thus the essence of a restriction on market access that it distorts the market somehow, affecting relative competitive positions.[23] If, by contrast, a measure merely imposes a cost but in a way that affects all competitors equally, and does not drive consumers to other products, then there is no reason why it should deter market access. The idea of a restriction on market access which affects everyone equally is oxymoronic.[24]

Restricting market access is thus a specific form of discrimination.[25] It benefits some at the expense of others but, unlike nationality discrimination, the distinction does not necessarily correspond to the nationality of the actors. Having said that, in practice, when access to a market is limited it tends to be incumbents who benefit and they tend to be national.

It could be otherwise; market access for a national producer could be restricted if rules affected their business model negatively, for example. However, the Treaty rules on free movement only

---

[22] K. Nicolaides and G. Schaffer, 'Transnational Mutual Recognition Regimes: Governance Without Global Government' (2005) 68 *Michigan Review of International Law* 267; G. Davies, 'Is Mutual Recognition an Alternative to Harmonisation: Lessons on Trade and Tolerance of Diversity from the EU' in F. Ortino and L. Bartels (eds.), *Regional Trade Agreements and the WTO* (Oxford University Press, 2006) 265–80; S. Schmidt (ed.), 'Mutual Recognition as a New Mode of Governance' (2007) 14(5) *JEPP*; K. Armstrong, 'Mutual Recognition' in C. Barnard and J. Scott (eds.), *The Law of the European Single Market* (Oxford, Hart, 2002) 225.

[23] J. Snell, 'The Notion of Market Access: A Concept or a Slogan?' (2010) 47 *CMLRev* 437; G. Davies. 'Understanding Market Access' 11 (2010) *German LJ* 671–704.

[24] *Ibid.*   [25] G. Davies, 'Discrimination and beyond in European Economic and Social Law' (2011) 18 *MJECL* 7.

apply to imports and foreign service providers, so such a person could not bring a lawsuit using free movement law.

When a person claims that a measure is restricting their market access they are therefore saying 'this measure affects my competitive position negatively, and I am foreign'. Where, by contrast, measures merely impose costs on all market actors without affecting their relative positions, the Court does not find a restriction on market access to exist.[26]

4 COMPETENCE TO LEGISLATE

There are a number of Treaty Articles which provide a legal basis for legislation relevant to the internal market. However, the most important is Article 114 TFEU.

Article 114 TFEU

(1) Save where otherwise provided in the Treaties, the following provisions shall apply for the achievement of the objectives set out in Article 26. The European Parliament and the Council shall, acting in accordance with the ordinary legislative procedure and after consulting the Economic and Social Committee, adopt the measures for the approximation of the provisions laid down by law, regulation or administrative action in Member States which have as their object the establishment and functioning of the internal market.

(2) Paragraph 1 shall not apply to fiscal provisions, to those relating to the free movement of persons nor to those relating to the rights and interests of employed persons.

Article 115 provides analogous powers for harmonisation concerning free movement of persons and direct taxation, but by unanimity in the Council.

The leading case interpreting Article 114 continues to be the first Tobacco Directive case, *Tobacco Advertising I*.[27] In this case, the Court of Justice annulled a Directive based on Article 114 for the first time, on the grounds that the Directive exceeded what the legal basis allowed.[28] The Directive amounted to a ban on all tobacco advertising in media other than television (which was addressed in an earlier Directive). This included sponsorship of sport by tobacco firms, tobacco advertising in magazines, and even tobacco advertising on ashtrays, parasols and posters in cafés. The argument put forward for the Directive was that the laws on tobacco advertising varied from State to State, which resulted in obstacles to free movement and distortions of competition. A magazine with tobacco advertisements could be printed and sold in one State, but not exported to another. Advertising firms based in States which permitted tobacco advertising had a source of revenue denied to firms in other States, giving them a competitive advantage, as did sports competitions and teams in those States. The development of pan-European advertising campaigns was prevented by the different rules in different States.

However, there were a number of forceful objections to the Directive. First, the distortions of competition were claimed to be marginal. Theoretically, there might be advantages for firms in one State or another but these did not reach the level of a serious market problem. Secondly, while there were certainly some obstacles to movement resulting from different advertising laws,

---

[26] See p. 742.   [27] *Germany* v. *Parliament and Council (Tobacco Advertising I)*, C-376/98, EU:C:2000:544.
[28] See generally J. Usher, annotation at (2001) 38 *CMLRev* 1520; T. Hervey, 'Up in Smoke? Community (Anti)-Tobacco Law and Policy' (2001) 7 *ELRev* 101.

notably where magazines were concerned, the Directive went beyond addressing these and banned advertising in contexts where it was not obvious that this made any contribution at all to interstate trade. For example, it was unclear in what way the banning of tobacco advertisements in cinemas or cigar shops would make any kind of movement easier. Thirdly, for some of the goods on which advertising was banned, such as ashtrays and parasols, the level of interstate trade was negligible. Finally, the Directive was claimed to be a covert health protection measure. Rather than being primarily aimed at improving the operation of the market, it was really aimed at improving public health. Not only was this outside the remit of Article 114, but it was in fact prohibited, it was claimed, elsewhere in the Treaty, in Article 168(5) TFEU. This article permits the Union to take public health measures but 'excluding harmonisation'.

Germany v. Parliament and Council (Tobacco Advertising I), C–376/98, EU:C:2000:544

80 In this case, the approximation of national laws on the advertising and sponsorship of tobacco products provided for by the Directive was based on Articles [114, 53 and 62 TFEU] of the Treaty . . .

83 Those provisions, read together, make it clear that the measures referred to in Article [114(1) TFEU] of the Treaty are intended to improve the conditions for the establishment and functioning of the internal market. To construe that article as meaning that it vests in the Community legislature a general power to regulate the internal market would not only be contrary to the express wording of the provisions cited above but would also be incompatible with the principle embodied in Article [5 TEU] that the powers of the Community are limited to those specifically conferred on it.

84 Moreover, a measure adopted on the basis of Article [114 TFEU] of the Treaty must genuinely have as its object the improvement of the conditions for the establishment and functioning of the internal market. If a mere finding of disparities between national rules and of the abstract risk of obstacles to the exercise of fundamental freedoms or of distortions of competition liable to result therefrom were sufficient to justify the choice of Article [114 TFEU] as a legal basis, judicial review of compliance with the proper legal basis might be rendered nugatory. The Court would then be prevented from discharging the function entrusted to it by Article [19 TEU] of ensuring that the law is observed in the interpretation and application of the Treaty.

85 So, in considering whether Article [114 TFEU] was the proper legal basis, the Court must verify whether the measure whose validity is at issue in fact pursues the objectives stated by the Community legislature.

86 It is true, that recourse to Article [114 TFEU] as a legal basis is possible if the aim is to prevent the emergence of future obstacles to trade resulting from multifarious development of national laws. However, the emergence of such obstacles must be likely and the measure in question must be designed to prevent them . . .

88 Furthermore, provided that the conditions for recourse to Articles [114, 53 and 62 TFEU] as a legal basis are fulfilled, the Community legislature cannot be prevented from relying on that legal basis on the ground that public health protection is a decisive factor in the choices to be made. On the contrary, [Article 168 TFEU] provides that health requirements are to form a constituent part of the Community's other policies and Article [114(3) TFEU] expressly requires that, in the process of harmonisation, a high level of human health protection is to be ensured . . .

Elimination of Obstacles to the Free Movement of Goods and the Freedom to Provide Services

96 It is clear that, as a result of disparities between national laws on the advertising of tobacco products, obstacles to the free movement of goods or the freedom to provide services exist or may well arise.

97　In the case, for example, of periodicals, magazines and newspapers which contain advertising for tobacco products, it is true, as the applicant has demonstrated, that no obstacle exists at present to their importation into Member States which prohibit such advertising. However, in view of the trend in national legislation towards ever greater restrictions on advertising of tobacco products, reflecting the belief that such advertising gives rise to an appreciable increase in tobacco consumption, it is probable that obstacles to the free movement of press products will arise in the future.

98　In principle, therefore, a Directive prohibiting the advertising of tobacco products in periodicals, magazines and newspapers could be adopted on the basis of Article [114 TFEU] with a view to ensuring the free movement of press products, on the lines of Directive 89/552, Article 13 of which prohibits television advertising of tobacco products in order to promote the free broadcasting of television programmes.

99　However, for numerous types of advertising of tobacco products, the prohibition under Article 3(1) of the Directive cannot be justified by the need to eliminate obstacles to the free movement of advertising media or the freedom to provide services in the field of advertising. That applies, in particular, to the prohibition of advertising on posters, parasols, ashtrays and other articles used in hotels, restaurants and cafés, and the prohibition of advertising spots in cinemas, prohibitions which in no way help to facilitate trade in the products concerned.

100　Admittedly, a measure adopted on the basis of Articles [114, 53 and 62 TFEU] of the Treaty may incorporate provisions which do not contribute to the elimination of obstacles to exercise of the fundamental freedoms provided that they are necessary to ensure that certain prohibitions imposed in pursuit of that purpose are not circumvented. It is, however, quite clear that the prohibitions mentioned in the previous paragraph do not fall into that category . . .

Elimination of Distortion of Competition

106　In examining the lawfulness of a directive adopted on the basis of Article [114 TFEU] of the Treaty, the Court is required to verify whether the distortion of competition which the measure purports to eliminate is appreciable (*Titanium Dioxide*, Case C-300/89, EU:C:1991:244).

107　In the absence of such a requirement, the powers of the Community legislature would be practically unlimited. National laws often differ regarding the conditions under which the activities they regulate may be carried on, and this impacts directly or indirectly on the conditions of competition for the undertakings concerned. It follows that to interpret Articles [114, 53 and 62 TFEU] as meaning that the Community legislature may rely on those articles with a view to eliminating the smallest distortions of competition would be incompatible with the principle, already referred to in paragraph 83 of this judgment, that the powers of the Community are those specifically conferred on it.

108　It is therefore necessary to verify whether the Directive actually contributes to eliminating appreciable distortions of competition.

109　First, as regards advertising agencies and producers of advertising media, undertakings established in Member States which impose fewer restrictions on tobacco advertising are unquestionably at an advantage in terms of economies of scale and increase in profits. The effects of such advantages on competition are, however, remote and indirect and do not constitute distortions which could be described as appreciable. They are not comparable to the distortions of competition caused by differences in production costs . . . [such as those in *Titanium Dioxide*, Case C-300/89, EU:C:1991:244].

110　It is true that the differences between certain regulations on tobacco advertising may give rise to appreciable distortions of competition. As the Commission and the Finnish and United Kingdom Governments have submitted, the fact that sponsorship is prohibited in some Member States and authorised in others gives rise, in particular, to certain sports events being relocated, with considerable repercussions on the conditions of competition for undertakings associated with such events.

111 However, such distortions, which could be a basis for recourse to Article [114 TFEU] of the Treaty in order to prohibit certain forms of sponsorship, are not such as to justify the use of that legal basis for an outright prohibition of advertising of the kind imposed by the Directive.

The Court of Justice provides a framework of legal principle which continues to define the scope of Article 114:[29]

(1) Measures based on that article must contribute to removing obstacles to interstate trade, or to removing distortions of competition.

(2) While there is no *de minimis* for obstacles to movement (even minor ones may be harmonised away), harmonisation to remove distortions is only possible when those distortions are 'appreciable'. The reason for this is that almost any differences between national laws have some kind of effect on business, and so could be claimed to cause some degree of market distortion. Without a minimum threshold for harmonisation, Article 114 would amount to an open-ended harmonisation power, which would be contrary to the principle that the Union only has conferred powers.[30]

(3) It is acceptable to harmonise to prevent obstacles arising, rather than removing already existing problems, but those future problems must be likely. One cannot harmonise on the basis of a theoretical possibility.

(4) Provided that a measure does in fact contribute to free movement or undistorted competition, it is not rendered invalid because it also contributes to public health. On the contrary, the Union is required to take other interests into account when deciding how obstacles and distortions should be removed. Article 168(5) TFEU is only a ban on harmonising public health using that Article, not on integrating public health considerations into internal market rules.

The Court of Justice applied these thoughts to the Directive on the basis of several findings of fact. First, the claimed distortions of competition were not significant. Secondly, a number of provisions of the Directive did not in fact contribute to free movement. The Court was unable to see how, for example, banning tobacco advertising in cinemas, or cigar shops, or on ashtrays or parasols – which were usually supplied free by tobacco companies, rather than sold – facilitated interstate trade.

Tobacco Advertising I has since been followed by a number of other cases also addressing the scope of Article 114 TFEU. These cases confirm the principles *of Tobacco Advertising I*, and clear up some ambiguities.

---

[29] See for commentary e.g. M. Kumm, 'Constitutionalising Subsidiarity in Integrated Markets: The Case of Tobacco Regulation in the European Union' (2006) 12 *ELJ* 503; F. Duina and P. Kurzer, 'Smoke in Your Eyes: The Struggle over Tobacco Control in the European Union' (2004) 11 *JEPP* 57; J. Snell, 'Who Has Got the Power: Free Movement and Allocation of Competences' (2003) 22 *YBEL* 323; A. Somek, *Individualism: An Essay on the Authority of EU Law* (Oxford University Press, 2008) ch. 7; S. Weatherill, 'Competence Creep and Competence Control' (2004) 23 *YBEL* 1; T. Hervey, 'Up in Smoke? Community (Anti) Tobacco Law and Policy' (2001) 26 *ELRev* 101.

[30] See Ch. 5.

Tobacco Advertising II addressed the Directive adopted to replace the one annulled in *Tobacco Advertising I*.[31] The broad idea of the replacement Directive was the same, but it was more limited, confining itself generally to matters that were genuinely cross-border, although its general ban on tobacco advertisement in printed media and radio extended even to local publications and local radio, which raised some concern. However, the Court found that to try and distinguish between which media might be traded or heard across the border and which would not be was practically impossible and would distort the market in itself. Therefore, a general approach was justified. An internal market Directive may regulate purely internal matters if this is an inseparable part of regulating cross-border ones.

The judgment also clarifies two further matters. First, a Directive does not have to pursue both the removal of obstacles to movement and undistorted competition. Either is enough. The first *Tobacco Advertising I* judgment had been a little unclear on this. Secondly, it is possible to harmonise public health matters under Article 114 TFEU provided this is part of genuine internal market regulation. *Tobacco Advertising I* had made clear that a contribution to public health was not excluded, but it might have been argued that this could not go so far as harmonisation. However, tobacco advertising rules *are* intended to protect public health, and they *were* harmonised in the second Tobacco Directive, and the Court found this to be acceptable. The Article 168 TFEU ban on harmonisation prevents that article being used for this purpose, but it does not prevent incidental harmonisation within the context of the internal market.

The second post-*Tobacco Advertising I* case was *Swedish Match*.[32] This concerned a Directive banning tobacco for chewing. Sweden enjoys an exemption from this ban, as a result of the particular popularity of chewing tobacco in that country. However, this was not enough for the complainants in this case who wished to market the chewing tobacco in the United Kingdom and, in a parallel case decided on the same day, Germany.[33] The Directive prevented this. They therefore challenged the validity of the Directive, saying a ban on a product did not contribute to the internal market. The Court of Justice disagreed, pointing out that without the Directive it was very likely that States would adopt different laws on the product, creating obstacles to trade. A pre-emptive approach, preventing these obstacles from arising, was appropriate.[34]

This was taken further in *Vodafone*, which concerned the validity of a regulation setting a maximum on mobile phone roaming charges within the European Union.[35] It was argued that this was not harmonisation, since none of the Member States had attempted to regulate these charges – there was no national law which could be said to be creating market problems. On the contrary, critics argued that the regulation was just an attempt to regulate the behaviour of mobile phone companies, whose commercial choices were making mobile phone use abroad very expensive. As such, it was not harmonisation of national laws and therefore should not be based on Article 114.[36]

---

[31] *Germany* v. *Parliament and Council (Tobacco Advertising II)*, C-380/03, EU:C:2006:772.

[32] *R* v. *Secretary of State for Health, ex parte Swedish Match*, C-210/03, EU:C:2004:802.

[33] *Arnold André GmBH & Co. KG* v. *Landrat des Kreises Herford*, C-434/02. EU:C:2004:800.

[34] See also *Philip Morris*, C- 547/14, ECLI:EU:C:2016:325; *Pillbox 38*, C-477/14, ECLI:EU:C:2016:324.

[35] *Vodafone*, C-58/8, EU:C:2010:321. See M. Brenncke, 'Annotation of *Vodafone*' (2010) 47 *CMLRev* 1793; S. Weatherill, 'The Limits of Legislative Harmonization Ten Years after *Tobacco Advertising*: How the Court's Case Law has become a "Drafting Guide"' (2011) 12 *German LJ* 827, 841–2.

[36] See also *United Kingdom* v. *Parliament and Council*, C-270/12, EU:C:2014:18.

The Court of Justice, however, accepted the Commission's argument that it was likely that individual Member States would regulate such charges in the future. That would create distortions of competition, and therefore pre-emptive harmonisation could be adopted using Article 114. A notable aspect of the case is that the Advocate General had concluded that there was no evidence that Member States were planning to adopt laws, so the test of 'likelihood' was not satisfied. As has been commented, it is extremely hard to know what kinds of laws Member States are going to adopt and, unless concrete plans and proposals are already in existence, the likelihood test becomes a very subjective and imprecise one.[37]

The other aspect of *Swedish Match* was that it involved a ban on a product. It is not obvious how banning something can facilitate trade in that product. This same point can be made about the *Seal Products* case, which concerned a Regulation prohibiting the import of seal products into the European Union.[38] If the point of that Regulation was just to protect seals, then, however worthy, it should not have been based on Article 114. The General Court nevertheless accepted that it was a legitimate internal market measure: some Member States felt very strongly about the ethics of seal culling and banned seal products on their national markets, while others did not, resulting in a situation where the internal market would effectively be divided. Any seal products that were imported would be saleable in some parts of the EU, and not others. The situation was complicated by the fact that it was not always easy to distinguish seal products from others. A ban therefore contributed to free trade, because it helped ensure that all products on sale in the internal market could be sold throughout that market. In its judgment the General Court allows a great deal of room for animal welfare considerations, yet integrates these smoothly with the core validity requirement that obstacles to trade should be removed.

Inuit Tapiriit Kanatami, Case T–526/10, EU:T:2013:215

41 In that regard, it must be borne in mind that, according to case-law, provided that the conditions for recourse to Article [114 TFEU] as a legal basis are fulfilled, the Union legislature cannot be prevented from relying on that legal basis on the ground that the protection of animal welfare is a decisive factor in the choices to be made. Such a situation may be found, by analogy, in relation to public health protection (*Germany* v. *Parliament and Council*, Case C–376/98 . . .), and as regards consumer protection (*Vodafone* . . .).

42 Moreover, it should be noted that the protection of animal welfare is a legitimate objective in the public interest, the importance of which was reflected, in particular, in the adoption by the Member States of the Protocol on the Protection and Welfare of Animals, annexed to the EC Treaty. Moreover, the Court has held on a number of occasions that the interests of the Union include the health and protection of animals.

43 As is apparent from recitals 9 and 10 in the preamble to the basic regulation, it is against that background that, aware of its obligations to pay full regard to the welfare requirements of animals when formulating and implementing its internal market policy under the Protocol, the Union legislature concluded that, to eliminate the present fragmentation of the internal market, it was necessary to provide for harmonised rules while taking into account animal welfare considerations.

---

[37] Brenncke, n. 35 above, 1802; Weatherill, n. 35 above, 833.
[38] Regulation 2065/2003 [2003] OJ L 309/1. *Inuit Tapiriit Kanatami*, T–526/10, EU:T:2013:215.

44 In order to be effective, the measure envisaged in the present case had to constitute an appropriate response taking into account the reasons which led to the rules which existed or were planned in the various Member States. In that connection, it appears from recital 10 in the preamble to the basic regulation that, to restore consumer confidence while, at the same time, ensuring that animal welfare concerns are fully met, 'the placing on the market of seal products should, as a general rule, not be allowed'. In addition, the Union legislature took the view that, to allay the concerns of citizens and consumers regarding 'the killing and skinning of seals as such, it [was] also necessary to take action to reduce the demand leading to the marketing of seal products and, hence, the economic demand driving the commercial hunting of seals'.

45 As is apparent from recital 13 in the preamble to the basic regulation, the Union legislature took the view that the most effective means of preventing existing and expected disturbances of the operation of the internal market in the products concerned was to reassure consumers by offering them a general guarantee that no seal product would be marketed on the Union market, *inter alia* by banning the import of such products from third countries.

The case was later confirmed on appeal to the Court of Justice.[39]

Banning products nevertheless remains a counter-intuitive contribution to market-building. It can best be understood by recognising that all products are part of a wider market, meaning that there are alternatives for the consumer: other tobacco products, or other forms of leather, in the examples above. Any product regulation limits what can be sold, and so entails a ban on non-complying products, but if the effect of that product delimitation is to steer consumers to freely tradeable alternatives then the regulation can be said to contribute to removing obstacles to trade and creating an open market.

The other major question on Article 114 arising in the case law concerns the meaning and scope of 'approximation'. Can this article be used only for legislation which actually harmonises, or can it be used for measures which contribute to the process of harmonising, without engaging in it as such? The latter position appears to be correct, following the *Smoke Flavourings* case and the *ENISA* case.[40]

The first of these concerned the British passion for chemically flavoured potato crisps, some varieties of which used flavourings which were likely to be banned under EU food safety rules. Faced with this sacrifice of national culture at the altar of mere safety, the British claimed that the procedure which had been created to decide on such bans lacked a legal basis. This procedure was found in Regulation 1007/2009, which enabled the Commission to regulate food additives according to a number of principles and processes, of which an important element was that they would receive advice from the European Food Safety Authority. The Regulation was based on Article 114. The British Government argued that this article could only be used to actually approximate national rules directly, not to create a system leading to such approximation, as the Regulation did.

---

[39] *Inuit Tapiriit Kanatami*, C-398/13 P, EU:C:2015:535.
[40] *United Kingdom* v. *Parliament and Council (ENISA)*, C-217/04, EU:C:2006:279.

United Kingdom v. Parliament and Council (Smoke Flavourings), C–66/04, EU:C:2005:743

45 ... in Article [114 TFEU] the authors of the Treaty intended to confer on the Community legislature a discretion, depending on the general context and the specific circumstances of the matter to be harmonised, as regards the harmonisation technique most appropriate for achieving the desired result, in particular in fields which are characterised by complex technical features.

46 That discretion may be used in particular to choose the most appropriate harmonisation technique where the proposed approximation requires physical, chemical or biological analyses to be made and scientific developments in the field concerned to be taken into account. Such evaluations relating to the safety of products correspond to the objective imposed on the Community legislature by Article [114(3) TFEU] of ensuring a high level of protection of health.

47 Finally, it should be added that where the Community legislature provides for a harmonisation which comprises several stages, for instance the fixing of a number of essential criteria set out in a basic regulation followed by scientific evaluation of the substances concerned and the adoption of a positive list of substances authorised throughout the Community, two conditions must be satisfied.

48 First, the Community legislature must determine in the basic act the essential elements of the harmonising measure in question.

49 Second, the mechanism for implementing those elements must be designed in such a way that it leads to a harmonisation within the meaning of Article [114 TFEU]. That is the case where the Community legislature establishes the detailed rules for making decisions at each stage of such an authorisation procedure, and determines and circumscribes precisely the powers of the Commission as the body which has to take the final decision. That applies in particular where the harmonisation in question consists in drawing up a list of products authorised throughout the Community to the exclusion of all other products.

Article 114 can therefore be used to create mechanisms leading to harmonisation, as well as for immediate harmonisation.

This was taken a step further in *ENISA*. The European Network and Information Society Agency provided non-binding advice on technical matters concerning electronic communications, for example, on current threats, or techniques for using electronic signatures, and so on. It was created by secondary legislation based on Article 114 and again the British Government argued that this went beyond approximation.

United Kingdom v. Parliament and Council (ENISA), C–217/04, EU:C:2006:279

44 It must be added in that regard that nothing in the wording of Article [114 TFEU] implies that the addressees of the measures adopted by the Community legislature on the basis of that provision can only be the individual Member States. The legislature may deem it necessary to provide for the establishment of a Community body responsible for contributing to the implementation of a process of harmonisation in situations where, in order to facilitate the uniform implementation and application of acts based on that provision, the adoption of non-binding supporting and framework measures seems appropriate.

45 It must be emphasised, however, that the tasks conferred on such a body must be closely linked to the subject-matter of the acts approximating the laws, regulations and administrative provisions of the Member States. Such is the case in particular where the Community body thus established provides services to national authorities and/or operators which affect the homogeneous implementation of harmonising instruments and which are likely to facilitate their application.

The activities of ENISA took place in the context of a number of Directives on electronic communication and networks. These outlined the functions and goals which Member State agencies were to adopt and pursue for the objective of creating compatible and secure European information systems and networks. However, much detailed implementation was left to the national agencies. The Court of Justice therefore found that ENISA, by providing information on common approaches and problems, even in a non-binding way, helped States to develop standardised and compatible systems, and therefore made a contribution to a harmonisation process. Provided the activities of ENISA were closely linked to the matter being harmonised, this was sufficient to justify Article 114 as a legal base.[41]

The scope of Article 114 is now reasonably clear. However, what is unaddressed is the ambiguity of the term 'appreciable' in *Tobacco Advertising I*. This is really the only word which prevents Article 114 from becoming a general power to harmonise national laws.[42] On the one hand, there seems no particular reason to fear that Article 114 will spiral out of control. Both the Council and Parliament must agree to legislation, and the Court of Justice is also likely to annul Directives which go too far.[43] Nevertheless, it is striking and, for many, problematic that the legal limit on harmonisation is so vague. One may still talk of limited Union powers, but hardly of well-defined ones.

Nor is 'appreciable' always an adequate limit. There are matters which cause very appreciable distortions of competition yet which we would not expect to see harmonised. The existence of different languages hinders trade and distorts competition in many and significant ways. It is beyond doubt that a common European language would contribute hugely to the internal market. Nothing in 'appreciable' provides an argument against a Directive legislating to make French the language of Europe.[44] Moreover, the appreciability threshold does not apply to the removal of obstacles to free movement. A fierce academic debate rages over whether the use of Article 114 to create a common European Contract Code would be appropriate.[45] There is much discussion over the extent to which differing laws on contracts hinder firms and individuals from doing business across borders, and whether a common code would make a significant difference. However, it seems likely that a common code would facilitate interstate contracts and business to at least some extent, and thus is prima facie possible under Article 114.

The objection to both these measures would be that they are disproportionate: the benefits to trade do not justify the cultural and social cost.[46] While the Court of Justice did not find the measures in *Tobacco Advertising II* or *Swedish Match* disproportionate, it is significant that it gave the matter explicit consideration. Proportionality is the other barrier to an open-ended Article 114.

---

[41] Similarly, *United Kingdom* v. *Parliament and Council*, C-270/12, EU:C:2014:18 on 'individual measures'.

[42] A. Dashwood, 'The Limits of European Community Powers' (1996) 21 *ELRev* 113.   [43] *Ibid.*

[44] G. Davies, 'Subsidiarity: The Wrong Idea, in the Wrong Place, at the Wrong Time' (2006) 43 *CMLRev* 63.

[45] S. Weatherill, 'Why Object to the Harmonisation of Private Law by the EC?' (2004) 12(5) *European Review of Private Law* 633; S. Weatherill and Stefan Vogenauer (eds.), *The Harmonisation of European Contract Law: Implications for European Private Laws, Business and Legal Practice* (Oxford, Hart, 2006); P. van den Bergh, 'Forced Harmonisation of Contract Law in Europe: Not to be Continued' in S. Grundmann and J. Stuyck (eds.), *An Academic Green Paper on European Contract Law* (The Hague, Kluwer, 2002) 245–64; M. van Hoecke and F. Ost (eds.), *The Harmonisation of European Private Law* (Oxford, Hart, 2000); A. Hartkamp *et al.*, *Towards a European Civil Code*, 3rd edn (The Hague, Kluwer Law International, 2004); P. Legrand, 'Against a European Civil Code' (1997) 60 *MLR* 44; M. Hesselink, *The Politics of a European Civil Code* (The Hague, Kluwer Law International, 2006); J.-J. Kuipers, 'The Legal Basis for a European Optional Instrument' (2011) 5 *European Review of Private Law* 545.

[46] G. Davies, 'Internal Market Adjudication and the Quality of Life in Europe' (2015) 21(2) *Columbia Journal of European Law* 289.

What this all shows is the problem of containing purposive powers. Article 114 is not defined in terms of a particular area of activity – health, education, foodstuffs – but in terms of the achievement of goals – free movement and undistorted competition. These cut across other areas of activity, because so many different kinds of law may impact upon them. Areas of law which are not conventionally 'economic' may still affect cross-border trade or the costs of doing business, and so be subject to harmonisation using Article 114. Goal-oriented powers have thus an inherent tendency to spread.[47] As governments have always known, if the end justifies the means then much can be achieved.

It may be noted that most of the above judgments took place in the context of the EC Treaty in which Article 3(g) provided that the Union would have 'a system ensuring that competition in the internal market is not distorted'. This provided the traditional intellectual background and support for the thesis that the 'establishment and functioning' of the internal market encompassed not only removing obstacles to movement, as explicitly mentioned in Article 26 TFEU, but also removing distortions of competition. However, the Lisbon Treaty cut this clause from the main Treaties and moved it to a Protocol.

Protocol No. 27 on the Internal Market and Competition

THE HIGH CONTRACTING PARTIES,

CONSIDERING that the internal market as set out in Article 3 of the Treaty on European Union includes a system ensuring that competition is not distorted,

HAVE AGREED that:
To this end, the Union shall, if necessary, take action under the provisions of the Treaties, including under Article 352 of the Treaty on the Functioning of the European Union. This protocol shall be annexed to the Treaty on European Union and to the Treaty on the Functioning of the European Union.

The intention appears to be that distortions of competition should be addressed via Article 352, which requires unanimity. However, the Court of Justice relies on its pre-Lisbon competence case law as if nothing has changed, and has even said that Article 114 'corresponds' to Article 95 EC, suggesting that the Protocol has had no legal effects on the scope of Article 114.[48]

5 TECHNIQUES OF REGULATION

(i) Old and New Approaches

One of the fundamental obstacles to free trade between States is technical standards. These vary from State to State, with the result that a product made according to French law probably does not conform to the requirements of German or UK law. Manufacturers thus have a difficult time making products that they can freely trade throughout the European Union.

In the early days of the Union (when it was the European Economic Community), the approach to this problem was relatively straightforward. Wherever necessary, the Commission sought to

---

[47] G. Davies, 'Democracy and Legitimacy in the Shadow of Purposive Competence' (2015) 21(1) *ELJ* 2.
[48] *UsedSoft*, C-128/11, EU:C:2012:407, para. 41.

propose legislation replacing national product standards with equivalent European ones. Common standards, combined with mutual recognition of inspections, removed the trade problem.[49] However, standards are a complex business, not only for complicated technical products, but even for apparently simple ones, such as toys, where one may have to think about paint types, strength, resistance to dismantling and so on. Each piece of legislation was a time-consuming business, and the Community was simply not able to produce enough legislation to create a single market, particularly given the pace of product development and the constant introduction of new product types.[50]

In the mid-1980s a new approach was introduced, still called 'the new approach' today.[51] This was based on a much more minimalist legislative approach. Instead of detailed and technical legislation for each product type, Directives would be adopted for broad product categories, toys, machinery, and so on. These would lay down, at a high level of abstraction, general demands concerning the essential health and safety requirements that such products should meet. A selection of the requirements from Directive 2009/48/EC on toy safety provides a flavour of the style of these requirements, abstract almost to the point of being banal.

Directive 2009/48/EC of the European Parliament and of the Council of 18 June 2009 on the safety of toys, Annex II, Particular Safety Requirements

I Physical and Mechanical Properties

(1) Toys and their parts and, in the case of fixed toys, their anchorages, must have the requisite mechanical strength and, where appropriate, stability to withstand the stresses to which they are subjected during use without breaking or becoming liable to distortion at the risk of causing physical injury.

(2) Accessible edges, protrusions, cords, cables and fastenings on toys must be designed and manufactured in such a way that the risks of physical injury from contact with them are reduced as far as possible.

(3) Toys must be designed and manufactured in such a way as not to present any risk or only the minimum risk inherent to their use which could be caused by the movement of their parts . . .

(5) Aquatic toys must be designed and manufactured so as to reduce as far as possible, taking into account the recommended use of the toy, any risk of loss of buoyancy of the toy and loss of support afforded to the child.

(6) Toys which it is possible to get inside and which thereby constitute an enclosed space for occupants must have a means of exit which the intended user can open easily from the inside.

The responsibility of the Member States under new approach Directives is to ensure that products placed onto their domestic markets conform to the essential requirements in the Directive.[52] How

---

[49] See General Programme on the Removal of Technical Obstacles to Trade [1969] OJ C 76/1.

[50] Commission White Paper, 'Completing the Single Market', COM(85)310; 'The Development of Standardisation: Action for Faster Technical Integration in Europe', COM(90)456.

[51] For policy documents, details of legislation and background, see www.newapproach.eu and http://ec.europa.eu/enterprise/policies/european-standards/harmonised-standards/new-approach_en.htm.

[52] On the new approach, see J. Pelkmans, 'The New Approach to Technical Harmonization and Standardization' (1987) 25 JCMS 249; European Commission, 'Enhancing the Implementation of New Approach Directives', COM(2003)240; A. McGee and S. Weatherill, 'The Evolution of the Single Market: Harmonisation or Liberalisation?' (1990) 53 MLR 578. See further M. Egan, Constructing a European Market (Oxford University Press, 2001) ch. 4; S. Weatherill, 'Pre-Emption, Harmonisation and the Distribution of Competence to Regulate the Internal Market' in C. Barnard and J. Scott (eds.), The Law of the Single European Market: Unpacking the Premises (Oxford-Portland, Hart, 2002); K. Armstrong, 'Governance and the Single European Market' in P. Craig and G. de Búrca (eds.), The Evolution of EU Law (Oxford University Press, 1998).

exactly they do this is up to them. There are two important differences from the old approach. First, the new approach gives States a considerable freedom to standardise in different ways. There is no uniform approach. Thus, the virtues of experiment and diversity are maintained. Essential health and safety requirements can be satisfied by different regulatory styles and methods according to the traditions and preferences of the State. Secondly, the legislation only deals with essential health and safety requirements. Matters that are purely concerned with quality are not harmonised. Thus, the Union may legislate to ensure that sausages are safe, but under the new approach will not be concerned with how much meat a sausage has to contain.

This decision not to harmonise quality standards was made possible by the decision in *Cassis de Dijon*, where the Court of Justice decided that pure quality issues are not a sufficient reason to exclude foreign products from the market.[53] Germany may decide that German-made sausages should have more than 50 per cent meat, but it cannot use this requirement to exclude British ones that may have much less. The EU approach to quality requirements is now no longer based on compulsory quality standards, but on informing the consumers, who then decide for themselves what they prefer: Germany may, for example, require sausages to indicate on the packaging how much meat they contain. Since quality standards therefore no longer create (in principle) obstacles to trade, there is no need to harmonise them. This is the core insight of the new approach.

(ii) Mechanics of the New Approach

The new approach does not rest on the broad-spectrum Directives alone. There are two other aspects which are in practice essential to its success. First, European standardisation is not abandoned. Rather, it is moved away from the legislative process to specialist standardisation agencies.[54] These create technical standards of a more detailed and specific type, although often less specific and detailed than under the old approach, still leaving a certain discretion and freedom in how to meet substantive requirements. The advantage of this outsourcing is that it decouples the making of standards (which can be slow and difficult) from the legislative process, so that the latter is no longer seized up. The Council and Parliament can agree on a general framework, and then let the experts deal with the details at their own pace. Moreover, the new European standards are voluntary: there is no obligation to adopt them. A State, or a manufacturer, may prefer to meet the requirements of the Directive in another way, and they are free to do so. However, they will then have to show that their products do in fact meet the health and safety requirements. It may be easier to simply follow the European standards, since if a producer does this it creates a strong presumption that the product conforms to the Directive. She should then be able to sell her goods throughout the Union without problem. The idea of a new European standard is therefore that it shows one way of manufacturing a product so that it is

---

[53] *Rewe-Zentral AG* v. *Bundesmonopolverwaltung für Branntwein (Cassis de Dijon)*, 120/78, EU:C:1979:42. See p. 721.

[54] E.g. European Committee for Standardisation (CEN), European Committee for Electrotechnical Standardisation (CENELEC) and European Telecommunication Standards Institute (ETSI). See European Commission Communication, 'The Role of European Standardisation in the Framework of European Policies and Legislation', COM(2004)674 final (18 October 2004); H. Schepel, *The Constitution of Private Governance* (Oxford-Portland, Hart, 2005) ch. 4; C. Frankel and E. Højbjerg, 'The Constitution of a Transnational Policy Field: Negotiating the EU Internal Market for Products' (2007) 14 *JEPP* 96; M. Austin and H. Milner, 'Strategies of European Standardization' (2001) 8 *JEPP* 411.

sufficiently safe and conforms to the relevant Directive, but it does not insist that this is the only way. Room for production-method innovation and deviation is allowed.

The second additional aspect of the new approach is its procedural requirements concerning certification. It is all very well to say that products conforming to the European standard, or complying with the Directive by another method, must be accepted by all Member States. This begs the question of who establishes that there actually is such conformity.

The new approach requires Member States to authorise 'notified bodies' to carry out testing and accreditation of products, and certify that they comply with EU law. These bodies, which may be private, should be selected according to the competence and expertise, so that their certification is trusted and accepted. However, a major weakness of the new approach is a lack of trust between States on the performance and reliability of these bodies, leading to a reluctance to accept their results as proof of compliance.[55]

The underlying problem is that if standards leave room for variety, then it becomes a harder and less objective process to assess whether they are met. It is easier to objectively certify a teddy bear if every detail of its manufacture is specified than if the rules say 'it must be able to resist normal use by a child'. Clearly, bodies will take different approaches to measuring compliance. The problems this creates are magnified by the fact that there is no uniform European approach to accreditation of notified bodies, and these vary greatly in character and quality. They may be private companies, public authorities or quasi-public agencies. There are repeated complaints that the bodies are not of consistent quality, that market pressures encourage them to be over-easy with their certification, that not all Member States adequately supervise the notified bodies or are strict enough about accreditation.

Thus, the principle of the new approach is attractively easy: a producer contracts with a notified body to have her products tested and certified to show they comply with the Directive; the body does this, whereupon the producer attaches a CE mark to her product, and supplies the certification documents to the authorities of the State to which she is exporting and the goods are accepted onto their market. However, this relies on these authorities trusting the notified bodies of other States, which they often do not. Thus, despite a CE mark and evidence of certification, it is not at all uncommon for States to block market access on the grounds that the products are not in fact sufficiently safe. They may take the view that the way the producer has chosen to meet the Directive's requirements is not adequate, or that there is insufficient evidence of such compliance.

It may well be that if the producer litigates, then ultimately she will win.[56] National authorities are still often over-suspicious of foreign standards and notifying bodies and their refusals may be unjustified. However, litigation is slow and expensive. If producers have to use the courts regularly to gain market access, then the new approach has failed. In fact the picture is mixed; in many cases it works well, but too often it does not.[57]

As a result of these concerns, the new approach has been updated. While trying to maintain its light legislative touch and flexibility, legislation has been adopted aiming to improve trust

---

[55] See G. Majone, 'Mutual Trust, Credible Commitments and the Evolution of the Rules of the Single Market', EUI Working Paper RSC 1995/1; J. Pelkmans, 'The New Approach to Technical Harmonization and Standardization' (1987) 25 *JCMS* 249.

[56] See e.g. *Commission* v. *Belgium*, C-254/05, EU:C:2012:539.

[57] See J. Pelkmans, Mutual Recognition in Goods and Services: An Economic Perspective, ENEPRI Working Paper No. 16/2003 (Brussels, ENEPRI, 2003).

surrounding the certification process. Regulation 765/2008/EC creates a Union framework for the operation, accreditation and supervision of conformity assessment bodies (notified bodies) in the hope that this will create a more uniform quality and approach, and therefore more trust and more effective interstate mutual recognition of certification.[58] It is perhaps an irony that minimising the harmonisation of products is only possible by increasing the harmonisation of procedure.

Alongside this, the old approach is not dead. Technical legislation usually provided for updating by the comitology process, so that it would survive product development.[59] A significant number of products are therefore still subject to 'old style' Directives.

(iii) Minimum Harmonisation

The new and old approaches are both about technical product standards, but much internal market harmonisation concerns production processes and the ironing out of distortions of competition, or less urgent aspects of product regulation such as consumer protection. Here the Union has other techniques which it uses to try and reach the right balance between harmonisation and local autonomy.

An approach often used is minimum harmonisation.[60] This lays down a minimum standard, but leaves Member States free to have stricter standards if they wish. Where this is applied to harmonisation of the conditions of competition it is relatively unproblematic in principle. The competitive impact of legal differences is not eliminated, but it is reduced. However, where minimum harmonisation is applied to matters related to tradable goods or services it raises legal problems. If a Member State chooses to maintain higher standards, is it entitled to apply these to imports or not? If so, then the Directive does not ensure free movement, and its purpose and validity may be questioned (if it is based on Article 114 TFEU at least; where it is based on other Treaty Articles such as those providing for environmental legislation, the matter becomes more complex).[61] Yet if not, then Member States are not in fact able to guarantee a higher level of protection on their territory, since they may only apply the higher standard to domestic producers, and not to imports. The minimum level may in practice become the actual level prevailing in the marketplace, rendering the option to maintain higher standards a little hollow.

The answer turns on the wording and context of each Directive. However, in general, the imperative that measures based on Article 114 facilitate free movement means that internal market Directives usually require Member States to admit products that meet the minimum standards. Thus, Member States may usually only apply stricter requirements to domestic production, and not to imports. One consequence of this is that domestic production may bear a heavier regulatory burden than imported goods. The Court of Justice confirmed in *Gallaher* that this is not to be seen as prohibited discrimination, but simply as an inevitable and acceptable result of the choice for minimum harmonisation.[62] *Gallaher* concerned the size of health warnings on cigarette packets. Directive 89/622/EC required these to cover at least 4 per cent of the packet, but allowed Member States to be stricter. The United Kingdom required 6 per cent

---

[58] Regulation 765/2008 setting out the requirements for accreditation and market surveillance relating to the marketing of products [2008] OJ L 218/30.
[59] See pp. 146–51.   [60] M. Dougan, 'Minimum Harmonization and the Internal Market' (2000) 37 *CMLRev* 853.
[61] *Ibid.*; J. Jans and H. H. B. Vedder, *European Environmental Law*, 3rd edn (Groningen, Europa Law Publishing, 2008).
[62] *R* v. *Secretary of State for Health, ex parte Gallaher Ltd*, C-11/92, EU:C:1993:262.

but, as the Directive required, did not enforce this against imports. UK producers complained, without avail, that they were unfairly disadvantaged.

6 NON-ECONOMIC INTERESTS IN THE INTERNAL MARKET

Economic and non-economic interests cannot feasibly be separated. Economic activity inevitably impacts on the environment, society and individual safety and security. Nor does the Treaty intend that such matters should be considered in isolation. It explicitly demands an integrated approach. Article 7 TFEU provides that the Union shall ensure consistency between all its policies, and Articles 8–12 require anti-discrimination goals, social policy, the environment and consumer protection to be integrated into all other policies. Moreover, Article 114 TFEU enables both the Commission, in its proposals, and Member States, by means of derogations from harmonisation measures, to take into account and react to health, safety and environmental concerns.

Article 114 TFEU

(3) The Commission, in its proposals envisaged in paragraph 1 concerning health, safety, environmental protection and consumer protection, will take as a base a high level of protection, taking account in particular of any new development based on scientific facts. Within their respective powers, the European Parliament and the Council will also seek to achieve this objective.

(4) If, after the adoption of a harmonisation measure by the European Parliament and the Council, by the Council or by the Commission, a Member State deems it necessary to maintain national provisions on grounds of major needs referred to in Article 36, or relating to the protection of the environment or the working environment, it shall notify the Commission of these provisions as well as the grounds for maintaining them.

(5) Moreover, without prejudice to paragraph 4, if, after the adoption of a harmonisation measure by the European Parliament and the Council, by the Council or by the Commission, a Member State deems it necessary to introduce national provisions based on new scientific evidence relating to the protection of the environment or the working environment on grounds of a problem specific to that Member State arising after the adoption of the harmonisation measure, it shall notify the Commission of the envisaged provisions as well as the grounds for introducing them.

The remainder of the article provides for procedures to assess and police the derogations above. The right balance between interests is, of course, always contested. This is the stuff of politics. However, an issue of current concern is the process of achieving that balance. An accusation levelled at the Union is that it is deaf to voices other than scientific ones, and presents scientific analyses of health and safety and environmental issues as more objective and less contested than they in fact are, and also as more important: scientific perspectives are only a part of a picture in which moral and social and democratic preferences are also relevant.[63]

---

[63] M. Kritikos, 'Traditional Risk Analysis and Releases of GMOs into the European Union: Space for Non-Scientific Factors' (2009) 44 *ELRev* 405; C. Joerges, 'The Law's Problems with the Governance of the Single European Market' in C. Joerges and R. Dehousse (eds.), *Good Governance in Europe's Integrated Market* (Oxford University Press, 2002) 1.

This is part of a wider debate about what the Union should be. While for some it is intended to be a technocratic regulator, and expert decisions on technical matters should be welcomed for their efficiency, others take the view that since these matters are emotionally or politically salient – whatever the experts might say – that means they should be part of the political process.[64] Delegating regulation to experts then creates a democratic deficit.

These issues arose in the *Austrian GMOs* case, in which the region of Upper Austria sought to ban the release of GMOs on its territory.[65] To do this it needed a derogation from Directive 2001/18/EC, which it sought on the basis of Article 114(5) TFEU. This was refused by the Commission, and the Commission's view was upheld in both the General Court and Court of Justice. The Court emphasised that Article 114(5) TFEU could only be relied upon where there was new scientific evidence, problems specific to a Member State arose after the harmonisation measure had been adopted and those problems related to the working or natural environment. These were cumulative requirements: a failure on any ground made derogation impossible. The Austrian view was that its unique eco-systems, sizeable organic production and large number of small farms made it a special case. It was not so much that they had new evidence on the science, as that the consequences for an industry and society where naturalness and purity are especially important were particularly frightening. There was no room for this within Article 114(5). The Court of Justice's view is textually understandable – the article is fairly clear – but it raises the question whether EU law is adapted to modern risk management, which has to face situations where threats to health and safety are bound up with ethics and social norms, or whether it is only suited for less controversial and more lumpen issues.[66]

This same bias towards the measurable and material may be seen in free movement law. The greatest changes which it has wrought in Member States are not to do with safety, health or the environment, but the way it has changed the quality of national life, replacing traditional but inefficient businesses by bigger, cheaper and more alien ones, bringing diversity into communities that were homogeneous, and replacing the shared experience of common goods and services with the primacy of individual choice.[67] The market is not just a way of allocating goods to those most prepared to pay, but a way of life. Yet in the case law of the Court on derogations, discussed in Chapter 19, we see extensive discussion of, and deference to, the concrete threats raised by free movement, but almost no mention of the social changes it causes, and whether these might justify restrictions – whether social discomfort with the pace or extent of change might deserve recognition as legitimate.

Partly this is because States are traditionally poor at explaining what the value of their laws really is, as some of the more laughable attempts at justification show.[68] However, these complex social issues are hard to render objectively and so hard for judges to deal with – which raises the question whether free movement law is being used to do too much.

As well as challenging societies' entrenched ways of production, sale and service, free movement law also redistributes power from the static to the mobile. One mobile individual has the right to challenge a law reflecting a collective choice. Of course, this is an inevitable corollary of accepting binding Treaty arrangements – that national political freedom is limited.

---

[64] G. Majone, 'The Credibility Crisis of Community Regulation' (2002) 38 *JCMS* 273; A. Føllesdal and S. Hix, 'Why There Is a Democratic Deficit in the EU: A Response to Majone and Moravcsik' (2006) 44 *JCMS* 533.
[65] *Land Oberösterreich and Austria* v. *Commission*, C-439/05 P and C-454/05 P, EU:C:2007:510.
[66] See now Regulation 2018/412.   [67] Davies, n. 46 above.   [68] *Ibid.*

Nevertheless, the democratic costs mean that its extent and mechanism need to be monitored nervously. That is sometimes hard when free movement justifies itself in high moral terms, such as non-discrimination. Nevertheless, despite the great value of this principle, its meaning leaves so much space for political choices that its use will rarely be an uncontested good.

F. De Witte, 'Transnational Solidarity and the Mediation of Conflicts of Justice in Europe' (2012) 18 *European Law Journal* 694, 702–3

[The exercise of free movement rights] structurally favours (in the most general terms) the much more mobile capital and the richer citizens over immobile labour and poorer citizens by making policy choices that go against the interests of such mobile actors unavailable. This process has been described in company law, labour law and regulation of the marketing of goods – where policy outcomes are structurally biased towards the interests of global (and mobile) capital. In those fields, collective choices are restricted by the need to respect individual agency of those who actually move. Such partial de-politicisation is problematic as such, given that collective agency was exactly meant to tame such (often the very same) particularistic interests, but more fundamentally because it shows that obligation of non-discrimination is not normatively neutral and may dislocate normative and redistributive commitments on the national level.

As well as its immediate effects in specific cases, the internal market has also been argued by Somek to embody a commitment to individualism which challenges the very fabric of social-democratic societies, tending to break the bonds of solidarity between citizens.[69] He makes a claim about the conflict between economic and social policy which goes to the heart of the internal market. Yet, by contrast with domestic politics, it has been argued that the European Union prefers to deny such conflicts rather than to debate, or even accept, them.[70] Neither in the legislative process nor before the Court of Justice when it adjudicates on free movement is there an open enough expression of all the interests at stake, which go beyond the merely concrete and include questions of identity, justice and views about 'the good life', as de Witte has put it: rules about products, services and migration are also rules about how we want to live together.[71] This depoliticisation of value-laden policy choices challenges the legitimacy of the internal market, and of the Union as a whole.[72]

7 REGULATORY COMPETITION

Where free movement is based on mutual recognition, rather than on harmonisation, this means that businesses in different States are subject to substantively different rules. It is a short step for them to consider moving to the State whose rules are the most attractive, often meaning that they impose the lowest costs and regulatory burdens. They can do this because irrespective of the State they are based in, they still have access to all other Member State markets, thanks to free movement.

---

[69] Somek, n. 29 above; A. Somek, 'From Workers to Migrants, from Distributive Justice to Inclusion: Exploring the Changing Social Democratic Imagination' (2012) 18 *ELJ* 711.

[70] M. Dani, 'Rehabilitating Social Conflicts in European Public Law' (2012) 18 *ELJ* 621.

[71] F. de Witte, 'Sex, Drugs and EU Law: The Regulation of Moral and Ethical Diversity in EU Law' (2013) 6 *CMLRev* 1545; Dani, n. 70 above; Davies, n. 46 above.

[72] G. Davies, 'Democracy and Legitimacy in the Shadow of Purposive Competence' (2015) 21(1) *ELJ* 2.

It is another short step for States to start adapting their rules to make them attractive to business – for if they do not, business may leave, and if they do, then they may benefit from new businesses coming.

Thus States begin to use their laws as tools of competition in a battle to attract mobile factors of production – sometimes highly skilled individuals, sometimes investors, but most often productive businesses. Law is here the product, and the mobile actors are the consumers. This is often called regulatory competition.[73]

S. Deakin, 'Legal Diversity and Regulatory Competition: Which Model for Europe?' (2006) 12 _European Law Journal_ 440, 441–3

Regulatory competition can be defined as a process whereby legal rules are selected and de-selected through competition between decentralised, rule-making entities, which could be nation states, or other political units, such as regions or localities. A number of beneficial effects are expected to flow from this process. Insofar as it avoids the imposition of rules by a centralised, 'monopoly' regulator, it promotes diversity and experimentation in the search for effective laws. In addition, by providing mechanisms for the preferences of the different users of laws to be expressed and for alternative solutions to common problems to be compared, it enhances the flow of information on what works in practice. Above all, it allows the content of rules to be matched more effectively to the preferences or _wants_ of those consumers, that is, the citizens of the polities concerned. In some versions of the theory, the first two of these goals are, in essence, simply the means by which the third is achieved.

Regulatory competition is sometimes welcomed as a force which disciplines States into making more economically efficient law, and which also encourages legal experiment, rewarding good laws and punishing bad ones. Like any market, in a fictive world of frictionless rationality, it would lead to better products.

Yet, there are also downsides attributed to regulatory competition. One is that it forces States to take account of only some of those who are affected by regulation: mobile economic actors. The citizen's voice is lost. Laws become tailored to those who are able to threaten exit, while others are ignored.[74]

Another, closely related, risk is that it leads to a 'race to the bottom' as States impose ever lighter regulatory standards to attract businesses. They cannot afford to regulate as protectively as their populations might like, because businesses will move away, causing economic harm.[75] As one State cuts environmental or social obligations, other States will be forced to do the same, or even go further, or they will lose their tax and employment base. A general lowering of

---

[73] See generally in the European context J.-M. Sun and J. Pelkmans, 'Regulatory Competition in the Single Market' (1995) 33 _JCMS_ 67; C. Barnard and S. Deakin, 'Market Access and Regulatory Competition' in C. Barnard and S. Deakin (eds.), _The Law of the European Single Market_ (Oxford-Portland, Hart, 2005); N. Reich, 'Competition between Legal Orders: A New Paradigm of EC Law?' (1992) 29 _CMLRev_ 459; A. Ogus, 'Competition between National Legal Systems: A Contribution of Economic Analysis to Comparative Law' (1999) 48 _ICLQ_ 405; S. Deakin, 'Legal Diversity and Regulatory Competition: Which Model for Europe?' (2006) 12 _ELJ_ 440; H. Søndergaard Birkmose, 'Regulatory Competition and the European Harmonisation Process' (2006) _EBLRev_ 1075.

[74] See A. O. Hirschmann, _Exit, Voice and Loyalty: Responses to Decline in Firms, Organizations and States_ (Cambridge, MA, Harvard University Press, 1970); F. De Witte, 'Transnational Solidarity and the Mediation of Conflicts of Justice in Europe' (2012) 18 _ELJ_ 694.

[75] See Barnard and Deakin, n. 73 above.

standards results, despite the fact that this may not reflect the majority preference in any individual Member State.

Harmonisation of the conditions of competition is seen as an essential balance to prevent this happening. Binding EU rules or standards prevent competitive deregulation. However, harmonisation also deprives Member States of regulatory autonomy, sometimes eliminates local particularities and also entails a convergence of regulatory standards and methods which may upset liberal and highly regulated States equally. It is not surprising that the optimal amount of EU harmonisation is a highly contested matter, with claims that the EU over-regulates existing alongside claims that it is a deregulatory, 'neoliberal' force.[76] The dilemma can be expressed as a choice between positive and negative harmonisation. Fritz Scharpf has argued that the latter of these tends to dominate, because it can be achieved by litigation, while the former requires difficult political consensus. There is thus a deregulatory bias in the system. This, he has suggested, along with the other disciplines of economic liberalism, takes away the capacity of States to maintain expensive welfare institutions. They are no longer able to impose the legal framework necessary to maintain these. Firms will migrate rather than pay for luxurious welfare systems via taxation or via worker-friendly social legislation. States are therefore forced to cut regulatory burdens.

F. Scharpf, 'The European Social Model: Coping with the Challenges of Diversity' (2002) 40 *Journal of Common Market Studies* 645, 648–9

[Having discussed the constraints on national policy resulting from the Euro rules, free movement, and state aid law] . . . compared to the repertoire of policy choices that was available two or three decades ago, European *legal* constraints have greatly reduced the capacity of national governments to influence growth and employment in the economies for whose performance they are politically accountable. In principle, the only national options which under European law remain freely available are supply-side strategies involving lower tax burdens, further deregulation and flexibilization of employment conditions, increasing wage differentiation and welfare cutbacks to reduce reservation wages. At the same time, governments face strong *economic* incentives to resort to just such strategies of competitive deregulation and tax cuts in order to attract or retain mobile firms and investments that might otherwise seek locations with lower production costs and higher post-tax incomes from capital. By the same token, unions find themselves compelled to accept lower wages or less attractive employment conditions in order to save existing jobs. Conversely, welfare states are tempted to reduce the generosity or tighten the eligibility rules of tax-financed social transfers and social services in order to discourage the immigration of potential welfare clients.

Scharpf goes on to argue that the only way to prevent economic freedom impacting destructively on welfare systems is to move welfare to a European level, but that this is not possible because of

---

[76] See for overviews e.g. S. Woolcock, 'Competition among Rules in the Single European Market' in W. Bratton *et al.* (eds.), *International Regulatory Competition and Coordination: Perspectives on Economic Regulation in Europe and the United States* (Oxford University Press, 1996); R. van den Bergh, 'Regulatory Competition or Harmonization of Laws? Guidelines for the European Regulator' in A. Marciano and J.-M. Josselin (eds.), *The Economics of Harmonizing European Law* (Cheltenham, Edward Elgar, 2002); Z. Drabak, 'Limits to the Harmonisation of Domestic Regulations' (2008) 2 *Journal of International Trade and Diplomacy* 47; G. Wagner, 'The Economics of Harmonisation: The Case of Contracts' (2002) 39 *CMLRev* 995.

the diversity of different national systems. For him, if the European Union is to retain its social character, it faces a choice between a less demanding internal market and more social integration.[77] He contrasts the situation with the United States, where the development of State welfare systems was initially prevented by regulatory competition considerations similar to those at work in Europe today.[78] However, after the New Deal in the 1930s, it became possible for the federal government to play a significant role in welfare, limiting the local competitive element. It is that federal involvement which is neither existent, nor currently possible, in the Union today, he suggests.

Yet, many consider his fears exaggerated. The empirical evidence to date is ambiguous, and economists never tire of pointing out that there is very limited evidence that a race to the bottom often takes place. Whether or not it will depends on the specific circumstances.[79] It may well be that States consider it in their national interest to maintain high standards and that certain kinds of industry are even attracted by this. There is certainly plenty of evidence that a high-tax high-standard economic model can work. It may be easier to attract good employees to a State with high environmental and social standards, and a generous welfare net may not be a net burden on firms: otherwise they would perhaps be forced by the employment market to offer even more expensive private facilities and protection. On the whole, solidarity can be cost-effective.

Other writers try to move beyond the simple opposition of a race to the bottom and regulatory diversity. The goal of policy should be to seek the ideal mix between competition and cooperation between States, summed up in an article by Esty and Gerardin as 'regulatory co-opetition'.[80] Deakin has, similarly, emphasised that harmonisation which reduces diversity so much that States can no longer experiment would be destructive. He introduces the idea of 'reflexive harmonisation' in which States learn from each other, and develop their own laws in the light of their neighbours. He sees a role for EU harmonisation as framing this process, facilitating communication between States and preventing competition which would, in practice, reduce State autonomy and ultimately diversity.

S. Deakin, 'Legal Diversity and Regulatory Competition: Which Model for Europe?' (2006) 12 *European Law Journal* 440, 444–5

The model of reflexive harmonisation holds that the principal objectives of judicial intervention and legislative harmonisation alike are two-fold: first, to protect the autonomy and diversity of national or local rule-making systems, while, second, seeking to 'steer' or channel the process of adaptation of rules at State level away from 'spontaneous' solutions that would lock in sub-optimal outcomes, such as a 'race to the bottom'. In this model, the process by which States may observe and emulate practices in jurisdictions to which they are closely related by trade and by institutional connections is more akin to the concept of 'co-evolution' than to convergence around the 'evolutionary peak' or end-state envisaged by Tiebout's general equilibrium model. The idea of co-evolution, borrowed from the modern evolutionary synthesis in

---

[77] Also see G. Majone, 'From Regulatory State to a Democratic Default' (2014) 52 *JCMS* 1216.

[78] F. Scharpf, 'Democratic Legitimacy under Conditions of Regulatory Competition: Why Europe Differs from the United States' in K. Nicolaidis and R. Howse, *The Federal Vision* (Oxford University Press, 2001) 355.

[79] See e.g. Ogus, n. 73 above; J.-M. Sun and J. Pelkmans, 'Regulatory Competition in the Single Market' (1995) 33 *JCMS* 67.

[80] D. Esty and D. Gerardin, 'Regulatory Co-opetition' (2000) 3 *JIEL* 235.

the biological sciences, argues that a variety of diverse systems can coexist within an environment, with each one retaining its viability. It thereby combines diversity and autonomy of systems with their interdependence within a single, overarching set of environmental parameters.

Nevertheless, any legislative framework has to correspond to popular notions of fairness if it is to be legitimate and politically stable. There is only a limited tolerance for diverse conditions of competition within the Union, and harmonisation is often driven by a desire for uniformity that transcends nuanced policy thinking and comes from a much deeper constitutional and cultural place.[81]

FURTHER READING

F. Amtenbrink, G. Davies, D. Kochenov and J. Lindeboom (eds.), *The Internal Market and the Future of European Integration* (Cambridge University Press, 2019).

C. Barnard and S. Deakin, 'Market Access and Regulatory Competition' in C. Barnard and J. Scott (eds.), *The Law of the European Single Market* (Oxford-Portland, Hart, 2005).

D. Chalmers, 'Risk, Anxiety and the European Mediation of the Politics of Life' (2005) 30 *European Law Review* 649.

G. Davies, 'Democracy and Legitimacy in the Shadow of Purposive Competence' (2015) 21(1) *European Law Journal* 2.

S. Garben and I. Govaere, *The EU Better Regulation Agenda: A Critical Assessment* (Oxford, Hart, 2018).

D. Gerber, *Law and Competition in Twentieth Century Europe: Protecting Prometheus* (Oxford University Press, 1998).

A. O. Hirschmann, *Exit, Voice and Loyalty: Responses to Decline in Firms, Organizations and States* (Cambridge, MA, Harvard University Press, 1970).

P. Koutrakos and J. Snell, *Research Handbook on the Law of the EU's Internal Market* (Cheltenham, Edward Elgar, 2017).

N. Nic Shuibhne, *The Coherence of EU Free Movement Law* (Oxford University Press, 2013).

K. Nicolaides and G. Schaffer, 'Transnational Mutual Recognition Regimes: Governance Without Global Government' (2005) 68 *Michigan Review of International Law* 267.

F. Scharpf, 'Democratic Legitimacy under Conditions of Regulatory Competition: Why Europe Differs from the United States' in K. Nicolaidis and R. Howse (eds.), *The Federal Vision* (Oxford University Press, 2001).

A. Somek, *Individualism: An Essay on the Authority of EU Law* (Oxford University Press, 2008).

S. Weatherill, 'Why Harmonise?' in T. Tridimas and P. Nebbia (eds.), *European Union Law for the Twenty-First Century* (Oxford-Portland, Hart, 2004).

S. Weatherill, 'The Limits of Legislative Harmonization Ten Years after Tobacco Advertising: How the Court's Case Law Has Become a "Drafting Guide"' (2011) 12 *German Law Journal* 827.

F. de Witte, 'Sex, Drugs and EU Law: The Regulation of Moral and Ethical Diversity in EU Law' (2013) 6 *Common Market Law Review* 1545.

---

[81] See J. Weiler, 'The State "Uber Alles": Demos, Telos and the German Maastricht Decision', Jean Monnet Working Paper No. 6/95 (1995).

15

Economic and Monetary Union

CONTENTS

1 INTRODUCTION

This chapter considers economic and monetary union. It is organised in the following manner.

Section 2 considers the central template for economic and monetary union set out in the Treaties. It is to secure stable prices, sound public finances and monetary conditions, and a sustainable balance of payments. To that end, it is built around four pillars. There is to be, first, free movement of capital. Secondly, an independent European Central Bank (ECB) is to have the exclusive right to authorise the issue of a single currency, the euro. Thirdly, States commit not to incur excessive government deficits. Fourthly, there is to be coordination of economic policy.

Section 3 looks at the differentiated rights and obligations of Member States within Economic and Monetary Union. As of 1 December 2018, nineteen Member States have the euro as their currency. Other Member States are formally committed to joining the euro but have to meet certain economic and fiscal criteria, Convergence Criteria, to do so. The only exception is Denmark, which has an option rather than a formal commitment to join. Non-euro area States do not participate in ECB decision-making nor in the Euro Group, a body comprising Euro area finance ministers that considers coordination of economic policies within the euro area. Conversely, ECB measures do not bind these States, and sanctions cannot be applied against them for weak economic or fiscal performance.

Section 4 outlines the institutional effects of the sovereign debt crisis. The crisis overwhelmed the public finances of a number of Member States, imposed significant damage on the banking sector, and generated extensive economic and social costs many of which still endure, particular in the south of the Union, in 2018. It generated four institutional responses. First, significant financial support was provided to euro area States experiencing public financing differences on condition that they comply with swingeing programmes of economic and fiscal reform. These programmes have now finished. Secondly, more extensive and intensive Union oversight of national economic and fiscal performance was established. Thirdly, the Union became tightly involved with the formulation of domestic budgets. Finally, the powers of the ECB were extended.

Section 5 considers Union oversight of domestic economic and fiscal performance. The Union is concerned that Member States do not run excessive deficits, run balanced budgets over the medium term, with each State agreeing a Medium-Term Budgetary Objective (MTBO), and that they correct macroeconomic imbalances. The central arena for oversight is the European Semester for Economic Policy Coordination. The Commission assesses domestic economic, fiscal and employment performance. Member States set out their future fiscal and reform programmes, and the Union adopts country-specific recommendations (CSRs) for each Member State. These CSRs are to feed into the draft budgets of euro area States, which must be presented for assessment by the Commission before adoption domestically. This disciplining of domestic fiscal and economic performance is reinforced by the possibility of sanctions for euro area States if they run excessive deficits or fail to correct either excessive macroeconomic imbalances or a significant observed deviation from their path towards meeting their MTBO. A prohibition on the ECB and other Member States offering finance to a Member State is intended to reinforce these disciplines still further. However, this prohibition has been relaxed since the crisis with such support permitted if it induces the Member State to pursue sound budget policy objectives.

Section 6 looks at the ECB and the European System of Central Banks (ESCB). The Governing Council of the ECB adopts laws, guidelines and interest rates. Its Executive Board manages day-to-day relations with national central banks (NCBs). The Governing Council comprises the Executive Board plus the Governors of the NCBs who participate in the euro. The Executive Board comprises the President and Vice-President of the ECB and four other members. The Supervisory Board prepares draft Decisions for the Governing Council in the field of prudential supervision, which are adopted unless the latter votes against them. The ESCB is a network comprising the ECB and NCBs with responsibility for implementing monetary policy. The ECB has two main tasks. It is responsible, first, for monetary policy. This has always involved authorisation of the issue of euros. Since the crisis, it has included being a lender of last resort to euro area States whose public finances are in crisis, and stimulating euro area economies through the purchase of securities when these face a deflationary threat. Secondly, it is responsible for prudential supervision of all credit institutions within the euro area, assessing the financial soundness of these and the levels of risk taken on these. The ECB only directly supervises those credit institutions considered significant. This always includes, however, the three largest credit institutions in each euro area State.

2 THE CENTRAL PILLARS OF ECONOMIC AND MONETARY UNION

Heads of Government first considered a single currency at The Hague in 1969. They established a working group, which produced a fully fledged blueprint for the establishment of economic and monetary union by 1980 (the 'Werner Report').[1] This came to nothing. Instead, efforts turned to managing exchange rates. An initial attempt to manage exchange rates in 1972, the so-called 'Snake', failed.[2] In 1979, the European Monetary System (EMS) and its exchange rate mechanism (ERM) was established.[3] Participating currencies fluctuated within a band (generally, of +/- 2.5 per cent around a central rate) with national central banks intervening to secure this. The seminal moment for the establishment of economic and monetary union was the Hanover European Council in June 1988.[4] Flushed with the success of the Single European Act, the European Council set up a committee of national central bank governors chaired by the President of the Commission, Jacques Delors, to set out a roadmap. The report, adopted at the Madrid European Council in 1990, set out the blueprint for the economic and monetary union we have today.

Committee for the Study of Economic and Monetary Union, 'Report on Economic and Monetary Union in the European Community' (Luxembourg, Official Office of Publications for the European Communities, 1989)

22 A *monetary union* constitutes a currency area in which policies are managed jointly with a view to attaining common macroeconomic objectives. As already stated in the 1970 Werner Report, there are three necessary conditions for a monetary union:
- the assurance of total and irreversible convertibility of currencies;
- the complete liberalization of capital transactions and full integration of banking and other financial markets; and
- the elimination of margins of fluctuation and the irrevocable locking of exchange rate parities . . .
23 . . . The adoption of *a single currency*, while not strictly necessary for the creation of a monetary union, might be seen – for economic as well as psychological and political reasons – as a natural and desirable further development of the monetary union. A single currency would clearly demonstrate the irreversibility

---

[1] Supplement to *Bull. EC* 11–1970. On the history of economic and monetary union see the magisterial H. James, *Making the European Monetary Union* (Cambridge, MA, Harvard University Press, 2012).

[2] The Basel Agreement created a multilateral intervention mechanism in the foreign exchange market and the European Monetary Co-operation Fund the following year; Regulation 907/73 establishing a European Monetary Cooperation Fund, OJ 1973, L 89/2.

[3] *Bull. EC* 6–1978, 1.5.2. See also J. van Ypersele and J.-C. Koeune, *The European Monetary System: Origins, Operation and Outlook* (Brussels, European Communities, 1984).

[4] On the conditions which allowed this see K. McNamara, *The Currency of Ideas: Monetary Politics in the European Union* (Ithaca, Cornell University Press, 1999).

of the move to monetary union, considerably facilitate the monetary management of the Community and avoid the transactions costs of converting currencies. A single currency, provided that its stability is ensured, would also have a much greater weight relative to other major currencies than any individual Community currency . . .

25 *Economic union* – in conjunction with a monetary union – combines the characteristics of an unrestricted common market with a set of rules which are indispensable to its proper working. In this sense economic union can be described in terms of four basic elements: the single market within which persons, goods, services and capital can move freely; competition policy and other measures aimed at strengthening market mechanisms; common policies aimed at structural change and regional development; and macroeconomic policy coordination, including binding rules for budgetary policies . . .

. . . A coherent set of economic policies at the Community and national levels would be necessary to maintain permanently fixed exchange rates between Community currencies and, conversely, a common monetary policy, in support of a single currency area, would be necessary for the Community to develop into an economic union . . .

30 *Macroeconomic policy* is the third area in which action would be necessary for a viable economic and monetary union. This would require an appropriate definition of the role of the Community in promoting price stability and economic growth through the coordination of economic policies. Many developments in macroeconomic conditions would continue to be determined by factors and decisions operating at the national or local level. This would include not only wage negotiations and other economic decisions in the fields of production, savings and investment, but also the action of public authorities in the economic and social spheres. Apart from the system of binding rules governing the size and the financing of national budget deficits, decisions on the main components of public policy in such areas as internal and external security, justice, social security, education, and hence on the level and composition of government spending, as well as many revenue measures, would remain the preserve of Member States even at the final stage of economic and monetary union.

However, an economic and monetary union could only operate on the basis of mutually consistent and sound behaviour by governments and other economic agents in all member countries. In particular, uncoordinated and divergent national budgetary policies would undermine monetary stability and generate imbalances in the real and financial sectors of the Community . . .

32 A new monetary institution would be needed because a single monetary policy cannot result from independent decisions and actions by different central banks. Moreover, day-to-day monetary policy operations cannot respond quickly to changing market conditions unless they are decided centrally. Considering the political structure of the Community and the advantages of making existing central banks part of a new system, the domestic and international monetary policy-making of the Community should be organized in a federal form, in what might be called a *European System of Central Banks* (ESCB). This new System would have to be given the full status of an autonomous Community institution . . .

The institutional architecture of economic and monetary union largely replicates these elements.

Free movement of capital: A currency union requires that people have freedom to invest within it. An investor in one part of the Union can invest in another part of the Union. Free movement of payments is necessary for this. It has to be possible for people to make payments for assets in different parts of the Union, and to transfer these payments across the Union. To this end, Article 63 TFEU prohibits, subject to certain limited exceptions, restrictions on the free movement of capital and payments.

> **Article 63 TFEU**
>
> (1) Within the framework of the provisions set out in this Chapter, all restrictions on the movement of capital between Member States and between Member States and third countries shall be prohibited.
> (2) Within the framework of the provisions set out in this Chapter, all restrictions on payments between Member States and between Member States and third countries shall be prohibited.

The provision is interpreted in similar fashion to other economic freedoms. It catches national measures liable to prevent or deter investment from one Member State to another: be these measures deterring non-residents from investing in a Member State or measures deterring the residents of a particular Member State from investing in another State.[5] National measures will be lawful only if they pursue a legitimate public interest in a manner that is both proportionate and does not arbitrarily discriminate between residents and non-residents.[6]

A single currency whose issue is authorised only by the European Central Bank: The model of monetary union adopted by the Union requires a single currency issued by a central bank, the ECB. Based in Frankfurt, this bank has a monopoly over authorising the issue of euros.[7] This monopoly also grants the ECB the power to set the terms on which it offers euros to financial institutions. Consequently, it also enjoys a monopoly over the setting of short-term interest rates as these constitute the terms at which it will offer these euros.

Controls on national budget deficits: Excessive borrowing by one government within a currency union creates costs for other governments.[8] At its mildest, it can generate inflationary pressures, with the consequence that the central bank has to raise interest rates to curb this, thereby penalising everybody. More dramatically, excessive borrowing can lead to one State going bankrupt. As it cannot print money to service its needs, the only possibilities are for it either to leave the monetary union to enable this, which will be difficult and costly, or for other States to bail it out (also expensive).[9] The TFEU therefore prohibits excessive government deficits.

> **Article 126 TFEU**
>
> (1) Member States shall avoid excessive government deficits.

---

[5] *SEGRO*, C-52/16 and C-113/16, EU:C:2018:157; *Jahin* v. *Ministre de l'Économie et des Finances*, C-45/17, EU:C:2018:18.

[6] E.g. *Sofina and Others* v. *Ministre de l'Action et des Comptes publics*, C-575/17, EU:C:2018:943. Article 65 TFEU also sets out a number of explicit justifications for restricting capital movements. These include public policy and security grounds, prudential supervision of financial institutions and protection of tax laws distinguishing between residents and non-residents. Most of the case law has focussed on the last heading.

[7] Article 128 TFEU.

[8] A government or budget deficit is the amount by which government expenditure exceeds government income in a given year.

[9] For an accessible explanation see W. Buiter, 'The "Sense and Nonsense of Maastricht" Revisited: What Have We Learnt about Stabilization in EMU?' (2006) 44 *JCMS* 687, 693–705.

A deficit is, in principle, excessive if it involves (a) an annual government deficit (the difference between expenditure incurred and revenue generated) of more than 3 per cent of GDP or (b) a government debt of more than 60 per cent of GDP.[10] A simple injunction was not seen as sufficient to prevent these. The Treaties established institutional arrangements, known as the Stability and Growth Pact, therefore, to discipline and sanction national budget policy.[11] There is a preventive arm to discipline budgetary policy. Each State is provided a MTBO, a target for its public finances, typically over three years. States formulate programmes to meet their MTBOs, and the Commission and the Council assess these annually.[12] There is a corrective arm: the Excessive Deficit Procedure. If the Commission and the Council find that a State's deficit is excessive, this procedure allows proceedings which can result in the Council imposing heavy financial sanctions on that State.[13]

Coordination and surveillance of national economic policy: Other national economic policies can disrupt monetary union. If a State fails to make its industry competitive or allows too much of industry to be concentrated in sectors vulnerable to shocks, this might lead to that economy having very different needs from other parts of the currency union. Equally, if national economic policies are too different, it may be difficult for the ECB to institute a policy which works for all parts of the currency union. Coordination of economic policy is, therefore, to take place within the Council.[14]

Article 121 TFEU

(1) Member States shall regard their economic policies as a matter of common concern and shall coordinate them within the Council, in accordance with the provisions of Article 120.

(2) The Council shall, on a recommendation from the Commission, formulate a draft for the broad guidelines of the economic policies of the member States and of the Union, and shall report its findings to the European Council.

The European Council shall, acting on the basis of the report from the Council, discuss a conclusion on the broad guidelines of the economic policies of the Member States and of the Union.

On the basis of this conclusion, the Council shall adopt a recommendation setting out these broad guidelines. The Council shall inform the European Parliament of its recommendation.

The central Union instruments in this field are those set out in Article 121(2) TFEU, the Broad Economic Policy Guidelines (BEPGs). These are developed both for each of the Member States individually and for the Union as a whole.

A vision of what economic and monetary policy should be doing underpins all this. It is set out in Article 128(3) TFEU.[15]

---

[10] Article 126(2) TFEU, Protocol on the Excessive Deficit Procedure, Article 1.

[11] Resolution of the European Council on the Stability and Growth Pact, OJ 1997, C 236/1. For discussion see M. Heipertz and A. Verdun, *Ruling Europe: The Politics of the Stability and Growth Pact* (Cambridge University Press, 2010).

[12] Regulation 1466/97/EC on the strengthening of the surveillance of budgetary positions and the surveillance and coordination of economic policies, OJ 1997, L 209/1 as amended by Regulation 1055/2005/EC, OJ 2005, L 174/1 and Regulation 1175/2011/EU, OJ 2011, L 306/12.

[13] Regulation 1467/97/EC on speeding up and clarifying the implementation of the Excessive Deficit Procedure, OJ 1997, L 209/6 as amended by Regulation 1056/2005/EC, OJ 2005, L 174/5 and Regulation 1177/2011/EU, OJ 2011, L 306/33.

[14] On the weakness of this coordination see D. Hodson, *Governing the Euro Area in Good Times and Bad* (Oxford University Press, 2011) ch. 5.

[15] See also Articles 119(2) TFEU and 219 TFEU which make it a norm of exchange rate and monetary policy, and Article 127 TFEU which makes it the central objective of the ESCB.

> ### Article 128(3) TFEU
>
> These activities of the Member States and the Union shall entail compliance with the following guiding principles: stable prices, sound public finances and monetary conditions and a sustainable balance of payments.

The commitments in Article 128(3) TFEU were made to secure credibility for the euro, and, to that end, the Treaties borrowed heavily from the successful post-War German monetary model. However, a feature of this German model was the commitment to low inflation was not a constitutional requirement.[16] However, entrenching economic objectives – be it low inflation, sound public finances or sustainable balance of payment – as quasi-constitutional commitments has highly authoritarian qualities.[17] It suppresses political debate and generates inflexibilities if circumstances arise which lead to other imperatives becoming more pressing.

3 THE DIFFERENTIATED OBLIGATIONS OF ECONOMIC AND MONETARY UNION

On 1 January 1999, eleven Member States adopted the euro as their currency. They have since been joined by a further eight Member States, so that nineteen Member States currently form the euro area. To adopt the euro, each Member State must meet a series of economic conditions known as the convergence criteria. These are currently:

- They are not subject to a Council decision that they have an excessive deficit.
- They have an annual rate of inflation not more than 1½ percentage points above the three best performing Member States.
- They have participated within the exchange-rate mechanism for at least two years, without devaluing against the euro.
- They have long-term nominal interest rates that are not more than 2 percentage points above the three best performing States in terms of price stability.[18]

States adjudged not to meet these criteria are described as 'States with a derogation'.[19] They are currently Bulgaria, Croatia, the Czech Republic, Hungary, Poland, Romania and Sweden. At least every two years or at their own request, they are assessed as to whether they meet the criteria and should be invited to join the euro.[20] In principle, the question is simply one of whether these States meet the above criteria, and they are, therefore, obliged to join the euro when they do. In practice, there is little that the Union can do to force a State to join the euro and, furthermore, it would be politically disastrous to have an unwilling participant as a member of the euro. Consequently, the decision whether to join the euro is also a matter of political choice for these Member States.

---

[16] This point is powerfully made in M. Herdegen, 'Price Stability and Budgetary Restraints in the Economic and Monetary Union: The Law as Guardian of Economic Wisdom' (1998) 35 *CMLRev* 9, 11–15.

[17] M. Wilkinson, 'Authoritarian Liberalism in the European Constitutional Imagination: Second Time as Farce?' (2015) 21 *ELJ* 313.

[18] Article 140(1) TFEU; Protocol on the Convergence Criteria.   [19] Article 139(1) TFEU.   [20] Article 140 TFEU.

This is not the case for Denmark. At Maastricht, it notified the other States that it would not participate in the euro, and there is no formal legal obligation to do so, although it can still request that.[21] Otherwise, its obligations are identical to those of States with a derogation.[22] The key obligations not applying to States with a derogation are:

- The Broad Economic Policy Guidelines apply to them unless these relate specifically to the euro area.[23]
- They cannot be sanctioned under the Excessive Deficit Procedure.[24]
- They are not bound by measures concerning use of the euro nor acts of the ECB.[25]

These States also do not participate in the governing arrangements of the European Central Bank or the appointment of its members,[26] and the ESCB, the institutional arrangement involving the ECB and national central banks that administers the euro.[27] Finally, they are excluded from the Euro Group. Comprising the finance ministers of the euro area States, with the ECB and the Commission invited to participate, this Group discusses questions regarding shared responsibilities concerning the euro.[28] It is extremely powerful. It meets before Council meetings, and this leads to concerns that it pre-empts decisions subsequently taken in the Council.[29]

4 THE INSTITUTIONAL SHOCK OF THE EUROPEAN SOVEREIGN DEBT CRISIS

The European Union's sovereign debt crisis was triggered by the dislocation in global financial markets which followed the collapse of Lehmann Brothers in Autumn 2008.[30] This dislocation simultaneously made it much more difficult for governments to borrow; switched off sectors of economic activity for many member States, notably finance and property, thereby depriving governments of tax receipts; forced many governments to buy out bankrupt banks; and, finally, pushed down on economic growth by making it very difficult for commercial actors to borrow. Average total debt and annual budget deficits (as proportions of GDP) within the Union increased, therefore, from 62.3 per cent and 2.4 per cent in 2008, to 80 per cent and 6.4 per cent in 2010. The first States to encounter serious problems were a number of European States outside the euro area. Hungary, Latvia Romania and Iceland all experienced catastrophic collapses in their public finances in 2008 and had to seek help from the Union and/or international organisations.

The crisis threatened the Union when, in October 2009, the Greek authorities announced that the Greek budget deficit had been massively underestimated. It was not 3.7 per cent of GDP but 12.5 per cent of GDP. This prompted concerns in financial markets through late 2009 and early 2010 that Greece would not be able to sustain its public finances. Despite the adoption of an austerity plan by Greece in early 2010 seen as sufficient by the European Council, concerns continued to mount with borrowing becoming increasingly expensive for Greece. Unable to meet

---

[21] Protocol No. 16 on Certain Provisions Relating to Denmark, para. 2. [22] *Ibid.* para. 1.
[23] Article 139(2)(a) TFEU. [24] Article 139(2)(b) TFEU. [25] Article 139(2)(d), (e) and (f) TFEU.
[26] Article 139(2)(h) TFEU. [27] Article 139(3) TFEU. [28] Article 137 TFEU; Protocol on the Euro Group.
[29] U. Puetter, *The Eurogroup: How a Secretive Group of Finance Ministers Shapes European Economic Governance* (Manchester University Press, 2006).
[30] On the stages of the crisis see F. Scharpf, 'Monetary Union, Fiscal Crisis and the Disabling of Democratic Accountability' in A. Schäfer and W. Streeck (eds.), *Politics in the Age of Austerity* (Cambridge, Polity Press, 2013); M. Drudi *et al.*, 'The Interplay of Economic Reforms and Monetary Policy: The Case of the Eurozone' (2012) 50 *JCMS* 881.

the demands of lenders, Greece was granted a loan of €110 billion by Eurozone States and the International Monetary Fund (IMF) in May 2010.

This heralded the beginning of financial market anxiety about whether many euro area States could service their public finances. A pattern repeated itself whereby lending costs to certain euro area States would escalate to the point where they would be unaffordable. These States would be offered financial support through a variety of mechanisms by the other euro area States and the IMF dependent on their meeting conditions aimed at rebalancing their public finances. These conditions typically involved tax increases, dramatic reductions in public spending often leading to considerable social hardship, and administrative and labour law reforms. Therefore, Ireland received a support package of €85 billion in November 2010; Portugal, €78 billion in May 2011; Greece a second support package of €130 billion in March 2012; Spain up to €100 billion in July to recapitalise its banks; Cyprus up to €10 billion in April 2013; and Greece a further support package of up to €86 billion in August 2015. In the initial years, these measures were insufficient to shore up national public finances. From May 2010 to August 2012, the ECB supported governments experiencing public financing difficulties through purchasing €220 billion of their bonds.[31]

The economic and social costs were severe for the States seeking financial support. In 2010, poverty increased in Greece from 20 per cent of all Greeks to 25.8 per cent: an increase of over a quarter.[32] Alongside this, welfare provision was reduced just as need increased. HIV infection arose in Greece by 52 per cent in 2011 with much of this rise due to increases in prostitution, and the lack of rehabilitation programmes for drug users (85 per cent were recorded as not on any programme).[33]

The easing of crisis in public finances from 2013 onwards left economic stagnation. The Greek economy reduced in size by nearly a quarter between 2008 and 2013. If this was particularly acute, both the Italian and Portuguese economies reduced in size by 8 per cent during those years. In the next four years, they only grew respectively by about 1.5, 3.7 and 7.4 per cent.[34] All their economies were, thus, smaller in 2017 than in 2008. This led to enduring social deprivation. Youth unemployment, for example, went from 18.1, 20.4 and 22.7 per cent in 2007 in Spain, Italy and Greece respectively to 36.4, 34.7 and 43.6 per cent in 2017.[35] It also generated problems in the commercial banking sector as banks had both fewer lending opportunities and were saddled with many bad debts: estimated in 2016 at 16.4 per cent of all loans in Italy and 47 per cent in Greece and Cyprus.[36] This has raised questions about the viability of a number of banks, and made them less able to lend, further slowing down the economies.

---

[31] Decision 2010/5/ECB establishing a securities markets programme, OJ 2010, L 124/8. On this programme see F. Eser and B. Schwab, 'Assessing Asset Purchases within the ECB's Securities Markets Programme', ECB, Working Paper 1587 (2013). This programme was discontinued in September 2012.

[32] M. Matsaganis and C. Leventi, 'The Distributional Impact of the Greek Crisis in 2010' (2013) 34 *Fiscal Studies* 83.

[33] A. Kentikelenis *et al.*, 'Health Effects of Financial Crisis: Omens of a Greek Tragedy' (2011) 378 *The Lancet* 1457. See also G. Quaglio *et al.*, 'Austerity and Health in Europe' (2013) 113 *Health Policy* 13. These effects were not confined to Greece. Health-care spending declined by 6.5% in Ireland and 7.3% in Estonia in 2010, OECD, *Health at a Glance: Europe 2012* (Paris, OECD, 2012) 120. On the legal consequences of these programmes within these States see T. Beukers, C. Kilpatrick and B. de Witte (eds.), *Constitutional Change through Euro-Crisis Law: Taking Stock, New Perspectives and Looking Ahead* (Cambridge University Press, 2017).

[34] https://ec.europa.eu/eurostat/tgm/table.do?tab=table&init=1&language=en&pcode=tec00115&plugin=1.

[35] https://ec.europa.eu/eurostat/statistics-explained/index.php/Unemployment_statistics#Youth_unemployment.

[36] T. Humblot, *The Value of Italian Non-Performing Loans* (Paris, BNP Paribas, 2017), http://economic-research.bnpparibas.com/Views/DisplayPublication.aspx?type=document&IdPdf=29943.

These developments led to a common perception amongst policy-makers that the institutional architecture established at Maastricht was inadequate. Reforms constellated around four trajectories: significant financial support for States experiencing public financing difficulties by other euro area States; more extensive and intensive Union oversight of national economic and fiscal performance; increasing Union involvement with the formulation of domestic budgets; and increased powers for the ECB.

Of these, the first, the provision of financial support by other euro area States, is now only of historical significance. The central vehicle was the European Stability Mechanism (ESM), a private company established by two international treaties between the euro area States in 2011 and 2012.[37] It was run by a Board of Governors, comprising euro area finance ministers, who could offer financial guarantees from a shared commitment of €500 billion to States experiencing difficulties.[38] Support could only be offered to States requesting it and was conditional on that State agreeing a series of conditions set out in a Memorandum of Understanding between that State and the ESM. Implementation of these conditions was overseen by a troika of the Commission, ECB and IMF with financial support tapered so that it became available as that State was adjudged to have made satisfactory progress in meeting these conditions.[39] Cyprus, Greece, Ireland, Portugal and Spain all received support from the ESM, with Greece the last State to exit its programme in August 2018.

It is, now, time to examine the other three developments: Union oversight of national economic and fiscal performance, its involvement with the formulation of domestic budgets, and the powers of the ECB – in more detail, looking at how these built on earlier law.

5 UNION OVERSIGHT OF NATIONAL FISCAL AND ECONOMIC PERFORMANCE

All Union governments believed that the narrowness and weakness of the Stability and Growth Pact had contributed to the crisis. Its focus was too narrow as it centred on the annual budget deficits of Member States. Insufficient attention was paid to their total debt, the sustainability of their public finance over the medium-term and whether their economic performance was exposing them to unnecessary or significant risks. Further, it was too weak because Union sanctions had never been used against non-compliant States[40] and no attention had been paid to the quality of domestic rules and processes to check against poor policy-making.[41]

Three sets of measures were put in place to rectify this.

---

[37] The consolidated versions of the treaties can be found at www.esm.europa.eu/sites/default/files/20150203_-_esm_treaty_-_en.pdf.

[38] For a critical account of the decision-making processes see M. Dawson and F. de Witte, 'Constitutional Balance in the EU after the Euro-Crisis' (2013) 76 *MLR* 817; M. Schwarz, 'A Memorandum of Misunderstanding – The Doomed Road of the European Stability Mechanism and a Possible Way Out: Enhanced Cooperation' (2014) 51 *CMLRev* 389.

[39] On these programmes see C. Henning, *Tangled Governance: International Regime Complexity, the Troika, and the Euro Crisis* (Oxford University Press, 2017).

[40] Subsequent research suggests that this is because governments were able to lean on the Commission, something unaddressed by the reforms, N. Baerg and M. Hallerberg, 'Explaining Instability in the Stability and Growth Pact: The Contribution of Member State Power and Euroskepticism to the Euro Crisis' (2016) 49 *Comparative Political Studies* 968. Failure to comply was, moreover, more usually driven by economic need rather than wilfulness or ideology, M. Hansen, 'Explaining Deviations from the Stability and Growth Pact: Power, Ideology, Economic Need or Diffusion' (2015) 35 *Journal of Public Policy* 477.

[41] All these criticisms are contained in the Report of the Task Force to the European Council, *Strengthening Economic Governance in the EU* (Brussels, European Council, 2010). This was co-authored by all national finance ministers as well as the Commission and the President of the Euro Group, ECB and European Council. In like vein, by two senior Commission officials, see M. Buti and N. Carnot, 'The EMU Debt Crisis: Early Lessons and Reforms' (2012) 50 *JCMS* 899.

The first was the *six-pack*, five Regulations and a Directive.[42] This strengthened Union surveillance and disciplines across all these fields of activity. It also widened the types of national behaviour that were subject to sanction, and made it easier for the Union to sanction such behaviour. Finally, Member States had to put extensive systems in place that allow reliable budgetary forecasting and planning and ensure their statistics and public accounts are in order.[43]

A concern remained that it would prove practically difficult for the Union to apply sanctions against States. The second measure, the *fiscal compact*, addressed this. The Treaty on Stability, Coordination and Governance in the Economic and Monetary Union (TSCG), informally known as the fiscal compact, was adopted as an international treaty because the Czech and United Kingdom Governments were unwilling to amend the EU Treaties. It required States to adopt rules ensuring that their budget is balanced or in surplus.[44] These rules are to be granted an elevated domestic legal status.

Article 3 TSCG

(2) The rules set out in paragraph 1 shall take effect in the national law of the Contracting Parties at the latest one year after the entry into force of this Treaty through provisions of binding force and permanent character, preferably constitutional, or otherwise guaranteed to be fully respected and adhered to throughout the national budgetary processes.[[45]]

The final concern was that too many of these measures focused on correcting or sanctioning domestic behaviour. *Ex ante* Union intervention had to be strengthened so that this was not necessary. The *two-pack* comprises two Regulations which provide for greater Union input in national budgets: one for States receiving financial support or experiencing severe financial difficulties[46] and the other for all other euro area States.[47]

These measures criss-cross but it is now time to examine in more detail the regime that they combine to put in place.

---

[42] Regulation 1173/2011 on the effective enforcement of budgetary surveillance in the euro area, OJ 2011, L 306/1; Regulation 1174/2011 on enforcement measures to correct excessive macroeconomic imbalances in the euro area, OJ 2011, L 306/8; Regulation 1175/2011 amending Regulation 1466/97 on the strengthening of the surveillance of budgetary positions and the surveillance and coordination of economic policies, OJ 2011, L 306/12; Regulation 1176/2011 on the prevention and correction of macroeconomic imbalances, OJ 2011, L 306/25; Regulation 1177/2011 amending Regulation 1467/97 on speeding up and clarifying the implementation of the Excessive Deficit Procedure, OJ 2011, L 306/33; Directive 2011/85/EU on requirements for budgetary frameworks of the Member States, OJ 2011, L 306/41.

[43] For an overview see D. Chalmers, 'The European Redistributive State and a European Law of Struggle' (2012) 18 *ELJ* 667; B. Laffan and P. Schlosser, 'Public Finances in Europe: Fortifying EU Economic Governance in the Shadow of the Crisis' (2016) 38 *Journal of European Integration* 237.

[44] All Member States, except the Czech Republic, are party to it. The Treaty can be found at OJ 2012, C 219/95. See P. Craig, 'The Stability, Coordination and Governance Treaty: Principle, Politics and Pragmatism' (2012) 37 *ELRev* 231.

[45] All States implemented this requirement through a formally binding law. Only eleven States gave it formal constitutional status (Austria, Belgium, Germany, Estonia, Spain, Finland, Italy, Lithuania, Latvia, Portugal and Slovakia). European Commission, *Report presented under Article 8 of the Treaty on Stability, Coordination and Governance in the Economic and Monetary Union,* C(2017)1201 final, 3–4.

[46] Regulation 472/2013/EU on the strengthening of economic and budgetary surveillance of Member States in the euro area experiencing or threatened with serious difficulties with respect to their financial stability, OJ 2013, L 140/1.

[47] Regulation 473/2013/EU on common provisions for monitoring and assessing draft budgetary plans and ensuring the correction of excessive deficit of the Member States in the euro area, OJ 2013, L 140/11.

(i) The Ambit of Union Surveillance: Excessive Deficits, Balanced Budgets and Macroeconomic Imbalances

The post-crisis reforms widened the horizons of Union policing considerably. The Union now required domestic policy-makers to realise three things: prevent excessive deficits; secure balanced budgets; and moderate macroeconomic imbalances. These three headings, in turn, paved the way for three types of sanction procedure to protect each of these ambitions. States can be sanctioned for incurring an excessive deficit; significantly diverging from their agreed Medium-Term Budgetary Objective (of a balanced budget); and failing to correct excessive macroeconomic imbalances.

Avoidance of excessive deficits: As mentioned earlier, Article 126 TFEU requires Member States to avoid excessive government deficits.[48] There is some flexibility about when a deficit will be regarded as requiring intervention.

Annual budget deficits can be higher than 3 per cent if this is because of a severe economic downturn[49] or they are close to it, and they are coming down in a substantial and continuous manner or are exceptional and temporary.[50] However, prior to the crisis, levels of total debt were barely policed. There was only a loose requirement that it was sufficiently diminishing and approaching the requirement of 60 per cent of GDP at a satisfactory pace.[51] This changed after the crisis. States are considered to be running an excessive deficit if, measured over a three-year period, they do not bring down their excess debt by one-twentieth of the difference between it and the 60 per cent value.[52] A State with a debt of 100 per cent of GDP would, for example, have to find 2 per cent of GDP per year to pay down its debt, in addition to its all other needs.

Securing a balanced budget: Member States are required to have balanced budgets.

Article 3 TSCG

(1) The Contracting Parties shall apply the rules set out in this paragraph in addition and without prejudice to their obligations under European Union law:

(a) the budgetary position of the general government of a Contracting Party shall be balanced or in surplus;

(b) the rule under point (a) shall be deemed to be respected if the annual structural balance of the general government is at its country-specific medium-term objective, as defined in the revised Stability and Growth Pact, with a lower limit of a structural deficit of 0.5% of the gross domestic product at market prices. The Contracting Parties shall ensure rapid convergence towards their respective medium-term objective.[53]

To a non-economist, this provision is a little obscure. An annual structural balance is the budgetary position of the State once it has been cyclically adjusted.[54] In recessions, welfare spending will increase and tax receipts fall, whilst the opposite is true in moments of economic boom. This balance is thus adjusted for where the State is on the economic cycle but the intention is that across the cycle there should not be a deficit lower than 0.5 per cent of GDP.

The requirement of a balanced budget imposes duties of medium-term planning on Member States. EU law requires each to have an MTBO of a 'budgetary position of close to balance or in surplus'.[55] To

---

[48] Regulation 1467/97/EC, Articles 3–16.   [49] Regulation 1467/97/EC, Article 2(2).   [50] Article 126(2)(a) TFEU.
[51] Article 126(2)(b) TFEU.   [52] Regulation 1467/97/EC, Article 2(1a). This is reiterated in Article 4, TSCG.
[53] The Czech Republic is not party to the TSCG.   [54] Article 3(3)(a) TSCG.
[55] Regulation 1466/97/EC, Article 3(1)(a).

that end, they must elaborate five-year programmes, annually updated, covering the previous and current years as well as the three subsequent years, which detail how they will secure this and the assumptions underpinning their calculations.[56] Member States are required to keep to these programmes. In particular, there must be no 'significant observed deviation' from the MTBO.[57] Such a deviation can lead to the application of the sanctions procedure against the State concerned.[58]

Moderating macroeconomic imbalances and correcting excessive macroeconomic imbalances: A number of States ran into difficulties during the sovereign debt crisis not because their public finances were weak but because of wider vulnerabilities in their economies.[59] A regime was therefore established to regulate macroeconomic imbalances. These are:

> any trend giving rise to macroeconomic developments which are adversely affecting, or have the potential adversely to affect, the proper functioning of the economy of a Member State or of the economic and monetary union, or of the Union as a whole.[60]

Examples can be:

> internal imbalances, including those that can arise from public and private indebtedness; financial and asset market developments, including housing; the evolution of private sector credit flow; and the evolution of unemployment;
>   ... external imbalances, including those that can arise from the evolution of current account and net investment positions of Member States; real effective exchange rates; export market shares; changes in price and cost developments; and non-price competitiveness, taking into account the different components of productivity.[61]

There is no duty on Member States to avoid macroeconomic imbalances or have a balanced economy. This would be impossible to police as it would involve Union intervention whenever a national economy was not in perfect equilibrium. Instead, the Commission is to watch out for imbalances. Taking due account of discussions within the Council and the Euro Group on multilateral surveillance of domestic economies or in the event of unexpected significant economic developments, it must undertake an in-depth review of any Member State that it considers may be affected by, or may be at risk of being affected by, these imbalances.[62] If it identifies imbalances, it should make a Recommendation to the State.[63] There is particular concern that States should not run excessive imbalances. These are:

> severe imbalances, including imbalances that jeopardise or risks jeopardising the proper functioning of the economic and monetary union.[64]

---

[56] These are called stability programmes for euro area States and convergence programmes for non-euro area States. The obligations are contained, respectively in Regulation 1466/97/EC, Articles 3 and 4, and Regulation 1466/97EC, Articles 7 and 8.

[57] Regulation 1466/97, Article 6(2) and (3).   [58] Regulation 1173/2011/EU, Article 4.

[59] A 2008 Commission report prior to the crisis presaged this by observing significant imbalances in the economies of the euro area States and pressed the case for greater economic policy coordination, European Commission, *EMU@10: Successes and Challenges after 10 Years of Economic and Monetary Union: European Economy 2* (Luxembourg, European Commission, 2008) 8–9 and 64.

[60] Regulation 1176/2011/EU, Article 2(1). On these criteria see M. Moschella, 'Monitoring Macroeconomic Imbalances: Is EU Surveillance More Effective than IMF Surveillance' (2014) 52 *JCMS* 1273; D. Hodson, 'The Macroeconomic Imbalance Procedure as European Integration: A Legalization Perspective' (2018) 25 *JEPP* 1610.

[61] Regulation 1176/2011/EU, Article 4(3).   [62] *Ibid*. Article 5(1).   [63] *Ibid*. Article 6(1).   [64] *Ibid*. Article 2(2).

If a State does not correct these excessive imbalances, this can trigger procedures imposing sanctions on it.[65]

(ii) The European Semester and Collective Guidance over Domestic and Fiscal Economic Policy

The crisis led to a perception that Union oversight did not look sufficiently at how different elements of economic and fiscal performance affected each other. It also happened too late in the day. This prevented early planning and only allowed for correction when matters had gone awry.[66] To rectify this, the annual European Semester for Economic Policy Coordination was established in September 2010, with the legal basis provided through an amendment to Regulation 1466/97/EC.

> ### Regulation 1466/97, Article 2-a(1)
>
> In order to ensure closer coordination of economic policies and sustained convergence of the economic performance of the Member States, the Council shall conduct multilateral surveillance as an integral part of the European Semester for economic policy coordination in accordance with the objectives and requirements set out in the TFEU.

The range of activities considered at the Semester is considerable. It covers all aspects of fiscal, economic and social policy, as well as commitments on matters such as climate change policy (handled in national reform plans):

- the formulation of guidelines in the fields of economic and employment policy and assessment of national performance and implementation of prior guidelines
- the submission of plans to meet each State's MTBO and assessment of national performance
- the submission and assessment of national reform plans (The Union growth strategy, Europe 2020, involves an Annual Growth Survey setting out challenges and priorities for the Union economy. Each State adopts a national reform programme indicating the measures it will take to support the objectives set out in this Survey.)
- assessment of national macroeconomic imbalances.[67]

A terse description of the procedure is set out in Article 2-a(3) of Regulation 1466/97.

> ### Regulation 1466/97, Article 2-a(3)
>
> In the course of the European Semester, in order to provide timely and integrated policy advice on macrofiscal and macrostructural policy intentions, the Council shall, as a rule, following the assessment of these programmes on the basis of recommendations from the Commission, address guidance to the Member States . . .

---

[65] *Ibid*. Article 10(4); Regulation 1174/2011/EU, Article 3.
[66] European Commission, 'Reinforcing Economic Policy Coordination', COM(2010)250 final.
[67] Regulation 1466/97, Article 2-a(2).

This article neither captures the full process nor explains it particularly clearly.[68] The European Semester involves five stages each year, starting in November and finishing the following October.

- *The Commission framing of the process*: The Commission publishes three documents intended to structure subsequent debate. The first, the Annual Growth Survey, sets out economic priorities and guidance for the Union as a whole. It focuses on public finances, structural reforms and investment. The second, the Alert Mechanism Report, identifies States who may be subject to macroeconomic imbalances and therefore should be subject to reviews. The third, the joint Employment Report, looks at the employment and social situation within the Union.
- *Commission assessment of domestic economic, fiscal and employment performance*: The Commission publishes in-depth reports which look at whether the State is experiencing any macroeconomic imbalances, its general economic, fiscal and employment performance as well as how it complied with previous Recommendations.
- *Development of fiscal and reform programmes*: The Member States set out their programmes for realising their respective MTBOs as well as their national reform plans.
- *Country-specific recommendations (CSRs)*: The Commission publishes detailed recommendations for the economic and fiscal performance of each State. These Recommendations are intended to set out realistic timetables of action for the next twelve to eighteen months aligning domestic performance with the Union objectives set out by the Commission at the beginning of the process. They are endorsed by the Council as guidance addressed to the Member States, as set out in Article 2-a3 above.
- *Member States take account of the CSR in the formulation of their budgets and national reform plans*: The CSRs sit at the heart of the European Semester. They structure economic and fiscal policy-making by setting out what Member States should do and establishing parameters against which their performance is assessed. There has, however, been poor compliance with CSRs.[69] Furthermore, they have been criticised for a 'one-size fits all approach' to policy-making.

M. Dawson, 'The Legal and Political Accountability Structure of "Post-Crisis" EU Economic Governance' (2015) 53 *Journal of Common Market Studies* 976, 984–5

While states are subject to different procedural obligations, substantive recommendations issued to them are surprisingly similar.

This begins with the economic model through which recommendations are produced. In examining the CSRs issued since 2011, one can consistently identify a strong focus on budgetary consolidation as an anchor point for recommendations across a wide range of policy areas. While this policy focus is to be expected in recommendations relating to fiscal policy, it is also apparent in other areas. This can best be

---

[68] On the process see K. Armstrong, 'The New Governance of EU Fiscal Discipline' (2013) 38 *ELRev* 601; A. Verdun and J. Zeitlin, 'Introduction: The European Semester as a New Architecture of EU Socioeconomic Governance in Theory and Practice' (2018) 25 *JEPP* 137.

[69] Z. Darvas and Á. Leandro, 'The Limitations of Policy Coordination in the Euro Area under the European Semester', Policy Contribution 2015/19, Bruegel (2015); K. Efstathiou and G. Wolf, 'Is the European Semester Effective and Useful?', Policy Contribution 2018/9, Bruegel (2018).

exemplified by examining two fields in more depth. One is the field of pensions policy – a field clearly outwith the normal confines of EU competence. Of the 24 countries for which the Commission compiled specific recommendations from 2011 to 2013, 17 receive recommendations on pensions reform; 15 are detailed. What is remarkable concerning these recommendations is their degree of uniformity. While systems of pension delivery vary significantly between the states to which recommendations are made, similar recommendations are made in the period 2011–13 to all 15 Member States.

Recommendations aimed at all 15 recommend increasing the statutory retirement age and linking retirement age to life expectancy. At the same time, aspects of the national pension regime which could inhibit long-term fiscal sustainability are rejected. Recommendations on invalidity pension schemes (a regular way to take into account different capabilities, especially when increasing the pension age) emphasize their possible abuse, and call for their restriction (Austria, Bulgaria). Where differentiated retirement ages for men and women (Bulgaria, Slovenia, Poland) exist, their abandonment is demanded. Finally, countries which carry income indexation of pensions, designed to ensure that they rise along with general incomes (Slovakia and Slovenia), are criticized. The emphasis on fiscal consolidation – and its elevation above other objectives of the pension system (such as poverty reduction and adequacy, mentioned in only three recommendations) – is clear.

Uniformity is also apparent in other areas of policy covered by the CSRs. Recommendations on tax and social security also display a common core. 23 Member States received recommendations in this area between 2011 and 2013. Of these states, 19 were asked to change their tax system in order to boost its 'growth-friendliness' and ability to contribute to fiscal consolidation. The Commission's favoured method of doing so is to alter the burden of taxation– Member States consistently received recommendations on shifting tax from labour to consumption (e.g. of energy, property and other goods). Little mention is made of the distributional impact of this choice (consumption taxes tend of course to fall far harder on the poor than labour taxes). In the place of the OMC's emphasis on diversity and flexible implementation, recommendations under the European Semester seem to advance a highly uniform policy agenda.

Finally, the recommendations promoted through the CSRs are not only relatively uniform but also highly prescriptive. This has previously been noted by Sonja Bekker, who has observed the tendency of CSRs to become more numerous and precise over time.[70] Recommendations increasingly point to specific programmes and reforms rather than aiming at general changes, such as improving 'labour activation', 'gender equality', 'pension sustainability' and so on.

Pushback has led, since 2015, to the Commission issuing fewer, less detailed CSRs and involving national representatives more in prior discussions before adopting any CSR. It appears that this has tempered some of the problems of over-prescriptiveness.[71] However, it generated other problems, as it has been accompanied by a further deterioration in implementation.[72]

The other big debate about the European Semester is how democratic it is. At a central level, parliamentary powers are weak. The European Parliament can ask the Presidents of the Commission, Council, European Council and Euro Group to appear before its relevant Committees to

[70] S. Bekker, 'The EU's Stricter Economic Governance: A Step Towards a More Binding Coordination of Social Policies?', WZB Discussion Paper No. 501, (2013) 15–16.

[71] J. Zeitlin and B. Vanhercke, 'Socializing the European Semester: EU Social and Economic Policy Co-Ordination in Crisis and Beyond' (2018) 25 JEPP 149, 162–3.

[72] Efstathiou and Wolf, n. 69 above, 4.

discuss the results and recommendations of the Semester.[73] This is only an *ex post control*. The Parliament must, furthermore, request their appearance as there is no duty for other Union Institutions to report to it.[74] At the national level, although there is no formal requirement for their involvement, the majority of national parliaments have exercised some oversight, most notably over domestic reform plans and plans to meet MTBOs.[75] In the vast majority of Member States, the budget committees of national parliaments seek input into the plans and scrutinise them after their adoption.[76] Their level of influence is, however, debatable. Parliamentary committees have been found to be most active if they are in non-euro area States or the matters are politically controversial.[77] However, the latter circumstance is also when domestic compliance with the European Semester is at its weakest.[78] Parliamentary input may be associated with defiance of the process, therefore, rather than contributing towards it. If this suggests some parliamentary influence, the overall picture may still be bleak. The European Semester centralises power within the Union by making the Commission the dominant actor in the Semester. Consequently, it exercises considerable influence over domestic economic and fiscal policy. However, national parliaments have no input into what it does. Nor can they hold it to account.[79]

(iii) The Commission and National Budgets

The European Semester does not merely secure Union input and oversight over Member State economic and fiscal planning; it also provides for Union involvement with the drafting of euro area State budgets.

Regulation 1466/97, Article 2-a(3)

Member States shall take due account of the guidance addressed to them in the development of their economic, employment and budgetary policies before taking key decisions on their national budgets for the succeeding years. Progress shall be monitored by the Commission.

Failure by a Member State to act upon the guidance received may result in:

(a) further recommendations to take specific measures;

---

[73] Regulation 1466/97/EC, Article 2-a(4).

[74] D. Fromage, 'The European Parliament in the Post-Crisis Era: An Institution Empowered on Paper Only?' (2018) 40 *JEI* 281, 287–8.

[75] D. Jančić, 'National Parliaments and EU Fiscal Integration' (2016) 22 *ELJ* 225.

[76] M. Hallerberg, B. Marzinotto and G. Wolff, 'Explaining the Evolving Role of National Parliaments under the European Semester' (2018) 25 *JEPP* 250, 255–8.

[77] *Ibid.* 258–63.

[78] A. Maatsch, 'European Semester Compliance and National Political Party Ownership' in D. Jančić (ed.), *National Parliaments after the Lisbon Treaty and the Euro Crisis: Resilience or Resignation* (Oxford University Press, 2017).

[79] B. Crum, 'Parliamentary Accountability in Multilevel Governance: What Role for Parliaments in Post Crisis EU Economic Governance?' (2018) 25 *JEPP* 268, 274–5; M. Rasmussen, 'Accountability Challenges in EU Economic Governance? Parliamentary Scrutiny of the European Semester' (2018) 40 *JEI* 341. Coordinated scrutiny between the European Parliament and national parliaments has, therefore, been suggested, C. Fasone, 'Towards a Strengthened Coordination between the EU and National Budgets: A Complementary Role and a Joint Control for Parliaments?' (2018) 40 *JEI* 265.

(b) a warning by the Commission under Article 121(4) TFEU;[80]

(c) measures under this Regulation, Regulation 1467/97 or Regulation 1176/2011.[81]

Implementation of the measures shall be subject to reinforced monitoring by the Commission and may include surveillance missions under Article -11 of this Regulation.[82]

Following adoption of the CSRs, usually in the late summer, euro area States are required to make public a draft budget for the forthcoming year by no later than 15 October.[83] This is to be presented to the Commission and the Euro Group.[84] The Commission shall then present an assessment of the draft Budget by 30 November to the Euro Group for discussion.[85] Following this assessment, the State should adopt the budget by no later than 31 December of that year.[86]

One challenge with the procedure is that it telescopes national parliament consideration of the budget. The budget must remain a plan until 30 November, and must then be ratified by the parliament within a month. There is, thus, little time for that parliament to consider the draft budget in the light of the Commission's assessment and Euro Group discussions. This weakens domestic parliamentary influence over the budget. There is, in particular, a danger that a national government will use the support of the Commission and other euro area States to push through last-minute changes in its budget during this rushed period of parliamentary consideration.

The other challenge for domestic democracy is the force of the Commission assessment. Formally, it is just an opinion. However, the backdrop, set out in Article 2-a(3) above, is that the sanctions procedures might be instigated against a State which responds inappropriately to the guidance provided within the European Semester. The Commission opinion on the draft budget builds on that. It carries with it a veiled threat. Inevitably, governments, particularly those with weak public finances, thus serve two masters: the Commission and their domestic parliament.

An example occurred in November 2018. The CSR for Italy in July 2018 recommended that it increase expenditure by only 0.1 per cent of GDP on account of its large debt, 131.8 per cent of GDP.[87] Italy planned to introduce a budget which would increase its annual budget deficit to 2.4 per cent of GDP. The reason was that the Italian Government wished to reduce VAT, increase some provision for early retirement and introduce an allowance for low-income or unemployed Italians. The Commission believed that if Italy was to maintain its path towards its MTBO, the deficit should only be 0.8 per cent of GDP. It passed a negative opinion on the draft budget with

---

[80] This provision allows the Commission to issue a warning to a Member State that it is not complying with the BEPG.

[81] These are the sanction procedures for, respectively, significantly diverging from the MTBO, incurring an excessive deficit and failing to correct an excessive macroeconomic imbalance.

[82] Article 11 provides for a permanent between the Commission and national authorities, and for it to carry out missions to the Member State to carry out economic assessments.

[83] Regulation 473/2013/EU on common provisions for monitoring and assessing draft budgetary plans and ensuring the correction of excessive deficit of the Member States in the euro area, OJ 2013, L 140/11, Article 4(2).

[84] *Ibid.* Article 6(1).

[85] *Ibid.* Article 7(1). The European Parliament or the parliament of the State concerned can also ask for this assessment to be presented to it, *ibid.* Article 7(3).

[86] *Ibid.* Article 4(3).

[87] Council Recommendation on the 2018 National Reform Programme of Italy and delivering a Council opinion on the 2018 Stability Programme of Italy, OJ 2018, C 320/48.

the Italian Government resubmitting essentially the same plans.[88] At this point, the Commission threatened to instigate the procedure for sanctions unless Italy revised its budget.[89] Notwithstanding previous insistence that it would not change its budget, the Italian Government negotiated a deal with the Commission as it was well aware that the instigation of sanction proceedings would affect its ability to borrow on capital markets.[90]

(iv) The Sanctions Procedures

The three most high-profile grounds for sanctions are:

- A Member State has failed to comply with a Council Decision to take effective action to rectify a significant observed deviation from its MTBO (its balanced budget commitment).
- It has failed to implement a correction action plan to correct excessive macroeconomic imbalances.
- It has failed to comply with a Council Decision to take necessary measures to reduce an excessive deficit.

All procedures involve a series of convoluted institutional steps.

The first procedure, sanctions for taking no effective action to counter a significant observed deviation from the MTBO, starts with the assessment of States' plans for realising their MTBO of a balanced budget during the European Semester. If the Commission identifies a 'significant observed deviation' from the State's adjustment path towards its MTBO, it is to issue a warning which can lead to a finding of no effective action by the State concerned.

Regulation 1466/97, Article 6(2)

In the event of a significant observed deviation from the adjustment path towards the medium-term budgetary objective . . . and in order to prevent the occurrence of an excessive deficit, the Commission shall address a warning to the Member State concerned . . .

The Council shall, within 1 month of the date of adoption of the warning referred to in the first subparagraph, examine the situation and adopt a recommendation for the necessary policy measures, on the basis of a Commission recommendation . . . The recommendation shall set a deadline of no more than 5 months for addressing the deviation. The deadline shall be reduced to 3 months if the Commission, in its warning, considers that the situation is particularly serious and warrants urgent action. The Council, on a proposal from the Commission, shall make the recommendation public.

Within the deadline set by the Council in the recommendation . . . the Member State concerned shall report to the Council on action taken in response to the recommendation.

If the Member State concerned fails to take appropriate action within the deadline specified in a Council recommendation under the second subparagraph, the Commission shall immediately recommend to the Council to adopt, by qualified majority, a decision establishing that no effective action has been taken. At the same time, the Commission may recommend to the Council to adopt a revised recommendation . . . on necessary policy measures.

---

[88] European Commission, *Opinion on the Revised Draft Budgetary Plan of Italy*, SWD(2018)528 final.
[89] 'Commission Calls for Disciplinary Action against Italy over Budget Plans: Brussels Says Door Remains Open for Further Dialogue', *Politico*, 24 November 2018.
[90] 'Commission Reaches Budget Deal with Italy', *Politico*, 19 December 2018.

The sequence, therefore, is, first, a warning by the Commission; secondly, a Council recommendation with a deadline for action from the Member State; thirdly, a recommendation by the Commission for the Council to take a decision that no effective action has been taken. There is a fourth stage if the Council does not adopt the Recommendation and the Member State concerned still takes no effective action. After one month, the Commission can recommend to the Council that it adopt the Decision. The Decision that no effective action has been taken shall be deemed to be adopted by the Council unless it votes against the Recommendation by simple majority within ten days.[91]

The second procedure, concerning a failure to correct excessive macroeconomic imbalances, is analogous. During the European Semester, the Commission carries out 'in-depth reviews' of States affected or at risk of being affected by imbalances.[92] The first step of the process is that it finds the State affected by excessive imbalances, and informs the Parliament, the Euro Group and the Council.[93] The second step is that the Council may adopt a recommendation establishing an excessive imbalance and recommending corrective action with a deadline.[94] This requires the State concerned to set out a corrective action plan with a timetable for action[95] whose adequacy the Council assesses following a report by the Commission.[96] If the Council considers the plan insufficient, it can ask for a new plan.[97] The third step involves the Commission monitoring national implementation of the correction action plan.[98] The fourth step involves assessment of that implementation. If the Commission makes a recommendation that there has been non-compliance, it will be deemed to be the Decision of the Council unless the latter rejects the Recommendation by qualified majority vote (QMV) within ten days.[99]

The third main sanctions procedure, the Excessive Deficit Procedure does not rely on the European Semester but can begin at any time.

The Commission must first write a report if it believes there is an excessive deficit or a risk of an excessive deficit.[100] Secondly, if the Commission, having written the report, still believes an excessive deficit exists or may occur, it must address an opinion to the Member State concerned and inform the Council.[101] The third stage involves the Council taking a decision on whether there is an excessive deficit after hearing the Member State.[102] If it finds an excessive deficit, it will make recommendations (on a recommendation from the Commission) to the State to take measures to bring the deficit to an end.[103] If no effective action is taken, these recommendations will be made public.[104] The fourth stage occurs if the State persists in failing to implement the Recommendations. In such circumstances, the Council takes a Decision requiring the State to take the action necessary to reduce the deficit within a time-frame.[105] Sanctions may be applied for as long as there is no compliance with this Decision.[106]

The Treaty requires that the Council adopt measures by QMV for the Excessive Deficit Procedure. As this threshold was felt to be too high for effective policing, the TSCG provided that the Council would follow Commission Recommendations unless a QMV of Member States opposed them.[107] The legal force of this commitment is uncertain. The TSCG cannot amend the Treaties. If the Council decides to follow the Treaty requirements that a QMV of Member States needs to be in favour for a Decision to be adopted, this would become the *modus operandi*.

---

[91] Regulation 1466/97, Article 6(2) fifth para.   [92] Regulation 1176/2011, Article 5(1).   [93] *Ibid*. Article 7(1).
[94] *Ibid*. Article 7(2).   [95] *Ibid*. Article 8(1).   [96] *Ibid*. Article 8(2).   [97] *Ibid*. Article 8(3).
[98] *Ibid*. Article 9.   [99] *Ibid*. Article 10(4).   [100] Article 126(3) TFEU.   [101] Article 126(5) TFEU.
[102] Article 126(6) TFEU.   [103] Article 126(7) TFEU.   [104] Article 126(8) TFEU.   [105] Article 126(9) TFEU.
[106] Article 126(11) TFEU.   [107] Article 7 TSCG.

However, the TSCG represents a powerful indication of how States expect to vote, namely that they will follow Commission Recommendations.

All three procedures lead to the possibility of sizeable sanctions.

The significant observed deviation and Excessive Deficit Procedures both require a further Council Decision for sanctions to be adopted after the respective Council Decisions that the State has taken no effective action or failed to comply with the Decision requiring measures to reduce the excessive deficit. In both instances, the Commission proposal for a Decision is adopted unless the Council votes against it by QMV within twenty days.[108] The consequences are, however, different. The former leads to the Member State having to lodge an interest-bearing deposit of 0.2 per cent of its GDP with the Commission whilst the latter leads to a fine of that amount.[109] By contrast, the Council Decision finding that non-compliance with the correction action plan in the case of the macroeconomic imbalance procedure leads automatically to the payment of an interest-bearing deposit of 0.1 per cent of GDP.[110]

Continued breach leads to further sanctions. States already punished under the significant observed deviation procedure or where the Commission has identified 'particularly serious non-compliance with their budgetary obligations' have to pay a non-interest bearing deposit of 0.2 per cent of GDP on the simple finding of an excessive deficit by the Council.[111] Under the excessive imbalance procedure, States subject to either two successive decisions of non-compliance with a correction action plan or two failures to provide a corrective action plan shall have their deposit converted into a fine.[112] Under the Excessive Deficit Procedure, continuance of an excessive deficit by a Member State can lead to further fines up to a ceiling of 0.5 per cent of GDP.[113]

The potential size of these fines is eye-watering, running into billions of euros. This creates an implausibility about the sanctions procedures. It is difficult to believe that national governments would impose these fines on one another or that citizens of that State would tolerate them. States incurring them are likely to be in financial difficulties, and there is, therefore, something paradoxical about fining a bankrupt State. The only fine imposed on a State, just under €19 million levied on Spain in 2015, was for manipulation of statistics.[114]

Focusing on the imposition of fines may be missing the point, however. It has been suggested that these procedures are not about States punishing other States but act as a 'focal point or coordination device that facilitates decentralized punishment of sovereigns by bond markets'.[115] Their instigation, according to this argument, should trigger a lack of faith in a State's fiscal and economic policies in international capital markets with the result that it will be harder and more expensive to finance its policies. This serves as the punishment for deviant policies, and the threat of this punishment disciplines policy-makers. Two problems stand in the way of this working effectively in the Union, however.

---

[108] Regulation 1173/2011/EU, Articles 4(1) and (2) and 6(1) and (2) respectively.   [109] *Ibid.* Articles 4(1) and 6(1).

[110] Regulation 1174/2011/EU, Article 3(1) and (5).

[111] Regulation 1173/2011/EU, Article 5(1). The Commission can recommend that this be reduced, article 5(4).

[112] Regulation 1174/2011/EU, Article 3(2). These sanctions can be reduced or cancelled upon a Commission request, Article 3(6).

[113] Regulation 1467/97/EC, Article 12.

[114] Decision 2015/1289/EU imposing a fine on Spain for the manipulation of deficit data in the Autonomous Community of Valencia, OJ 2015, L 198/19. Provision for fines for manipulation of statistics is provided in Regulation 1173/2011/EU, Article 8. The Decision was challenged unsuccessfully in *Spain* v. *Council*, C-521/15, EU:C:2017:982.

[115] D. Kelemen and T. Teo, 'Law, Focal Points, and Fiscal Discipline in the United States and the European Union' (2014) 108 *American Political Science Review* 355, 356.

> **D. Kelemen and T. Teo, 'Law, Focal Points, and Fiscal Discipline in the United States and the European Union' (2014) 108 *American Political Science Review* 355, 366 and 367**
>
> First, our argument suggests that balanced budget laws can work because they provide a focal point that enables investors to coordinate on when to punish governments for running excessive deficits – not because they establish a credible threat that the judiciary will step in to force governments to balance their budgets. From this perspective, the crucial attribute of a balanced budget rule is not the strength of its legal enforcement mechanisms, but rather its clarity. The clearer the rule in question, the more obvious it is when a government violates that rule and the better investors can coordinate on enforcing the rule ... However, the 'structurally balanced budget' rules called for in the Fiscal Compact Treaty are anything but clear. The Treaty focuses on the legal enforceability of the rules, but leaves the rules themselves extremely vague. Therefore, they are unlikely to help coordinate decentralized punishment of irresponsible governments ...
>
> Secondly, in the EU the background conditions that surround these balanced budget rules undermine the credibility of the rules. Scholars of fiscal federalism emphasize that market forces can only effectively discipline subnational borrowing if there is no perceived chance of a bailout by the central government or central bank ... Thus, for instance, in the U.S., state level balanced budget rules have been able to restrain state deficits because the federal government had established a credible commitment not to bailout states. With the establishment of the ESM, there is now a permanent structure in place designed to provide bailouts to E.U. member states. The possibility of bailouts under the ESM is likely to undermine the effectiveness of market disciplines.

The use of the sanction procedures to allow investors to patrol economic and fiscal policy-making is controversial. It seems to subvert local democracy. The arguments about its ineffect-iveness, on its own terms, in instilling good policy-making apply broadly within the Union context, moreover. It is not only the balanced budget rule, which lacks legal clarity but also other EU laws, notably those on excessive deficits and macroeconomic imbalances. Bail-outs have been provided mostly by ongoing ECB intervention in recent years rather than through support between euro area States.

(v) The Prohibition on Cross Financing unless for Sound Budgetary Policy Reasons

There is, finally, the question of what legal controls apply to those supervising States' economic and fiscal performance. The article by Kelemen and Teo above alludes to a particular issue, namely whether they can cross-finance each other. Can Member States or, for that matter, EU Institutions help out those in trouble by providing them finance? The Treaties appear to indicate that this is not possible.

The 'no bail-out' provision, Article 125 TFEU prohibits the Union or Member States from taking on the liabilities of other Member States.

> **Article 125 TFEU**
>
> (1) The Union shall not be liable for or assume the commitments of central governments, regional, local or other public authorities, other bodies governed by public law, or public undertakings of any Member State,

> without prejudice to mutual financial guarantees for the joint execution of a specific project. A Member State shall not be liable for or assume the commitments of central governments, regional, local or other public authorities, other bodies governed by public law, or public undertakings of another Member State, without prejudice to mutual financial guarantees for the joint execution of a specific project.

This posed particular challenges during the sovereign debt crisis. A number of Member States were unable to secure finance on international capital markets. The only realistic available source of revenue that would allow them to keep running their governments was from other States or the ECB. As has been described earlier,[116] the European Stability Mechanism established a fund of €500 billion, financed by the euro area States, which offered financial support to States in difficulties by purchasing their bonds from third parties. This support generated a new debt for these States, as they had to repay it plus interest. It was only offered if they entered an agreed programme of fiscal, economic and welfare measures that would seek to resolve their budgetary difficulties. A challenge was brought in Ireland on the ground, *inter alia*, that the ESM violated Article 125 TFEU.

Pringle v. *Government of Ireland*, C-370/12, EU:C:2012:756

133 . . . to determine which forms of financial assistance are compatible with Article 125 TFEU, it is necessary to have regard to the objective pursued by that article.

134 To that end, it must be recalled that the origin of the prohibition stated in Article 125 TFEU is to be found in Article 104b of the EC Treaty (which became Article 103 EC), which was inserted in the EC Treaty by the Treaty of Maastricht.

135 It is apparent from the preparatory work relating to the Treaty of Maastricht that the aim of Article 125 TFEU is to ensure that the Member States follow a sound budgetary policy (see Draft treaty amending the Treaty establishing the European Economic Community with a view to achieving economic and monetary union, *Bulletin of the European Communities*, Supplement 2/91, pp. 24 and 54). The prohibition laid down in Article 125 TFEU ensures that the Member States remain subject to the logic of the market when they enter into debt, since that ought to prompt them to maintain budgetary discipline. Compliance with such discipline contributes at Union level to the attainment of a higher objective, namely maintaining the financial stability of the monetary union.

136 Given that that is the objective pursued by Article 125 TFEU, it must be held that that provision prohibits the Union and the Member States from granting financial assistance as a result of which the incentive of the recipient Member State to conduct a sound budgetary policy is diminished. As is apparent from paragraph 5 of the ECB opinion on the draft European Council Decision amending Article 136 of the Treaty on the Functioning of the European Union with regard to a stability mechanism for Member States whose currency is the euro, the activation of financial assistance by means of a stability mechanism such as the ESM is not compatible with Article 125 TFEU unless it is indispensable for the safeguarding of the financial stability of the euro area as a whole and subject to strict conditions.

137 However, Article 125 TFEU does not prohibit the granting of financial assistance by one or more Member States to a Member State which remains responsible for its commitments to its creditors provided that the conditions attached to such assistance are such as to prompt that Member State to implement a sound budgetary policy.

[116] See p. 665.

The Court found the ESM prompted States receiving its support to implement sound budgetary policies in two ways: it required them, first, to implement a series of fiscal, economic and welfare reforms to achieve sound budgets, and, secondly, it did not underwrite or assume their debts to other parties. If this judgment had gone the other way, there is no doubt the sovereign debt crisis would have taken a dramatic turn as a number of euro area States would, in all likelihood, have had to default on their debts and leave the euro. However, the judgment poses two challenges. First, the reasoning is fairly elastic. It gets around the categorical wording of Article 125 TFEU which prohibits such support absolutely, and introduces a qualification that is absent from the explicit language of the provision extent, namely that it can be provided if a State implements sound budgetary policies, by referring back to earlier debates. Secondly, the new test inevitably requires courts to assess when States are pursuing sound budgetary policies to determine whether the support is lawful, and this is difficult for a court to do.

The issue raised its head in relation to the other prohibition on cross-financing in the Treaties, the prohibition on monetary financing imposed on the ECB in Article 123 TFEU.

Article 123 TFEU

(1) Overdraft facilities or any other type of credit facility with the European Central Bank or with the central banks of the Member States (hereinafter referred to as 'national central banks') in favour of Union institutions, bodies, offices or agencies, central governments, regional, local or other public authorities, other bodies governed by public law, or public undertakings of Member States shall be prohibited, as shall the purchase directly from them by the European Central Bank or national central banks of debt instruments.

In September 2012, as it became clear that the ESM support might not be enough to support the economies of a number of euro area States, the ECB announced the Outright Monetary Transactions Programme. This was an open-ended commitment to buy from third parties bonds of euro area States, which were in and complying with an ESM programme. No purchases ever took place but the commitment was challenged before the German Constitutional Court on the ground, *inter alia*, that it violated Article 123 TFEU. The German Constitutional Court considered that it might do so, but also referred the matter to the Court of Justice.[117]

Gauweiler v. *Deutscher Bundestag*, C–62/14, EU:C:2015:400

94 It is clear from its wording that Article 123(1) TFEU prohibits the ECB and the central banks of the Member States from granting overdraft facilities or any other type of credit facility to public authorities and bodies of the Union and of Member States and from purchasing directly from them their debt instruments . . .

95 It follows that that provision prohibits all financial assistance from the ESCB to a Member State . . . but does not preclude, generally, the possibility of the ESCB purchasing from the creditors of such a State, bonds previously issued by that State . . .

---

[117] 2 BvR 2728/13, *ESM/OMT*, Order of 14 January 2014. On this judgment see C. Gerner-Beuerle, E. Küçük and E. Schuster, 'Law Meets Economics in the German Federal Constitutional Court: Outright Monetary Transactions on Trial' (2014) 15 *German LJ* 281; M. Payandeh, 'The OMT Judgment of the German Federal Constitutional Court: Repositioning the Court within the European Constitutional Architecture' (2017) 13 *EuConst* 400.

97 Nevertheless, the ESCB does not have authority to purchase government bonds on secondary markets under conditions which would, in practice, mean that its action has an effect equivalent to that of a direct purchase of government bonds from the public authorities and bodies of the Member States, thereby undermining the effectiveness of the prohibition in Article 123(1) TFEU.

98 In addition, in order to determine which forms of purchases of government bonds are compatible with Article 123(1) TFEU, it is necessary to take account of the objective pursued by that provision . . .

99 To that end, it must be recalled that the origin of the prohibition laid down in Article 123 TFEU is to be found in Article 104 of the EC Treaty (which became Article 101 EC), which was inserted in the EC Treaty by the Treaty of Maastricht.

100 It is apparent from the preparatory work relating to the Treaty of Maastricht that the aim of Article 123 TFEU is to encourage the Member States to follow a sound budgetary policy, not allowing monetary financing of public deficits or privileged access by public authorities to the financial markets to lead to excessively high levels of debt or excessive Member State deficits (see the Draft Treaty amending the Treaty establishing the European Economic Community with a view to achieving economic and monetary union, *Bulletin of the European Communities*, Supplement 2/91, pp. 24 and 54).

101 Thus, as is stated in the seventh recital in the preamble to Council Regulation (EC) No 3603/93 of 13 December 1993 specifying definitions for the application of the prohibitions referred to in Articles [123 TFEU] and [125(1) TFEU] (OJ 1993 L 332, p. 1), purchases made on the secondary market may not be used to circumvent the objective of Article 123 TFEU.

102 It follows that . . . when the ECB purchases government bonds on secondary markets, sufficient safeguards must be built into its intervention to ensure that the latter does not fall foul of the prohibition of monetary financing in Article 123(1) TFEU.

The Court found that these safeguards were present here. The ECB only purchased bonds from third parties and not directly from the States themselves. It also left open when and if it would make these purchases. This created enough uncertainty that neither market players nor States could have sufficient confidence that the ECB was simply acting as an underwriter for a State's debts. In addition, purchases would only be made if the State were in the ESM and adopting policies that would allow a return to international capital markets. These conditions meant States had to pursue sound budget policies for financial support to be offered.[118]

6 THE EUROPEAN CENTRAL BANK

If one half of euro area policy-making has been about disciplining domestic economic and fiscal policy, the other half has involved the development of substantive policies by the ECB. These have expanded over time. To understand the possibilities and limits of these, it is necessary, first, to understand the nature of the institution pursuing them.

(i) The European Central Bank and its Decision-Making Bodies

The ECB comprises two formal decision-making bodies, the Governing Council and the Executive Board,[119] and one, body, the Supervisory Board, that has significant decision-making influence.

---

[118] On the judgment see the Special Section on 'The CJEU's OMT Decision' in (2015) 16(4) *German LJ*.
[119] Article 129(1) TFEU. See also Article 282(2) TFEU.

The Governing Council and Executive Board: Membership of these two bodies is set out in Article 2832 TFEU.

Article 283 TFEU

(1) The Governing Council of the European Central Bank shall comprise the members of the Executive Board of the European Central Bank and the Governors of the national central banks of the Member States whose currency is the euro.

(2) The Executive Board shall comprise the President, the Vice-President and four other members. The President, the Vice-President and the other members of the Executive Board shall be appointed by the European Council, acting by a qualified majority, from among persons of recognised standing and professional experience in monetary or banking matters, on a recommendation from the Council, after it has consulted the European Parliament and the Governing Council of the European Central Bank.

The respective tasks of the two bodies are set out below.

Protocol on the Statute of the European System of Central Banks

12.1 The Governing Council shall adopt the guidelines and take the decisions necessary to ensure the performance of the tasks entrusted to the ESCB under these Treaties and this Statute.[120] The Governing Council shall formulate the monetary policy of the Union including, as appropriate, decisions relating to intermediate monetary objectives, key interest rates and the supply of reserves in the ESCB, and shall establish the necessary guidelines for their implementation.

The Executive Board shall implement monetary policy in accordance with the guidelines and decisions laid down by the Governing Council. In doing so the Executive Board shall give the necessary instructions to national central banks. In addition the Executive Board may have certain powers delegated to it where the Governing Council so decides.

To the extent deemed possible and appropriate and without prejudice to the provisions of this Article, the ECB shall have recourse to the national central banks to carry out operations which form part of the tasks of the ESCB.

The supreme decision-making body is, therefore, the Governing Council. It takes the decisions most readily associated with the ECB, notably the setting of short-term interest rates. The Executive Board, by contrast, is responsible for the preparation of the Governing Council meetings, the management of the daily business and implementing policy through giving instructions to NCBs.

This leads to complicated decision-making dynamics. The NCB governors comprise a large majority on the Governing Council, and they are subject to national societal pressures and rely for their briefings primarily on their own staff.[121] Potentially, a coalition could exercise a strong influence over the direction of the single monetary policy.[122] The counterbalance to this is that the Executive Board prepares the agenda for the meetings and its President chairs those meetings.[123]

---

[120] The ESCB is described in more detail later. See p. 686.

[121] Buiter observes the 'collegiate' presentation of the Governing Council's decisions does not provide effective protection from pressures being exercised by governments who may find out what has gone on behind the curtains. W. Buiter, 'Alice in Euroland' (1999) 37 *JCMS* 191, 195–6.

[122] C. Zilioli and M. Selmayr, 'The Constitutional Status of the European Central Bank' (2007) 44 *CMLRev* 355, 359–60.

[123] Protocol on the Statute of the ESCB, Articles 12(2) and 13 respectively.

The Supervisory Board: The Supervisory Board carries out the preparatory work for the Governing Council when it exercises its supervisory powers over euro area banks.[124] Formally, it does not have decision-making power as it merely submits draft Decisions to the Governing Council which are adopted by the latter. However, these draft Decisions are adopted unless the Governing Council objects within a period, which shall in no circumstances exceed ten working days.[125] As the draft Decision is, thus, the default Decision which requires a majority in the Governing Council to overturn it, the Supervisory Board is, in most cases, the substantive decision-maker.

The Supervisory Board comprises four ECB members chosen by the Governing Council of the ECB, and one representative from each of the competent authorities of the euro area States.[126] In addition, it has a Chair and a Vice Chair chosen from the members of the ECB Executive Board.[127] All members must act in the interest of the Union as a whole.[128] Decisions are taken by simple majority,[129] other than where the ECB is adopting Regulations which have to be adopted by QMV. In these cases, the Supervisory Board acts by QMV.[130]

(ii) The Independence and Accountability of the European Central Bank

Academic literature drawing a link between strong price stability and independent central banks influenced the framers of the Treaties.[131] Thus, they modelled the institutional settlement for the ECB on that of the German *Bundesbank*, with its federal structure and strong tradition of independence.[132] The central provision is Article 130 TFEU.

Article 130 TFEU

When exercising the powers and carrying out the tasks and duties conferred upon them by the Treaties and the Statute of the ESCB and of the ECB, neither the ECB, nor a national central bank, nor any member of their decision-making bodies shall seek or take instructions from Union institutions, bodies, offices or agencies, from any government of a Member State or from any other body. The Union institutions, bodies, offices or agencies and the governments of the Member States undertake to respect this principle and not to seek to influence the members of the decision-making bodies of the ECB or of the national central banks in the performance of their tasks.[133]

---

[124] These powers are set out in the Single Supervisory Mechanism Regulation 1024/2013/EU conferring specific tasks on the European Central Bank concerning policies relating to the prudential supervision of credit institutions, OJ 2013, L 287/63.

[125] *Ibid*. Article 26(8).

[126] *Ibid*. Article 26(1). The four ECB members cannot participate in the monetary functions of the ECB, Article 26(5). On the discussions surrounding the inception of the Supervisory Board see T. Beck and D. Gros, 'Monetary Policy and Banking Supervision: Coordination Instead of Separation' (2012) 13(4) *CESifo Forum* 33.

[127] Single Supervisory Mechanism Regulation 1024/2013/EU, Article 26(3).   [128] *Ibid*. Article 26(1).

[129] *Ibid*. Article 26(6).   [130] *Ibid*. Article 26(7).

[131] A review of the arguments can be found in R. Burdekin *et al.*, 'A Monetary Constitution Case for an Independent European Central Bank' (1992) 15 *World Economy* 231.

[132] On the institutional design of the ECB and the ESCB see R. Smits, *The European Central Bank: Institutional Aspects* (The Hague, Kluwer Law International, 1997); F. Amtenbrink, *The Democratic Accountability of Central Banks: A Comparative Study of the European Central Bank* (Oxford, Hart Publishing, 1999).

[133] The same text also appears in the Protocol on the Statute of the ESCB, Article 7.

The Treaty sets out a series of institutional guarantees to protect this independence. The ECB has its own legal personality,[134] and financial and accounting independence.[135] There are also guarantees to protect the personal independence of its decision-makers. Members of the Executive Board are to avoid conflicts of interest and to take the job on a full-time basis.[136] They are appointed for one eight-year non-renewable term.[137] Hope of reappointment will, thus, not be a factor which might lead the Board's members to heed to political pressures in their decision-making.[138]

In line with this, the TFEU confines contacts between the political institutions and the ECB to those necessary to ensure mutual understanding of their respective policy stances. The President of the Council and a member of the Commission can participate, without a vote, in meetings of the ECB's Governing Council.[139] Conversely, the President of the ECB must be invited to meetings of the Euro Group[140] and to Council meetings whenever matters relating to the ESCB's field of competence are discussed.[141]

The flip side of this independence is the ECB's weak accountability and limited transparency. Whilst Governing Council meetings are confidential, the ECB can make its deliberations public.[142] Since 2014, it has published very general summaries of its meetings, which are of limited informative value.[143] Alongside this, there are certain reporting duties. The ECB must publish quarterly reports and present an Annual Report to the Parliament, European Council, Commission and Council.[144] Finally, there is the 'Monetary Dialogue'. The competent Committees of the European Parliament also hear the President and other members of the Executive Board at the request of the European Parliament or at their own initiative.[145] This has led, in practice, to their appearing before the European Parliament four times a year.[146] This dialogue has, however, been described as a 'soft and relatively harmless' instrument, which provides little effective control.[147]

Amtenbrink compared this accountability to seven other central banking systems.[148] There is no clear legal yardstick against which the ECB's monetary performance may be judged. Institutionalised contacts with the EU Institutions are scarce. There is no override mechanism which allows political branches of government to intervene in the conduct of monetary policy or suspend the legal objectives of the central bank. The reporting requirements are weak and

---

[134] Article 282(3) TFEU; Protocol on the Statute of the ESCB, Article 9(1).

[135] See, generally, Protocol on the Statute of the ESCB, Articles 26–33.

[136] Protocol on the Statute of the ESCB, Article 11(2).

[137] Article 283(2) TFEU; Protocol on the Statute of the ESCB, Article 11(1).

[138] The Supervisory Board and its members are required to act independently, and not take instructions from third parties, Regulation 1024/2013/EU, Article 19(1). There are, however, none of the guarantees which exist in relation to the Executive Board.

[139] Article 284(1) TFEU.   [140] Protocol on the Euro Group.   [141] Article 284(2) TFEU.

[142] Protocol on the Statute of the ESCB, Article 10(4).

[143] www.ecb.europa.eu/press/pr/date/2018/html/ecb.mp181025.en.html. On this see A. Belke, 'Central Bank Communication: Managing Expectations through the Monetary Dialogue', Ruhr Economic Papers 692, RWI (2017).

[144] Protocol on the Statute of the ESCB, Article 15(1) and (3) respectively. On the latter see also Article 284(3) TFEU.

[145] Article 284(3) TFEU.

[146] D. Fromage and R. Ibrido, 'The 'Banking Dialogue' as a Model to Improve Parliamentary Involvement in the Monetary Dialogue?' (2018) 40 *JEI* 295, 299–301.

[147] *Ibid.* 301.

[148] Amtenbrink, n. 132 above, esp. ch. 4. See also J. de Haan, F. Amtenbrink and S. Eijffinger, 'Accountability of Central Banks: Aspects and Quantifications', Tilburg University, Center for Economic Research Discussion Paper 98–54 (1998).

performance-based disciplining or dismissal of ECB members largely excluded. This combination of features was not present in other independent central banks.

In monetary policy, this lack of accountability is borne out of a tradition prizing the independence of central banks. There is no such tradition in the field of banking supervision.[149] The British House of Lords described the issues in the following terms.

> **House of Lords, European Union Committee, *European Banking Union: Key Issues and Challenges*, 7th Report (London, Stationery Office, 2012–13)**
>
> 55 The principle of ECB independence is a necessary one in terms of the ECB's core monetary policy role. Effective banking supervision also requires independence, but independence in the supervisory context must be balanced by strong accountability mechanisms.
>
> 56 The ECB will become an exceptionally powerful institution if it takes on the proposed supervisory powers. Four principles of accountability need to be borne in mind:
>
> That the ECB should be fully answerable to the Council and European Parliament for the supervisory decisions that it undertakes;
>
> That an effective, calibrated and streamlined mechanism of accountability to national parliaments should be established, in particular in relation to individual supervision decisions that have a significant impact on an individual Member State's banking sector. It must be for national Parliaments to set out how any new accountability structures and frameworks should operate in practice;
>
> That an effective appeals system should be established within the ECB, with a timely and appropriate system of external legal challenge;
>
> That the accountability mechanism should be able to operate speedily and effectively at moments of acute crisis.

When the ECB acquired significant powers of banking supervision, there was some responsiveness to these concerns.[150]

First, the ECB must present an Annual Report on its supervisory activities and the development of supervisory structures to the European Parliament, the Council, the Commission and the Euro Group.[151] The Euro Group and European Parliament can request the Chair of the Supervisory Board to appear before either of them,[152] and the ECB must answer questions put by either of them.[153]

Secondly, the European Parliament holds hearings scrutinising the supervisory activities of the ECB twice per year.[154] Such hearings are public, and thus allow for greater transparency. This

---

[149] On controls over financial regulators see M. Quintyn *et al.*, 'The Fear of Freedom: Politicians and the Independence and Accountability of Financial Sector Supervisors', IMF Working Paper 7/25 (2007).

[150] G. Ter Kuile, L. Wissink and W. Bovenschen, 'Tailor Made Accountability Within the Single Supervisory Mechanism' (2015) 52 *CMLRev* 155; D. Jančić, 'Accountability of the European Central Bank in a Deepening Economic and Monetary Union' in D. Jančić (ed.), *National Parliaments after the Lisbon Treaty and the Euro Crisis: Resilience or Resignation?* (Oxford University Press, 2017).

[151] Regulation 1024/2013/EU, Article 20(2).   [152] *Ibid.* Article 20(4) and (5).   [153] *Ibid.* Article 20(6).

[154] *Ibid.* Article 20(8) and (9). Inter-institutional Agreement between the European Parliament and the European Central Bank on the practical modalities of the exercise of democratic accountability and oversight over the exercise of the tasks conferred on the ECB within the framework of the Single Supervisory Mechanism, OJ 2013, L 320/1.

transparency is reinforced by the ECB having to provide the relevant Parliament Committee with a comprehensive and meaningful record of Supervisory Board proceedings. The only caveat is that if the Governing Council opposes a draft Decision of the Supervisory Board, the Supervisory Board must only supply the Committee with the reasons for the latter's objection and not the content of its debate.[155] The Chair of the European Parliamentary Committee may also require additional confidential meetings with the Chair of the Supervisory Board. If these bear on confidential matters, MEPs attending will be bound by duties of confidentiality.[156]

There is also some accountability to national parliaments. The ECB must present its Annual Report to these[157] and answer questions put by these.[158] The Chair or other members of the Supervisory Board can also appear before a national parliament for an exchange of views.[159] This still all amounts to little more than a duty to report. The House of Lords, thus, found the accountability mechanisms to be 'patently weak'.[160] Individual decisions are likely to affect particular States insofar as they regulate a bank based in that State. National parliaments have little comeback in such circumstances other than an *ex post* report which includes no duty to provide a full record of what took place.[161]

(iii) The Expansion of the European Central Bank's Monetary Powers

The ECB enjoys a monopoly over use of the central tool of monetary policy, the authorisation of the issue of euros and, with it, the setting of short-term interest rates.

Article 128 TFEU

(1) The European Central Bank shall have the exclusive right to authorise the issue of euro banknotes within the Union. The European Central Bank and the national central banks may issue such notes. The banknotes issued by the European Central Bank and the national central banks shall be the only such notes to have the status of legal tender within the Union.

(2) Member States may issue euro coins subject to approval by the European Central Bank of the volume of the issue . . .

If decisions about how many euros are issued and the interest rates at which they are to be offered to commercial banks is a matter for the ECB, the implementation of monetary policy is a matter for the ESCB.[162] This is a composite organisation comprising the ECB and the NCBs of all twenty-eight Member States.[163]

---

[155] Inter-institutional Agreement, para. 4.   [156] *Ibid*. para. 2.   [157] Regulation 1024/2013/EU, Article 21(1).
[158] *Ibid*. Article 21(2).   [159] *Ibid*. Article 21(3). On practice here see Fromage and Ibrido, n. 146 above, 305.
[160] House of Lords, European Union Committee, *European Banking Union: Key Issues and Challenges*, 7th Report (London, Stationery Office, 2012–13) para. 57.
[161] The head of the legal service has, by contrast, argued that this accountability might obstruct the ECB from having regard to the Union interest, C. Zilioli, 'The Independence of the European Central Bank and its New Banking Supervisory Competences' in D. Ritleng (ed.), *Independence and Legitimacy in the Institutional System of the European Union* (Oxford University Press, 2017).
[162] Article 127 TFEU.
[163] Article 282 TFEU; Protocol on the Statute of the ESCB, Article 1. On the legal arrangements see B. Krauskopf and C. Steven, 'The Institutional Framework of the European System of Central Banks: Legal Issues in the Practice of the First Ten Years of Its Existence' (2009) 46 *CMLRev* 1143.

Article 127 TFEU

(1) The primary objective of the European System of Central Banks, hereinafter referred to as 'ESCB', shall be to maintain price stability. Without prejudice to the objective of price stability, the ESCB shall support the general economic policies in the Union with a view to contributing to the achievement of the objectives of the Union as laid down in Article 3 of the Treaty on European Union. The ESCB shall act in accordance with the principle of an open market economy with free competition, favouring an efficient allocation of resources, and in compliance with the principles set out in Article 119.[164]

(2) The basic tasks to be carried out through the ESCB shall be:
   – to define and implement the monetary policy of the Union,
   – to conduct foreign-exchange operations consistent with the provisions of Article 219;[165]
   – to hold and manage the official foreign reserves of the Member States,
   – to promote the smooth operation of payment systems.

The ECB is the central decision-maker within the ESCB. It adopts the guidelines and takes the decisions necessary to ensure that the ESCB realises its tasks. NCBs are, thus, required, when acting within the framework of the ESCB, to act in accordance with the guidelines and under the instructions of the ECB.[166] Furthermore, they are constrained even when they act outside that framework, as the ECB can require them not to carry out these activities if it believes these interfere with the objectives and tasks of ESCB.[167]

There are, however, two particular constraints on the ECB's power.

The first is the decentralised nature of the ESCB. This has led to increased dependence on formal legal techniques, be these instructions or guidelines, to implement monetary policy, in situations where a unitary central bank would treat similar issues as purely internal affairs. The Treaties, consequently, empower the ECB to commence enforcement proceedings before the Court of Justice against NCBs which fail to fulfil their ESCB-related obligations.[168] Conversely, ECB measures may be challenged by NCBs where these are addressed to them or of direct and individual concern to them.[169] Such legal challenges have not happened, but the system relies on significant cooperation and goodwill between the ECB and NCBs.

The second constraint lies in the external relations of the euro. Notwithstanding the strong relationship between exchange rate policy and monetary policy, the Council can intervene extensively here.[170] It can conclude formal agreements establishing exchange-rate systems between the euro and non-Union currencies,[171] adopt general orientations for exchange rate

---

[164] Article 119(2) TFEU states the activities of the Union should include a single monetary policy and exchange rate policy whose primary objective is to maintain price stability and to support the general policies in the Union in accordance with the principle of an open market economy with free competition.

[165] This provision governs exchange rate policy between the euro and other currencies.

[166] Protocol on the Statute of the ESCB, Article 14.3.

[167] If the Governing Council can only do this with a two-thirds vote cast, Protocol on the Statute of the ESCB, Article 14.4.

[168] Article 271 TFEU; Protocol on the Statute of the ESCB, Article 35.6.

[169] Article 263(1) and (4) TFEU; Protocol on the Statute of the ESCB, Article 35(1).

[170] On the possibility of conflict see C. Zilioli and M. Selmayr, 'The External Relations of the Euro Area: Legal Aspects' (1999) 36 *CMLRev* 273; the same authors' *The Law of the European Central Bank* (Oxford, Hart Publishing, 2001) ch. 5; Smits, n. 132 above, Part III.

[171] Article 219(1) TFEU. The Council acts unanimously and has to consult the Parliament.

policy,[172] and establish common positions on matters of particular interest for economic and monetary union within international financial institutions and conferences.[173] By contrast, the ECB competences are modest. It can establish 'relations with central banks and financial institutions in other countries and, where appropriate, with international organisations'.[174] It is also responsible for the management of the revamped exchange rate mechanism (ERM II), which manages exchange rates with non-euro area Member State currencies.[175]

These monetary powers rested on two assumptions: no euro area State would go bankrupt and significant inflationary pressures would continue to confront the euro area. For this reason, the central power granted to the ECB in Article 128 TFEU was the raising or lowering of short interest rates. Raising these would counteract inflation whilst lowering them would give economies a boost in leaner times. However, in the case of States who cannot service their debts, the central problem is that private lenders are unwilling to lend them money because they do not believe that they will be repaid. In moments of crisis, changing interest rates will not affect their calculations as these are simply too firmly held. Equally, changing interest rates does not help much in a world of deflation where the problem is falling prices rather than rising problems. In such cases, even an interest rate of zero percent will not encourage people to spend – since deflation means that things will be cheaper tomorrow, it is better to save and to wait.

The crisis shattered both these assumptions. Many euro area States could not service their public finances and were, therefore, in danger of defaulting on their loans and being effectively bankrupt. Furthermore, as the crisis wore on, the central concern in a number of States was falling demand and deflation.

The ECB responded to both problems.

From May 2010 to August 2012, it provided financial support to euro area States experiencing difficulties borrowing on capital markets through the Securities Market Programme, which bought these governments' bonds from third parties. The intervention was considerable. The ECB purchased €220 billion of bonds during this period.[176] This programme was still seen as too limited in scale and *ad hoc*. The Outright Market Transactions (OMT) programme, therefore, replaced it. This programme, discussed earlier,[177] allowed for the unlimited purchase from third parties of securities of those euro area States who had entered a programme of support under the ESM Treaty.[178] It offered, in other words, the possibility of indefinite and open-ended financial support.

The extent of the financial support offered led some to argue that the ECB had acquired a new power. It had become a lender of last resort. If nobody else offers finances to a euro area State,

---

[172] Article 219(2) TFEU. [173] Article 138 (1) TFEU.

[174] Protocol on the Statute of the ESCB, Article 23, first indent.

[175] Resolution of the European Council on the establishment of an exchange-rate mechanism in the third stage of economic and monetary union, OJ 1997, C 236/5. An agreement between the European Central Bank (ECB) and non-euro area NCBs requires collective intervention to keep actual rates within these bands, Agreement between the ECB and the national central banks of the Member States outside the euro area laying down the operating procedures for an exchange rate mechanism in stage three of Economic and Monetary Union, OJ 2006, C 73/9.

[176] Decision 2010/5/ECB establishing a securities markets programme, OJ 2010, L124/8. On this programme see F. Eser and B. Schwab, 'Assessing Asset Purchases within the ECB's Securities Markets Programme', ECB, Working Paper 1587 (2013).

[177] See p. 679.

[178] European Central Bank, *Technical features of Outright Monetary Transactions*, www.ecb.europa.eu/press/pr/date/2012/html/pr120906_1.en.html.

according to this argument, the ECB steps in to lend as much as it takes to sustain that State's finances.[179] The German Constitutional Court took a similar view when the OMT programme was challenged on the ground, *inter alia*, that it was an economic policy measure which the ECB had no power to adopt. The German court agreed. It found that the granting of financial assistance was economic policy and that control of budget policy through the requirement of State participation in the ESM was not monetary policy either.[180] The court, nevertheless, referred the matter to the Court of Justice, who disagreed and held the programme to be a monetary policy measure.

Gauweiler v. *Deutscher Bundestag*, C–62/14, EU:C:2015:400

46 ... to determine whether a measure falls within the area of monetary policy it is appropriate to refer principally to the objectives of that measure. The instruments which the measure employs in order to attain those objectives are also relevant ...

47 In the first place, as regards the objectives of a programme such as that at issue in the main proceedings, it can be seen from the press release that the aim of the programme is to safeguard both 'an appropriate monetary policy transmission and the singleness of the monetary policy'.

48 First, the objective of safeguarding the singleness of monetary policy contributes to achieving the objectives of that policy inasmuch as, under Article 119(2) TFEU, monetary policy must be 'single'.

49 Secondly, the objective of safeguarding an appropriate transmission of monetary policy is likely both to preserve the singleness of monetary policy and to contribute to its primary objective, which is to maintain price stability.

50 The ability of the ESCB to influence price developments by means of its monetary policy decisions in fact depends, to a great extent, on the transmission of the 'impulses' which the ESCB sends out across the money market to the various sectors of the economy. Consequently, if the monetary policy transmission mechanism is disrupted, that is likely to render the ESCB's decisions ineffective in a part of the euro area and, accordingly, to undermine the singleness of monetary policy. Moreover, since disruption of the transmission mechanism undermines the effectiveness of the measures adopted by the ESCB, that necessarily affects the ESCB's ability to guarantee price stability. Accordingly, measures that are intended to preserve that transmission mechanism may be regarded as pertaining to the primary objective laid down in Article 127(1) TFEU.

51 The fact that a programme such as that announced in the press release might also be capable of contributing to the stability of the euro area, which is a matter of economic policy ... does not call that assessment into question.

52 Indeed, a monetary policy measure cannot be treated as equivalent to an economic policy measure merely because it may have indirect effects on the stability of the euro area ...

53 In the second place, as regards the means to be used for achieving the objectives sought by a programme such as that announced in the press release, it is not disputed that the implementation of such a programme will entail outright monetary transactions on secondary sovereign debt markets.

54 It is clear from Article 18.1 of the Protocol on the ESCB and the ECB, which forms part of Chapter IV thereof, that in order to achieve the objectives of the ESCB and to carry out its tasks, as provided for in primary law,

---

[179] W. Buiter and E. Rahbari, 'The European Central Bank as Lender of Last Resort for Sovereigns in the Eurozone' (2012) 50 *JCMS* 5 (Annual Review).

[180] 2 BvR 2728/13 *OMT/ESM*, Order of 14 January 2014, paras. 65–7 (German Constitutional Court).

the ECB and the national central banks may, in principle, operate in the financial markets by buying and selling outright marketable instruments in euro. Accordingly, the transactions which the Governing Council has in mind in the press release use one of the monetary policy instruments provided for by primary law . . .

56 In the light of those considerations, it is apparent that a programme such as that announced in the press release, in view of its objectives and the instruments provided for achieving them, falls within the area of monetary policy. . .

66 It follows from Articles 119(2) TFEU and 127(1) TFEU, read in conjunction with Article 5(4) TEU, that a bond-buying programme forming part of monetary policy may be validly adopted and implemented only in so far as the measures that it entails are proportionate to the objectives of that policy.

67 In that regard, it should be borne in mind that, according to the settled case-law of the Court, the principle of proportionality requires that acts of the EU institutions be appropriate for attaining the legitimate objectives pursued by the legislation at issue and do not go beyond what is necessary in order to achieve those objectives . . .

The remit of monetary policy, and therefore of the ECB's monetary powers, is, thus, determined primarily by looking at the objective of the measure: whether it seeks to contribute to the singleness of monetary policy and to maintaining price stability. The OMT programme did this, the Court argued, because it sought to restore the pan-Union effectiveness of interest rates. At that time, these worked in those parts of the euro area which were doing satisfactorily but had no positive effect in States whose economies were on their knees. Protecting the public finances of these States through offering to be a lender of last resort was a first step to restoring their economies so that the raising and lowering of interest rates would work for them too.

Having regard to the objective of a measure rather than to its form to determine the extent of the ECB's monetary powers gives these powers an open-ended quality with the consequence that the ECB could become the main actor governing the economies of the euro area. The *Gauweiler* judgment placed a constraint on this by only allowing the ECB to have these powers if they were proportionate to the monetary objectives sought by it.

The German Constitutional Court has seen this as insufficient and argued that an instrument's impact on the economy and on parties' behaviour can make it an economic policy instrument, irrespective of its objectives. In January 2015, the ECB announced that it would buy securities to counteract deflation in the south of the euro area. As part of this process, the Public Sector Purchase Programme (PSPP) would buy government debt securities from third parties. The sums were enormous. By May 2017, the ECB had purchased over €1.5 trillion of government debt securities under the PSPP. The German Constitutional Court, once again, referred the matter to the Court of Justice. However, in its judgment, the German Constitutional Court noted that even if the objectives of PSPP were monetary policy ones, that was insufficient to make it monetary policy. The nature and impact of a measure could make it an economic policy measure, which the ECB was not empowered to take. And that might well be the case in this instance.

2 BvR 859/15, *Weiss*, Order of 18 July 2017 (German Constitutional Court)

119 . . . While solely indirect effects of monetary policy measures on economic policy may not per se suffice to qualify the measure in question as falling entirely within the area of economic policy . . . such effects can

only be considered 'indirect' when they are connected to the challenged measure only through additional intermediate measures and when they do not constitute consequences that are foreseeable with certainty. It might be untenable, however, to still consider economic policy effects to be 'indirect' in nature if the economic policy effects of a measure are intended or deliberately accepted, and these effects are at least comparable in weight to the monetary policy objective pursued. Accepting the proclaimed objectives of the competent EU institutions and bodies, while granting wide margins of assessment to the entities and decreasing the intensity of judicial review, appears capable of enabling institutions, bodies, offices, and agencies of the European Union to decide autonomously upon the scope of the competences that the Member States have transferred to them ...

120   Beyond its proclaimed monetary policy objectives, and irrespective of the extent to which such objectives are achieved, the PSPP has considerable economic policy effects. Based on its sheer volume alone, the inevitable consequences of its monetary policy objectives are its considerable steering effects on the economy. The PSPP affects balance sheet structures in the commercial banking sector by transferring large quantities of Member State bonds, including high-risk ones, from the balance sheets of the Member States to the balance sheets of the ECB and national central banks. As a result, the economic situation of the banks is improved significantly and their credit rating increases. The mechanism allows banks to sell the Eurosystem high-risk securities that otherwise could have only been unloaded at a loss, if at all. The factual preponderance of economic policy that this brings about, could potentially result in the ECB exercising a steering influence in economic matters, thus undermining the distribution of competences of [the TFEU].

121   Moreover, the PSPP improves the refinancing conditions for the Member States. It enables the Member States to obtain loans on the capital market at much better conditions than would be available to them without the programme. Of course, the conduct of monetary policy will generally entail an impact on interest rates and bank refinancing conditions, which necessarily has consequences for the financing conditions of the public deficit of the Member States ... Moreover, Art. 18 ESCB Statute expressly refers to the purchase of government bonds as a legitimate instrument of monetary policy ... Yet the question arises whether and to what extent the particularly large volume of the PSPP and the rather considerable economic policy effects resulting therefrom, as described above, could mean that the programme is to be qualified as predominantly of an economic policy nature. With an average monthly purchase pace of approximately EUR 48 billion starting in March 2015, and EUR 64 billion as of April 2016, it appears as though the impact on the refinancing conditions of the individual Member States were a deliberately accepted consequence of the PSPP. This impact is furthermore of such weight that it might be seen as superseding the monetary policy objectives. This applies all the more given that there is largely factual certainty ... that the government bonds will indeed be purchased and that the euro area Member States are aware that these purchases improve the refinancing conditions available to them. In addition, it should be foreseeable for the ECB that the States will increase their borrowing in order to stimulate the economy by means of investment programmes; as discussed above, this is indeed largely what occurred ... Thus, it could be concluded that the economic policy effects of the PSPP were not mere indirect effects of the monetary policy objectives pursued, but rather constituted an at least equally weighty aim pursued by the programme.

(iv) Banking Union and the European Central Bank as a Financial Supervisor

An ongoing concern during the crisis was that weaknesses in the banking sector would undermine States' attempts to restore their public finances as they would be forced to spend large amounts recapitalising their banks. In June 2012, the Commission proposed a banking union for the euro area.[181]

European Commission, 'A Roadmap towards a Banking Union', COM(2012)510, 3

Further steps are needed to tackle the specific risks within the Euro Area, where pooled monetary responsibilities have spurred close economic and financial integration and increased the possibility of cross-border spill-over effects in the event of bank crises, and to break the link between sovereign debt and bank debt and the vicious circle which has led to over €4,5 trillion of taxpayer's money being used to rescue banks in the EU. Coordination between supervisors is vital but the crisis has shown that mere coordination is not enough, in particular in the context of a single currency and that there is a need for common decision-making. It is also important to curtail the increasing risk of fragmentation of EU banking markets, which significantly undermines the single market for financial services and impairs the effective transmission of monetary policy to the real economy throughout the Euro Area.

The Commission has therefore called for a banking union to place the banking sector on a more sound footing and restore confidence in the Euro as part of a longer term vision for economic and fiscal integration. Shifting the supervision of banks to the European level is a key part of this process, which must subsequently be combined with other steps such as a common system for deposit protection, and integrated bank crisis management.

The banking union has three pillars.[182]

The first is 'a European single rule book applicable to all financial institutions in the Single Market'.[183] There was already considerable EU financial services legislation, and the single rule book comprises, in practice, a small number of pieces of legislation: on the capital credit institutions must hold, as well as requirements on bankers' remuneration and corporate governance;[184] on deposit guarantee schemes protecting depositors up to €100,000 per bank;[185] and providing a process and financial resources for the orderly resolution of credit institutions.[186]

The second is the Single Resolution Mechanism (SRM).[187] Resolution can involve a number of things: selling the credit institution or its assets to a third party, breaking it up or recapitalising it. In all cases, the central objectives must be to protect depositors, client funds and client assets; ensure minimal effects on the stability of the financial system or taxpayers; and secure the

---

[181] On the banking union see N. Moloney, 'European Banking Union: Assessing its Risks and Resilience' (2014) 51 *CMLRev* 1609; D. Howarth and L. Quaglia, *The Political Economy of European Banking Union* (Oxford University Press, 2016) chs. 5–9; E. Jones, D. Kelemen and S. Meunier, 'Failing Forward? The Euro Crisis and the Incomplete Nature of European Integration' (2016) 49 *Comparative Political Studies* 1010.

[182] The banking union is also believed to require a single rule book providing a single set of rules for financial services, a single resolution mechanism to provide for the orderly winding up of a bankrupt bank, and strong guarantees for depositors, European Commission, 'A Roadmap towards a Banking Union', COM(2012)510.

[183] Conclusions of the Presidency of the European Council, 18 and 19 June 2009, para. 20.

[184] Regulation 573/2013/EU on prudential requirements for credit institutions and investment firms, OJ 2013, L 176/1; Directive 2013/36/EU on access to the activity of credit institutions and the prudential supervision of credit institutions and investment firms, OJ 2013, L 176/338.

[185] Directive 2014/49/EU on deposit guarantee schemes, OJ 2014, L 173/49.

[186] Directive 2014/59/EU establishing a framework for the recovery and resolution of credit institutions and investment firms, OJ 2014, L 173/190.

[187] Regulation 806/2014/EU establishing uniform rules and a uniform procedure for the resolution of credit institutions and certain investment firms in the framework of a Single Resolution Mechanism and a Single Resolution Fund, OJ 2014, L 225/1.

continuity of the critical functions of the credit institution.[188] An independent EU agency, the Single Resolution Board, is to plan the resolution of large euro area credit institutions which are about to fail or are failing, put them into resolution when necessary, and, finally, secure their orderly resolution.[189] Alongside this, an international agreement established a fund, financed by the banking sector, the Single Resolution Fund, to provide the financial resources for resolution in such cases.[190] The ECB has only one significant power here. It can make an assessment when a credit institution is failing or likely to fail, and the SRB must provide for resolution of that institution.[191]

By contrast, the ECB enjoys a powerful role within the third pillar, the Single Supervisory Mechanism. Historically, the ECB enjoyed limited regulatory powers, notably on minimum reserves[192] and clearing and payment systems.[193] The Single Supervisory Mechanism changes that by granting the ECB significant powers of prudential supervision over large banks in the euro area.[194] These powers are wide-ranging but the most significant include powers to:

- veto the authorisation to establish a credit institution within the euro area[195] and the acquisition and disposal of qualifying holdings (typically 10 or more per cent of voting rights or shares) of any credit institution within the euro area[196]
- supervise the compliance of *significant* credit institutions compliance with EU law and national law requirements on, *inter alia*, exposure limits, liquidity, leverage, reporting and public disclosure as well as remuneration, risk management arrangements and internal control mechanisms[197]
- carry out stress tests to assess the financial robustness of *significant* credit institutions.[198]

The ECB has some powers vis-á-vis all credit institutions within the euro area (first bullet point above), but exercises wide-ranging supervisory tasks only over those credit institutions which are significant (second and third bullet points). Significance is measured by a variety of criteria:

---

[188] *Ibid*. Article 14(2).

[189] It has the power to do this for significant credit institutions supervised by the ECB under the Single Supervisory Mechanism and for 'large cross border groups'. *Ibid*. Article 7(2). Resolution of other credit institutions is done by national authorities. *Ibid*. Article 7(3). K. Alexander, 'European Banking Union: A Legal and Institutional Analysis of the Single Supervisory Mechanism and the Single Resolution Mechanism' (2015) 40 *ELRev* 154; M. Božina Beroš, 'Some Reflections on the Governance Framework of the Single Resolution Board' (2018) 56 *JCMS* 646.

[190] EU Council, *Agreement on the transfer and mutualisation of contributions to the Single Resolution Fund*, 14 May 2014, 8457/14.

[191] Regulation 806/2014/EU, Article 18(1)(a).

[192] Regulation 1745/2003/EC on the application of minimum reserves, OJ 2003, L 250/10.

[193] Decision 2007/601/EC concerning the terms and conditions of TARGET2-ECB, OJ 2007, L 237/71.

[194] Regulation 1024/2013/EU conferring specific tasks on the European Central Bank concerning policies relating to the prudential supervision of credit institutions, OJ 2013, L 287/63. There is provision for non-euro area States to engage with this, Article 7(2). None have. For the reasons why not and the problems caused, see p. 143. On the SSM see E. Ferran and V. Babis, 'The European Single Supervisory Mechanism' (2013) 13 *Journal of Corporate Law Studies* 255; T. Tröger, 'The Single Supervisory Mechanism: Panacea or Quack Banking Regulation? Preliminary Assessment of the New Regime for the Prudential Supervision of Banks with ECB Involvement' (2014) 15 *European Business Organization L Rev* 449; A. Pizzolla, 'The Role of the European Central Bank in the Single Supervisory Mechanism: A New Paradigm for EU Governance' (2018) 44 *ELRev*. 3.

[195] Decision 2007/601/EC, Articles 4(1)(a) and 14.

[196] *Ibid*. Articles 4(1)(c) and 15. Regulation 468/2014/EU establishing the framework for cooperation within the Single Supervisory Mechanism between the European Central Bank and national competent authorities and with national designated authorities, OJ 2014, L 141/1, Articles 85-87.

[197] Decision 2007/601/EC, Article 4(1)(d) and (e).

[198] Regulation 1024/2013/EU, Article 4(1)(f). The full range of powers are set out in Articles 4(1) and 5(2).

- the size of the credit institution and whether the total value of its assets exceeds €30 billion
- its importance for the economy of the Union or national economic imbalance and whether the value of its assets exceeds the GDP of its State establishment by 20 per cent (unless their value is below €5 billion)
- the significance of its cross-border activities, namely whether its ratio of cross-border liabilities or assets is more than 20 per cent of total assets and liabilities (unless the value of the latter is below €5 billion)
- it is one of the three largest credit institutions in the participating State.[199]

The ECB has wide-ranging supervisory powers over these. Most significantly, it can require these credit institutions to meet substantive prudential requirements set by it in those fields of activity that it supervises.[200] To enable it to perform its tasks, it also may request information from credit institutions,[201] carry out investigations,[202] carry out on-site inspections of credit institutions (with authorisation from the relevant judicial authority),[203] and fine credit institutions up to 10 per cent of their annual turnover where they wilfully or negligently breach EU law.[204] The ECB can issue guidelines, Regulations and Decisions in the exercise of these powers.[205] In addition, where it does not have the necessary supervisory or investigatory powers, the ECB can require these national authorities to use their powers under domestic law, so they are effectively acting on its behalf.[206] However, the thrust of the SSM is that authorities should work in tandem with one another. Thus, joint supervisory teams made up of members from both the ECB and relevant national authorities carry out supervision.[207]

The consequence is that the ECB has become one of the world's largest financial regulators. In November 2018, the ECB was directly supervising 118 banks, which accounted for 82 per cent of all banking assets within the euro area.[208] This has involved not simply the acquisition of extensive new powers for the ECB, making it as much of a supervisory institution as it is a monetary one. It has redrawn the architecture for financial regulation within the European Union with national regulators displaced by it. This has led to significant credit institutions having to deal not only with a new boss but also a new regulatory culture.

J. Binder, 'The Banking Union and National Authorities 2 Years Down the Line: Some Observations from Germany' (2017) 18 *European Business Organisation Law Review* 401, 403–4

German bankers tend to be rather cautious in off-the-record statements when it comes to their views on the quality of supervisory standards developed so far (which may or may not be entirely objective). One would probably not find representatives of German banks who would admit in public that they are happy with the new world. In particular, representatives of smaller institutions frequently express concerns about what they perceive as a growing trend towards over-regulation and excessive compliance costs. Compared

---

[199] Decision 2007/601/EC, Article 6(4); Regulation 468/2014/EU, Articles 50–60.
[200] Regulation 1024/2013/EU, Article 16.   [201] *Ibid*. Article 10(1).   [202] *Ibid*. Article 11(1).
[203] *Ibid*. Articles 12 and 13.   [204] *Ibid*. Article 18(1).   [205] *Ibid*. Article 4(3).
[206] Regulation 1024/2013/EU, Article 9(1).
[207] Regulation 468/2014/EU, Article 4. Rights of defence are also provided for the credit institutions, Articles 31 and 32.
[208] www.bankingsupervision.europa.eu/about/thessm/html/index.en.html.

with the national regime, where supervision by the Bundesanstalt für Finanzdienstleistungsaufsicht (BaFin) used to be open to individual contacts, less transparent with regard to supervisory strategies but more flexible in terms of direct communication of technical approaches and perhaps also less ambitious in terms of making the most of a discretionary regulatory framework, the ECB's concept of 'independent, intrusive and forward-looking supervision', certainly looks different. This shift in supervisory regime naturally comes with uncertainties, which are augmented by the fact that individual contacts between banks, their advisers and the supervisor have yet to be (re-)established. However, a more formal and less personal relationship between the supervisor and the supervised entities may well prove beneficial in terms of supervisory effectiveness and protection against capture. Given the evolutionary character of the new supervisory arrangements, it is perhaps not surprising that critical voices note a lack of transparency with regard to the ECB's approach to technical aspects, such as capital charges and the determination of minimum requirements on capital and bail-inable debt, or the calculation of scores for the purposes of the Supervisory Review Process (SREP). Open and detailed criticism of the technical approaches adopted so far has rarely been heard, however. All in all, the German perspective thus seems to corroborate general analyses according to which supervision by the SSM is widely perceived to be tough but generally fair, while day-to-day management certainly could be improved in some respects.

FURTHER READING

F. Amtenbrink, *The Democratic Accountability of Central Banks: A Comparative Study of the European Central Bank* (Oxford, Hart Publishing, 1999).

D. Chalmers, 'The European Redistributive State and a European Law of Struggle' (2012) 18 *European Law Journal* 667.

B. Crum, 'Parliamentary Accountability in Multilevel Governance: What Role for Parliaments in Post Crisis EU Economic Governance?' (2018) 25 *Journal of European Public Policy* 268.

E. Ferran and V. Babis, 'The European Single Supervisory Mechanism' (2013) 13 *Journal of Corporate Law Studies* 255.

D. Fromage and R. Ibrido, 'The "Banking Dialogue" as a Model to Improve Parliamentary Involvement in the Monetary Dialogue?' (2018) 40 *Journal of European Integration* 295.

N. Baerg and M. Hallerberg, 'Explaining Instability in the Stability and Growth Pact: The Contribution of Member State Power and Euroskepticism to the Euro Crisis' (2016) 49 *Comparative Political Studies* 968.

D. Howarth and L. Quaglia, *The Political Economy of European Banking Union* (Oxford University Press, 2016).

N. Moloney, 'European Banking Union: Assessing its Risks and Resilience' (2014) 51 *Common Market Law Review* 1609.

A. Verdun and J. Zeitlin, 'Introduction: The European Semester as a New Architecture of EU Socioeconomic Governance in Theory and Practice' (2018) 25 *Journal of European Public Policy* 137.

C. Zilioli and M. Selmayr, 'The Constitutional Status of the European Central Bank' (2007) 44 *Common Market Law Review* 355.

16

The Free Movement of Goods

CONTENTS

1 INTRODUCTION

Article 34 TFEU prohibits restrictions on the import of goods from other Member States. Case law has divided measures which may be restrictions into three categories, governed by three important cases, *Dassonville*, *Cassis de Dijon* and *Keck*. The structure of the chapter reflects this.

Section 2 discusses the umbrella notion of a restriction on imports, or Measure Equivalent to a Quantitative Restriction (MEQR), which is provided in *Dassonville*. This case established a very broad scope to Article 34, applying to any measure which impedes imports, however that effect is achieved. Rules limiting the use of goods, for example, may well hinder their sale, and therefore their importation, and so be MEQRs.

Section 3 discusses the application of Article 34 to product rules. The basis for this application is provided in *Cassis de Dion*. Product rules are rules which require producers to change some aspect of the physical product or its packaging before it may be sold. Examples are rules which only allow the sale of foodstuffs made in certain ways, or which limit the kinds of containers that can be used for soft drinks. The Court of Justice held in *Cassis de Dijon* that even if these rules apply equally to imports and domestic products, they are nevertheless restrictions on imports.

(a) The reason for the ruling was that in practice it is very difficult to export to other Member States if one has to amend products to adapt to the different rules in each State.

(b) The judgment created a principle of 'mutual recognition' of the adequacy of other Member State laws. It established that goods should only be subject to the regulation of their country of production. The principles of country of origin regulation and mutual recognition are now applied throughout free movement law.

(c) It is possible to derogate from mutual recognition for legitimate and proportionate reasons, but this is strictly policed. It is often argued, for example, that permitting foreign products to be sold when these do not conform to national rules and expectations undermines consumer protection. However, the Court usually finds that labelling provides the consumer with sufficient information and protection, and is a lesser hindrance to trade.

Section 4 discusses *Keck* and the idea of 'selling arrangements'. These are rules which regulate the way products are sold. Examples are advertising and rules on shop opening times. As long as these rules do not have a greater effect on imports than on domestic products they will not be treated as MEQRs. Member States may therefore regulate selling arrangements however they like, so long as the effect on imports and domestic products is the same.

Some principles are common to all categories of restrictions on imports.

(a) MEQRs which discriminate directly between national and foreign goods may only be saved by Article 36 TFEU. This is discussed in Chapter 19.

(b) MEQRs which are equally applicable (equal on their face, although they may have some unequal effect) will not be prohibited if they are necessary for some legitimate public interest objective (often called a 'mandatory requirement') and are proportionate.

(c) Article 34 only applies insofar as measures affect imports. If Member States wish to burden domestic producers with heavy regulation this is a matter of purely national law. However, in exceptional situations stricter regulation of domestic production may actually give it a reputational advantage, and so be a hindrance to imports.

(d) Article 34 TFEU has never been clearly applied to a purely private measure, only to broadly public ones. However, the notion of 'public' catches all bodies and measures in which the State is implicated or has control, or which carry out public functions, even if they are formally private. Moreover, the Member State has a positive obligation to prevent private parties from obstructing free movement, for example, where demonstrators block roads. This may entail sensitive balancing between free movement and fundamental rights to free expression and to demonstrate.

Section 5 discusses Article 35 TFEU, which prohibits restrictions on exports. It has a different logic from Article 34 TFEU. It only applies to measures which have some greater negative effect on export sales than on domestic sales. As with Article 34, if these measures are equally applicable and serve a legitimate aim in a proportionate way, then they may be permitted.

2 GENERAL DEFINITION OF A MEASURE EQUIVALENT TO A QUANTITATIVE RESTRICTION

Article 34 TFEU provides that:

> Quantitative restrictions on imports and all measures having equivalent effect shall be prohibited between Member States.

A quantitative restriction is a limit on the amount of imports.[1] That limit may be constructed in various ways, by reference to value, or physical quantity or some other factor. Examples could be a rule permitting only so many cars to be imported per year or limiting imports of cheese to a percentage of total domestic sales. Quantitative restrictions do not arise often any more: their prohibition is too clear. The second part of Article 34 is rather more important in practice. This prohibits measures which do not actually set a limit to imports, but have the same effect as such a limit. These 'measures of equivalent effect' (MEQRs), as they are often called, result in imports being reduced just as if there was in fact an explicit limit.

The case law on Article 34 consists of attempts to define and explain what constitutes a MEQR. The problems of such a definition are twofold. First, a MEQR, by definition, produces its import-reducing effects by a more or less indirect path. That can make causation difficult to establish. The first problem is therefore to know, as a matter of fact, which measures actually do result in imports being reduced or are likely to do so. In some cases it may be obvious, but other cases are difficult. The Court of Justice has dealt with this by drawing broad-brush distinctions of convenience between the types of measures that may be expected to obstruct trade or not, as will be seen below in the discussions of *Dassonville* and *Keck*.[2] The second problem is to decide whether Article 34 is about combating rules with a protectionist effect or about deregulating economic activity.[3] Many measures restrict or reduce economic activity generally: tax rises, rules on transport and advertising, labour regulation. Such measures are likely, therefore, to reduce imports too. However, they do not *specifically* reduce imports. They do not have any effect on imports that they do not also have on domestic production. On the whole, as will be seen below, the Court of Justice excludes such measures from Article 34, although the position is far from entirely clear and recent cases suggest a rethinking may be underway.[4]

In the current state of the law, measures potentially within Article 34 can be divided into three groups, each falling within a distinct legal regime. The most recent group consists of measures which concern the way goods are marketed or sold. Whether or not this type of measure is prohibited is decided according to the principles laid down in *Keck*, discussed later in this chapter.[5] Perhaps the most important group in practice consists of measures concerning the way products are produced or packaged – their physical specifications. Whether or not these measures contravene Article 34 is decided according to the principles laid down in *Cassis de Dijon*, also discussed below.[6] The third group consists of measures which affect imports or trade in some way, but do not fall within the other groups. These are measures which cannot be easily captured by the *Cassis* definition of a product rule or the *Keck* definition of a selling arrangement. The legality of this third group of measures is decided according to the principles in *Dassonville*.[7] In fact, this is the oldest of the three central goods cases, and is the case which provides the general umbrella definition of a MEQR. In the years immediately after it was

---

[1] See *Riseria Luigi Geddo* v. *Ente Nazionale Risi*, 2/73, EU:C:1973:89.

[2] *Procureur du Roi* v. *Benoît and Gustave Dassonville*, 8/74, EU:C:1974:82; *Keck and Mithouard*, C-267–8/91, EU:C:1993:905. See also G. Davies, 'The Court's Jurisprudence on Free Movement of Goods: Pragmatic Presumptions, Not Philosophical Principles' (2012) 2 *EJCL/REDC* 25.

[3] See Ch. 15; Advocate General Tesauro in *Ruth Hünermund and Others* v. *Landesapothekerkammer Baden-Württemberg*, C-292/92, EU:C:1993:932.

[4] See pp. 730–1.   [5] See pp. 724–31.

[6] *Rewe-Zentral AG* v. *Bundesmonopolverwaltung für Branntwein*, 120/78, EU:C:1979:42, discussed at pp. 713–24.

[7] *Riseria Luigi Geddo* v. *Ente Nazionale Risi*, 2/73, EU:C:1973:89.

decided, it was the starting point for all questions of free movement of goods. However, now that the specialised sub-regimes of *Cassis* and *Keck* are well-established, *Dassonville* has become less important in practice. Nevertheless, a wave of recent cases relying on it to extend Article 34 to new areas shows that its principles are in no way defunct.

(i) *Dassonville*

Mr Dassonville was a Belgian trader who bought Scotch whisky in France and imported it to Belgium for sale there. The reason why he did this was that whisky was much cheaper in France than in Belgium. The French, at the time of the case, did not have as high a disposable income as Belgians, and could not be persuaded to pay as much for whisky. Moreover, while whisky was a fairly well-established tipple in Belgium, it was less so in France, where it had to compete against domestic spirits and aperitifs. A common technique used to enter a new market is to sell the product at a low price initially, and whisky producers and retailers did precisely this. The hope was, of course, that eventually the French would come to love whisky and the price could be raised, and large profits finally made.

However, such market-specific pricing is made very difficult by Article 34, since what is called parallel trading quickly reduces the price differences. People like Mr Dassonville go and buy the goods in the cheap market and sell in the expensive one, until the prices converge. This is possible because, given Article 34, there should be no obstacles to the trading of goods between States.

Nevertheless, Mr Dassonville encountered a problem in the form of a Belgian law on 'designations of origin'. The law prohibited the import of products bearing such a 'designation of origin' without a certificate from the authorities of the State of production to prove that this designation was correct. Thus, whisky labelled as Scotch (from Scotland) could not be imported to Belgium without a certificate of origin from the British customs.

For retailers who imported their whisky directly from the United Kingdom this was not a problem, since the whisky would be delivered with the appropriate certificate if desired. However, such certificates were typically removed at the point of importation, and were no longer attached to the whisky by the time it was on sale within the country. Thus, when Mr Dassonville bought his whisky for a good price in France it came without a certificate. Moreover, it was difficult for him to obtain such a certificate since the goods had already left the United Kingdom. He was therefore in possession of Scotch whisky which could not be lawfully sold in Belgium according to Belgian law. He claimed that this law was a MEQR, and in the Court of Justice's judgment gave what continues to be the standard description of what a MEQR is.

Procureur du Roi v. *Benoît and Gustave Dassonville*, 8/74, EU:C:1974:82

5 All trading rules enacted by Member States which are capable of hindering, directly or indirectly, actually or potentially, intra-community trade are to be considered as measures having an effect equivalent to quantitative restrictions.

6 In the absence of a community system guaranteeing for consumers the authenticity of a product's designation of origin, if a Member State takes measures to prevent unfair practices in this connection, it is however subject to the condition that these measures should be reasonable and that the means of proof

required should not act as a hindrance to trade between Member States and should, in consequence, be accessible to all community nationals.

7 Even without having to examine whether or not such measures are covered by Article [34 TFEU], they must not, in any case, by virtue of the principle expressed in the second sentence of that article, constitute a means of arbitrary discrimination or a disguised restriction on trade between Member States.

8 That may be the case with formalities, required by a Member State for the purpose of proving the origin of a product, which only direct importers are really in a position to satisfy without facing serious difficulties.

9 Consequently, the requirement by a Member State of a certificate of authenticity which is less easily obtainable by importers of an authentic product which has been put into free circulation in a regular manner in another Member State than by importers of the same product coming directly from the country of origin constitutes a measure having an effect equivalent to a quantitative restriction as prohibited by the Treaty.

There are four elements of this judgment worth noting: first, the definition in paragraph 5, which continues to be cited in almost unchanged terms, although with the words 'all trading rules' replaced in some judgments by the words 'all rules' or 'all measures'.[8] This definition is very broad. It extends a MEQR to include measures which have not yet had any actual effect, but may potentially do so, as well as those whose effect on trade is indirect. Article 34 TFEU applies to any measure which may somehow hinder interstate trade. Yet, the second aspect of the judgment mitigates this. The Court of Justice appears to accept in paragraph 6 that even measures which might fall within its own definition may be permitted if they are 'reasonable'. This notion was later developed and brought to fruition in *Cassis de Dijon*. As a result, even though paragraph 5 of the judgment establishes a broad scope of supervision of Article 34, some of the measures caught may in fact ultimately escape its prohibition.

Thirdly, the breadth of the definition can then be understood as an establishment of jurisdiction. By making Article 34 broad, the Court is granting itself equally broad powers to supervise national measures via the preliminary reference procedure, even if in some cases it will find those measures compatible with the Treaty. This was particularly important in a time where the internal market was in its infancy and national protectionist traditions were well-entrenched, while national judges were still often unfamiliar with EU law. Finally, one may note the emphasis in paragraphs 7–9 on discrimination. There is no mention of this in the paragraph 5 definition, and yet the Belgian rule is finally ruled incompatible not because it makes all imports difficult, but because it makes imports from France harder than those from the United Kingdom (para. 9). The traditional view of free trade agreements, and of Article 34, that they are fundamentally about equal treatment of goods from different States,[9] is clearly influential here.

In practice, subsequent case law reflects much of this nuance, and the headline rule of *Dassonville* is not a complete representation of the law on Article 34 TFEU. Nevertheless, it

---

[8] See e.g. *Commission* v. *Spain*, C-88/07, EU:C:2008:567; *Commission* v. *Germany*, C-319/05, EU:C:2007:678; *Alfa Vita Vassilopoulos AE and Carrefour Marinopoulos AE* v. *Elliniko Dimosio and Nomarchiaki Aftodioikisi Ioanninon*, C-158–9/04, EU:C:2006:562; *Van der Laan*, C-383/97, EU:C:1999:64. See for discussion, R. Schütze, *From International to Federal Market* (Oxford University Press, 2017) ch. 3.

[9] See G. de Búrea, 'Unpacking the Concept of Discrimination in EC and International Trade Law' in C. Barnard and J. Scott (eds.), *The Law of the European Single Market* (Oxford, Hart, 2002) 181.

has been influential, and Regan argues that it should never have been used, since it offers an interpretation which does not fit the text of the article, or the intention of the Treaty authors.

D. Regan, 'An Outsider's View of "Dassonville" and "Cassis de Dijon": On Interpretation and Policy' in M. Poiares Maduro and L. Azoulai (eds.), _The Past and Future of EU Law_ (Oxford, Hart, 2010) 465, 465–6

In _Dassonville_, the Court simply announces that all measures that have any tendency to reduce imports are 'measures having equivalent effect' to quantitative restrictions. The implicit argument seems to be: 'Quantitative restrictions reduce imports. Therefore any sort of measure that reduces imports has "equivalent effect"'. This is a bad argument. There are many ways to describe the effects of traditional quantitative restrictions (embargoes and quotas). They do reduce imports. More particularly still, they reduce imports, without reducing domestic production or sales, and their form is such as to ground a (rebuttable) presumption that they are not justified by any positive effects they may have on domestic non-economic values. We now have three descriptions of quantitative restrictions in terms of their effects. Which should the Court choose? The third, the most complete. The Court is going to condemn (presumptively) any measure whose effects fall within its chosen description of quantitative restrictions. So the description it chooses should be complete enough to explain why quantitative restrictions themselves are condemned (presumptively). The description the Court chooses in _Dassonville_ fails this test. Only the third description passes this test. And even though it covers many fewer measures than _Dassonville_, the third description still encompasses not only border measures other than core quantitative restrictions (which Articles 31 and 32 of the Treaty of Rome, now repealed, suggest were probably the main thing the drafters were thinking about), but also facially discriminatory internal measures (which they may have been thinking about, with GATT Article III in mind), and arguably even the sort of facially neutral measures on products/packaging/labeling covered by _Cassis de Dijon_.

(ii) Limits of the Notion of a MEQR

Most situations to which _Dassonville_ has been applied involve some kind of discrimination or protectionism: either they discriminate against imported products directly, or they create some specific hindrance to cross-border trade which they do not create for internal trade. Examples of this type of measure which have been caught by Article 34 include government campaigns encouraging consumers to purchase domestic goods;[10] rules requiring electricity suppliers to purchase a percentage of their electricity from domestic wind farms;[11] obligations on petrol importers to maintain a reserve store;[12] requirements to obtain a licence to import certain goods,[13] even where the licence is a formality granted as of right;[14] public tenders requiring goods made according to national standards;[15] and procedures whereby alcoholic drinks could

---

[10] _Commission_ v. _Ireland_, 249/81, EU:C:1982:402; _Commission_ v. _United Kingdom of Great Britain and Northern Ireland (Marks of Origin)_, EU:C:1985:161.

[11] _PreussenElektra_, C-379/98, EU:C:2001:160; _Ålands vindkraft AB_, C-573/12, EU:C:2014:2037.

[12] _Commission_ v. _Greece_, C-398/98, EU:C:2001:565.

[13] _Commission_ v. _Finland_, C-265/06, EU:C:2008:210. See also _Philippe Bonnarde_ v. _Agence de Services et de Paiement_, C-433/10, EU:C:2011:641.

[14] _Ahokkainen_, C-434/04, EU:C:2006:609.   [15] _Commission_ v. _Ireland_, 45/87, EU:C:1997:435.

only be imported via certain State-controlled channels.[16] It is not necessary that such measures actually exclude imports, as long as they make import harder. As the Court said in *Fra.Bo*, 'the mere fact that an importer might be dissuaded from introducing or marketing the products in question in the Member State concerned constitutes a restriction on the free movement of goods for the importer'.[17]

Other measures appear to be neutral between domestic and foreign goods, but closer examination reveals an unequal effect. An example is *Commission* v. *Austria*, an Austrian rule prohibiting heavy goods traffic from an alpine motorway, on environmental grounds.[18] The rule applied without reference to nationality, to all trucks, but the Commission argued, without being contradicted, that most of the heavy trucks on that road were in fact transiting Austria, and were likely to be foreign or to be carrying foreign goods, while local freight traffic tended to use smaller vehicles.

Another example is rules on pricing, typically setting a minimum price.[19] This may be to protect the market structure, by preventing large, low-cost, firms driving out small ones, or it may be to influence consumer behaviour. In *Scotch Whisky* minimum alcohol unit prices were intended to reduce binge drinking by eliminating very low-priced alcohol from the market.[20] Yet such measures also prevent foreign goods coming from lower-priced countries from exploiting their cost-advantage, and so protect domestic production from imports. Such price controls do thus specifically hinder imports, at least potentially, and are MEQRs.

Recent cases have placed less emphasis on inequality or protectionism, and more reliance on the idea of 'market access'.[21] One of the leading examples is *Commission* v. *Italy*, in which a challenge was brought to Italian rules prohibiting the towing of a trailer behind a motorcycle.[22] It was thus not the form of a good, or its sale, that was regulated, but its *use* by the end purchaser, something that has recurred in several cases since.[23] Could that amount to an MEQR?

Commission v. Italy, C–110/05, EU:C:2009:66

33 It should be recalled that, according to settled case-law, all trading rules enacted by Member States which are capable of hindering, directly or indirectly, actually or potentially, intra-Community trade are to be considered as measures having an effect equivalent to quantitative restrictions and are, on that basis, prohibited by Article [34 TFEU].

---

[16] *Klas Rosengren and Others* v. *Riksåklagaren*, C-170/04, EU:C:2007:313. Also *ANETT*, C-456/10, EU:C:2012:241.

[17] *Fra.Bo*, C-171/11, EU:C:2012:453, para. 22; *Philippe Bonnarde* v. *Agence de Services et de Paiement*, C-433/10, EU: C:2011:641, para. 26.

[18] *Commission* v. *Austria*, C-320/03, EU:C:2005:684.

[19] *Fachverband der Buchund Medienwirtschafl*, C-531/07, EU:C:2009:276; *Deutsche Parkinson*, C-148/15, EU: C:2016:776; *Van Tiggele*, 82/77, EU:C:1978:10.

[20] *Scotch Whisky*, C-333/14, EU:C:2015:845.

[21] J. Snell, 'The Notion of Market Access: A Concept or a Slogan?' (2010) 47 *CMLRev* 437; G. Davies, 'Understanding Market Access: Exploring the Economic Rationality of Different Conceptions of Free Movement Law' (2010) 11 *German LJ* 671.

[22] *Commission* v. *Italy*, C-110/05, EU:C:2009:66. See also *Commission* v. *Portugal*, C-265/06, EU:C:2008:210; *Åklagaren* v. *Mickelsson and Roos*, C-142/05, EU:C:2009:336; *Lahousse*, C-142/09, EU:C:2010:694; *Sandström*, C-433/05, EU: C:2010:184. See also the special edition of the *European Journal of Consumer Law* dedicated to these cases, Gormley, Nihoul and Nieuwenhuyze (eds.), (2012) 2 *EJCL/REDC*.

[23] *Ibid*.

34 It is also apparent from settled case-law that Article [34 TFEU] reflects the obligation to respect the principles of non-discrimination and of mutual recognition of products lawfully manufactured and marketed in other Member States, as well as the principle of ensuring free access of Community products to national markets . . .

35 Hence, in the absence of harmonisation of national legislation, obstacles to the free movement of goods which are the consequence of applying, to goods coming from other Member States where they are lawfully manufactured and marketed, rules that lay down requirements to be met by such goods constitute measures of equivalent effect to quantitative restrictions even if those rules apply to all products alike (see, to that effect, 'Cassis de Dijon', paragraphs 6, 14 and 15; Case C-368/95 Familiapress [1997] ECR I-3689, paragraph 8; and Case C-322/01 Deutscher Apothekerverband [2003] ECR I-14887, paragraph 67).

36 By contrast, the application to products from other Member States of national provisions restricting or prohibiting certain selling arrangements is not such as to hinder directly or indirectly, actually or potentially, trade between Member States for the purposes of the case-law flowing from Dassonville, on condition that those provisions apply to all relevant traders operating within the national territory and that they affect in the same manner, in law and in fact, the marketing of domestic products and of those from other Member States. Provided that those conditions are fulfilled, the application of such rules to the sale of products from another Member State meeting the requirements laid down by that State is not by nature such as to prevent their access to the market or to impede access any more than it impedes the access of domestic products (see Keck and Mithouard, paragraphs 16 and 17).

37 Consequently, measures adopted by a Member State the object or effect of which is to treat products coming from other Member States less favourably are to be regarded as measures having equivalent effect to quantitative restrictions on imports within the meaning of Article 28 EC, as are the measures referred to in paragraph 35 of the present judgment. Any other measure which hinders access of products originating in other Member States to the market of a Member State is also covered by that concept.

. . .

55 In its reply to the Court's written question, the Commission claimed, without being contradicted by the Italian Republic, that, in the case of trailers specially designed for motorcycles, the possibilities for their use other than with motorcycles are very limited. It considers that, although it is not inconceivable that they could, in certain circumstances, be towed by other vehicles, in particular, by automobiles, such use is inappropriate and remains at least insignificant, if not hypothetical.

56 It should be noted in that regard that a prohibition on the use of a product in the territory of a Member State has a considerable influence on the behaviour of consumers, which, in its turn, affects the access of that product to the market of that Member State.

57 Consumers, knowing that they are not permitted to use their motorcycle with a trailer specially designed for it, have practically no interest in buying such a trailer. Thus, Article 56 of the Highway Code prevents a demand from existing in the market at issue for such trailers and therefore hinders their importation.

58 It follows that the prohibition laid down in Article 56 of the Highway Code, to the extent that its effect is to hinder access to the Italian market for trailers which are specially designed for motorcycles and are lawfully produced and marketed in Member States other than the Italian Republic, constitutes a measure having equivalent effect to quantitative restrictions on imports within the meaning of Article [34 TFEU], unless it can be justified objectively.

In the first part of this extract the Court restates its case law on Article 34 and concludes that three kinds of measures are to be seen as MEQRs:

(i)   measures which create a disadvantage for imports or foreign goods – the examples discussed above in this section

(ii) measures which fail to comply with the principle of mutual recognition – these are the product rules addressed in *Cassis de Dijon*, discussed later in this chapter

(iii) measures which hinder access to the market for imports.

This third category is the most problematic. What does it mean? What is a hindrance or restriction on market access?[24] In *Commission* v. *Italy* the Court finds that if use of a product is banned, then consumers will have no reason to buy it, and so import will be made much harder – market access restricted. The reasoning seems like common sense, but could be far-reaching, as it applies just as well to gun licences and driving licences. Of course, these would not be prohibited by Article 34, as there are derogations possible, and they would undoubtedly be found justified, as in fact was the rule in *Commission* v. *Italy*, by road safety. However, including rules on how goods are used within the scope of Article 34 makes it possible for a court to test whether these rules are genuine public interest measures or covert exclusion of selected, probably foreign, products.[25]

Alfa Vita goes a step further.[26] Greek law required all bakeries to have an area for kneading bread and a flour store, and laid down compulsory specifications for these. A number of supermarkets were prosecuted because they had bakery sections, but did not have these specific rooms. Their defence was that they had no flour and did no kneading: the bread they sold was made from frozen dough, or frozen part-cooked bread, which the supermarket merely had to place in its ovens for a while. The bakery requirements were completely inappropriate to their activities.

The Court found the rules to be an MEQR: the measures imposed a cost on a specific product, effectively making it more expensive, and so making sale, and therefore import, harder. The costs in this case could obviously not be justified. It was not discussed whether the frozen dough actually was imported, but it could well have been, and it was certainly in competition with fresh bread, which generally could not be.

As with the use cases the idea is that if a rule inhibits sale of goods – by making them more expensive, or less useful, or by restricting advertisements for them, perhaps – then that will in turn inhibit their import. Access to the market will then be hindered. However, this idea needs some boundaries in order to be workable: income tax reduces disposable income, and also inhibits consumer purchases; speed limits or environmental rules may affect deliveries, and make them slower or more expensive, also affecting sales; mortgage rules affect house prices and so may also impact on house size and purchase of garden furniture; many kinds of measure affect the market for consumer goods somehow.

The cases on market access to date suggest two limits. Those cases are of two sorts: either the sale of a specific kind of good is effectively stopped completely, as in the trailers case, or where sale is merely reduced as a result of some regulatory cost or burden, that burden is not applied to all goods in the market equally, but only to some, creating a competitive disadvantage. The

---

[24] See pp. 744–7; n. 21 above; L. W. Gormley, 'Inconsistencies and Misconceptions in the Free Movement of Goods' (2015) *ELRev* 40(6) 925–93.

[25] G. Davies, 'The Court's Jurisprudence on Free Movement of Goods: Pragmatic Presumptions, Not Philosophical Principles' (2012) 2 *EJCL/REDC* 25.

[26] *Alfa Vita* v. *Elliniko Dimosio and Nomarchiaki Aftodioikisi Ioanninon*, C-158–9/04, EU:C:2006:212.

disadvantaged goods might not necessarily be imported – for example, where use of jet-skis was restricted, it was not shown that the jet-skis were imported[27] – but they could be. The 'potential' of *Dassonville* comes to fruition here. It is the fact that the measure is creating inequality between competing goods, for example encouraging consumers to buy boats rather than jet-skis, or fresh rather than bake-off bread, which raises the spectre of protectionism, and engages Article 34 – after which a court must consider if the measure is justified or not.

A hindrance to market access is thus a measure which either excludes a product from the market altogether, or creates advantages or disadvantages for certain products. It is a market-distorting measure. This idea has been applied most explicitly by the Court in its case law on selling arrangements, discussed later in this chapter, but it is implicit throughout the law on goods and indeed all of free movement law:[28] there are no examples of measures being found to be MEQR when they impact on all market actors equally, and exclude none. To identify a hindrance to market access one must ask whether a measure steers the consumer away from certain products, and towards others.

(iii) Form of a MEQR

The form of a MEQR has never been something of great significance. The Court of Justice looks at the effects, and does not limit Article 34 to any particular type of legal measure. National laws and regulations may be caught, but so may administrative practices without a formal legal basis.[29] Most notably, in the *AGM* case, the Court found a mere pronouncement by a public official to comprise a MEQR.[30] AGM, an Italian company, exported lifting machines to Finland. There was some doubt in Finland as to whether they complied with the safety requirements of Finnish law and of the relevant European standards. After negotiations with AGM, which agreed to make some alterations to the machines, the Finnish Government decided that no further action was necessary. However, there were clearly differences of opinion within the safety authorities, because the safety official who had initially investigated the machines, Mr Lehtinen, went on television in an interview and declared that the machines were dangerous and did not comply with the relevant Directive. A storm of media interest followed, with newspaper reports about 'treacherous vehicle lifts', concern from the Finnish metalworkers union and so on. Inevitably, sales of AGM machines were badly affected.

The Court was asked to consider whether Mr Lehtinen's statements could be a MEQR. It took into account the fact that he had initially been authorised by his superiors to appear in the interview, but that he was later removed from the case and disciplined for making public statements which did not conform to the official position. The extent to which his statements should therefore be attributed to the State was therefore arguable.

---

[27] *Åklagaren* v. *Mickelsson and Roos*, C-142/05, EU:C:2009:336; *Sandström*, C-433/05, EU:C:2010:184.
[28] See p. 634.
[29] *Commission* v. *France*, 21/84, EU:C:1985:184; *Commission* v. *Denmark*, C-192/01, EU:C:2003:492; *Commission* v. *France*, C-212/03, EU:C:2005:313.
[30] *AGM-COS.MET Srl* v. *Suomen Valtio and Tarmo Lehtinen*, C-470/03, EU:C:2007:213; see N. Reich, '*AGMCOS.MET* or Who is Protected by EC Safety Regulation?' (2008) 31 *ELRev* 85; S. de Vries, 'Annotation of *AGM*' (2008) 45 *CMLRev* 569.

The discussion in the case took place in the context of Article 4(1) of the relevant harmonisation Directive. That article provided that machinery complying with the Directive should benefit from free movement. It essentially translates Article 34 TFEU to this particular context.

AGM-COS.MET Srl v. Suomen Valtio and Tarmo Lehtinen, C-470/03, EU:C:2007:213

55 ... the referring court's first question should be reformulated so that the court essentially asks whether it is possible to classify the opinions expressed publicly by Mr Lehtinen as obstacles to the free movement of goods for the purposes of Article 4(1) of the Directive, attributable to the Finnish State.

56 Whether the statements of an official are attributable to the State depends in particular on how those statements may have been perceived by the persons to whom they were addressed.

57 The decisive factor for attributing the statements of an official to the State is whether the persons to whom the statements are addressed can reasonably suppose, in the given context, that they are positions taken by the official with the authority of his office.

58 In this respect, it is for the national court to assess in particular whether:
   - the official has authority generally within the sector in question;
   - the official sends out his statements in writing under the official letterhead of the competent department;
   - the official gives television interviews on his department's premises;
   - the official does not indicate that his statements are personal or that they differ from the official position of the competent department; and
   - the competent State departments do not take the necessary steps as soon as possible to dispel the impression on the part of the persons to whom the official's statements are addressed that they are official positions taken by the State.

59 It remains to examine whether the statements at issue in the main proceedings, on the assumption that they are attributable to the Finnish State, infringe Article 4(1) of the Directive.

60 Any measure capable of hindering, directly or indirectly, actually or potentially, intra-Community trade is to be considered as an obstacle. That principle applies also where the interpretation of Article 4(1) of the Directive is concerned ...

65 Since the statements at issue described the vehicle lifts, in various media and in widely circulated reports, as contrary to standard EN 1493:1998 and dangerous, they are capable of hindering, at least indirectly and potentially, the placing on the market of the machinery.

It is long established that if the State were to campaign in favour of national products, using appeals to patriotism or chauvinism, or criticising foreign products, this would contravene Article 34 TFEU.[31] It seems, following *AGM*, that the same principles apply to statements by individual officials where these are reasonably attributed to the State by their addressees, something which will encourage official organs to keep an even stricter rein on their functionaries. The Court went on to find that the normal principles of State liability applied, so that it was open to the national court to find the State liable to compensate AGM. EU law also permitted, but did not require, that officials such as Mr Lehtinen attract personal liability for behaviour amounting to a MEQR.

---

[31] *Commission* v. *Ireland*, 249/81, EU:C:1982:402; *Commission* v. *United Kingdom of Great Britain and Northern Ireland (Marks of Origin)*, 207/83, EU:C:1985:161.

Cases such as *AGM* beg the question whether Article 34 TFEU has a *de minimis* threshold. Not every comment by a civil servant causes as much excitement as Mr Lehtinen's did. One can imagine discriminatory statements or acts by individuals or authorities that are wrongful in principle, but simply too insignificant to merit much concern. Does Article 34 apply?

(iv) *De Minimis*

The Court of Justice's formal position has always been that there is no *de minimis* for the application of Article 34.

Van de Haar, 177/82 and 178/82, EU:C:1984:144

13 It must be emphasized in that connection that Article [34 TFEU] does not distinguish between measures having an effect equivalent to quantitative restrictions according to the degree to which trade between Member States is affected. If a national measure is capable of hindering imports it must be regarded as a measure having an effect equivalent to a quantitative restriction, even though the hindrance is slight and even though it is possible for imported products to be marketed in other ways.

Thus, if a measure is a MEQR within the *Dassonville* definition, it is not important that its effect is in fact very small.

However, a quasi-*de minimis* rule is introduced by the doctrine, consistently present in the case law on goods and on the other freedoms, that measures whose effect is too 'uncertain and indirect' will not be caught by the Treaty.[32]

Peralta, C–379/92, EU:C:1994:296

23 The national court enquires about the compatibility of the Italian legislation with Article [34 TFEU] insofar as it requires Italian vessels to carry costly equipment. It asks itself whether this makes imports of chemical products into Italy more expensive and therefore creates an obstacle prohibited by that article.

24 On this point, it is sufficient to observe that legislation like the legislation in question makes no distinction according to the origin of the substances transported, its purpose is not to regulate trade in goods with other Member States and the restrictive effects which it might have on the free movement of goods are too uncertain and indirect for the obligation which it lays down to be regarded as being of a nature to hinder trade between Member States.

This is potentially important in the light of the recent market access cases discussed above.[33] In the event that Article 34 is increasingly applied in the future on the basis that a measure has the effect of reducing sales, the rule in *Peralta* could provide a useful counterbalance, preventing every tax rise or change to public transport becoming subject to Article 34.

---

[32] *Volksbank Romania*, C-602/10, EU:C:2012:443; *Graf*, C-190/98, C-190/98, EU:C:2000:49; cf. Gormley, n. 24 above.

[33] T. Horsley, 'Unearthing Buried Treasure: Art. 34 TFEU and the Exclusionary Rules' (2012) 37 *ELRev* 734; M. Jansson and H. Kalimo, 'De Minimis Meets Market Access: Transformations in the Substance – and the Syntax – of EU Free Movement Law' (2014) 51 *CMLRev* 523.

(v) Internal Situation

Article 34 TFEU only applies to measures hindering imports. If a measure does not apply to imports but only to domestic producers, then in general it will be outside Article 34.[34] Thus, in *Dassonville*, the Court of Justice found that applying the origin-certificates rule to imports was contrary to Article 34, but if the Belgian State had continued to apply that rule only to Belgian drinks brewed in Belgium and bearing origin marks from Belgian towns or regions, this would have been of no interest to EU law. It is true that this approach can lead to reverse discrimination, whereby EU law tolerates a situation in which domestic producers are more heavily burdened by law than importers. However, the Court is unconcerned by this:

> As regards the general principle of non-discrimination, it must be observed that community law does not apply to treatment which works to the detriment of national products as compared with imported products or to the detriment of retailers who sell national products.[35]

In some, relatively unusual, circumstances even though a measure does not apply to imports it may nevertheless create a problem or disadvantage for them and so comprise a MEQR. *Pistre* concerned French law on product designations, and the particular designation 'mountain ham'.[36] Apparently ham from pigs that have lived in the mountains is often particularly good, and so in marketing such ham, specific reference is made to its high-altitude origin. To protect the consumer, French law regulated the use of such references. Ham could only be called 'mountain ham' if its production complied with a number of rules. However, in practice it was only possible to comply with these rules if the ham was French. They were so formulated that ham even from very high places in other countries would not comply.

Realising that this amounted to discrimination against imported goods, the French Government chose not to apply the rules to imports. It was therefore possible to sell Spanish or Scottish ham in France which bore the word 'mountain' on the package, or reference to a specific mountain area, without legal problems. In the case, therefore, it was not an importer, but a French producer who complained. He was being prosecuted for selling French ham bearing the word 'mountain' without complying with the rules associated with that name. In his defence he challenged the legality of the French rules. The French Government claimed that since these rules did not apply to imports, Article 34 was not relevant. The Court of Justice disagreed.

Pistre, C–321/94, EU:C:1997:229

43 According to settled case-law, the prohibition laid down in Article [34 TFEU] covers all trading rules enacted by Member States which are capable of hindering, directly or indirectly, actually or potentially, intra-Community trade.

44 Accordingly, whilst the application of a national measure having no actual link to the importation of goods does not fall within the ambit of Article [34 TFEU], Article [34 TFEU] cannot be considered inapplicable simply because all the facts of the specific case before the national court are confined to a single Member State.

---

[34] *Mathot*, 98/86, EU:C:2000:663.   [35] *Driancourt* v. *Cognet*, 355/85, EU:C:1986:410, para. 11.
[36] *Pistre*, C–321/94, EU:C:1997:229.

45 In such a situation, the application of the national measure may also have effects on the free movement of goods between Member States, in particular when the measure in question facilitates the marketing of goods of domestic origin to the detriment of imported goods. In such circumstances, the application of the measure, even if restricted to domestic producers, in itself creates and maintains a difference of treatment between those two categories of goods, hindering, at least potentially, intra-Community trade.

The Court found that the measure contravened Article 34 even though it only applied to domestic products – in fact precisely because it only applied to domestic products. By having a designation with which only domestic ham could comply, French law provided a marketing advantage to national ham over foreign ham. What appeared to be an advantage for imports – not having to comply with national rules – turned out to be a disadvantage when it came to marketing and sale. The mere creation of a distinction between national and foreign products may itself amount to a barrier to imports.[37]

EU law often also applies indirectly to internal situations, via national law. Sometimes national law prohibits reverse discrimination, meaning that a court faced with internal facts, as in *Pistre*, is required by national law to treat the litigant in the same way as they would were she an importer. This means that the court needs to know what EU law would say in the hypothetical situation that the measure is applied to imports. The Court often answers such questions, because the answer is necessary for the national judge if she is to reach her decision. However, the actual situation in question, being internal, is not within the scope of EU law.[38]

A variation on the internal situation is the U-turn, whereby goods are exported and then reimported. This may simply be the result of several sales, from party to party. Sometimes goods are traded quite extensively before reaching the final consumer. However, it may be a deliberate construction, aimed at bringing the goods within Article 34 so that they can benefit from EU law and be exempted from burdensome national rules. In *Au Blé Vert*, the Court of Justice decided that reimports must be treated as imports, unless it could be shown that the goods were exported for the sole purpose of reimportation, in order to circumvent national legislation. This is doctrinally quite straightforward, but raises very difficult questions of evidence.[39] Where goods are sold to a trader abroad, and then resold to a new domestic trader, it is a considerable challenge to demonstrate that these were working together.[40]

(vi) Article 34 TFEU and Private Actors

In contrast to the other fundamental freedoms in the Treaty, the Court of Justice has never clearly applied Article 34 to a purely private measure.[41] Indeed, its usual position is that 'Articles

---

[37] See G. Davies, 'Consumer Protection as an Obstacle to the Free Movement of Goods' (2007) 4 *ERA-Forum* 55.

[38] *Guimont*, C-448/98, EU:C:2000:663; see C. Ritter, 'Purely Internal Situations, Reverse Discrimination, *Guimont*, *Dzodzi* and Article 234' (2006) 31 *ELRev* 690.

[39] *Leclerc* v. *Au Blé Vert*, 299/83, EU:C:1985:1.

[40] *Deutscher Apothekerverband* v. *DocMorris*, C-322/01, EU:C:2003:664.

[41] See generally H. Schepel, 'Annotation of *Fra.Bo*' (2013) 9 *European Review of Contract Law* 186; V. Trstenjak and E. Beysen, 'The Growing Overlap of Fundamental Freedoms and Fundamental Rights in the Case-Law of the CJEU' (2013) 38 *ELRev* 293; C. Krenn, 'A Missing Piece in the Horizontal Effect "Jigsaw": Horizontal Direct Effect and the Free Movement of Goods' (2012) 49 *CMLR* 177; E. Lohse, 'Fundamental Freedoms and Private Actors' (2007) 13 *EPL* 159; R. Babayev, 'Private Autonomy at Union Level: On Article 16 CFREU and Free Movement Rights' (2016) 53 *CMLR* 979–1005, 813–20 and 859.

[34 and 35 TFEU] concern only public measures and not the conduct of undertakings.'[42] Where companies or individuals act in a way that excludes foreign products, the Court has usually seen this as a matter for competition law.[43]

This apparent limit to Article 34 is mitigated somewhat by a broad conception of the public. For Article 34 to apply, a body does not have to be formally a part of the government. It is sufficient that it is carrying out a public duty on behalf of the State, or that it is controlled by the State. In *Apple and Pear Development Council*, a body representing fruit growers ran a 'buy English apples and pears' campaign. The council was not a public body, but it enjoyed public law privileges, such as the power to levy fruit growers.

Apple and Pear Development Council, 222/82, EU:C:1983:370

17 As the Court held in its judgment of 24 November 1982 in Case 249/81 *Commission* v. *Ireland*, a publicity campaign to promote the sale and purchase of domestic products may, in certain circumstances, fall within the prohibition contained in Article [34 TFEU] . . . , if the campaign is supported by the public authorities . . . [I]n fact, a body such as the development council, which is set up by the government of a Member State and is financed by a charge imposed on growers, cannot under Community law enjoy the same freedom as regards the methods of advertising used as that enjoyed by producers themselves or producers' associations of a voluntary character.

The Court refers here to the *Buy Irish* case, in which the Irish Government set up a marketing organisation to promote Irish goods.[44] This was clearly discrimination against foreign goods, but was it attributable to the Irish State? They argued that the body was incorporated as an independent company, acting on behalf of Irish producers, for whose actions the State could not be held accountable.

Commission v. Ireland, 249/81, EU:C:1982:402

23 The first observation to be made is that the campaign cannot be likened to advertising by private or public undertakings . . . , or by a group of undertakings, to encourage people to buy goods produced by those undertakings. Regardless of the means used to implement it, the campaign is a reflection of the Irish government's considered intention to substitute domestic products for imported products on the Irish market and thereby to check the flow of imports from other Member States.

It is clear that the link between State and organisation does not need to be legally watertight, as long as it is demonstrably real. In this case it was the Irish State that was the object of the Commission's enforcement action, but given the way the Court in *Apples and Pears* draws a parallel between that case and the *Buy Irish* case, it seems likely that it would have been possible

---

[42] *Vereniging van Vlaamse Reisbureaus* v. *ASBL Sociale Dienst van de Plaatselijke en Gewestelijke Overheidsdiensten*, 311/85, EU:C:1987:418.

[43] See generally on the competition/free movement boundary: W. Sauter and H. Schepel, *State and Market in EU Law* (Cambridge University Press, 2008) ch. 4; K. Mortelmans, 'Towards Convergence in the Application of the Rules on Free Movement and on Competition' (2001) 38 *CMLRev* 613.

[44] *Commission* v. *Ireland*, 249/81, EU:C:1982:402.

to apply Article 34 directly to the Buy Irish organisation itself. This is what happened in the *German Quality Products* case.[45] German producers complying with various quality rules were able to apply for the right to affix a mark to their goods, 'German Quality Product'. This was clearly not available to foreign goods, and so amounted to a discriminatory marketing scheme. It was found to violate Article 34 even though the scheme was operated by a non-governmental body, because that body was a product of statute, and so was essentially acting on behalf of and under the auspices of the State.

Fra.Bo is in several ways similar to *German Quality Products*.[46] It concerned a German body, DVGW, which certified water and gas pipe components as being fit for use and in compliance with the relevant German laws. The complaint was that part of its certification procedure was particularly inaccessible to foreign producers, including Fra.Bo, an Italian producer, making it harder for them to get certified and gain access to the German market. While the body in question was undoubtedly a private organisation, its certificates were recognised in German law, and it was the only body authorised to issue such certificates.

Fra.Bo v. *DVGW*, C–171/11, EU:C:2012:453

24 It is common ground that the DVGW is a non-profit, private-law body whose activities are not financed by the Federal Republic of Germany. It is, moreover, uncontested that that Member State has no decisive influence over the DVGW's standardisation and certification activities, although some of its members are public bodies.

25 The DVGW contends that, accordingly, Article [34 TFEU] is not applicable to it, as it is a private body. The other parties concerned consider that private-law bodies are, in certain circumstances, bound to observe the free movement of goods as guaranteed by Article [34 TFEU].

26 It must therefore be determined whether, in the light of *inter alia* the legislative and regulatory context in which it operates, the activities of a private-law body such as the DVGW has the effect of giving rise to restrictions on the free movement of goods in the same manner as do measures imposed by the State.

27 In the present case, it should be observed, firstly, that the German legislature has established, in Paragraph 12(4) of the ABVWasserV, that products certified by the DVGW are compliant with national legislation.

28 Secondly, it is not disputed by the parties to the main proceedings that the DVGW is the only body able to certify the copper fittings at issue in the main proceedings for the purposes of Paragraph 12(4) of the ABVWasserV. In other words, the DVGW offers the only possibility for obtaining a compliance certificate for such products . . .

30 Thirdly, the referring court takes the view that, in practice, the lack of certification by the DVGW places a considerable restriction on the marketing of the products concerned on the German market. Although the ABVWasserV merely lays down the general sales conditions as between water supply undertakings and their customers, from which the parties are free to depart, it is apparent from the case-file that, in practice, almost all German consumers purchase copper fittings certified by the DVGW.

31 In such circumstances, it is clear that a body such as the DVGW, by virtue of its authority to certify the products, in reality holds the power to regulate the entry into the German market of products such as the copper fittings at issue in the main proceedings.

32 Accordingly, the answer to the first question is that Article [34 TFEU] must be interpreted as meaning that it applies to standardisation and certification activities of a private-law body, where the national legislation considers the products certified by that body to be compliant with national law and that has the effect of restricting the marketing of products which are not certified by that body.

---

[45] *Commission* v. *Germany*, C-325/00, EU:C:2002:633.   [46] See Schepel, n. 41 above.

Notwithstanding its private origins, DVGW was the bearer of public law privileges and power, in the form of unique certification rights, and it was these legal supports which gave it such power over access to the market. The result is thus quite consistent with previous case law. However, it is notable that the Court of Justice is ambiguous in its reasoning. Paragraphs 25 and 26 suggest that private law bodies are subject to Article 34 TFEU whenever they restrict free movement 'in the same manner as do measures imposed by the state' which seems like a broadening of the law – albeit not a clear one. When are private measures similar to public measures? If this just means that Article 34 applies when private bodies are linked to the State then the case adds nothing new. However, it could also be suggesting an effects-based approach, in which not the actor but the consequence of their actions is central, as appears to be the case in the other freedoms.[47] It may be that even private parties are subject to Article 34 if they have the power to do what laws so often do, and restrain or discourage other parties from engaging in cross-border contracts with each other.[48]

A different kind of situation, sometimes called indirect horizontal effect, arises where the State does not actively support market-closing measures, but simply refrains from taking action against them. This first occurred in *Commission* v. *France*, in which the Court found that France had violated a combination of Articles 34 and 4(3) TEU (the duty of loyalty) by failing to remove French farmers who were blocking border crossings to prevent imported agricultural goods from reaching the French market.[49] The leading case, however, is now *Schmidberger*, in which the relevant principles have been most clearly developed. In *Schmidberger*, a group of Austrian demonstrators blocked motorways coming into Austria from Italy, as a protest against the pollution caused by transit traffic in Alpine valleys. This clearly restricted the import of goods by blocking freight traffic, and the Austrian Government therefore had an obligation as in *Commission* v. *France* to clear the roads. However, this obligation had to be balanced against the fundamental right to association, which the protesters claimed would be violated by an unmitigated application of Article 34. The question, ultimately, was whether the Austrian Government had behaved in a proportionate and reasonable way in the light of the balance which needed to be struck. The Court found that it had, and provided a very clear framework for the balancing of free movement and fundamental rights.

Schmidberger v. *Republic of Austria*, C–112/00, EU:C:2003:333

58 The fact that a Member State abstains from taking action or, as the case may be, fails to adopt adequate measures to prevent obstacles to the free movement of goods that are created, in particular, by actions by private individuals on its territory aimed at products originating in other Member States is just as likely to obstruct intra-Community trade as is a positive act.

59 Consequently, Articles [34 and 35 TFEU] require the Member States not merely themselves to refrain from adopting measures or engaging in conduct liable to constitute an obstacle to trade but also, when read with Article [4(3) TEU], to take all necessary and appropriate measures to ensure that that fundamental

---

[47] See p. 752.

[48] G. Davies, 'Freedom of Movement, Horizontal Effect, and Freedom of Contract' (2012) 20 *European Review of Private Law* 805; R. Babayev, 'Private Autonomy at Union Level: On Article 16 CFREU and Free Movement Rights' (2016) 53 *CMLR* 979–1005.

[49] *Commission* v. *France (Spanish Strawberries)*, C–265/95, EU:C:1997:595.

freedom is respected on their territory. Article [4(3) TEU] requires the Member States to take all appropriate measures, whether general or particular, to ensure fulfilment of the obligations arising out of the Treaty and to refrain from any measures which could jeopardise the attainment of the objectives of that Treaty.

. . .

69 It is apparent from the file in the main case that the Austrian authorities were inspired by considerations linked to respect of the fundamental rights of the demonstrators to freedom of expression and freedom of assembly, which are enshrined in and guaranteed by the ECHR and the Austrian Constitution . . .

77 The case thus raises the question of the need to reconcile the requirements of the protection of fundamental rights in the Community with those arising from a fundamental freedom enshrined in the Treaty and, more particularly, the question of the respective scope of freedom of expression and freedom of assembly, guaranteed by Articles 10 and 11 of the ECHR, and of the free movement of goods, where the former are relied upon as justification for a restriction of the latter.

78 First, whilst the free movement of goods constitutes one of the fundamental principles in the scheme of the Treaty, it may, in certain circumstances, be subject to restrictions for the reasons laid down in Article [36 TFEU] or for overriding requirements relating to the public interest, in accordance with the Court's consistent case-law since the judgment in Case 120/78 *Rewe-Zentral* ('*Cassis de Dijon*') [1979] ECR 649.

79 Second, whilst the fundamental rights at issue in the main proceedings are expressly recognised by the ECHR and constitute the fundamental pillars of a democratic society, it nevertheless follows from the express wording of paragraph 2 of Articles 10 and 11 of the Convention that freedom of expression and freedom of assembly are also subject to certain limitations justified by objectives in the public interest, insofar as those derogations are in accordance with the law, motivated by one or more of the legitimate aims under those provisions and necessary in a democratic society, that is to say justified by a pressing social need and, in particular, proportionate to the legitimate aim pursued.

80 Thus, unlike other fundamental rights enshrined in that Convention, such as the right to life or the prohibition of torture and inhuman or degrading treatment or punishment, which admit of no restriction, neither the freedom of expression nor the freedom of assembly guaranteed by the ECHR appears to be absolute but must be viewed in relation to its social purpose. Consequently, the exercise of those rights may be restricted, provided that the restrictions in fact correspond to objectives of general interest and do not, taking account of the aim of the restrictions, constitute disproportionate and unacceptable interference, impairing the very substance of the rights guaranteed.

81 In those circumstances, the interests involved must be weighed having regard to all the circumstances of the case in order to determine whether a fair balance was struck between those interests.

82 The competent authorities enjoy a wide margin of discretion in that regard. Nevertheless, it is necessary to determine whether the restrictions placed upon intra-Community trade are proportionate in the light of the legitimate objective pursued, namely, in the present case, the protection of fundamental rights.

The Court of Justice went on to find that the Austrian authorities had not violated Article 34 TFEU. Their actions reflected a justified and proportionate approach to balancing free movement of goods and the right to demonstrate. The factors which influenced the Court in particular were that this was a lawful and peaceful demonstration, approved in advance, for a limited period of time (around thirty hours), and for the purpose of demonstrating a legitimate concern – the protection of the environment. Moreover, the authorities could show that they had considered whether limiting the place and time of the demonstration so that the effect on goods traffic was reduced was a realistic alternative, but had for reasonable grounds come to the conclusion that these would deprive the demonstration of its very purpose and so be an excessive restriction on the right to demonstrate. Finally, once the demonstration was approved the authorities tried to minimise disruption by diverting traffic to other possible routes. In short, the Austrian authorities were a model of good governance, balancing interests in a carefully reasoned way. *Schmidberger* can be contrasted with *Commission* v. *France*, in which the demonstration was explicitly aimed at preventing imports as such yet the French authorities tolerated border closure for an extended and open-ended period, showed little concern about occasional violence by those involved, allowed a climate of fear and hostility to trade to develop and expressed complete passivity over the consequences.

Schmidberger has been criticised because the Court of Justice appears to put the 'fundamental freedom' embodied in Article 34, which is essentially about trade, on an equal level with the fundamental rights to free association and expression.[50] Despite the actual result, it has been argued that the case opens the door to a degradation of the status of fundamental rights. However, as the Court noted, the rights to free expression and assembly are not absolute, and neither is Article 34, so it is hard to see what the Court could have done other than look for an appropriate balance. However, whether the Court always takes such a rights-friendly stance needs to be considered in the light of recent cases in the field of services, *Laval* and *Viking*, discussed in Chapter 17.[51]

3 PRODUCT STANDARDS AND *CASSIS DE DIJON*

Germany, like a number of EU Member States, traditionally regulates products strictly, leading to a marketplace with a limited range of goods but high quality. This creates problems for importers located in less demanding States. Their goods, made according to different, or laxer, standards do not comply with local rules in many other States and so cannot gain access to the markets of these States. In the early days of European integration this was not seen as unfair. A 'when in Rome' approach was taken.[52] If importers wished to sell in State X they should comply with its rules. *Dassonville* was not generally considered to prohibit product standards if these were equally applicable to domestic and to foreign products.

However, this approach brings with it a number of problems. First, it requires producers to make their products according to a number of different standards, depending upon where they wish to export to. The idea that the internal market will enable consolidation of industry and economies of scale is undermined if factories have to run numerous separate production lines for different markets. Moreover, in practice, producers will not always do this, so that the realisation of an undivided European market will be impeded. Markets will remain local, as producers decide that it is too difficult or expensive to rework their goods to comply with local rules. The markets in smaller States will be particularly isolated, as potential profits are less and may not justify adapting production.

Traditionally such issues were to be dealt with by harmonisation. However, this did not turn out to be the easy and effective market-building tool that some had hoped, as product

---

[50] J. Morijn, 'Balancing Fundamental Rights and Common Market Freedoms in Union Law' (2006) 12 *ELJ* 15.

[51] See N. Nic Shuibhne, 'Margins of Appreciation: National Values, Fundamental Rights and EC Free Movement Law' (2009) 34 *ELRev* 230; C. Kombas, 'Fundamental Rights and Fundamental Freedoms: A Symbiosis on the Basis of Subsidiarity' (2006) 12 *EPL* 433.

[52] The use of the phrase in this context is borrowed from K. Nicolaidis and G. Shaffer, 'Managed Mutual Recognition Regimes: Governance Without Global Government' (2005) 68 *Law and Contemporary Problems* 263.

development and national regulation outpaced the capacity of the European institutions to harmonise.[53] It was in this context, and during a period of European political stagnation, that the Court of Justice intervened with its judgment in *Cassis de Dijon*.

German law required fruit liqueurs to possess at least 25 per cent alcohol. Cassis de Dijon, a blackcurrant liqueur, was made in France and typically contained between 15 and 20 per cent alcohol. As a result it could not be sold in Germany. A German importer, refused authorisation to import and sell Cassis, challenged this decision on the basis that it contravened Article 34 TFEU.

Rewe–Zentral AG v. Bundesmonopolverwaltung für Branntwein (Cassis de Dijon), 120/78, EU:C:1979:42

8 In the absence of common rules relating to the production and marketing of alcohol . . . it is for the Member States to regulate all matters relating to the production and marketing of alcohol and alcoholic beverages on their own territory.

Obstacles to movement within the community resulting from disparities between the national laws relating to the marketing of the products in question must be accepted insofar as those provisions may be recognized as being necessary in order to satisfy mandatory requirements relating in particular to the effectiveness of fiscal supervision, the protection of public health, the fairness of commercial transactions and the defence of the consumer.

9 The government of the Federal Republic of Germany, intervening in the proceedings, put forward various arguments which, in its view, justify the application of provisions relating to the minimum alcohol content of alcoholic beverages, adducing considerations relating on the one hand to the protection of public health and on the other to the protection of the consumer against unfair commercial practices.

10 As regards the protection of public health the German government states that the purpose of the fixing of minimum alcohol contents by national legislation is to avoid the proliferation of alcoholic beverages on the national market, in particular alcoholic beverages with a low alcohol content, since, in its view, such products may more easily induce a tolerance towards alcohol than more highly alcoholic beverages.

11 Such considerations are not decisive since the consumer can obtain on the market an extremely wide range of weakly or moderately alcoholic products and furthermore a large proportion of alcoholic beverages with a high alcohol content freely sold on the German market is generally consumed in a diluted form.

12 The German government also claims that the fixing of a lower limit for the alcohol content of certain liqueurs is designed to protect the consumer against unfair practices on the part of producers and distributors of alcoholic beverages.

This argument is based on the consideration that the lowering of the alcohol content secures a competitive advantage in relation to beverages with a higher alcohol content, since alcohol constitutes by far the most expensive constituent of beverages by reason of the high rate of tax to which it is subject.

Furthermore, according to the German government, to allow alcoholic products into free circulation wherever, as regards their alcohol content, they comply with the rules laid down in the country of production would have the effect of imposing as a common standard within the community the lowest alcohol content permitted in any of the Member States, and even of rendering any requirements in this field inoperative since a lower limit of this nature is foreign to the rules of several Member States.

---

[53] See Ch. 14.

13 As the Commission rightly observed, the fixing of limits in relation to the alcohol content of beverages may lead to the standardization of products placed on the market and of their designations, in the interests of a greater transparency of commercial transactions and offers for sale to the public.

    However, this line of argument cannot be taken so far as to regard the mandatory fixing of minimum alcohol contents as being an essential guarantee of the fairness of commercial transactions, since it is a simple matter to ensure that suitable information is conveyed to the purchaser by requiring the display of an indication of origin and of the alcohol content on the packaging of products.

14 It is clear from the foregoing that the requirements relating to the minimum alcohol content of alcoholic beverages do not serve a purpose which is in the general interest and such as to take precedence over the requirements of the free movement of goods, which constitutes one of the fundamental rules of the Community.

    In practice, the principal effect of requirements of this nature is to promote alcoholic beverages having a high alcohol content by excluding from the national market products of other Member States which do not answer that description.

    It therefore appears that the unilateral requirement imposed by the rules of a Member State of a minimum alcohol content for the purposes of the sale of alcoholic beverages constitutes an obstacle to trade which is incompatible with the provisions of Article [34 TFEU].

    There is therefore no valid reason why, provided that they have been lawfully produced and marketed in one of the Member States, alcoholic beverages should not be introduced into any other Member State; the sale of such products may not be subject to a legal prohibition on the marketing of beverages with an alcohol content lower than the limit set by the national rules.

15 Consequently, the first question should be answered to the effect that the concept of 'measures having an effect equivalent to quantitative restrictions on imports' contained in Article [34 TFEU] is to be understood to mean that the fixing of a minimum alcohol content for alcoholic beverages intended for human consumption by the legislation of a Member State also falls within the prohibition laid down in that provision where the importation of alcoholic beverages lawfully produced and marketed in another Member State is concerned.

The Court finds that the application of product standards to imports hinders their importation, as is obviously correct. Therefore such rules, applied to imports, are MEQRs.

    The solution, however, is not to prohibit product standards as such. This would result in an unregulated European product market, undesirable for many reasons. By contrast, the Court begins paragraph 8 by noting that since there is no EU legislation harmonising alcohol levels (there is now, there was not then), it is quite legitimate for Member States to regulate this matter. Thus, it is not the existence of product standards as such that is the problem, but just their application to products imported from other Member States.

    The trade-restricting effects of such application are dealt with by developing two ideas, which are the major contribution of *Cassis de Dijon* to EU law, and which are both among the most important legal developments since the Union's foundation.

    The first of these is mutual recognition. The Court finds in paragraph 14 that if products comply with the laws of the Member State where they are produced, then there is no reason why they should not be sold in all other Member States. Each Member State is required to accept products made according to the laws of other Member States. What is good enough for France is good enough for Germany. The name subsequently given to this idea is 'mutual recognition', because Member States recognise as adequate each other's laws and regulations, and therefore do not impose additional requirements on products complying with these. This idea is immensely powerful and has become a general principle of EU law, applied not only to the free movement of goods, but throughout the internal market.[54] It provides a conceptual basis for accepting not just foreign products, but foreign qualifications, tests and certificates, official documents and so on.[55] As a general rule, the foreign (from another Member State) must be recognised as functionally equivalent, at least in all really important respects, to the domestic.

The second idea is that of mandatory requirements. While the Court states that in principle goods from one State should be marketable in all others, it also concedes in paragraph 8 that there may sometimes be a need for derogation from this general principle. Sometimes the application of standards to imports may be necessary to protect important interests such as consumer protection or public health. The name given to these, 'mandatory requirements', sounds somewhat odd in English, but has stuck and is still used, although the phrase 'public interest objectives' is now also used.

It is therefore the case that an equally applicable rule which would otherwise violate Article 34 may be saved if it can be shown that it is necessary to protect some public interest objective. There is therefore a balancing process involved, in which proportionality is the central concept. Cases subsequent to *Cassis* are in fact a litany of judicial attempts to decide whether a given general interest is, on the facts, sufficient to justify derogation from the mutual recognition rule. The following two sections go into more detail first on the general rule, and then the application of the mandatory requirement exceptions.

(i) Mutual Recognition

It seems fairly intuitive that a factory located in a certain Member State should be subject to the rules and regulations of that State. It also seems fairly intuitive that a product on the supermarket shelves in a Member State should be subject to the rules and regulation in that State. Yet, if products are required to comply with the laws of both the State of production and the State of sale this can create impossible burdens. Imagine, for example, that France had a maximum alcohol limit of 20 per cent and Germany a minimum of 25 per cent; it would be impossible to manufacture in France for sale in Germany. Even without such extreme situations, the burden of complying with two sets of laws would impose cost and inconvenience on producers.

This is, of course, an import-specific problem. Goods sold domestically would face no problem because the State of production and State of sale would be the same. They would only have one set of laws to comply with. However, any goods traded between States would face at least two.[56] The application of product standards to imports would therefore not just make trade difficult, but it would often disadvantage imports relative to domestic production.

The solution is to construct a regime in which a given product (or service, the principle is generalised now) is only subject to one set of rules. If there has been harmonisation then this will provide that unique regulatory framework. However, in the absence of harmonisation the question is whether it is better to apply the rules of the State of sale or of production.

Given that product standards exist to protect the consumers of the products, and that the relevant consumers are in the State of sale, it might seem most logical to make these the relevant laws. On such a model, a factory located in France could gain exemption from local product

---

[54] See Ch. 14.   [55] See Chs. 17 and 18.
[56] See *Verein gegen Unwesen in Handel und Gewerbe Köln* v. *Mars GmbH*, C-470/93, EU:C:1995:224.

regulations by declaring that it was manufacturing for export. However, this approach has great practical difficulties. First, it fragments the production process, by requiring producers to make different goods for different markets, as discussed above, and since those goods could not be resold to other States with different rules it fragments the internal market too. Secondly, it is hard to supervise. On the whole, supervision of production facilities is easier than of the marketplace. A factory is fixed, hard to hide and easy to inspect. By contrast, if liqueurs have not been subject to any French laws or control because they were declared to be destined for the German market, then the German authorities will want to conduct very thorough controls before admitting them, creating new and significant barriers to movement which, given the openness of borders, may be hard to enforce. There is a real risk that a choice for State of destination regulation would result in products or services actually escaping any effective supervision.

The Court of Justice in *Cassis* therefore made a choice for regulation by the country of origin. It is now a general rule of free movement law that products or services are primarily subject to the laws of their origin State, and should not, except where mandatory requirements apply, be subjected to further requirements based on destination State law.[57] Joerges has described *Cassis de Dijon* as creating a meta-norm which both parties to a free movement conflict (France and Germany in this case) can accept, and which mediates between their different laws.[58]

This approach has great legal elegance. It has been described as a principle of tolerance, akin to multiculturalism in products, because it requires Member States to accept products that are different from those they are used to domestically.[59] It embodies an idea of 'different but equal'. Moreover, in a few lines it provides a framework for an entire internal market.[60] Using the ideas in *Cassis* it is possible to implement trade between States while still allowing Member States to maintain their own laws and avoiding the need for harmonisation.

Yet, it is open to powerful criticism from various perspectives. It has been claimed that applying mutual recognition results in non-economic concerns being trumped by free trade; that it crushes diversity and replaces it by a deregulated and uniform marketplace;[61] and yet also that it is ineffective in creating free trade, that mutual recognition is too open-ended and abstract to be effectively applied by national courts and authorities.[62] It can even therefore be seen as a stalking horse for harmonisation, an approach to free movement that is apparently based on local diversity of regulation but by its very failure to create a market turns into a justification for centralised rules.[63]

---

[57] See *Gouda* v. *Commissariat voor de Media*, C-288/89, EU:C:1991:323; Directive 2006/123/EC on services in the internal market [2006] OJ L 376/36; see Ch. 17.

[58] See C. Joerges and J. Neyer, 'Deliberative Supranationalism Revisited', EUI Working Paper 2006/20, 25.

[59] See Nicolaidis and Shaffer, n. 52 above, 317; G. Davies, 'Is Mutual Recognition an Alternative to Harmonisation: Lessons on Trade and Tolerance of Diversity from the EU' in F. Ortino and L. Bartels (eds.), *Regional Trade Agreements and the WTO* (Oxford University Press, 2006) 265–80.

[60] For a very thorough discussion of the policy issues, see the special edition of the *Journal of European Public Policy* on mutual recognition: S. Schmidt (ed.), 'Mutual Recognition as a New Mode of Governance' (2007) 14(5) *JEPP*; K. Armstrong, 'Mutual Recognition' in C. Barnard and J. Scott (eds.), *The Law of the European Single Market* (Oxford, Hart, 2002) 225.

[61] See K. Alter and S. Meunier-Aitsahalia, 'Judicial Politics in the European Community: European Integration and the Pathbreaking Cassis de Dijon Decision' (1994) 26 *Comparative Political Studies* 535.

[62] See J. Pelkmans, 'Mutual Recognition in Goods: On Promises and Disillusions' (2007) 14 *JEPP* 699; Commission Report to the Council, Parliament and ESC, 'Second Biennial Report on the Application of the Principle of Mutual Recognition in the Single Market', COM(2002)419 final, 23 July 2002.

[63] See Davies, n. 59 above; W. Kerber and R. van den Bergh, 'Mutual Recognition Revisited: Misunderstandings, Inconsistencies, and a Suggested Reinterpretation' (2008) 61 *Kyklos* 447.

The first criticism is that standards are not in fact equal in different States. While it may be true that all Member States generally ensure that their products are adequately safe, it is a fantasy to think that the quality guaranteed by different standards is the same. Some States have a *laissez-faire* approach to quality regulation, and are content to let the consumer decide what she is prepared to pay for. Others are strict, as will be seen in the subsequent section. Admitting goods made according to foreign laws therefore undermines the quality standards in force in strict States. The populations of those countries are no longer able to express their collective preference for a certain kind of strictly regulated market in which low quality goods are prohibited. Trade trumps both local democracy and product quality.[64]

Moreover, mutual recognition has potential economic effects. The Court of Justice is quite clear that it is not the product rule as such which is contrary to Article 34 TFEU, but its application to imports. Thus, Germany is able to apply its 25 per cent rule to domestically made liqueurs, just not to foreign ones. But this puts German producers at a distinct disadvantage. Alcohol is a significant part of the cost of such liqueurs (one of the reasons for the conflict), so foreign liqueur will probably be cheaper. The German Government is then faced with the choice between abandoning its rule for domestic producers, and moving to a *laissez-faire* marketplace, or continuing to enforce the rule and risking domestic producers being priced out of the market. Ultimately, as the German Government argued in the case, there is a risk that the lowest standard State provides the *de facto* standard everywhere; their exports are the cheapest products in every shop in Europe. A regulatory race to the bottom is then feared as other States abandon their own rules. In fact, as discussed in Chapter 14, it is notable that this does not always, or even often, happen but the risk is real in some circumstances.

The discussion above may suggest that mutual recognition tends to sacrifice non-economic concerns in the cause of free trade. However, the principle is also criticised from a free trade perspective, with the claim being that in practice it is ineffective.[65] The problem is that applying *Cassis* entails balancing interests, since the possibility of derogations, the mandatory requirements, does exist. This balancing is so politically laden that it is seen as a heavy burden on national judges and authorities, who may well be inclined to defer to national laws and quickly concede their necessity when faced with governmental arguments to that effect.[66] Expecting national bodies to set aside national law to an extent sufficient to really create a single market is perhaps unrealistic. Thus, it can be argued that mutual recognition has not turned out to be the legal panacea it may seem, and leaves many obstacles to movement in place.[67] In practice, what often happens is that litigation over national product rules identifies a particular problem, at which point the Commission may begin the process of harmonisation. *Cassis de Dijon* itself did not lead to a European market in which alcohol products are freely traded on the basis of that mutual recognition. On the contrary, shortly afterwards harmonising legislation on alcohol levels was adopted.

---

[64] Kerber and van den Bergh, n. 63 above; H.-C. von Heydebrand u.d. Lasa, 'Free Movement of Foodstuffs, Consumer Protection and Food Standards in the European Community: Has the Court Got it Wrong?' (1991) *ELRev* 391.

[65] See Pelkmans, n. 62 above.

[66] See M. Jarvis, *The Application of EC Law by National Courts: The Free Movement of Goods* (Oxford University Press, 1998) 220–1.

[67] See particularly N. Bernard, 'On the Art of Not Mixing One's Drinks: *Dassonville* and *Cassis de Dijon* Revisited' in M. Poiares Maduro and L. Azoulai (eds.), *The Past and Future of EU Law* (Oxford, Hart, 2010) 456.

Most of these abstract criticisms depend for their force upon the extent to which mandatory requirements actually limit the general rule of mutual recognition. It is thus these requirements, rather than the general principle, which have been the concrete subject matter of post-*Cassis* legal debate.

(ii) Mandatory Requirements

In *Cassis de Dijon*, the Court of Justice provided a list of the sorts of reasons which might justify restricting the free movement of goods. It mentioned the 'effectiveness of fiscal supervision, the protection of public health, the fairness of commercial transactions and the defence of the consumer'. This list was broadened in subsequent cases, and the category of mandatory requirements is now considered to be open-ended. A formulation which is often cited by the Court was used in *Bellamy and English Shop*, where the Court had to consider whether Belgium was justified in applying its food labelling laws to imported English foodstuffs, which the Belgians claimed was necessary to protect the consumer.

> ### *Criminal Proceedings Against Bellamy and English Shop Wholesale*, C-123/00, EU: C:2001:214
>
> 18   In that regard, it should be borne in mind that, in the absence of harmonisation of legislation, obstacles to free movement of goods which are the consequence of applying, to goods coming from other Member States where they are lawfully manufactured and marketed, rules that lay down requirements to be met by such goods (such as those relating to designation, form, size, weight, composition, presentation, labelling, packaging) constitute measures having equivalent effect which are prohibited by Article [34 TFEU], even if those rules apply without distinction to all products, unless their application can be justified by a public-interest objective taking precedence over the free movement of goods

An equally applicable rule restricting movement may therefore be justified by any reason within the umbrella concept of the 'public interest'. The Court of Justice has set certain limits to this concept, such as the rule that purely economic reasons may not be relied upon,[68] and these limits are discussed further in Chapter 19. However, the class of legitimate justifications remains broad. Nevertheless, in practice the majority of cases have concerned consumer protection, while those concerning environmental protection also form an important group. These are looked at in the next two sections, to show how the Court determines what is justified and, in particular, what is proportionate.

The legal status of these judicially invented derogations is odd. Article 36 TFEU provides for exceptions to Article 34 where necessary to protect really important interests such as public health or security.[69] Yet when the Court of Justice referred to mandatory requirements in *Cassis*, it was not offering a broad interpretation of Article 36. On the contrary, it was creating a new class of exception to free movement, existing alongside and in addition to the exceptions in the Treaty.[70]

---

[68] *Campus Oil* v. *Minister for Industry and Energy*, 72/83, EU:C:1984:256; J. Snell, 'Economic Aims as Justifications for Restrictions on Free Movement' in A. Schrauwen (ed.), *The Rule of Reason: Rethinking Another Classic of European Legal Doctrine* (Groningen, Europa Law Publishing, 2005).

[69] See Ch. 19.   [70] See P. Craig and G. de Búrca, *EU Law*, 4th edn (Oxford University Press, 2006) 706–7.

These exceptions are in one sense broader than Article 36: they cover a wider range of interests. However, they are narrower than Article 36 in that they only apply to equally applicable measures.[71] Where a measure discriminates directly, an appeal to the doctrine of mandatory requirements may not be made.

(a) Consumer Protection

The most common justification for applying national product rules to imports is the protection of the consumer. One of the most well-known examples is the *German Beer* case.[72] The Reinheitsgebot, a centuries-old German rule defining the ingredients permitted in beer, was challenged as contrary to Article 34. Many foreign beers used ingredients not on the list, varying from rice to various chemical additives, and so were denied access to the German market under the name beer – they could be sold under some other name, say 'rice-chemical alcoholic beverage', but this was clearly unattractive. The German Government claimed that the rule was necessary to prevent consumers being deceived about what they were buying: the German consumer had certain expectations, which beers made from non-conforming ingredients did not fulfil. The impure brew was simply not, in German eyes, beer.

Commission v. *Germany (German Beer)*, 178/84, EU:C:2001:214

29 It is not contested that the application of article 10 of the Biersteuergesetz to beers from other Member States in whose manufacture raw materials other than malted barley have been lawfully used, in particular rice and maize, is liable to constitute an obstacle to their importation into the Federal Republic of Germany.

30 Accordingly, it must be established whether the application of that provision may be justified by imperative requirements relating to consumer protection.

31 The German government's argument that article 10 of the Biersteuergesetz is essential in order to protect German consumers because, in their minds, the designation 'Bier' is inseparably linked to the beverage manufactured solely from the ingredients laid down in article 9 of the Biersteuergesetz must be rejected.

32 Firstly, consumers' conceptions which vary from one Member State to the other are also likely to evolve in the course of time within a Member State. The establishment of the common market is, it should be added, one of the factors that may play a major contributory role in that development. Whereas rules protecting consumers against misleading practices enable such a development to be taken into account, legislation of the kind contained in article 10 of the Biersteuergesetz prevents it from taking place. As the court has already held in another context (Case 170/78 *Commission* v. *United Kingdom*), the legislation of a Member State must not 'crystallize given consumer habits so as to consolidate an advantage acquired by national industries concerned to comply with them'.

33 Secondly, in the other Member States of the Community the designations corresponding to the German designation 'Bier' are generic designations for a fermented beverage manufactured from malted barley, whether malted barley on its own or with the addition of rice or maize. The same approach is taken in Community law as can be seen from heading no. 22.03 of the common customs tariff. The German legislature itself utilizes the designation 'Bier' in that way in article 9(7) and (8) of the Biersteuergesetz in order to refer to beverages not complying with the manufacturing rules laid down in article 9(1) and (2).

---

[71] *Gilli and Andres*, 788/79, EU:C:1980:171. [72] *Commission* v. *Germany (German Beer)*, 178/84, EU:C:1987:126.

34 The German designation 'Bier' and its equivalents in the languages of the other Member States of the Community may therefore not be restricted to beers manufactured in accordance with the rules in force in the Federal Republic of Germany.

35 It is admittedly legitimate to seek to enable consumers who attribute specific qualities to beers manufactured from particular raw materials to make their choice in the light of that consideration. However, as the court has already emphasized, that possibility may be ensured by means which do not prevent the importation of products which have been lawfully manufactured and marketed in other Member States and, in particular, 'by the compulsory affixing of suitable labels giving the nature of the product sold'. By indicating the raw materials utilized in the manufacture of beer 'such a course would enable the consumer to make his choice in full knowledge of the facts and would guarantee transparency in trading and in offers to the public'. It must be added that such a system of mandatory consumer information must not entail negative assessments for beers not complying with the requirements of article 9 of the Biersteuergesetz.

The Court of Justice accepted that consumers may have preferences, for example for pure beer, and that their ability to satisfy these preferences was important and deserved protection. However, it took the view that prohibiting the sale as 'beer' of any non-conforming product was disproportionate. Consumers could be adequately protected by a labelling requirement: if it was clear from the label which ingredients the beer contained and whether it was made according to the purity rules then this was sufficient consumer protection, and was more proportionate because it had far less effect on interstate trade. It is easier for foreign beer producers to amend their labels than their product.

This is the Court's consistent approach. It insists that matters of quality and preference, rather than safety or health, do not need to be dealt with by bans, but can be more proportionately addressed by rules on labels.[73] Indeed, its usual standpoint is that protecting the quality of goods as such does not justify a restriction on free movement.[74] This is a coherent part of the Court's relatively liberal philosophy of consumer protection, which assumes that if adequate information is available to consumers they are then able to make their own decisions about quality.[75] This contrasts with the more paternalistic approach reflected in the rules challenged in *Cassis* and *German Beer*, where the State determined what consumers could buy and what they could not.

This information-based approach assumes that consumers read labels, and are reasonably circumspect.[76] It is vulnerable to the criticism that in fact these assumptions are not true, and consumers will simply seize a product without realising that it is not quite what they are used to.[77] On the other hand, this law does not just aim to protect consumers, but also to construct them. The

---

[73] See e.g. *Ran* v. *De Schmedt*, 261/81, EU:C:1982:382; *Drei Glocken*, 407/85, EU:C:1988:401; see also *Gilli and Andres*, 788/79, EU:C:1980:171. See also *Alfa Vita Vassilopoulos AE and Carrefour Marinopoulos AE* v. *Elliniko Dimosio and Nomarchiaki Aftodioikisi Ioanninon*, C-158–9/04, EU:C:2006:562, para. 23.

[74] *Kakavetsos-Fragkopoulos*, C-161/09, EU:C:2011:110, para. 54; *Alfa Vita Vassilopoulos AE and Carrefour Marinopoulos AE* v. *Elliniko Dimosio and Nomarchiaki Aftodioikisi Ioanninon*, C-158–9/04, EU:C:2006:562, para. 23.

[75] See S. Weatherill, *EU Consumer Law and Policy* (Northampton, Edward Elgar, 2005); M. Radeideh, *Fair Trading in EC Law: Information and Consumer Choice in the Internal Market* (Groningen, Europa Law Publishing, 2005).

[76] See *Gut Springenheide*, C-210/96, EU:C:1988:369; *Commission* v. *Germany*, C-51/94, EU:C:1995352; *Fietje*, 27/80, EU:C:1980:293.

[77] See L. W. Gormley, 'The Consumer Acquis and the Internal Market' (2009) 20 *EBLRev* 409; von Heydebrand u.d. Lasa, n. 64 above; C. Macmaolain, 'Waiter, There's a Fly in my Soup. Yes Sir, that's E120: Disparities between Actual Individual Behaviour and Regulating Labelling for the Average Consumer in EU Law' (2008) 45 *CMLRev* 1147; Radeideh, n. 75 above; H. Unberath and A. Johnston, 'The Double-Headed Approach of the ECJ Concerning Consumer Protection'

European consumer may not be used to diversity, but the goals of the internal market are that she should become so. This means she will need to get used to making decisions on the basis of information, rather than having products selected for her by the State. Whether this is necessarily an improvement in quality of life is another issue, but it is a plausible corollary of the free trade agreement which Article 34 TFEU represents.[78] It may also be remembered that this approach only applies to quality: where there is a genuine health risk, the Court of Justice is much more deferential to national rules.[79]

This tension between the consumer as she is, and as she must become, is often made visible by questions of naming. The German Government had argued that foreign beer, using different ingredients, was not 'beer' as Germans understood it. Similar arguments have been made about products including pasta, chocolate and foie gras.[80] Yet as paragraph 32 of the judgment above notes, consumer behaviour and expectations are not fixed, but changing, and so the law should not try to entrench them as they are, but provide a framework within which they can develop.

The Court preferred to understand 'beer' in the context of other national definitions and the EU customs definition. It explained the limits of this naming cosmopolitanism in the foie gras case.

Commission v. France, C–184/96, EU:C:1998:495

23 So far as concerns the argument based on the necessity to prevent offences with respect to false descriptions, the Court, in its judgment in *Deserbais*, did not exclude the possibility that Member States could require those concerned to alter the denomination of a foodstuff where a product presented under a particular denomination is so different, as regards its composition or production, from the products generally known under that denomination in the Community that it cannot be regarded as falling within the same category (Case 286/86 *Ministère Public* v. *Deserbais* [1988] ECR 4907).

24 Nonetheless, the mere fact that a product does not wholly conform to the requirements laid down in national legislation on the composition of certain foodstuffs with a particular denomination does not mean that its marketing can be prohibited.

If someone tried to market a generic paté as foie gras, it would be justifiable to prevent this on consumer protection grounds. However, the fact that foie gras is made in slightly different ways in other places is not enough to justify a prohibition on using the name.

The concept of the informed and circumspect consumer is central to the Court's thinking about consumer protection, and leads naturally to labelling as the most appropriate method for addressing consumer quality concerns. Yet even labelling requirements may be disproportionate. Because the label is a physical part of the product, national labelling rules are themselves product

---

(2007) 44 *CMLRev* 1237; S. Weatherill, 'Recent Case Law Concerning the Free Movement of Goods: Mapping the Frontiers of Market Deregulation' (1999) 36 *CMLRev* 51; Weatherill, n. 75 above.

[78] G. Davies, 'Internal Market Adjudication and the Quality of Life in Europe' (2015) 21(2) *Columbia Journal of European Law*, 289.

[79] See p. 836.

[80] *Gilli and Andres*, 788/79, EU:C:1980:171; *Commission* v. *France (Gold)*, C–166/03, EU:C:2004:422; *Commission* v. *Spain (Spanish Chocolate)*, C–12/00, EU:C:2003:21; *Commission* v. *Italy (Chocolate)*, C–14/00, EU:C:2003:22; *Commission* v. *Spain*, C–358/01, EU:C:2003:599; see also *Commission* v. *France*, C–6/02, EU:C:2003:136.

rules in the *Cassis* sense, and so must still be justified. That means that the requirements imposed on a product label must not go beyond what is genuinely required.[81]

Where the traditionally protective European approach to product regulation is translated to labels this can be a challenge. In *Clinique*, for example, the German Government objected to the marketing of cosmetics under that name, because it was too similar to *Klinik*, the German word for hospital.[82] Consumers might therefore think that the products were medically approved, and believe that they really would look younger or more beautiful if they used them. The Court of Justice disagreed. In the circumstances (the products were sold not by pharmacists but in shops selling make-up), it felt the dangers did not justify the trade-hindering effects of the rule.

Most labelling challenges have, however, arisen where the requirements were discriminatory in some way, diminishing the marketing appeal of foreign goods. For example, in the *Irish Souvenirs* case, Ireland proposed that souvenirs not made in Ireland be stamped with their country of production or with the word 'foreign'.[83] The Court has found in several cases that a requirement to indicate the country of production, even if it applies to all goods, may have the effect of steering consumers towards national goods, while it is not in fact necessary information.[84]

(b) Protection of the Environment

Environmental issues are often dealt with under Article 36 TFEU, and are discussed further in Chapter 19. However, the protection of the environment has also been recognised as a mandatory requirement, especially in the context of recycling schemes and their effect on trade.

These recycling cases have been about soft drinks containers. In each case a State has imposed obligations on producers related to the types of containers they used for their drinks. In *Commission* v. *Denmark*, a system was successfully challenged in which only certain types of soft drinks containers were permitted in Denmark, the goal being to make recycling more efficient and practical.[85] Since this dramatically limited the possibilities for importing soft drinks from elsewhere in Europe where many different kinds of containers were in use, the rule was disproportionate. The reasoning of the Court of Justice was that it was not necessary to limit the types of containers, since the goal of promoting recycling could be met by other means.

The case was heavily criticised.[86] While many different kinds of containers can be recycled, this is expensive. A recycling scheme is most efficient if it only has to deal with a limited range of packaging types. In reality, recycling will be successful if it is not too expensive, and so the Danish considered that their strict limits on container types were an essential part of increasing the amount of recycling. The Court, however, simply ignored this, suggesting that environmental protection was not being taken seriously, and would be subordinated to trade.

---

[81] *Commission* v. *Belgium*, C-217/99, EU:C:2000:638; *Commission* v. *France*, C-55/99, EU:C:2000:693.
[82] *Verband Sozialer Wettbewerb* v. *Clinique Laboratories*, C-315/92, EU:C:1994:34.
[83] *Commission* v. *Ireland (Irish Souvenirs)*, 113/80, EU:C:1981:139.
[84] *Ibid.*; *Commission* v. *United Kingdom of Great Britain and Northern Ireland (Marks of Origin)*, 207/83, EU:C:1985:161.
[85] *Commission* v. *Denmark*, 302/86, EU:C:1988:421.
[86] See J. Scott, *EC Environmental Law* (London, Longman, 1998) 69–72, quoted in J. Holder and M. Lee, *Environmental Protection: Law and Policy* (Cambridge University Press, 2007) 179; H. Temmink, 'From Danish Bottles to Danish Bees: The Dynamics of Free Movement of Goods and Environmental Protection – A Case Law Analysis' (2000) 1 *YEEL* 61.

Recently, however, it has been more deferential to environmental claims. In *Radlberger Getränkegesellschaft*, Germany required producers selling soft drinks in non-reusable containers to set up a deposit-and-return scheme, whereby they would take back the waste packaging they generated, and deal with it themselves.[87] This probably burdened non-German producers more, since they used a higher proportion of non-recyclable packaging than German ones, and because returning containers to a foreign production site would probably be more expensive.

Nevertheless, the Court accepted the rules because they served an important environmental goal. It did insist, in the name of proportionality, that producers be given a reasonable amount of time to adapt to the new rules and that the system be so constructed that producers were in practice able to participate and comply. This rather procedural approach to proportionality is also found in other cases, where the Court has preferred to examine whether the State has taken account of all interests and considered alternatives, rather than engaging too deeply in the substantive policy choice.[88]

4 SELLING ARRANGEMENTS AND *KECK*

The acceptance in *Cassis* that equally applicable rules could be MEQRs led to cases testing the limits of this principle, applying it to any kind of measure which could be argued to have a negative effect on import quantities. Most well-known, the rules on Sunday trading in the United Kingdom were challenged as contrary to Article 34 TFEU: if shops could open on Sundays they could sell more goods, and some of those goods would be imported.[89] *Ergo*, requiring shops to close on Sundays limited imports.

This turns a Treaty Article that is apparently about goods into a tool for policing wider socio-economic regulation, which brings with it risks of constitutional discontent among the Member States. Moreover, it is inefficient. In the Sunday trading cases, the Court of Justice unsurprisingly found that the measures were justified by legitimate social goals, and therefore not contrary to the Treaty. All that was happening was that many creative cases were being brought, but they were not being won. Such a broad reading of the Treaty was not therefore opening up the internal market or increasing trade. It was just increasing work for the Court.

In *Keck*, the Court of Justice finally set a limit to the kinds of equally applicable rules which could be MEQRs. It excluded one group, which it called selling arrangements. These, it said, were simply outside the scope of the Treaty, as long as they were in fact equal in impact on both domestic goods and imports.

---

[87] *Radlberger Getränkegesellschaft* v. *Land Baden-Württemberg*, C-309/02, EU:C:2004:799; see also the almost identical *Commission* v. *Germany*, C-463/01, EU:C:2004:797, decided on the same day.

[88] *Commission* v. *Austria*, C-28/09, EU:C:2011:854; *Philippe Bonnarde* v. *Agence de Services et de Paiement*, C-433/10, EU:C:2011:641. S. Prechal, 'Free Movement and Procedural Requirements: Proportionality Reconsidered' (2008) 35 *LIEI* 201.

[89] See e.g. *Torfaen Borough Council* v. *B & Q*, C-145/88, EU:C:1989:593; *Stoke-on-Trent and Norwich City Council* v. *B & Q*, C-169/91, EU:C:1992:519; for full discussion see C. Barnard, *The Substantive Law of the EU*, 3rd edn (Oxford University Press, 2010) 117–23.

Keck and Mithouard, C–267–8/91, EU:C:1993:905

11 By virtue of Article [34 TFEU], quantitative restrictions on imports and all measures having equivalent effect are prohibited between Member States. The Court has consistently held that any measure which is capable of directly or indirectly, actually or potentially, hindering intra-Community trade constitutes a measure having equivalent effect to a quantitative restriction.

12 National legislation imposing a general prohibition on resale at a loss is not designed to regulate trade in goods between Member States.

13 Such legislation may, admittedly, restrict the volume of sales, and hence the volume of sales of products from other Member States, insofar as it deprives traders of a method of sales promotion. But the question remains whether such a possibility is sufficient to characterize the legislation in question as a measure having equivalent effect to a quantitative restriction on imports.

14 In view of the increasing tendency of traders to invoke Article [34 TFEU] as a means of challenging any rules whose effect is to limit their commercial freedom even where such rules are not aimed at products from other Member States, the Court considers it necessary to re-examine and clarify its case-law on this matter.

15 It is established by the case-law beginning with '*Cassis de Dijon*' that, in the absence of harmonization of legislation, obstacles to free movement of goods which are the consequence of applying, to goods coming from other Member States where they are lawfully manufactured and marketed, rules that lay down requirements to be met by such goods (such as those relating to designation, form, size, weight, composition, presentation, labelling, packaging) constitute measures of equivalent effect prohibited by Article [34 TFEU].

   This is so even if those rules apply without distinction to all products unless their application can be justified by a public-interest objective taking precedence over the free movement of goods.

16 By contrast, contrary to what has previously been decided, the application to products from other Member States of national provisions restricting or prohibiting certain selling arrangements is not such as to hinder directly or indirectly, actually or potentially, trade between Member States within the meaning of the *Dassonville* judgment, so long as those provisions apply to all relevant traders operating within the national territory and so long as they affect in the same manner, in law and in fact, the marketing of domestic products and of those from other Member States.

17 Provided that those conditions are fulfilled, the application of such rules to the sale of products from another Member State meeting the requirements laid down by that State is not by nature such as to prevent their access to the market or to impede access any more than it impedes the access of domestic products. Such rules therefore fall outside the scope of Article [34 TFEU].

18 Accordingly, the reply to be given to the national court is that Article [34 TFEU] of the EEC Treaty is to be interpreted as not applying to legislation of a Member State imposing a general prohibition on resale at a loss.

The rule that the Court of Justice lays down is that rules governing the way products are sold are not MEQRs within the meaning of *Dassonville* and Article 34 TFEU. Member States may therefore legislate however they like on matters such as advertising, shop opening hours, and sales techniques.[90] However, this is subject to the proviso that the measures taken must apply to all the traders in the relevant market, and must not have a greater effect on imports than they do on domestic goods or producers. If this is the case, then even measures concerning selling

---

[90] See n. 105 below for examples of the range of selling arrangements.

arrangements will be MEQRs. The usual approach then applies: such measures will be prohibited unless they are justified by a mandatory requirement or a Treaty exception.[91]

The reasoning provided by the Court for this position is that, it says, rules on selling arrangements do not generally have the effect of preventing access to the market for imports, nor of impeding it any more than is the case for domestic products. If a shop has to close on Sundays, or advertising of certain goods is prohibited, this does not actually prevent those goods being sold. It may have some effect on their sales, but in general this effect is the same for domestic and foreign goods. The implicit contrast is with product rules, which do tend to prevent non-conforming products reaching the market, and which tend to protect domestic goods from foreign competition.

Keck therefore interprets Article 34 to prohibit two things: (i) measures which have a greater effect on imports than on domestic products; and (ii) measures which effectively prevent certain imports from being sold.[92] This is compatible with the other goods case law, product rules and bans on use being examples of group (ii), and the other *Dassonville* unequal-effect cases falling within group (i).[93] Selective burdens, as in *Alfa Vita*, or *Sandström*, where use of jet-skis was restricted, would also presumptively fall within group (i) if the burden is in fact imposed on imports. The use of language by the Court, particularly market access, is sometimes inconsistent,[94] but the underlying idea of preventing Member States adopting measures which favour certain actors over others within the internal market is clear.

Keck is a controversial case, partly because it sets limits to Article 34, but also because its business sense has been doubted.[95] In reality, it has been argued, rules on advertising may have a greater effect on sales of goods than some product rules do. Adapting a product is not always expensive or difficult, while there may be contexts where an inability to advertise, or to sell via certain channels, or to offer certain kinds of discounts (all of which are selling arrangements) might seriously undermine a marketing campaign and make market access impractical. *Keck* is often considered to be a very formalistic approach to Article 34 TFEU. Instead of trying to distinguish between rules according to their actual effect on trade, it divides them into convenient, but somewhat arbitrary, groups which do not correspond to practical importance for the trader.

The advantage of this division is that it is relatively clear. In most cases it is easy to distinguish between a selling arrangement and a product rule, and both States and market actors are able to determine what their legal position is. An alternative interpretation of Article 34 which is sometimes put forward is that it should prohibit all measures which substantially restrict market access, relying on this effect to engage Article 34 and not *a priori* categories of measure. This interpretation is very close to the goals of the article, and has an obvious integrationist appeal, but would result in a very open and vague rule. It is, moreover, open to question whether such an

---

[91] See e.g. *Burmanjer*, C-20/03, EU:C:2005:307; *A-Punckt Schmuckhandels*, C-441/04, EU:C:2006:141.

[92] *Keck and Mithouard*, C-267–8/91, EU:C:1993:905, paras. 16 and 17.   [93] Gormley, n. 24 above.

[94] P. Pecho, 'Good-Bye *Keck*: A Comment on the Remarkable Judgment in *Commission v. Italy*' (2009) 36 *LIEI* 257; R. Schutze, 'Of Types and Tests: Towards a Unitary Doctrinal Framework for Article 34 TFEU?' (2016) 41 *ELRev* 826.

[95] L. W. Gormley, 'Two Years after *Keck*' (1996) 19 *Fordham Int'l LJ* 866; S. Weatherill, 'After *Keck*: Some Thoughts on How to Clarify the Clarification' (1996) 33 *CMLRev* 885; C. Barnard, 'Fitting the Remaining Pieces into the Goods and Persons Jigsaw' (2001) 26 *ELRev* 35; A. Tryfonidou, 'Was *Keck* a Half-Baked Solution after All?' (2007) 34 *LIEI* 167. Cf. L. Rossi, 'Economic Analysis of Article 28 after the *Keck* Judgment' (2006) 7(5) *German LJ* 479.

open norm would be effective in practice because it would be so difficult to apply in an apparently apolitical way, perhaps causing national judges to be shy of using it forcefully.[96]

There is also a market logic to the categorisation created by *Keck*. Unlike product rules, selling arrangements do not impose a double burden on imports, nor do selling arrangements require products to be adapted at all, so there is no question of excluding non-conforming goods. There is a fundamental difference between the market effects of selling arrangements and the market effects of product rules, which explains why the Court chose the State of production as the default regulatory State for rules concerning product composition, but the State of sale as the default regulator for rules concerning sale.[97]

In any case, *Keck* has resisted criticism from many commentators and is still part of the law.[98] Its apparent clarity and ease of use are among the major reasons for its resilience. Yet, while most of the time it is fairly easy to see whether a measure is a selling arrangement and whether it has an unequal effect, there are cases where this becomes very difficult.

(i) Notion of a Selling Arrangement

The distinction between a selling arrangement and a product rule was laid down in *Familia-press*.[99] A product rule is a measure which requires some physical aspect of the product or its packaging or labelling to be changed, while a selling arrangement is concerned only with the way in which goods are sold or marketed. Measures conforming to neither definition are to be considered under *Dassonville*.

The boundary between categories becomes difficult when measures are concerned with the sale of particular types of products, for example a rule restricting sale of alcohol with a percentage above 25 per cent to licensed shops. Is that a product rule, because it is to do with the amount of alcohol in the drink, or a selling arrangement, because it regulates the place where the product is sold? The Court of Justice seems to find rules like this to be product rules, because the obligation or burden that they contain is specifically linked to the physical characteristics of the product. There is thus a pressure, if not an absolute requirement, on producers to amend their product to avoid the burdensome rule.

For example, in *Schwarz*, an Austrian rule was in issue which prohibited the sale of unwrapped bubble gum from vending machines.[100] This was said to be unhygienic. The Court found that this was a product rule because those 'importers wishing to put those goods up for sale in Austria have to package them'. A producer who wanted to sell bubble gum to vending machine operators in Austria would have to make adjustments to her production process. Similarly, in *Dynamic Medien*, a rule prohibiting the sale by mail order of DVDs without an age-classification sticker was found to be a product rule, because the rule, while restricting the method of sale, was linked to a physical part of the packaging.[101]

---

[96] See D. Wilsher, 'Does *Keck* Discrimination Make Any Sense? An Assessment of the Non-discrimination Principle within the European Single Market' (2008) 33 *ELRev* 3.

[97] See also M. Poiares Maduro, *We the Court* (Oxford, Hart, 1998); Cf. D. Regan, 'An Outsider's View of "Dassonville" and "Cassis de Dijon": On Interpretation and Policy' in M. Poiares Maduro and L. Azoulai (eds.), *The Past and Future of EU Law* (Oxford, Hart, 2010) 465.

[98] *Pelckmans Turnhout*, C-483/12, EU:C:2014:304. See also I. Lianos, 'In Memoriam *Keck*: The Reformation of the EU Law on the Free Movement of Goods' (2015) 40 *ELRev* 225.

[99] *Familiapress* v. *Heinrich Bauer Verlag*, C-368/95, EU:C:1997:325. See also *Sapod Audic*, C-159/00, EU:C:2002:343.

[100] *Georg Schwarz* v. *Bürgermeister der Landeshauptstadt Salzburg*, C-366/04, EU:C:2005:719.

[101] *Dynamic Medien Vertriebs GmbH* v. *Avides Media AG*, C-244/06, EU:C:2008:85.

By contrast, *Morellato* concerned an Italian law on semi-baked bread.[102] This is bread that is bought by shops as half-baked frozen dough. The shops then finish baking it in their own ovens. This enables them to sell warm fresh bread, without having all the facilities for making bread from scratch. The process is quite controversial in some countries, because it threatens the traditional artisanal baker, and enables all kinds of shops to apparently sell their own freshly baked bread. It was in this context that Italy required shops selling bread made by this process to prepackage it in bags with labels clearly indicating its nature. The measures informed the consumer, but also distinguished the bread from bread made on the premises, which did not need to be packaged, allowing this latter to preserve some distinctive aura of naturalness.

The Court of Justice found that the measure was a selling arrangement.

Morellato, C–416/00, EU:C:2003:475

32 The distinctive feature of the main proceedings is that the product put on sale by Mr Morellato was imported at a stage when its production process was not yet finished. In order to be able to market the product in Italy as bread ready for consumption, it was necessary to complete the baking of the pre-baked bread imported from France.

33 The fact that a product must, to a certain extent, be transformed after importation does not in itself preclude a requirement relating to its marketing from falling within the scope of application of Article [34 TFEU]. It is possible that, as in the main proceedings, the imported product is not simply a component or ingredient of another product but in reality constitutes the product that is intended for marketing as soon as a simple transformation process has been carried out.

34 In such a situation, the relevant question is whether the requirement for prior packaging laid down in the legislation of the Member State of import makes it necessary to alter the product in order to comply with that requirement.

35 In the present case, nothing in the file indicates that it was necessary for the pre-baked bread, as imported into Italy, to be altered in order to comply with that requirement.

36 In those circumstances, the requirement for prior packaging, since it relates only to the marketing of the bread which results from the final baking of pre-baked bread, is in principle such as to fall outside the scope of Article [34 TFEU], provided that it does not in reality constitute discrimination against imported products.

As in *Schwarz* the product had to be packaged before it could be sold. There was thus a physical adjustment necessary. However, the difference was that in *Schwarz* the nature of the adjustment was such that it could only realistically be done by the producer. One could not expect vending machine operators to put balls of bubble gum in individual sealed plastic bags. *Schwarz* therefore imposed a production burden. However, in *Morellato*, there was no need for the producer of the semi-baked dough to change anything at all. While shops had to put the bread in bags, they had no need to get those bags from the dough producers, and the packaging had to be done by the shops, not by the producers, since, as the Court said, the production process was incomplete when the dough was delivered – it still had to be partly baked. Thus, although *Morellato* is superficially similar to *Schwarz* and *Dynamic Medien*, it is very different from the perspective of the producer of the imported product. These cases highlight that the question determining

---

[102] *Morellato*, C–416/00, EU:C:2003:475.

whether a measure is a selling arrangement or a product rule is whether that producer is required, or pressured, to change some physical aspect of the product that she ships.

On the other hand, the rule in *Alfa Vita* requiring bakery facilities, or the rules at issue in the use cases, were not selling arrangements. Although they were not to do with the composition of products, and so were not product rules, they were also not about circumstances of sale either – *Alfa Vita* was about pre-sale circumstances, and the use cases about, well, use. The residual, catch-all category in free movement of goods is not the selling arrangement but the general, *Dassonville*-based, MEQR.[103]

(ii) Unequal Effect of Selling Arrangements

Where a selling arrangement has a greater effect on imported products than on domestic ones, it will fall within Article 34 TFEU, and will be prohibited unless justified. If it discriminates directly a justification must be sought in Article 36 TFEU, while if it is equally applicable but tends as a matter of fact to burden imports more then it may be saved by proportionate reliance on a mandatory requirement.

For some years after *Keck* was decided, this proviso was largely theoretical, with the Court of Justice being reluctant to investigate whether a measure might have some unequal effect.[104] There are good reasons for this. Restrictions on selling arrangements tend to keep markets static, but this tends to be to the advantage of incumbents and the disadvantage of market newcomers. Since the former are often national it can be argued that most selling arrangements in fact hurt importers most. An over-realistic approach to the proviso might therefore bring most selling arrangements back within Article 34 and once again extend that article beyond the judicial and constitutional comfort zone.

Nevertheless, in a growing number of recent cases the Court has recognised that the above logic could apply. Initial examples, including *De Agostini* and *Gourmet International*, involved advertising.[105] The former case concerned television advertising aimed at children, and the latter case concerned advertising of alcohol in Sweden. Bans on these, claimed the litigants, preserved domestic incumbents at the expense of foreign 'wannabe' market entrants. In *De Agostini*, the Court left it to the national court to decide whether the rule did, as a matter of fact, affect importers more. By contrast, in *Gourmet*, it felt able to take a view itself.

Konsumentombudsmannen (KO) v. *Gourmet International Products AB*, C–405/98, EU:C:2001:135

21 Even without its being necessary to carry out a precise analysis of the facts characteristic of the Swedish situation, which it is for the national court to do, the Court is able to conclude that, in the case of products like alcoholic beverages, the consumption of which is linked to traditional social practices and to local habits and customs, a prohibition of all advertising directed at consumers in the form of advertisements in

---

[103] See also *Klas Rosengren and Others* v. *Riksåklagaren*, C-170/04, EU:C:2007:313.

[104] See e.g. *Commission* v. *Greece (Greek Milk)*, C-391/92, EU:C:1995:199; *Punto Casa* v. *Sindaco del Comune di Capena*, C-69/93 and C-258/93, EU:C:1994:226.

[105] See also *Schutzverband* v. *TK-Heimdienst*, C-254/98, EU:C:2000:12; *Fachverband der Buchund Medienwirtschafl*, EU:C:2009:276; *Burmanjer*, C-20/03, EU:C:2006:307; *A-Punckt Schmuckhandels*, C-441/04, EU:C:2006:141; *Deutscher Apothekerverband* v. *DocMorris*, C-322/01, EU:C:2003:664; see also *Karner*, C-71/02, EU:C:2004:181.

the press, on the radio and on television, the direct mailing of unsolicited material or the placing of posters on the public highway is liable to impede access to the market by products from other Member States more than it impedes access by domestic products, with which consumers are instantly more familiar.

The key factor was the nature of the product. Alcoholic drinks are not usually bought only on price, but also on the basis of tradition, reputation, image and brand. Market entry is very difficult without the chance to speak directly to consumers via advertising.

Other recent examples of unequal selling arrangements include *Fachverband*, where the Court found that minimum book prices deprived imports, which might otherwise be cheaper than domestic goods, of an important competitive advantage.[106] Although the goal of the rule, protecting cultural diversity, was legitimate, a uniform price for domestic books and imports was disproportionate. The Court found that a minimum price could be set for imports, but it had to be one which reflected the possibility of cheaper production abroad. Although prices may seem obviously to be selling arrangements, in other recent cases the Court has addressed them without mentioning *Keck*, probably because with such rules the unequal effect is the norm, and so the presumption that Article 34 does not apply is no longer appropriate.[107]

Indeed, the exception may now be the rule, largely because of cases concerning restrictions on Internet sales. An example is *DocMorris*, in which the Court of Justice found that a prohibition on Internet sales of pharmaceutical products had an unequal effect because it was inevitably pharmacies at a distance who would be most affected, and these were most likely to be foreign.[108] Such a disadvantage for foreign traders will generally be the case where Internet restrictions are involved, so that the original idea of *Keck*, that in most cases there is no need to examine selling arrangements in the light of Article 34, is now open to question. As a result, the Court in *Ker-Optika* reversed its presentation of the law.

Ker-Optika, C-108/09, EU:C:2010:725

51   For that reason, the application to products from other Member States of national provisions restricting or prohibiting certain selling arrangements is such as to hinder directly or indirectly, actually or potentially, trade between Member States for the purposes of the case-law flowing from *Dassonville*, unless those provisions apply to all relevant traders operating within the national territory and affect in the same manner, in law and in fact, the selling of domestic products and of those from other Member States. The application of such rules to the sale of products from another Member State meeting the requirements laid down by that State is by nature such as to prevent their access to the market or to impede such access more than it impedes the access of domestic products.

The Court here finds that selling arrangements *are* generally MEQRs unless they are equal in law and fact. That does not change the substance of the rule, but it implies that the evidential

---

[106] *Fachverband der Buch und Medienwirtschaft*, C-531/07, EU:C:2009:276.

[107] *Scotch Whisky*, C-333/14, EU:C:2015:845; *Deutsche Parkinson*, C-148/15, EU:C:2016:776; see generally A. MacCulloch, 'State Intervention in Pricing: An Intersection of EU Free Movement and Competition Law' (2017) 42 *ELRev* 190.

[108] *Deutscher Apothekerverband* v. *DocMorris*, C-322/01, EU:C:2003:664.

presumption may be changed: selling arrangements are to be seen as hindering trade unless the State shows that they affect everyone equally. The burden of proof is now probably on the State if it wishes to escape Article 34.[109]

5 ARTICLE 35 TFEU AND RESTRICTIONS ON EXPORTS

Article 35 TFEU is the equivalent of Article 34 for exports, and provides:

> Quantitative restrictions on exports, and all measures having equivalent effect, shall be prohibited between Member States.

The leading case, until recently, was *Groenveld*, which concerned a ban on the possession of horsemeat by sausage-makers in the Netherlands.[110] This was to make Dutch sausages acceptable in States where horsemeat was prohibited, by removing any risk of contamination. The measure was therefore aimed at protecting exports. However, a sausage producer who wanted to branch out into horsemeat sausages attempted to overturn the rule by claiming that it contravened Article 35. Since he could not possess horsemeat, he could not export horsemeat sausages.

Although the Dutch rule could be conceived of as a product rule in the *Cassis* sense, limiting the way sausages are produced, the Court of Justice found that the measure fell outside Article 35, since it applied to all producers and products, whether aimed for the domestic market or for export.

Case 15/79 *Groenveld BV* v. *Produktschap voor Vee en Vlees* [1979] ECR 3409

7 That provision concerns national measures which have as their specific object or effect the restriction of patterns of exports and thereby the establishment of a difference in treatment between the domestic trade of a Member State and its export trade in such a way as to provide a particular advantage for national production or for the domestic market of the state in question at the expense of the production or of the trade of other Member States.

This made clear that Article 35 has its own logic, and Article 34 reasoning cannot simply be transposed. A measure within Article 35 must provide some specific disadvantage for exports, by comparison with goods sold domestically, thereby encouraging domestic sales at the expense of export sales.

An example is *Ravil*, which concerned Italian rules on the sale of grated cheese.[111] The specific cheese in question, 'Grana Padano', could only be sold under that name in grated form if it had been grated within the region of production. If it was exported whole, and grated abroad, the name could not be used. This rule was enforced by means of bilateral conventions with other States, and it was one such with France that was at the centre of the case. The Court of Justice found that this was an Article 35 MEQR because it treated cheese which had been transported across a border for grating differently from cheese which had been transported within the Grana Padano region of Italy for grating, grating often being done not by the cheese producer but by the large retail firms who package and sell the grated cheese to consumers.

---

[109] But see *Pelckmans Turnhout*, C-483/12, EU:C:2014:304; *Visser Vastgoed*, C-360/15 and C-31/16, EU:C:2018:44, paras. 84–97.
[110] *Groenveld BV* v. *Produktschap voor Vee en Vlees*, 15/79, EU:C:1979:253.
[111] *Ravil* v. *Bellon Import*, C-469/00, EU:C:2003:295; see also *Belgium* v. *Spain*, C-388/95, EU:C:2000:244.

By contrast, *Gysbrechts* concerned a rule which applied without distinction between domestic sale and exports yet which the Court nevertheless found to be within Article 35.[112] It had long been assumed that equally applicable rules were not within Article 35, as a result of comments in *Groenveld* and the result in that case. It is now clear that this assumption was mistaken. Even an equally applicable rule may, as a matter of fact, disadvantage exports relative to domestic sales, contrary to Article 35.[113]

The rule in *Gysbrechts* prohibited those selling goods at a distance, for example by Internet, from requiring buyers to pay in advance or even to provide details of their payment card. Buyers were only required to pay once they had received the goods. This, of course, created a significant risk of non-payment. However, it is far simpler and cheaper for a firm to pursue a domestic customer for payment than one abroad. Thus, this rule had a more discouraging effect on sales abroad than on domestic sales.

Gysbrechts, C-205/07, EUC:2008:730

40 In that regard, the Court has classified as measures having equivalent effect to quantitative restrictions on exports national measures which have as their specific object or effect the restriction of patterns of exports and thereby the establishment of a difference in treatment between the domestic trade of a Member State and its export trade in such a way as to provide a particular advantage for national production or for the domestic market of the State in question, at the expense of the production or of the trade of other Member States.

41 In the main proceedings, it is clear, as the Belgian Government has moreover noted in its written observations, that the prohibition on requiring an advance payment deprives the traders concerned of an efficient tool with which to guard against the risk of non-payment. That is even more the case when the national provision at issue is interpreted as prohibiting suppliers from requesting that consumers provide their payment card number even if they undertake not to use it to collect payment before expiry of the period for withdrawal.

42 As is clear from the order for reference, the consequences of such a prohibition are generally more significant in cross-border sales made directly to consumers, in particular, in sales made by means of the Internet, by reason, *inter alia*, of the obstacles to bringing any legal proceedings in another Member State against consumers who default, especially when the sales involve relatively small sums.

43 Consequently, even if a prohibition such as that at issue in the main proceedings is applicable to all traders active in the national territory, its actual effect is nonetheless greater on goods leaving the market of the exporting Member State than on the marketing of goods in the domestic market of that Member State.

Article 35 therefore applies to all national measures which tend to make export sales more difficult or burdensome than domestic sales, whether or not this is by direct discrimination or simply as a matter of fact.[114] However, as with Article 34, equally applicable measures hindering exports may in principle be permitted if they are necessary to meet some mandatory requirement and are proportionate. In *Gysbrechts*, the Court found the prohibition on advance payment to be justified by consumer protection, while the prohibition on even asking for a payment card number was held to be disproportionate.

---

[112] *Gysbrechts*, C-205/07, EU:C:2008:730.
[113] A. Dawes, 'A Freedom Reborn? The New Yet Unclear Scope of Article 29' (2009) 34 *ELRev* 639.
[114] See *Grilli*, C-12/02, EU:C:2003:538; *New Valmar*, C-15/15, EU:C:2016:464.

Finally, in *Jersey Potatoes*, the Court of Justice ruled that measures hindering the movement of potatoes from Jersey to the United Kingdom were contrary to Article 35.[115] The oddity of the case is that Jersey is not an independent Member State, and free movement of goods law only applies to it via a Protocol as a result of its special ties with the United Kingdom. For the purposes of EU law, United Kingdom–Jersey trade is not cross-border.[116] However, the Court's reasoning was that the potatoes sent to the United Kingdom might in some cases be exported on to other Member States. Extrapolating the reasoning it would seem that internal barriers to movement may fall within Article 35 where they may hinder export by, for example, making access to ports or roads more difficult.[117]

FURTHER READING

B. Akkermans and E. Ramaekers, 'Free Movement of Goods and Property Law' (2013) 19 *European Law Journal* 237–66.

C. Barnard, 'What the *Keck* ? Balancing the Needs of the Single Market with State Regulatory Autonomy in the EU (and the US)' (2012) 2 *European Journal of Consumer Law/Revue Européenne de Droit de la Consommation* 201.

G. Davies, 'Understanding Market Access: Exploring the Economic Rationality of Different Conceptions of Free Movement Law' (2010) 11 *German Law Journal* 671.

G. Davies, 'The Court's Jurisprudence on Free Movement of Goods: Pragmatic Presumptions, Not Philosophical Principles' (2012) 2 *European Journal of Consumer Law/Revue Européenne de Droit de la Consommation* 25.

S. Enchelmaier, 'The Awkward Selling of a Good Idea, or a Traditionalist Interpretation of *Keck*' (2003) 22 *Yearbook of European Law* 259.

S. Enchelmaier, 'Horizontality: The Application of the Four Freedoms to Restrictions Imposed by Private Parties' in G. T. Davies, P. Koutrakos and J. Snell (eds,), *Research Handbook on EU Internal Market Law* (Cheltenham, Edward Elgar, 2017) 54.

L. W. Gormley, 'Inconsistencies and Misconceptions in the Free Movement of Goods' (2015) 6 *European Law Review* 925–39.

H.-C. von Heydebrand u.d. Lasa, 'Free Movement of Foodstuffs, Consumer Protection and Food Standards in the European Community: Has the Court Got it Wrong?' (1991) 16 *European Law Review* 391.

T. Horsley, 'Unearthing Buried Treasure: Art. 34 TFEU and the Exclusionary Rules' (2012) 37 *European Law Review* 734.

D. Regan, 'An Outsider's View of "Dassonville" and "Cassis de Dijon": On Interpretation and Policy' in M. Poiares Maduro and L. Azoulai (eds.), *The Past and Future of EU Law* (Oxford, Hart, 2010) 465.

J. Snell, 'The Notion of Market Access: A Concept or a Slogan?' (2010) 47 *Common Market Law Review* 437.

E. Spaventa, 'Leaving *Keck* Behind? The Free Movement of Goods after the Rulings in *Commission* v. *Italy* and *Mickelsson and Roos*' (2009) *European Law Review* 914.

S. Weatherill, *The Internal Market as a Legal Concept* (Oxford University Press, 2017).

---

[115] *Jersey Potatoes*, C-293/02, EU:C:2005:664.

[116] See P. Oliver and S. Enchelmaier, 'Free Movement of Goods: Recent Developments in the Case Law' (2007) 44 *CMLRev* 649.

[117] See similarly *Kakavetsos-Fragkopoulos*, C-161/09, EU:C:2011:110; *Aragonesa*, C-1/90 and C-176/90, EU:C:1991:327; *Carbonati Apuani*, C-72/03, EU:C:2004:506. See I. Kvesko, 'Is There Anything Left Outside the Reach of the European Court of Justice?' (2006) 33 *LIEI* 405.

17

The Free Movement of Services

CONTENTS

1 INTRODUCTION

Article 56 TFEU prohibits restrictions on the provision of services between Member States. Trade in services comprises the largest part of a modern economy, yet interstate trade is hindered by the high level of regulation applying to many service activities. EU law has taken a threefold approach to breaking down these barriers: the direct application of Article 56 by courts is now complemented by Directive 2006/123/EC on services in the internal market (Services Directive), and by sector-specific regulation for many complex services of particular social or economic importance. This chapter addresses Article 56 and the Services Directive. It is organised as follows.

Section 2 provides an overview of why services markets are hard to integrate. Because services involve people interacting, they raise issues of power and knowledge inequalities, requiring protective legislation. Also, services are often of great social importance and some services arouse strong moral feelings.

Section 3 is concerned with defining the services to which Article 56 applies. A core aspect is that the services must be provided for remuneration. Genuinely non-economic services, such as free public education, are excluded. Yet, where the service consumer, or an insurer acting on her behalf, does pay for services, Article 56 applies, however socially sensitive the services may be. Health care has been subjected to Article 56 on this basis.

Section 4 considers prohibited restrictions on the free movement of services. The range of these is broad. The Court of Justice applies Article 56 to any measure which makes access to the service market of a State more difficult. Since *Gebhard* and *Alpine Investments*, it does not appear to be necessary to show that the measure promotes either domestic service providers or domestic transactions. Yet in *Mobistar*, the Court said that measures which merely impose costs, but have no unequal impact, are outside Article 56. A certain ambiguity about the limits of Article 56 remains.

Section 4(ii) is devoted to the application of Article 56 to non-State actors. The powers of the bodies governing sport, and of trade unions, have both been subjected to the principle that they must not be exercised in a way that unjustifiably hinders the movement of services. This has been deeply controversial. In particular, the right of trade unions to both protect their members against low-cost competition from other Member States and preserve levels of worker protection in their home State are seen as threatened. Yet, the Court of Justice notes that if non-State bodies do not have to respect Article 56, this greatly reduces its effectiveness, and allows an opening for nationality discrimination and protectionism.

Section 5 is about justifying restrictions on the movement of services. This is possible where the restrictions are equally applicable, and the restrictive measure is necessary for a good public interest reason. However, service providers cannot be subjected to all host State legislation. First, account must be taken of whether the interest concerned is already protected by measures in the home State. Secondly, in deciding whether a regulatory burden is proportionate it is important to remember that a service provider may only have weak bonds with the host State market, perhaps just a few clients. Over-regulation of them would then be disproportionate, the Court has found.

Section 6 considers the way Article 56 impacts on society beyond business. In particular, the free movement of services requires that many sensitive and important activities be looked at through an economic lens. Abortion, gambling and prostitution are legally provided for remuneration in some States, enabling reliance on Article 56 to challenge restrictive measures. These challenges will not necessarily be successful, but the mere fact that courts must place non-economic concerns in the context of a right to trade in services has been offensive to some, and may rebalance public reasoning so that the non-economic interests are marginalised.

Section 6(iii) focuses in more detail on Article 56 and Welfare States. The case law on health care has been the most significant here, and provides patients with a right to go abroad to receive medical treatment at the expense of their home State. States claim this may add to the cost of health care and threaten budgets, and in response limited restrictions are permitted where hospital treatment is concerned. Nevertheless, both the general principle, and the procedural and transparency requirements which the Court has attached to it, are transformative, and are causing health-care systems to rethink their financing and organisation. Some of the Court's reasoning has now been adopted in a Directive on patients' rights to cross-border health care.

Section 7 is about the Services Directive. This is the most significant recent development in the law on services. The Directive applies a strict country of origin principle to services, so that providers need hardly concern themselves with the rules of their host State. The only exceptions are the narrowly interpreted grounds of public policy, public security, public health and the environment. Yet, the Directive, the product of a dramatically controversial legislative process, is full of exclusions and limitations, so that there will be just as many situations to which it does not apply as to which it does, and the direct application of Article 56 will remain important.

2 REGULATING THE SERVICES MARKET

Creating a single market for services is difficult.[1] Service providers are people, or companies, and when they are active in host States they interact with a wide range of regulations. These may be to do with the actual service, but may also be to do with the nature of the provider: their qualifications, legal form or financial position. A comparison with goods may be helpful: imagine if sale of goods were to be made conditional not just on aspects of the product, but on aspects of the company producing it, their factory and work methods. The creation of free movement would become even more of a challenge.

It is, of course, natural for a State to apply their laws to all on their territory. The EU law rejection of this is counter-intuitive from a national perspective. Yet, it is equally natural for a service provider to find it deeply frustrating when she is forced to demonstrate compliance with all kinds of professional and technical regulation which essentially duplicates similar demands in her State of establishment. Nor is such duplication the only problem. Other local rules may impose costs and make it harder for her to do business in the way she is used to – according to her business model, as the Court of Justice has recently put it.[2] Examples might be a prohibition on a particular marketing method, such as cold-calling, or a tax on the equipment necessary for the service, advertising rules, or rules about the legal form of the service provider. These rules might not discriminate, nor have any protectionist intent, but they might nevertheless have the effect that some service providers decide it is just not worth entering that market, or that market entry should be on a smaller scale. Trade is inhibited.

When law is potentially this broad in its impact, politically acceptable regulation becomes a challenge for courts and legislatures. That challenge is increased by the fact that services can be both economically and socially extremely sensitive. Partly this is a matter of scale. At one extreme, huge service industries like banking, Internet services, telecoms and transport are of such importance to the wider economy that they demand intensive regulation and control. This makes transnational integration even harder, for it is difficult for a generalist court to tamper with complex national supervisory systems. In practice, free movement in this kind of industry is usually pursued via sector-specific legislation. Yet, services can equally be very local, very small-scale, and sometimes very traditional, which raises its own problems, often political. In France, the debate around the Services Directive focused on the image of a French plumber threatened by Polish competition. The ability to remain established in Poland, with associated low costs, while providing services in France, would enable the Polish plumbers to undercut the French, plunder

---

[1] European Commission, 'The State of the Internal Market in Services', COM(2002)441 final.
[2] *Commission* v. *Italy*, C-518/06, EU:C:2009:270.

the local market and wipe out a class of small-scale artisanal service providers, it was claimed by opponents. This is globalisation brought down to a human scale, and all the more politically potent as a result.

Other services are hard to integrate, or adjudicate, because they are part of the structure of the State, or the fabric of national society. Health care, education and sport are examples. Breaking down national barriers to these affects the sense of national community and identity[3] and so free movement has to be balanced against factors which are hard to voice, hard to weigh, impossible to quantify and sometimes not easy to distinguish from unacceptable nationalism.[4]

Finally, services are about people doing things to, or for, each other. Some of the things people do enrage others: abortion, gambling, prostitution.[5] Adjudicating the free movement of these is always controversial. Other things that people do involve risk for others: lay clients buying complex professional services are vulnerable to exploitation by their provider, while providers of sex services may be vulnerable to their clients; services tend to involve unequal relationships. In all these cases, the Court of Justice is faced with human, moral and social concerns and interests which complicate its decision-making but cannot be ignored.

The Court is not the primary regulator of such issues: it supervises Member State legislation, and acknowledges the national margin of appreciation where choices of social or moral policy are concerned.[6] However, since free movement and non-discrimination are also values within the European legal system, it is forced to balance national priorities against EU priorities. Where matters such as the opening of the Welfare State or trade in morally controversial services are concerned, there is no safe neutral position, only value-laden choices to be made.

3 CROSS-BORDER SERVICES

The free movement of services is regulated by Article 56 TFEU, which provides in its first paragraph:

> Within the framework of the provisions set out below, restrictions on freedom to provide services within the Union shall be prohibited in respect of nationals of Member States who are established in a Member State other than that of the person for whom the services are intended.

Article 57 TFEU then provides that:

> Services shall be considered to be 'services' within the meaning of the Treaties where they are normally provided for remuneration.

Subsequent Articles address aspects of certain specific services (transport, banking and insurance services) and aspects of the process of harmonisation and liberalisation.

A number of derogations are also provided. The free movement of services may be restricted on grounds of public policy, public security or public health, and it does not apply at all to the

---

[3] See M. Wright and T. Reeskens, 'Of What Cloth are the Ties that Bind? National Identity and Support for the Welfare State Across 29 European Countries' (2013) 20 *JEPP* 1443.

[4] See C. Hilson, 'The Unpatriotism of the Economic Constitution? Rights to Free Movement and the Impact on National and European Identity' (2008) 14 *ELJ* 156.

[5] See *Jany* v. *Staatssecretaris van Justitie*, C-268/99, EU:C:2001:616.

[6] See N. Nic Shuibhne, 'Margins of Appreciation: National Values, Fundamental Rights and EC Free Movement Law' (2009) 34 *ELRev* 230.

exercise of official authority. These derogations are found in the Treaty Chapter on freedom of establishment, and are applied to the services Chapter by Article 61 TFEU. They are discussed further in Chapter 19.

The free movement of services raises several issues of definition. What is a service? What is 'remuneration'? And, when does a service have a sufficient cross-border element to fall within Article 56 TFEU? These questions are addressed below.

(i) What Is a Service?

The distinction between goods and services is relatively simple. Goods are things that one can feel. Hence, electricity is treated by the Court of Justice as goods. The sale of e-books, however, would fall within the provision of services, since there is no tactile object being traded. If the book were on a CD, by contrast, then this CD would be a good.[7]

Sometimes the provision of a service is attached to the provision of a physical thing. Most notably, in *Schindler*, the Court found that buying a lottery ticket fell within the free movement of services, not goods, because the physical ticket was purely ancillary to the real substance of the transaction, which was the chance of winning a prize.[8] The customer paid in order to participate in the lottery – a service – not in order to own a piece of paper. On the other hand, the Court ruled in *Visser*, considering rules restricting shop location, that the retail sale of goods is a service.[9] The decision was in the context of the Services Directive, and the Court emphasised in the judgment that terms in that Directive may have autonomous meanings, not simply copied from jurisprudence interpreting the Treaty. This makes the application of this finding to Article 49 and 56 unclear.[10] At the same time, one would perhaps expect the underlying concept of a service to be one that is shared.

Visser shows how a single measure might genuinely impact on multiple freedoms, in that case goods and establishment, but most often on establishment and services. They will then both be considered by the Court, unless one is clearly 'entirely secondary' to the other, in which case it will not be addressed.[11]

The distinction between services and establishment is far from precise. If a person or company has a number of customers in another Member State to which they provide services, this will fall within Article 56. However, if their position in that Member State reaches a sufficient level of permanence and solidity that one might speak of them being 'established' there, then any restrictions on their activities will be seen as restrictions on freedom of establishment, not of services.[12] Deciding when a service provider is embedded enough that they become established entails looking at several factors.[13]

---

[7] *Giuseppe Sacchi*, 155/73, EU:C:1974:40; L. Woods, *Free Movement of Goods and Services within the European Community* (Aldershot, Ashgate, 2004) 19.

[8] *HM Customs and Excise* v. *Schindler*, C-275/92, EU:C:1994:119. See also *Van Schaik*, C-55/93, EU:C: 1994:363; *Karner* v. *Troostwijk*, C-71/02, EU:C:2004:181; *Omega Spielhallen-und Automatenaufstellungs* v. *Oberbürgermeisterin der Bundesstadt Bonn*, C-36/02, EU:C:2004:614; *Jägerskiöld* v. *Gustafsson*, C-97/98, EU:C:1999:515; *Cura Anlagen* v. *Auto Source Leasing*, C-451/99, EU:C:2002:195.

[9] *Visser Vastgoed*, C-360/15 and C-31/16, EU:C:2018:44.   [10] Cf. *Pelckmans Turnhout*, C-483/12, EU:C:2014:304.

[11] *Vanderborght*, C-339/15, EU:C:2017:335, para. 58; *NN*, C-48/15, EU:C:2016:356.

[12] *Reyners* v. *Belgium*, 2/74, EU:C:1974:69; *Gebhard* v. *Consiglio dell'ordine degli avvocati eprocuratori di Milano*, C-55/94, EU:C:1995:411.

[13] See also *Google Spain*, C-131/12, EU:C:2014:317.

Schnitzer, C–215/01, EU:C:2003:662

27 The third paragraph of Article [57 TFEU] states that the person providing a service may, in order to do so, temporarily pursue his activity in the Member State where the service is provided, under the same conditions as are imposed by that State on its own nationals. Insofar as pursuit of the activity in that Member State remains temporary, such a person thus continues to come under the provisions of the chapter relating to services.

28 The Court has held that the temporary nature of the activity of the person providing the service in the host Member State has to be determined in the light not only of the duration of the provision of the service but also of its regularity, periodical nature or continuity. The fact that the activity is temporary does not mean that the provider of services within the meaning of the Treaty may not equip himself with some form of infrastructure in the host Member State (including an office, chambers or consulting rooms) insofar as such infrastructure is necessary for the purposes of performing the services in question.

(ii) Cross-Border Element

Article 56 TFEU provides that it applies whenever the service provider and service recipient are established in different Member States.[14] This covers several situations.[15] The most obvious is where the service provider (who must be an EU company or an EU citizen established in a Member State)[16] travels to another State, as in *van Binsbergen*, where a Dutch lawyer established in Belgium travelled to the Netherlands to see and represent clients.[17] However, Article 56 also applies where it is the recipient who travels. This was established in *Luisi and Carbone*, where two Italians wanted to go to Germany to receive medical services. Italian laws which obstructed this fell within Article 56.[18] It may even be the case that recipient and provider both travel, and meet in a third Member State.[19]

Equally important today is the situation where the service itself moves. Services provided over the Internet, telesales and the cross-border provision of telecoms and television are all commercially important examples of cross-border service provision in which neither provider nor recipient has to physically move. Thus, measures which prevent companies from cold-calling customers abroad, or which impose restrictions on the supply or receipt of television programmes from abroad, and many other examples of this type, have been found to fall within Article 56.[20]

---

[14] Wholly internal situations are thus excluded: see *RI-SAN* v. *Commune de Ischia*, C–108/98, EU:C:1999:400; *Procureur du Roi* v. *Debauve*, 52/79, EU:C:1980:83. Cf. *SG Alsacienne* v. *Koestler*, 15/78, EU:C:1978:184.

[15] See G. Sampson and R. Snape, 'Identifying the Issues in Trade in Services' (1985) 8 *World Economy* 171, 172–3; P. Eeckhout, *The European Internal Market and International Trade: A Legal Analysis* (Oxford, Clarendon Press, 1994) 10; J. Snell, *Goods and Services in EC Law: A Study of the Relationship Between the Freedoms* (Oxford University Press, 2002) 16–17. The situation is very similar in the central treaty regulating international trade in services, the General Agreement on Trade in Services (GATS), Article I(2).

[16] *FKP Scorpio*, C–290/04, EU:C:2006:630; *Fidium Finanz* v. *Bundesanstalt für Finanzdienstleistnugsaufsicht*, C–452/04, EU:C:2006:182. As EU citizens, service providers and recipients enjoy the citizenship rights discussed in Ch. 11.

[17] *Van Binsbergen* v. *Bestuur van de Bedrijsvereniging voor de Metaalnijverheid*, 33/74, EU:C:1974:131.

[18] *Luisi and Carbone* v. *Ministero del Tesoro*, 286/82 and 26/83, EU:C:1984:35. Also *Cowan* v. *Trésor Public*, 186/87, EU:C:1989:47.

[19] As is often the case with tour guides. See e.g. *Commission* v. *Italy*, 180/89, EU:C:1991:78; *Syndesmos ton en Elladi Touristikon kai Taxidiotikon Grafeion* v. *Ypourgos Ergasias*, C–398/95, EU:C:1997:282.

[20] See e.g. *Bond van Adverteerders* v. *Netherlands*, 352/85, EU:C:1988:196; *Försäkringsaktiebolaget Skandia* v. *Riksskatteverket*, C–422/01, EU:C:2003:380; *Gambelli*, C–243/01, EU:C:2003:156; *Commission* v. *Portugal (Flight*

The Court has also extended Article 56 beyond its literal wording. In *Vestergard*, a Danish company organised training courses for Danish workers on Greek islands. On the one hand, provider and recipients all travelled to another Member State, so there was clearly an international element to the service provision. However, both provider and recipient were established in Denmark, so the transaction was domestic.[21] Nevertheless, the Court applied Article 56.

Skatteministeriet v. Vestergard, C–55/98, EU:C:1999:533

18 Thirdly, it is important to point out that in order for services such as those in question in the main proceedings, namely the organisation of professional training courses, to fall within the scope of Article [56 TFEU], it is sufficient for them to be provided to nationals of a Member State on the territory of another Member State, irrespective of the place of establishment of the provider or recipient of the services.

19 Article [56 TFEU] applies not only where a person providing a service and the recipient are established in different Member States, but also whenever a provider of services offers those services in a Member State other than the one in which he is established, wherever the recipients of those services may be established.

This was taken a step further in *ITC*, where a German employment agency found a job in the Netherlands for its German client, who at that time lived in Germany. The Court of Justice found that Article 56 applied even though client, provider and payment all took place in Germany. The judgment does not indicate very clearly what reasoning was behind this, but the Advocate General, whose opinion was followed, provides a useful analysis.

ITC Innovative Technology Center GmbH v. Bundesagentur für Arbeit, C–208/05. EU:C:2006:649, Opinion of Advocate General Léger

118 Next, unlike the German Government, I am of the view that the situation at issue in the main proceedings does indeed involve a sufficient cross-border extraneous element.

119 I would point out in that regard that the Court of Justice has held that Article [56 TFEU] applies even where the provider and the recipient of the services are established in the same Member State, on condition that the services are being provided in another Member State.

120 In the case in the main proceedings, the cross-border dimension is made clear by the fact that the job searching, which forms an integral part of the activity of recruitment, was done by the private-sector agency in another Member State. It is, moreover, to be expected that, as part of the performance of a recruitment contract the service provider will have contacts with potential employers based in other Member States, in order to increase the chances of a successful recruitment.

121 Thus, the fact that a recruitment contract was concluded between a person seeking employment and a private-sector recruitment agency each of which are located in the same Member State does not in my view preclude the applicability of Article [56 TFEU] since the job searching, which is the main purpose of the recruitment activity, was undertaken in another Member State.

Taxes), C-70/99, EU:C:2001:125. See also *Corsica Ferries France*, C-18/93, EU:C:1994:195; *Commission v. France*, C-381/93, EU:C:1994:370; *Alpine Investments v. Minister van Financiën*, C-384/93, EU:C:1995:15.

[21] See also *Commission v. France*, C-381/93, EU:C:1994:370.

The Advocate General took the view that the actual service was the finding of a job, and this was done in the Netherlands – that was where the company went to look. It therefore appears, following *Vestergard* and *ITC*, that even a domestic service contract falls within Article 56 if an important part of the work for which the service provider is paid takes place abroad.

It is not necessary that the cross-border element be already realised. As is the case in goods, if a measure could restrict cross-border service provision, then the fact that no actual complainant can be found does not exclude a reference or an answer. Potential restrictions are also caught by Article 56.[22]

However, as with the other freedoms, if 'the relevant facts are confined within a single Member State' the Treaty will not apply to those facts.[23] Nevertheless, questions are sometimes referred in such cases, where a national judge is required by national law to 'grant the same rights to a national of a given Member State as those which a national of another Member State in the same situation would derive from European Union law'.[24] In such situations it is necessary to know the EU law position, and the Court of Justice therefore answers the question.[25]

(iii) Remuneration

Services provided out of charity, or without any desire for payment, are not covered by Article 56 TFEU. It is concerned with economic activity, and Article 57 TFEU provides that services must be 'normally provided for remuneration'. The word 'normally', although it has not been discussed by the Court of Justice, is probably intended to ensure that the occasional provision of a service for free in a generally commercial context (as part of a sales promotion, for example) does not result in essentially economic activities falling outside the Treaty.

Remuneration need not be money, as long as it can be valued in money.[26] Food and lodging has been found by the Court to be remuneration in the context of employment, and there is no reason why it should take a different stance on services.[27] Nor does remuneration need to be paid by the recipient of the service.[28] If an insurance company pays for medical care abroad this is remuneration just as much as if the patient had paid herself, and is sufficient to bring that care within Article 56. One potentially important consequence is that users of free websites, including search engines, should be able to rely on Article 56 where that use is restricted, even though the payment for the websites is from advertisers: the user is an essential part of the economic activity, and so this falls within its scope.[29]

---

[22] *Anomar* v. *Estado Português*, C-6/01, EU:C:2003:446; *Syndesmos ton en Elladi Touristikon kai Taxidiotikon Grafeion* v. *Ypourgos Ergasias*, C-398/95, EU:C:1997:282; *Blanco Pérez*, C-570/07, EU:C:2010:300. In like vein, C-384/93 *Alpine Investments* v. *Minister van Financiën* C-384/93, EU:C:1995:15. See annotation by V. Hatzopoulos, 'Annotation of *Alpine Investments*' (1995) 29 *CMLRev* 1427.

[23] *Omalet*, C-245/09, EU:C:2010:808, para. 12; *RI.SAN*, C-108/98, EU:C:1999:400.

[24] *Omalet*, C-245/09, EU:C:2010:808, para. 12, para. 15.

[25] See also *Volksbank Romania*, C-602/10, EU:C:2012:443, 12 July 2012.

[26] *Staatsecretaris van Financiëen* v. *Coöperative Aardappelenbewaarplaats*, 154/80, EU:C:1981:38; *Commission* v. *Belgium*, 324/82, EU:C:1984:152; *Argos Distributors Ltd* v. *CCE*, C-288/94, EU:C:1996:253; *Söhne* v. *Finanzamt Neustadt*, C-258/95, EU:C:1997:491.

[27] *Steymann* v. *Staatssecretaris van Justitie*, 196/87, EU:C:1988:475.

[28] *Bond van Adverteerders*, 352/85 EU:C:1988:196, at 16.

[29] See *Deliege* v. *Asbl Ligue Francophone de Judo*, C-51/96, EU:C:2000:199.

However, not every payment to the service provider is remuneration. In *Humbel*, the Court of Justice had to consider whether university education was a Treaty service.[30] Universities receive most of their funding from the State, but students paid a small contribution.

Humbel v. *Belgium*, 263/86, EU:C:1988:451

17 The essential characteristic of remuneration thus lies in the fact that it constitutes consideration for the service in question, and is normally agreed upon between the provider and the recipient of the service.

18 That characteristic is, however, absent in the case of courses provided under the national education system . . . First of all, the State, in establishing and maintaining such a system, is not seeking to engage in gainful activity but is fulfilling its duties towards its own population in the social, cultural and educational fields . . . Secondly, the system in question is, as a general rule, funded from the public purse and not by pupils or their parents . . .

19 The nature of the activity is not affected by the fact that pupils or their parents must sometimes pay teaching or enrolment fees in order to make a certain contribution to the operating expenses of the system.

The Court makes an implicit contrast between payments which are essentially consideration for the services – where there is a transaction between payer and provider – and payments which are intended to fund or support the provider, for non-commercial motives.[31] One way of looking at this is to ask whether the service provider would consider the payer (here the State) to be her 'client', or to be acting on behalf of her client. In the case of free public education this would usually be a somewhat artificial perspective.

It is arguable that there must be some legal obligation to pay. In *Tolsma*, the Court of Justice had to consider whether busking on the highway fell within the ambit of Article 2 of the Sixth VAT Directive.[32] This is similarly phrased to Article 57 TFEU, as it provides that services provided by a taxable person must, in principle, be taxed if they are made for payment or consideration.[33] The Court of Justice held that money given by passers-by could not be seen as value provided for a service. Donations were voluntary and the passers-by did not request the music. Thus, it was difficult to find any legal relationship that provided a context for remuneration.

It should also be noted that in *Humbel*, the Court suggested that very small payments will not amount to remuneration. The function of the essentially symbolic fees which many States require students to pay is not really to pay for the education they receive, but to encourage the students to take their education seriously.

In later cases, notably *Wirth*, the Court has suggested that as long as the State 'essentially' funds public education, this will fall outside Article 56 TFEU.[34] This suggests that if private payments, from students or their parents, or from scholarship funds, for example, amount to more than half of the total funds received for the service provided, then these payments will be remuneration and Article 56 will apply.

---

[30] *Humbel* v. *Belgium*, 263/86, EU:C:1988:151.

[31] See also EFTA Case E-5/07, *Private Barnehagers Landsforbund* v. *EFTA Surveillance Authority*, Judgment of 21 February 2008, www.eftacourt.int/press-publications/detail/article/case-e-507-private-barnehagers-landsforbund-v-efta-surveillance-authority/.

[32] *Tolsma* v. *Inspecteur der Omzelbelastingen Leeuwarden*, C-16/93, EU:C:1994:80 on busking.

[33] Directive 77/388/EEC [1977] OJ L 145/1.

[34] *Wirth* v. *Landeshauptstadt Hannover*, C-109/92, EU:C:1993:916; *Commission* v. *Germany*, C-318/05, EU:C:2007:495.

In education it is increasingly common for universities to have some courses, often Masters courses, which are paid for by students and run at a profit, while other courses are State-funded. This raises the question whether a specific course may fall within Article 56 even if most other courses provided by that institution do not. Will a generally non-economic organisation that dabbles in the market find itself subject to Article 56? Following the approach in competition law, one would expect that it is the nature of the particular activity or service which matters, rather than the institution as a whole.[35] The alternative would allow largely non-economic institutions to enter markets without being subject to their rules, creating quite serious risks of competitive distortions. In *Zanotti*, an LLM at a public Dutch university was involved, which had been paid for by the Italian student.

Zanotti, C–56/09, EU:C:2010:288

32 [T]he Court has held that courses offered by educational establishments essentially financed by private funds, in particular by students and their parents, constitute services within the meaning of Article [57 TFEU] since the aim of those establishments is to offer a service for remuneration.

33 Therefore, courses essentially financed by persons seeking training or professional specialisation must be regarded as constituting services within the meaning of Article [57 TFEU].

34 It is for the national court to assess the facts and, in particular, the terms and conditions of the specialist course attended by the applicant in the main proceedings.

35 It follows that Article [56 TFEU] is applicable to facts such as those in the main proceedings where a taxpayer of a given Member State attends a university in another Member State which may be regarded as providing services for remuneration, that is to say, which is essentially financed by private funds, which it is for the national court to verify.

Although there is ambiguity in this extract, with some references apparently to the nature of the institution as a whole, on balance it seems to suggest that even in a largely State-financed institution individual courses which are provided for remuneration will be within Article 56. This is confirmed by the ultimate finding: the University of Leiden is State-owned and largely State financed, and most students just pay *Humbel*-type 'contributions'. However, this still leaves other constellations open to some doubt: whether Article 56 would apply – for example, if half the students on the course are being paid for by the State, while the other half are paying fees. On the one hand, a service paid for by an individual should not cease to be a service because someone else gets it free. On the other hand, the word 'normally' in Article 57 might conceivably play a role here.

An odd tension in the case law is that while the motivation of the payer appears to be important in characterising services, the motivation of the provider is not.[36] The Court of Justice has ruled that there is no need for service providers to seek to make a profit, and the mere fact that they are providing very important public services, such as health or education, does not as such take them outside of Article 56.[37] Nor does it matter what legal or institutional form they

---

[35] *Commission* v. *Italy*, 118/85, EU:C:1987:283; *FENIN*, T-319/99, EU:T:2003:50.

[36] Cf. *Zanotti*, C-56/09, EU:C:2010:288, para. 32.

[37] *Geraets-Smits* v. *Stichting Ziekenfonds*; *Peerbooms* v. *Stichting CZ Groep Zorgverzekeringen*, C-157/99, EU:C:2001:404; *Kohll* v. *Union des Caisses de Maladie*, C-158/96, EU:C:1998:171. Cf. Articles 54 and 62 TFEU. See pp. 763–4.

have: they need not be a company or a business, but might be, for example, a school or a foundation.[38] They do not even have to be 'doing it for the money'. In *Jundt*, a university teacher received a fee for a guest lecture.[39] It was argued that his post was 'quasi-honorary'. The Court found this to be irrelevant, since he did in fact receive a payment in return for his teaching. The only question appears to be whether the service provider receives consideration for their activities.

One of the consequences of this case law is that the mechanism of funding public services becomes very important. In some Member States, health care is provided free on the basis of need, and is probably not therefore a Treaty service. In other Member States, the State guarantees universal health care by requiring residents to purchase medical insurance from private companies, in the context of a legislative framework in which insurance for the poor or sick is cross-subsidised by the richer and healthier. Because the actual medical care in such a system is paid for by insurers, Article 56 TFEU will apply. Similarly, if universities have high fees, but students can take out subsidised loans to pay them, then university education will probably be remunerated. If, on the other hand, the State funds universities directly, there will be no remuneration. In both cases the State ultimately pays, but the choice of mechanism determines the extent to which the Treaty applies.

This interaction of Article 56 and aspects of the Welfare State is of great current importance, and has been the source of much case law. It is discussed further in section 6 below.

4 RESTRICTIONS ON THE MOVEMENT OF SERVICES

(i) Notion of a Restriction on the Provision of Services

It has never been in doubt that direct and indirect nationality discrimination is prohibited within the sphere of Article 56 TFEU,[40] but the Court's most commonly used definition of the freedom makes other concepts central. In *Gebhard*, it stated that all national measures 'liable to hinder or make less attractive the exercise of fundamental freedoms' are to be seen as restrictions on movement.[41] The case was actually about establishment, but the formulation was general, and is very often cited for services too.

This suggests a broad scope for services law, and the cases bear that out. As the chapter will show, restrictions have been found in diverse situations, such as where national law restricts matters such as the way a service is provided,[42] advertising of the service,[43] the qualifications or legal form of the service provider,[44] the use of premises,[45] access to information on permits[46] or

---

[38] *Wirth* v. *Landeshauptstadt Hannover*, C-109/92, EU:C:1993:916; *Commission* v. *Germany*, C-318/05, EU:C:2007:495; G. Davies, 'Welfare as a Service' (2002) 29 *LIEI* 27, 29–30.

[39] *Jundt and Jundt* v. *Finanzamt Offenburg*, C-281/06, EU:C:2007:816.

[40] Article 57 TFEU, last paragraph; see e.g. *Van Binsbergen* v. *Bestuur van de Bedrijsvereniging voor de Metaalnijverheid*, 33/74, EU:C:1974:131; *Coenen* v. *Sociaal-Economische Raad*, 39/75, EU:C:1975:155; *Gouda* v. *Commissariat voor de Media*, C-288/89, EU:C:1991:157; *FDC* v. *Estado Español and UPCT*, C-17/92, EU:C:1993:172; *Eurowings* v. *Finanzamt Dortmund-Unna*, C-294/97, EU:C:1999:524. For definitions of discrimination in EU law, see p. 485.

[41] *Gebhard* v. *Consiglio dell'ordine degli avvocati eprocuratori di Milano*, C-55/94, EU:C:1995:411.

[42] *Alpine Investments* v. *Minister van Financiën*, C-384/93, EU:C:1995:15.

[43] *Corporacion Dermoestetica*, C-500/06, EU:C:2008:62.   [44] *Säger* v. *Dennemeyer*, C-76/90, EU:C:1991:331.

[45] *Commission* v. *Italy*, C-134/05, EU:C:2007:435.   [46] *UNIS*, C-25/14, EU:C:2015:821.

the price at which the service is offered.[47] Yet a systematic definition of what is meant by hindering free movement is absent.[48]

An important and useful restatement is however found in *Commission* v. *Italy*. This concerned a national rule which prohibited motor insurers from rejecting a client.[49] Such rules are quite common where socially important insurance is concerned, as they ensure universal access, even for individuals who may be bad risks, and who would be refused cover in a free market. However, insurance companies are not always happy, since they are obliged to accept clients who are likely to cost them money. In *Commission* v. *Italy*, it was argued that foreign insurance companies would be deterred from offering insurance services in Italy by the acceptance obligation, and that it therefore amounted to a restriction on the free movement of services.

***Commission* v. *Italy*, C–518/06, EU:C:2009:270, Judgment of 28 April 2009**

62 It is settled case-law that the term 'restriction' within the meaning of Articles [49 TFEU] and [56 TFEU] covers all measures which prohibit, impede or render less attractive the freedom of establishment or the freedom to provide services.

63 As regards the question of the circumstances in which a measure applicable without distinction, such as the obligation to contract at issue in the present case, may come within that concept, it should be borne in mind that rules of a Member State do not constitute a restriction within the meaning of the EC Treaty solely by virtue of the fact that other Member States apply less strict, or more commercially favourable, rules to providers of similar services established in their territory.

64 By contrast, the concept of restriction covers measures taken by a Member State which, although applicable without distinction, affect access to the market for undertakings from other Member States and thereby hinder intra-Community trade.

65 In the present case, it is common ground that the obligation to contract does not have any repercussions for the acceptance by the Italian authorities of the administrative authorisation, referred to in paragraph 13 of this judgment, which insurance undertakings having their head office in a Member State other than the Italian Republic obtain in the Member State in which they have their head office. It therefore leaves intact the right of access to the Italian market as regards third-party liability motor insurance resulting from that authorisation.

66 Nevertheless, the imposition by a Member State of an obligation to contract such as that at issue constitutes a substantial interference in the freedom to contract which economic operators, in principle, enjoy.

67 In a sector like that of insurance, such a measure affects the relevant operators' access to the market, in particular where it subjects insurance undertakings not only to an obligation to cover any risks which are proposed to them, but also to requirements to moderate premium rates.

68 Inasmuch as it obliges insurance undertakings which enter the Italian market to accept every potential customer, that obligation to contract is likely to lead, in terms of organisation and investment, to significant additional costs for such undertakings.

---

[47] *Federico Cipolla*, C–94/04 and C–202/04, EU:C:2006:758.
[48] See generally S. Enchelmeier, 'Always at Your Service (Within Limits): The ECJ's Case Law on Article 56 TFEU (2006–11)' (2011) 36 *ELRev* 615.
[49] *Commission* v. *Italy*, C–518/06, EU:C:2009:270.

> 69 If they wish to enter the Italian market under conditions which comply with Italian legislation, such undertakings will be required to re-think their business policy and strategy, *inter alia*, by considerably expanding the range of insurance services offered.
>
> 70 Inasmuch as it involves changes and costs on such a scale for those undertakings, the obligation to contract renders access to the Italian market less attractive and, if they obtain access to that market, reduces the ability of the undertakings concerned to compete effectively, from the outset, against undertakings traditionally established in Italy.
>
> 71 Therefore, the obligation to contract restricts the freedom of establishment and the freedom to provide services.

Market access is now the buzzword, and the Court finds that if a company has to change their business model in order to enter a new market that makes it less attractive to do so, and therefore affects their market access, engaging Article 56. The mere fact that a national law requires a foreign company to do something differently (if this imposes costs – or at least significant costs) creates a restriction on movement.

Yet the Court also hints at limits. The reason for its finding is that cost increases limit the capacity of the undertaking to compete against established undertakings. The implication here is that the Italian rule is protecting incumbents, and is not market-neutral. That need not necessarily be the case for all market rules.

Other cases confirm that the mere fact of having to comply with host State law will not be enough to demonstrate a market access restriction.[50] In *Commission* v. *Italy (Lawyers' Fees)* Italian rules setting maximum lawyers' fees were challenged with reference to *Commission* v. *Italy*, and in *Volksbank Romania* a similar challenge was made to Romanian rules limiting the kinds of charges that credit organisations could apply.[51] While it would seem that both of these rules could in principle affect a business model, the Court of Justice found that there was no evidence that they actually did have this effect. Nor was it clear that they were even liable to, partly because the rules were, in both cases, less strict than they first seemed. As a result, in *Volksbank Romania*, it found the impact of the measures to be too 'uncertain and indirect' to fall within Article 56. In both cases the Court used the language of competition in its reasoning and, as in *Commission* v. *Italy*, seemed to be looking for evidence that the rules affected the ability of the foreign provider to compete on the host State market.[52] Minimum fees, it is well established, can have this effect by taking away a competitive advantage which lower-cost foreign providers would otherwise enjoy.[53] Maximum fees, by contrast, can exclude market entry at the high end. However, there needs to be evidence that this is actually the case.

Principled summaries of these limits are found in *Viacom* and *Mobistar*.[54] The first of these concerned a tax on outdoor advertising. This put up the cost of such advertising, and local agencies complained that it had become harder to attract foreign clients. The Court found that because the measure was equally applicable to all persons, and the tax was not so high that it

---

[50] *Konstantinides*, C-475/11, EU:C:2013:542.

[51] *Commission* v. *Italy*, C-565/08, EU:C:2011:188; *Volksbank Romania*, C-602/10, EU:C:2012:443, Judgment of 12 July 2012.

[52] See *Commission* v. *Italy*, C-565/08, EU:C:2011:188, paras. 48–52; *Volksbank Romania*, C-602/10, EU:C:2012:443, Judgment of 12 July 2012, para. 80; *Commission* v. *Italy*, C-518/06, EU:C:2009:270, para. 70.

[53] *Cipolla and Others*, C-94/04 and C-202/04, EU:C:2006:758.   [54] See also *Perfili*, C-177/94, EU:C:1996:24.

might exclude anyone, it was 'not liable to prohibit, impede or otherwise make less attractive the provision of advertising services'. The idea that a measure falls outside Article 56 when it neither excludes, nor impacts unequally, is reminiscent of the law on goods.

The same spirit is abroad in *Mobistar*. This was about a tax on telecoms masts and pylons, necessary for the transmission of phone calls. It was argued that this hindered the provision of cross-border telecoms services, by imposing an additional cost on the necessary infrastructure. But the masts were just as necessary for domestic phone calls as for cross-border ones.

Mobistar v. *Commune de Fléron*, C–544/03, EU:C:2005:518

30 Furthermore, the Court has already held that Article [56 TFEU] precludes the application of any national rules which have the effect of making the provision of services between Member States more difficult than the provision of services purely within one Member State.

31 By contrast, measures, the only effect of which is to create additional costs in respect of the service in question and which affect in the same way the provision of services between Member States and that within one Member State, do not fall within the scope of Article [56 TFEU].

The insistence that Article 56 only applies to measures which (potentially) steer the consumer towards domestic rather than cross-border services is consistent with *Commission* v. *Italy* as well as the goods law.[55] Considering that analogy it may be noted that whereas *Commission* v. *Italy* concerned what could be seen as a product rule, requiring the nature of the service to be changed, *Volksbank*, *Viacom* and *Mobistar* all concerned what the Court would call selling arrangements – although the Court does not use those categories outside of the law on goods.

Finally, Article 56 does apply to restrictions on export of services.[56] In *Alpine Investments*, a Dutch law prohibited Dutch companies from cold-calling customers, even those in other Member States where cold-calling was not prohibited.[57] The aim was to prevent the Dutch financial services industry from getting a bad reputation, but frustrated Dutch providers who wanted to cold-call German clients claimed that the measure was a restriction on services. The Court of Justice agreed, for the very straightforward reason that:

28 . . . such a prohibition deprives the operators concerned of a rapid and direct technique for marketing and for contacting potential clients in other Member States. It can therefore constitute a restriction on the freedom to provide cross-border services.

This fits the general effects-orientation of free movement law. It should not matter which State, or perhaps even which person or organisation, creates the restriction if it in fact impedes free movement.

(ii) Horizontal Application of Article 56 TFEU

Article 56 TFEU is, like the other free movement articles, apparently addressed primarily to Member States. However, unlike the case with goods, Article 56 may also be directly applied to

---

[55] Cf. *Mazzoleni and ISA*, C–165/98, EU:C:2001:162.
[56] *Corsica Ferries France*, C–18/93, EU:C:1994:195; *Peralta*, C–379/92, EU:C:1994:296.
[57] *Alpine Investments* v. *Minister van Financiën*, C–384/93, EU:C:1995:15.

private actors under certain circumstances.[58] The reason why the Court of Justice allows this is that the article would be deprived of some of its effectiveness if private actors were permitted to act in ways obstructing service provision by others. This is even more so as the trend of recent decades has been for States to outsource ever more of their regulatory functions to non-governmental bodies of different types. Yet, many private organisations represent the views and interests of individuals so constraining their freedom of choice and action raises issues of fundamental rights.

The most common situation to have occurred in practice is where a private organisation is involved in regulating some area of activity. In *Walrave and Koch*, the rules of the International Cycling Union (ICU) were involved.[59] This non-governmental body organised and regulated international bicycling competitions, and made certain demands concerning the nationality of members of the support team. Because these team members received payment for their work, the matter fell within free movement law, and it was decided that they were self-employed providers of services rather than employed people. The claim was therefore made that the ICU rules restricted the freedom to provide services in other Member States, by preventing team members with the wrong nationality from taking part in international competitions. However, it was disputed whether Article 56 could be applied to the ICU, since it was a private body.

Walrave and Koch v. *Association Union Cycliste Internationale*, 36/74, EU:C:1974:140

19 Since, moreover, working conditions in the various Member States are governed sometimes by means of provisions laid down by law or regulation and sometimes by agreements and other acts concluded or adopted by private persons, to limit the prohibitions in question to acts of a public authority would risk creating inequality in their application.

20 Although the third paragraph of Article [57 TFEU], and Articles [59 and 61 TFEU], specifically relate, as regards the provision of services, to the abolition of measures by the state, this fact does not defeat the general nature of the terms of Article [56 TFEU], which makes no distinction between the source of the restrictions to be abolished . . .

21 It is established, moreover, that Article [45 TFEU], relating to the abolition of any discrimination based on nationality as regards gainful employment, extends likewise to agreements and rules which do not emanate from public authorities.

22 Article 7(4) of Regulation No. 1612/68 in consequence provides that the prohibition on discrimination shall apply to agreements and any other collective regulations concerning employment . . .

23 The activities referred to in Article [56] are not to be distinguished by their nature from those in Article [45 TFEU], but only by the fact that they are performed outside the ties of a contract of employment.

24 This single distinction cannot justify a more restrictive interpretation of the scope of the freedom to be ensured . . .

Several points emerge. First, Article 56 TFEU is applied to the rules of the ICU because these are part of the regulation of an area of economic activity. To exclude private agreements and rules, which are often an important part of the employment context, from the scope of Article 56 would

---

[58] See generally J. Snell, 'Private Parties and Free Movement of Goods and Services' in M. Andenas and W.-H. Roth (eds.), *Services and Free Movement in EU Law* (Oxford University Press, 2002) 211; S. Prechal and S. de Vries, 'Seamless Web of Judicial Protection in the Internal Market?' (2009) 34 *ELRev* 5.

[59] *Walrave and Koch* v. *Association Union Cycliste Internationale*, 36/74, EU:C:1974:140.

allow private parties to create obstacles to movement, and create an arbitrary distinction between the rights of economic actors according to the particular mode of regulation prevailing in their industry and State. This view has particular force as States privatise ever more of their regulatory functions, and the distinction between public and private becomes ever less clear and principled.[60]

Secondly, the Court of Justice sees no reason to make a principled distinction between the free movement of workers and services. It is a technical matter whether an economic relationship is structured as one of employment or self-employed service provision, and this should not affect the scope of the freedom or the degree to which it may be restricted. Since the free movement of workers applies to all aspects of employment regulation and agreements, private or public, it would be arbitrary to exclude such matters from Article 56. This approach has continued in later cases, and the principles of horizontal application appear to be the same whether workers, services or establishment are concerned.[61]

This application of Article 56 TFEU to sport has been very controversial. Sport is, for many people, a matter of social and cultural importance. It can be socially cohesive, and provides a relatively harmless outlet for national identity and the urge to sublimate oneself to a greater whole. To subject it to economic law is not just to miss the point, but to actively threaten the values it embodies and the positive role that it can play in society.[62] Yet, sport is also economic: modern sporting competitions involve large amounts of money, and sportspeople are often well paid for their services.

The case law shows the Court of Justice trying to maintain a distinction between rules which are an inherent part of the regulation of sport, and should not be seen as restrictions on free movement, and those that are to do with the economic aspects of sporting activity and may be assessed in the light of free movement law. In *Deliège*, a judoka who had not been selected by the Belgian judo association to represent Belgium in the Olympics claimed that this restricted her freedom to provide services in another Member State. The process of selection limited participation, she argued, and thereby restricted the provision of services.[63] Clearly, she could not win, as this would have created sporting chaos, but rather than finding that there was a restriction which was justified, the Court of Justice found there to be no restriction at all. Its reasoning was that restrictions on participation were inherent to the organisation of a sporting event, and as such did not fall within Article 56.

The General Court explained this idea in more detail in *Meca Medina*.[64] A Spanish and a Slovenian long-distance swimmer both tested positive for nandrolone, a banned substance. They

---

[60] *Van Ameyde* v. *UCI*, 90/76, EU:C:1977:76; J. Baquero Cruz, *Between Competition and Free Movement: The Economic Constitutional Law of the European Community* (Oxford-Portland, Hart, 2002) 123.

[61] *Roman Angonese* v. *Cassa di Risparmio di Bolzano*, C-281/98, EU:C:2000:296; *Union Royale Belge des Sociétés de Football Association and Others* v. *Bosman and Others*, C-415/93, EU:C:1995:463; *Jyri Lehtonen and Castors Canada Dry Namur-Braine Asbl* v. *Fédération royale belge des sociétés de basket-ball Asbl (FRBSB)*, C-176/96, EU:C:2000:201; *International Transport Workers' Federation and Finnish Seamen's Union* v. *Viking Line ABP and OÜ Viking Line Eesti*, C-438/05, EU:C:2007:772.

[62] The Declaration on Sport attached to the Treaty of Amsterdam. See also the 'Helsinki Report' by the Commission. European Commission, 'Report to the European Council with a View to Safeguarding Current Sports Structures and Maintaining the Social Function of Sport within the Community Framework', COM(1999)644. For discussion, see S. Weatherill, 'European Football Law' in Collected Courses of the 7th Session of the Academy of European Law (Florence, Kluwer/European Union Institute, 1999) 339–82; S. Weatherill, 'The Helsinki Report on Sport' (2000) 25 ELRev 282.

[63] *Deliège* v. *Asbl Ligue Francophone de Judo*, C-51/96 and C-191/97, EU:C:1999:147.   [64] See also p. 925.

were suspended for four years by FINA, the International Swimming Federation, acting under the rules of the International Olympic Committee, reduced on appeal to two years. The swimmers appealed to the Commission that the ban breached EU competition law and what is now Article 56 TFEU. When the Commission took no action, they brought their case before the General Court.

Meca Medina and Majcen v. *Commission*, T–313/02, EU:T:2004:282

37 ... having regard to the objectives of the Community, sport is subject to Community law only insofar as it constitutes an economic activity within the meaning of Article 2 EC ...

38 That is also borne out by Declaration on Sport No. 29, annexed to the final act of the Conference which adopted the text of the Amsterdam Treaty, which emphasises the social significance of sport and calls on the bodies of the European Union to give special consideration to the particular characteristics of amateur sport. In particular, that Declaration is consistent with the abovementioned case law insofar as it relates to situations in which sport constitutes an economic activity.

39 Where a sporting activity takes the form of paid employment or a provision of remunerated service, it falls, more particularly, within the scope of Article [45 TFEU] *et seq.* or of Article [56 TFEU] *et seq.*, respectively ...

40 Therefore ... the prohibitions laid down by those provisions of the Treaty apply to the rules adopted in the field of sport which concern the economic aspect which sporting activity can present. In that context, the Court has held that the rules providing for the payment of fees for the transfer of professional players between clubs (transfer clauses) or limiting the number of professional players who are nationals of other Member States which those clubs may field in matches (rules on the composition of club teams), or fixing, without objective reasons concerning only the sport or justified by differences in the circumstances between players, different transfer deadlines for players coming from other Member States (clauses on transfer deadlines) fall within the scope of those provisions of the Treaty and are subject to the prohibitions which they enact ...

41 On the other hand, the prohibitions enacted by those provisions of the Treaty do not affect purely sporting rules, that is to say rules concerning questions of purely sporting interest and, as such, having nothing to do with economic activity ... In fact, such regulations, which relate to the particular nature and context of sporting events, are inherent in the organisation and proper conduct of sporting competition and cannot be regarded as constituting a restriction on the Community rules on the freedom of movement of workers and the freedom to provide services. In that context, it has been held that the rules on the composition of national teams ... or the rules relating to the selection by sports federations of those of their members who may participate in high-level international competitions ... constitute purely sporting rules which therefore, by their nature, fall outside the scope of Articles [45 TFEU] and [56 TFEU]. Also among such rules are 'the rules of the game' in the strict sense, such as, for example, the rules fixing the length of matches or the number of players on the field, given that sport can exist and be practised only in accordance with specific rules. That restriction on the scope of the above provisions of the Treaty must however remain limited to its proper objective ...

44 It is appropriate to point out that, while it is true that high-level sport has become, to a great extent, an economic activity, the campaign against doping does not pursue any economic objective. It is intended to preserve, first, the spirit of fair play, without which sport, be it amateur or professional, is no longer sport. That purely social objective is sufficient to justify the campaign against doping. Secondly, since doping products are not without their negative physiological effects, that campaign is intended to safeguard the health of athletes. Thus, the prohibition of doping, as a particular expression of the requirement of fair play, forms part of the cardinal rule of sport.

45 It must also be made clear that sport is essentially a gratuitous and not an economic act, even when the athlete performs it in the course of professional sport. In other words, the prohibition of doping and the anti-doping legislation concern exclusively, even when the sporting action is performed by a professional, a non-economic aspect of that sporting action, which constitutes its very essence . . .

47 In view of the foregoing, it must be held that the prohibition of doping is based on purely sporting considerations and therefore has nothing to do with any economic consideration. That means, in the light of the case law and the considerations set out . . . above, that the rules to combat doping cannot . . . come within the scope of the Treaty provisions on the economic freedoms.

The General Court's judgment was later overturned by the Court of Justice, but not on grounds relevant to the extract above.

The other area where horizontal application of services law has been applied to significant effect, perhaps even more controversially, is labour regulation, in particular the activities of trade unions. This is the result of *Laval* and *Viking Line*.[65]

Of the two, *Laval* was decided a week later, but is the more concerned with service provision, whereas *Viking* is primarily about establishment. In *Laval*, the Court of Justice applied Article 56 TFEU to the law concerning trade unions. Swedish unions took industrial action against foreign employers using posted workers. The unions were trying to force the employers to sign Swedish collective agreements. The union fear was that otherwise the posted workers would receive lower pay and worse conditions, and would undercut local workers and undermine local standards. The employers, however, considered that their freedom to provide services was being restricted by the industrial action, which was effectively preventing them from carrying out their building projects. Citing cases on services, workers and establishment, the Court ruled as follows.

Laval un Partneri Ltd v. *Svenska Byggnadsarbetareförbundet, Svenska Byggnadsarbetareförbundets avdelning 1, Byggettan and Svenska Elektrikerförbundet,* C–341/05, EU:C:2007:291

98 Furthermore, compliance with Article [56 TFEU] is also required in the case of rules which are not public in nature but which are designed to regulate, collectively, the provision of services. The abolition, as between Member States, of obstacles to the freedom to provide services would be compromised if the abolition of State barriers could be neutralised by obstacles resulting from the exercise of their legal autonomy by associations or organisations not governed by public law . . .

This application of Article 56 TFEU to trade unions raised fears because of its implications for union autonomy and the freedom of workers to fight for their interests, not least because they might perhaps be sued for damages if their action violated Article 56.[66] However, it was

---

[65] *Laval un Partneri Ltd* v. *Svenska Byggnadsarbetareförbundet, Svenska Byggnadsarbetareförbundets avdelning 1, Byggettan and Svenska Elektrikerförbundet,* C–341/05, EU:C:2007:291; *International Transport Workers' Federation and Finnish Seamen's Union* v. *Viking Line ABP and OÜ Viking Line Eesti,* C–438/05, EU:C:2007:772.

[66] See C. Barnard, *Employment Rights, Free Movement under the EC Treaty and the Services Directive,* Mitchell Working Paper No. 5/08 (2008); N. Reich, 'Free Movement v. Social Rights in an Enlarged Union: The *Laval* and *Viking* Cases before the ECJ' (2008) 9 *German LJ* 125; J. Malmberg and T. Sigeman, 'Industrial Actors and EU Economic Freedoms: The Autonomous Collective Bargaining Model Curtailed by the European Court of Justice' (2008) 43 *CMLRev* 1115;

doctrinally hardly different from *Walrave*.[67] In the Swedish employment system, trade unions were an important part of the system of employment regulation, and via their role in collective bargaining, contributed to *de facto* regulation of labour terms and conditions.

However, in *Viking Line*, the Court of Justice appeared to go further, and suggest that the application of free movement law to private bodies is not dependent upon them playing some quasi-regulatory role. In *Viking Line*, it was Finnish trade unions that were objecting to free movement, but in this case they took industrial action to try and prevent a Finnish shipping company from reflagging a ship under a Latvian flag. The company wanted to employ workers under cheaper Latvian terms and conditions. It was therefore the freedom of the shipping company to choose their State of establishment that was being restricted by the unions. The Court reaffirmed that Article 49 TFEU must be interpreted to apply to private bodies, in terms almost identical to those in the paragraph above from *Laval*, and then continued as follows.

International Transport Workers' Federation and Finnish Seamen's Union v. Viking Line ABP and OÜ Viking Line Eesti, C–438/05, EU:C:2007:772

64 It must be added that, contrary to the claims, in particular, of ITF, it does not follow from the case-law of the Court . . . that that interpretation applies only to quasi-public organisations or to associations exercising a regulatory task and having quasi-legislative powers.

65 There is no indication in that case-law that could validly support the view that it applies only to associations or to organisations exercising a regulatory task or having quasi-legislative powers. Furthermore, it must be pointed out that, in exercising their autonomous power, pursuant to their trade union rights, to negotiate with employers or professional organisations the conditions of employment and pay of workers, trade unions participate in the drawing up of agreements seeking to regulate paid work collectively.

This is an important clarification *of Laval* and *Walrave*. Although there is a certain tension between paragraph 64 and the comment in the next paragraph that trade unions do in fact contribute to labour regulation, it appears that the Court is saying that Article 49 does not apply to private parties because they have some specific legally assigned role in economic activity, but merely because as a matter of fact they have the power to obstruct free movement.

The application to unions is therefore not because of any particular legal status that they may enjoy, but because as a matter of fact the action they were undertaking was making establishment in Latvia harder. There seems no reason why the Court should take a different approach in the context of services.

Schepel has made two powerful criticisms of the doctrine in *Viking* and *Laval*. One is that the kind of balancing of interests that courts will have to make in order to see whether industrial action is justified is so imprecise that it will lead to legal uncertainty, which will result in poor application of the law, which will in turn lead ultimately to a reduced effectiveness of

---

C. Barnard, '*Viking* and *Laval*: An Introduction' in C. Barnard (ed.), (2007–8) 10 *CYELS* 463; A. Dashwood, '*Viking* and *Laval*: Issues of Horizontal Direct Effect' in C. Barnard (ed.), (2007–08) 10 *CYELS* 525; T. Novitz, 'A Human Rights Analysis of the *Viking* and *Laval* Judgments' in C. Barnard (ed.), (2007–08) 10 *CYELS* 541; S. Sciarra, '*Viking* and *Laval*: Collective Labour Rights and Market Freedoms in the Enlarged EU' in C. Barnard (ed.), (2007–08) 10 *CYELS* 563; C. Kaupa, 'Maybe Not Activist Enough? On the Court's Alleged Neoliberal Bias in its Recent Labor Cases' in M. Dawson, B. de Witte and E. Muir (eds.), *Judicial Activism at the European Court of Justice* (Cheltenham, Edward Elgar, 2013) 56.

[67] Cf. H. Schepel, 'Constitutionalising the Market, Marketising the Constitution, and to Tell the Difference: On the Horizontal Application of the Free Movement Provisions in EU Law' (2012) 18 *ELJ* 177.

Article 56 – even though, ironically, effectiveness is the primary rationale for the decision that the Court of Justice provides. As well as this, the uncertainty may create a 'chilling' effect on the right to strike: unions will hesitate to take industrial action if they cannot be sure it is legal, because illegal strikes could lead to devastating compensation claims.

The other criticism is that it is wrong to see *Viking* and *Laval* as following on from *Walrave*: as he argues in the extract below, they have a quite different underlying philosophy.

H. Schepel, 'Constitutionalising the Market, Marketising the Constitution, and to Tell the Difference: On the Horizontal Application of the Free Movement Provisions in EU Law' (2012) 18 *European Law Journal* 177, 177–8

In constitutional scholarship, the issue of horizontal effect of fundamental rights is usually thought to arise when market outcomes seem to conflict with constitutional norms. Put this way, it is easy to see the trouble the concept gets into when entitlements to market outcomes are elevated to the status of fundamental rights. In a string of cases starting with the 1974 decision in *Walrave*, the Court of Justice has held that the economic freedom of private employers and other powerful organisations are limited by the free movement provisions of the Treaty that protect individuals from discrimination on grounds of nationality. In 2007, the Court held in *Viking* and *Laval* that the fundamental right of collective action of trade unions is limited by the provisions of the Treaty that guarantee employers the economic freedom to provide services and to establish themselves in other Member States. One could be forgiven for thinking that these cases represent radically different conceptions of the internal market: the first as the expression of the primacy of the polity over 'the market' through the imposition of public law values on principles of private law, the second as an act of neoliberal faith in imposing economic freedom on constitutionally protected social rights. Where the former cases seem to foreshadow the 'social market economy', the latter hark back to the days when the Treaty could be described as the 'most strongly free market-oriented constitution in the world'.[68] And yet, the Court decided the latter cases largely on the authority of the former under the same rubric of the 'horizontal direct effect of the fundamental freedoms'.

Non-discrimination can thus achieve different social and economic ends, depending how it is used. Nevertheless, it is wrong to think that *Viking* and *Laval* express no more than 'neoliberalism'. There is not just a conflict of interest between corporate and labour interests in these cases, but also between different groups of workers: those from poorer Member States, who want to work in richer ones, even on terms that locals would not accept, and those from the richer States, who want to protect their labour and social rights from the hollowing-out effects of such competition. The resolution of this conflict will only occur when socio-economic inequalities between States are reduced. In the meantime the cases should be seen as part of a broader legal search for an acceptable compromise. In achieving that, legislation is at least as important as case law.

All of the cases discussed in this section have concerned a private party who was not themselves engaged in cross-border provision of services, but was taking measures which prevented two other parties from doing so. Could the Treaty also be applied to one of the parties to the service provision, the recipient or the provider?[69] It seems now to be clear that if a private

---

[68] C.-D. Ehlermann, 'The Contribution of EC Competition Policy to the Single Market' (1992) 29 *CMLRev* 257, 273.

[69] See G. Davies, 'Freedom of Movement, Horizontal Effect, and Freedom of Contract' (2012) 20 *European Review of Private Law*, 805.

party prevents an Italian hairdresser from accessing Belgian clients then that private party will be subject to the Treaty. But what if the Italian hairdresser herself refuses Belgian clients, or if a Belgian client refuses to go to an Italian hairdresser? Is this a restriction on free movement of services? On the one hand, a cross-border provision of services is being prevented by a directly discriminatory choice. On the other hand, applying the Treaty to individual preferences like this would have a huge impact on individual autonomy, as well as being practically impossible to police. Moreover, if we cannot choose an Italian hairdresser, does this mean that the time will come when we cannot choose French cheese without discriminating illegally?

It is suggested that it is possible to draw a distinction between areas of free movement: people are different, and a rejection of discrimination against them is not new to policy. Discrimination in employment is prohibited already and where service relationships come close to employment in their substance it would make sense to take the same approach.[70] Yet could this go so far as to prohibit a private preference to do business with a national bank, or an Italian hairdresser? Conceptual tools which may help answer this difficult question could include the presence of market power, and the effect on the dignity of the individual.[71] It may be noted that Directives have already been adopted prohibiting discrimination on grounds of sex and race in the supply of goods and services.[72] The application of normative constraints to individual choices is something EU law has already begun to embrace.

5 JUSTIFYING RESTRICTIONS ON SERVICES

The analytical structure of the law on services is summarised in *Gebhard*:[73]

> 37 It follows, however, from the Court's case-law that national measures liable to hinder or make less attractive the exercise of fundamental freedoms guaranteed by the Treaty must fulfil four conditions: they must be applied in a non-discriminatory manner; they must be justified by imperative requirements in the general interest; they must be suitable for securing the attainment of the objective which they pursue; and they must not go beyond what is necessary in order to attain it.

Rephrasing this, it can be said that as with the law on the other freedoms, a restriction on services will be permitted if it is:

(i) equally applicable to the national and the foreign
(ii) justified by some legitimate public interest objective and
(iii) proportionate to that objective.

If a restriction on services is not equally applicable, but discriminates on its face, then it may only be saved by reliance on one of the Treaty exceptions.[74]

---

[70] *Roman Angonese* v. *Cassa di Risparmio di Bolzano*, C-281/98, EU:C:2000:296.

[71] See generally Davies, n. 69 above.

[72] Council Directive 2004/113/EC of 13 December 2004 implementing the principle of equal treatment between men and women in the access to and supply of goods and services [2004] OJ L 373/37–43; Council Directive 2000/43/ EC of 29 June 2000 implementing the principle of equal treatment between persons irrespective of racial or ethnic origin [2000] OJ L 180/22–6.

[73] *Gebhard* v. *Consiglio dell'ordine degli avvocati eprocuratori di Milano*, C-55/94, EU:C:1995:411.

[74] *Gouda* v. *Commissariat voor de Media*, C-288/89, EU:C:1991:157; see also p. 827.

The justifications which may be put forward for equally applicable measures are diverse, and the list is not closed.[75] Any good policy reason that is not discriminatory or purely economic is acceptable. The need to regulate a profession in the public interest, consumer protection and the protection of workers are examples.[76] However, the imposition of national laws on service providers is not justified where the interest concerned is protected by legislation in the State of establishment.[77] In *Guiot*, employers were required to pay social security payments for workers in Belgium. However, this applied not only if the company and its workers were established in Belgium, but also if the company was established in another Member State and had temporarily posted workers to Belgium to supply services there. The Court of Justice found that compulsory social security payments could be justified in general by the protection of workers, but imposing them on companies that might be making similar contributions in their home States, without taking any account of this, was disproportionate.[78]

Guiot, C-272/94, EU:C:1996:147

14 National legislation which requires an employer, as a person providing a service within the meaning of the Treaty, to pay employer's contributions to the social security fund of the host Member State in addition to the contributions already paid by him to the social security fund of the State where he is established places an additional financial burden on him, so that he is not, so far as competition is concerned, on an equal footing with employers established in the host State.

15 Such legislation, even if it applies without distinction to national providers of services and to those of other Member States, is liable to restrict the freedom to provide services within the meaning of Article [56 TFEU].

16 The public interest relating to the social protection of workers in the construction industry may however, because of conditions specific to that sector, constitute an overriding requirement justifying such a restriction on the freedom to provide services.

17 However, that is not the case where the workers in question enjoy the same protection, or essentially similar protection, by virtue of employer's contributions already paid by the employer in the Member State of establishment.

Requiring a service provider to undergo police checks when similar ones have been performed in the home State is another example of an attempt to make a foreign provider jump through two sets of hoops, in violation of mutual recognition.[79]

It is also disproportionate to subject service providers to all the rules which would apply to them if they were established.[80] The logic of the internal market is that as far as possible each economic actor should be subject to the law of their home State, and mutual recognition should ensure that other States recognise the adequacy of this law and permit that actor to do business on their national markets without further ado. Thus, if a company chooses to establish in State X it is

---

[75] S. O'Leary and J. Fernández-Mártin, 'Judicially Created Exceptions to Free Provision of Services' in M. Andenas and W.-H. Roth (eds.), *Services and Free Movement in EU Law* (Oxford University Press, 2002); Snell, n. 15 above, 169–219.

[76] See *Gouda* v. *Commissariat voor de Media*, C-288/89, EU:C:1991:157, para. 14 for a long list.

[77] *Ibid.*; *Commission* v. *Germany (German Insurance)*, 205/84, EU:C:1986:463; *Commission* v. *Italy (Trade Fairs)*, C-439/99, EU:C:2002:14. See also *Jyske Bank*, C-212/11, EU:C:2013:270, 25 April 2013.

[78] Similarly, *Seco* v. *Etablissement d'assurance contre la vieillesse et l'invalidité*, 62–3/81, EU:C:1982:34; *Commission* v. *Italy*, 3/88, EU:C:1992:49. See also *Bundesdruckerei GmbH* v. *Stadt Dortmund*, C-549/13, EU:C:2014:2235.

[79] *Webb*, 279/80, EU:C:1981:314; *Commission* v. *Portugal*, C-458/08, EU:C:2010:692. See also *Jyske Bank*, C-212/11, EU:C:2013:270; *X-Steuerberatungsgesellschaft* v. *Finanzamt Hannover-Nord*, C-342/14, EU:C:2015:827.

[80] *Commission* v. *Germany (German Insurance)*, 205/84, EU:C:1986:463. See also *Essent*, C-91/13, EU:C:2014:2206.

reasonable that in principle it should comply fully with the regulation of X. However, if it is merely providing temporary services in X, then full compliance with the laws of X will almost always be a disproportionate demand. This would take away the regulatory distinction between services and establishment, and undermine the capacity of service providers to choose where to establish. In *Säger*, the German Government obstructed the provision of patent services in Germany by patent agents based in the United Kingdom.[81] They did not possess the qualifications required in Germany for the service they were providing. The Court of Justice did not object to the German rules as such: appropriate rules on qualifications are a way of protecting the consumer in a complex and technical field. However, it went on to hold as follows.

> ### Säger v. Dennemeyer, C-76/90, EU:C:1991:331
>
> [A] Member State may not make the provision of services in its territory subject to compliance with all the conditions required for establishment and thereby deprive of all practical effectiveness the provisions of the Treaty whose object is, precisely, to guarantee the freedom to provide services. Such a restriction is all the less permissible where, as in the main proceedings, and unlike the situation governed by the third paragraph of Article [57 TFEU], the service is supplied without its being necessary for the person providing it to visit the territory of the Member State where it is provided.

A step further is to actually require a service provider to establish: some cases have involved national rules which restrict certain service activities to those who are established in that Member State, or have physical premises there, or who live there. In *Van Binsbergen*, a Dutch requirement that lawyers be established in the Netherlands in order to provide legal services was in issue, and in *Commission* v. *Italy* a rule was challenged requiring debt collectors to have physical premises in each province where they were licensed.[82] The argument for such rules is usually about the need for supervision, but they are rarely justified. Given the fact that they effectively ban all cross-border provision of the service in question, and given that the requirements in question do not really do much to guarantee effective supervision in a world of modern communication, the general position is that a less restrictive and more proportionate approach should be found.

(i) Restrictions on Marketing and Prices

The way that a service is marketed and priced may be just as important to the commercial success of the service provider as the content or quality of the service. Moreover, where a market is dominated by established providers, an innovative marketing or pricing policy can help a new market player break in. The Court of Justice has therefore acknowledged that rules which limit price competition may restrict trade.[83] Most notably, in *Cipolla*, it considered regional rules in Italy which fixed legal fees at a set level, and prohibited lawyers from charging less.[84]

---

[81] *Säger* v. *Dennemeyer*, C-76/90, EU:C:1991:331.

[82] *Van Binsbergen* v. *Bestuur van de Bedrijsvereniging voor de Metaalnijverheid*, 33/74, EU:C:1974:131; *Commission* v. *Italy*, C-134/05, EU:C:2007:435.

[83] *Van Tiggele*, 82/77, EU:C:1978:10; *Cullet*, 231/83, EU:C:1985:29; *Caixabank France*, C-442/02, EU:C:2004:586; *DKV*, C-577/11, EU:C:2013:146, 7 March 2013.

[84] See M. J. Frese and H. J. van Harten, 'How Extravagant the Fees of Counselors at Law Sometimes Appear: Competition Law and Internal Market Constraints to Fixed Remuneration Schemes' (2007) 34 *LIEI* 393. See also *Commission* v. *Italy*, C-565/08, EU:C:2011:188.

Federico Cipolla and Others v. _Rosaria Fazari, née Portolese and Roberto Meloni_, C–94/04 and C–202/04, EU:C:2006:758

59 That prohibition deprives lawyers established in a Member State other than the Italian Republic of the possibility, by requesting fees lower than those set by the scale, of competing more effectively with lawyers established on a stable basis in the Member State concerned and who therefore have greater opportunities for winning clients than lawyers established abroad ...

60 Likewise, the prohibition thus laid down limits the choice of service recipients in Italy, because they cannot resort to the services of lawyers established in other Member States who would offer their services in Italy at a lower rate than the minimum fees set by the scale ...

62 In order to justify the restriction on freedom to provide services which stems from the prohibition at issue, the Italian Government submits that excessive competition between lawyers might lead to price competition which would result in a deterioration in the quality of the services provided to the detriment of consumers, in particular as individuals in need of quality advice in court proceedings ...

64 In that respect, it must be pointed out that, first, the protection of consumers, in particular recipients of the legal services provided by persons concerned in the administration of justice and, secondly, the safeguarding of the proper administration of justice, are objectives to be included among those which may be regarded as overriding requirements relating to the public interest capable of justifying a restriction on freedom to provide services, on condition, first, that the national measure at issue in the main proceedings is suitable for securing the attainment of the objective pursued and, secondly, it does not go beyond what is necessary in order to attain that objective.

65 It is a matter for the national court to decide whether, in the main proceedings, the restriction on freedom to provide services introduced by that national legislation fulfils those conditions. For that purpose, it is for that court to take account of the factors set out in the following paragraphs.

66 Thus, it must be determined, in particular, whether there is a correlation between the level of fees and the quality of the services provided by lawyers and whether, in particular, the setting of such minimum fees constitutes an appropriate measure for attaining the objectives pursued, namely the protection of consumers and the proper administration of justice.

67 Although it is true that a scale imposing minimum fees cannot prevent members of the profession from offering services of mediocre quality, it is conceivable that such a scale does serve to prevent lawyers, in a context such as that of the Italian market which, as indicated in the decision making the reference, is characterised by an extremely large number of lawyers who are enrolled and practising, from being encouraged to compete against each other by possibly offering services at a discount, with the risk of deterioration in the quality of the services provided.

68 Account must also be taken of the specific features both of the market in question, as noted in the preceding paragraph, and the services in question and, in particular, of the fact that, in the field of lawyers' services, there is usually an asymmetry of information between 'client-consumers' and lawyers. Lawyers display a high level of technical knowledge which consumers may not have and the latter therefore find it difficult to judge the quality of the services provided to them.

69 However, the national court will have to determine whether professional rules in respect of lawyers, in particular rules relating to organisation, qualifications, professional ethics, supervision and liability, suffice in themselves to attain the objectives of the protection of consumers and the proper administration of justice.

The argument that minimum prices prevent excessive competition leading to lower standards and thereby protect the consumer is a very common one, used in most professional contexts. What is striking about *Cipolla* is the extent to which the Court of Justice is prepared to critically examine this argument on the particular facts, and to question whether professional quality could be protected by less restrictive means. What is also interesting is that while it leaves the final answer to the national court to decide, the Court implies that facts specific to Italy or the local legal market may be relevant to that answer. It is therefore possible that a minimum price might be justified and proportionate in Italy, but not in another Member State, or even in one region of Italy but not in another, because of the different characteristics of the market for legal services in each area. Such a market-specific approach to proportionality is only politically sustainable because it is local judges who finally decide whether local rules are proportionate. Were the Court of Justice to rule that, for example, minimum prices were permissible in Italy but not in Germany, this would probably be seen as grossly unfair.

Other marketing restrictions concern advertising and methods of sale. For example, in *Alpine Investments* the Court allowed the Netherlands to stop Dutch financial services companies from cold-calling German consumers.[85] One might think this was a matter for the German Government to worry about, but the Court accepted that the reputation of the Dutch finance industry was at stake – cold-calling being associated with the exploitation of vulnerable consumers – and the measure was a proportionate way of protecting it.[86]

By contrast, it has been hostile to advertising restrictions, even in sensitive fields. *Dermoestetica* concerned a prohibition on advertising private medical or surgical care on national television. Advertising is particularly important for cross-border services, where the foreign provider, who may not have a local physical presence, has no other means of coming into contact with local clients. This suggests one reason why there is no *Keck* for services – because the effect of selling arrangements on goods and services is not necessarily the same.[87] Nevertheless, the Court of Justice would have been prepared to find the restriction justified by public health were it not that similar advertising was permitted on local television. This inconsistency undermined the effectiveness of the measure, so that it was no longer, the Court found 'appropriate for the purpose of securing the attainment of the objective of public health'.[88] That would seem to be second-guessing quite complex policy choices – local advertisers are not, for example, always the same people as national ones. Similarly, in *Vanderborght* the Court indicated that an absolute ban on advertising dental services could not be proportionate – the consumer and social interests at stake could be just as well protected by having rules on advertising and policing them well.[89] Really?

---

[85] *Alpine Investments* v. *Minister van Financiën*, C-384/93, EU:C:1995:15.

[86] *Corsica Ferries France*, C-18/93, EU:C:1994:195; *Peralta*, C-379/92, EU:C:1994:296.

[87] Although see the parallels drawn in W.-H. Roth, 'The European Court of Justice's Case Law on Freedom to Provide Services: Is *Keck* Relevant?' in M. Andenas and W.-H. Roth (eds.), *Services and Free Movement in EU Law* (Oxford University Press, 2002) 1; Hatzopoulos, n. 22 above; J. L. Da Cruz Vilaca, 'On the Application of *Keck* in the Field of Free Provision of Services' in M. Andenas and W.-H. Roth (eds.), *Services and Free Movement in EU Law* (Oxford University Press, 2002) 25.

[88] *Corporacion Dermoestetica*, EU:C:2008:421, C-500/06, para. 40.   [89] *Vanderborght*, C-339/15, EU:C:2016:660.

(ii) Access to Regulated Industries and Professions

Many cases on services concern access to regulated professions and industries. Foreign service providers wishing to provide services in a highly regulated industry, such as the law, medicine, gambling or private security, typically find that many measures stand in their way. One of the most common problems is obtaining recognition of foreign qualifications, which is dealt with in Chapter 18.[90] However, other aspects of authorisation and regulation have also been the subject of much case law.

Corsten is a relatively simple example. An architect working from the Netherlands contracted to arrange floor-laying in Germany, but was fined when he did the work because he was not entered on the local German register of skilled traders. In order to go on this register, he had to submit various documents, pay a fee and become a member of the local chamber of skilled trades, which entailed paying a subscription. The process also took some time, and he was not permitted to practise his trade in the area until it was completed.

Corsten, C–58/98, EU:C:2000:527

45 Even if the requirement of entry on that Register, entailing compulsory membership of the Chamber of Skilled Trades for the undertakings concerned and therefore payment of the related subscription, could be justified in the case of establishment in the host Member State, which is not the situation in the main proceedings, the same is not true for undertakings which intend to provide services in the host Member State only on an occasional basis, indeed perhaps only once.

46 The latter are liable to be dissuaded from going ahead with their plans if, because of the compulsory requirement that they be entered on the Register, the authorisation procedure is made lengthier and more expensive, so that the profit anticipated, at least for small contracts, is no longer economically worthwhile. For those undertakings, therefore, the freedom to provide services, a fundamental principle of the Treaty, and likewise Directive 64/427 are liable to become ineffective.

47 In consequence, the authorisation procedure instituted by the host Member State should neither delay nor complicate exercise of the right of persons established in another Member State to provide their services on the territory of the first State where examination of the conditions governing access to the activities concerned has been carried out and it has been established that those conditions are satisfied.

48 Moreover, any requirement of entry on the trades Register of the host Member State, assuming it was justified, should neither give rise to additional administrative expense nor entail compulsory payment of subscriptions to the chamber of trades.

The Court of Justice highlights the importance of distinguishing between established persons and those providing services. Service providers may do very little business in their host State, and so even relatively light administrative burdens wipe out their profit and deter them from entering the market. The aim of the register was to ensure the quality of traders and protect consumers, which was legitimate, but proportionality demanded that where a service provider was concerned the procedure for register entry be as minimal and simple as possible. In particular, it must not add 'administrative expense' and nor must it delay the start of work – meaning that either a trader can begin work while the process of registration is underway, or registration must be available

---

[90] See pp. 796–802.

immediately. In *Commission* v. *Belgium*, an apparently very simple administrative procedure was found to violate Article 56: all those providing services in Belgium who were established elsewhere were required to fill in a form once a year indicating their identity and the services they were providing.[91] The form was available online, and the procedure was free, and the Belgian Government estimated it took about half an hour per year to fill in. Nevertheless, since the Belgian Government could not show that the information was actually necessary to safeguard some public interest, it was disproportionate. It may have been relevant that although not much was being asked of service providers, there were criminal sanctions for a failure to comply.

Somewhat more burdensome demands have been involved in the considerable number of cases concerning private security firms.[92] These are highly regulated for understandable reasons, but the nature of the regulation is at times bizarre, and very often disproportionate. In *Commission* v. *Italy*, security guards were required to swear an oath of allegiance to the Italian State, obviously disproportionate, and particularly irksome for the temporary service provider; while in *Commission* v. *Belgium*, private security firms were required to be established in Belgium, and the managers and employees were required to live in Belgium.[93] Such territorial requirements have been the subject of many cases over the years, and are invariably disproportionate.[94] The proposed justification is that it enables better supervision of the firms and individuals by the national authorities, but the Court has found that this can be achieved by less restrictive means. It is possible to communicate with authorities in other States, and it is possible to carry out checks on firms and individuals wherever they live or are established.[95]

A number of recent gambling cases have concerned the right to offer gambling services, such as lotteries or betting on horse-races, at a distance, usually over the Internet.[96] The Court of Justice accepts that this kind of service requires strict controls in the cause of preventing crimes such as fraud and money-laundering and preventing addiction to gambling by the public. These issues are discussed further in Chapter 19.[97] However, even justifiably protective measures can be prohibited restrictions on free movement if they have some discriminatory or protectionist element in the way they are applied. This was the case with horse-betting licences in *Commission* v. *Italy*. Italy permitted a fixed number of these, but they were awarded and renewed without any

---

[91] *Commission* v. *Belgium*, C-577/10, EU:C:2012:814, 19 December 2012.

[92] *Commission* v. *Belgium*, C-355/98, EU:C:2000:113; *Commission* v. *Portugal*, C-171/02, EU:C:2004:270; *Commission* v. *Spain*, C-514/03, EU:C:2006:63; *Commission* v. *Italy*, C-465/05, EU:C:2007:781.

[93] *Commission* v. *Italy*, C-465/05, EU:C:2007:781; *Commission* v. *Belgium*, C-355/98, EU:C:2000:113.

[94] *Van Binsbergen* v. *Bestuur van de Bedrijsvereniging voor de Metaalnijverheid*, 33/74, EU:C:1974:131; *Coenen* v. *Sociaal-Economische Raad*, 39/75, EU:C:1975:155; *Commission* v. *Germany (German Insurance)*, 205/84, EU:C:1986:463. Similarly, *Commission* v. *Netherlands*, C-299/02, EU:C:2004:620.

[95] *Commission* v. *Austria*, C-393/05, EU:C:2007:428; *Commission* v. *Germany*, C-404/05, EU:C:2007:428; *Talotta* v. *Belgium*, C-383/05, EU:C:2007:181; *Ordre des Avocats au Barreau de Paris* v. *Klopp*, 107/83, EU:C:1984:270; *Van Binsbergen* v. *Bestuur van de Bedrijsvereniging voor de Metaalnijverheid*, 33/74, EU:C:1974:13.

[96] E.g. *Stanleybet*, C-186/11, EU:C:2012:582, Judgment of 24 January 2013; *Carmen Media*, C-46/08, EU:C:2010:505; *Stoß*, C-316/07, EU:C:2010:504; C-258/08 *Ladbrokes*, EU:C:2010:308; *Questore di Verona* v. *Zenatti*, C-67/98, EU:C:1999:514; *Lindman*, C-42/02, EU:C:2003:613; *Anomar* v. *Estado Português*, C-6/01, EU:C:2003:446; *Gambelli*, C-243/01, EU:C:2003:597; *Placanica, Palazzese and Sorricchio*, C-338/04, C-359–60/04, EU:C:2007:133; *Liga Portuguesa de Futebol Profissional and Bwin International Ltd* v. *Departamento de Jogos da Santa Casa da Misericórdia de Lisboa*, C-42/07, EU:C:2009:519, Judgment of 8 September 2009. See D. Doukas, 'In a Bet There Is a Fool and a State Monopoly: Are the Odds Stacked Against Cross-border Gambling?' (2011) 36 *ELRev* 243; S. Van den Bogaert and A. Cuyvers, '"Money for Nothing": The Case Law of the EU Court of Justice on the Regulation of Gambling' (2011) 48 *CMLRev* 1175; J. Mulder, 'A New Chapter in the European Court of Justice Gambling Saga: A Stacked Deck?' (2011) 38 *LIEI* 243.

[97] See esp. pp. 829–38.

publicity so that there was little turnover of licence holders, and for a new entrant it was difficult to obtain a licence. The Court found an obligation of transparency to be imposed on public authorities by Article 56 TFEU.[98]

Commission v. Italy, C–260/04, EU:C:2007:508

22 The Court has held that, notwithstanding the fact that public service concession contracts are, as Community law stands at present, excluded from the scope of Directive 92/50 [on public procurement] the public authorities concluding them are, nonetheless, bound to comply with the fundamental rules of the EC Treaty, in general, and the principle of non-discrimination on the grounds of nationality, in particular.

23 The Court then stated that the provisions of the Treaty applying to public service concessions, in particular Articles [49 and 56 TFEU], and the prohibition of discrimination on grounds of nationality are specific expressions of the principle of equal treatment.

24 In that regard, the principles of equal treatment and non-discrimination on grounds of nationality imply, in particular, a duty of transparency which enables the concession-granting public authority to ensure that those principles are complied with. That obligation of transparency which is imposed on the public authority consists in ensuring, for the benefit of any potential tenderer, a degree of advertising sufficient to enable the service concession to be opened up to competition and the impartiality of procurement procedures to be reviewed.

A final group of cases concern measures which set restrictions on the nature of the service provider, rather than on their activities. For example, in *Sjöberg*, Sweden only allowed non-profit and public organisations to offer gambling services, and did not allow advertising of foreign gambling providers in Sweden unless these were also non-profit or public.[99] The Court of Justice found that the principle that profit and gambling should not be mixed was a fundamental part of the Swedish system of gambling regulation, served legitimate policy goals and justified the measure. *Duomo*, by contrast, concerned an Italian rule that companies involved in tax collection (there was some outsourcing of this to the private sector) must have a minimum size.[100]

Reasons were put forward for this, mainly that larger companies were less likely to go bankrupt with resulting loss of the collected revenue. However, the Court found that other measures could be found which were less restrictive, and did not absolutely exclude smaller actors.

(iii) Tax and Investment Issues

Tax is still a very national matter. In the current state of European integration, it can neither be levied nor spent in a way that takes no account of national boundaries, creating an unavoidable tension with free movement law, which pursues a Europe in which those boundaries are gone. What is simply practical and responsible tax policy, focused on those living and working in a given Member State, may look like nationality discrimination from another perspective. The necessary compromises have created a complex body of EU law which cannot be fully addressed here.

The underlying principles are no different from those applicable to other measures discussed above. It is just that in deciding what is justified, it is often necessary to have a detailed

---

[98] See M. Szydlo, 'The Process of Granting Exclusive Rights in the Light of Treaty Rules on Free Movement' (2011) 12 *German LJ* 1408.

[99] *Sjöberg*, C-447/08, EU:C:2010:415.   [100] *Duomo*, C-357/10, EU:C:2012:283, 10 May 2012.

knowledge of how the tax system works. However, in some cases the facts are more accessible, and these provide a taste of how tax and the free movement of services interact.

Tax discrimination based on location is the most common problem.[101] The Spanish Government exempted winnings from a number of lotteries from tax, but all the relevant lotteries were organised by Spanish organisations.[102] Lottery winnings from lotteries established abroad were not exempted. This placed lotteries established abroad at a disadvantage on the Spanish market and discouraged them from offering their services there. The case is also an example of the well-established principle that it is not necessary to advantage every national operator in order to discriminate: advantaging some national businesses at the expense of foreign ones will suffice.[103]

In *Jundt*, it was tax on the provider rather than the recipient that was in issue.[104] The German Government exempted expense payments to part-time university teachers from tax, but only if the university in question was established in Germany. This was prohibited because it made the provision of services abroad less attractive than equivalent domestic provision and so amounted to a restriction on cross-border service provision.

Commission v. *Belgium* is the mirror of *Jundt*.[105] Belgian laws required those employing building contractors not established in Belgium to withhold 15 per cent of any payment to them against possible tax liabilities of those contractors in Belgium. The contractors had to go through an administrative procedure to show they owed no tax before they could get this money. This deterred foreign contractors from working in Belgium. The justification of preventing tax fraud was not enough to convince the Court of Justice, which suggested, quite consistently with its case law, that a more proportionate approach would be for the authorities to exchange information with employers and contractors so that tax obligations could be enforced.

De Coster concerned indirect discrimination.[106] A tax was imposed on satellite dishes by the municipal authorities in a town in Belgium. This was claimed to be largely on aesthetic grounds: dishes are not pretty, and the tax was intended to discourage them. However, satellite dishes tend to be used to receive cross-border television transmissions, whereas most national programmes are transmitted by cable. Since there was no analogous tax on cable connections, the measure disadvantaged foreign television providers. The Court found that it could not be justified.

De Coster v. *Collège des bourgmestre et échevins de Watermael-Boitsfort*, C-17/00, EU:C:2001:651

38 As the Commission observed, there are methods other than the tax in question in the main proceedings, less restrictive of the freedom to provide services, which could achieve an objective such as the protection of the urban environment, for instance the adoption of requirements concerning the size of the dishes, their

---

[101] *Laboratoires Fournier SA* v. *Direction des vérifications nationales et internationales*, C-39/04, EU:C:2005:161; *Talotta* v. *Belgium*, C-383/05, EU:C:2007:181; *Jobra VermögensverwaltungsGesellschaft mbH* v. *Finanzamt Amstetten Melk Scheibbs*, C-330/07, EU:C:2008:685, 4 December 2008.
[102] *Commission* v. *Spain*, C-153/08, EU:C:2009:618, 6 October 2009.
[103] *Presidente del Consiglio dei Ministri* v. *Regione Sardegna*, C-169/08, EU:C:2009:709, 17 November 2009.
[104] *Jundt and Jundt* v. *Finanzamt Offenburg*, C-281/06, EU:C:2007:816.
[105] *Commission* v. *Belgium*, C-433/04, EU:C:2006:702.
[106] *De Coster* v. *Collège des bourgmestre et échevins de Watermael-Boitsfort*, C-17/00, EU:C:2001:651.

position and the way in which they are fixed to the building or its surroundings or the use of communal dishes. Moreover, such requirements have been adopted by the municipality of Watermael-Boitsfort, as is apparent from the planning rules on outdoor aerials adopted by that municipality and approved by regulation of 27 February 1997 of the government of the Brussels-Capital region.

The odd thing here is that the municipality had already adopted the measures proposed by the Court of Justice, and clearly considered that they were not enough. Yet, the Court uses their adoption as an argument against the tax. This perhaps shows two things. One is that the Court is very strict where unequal effects are involved, particularly if there is the suspicion of deliberate discrimination against foreign service providers. The other is that the Court may have been aware of the considerable unspoken social background to taxes such as these: satellite dishes are most popular among immigrant groups, and this colours the aesthetic arguments against them, however real these may be.

6 SERVICES AND THE MARKET SOCIETY

(i) Right to Trade and Socially Sensitive Services

Article 56 TFEU embodies a right to trade services. This applies even to services which have not traditionally been seen as tradeable or as primarily economic. Health care, education, sport and ethically sensitive services like abortion or gambling have traditionally been regulated from a primarily non-economic perspective.

It has been put to the Court of Justice that such services should not fall within Article 56 because of their special social, cultural or ethical importance. The Court has consistently rejected this.[107] In *Kohll*, speaking of rules on social security and health care, it said: 'The Court has held that the special nature of certain services does not remove them from the ambit of the fundamental principle of freedom of movement.'[108] Similarly, when it was argued in *Schindler* that gambling could not be regarded as a service because in some States it was illegal, the Court refused to take a moral stance.

HM Customs and Excise v. *Schindler*, C–275/92, EU:C:1994:119

32 In these circumstances, lotteries cannot be regarded as activities whose harmful nature causes them to be prohibited in all the Member States and whose position under Community law may be likened to that of activities involving illegal products (see, in relation to drugs, the judgment in Case 294/82 *Einberger* v. *Hauptzollamt Freiburg* [1984] ECR 1177) even though, as the Belgian and Luxembourg Governments point out, the law of certain Member States treats gaming contracts as void. Even if the morality of lotteries is at least questionable, it is not for the Court to substitute its assessment for that of the legislatures of the Member States where that activity is practised legally . . .

---

[107] By contrast, it has been more reluctant to apply competition law. See *Poucet* v. *Assurances Générales de France and Caisse Mutuelle Régionale du Languedoc-Roussillon*, C–159–60/91, EU:C:1993:63. See generally W. Sauter and H. Schepel, *State and Market in European Union Law* (Cambridge University Press, 2009).

[108] *Kohll* v. *Union des Caisses de Maladie*, C–158/96, EU:C:1997:399.

It has applied the same logic to prostitution,[109] and most famously to abortion, in *Grogan*. A group of students in Ireland distributed pamphlets providing information on how to get an abortion in the United Kingdom. Abortion was at that time constitutionally prohibited in Ireland.[110] The Irish authorities took steps to prohibit the distribution of the pamphlets, and the question was whether this amounted to a restriction on the free movement of services.

Society for the Protection of the Unborn Child (SPUC) v. Grogan, C-159/90, EU:C:1991:378

18 It must be held that termination of pregnancy, as lawfully practised in several Member States, is a medical activity which is normally provided for remuneration and may be carried out as part of a professional activity. In any event, the Court has already held in the judgment in *Luisi and Carbone* that medical activities fall within the scope of Article [57] of the Treaty.[111]

19 SPUC, however, maintains that the provision of abortion cannot be regarded as being a service, on the grounds that it is grossly immoral and involves the destruction of the life of a human being, namely the unborn child.

20 Whatever the merits of those arguments on the moral plane, they cannot influence the answer to the national court's first question. It is not for the Court to substitute its assessment for that of the legislature in those Member States where the activities in question are practised legally.

21 Consequently, the answer to the national court's first question must be that medical termination of pregnancy, performed in accordance with the law of the State in which it is carried out, constitutes a service within the meaning of Article [57] of the Treaty ...

24 As regards, first, the provisions of Article [56] of the Treaty, which prohibit any restriction on the freedom to supply services, it is apparent from the facts of the case that the link between the activity of the students associations of which Mr Grogan and the other defendants are officers and medical terminations of pregnancies carried out in clinics in another Member State is too tenuous for the prohibition on the distribution of information to be capable of being regarded as a restriction within the meaning of Article [56] of the Treaty.

In the last paragraph above the Court of Justice managed to avoid a major conflict of values by finding that Article 56 did not apply because the students had no connection with the service providers.[112] They were acting out of non-commercial motives on their own initiative. The case implicitly introduces a 'directness' criterion into the concept of a restriction on services,[113] but the context was so politically sensitive and the facts so unusual that this extrapolation must remain uncertain.

However, the lasting importance of the case is in the confirmation that, however offensive or illegal a service may be in one State, if it is permitted in others then providers in those States can rely on Article 56. Had the Irish Government taken sufficiently concrete steps to prevent Irish women going to the United Kingdom for paid abortions, Article 56 TFEU would have applied, the Irish Constitution notwithstanding.

---

[109] See also *Jany* v. *Staatssecretaris van Justitie*, C-268/99, EU:C:2001:616.

[110] With nuances: see e.g. I. Bacik, 'The Irish Constitution and Gender Politics: Developments in the Law on Abortion' (2013) 28 *Irish Political Studies* 380.

[111] *Luisi and Carbone* v. *Ministero del Tesoro*, 286/82 and 26/83, EU:C:1984:35, para. 16.

[112] See D. R. Phelan, 'The Right to Life of the Unborn v. Promotion of Trade in Services: The European Court and the Normative Shaping of the European Union' (1992) 55 *MLR* 670. Shortly after this case a Protocol was adopted protecting the Irish ban on abortion from EU law. See C. Barnard, *The Substantive Law of the EU*, 5th edn (Oxford University Press, 2016) 297–301.

[113] Barnard, n. 112, 296.

This is not to say that national constitutional values will not be respected, or may not prevail. Both mandatory requirements and Treaty exceptions may justify a restriction on free movement and it is undoubtedly the case that where there is such strong national feeling as exists in Ireland over abortion, the Court of Justice will weigh this heavily.[114] However, the structure of the normative framework has been changed. After *Kohll*, *Grogan* and *Schindler*, moral, social and cultural perspectives are tested against economic rights, rather than economic rights being clearly subordinated to higher norms. This does not necessarily lead to different outcomes in cases, but it may encourage them: rhetorical reordering does influence the reasoning process, both in public debate and in judicial proceedings. Hervey has expressed this point.

> **T. Hervey, 'Buy Baby: The European Union and the Regulation of Human Reproduction'**
> **(1998) 18 *Oxford Journal of Legal Studies* 207, 230**
>
> [T]he ability and indeed duty to apply EC law hinders national courts from explicitly approaching issues concerned with moral or ethical choices. Rather, the application of EC law may encourage or at least enable national courts to resolve cases by applying economic concepts, for example, relating to trade in goods and services. The EU legal order, with its underlying principles of market openness, and conceptualization of individuals as market actors, might aid this type of approach.[115]

(ii) Article 56 TFEU and the Welfare State

The fundamental fear – for others the hope – is that Article 56 TFEU will create a market society, in Polanyi's famous term, which inverts the relationship between the market and society.[116] Instead of the economy being embedded in social relations, social relations are embedded in the economic system.

If that is indeed to be observed, then one promising context is where Article 56 TFEU has interacted with the Welfare State, and in particular health care.[117] This is the area where the law has intruded the furthest into a sensitive service area, embodying many non-economic values. The cases show, as suggested above, an increasing centrality for individual transactions and preferences above systemic considerations.[118] However, they also show pragmatism and compromise, and a willingness at least to listen to Member State fears, if not always to accept them. Nor can they be seen as a simple triumph of economic freedom over other values: in most cases, States oppose the use of Article 56 on largely budgetary (economic) grounds, while individuals plead for free movement using a normative and non-economic language in which their personal and medical circumstances are more central than any notion of economic liberty. Perhaps the far-reaching scope of the health-care cases has been partly possible because it is the patients,

---

[114] See pp. 830–1.

[115] T. Hervey, 'Buy Baby: The European Union and the Regulation of Human Reproduction' (1998) 18 *OJLS* 207, 230.

[116] The term was first used in K. Polanyi, *The Great Transformation*, 2nd edn (Boston, MA, Beacon, 2001).

[117] See e.g. G. de Búrca (ed.), *EU Law and the Welfare State* (Oxford University Press, 2005); M. Dougan and E. Spaventa, *Social Welfare and EU Law* (Oxford, Hart, 2005); E. Spaventa, 'Public Services and European Law: Looking for Boundaries' (2002) *CYELS* 271; G. Davies, 'The Process and Side-effects of Harmonisation of European Welfare States', Jean Monnet Working Paper No. 2/06 (2006); M. Ross and Y. Borgmann-Prebil, *Promoting Solidarity in the European Union* (Oxford University Press, 2010).

[118] See C. Newdick, 'Citizenship, Free Movement and Healthcare: Cementing Individual Rights by Corroding Social Solidarity' (2006) 43 *CMLRev* 1645.

rather than the providers, who have led the litigation, and have more easily claimed the moral high ground than a commercial service provider could have done.[119]

In any event, the law discussed below is leading to a reorganising of welfare structures and a redrawing of the boundaries of solidarity.[120] Individuals have been granted rights to exit their national system and receive services in other Member States, with consequences for the budgets of their home State and the State they travel to. As well as this, institutions have also been granted the right to offer welfare services in other Member States, with consequences for the integrity and stability of pre-existing national institutions. This is primarily an issue of establishment, and is addressed in Chapter 18.[121] What follows focuses on the rights of individuals to seek services such as health care and education abroad.

This right took some time to emerge. Many public services are provided free and the Court of Justice has found these not to be remunerated, and so not to be Treaty services.[122] This was enough to prevent Article 56 and the Welfare State meeting, and to raise a perception that this meeting would not occur.

One reason that this has changed in recent years is that public institutions such as schools, universities and hospitals are increasingly funded by private insurance or by the consumers of their services, so that Article 56 applies to at least some of their activities.[123] Yet another reason, which has been more important in the case law, is that the type of migration has changed: instead of individuals going abroad to receive free public services, in recent years individuals have been exiting their (free) domestic systems in order to pay for services abroad. Instead of the non-economic Welfare State being a destination, it has become a hindrance.

This creates a role for Article 56. Whatever the character of the domestic Welfare State, economic or not, where migrants pay for services abroad there is obviously a remunerated cross-border service in issue. The nature of the domestic system becomes quite irrelevant to this point. For example, in *Commission* v. *Germany*, the Commission challenged German rules which made school fees tax deductible, but only if the school was in Germany.[124] This, of course, discouraged the sending of children to schools abroad. Germany argued that school education was not a service.

Commission v. Germany, C–318/05, EU:C:2007:495

71 It is undisputed that, in parallel with schools belonging to a public educational system whereby the State performs its task in the social, educational and cultural areas, the financing of which is essentially from public funds, there are schools in certain Member States which do not belong to such a system of public education and which are financed essentially from private funds.

72 The education provided by such schools must be regarded as a service provided for remuneration.

---

[119] But see pp. 772–3.
[120] See e.g. D. S. Martinsen and V. Vrangbaek, 'The Europeanisation of Health Care Governance: Implementing the Market Imperatives of Europe' (2008) 86 *Public Administration* 169; Davies, n. 117 above; J. Montgomery, 'The Impact of European Union Law on English Healthcare Law' in M. Dougan and E. Spaventa, *Social Welfare and EU Law* (Oxford, Hart, 2005) 145; M. Ferrera, 'Towards an Open Social Citizenship? The New Boundaries of Welfare in the European Union' in G. de Búrca (ed.), *EU Law and the Welfare State* (Oxford University Press, 2005) 11.
[121] See pp. 808–9.   [122] See pp. 741–4.   [123] *Ibid.*
[124] See also *Schwarz and Gootjes-Schwarz* v. *Finanzamt Bergisch Gladbach*, C-76/05, EU:C:2007:492.

> 73 It should be added that, for the purposes of determining whether Article [56 TFEU] applies to the national legislation at issue, it is irrelevant whether or not the schools established in the Member State of the user of the service – in this case the Federal Republic of Germany – which are approved, authorised or recognised in that Member State within the meaning of that legislation, provide services within the meaning of the first paragraph of Article [57 TFEU]. All that matters is that the private school established in another Member State may be regarded as providing services for remuneration.

The mere fact that a State organises its public services in a non-economic way does not therefore protect that State from Article 56 TFEU: its citizens still have a right to go to other States where the services may be economic in character, and this right of exit may have far-reaching organisational consequences for the systems at home.[125] This has been above all the case in the context of health care. The Dutch and UK Governments have both argued in the past that Article 56 could not be used by patients who wished to leave the Netherlands or United Kingdom for health care abroad, because those countries provided health care to their citizens within a non-remunerated framework to which Article 56 did not apply (this has now changed in the Netherlands). In both cases, this argument was just as irrelevant as above.[126]

A right to go abroad for health care is, however, only half the story. The real question, which determines the domestic impact of that right, is what kind of national measures will be seen as impeding it. In particular, most national health systems or insurers have traditionally only paid for health care at home, and refused to cover the cost of treatment abroad, except perhaps in exceptional situations. A policy such as this discourages patients from exiting the system and encourages them to receive their health care at home. Is that sufficient to say that not paying for foreign treatment is a restriction on services?

In *Kohll*, the Court of Justice ruled that this is the case. Kohll, a Luxembourgeois national, applied for his daughter to have dental treatment in Germany. Under Luxembourg law, such treatment could be received free if provided in Luxembourg, but required prior authorisation from the sickness insurance fund if it were to be provided outside the country. Authorisation was refused on the grounds that the treatment was not urgent and could, in any case, be provided within Luxembourg. Kohll argued that this breached Article 56 as the dental treatment constituted a service under that provision.

Kohll v. *Union des Caisses de Maladie*, C-158/96, EU:C:1997:399

> 32 The Member States which have submitted observations consider, on the contrary, that the rules at issue do not have as their purpose or effect to restrict freedom to provide services, but merely lay down the conditions for the reimbursement of medical expenses.
>
> 33 It should be noted that, according to the Court's case law, [Article 56 TFEU] precludes the application of any national rules which have the effect of making the provision of services between Member States more difficult than the provision of services purely within one Member State.

---

[125] Cf. The limitation of establishment rights to profit-seeking actors. See pp. 808–9; *No. 5 Spezzino*, C-113/13, EU:C:2014:291.

[126] *Geraets-Smits* v. *Stichting Ziekenfonds*, C-157/99, EU:C:2001:404; *Peerbooms* v. *Stichting CZ Groep Zorgverzekeringen*, C-157/99, EU:C:2001:404; *Watts* v. *Bedford Primary Care Trust*, C-372/04, EU:C:2006:325.

34 While the national rules at issue in the main proceedings do not deprive insured persons of the possibility of approaching a provider of services established in another Member State, they do nevertheless make reimbursement of the costs incurred in that Member State subject to prior authorisation, and deny such reimbursement to insured persons who have not obtained that authorisation. Costs incurred in the State of insurance are not, however, subject to that authorisation.

35 Consequently, such rules deter insured persons from approaching providers of medical services established in another Member State and constitute, for them and their patients, a barrier to freedom to provide services.

The practical consequences of this judgment are displayed in the series of post-*Kohll* cases on health care, which have now been consolidated into Directive 2011/24 on patients' rights in cross-border health care (Patients' Rights Directive).[127] The cases and Directive confirm a patient's right to exit the national system of health care and choose treatment abroad, subject to certain limitations.[128]

The three cases which substantially formed the law in this area, *Geraets-Smits and Peerbooms*, *Müller-Fauré* and *Watts*, share essentially the same fact pattern as *Kohll*.[129] A patient (Dutch in the first two cases, British in the third) approached their health insurer or health authority to ask for authorisation to go abroad for treatment, to ask for confirmation that the insurer or authority would pay the costs. This was refused in each case, whereupon the patient went anyway, and submitted the bill. The insurers or authorities refused to pay, the patient litigated, and the Court of Justice was ultimately asked to adjudicate on exactly when a State or insurer was permitted to refuse payment for treatment abroad and exactly when a patient could obtain it.

In all of these cases, the Member States argued that restrictions on treatment abroad could be justified by public health reasons. They claimed that the cost increases which might result from

---

[127] Directive 2011/24/EU on the application of patients' rights in cross-border health care. The cases in this area and the Directive need to be seen alongside Regulation 883/2004 which provides for a parallel regime, in which instead of being reimbursed as if they were being treated at home, a migrant patient is treated as if they were insured under the law of the treating State. See generally S. de la Rosa, 'The Directive on Cross-border Healthcare or the Art of Codifying Complex Case Law' (2012) 49 *CMLRev* 15; M. Peeters, 'Free Movement of Patients: Directive 2011/24 on the Application of Patients' Rights in Cross-Border Healthcare' (2012) 19 *European Journal of Health Law* 29; A. den Exter, 'One Year after the EU Patient Mobility Directive: A Three-Country Analysis' (2015) 40 *ELRev* 279.

[128] See A.-P. van der Mei, 'Annotation of *Commission* v. *France* and *Elchinov*' (2011) 48 *CMLRev* 1297; V. Hatzopoulos, 'Killing National Health and Insurance Systems but Healing Patients? The European Market for Health Care Services after the Judgments of the ECJ in *Van Braekel* and *Peerbooms*' (2002) 39 *CMLRev* 683; M. Flear, 'Note on Müller-Fauré' (2004) 41 *CMLRev* 209; M. Cousins, 'Patient Mobility and National Health Systems' (2007) 34 *LIEI* 183; K. Stoger, 'Freedom of Establishment and the Market Access of Hospital Operators' (2006) *EBLRev* 1545; V. Hatzopoulos, 'Health Law and Policy: The Impact of the EU' in G. de Búrca (ed.), *EU Law and the Welfare State* (Oxford University Press, 2005) 111; P. Koutrakos, 'Healthcare as an Economic Service under EC Law' in M. Dougan and E. Spaventa (eds.), *Social Welfare and EU Law* (Oxford, Hart, 2005) 105; Davies, n. 117 above.

[129] *Geraets-Smits* v. *Stichting Ziekenfonds*; *Peerbooms* v. *Stichting CZ Groep Zorgverzekeringen*, C-157/99, EU:C:2001:404; *Müller-Fauré* v. *Onderlinge Waarborgmaatschappij OZ Zorgverzekeringen*, C-385/99, EU:C:2003:270; *Watts* v. *Bedford Primary Care Trust*, C-372/04, EU:C:2006:325; see also *Commission* v. *Spain*, C-211/08, EU:C:2010:340; *Elchinov*, C-173/09, EU:C:2010:336; *Commission* v. *France*, C-512/08, EU:C:2010:579; *Leichtle* v. *Bundesanstalt für Arbeit*, C-8/02, EU:C:2004:161; *Vanbraekel* v. *ANMC*, C-368/98, EU:C:2001:400; *Stamatelaki* v. *OAEE*, C-444/05, EU:C:2007:231; *Inizan* v. *Caisse Primaire d'Assurance Maladie des Hauts-de-Seine*, C-56/01, EU:C:2003:578.

patient migration could be so dramatic that the stability and sustainability of the public health system would be threatened.

The reasons why costs might increase are several. First, the costs of treatment abroad may be higher than the cost of equivalent treatment domestically. Secondly, patients may go abroad for treatment that is not in fact medically effective, following their whims rather than medical science. Thirdly, a good domestic health system requires the maintenance of an expensive medical infrastructure. For the most efficient use of this there must be a stable and continuous flow of clients. If patients can go abroad then domestic hospitals may run at less than full capacity. Yet, States cannot close them, because each State wants to maintain the domestic capacity to treat its citizens. Hence, States may be forced effectively to pay twice, once for the unused domestic capacity, and once for the actual treatment abroad.

In all of the cases, the Court of Justice took the same approach: merely budgetary or economic arguments do not justify a restriction on free movement.[130] However, if States could show that the financial consequences would be so great that they would indeed threaten the stability and quality of the system, then this would justify restrictions. The question is when this would be the case. The first two arguments for cost increase – expensive foreign treatment and luxury treatment – have not been accepted. The Court has noted that Member States are free to define the scope of health care for which their system will pay, and the rates that they will pay.[131] Provided they do this in a non-discriminatory, transparent and rational way, the existence of a defined health package will not in itself contravene Article 56.[132] These limits then apply equally to treatment abroad, so that the cost risk is avoided. If States determine that a hip operation costs €3,000 in their domestic system, they may, for example, rule that they will pay a maximum of €3,000 for the same operation abroad. They must not have a lower reimbursement tariff for foreign treatment, but it need not be higher. This is now the approach taken in the Patients' Rights Directive.[133]

This sounds reasonable, but defining the domestic health-care package imposes considerable administrative burdens on States.[134] In *Geraets-Smits and Peerbooms*, a Dutch coma patient was refused authorisation for a treatment in Austria on the grounds that it was experimental and had not been proven to be effective. The Dutch system only paid for treatment that was considered 'normal'. Even after the patient had been cured by the Austrian treatment, the Dutch insurance fund continued to refuse reimbursement on this ground. They lost before the Court of Justice because the definition of 'normal' treatment appeared to be one deriving exclusively from domestic medical practice, rather than from medical science, which, as the Court noted, is inherently international. 'Only an interpretation on the basis of what is sufficiently tried and tested by international medical science' was compatible with Article 56. Thus, Member States which wish to effectively limit the treatment their patients can receive abroad must define the scope of their domestic care with reasonable precision and care.[135]

---

[130] See pp. 825–6.
[131] *Geraets-Smits* v. *Stichting Ziekenfonds*; *Peerbooms* v. *Stichting CZ Groep Zorgverzekeringen*, C-157/99, EU:C:2001:404; *Müller-Fauré* v. *Onderlinge Waarborgmaatschappij OZ Zorgverzekeringen*, C-385/99, EU:C:2003:270; *Watts* v. *Bedford Primary Care Trust*, C-372/04, EU:C:2006:325.
[132] *Ibid.* [133] Patients' Rights Directive, Article 7.
[134] G. Davies, 'The Effect of Mrs Watts' Trip to France on the National Health Service' (2007) 18 *Kings LJ* 158; *Elchinov*, C-173/09, EU:C:2010:336.
[135] *Elchinov*, C-173/09, EU:C:2010:336.

This applies also to costs. Treatment abroad may be limited to the costs of equivalent domestic care, but this requires establishing what domestic care actually costs. In many systems, this is no easy task. Where hospitals receive lump-sum funding, or a mix of lump-sum funding and per-patient or per-treatment funding, establishing what a given operation or treatment costs is extremely difficult, and any sum is likely to be open to legal challenge. If it is artificially low it will prevent patients going abroad, but attract foreign patients, burdening the domestic system. If it is artificially high, then patients will be able to accumulate large bills abroad. The Directive requires Member States to base both the amount they reimburse and the prices they charge on objective, non-discriminatory criteria, but this is more easily said than done.[136] Moreover, States are likely to find that compliance has consequences: as they establish transparent price lists and lists of available treatment, this will reveal the efficiencies and weaknesses of the system, and enable international comparison, with possible political impact.

The third argument for cost increase – the cost of infrastructure – was recognised by the Court of Justice in *Müller-Fauré*. Here it made a distinction between hospital care and non-hospital care. Where non-hospital care is concerned, it ruled that the infrastructure argument did not apply, and there is no justification for restricting foreign treatment. EU patients may now go wherever they want in the European Union for their consultations or minor treatments and expect costs to be covered by their domestic system just as if they had had the treatment at home. By contrast, where hospital care is concerned the Court conceded that the potential cost risks were indeed far greater, and certain restrictions could be justified. This approach has been incorporated in the Directive, which provides that where treatment involves at least one night in hospital, or the use of expensive medical infrastructure, Member States may require patients to seek authorisation before treatment abroad.[137] That authorisation may be refused on various grounds, of which the most important, provided for in Article 8, is that the treatment can be provided domestically within a 'medically justifiable' time.

This is particularly important because the most common reason for patient migration is not to receive better or different treatment but to avoid domestic waiting lists. Member States have a particular objection to this which is not to do with absolute cost increases, but to do with cost control. The UK Government's position in *Watts*, and as intervener in *Müller-Fauré*, was that it had a finite annual health-care budget, and so needed to control the rate of treatment. If patients could avoid waiting lists, then apart from this being unethical (queue jumping) it would make this annual budget control impossible. It would also undermine planning: with a finite budget the State may wish to determine which treatments get priority, and make hip patients wait longer than heart patients, for example. Waiting lists, in the view of the United Kingdom, were part of a fair and effective health-care system.[138]

The question of when a waiting time is 'medically justifiable' is thus very much at the heart of the law and policy. In the pre-Patients' Rights Directive case law, the Court of Justice had ruled that authorisation could be refused if treatment could not be provided without 'undue delay' and had interpreted this in a way which put the concerns of the patient, not the health-care system, central.

---

[136] Patients' Rights Directive, Articles 4 and 7.   [137] *Ibid.* Article 8.   [138] See Newdick, n. 118 above.

Müller-Fauré v. *Onderlinge Waarborgmaatschappij OZ Zorgverzekeringen*, C–385/99, EU: C:2003:270

90 In order to determine whether treatment which is equally effective for the patient can be obtained without undue delay in an establishment having an agreement with the insured person's fund, the national authorities are required to have regard to all the circumstances of each specific case and to take due account not only of the patient's medical condition at the time when authorisation is sought and, where appropriate, of the degree of pain or the nature of the patient's disability which might, for example, make it impossible or extremely difficult for him to carry out a professional activity, but also of his medical history . . .

Putting the effect of illness on the patient's broader health, and on their career, into the concept of undue delay makes it fluid and contestable. Each case has to be looked at on its own facts, and it would no longer be possible for States or insurers to decide authorisation applications purely by looking at a tariff or standard times.[139] This makes it significant that the Patients' Rights Directive appears to have moved back to the narrower 'medically justifiable', which would seem to exclude wider considerations. Yet in Article 9, which is about the administrative procedures for authorisations, the Directive provides that when considering applications for authorisation Member States shall take into account (a) the specific medical condition, and (b) urgency and individual circumstances. This seems somewhat broader than the substantive rule in Article 8. There is certainly room here for the Court of Justice to maintain the *Müller-Fauré* line that even non-medical factors should be taken into account. At any rate it is clear that the mere fact that a patient does not have to wait any longer than other national patients is not decisive: medical justification is not determined purely by the institutional status quo.

Litigation on these points matters because both waiting times for treatment and attitudes towards what is an acceptable waiting period vary widely between Member States. The UK Government considered it not undue, nor medically problematic, to make the elderly Mrs Watts wait months for a hip replacement, largely because this was normal in the United Kingdom. Some doctors in other States will be shocked by this. The fact that perceptions of what is medically, and above all humanly, acceptable vary so much make it significant that this matter is now within the scope of EU law. Applying the logic of *Geraets-Smits* one might argue that it should not be answered just by reference to local habits and expectations, but also by reference to international scientific best practice. That would be demanding for Member States with long, and long-established, waiting times.

All of these points will, however, be academic if patients cannot enforce their rights, and this is why the Court of Justice and now the Patients' Rights Directive give procedural requirements a prominent place. The Directive contains a number of provisions ensuring that Member States publish clear and accessible information on what and how much will be reimbursed, that they provide speedy decisions based on objective criteria and that they make it possible for patients to challenge these decisions in court.[140] The core ideas are still summarised best by the Court, whose approach has been adopted wholesale in the Directive.

---

[139] Davies, n. 117 above.   [140] Patients' Rights Directive, Articles 5 and 9.

Geraets-Smits v. Stichting Ziekenfonds; Peerbooms v. Stichting CZ Groep Zorgverzekeringen, C-157/99, EU:C:2001:404

90   ... a scheme of prior authorisation cannot legitimise discretionary decisions taken by the national authorities which are liable to negate the effectiveness of provisions of Community law, in particular those relating to a fundamental freedom such as that at issue in the main proceedings ... Therefore, in order for a prior administrative authorisation scheme to be justified even though it derogates from such a fundamental freedom, it must, in any event, be based on objective, non-discriminatory criteria which are known in advance, in such a way as to circumscribe the exercise of the national authorities' discretion, so that it is not used arbitrarily ... Such a prior administrative authorisation scheme must likewise be based on a procedural system which is easily accessible and capable of ensuring that a request for authorisation will be dealt with objectively and impartially within a reasonable time and refusals to grant authorisation must also be capable of being challenged in judicial or quasi-judicial proceedings.

As ever, the Court of Justice is concerned not just with abstract principle but with the effectiveness of EU law. Member States are likely to be just as concerned about these procedural demands as about the substantive rights of patients. As long as the number of patients migrating is small the issue is manageable, but the requirement for quick, objective and transparent decision-making is precisely what may make the right to receive medical services abroad a reality for the many rather than the few. Whether this will happen continues to be the object of research. The factors which are likely to influence this include cultural and linguistic barriers (border areas between States sharing a language may see significant cross-border health care), physical distance (distant States such as the United Kingdom or Greece may see less for this reason), but also the presence of domestic waiting lists (so States with national health systems, which tend to have waiting lists, may have the greatest outflow). Views on the likely extent of patient migration in the future vary widely and remain speculative.[141]

As well as the above, the Directive contains provisions aimed at helping patients find their way in the foreign legal system, and protecting their rights to privacy and information. Contact points, cooperation between national medical authorities and domestic follow-up treatment after initial treatment abroad are all addressed.[142] It is a fairly comprehensive package, clearly aimed at promoting patient movement, not merely regulating it.

That has invited criticism that the character of national welfare organisation is being undermined. The promotion of exit benefits the elite who can use this right, and reduces their commitment to the national system, to the detriment of the mass; the prioritising of individual rights is essentially the pre-emption of a value choice about the right balance between the collective and the individual good, going beyond a guarantee of essential medical care and protecting individual choice, time and convenience in a way that brings costs for others; and the locus of all this within the law on services, and the free movement logic of economic exchange, makes the patient into a consumer, with a consequent change in the nature of their relationship

[141] See the special edition of the *European Journal of Public Health* on cross-border health care: (1997) 7 *EJPub Health Supplement* 3, 1–50; see e.g. G. France, 'Cross-Border Flows of Italian Patients within the European Union' (1997) 7 *EJPub Health Supplement* 3, 18 (Italians were then the largest group of users of cross-border health care in the Union).

[142] Patients' Rights Directive, Articles 4, 5 and 6.

with their doctors – treatment becomes more business than care.[143] While not uncontested,[144] these arguments highlight how the apparently reasonable step-by-step progress of the case law can be seen as threatening to certain visions of social order, importing economic and individual values to places where they do not belong. The question now is whether the same process will be seen in education, where mobile individuals who are prepared to pay and entrepreneurial institutions prepared to sell combine to put pressure on traditional systems in an analogous way to the law on patients and health.[145] The dynamic there is more difficult, as most education is not provided for payment, even to foreign recipients, so that citizenship rights have been more important to this field than Article 56. However, the movement of institutions, taking on a role as transnational educational entrepreneurs, as discussed in Chapter 18, may yet bring economic law to the educational field on a large scale.

7 SERVICES DIRECTIVE

Directive 2006/123/EC on services in the internal market (Services Directive) is the product of one of the most publicised and controversial legislative processes that the Union has enjoyed.[146] The aim of the Directive is to finally break down the many barriers to interstate service provision and establishment. There is a perception that the complexity and sensitivity of many services has meant that case law has not succeeded in this task.[147] Member States continue to rely on mandatory requirements to obstruct services, and providers must fight for their rights on a case-by-case basis. Nevertheless, the impact of the Directive is limited by its numerous exclusions and limitations.

The Services Directive has three aspects. First, it regulates the administrative and bureaucratic procedures relevant to services and establishment. Secondly, it elaborates the scope of the rights to provide and receive services and to establish in another Member State. Articles 9–15 deal with the right to establish, while Articles 16–20 deal with cross-border service provision. Thirdly, it contains coordination provisions allowing and requiring States to exchange the information necessary for an effective regulation of service providers.

---

[143] See D. da Costa Leite Borges, 'Making Sense of Human Rights in the Context of European Union Health-Care Policy: Individualist and Communitarian Views' (2011) 7 *International Journal of Law in Context* 335; V. Hatzopoulos, 'Some Thoughts on the Fate of Poorer Member States' Healthcare Systems after the Ruling in Elena Petru' (2016) 41 *ELRev* 424.

[144] See e.g. C. Rieder, 'When Patients Exit, What Happens to Solidarity?' in M. Ross and Y. Borgmann-Prebil (eds.), *Promoting Solidarity in the European Union* (Oxford University Press, 2010) 122; B. van Leeuwen, 'The Doctor, the Patient, and EU Law: The Impact of Free Movement Law on Quality Standards in the Healthcare Sector' (2016) 41 *ELRev* 638; G. Davies, 'Health and Efficiency: Community Law and National Health Systems in the Light of *Müller-Fauré*' (2004) 67 *MLR* 94.

[145] A. Gideon, 'Higher Education Institutions and EU Competition Law' (2012) 8 *Competition L Rev* 169.

[146] See M. Klamert, 'Of Empty Glasses and Double Burdens: Approaches to Regulating the Services Market à propos the Implementation of the Services Directive' (2010) 37 *LIEI* 111; C. Barnard, 'Unravelling the Services Directive' (2008) 41 *CMLRev* 323; V. Hatzopoulos, 'Assessing the Services Directive' in C. Barnard (ed.), (2007–8) 10 *CYELS* 215; U. Neergaard, R. Nielsen and L. M. Roseberry (eds.), *The Services Directive: Consequences for the Welfare State and the European Social Model* (Copenhagen, DJØF Publishing, 2008); G. Davies, 'The Services Directive: Extending the Country of Origin Principle and Reforming Public Administration' (2007) 32 *ELRev* 232; B. De Witte, 'Setting the Scene: How Did Services Get to Bolkestein and Why?', Mitchell Working Paper No. 3/2007 (2007); R. Craufurd Smith, 'Old Wine in New Bottles? From the "Country of Origin Principle" to "Freedom to Provide Services" in the European Community Directive on Services in the Internal Market', Mitchell Working Paper No. 6/2007 (2007).

[147] *Visser Vastgoed*, C-360/15 and C-31/16, EU:C:2017:397.

(i) Scope of Application of Services Directive

The Directive applies to all services except those specifically excluded. However, these exclusions are so impressively numerous that it is almost easier to think about what the Directive does apply to. A list of examples is provided in recital 33: management consultancy; facilities management; advertising; recruitment services; real estate services; legal and fiscal advice; car rental; travel agencies; and tourism services such as those provided by tour guides or amusement parks.

By contrast, it does not apply to: financial services; electronic communications services; transport services;[148] temporary work agencies; health-care services;[149] gambling; private security; most social services such as social housing or child care; notaries and bailiffs; services connected with official authority; or audio-visual services.[150] In addition, there are specific exclusions relating only to services, but not to establishment.[151] These include waste treatment; posted workers; social security; water distribution; the registration of vehicles in other States, and activities reserved for particular professions.[152]

There are also several areas upon which the Services Directive is said not to impinge or not to affect or not to concern: taxation; labour law; fundamental rights; criminal law; cultural or linguistic diversity; and the liberalisation of services of general economic interest or private international law.[153] As a description of the Services Directive, these provisions are rather dubious. It is quite imaginable that the rest of the Directive could have significant implications for these matters. Education provided for remuneration, by example, is not excluded, and the free movement of educational services has obvious implications for cultural diversity. If these provisions are to have meaning, then presumably where the application of the Directive would have implications for such matters, for example labour law or fundamental rights, this would be a reason to set the Directive aside, or to interpret it differently.

In addition, the Services Directive is expressed to be residual. Article 3(1) provides that if it conflicts with other EU legislation concerning a specific service activity, the specific legislation will take precedence. Examples given include legislation on posted workers, social security and television broadcasting.

The Services Directive's limited scope means that services now fall broadly into one of three categories: those governed by the Directive, those governed by specific legislation and those governed by the case law and Article 56 TFEU directly. However, the situation is actually more complex than this. Even if a service falls within the Directive, then it will be necessary to look at the particular measure which is being challenged. It may be that this is addressed by the Directive, in which case that will apply and the case law will be of purely interpretative or contextual relevance. On the other hand, it may be that a service is involved which in itself is within the Directive (say management consultancy), but the measure being challenged involves labour law or taxation or the registration of a vehicle abroad, or is addressed by specific legislation, so that the Directive cannot be relied upon and the cases or the specific legislation are the proper source of law. Given that many cases involve a long list of measures which impede a particular services activity, it is quite likely that some will fall within the Directive and some without, so that we will see a body of case law in which the Directive and Article 56 are used

---

[148] *Uber*, C-434/15, EU:C:2017:364. [149] *Femarbel*, C-57/12, EU:C:2013:171, 11 July 2013.
[150] Directive 2006/123/EC, Article 2. [151] *Ibid.* Article 17.
[152] *X-Steuerberatungsgesellschaft* v. *Finanzamt Hannover-Nord*, C-342/14, EU:C:2015:827.
[153] Directive 2006/123/EC, Articles 1–3.

alongside each other. This only increases the likelihood that they will exert an interpretative influence on each other.

(ii) Administrative Simplification

Bureaucratic and administrative procedures have long been identified as a major obstacle to the free movement of services. A Commission survey of small and medium-sized enterprises found that 91 per cent of these believed that the highest priority should be given to simplification of these.[154] The time taken to complete the certification of translation, the fees, the non-constructive attitude of the authorities and the difficulties in lodging appeals were all seen as hindering the provision of services.[155]

Article 5(1) of the Services Directive accordingly provides that:

> Member States shall examine the procedure and formalities applicable to access to a service activity and to the exercise thereof. Where procedures and formalities examined under this paragraph are not sufficiently simple, Member States shall simplify them.

Articles 6, 7 and 8 go on to provide that service providers must be able to complete all formalities and procedures via a single point of contact, and that this must be possible electronically and at a distance. Thus, the vision of the Services Directive is that where an activity is legitimately regulated and service providers must complete formalities, instead of going from office to office filling in forms they can simply visit a single website or office and complete everything once.

It appears since *Visser*[156] that these provisions should apply not just to foreign service providers or established persons, but also to the national starting a business in her own State.[157] She is also engaging in a service activity in that State. These provisions are therefore a limited harmonisation of the government–citizen relationship, changing the balance of power towards the citizen, and moving the mode of interaction from face-to-face towards the electronic.[158] The notion of 'access to a service activity', not entirely transparent, is discussed in the next section.

(iii) Right to Provide and Receive Services

The Services Directive has a Chapter on establishment and one on services. The establishment provisions are discussed in Chapter 18.[159] The central provision on the free movement of services is Article 16.

Services Directive, Article 16

Freedom to provide services
1. Member States shall respect the right of providers to provide services in a Member State other than that in which they are established. The Member State in which the service is provided shall ensure free access to and free exercise of a service activity within its territory.

---

[154] European Commission, Internal Market and Services Directorate General, *Internal Market Scoreboard November 2000* (Brussels, 2000) 10–12.
[155] European Commission, 'The State of the Internal Market for Services', COM(2004)441 final, 18.
[156] Discussed in Ch. 18. [157] Davies, n. 146 above. See also Barnard, n. 146 above, 341–2.
[158] Davies, n. 146 above. [159] See pp. 817–18.

Member States shall not make access to or exercise of a service activity in their territory subject to compliance with any requirements which do not respect the following principles:

(a) non-discrimination: the requirement may be neither directly nor indirectly discriminatory with regard to nationality or, in the case of legal persons, with regard to the Member State in which they are established;

(b) necessity: the requirement must be justified for reasons of public policy, public security, public health or the protection of the environment;

(c) proportionality: the requirement must be suitable for attaining the objective pursued, and must not go beyond what is necessary to attain that objective . . .

Examples of prohibited requirements are included in Article 16(2) and include the obligation to have an establishment within the Member State, to register with a professional body in that State, or to possess an identity document issued by that State.

This article therefore applies to any public measure imposing conditions on access to or exercise of a service activity. This concept of 'access to or exercise of a service activity', and 'requirements' affecting such access, is one of the central ones in the Directive, occurring in the administrative provisions, and the establishment chapter, as well as in Article 16. What is meant by the phrase? It could be read, in the light of the case law, to include anything 'hindering or making less attractive' establishment or the provision of services. However, in *Visser* the Court appears to give it a more precise meaning. At issue were zoning rules which limited the opening of shops in certain parts of the city of Appingedam. It was therefore establishment which was at stake, but the Court took a more global view. Having found that the retail sale of goods comprised a service, it went on:

Visser Vastgoed, C–360/15 and C–31/16, EU:C:2018:44

120 In this case, it is undisputed that the effect of the rules of the zoning plan at issue in the main proceedings is to prohibit the activity of retail trade in goods that are not bulky goods, goods such as shoes and clothing, in a geographical zone situated outside the city centre of the municipality of Appingedam.

121 The referring court observes however that recital 9 of Directive 2006/123 states that that directive 'applies only to requirements which affect the access to, or the exercise of, a service activity', which excludes, consequently, 'requirements, such as . . . rules concerning the development or use of land, town and country planning, . . . as well as administrative penalties imposed for non-compliance with such rules which do not specifically regulate or specifically affect the service activity but have to be respected by providers in the course of carrying out their economic activity in the same way as by individuals acting in their private capacity'.

122 It must be observed that recital 9 of Directive 2006/123 is wholly consistent with the legal framework established by that directive, which, as is stated in paragraphs 104 to 106 of the present judgment, has the objective of eliminating restrictions on freedom of establishment of service providers in Member States and on the free movement of services between the Member States, with the aim of contributing to the achievement of a genuine internal market in services.

123 Directive 2006/123 is not therefore applicable to requirements which cannot be regarded as constituting such restrictions, since those requirements do not regulate or do not specifically affect the taking up or the

124 pursuit of a service activity, but have to be respected by providers in the course of carrying out their economic activity in the same way as by individuals acting in their private capacity.

124 That said, it is clear that the specific subject matter of the rules at issue in the main proceedings, even if their objective, as is stated in the order for reference, is to maintain the viability of the city centre of the municipality of Appingedam and to avoid there being vacant premises within the city as part of a town and county planning policy, remains that of determining the geographical zones where certain retail trade activities can be established. Those rules are therefore addressed only to persons who are contemplating the development of those activities in those geographical zones, and not to individuals acting in their private capacity.

The Directive therefore does not apply to matters such as private car parking permits or school access or rules on renting a private home, even though these might affect service providers, because such matters are not to do with the service activity but to do with the actions of the service provider in their 'private capacity'. This would appear to make the scope of the Directive importantly narrower than Article 56.

The next question is whether this is also true of the justifications which the Directive allows. According to Article 16 restrictions may only be justified by public policy, security, health or the environment. That appears to exclude mandatory requirements, such as consumer protection. That impression is strengthened by contrasting Article 16 with Article 9 on establishment, which specifically includes the possibility to restrict establishment for an 'overriding reason relating to the public interest'. This suggests persuasively that Article 16 is intended to be narrower, and not to encompass public interest derogations beyond the short list in Article 16(l)(b).

On the other hand, it may be noted that Article 16 largely reproduces the words of the Treaty, which also does not mention mandatory requirements. This did not prevent the Court of Justice discovering them to be implicit. Why should it not do the same here?[160]

In *Rina Services* the Court had to consider Article 14 of the Directive, which contains a list of prohibited requirements. It was argued that a Member State should nevertheless be able to rely on Treaty derogations such as public policy and security to deviate from these. The Court noted however that the very point of the Directive was to lay down clear rules that would make it unnecessary to consider each situation in an *ad hoc* way in the light of general Treaty principles: that is the added value of legislation. It said 'To concede that the "prohibited" requirements under Article 14 of that directive may nevertheless be justified on the basis of primary law would in fact be tantamount to reintroducing such case-by-case examination, under the FEU Treaty, for all restrictions on freedom of establishment', which it considered would deprive the article of any practical effect.[161] This approach suggests that the derogations in Article 16 should indeed be read as exhaustive.

However, in *Commission* v. *Hungary*, where precisely this question came up, the Court refused to settle the matter definitively. It noted that 'regardless' of whether it was possible to introduce new overriding reasons of public interest into Article 16, the measure in question was disproportionate anyway.[162] If the judicially created doctrine of mandatory requirements has been abolished by the Services Directive, at least regarding the free movement of services and matters where the Directive applies, then this is the Directive's biggest substantive innovation. It is not yet clear however that this is the case.

---

[160] Which appeared to be accepted in *Commission* v. *Portugal*, C-458/08, EU:C:2010:692.
[161] *Rina Services*, C-593/13, EU:C:2015:399.   [162] *Commission* v. *Hungary*, C-179/14, EU:C:2016:108.

(iv) Administrative Cooperation

The risks to the consumer which home State regulation entails are twofold. One is that the consumer will contract with a foreign provider, not realising that this provider is subject to laxer regulation than providers established in the consumer's home State. They may not receive the quality of service they expect from the type of provider they expected. The second risk is that providers in fact slip through the supervisory net. Their home State regulators have little idea exactly what the provider is doing when providing services abroad, and may not be very interested, while host State regulators are prohibited from interfering and imposing their own rules.

These fears are addressed by the later parts of the Services Directive. The Chapter on quality of services requires Member States to ensure that providers make a range of information available to service recipients, from the legal form and address of the provider to their indemnity insurance, where relevant, so that the recipient can have a clear idea of exactly what she is paying for, and from whom.[163] It also, quietly but importantly, requires Member States to remove all total prohibitions on commercial communication (broadly, advertising) by the regulated professions, although it permits continued regulation of this.[164] The philosophy is, just as with the Court of Justice's consumer case law, that consumer protection should primarily be achieved by clear and fair communication between all parties.[165]

Chapter VI of the Services Directive addresses administrative cooperation between national supervisory authorities. It requires these bodies to communicate with each other about service providers, providing information on those who might be a threat to recipients, for example because they are struck off or convicted or bankrupt.[166] This may raise human rights issues where concerns are communicated that later turn out to be misplaced: getting off the watch-list in other Member States will probably be harder than getting onto it. There is also a specific obligation on authorities not to relax their supervision of those established in their State merely because services are being provided in another State.[167] The logic of home State regulation requires that national authorities now protect the interests of consumers in other States.

The supervisory challenge raised by cross-border services is also addressed by a special emergency procedure, provided for in Articles 18 and 35. This permits host States to take measures necessary for the safety of consumers, in exceptional circumstances. However, rather than acting unilaterally against service providers, they are to follow a mutual assistance procedure in which they ask the State of establishment to investigate the service provider and take appropriate measures. The State of establishment is obliged to do this 'within the shortest possible period'.[168] The host State may then take additional measures, but only if it can show that the measures taken by the State of establishment are insufficient. The Commission is to be informed, and will take a decision either confirming or rejecting the host State measures.

This procedure is an attempt to reconcile the country of origin principle with high levels of service safety. It concedes that host States need to be able to guarantee service safety on their territory, but creates a communicative and cooperative mechanism which attempts to achieve this goal as much as possible via home State control.

---

[163] Services Directive, Article 22.   [164] *Ibid.* Article 24.   [165] See pp. 720–3.
[166] Services Directive, Articles 28–33.   [167] *Ibid.* Article 30.   [168] *Ibid.* Article 35(2).

FURTHER READING

C. Barnard, 'Employment Rights, Free Movement under the EC Treaty and the Services Directive', Mitchell Working Paper No. 5/08 (2008).

C. Barnard, 'Unravelling the Services Directive' (2008) 41 *Common Market Law Review* 323.

C. Barnard, 'Viking and Laval: An Introduction' in C. Barnard (ed.), *Cambridge Yearbook of European Legal Studies 2007–8* (Oxford, Hart, 2008) 463.

A. Biondi, 'Recurring Cycles in the Internal Market: Some Reflections on the Free Movement of Services' in A. Arnull, P. Eeckhout and T. Tridimas (eds.), *Continuity and Change in EU Law* (Oxford University Press, 2008) 228.

A. Dashwood, 'Viking and Laval: Issues of Direct Horizontal Effect' in C. Barnard (ed.), *Cambridge Yearbook of European Legal Studies 2007–8* (Oxford, Hart, 2008) 525.

G. Davies, 'The Process and Side-effects of Harmonisation of European Welfare States', Jean Monnet Working Paper No. 02/06 (2006).

S. Enchelmaier, 'Always at Your Service (Within Limits): The ECJ's Case Law on Article 56 TFEU (2006–11)' (2011) 36 *European Law Review* 615.

V. Hatzopoulos, 'The Court's Approach to Services (2006–2012): From Case Law to Case Load?' (2013) 50 *Common Market Law Review* 459.

V. Hatzopoulos, *Regulating Services in the European Union* (Oxford University Press, 2012).

V. Hatzopoulos and S. Roma, 'Caring for Sharing? The Collaborative Economy under EU Law' (2017) 54 *Common Market Law Review*, 81.

T. Hervey, 'Buy Baby: The European Union and Regulation of Human Reproduction' (1998) 18 *Oxford Journal of Legal Studies* 207.

G. Marenco, 'The Notion of Restriction on the Freedom of Establishment and Provision of Services in the Case-Law of the Court' (1991) 11 *Yearbook of European Law* 111.

S. de la Rosa, 'The Directive on Cross-Border Healthcare or the Art of Codifying Complex Case Law' (2012) 49 *Common Market Law Review* 15.

H. Schepel, 'Constitutionalising the Market, Marketising the Constitution, and to Tell the Difference: On the Horizontal Application of the Free Movement Provisions in EU Law' (2012) 18 *European Law Journal* 177.

E. Spaventa, 'From Gebhard to Carpenter: Towards a (Non)-Economic European Constitution' (2004) 41 *Common Market Law Review* 743.

B. de Witte, 'Setting the Scene: How Did Services Get to Bolkestein and Why?', Mitchell Working Paper No. 3/07 (2007).

R. Zahn, 'Revision of the Posted Workers Directive: A Europeanisation Perspective' (2017) 19 *Cambridge Yearbook of European Legal Studies*, 187.

18

The Pursuit of an Occupation in Another Member State

CONTENTS

1 INTRODUCTION

This chapter is about the right to pursue an occupation in another Member State. It is organised as follows.

Section 2 outlines the scope of this right. Article 45 TFEU provides a right to work in other Member States, while Article 49 TFEU provides a right to self-employment in other Member

States. While these are separate Treaty provisions, the Court of Justice often interprets them in parallel. Beneficiaries are EU citizens (and companies in the case of Article 49) who engage in a more than marginal economic activity with some cross-border element. If the subject lives in one State and works in another, this is sufficiently cross-border.

Section 3 considers national measures which restrict access to an occupation. In the past, certain professions were often restricted to nationals, but more recent cases tend to concern refusals to recognise foreign qualifications, or measures which make establishment of a business or professional practice subject to various requirements: these may be to do with the legal form of the business, the qualifications of the owner or shareholders, local economic need or limits on the number of establishments which one person or company may run. The Court of Justice's approach, as ever, is to permit only those justified by the public interest and proportionate. It tends to apply this strictly, because of the highly exclusionary effect of access requirements.

Section 4 analyses restrictions on the exercise of an occupation. Discrimination in pay and conditions, in union rights and in tax benefits, are all prohibited by case law and secondary legislation. The Court of Justice also examines measures critically for proportionality where they are equally applicable but tend to protect incumbents and disadvantage market entrants. However, it has been reluctant to engage with national measures whose only effect is to hinder economic effect generally, without any inequality in their impact.

Section 5 discusses the free movement of companies. Freedom of establishment enables companies to incorporate in one State while doing all their business in another. They can then avoid burdensome company laws in their State of business. Member States have argued that this is an abuse of free movement, but the Court of Justice disagrees. It is part of free movement that economic actors can choose to establish themselves in the jurisdiction most advantageous for them.

Section 6 is about the Services Directive, which also addresses establishment. Its Chapter on establishment addresses a limited number of national measures, but takes a similar approach to the case law; States may not discriminate, and measures restricting the business activities of established persons must be justified and proportionate. However, the Directive applies these principles not only where the measures impact on cross-border establishment, but generally, so that those starting a business in their own State will also benefit.

2 TAKING UP AND PURSUIT OF AN OCCUPATION IN ANOTHER MEMBER STATE

A central feature of any market is the possibility for individuals and companies to relocate to any part of its territory which offers them economic opportunities. Two economic freedoms in EU law are pivotal to the realisation of this. The first is free movement of workers, for which the central provision is Article 45 TFEU.

Article 45 TFEU

(1) Freedom of movement for workers shall be secured within the Union.
(2) Such freedom of movement shall entail the abolition of any discrimination based on nationality between workers of the Member States as regards employment, remuneration and other conditions of work and employment.

(3) It shall entail the right, subject to limitations justified on grounds of public policy, public security or public health:

(a) to accept offers of employment actually made;

(b) to move freely within the territory of Member States for this purpose;

(c) to stay in a Member State for the purpose of employment in accordance with the provisions governing the employment of nationals of that State laid down by law, regulation or administrative action;

(d) to remain in the territory of a Member State after having been employed in that State, subject to conditions which shall be embodied in regulations to be drawn up by the Commission.

(4) The provisions of this Article shall not apply to employment in the public service.

The second freedom is that of establishment. The central provision governing this is Article 49 TFEU.

Article 49 TFEU

Within the framework of the provisions set out below, restrictions on the freedom of establishment of nationals of a Member State in the territory of another Member State shall be prohibited. Such prohibition shall also apply to restrictions on the setting-up of agencies, branches or subsidiaries by nationals of any Member State established in the territory of any Member State.

Freedom of establishment shall include the right to take up and pursue activities as self-employed persons and to set up and manage undertakings, in particular companies or firms within the meaning of the second paragraph of Article 54, under the conditions laid down for its own nationals by the law of the country where such establishment is effected, subject to the provisions of the Chapter relating to capital.

An important difference between the articles is that Article 45 only applies to natural persons, whereas Article 49 also applies to legal persons such as companies, provided they fall within the definition in Article 54 TFEU: that they are formed according to the law of a Member State and they are profit-seeking.[1]

Regarding natural persons, the reason for treating the employed and self-employed separately is not obvious, and this chapter will suggest that the two groups are best considered in parallel. Their separateness in the Treaty is a historical artefact which does not fully correspond to the current state of the law or of society.

The origins of the distinction lie in the circumstances surrounding the original European Economic Community (EEC) Treaty. At a time of full employment, there were no concerns about the labour market and thus an assumption that free movement of labour was unproblematic. By contrast, there was concern that free movement might undermine professionals, such as lawyers, accountants and doctors, much of whose activity was carried out on a self-employed basis. Legislative harmonisation was thus seen as a precondition for free movement of the self-employed.

However, in today's world the distinction appears anachronistic, and often problematic in practice. People move interchangeably between employment and self-employment, each being

---

[1] *Kronos*, C-47/12, EU:C:2014:2200; Article 54(2) TFEU; see also *Spezzino*, C-113/13, EU:C:2014:2440.

economically substitutable for the other. In addition, companies have a range of contracts with individuals working for them, of which only some fit easily into the traditional model of the contract of employment.[2]

Moreover, the legal distinctiveness of the two categories has been eroded by EU citizenship. Regulation 492/211 confers on workers certain advantages and restrictions, most notably in the field of social benefits, but does not extend these to the self-employed.[3] However, both workers and the self-employed are EU citizens, and this fact has been used in recent years by both the Court of Justice and the EU legislature to assimilate their rights. In particular, the Citizenship Directive 2004/38/EC ensures that rights of entry, residence and expulsion, and rights to social benefits are now the same for all categories of economically active migrant.[4] The distinction between economically active and non-active is more important today than the distinction between employed and self-employed.[5]

This constitutional and social convergence of the worker and the self-employed person may have influenced the Court of Justice, which interprets Articles 45 and 49 TFEU in a similar manner, using the same concepts and limits. In particular, both these provisions are interpreted as being part of a more general right to pursue an occupation in another Member State.

Nevertheless, the free movement of persons, established or employed, cannot be understood in isolation from the free movement of services. The situations to which they are relevant often overlap: a measure which makes service provision from State X to other States harder will deter establishment in State X, and vice versa. Unsurprisingly, therefore, the Court has interpreted the law on services, establishment and workers largely in parallel. This chapter is therefore complemented by the chapter on free movement of services. In particular, the discussion of horizontal application of Article 56 TFEU is just as relevant to Articles 45 and 49,[6] while the discussion of abuse later in this chapter is applicable to the law on services.[7]

(i) Employment and Self-Employment

Article 45 governs movement of the employed, whereas Article 49 performs the same function for the self-employed.[8] The distinction between the two was explored in some depth in *Trojani*. Trojani, a French man, was given accommodation in a Salvation Army hostel in Brussels and some pocket money, in return for which he carried out approximately thirty hours of work each week for the hostel. This arrangement had a social purpose, as it was perceived to be a rehabilitation programme. After two years, Trojani approached the Belgian authorities for social assistance. On refusal, he argued that he was a worker under Article 45 and therefore entitled to social assistance.

---

[2] *Uber*, C-434/15, EU:C:2017:981.
[3] Regulation 492/2011 on freedom of movement for workers, replacing Regulation 1612/68, [1968] OJ Special Edn, L 257/2, 475.
[4] See pp. 475–518.
[5] Although see *Czop and Punakova*, C-147–8/11, EU:C:2012:538 and C. O'Brien, 'Social Blind Spots and Monocular Policy Making: The ECJ's Migrant Worker Model' (2009) 46 *CMLRev* 1107.
[6] See pp. 747–54.   [7] See pp. 802–4.
[8] *Laurie-Blum*, 66/85, EU:C:1986:284; *Gebhard* v. *Consiglio dell'ordine degli avvocati e procuratori di Milano*, C-55/94, EU:C:1995:411.

C-456/02 *Trojani* v. *Centre public d'aide sociale* [2004] ECR 1–7573

15 . . . the concept of 'worker' within the meaning of Article [45 TFEU] has a specific Community meaning and must not be interpreted narrowly. Any person who pursues activities which are real and genuine, to the exclusion of activities on such a small scale as to be regarded as purely marginal and ancillary, must be regarded as a 'worker'. The essential feature of an employment relationship is, according to that case law, that for a certain period of time a person performs services for and under the direction of another person in return for which he receives remuneration . . .

16 Moreover, neither the sui generis nature of the employment relationship under national law, nor the level of productivity of the person concerned, the origin of the funds from which the remuneration is paid or the limited amount of the remuneration can have any consequence in regard to whether or not the person is a worker for the purposes of Community law . . .

17 With respect more particularly to establishing whether the condition of the pursuit of real and genuine activity for remuneration is satisfied, the national court must base its examination on objective criteria and make an overall assessment of all the circumstances of the case relating to the nature both of the activities concerned and of the employment relationship at issue . . .

18 In this respect, the Court has held that activities cannot be regarded as a real and genuine economic activity if they constitute merely a means of rehabilitation or reintegration for the persons concerned . . .

19 However, that conclusion can be explained only by the particular characteristics of the case in question,[9] which concerned the situation of a person who, by reason of his addiction to drugs, had been recruited on the basis of a national law intended to provide work for persons who, for an indefinite period, are unable, by reason of circumstances related to their situation, to work under normal conditions . . .

20 In the present case, as is apparent from the decision making the reference, Mr Trojani performs, for the Salvation Army and under its direction, various jobs for approximately 30 hours a week, as part of a personal reintegration programme, in return for which he receives benefits in kind and some pocket money.

21 Under the relevant provisions [the national law] the Salvation Army has the task of receiving, accommodating and providing psycho-social assistance appropriate to the recipients in order to promote their autonomy, physical well-being and reintegration in society. For that purpose it must agree with each person concerned a personal reintegration programme setting out the objectives to be attained and the means to be employed to attain them.

22 Having established that the benefits in kind and money provided by the Salvation Army to Mr Trojani constitute the consideration for the services performed by him for and under the direction of the hostel, the national court has thereby established the existence of the constituent elements of any paid employment relationship, namely subordination and the payment of remuneration.

23 For the claimant in the main proceedings to have the status of worker, however, the national court, in the assessment of the facts which is within its exclusive jurisdiction, would have to establish that the paid activity in question is real and genuine.

24 The national court must in particular ascertain whether the services actually performed by Mr Trojani are capable of being regarded as forming part of the normal labour market. For that purpose, account may be taken of the status and practices of the hostel, the content of the social reintegration programme, and the nature and details of performance of the services . . .

27 . . . the freedom of establishment provided for in Articles [49 TFEU] to [54 TFEU] includes only the right to take up and pursue all types of self-employed activity, to set up and manage undertakings, and to set up agencies, branches or subsidiaries . . . Paid activities are therefore excluded.

---

9 *Laurie-Blum*, 66/85, EU:C:1986:284; *Gebhard* v. *Consiglio dell'ordinedegli avvocati e procuratori di Milano*, C-55/94, EU:C:1995:411.

Trojani provides a useful and oft-cited summary of the preceding case law on the application of Article 45. The extract above should also be read alongside the following section.

The judgment makes clear that where a migrant works under the direction of another person in return for payment, she is regarded as an employee and falls under Article 45. The essence of a worker is that she has a boss and a wage. By contrast, if she earns her living independently through supplying goods or services to other persons, she is treated as self-employed and falls under Article 49.

The motivation for working in another Member State is irrelevant as long as a person is in fact engaging in sufficient economic activity. In *Levin* the claim was that the work was only performed in order to obtain associated family rights, and in *L.N.* the claim was that it was done in order to obtain a right to study finance. The Court dismissed the claims as irrelevant.

L.N., C–46/12, EU:C:2013:97

47 It should be noted that the definition of the concept of 'worker' within the meaning of Article 45 TFEU expresses the requirement, which is inherent in the very principle of the free movement of workers, that the advantages conferred by European Union law under that freedom may be relied on only by people genuinely pursuing or genuinely wishing to pursue employment activities. It does not mean, however, that the enjoyment of that freedom may be made contingent on which objectives are being pursued by a national of a Member State in applying to enter the territory of a host Member State, provided that he pursues or wishes to pursue effective and genuine employment activities. Once that condition is satisfied, the motives which may have prompted a worker of a Member State to seek employment in another Member State are of no account and must not be taken into consideration.

(ii) Performance of Significant Economic Activity in Another Member State

To fall within either Articles 45 or 49 TFEU, the migrant must be engaging in activity which is economic in nature. Economic activity involves her 'satisfying a request by the beneficiary in return for consideration'.[10] In the case of employment, the migrant will be receiving consideration from the employer and providing services under the direction of the employer. In the case of the self-employed, the remuneration is usually received from the customer for whom the service is carried out.

The Court of Justice has enlarged this notion of economic activity in two ways. In *Steymann*, a migrant lived in a Bhagwan community and received food and lodging and pocket money in return for doing tasks and duties within the community. The Court accepted that remuneration need not be financial, but could be in kind, so that Steymann was a worker in the Treaty sense.[11]

A similarly substantive approach was taken in *Raccanelli*, where the Court of Justice found that a PhD student may or may not be a worker.[12] It depends on whether the key elements of the worker relationship are present: remuneration and subordination. A grant may count as

---

[10] *Laurie-Blum, 66/85, EU:C:1986:284; Gebhard v. Consiglio dell'ordinedegli avvocati e procuratori di Milano*, C-55/94, EU:C:1995:411.

[11] *Steymann v. Staatssecretaris van Justitie*, 196/87, EU:C:1988:475. See also *Trojani v. Centre public d'aide sociale*, C-456/02, EU:C:2004:488.

[12] *Raccanelli v. Max-Planck-Gesellschaft zur Förderung der*, C-94/07, C:2008:425.

remuneration, but whether the researcher is under the direction of the faculty in question or is independent in their activities is a question of fact for the national court.

The work must, however, be part of the 'normal labour market'.[13] That is to say, it must be an essentially economic transaction, rather than an activity existing purely for therapeutic or social reasons. However, an element of guardianship or social welfare does not necessarily prevent a finding of economic activity if the context suggests a labour market orientation. Thus training has been found to be an economic activity if it is regarded as practical preparation directly related to the actual pursuit of an occupation, and the training period itself takes the form of economic activity.[14] Similarly, jobs which would otherwise be unviable, sponsored with public funds to enable individuals to enter or re-enter working life, have been classified as economic activity.[15] Within such schemes, however, the person must have been chosen on the basis of their ability to perform a particular activity, rather than the work found to fit the person. In *Bettray*,[16] a Dutch drug rehabilitation scheme which offered individuals employment as part of the treatment of weaning them off drugs was not considered economic activity. It was regarded instead as a form of treatment because the jobs were adapted to the physical and mental capabilities of each person.

To fall within the provisions, the degree of economic activity must be more than minimal. In *Levin*, the Court of Justice ruled that to fall within Article 45 a migrant had to pursue 'effective and genuine activities, to the exclusion of activities on such a small scale as to be purely marginal and ancillary'.[17] But this does not exclude work under a short-term contract,[18] part-time work or low-paid work.[19] In the same case the Court offered an interpretation of Article 45 in its broader context which still stands:

> 15 . . . Since part-time employment, although it may provide an income lower than what is considered to be the minimum required for subsistence, constitutes for a large number of persons an effective means of improving their living conditions, the effectiveness of Community law would be jeopardized if the enjoyment of rights conferred by the principle of freedom of movement for workers were reserved solely to persons engaged in full-time employment and earning, as a result, a wage at least equivalent to the guaranteed minimum wage in the sector under consideration.

Following this, in *Kempf*,[20] the Court held that a part-time music teacher who gave twelve hours of lessons a week was doing sufficient work to be covered by Article 45, even though she earned so little that she was forced to apply for benefits. The question whether work is more than 'marginal and ancillary' is one for the national judge.[21]

The minimum threshold for engaging Article 49 is a little more complex. In some cases, the question may be whether an individual is established in a host State or providing services, and

---

[13] *Trojani* v. *Centre public d'aide sociale*, C-456/02, EU:C:2004:488.

[14] *Kranemann* v. *Land Nordrhein-Westfalen*, C-109/04, EU:C:2005:68.

[15] *Birden* v. *Stadtgemeinde Bremen*, C-1/97, EU:C:1998:568.

[16] *Bettray* v. *Staatssecretaris van Justitie*, 344/87, EU:C:1989:226.

[17] *Levin* v. *Staatssecretaris van Justitie*, 53/81, EU:C:1982:105.

[18] *Franca Ninni-Orasche* v. *Bundesminister für Wissenschaft, Verkehr und Kunst*, C-413/01, EU:C:2003:600.

[19] Although see C. O'Brien, 'Civis Capitalis Sum: Class as the New Guiding Principle of EU Free Movement Rights' (2016) 53 *CMLR* 937.

[20] *Kempf* v. *Staatssecretaris van Justitie*, 139/85, EU:C:1986:223.   [21] *L.N.*, C-46/12, EU:C:2013:97.

the intensity and scale of their economic activity will be relevant to this determination. This was discussed in Chapter 17.[22] However, if an individual is resident in a host State, so that there is no question that this is the centre of her activities, then the question may arise, as with Article 45, whether those activities are of a sufficient scale to classify her as economically active. The only words of guidance that the Court of Justice has provided are in *Gebhard*, in which it said that:

> 25. The concept of establishment within the meaning of the Treaty is therefore a very broad one, allowing a Community national to participate, on a stable and continuous basis, in the economic life of a Member State other than his State of origin and to profit therefrom, so contributing to economic and social interpenetration within the Community in the sphere of activities as self-employed persons.[23]

This was intended to distinguish establishment from services, but may also indicate the minimum criteria for establishment per se. There must be some non-trivial stability and continuity in the activities: one small or brief job performed for one client is not enough. In substance, it is suggested that the minimum level of economic activity will be interpreted in the same way as for Article 45.

The definition of 'worker' which emerges from these cases is unusual in EU law in not taking account of the personal circumstances of the individual, instead imposing a fixed test. That may have the consequence that a disabled person, working as much as they can, will have to cross the same threshold of 'genuine and effective activity' as an able-bodied person, and that someone engaging in informal, but arduous and necessary, care may not be a worker while someone who receives payment for the same work will be. This may seem quite reasonable from an economic point of view, but it fits somewhat uneasily with cases such as *Levin* and *Kempf*, where the Court of Justice seems to be focusing far less on the economic contribution of the individual, and rather on what has been described as their 'genuine intention to work', treating worker status as recognition of effort and attitude rather than success.[24] It also fits uneasily with current anti-discrimination law, which generally requires recognition of the particular position of disabled people in the labour market.

C. O'Brien, 'Social Blind Spots and Monocular Policy Making: The ECJ's Migrant Worker Model' (2009) 46 *Common Market Law Review* 1107

It is here suggested that the application of the same 'worker' test to all people is inappropriate, and actually discriminatory. This problem is not solved by 'refining' the test by continually adding conditions. Instead, these entrench the problem by introducing extra sources of discrimination, as exemplified by the 'genuine and effective' requirement, and its refinement, that work be part of the 'normal labour market'. The meaning of 'genuine and effective' has been somewhat shrouded in ambiguity, with no suggestion that it may vary as between workers. If anything, the 'normal labour market' stipulation makes clear that there is

---

[22] See pp. 738–9.

[23] *Gebhard* v. *Consiglio dell'ordine degli avvocati e procuratori di Milano*, C-55/94, EU:C:1995:411.

[24] E. Johnson and D. O'Keeffe, 'The Free Movement of Workers 1989–1994' (1994) 31 *CMLRev* 1318, quoted in C. O'Brien, 'Social Blind Spots and Monocular Policy Making: The ECJ's Migrant Worker Model' (2009) 46 *CMLRev* 1107, 1117.

no room for accommodating such differences. It squeezes social concerns out of the definitional process and shuts out any positive equality duty. It was possibly a knee-jerk reaction, to avoid the social obligations of host Member States 'going too far' after the widening application of the term 'worker' reached its fullest compass in *Steymann*. A German national who had worked as a plumber in the Netherlands, joined a religious community that provided for the material needs of its members, where he contributed to the life of the community through activities, including its fundraising activities. The community preserved an independence from surrounding society. This was clearly not a 'classic' employment relationship, yet it was 'impossible to rule out a priori the possibility that [the] work ... in question constitutes an economic activity within the meaning of Article 2 of the Treaty'. The Court was soon faced with a 'less attractive' claimant than a religious plumber seeking a right to reside, this time an ex-drug addict, and circumvented its own reasoning.

The consequence was the *Bettray* principle that work should be part of the 'normal labour market'. That it departed from previous case law was implied in the Advocate General's statement that he did 'not think that [previous] case law can be directly transposed to the unusual circumstances of the present case'. It is a poorly elaborated, apparently foundation-free principle, applied without substantiating evidence. Bettray's activity under the Social Employment Law did exhibit 'the essential feature of an employment relationship', as he performed services under the direction of another person in return for remuneration, and Advocate General Jacobs did actually acknowledge his activities to have been 'substantial'. Furthermore, Bettray was classed under the Social Employment Law as a person whose productivity is expected to be a third of a 'normal' worker's. If working full time, that still suggests productivity capable of being compared to that of a 'normal' part time worker. This contrasts considerably with the (undetermined) amount of activity in *Steymann*.

The various elements called upon in 'abnormalizing' Bettray's work include: physical/mental adaptations to work; unavailability for 'normal' work; selection of the work rather than the worker; and speculation about the noncommerciality of the labour. Each criterion makes clear that all workers are to be subjected to the same test for genuine and effective work; a test against which non-normal work is not valued, exacerbating the danger of disability discrimination. The significance attributed to the fact that the work had been adapted to the physical and mental possibilities of the persons in question is difficult to reconcile with notions of reasonable adjustments and positive discrimination as regards disability discrimination. Rather than allowing notions of genuine work to be altered to accommodate adapted work, it actually uses such adaptations as an indicator to rule out that work.

(iii) Cross-Border Element

In an analogous manner to the other freedoms, Articles 45 and 49 TFEU apply only to work or establishment with a cross-border aspect.[25] The usual situation is where the individual physically relocates to another Member State. However, Article 45 also includes the situation where the worker works in their home State, but lives in another. In *Hartmann*, a German worker living and working in Germany moved house, but not job, to France. The Court of Justice found that this was enough to give him the status of migrant worker.[26] In similar fashion, the Court has stated that

---

[25] *Saunders*, 175/78, EU:C: 1979:88; *Uecker and Jacquet*, C-65/96, EU:C:1997:285; *Asscher*, C-107/94, EU:C:1996:251.

[26] *Hartmann* v. *Freistaat Bayern*, C-212/05, EU:C:2007:437; see also *Gilly* v. *Directeur des services fiscaux du Bas-Rhin*, C-336/96, EU:C:1998:221; *Geven* v. *Land Nordrhein-Westfalen*, C-213/03, EU:C:2007:438; A. Tryonidou, 'In Search of the Aim of the EC Free Movement of Persons Provisions: Has the Court of Justice Missed the Point?' (2009) 46 *CMLRev* 1591.

where the economic activity of a person or company based in one Member State is entirely or principally directed towards the territory of another Member State, they fall within Article 49.[27]

The cross-border economic activity need not already be underway to engage Articles 45 and 49. Measures which prevent it starting are also caught, provided their effect is not too hypothetical.[28] These Articles therefore involve not merely the right to pursue an occupation in another Member State but also the right to *take up* that occupation. Article 45 therefore protects both workers and work-seekers.[29] In like vein, Article 49 covers restrictions on those who are self-employed as well as restrictions preventing EU citizens wishing to take up self-employment, but not yet self-employed. For example, in *Reyners*,[30] a Dutch national successfully challenged a Belgian measure permitting only Belgian nationals to practise as advocates in Belgium, which was preventing him practising as a lawyer in that State.

(iv) Right to Pursue an Occupation in Another Member State

The common themes present in employment and self-employment, and the Court of Justice's clear inclination towards parallel development of the four freedoms,[31] suggest room for an explicit overarching right to take up and pursue an occupation in another Member State, which encompasses and structures both Articles 45 and 49. Such reasoning is present in the recent case of *Danish Company Cars*.[32] To avoid tax evasion, Denmark prohibited Danish residents from using company cars registered abroad for private purposes in Denmark. The Commission considered this to penalise those working abroad and therefore to breach Article 45, as Danish residents could use company cars registered in Denmark for private purposes. The Danish Government argued that the measure fell outside Article 45 as this article related solely to conditions of employment.

Commission v. Denmark (Danish Company Cars), C-464/02, EU:C:2005:38

34 The provisions of the Treaty on freedom of movement for persons are intended to facilitate the pursuit by Community citizens of occupational activities of all kinds throughout the Community, and preclude measures which might place Community citizens at a disadvantage when they wish to pursue an economic activity in the territory of another Member State . . .

35 Provisions which preclude or deter a national of a Member State from leaving his country of origin in order to exercise his right to freedom of movement therefore constitute an obstacle to that freedom even if they apply without regard to the nationality of the workers concerned . . .

36 However, in order to be capable of constituting such an obstacle, they must affect access of workers to the labour market . . .

37 The manner in which an activity is pursued is liable also to affect access to that activity. Consequently, legislation which relates to the conditions in which an economic activity is pursued may constitute an obstacle to freedom of movement within the meaning of that case law.

38 It follows that the Danish legislation at issue in this case is not excluded from the outset from the scope of Article [45 TFEU].

---

[27] *Commission* v. *Germany (German Insurance)*, 205/84, EU:C:1986:463. [28] See pp. pp. 794–5.

[29] *Levin* v. *Staatssecretaris van Justitie*, 53/81, EU:C:1982:105; *Roman Angonese* v. *Cassa di Risparmio di Bolzano SpA*, C-281/98, EU:C:1999:583.

[30] *Reyners* v. *Belgium*, 2/74, EU:C:1974:68.

[31] See A. Tryfonidou, 'Further Steps on the Road to Convergence Among the Market Freedoms' (2010) 35 *ELRev* 35.

[32] For similar reasoning in respect of Article 56 TFEU, see *Stanton* v. *INASTI*, 143/87, EU:C:1988:378, paras. 13 and 14.

The case is, like *Alpine Investments, Rüffler, Bosman*[33] and the case law on Article 35 TFEU, about a restriction on exit, imposed by the home State. These are legally interesting because they can rarely be seen in terms of nationality discrimination. As a result, the Court of Justice is often forced into innovative legal formulations, usually relying on the fact that a measure makes cross-border movement less attractive than staying at home.[34] Accordingly, in the extract above the central objection is that the measure discouraged Danes from going abroad to work, since a job abroad would be relatively less advantageous for them.[35] In paragraph 34, the Court places this in a cross-category context. The extract implies a right to pursue an occupation abroad which encompasses both Articles 45 and 49, and extends beyond mere equal treatment.

As a matter of convenience, the right to pursue an occupation abroad can be considered to have two aspects: the right to *take up* economic activities and the right to *pursue* these activities. This distinction often occurs in the language of the Court of Justice,[36] and is useful in understanding the kinds of situations which may arise.

The right to take up activities concerns entry onto the market of another Member State. At its crudest, this would capture restrictions on residence in another Member State. It would also comprise anything that might prevent the migrant from commencing activity in that Member State. This would include restrictions on secondary establishment, which prevent traders with a central place of business opening up branches, agencies or subsidiaries in other Member States, restrictions on entering the labour market, such as prerequisites that one have a licence or join a trade union, which may be difficult to meet or, finally, requirements that a migrant have a qualification before she can pursue a particular activity. The nature of all these rules is that they reserve the occupation in question for those complying with certain criteria.

Restrictions on the pursuit of economic activity are restrictions on activities of the migrant once she is on the market of the host Member State. They do not determine who may engage in the occupation in question, but they create disadvantages for some of those who do so. They might involve discriminatory conditions of employment, discriminatory planning restrictions for the location of a business, or discrimination in the tax system or in access to credit. They may also include non-discriminatory regulation of economic activity which, because it imposes disproportionate burdens, hinders that activity.[37]

The distinction between restrictions on the taking up of activities and restrictions on the pursuit of activities is not always clear-cut. As *Danish Company Cars* suggests, restrictions on the pursuit of economic activity may be so onerous for the trader that they make it unviable for her to enter the market, and so perform the same role as restrictions on the taking up of activity. Nevertheless, in many cases the distinction is real and useful. Being told by a State 'You cannot practise that profession' is different from being permitted to do so but to find that some of the State's regulation is burdensome.

---

[33] *Alpine Investments* v. *Minister van Financiën*, C-384/93, EU:C:1995:15; *Rüffler*, C-544/07, EU:C:2009:258; *Union Royale Belge des Sociétés de Football Association and Others* v. *Bosman and Others*, C-415/93, EU:C:1995:463.

[34] See pp. 495–8.

[35] See also *Federspiel*, C-419/16, EU:C:2017:677; *Home Credit Slovakia*, C-42/15, EU:C:2016:842; *Commission* v. *Cyprus*, C-515/14, EU:C:2016:30.

[36] *Steinhauser* v. *City of Biarritz*, 197/84, EU:C:1985:260; *Consiglio Nazionale degli Ingegneri* v. *Ministero della Giustizia and Marco Cavallera*, C-311/06, EU:C:2009:37; *Commission* v. *Denmark (Danish Company Cars)*, C-464/02, EU:C:2005:38.

[37] See pp. 807–10.

3 RESTRICTIONS ON THE TAKING UP OF AN OCCUPATION

(i) Discriminatory Restrictions on Taking Up an Occupation

In some instances, Member States have reserved certain occupations to their own nationals. Because of the obvious discriminatory intent of such measures, the Court of Justice has chosen to strike them down as a violation of the non-discrimination principle. In *Reyners*,[38] a Belgian requirement that one have Belgian nationality to practise as an advocate was therefore condemned as a breach of Article 49 TFEU on the grounds that it discriminated against other EU nationals. Similar reasoning has been applied to companies,[39] and in respect of Article 45. In *French Merchant Navy*,[40] a French restriction limiting the proportion of non-national French merchant navy employees was found to breach Article 45 on the grounds of its discriminatory nature.

There are also slightly less direct requirements, which still work to protect locals. In *Angonese*, a bank in the German-speaking part of Italy made employment conditional upon a particular local certificate of bilingualism, refusing to accept other evidence.[41] The Court of Justice found this a violation of Article 45 because of its discriminatory effect on access to the posts, notwithstanding that instead of a public measure, a rule imposed by a private company was in issue. Article 45 is general, and applies equally to private and public employers and measures. More recently, in *Las*, the Court found it disproportionate to require by law that all employment contracts with companies established in the Flemish-speaking part of Belgium be drafted exclusively in Flemish.[42] Legal requirements that an employee actually speak the local language are in practice even more exclusionary. They could be argued to fall within Article 3 of Regulation 492/2011, which declares that Member State laws or practices shall not apply if their exclusive aim or effect is to limit the access of non-nationals to employment.[43] However, such requirements may of course be reasonable, and Article 3 goes on to explicitly permit language requirements where the linguistic knowledge is required by reason of the nature of the post. In such a case, although the requirement may adversely affect foreign applicants, it will not be treated as prohibited discrimination. In *Groener*,[44] a Dutch teacher challenged an Irish requirement that all full-time teachers in Irish State colleges were proficient in the Irish language. She argued that this did not fall within the exception, as teaching could be done in English. The Court of Justice nevertheless found the requirement to be lawful. It stated that any requirement of linguistic proficiency would be lawful if it was necessary for the implementation of a policy to protect and promote a language which is both the national language and the first official language, and the restriction was neither disproportionate to the aim pursued nor unnecessarily discriminatory towards other Member State nationals. In this case, the restriction was not disproportionate, as education was seen by the Court as central to the implementation of such a policy. In this instance, education included not merely teaching but also participation in the daily life of the school and the forging of relations with pupils. In such circumstances, the Court

---

[38] *Reyners* v. *Belgium*, 2/74, EU:C:1974:68.   [39] *Commission* v. *Netherlands*, C-299/02, EU:C:2004:620.

[40] *Commission* v. *France (French Merchant Navy)*, 167/73, EU:C:1974:35.

[41] *Roman Angonese* v. *Cassa di Risparmio di Bolzano SpA*, C-281/98, EU:C:2000:296. See also *Commission* v. *Belgium*, C-317/14, EU:C:2015:63.

[42] *Las*, C-202/11, EU:C:2013:239.

[43] Cf. posted workers in a recent situation: C. Barnard, '"British Jobs for British Workers": The Lindsey Oil Refinery Dispute and the Future of Local Labour Clauses in an Integrated EU Market' (2009) 38 *ILJ* 245.

[44] *Groener* v. *Minister for Education and the City of Dublin Vocational Educational Committee*, 379/87, EU:C:1989:599.

considered that even though teaching did not have to be done in Irish, the language could be central to other parts of school life.[45]

The vast majority of restrictions on the taking up of activity in another Member State are not explicitly directed at foreigners. In such instances, the Court looks at the restrictive effects of the measure rather than its discriminatory effects. We look at these below.

(ii) Equally Applicable Restrictions on Taking Up an Occupation

One of the best-known cases in EU law is that of *Bosman*, which revolutionalised the European football industry. Bosman played football for Liège in Belgium. Following the end of his contract, relations between him and the club broke down. Under the footballing rules of the time, the club held on to the registration card that entitled him to play as a footballer. They sought to transfer him, with his consent, to Dunkerque in France. The sale broke down because there were doubts about Dunkerque's solvency and its ability to pay the transfer fee demanded by Liège. Despite his being out of contract, Liège refused to allow Bosman to move to Dunkerque until its demand for a transfer fee had been met. Bosman was therefore unable to work as a footballer: Liège would not use him, but they would not let him go to another team. He challenged the transfer system operating in football, which allowed clubs to restrict the movement of players post-contract by holding on to their registration card, arguing it violated Article 45 TFEU. UEFA argued that the system was in no way discriminatory, applying to all transfers, irrespective of whether they were cross-border or not.

Union Royale Belge des Sociétés de Football Association and Others v. *Bosman and Others*, C-415/93, EU:C:1995:463

98 It is true that the transfer rules in issue in the main proceedings apply also to transfers of players between clubs belonging to different national associations within the same Member State and that similar rules govern transfers between clubs belonging to the same national association.

99 However ... those rules are likely to restrict the freedom of movement of players who wish to pursue their activity in another Member State by preventing or deterring them from leaving the clubs to which they belong even after the expiry of their contracts of employment with those clubs.

100 Since they provide that a professional footballer may not pursue his activity with a new club established in another Member State unless it has paid his former club a transfer fee agreed upon between the two clubs or determined in accordance with the regulations of the sporting associations, the said rules constitute an obstacle to freedom of movement for workers ...

104 Consequently, the transfer rules constitute an obstacle to freedom of movement for workers prohibited in principle by Article [45 TFEU]. It could only be otherwise if those rules pursued a legitimate aim compatible with the Treaty and were justified by pressing reasons of public interest. But even if that were so, application of those rules would still have to be such as to ensure achievement of the aim in question and not go beyond what is necessary for that purpose.

The Court went on to find that the rules could not be justified by the need to maintain the financial and competitive balance between clubs, nor by the need to find and support young

---

[45] See also *Salomone Haim* v. *Kassenzahnärztliche Vereinigung Nordrhein*, C-424/97, EU:C:2000:357; *Wilson* v. *Ordre des avocats du barreau de Luxembourg*, C-506/04, EU:C:2006:587.

talent. These were good goals, but the Court was convinced they could be achieved by means less restrictive of free movement.[46]

Bosman applies the same logic to Articles 45 and 49[47] as has been applied, since *Cassis de Dijon*, to the case law on free movement of goods and freedom to provide services.[48] The provisions will not only catch measures which distinguish between nationals of different Member States. They will also catch certain equally applicable restrictions on employment and establishment. In cases where such a measure falls within either provision, it will only be lawful if it meets a number of conditions. It must be justified in the public interest; it must be applied in a non-discriminatory manner, it must be suitable for securing the attainment of the objective pursued; and it must not go beyond what is necessary to attain this objective.[49]

The same reasoning has been applied in the context of Article 49 in *Gebhard*, where the Court pronounced that any measure 'liable to hinder or make less attractive the exercise of fundamental freedoms' would be prohibited, unless it complied with the same justificatory requirements outlined in *Bosman*.[50]

The application of Article 49 to equally applicable measures has, as with the other freedoms, been a powerful tool for opening up regulated professions to new competition. In *Hartlauer*, an Austrian rule made the setting up of an outpatient dental clinic conditional upon local 'need', which was determined by the relevant authority.[51] This was found to be a restriction on establishment which ultimately, because of various arbitrary elements in the authorisation procedure, was not justified. Similarly, rules in Greece permitting opticians to own only one shop, and Italian laws which prohibited either companies or non-pharmacists from owning pharmacies, were both found to comprise restrictions on establishment, albeit in the latter case justified.[52] Other unjustified restrictions have included those requiring businesses carrying on certain activities to have a certain minimum size,[53] and planning rules, such as those in *Commission* v. *Spain*, which set a maximum size for shopping malls.[54]

As in *Bosman*, these cases concern rules which do not discriminate explicitly, and do not seem to have any greater effect, in general. on cross-border movement than domestic movement.[55] However, they have a feature which they share with goods cases such as *Commission* v. *Italy*:[56]

---

[46] See also *Olympique Lyonnais*, C-325/08, EU:C:2010:143.

[47] Similar reasoning was first used in relation to Article 49 TFEU in *Ordre des Avocats au Barreau de Paris* v. *Klopp*, 107/83, EU:C:1984:270.

[48] See pp. 713 et seq.

[49] *Gebhard* v. *Consiglio dell'ordine degli avvocati e procuratori di Milano*, C-55/94, EU:C:1995:411; *Commission* v. *Netherlands*, EU:C:2004:620.

[50] *Gebhard* v. *Consiglio dell'ordine degli avvocati e procuratori di Milano*, C-55/94, EU:C:1995:411.

[51] *Hartlauer Handelsgesellschaft mbH* v. *Wiener Landesregierung, Oberösterreichische Landesregierung*, C-169/07, EU:C:2009:141. See also *Grisoli*, C-315/08, EU:C:2011:618; *Polliseni*, C-217/09, EU:C:2010:796; *Blanco Perez*, C-570/07, EU:C:2010:300; *Costa*, C-72/10, EU:C:2012:80; *Ottica*, C-539/11, EU:C:2013:591; *Italevesa*, C-168/14, EU:C:2015:685; *Venturini*, C-159/12, EU:C:2013:791. See for discussion R. Cisotta, 'Limits to Rights to Health Care and the Extent of Member States' Discretion to Decide on the Parameters of their Public Health Policies' in F. Benyon (ed.), *Services and the EU Citizen* (Oxford, Hart, 2013) 113.

[52] *Commission* v. *Greece*, C-140/03, EU:C:2005:242; *Commission* v. *Italy*, C-531/06, EU:C:2009:315; see also *Apothekerkammer des Saarlandes*, C-171–2/07, EU:C:2009:316.

[53] *Duomo*, C-357/10, EU:C:2012:283.

[54] *Commission* v. *Spain*, C-400/08, EU:C:2011:172; *Yellow Cab*, C-338/09, EU:C:2010:814.

[55] See C. Costello, 'Market Access All Areas? The Treatment of Non-Discriminatory Barriers to the Free Movement of Workers' (2000) 27(3) *LIEI* 267.

[56] *Commission* v. *Italy*, C-110/05, EU:C:2009:66.

they do more than just burden free movers – they *de facto* exclude them. The individuals or companies could not solve their problem by paying a fee or getting a permit. They were just told 'no, you may not move clubs' or 'no, you may not open a clinic in this town' or 'no, you may not purchase this pharmacy'. Where access is prevented, rather than hindered, the Court is consistently strict. Another feature that they share is that they do not affect all market actors equally: in each of the cases mentioned above there is protection of established incumbents from new competition.

(iii) *De Minimis*: Limits of the Right to Take Up an Occupation

Bosman and the other cases in the preceding section concerned measures with a very direct and powerful effect. In *Graf*, the Court of Justice stated that measures affecting the taking up of economic activities in another Member State would not fall within Article 45 TFEU if their restrictive effects were too indirect or uncertain.[57] In that instance, an Austrian law entitling employees to two months' pay as compensation for loss of employment where they had been working for their employer for at least three years was challenged. This entitlement did not exist where it was the employee who gave notice. Graf left his company to work in Germany. He sued for the compensation, claiming that its absence acted as a disincentive to move job, and thus fell within Article 45. The Court disagreed.

Graf v. *Filzmoser Maschinenbau*, C–190/98, EU:C:2000:49

22 Nationals of Member States have in particular the right, which they derive directly from the Treaty, to leave their country of origin to enter the territory of another Member State and reside there in order to pursue an economic activity.

23 Provisions which, even if they are applicable without distinction, preclude or deter a national of a Member State from leaving his country of origin in order to exercise his right to freedom of movement therefore constitute an obstacle to that freedom. However, in order to be capable of constituting such an obstacle, they must affect acces of workers to the labour market.

24 Legislation of the kind at issue in the main proceedings is not such as to preclude or deter a worker from ending his contract of employment in order to take a job with another employer, because the entitlement to compensation on termination of employment is not dependent on the worker's choosing whether or not to stay with his current employer but on a future and hypothetical event, namely the subsequent termination of his contract without such termination being at his own initiative or attributable to him.

25 Such an event is too uncertain and indirect a possibility for legislation to be capable of being regarded as liable to hinder freedom of movement for workers where it does not attach to termination of a contract of employment by the worker himself the same consequence as it attaches to termination which was not at his initiative or is not attributable to him.

Graf may be contrasted with *Kranemann*,[58] where there was a challenge to the regulations governing travel expenses for trainee civil servants in the German state of Nordrhein-Westfalen. Travel expenses were reimbursed where the training was carried out within Germany, but not for

---

[57] *Graf* v. *Filzmoser Maschinenbau*, C–190/98, EU:C:2000:49; see also Costello, n. 55 above; *Pelckmans Turnhout*, C–483/12, EU:C:2014:304.

[58] *Kranemann* v. *Land Nordrhein-Westfalen*, C–109/04, EU:C:2005:187.

that outside Germany. It was not clear whether this would dissuade many trainees from taking up training abroad. The Court of Justice, nevertheless, considered that the measure violated Article 45 TFEU, as it considered that it might deter trainees with limited financial resources from taking up training abroad. As with the other freedoms, there is no *de minimis* where measures are discriminatory, or specifically disadvantageous for cross-border movement.[59]

(iv) Restrictions on Secondary Establishment

The taking up of business activity in another Member State can occur either through primary or secondary establishment. The former is where a trader relocates her central place of business to another Member State. By contrast, with secondary establishment, the trader remains in her home State, but sets up branches, agencies or subsidiaries in other Member States. Restrictions on secondary establishment inevitably prevent traders from other Member States setting up a business in the host State, as to do so would involve their having to abandon their place of business in their home State. This question was raised in *Klopp*, concerning a German lawyer practising law in Dusseldorf. He applied to register with the Paris Bar Council in order to practise in Paris, but was refused because of a general prohibition on anyone practising at the Paris Bar unless their principal office was in Paris and the other offices they worked from were in the environs of Paris.

Ordre des Avocats au Barreau de Paris v. Klopp, 107/83, EU:C:1984:270

17 ... under [the second paragraph of Article 49 TFEU] freedom of establishment includes access to and the pursuit of the activities of self-employed persons 'under the conditions laid down for its own nationals by the law of the country where such establishment is effected'. It follows from that provision and its context that in the absence of specific Community rules in the matter each Member State is free to regulate the exercise of the legal profession in its territory

18 Nevertheless that rule does not mean that the legislation of a Member State may require a lawyer to have only one establishment throughout the Community territory. Such a restrictive interpretation would mean that a lawyer once established in a particular Member State would be able to enjoy the freedom of the Treaty to establish himself in another Member State only at the price of abandoning the establishment he already had.

19 That freedom of establishment is not confined to the right to create a single establishment within the Community is confirmed by the very words of Article [49 TFEU], according to which the progressive abolition of the restrictions on freedom of establishment applies to restrictions on the setting up of agencies, branches or subsidiaries by nationals of any Member State established in the territory of another Member State. That rule must be regarded as a specific statement of a general principle, applicable equally to the liberal professions, according to which the right of establishment includes freedom to set up and maintain, subject to observance of the professional rules of conduct, more than one place of work within the Community.

20 In view of the special nature of the legal profession, however, the second Member State must have the right, in the interests of the due administration of justice, to require that lawyers enrolled at a bar in its territory should practise in such a way as to maintain sufficient contact with their clients and the judicial authorities

---

[59] See pp.706–7.

and abide by the rules of the profession. Nevertheless such requirements must not prevent the nationals of other Member States from exercising properly the right of establishment guaranteed them by the Treaty.

21 In that respect it must be pointed out that modern methods of transport and telecommunications facilitate proper contact with clients and the judicial authorities. Similarly, the existence of a second set of chambers in another Member State does not prevent the application of the rules of ethics in the host Member State.

The argument in *Klopp* that effective supervision does not in fact require physical presence has been reinforced in the context of taxation in *Commission* v. *Denmark*, where the Court pointed out that a Directive existed specifically to regulate mutual assistance between national tax authorities.[60] Denmark made certain tax breaks conditional upon incorporation in Denmark, saying this was necessary to prevent fraud, because the authorities could not verify tax claims made by companies based abroad. In a judgment entirely consistent with its information-based approach to the internal market, and with the philosophy of the Services Directive, the Court found this to be disproportionate.[61] If checking of claims was necessary, Denmark should seek to find ways to do this abroad, with the help of local authorities, rather than washing its hands of the matter. The case shows that Member States should not regard foreign establishments as beyond the supervisory pale, but rather should engage with authorities in other States to obtain the information that they need.

Most cases have concerned more hidden restrictions on secondary establishment. In *Stanton*,[62] a challenge was made to a Belgian requirement for the self-employed to pay social security contributions unless they were also employed in Belgium. The Court of Justice considered that such an exemption penalised those who extended their business activities across more than one Member State and whilst it was not discriminatory, as more Belgians were affected by it than any other nationality, it was nevertheless illegal as it restricted free movement. In *Commission* v. *Portugal*,[63] a Portuguese requirement that private security firms be legally incorporated in Portugal was held to be an illegal restriction on secondary establishment as it prevented natural persons from other Member States setting up in Portugal.

In general, it is hard to justify restrictions on secondary establishment. The fact that an actor is established in one State is a strong argument that they should be allowed to work in others. Quality-based arguments against multiple establishments, to do with supervision or customer access, are often archaic and tend to fail for lack of genuine need.[64]

(v) Restrictions on the Use of Diplomas and Qualifications

By definition, professions deny access to an occupation, for they prevent that activity being pursued unless the individual submits to oversight of the professional body governing the activity in question and has the qualifications required for exercise of the profession. It might, therefore, be that the very presence of a profession is challenged under Articles 45 and 49 TFEU on the grounds that it prevents an individual taking up an economic activity. Early on, however,

---

[60] *Commission* v. *Denmark*, C-150/04, EU:C:2007:69.   [61] See pp. 720–3.

[62] *Stanton* v. *INASTI*, 143/87, EU:C:1988:378. See also *Rijksinstituut voor de sociale verzekering des zelfstandigen* v. *Wolf*, 154–5/87, EU:C:1988:379; *INASTI* v. *Kammler*, C-53/95, EU:C:1996:58; *Iraklis*, C-201/15, EU:C:2016:972.

[63] *Commission* v. *Portugal*, C-171/02, EU:C:2004:270.

[64] *Commission* v. *France*, 96/85, [1986] ECR 1475. See also *Commission* v. *Luxembourg*, C-351/90, [1992] ECR I-3945.

the Court of Justice ruled that Member States may be permitted to lay down professional rules relating to organisation, qualifications, professional ethics, supervision and liability,[65] and this has been repeated on a number of occasions since.[66] The Court has, instead, scrutinised the conditions imposed by these rules for the taking up of a profession, most notably the qualifications required before a migrant can enter a particular profession.

The central case is *Vlassopoulou*, concerning a Greek lawyer who completed her doctorate at the University of Tübingen, Germany, in 1982, and from 1983 until 1988 worked at a German law firm in Mannheim. In 1988 she applied to become a Rechtsanwalt, a German lawyer, but was refused on the grounds that she had neither studied law at a German university for two years, nor completed the First State exams, nor undergone the relevant period of training in Germany. She argued that this violated Article 49 as no account was taken of her Greek qualifications or her work experience in Germany.

Vlassopoulou v. *Ministerium für Justiz Bundes- und Europaangelegenheiten Baden-Wurttemberg*, C-340/89, EU:C:1991:193

14 ... insofar as Community law makes no special provision, the objectives of the Treaty, and in particular freedom of establishment, may be achieved by measures enacted by the Member States, which, under Article [4(3) TEU], must take 'all appropriate measures, whether general or particular, to ensure fulfilment of the obligations arising out of this Treaty or resulting from action taken by the institutions of the Community' and abstain from 'any measure which could jeopardize the attainment of the objectives of this Treaty'. [The wording of this provision has since been slightly amended by the Lisbon Treaty.]

15 It must be stated in this regard that, even if applied without any discrimination on the basis of nationality, national requirements concerning qualifications may have the effect of hindering nationals of the other Member States in the exercise of their right of establishment guaranteed to them by Article [49 TFEU]. That could be the case if the national rules in question took no account of the knowledge and qualifications already acquired by the person concerned in another Member State.

16 Consequently, a Member State which receives a request to admit a person to a profession to which access, under national law, depends upon the possession of a diploma or a professional qualification must take into consideration the diplomas, certificates and other evidence of qualifications which the person concerned has acquired in order to exercise the same profession in another Member State by making a comparison between the specialized knowledge and abilities certified by those diplomas and the knowledge and qualifications required by the national rules.

17 That examination procedure must enable the authorities of the host Member State to assure themselves, on an objective basis, that the foreign diploma certifies that its holder has knowledge and qualifications which are, if not identical, at least equivalent to those certified by the national diploma. That assessment of the equivalence of the foreign diploma must be carried out exclusively in the light of the level of knowledge and qualifications which its holder can be assumed to possess in the light of that diploma, having regard to the nature and duration of the studies and practical training to which the diploma relates ...

18 In the course of that examination, a Member State may, however, take into consideration objective differences relating to both the legal framework of the profession in question in the Member State of origin

---

[65] *Thieffry* v. *Conseil de l'Ordre des Avocats à la Cour de Paris*, 71/76, EU:C:1977:65.

[66] *Gullung* v. *Conseil de l'Ordre des Avocats*, 292/86, EU:C:1988:15; *Gebhard* v. *Consiglio dell'ordine degli avvocati e procuratori di Milano*, C-55/94, EU:C:1995:411.

and to its field of activity. In the case of the profession of lawyer, a Member State may therefore carry out a comparative examination of diplomas, taking account of the differences identified between the national legal systems concerned.

19 If that comparative examination of diplomas results in the finding that the knowledge and qualifications certified by the foreign diploma correspond to those required by the national provisions, the Member State must recognize that diploma as fulfilling the requirements laid down by its national provisions. If, on the other hand, the comparison reveals that the knowledge and qualifications certified by the foreign diploma and those required by the national provisions correspond only partially, the host Member State is entitled to require the person concerned to show that he has acquired the knowledge and qualifications which are lacking.

20 In this regard, the competent national authorities must assess whether the knowledge acquired in the host Member State, either during a course of study or by way of practical experience, is sufficient in order to prove possession of the knowledge which is lacking.

21 If completion of a period of preparation or training for entry into the profession is required by the rules applying in the host Member State, those national authorities must determine whether professional experience acquired in the Member State of origin or in the host Member State may be regarded as satisfying that requirement in full or in part.

22 Finally, it must be pointed out that the examination made to determine whether the knowledge and qualifications certified by the foreign diploma and those required by the legislation of the host Member State correspond must be carried out by the national authorities in accordance with a procedure which is in conformity with the requirements of Community law concerning the effective protection of the fundamental rights conferred by the Treaty on Community subjects. It follows that any decision taken must be capable of being made the subject of judicial proceedings in which its legality under Community law can be reviewed and that the person concerned must be able to ascertain the reasons for the decision taken in his regard.

There is a duty to take account of the qualifications and experience of the migrant in deciding whether to grant her access to the market.[67] A question emerging from *Vlassopoulou* is that concerning the types of proof that may be furnished by the migrant in order to demonstrate that she meets the required standard. The host State can only refuse access to the profession if there are 'objective differences' between its qualifications and the practical experience and qualifications of the migrant. Such an approach assumes a substitutability of knowledge, whereby if the migrant has the requisite standard of knowledge, no matter the source, she should be allowed to practise.

Subsequent case law has expounded on which knowledge and training must be taken into account by the host State authorities. In *Hocsman*,[68] a Spaniard applied to practise as a doctor in France. All his university training was from Argentina, whose diplomas France did not recognise as equivalent to its own. He had, however, worked for a number of years as a doctor in Spanish hospitals and as a urologist in French hospitals. The Court of Justice held that in making their decision the French authorities should have considered all the practical experience acquired by Hocsman not only in France, but also in Spain. They were also required to take into account all

---

[67] *Pesla*, C-345/08, EU:C:2009:771; *Vandorou*, C-422/09, EU:C:2010:732; *Koller*, C-118/09, EU:C:2010:805; *X-Steuerberatungsgesellschaft*, C-342/14, EU:C:2015:827.

[68] *Hocsman* v. *Ministre de l'Emploi et de la Solidarité*, C-238/98, EU:C:2000:440.

the diplomas and qualifications that certified a specialised knowledge, notwithstanding that these came from outside the European Union. The test imposes severe demands on the professional bodies. It will be difficult to vet the quality of practical experience not gained on their territory. It is even more difficult to know how to evaluate certification of an expertise from an institution whose standards are not trusted. Finally, they are required to provide some overall assessment on what may be a set of heterogeneous and eclectic experiences. Any decision will be difficult for the authority to make. Such requirements are not necessarily advantageous to the migrant, as this complexity results in any decision being difficult to review as it is difficult to point to a clear standard which is being breached.

Professional qualifications also facilitate the pursuit of an activity by demonstrating certification of a skill, thereby making the holder more marketable. It would be extremely complicated if different constraints were to apply to how Member States regulated access to a profession and how they regulated the broader use of professional qualifications. The Court of Justice has, therefore, a similar logic on all non-discriminatory restrictions on the recognition of non-national professional qualifications. In *Kraus*,[69] a German, who had completed an LLM at Edinburgh University, challenged a German requirement that administrative authorisation was necessary for use of higher education titles acquired abroad. The Court noted that qualifications were necessary both for access to a profession and, more generally, to facilitate the exercise of economic activity. Any conditions on the use of a title which hindered or made more difficult the exercise of the economic freedoms fell, in its view, within Article 49 TFEU. It refused to draw a distinction between titles necessary for access to a profession and other titles, but held that Member States could impose non-discriminatory restrictions on the use of titles to prevent fraud. An administrative authorisation for these purposes was lawful provided it was accessible, susceptible to judicial review, reasons were given for any refusal to approve a title, the administrative costs charged were not excessive and any sanctions imposed for the use of the title without authorisation were not disproportionately heavy.[70]

Vlassopoulou now coexists alongside Directive 2005/36/EC on the recognition of professional qualifications, which consolidates what had previously been a number of different Directives.[71] There are situations which do not fall within the Directive, to which the case law principles continue to apply, but it provides a fairly comprehensive regime.

The Directive governs the pursuit, either in an employed or self-employed capacity, of a regulated profession by EU nationals in a Member State other than that where they acquired their qualifications.[72] The Directive gives a nigh exhaustive definition of regulated professions, taking these to include any professional activity access to or the pursuit of which is subject to the possession of specific professional qualifications.[73] These professional qualifications may be attested by formal qualifications, a confirmation of competence or professional experience.[74] The central provision of the Directive, Article 4(1), states that an EU national who has qualified abroad will have access to the host State market where her qualifications are recognised by that State.

---

[69] *Kraus* v. *Land Baden-Württemberg*, C-19/92, EU:C:1993:125.   [70] See also *Iraklis*, C-201/15, EU:C:2016:972.
[71] [2005] OJ L 255/22.   [72] *Ibid.* Article 2(1).
[73] *Ibid.* Article 3(1). The Directive also applies to a large number of occupations not fitting neatly into this definition. These are set out in Annex I.
[74] *Ibid.* Article 3(1)(b).

> ### Directive 2005/36/EC, Article 4
>
> (1) The recognition of professional qualifications by the host Member State allows the beneficiary to gain access in that Member State to the same profession as that for which he is qualified in the home Member State and to pursue it in the host Member State under the same conditions as its nationals.

The Directive provides three routes to recognition, depending upon the professional activity being undertaken.

The first is the 'general system for the recognition of evidence of training'.[75] This applies where access to or pursuit of a regulated profession in the host State is contingent upon possession of specific qualifications. The general rule here is mutual recognition of qualifications. However, where the duration of the training undertaken is at least one year shorter than that in the host State, where the training is substantially different from that in the host State, or where the regulated profession in the host State comprises one or more regulated activities which do not exist in the corresponding home State and which involve specific training, there are deviations from the rule. Then Member States may require applicants to take an aptitude test or complete an adaptation period – a period of supervised and assessed work – of up to three years but the applicant must be able to choose which, except where the activity requires precise knowledge of national law, in which case the host State may choose.[76]

A difficult situation occurs where qualifications and training are not merely different in detail, but so fundamentally divergent that differences cannot just be made up by a little extra training. In this case the Directive does not provide a solution, but the Court of Justice has found that Member States must still consider how free movement can be protected, and a good solution may be to allow the migrant to practise a specific part of the protected profession, perhaps under their home title, to avoid confusion. Mr Nasiopoulos had qualified as a medical masseur-hydrotherapist in Germany, but this particular form of therapy was conducted in Greece, where he wished to establish, by physiotherapists, and reserved to them. Mr Nasiopoulos did not claim that he should be recognised as a physiotherapist or allowed to do all the things that they do, but argued that he should be allowed to carry out the specific therapy for which he was trained: he wanted what the Court has called 'partial recognition'.

> ### *Nasiopoulos*, C-573/11, EU:C:2013:564
>
> 20 Since the conditions for access to the profession of physiotherapist have not, to date, been harmonised at European Union level, the Member States remain competent to define such conditions since Directive 2005/36 does not restrict their powers on that point. They must, however, exercise their powers in this area in a manner which respects the basic freedoms guaranteed by the Treaty.
>
> 21 Thus, legislation of a host Member State which excludes all partial access to a regulated profession and, accordingly, is liable to hinder or make less attractive the exercise of freedom of establishment may be justified, *inter alia*, by overriding reasons relating to the public interest, provided that it does not go beyond what is necessary in order to attain the objective which it pursues.

---

[75] *Ibid.* Articles 10–15.   [76] *Ibid.* Article 14.

22 With regard to the objective of legislation such as that at issue in the main proceedings, the overriding reasons relating to the public interest relied upon by the Governments which submitted observations are, firstly, consumer protection and, secondly, health protection.

23 As regards consumer protection, it must be noted that, indeed, partial recognition of professional qualifications could, theoretically, have the effect of fragmenting the professions regulated in a Member State into various activities. That would lead essentially to a risk of confusion in the minds of the recipients of services provided by professionals established in that Member State, which recipients might well be misled as to the scope of the qualifications associated with the profession of physiotherapist.

24 However, exclusion from even partial access to the profession of physiotherapist goes beyond what is necessary to achieve the objective of consumer protection.

25 As the Court has already pointed out in the judgment in [C-330/02] *Colegio de Ingenieros de Caminos, Canales y Puertos*, the legitimate objective of protection of consumers may be achieved through less restrictive means than total exclusion of even partial access to a profession, particularly the obligation to use the professional title of origin or the academic title both in the language in which it was awarded and in its original form, and in the official language of the host Member State.

The Court went on to make clear that these principles only applied where training was so different that the title acquired and the relevant host State title did not belong to the 'same profession', so that the Directive could not be applied. Partial recognition cannot be used as a path to avoid acquiring necessary extra knowledge where similar professional qualifications differ in content, thereby undermining the host State profession. It is also necessary, before engaging in partial recognition, to consider whether a particular aspect of a profession can safely and coherently be separated from the whole. In Mr Nasiopoulos's case that seemed to be so.

The second route concerns activities which require only general commercial or professional knowledge.[77] These are listed in Annex IV of the Directive and include activities involving mainly industrial experience. Access to the market is premised upon mutual recognition of experience.

Directive 2005/36/EC, Article 16

If, in a Member State, access to or pursuit of one of the activities listed in Annex IV is contingent upon possession of general, commercial or professional knowledge and aptitudes, that Member State shall recognise previous pursuit of the activity in another Member State as sufficient proof of such knowledge and aptitudes.

The length of time depends on the activity in question and whether any prior training has been carried out. There is less protection for these activities than for those in the first category. There are no checks on the equivalence of the experience or any exceptions to this requirement of mutual recognition.

The third category covers those professionals (doctors, vets, nurses, midwives, pharmacists, architects and dentists) who were previously regulated by sectoral Directives.[78] These require not only evidence of formal qualifications, but also evidence that the applicant has satisfied

---

[77] *Ibid.* Articles 16–20.   [78] *Ibid.* Articles 21–52.

minimum training conditions which are set out in the Directive.[79] There is thus a degree of harmonisation of the training of these professions, primarily concerning length of training and of internships.

(vi) Restrictions on Grounds of Abuse of Free Movement

In a number of situations individuals may be motivated to go abroad in order to avoid inconvenient rules in their home State. This occurs where individuals migrate in order to benefit from the family rights awarded to migrant citizens, and then come home at a later date, continuing to rely on their migrant status. It also occurs where companies relocate to a Member State with more convenient tax or incorporation rules, but continue to do business in their original State. In both these cases, the original State is inclined to regard the use of free movement as 'abusive' and to claim that reliance on free movement rights merely to avoid national law should not be permitted. As is discussed in Chapter 11, and below, the Court of Justice has not been sympathetic.[80] It is not abusive to allow the legal advantages of a particular location or relocation to influence decision-making, and nor is it abusive to engage in economic activity purely in order to benefit from the associated rights, as may happen where a student gets a job in order to obtain finance for their study: the reasons why someone migrates or works are irrelevant to their rights.[81]

Abuse arguments have also been important in the field of education and training. An early example was *Knoors*, where a Dutch citizen worked as a plumber in Belgium, and on his return to the Netherlands applied to have his experience recognised as equivalent to the Dutch plumbing qualification, as the Directive then in force permitted. The Dutch Government claimed that he had migrated purely to avoid having to study for the plumbing qualification which in the Netherlands was compulsory.

J. Knoors v. *Staatssecretaris van Economische Zaken*, 115/78, EU:C:1979:31

24 Although it is true that the provisions of the Treaty relating to establishment and the provision of services cannot be applied to situations which are purely internal to a Member State, the position nevertheless remains that the reference in Article [49 TFEU] to 'nationals of a Member State' who wish to establish themselves 'in the territory of another Member State' cannot be interpreted in such a way as to exclude from the benefit of Community law a given Member State's own nationals when the latter, owing to the fact that they have lawfully resided on the territory of another Member State and have there acquired a trade qualification which is recognized by the provisions of Community law, are, with regard to their state

---

[79] *Ibid.* Article 21.

[80] See pp. 511–14; see also *O and B*, C-456/12, EU:C:2014:135; *Torresi*, C-58–9/13, EU:C:2014:2088; K. Engsig Sørensen, 'Abuse of Rights in Community Law: A Principle of Substance or Merely Rhetoric?' (2006) 43 *CMLRev* 423; A. Kjellgren, 'On the Border of Abuse: The Jurisprudence of the European Court of Justice on Circumvention, Fraud and Other Misuses of Community Law' (2000) 11 *EBLRev* 179; M. Evers and A. de Graaf, 'Limiting Benefit Shopping: Use and Abuse of EC Law' (2009) 18 *EC Tax Review* 279; R. de la Feria, 'Prohibition of Abuse of (Community) Law: The Creation of a New General Principle of EC Law Through Tax' (2008) 45 *CMLRev* 395; K. Ziegler, '"Abuse of Law" in the Context of the Free Movement of Workers' in R. de la Feria and S. Vogenauer (eds.), *Prohibition of Abuse of Law: A New General Principle of EU Law?* (Oxford, Hart, 2011).

[81] *L.N.*, C-46/12, EU:C:2013:97; *Levin*, 53/81, EU:C:1982:105; *Torresi*, C-58–9/13, EU:C:2014:2088.

of origin, in a situation which may be assimilated to that of any other persons enjoying the rights and liberties guaranteed by the Treaty.

25 However, it is not possible to disregard the legitimate interest which a Member State may have in preventing certain of its nationals, by means of facilities created under the Treaty, from attempting wrongly to evade the application of their national legislation as regards training for a trade.

The suggestion in this last paragraph, that there may be limits to the extent to which individuals can choose the jurisdiction that suits them best, has not been realised in practice.[82] Just as a State may, sometimes, be able to justify applying rules to migrants which restrict their movement, if necessary in order to protect important interests, they may in principle do this also to citizens engaging in U-turns. However, that does not mean that self-interested choices somehow nullify rights, and in practice the Court of Justice continues to respect the individual freedom of choice which is inherent in free movement.

Centros, a case on company migration which is discussed later in this chapter,[83] has become a central authority on this and contains the clear statement that 'the fact that a national of a Member State who wishes to set up a company chooses to form it in the Member State whose rules of company law seem to him the least restrictive and to set up branches in other Member States cannot, in itself, constitute an abuse of the right of establishment'.[84] That appears to reflect the Court's general approach to 'instrumental' use of free movement law.

N. Nic Shuibhne, *The Coherence of EU Free Movement Law* (Oxford University Press, 2013) 91

The Court's sanctioning of the instrumental use of EU law short of fraudulent conduct – i.e. simply taking advantage of the possibilities created by free movement – was widely transposed from *Centros* to the case law on personal free movement. While some Advocates General did consider the relevance of intention or motivation, the Court's approach becomes more consciously consistent with the view that instrumental exercise (or 'legitimate circumvention'[85]) of free movement rights does not constitute abuse. For example, in *Ninni-Orasche*, the applicant, an Italian national living in Austria and married to an Austrian national, had worked for a short period in order to generate eligibility for study finance benefits in the host state.[86] To determine whether she was a worker within the meaning of EU law the national court was empowered by the Court of Justice to determine whether the relevant activity was purely marginal and ancillary. It was also emphasized that 'factors relating to the conduct of the person concerned before and after the period of employment are not relevant in establishing the status of worker'.

In recent years entrepreneurial higher education institutions have created a new locus for abuse arguments. The European School of Economics (ESE) was a UK institution which awarded degrees according to UK law, but which provided classes at a campus in Italy. Italian law, however, only recognised foreign degrees if the study for that degree had actually been undertaken in the degree-awarding State. In *Neri*, the Court of Justice found that this was an

---

[82] See N. Nic Shuibhne, *The Coherence of EU Free Movement Law* (Oxford University Press, 2013) 85–100.
[83] See pp. 813–15.   [84] *Centros*, C-212/97, EU:C:1999:126, para. 27.   [85] De la Feria, n. 80 above, 403.
[86] *Franca Ninni-Orasche* v. *Bundesminister für Wissenschaft, Verkehr und Kunst*, C-413/01, EU:C:2003:600.

unlawful restriction on the freedom of establishment of the ESE.[87] In *Khatzithanasis* and *Commission* v. *Spain*, the Court took the same approach in similar situations, ruling that a failure to recognise qualifications as an optician or engineer just because the actual study was done in the home State was contrary to the Directive on professional qualifications then in force.[88]

The requirement to recognise qualifications awarded by bodies in other Member States is not subject to an exception or condition to do with the physical place of study.

A limit was, however, reached in *Cavallera*.[89] In Italy, one may practise as an engineer after a university course in engineering, and the taking of a State exam. In Spain, a university course in engineering suffices. Mr Cavallera attempted to leverage this difference: he had obtained a university degree in engineering in Italy, and successfully obtained recognition of this in Spain as equivalent to a Spanish degree. This entitled him to practise as an engineer in Spain and he obtained certification to this effect. He then returned to Italy and argued that since he was entitled to practise as an engineer in Spain, his Spanish authorisation should be recognised and translated to an authorisation to practise in Italy, pursuant to the Directive on professional qualifications then in force. He would then have successfully avoided the Italian State examination. However, he lost his case. The Court of Justice found that the Directive did not grant any right to rely on a certificate authorising a person to practise a profession when that certificate did not attest to any course of study or examination at an institution in that State.[90] One may choose one's State of study, for whatever reasons one wants, but that choice must be genuinely exercised if it is to found further rights.

4 RESTRICTIONS ON THE PURSUIT OF AN OCCUPATION

The law requires a migrant to be able to pursue their profession in a host State free of direct (overt) or indirect (covert) discrimination. Alongside this, the question arises whether a person or business can challenge host State regulation merely because it obstructs their activities, even without showing that national or local businesses suffer less harm. The law and policy surrounding this question is addressed in section (iii) below.

(i) Discrimination in Labour Markets

Discrimination is prohibited by Article 45(2) in all aspects of employment, specifically including remuneration and conditions of employment, but covering any other aspects of the employment process too.[91] Regulation 492/2011 elaborates on this, and provides in Article 7(4) that:

> Any clause of a collective or individual agreement or of any other collective regulation concerning eligibility for employment, employment, remuneration and other conditions of work or dismissal shall be null and void insofar as it lays down or authorises discriminatory conditions in respect of workers who are nationals of the other Member States.

---

[87] *Neri* v. *European School of Economics*, C-153/02, EU:C:2003:614.

[88] *Theologos-Grigorios Khatzithanasis* v. *Ypourgos Ygeias kai Koinonikis Allilengyis and Organismos Epangelmatikis Ekpaidefsis kai Katartisis (OEEK)*, C-151/07, EU:C:2008:680; *Commission* v. *Spain*, C-286/06, EU:C:2008:586. See also *Commission* v. *Greece*, C-274/05, EU:C:2008:585.

[89] *Consiglio Nazionale degli Ingegneri* v. *Ministero della Giustizia and Marco Cavallera*, C-311/06, EU:C:2009:37.

[90] See e.g. *Koller*, C-118/09, EU:C:2010:805.

[91] *Roman Angonese* v. *Cassa di Risparmio di Bolzano SpA*, C-281/98, EU:C:2000:296.

An example of this in action is *Erny*.[92] German employers provided extra contributions to part-time workers nearing retirement, and did so according to a formula which took account of their salary and the amount of tax they paid. However, frontier workers living in France were treated as if they were taxed at the German level, even though they in fact paid tax in France, and this had disadvantageous consequences for them. The contributions had come into being as part of a collective agreement, but the Court of Justice considered that neither the autonomy of the social partners, nor the practical difficulties of taking into account foreign tax levels, provided sufficient justification for the discriminatory effect. The clauses of the agreement were therefore null and void. What is notable is that the Court did not prescribe an alternative, but left it to the Member State or the social partners to come up with a better solution. On the one hand, this respects the autonomy of labour processes, but on the other it means that negotiations towards a collective agreement are framed by stringent Treaty obligations and the case law of the Court.

A good example of discrimination in work is *Köbler*.[93] Austrian law granted university professors an increased salary once they had completed fifteen years' service in the Austrian university system. This was not available to university professors who had served part of that time at universities outside Austria. Köbler was denied the increase on the grounds that he had spent some of this period in a German university and, as the scheme was designed to reward loyalty to the Austrian university system, it was considered that this period away meant he did not qualify. The Court of Justice found the measure to be illegal, as it discriminated in two ways. First, it penalised non-Austrians who were likely to have spent some time in universities elsewhere in the European Union. Secondly, it discriminated against Austrians who had exercised their rights under Article 45 TFEU and spent time abroad. Similar failures to take account of experience abroad, when domestic experience is rewarded, have been repeatedly condemned by the Court.[94] A variation on this theme was found in *Delay*, where a failure to take into account years of experience in a particular domestic job was also discriminatory, where that job was one that was primarily done by foreigners.[95] The case concerned language assistants in Italian universities. If they were lucky enough to obtain a permanent post, their years as a language assistant did not count towards their seniority, whereas under the Italian university rules experience in other comparable posts would have done.

Several types of discrimination have been the recurring subject of litigation before the Court of Justice: trade union rights, tax advantages and social advantages. With regard to trade union rights, provision is made in Article 8 of Regulation 1612/68 for migrants to enjoy equality of treatment in respect of both membership of trade unions and exercise of those trade union rights.[96] A broad interpretation has been taken, so this right to equal treatment applies not merely to formally recognised trade unions, but also to any body to which workers pay contributions in return for defence and representation of their interests.[97] It also confers the right not only to equal protection from the union, but also the equal opportunity to govern the trade union, by standing for election for office.[98]

---

[92] *Erny*, C-172/11, EU:C:2012:399.   [93] *Köbler v. Austria*, C-224/01, EU:C:2003:513.

[94] *Ingetraut Scholz v. Opera Universitaria di Cagliari and Cinzia Porcedda*, C-419/92, EU:C:1994:62; *Commission v. Italy*, C-371/04, EU:C:2006:668; *Landeskliniken*, C-514/12, EU:C:2013:799.

[95] *Nancy Delay v. Università degli studi di Firenze, Istituto nazionale della previdenza sociale*, C-276/07, EU:C:2008:282.

[96] [1968] OJ Special Edn, L 257/2, 475.

[97] *Association de Soutien aux Travailleurs Immigrés (ASTI) v. Chambre des employés privés*, C-213/90, EU:C:1991:291.

[98] *Ibid.*; *Commission v. Austria*, C-465/01, EU:C:2004:530; *Erzberger*, C-566/15, ECLI:EU:C:2017:562.

The migrant is entitled, by virtue of both Article 45(2) TFEU and secondary legislation,[99] to the same tax benefits in a Member State as its nationals who are working there.[100] This principle has not proved straightforward to apply. Tax benefits are intended to compensate for or diminish tax burdens. However, individuals are usually taxed in their place of residence. As a result, tax benefits are often also awarded only to residents. Yet, this is likely to especially adversely affect migrant workers, particularly frontier workers, and so may be indirectly discriminatory.

The Court of Justice addressed this problem in *Schumacker*, and found that since, in general, residents and non-residents were in objectively different positions with regard to taxation, differences in treatment with regard to tax benefits were not generally wrongful.[101] However, they found that there could be exceptions to this rule. Mr Schumacker earned the major part of his income in Germany, and it was taxed in Germany, while he earned no significant income in Belgium, where he lived. In those circumstances he should have the right to the same tax benefits as a German resident. This lays down a rule of thumb for a particular problem, but serves more to demonstrate the complexities of taxation than to provide a general framework for addressing them.[102]

Other prohibited practices include discrimination between workers from different States – travel costs which in practice favoured those living further away – and discrimination based on the location of one's employer.[103] Article 45 goes beyond mere host State treatment.

Finally, Regulation 492/2011 also prohibits discrimination in 'social advantages' and housing.[104] However, these clauses have become considerably less important since the development of citizenship. Those relying on Articles 45 and 49 TFEU are also EU citizens, and can rely on Article 18 TFEU and the Citizenship Directive 2004/38/EC to obtain equal treatment in matters relating to their life outside work.[105]

(ii) Discrimination in the Pursuit of a Business

Freedom of establishment includes the right to pursue business activities. The Court of Justice has understood this as involving anything connected with the running of the business. There must be no discrimination in anything which affects the running of the migrant's business in any way at all. In *Steinhauser*,[106] a German artist living in Biarritz in France applied to rent a fisherman's shed from the local authority but was refused on the grounds that he was not a French national. In its reference the national court noted that the letting of premises did not relate to a specific business activity and, therefore, implicitly raised the question of whether it fell outside Article 49 TFEU. The Court held that the measure constituted illegal discrimination within Article 49. It stated that as the renting of premises for business purposes furthers the pursuit of a business, it falls within Article 49. Insofar as the measure was discriminatory, it was illegal. The remit of Article 49 in particular is, therefore, very wide. Planning, tax, health and

---

[99] Regulation 1612/68, Article 7(2).
[100] *Biehl* v. *Administration des contributions du grand-duché de Luxembourg*, C-175/88, EU:C:1990:186.
[101] *Finanzamt Köln-Altstadt* v. *Schumacker*, C-279/93, EU:C:1995:31.
[102] I. Roxan, 'Assuring Real Freedom of Movement in EU Direct Taxation' (2000) 63 *MLR* 831, 847–50. See e.g. *Eschenbrenner*, C-496/15, EU:C:2017:152; *X*, C-283/15, EU:C:2017:102.
[103] *Sopora*, C-512/13, EU:C:2015:108; *Petersen*, C-544/11, EU:C:2013:124.
[104] Regulation 492/2011, Articles 7(2), 9. See e.g. *Anita Cristini* v. *Société nationale des chemins de fer français*, 32/75, EU:C:1975:120.
[105] See Ch. 11.   [106] *Steinhauser* v. *City of Biarritz*, 197/84, EU:C:1985:260.

safety, environmental and labour laws all affect the running of a business. They must all be couched and applied in a manner that does not discriminate against non-nationals or foreign companies.

In most cases it is indirect discrimination that is in issue, commonly as a result of rules referring to the location of establishment or employment. In *CIBA*, a Hungarian law was challenged which required companies to pay a training levy on all their employees, including those employed abroad, but which granted those companies a discount if they provided in-house training.[107] However, the discount was only granted where the training took place in Hungary. That disparity between benefit and burden might discourage companies from establishing subsidiaries abroad, the Court found, and so restricted secondary establishment.[108]

(iii) Equally Applicable Restrictions on the Pursuit of an Occupation

Some measures do not obviously discriminate on grounds of nationality, either directly or indirectly, and yet do disadvantage those who move across borders. In *Danish Company Cars* it will be remembered that Denmark prohibited residents using company cars registered abroad in Denmark, to quell the fear that many of its residents would use this as a way of not paying Danish motor vehicle tax. Company cars are an employment benefit and therefore relate to the pursuit of employment rather than the taking up of employment. In the excerpt quoted earlier,[109] the Court stated that such restrictions could fall within Article 45 if they affected access to the labour market. It then considered whether this was the case.

Commission v. Denmark (Danish Company Cars), C-464/02, EU:C:2005:38

45 It is settled case law that Article [45 TFEU] prohibits not only all discrimination, direct or indirect, based on nationality, but also national rules which are applicable irrespective of the nationality of the workers concerned but impede their freedom of movement.

46 It is clear that the original scheme, insofar as it remains applicable, could, on account of the obligation to register in Denmark a company car made available to the employee by an employer established in another Member State, deter such an employer from taking on an employee resident in Denmark for work which is not the employee's principal employment and, consequently, impede access to such employment by residents in Denmark.

47 As regards employees resident in Denmark who wish to pursue their principal employment in an undertaking established in another Member State, the amended scheme also impedes freedom of movement for those workers since it imposes additional costs in the form of a temporary registration tax.

48 Insofar as the undertaking established in another Member State bears those costs without being compensated, it is deterred from taking on an employee resident in Denmark in respect of whom the costs are higher than those borne for an employee who does not reside in that State.

49 It is true, as the Danish Government asserts, that the employer could attempt to adjust the salary of an employee resident in Denmark in order to offset the additional expense in question. In other words, he could try to pay to that employee a salary lower than that paid to an employee engaged in the same activity, but who resides in another Member State.

---

[107] *CIBA*, C-96/08, EU:C:2010:185.   [108] Cf. *Impacto Azul*, C-186/12, EU:C:2013:412.   [109] See p. 789.

50 However, an employee resident in Denmark might already be deterred from seeking employment in another Member State faced with the prospect of receiving a salary lower than that of a comparable employee resident in that other Member State. As the Court ruled in paragraph 18 of Case 121/86 *Ledoux* [1988] ECR 3741, the fact that an employee is placed at a disadvantage in regard to working conditions compared to his colleagues residing in the country of their employer has a direct effect on the exercise of his right to freedom of movement within the Community . . .

52 Consequently, it must be held that the Danish legislation, both in its original version and in its amended version, constitutes a restriction on freedom of movement for workers.

The same reasoning has been applied to an analogous rule in the context of self-employed workers in *Nadin*.[110] In neither case was it possible to speak of nationality discrimination, but rather discrimination against migrants, against those who had exercised their EU rights to engage in economic activity in another Member State. This has been one of the major themes of the case law on equally applicable restrictions on employment and establishment.[111]

However, where a measure does not specifically disadvantage movement, and in the absence of an argument that it disadvantages foreigners and is therefore discriminatory, the Court of Justice has tended to find no restriction to be present. An example is *Sodemare*.[112] Sodemare was a Luxembourg company, which, amongst other things, provided sheltered accommodation for elderly residents. It was refused approval to enter into contracts with public authorities in the region of Lombardy in Italy, which would have allowed it to be reimbursed for some of the health-care services it provided. The reason was that under Lombard law, such contracts were only available to non-profit-making bodies.[113] Sodemare challenged this, claiming that it violated Article 49 as it affected its ability to run its business in Italy.

C–70/95 *Sodemare* v. *Regione Lombardia* [1997] ECR I-3395

32 . . . as Community law stands at present, a Member State may, in the exercise of the powers it retains to organize its social security system, consider that a social welfare system of the kind at issue in this case necessarily implies, with a view to attaining its objectives, that the admission of private operators to that system as providers of social welfare services is to be made subject to the condition that they are non-profit-making.

33 Moreover, the fact that it is impossible for profit-making companies automatically to participate in the running of a statutory social welfare system of a Member State by concluding a contract which entitles them to be reimbursed by the public authorities for the costs of providing social welfare services of a health-care nature is not liable to place profit-making companies from other Member States in a less favourable factual or legal situation than profit-making companies in the Member State in which they are established.

34 In view of the foregoing, the non-profit condition cannot be regarded as contrary to Article [49 TFEU].

---

[110] *Nadin, Nadin-Lux and Durré*, C-151–2/04, EU:C:2005:775.

[111] See e.g. *Geurts and Vogten* v. *Administratie van de BTW, registratie en domeinen, Belgische Staat*, C-464/05, EU:C:2007:631.

[112] See also *Commission* v. *Belgium*, 221/85, EU:C:1986:456; *Conradi and Others*, 198/86, EU:C:1987:489; L. Hancher, and W. Sauter, 'One Step Beyond? From Sodemare to Docmorris: The EU's Freedom of Establishment Case Law Concerning Healthcare' (2010) 47 *CMLRev* 117.

[113] *Spezzino*, C-113/13, EU:C:2014:2440.

It has therefore been argued that Articles 45 and 49 TFEU are fundamentally, perhaps only, concerned with prohibiting discrimination. The first set of cases in this chapter, concerning restrictions on the taking up of an activity, are (arguably) in reality about discrimination since, by preventing migrants entering the market, these measures protect the Member State's own nationals from competition. The second set of cases, concerning restrictions on the pursuit of economic activity, are also about discrimination since they specifically disadvantage either nationals of other Member States, or those who have exercised their cross-border EU rights.[114]

However, recent cases fit this framework a little uncomfortably. In *Caixa Bank France*, a challenge was made by the subsidiary of a Spanish bank to a French prohibition on the offering of certain types of bank account. French law prohibited remuneration or interest being offered on 'sight accounts'. These are accounts that allow instant withdrawals. The restriction applied to all banks and although it did not prevent foreign banks setting up in France, it did prevent them from carrying out these types of activity.

CaixaBank France v. Ministère de l'Économie, des Finances et de l'Industrie, C–442/02, EU:C:2004:586

11 Article [49 TFEU] requires the elimination of restrictions on the freedom of establishment. All measures which prohibit, impede or render less attractive the exercise of that freedom must be regarded as such restrictions.

12 A prohibition on the remuneration of sight accounts such as that laid down by the French legislation constitutes, for companies from Member States other than the French Republic, a serious obstacle to the pursuit of their activities via a subsidiary in the latter Member State, affecting their access to the market. That prohibition is therefore to be regarded as a restriction within the meaning of Article [49 TFEU].

13 That prohibition hinders credit institutions which are subsidiaries of foreign companies in raising capital from the public, by depriving them of the possibility of competing more effectively, by paying remuneration on sight accounts, with the credit institutions traditionally established in the Member State of establishment, which have an extensive network of branches and therefore greater opportunities than those subsidiaries for raising capital from the public.

14 Where credit institutions which are subsidiaries of foreign companies seek to enter the market of a Member State, competing by means of the rate of remuneration paid on sight accounts constitutes one of the most effective methods to that end. Access to the market by those establishments is thus made more difficult by such a prohibition . . .

17 It is clear from settled case law that where, as in the case at issue in the main proceedings, such a measure applies to any person or undertaking carrying on an activity in the territory of the host Member State, it may be justified where it serves overriding requirements relating to the public interest, is suitable for securing the attainment of the objective it pursues and does not go beyond what is necessary to attain it . . .

The Court nevertheless found that the restriction could not be justified by the protection of consumers or the need to encourage long-term saving. These admirable goals, it asserted, could be met by less restrictive measures.

On the one hand, the rule in question in this case does not, at first glance, appear to have any discriminatory element. Might a French bank not also be frustrated that it cannot attract

---

[114] G. Marenco, 'The Notion of Restriction on the Freedom of Establishment and Provision of Services in the Case-Law of the Court' (1991) 11 *YBEL* 111.

customers by paying interest on their current account? Yet, on the other hand, as the Court implicitly notes, the rule excludes a certain business model from the French market, and that will inevitably work to the advantage of incumbents and inhibit new entrants, particularly from banks established in Member States where they are using that particular model.[115] What this shows is that where regulation has a significant impact, as the Court found that this rule would, the distinction between discriminatory and non-discriminatory rules evaporates: the mere fact of freezing the market in a particular form will generally be exclusionary.

Caixa Bank may be contrasted with *DHL*, in which Belgium required operators of postal services to submit to an external complaints procedure. The Court of Justice took the view that imposition of such a procedure could not be said to hinder or discourage establishment in Belgium.

DHL, C-148/10, EU:C:2011:654

62 First, that measure is applied, without discrimination on grounds of nationality, to all providers established in Belgium of postal services which are outside the scope of the universal service. Secondly, as the Advocate General stated in point 77 of his Opinion, operators cannot expect Member States not to have structures in place which afford legal protection for the interests of their customers and provide out-of-court procedures for settling disputes. Lastly, nearly all Member States have extended the external complaints schemes to providers of postal services which are outside the scope of the universal service.

The fact that DHL considered the procedure to some extent burdensome and costly is suggested by the fact that they fought it in the Belgian courts. Nevertheless, the Court of Justice was clearly more influenced by the fact that the procedure seemed reasonable, probably of marginal impact on business, and common. Unlike the rule in *Caixa Bank*, this requirement in *DHL* was not plausibly likely to discourage anyone from entering the market, nor to disadvantage them relative to competitors if they did. This is a *de minimis* ruling in all but name.

5 FREE MOVEMENT OF COMPANIES

(i) Discrimination and Foreign Companies

Freedom of establishment is granted not merely to EU citizens, but also to non-natural legal persons. The beneficiaries of the right to establishment are set out in Article 54 TFEU.

Article 54 TFEU

Companies or firms formed in accordance with the law of a Member State and having their registered office, central administration or principal place of business within the Community shall, for the purposes of this Chapter, be treated in the same way as natural persons who are nationals of Member States.

'Companies or firms' means companies or firms constituted under civil or commercial law, including cooperative societies, and other legal persons governed by public or private law, save for those which are non-profit-making.

---

[115] See *Commission* v. *Italy*, C-518/06, EU:C:2009:270.

Companies have to be formed in accordance with the laws of one of the Member States and have their registered office, central administration or principal place of business within the European Union if they are to have the right to freedom of establishment.[116] Therefore, whilst the prohibition on discrimination in Article 49 forbids discrimination on the grounds of nationality in the case of individuals, it forbids discrimination on the grounds of the place of registered office, central administration or principal place of business in the case of companies.[117]

(ii) Movement of Companies and Reincorporation

Companies may wish to move their principal place of business or head office to another Member State or to reincorporate in another Member State. This is something more than establishing a secondary establishment, which has been addressed in the previous sections. Such fundamental movement is about a company changing its core legal nature, going from incorporation in one Member State, under that Member State's laws, to incorporation in another Member State, in effect recreating itself. This is nevertheless a form of movement, and since it takes place for the same kind of economic reasons that companies engage in other cross-border activities and arrangements it would seem the type of relocation of business activity that the single market is intended to stimulate. However, there is a double context which complicates matters.

The first difficulty is a formal legal one. The company's incorporation within its home Member State is the feature which allows it to claim rights under Article 49.[118] If companies lose their legal personality within that State, either by dissolving or not meeting its corporate law requirements, they would lose their right to establish under Article 49.

The second is the policy context. Companies may wish to evade their fiscal and corporate responsibilities in Member States where they carry out their principal business by creating a legal shell in another Member State, which has lower fiscal obligations and less demanding corporate law (e.g. lower minimum capital requirements or less protection of minority shareholders). There are, moreover, incentives for Member States to attract these legal shells because, at very little cost to themselves, they can attract taxes that would otherwise go to the State where the company carries out its principal place of business. This can lead to a 'race to the bottom' where the tax base and basic company law requirements are eroded as States compete to attract investment.[119]

These issues were first addressed in the *Daily Mail* judgment. Under UK law, companies could not transfer their central management from the United Kingdom and still retain their legal personality without first obtaining the consent of the Treasury. The *Daily Mail* newspaper wished to transfer its central management to the Netherlands so that it might sell off some of its shares without being subject to UK capital gains tax. After negotiations with the Treasury broke down, it brought an action claiming that the UK regime breached Article 49. The case therefore raised both of the concerns outlined above.

---

[116] Article 54(1) TFEU; *Kronos*, C-47/12, EU:C:2014:2200.   [117] *Commission* v. *France*, 270/83, EU:C:1986:37.
[118] *Kronos*, C-47/12, EU:C:2014:2200.
[119] This is sometimes called the 'Delaware effect' after a so-called 'race to the bottom' in state company laws in the United States was believed to have been initiated by the state of Delaware in the 1960s. W. Gary, 'Federalism and Corporate Law: Reflections upon Delaware' (1974) 83 *Yale LJ* 663. On this within the European Union, see C. Barnard, 'Social Dumping and the Race to the Bottom: Some Lessons for the European Union from Delaware?' (2000) 25 *ELRev* 57. See also pp. 651–5.

The Court of Justice found that there was no violation of Article 49. The United Kingdom was not preventing the *Daily Mail* from emigrating and becoming a Dutch company, if it so wanted. Rather, the *Mail* wanted to remain a UK company, while moving its headquarters abroad, whereas UK law said that to be a UK company entailed that its headquarters were in the United Kingdom. Thus the case, in the view of the Court, was not so much about whether the *Daily Mail* could move, as about the right of the United Kingdom to define what it meant to be a UK company. In the absence of harmonisation of the rules concerning incorporation, this was for the United Kingdom to decide.

R v. HM Treasury, ex parte Daily Mail, 81/87, EU:C:1988:456

18 The provision of United Kingdom law at issue in the main proceedings imposes no restriction on transactions such as those described above [reincorporation in another Member State]. Nor does it stand in the way of a partial or total transfer of the activities of a company incorporated in the United Kingdom to a company newly incorporated in another Member State, if necessary after winding-up and, consequently, the settlement of the tax position of the United Kingdom company. It requires Treasury consent only where such a company seeks to transfer its central management and control out of the United Kingdom while maintaining its legal personality and its status as a United Kingdom company.

19 In that regard it should be borne in mind that, unlike natural persons, companies are creatures of the law and, in the present state of Community law, creatures of national law. They exist only by virtue of the varying national legislation which determines their incorporation and functioning.

20 As the Commission has emphasized, the legislation of the Member States varies widely in regard to both the factor providing a connection to the national territory required for the incorporation of a company and the question whether a company incorporated under the legislation of a Member State may subsequently modify that connecting factor. Certain States require that not merely the registered office but also the real head office, that is to say the central administration of the company, should be situated on their territory, and the removal of the central administration from that territory thus presupposes the winding-up of the company with all the consequences that winding-up entails in company law and tax law. The legislation of other states permits companies to transfer their central administration to a foreign country but certain of them, such as the United Kingdom, make that right subject to certain restrictions, and the legal consequences of a transfer, particularly in regard to taxation, vary from one Member State to another.

21 The Treaty has taken account of that variety in national legislation. In defining, in Article [54 TFEU], the companies which enjoy the right of establishment, the Treaty places on the same footing, as connecting factors, the registered office, central administration and principal place of business of a company . . .

22 It should be added that none of the Directives on the coordination of company law adopted under Article 54 (3)(g) of the Treaty deal with the differences at issue here.

23 It must therefore be held that the Treaty regards the differences in national legislation concerning the required connecting factor and the question whether – and if so how – the registered office or real head office of a company incorporated under national law may be transferred from one Member State to another as problems which are not resolved by the rules concerning the right of establishment but must be dealt with by future legislation or conventions.

24 Under those circumstances, Articles [49 and 54 TFEU] cannot be interpreted as conferring on companies incorporated under the law of a Member State a right to transfer their central management and control and their central administration to another Member State while retaining their status as companies incorporated under the legislation of the first Member State.

Daily Mail has been confirmed in *Cartesio*.[120] The facts were similar, but concerned Hungary and Italy rather than the United Kingdom and the Netherlands. The company Cartesio argued that *Daily Mail* was no longer good law in the light of subsequent cases, but the Court of Justice rejected this, repeating its arguments above in almost identical terms, and emphasising that it was for Member States to determine the conditions for incorporation in their jurisdiction, and the presence of headquarters was a perfectly legitimate condition. Nevertheless, although this did not arise in *Cartesio*, it would be wrong to think that conditions for incorporation are outside the scope of Article 49. If, for example, they discriminate, they will still violate the Treaty.[121]

This was the case in *VALE*, which concerned the Hungarian law on company conversion. Conversion is where one company ceases to exist, and a new one is formed, but it is recorded in the incorporation that the old company is the predecessor in law of the new one.[122] This can be important for matters such as the continuity of debts which the old company may have had. VALE was an Italian company originally, which removed itself from the Italian company register with the intention of converting to a Hungarian company, incorporated under Hungarian law. It was prepared to comply with all the requirement of Hungarian law, but conversion was still not possible, because Hungarian law simply did not allow cross-border conversions. Only a Hungarian company could convert to a new Hungarian company. The directors could start a new Hungarian company, but they could not have the old Italian VALE recorded as its predecessor in law. This time the Court of Justice found the rules contrary to Article 49. While it was for Member States to determine whether and under what conditions company conversion was possible, 'Articles 49 TFEU and 54 TFEU require Member States which make provision for the conversion of companies governed by national law to grant that same possibility to companies governed by the law of another Member State which are seeking to convert to companies governed by the law of the first Member State.'[123] It went on to reject the force of the Hungarian Government's arguments about the procedural and documentary difficulties that a conversion from a non-Hungarian company would entail. *Polbud* was a similar story, but with the obstacles to cross-border conversion coming from the State it was leaving, rather than the State it was going to.[124] They were similarly unjustified.

Most cases involve a different scenario however: where a company is incorporated in State X, but does most of its business in State Y. The reason for such a construction is often to avoid strict rules on incorporation in Y, and for this same reason State Y is usually inclined to view the incorporation in X as an abusive attempt to avoid its rules. These cases raise the concerns about regulatory competition raised above.

This scenario was addressed in *Centros*. Two Danish nationals registered a company in the United Kingdom. Although it never traded from the United Kingdom, it was registered there because the UK authorities impose no minimum share capital requirement for companies, whilst in Denmark there was a requirement of a minimum of 100,000 Danish kroner. They were refused

---

[120] *Cartesio*, C-210/06, ECLI:EU:C:2008:723.

[121] *Commission v. Netherlands*, C-299/02, EU:C:2004:620. See generally O. Mörsdorf, 'The Legal Mobility of Companies Within the European Union Through Cross-border Conversion' (2012) 49 *CMLRev* 629.

[122] *VALE*, C-378/10, EU:C:2012:440. See S. Rammeloo, 'Case C-378/10 *VALE Építési Kft*, Freedom of Establishment: Cross-border Transfer of Company "Seat": The Last Piece of the Puzzle?' (2012) 19 *MJECL* 563; Thomas Biermeyer, 'Case C-378/10, *VALE Építési Kft*, Judgment of the Court of Justice (Third Chamber) of 12 July 2012' (2013) 50 *CMLRev* 571; O. Morsdorf, 'The Legal Mobility of Companies within the European Union through Cross-Border Conversion' (2012) 49 *CMLRev* 629.

[123] *VALE*, C-378/10, EU:C:2012:440, para. 46.   [124] *Polbud*, C-106/16, ECLI:EU:C:2017:804.

permission to register a branch in Denmark and challenged this under Article 49. The Danish Government argued that there was no violation as they were simply refusing the setting up of a primary establishment and not the setting up of a branch. The Court of Justice disagreed.

Centros v. Erhvervs–og Selskabsstyrelsen, C–212/97, EU:C:1999:126

21 Where it is the practice of a Member State, in certain circumstances, to refuse to register a branch of a company having its registered office in another Member State, the result is that companies formed in accordance with the law of that other Member State are prevented from exercising the freedom of establishment conferred on them by Articles [49 and 54 TFEU].

22 Consequently, that practice constitutes an obstacle to the exercise of the freedoms guaranteed by those provisions.

23 According to the Danish authorities, however, Mr and Mrs Bryde cannot rely on those provisions, since the sole purpose of the company formation which they have in mind is to circumvent the application of the national law governing formation of private limited companies and therefore constitutes abuse of the freedom of establishment. In their submission, the Kingdom of Denmark is therefore entitled to take steps to prevent such abuse by refusing to register the branch.

24 It is true that according to the case law of the Court a Member State is entitled to take measures designed to prevent certain of its nationals from attempting, under cover of the rights created by the Treaty, improperly to circumvent their national legislation or to prevent individuals from improperly or fraudulently taking advantage of provisions of Community law . . .

25 However, although, in such circumstances, the national courts may, case by case, take account – on the basis of objective evidence – of abuse or fraudulent conduct on the part of the persons concerned in order, where appropriate, to deny them the benefit of the provisions of Community law on which they seek to rely, they must nevertheless assess such conduct in the light of the objectives pursued by those provisions . . .

26 In the present case, the provisions of national law, application of which the parties concerned have sought to avoid, are rules governing the formation of companies and not rules concerning the carrying on of certain trades, professions or businesses. The provisions of the Treaty on freedom of establishment are intended specifically to enable companies formed in accordance with the law of a Member State and having their registered office, central administration or principal place of business within the Community to pursue activities in other Member States through an agency, branch or subsidiary.

27 That being so, the fact that a national of a Member State who wishes to set up a company chooses to form it in the Member State whose rules of company law seem to him the least restrictive and to set up branches in other Member States cannot, in itself, constitute an abuse of the right of establishment. The right to form a company in accordance with the law of a Member State and to set up branches in other Member States is inherent in the exercise, in a single market, of the freedom of establishment guaranteed by the Treaty.

28 In this connection, the fact that company law is not completely harmonised in the Community is of little consequence. Moreover, it is always open to the Council, on the basis of the powers conferred upon it by Article [50(3)(g) TFEU], to achieve complete harmonisation.

29 In addition . . . the fact that a company does not conduct any business in the Member State in which it has its registered office and pursues its activities only in the Member State where its branch is established is not sufficient to prove the existence of abuse or fraudulent conduct which would entitle the latter Member State to deny that company the benefit of the provisions of Community law relating to the right of establishment.

> 30   Accordingly, the refusal of a Member State to register a branch of a company formed in accordance with the law of another Member State in which it has its registered office on the grounds that the branch is intended to enable the company to carry on all its economic activity in the host State, with the result that the secondary establishment escapes national rules on the provision for and the paying-up of a minimum capital, is incompatible with Articles [49 and 54 TFEU], insofar as it prevents any exercise of the right freely to set up a secondary establishment which Articles [49 and 54 TFEU] are specifically intended to guarantee.

Centros reaffirms the right of companies to secondary establishment in other States. Whilst a company retains corporate status within its home Member State, other Member States must recognise it as validly incorporated under Article 54 TFEU and therefore entitled to the benefits of Article 49 TFEU. The argument about abuse was dismissed by the Court: companies, like individuals, have the right to choose the Member State with the most convenient laws.

Needless to say, this does not meet the policy concerns about regulatory competition whereby companies will simply incorporate in the State whose fiscal and corporate regime is most favourable to them. Member States have attempted to prevent this practice in a number of cases before the Court of Justice.

In *Überseering*,[125] a challenge was made to the German law which stated that a company's legal capacity is governed by the law of the territory in which its central place of administration is based. What this meant in substance was that German law would only recognise the existence of a company whose administration and incorporation were in the same State. Überseering, however, had its central administration in Germany, but was incorporated in the Netherlands. Dutch law permitted this, but when Überseering sought to bring legal action in Germany over a business dispute it discovered that it had no standing because in the eyes of German law it did not exist. The Court of Justice found this to be a violation of Article 49. Where a company is validly incorporated in one Member State according to the laws of that State, other Member States are required to recognise that incorporation, notwithstanding that their own conditions for incorporation may be different. Not to recognise Überseering's Dutch legal status would be to greatly deter establishment in the Netherlands.

In *Inspire Art*,[126] the Netherlands rather clumsily attempted to avoid *Centros*. Companies incorporated abroad, but which conducted almost all their business in the Netherlands through branches or agencies, had to register their agencies or branches in the Netherlands as 'foreign companies'. These were then required to meet Dutch company law requirements on directors' duties and minimum share capital for companies. Inspire Art was a company which conducted almost all its business in *objets d'art*, but which had incorporated in the United Kingdom specifically to avoid these requirements. It challenged the obligation to satisfy them under Article 49 TFEU. The Dutch Government argued that Inspire Art was engaged in an abuse of Article 49 as it was deliberately incorporating in another Member State in which it did no business to evade and thereby undermine Dutch company law. The Court of Justice disagreed. It found that the formation of a company in one Member State for the sole purpose of enjoying the benefit of more favourable legislation was not abusive behaviour even where that company conducted all its activities in another Member State. Thus, insofar as the Dutch Government was

---

[125] *Überseering v. NCC,* C-208/00, EU:C:2002:632.
[126] *Kamer van Koophandel en Fabrieken voor Amsterdam v. Inspire Art,* C-167/01, EU:C:2003:512.

imposing restrictions on companies validly incorporated within the European Union and thereby preventing them from trading in the Netherlands unless they met certain conditions concerning directors' duties and minimum share capital, it was engaged in a breach of Article 49.[127]

This case law reflects two potent dangers between which it is difficult to navigate. On the one hand, if companies could only trade in another Member State where they met all that State's company law requirements, there would be a grinding halt to economic activity across the Union. In effect, no foreign companies could operate in the State with the most restrictive company law as they would not meet these standards. On the other hand, allowing foreign companies who do not meet the Member State's company law standards to operate on local markets can undermine local company and tax laws, as it is easy and inexpensive for companies to locate in the State with the least onerous requirements.

An alternative way of addressing some of these concerns, which is more likely to be successful than the attempts above to deny recognition to a company, or exclude its establishment, is to adopt proportionate laws concerning company obligations and taxation: it is not the movement which is combatted, but the avoidance. For example, where UK companies moved profits abroad to subsidiaries that existed solely in order to receive those profits, with the aim of avoiding UK tax, the UK considered that the 'profits' of those subsidiaries were taxable. *Cadbury Schweppes* argued that this discouraged setting up those subsidiaries and so hindered establishment.

Cadbury Schweppes, C–196/04, EU:C:2006:544

50 It is also apparent from case-law that the mere fact that a resident company establishes a secondary establishment, such as a subsidiary, in another Member State cannot set up a general presumption of tax evasion and justify a measure which compromises the exercise of a fundamental freedom guaranteed by the Treaty.

51 On the other hand, a national measure restricting freedom of establishment may be justified where it specifically relates to wholly artificial arrangements aimed at circumventing the application of the legislation of the Member State concerned.

52 It is necessary, in assessing the conduct of the taxable person, to take particular account of the objective pursued by the freedom of establishment.

53 That objective is to allow a national of a Member State to set up a secondary establishment in another Member State to carry on his activities there and thus assist economic and social interpenetration within the Community in the sphere of activities as self-employed persons. To that end, freedom of establishment is intended to allow a Community national to participate, on a stable and continuing basis, in the economic life of a Member State other than his State of origin and to profit therefrom.

54 Having regard to that objective of integration in the host Member State, the concept of establishment within the meaning of the Treaty provisions on freedom of establishment involves the actual pursuit of an economic activity through a fixed establishment in that State for an indefinite period. Consequently, it

---

[127] There is substantial literature on this case law. See particularly M. Siems, 'Convergence, Competition, *Centros* and Conflicts of Law: European Company Law in the 21st Century' (2002) 27 *ELRev* 47; W.-H. Roth, 'From *Centros* to *Überseering*: Free Movement of Companies, Private International Law, and Community Law' (2003) 52 *ICLQ* 177; E. Micheler, 'Recognition of Companies Incorporated in Other EU Member States' (2003) 52 *ICLQ* 521; C. Kersting and C. Philipp Schindler, 'The ECJ's *Inspire Art* Decision of 30 September 2003 and its Effects on Practice' (2003) 4(12) *German LJ* 1277.

> presupposes actual establishment of the company concerned in the host Member State and the pursuit of genuine economic activity there.
>
> 55 It follows that, in order for a restriction on the freedom of establishment to be justified on the ground of prevention of abusive practices, the specific objective of such a restriction must be to prevent conduct involving the creation of wholly artificial arrangements which do not reflect economic reality, with a view to escaping the tax normally due on the profits generated by activities carried out on national territory.

This leaves companies free to set up foreign branches, but gives Member States some space to chase their profits for tax. The core distinction is between genuine exercise of free movement rights and 'wholly artificial arrangements'.

6 SERVICES DIRECTIVE AND FREEDOM OF ESTABLISHMENT

Directive 2006/123/EC (Services Directive) applies not only to cross-border service provision but also to those establishing in a Member State. They benefit from the Directive's Chapter on establishment, as well as from its rules on administrative simplification. These latter, and the material scope of the Services Directive, were discussed in Chapter 17.[128]

The Chapter on freedom of establishment addresses three categories of national measures.[129]

The first articles in this Chapter deal with authorisation schemes – rules which require that a person cannot establish or begin their activity without an authorisation. Such rules are fairly common in some Member States. Article 9 provides that such schemes are only permitted where they are non-discriminatory, justified by a public interest objective and the goal cannot be met by a less restrictive measure. As is evident, this is neither more nor less than the existing case law would suggest. However, Articles 9 to 13 provide some detail on the operation of authorisation schemes, with procedural requirements aimed at ensuring that they function in an accessible, fair, reasonably quick, transparent and non-discriminatory way. Any fees must also be no more than reasonable and proportionate, which the Court in *Hemming* found to mean that they must not exceed the actual cost of processing the application and could not include a contribution to the wider costs of the administering institution.[130] In a similar spirit of proportionality, when the number of authorisations is limited, for legitimate reasons, as was the case with canal boat operators in Amsterdam, the authorisations may not be for an unlimited period – this obviously undermines the openness that the Directive aims to achieve.[131]

Article 14 then lists certain kinds of measure concerning established persons which are prohibited. These include discriminatory requirements, requirements concerning the nationality of shareholders or company directors, restrictions on secondary establishment or requirements that the establishment in the State be the primary establishment and market-need based restrictions.[132] The Court of Justice has tended to prohibit such restrictions anyway, but the absence of grounds for derogation may make the Directive stricter, although this has to be weighed against the many exclusions from the Directive's scope.

---

[128] See pp. 773–9.   [129] Directive 2006/123/EC on services in the internal market, Articles 9–15.
[130] *Hemming*, C-316/15, EU:C:2016:879.   [131] *Trijber and Harmsen*, C-340–1/14, EU:C:2015:641.
[132] *Rina Services*, C-593/13, EU:C:2015:399.

Finally, Article 15 provides a list of 'requirements to be evaluated'. These include limits on employee numbers or tariffs, requirements to have a particular legal form or 'quantitative or territorial restrictions'. Any such requirements are only permitted if they are non-discriminatory, justified and proportionate. Once again, the Directive follows the case law of the Court.

The establishment Chapter is apparently weaker than the services Chapter. It only applies to certain specifically listed national requirements, and, apart from Article 14, it permits these to be justified by any good public interest objective. Its approach to the legality of national measures is essentially a summary of the case law.

This difference between the approach to service and establishment reflects their different roles in the wider structure of the internal market. Home State regulation, which is the philosophy of the cases and of the Directive, entails that requirements imposed on service providers by their host State should be the exception, and so are subject to strict limits. By contrast, the home State approach entails that the established person has in principle made a choice to subject herself to the rules of her State of new establishment, and EU intervention should confine itself to rooting out discrimination against her, or particularly obstructive and disproportionate rules.

However, the Chapter on establishment does add to the law in another way: it applies to those establishing in their own State, as well as those coming from other States.[133] Thus, while the law on establishment is not made stricter by the Directive, it has been broadened. The defined group of national rules to which this Chapter applies is now subject to proportionality review at the request of any economic actor suffering disadvantage from them.

This is understandable. The alternative would be that the foreigner wishing to start his business would be exempted from all kinds of authorisation procedures and administrative requirements with which the national would still have to comply. This would create reverse discrimination. That may sometimes be an unavoidable side-effect of the case law, but it is bad policy to entrench it in legislation.[134] Secondly, any such entrenched distinction would create a motivation for artificial cross-border constructions: the Frenchman wanting to start a business in France would be better first starting a nominal business abroad and then coming home, or looking for a foreign 'partner'. As is usually the case with harmonising legislation, the Directive tries to avoid such problems by creating a uniform structure of rights for all economic actors, albeit within a limited sphere.

FURTHER READING

D. Ashiagbor, 'Unravelling the Embedded Liberal Bargain: Labour and Social Welfare Law in the Context of EU Market Integration' (2013) 19 *European Law Journal* 303.

S. Deakin, 'Reflexive Governance and European Company Law' (2009) 15 *European Law Journal* 224.

L. Hancher and W. Sauter, 'One Step Beyond? From *Sodemare* to *Docmorris*: The EU's Freedom of Establishment Case Law Concerning Healthcare'(2010) 47 *Common Market Law Review* 117.

A. Johnston and P. Syrpis, 'Regulatory Competition in European Company Law after *Cartesio*' (2009) 34 *European Law Review* 378.

D. Kramer, 'From Worker to Self-Entrepreneur: The Transformation of Homo Economicus and the Freedom of Movement in the European Union' (2017) 23 *European Law Journal* 172–88.

---

[133] *Visser Vastgoed*, C-360/15 and C-31/16, EU:C:2018:44.
[134] See G. Davies, 'Services, Citizenship and the Country of Origin Principle', Mitchell Working Paper No. 2/07 (2007).

A. Kranz, 'The *Bosman* Case: The Relationship Between European Union Law and the Transfer System in European Football' (1999) 5 *Cambridge Journal of European Law* 431.

G. Marenco, 'The Notion of Restriction on the Freedom of Establishment and Provision of Services in the Case-Law of the Court' (1991) 11 *Yearbook of European Law* 111.

C. O'Brien, 'Social Blind Spots and Monocular Policy Making: The ECJ's Migrant Worker Model' (2009) 46 *Common Market Law Review* 1107.

A. Tryfonidou, 'In Search of the Aim of the EC Free Movement of Persons Provisions: Has the Court of Justice Missed the Point?' (2009) 46 *Common Market Law Review* 1591.

19

Trade Restrictions and Public Goods

1 INTRODUCTION

This chapter is about derogations from free movement, and their review by the Court of Justice. These derogations exist to protect important national interests – public goods – but they can also be used to disguise protectionism, which is why they are usually quite strictly reviewed.

Section 2 provides an introduction to the themes and context of the Treaty derogations. These articles are at the heart of one of the most important current debates: whether globalisation unavoidably threatens non-economic interests and values, or whether reconciliation or compromise is possible. The Court uses a range of ideas and principles, from transparency to a margin of appreciation, in its search for the right approach.

Section 3 addresses the range of public goods which the Treaty protects. The explicit derogations are brief and limited, but the Court has extended them with its invention of the mandatory requirement, or the general public interest objective. The range of justifications which may be relied upon to restrict movement is now very broad, and only protectionist reasons, or purely economic reasons, have been excluded. This latter category is problematic: the distinction between an economic and a non-economic interest is often not clear. For example, protecting national budgets protects the health of public institutions, and so also protects interests such as public health and public security.

Section 4 is about the principles governing derogations. The Court will critically examine whether they are truly necessary, or whether the goals could be achieved by less restrictive measures. In making this decision it is influenced by the coherence of national policy: if the Member State shows itself to be inconsistent in protecting a particular interest then this undermines its claim that the threat is serious and action is necessary. This, however, ignores the political compromises which legislation and policy-making entail. Consistency may not always be a feasible governmental goal. In deciding whether less restrictive measures could be adopted the Court may itself investigate the question, or instruct the national court to, or it may adopt a procedural approach and ask whether the Member State adequately investigated other possibilities before it acted.

Sections 5 to 8 are about specific Treaty derogations and provide examples of how the Court applies them. It becomes apparent that while, for example, public health claims are often critically examined and tested strictly for proportionality, where public policy and security are involved the Court may be more deferential. Environmental reasons occupy their own unique position. The environment is not specifically mentioned in the Treaty derogations, but the Court is aware that current concerns require it to be taken seriously and measures protecting the environment are weighed heavily in the balance when they impact on trade.

2 BALANCING FREE MOVEMENT AGAINST OTHER INTERESTS

At the heart of many globalisation debates is the fear that we are living in a runaway world.[1] In this world, the free movement of different factors of production undermines local democracy. Investment and companies simply move elsewhere whenever faced with unattractive demands by the local population. The dedication to the pursuit of wealth means that insufficient attention is paid to damaging side-effects, such as harm to the environment, further impoverishment of poor regions or the marketing of unsafe food. Finally, local forms of culture become swamped by the pervasiveness of global branding. Such a view is a distortion of what generally takes place, yet, if there is a setting to provide a stage for these fears, it is that offered by the economic freedoms. These freedoms institutionalise such concerns by giving capital, goods, services and labour a legal right to move across borders. This is not an unfettered right. Even in the early European Economic Community (EEC) Treaty, there were a number of grounds on which Member States were permitted to restrict trade. As attitudes evolved and conflicts have become more diverse, the Court of Justice has extended the grounds on which Member States may restrict trade to include an extremely wide array of justifications. The accommodation of so many interests and values has prompted further challenges. Everything turns on the way the Court of Justice mediates between the economic freedom and the exception in question. As we shall see, it has used a few generic principles to do this. Measures must be effective. They must not arbitrarily discriminate. They must take account of the regulatory requirements that have already been met in other Member States. They must be the least restrictive of trade necessary to secure their objectives. However, the sheer diversity of the

---

[1] See e.g. K. Ohmae, *The Borderless World: Power and Strategy in the Interlinked Economy* (New York, Harper, 1990); J. Habermas, *The Postnational Constellation* (London, Polity, 2001) ch. 4.

disputes and issues involved has inevitably led to the partial breakdown of these general principles, so that they are applied in different ways in different areas and cases. This has generated its own uncertainties, leading to doubt about the relationship between the general principles that are supposed to apply across the board and the specialised case law that predominates in certain areas.

Alongside a substantive investigation, or instead of it, the Court of Justice increasingly relies on procedural principles to determine the legitimacy of derogations. The Court now regularly asks whether the Member State has taken appropriate measures in the process leading to its decision, and whether that decision is adequately open to challenge by those affected: was there a detailed risk assessment; was international scientific opinion taken into account; are authorisation procedures transparent, quick and accessible, and can decisions be challenged in court? This proceduralisation reflects broader themes in market regulation, especially the ever more central role of risk management, and the emphasis of recent years on good governance.

In general, the trend in many technocratic areas of the internal market seems to be towards more intrusive review and a heavier evidential burden on Member States to prove their case. Yet, in more subjective and value-laden fields the notion of a national margin of appreciation has become ever more central. Here, the Court of Justice looks for signs of honest intent, but emphasises the continuing freedom of States to define their own values and public norms. Perhaps the broadest overarching theme is that, within a framework of common principles, there is a differentiated approach to their application and an ever-greater repertoire of rules and ideas which the Court can use.

3 PUBLIC GOODS PROTECTED UNDER EU LAW

The TFEU makes only limited provision for the protection of public goods from free trade, such as the environment, public morality and public health. The most extensive provision is that in relation to free movement of goods.

Article 36 TFEU

The provisions of Articles 34 and 35 shall not preclude prohibitions or restrictions on imports, exports or goods in transit justified on grounds of public morality, public policy or public security; the protection of health and life of humans, animals or plants; the protection of national treasures possessing artistic, historic or archaeological value; or the protection of industrial and commercial property. Such prohibitions or restrictions shall not, however, constitute a means of arbitrary discrimination or a disguised restriction on trade between Member States.

In addition, Article 65 TFEU sets out circumstances in which Member States may derogate from Article 63, which provides for free movement of capital.

Article 65 TFEU

(1) The provisions of Article 63 shall be without prejudice to the right of Member States:
   (a) to apply the relevant provisions of their tax law which distinguish between taxpayers who are not in the same situation with regard to their place of residence or with regard to the place where their capital is invested;

(b) to take all requisite measures to prevent infringements of national law and regulations, in particular in the field of taxation and the prudential supervision of financial institutions, or to lay down procedures for the declaration of capital movements for purposes of administrative or statistical information, or to take measures which are justified on grounds of public policy or public security.

In both instances, the grounds on which Member States can restrict trade are fairly limited. They are, however, more extensive than those provided for the other economic freedoms. Derogations from the articles on free movement of workers, establishment and services are only provided for on grounds of public policy, public security and public health.[2] These, however, have been used more commonly as a form of migration control, to prevent persons entering the territory, than to stop undesirable economic activities.

Two more derogations allow for the protection of the special link between a Member State and its own nationals, reserving them an exclusive role in some aspects of the business of government. With regard to workers, therefore:

Article 45 TFEU

(4) The provisions of this Article shall not apply to employment in the public service.

A parallel provision exists for services and establishment.

Article 51 TFEU

The provisions of this chapter [on establishment] shall not apply, so far as any given Member State is concerned, to activities which in that State are connected, even occasionally, with the exercise of official authority.

All the provisions above are both limited and static. Largely unchanged since they were first introduced into the EEC Treaty in 1957, it has been left to the Court of Justice to protect the mixed economy in a dynamic fashion that takes account of the changing nature of the integration process, developments in political value and the challenges posed by new technologies. In the *Cassis de Dijon* judgment, the Court of Justice indicated that a quid pro quo for the extension of the economic freedoms was an acceptance that Member States should be able to take measures to protect a wide array of public interests, which would otherwise be threatened by these provisions, on condition that the measures did not arbitrarily discriminate and were proportionate and necessary to securing the objective they pursued.[3] The 'mandatory requirements' established in *Cassis de Dijon* to protect these interests from erosion by Article 34 TFEU have

---

[2] Articles 45(3), 52(1) and 62 TFEU.

[3] *Rewe-Zentrale AG* v. *Bundesmonopolverwaltung für Branntwein (Cassis de Dijon)*, 120/78, EU:C:1979:42.

been applied in various guises to all the other economic freedoms.[4] The array of interests that have been successfully invoked to safeguard national legislation, using Treaty exceptions or mandatory requirements, may be grouped for convenience under four headings.

(i) *Market externalities.* Market externalities arise where a transaction fails to take account of somebody's interests and that person was not deemed to have a choice in the matter. Most obviously, these interests are third party interests, such as those of the wider public. Market externalities can also affect the interests of one of the parties directly involved in the transaction. The sale of a dangerous product is an example. Such a transaction is associated with the risk of some undesirable physical impact. The Court of Justice has moved to protect against a wide variety of market externalities. These include damage to public health;[5] harm to the consumer;[6] destruction of the environment;[7] unfair competition; fraud;[8] abuse of creditors;[9] dangers to road safety;[10] violation of intellectual property rights;[11] harm to the health and safety of workers;[12] and damage to the national historic and artistic heritage and to cultural policy.[13]

(ii) *Civil liberties.* The Court of Justice has also moved to ensure that the economic freedoms do not compromise those political values which are central to protecting human dignity, autonomy and equality. In such circumstances, the Court is concerned not only with the material impacts of trade but also its symbolic impacts, namely, whether it is seen to undermine the standing of important constitutional values.[14] To this end, the Court has indicated that matters such as human dignity,[15] freedom of expression,[16] freedom of assembly,[17] the right to strike,[18] the sanctity of religious beliefs[19] and cultural pluralism[20] are all capable of justifying derogations.

(iii) *Socio-cultural preferences.* Many rules may reflect or embody societal and cultural preferences or traditions. For example, rules concerning the role of professional organisations in regulating local markets are not just about the maintenance of objective standards, but about the place of the skilled person and of non-governmental bodies in society.[21] Such rules are seen as

---

[4] *Union Royale Belge des Sociétés de Football Association and Others* v. *Bosman and Others*, C-415/93, EU:C:1995:463; *Commission* v. *Germany (German Insurance)*, 205/84, EU:C:1986:463 (services); *Ordre des Avocats au Barreau de Paris* v. *Klopp*, 107/83, EU:C:1984:270 (establishment); *Reisch and Others* v. *Bürgermeister der Landeshauptstadt Salzburg*, C-515/99 and C-527–40/99, EU:C:2002:135 (capital).

[5] See e.g. *Bacardi France* v. *Télévision française*, C-429/02, EU:C:2004:432.

[6] *Commission* v. *France*, 220/83, EU:C:1986:461; *Commission* v. *France*, C-262/02, EU:C:2004:431.

[7] *Commission* v. *Denmark*, 302/86, EU:C:1988:421; *De Coster* v. *Collège des bourgmestre et échevins de Watermael-Boitsfort*, C-17/00, EU:C:2001:651.

[8] *Gambelli*, C-243/01, EU:C:2003:597.   [9] *Centros* v. *Erhvervs- og Selskabsstyrelsen*, C-212/97, EU:C:1999:126.

[10] *Van Schaik*, C-55/93, EU:C:1994:363; *Cura Anlagen* v. *Auto Service Leasing*, C-451/99, EU:C:2002:195; *Commission* v. *Italy*, C-110/05, EU:C:2009:66.

[11] *Coditel* v. *Ciné-Vog Films*, 262/81, EU:C:1982:334.

[12] *Oebel*, 155/80, EU:C:1981:177; *Rush Portuguesa* v. *Office national d'immigration*, C-113/89, EU:C:1990:142; *Portugaia Construções*, C-164/99, EU:C:2002:40; *Commission* v. *Luxembourg (Employment of Foreign Workers)*, C-445/03, EU:C:2004:655.

[13] *Commission* v. *Italy*, C-180/89, EU:C:1991:78 *Metronome Musik* v. *Music Point Hokamp*, C-200/96, EU:C:1998:172.

[14] See *Sayn Wittgenstein*, C-208/09, EU:C:2010:806.

[15] *Omega Spielhallen -und Automatenaufstellungs-GmbH* v. *Oberbürgermeisterin der Bundesstadt Bonn*, C-36/02, EU:C:2004:614.

[16] *Karner* v. *Troostwijk*, C-71/02, EU:C:2004:181.   [17] *Schmidberger* v. *Republic of Austria*, C-112/00, EU:C:2003:333.

[18] *Viking*, C-438/05, EU:C:2007:772; *Laval*, C-341/05, EU:C:2007:809; but see pp. 751–4.

[19] *HM Customs and Excise* v. *Schindler*, C-275/92, EU:C:1994:119.

[20] *Gouda* v. *Commissariat voor de Media*, C-288/89, EU:C:1991:323.

[21] *Van Binsbergen* v. *Bestuur van de Bedrijsvereniging voor de Metaalnijverheid*, 33/74, EU:C:1974:131; *Thieffry* v. *Conseil de l'Ordre des Avocats à la Cour de Paris*, 71/76, EU:C:1977:65; *Corsten*, C-58/98, EU:C:2000:527; *Wouters and Others* v. *Algemene Raad van de Nederlandse Orde van Advocaten*, C-309/99, EU:C:2002:98.

contributing to trust and stability. Rules on the opening hours of shops, such as Sunday opening, are not just economic policy, but reflect choices about the place of economic activity in the national lifestyle.[22] The autonomy of sporting organisations and their freedom to determine rules is also the product of the particular role of sport in society and attitudes towards it,[23] just as the rules on ownership of land, which have often been the subject of litigation, have much to do with the societal desire to nurture rural communities and protect a particular quality of life.[24] Measures aimed at guaranteeing the availability of housing for the local poor, as in issue in *Libert*, would also fall within this group, and show that while preferences must be compatible with the Treaty if they are to justify derogation (so they may not be nationalistic or protectionist) the specific responsibility of a Member State for those within its territory is acknowledged.[25] The Court of Justice has recognised the legitimacy of a wide range of rules within this group, varying from those which are deeply rooted in culture, such as traditions on naming of children,[26] to mere policy choices, such as the internationalisation of the labour market.[27]

(iv) *Preservation of the machinery of the State.* The final category of cases relates to the Member State's capacity to supply the services that are necessary for the government of its territory. In such cases, the Court of Justice is not so much concerned to protect certain values or interests per se but, rather, it aims to safeguard the machinery of government that enables such protection. Member States may, therefore, keep in place measures derogating from the economic freedoms to maintain internal and external security;[28] cohesion of their tax systems;[29] order in society;[30] their systems of administration of justice;[31] and financial balance in their systems of education or social security.[32]

There is one group of interests that the Court of Justice will not protect: interests of a purely economic nature. In numerous cases it has repeated that purely economic reasons cannot justify restrictions on free movement.[33] The implication is that the type of interests protected by free movement are qualitatively of a higher order than purely economic matters, so these latter can never serve to restrict the former. However, in practice the idea of a purely economic reason is not tidily defined, since money impacts on other interests. Indeed, since the Member State's capacity to carry out policy is dependent to a large extent on its budget, and since the wellbeing of its citizens is dependent to a large extent on the state of the national economy, any economic reason can be repackaged as being about other interests, such as good public services, employee protection or even public order, as the cases below show.

---

[22] *Torfaen Borough Council* v. *B & Q*, C-145/88, EU:C:1989:593; G. Davies, 'Internal Market Adjudication and the Quality of Life in Europe' (2015) 21(2) *Columbia Journal of European Law* 289.

[23] *Union Royale Belge des Sociétés de Football Association and Others* v. *Bosman and Others*, C-415/93, EU:C:1995:463.

[24] *Festersen*, C-370/05, EU:C:2007:59.   [25] *Libert*, C-197/11, EU:C:2013:288.

[26] *Runevic*, C-391/09, EU:C:2011:291.   [27] *Commission* v. *Netherlands*, C-542/09, EU:C:2012:346.

[28] *Campus Oil* v. *Minister for Industry and Energy*, 72/83, EU:C:1984:256.

[29] *Bachmann* v. *Belgian State*, C-204/90, EU:C:1992:35; *Commission* v. *Belgium*, C-300/90, EU:C:1992:37.

[30] *HM Customs and Excise* v. *Schindler*, C-275/92, EU:C:1994:119.

[31] *Reisebüro Broede* v. *Sandker*, C-3/95, EU:C:1996:487.

[32] *Commission* v. *Austria*, C-147/03, EU:C:2005:427; *Bressol*, C-73/08, EU:C:2010:181; *Kohll* v. *Union des Caisses de Maladie*, C-158/96, EU:C:1998:171; see also *Federspiel*, C-419/16, EU:C:2017:997.

[33] *Bond van Adverteerders*, 352/85, EU:C:1988:196; *Kohll* v. *Union des Caisses de Maladie*, C-158/96, EU:C:1998:171; *Syndesmos ton en Elladi Touristikon kai Taxidiotikon Grafeion* v. *Ypourgos Ergasias*, C-398/95, EU:C:1997:282; *Commission* v. *Portugal*, C-171/08, EU:C:2010:412; *Erny*, C-172/11, EU:C:2014:157; J. Snell, 'Economic Aims as Justifications for Restrictions on Free Movement' in A. Schrauwen (ed.), *The Rule of Reason: Rethinking Another Classic of Community Law* (Groningen, Europa Law Publishing, 2005) 37.

Within the concept of the economic reason there are two distinct types of reason, both unacceptable. One reason sometimes put forward for a measure is the desire to protect local businesses or industry, or the national or local economy.[34] The main reason to object to such measures is that they are implicitly protectionist. They aim to ensure that national economic actors are protected from foreign intrusion. This aim is not legitimate in the context of a market where Member States have committed to openness and non-discrimination. However, there is a very fine line between a quasi-protectionist measure and one serving legitimate goals. For example, in *Wolff and Müller*, a German law requiring foreign service providers to pay their employees the German minimum wage whilst providing services in Germany was claimed to breach Article 56 TFEU.[35] The Explanatory Memorandum made clear that the purpose of the law was to protect small and medium-sized enterprises from cheap competition. Yet, the measure also protected the employees of the service providers, and employees on the German market in general. For this reason, the Court of Justice ruled the measure to be lawful. The fact that one justification – protection from cheap competition – fails, does not mean that another justification – employee protection – cannot be put forward.

The other type of economic interest is where the Member State is trying to protect its own budget. For example, in *Kranemann*, the German Government paid travel expenses for trips taken by trainee civil servants only if these trips were within Germany, and claimed that this was necessary for budgetary reasons.[36] Similarly, in *Kohll* and the other health-care cases, governments have argued that restrictions on patient migration should be imposed to prevent strain on health-care budgets.[37] Neither argument was acceptable as such, since they posed purely economic interests against a fundamental freedom. However, in *Kohll* the Court of Justice acknowledged that if the economic effects were such that the health-care system was threatened, then the economic concern in fact became a public health concern, which would be a legitimate reason for a restriction.[38] Analogously, in *Campus Oil* the Court permitted the Irish Government to require oil companies to purchase some of their oil from a national refinery.[39]

This measure reduced imports, and its immediate reason was to ensure the viability of the State refinery – an economic reason. However, the Irish Government successfully argued that keeping the refinery operating was of strategic and security importance – legitimate reasons – and such operation could only be guaranteed by ensuring customers. Other interests which have been used to make concerns about money acceptable by presenting them as social, systemic or moral concerns, are the cohesion of the tax system, the protection of local agricultural communities and the effectiveness of fiscal supervision (prevention of tax avoidance).[40] The lack of clarity in all this is reflected in the Court of Justice's ruling that preventing a reduction in tax revenue, by

---

[34] *Commission v. Portugal (Free Movement of Capital)*, C-367/98, EU:C:2001:326; *Ospelt v. Schössle Weissenberg Familienstiftung*, C-452/01, EU:C:2003:493.

[35] *Wolff and Müller v. Felix*, C-60/03, EU:C:2004:610; see also *Festersen*, C-370/05, EU:C:2007:59.

[36] *Kranemann v. Land Nordrhein-Westfalen*, C-109/04, EU:C:2005:187.

[37] *Kohll v. Union des Caisses de Maladie*, C-158/96, EU:C:1998:171.

[38] *Ibid.*; see also *Commission v. Germany*, C-141/07, EU:C:2008:492.

[39] *Campus Oil v. Minister for Industry and Energy*, 72/83, EU:C:1984:256.

[40] *Bachmann*, C-204/90, EU:C:1992:35; *Futura Participations and Singer v. Administration des contributions*, C-250/95, EU:C:1997:239; *Ospelt v. Schössle Weissenberg Familienstiftung*, C-452/01, EU:C:2003:493; see also *Petersen*, C-544/11, EU:C:2013:124.

contrast with avoidance, is in pursuit of an economic interest and cannot, therefore, justify restrictions.[41]

4 PRINCIPLES MEDIATING CONFLICTS BETWEEN FREE MOVEMENT AND PUBLIC GOODS

When applying Treaty exceptions, the starting point is that these are to be strictly and narrowly interpreted, and that they are EU law concepts. Member States cannot play a Treaty exception as a trump card. By contrast, it is for national judges and ultimately the Court of Justice to assess the State measure in the light of the constraints imposed by EU law. These points were made clear in *Van Duyn*, in which the United Kingdom wished to restrict the entry of a Dutch national on the grounds that she was a scientologist, and therefore a threat to public policy.

> ### Van Duyn v. Home Office, 41/74, EU:C:1974:133
>
> 18 ... It should be emphasized that the concept of public policy in the context of the Community and where, in particular, it is used as a justification for derogating from the fundamental principle of freedom of movement for workers, must be interpreted strictly, so that its scope cannot be determined unilaterally by each Member State without being subject to control by the institutions of the Community. Nevertheless, the particular circumstances justifying recourse to the concept of public policy may vary from one country to another and from one period to another, and it is therefore necessary in this matter to allow the competent national authorities an area of discretion within the limits imposed by the Treaty.

A strict review can only mean that the Court of Justice assesses the proportionality of the measure, rather than just looking at formal correctness. In that sense, *Van Duyn* embodies similar principles to those which *Gebhard* and other cases have applied to mandatory requirements. It will be remembered that in this latter context, the Court found that restrictions on free movement could be justified by public interest objectives provided that the measures were equally applicable and proportionate.[42]

The fundamental difference between relying on a Treaty exception and relying on a mandatory requirement/general public interest objective is therefore that mandatory requirements are only available for equally applicable measures, whereas Treaty exceptions do not have this restriction – although overt discrimination will still require explanation, which may be a significant hurdle.

This distinction is often regarded as somewhat arbitrary.[43] Why not just merge the two classes of exception into one? In *Danner*, a case concerning Finnish rules which applied a more generous fiscal regime to pension insurance schemes based in Finland, Advocate General Jacobs put the case for this:

> Once it is accepted that justifications other than those set out in the Treaty may be invoked, there seems no reason to apply one category of justification to discriminatory measures and another

---

[41] *Staatssecretaris van Financiën* v. *Verkooijen*, C-35/98, EU:C:2000:294; *X and Y* v. *Riksskatteverket*, C-436/00, EU:C:2002:704.

[42] See p. 754.

[43] P. Oliver, 'Some Further Reflections on the Scope of Articles 28–30 (ex 30–36) EC' (1999) 36 *CMLRev* 783, 804–5; N. Notaro, 'The New Generation of Case Law on Trade and the Environment' (2000) 25 *ELRev* 467, 489–91.

category to non-discriminatory restrictions. Certainly the text of the Treaty provides no reason to do so: Article [56 TFEU] does not refer to discrimination but speaks generally of restrictions on freedom to provide services. In any event, it is difficult to apply rigorously the distinction between (directly or indirectly) discriminatory and non-discriminatory measures. Moreover, there are general interest aims not expressly provided for in the Treaty (e.g. protection of the environment, consumer protection) which may in given circumstances be no less legitimate and no less powerful than those mentioned in the Treaty. The analysis should therefore be based on whether the ground invoked is a legitimate aim of general interest and if so whether the restriction can properly be justified under the principle of proportionality. In any event, the more discriminatory the measure, the more unlikely it is that the measure complies with the principle of proportionality.[44]

This line of reasoning is present in opinions from other Advocates General too,[45] but the Court of Justice nevertheless maintains the distinction. Usually this is of little importance: measures which are not equally applicable are very hard to justify anyway, so the theoretical possibility of relying on mandatory exceptions would be unlikely to change the outcome of many cases. Moreover, there is a good symbolic argument for restricting the justifications open to overtly discriminatory measures. These are, after all, an affront to the basic principles of the Union. Yet, in some exceptional contexts an overt distinction between people, products or providers from different States may apparently serve a legitimate policy aim which is not comfortably within the Treaty exceptions. In these situations, the Court has been known to overlook its general rule and permit non-Treaty justifications to be invoked.[46]

In any case, whichever type of justification is invoked, the Member State or organisation pleading it must show that the measure in question is the right way of addressing the problem.

Broadly speaking this means that the measure must be a proportionate, non-discriminatory and procedurally fair response to the policy concern raised. The specific questions which the Court tends to pose are, however, whether it has been shown that action is necessary; whether the measure is effective; whether the measure respects non-discrimination and mutual recognition; whether a less restrictive policy option would also be possible; and whether the procedural rights of those affected are guaranteed. All of these are considered at the time when the measure is applied in the case. Thus, a measure adopted for bad reasons will nevertheless be accepted if, at the time of challenge, the Member State is able to put forward good ones.[47] It is not the motivation or competence of the legislature which is being assessed, but the actual effects and necessity of the measure at the moment of its claimed obstructive effects.

[44] *Danner*, C-136/00, EU:C:2002:558.
[45] Opinion of Advocate General Leger in *Wielockx* v. *Inspecteur der Directe Belastingen*, C-80/94, EU:C:1995:156; Opinion of Advocate General Tesauro in *Decker* v. *Caisse de maladie des employés privés*, C-120/95, EU:C:1997:399; Opinion of Advocate General Poiares Maduro in *Marks & Spencer* v. *Halsey*, C-446/03, EU:C:2005:201.
[46] *Commission* v. *Belgium (Walloon Waste)*, C-2/90, EU:C:1992:310; *PreussenElektra*, C-379/98, EU:C:2001:160; *Chemische Afvalstoffen Dusseldorp BV and Others* v. *Minister van Volkhuisvesting, Ruimtelijke Ordening en Milieubeheer*, C-203/96, EU:C:1998:316; *Commission* v. *Ireland (Irish Souvenirs)*, 113/80, EU:C:1981:139; *Decker*, C-120/95, EU:C:1998:167; *Kohll* v. *Union des Caisses de Maladie*, C-158/96, EU:C:1998:171.
[47] *Admiral Casinos*, C-464/15, EU:C:2016:500; *Scotch Whisky*, C-333/14, EU:C:2015:845.

(i) The Measure Must Be Necessary

Any measure must meet a real rather than imagined threat to the public good in question.[48] In *Commission* v. *Denmark*,[49] Denmark prohibited foods being enriched with vitamins and minerals unless there was a nutritional need on the part of the Danish population for these additives. The Court of Justice held that such a restriction would only be lawful if it could be shown that the products posed a real risk to public health. The Court ruled that without the presence of a prior risk assessment to appraise the probability of the danger to public health, the products could not be shown to pose a real risk to public health.

In many cases there may be genuine scientific uncertainty about whether protective measures are necessary. Numerous health cases have, like *Commission* v. *Denmark*, concerned the addition of vitamins to food, about the safety of which opinions vary widely. In *Greenham and Abel*, the Court of Justice followed positions it had taken in *Commission* v. *Denmark* and *Sandoz*, and confirmed that in a situation of scientific uncertainty Member States may take legitimately varying positions, but are not relieved of the obligation to provide evidence for the position they choose.[50]

Greenham and Abel, C-95/01, EU:C:2004:71

37 It is of course for the Member States, in the absence of harmonisation and to the extent that there is still uncertainty in the current state of scientific research, to decide on the level of protection of human health and life they wish to ensure and whether to require prior authorisation for the marketing of foodstuffs, taking into account the requirements of the free movement of goods within the Community.

38 That discretion relating to the protection of public health is particularly wide where it is shown that there is still uncertainty in the current state of scientific research as to certain nutrients, such as vitamins, which are not as a general rule harmful in themselves but may have special harmful effects solely if taken to excess as part of the general diet, the composition of which cannot be foreseen or monitored.

39 However, in exercising their discretion relating to the protection of public health, the Member States must comply with the principle of proportionality. The means which they choose must therefore be confined to what is actually necessary to ensure the safeguarding of public health; they must be proportionate to the objective thus pursued, which could not have been attained by measures less restrictive of intra-Community trade.

40 Furthermore, since Article [36 TFEU] provides for an exception, to be interpreted strictly, to the rule of free movement of goods within the Community, it is for the national authorities which invoke it to show in each case, in the light of national nutritional habits and in the light of the results of international scientific research, that their rules are necessary to give effective protection to the interests referred to in that provision and, in particular, that the marketing of the products in question poses a real risk to public health.

41 A prohibition on the marketing of foodstuffs to which nutrients have been added must therefore be based on a detailed assessment of the risk alleged by the Member State invoking Article [36 TFEU].

---

[48] *Zetur*, C-212/08, EU:C:2011:437.   [49] *Commission* v. *Denmark*, C-192/01, EU:C:2003:492.

[50] *Ibid.*; *Sandoz*, 174/82, EU:C:1983:213; see also *Solgar*, C-446/08, EU:C:2010:233; *Commission* v. *France*, C-333/08, EU:C:2010:44; see N. Nic Shuibhne and M. Maci, 'Proving Public Interest: The Growing Impact of Evidence in Free Movement Case Law' (2013) 50 *CMLRev* 965.

The judgment refers to public health, but the procedural and substantive principles above should apply to any area where the underlying issue is one of scientific fact, rather than preference. The details of the risk assessment process and its consequences are discussed in the section on public health, below.

By contrast, the question of necessity is less amenable to a scientific approach where moral or social values and interests are concerned. There may be fundamental disagreements not just about evidence, but about what is threatening to the public interest. *Omega Spielhallen* concerned a German ban on laser game arcades which involved 'playing at killing'. This ban restricted the free movement of goods and services. Most other Member States allowed these games, and the German measure reflected a particular national sensitivity to the moral issues involved.

Omega Spielhallen, C–36/02, EU:C:2004:614

32 In this case, the competent authorities took the view that the activity concerned by the prohibition order was a threat to public policy by reason of the fact that, in accordance with the conception prevailing in public opinion, the commercial exploitation of games involving the simulated killing of human beings infringed a fundamental value enshrined in the national constitution, namely human dignity ...

33 It should be recalled in that context that, according to settled case-law, fundamental rights form an integral part of the general principles of law the observance of which the Court ensures, and that, for that purpose, the Court draws inspiration from the constitutional traditions common to the Member States and from the guidelines supplied by international treaties for the protection of human rights on which the Member States have collaborated or to which they are signatories. The European Convention on Human Rights and Fundamental Freedoms has special significance in that respect.

34 As the Advocate General argues in paragraphs 82 to 91 of her Opinion, the Community legal order undeniably strives to ensure respect for human dignity as a general principle of law. There can therefore be no doubt that the objective of protecting human dignity is compatible with Community law, it being immaterial in that respect that, in Germany, the principle of respect for human dignity has a particular status as an independent fundamental right.

35 Since both the Community and its Member States are required to respect fundamental rights, the protection of those rights is a legitimate interest which, in principle, justifies a restriction of the obligations imposed by Community law, even under a fundamental freedom guaranteed by the Treaty such as the freedom to provide services.

36 However, measures which restrict the freedom to provide services may be justified on public policy grounds only if they are necessary for the protection of the interests which they are intended to guarantee and only in so far as those objectives cannot be attained by less restrictive measures.

37 It is not indispensable in that respect for the restrictive measure issued by the authorities of a Member State to correspond to a conception shared by all Member States as regards the precise way in which the fundamental right or legitimate interest in question is to be protected. Although, in paragraph 60 of *Schindler*, the Court referred to moral, religious or cultural considerations which lead all Member States to make the organisation of lotteries and other games with money subject to restrictions, it was not its intention, by mentioning that common conception, to formulate a general criterion for assessing the proportionality of any national measure which restricts the exercise of an economic activity.

38 On the contrary, as is apparent from well-established case-law subsequent to *Schindler*, the need for, and proportionality of, the provisions adopted are not excluded merely because one Member State has chosen a system of protection different from that adopted by another State.

The Court of Justice strives here to bring the German ban within a wider European framework of respect for rights, to present it as a particular embodiment of a shared norm, rather than a fundamental value difference with other Member States. Yet at the same time, it accepts the German right to interpret and protect such fundamental values in their own way, even if other States do so differently.

This respect for Member State peculiarities is vital if derogations are to serve their goal of protecting the things that States legitimately care about. However, if the need for a measure is based on local and subjective preferences it can make that need hard to police, and could invite misuse of the exceptions. The central concept in preventing this is consistency.[51] Consistent policy is increasingly taken as a reasonable proxy for genuineness. Thus, where a Member State attempts to prevent the entry of goods or persons, claiming they are a threat to some domestic interest, but takes no measures against similar domestically made goods, or nationals with the same allegedly dangerous characteristic, then it undermines its own claim of a serious threat, and will no longer be taken seriously.

In *Conegate*,[52] pornographic rubber dolls were seized under the Customs Consolidation Act 1976, which prohibited the importation of obscene or indecent articles. However, British law on their domestic equivalents varied. In the Isle of Man and Scotland, the manufacture, sale and distribution of such articles were prohibited. In England and Wales, however, neither the manufacture nor sale was prohibited. The only controls were that such items could not be sold through the post, could not be displayed in a public place and had to be sold from licensed premises.

Conegate v. *Customs and Excise Commissioners*, 121/85, EU:C:1986:114

14 ... In principle it is for each Member State to determine in accordance with its own scale of values and in the form selected by it the requirements of public morality in its territory.

15 However, although Community law leaves the Member States free to make their own assessments of the indecent or obscene character of certain articles, it must be pointed out that the fact that goods cause offence cannot be regarded as sufficiently serious to justify restrictions on the free movement of goods where the Member State concerned does not adopt, with respect to the same goods manufactured or marketed within its territory, penal measures or other serious and effective measures intended to prevent the distribution of such goods in its territory.

16 It follows that a Member State may not rely on grounds of public morality in order to prohibit the importation of goods from other Member States when its legislation contains no prohibition on the manufacture or marketing of the same goods on its territory.

17 It is not for the Court ... to consider whether, and to what extent, the United Kingdom legislation contains such a prohibition. However, the question whether or not such a prohibition exists in a state comprised of different constituent parts which have their own internal legislation, can be resolved only by taking into consideration all the relevant legislation. Although it is not necessary, for the purposes of the application of the above-mentioned rule, that the manufacture and marketing of the products whose importation has been prohibited should be prohibited in the territory of all the constituent parts, it must at least be possible to conclude from the applicable rules, taken as a whole, that their purpose is, in substance, to prohibit the manufacture and marketing of those products.

---

[51] See G. Mathisen, 'Consistency and Coherence as Conditions for Justification of Member State Measures Restricting Free Movement' (2010) 47 *CMLRev* 1021.

[52] *Conegate* v. *Customs and Excise Commissioners*, 121/85, EU:C:1986:114.

The same logic has been applied in numerous cases, but with varying results. In *Henn and Darby*, the United Kingdom was able to restrict the import of pornographic magazines, because the Court of Justice took the view that production of similar domestic ones was also prohibited.[53] However, in *Adoui and Cornuaille*, Belgium could not deport French prostitutes because even though prostitution was illegal in Belgium, repressive measures were not in fact taken.[54] The comparison between the domestic and the foreign must clearly be one of substance, not just legal form. Yet, this does not mean they need to be treated identically. In *Van Duyn*, the Court pointed out that Member States could not deport their own nationals, so one could not demand identical treatment of foreign and domestic scientologists.[55] What is necessary, if the State is to make good its claim of a serious threat against which action is necessary, is evidence of a consistent policy reflecting that view.

Consistency has also been at the heart of the very large number of cases concerning gambling restrictions.[56] Gambling is sometimes reserved to national monopolies, or to providers who have obtained one of a limited number of licences. The reasons put forward are usually to do with preventing crime, money laundering and gambling addiction, and the general desire to limit what is seen as a socially undesirable activity. However, the suspicion is always present that the Member State is merely trying to keep the profit from gambling for itself, or for a few chosen partners. First, the Court of Justice repeatedly finds that the ambition to reduce gambling, while legitimate, will not justify restrictions if Member States simultaneously allow, for example, a national lottery to advertise widely. Secondly, claims about the need to exert control over a business often closely linked to criminal activities, while potentially acceptable, must actually be based on factual problems, and not be mere assertions. *Zeturf* is but one example among many, but the judgment captures the issues fairly clearly. At issue was the exclusive right of the PMU, a State-controlled organisation, to take bets on horse racing in France.[57]

Zeturf, C-212/08, EU:C:2011:437

66 It must be recalled at the outset in that context that, in so far as the authorities of a Member State incite and encourage consumers to participate in games of chance to the financial benefit of the public purse, the authorities of that State cannot invoke public and social policy concerns relating to the need to reduce opportunities for gambling in order to justify restrictions on the freedom to provide services.

67 The Court has nevertheless held that a policy of controlled expansion of gambling activities may be consistent with the objective of channelling them into controlled circuits by drawing bettors away from clandestine, prohibited betting and gaming to activities which are authorised and regulated. Such a policy

---

[53] *R* v. *Henn and Darby*, 34/79, EU:C:1979:295.

[54] *Rezguia Adoui* v. *Belgian State and City of Liège*; *Dominique Cornuaille* v. *Belgian State*, 115–16/81, EU:C:1982:183; see *also Jany* v. *Staatssecretaris van Justitie*, C-268/99, EU:C:2001:616.

[55] *Van Duyn* v. *Home Office*, 41/74, EU:C:1974:133 v.

[56] *HM Customs and Excise* v. *Schindler*, C-275/92, EU:C:1994:119; *Läärä* v. *Kihlakunnansyyttäjä*, C-124/97, EU:C:1999:435; *Gambelli*, C-243/01, EU:C:2003:597; *Carmen Media*, C-46/08, EU:C:2010:505; *Placanica, Palazzese and Soricchio*, C-338/04, C-359–60/04, EU:C:2007:133; *Ladbrokes*, C-258/08, EU:C:2010:308; *Stoß*, C-316/07, EU:C:2010:504; *Stanleybet*, C-186/11, EU:C:2013:33; *Liga Portuguesa de Futebol Profissional and Bwin International Ltd* v. *Departamento de Jogos da Santa Casa da Misericórdia de Lisboa*, C-42/07, EU:C:2009:519; D. Doukas, 'In a Bet there is a Fool and a State Monopoly: Are the Odds Stacked Against Cross-border Gambling?' (2011) 36 *ELRev* 243.

[57] See G. Anagnostaras, 'Les Jeux Sont Faits: Mutual Recognition and the Specificities of Online Gambling' (2012) 37 *ELRev* 191; *Berlington Hungary*, C-98/14, EU:C:2015:386.

may indeed be consistent both with the objective of preventing the use of gambling activities for criminal or fraudulent purposes and that of preventing incitement to squander money on gambling and of combating addiction to the latter, by directing consumers towards the offer emanating from the holder of the public monopoly, that offer being deemed to be protected from criminal elements and also designed to safeguard consumers more effectively against squandering of money and addiction to gambling.

68   In order to achieve that objective of channelling into controlled activities, it is common ground that authorised operators must represent a reliable, but at the same time attractive, alternative to non-regulated activities, which may as such necessitate the offer of an extensive range of games, advertising on a certain scale and the use of new distribution techniques.

69   It is specifically for the national court to determine, in the light of the facts of the dispute before it, whether the commercial policy of the PMU may be regarded, both with regard to the scale of advertising undertaken and with regard to its creation of new games, as forming part of a policy of controlled expansion in the betting and gaming sector, aiming, in fact, to channel the propensity to gamble into controlled activities.

70   In the context of that assessment, it is for the national court to determine, in particular, whether, first, criminal and fraudulent activities linked to gambling and, second, gambling addiction might have been a problem in France at the material time and whether the expansion of authorised and regulated activities would have been capable of solving such a problem. In particular, the Court has stated that if a Member State wishes to rely on an objective capable of justifying an obstacle to the freedom to provide services arising from a national restrictive measure, it is under a duty to supply the court called upon to rule on that question with all the evidence of such a kind as to enable the latter to be satisfied that the said measure does indeed fulfil the requirements arising from the principle of proportionality. In that regard the Commission argues that the national authorities have not, in contrast to the situation in *Placanica and Others* and *Liga Portuguesa de Futebol Profissional and Bwin International*, demonstrated the reality of a black market for betting on horse racing.

71   In any event, any advertising issued by the holder of a public monopoly must remain measured and strictly limited to what is necessary in order thus to channel consumers towards controlled gaming networks. Such advertising cannot, on the other hand, specifically aim to encourage consumers' natural propensity to gamble by stimulating their active participation in it, such as by trivialising gambling or giving it a positive image owing to the fact that revenues derived from it are used for activities in the public interest, or by increasing the attractiveness of gambling by means of enticing advertising messages holding out the prospect of major winnings.

A quite different conceptual issue arose in *Compassion in World Farming*.[58] The United Kingdom wished to restrict the export of young calves to Spain on grounds of animal welfare: they were destined to be reared in boxes for veal, which is prohibited in the United Kingdom. The United Kingdom lost because minimum conditions for the welfare of calves were laid down in secondary legislation, and Spain complied with this legislation. The United Kingdom was free to have stricter standards, but where legislation of this type exists a Member State must accept as adequate the standards of any Member State complying with it, notwithstanding that the first State may be stricter.

Yet, the case could have been resolved on other grounds: the threat to animal welfare was to occur in Spain, and was none of the United Kingdom's business. The Advocate General hinted at

---

[58] *Compassion in World Farming*, C-1/96, EU:C:1998:113.

this, but the Court of Justice did not raise the issue, and implicitly accepted that in principle the threat against which action is necessary need not be domestic. This principle is of particular importance where environmental measures are concerned, and the Court has indeed accepted measures which aim to protect the environment in other Member States, as well as the global environment.[59] Action may be necessary to protect interests beyond the borders of the acting Member State.

(ii) The Measure Must Be Effective

In addition to addressing a genuine need, the measure must effectively protect the public good in question. The Court of Justice will generally not look to whether there are more effective instruments available but, rather, will be concerned merely that the measure contributes to protection of the public good. In *Commission* v. *Belgium*, the Court of Justice ruled illegal a Belgian law stipulating that all goods to which nutrients had been added must be labelled with a notification number allocated to them by the Belgian authorities.[60] The Court contemplated that labelling a product with a notification number did not protect public health or the consumer as it did not inform the consumer of the nutritional content of the goods or whether the appropriate checks had been carried out. The measure was, measured against its stated goals, useless.[61]

A situation which has recurred in several cases is where a measure could be effective, but in fact is not, as a result of other aspects of national law and policy. For example, *Hartlauer* concerned Austrian rules which required new out-patient dental clinics to be authorised. This was said to be necessary to prevent an over-supply of dentists in a given area, which might have implications for quality and for local health budgets, and so ultimately for access to good dental care. However, the rules only applied to clinics which employed dentists, not to group practices, which were usually partnerships. The difference between a clinic and a partnership is one of business model – the employment model being traditionally regarded as threatening by professionals – but not of obvious importance to the customer.

Hartlauer Handelsgesellschaft mbH v. *Wiener Landesregierung and Oberösterreichische Landesregierung*, C-169/07, EU:C:2009:141

50 Consequently, it must be ascertained whether the restrictions at issue in the main proceedings are appropriate for ensuring attainment of the objectives of maintaining a balanced high-quality medical service open to all and preventing the risk of serious harm to the financial balance of the social security system. [The Court then accepted that a planning and authorisation system could in principle be a part of achieving these goals.] . . .

54 In the present case, however, two series of considerations prevent the legislation in question from being accepted as appropriate for ensuring attainment of the above objectives.

55 First, it must be recalled that national legislation is appropriate for ensuring attainment of the objective pursued only if it genuinely reflects a concern to attain it in a consistent and systematic manner.

---

[59] See p. 849; see also G. Davies, 'Process and Production Method-Based Restrictions on Trade in the EU' in C. Barnard (ed.), *CYELS* (Oxford, Hart, 2008) 69.

[60] *Commission* v. *Belgium*, C-217/99, EU:C:2000:638. [61] See also *Commission* v. *France*, C-55/99, EU:C:2000:693.

56 However, it follows from [national law], that a prior authorisation based on an assessment of the needs of the market is required for setting up and operating new independent outpatient dental clinics, whatever their size, and that the setting up of new group practices, by contrast, is not subject to any system of authorisation, regardless of their size.

57 Yet it appears from the order for reference that the premises and equipment of group practices and those of outpatient dental clinics may have comparable features and that in many cases the patient will not notice any difference between them.

58 Moreover, group practices generally offer the same medical services as outpatient dental clinics and are subject to the same market conditions.

59 Similarly, group practices and outpatient dental clinics may have comparable numbers of practitioners. It is true that the practitioners who provide medical services within group practices have the status of personally liable partner and are authorised to practise independently as dental practitioners, whereas the practitioners in an outpatient clinic have the status of employee. However, the documents before the Court do not show that that circumstance has any definite effect on the nature or volume of the services provided.

60 Since those two categories of providers of services may have comparable features and a comparable number of practitioners and provide medical services of equivalent volume, they may therefore have a similar impact on the market in medical services, and are thus liable to affect in an equivalent manner the economic situation of contractual practitioners in certain geographical areas and, in consequence, the attainment of the planning objectives pursued by the competent authorities.

61 That inconsistency also affects the attainment of the objective of preventing a risk of serious harm to the financial balance of the national social security system. Even supposing that the uncontrolled establishment of independent outpatient dental clinics may lead to a considerable increase in the volume of medical services at constant prices to be paid for by that system, the Austrian Government has not put forward anything capable of explaining why the establishment of those clinics but not of group practices could have such an effect.

62 Moreover, the provision of dental care in those independent outpatient clinics is liable to prove more rational, in view of the way they are organised, the fact of having several practitioners, and the use in common of medical installations and equipment, which enable them to reduce their operating costs. They will thus be able to provide medical services in conditions that are less costly than those, in particular, of independent practitioners who do not have such opportunities. The provision of care services by those institutions may have the consequence of more efficient use of the public funds allocated to the statutory health insurance system.

63 In those circumstances, it must be concluded that the national legislation at issue in the main proceedings does not pursue the stated objectives in a consistent and systematic manner, since it does not make the setting up of group practices subject to a system of prior authorisation, as is the case with new outpatient dental clinics.

Hartlauer, with its emphasis on consistency, is very close in principle to the cases in the previous section. However, the Court of Justice's argument is slightly different. In this case it does not regard inconsistency as demonstrating that there is no real problem to be addressed, but rather that the measure is not actually going to effectively achieve its goal.[62] Nevertheless,

---

[62] See also *Dermoestetica*, C-500/06, EU:C:2008:421; *Blanco Perez*, C-570/07, EU:C:2010:300.

the two issues blur into each other in many judgments, and this is not unreasonable: if a Member State undermines the effectiveness of its own measures, by acting in a way that conflicts with their stated policy goals, then this must also raise the question whether that State genuinely considers action to meet those goals to be necessary. Where inconsistency is taken as showing measures are not necessary the implicit accusation is that the Member State is being dishonest. Where inconsistency is taken as showing that measures will not be effective the implicit accusation is that the Member State is incompetent. Which of these is closer to the truth may vary from case to case. However, the basis of either is an assessment of the measure in its wider policy context. *Hartlauer* is an example of a moderately penetrating review of this.

A similar level of intensity was shown by the Court of Justice in *Festersen*.[63] Denmark wanted to stop yuppies and foreigners from buying up rural housing for use as holiday homes, which both hollowed out local communities and priced locals out of the housing market. The Court accepted the aim of protecting the agricultural community but did quite a detailed second-guessing of how the law actually worked, its loopholes and whether it was likely to be effective.[64] What about yuppies who bought farms to live in, but not to farm? Was that problem addressed? What about neighbouring farmers who bought land and merged it with their own, thereby effectively removing housing from the market?

The confidence with which the Court critically examines these national policy choices is typical of cases which are dominated neither by science, as in food safety, nor by sensitive values, as where morality arguments are made. Rather, *Hartlauer* and *Festersen* concern practical, reasonably comprehensible policy fields which lie within the judicial comfort zone, so we see the Court of Justice engaging in a factual analysis, and conclusion, which is slightly at odds with its role in the reference procedure. There is a risk with these apparently accessible national policy areas that the common-sense judicial approach does not do justice to the full complexity of the policy and the factors involved. Both housing policy, and the structure of local competition, are considerably more constrained by rights, history, other policies, and political ideologies than the judgments recognize. Member States are often compelled to compromise, but their choices are nevertheless measured against a technocratic ideal.

Carmen Media shows how that complexity may be not just a policy matter, but a political one. The German region of Schleswig-Holstein had established a regional betting monopoly, with the aim of controlling the supply of gambling in order to prevent addiction and 'squandering' money. This might have been fine, but was undermined by the fact that it did not cover all forms of gambling, and the rules on casinos and arcade games were actually being relaxed, with a significant increase in supply in recent years. Yet Schleswig-Holstein argued that this could not be blamed on them: some forms of gambling were regulated by the German Länder, but others were at least partly under the control of the federal government. The conflicting policies came from different levels of government, which had constitutionally protected spheres of competence. The Court of Justice acknowledged this, but found it irrelevant.

---

[63] *Festersen*, C-370/05, EU:C:2007:59.

[64] *Konle*, C-302/97, EU:C:1999:271; *Reisch and Others* v. *Bürgermeister der Landeshauptstadt Salzburg*, C-515/99 and C-527–540/99, EU:C:2002:135; *Ospelt* v. *Schössle Weissenberg Familienstiftung*, C-452/01, EU:C:2003:493.

Carmen Media, C–46/08, EU:C:2010:505

64 ... the case-law of the Court of Justice also shows that the establishment, by a Member State, of a restriction on the freedom to provide services and the freedom of establishment on the grounds of such an objective is capable of being justified only on condition that the said restrictive measure is suitable for ensuring the achievement of the said objective by contributing to limiting betting activities in a consistent and systematic manner ...

67 In the present case, after stating that bets on competitions involving horses and automated games can be exploited by private operators which hold an authorisation, the referring court has also established that, in regard to casino games and automated games, even though such games present a higher risk of addiction than bets on sporting competitions, the competent public authorities are pursuing a policy of expanding supply. Thus, the number of casinos has risen from 66 to 81 between 2000 and 2006, while the conditions under which automated games may be exploited in establishments other than casinos, such as gaming arcades, restaurants, cafes and places of accommodation, have recently been the subject of major relaxations.

68 In that respect, on the basis of such findings, it must be acknowledged that the referring court may legitimately be led to consider that the fact that, in relation to games of chance other than those covered by the public monopoly at issue in the main proceedings, the competent authorities thus pursue policies seeking to encourage participation in those games rather than to reduce opportunities for gambling and to limit activities in that area in a consistent and systematic manner has the effect that the aim of preventing incitement to squander money on gambling and of combating addiction to the latter, which was at the root of the establishment of the said monopoly, can no longer be effectively pursued by means of the monopoly, with the result that the latter can no longer be justified having regard to Article [56 TFEU].

69 As for the fact that the various games of chance concerned are partially within the competence of the Länder and partially within the competence of the federal State, it should be recalled that, according to consistent case-law, a Member State may not rely on provisions, practices or situations of its internal legal order in order to justify non-compliance with its obligations under EU law. The internal allocation of competences within a Member State, such as between central, regional or local authorities, cannot, for example, release that Member State from its obligation to fulfil those obligations.

70 It follows from the above that, whilst EU law does not preclude an internal allocation of competences whereby certain games of chance are a matter for the Länder and others for the federal authority, the fact remains that, in such a case, the authorities of the Land concerned and the federal authorities are jointly required to fulfil the obligation on the Federal Republic of Germany not to infringe Article [56 TFEU]. It follows that, in the full measure to which compliance with that obligation requires it, those various authorities are bound, for that purpose, to coordinate the exercise of their respective competences.

The demand that levels of government coordinate their policies before they can legitimately rely on a derogation from the Treaty is substantively understandable, but has potentially far-reaching implications for the domestic political order.

The Court seemed to soften Carmen Media a little in *Digibet*, where it found that the mere fact that a single Land had deviated from the national policy approach, and for a limited period, was not enough to show the policy was too inconsistent to be effective.[65] Nevertheless, it seems that

---

[65] *Digibet*, C-156/13, EU:C:2014:1756; see also *Berlington Hungary*, C-98/14, EU:C:2015:386.

internal policy diversity – local democracy – makes all levels of policy less legitimate in the eyes of the Court.

(iii) Arbitrary Discrimination and Mutual Recognition

Measures taken in derogation from the freedoms must of course comply with general principles of EU law, such as fundamental rights.[66] One of the most important of these in practice is the principle of non-discrimination. This is expressly referred to in the second sentence of Article 36 TFEU, which prevents 'arbitrary discrimination', but the principle applies across the freedoms.[67] It entails that Member States may not use derogations for covert protectionism, and requires them to take full account of protective measures which may be in place in other Member States, and which may make their own measures less necessary.

An extreme example is found in the *Newcastle Disease* case. This highly infectious viral disease affects birds including chickens and turkeys, and after an outbreak on the Continent the British Government imposed restrictions on the import of poultry products from mainland Europe. At first glance this seemed like a reasonable animal health measure. However, the Commission and France presented the facts in a way which told a different story. The timing of the measure, the political pressure preceding it, the absence of any scientific basis for it and the fact that measures taken by France to combat Newcastle Disease had been summarily dismissed as inadequate by the United Kingdom were all relevant.

Commission v. United Kingdom (Newcastle Disease), 40/82, EU:C:1984:33

36 As the Court has already observed . . . in Case 34/79 *Henn and Darby*, the second sentence of Article [36 TFEU] is designed to prevent restrictions on trade mentioned in the first sentence of that article from being diverted from their proper purpose and used in such a way as either to create discrimination in respect of goods originating in other Member States or indirectly to protect certain national products.

37 Certain established facts suggest that the real aim of the 1981 measures was to block, for commercial and economic reasons, imports of poultry products from other Member States, in particular from France. The United Kingdom Government had been subject to pressure from British poultry producers to block these imports. It hurriedly introduced its new policy with the result that French Christmas turkeys were excluded from the British market for the 1981 season. It did not inform the Commission and the Member States concerned in good time, as the letter in which the Commission was informed of the new measures – which took effect on 1 September 1981 – was dated 27 August 1981. It did not find it necessary to discuss the effects of the new measures on imports with the Community Institutions, with the Standing Veterinary Committee or with the Member States concerned.

38 It should be noted, in this context, that when the United Kingdom abandoned, in 1964, the policy of non-vaccination and compulsory slaughter conducted till then in Great Britain, in order to adopt a policy of control of Newcastle disease by vaccination, this change of policy was thoroughly prepared by an elaborate report of a committee of experts, by various studies and by prolonged discussions among veterinary experts. The evidence available in the present case does not suggest that any comparable effort was made before the

---

[66] *ERT* v. *DEP*, C-260/89, EU:C:1991:254; see Ch. 6.
[67] See Article 18 TFEU; *Sjöberg and Gerdin*, C-447/08, EU:C:2010:415.

Government decided, in 1981, to reintroduce the policy which it had applied before 1964. The deduction must be made that the 1981 measures did not form part of a seriously considered health policy.

39 This conclusion is reinforced by the way in which the United Kingdom dealt with French demands that French poultry products should be readmitted to Great Britain after the French Republic had fulfilled the three conditions laid down by the United Kingdom Government, namely that the exporting country should be totally free from outbreaks of Newcastle disease, should prohibit vaccination and should apply a policy of compulsory slaughter in the event of any future outbreak of the disease. By refusing French imports on the ground that France had not closed its frontiers to poultry imports from non-member countries where vaccine was still in use, the United Kingdom added in fact a fourth condition to the three which it had previously stated in its letter to the Commission of 27 August 1981, and which it still states in its defence in the present case as the only applicable conditions.

The ban on arbitrary discrimination also covers less colourful stories.[68] In *Rewe*, a German policy on apple disease was examined, which subjected imported apples to phytosanitary checks, while German apples were subjected to a different regime in which the trees were checked.[69] This resulted in different cost burdens on German and imported apples. However, the Court of Justice found this to be permitted differentiation, not arbitrary discrimination: the fact was that it was not possible to conduct checks on trees outside Germany, and this difference justified the different approach to controls.

Nevertheless, had the Member States of origin conducted such tree checks and offered evidence of the results Germany would have been obliged to accept them. The principle of mutual recognition is a specific expression of non-discrimination, and is often relevant to derogations, particularly where testing and certification are concerned. This principle prevents the importing State duplicating measures which have already been taken by the exporting State. This principle was confirmed in *Biologische Producten*,[70] where a Dutch law requiring prior authorisation for the marketing of all toxic plant protection products by the Dutch authorities was challenged on the grounds that the product in question had already been subject to extensive laboratory analyses in France. The Court reminded the parties that Member States 'are not entitled unnecessarily to require technical or chemical analyses or laboratory tests where those analyses and tests have already been carried out in another Member State and their results are available to those authorities, or may at their request be placed at their disposal'.

The requirement to accept foreign tests as adequate is premised on them being equivalent to the national ones. This may not always be so. If the Member State can establish that there are important differences, so that the tests do not in fact satisfy the (legitimate and proportionate) domestic needs, then they may impose additional tests. But while this is simple in principle it may be complex in practice.[71] The procedures used by different Member States will rarely be identical. Thus, establishing equivalence between different standards in often highly complex

---

[68] *Costa and Cifone*, C-72/10 and C-77/10, EU:C:2012:80; *Biasci and Others*, C-660/11 and C-8/12, EU:C:2013:550; *Pfleger*, C-390/12, EU:C:2014:281.

[69] *Rewe-Zentralfinanz GmbH* v. *Landwirtschaftskammer Bonn*, 4/75, EU:C:1975:98.

[70] *Frans-Nederlandse Maatschappij voor Biologische Producten*, 272/80, EU:C:1981:312; see also *Commission* v. *Portugal*, C-432/03, EU:C:2005:669.

[71] See pp. 646–8.

and technical areas will be difficult.[72] The principle of equivalence places an exacting burden on the national judge. This is not only true where product standards are concerned, but also where the adequacy of supervision by other Member State regulatory authorities is in issue. Member States should regard supervision by the home State as rendering their own supervision superfluous unless they can show that it leaves gaps in protection which must be filled, but this is once again often a complex matter.[73] One response to that complexity is to take a procedural approach to reviewing Member State measures, asking primarily whether they have complied with principles of good governance in their approach to issues of equivalence. This is increasingly adopted by the Court of Justice, and discussed further below.[74]

Mutual recognition is at its most powerful where objective, factual issues are concerned and documents from different States can be easily compared. By contrast, where authorisations are concerned these may be based on different policy considerations, making them non-comparable. In the gambling cases the issue has arisen whether an authorisation to provide gambling services from one Member State should automatically entitle the holder to offer these in other Member States. The Court of Justice in *Stoß* explains why mutual recognition should not apply in this case.

Stoß, C–316/07, EU:C:2010:504

111   In that respect, it should however be noted that, having regard to the discretion ... which Member States have in determining, according to their own scale of values, the level of protection which they intend to ensure and the requirements which that protection entails, the Court had regularly held that assessment of the proportionality of the system of protection established by a Member State cannot, in particular, be influenced by the fact that another Member State has chosen a different system of protection.

112   Having regard to that margin of discretion and the absence of any Community harmonisation in the matter, a duty mutually to recognise authorisations issued by the various Member States cannot exist having regard to the current state of EU law.

113   It follows in particular that each Member State retains the right to require any operator wishing to offer games of chance to consumers in its territory to hold an authorisation issued by its competent authorities, without the fact that a particular operator already holds an authorisation issued in another Member State being capable of constituting an obstacle.

Because the underlying conditions for obtaining a licence may vary significantly from State to State they cannot be treated as interchangeable or equivalent.[75] Mutual recognition, at least in the context of Treaty derogations, is not intended to undermine the substantive policy choices of Member States.[76]

(iv) The Measure Must Be the Least Restrictive Option

Even if action has been shown to be necessary, and the measure has been shown to be effective, it must still be no more restrictive of movement than is necessary.[77] The definitive statement on

---

[72] European Commission, 'Second Biennial Report on the Application of the Principle of Mutual Recognition in the Single Market', COM(2002)419 final, 17–21.

[73] *Gambelli*, C-243/01, EU:C:2003:597; *Commission* v. *Austria*, C-393/05, EU:C:2007:722; *Commission* v. *Germany*, C-404/05, EU:C:2007:723.

[74] See pp. 845–8; also *Commission* v. *France*, C-333/08, EU:C:2010:44 v.

[75] See Doukas, n. 56 above; Anagnostaras, n. 57 above.   [76] Cf. pp. 717–18.

[77] *Officier van Justitie* v. *De Peijper*, 104/75, EU:C:1976:67.

this is now found in *Scotch Whisky*. The Scottish Parliament had decided to impose a minimum price on alcohol, fixed per alcohol unit (MPU – minimum price per unit). This would prevent very cheap alcohol being sold and so combat excessive drinking, particularly by young people. However, it was argued that an MPU would disproportionately affect cheap alcohol, and so particularly effect imports from low-cost States. A general increase in alcohol taxation, which would affect expensive drinks too, might be less protectionist in effect and so less trade-restrictive. On the other hand, it also went beyond what was necessary, as expensive drinks were not the social problem. The referring court asked how it was supposed to assess whether a less restrictive measure was possible.

Scotch Whisky, C–333/14, EU:C:2015:845

53 Since a prohibition such as that which arises from the national legislation at issue in the main proceedings amounts to a derogation from the principle of the free movement of goods, it is for the national authorities to demonstrate that that legislation is consistent with the principle of proportionality, that is to say, that it is necessary in order to achieve the declared objective, and that that objective could not be achieved by prohibitions or restrictions that are less extensive, or that are less disruptive of trade within the European Union.

54 In that regard, the reasons which may be invoked by a Member State by way of justification must be accompanied by appropriate evidence or by an analysis of the appropriateness and proportionality of the restrictive measure adopted by that State, and specific evidence substantiating its arguments.

55 It must however be stated that that burden of proof cannot extend to creating the requirement that, where the competent national authorities adopt national legislation imposing a measure such as the MPU, they must prove, positively, that no other conceivable measure could enable the legitimate objective pursued to be attained under the same conditions.

56 In that context, it is for the national court called on to review the legality of the national legislation concerned to determine the relevance of the evidence adduced by the competent national authorities in order to determine whether that legislation is compatible with the principle of proportionality. On the basis of that evidence, that court must, in particular, examine objectively whether it may reasonably be concluded from the evidence submitted by the Member State concerned that the means chosen are appropriate for the attainment of the objectives pursued and whether it is possible to attain those objectives by measures that are less restrictive of the free movement of goods.

57 In this case, in the course of such a review, the referring court may take into consideration the possible existence of scientific uncertainty as to the actual and specific effects on the consumption of alcohol of a measure such as the MPU for the purposes of attaining the objective pursued. As the Advocate General stated in point 85 of his Opinion, the fact that the national legislation provides that the setting of an MPU will expire six years after the entry into force of the MPU Order, unless the Scottish Parliament decides that it is to continue, is a factor that the referring court may also take into consideration.

58 That court must also assess the nature and scale of the restriction on the free movement of goods resulting from a measure such as the MPU, by comparison with other possible measures which are less disruptive of trade within the European Union ... that assessment being intrinsic to the examination of proportionality.

The Court made a number of other important points elsewhere in the judgment. It noted that the mere fact that an excise duty had broader effects on alcohol consumption, beyond the immediate policy need, did not as such justify its rejection. Moreover, the evidence which the national court should consider in making its assessment above was not just that which was available or relied upon when the measure was adopted but on the contrary, all the evidence and information available to the court at the time of its judgment.

Despite its extensive instructions to the national court, the Court also gave its own preliminary reviews on the substantive question, as it typically does in cases where the facts are amenable to judicial review – often where market externalities are involved, or the more practical aspects of State administration, as in the many gambling cases, tax and often in public health and consumer protection.[78] It strongly implied that a tax increase would be a more proportionate approach, while formally leaving it to the national court to see if this was the case. In fact, the national court ultimately decided that it was not.

This shows some of the risks of the Court engaging in intensive substantive review. The national court may legitimately disagree, with its better understanding of the facts, or the national court may disagree because it is committed to relatively marginal national traditions of judicial review and is reluctant to challenge the lawmaker. A way of steering between these problems is to focus less on which is the best policy, and more on whether the decisions were taken in an appropriate way. This quasi-procedural emphasis still constrains decision-makers, and is perhaps more likely to be applied by national courts.

For example, in *Leichtle*, concerning health-care rules which impacted on free movement of services, the Court said that 'the reasons which may be invoked by a Member State by way of justification must be accompanied by an analysis of the appropriateness and proportionality of the restrictive measure adopted by that State', and went on in the next paragraph to find that the Member State had failed to supply evidence demonstrating the necessity of its measures.[79] An even stronger statement is found in *Commission* v. *Austria*, where heavy goods trucks were prohibited on certain stretches of motorway, on air quality grounds.[80] Having accepted the need for measures, and that the measures in question were effective, the Court then said:

> As the Court stated in Case C-320/03 *Commission* v. *Austria*, paragraph 87, before adopting a measure so radical as a total traffic ban on a section of motorway constituting a vital route of communication between certain Member States, the Austrian authorities were under a duty to examine carefully the possibility of using measures less restrictive of freedom of movement, and discount them only if their inappropriateness to the objective pursued was clearly established.[81]

It went on to find that Austria was in breach of Article 28 TFEU purely because it had not demonstrated that alternative, less restrictive measures, could not be effective. This puts a strict burden of proof on Member States, and pressures them to incorporate free movement concerns into their decision-making.

Nevertheless, in other cases the Court has said that a failure to analyse the impact of and need for a measure when it was adopted does not automatically make it disproportionate, if the

---

[78] See e.g. *Gambelli*, C-243/01, EU:C:2003:597; *Commission* v. *United Kingdom*, 124/81, EU:C:1983:30; *Bluhme*, C-67/97, EU:C:1998:584; *Deutscher Apothekerverband* v. *DocMorris*, C-322/01, EU:C:2003:664; *Placanica, Palazzese and Soricchio*, C-338/04, C-359–60/04, EU:C:2007:133; *Ludwigs–Apotheke München Internationale Apotheke* v. *Juers Pharma Import-Export GmbH*, C-143/06, EU:C:2007:656; *Humanplasma*, C-421/09, EU:C:2010:760; *Jyske Bank*, C-212/11, EU:C:2013:270; *Commission* v. *Belgium*, C-383/10, EU:C:2013:364; *Passenheim-van Schoot*, C-155/08, EU:C:2009:368; *Partena*, C-137/11, EU:C:2012:593; G. de Búrca, 'The Principle of Proportionality and Its Application in EC Law' (1993) 13 *YBEL* 105.

[79] *Leichtle* v. *Bundesanstalt für Arbeit*, C-8/02, EU:C:2004:161.   [80] *Commission* v. *Austria*, C-28/09, EU:C:2011:854.

[81] *Ibid.* para. 140.

evidence available at trial – the burden of proof being on the State – does in fact justify it.[82] Following good decision-making procedure is a way for Member States to justify their actions, but not the only one possible: the question of justification remains ultimately substantive, and the relevant moment is when the obstruction occurs.

Where socio-cultural preferences are concerned, by contrast, the Court is often less demanding.[83] These are often quirky and particularistic. Their value lies not so much in realising some general goal, but in reinforcing the identity of a community or region. As a consequence, it is very difficult to separate the institutions and legislation protecting these traditions and preferences from the tradition itself. It is also very difficult for the Court of Justice to provide a general statement about the nature and value of the tradition to act as a standard for review.

In many cases in this field, a fairly marginal standard of review is adopted. In *UTECA*, concerning Spanish rules requiring film companies to reserve a percentage of their income for financing films in local languages, the Court asked itself whether the measure went beyond what was necessary to protect 'Spanish multilingualism' and noted '[t]he documents submitted to the Court do not contain any material which might lead to the conclusion that such a percentage is disproportionate in relation to the objective pursued', an apparent reversal of the usual burden of proof.[84] In *Sayn Wittgenstein*, where an Austrian ban on the use of noble titles was claimed to reflect a constitutional commitment to equality, the Court accepted the measure without discussion of evidence or alternatives, on the basis that it did not appear to go further than was necessary.[85] The symbolic value of the rule meant that a narrowly evidence-based or functional analysis of its effects would have been inappropriate. This respect for national symbols and constitutional values is now reinforced by the so-called constitutional identity clause in Article 4(2) TEU.

Similar deference is shown towards decisions concerning the more sensitive aspects of the State apparatus, such as national security. In *Campus Oil*, the Irish Government required importers of petroleum to obtain a minimum of 35 per cent of their needs from the one Irish refinery, which had been set up to ensure an orderly supply of petrol onto the Irish market.[86] The Court of Justice found this minimum purchasing requirement to be lawful on the grounds that securing non-interruption of petrol supplies was essential to a State's security. It had been argued, however, that refineries could not secure a supply of oil, and maintenance of reserves would be a less restrictive way of securing this. A less onerous system of supporting the refinery than through a purchasing commitment might have been for the Irish Government to subsidise the refinery directly. The Court was dismissive of these arguments. It noted that having an independent refining capacity prevented a State being dependent upon foreign refineries and thus removed one threat to its security.

This does not give Member States a *carte blanche*. In *Commission v. Greece*, the Court of Justice examined a Greek obligation on those marketing petrol to hold minimum stocks of petrol.

---

[82] *Sporting Odds*, C-3/17, EU:C:2018:130; *Pfleger*, C-390/12, EU:C:2014:281; *Admiral Casinos*, C-464/15, EU:C:2016:500.

[83] E.g. *UTECA* v. *Administración General del Estado*, C-222/07, EU:C:2009:124; *Groener* v. *Minister for Education and the City of Dublin Vocational Educational Committee*, 379/87, EU:C:1989:599; *Salomone Haim* v. *Kassenzahnärztliche Vereinigung Nordrhein*, C-424/97, EU:C:2000:357; *United Pan-Europe Communications Belgium SA and Others* v. *Belgian State*, C-250/06, EU:C:2007:783; see also *Graham J. Wilson* v. *Ordre des avocats du barreau de Luxembourg*, C-506/04, EU:C:2006:587.

[84] See e.g. *Ahokainen*, C-434/04, EU:C:2006:609; *Commission* v. *Denmark*, C-192/01, EU:C:2003:492.

[85] *Sayn Wittgenstein*, C-208/09, EU:C:2010:806.

[86] *Campus Oil* v. *Minister for Industry and Energy*, 72/83, EU:C:1984:256.

It was unimpressed by a provision that allowed companies to transfer these obligations to refineries, so long as they had purchased petrol from those refineries in the last year.[87] The Court found that this requirement of prior purchase was not the least restrictive means available to secure petrol supply and was therefore illegal. The explanation for this stricter measure of review can be found in the sheer protectionist nature of the measure and its lack of relationship to public security. It had less to do with ensuring stocks were maintained than with providing a subsidy to those who purchased petrol from Greek refineries.

Another field which is politically sensitive is higher education. Yet here the Court has been consistently rigorous in its review, perhaps because the aspects which have come before it have been more to do with financing than content, or perhaps because Member States have tried to defend their policies primarily in functional, rather than symbolic or value-based terms. As a result, they have invited functionally oriented review.

This has been apparent in the large number of cases involving student migration and grants, but also those involving small Member States trying to protect their universities from being flooded by students from a neighbouring large one.[88] This has been the situation faced, or feared, in Belgium and Austria. Belgium introduced a quota for medical students who were not resident in Belgium, claiming that otherwise there would be a shortage of medical personnel staying in Belgium after their studies, raising a public health issue. This was litigated in *Bressol*, where the Court of Justice referred the question back to the national court after giving it detailed instructions on the kinds of evidence of a serious threat that it should insist the Belgian Government present.[89] The Austrians introduced rules making it harder for those with foreign qualifications to obtain a place at Austrian universities, and justified this by, among other reasons, the desire to safeguard the 'homogeneity' of the Austrian higher education system. Again, the Court imposed a high burden of proof on the State.

Commission v. Austria (Access to Universities), C-147/03, EU:C:2005:427

63 Moreover, it is for the national authorities which invoke a derogation from the fundamental principle of freedom of movement for persons to show in each individual case that their rules are necessary and proportionate to attain the aim pursued. The reasons which may be invoked by a Member State by way of justification must be accompanied by an analysis of the appropriateness and proportionality of the restrictive measure adopted by that State and specific evidence substantiating its arguments.

64 In the present case, the Republic of Austria simply maintained at the hearing that the number of students registering for courses in medicine could be five times the number of available places, which would pose a risk to the financial equilibrium of the Austrian higher education system and, consequently, to its very existence.

65 It must be pointed out that no estimates relating to other courses have been submitted to the Court and that the Republic of Austria has conceded that it does not have any figures in that connection. Moreover, the Austrian authorities have accepted that the national legislation in question is essentially preventive in nature.

---

[87] *Commission* v. *Greece*, C-398/98, EU:C:2001:565.

[88] See pp. 892–5; *Commission* v. *Austria* (Access to Universities), C-147/03, EU:C:2005:427; *Bressol*, C-73/08, EU:C:2010:181.

[89] *Bressol*, C-73/08, EU:C:2010:181.

> **66** Consequently, it must be held that the Republic of Austria has failed to demonstrate that, in the absence of Paragraph 36 of the UnistG, the existence of the Austrian education system in general and the safeguarding of the homogeneity of higher education in particular would be jeopardised. The legislation in question is therefore incompatible with the objectives of the Treaty.

The Court of Justice is particularly critical of the fact that the Austrian Government is taking a 'preventive' measure, acting on the basis of a potential problem without showing quantitative evidence that this problem will be, or has been, realised.[90] Yet it can be difficult to produce convincing evidence of future flows of students. It is also hard for a Member State to accept that it should just wait and see, and only act once its higher education system is clearly struggling and failing to cope, since the reality of legislation and policy-making is that it cannot be put in place in an instant, and anticipating and preventing problems would normally be seen as good practice. On the other hand, one of the reasons why the Court is probably reluctant to be tolerant of State claims is that the risk of exclusionary and nationalistic action is quite real: if Member States are allowed to act on the basis of an unquantified potential risk then it is extremely likely that cross-border access to education – or indeed health, for the same evidential issues have arisen in that context[91] – will be widely restricted. Potential threats to movement justify limits to national policies,[92] but potential threats to national policy do not justify limits to movement.

Something which emerges from the cases above is that the proportionality principle is not always applied in the same way in the case law, which invites criticisms of inconsistency by the Court of Justice. Yet although the variation is real, it is inevitable that the interface between the economic freedoms and a great many diverse public interests will generate heterogeneous tensions. Variation in approach may be a price worth paying if the alternative is insensitivity to national concerns.

A more defining, and more precise, criticism is that the case law is too 'decisionistic', in that it is too preoccupied with outcomes,[93] and should be more concerned with the process of policy formation and decision-making. The emphasis on evidence and proof in cases such as *Leichtle*, *Commission* v. *Austria (Heavy Goods Trucks)* and *Commission* v. *Austria (Access to Universities)*, and the growing importance given to consistency in the judgments, both suggest that the Court is moving in this direction.[94] Majone explains below the merits of the procedural approach.

> ### G. Majone, *Evidence, Argument and Persuasion in the Policy Process* (New Haven, CT, Yale University Press, 1989) 17–18
>
> A . . . limitation of decisionism is its exclusive preoccupation with outcomes and lack of concern for the processes whereby the outcomes are produced. A lack of concern for process is justified in some situations. If the correctness or fairness of the outcome can be determined unambiguously, the manner in which the

---

[90] See N. Nic Shuibhne and M. Maci, 'Proving Public Interest: The Growing Impact of Evidence in Free Movement Case Law' (2013) 50 *CMLRev* 965.

[91] See p. 769. [92] See p. 741; *Dassonville*, 8/74, EU:C:1974:82.

[93] For more specific arguments that EU law should be concerned with process in this field, see J. Scott, 'Of Kith and Kine (and Crustaceans): Trade and Environment in the EU and WTO' in J. Weiler (ed.), *The EU, NAFTA and the WTO: Towards a Common Law of International Trade* (Oxford University Press, 2000).

[94] S. Prechal, 'Free Movement and Procedural Requirements: Proportionality Reconsidered' (2008) 35 *LIEI* 201.

decision is made is often immaterial; only results count. But when the factual or value premises are moot, when there are no generally accepted criteria of rightness, the procedure of decision-making acquires special significance and cannot be treated as purely instrumental.

Even in formal decision analysis the explicit recognition of uncertainty forces a significant departure from a strict orientation toward outcomes. Under conditions of uncertainty different alternatives correspond to different probability distributions of the consequences, so that it is no longer possible to determine unambiguously what the optimal decision is. Hence, the usual criterion of rationality – according to which an action is rational if it can be explained as the choosing of the best means to achieve given objectives – is replaced by the weaker notion of consistency. The rational decision maker is no longer an optimiser, strictly speaking. All that is required now, and all that the principle of maximising expected utility guarantees, is that the choice be consistent with the decision maker's valuations of the probability and utility of the various consequences. Notice that consistency is a procedural, not a substantive, criterion.

Exclusive preoccupation with outcomes is a serious limitation of decisionism, since social processes seldom have only instrumental value for the people who engage in them. In most areas of social activity, the processes and rules that constitute the enterprise and define the roles of its participants matter quite apart from any identifiable 'end state' that is ultimately produced. Indeed in many cases it is the process itself that matters most to those who take part in it.

(v) The Measure Must Be Procedurally Fair

A condition for the legitimacy of a restriction is that the rights of the parties affected are sufficiently protected: that the powers of the national authorities imposing the restriction are defined in an objective and transparent way; that the parties affected have access to sufficient information to assess and challenge the measures; that courts have jurisdiction to consider these challenges; and that the systems for doing all these are reasonably accessible and speedy. The logic of these principles is that rights are only meaningful if they can be enforced and defended. In this light they are no more than is necessary or sensible to make the law effective. Yet they can be quite constraining and troublesome for Member States.[95]

An example is *French Vitamins*. In this case the Commission challenged French legislation which provided that food containing added nutrients that were not on an approved list endorsed by the French authorities had to be subject to a procedure of prior authorisation before it could be marketed. The procedure for this authorisation was often lengthy and took no account of regulatory tests carried out in other Member States.

Commission v. France (French Vitamins), C–24/00, EU:C:2004:70

36 As is clear from paragraph 26 of this judgment, a procedure which requires prior authorisation, in the interest of public health, for the addition of a nutrient authorised in another Member State complies with Community law only if it is readily accessible and can be completed within a reasonable time and if, when it is refused, the refusal can be challenged before the courts.

---

[95] See the section on welfare states at pp. 765–72.

37 As regards first the accessibility of the procedure in question in this case, a Member State's obligation to provide for such a procedure in the case of any national rule which on grounds of public health makes the addition of nutrients subject to authorisation cannot be fulfilled if that procedure is not expressly provided for in a measure of general application which is binding on the national authorities ...

French Vitamins applies general principles of administrative due process, such as duties of transparency, efficiency and judicial accountability.[96] An important element is the idea of explicit regulation via a measure of general application. When decisions are taken in an *ad hoc* way, relying on some highly general decision-making authority, it becomes impossible for individuals or companies to know the legal situation in advance, and to effectively challenge decisions afterwards. Thus, it is necessary that the decision-maker be constrained by sufficiently precise and binding laws that their decisions are both predictable and reviewable.[97] For this reason, the Court of Justice has consistently objected to imprecise powers, even in sensitive policy fields.

In *Église de Scientologie de Paris*,[98] French law required any direct foreign investment, subject to highly limited exceptions, to have prior authorisation from the French authorities. The French Government argued that this was necessary on grounds of public policy. The French authorities were accused, however, of exercising their discretion in an arbitrary manner.

Église de Scientologie de Paris v. *Prime Minister*, C-54/99, EU:C:2000:124

20 In the case of direct foreign investments, the difficulty in identifying and blocking capital once it has entered a Member State may make it necessary to prevent, at the outset, transactions which would adversely affect public policy or public security. It follows that, in the case of direct foreign investments which constitute a genuine and sufficiently serious threat to public policy and public security, a system of prior declaration may prove to be inadequate to counter such a threat.

21 In the present case, however, the essence of the system in question is that prior authorisation is required for every direct foreign investment which is such as to represent a threat to public policy [and] public security, without any more detailed definition. Thus, the investors concerned are given no indication whatever as to the specific circumstances in which prior authorisation is required.

22 Such lack of precision does not enable individuals to be apprised of the extent of their rights and obligations deriving from [Article 63 TFEU]. That being so, the system established is contrary to the principle of legal certainty.

Analogous reasoning is found in a large number of cases concerning investment restrictions.[99] Concern over who may own or influence strategic industries is justifiable, but catch-all authorisation schemes are unacceptable: restrictions must be based on specific, objective criteria; these

---

[96] See also *Watts*, C-372/04, EU:C:2006:325; *Commission* v. *France*, C-333/08, EU:C:2010:44 v.

[97] *Ålands Vindkraft*, C-573/12, EU:C:2014:2037; *Iraklis*, C-201/15, EU:C:2016:972; *Unibet Hungary*, C-49/16, EU:C:2017:491.

[98] *Église de Scientologie de Paris* v. *Prime Minister*, C-54/99, EU:C:2000:124.

[99] *Trummer and Mayer*, C-222/97, EU:C:1999:143; *Commission* v. *France*, C-483/99, EU:C:2002:327; *Commission* v. *Belgium*, C-503/99, EU:C:2002:328; *Commission* v. *Italy (Free Movement of Capital)*, C-174/04, EU:C:2005:350; *Commission* v. *Netherlands (Direct and Portfolio Investments)*, C-282–3/04, EU:C:2006:608; *Woningstichting Sint Servatius*, C-567/07, EU:C:2009:593.

criteria must be known in advance; authorisations must be accessible and speedy, given the particular importance of time to investment issues; and they must be open to challenge in court.[100]

Nevertheless, it is not the case that the Court of Justice rejects any role for discretion in decision-making. Where interests are complex and non-quantifiable it may be unavoidable, and the test then is whether it is sufficiently constrained to ensure that it is exercised in a fair and non-discriminatory way.[101]

Garkalns, C–470/11, EU:C:2012:505

41 In those circumstances, it must be ascertained whether the restriction on the freedom to provide services imposed by the national legislation at issue in the main proceedings is appropriate for achieving the objective of protecting consumers against the risks linked to betting and gaming and whether it does not go beyond what is necessary to achieve that objective.

42 In addition, in order to be consistent with the principle of equal treatment and to meet the obligation of transparency which flows from that principle, an authorisation scheme for betting and gaming must be based on objective, non-discriminatory criteria known in advance, in such a way as to circumscribe the exercise by the authorities of their discretion so that it is not used arbitrarily.

43 In order to enable the impartiality of the authorisation procedures to be monitored, it is also necessary for the competent authorities to base each of their decisions on reasoning which is accessible to the public, stating precisely the reasons for which, as the case may be, authorisation has been refused.

44 In that connection, the Court has held that it is for the national courts to ensure, in the light, in particular, of the actual rules for applying the restrictive legislation concerned, that that legislation genuinely meets the concern to reduce opportunities for gambling and to limit activities in that domain in a consistent and systematic manner.

45 In the case under consideration, it cannot be denied that, as is apparent from the order for reference, in allowing authorisation to open an amusement arcade to be refused on grounds of substantial impairment of the interests of the State and of the residents of the administrative area concerned, the national legislation at issue in the main proceedings confers a broad discretion on the administrative authorities, particularly for the purposes of assessing the interests which that legislation is intended to protect.

46 Discretion, such as that at issue in the main proceedings, could be justified if the national legislation itself were genuinely intended to meet the concern to reduce opportunities for gambling and to limit activities in that domain in a consistent and systematic manner, or to ensure that local residents can live in peace or even, generally, to preserve public order, by conferring on the local authorities, for that purpose, a certain discretion in applying the rules relating to the organisation of betting and gaming.

47 In order to assess the proportionality of the national legislation at issue, it is therefore for the national court to verify, in particular, that the State strictly supervises the activities related to betting and gaming; that the refusal of the local authorities to authorise the opening of new establishments of that type genuinely pursues the declared objective of protecting consumers; and that the criterion of 'substantial impairment of the interests of the State and of the residents of the administrative area concerned' is applied without discrimination.

A slightly different kind of problem arose in *French Processing Aids*.[102] This case was very similar to *French Vitamins*, except that it concerned authorisation for foods containing additives

---

[100] *Ibid.*   [101] See also *Libert*, C–197/11, EU:C:2013:288; *Unibet Hungary*, C–49/16, EU:C:2017:491.
[102] *Commission* v. *France*, C–333/08, EU:C:2010:44 v.

to do with processing (e.g. preservatives), rather than vitamins. The particular problem in this case was that thanks to contradictory national legal measures it was not quite clear what the legal position was, and what those marketing imported foodstuffs were exactly required to do. The Court of Justice found that the various laws and decrees 'have created a situation of legal uncertainty which itself constitutes an unjustified obstacle to Article 28 EC'.[103] Once again, if people cannot know their rights, they will not be able to protect them.

5 ENVIRONMENTAL PROTECTION

Protection of the environment has been used to justify a number of types of national restriction.[104] Member States are permitted to take measures prohibiting environmentally harmful activities where the ecological costs of an activity are obvious and high. A French prohibition on the burning of waste oils was, therefore, found to be compatible with Article 56 TFEU on the grounds that it protected the environment. In like vein, the Court of Justice has approved measures that ban chlorofluorocarbons or other ozone-depleting substances.[105] Member States must still show, however, that there are no other, less restrictive means of protecting the environment. In *Aher-Waggon*, a challenge was made to German restrictions on permissible noise emissions from aircraft.[106] These measures were stricter than those permitted by EU legislation. It was argued that there were less restrictive means of limiting noise, such as restricting the amount of flights or planning restrictions on the sites of airports. The Court, nevertheless, upheld the German restriction because it was convinced that these other options were not in fact feasible.

Member States can also take measures to protect biodiversity. The most interesting case is *Bluhme*.[107] The case suggests that biodiversity is to be protected under the heading of protection of the health of animals rather than that of protection of the environment, and that Member States are to be given considerable leeway to protect fauna or flora. It concerned a Danish law allowing only Læsø brown bees to be kept on the island of Læsø in Denmark. Bluhme argued that this restriction, which was in order to protect the dissolution of the local brown bee population through mating with other bees, could not be justified ecologically as the brown bee was not a distinct species in its own right.

Bluhme, C–67/97, EU:C:1998:584

33   ... the Court considers that measures to preserve an indigenous animal population with distinct characteristics contribute to the maintenance of biodiversity by ensuring the survival of the population concerned. By so doing, they are aimed at protecting the life of those animals and are capable of being justified under Article [36 TFEU].

34   From the point of view of such conservation of biodiversity, it is immaterial whether the object of protection is a separate subspecies, a distinct strain within any given species or merely a local colony, so long as the

---

[103] *Ibid.* para. 111.   [104] See also pp. 723–4.
[105] *Bettati* v. *Safety Hi-Tech*, C–341/95, EU:C:1998:353; *Safety Hi-Tech* v. *S and T*, C–284/95, EU:C:1998:352.
[106] *Aher-Waggon* v. *Federal Republic of Germany*, C–389/96, EU:C:1998:357.   [107] *Bluhme*, C–67/97, EU:C:1998:584.

populations in question have characteristics distinguishing them from others and are therefore judged worthy of protection either to shelter them from a risk of extinction that is more or less imminent, or, even in the absence of such risk, on account of a scientific or other interest in preserving the pure population at the location concerned.

35 It does, however, have to be determined whether the national legislation was necessary and proportionate in relation to its aim of protection, or whether it would have been possible to achieve the same result by less stringent measures . . .

36 Conservation of biodiversity through the establishment of areas in which a population enjoys special protection, which is a method recognised in the Rio Convention, especially Article 8a thereof, is already put into practice in Community law [in particular, by means of the special protection areas provided for in Council Directive 79/409/EEC of 2 April 1979 on the conservation of wild birds [1979] OJ L103/1, or the special conservation areas provided for in Directive 92/43/EC].

37 As for the threat of [the disappearance] of the Læsø brown bee, it is undoubtedly genuine in the event of mating with golden bees by reason of the recessive nature of the genes of the brown bee. The establishment by the national legislation of a protection area within which the keeping of bees other than Læsø brown bees is prohibited, for the purpose of ensuring the survival of the latter, therefore constitutes an appropriate measure in relation to the aim pursued.

The judgment is unusual in placing the Member State restriction in the context of international conventions. Environmental protection is an atypical ground for derogation because it is also an EU goal. There is not always a simple balance to be made between the Union interest in movement and the national interest in a restriction. Rather, the Union may have as great an interest as the Member State in the restriction, particularly where the environmental concerns are not strictly local as is the case with biodiversity and climate change.

An example of this latter goal justifying an apparently discriminatory measure is *Preussen-Elektra*. The German Government required electricity retailers to buy a proportion of their electricity from wind farms in Germany, the aim being to stimulate such farms and make them viable, and so reduce global warming. Such a measure is clearly both protectionist and directly discriminatory, but it is also, arguably, one of the most practical ways of stimulating a domestic green energy sector, particularly since the law on State aids imposes constraints on direct subsidy. The Court of Justice's judgment was, like that in *Bluhme*, notably context-aware and discursive. The cases suggest that where current environmental crises are in issue, the Court may take a less hostile approach to Member State derogations than is normally the case.

PreussenElektra, C–379/98, EU:C:2001:160

73 The use of renewable energy sources for producing electricity, which a statute such as the amended Stromeinspeisungsgesetz is intended to promote, is useful for protecting the environment insofar as it contributes to the reduction in emissions of greenhouse gases which are amongst the main causes of climate change which the European Community and its Member States have pledged to combat.

74 Growth in that use is amongst the priority objectives which the Community and its Member States intend to pursue in implementing the obligations which they contracted by virtue of the United Nations Framework Convention on Climate Change, approved on behalf of the Community by Council Decision 94/69/EC of 15 December 1993 (OJ 1994 L 33, p. 11), and by virtue of the Protocol of the third conference of the parties

to that Convention, done in Kyoto on 11 December 1997, signed by the European Community and its Member States on 29 April 1998 (see *inter alia* Council Resolution 98/C 198/01 of 8 June 1998 on renewable sources of energy (OJ 1998 C 198, p. 1), and Decision No. 646/2000/EC of the European Parliament and of the Council of 28 February 2000 adopting a multiannual programme for the promotion of renewable energy sources in the Community (Altener) (1998 to 2002) (OJ 2000 L 79, p. 1)).

75 It should be noted that that policy is also designed to protect the health and life of humans, animals and plants.

76 Moreover, as stated in the third sentence of the first subparagraph of Article [11 TFEU], environmental protection requirements must be integrated into the definition and implementation of other Community policies . . .

It is not clear from the judgment whether a Treaty derogation or a mandatory requirement is being relied upon. This is partly because the Treaty does not in fact contain a clear environmental exception. The free movement of goods derogation, Article 36 TFEU, refers instead to the life and health of humans, animals and plants, an apparently narrow concept. Admittedly, it could be interpreted to cover all kinds of environmental harm, but it is sometimes an uncomfortable stretch, leading the Court of Justice in this case to choose studied ambiguity. The absence of a clear naming of the environment in Article 36 is distinctly old-fashioned, but the Court is clearly not going to allow this to have undesirable consequences. There are a number of cases now where measures specifically affecting cross-border movement have been justified by environmental protection, contrary to the general rule that mandatory requirements only excuse equally applicable rules.[108]

This can be explained by the repeated Treaty references to the importance of the environment generally, and within EU policies. Environmental protection is not an ordinary mandatory requirement, nor an ordinary Treaty derogation, but rather a condition for the legitimacy of all policies. *Commission* v. *Austria*, where a ban on heavy goods traffic on certain roads was in issue, makes this clear.

Commission v. Austria (Heavy Goods Trucks), C–28/09, EU:C:2011:854

119 It is settled case-law that national measures liable to obstruct intra-Community trade may be justified on one of the public-interest grounds set out in Article 30 EC, such as the protection of human health and life, or one of the overriding requirements relating *inter alia* to protection of the environment, provided that the measures in question are proportionate to the objective sought.

120 It should be recalled that the protection of health and the protection of the environment are essential objectives of the European Union. Article 2 EC states that the Community has, as one of its tasks, to promote 'a high level of protection and improvement of the quality of the environment' and Article 3(1)(p) EC states that the activities of the Community are to include a contribution to the attainment of 'a high level of health protection'.

---

[108] *Commission* v. *Belgium (Walloon Waste)*, C-2/90, EU:C:1992:310 v; *PreussenElektra*, C-379/98, EU:C:2001:160; *Chemische Afvalstoffen Dusseldorp BV and Others* v. *Minister van Volkhuisvesting, Ruimtelijke Ordening en Milieubeheer*, C-203/96, EU:C:1998:316; *Ålands Vindkraft*, C-573/12, EU:C:2014:2037.

121 Furthermore, in accordance with Articles 6 EC and 152(1) EC, the requirements of environmental protection and public health must be taken into account in the definition and implementation of Community policies and activities. The transversal and fundamental nature of those objectives is also reaffirmed in Articles 37 and 35 respectively of the Charter.

122 As to the relationship between the objectives of protection of the environment and protection of health, it is apparent from Article 174(1) EC that the protection of human health is one of the objectives of Community policy on the environment. Those objectives are closely linked, in particular in connection with the fight against air pollution, the purpose of which is to limit the dangers to health connected with the deterioration of the environment. The objective of protection of health is therefore already incorporated, in principle, in the objective of protection of the environment.

123 In those circumstances, the arguments of the Republic of Austria on protection of health need not be considered separately from those on protection of the environment.

The 'incorporation' of public health – a Treaty derogation – within environmental protection – a mandatory requirement – may not have been doctrinally important to the outcome of the case, but it is rhetorically striking.

Another type of environmental restriction which has been considered by the Court of Justice concerns the transportation of waste. In *Walloon Waste*, the Court considered a Wallonian ban on the import of waste from anywhere outside that region of Belgium.[109] The Court accepted the measure was justified on the basis of the proximity principle – namely, that waste should be disposed of as close to the place of production as possible. The ecological basis for such a principle is that it avoids the environmental costs and risks of transporting the waste and establishes a principle of environmental equity. Clean places are not to bear the environmental costs generated by dirty places. However, the judgment is contentious. The reach of the proximity principle is unclear. *Walloon Waste* covered a regional restriction, but it is far harder to justify a similar national restriction, as that would permit waste to be transported over long distances. More fundamentally, the principle is unsatisfactory as an instrument for allocating environmental costs.[110] Most industrial waste is produced in locations far away from where the good is consumed and, in an integrated European economy, it is not really fair to expect the people who live close to the factory to bear the full cost of disposal. The inevitable duplication of facilities associated with such a principle, in addition, increases the risk of waste facilities being placed in locations which, in ecological terms, are far from ideal and deprives operators of the most suitable sites for waste disposal.

The operation of the proximity principle is made more difficult by the use of different reasoning for waste for recovery. In *Afvalstoffen Dusseldorp*,[111] an application to export two loads of oil filters for processing was refused by the Dutch authorities on the grounds that, under Dutch law, export of waste for recovery was only permitted if there were superior processing techniques abroad or there was insufficient capacity in the Netherlands. The Court of Justice

---

[109] *Commission* v. *Belgium (Walloon Waste)*, C-2/90, EU:C:1992:310 v.

[110] P. von Wilmowsky, 'Waste Disposal in the Internal Market: The State of Play after the ECJ's Ruling on the Walloon Import Ban' (1993) 30 *CMLRev* 541, 547–7; D. Chalmers, 'Community Policy on Waste Management: Managing Environmental Decline Gently' (1994) 14 *YBEL* 257, 280–4.

[111] *Chemische Afvalstoffen Dusseldorp BV and Others* v. *Minister van Volkhuisvesting, Ruimtelijke Ordening en Milieubeheer*, C-203/96, EU:C:1998:316 v.

noted that such an export restriction provided an advantage for national facilities. It enabled the Dutch undertaking, AVR Chemie, which recovered the waste, to operate in a profitable manner and to use the filters as a cheap source of fuel. The Court found that there was no evidence of a health risk resulting from transport, and so no justification for the restriction on export of waste with an economic value. From an ecological perspective, however, the transport risks for both forms of waste are the same, and there is still the danger of dirty regions offloading waste onto clean regions. Advocates of the proximity principle have therefore been highly critical of *Dusseldorp*.[112] It may be that the reasons for the distinction are more pragmatic, economic ones. Waste recovery is a large and growing industry. Preventing its development on a European scale might bring some environmental benefits, but would also bring significant economic costs.[113]

6 PUBLIC HEALTH

In its initial case law on public health, the Court simply looked at the answers provided by international science. If there was doubt or international science ruled something unsafe, a Member State would be justified in banning the product. Increasingly, this test appeared unsatisfactory.[114] In many scenarios knowledge developed, so what had formerly appeared certain was now less so. In other scenarios, it would be unrealistic to assume zero risk as this would be something that science could never certify. Therefore, the Court of Justice has increasingly moved towards a proceduralist test of whether a sufficiently rigorous risk assessment has been carried out. An example of this new approach is *Dutch Vitamins*.[115] With a couple of exceptions, Dutch legislation prohibited the addition of a number of vitamins to foods. The Dutch argument was not that these vitamins were dangerous in themselves, but that ingestion of excess quantities could be dangerous. In this, they relied on general studies. There was no study that estimated the likelihood of risk. For this reason, the Court of Justice found the Dutch legislation to be illegal. It stated its general approach in the following manner.

Commission v. Netherlands (Dutch Vitamins), C-41/02, EU:C:2004:762

47 Furthermore, since [Article 36 TFEU] provides for an exception, to be interpreted strictly, to the rule of free movement of goods within the Community, it is for the national authorities which invoke it to show in each case, in the light of national nutritional habits and in the light of the results of international scientific research, that their rules are necessary to give effective protection to the interests referred to in that provision and, in particular, that the marketing of the products in question poses a real risk for public health . . .

---

[112] N. Notaro, 'The New Generation Case Law on Trade and Environment' (2000) 25 *ELRev* 467.

[113] Movements of waste within the European Union are now governed exclusively by Regulation 259/93 on the supervision and control of shipments of waste [1993] OJ L 30/11. This retains the distinction made in the case law, however: *DaimlerChrysler* v. *Land Baden-Württemberg*, C-324/99, EU:C:2001:682; for discussion, see G. van Calster, 'The Free Movement of Waste after *DaimlerChrysler*' (2002) 27 *ELRev* 610.

[114] *Frans-Nederlandse Maatschappij voor Biologische Producten*, 272/80, EU:C:1981:312.

[115] *Commission* v. *Netherlands (Dutch Vitamins)*, C-41/02, EU:C:2004:762. See also *Commission* v. *Germany*, C-319/05, EU:C:2007:678; *Commission* v. *Spain*, C-88/07, EU:C:2009:123.

48 A prohibition on the marketing of foodstuffs to which nutrients have been added must therefore be based on a detailed assessment of the risk alleged by the Member State invoking [Article 36 TFEU] . . .

49 A decision to prohibit the marketing of a fortified foodstuff, which indeed constitutes the most restrictive obstacle to trade in products lawfully manufactured and marketed in other Member States, can be adopted only if the real risk for public health alleged appears sufficiently established on the basis of the latest scientific data available at the date of the adoption of such decision. In such a context, the object of the risk assessment to be carried out by the Member State is to appraise the degree of probability of harmful effects on human health from the addition of certain nutrients to foodstuffs and the seriousness of those potential effects . . .

50 In assessing the risk in question, it is not only the particular effects of the marketing of an individual product containing a definite quantity of nutrients which are relevant. It could be appropriate to take into consideration the cumulative effect of the presence on the market of several sources, natural or artificial, of a particular nutrient and of the possible existence in the future of additional sources which can reasonably be foreseen . . .

51 In a number of cases, the assessment of those factors will demonstrate that there is much uncertainty, in science and in practice, in that regard. Such uncertainty, which is inseparable from the precautionary principle, affects the scope of the Member State's discretion and thus also the manner in which the precautionary principle is applied.

52 It must therefore be accepted that a Member State may, in accordance with the precautionary principle, take protective measures without having to wait until the existence and gravity of those risks become fully apparent . . . However, the risk assessment cannot be based on purely hypothetical considerations . . .

53 A proper application of the precautionary principle requires, in the first place, the identification of the potentially negative consequences for health of the proposed addition of nutrients, and, secondly, a comprehensive assessment of the risk for health based on the most reliable scientific data available and the most recent results of international research . . .

54 Where it proves to be impossible to determine with certainty the existence or extent of the alleged risk because of the insufficiency, inconclusiveness or imprecision of the results of studies conducted, but the likelihood of real harm to public health persists should the risk materialise, the precautionary principle justifies the adoption of restrictive measures.

Dutch Vitamins suggests that, following a risk assessment, if the Member State finds a likelihood of real harm then, based on the precautionary principle, it can ban the good.

This leaves open the question whether Member States may impose restrictions for reasons of nutrition. This is a particular concern as the dangers posed by obesity mount in the European population. In *Sandoz*, permission was sought to market muesli bars to which vitamins A and D had been added. Authorisation was refused on the grounds that although these vitamins were necessary for a healthy life, too much of them could be dangerous. The Court of Justice held that Member States could ban a substance if there was a danger that it could be taken to excess as part of the general nutrition, and the individual amounts consumed could neither be monitored nor foreseen.[116] In *French Vitamins*, a broader ban was involved. The French authorities refused to allow vitamins or nutrients to be added to food unless there was a nutritional need.[117] The

---

[116] *Sandoz*, 174/82, EU:C:1983:213.
[117] *Commission v. France (French Vitamins)*, C-24/00, EU:C:2004:70 v; see also *Commission v. Denmark*, C-192/01, EU:C:2003:492.

Court found this restriction to be unlawful. The blanket ban was not based on specific dangers, but just on the general view that such additives were not necessary. This fact could not, in itself, justify a ban. Even very small concrete risks can justify measures, but purely nutritional aspects of food are reserved to the sovereignty of the consumer.[118]

Restrictions on nutritional content can only be imposed, therefore, if the nutritional content of the good is felt to lead to some harm or be part of some threat to public health. An argument to this effect could certainly be made with respect to fat, salt or carbohydrate levels in food, and it would not be difficult to produce relevant scientific evidence. The approach in *Sandoz* could be used to justify regulation of food aimed at combating obesity. Just like vitamins A and D, fats, salt and carbohydrates are essential in some quantities, and dangerous in excess. Nevertheless, the politics and economics of such regulation would clearly be quite different, as the rules would have a far broader effect, and would also be difficult to adopt in a coherent and consistent way – many traditional and natural foods are as fatty, salty or sugary as processed ones. The Court of Justice has not closed the door to the use of food law to attack obesity, but the demands of proportionality and consistency would make such a policy challenging.

A criticism of the case law is that it is too narrow. By focusing exclusively on demonstrable threats, it chooses a test that is different from that chosen by many consumers when they decide whether food is safe or not. The latter weave in considerations such as how the food is produced, by whom and the effect on the environment. Trust in the producer, ideas about naturalness and purity, and mistrust of scientific progress, may all influence the consumer in her judgments about the risks food poses to her.[119] These may not be factors for which expert evidence can be produced, but they are relevant to consumers, so should they not be relevant to the law?[120]

Another question to arise is the administration of health restrictions. Whilst sampling of imports will often be permitted on grounds of public health, the Court of Justice has shown itself to be unsympathetic to systematic analysis. It was held disproportionate, in the absence of fraud or irregularities, for the French authorities to inspect three out of four consignments of Italian wine, and the Court, in its interim measures, ordered the French to inspect no more than 15 per cent of the consignments.[121] Conversely, a Directive authorising national authorities to check one in three consignments was not considered to be disproportionate.[122] This is an area, however, where there can clearly be very little certainty, as the number of inspections that may be permissible will depend upon the nature of the goods and other circumstances, such as whether there has been a recent outbreak of a particular disease.

7 PUBLIC POLICY, PUBLIC SECURITY AND PUBLIC MORALITY

Public policy, public security and public morality are treated as separate headings in the Treaty. Historically, they have also been treated differently in the case law. Public policy and public security have been treated, on the one hand, as interchangeably protecting the fundamental

---

[118] For a measure held lawful that constituted a minuscule risk to health, see *Hahn*, C-121/00, EU:C:2002:611.

[119] See G. Davies, 'Morality Clauses and Decision-making in Situations of Scientific Uncertainty: The Case of GMOs' (2007) 6 *World Trade Review* 249.

[120] B. Wynne, 'Scientific Knowledge and the Global Environment' in M. Redclift and T. Benton (eds.), *Social Theory and the Global Environment* (London, Routledge, 1994) 169, 175–6.

[121] *Commission* v. *France*, 42/82, EU:C:1983:88.

[122] Directive 77/93/EEC [1977] OJ L 26/20; *Rewe-Zentrale* v. *Landwirtschaftskammer Rheinland*, 37/83, EU:C:1984:89.

interests of a society.[123] Public morality has been concerned to secure the central values of a society.[124] However, there is no morality exception provided except for free movement of goods, so where morals questions arise in other fields they are treated as public policy matters. *Omega* concerned a German prohibition on a laser game, where people simulated killing each other, on the grounds that it violated the German constitutional provision protecting human dignity.[125] The measure was concerned with the protection of a fundamental value and was essentially about the moral standards of society. The Court of Justice, nevertheless, treated the matter as one of public policy, showing the fluidity and interchangeability of the concepts. Such fluidity is also evident in *Josemans*, where a Dutch policy restricting drugs tourism was in issue.[126] The Court noted the differing opinions of the parties on whether public policy or security were relevant grounds for the restriction, without actually settling the issue, merely noting that:

65 It must be pointed out that combating drug tourism and the accompanying public nuisance is part of combating drugs. It concerns both the maintenance of public order and the protection of the health of citizens, at the level of the Member States and also of the European Union.

66 Given the commitments entered into by the European Union and its Member States, there is no doubt that the abovementioned objectives constitute a legitimate interest which, in principle, justifies a restriction of the obligations imposed by European Union law.

The use of the phrase 'public order' is notable, since this has recurred in other cases, and it has been suggested that there is a move towards an umbrella 'European public order' exception whereby Member States are free to take measures to protect the central interests, symbols and values of their societies, and the Court of Justice engages in a more marginal form of appraisal.[127] An example of judicial rhetoric which might support this idea is found in *Ladbrokes*, yet another gambling case.[128]

Ladbrokes, C–258/08, EU:C:2010:308

18 Article 46(1) EC allows restrictions justified on grounds of public policy, public security or public health. A certain number of overriding reasons in the public interest which may also justify such restrictions have been recognised by the case-law of the Court, including, in particular, the objectives of consumer protection and the prevention of both fraud and incitement to squander money on gambling, as well as the general need to preserve public order.

19 In that context, moral, religious or cultural factors, as well as the morally and financially harmful consequences for the individual and for society associated with betting and gaming, may serve to justify a margin of discretion for the national authorities, sufficient to enable them to determine what is required in order to ensure consumer protection and the preservation of public order.

---

[123] *Ministre de l'Intérieur v. Olazabal*, C-100/01, EU:C:2002:712.   [124] *R v. Henn and Darby*, 34/79, EU:C:1979:295.

[125] *Omega Spielhallen- und Automatenaufstellungs v. Oberbürgermeisterin der Bundesstadt Bonn*, C-36/02, EU:C:2004:614; see p 830.

[126] *Josemans*, C-137/09, EU:C:2010:774.

[127] G. Straetmans, 'Note on Case C-124/97 *Läärä* and Case C-67/98 *Zenatti*' (2000) 37 *CMLRev* 991, 1002–5.

[128] *Ladbrokes*, C-258/08, EU:C:2010:308.

20 The Member States are free to set the objectives of their policy on betting and gambling according to their own scale of values and, where appropriate, to define in detail the level of protection sought. The restrictive measures that they impose must, however, satisfy the conditions laid down in the case-law of the Court, in particular as regards their proportionality.

The particular moral, cultural and religious particularities of the Member States are acknowledged as justifying unique standpoints, and yet the use of the 'margin of appreciation' concept makes clear that this is within a broader EU framework of what is acceptable, and the framing concept that the Court of Justice chooses (perhaps counter-intuitively for moral and religious questions) is that of public order, albeit coupled with consumer protection.

Despite any margins of discretion, there are still constraints which Member States must observe. The central issues are usually the necessity of the measure, and the coherence of the national policy, as discussed above. *Conegate, Adoui, Van Duyn, Henn and Darby* and the gambling cases were all about public policy or morality.[129]

Public security is an even stronger governmental card, which judges are traditionally shy of challenging. The Court of Justice is primarily concerned to establish that the measure actually serves the right aim. In *Commission* v. *Greece*, a challenge was brought to Greek rules on the storage of petroleum.[130] Oil companies operating in Greece were required to maintain a store of petroleum in Greece, which was justified by the national security interest in a domestic oil reserve. However, they could also transfer this reserve to a national refinery (that is to say, the refinery would maintain a store on their behalf) but only if and to the extent that they had purchased oil from this refinery in the last year. The Court was comfortable with the obligation to maintain national stores, but the creation of a system which protected and benefited national refineries appeared to have nothing to do with the storage goal, and could not be justified by Article 36 TFEU.

In *Commission* v. *France*, public policy was used, unusually, to justify inaction rather than action. French farmers had blocked cross-border roads and ports to prevent imports of agricultural products, which they regarded as unfair, or at any rate undesirable, competition. The French Government, to the despair of its trading partners, did nothing. The blockades happened several times over a period of years, sometimes going on for weeks at a time, and occasionally involving eruptions of violence against foreign trucks, goods and drivers. One of the arguments put forward by the French Government in its defence was that public feeling was so strong, particularly among the farmers but also in the general population, that if it were to use the police to clear roads and reopen ports this might lead to a breakdown of public order. The government was afraid of provoking demonstrations and riots and losing control.

Having found that the French Government had not taken sufficient measures to guarantee the free movement of goods, the Court of Justice went on to consider whether these arguments in defence could be accepted.

---

[129] See pp. 831–2.   [130] *Commission* v. *Greece*, C-398/98, EU:C:2001:565 v.

> **Commission v. France (Spanish Strawberries)**, C-265/95, EU:C:1997:595
>
> 54 The above finding is in no way affected by the French Government's argument that the situation of French farmers was so difficult that there were reasonable grounds for fearing that more determined action by the competent authorities might provoke violent reactions by those concerned, which would lead to still more serious breaches of public order or even to social conflict.
>
> 55 Apprehension of internal difficulties cannot justify a failure by a Member State to apply Community law correctly.
>
> 56 It is for the Member State concerned, unless it can show that action on its part would have consequences for public order with which it could not cope by using the means at its disposal, to adopt all appropriate measures to guarantee the full scope and effect of Community law so as to ensure its proper implementation in the interests of all economic operators.
>
> 57 In the present case the French Government has adduced no concrete evidence proving the existence of a danger to public order with which it could not cope.
>
> 58 Moreover, although it is not impossible that the threat of serious disruption to public order may, in appropriate cases, justify non-intervention by the police, that argument can, on any view, be put forward only with respect to a specific incident and not, as in this case, in a general way covering all the incidents cited by the Commission.
>
> 59 As regards the fact that the French Republic has assumed responsibility for the losses caused to the victims, this cannot be put forward as an argument by the French Government in order to escape its obligations under Community law.
>
> 60 Even though compensation can provide reparation for at least part of the loss or damage sustained by the economic operators concerned, the provision of such compensation does not mean that the Member State has fulfilled its obligations.

The Court of Justice suggests that if feeling on an issue is sufficiently strong that a Member State is essentially unable to enforce EU law, or would be unable to deal with the consequences of such enforcement, this might justify non-action. The same could presumably be translated to positive acts: if a Member State takes measures restricting free movement because it otherwise fears consequences with which it cannot cope, this could also be legitimate. However, the judgment shows that such arguments will be regarded with great suspicion, and measures will be very strictly limited to what is necessary. Such a breakdown of order justification will be truly exceptional.

Part of the reason for such strictness is not just the cost for EU policy of national derogations, but the cost for individuals. Free movement is presented as a 'fundamental freedom' of Europeans which must be valued, but traditional human rights can be equally relevant. Where Member States do derogate, a condition for the legitimacy of their action is that any measure should respect both fundamental rights[131] and general principles of law. This is often particularly relevant to procedural questions, where Member States make exercise of EU rights conditional upon procedures which may be inaccessible, arbitrary or otherwise unfair.[132]

8 PUBLIC SERVICE AND OFFICIAL AUTHORITY

The public service and official authority exceptions apply to the free movement of workers, and to establishment and services, respectively. They have long been interpreted in parallel. The core

---

[131] *Schmidberger v. Republic of Austria*, C-112/00, EU:C:2003:333. [132] See pp. 846–9.

question surrounding them has always been their scope – which kinds of jobs or activities fall within?

In early cases on public service Member States argued for a formalist approach, catching all those paid by the State, however menial or non-sensitive their role. They wanted to keep as much control as possible over their employees and employment policies.[133] One reason was that State employment has traditionally been used to manage unemployment, an increase in the number of State functionaries being a politically acceptable way to provide jobs. That made it convenient to be able to reserve these jobs for nationals.

In some cases, such jobs were also part of broader social engineering. State employees may be posted to various regions, so that public jobs were not only about reducing unemployment but also about redeploying the population to areas where their social or economic impact might be more beneficial – for example, taking unemployed urban youth and transferring them to aging and underpopulated rural areas.

Yet although those policy goals may be legitimate, total exclusion of foreigners from State employment is neither a necessary nor proportionate requirement for achieving them.[134] More-over, the post-war growth of Welfare States, and the increase in the size of the State generally, meant that quite soon after the founding of the EEC a large proportion of the workforce in most States was in some sense a State employee. Taking these out of the free movement of workers would have made an enormous hole in that policy and significantly limited its impact. It would also have created political tensions as the scope of public employment, and thus of access to the labour market for foreigners, varied from State to State.[135] There would also have been an incentive created for States to act via public employees or institutions rather than via the market.

As a result of these considerations the Court consistently rejected a broad interpretation of the exceptions, reading them in the way that they were probably originally intended, having been written in a time when the State was not ubiquitous. It found the exceptions to extend only to functions which go to the heart of public power, and which demand a particular loyalty to the State, such as the judiciary, armed forces and senior or sensitive posts in the national or regional administration. In *Commission* v. *Belgium* it gave its standard definition, that the public service included only

> posts which involve direct or indirect participation in the exercise of powers conferred by public law and duties designed to safeguard the general interests of the state or of other public authorities. Such posts in fact presume on the part of those occupying them the existence of a special relationship of allegiance to the state and reciprocity of rights and duties which form the foundation of the bond of nationality.[136]

The core element appears to be the exercise of power on behalf of the State, as well as particular obligations of loyalty or duty. Nevertheless, this is vague, and the Court has tended to give case-by-case decisions rather than expanding on the definition. Teachers, nurses and general municipal employees are not within the exception. Yet it found that night watchmen or those in

---

[133] See *Commission* v. *Belgium (No. 2)*, 149/79, EU:C:1982:195.
[134] Advocate General Mancini in *Commission* v. *France*, 307/84, EU:C:1986:150.
[135] *Commission* v. *Belgium (No. 2)*, 149/79, EU:C:1982:195.
[136] *Commission* v. *Belgium (No. 1)*, 149/79, EU:C:1980:297, para. 10.

charge of a railway yard, who clearly have safety responsibilities, might be.[137] These are, perhaps, bearers of public authority in a way that the others are not, authorised quite possibly to take coercive decisions in certain circumstances. No one has put it better than Advocate General Mancini:

> Those who occupy the post must don full battle dress: in non-metaphorical terms, their duties must involve acts of will which affect private individuals by requiring their obedience or, in the event of disobedience, by compelling them to comply.[138]

'Official authority' is built on similar ideas. A useful description of what it entails is found in *Commission* v. *Germany*. Here it was argued that the special traffic privileges granted to ambulances, and the nature of the working relationship they enjoyed with the police in emergency situations, meant that ambulance services should be considered to fall within official authority. The Court of Justice disagreed.

Commission v. *Germany (Ambulance Services)*, C-160/08, EU:C:2010:230

73 According to the first paragraph of Article 45 EC, in conjunction with Article 55 EC, the provisions relating to the freedom of establishment and the freedom to provide services do not extend to activities which in a Member State are connected, even occasionally, with the exercise of official authority.

74 As the Advocate General stated at point 51 of her Opinion, such activities are also excluded from the scope of directives which, like Directives 92/50 and 2004/18, are designed to implement the provisions of the Treaty relating to the freedom of establishment and the freedom to provide services.

75 It is necessary, therefore, to determine whether the ambulance service activities at issue in the present case are among the activities referred to in the first paragraph of Article 45 EC.

76 In that regard, it must be borne in mind that, as derogations from the fundamental rules of freedom of establishment and freedom to provide services, Articles 45 EC and 55 EC must be interpreted in a manner which limits their scope to what is strictly necessary in order to safeguard the interests which they allow the Member States to protect.

77 Moreover, it has consistently been held that the review of the possible application of the exceptions laid down in Articles 45 EC and 55 EC must take into account the fact that the limits imposed by those articles on the exceptions referred to fall within European Union law.

78 According to settled case-law, the derogation provided for under those articles must be restricted to activities which, in themselves, are directly and specifically connected with the exercise of official authority.

79 As the Advocate General noted at point 58 of her Opinion, such a connection requires a sufficiently qualified exercise of prerogatives outside the general law, privileges of official power or powers of coercion.

80 In the present case, it must first be observed that a contribution to the protection of public health, which any individual may be called upon to make, in particular by assisting a person whose life or health are in danger, is not sufficient for there to be a connection with the exercise of official authority.

81 As regards the right of ambulance service providers to use equipment such as flashing blue lights or sirens, and their acknowledged right of way with priority under the German Highway Code, they certainly reflect the overriding importance which the national legislature attaches to public health as against general road traffic rules.

---

[137] *Commission* v. *Belgium (No. 2)*, 149/79, EU:C:1982:195. v.   [138] *Commission* v. *France*, 307/84, EU:C:1986:222. v.

82 However, such rights cannot, as such, be regarded as having a direct and specific connection with the exercise of official authority in the absence, on the part of the providers concerned, of official powers or of powers of coercion falling outside the scope of the general law for the purposes of ensuring that those rights are observed, which, as the parties agree, is within the competence of the police and judicial authorities.

83 Nor can matters such as those raised by the Federal Republic of Germany – concerning special organisational powers in the field of the services delivered, the power to request information from third parties and the deployment of other specialist services, or even involvement in the appointment of civil service administrators in connection with the services at issue – be regarded as reflecting a sufficiently qualified exercise of official powers or of powers falling outside the scope of the general law.

84 As the Federal Republic of Germany also asserted, the fact that the provision of public ambulance services entails collaboration with the public authorities and with professional staff on whom official powers have been conferred, such as members of the police force, does not constitute evidence that the activities of those services have a connection with the exercise of official authority either.

85 The same applies to the fact, also maintained by the Federal Republic of Germany, that agreements relating to the service contracts at issue come within the scope of public law and that the activities concerned are carried out on behalf of those public-law bodies which take on responsibility for public emergency services.

86 It follows from this that the Court cannot accept that Articles 45 EC and 55 EC are applicable to the activities at issue in the present case.

The core concepts are clearly the possession of State-like powers or authorities, of which powers of coercion are the most obvious example. By contrast, the mere possession of privileges such as the right to break the highway code or have flashing lights on a car does not, alas, suffice. Nor will a purely marginal or theoretical exercise of public authority suffice: in *Haralambidis* the Court said:

> However, recourse to that derogation cannot be justified on the sole ground that powers of a public authority are attributed under national law to the President of a Port Authority. It is also necessary that those powers be in fact exercised on a regular basis by that holder and do not constitute a minor part of his duties.[139]

A related question which has arisen quite often is how close to that public power the activity has to be. In *Peñarroja Fa*, it was argued that a court translator, as part of the court system, producing documents with legal force on behalf of a judge, should be seen as part of official authority. The Court of Justice developed the idea that the connection with public power must be direct, and the activity must be truly a part of that power, not just ancillary to it.

Peñarroja Fa, C–372/09, EU:C:2011:156

43 In the case before the referring court, it is apparent from the documents placed before the Court that the duty of a court expert translator, at issue in the main proceedings, is to provide to a high standard an impartial translation from one language to another, not to give an opinion on the substance of the case.

---

[139] *Haralambidis*, C–270/13, EU:C:2014:2185, para. 58.

44 The translations carried out by such an expert are therefore merely ancillary steps and leave the discretion of judicial authority and the free exercise of judicial power intact, so that – as submitted by Mr Peñarroja Fa, the French Government, the European Commission and the EFTA Surveillance Authority – such translation services cannot be regarded as activities connected with the exercise of official authority.

Somewhat similarly, notaries do not exercise official authority, and nor are they in the public service when employed.[140] Their acts may help provoke the State to action, but they are not one of its arms.

In *Commission* v. *Portugal* it was argued that vehicle testing therefore did fall within official authority, since the businesses involved actually conducted the tests and issued certificates which were necessary if the vehicle was to be allowed on the road; their activities were the very stuff of State coercive power. Yet the Court of Justice disagreed, on the basis that they were directly supervised by a public authority, rendering them apparently mere servants of power, not bearers of it.[141]

Commission v. Portugal, C–438/08, EU:C:2009:651

36 Thus, according to settled case-law, the derogation for which that article provides must be restricted to activities which, in themselves, are directly and specifically connected with the exercise of official authority, which excludes from being regarded as 'connected with the exercise of official authority', within the meaning of that derogation, functions that are merely auxiliary and preparatory vis-à-vis an entity which effectively exercises official authority by taking the final decision.

37 The Court has defined further the distinction between activities of private bodies constituting simple preparatory tasks and those constituting a direct and specific connection with the exercise of official authority by finding that, even where private bodies exercise the powers of a public authority, drawing the conclusions from the inspections which they carry out, Article 45 EC cannot be relied on where the applicable legislation lays down that those private bodies are to be supervised by the public authority. The Court has found that private bodies carrying out their activities under the active supervision of the competent public authority, responsible, ultimately, for inspections and decisions of those bodies, cannot be considered to be 'connected directly and specifically with the exercise of official authority' within the meaning of Article 45 EC.

38 According to the indications contained in the application and in the defence, the carrying out of roadworthiness tests on vehicles in Portugal falls within the competence of a public establishment, the Public Institute for Mobility and Transport by Land, which can, however, have recourse to private bodies in order to carry out those inspections. The decision whether or not to certify the roadworthiness of vehicles is taken by the private vehicle inspection body without any intervention by the public administrative authority.

---

[140] E.g. *Commission* v. *Czech Republic*, C-575/16, EU:C:2018:186; *Commission* v. *Hungary*, C-392/15, EU:C:2017:73; *Commission* v. *Latvia*, C-151/14, EU:C:2015:577; *Commission* v. *Belgium*, C-47/08, EU:C:2011:334; *Commission* v. *France*, C-50/08, EU:C:2011:335; *Commission* v. *Luxembourg*, C-51/08, EU:C:2011:336; *Commission* v. *Austria*, C-53/08, EU:C:2011:338; *Commission* v. *Germany*, C-54/08, EU:C:2011:339; *Commission* v. *Greece*, C-61/08, EU:C:2011:340; *Commission* v. *Netherlands*, C-157/09, EU:C:2011:794; *Commission* v. *Portugal*, C-52/08, EU:C:2011:337.

[141] *Hiebler*, C-293/14, EU:C:2015:843.

39   As is moreover apparent from the defence, the activity of vehicle inspection establishments is organised in two stages. The first stage of that activity consists in carrying out technical inspections, that is, in verifying whether the vehicles inspected comply with the technical standards applicable and drawing up a report of the inspection recording the details of the tests carried out and the results obtained. The second stage of that activity includes certification of the inspection carried about by affixing a badge to the vehicle or, conversely, the refusal of such certification.

40   The tasks within the first stage are of a technical nature and thus unrelated to the exercise of official authority. On the other hand, the second stage, involving the certification of roadworthiness, includes the exercise of public authority powers, in that it concerns the drawing of legal conclusions from the roadworthiness test.

41   In that regard, it should, none the less, be pointed out that the decision whether or not to certify roadworthiness, which essentially only records the results of the roadworthiness test, on the one hand, lacks the decision-making independence inherent in the exercise of public authority powers and, on the other hand, is taken in the context of direct State supervision.

      . . .

44   In addition, as the Commission has pointed out, without being contradicted by the Portuguese Republic, the private vehicle inspection bodies, in connection with their activities, have no power of coercion, the right to impose penalties for failure to comply with the rules on vehicle inspection belonging to the police and judicial authorities.

45   Consequently, the activities of the private vehicle roadworthiness testing bodies concerned in this case do not fall within the exception provided for in Article 45 EC. It is thus necessary to examine whether the regime for access to vehicle inspection implemented by the Portuguese Republic can be justified.

The Court went on to find that the conditions imposed on businesses wanting to engage in vehicle testing were overly restrictive, and not justified.

As well as restricting the core concept of public service and official authority, which are interpreted in parallel, the Court of Justice has made clear that they must be applied to specific functions, rather than to institutions as a whole. *Commission* v. *Italy* concerned the Italian national research centre, in which all posts were reserved for Italians.[142] Part of the justification was that senior and management posts involved advising the government and contributing to policy formation. The Court accepted this, but found that it did not justify extending the exclusion to all researchers. The judgment had the consequence that foreign researchers might come up against a ceiling to their career, since unlike their Italian colleagues they could be legitimately denied promotion to the reserved senior posts. However, the Court emphasised that such discrimination must be kept to a minimum, and did not justify, for example, only employing foreigners on short-term contracts. Where foreigners were employed, they were entitled to equality of conditions, and this must be reconciled with their more limited promotion prospects to the greatest extent possible.

Finally, the concept of public service may include work for private employers, if these are engaged in the service of the State and exercising public law powers.[143] This is quite logical: if the activities of a private organisation may be official authority, then the employees carrying out

[142] *Commission* v. *Italy*, 225/85, EU:C:1987:284.
[143] *Anker*, C-47/02, EU:C:1987:284; *Colegio de Oficiales de la Marina Mercante Española* v. *Administración del Estado*, C-405/01, EU:C:2003:515.

those activities may be expected to fall within the concept of public service. However, the privatisation of public functions means there are many difficult lines now to be drawn, and adds another layer of complexity to this particular derogation. The preference for distinctions based on the interests at stake, rather than formal public or private status, is consistent with the wider approach of free movement law, and in particular with the ruling in *Bosman* that public policy derogations from free movement could, in principle, be relied upon by private parties.[144]

FURTHER READING

A. Arcuri, 'The Case for a Procedural Version of the Precautionary Principle: Erring on the Side of Environmental Protection' 10(4) *Global Law Working Paper* (New York, Hauser Global Law School, 2004).

C. Barnard, 'Derogations, Justifications and the Four Freedoms: Is State Interest Really Protected?' in C. Barnard and O. Odudu (eds.), *The Outer Limits of European Law* (Oxford, Hart, 2009).

G. Davies, 'Process and Production Method-based Restrictions on Trade in the EU' in C. Barnard (ed.), *Cambridge Yearbook of European Legal Studies* (Oxford, Hart, 2008).

N. Georgiadis, *Derogation Clauses: The Protection of National Interests in EC Law* (Brussels, Bruylant, 2006).

J. Gerards, 'Pluralism, Deference and the Margin of Appreciation Doctrine' (2011) 17 *European Law Review* 80.

W. Haslehner, '"Consistency" and Fundamental Freedoms: The Case of Direct Taxation' (2013) 50 *Common Market Law Review* 737.

P. Koutrakos, N. Nic Shuibhne and P. Syrpis, *Exceptions from EU Free Movement Law* (Oxford, Hart, 2016).

C. Macmaolain, 'Free Movement of Foodstuffs, Quality Requirements and Consumer Protection: Have the Court and the Commission Both Got it Wrong?' (2001) 26 *European Law Review* 413.

G. Mathisen, 'Consistency and Coherence as Conditions for Justification of Member State Measures Restricting Free Movement' (2010) 47 *Common Market Law Review* 1021.

N. Nic Shuibhne and M. Maci, 'Proving Public Interest: The Growing Impact of Evidence in Free Movement Case Law' (2013) 50 *Common Market Law Review* 965.

W. Sauter and J. Langer, 'The Consistency Requirement in EU Law' (2017) 24 *Columbia Journal of European Law* 39.

J. Scott, 'Of Kith and Kine (and Crustaceans): Trade and Environment in the EU and WTO' in J. Weiler (ed.), *The EU, NAFTA and the WTO: Towards a Common Law of International Trade* (Oxford University Press, 2000).

J. Scott, 'Mandatory or Imperative Requirements in the EU and WTO' in C. Barnard and J. Scott (eds.), *The Law of the European Single Market: Unpacking the Premises* (Oxford, Hart, 2002).

J. Snell, 'Economic Aims as Justifications for Restrictions on Free Movement' in A. Schrauwen (ed.), *The Rule of Reason: Rethinking Another Classic of Community Law* (Groningen, Europa Law Publishing, 2005).

---

[144] *Union Royale Belge des Sociétés de Football Association and Others* v. *Bosman and Others*, C-415/93, EU:C:1995:463.

20

EU Competition Law: Function and Enforcement

CONTENTS

1   INTRODUCTION

When the European Economic Community (EEC) Treaty was negotiated, there was considerable pressure by Americans, but also by segments of Europe's academic community, that competition law should be included in the Treaty.[1] However, at that time, the 'culture of competition' had yet to emerge in most Member States, who traditionally favoured cartel arrangements, State intervention and the promotion of national champions.[2] Indeed, some Member States only introduced national competition laws as late as the 1990s, and even today in some countries enforcement is emerging or unstable.[3] Thus, when provisions were first introduced to curb restrictive practices in the coal and steel sector (by Articles 65 and 66 of the European Coal and Steel Community Treaty), these were an innovation for the Member States.[4] Originally the purpose of introducing competition law into the EEC Treaty was to complement the internal market rules by preventing businesses from partitioning the internal market and by encouraging competition across borders.[5] Today, the need for EU competition law as a means of securing economic welfare is widely accepted and the rules are enforced robustly by the Commission.

The present chapter considers why competition law is important and how it is enforced. It is organised as follows.

Section 2 is a review of the debates about the objectives of EU competition law. It shows that there are divided opinions on two fronts: first, between those who consider that the application of competition law should focus on maximising economic welfare and those who take the view that competition law is about the pursuit of economic and non-economic considerations; and secondly that even among those who think that economics offers a superior paradigm for applying competition law, there are differences of opinion about how to best deploy economic thinking. This section of the chapter is essential reading for an understanding of the subject, because, as will be seen in Chapter 23, these differences can have a significant impact on how competition law is applied and enforced.

Section 3 examines the enforcement powers of the European Commission. It explains how the Commission investigates cases, the procedures for reaching a decision, and the penalties that may be imposed if an infringement is found. Attention is given to the effectiveness of the enforcement scheme as well as to its legitimacy, measured by how well it safeguards the fundamental rights of those under investigation.

Section 4 considers the significance of Regulation 1/2003. This Regulation 'entrusted the national competition authorities with a key role in ensuring that the EU competition rules are applied effectively and consistently, in conjunction with the Commission'.[6] It was a significant and controversial measure. It gave greater prominence to national competition authorities, and changed the role of the Commission.

---

[1] D. J. Gerber, *Law and Competition in Twentieth Century Europe* (Oxford University Press, 1998) ch. 9.

[2] H. G. Schröter, 'Cartelization and Decartelization in Europe, 1870–1995: Rise and Decline of an Economic Institution' (1996) 25 *Journal of European Economic History* 129. An exception was West Germany's competition law drafted in 1957.

[3] Examples of latecomers include: Ireland and Italy in 1990, the Netherlands in 1997, Luxembourg in 2004. The enforcement of competition law in Italy is advanced in part but certain markets remain closed to competition. See L. Berti and A. Pezzoli, *Le Stagioni dell'Antitrust* (Milan, EGEA, 2010). Furthermore, in exchange for receiving financial aid from the Union, a number of Member States have been required to strengthen their competition laws. For an overview see G. Monti, 'Independence, Interdependence and Legitimacy: The EU Commission, National Competition Authorities and the European Competition Network', EUI Department of Law Research Paper 2014/01.

[4] Jean Monnet, *Mémoires* (Paris, Fayard, 1976) 356–7, 411–13 (also noting US pressure to implement anti-cartel laws).

[5] G. Marenco, 'The Birth of Modern Competition Law in Europe' in A. von Bogdandy, P. Mavroidis and Y. Mény (eds.), *European Integration and International Coordination: Studies in Transnational Economic Law in Honour of C.-D. Ehlermann* (The Hague, Kluwer, 2002) esp. 297–8.

[6] European Commission, 'Report on the Functioning of Regulation 1/2003', COM(2009)206 final, para. 28.

Section 5 reviews the rules relating to the private enforcement of EU competition law. It considers the contribution of the Court of Justice, the Damages Directive and the value and role of private enforcement.

Section 6 discusses the possible impact of Brexit on competition law enforcement in the United Kingdom.

2 AIMS OF EU COMPETITION LAW

There is considerable debate regarding the functions of competition law. Today, the majority view is that competition law should be enforced against firms whose behaviour harms consumers. Against this, there are two alternative views. One is that competition law should not be concerned with an outcome (consumer welfare) but with maintaining the competitive process. Another view is that competition law can be enforced to attain a wider set of economic and non-economic ambitions; for example, it may be enforced to promote national industries, to safeguard employment or to protect the environment. In section (i) below, we sketch a justification of the role of competition law derived from the discipline of economics, which supports the majority view. In some jurisdictions (most notably the United States), scholars argue that competition law should be interpreted solely according to what economic theory dictates.[7] This mainstream view is contingent upon advances in economics, so that lawyers are called upon to reflect new learning in the application of the law. In section (ii), we consider the alternative points of view. In section (iii), we turn to explore how far these competing approaches have influenced EU competition law enforcement, and in section (iv) we discuss recent debates that stem from the great recession.

(i) Economics of Competition

From an economic perspective, competition law should prohibit commercial practices that damage the operation of markets. Accordingly, the principal measuring stick of a good competition law is how well it sustains an efficient economic order by prohibiting conduct that reduces efficiency.

> **M. de la Mano, 'For the Customer's Sake: The Competitive Effects of Efficiencies in European Merger Control', Enterprise Papers No. 11 (Brussels, Enterprise Directorate General, 2002) 8–14**
>
> Economists generally distinguish between three broad classes of efficiencies all of which are relevant for the analysis of competition: allocative, productive (or technical) and dynamic (or innovation) efficiency.
>
> *Allocative efficiency*: Allocative efficiency is achieved when the existing stock of (final and intermediate) goods are allocated through the price system to those buyers who value them most, in terms of willingness

---

[7] R. H. Bork, *The Antitrust Paradox* (New York, The Free Press, 1978, repr. 1993); R. A. Posner, *Antitrust Law*, 2nd edn (University of Chicago Press, 2000). The major debate here is whether this is best achieved with a consumer welfare standard or a total welfare standard. See e.g. R. D. Blair and D. D. Sokol, 'Welfare Standards in US and EU Antitrust Enforcement' (2003) 81 *Fordham L Rev* 2497.

to pay or willingness to forego other consumption possibilities. At an allocatively efficient outcome, market prices are equal to the real resource costs of producing and supplying the products.

Productive (or technical) efficiency: Productive efficiency is a narrower concept than allocative efficiency, and focuses on a particular firm or industry. It addresses the question of whether any given level of output is being produced by that firm/industry at least cost or, alternatively, whether any given combination of inputs is producing the maximum possible output. Productive efficiency depends on the existing technology and resource prices. The state of technology determines what alternative combinations of resources can produce a given amount of output. Resource prices determine which combination of resources is the most efficient one in that it gives rise to the lowest production cost. Productive efficiency is achieved when output is produced in plants of optimal scale (or minimum efficient scale) given the relative prices of production inputs.

Dynamic (or innovation) efficiency: Allocative and productive efficiency are static notions concerned with the performance of an economy, industry or firm at a given point in time, for a given technology and level of existing knowledge. Dynamic efficiency in antitrust economics is connected to whether appropriate incentives and ability exist to increase productivity and engage in innovative activity over time, which may yield cheaper or better goods or new products that afford consumers more satisfaction than previous consumption choices.

The distinction between static (allocative or productive) efficiency and dynamic efficiency is based on the idea that the latter leads to improvements in the available technology or the discovery of new production processes or products. In other words, dynamic efficiency is related to the ability of a firm, industry or economy to exploit its potential to innovate, develop new technologies and thus expand its production possibility frontier.

These definitions provide us with the main tools to evaluate the performance of industry. Suppose that manufacturers of escalators agree among each other to raise prices. The implementation of this agreement serves to raise prices well above cost (allocative inefficiency), it reduces demand so that the manufacturers are not using their resources optimally (productive inefficiency) and, since the firms cooperate in a way that is mutually beneficial, the incentive to innovate is reduced (dynamic inefficiency). This example typifies the kinds of considerations an economist makes to test if behaviour by firms is to be challenged as anti-competitive. It has also been suggested that there is a further economic harm: cartels are well-organised political players who can lobby successfully for legislative measures to exclude rivals.[8] This particular concern is also found in monopolies.

M. de la Mano, 'For the Customer's Sake: The Competitive Effects of Efficiencies in European Merger Control', Enterprise Papers No. 11 (Brussels, Enterprise Directorate General, 2002) 8–14

Further, monopoly rents will tend to be dissipated as firms, in order to establish or defend a dominant position, are willing to spend anything up to the value of their monopoly profits. Such expenditures may take various forms: excess advertising, research and development (R&D), investment in excess capacity or

---

[8] G. Amato, *Antitrust and the Bounds of Power* (Oxford, Hart, 1997).

brand proliferation in order to deter entry from rival firms, lobbying to secure government quotas or licences, etc. Often this expenditure is in itself entirely unproductive (e.g. lobbying) although other expenditures may partly lead to consumer benefits (as in the case of R&D that results in innovations). These examples imply that the costs of market power through weakened productive efficiency may be at least as important as its adverse impact on allocative efficiency.

The upshot is that competition law should be mostly concerned with manifestations of market power, where the likelihood of inefficient outcomes is higher. However, diagnosing market power and identifying harmful practices has evolved, and we trace this history briefly here.

In the 1960s, some economists believed that there was a direct causal relation between market structure and economic performance, whereby the fewer the firms (and thus the more concentrated the market), the less competitive the industry. This view (often labelled the 'Harvard School' view, as the main proponents were Harvard economists) influenced the development of US antitrust law (called antitrust rather than competition law, as its earliest actions were against cartels established in the form of trusts) until the 1970s, when the economic mood swung away from this exclusively structural understanding of markets.[9] One of the major policy consequences of this approach was that mergers were viewed with suspicion and conduct likely to exclude rivals was also of concern as both strategies would serve to exclude rivals, increasing concentration and thereby worsening economic performance. This led to aggressive antitrust enforcement.

In the 1970s, the 'Chicago School' championed a different set of opinions about how markets worked and advocated a more lax degree of scrutiny.[10] Their arguments can be summarised in the following manner. First, while it is true that a firm with a large market share may be tempted to behave anti-competitively by reducing output and increasing prices, this kind of behaviour will send a signal to other market players that there is unmet demand in the market, and invite the entry of new firms. This new entry will bring prices down and reintroduce the degree of competition necessary to satisfy consumer desires. In other words, while acknowledging that market structure may affect economic performance, the Chicago School added the rider that if economic performance led to unmet consumer demand, this would cause the entry of other firms. This economic dynamic meant that competition law was largely unnecessary unless new entry was hampered, and the greatest reason why entry was hampered was national legislation limiting business freedom, not the anti-competitive behaviour of business. Absent barriers for new competitors, the market would heal itself. Secondly, while the Harvard School lamented the increasing concentration of firms, the Chicago School argued that concentrated markets were more efficient because firms would be able to exploit economies of scale (that is, it is relatively cheaper for one firm to manufacture millions of cars than for several firms to manufacture a

[9] See F. M. Scherer and G. Ross, *Industrial Market Structure and Economic Performance*, 3rd edn (Boston, MA, Houghton Mifflin, 1990) ch. 1 for a review of this approach. See the policy prescriptions in C. Kaysen and D. F. Turner, *Antitrust Policy: An Economic and Legal Analysis* (Cambridge, MA, Harvard University Press, 1959).

[10] H. Hovenkamp, 'Antitrust Policy after Chicago' (1986) 84 *Mich L Rev* 213; F. H. Easterbrook, 'Workable Antitrust Policy' (1986) 84 *Mich L Rev* 1696; B. Hawk, 'The American Antitrust Revolution: Lessons for the EEC?' (1988) *ECLR* 53. For a more critical perspective see E. M. Fox and L. A. Sullivan, 'Antitrust – Retrospective and Prospective: Where Are We Coming From? Where Are We Going?' (1987) 62 *NYUL Rev* 936.

thousand cars each). Thirdly, the Chicagoans believed that law enforcers were more likely to damage the competitive process by their intervention because of their ignorance about how markets worked.

The Chicago and Harvard views can diverge significantly in their prescriptions for competition law enforcement. For example, a Harvard School approach would suggest that high prices by a monopoly are illegal but a Chicago School approach would indicate that high prices invite new entry, which would render the market competitive in the long run. The Chicago School is probably the most influential school of thought in competition law. It set out a coherent view of competition law enforcement, embedded in confidence that markets work best without excessive regulation by States or courts. It was contested by 'post-Chicago' economic theories.[11]

M. S. Jacobs, 'An Essay on the Normative Foundations of Antitrust Economics' (1995–6) 74 *North Carolina Law Review* 219, 222–5

A post-Chicago School of economics has arisen, working within the efficiency model, but starting from assumptions and ending with an enforcement methodology markedly different from Chicago's . . . Both agree that economics is 'the essence of antitrust' and that protecting consumer welfare, conceived in allocative efficiency terms, should be the exclusive goal of competition law. Both eschew the subjective inquiries that they ascribe to the overtly political approaches of the past, and both assert that unless business conduct raises prices or reduces output it should be left alone, regardless of the political or distributive consequences.

The new debate involves contending visions of the workings of the market mechanism and of the proper model for antitrust enforcement. Chicagoans believe that markets tend toward efficiency, that market imperfections are normally transitory, and that judicial enforcement should proceed cautiously, lest it mistakenly proscribe behavior that promotes consumer welfare. Post-Chicagoans, by contrast, believe that market failures are not necessarily self-correcting, and that firms can therefore take advantage of imperfections, such as information gaps or competitors' sunk costs, to produce inefficient results even in ostensibly competitive markets. They argue that the distortions to competition made possible by market imperfections should prompt enforcement authorities to scrutinize a wider variety of conduct than Chicagoans would examine. On the doctrinal level, this debate has produced conflicting answers to some of antitrust's most pressing questions: the relevant measures of market power, the competitive effects of tying arrangements and other vertical restraints, the economic plausibility of predatory pricing schemes, and the durability of cartels and oligopolies.

On its surface, the nature of this debate confirms the view that antitrust analysis has taken a decidedly technological turn . . . What apparently divide the parties are not their political ideologies or interpretations of history, but differing evaluations of the efficiency implications of their respective theories and methodologies. Indeed, some post-Chicagoans characterize their work not as an alternative to Chicago thinking but as a refinement of it, an effort to provide decisionmakers with a more accurate picture of the marketplace and more sensitive tools for detecting inefficient behavior.

---

[11] See H. Hovenkamp, 'Post-Chicago Antitrust: A Review and Critique' (2001) *Colum. Bus. L. Rev* 257; L. A. Sullivan and W. S. Grimes, *The Law of Antitrust: An Integrated Handbook*, 2nd edn (St Paul, MN, West Publishing, 2006), a textbook written taking into account many post-Chicago insights; R. Pitofsky (ed.), *How the Chicago School Overshot the Mark* (Oxford University Press, 2008).

These appearances, however, are deceptive. The parties' shared commitment to efficiency and the debate's specialized vocabulary mask deep divisions regarding the normative assumptions most appropriate to competition policy. The contending economic models reflect very different views of human nature, firm behavior, and judicial competence. While Chicagoans assume that the desire to maximize profits drives firms to compete away market imperfections and destabilizes collusive activity, post-Chicagoans believe that strategizing firms can create or perpetuate market imperfections that can seriously hamper competitive balance. Similarly, while Chicagoans presuppose that markets promote efficient business behavior and that judges untrained in economics are ill-equipped to identify and measure market imperfections, post-Chicagoans have less trust in markets and more confidence in the judiciary's ability to distinguish between competitive and anticompetitive conduct. Post-Chicagoans have shown that the neoclassical price model [based on assumptions that individuals have rational preferences and act based on all relevant information to maximise income (firms) or utility (consumers)] is not the only method for analyzing the efficiency questions central to antitrust. They have demonstrated that economists equally loyal to the goal of consumer welfare can disagree markedly with price theorists about the means most conducive to allocative efficiency. In doing so, however, they have revealed, albeit unintentionally, the inability of economics to furnish empirical or theoretical criteria for resolving the differences between their model and Chicago's. Their work has produced a stalemate in economic theory that effectively requires antitrust decisionmakers, most of whom accept the legitimacy of the economic model, to probe the technocratic surface of the current debate and evaluate the conflicting beliefs about firms, markets, and governments embedded in its foundation. Ironically, far from having marginalized the role of value choice in antitrust discourse, the ascendancy of economic models underscores its enduring importance.

The post-Chicago approach leads to suggestions for competition law enforcement that are different from the Chicago model. For example, under a Chicago approach, predatory pricing (that is, prices set at a level below the cost of production) is only unlawful when the predator is able to cause all rivals to exit and monopolise the market. In contrast, under post-Chicago theories, predatory pricing can be held to be unlawful even if the predator does not monopolise the market. Instead, predatory pricing may be a way of hurting competitors to 'discipline' them (e.g. if a firm is well-established in the United Kingdom and its competitor mainly sells in Germany, predatory pricing might be used by the UK firm should the German firm try to penetrate the UK market, the aim being not the destruction of the German competitor, but the maintenance of separate markets) or to establish a reputation as a tough competitor (e.g. in a market where entry is relatively easy, one bout of predatory pricing against a new entrant may discourage other firms from entering, even when it might be economically rational to enter).[12] Jacobs suggests that these differences of opinion about what is economically rational belie a series of value assumptions about how markets work. Therefore, competition law cannot be founded upon economics; rather it is premised upon the assumptions we make about how market players operate. On this argument, a competition authority chooses an economic theory that supports those assumptions.

[12] A. Kate and G. Neils, 'On the Rationality of Predatory Pricing: The Debate Between Chicago and Post-Chicago' (2002) *Antitrust Bulletin* 1. However, these new approaches have not been very successful. For a discussion of why this may be so, see N. Giocoli, 'Games Judges Don't Play: Predatory Pricing and Strategic Reasoning in US Antitrust' (2013) 21 *Supreme Court Economic Review* 271.

A further, similar, challenge to the Chicago School approach comes from behavioural economics. This approach to economics rejects the assumption of mainstream economic theory that actors behave rationally, and this has an effect on how one regulates markets. In the specific context of antitrust, irrationality may manifest itself on the side of consumers (who mishandle information, or make decisions based on factors like loyalty or an over-inflated perception of risk) and producers (who may similarly read market signals poorly). For instance, it has been suggested that firms entering new markets assume they will be successful, when in reality few manage to make any lasting inroads: this suggests that the Chicagoan view that low entry barriers reduce the risk of anti-competitive behaviour might be too limited if new entrants fail to bring discipline to the market. This means more sophisticated evidence is required to test if there is market power.[13]

A final economic issue to consider is the role of dynamic efficiency. We might object to the pharmaceutical sector being monopolised by one firm, but what if this is the only way to concentrate enough resources to obtain life-saving drugs in the future? How much can we suffocate competition today in favour of greater consumer benefits tomorrow? Some have taken the view that innovation requires large firms so that monopolies are more likely to innovate, while others have taken the view that innovation can only take place if new entrants are protected by competition law regulating the firms that monopolise the market.[14] There is no consensus on the best competition policy to facilitate innovation, although 'antitrust economists recognise that dynamic net efficiency gains from continuing innovation may far outweigh the static gains from marginal-cost pricing'.[15] However, competition authorities have tended to focus on allocative and productive efficiency.[16]

It is worth closing with the following consideration: the post-Chicago and behavioural antitrust approaches, and the concerns over dynamic efficiency pose sound qualifications to a Chicago-based perspective but they have not led to major changes in enforcement policy. The reason for this has largely to do with considerations of institutional design.

W. E. Kovacic, 'The Intellectual DNA of Modern Competition Law for Dominant Firm Conduct: The Chicago/Harvard Double Helix' (2007) 1(1) *Columbia Business Law Review* 1, 36–7, 72

Antitrust rules should not outrun the capabilities of implementing institutions. Among other points, Areeda and Turner [founding authors of the leading multi-volume treatise on US antitrust law] argued

---

[13] A. Tor, 'The Fable of Entry: Bounded Rationality, Market Discipline, and Legal Policy' (2002) 101 *Mich L Rev* 482.

[14] See D. S. Evans and R. Schmalensee, 'Some Economic Aspects of Antitrust Analysis in Dynamically Competitive Industries' in A. B. Jae, J. Lerner and S. Stern (eds.), *Innovation Policy and the Economy* (Cambridge, MA, NBER and MIT Press, 2002) vol. II; G. Monti, 'Article 82 EC and New Economy Markets' in C. Graham and F. Smith (eds.), *Competition, Regulation and the New Economy* (Oxford, Hart, 2004); J. D. Balto and R. Pitofsky, 'Challenges of the New Economy: Issues at the Intersection of Antitrust and the New Economy' (2001) 68 *Antitrust Bulletin* 913.

[15] M. de la Mano, 'For the Customer's Sake: The Competitive Effects of Efficiencies in European Merger Control', Enterprise Papers No. 11 (Brussels, Enterprise Directorate General, 2002) 14.

[16] Although dynamic efficiency considerations played a role in the *Microsoft* decision, where the firm indicated the risk that the European Commission's action would undermine dynamic efficiency (summary at: [2007] OJ L 32/23); and in *GlaxoSmithKline Services Unlimited* v. *Commission*, C-501/06 P, C-513/06 P, C-515/06 P and C-519/06 P, ECLI:EU:C:2009:610, where the ECJ confirmed that dynamic efficiencies may be pleaded under Article 101(3) TFEU.

that antitrust rules and decision-making tasks must be administrable for the central participants in the antitrust system (courts, enforcement agencies, the private bar, and business managers); that special substantive and procedural screens should be used to ensure that suits initiated by private antitrust plaintiffs were consistent with larger social aims; and that remedies should be carefully linked to the harm caused by the specific practices found to have constituted improper behaviour . . .

Post-Chicago scholars often falter because they make unduly hopeful assumptions about the capacity of the key implementing institutions of the antitrust system to apply the insights of Post-Chicago analysis skillfully. By this view, non-interventionist presumptions are endorsed not because they inevitably make sound assumptions about the harms of specific forms of business behavior, but instead because they make more accurate assumptions about the limitations of courts and enforcement agencies.

In other words, the conservative economic approach of the Chicago School is supported in large part because it is legally workable given the institutional setting for law enforcement in the United States. In particular, jury trials caution against the use of complex economic theories which may be misunderstood, punitive damages awards for antitrust offences often invite spurious claims that courts must ward off,[17] and the level of expertise and capacity of an antitrust authority limits the degree to which it can regulate certain complex markets where specific regulators have a comparative advantage.[18]

(ii) Politics of Competition Law

The debates about the economics of competition law often seem technical and non-political. However, as Jacobs argued above, there is an inherent political dimension to competition law, even when analysed through an economic perspective.

E. M. Fox and L. A. Sullivan, 'Antitrust – Retrospective and Prospective: Where are We Coming From? Where are We Going?' (1987) 62 *New York University Law Review* 936, 942, 956–9

Many economists, especially those with Chicago leanings, think that because antitrust is about markets, as is microeconomics, antitrust law should be economics. They react as though the law is out of kilter whenever it diverges from their particular economic insight; and they so react regardless of whether the law diverges because empirical processes have not validated factual assumptions, or because the law has identified social goals other than or in addition to allocative efficiency.

Law is not economics. Nor were the antitrust laws adopted to squeeze the greatest possible efficiency out of business.

Finally, the producer-plus-consumer-welfare paradigm presses the analyst to think only in terms of aggregate outcomes or wealth of the nation. But this concept is static and outcome-oriented, while the

---

[17] *Brunswick Corp.* v. *Pueblo Bowl-O-Mat, Inc.* 429 US 477 (1977), denying damages when the conduct in question was pro-competitive.

[18] E.g. *Verizon* v. *Trinko*, 540 US 398 (2004), refusing to extend the scope of antitrust law on the facts because there is a dedicated telecommunications regulator tasked with promoting competition.

antitrust laws are dynamic and process-oriented. They protect not an outcome, but a process – competition. Antitrust laws set fair rules of the game. They give rights of access and opportunity. The antitrust laws preserve and foster dynamic interactions among those in the market. They deal not with aggregate national wealth, but with the expectations and behavior of the people who participate in the markets.

The American debate is particularly instructive in setting out the values that animate competition policy. As Fox has suggested more recently, the real point of debate presently is between those who consider that antitrust law should only be enforced when one proves a harmful economic outcome (or at most the strong likelihood of a harmful economic outcome) and those who believe that it should also be enforced when certain actions weaken the competitive process, by weakening rivals.[19]

Moreover, Fox and Sullivan locate competition law within the perspective of a liberal economic order, which has a particular affinity to the origins of EU competition law. In its early years, EU competition law was influenced by German scholarship and German officials played a key role in the development of competition law. Underpinning the German approach to competition was a unique economic philosophy: ordoliberalism.[20]

W. Möschel, 'Competition Policy from an Ordo Point of View' in A. Peacock and H. Willgerodt (eds.), *German Neo-liberals and the Social Market Economy* (London, Macmillan, 1989) 146

The actual goal of the competition policy of Ordo-liberalism lies in the protection of individual economic freedom of action as a value in itself, or vice versa, in the restraint of undue economic power. Franz Böhm once illuminated this idea by the aphoristic formula, 'the one who has power has no right to be free and the one who wants to be free should have no power'. Economic efficiency as a generic term for growth, for the encouragement and development of technical progress and for allocative efficiency, is but an indirect and derived goal. It results generally from the realisation of individual freedom of action in a market system . . .

This is contrary to the various concepts of utilitarianism. In this respect the Ordo-liberal competition policy is obviously related to the intellectual traditions of idealist German philosophy, particularly that of Immanuel Kant . . . Modern currents in the American anti-trust law which lean directly upon wealth maximisation, [like] Richard Posner's constrained utilitarianism . . . are obviously incompatible with the Ordo-liberal system of values. Ordo-liberalism treats individuals as ends in themselves and not as means of another's welfare.

Here, the dislike of market power is not based primarily on fears of inefficiency, rather on concerns that firms with market power can stifle the freedom of other economic operators, and this leads to inefficiency. Like Fox and Sullivan, the process of competition, favouring access

---

[19] E. M. Fox, 'Against Goals' (2013) 81 *Fordham L Rev* 2157.

[20] See also D. J. Gerber, *Law and Competition in Twentieth Century Europe* (Oxford University Press, 1998) ch. 7; W. Möschel, 'The Proper Scope of Government Viewed from an Ordoliberal Perspective: The Example of Competition Policy' (2001) 157(1) *Journal of Institution and Theoretical Economics* 3.

and opportunities for new businesses, is valued. This vision has had a strong influence on the development of EU competition law.[21] Protecting the competitive process or competitive outcomes does not make a significant practical difference in most cases (e.g. both condemn cartels and mergers that create a dominant player). The major difference (as we will examine more closely in the following chapter) is over exclusionary conduct. Taking predatory pricing again, an economic approach would condemn it only if it is likely that the conduct harms welfare, while an approach protecting the competitive process would condemn it a step before: once it is likely that the conduct excludes market players. One criticism that may be made of the latter approach is that it is not always clear how to translate the notion of competitive process when faced with a set of facts: to a certain extent every contract reduces competition (if I agree to sell all my books to you, nobody else can buy them), but it is hard to find a test by which one decides what degree of reduction is sufficiently meaningful to merit prohibition, and there is a risk that one slides into taking a very formalistic approach which applies the prohibition too aggressively.[22]

Originally the Commission enforced competition law informed by this approach, but it is currently recalibrating its rules to focus more on examining the effects of suspicious conduct. Those that support the old policy have three major concerns: first, the absence of any debate at EU level about the choice to abandon the model of competition based on safeguarding the competitive process and favouring an economic approach; secondly, that an economic approach may lead to reduced enforcement, especially against the most powerful firms, while harming smaller players; and thirdly, that the mainstream economic approach focuses on allocative efficiency (i.e. measuring the direct impact on consumers today) at the expense of promoting dynamic efficiency.[23]

(iii) Aims of EU Competition Policy

It was only in the late 1980s that EU competition policy took shape. This happened as a result of five factors. First, the neoliberal economic policies championed by Reagan in the United States and Thatcher in the United Kingdom began to affect governments and industries across Europe, and the economic liberalisation called for by the Single European Act necessitated a stronger role for competition law to ensure that the transformation from a mixed economy to a free market occurred smoothly. Secondly, the Court of Justice, since the 1960s, had ruled on a number of competition law cases and established strong precedents that consolidated the Commission's powers. Thirdly, the staff morale at the Directorate General (DG) for Competition (charged with enforcing competition law in the Union) was considerably strengthened by the economic and legal backing that emerged in the 1980s. Fourthly, the personalities of the competition Commissioners were instrumental in strengthening this DG. Two competition commissioners, Peter

---

[21] D. Gerber, 'Constitutionalising the Economy: German Neo-Liberalism, Competition Law and the "New" Europe' (1994) 42 *AJCL* 25, 69–74.

[22] C. Ahlborn and C. Grave, 'Walter Eucken and Ordoliberalism: An Introduction from a Consumer Welfare Perspective' (2006) 2(2) *Competition Policy International* 197.

[23] I. L. O. Schmidt, 'The Suitability of the More Economic Approach for Competition Policy: Dynamic vs. Static Efficiency' (2007) *ECLR* 408; Bundeskartellamt/Competition Law Forum, 'A Bundeskartellamt/Competition Law Forum Debate on Reform of Article 82: A Dialectic on Competing Approaches' (2006) 2 *ECJ* 211; R. Zäch and A. Künzler, 'Freedom to Compete or Consumer Welfare: The Goal of Competition Law according to Constitutional Law' in R. Zäch, A. Heinemann and A. Kellerhals (eds.), *The Development of Competition Law* (Cheltenham, Edward Elgar, 2009).

Sutherland (1985–9) and Sir Leon Brittan (1989–93), were instrumental in pursuing and extending the free market logic, often leading to clashes between the views espoused by DG Competition and those of the Commission President, Jacques Delors. Finally, in 1990, the Commission obtained powers to regulate mergers in the Union. With the economic restructuring that was taking place as a result of economic liberalisation, this placed EU competition law at the heart of the Union's transformation to a neoliberal market economy.[24]

Two aspects of this evolution are worthy of note. First, the increased emphasis on the benefits of efficient markets undermined concerns about economic power and economic freedom that were seminal in the early development of EU competition law. Secondly, the Commissioner for competition policy can have a direct role in influencing the general direction of competition policy. For instance, Sir Leon Brittan's advocacy of free markets was instrumental in the early success of the implementation of the merger rules. His successor, Karel van Miert (1993–9), however, was less convinced than his predecessor about grounding competition law in free market terms, favouring an approach that considers the impact of competition law 'in other areas of Commission policy, such as industrial policy, regional policy, social policy and the environment'.[25] His replacement, Mario Monti (1999–2004), an economics professor, steered competition policy back along the lines taken by Sutherland and Brittan, and the Commissioners who have followed him have more or less continued to follow this policy line. In particular, the speeches of these Commissioners make regular reference to the benefits consumers obtain as a result of competition law enforcement, whether this is lower prices as a result of dismantling a cartel, or more choice as a result of removing certain contract terms.[26] However, it should be recalled that competition law (and indeed, the economic provisions in the Treaty) are there also for the development of a strong European industry.[27] And a closer study of the development of the Community shows that an even broader range of objectives have influenced EU competition law.

R. Wesseling, *The Modernisation of EC Antitrust Law* (Oxford–Portland, Hart, 2000) 48–9

Initially, the antitrust law provisions were inserted into the Treaty in view of their role in the process of market integration. The antitrust rules were no more than the private counterpart to the rules, enshrined in Arts 28–30 EC which guaranteed freedom to trade across borders without hindrance from the Community's Member States. The framers of the Treaty wanted to preclude private undertakings replacing the prohibited public obstacles to inter-State trade. The first period of Community antitrust policy [1958–1973][28] saw

---

[24] L. McGowan, 'Safeguarding the Economic Constitution: The Commission and Competition Policy' in N. Nugent (ed.), *At the Heart of the Union: Studies of the European Commission*, 2nd edn (Basingstoke, Macmillan Press, 2000) 151–3; R. Buch-Hansen and A. Wigger, *The Politics of European Competition Regulation: A Critical Political Economy Perspective* (Abingdon, Routledge, 2011).

[25] Karel van Miert, 'The Competition Policy of the New Commission', EGKartellrechtsforum der Studienvereinigung Kartellrecht Brussels 11/5/1995, http://europa.eu.int/comm/competition/index_en.html.

[26] See e.g. M. Monti, 'European Competition for the 21st Century' (2001) *Fordham Corporate Law Institute* 257, 257–8; M. Vestager, 'Introductory Statement to the European Parliament' 2 October 2014, https://ec.europa.eu/commission/commissioners/2014–2019/vestager_en.

[27] European Commission, 'A Pro-Active Competition Policy for a Competitive Europe', COM(2004)293 final, esp. ch. 2.

[28] The author uses the same time periods as J. Weiler, 'The Transformation of Europe' (1991) 100 *Yale LJ* 2403.

the Commission enforcing the rules with constant reference to ensuring the free flow of goods, thus promoting market integration.

Subsequently, in the second period [1973–1985], antitrust policy was employed to establish a broader Community industrial policy. Exemptions for the antitrust rules were granted to forms of (trans-national) co-operation between undertakings which the Commission considered desirable, to promote either integration (*Eurocheque*) or broader Community policy aims (e.g. employment in crisis sectors). Thus, a Community industrial policy was gradually developed on the basis of the Treaty's antitrust rules.

The momentum generated by the Commission's '1992 programme' then provided the occasion for expanding the scope of Community antitrust policy even further [in the third period commencing in 1985]. With continued reference to the needs of market integration, the Commission acquired powers under the Merger Regulation to regulate the structure of markets. Furthermore it extended the enforcement of the antitrust rules to the public sectors of the various Member States. While reference was still made to the underpinning of Community antitrust law in economic integration, the socio-political implications of integration by competition (law) became ever more apparent. In this respect the control of corporate mergers and the gradual liberalisation of public economic sectors, both highly political exercises, which commenced by the end of the 1980s, symbolise the altered character of Community antitrust law enforcement.

Although the system was originally devised for promoting market integration, antitrust policy is now also – and mainly – directed at promoting the various objectives of the Community enshrined in Article 2 EC. Absent a clear hierarchy between those objectives, priorities are selected on a case by case basis. Agreements between undertakings have been exempted from the prohibition in Article 81(1) EC when their negative effect on the intensity of competition on the relevant market was outweighed by positive consequences for European industry's competitiveness, or for social and economic cohesion. Likewise, mergers are sometimes held compatible with the common market, in spite of the significant reduction in the degree of competition they engender, when the Commission considers that they may contribute to one or more of the objectives laid down in Article 2 EC. While it is not submitted that the majority of antitrust issues is settled on the basis of extra-competition elements, it is evident from the Commission decisions, endorsed by the European Courts, that the Commission is able to pursue 'flanking' policies on the basis of its enforcement of the antitrust rules.

This review suggests that a wide range of policy issues affect competition law decisions, and that competition law objectives might at times take second place to other EU values. On the one hand, we might be sympathetic to the use of competition law to sustain other policies, but this would be to forget that there are other, direct means to achieve them. For example, if we wish to reduce pollution, we might prefer banning pollutants than tolerating an agreement among firms to phase out certain polluting equipment which might yield higher prices.[29] Secondly, legal certainty for market participants is undermined if competition law is modified to achieve other objectives. Lastly, there is a risk that by securing other policies, markets may not develop efficiently and thereby harm consumers. These concerns, among others, led the Commission to try and concentrate on regulating markets only when there was harm to consumer welfare.

[29] L. Kaplow, 'On the Choice of Welfare Standards in Competition Law' in D. Zimmer (ed.), *The Goals of Competition Law* (Cheltenham, Edward Elgar, 2012).

However, as we illustrate in this and the following chapters, there remain episodes where competition is enforced for the pursuit of other goals.

(iv) Impact of the Economic Crisis

The great recession which commenced in 2008 has led to two rounds of rethinking the objectives of competition law. During the crisis, the question arose whether competition law should be applied less strictly. The Commission refused maintaining that competition law enforcement is part of the solution to the economic crisis. Firms cannot be allowed to form cartels as a means of surviving the crisis: some firms should exit the market if they are not competitive, to allow the more efficient firms to serve consumers best. Nor can merger control be made more lenient to support politically important industries. The former Competition Commissioner, Neelie Kroes, described this approach as 'tough love'.[30] The one concession was reducing some cartel fines if this would lead to an 'increase in unemployment or deterioration in the economic sectors upstream and downstream of the undertaking concerned'.[31] The second was the application of the State aid rules to facilitate the rescue of banks.[32]

The justification of this stance is the following: first, in the aftermath of the recession of 1929 the US Government had supported a relaxation of antitrust laws but an influential study came to the conclusion that this made matters worse, not better.[33] Secondly, the Commission reflected back on its own management of the oil crisis in the 1970s and concluded that its lax approach to competition law, which included allowing the formation of so-called crisis cartels (i.e. agreements between manufacturers to reduce output collectively so as to ensure that all firms survived) was a failure because it did not force industries to adjust.[34] Furthermore, Wigger and Buch-Hansen have suggested that while crises normally lead to policy changes, the present crisis has not made an impression for five reasons. First, the policy approach has been to fix the current economic system rather than rethink it; secondly, this approach has the backing of major industrial and financial interest groups as well as politicians; thirdly, no concrete alternative to the current economic system has been identified. The fourth and fifth reasons are given in the extract below.

A. Wigger and H. Buch-Hansen, 'Explaining (Missing) Regulatory Paradigm Shifts: EU Competition Regulation in Times of Economic Crisis' (2013) *New Political Economy* 1, 18

Fourth, the Commission, enjoying significant powers and a considerable degree of operational autonomy from Member State governments, has been able to take a proactive approach in acting as a neoliberal crisis manager, interfering with national-level crisis management and prescribing ever more vigorous neoliberal

---

[30] Neelie Kroes, 'Competition, the Crisis and the Road to Recovery', address at Economic Club of Toronto, Speech/09/152, 30 March 2009.

[31] *Novácke chemické závody a.s.* v. *Commission*, T-352/09, ECLI:EU:T:2012:673, para. 192. P. Kienapfel and G. Wils, 'Inability to Pay: First Cases and Practical Experiences' (2010) 3 *Competition Policy Newsletter* 3.

[32] See Ch. 23.

[33] H. L. Cole and L. E. Ohanian, 'New Deal Policies and the Persistence of the Great Depression: A General Equilibrium Analysis' (2004) 112 *Journal of Political Economy* 779.

[34] OECD Global Forum on Competition, *Crisis Cartels* (DAF/COMP/GF(2011)11) 109–20.

policies. By being strategically selective, it has privileged the interests of organised financial capital and national crisis strategies compatible with neoliberal ideas. The relative strength of the DG, namely its institutional independence, discretionary powers and resources as well as ensuing business support, allowed it to oppose fundamental institutional change, thereby marginalising more radical solutions from the outset and thus the possibility for a regulatory paradigm shift.

The fifth and final factor relates to the absence of a wider shift in the regulation of economic activities . . . Recent studies in the fields of EU financial services regulation, EU trade policies and international tax policies as well as the budget austerity programmes orchestrated by the EU-IMF tandem more generally suggest that neoliberalism is currently being reworked and extended in various regulatory fields rather than being abandoned. Against the backdrop of the prevalence of a neoliberal crisis management filling merely regulatory gaps in the financial sector, a paradigm shift in the field of EU competition regulation is also unlikely at this stage.

After the crisis, however, with growing evidence of inequality and seeing that many industries are composed of a small number of large players, pressure is being exerted to invest in more rigorous competition law enforcement.[35] This challenge to antitrust is largely US-based at present, and has two major strands: the first is to use antitrust to fight against inequalities, however it is not easy to see how policy could be directed at this social problem other than by making a priority cases in markets that affect the more vulnerable members of society (e.g. prioritising a case that harms disabled consumers).[36] Others instead plead for a much more robust antitrust enforcement against large corporations.[37] This challenges the foundations of modern competition law, however it is not clear whether this debate is of relevance to the European Union for it appears to be largely directed at the very low levels of enforcement in the United States against firms that the European Union has instead pursued with vigour: e.g. Google, Facebook, Qualcomm.[38]

3 ENFORCEMENT BY THE COMMISSION

The Commission's powers are set in Regulation 1/2003, which is in force from 1 May 2004.[39] In the beginning, there was little expectation that competition policy would form a key part of EU law; today it has 'a kind of rock-star status' because of the active way these powers are exercised.[40]

The cases the Commission takes up have two sources. First, the Commission may start an investigation on its own initiative, triggered by press reports, or its investigation of an economic

---

[35] C. Shapiro, 'Antitrust in a Time of Populism' (2018) *International Journal of Industrial Organization*, https://faculty.haas.berkeley.edu/shapiro/antitrustpopulism.pdf.

[36] J. B. Baker and S. C. Salop, 'Antitrust, Competition Policy, and Inequality' (2015) 104 *Georgetown LJ* 1.

[37] L. Kahn and S. Vaheesan, 'Market Power and Inequality: The Antitrust Counterrevolution and Its Discontents' (2017) 11 *Harvard Law & Policy Review* 235.

[38] Thus, the present Commissioner does not believe that applying Article 102 to Google requires any fundamental reconsideration to guarantee fair markets. See speech by M. Vestager, 'Fair Markets in a Digital World', 9 March 2018.

[39] Regulation 17/62 First Regulation implementing Articles 81 and 82 [1959] OJ Special Edn, 062, 57; Regulation 1/2003 on the implementation of the rules on competition laid down in Articles 81 and 82 [2003] OJ L 1/1.

[40] R. D. Kelemen, *Eurolegalism: The Transformation of Law and Regulation in the European Union* (Cambridge, MA, Harvard University Press, 2011) 143.

sector under the powers provided in Regulation 1/2003, Article 17. Secondly, some cases arise from complaints made by private parties or applications for leniency brought by undertakings that have infringed the rules. However, the Commission has no obligation to reach a decision on every complaint or leniency application it receives: it may prioritise cases on the basis of whether there is a Union-wide interest.[41] This is so where the parties commit violations that have an impact in the EU market as a whole or, where the case gives rise to novel points of law, or where the practices in question have a significant effect on market integration.[42] Given that as a result of Regulation 1/2003 national competition authorities (NCAs) are required to apply EU competition law, this provides a further basis for declining to take up a case when this is best addressed at national level.[43]

The enforcement procedure, which is administrative in character, is divided into two stages.[44] In the first stage, the Commission gathers evidence to determine whether there has been an infringement. In the second stage, it makes its concerns known to the parties being investigated and after a hearing issues a decision.[45] The main challenge is balancing the effectiveness of competition law enforcement with the protection of fundamental rights found in the European Convention on Human Rights (ECHR) and the Charter of Fundamental Rights (EUCFR).

(i) First Stage: Investigation

In order to obtain information to determine whether an undertaking has infringed competition law, the Commission has two powers. First, it may require undertakings to hand over information and carry out interviews; secondly, it has power to inspect business premises and private homes to seize relevant documents.

(a) Requests for Information and Interviews

Regulation 1/2003, Article 18(1) empowers the Commission to require undertakings to hand over information related to the suspected infringement.[46] The Commission may make a simple request (to which reply is not compulsory, but a fine is payable if incorrect information is supplied intentionally or negligently),[47] or issue a decision requiring information to be provided. The Commission also relies on statements made to it by the parties.[48]

---

[41] *Automec Srl* v. *Commission (Automec II)*, T-24/90, ECLI:EU:T:1992:97; but reasons must be given, see *CEAHR* v. *Commission*, T-427/08, ECLI:EU:T:2010:517.

[42] Commission Notice on cooperation within the Network of Competition Authorities [2004] OJ C 101/42, paras. 14, 15 and 54.

[43] *easyJet Airline* v. *Commission*, T-355/13, ECLI:EU:T:2015:36. E. Rousseva, 'Article 13 of Regulation 1/2003 Animated' (2018) 2 *Concurrences* 1.

[44] For a detailed exposition, see C. S. Kerse and N. Kahn, *EU Antitrust Procedure*, 6th edn (London, Sweet & Maxwell, 2012). See also Commission Regulation 773/2004 of 7 April 2004 relating to the conduct of proceedings by the Commission pursuant to Articles 81–82 of the EC Treaty [2004] OJ L 123/18, setting out in more detail the practicalities of the proceedings; and a helpful guide is also DG Competition's *Manual of Procedure for the Application of Articles 101 and 102 TFEU* (March 2012).

[45] *Limburgse Vinyl Maatschappij NV and Others* v. *Commission*, C-238/99 P, C-244–5/99 P, C-247/99 P, C-250–2/99 P and C-254/99 P, ECLI:EU:C:2002:582, paras. 181–3.

[46] *SEP* v. *Commission*, C-36/92, ECLI:EU:C:1994:205, para. 21. [47] Regulation 1/2003, Article 23(1).

[48] E.g. *Pre-insulated Pipes* [1999] OJ L 24/1, para. 24; *Zinc Phosphate* [2003] OJ L 153/1, paras. 57 and 59. Now see Regulation 1/2003, Article 19(1).

In supplying information, there is a risk that the undertaking is providing proof that it has infringed competition law. This would run counter to the undertaking's privilege against self-incrimination and in a challenge to a request for information by the Commission, the Court of Justice recognised this in part. First, the right not to incriminate oneself only applies to requests where the addressee is required to reply, under pain of a fine; in cases of a simple request, this protection is not available, because the undertaking has no duty to reply.[49] Secondly, even in cases of requests made under pain of a fine, the right to remain silent is limited.

Orkem v. Commission, 374/87, ECLI:EU:C:1989:387

28 In the absence of any right to remain silent expressly embodied in Regulation No. 17 [now Regulation 1/2003], it is appropriate to consider whether and to what extent the general principles of Community law, of which fundamental rights form an integral part and in the light of which all Community legislation must be interpreted, require, as the applicant claims, recognition of the right not to supply information capable of being used in order to establish, against the person supplying it, the existence of an infringement of the competition rules . . .

33 In that connection, the Court observed recently that whilst it is true that the rights of the defence must be observed in administrative procedures which may lead to the imposition of penalties, it is necessary to prevent those rights from being irremediably impaired during preliminary inquiry procedures which may be decisive in providing evidence of the unlawful nature of conduct engaged in by undertakings and for which they may be liable. Consequently, although certain rights of the defence relate only to contentious proceedings which follow the delivery of the statement of objections, other rights must be respected even during the preliminary inquiry.

34 Accordingly, whilst the Commission is entitled, in order to preserve the useful effect of Article [18 of Regulation 1/2003], to compel an undertaking to provide all necessary information concerning such facts as may be known to it and to disclose to it, if necessary, such documents relating thereto as are in its possession, even if the latter may be used to establish, against it or another undertaking, the existence of anti-competitive conduct, it may not, by means of a decision calling for information, undermine the rights of defence of the undertaking concerned.

35 Thus, the Commission may not compel an undertaking to provide it with answers which might involve an admission on its part of the existence of an infringement which it is incumbent upon the Commission to prove.

On the facts of the case, the Court of Justice held that some of the information sought by the Commission infringed the applicant's rights. For example at paragraph 39, the Court held:

> [b]y requiring disclosure of the 'details of any system or method which made it possible to attribute sales targets or quotas to the participants' and details of 'any method facilitating annual monitoring of compliance with any system of targets in terms of volume or quotas', the Commission endeavoured to obtain from the applicant an acknowledgment of its participation in an agreement intended to limit or control production or outlets or to share markets.

Likewise, the Commission cannot ask parties how many meetings they had with their competitors that infringed Article 101 TFEU. However, it is possible to obtain documentary information

---

[49] *Damline SpA* v. *Commission*, C-407/04 P, ECLI:EU:C:2007:53, paras. 33–6.

concerning agreements entered into, or factual information – for example, about which under-takings were present in certain meetings.[50] Following *Orkem*, parties have challenged the Commission's requests for information as infringing the privilege against self-incrimination, with occasional success.[51] The Court of Justice has not changed the position taken in *Orkem*, and a helpful explanation is found in Advocate General Geelhoed's opinion.

Commission v. *SGL Carbon*, C-301/04 P, ECLI:EU:C:2006:53, Opinion of Advocate General Geelhoed

67 … the interplay between the fundamental rights of legal persons and competition enforcement remains a balancing exercise: at stake are the protection of fundamental rights versus effective enforcement of Community competition law. Article [101 TFEU] is a fundamental provision which is essential for the accomplishment of the tasks entrusted to the Community and, in particular, for the functioning of the internal market. Article [101 TFEU] forms part of public policy. If the Commission is no longer empowered to request the production of documents its enforcement of competition law in the Community legal order will become heavily dependent on either voluntary cooperation or on the use of other means of coercion as for example dawn raids. It is self-evident that the effective enforcement with reasonable means of the basic tenets of the Community public legal order should remain possible, just as it is evident that the rights of the defence should be respected too. In my view, the latter is the case. As case-law now stands, a defendant is still able, either during the administrative procedure or in the proceedings before the Community courts, to contend that the documents produced have a different meaning from that ascribed to them by the Commission.[52]

While the General Court considers that the approach reflects the jurisprudence of the European Court of Human Rights (ECtHR) on the right against self-incrimination, commentators have been less convinced.[53] There are two points of debate. The first is whether the judgments of the Court of Justice are in conformity with those of the ECtHR. Here the Court of Justice appears to take the view that they are, on the ground that when asking for documents one is seeking information which is available independently of the person. The second issue is whether the right against self-incrimination developed in the context of human rights law should apply with equal vigour to the enforcement of economic laws. According to Advocate General Geelhoed, 'it is not possible simply to transpose the findings of the European Court of Human Rights without more to legal persons or undertakings'.[54] This suggests that corporations may enjoy less protection from the fundamental rights.

---

[50] *Austrian Banks* [2002] OJ L 56/1, para. 488.

[51] E.g. *Mannesmannröhren-Werke AG* v. *Commission*, T-112/98, ECLI:EU:T:2001:61, para. 71.

[52] The ECJ took the same view; see paras. 39–49 of the judgment.

[53] *Mannesmannröhren-Werke AG* v. *Commission*, T-112/98, ECLI:EU:T:2001:61, para. 77. The leading cases are *Funke* v. *France* [1993] 16 EHRR 297; *Saunders* v. *United Kingdom* (1997) 23 EHRR 313. For comment see I. van Bael and J.-F. Bellis, *Competition Law of the European Community*, 4th edn (The Hague, Kluwer Law International, 2005) 107, opining that national courts which are signatories to the ECHR might interpret the ECHR more strictly than the ECJ; A. McCulloch, 'The Privilege against Self-incrimination in Competition Investigations' (2006) 26(2) *Legal Studies* 211, criticising the distinction between factual questions and admissions of infringement.

[54] *Commission* v. *SGL Carbon*, C-301/04 P, ECLI:EU:C:2006:53, Opinion of Advocate General Geelhoed, para. 63. See further S. Douglas-Scott, 'A Tale of Two Courts: Luxembourg, Strasbourg and the Growing Human Rights Acquis' (2006) 43 *CMLRev* 629.

The Court of Justice also protects the privacy of communications between an undertaking and its lawyers, and information passing between lawyer and client need not be disclosed. This rule is justified by the view that the lawyer collaborates in the administration of justice and is required to provide, independently and confidentially, any legal assistance the client needs.[55] However, the Court curtails lawyer–client privilege in one way: it only protects communication by independent lawyers, not in-house lawyers. The rationale for this is that in many Member States in-house lawyers are not subject to professional codes of discipline.[56] Furthermore, the information that is privileged only extends to matters linked with the subject matter of the investigation, which will normally be material written after the investigation.[57] It may include working documents prepared by the undertaking to aid the lawyers in preparing the defence.[58]

(b) Inspections

The Commission's most draconian means to secure information about a possible competition law infringement are its powers to enter business premises of the parties under investigation and seize the relevant information. These procedures are colloquially referred to as 'dawn raids'.[59]

Regulation 1/2003

Article 20

(1) In order to carry out the duties assigned to it by this Regulation, the Commission may conduct all necessary inspections of undertakings and associations of undertakings.

(2) The officials and other accompanying persons authorised by the Commission to conduct an inspection are empowered:
   (a) to enter any premises, land and means of transport of undertakings and associations of undertakings;
   (b) to examine the books and other records related to the business, irrespective of the medium on which they are stored;
   (c) to take or obtain in any form copies of or extracts from such books or records;
   (d) to seal any business premises and books or records for the period and to the extent necessary for the inspection;
   (e) to ask any representative or member of staff of the undertaking or association of undertakings for explanations on facts or documents relating to the subject-matter and purpose of the inspection and to record the answers . . .

(4) Undertakings and associations of undertakings are required to submit to inspections ordered by decision of the Commission.

---

[55] *AM&S Europe Ltd* v. *Commission*, 155/79, ECLI:EU:C:1982:157, para. 24. See generally J. Faull, 'Legal Professional Privilege: The Commission Proposes International Negotiations' (1985) 10 *ELRev* 119.

[56] The General Court has followed the approach of the ECJ in *Akzo Nobel Chemicals Ltd and Akcros Chemicals Ltd* v. *Commission*, T-125 and 253/03, ECLI:EU:T:2007:287.

[57] *AM&S Europe Ltd* v. *Commission*, 155/79, ECLI:EU:C:1982:157.

[58] *Akzo Nobel Chemicals Ltd and Akcros Chemicals Ltd* v. *Commission*, T-125 and 253/03, ECLI:EU:T:2007:287, paras. 123–4.

[59] J. Joshua, 'The Element of Surprise' (1983) 8 *ELRev* 3.

> **Article 21**
>
> (1) If a reasonable suspicion exists that books or other records related to the business and to the subject-matter of the inspection, which may be relevant to prove a serious violation of Article [101 TFEU] or Article [102 TFEU] ... are being kept in any other premises, land and means of transport, including the homes of directors, managers and other members of staff of the undertakings and associations of undertakings concerned, the Commission can by decision order an inspection to be conducted in such other premises, land and means of transport.

The Commission must specify the subject matter and purpose of its investigation 'not merely to show that the proposed entry onto the premises of the undertakings concerned is justified but also to enable those undertakings to assess the scope of their duty to cooperate whilst at the same time safeguarding their rights of defence'.[60] Article 21 is an innovation and provides for searches into private homes, but these require prior authorisation from a national court where the premises are located.

The Commission's power to search premises is controversial when judged against fundamental rights standards. Article 8 of the European Convention of Human Rights (ECHR) incorporates a right to private and family life. A derogation from this right is specified in Article 8(2) ECHR, which states that infringements of privacy are justified only when necessary, *inter alia*, for the economic wellbeing of the country or the prevention of crime. To benefit from the derogation in Article 8(2), the interference with the right to privacy must be based on accessible legal rules, the interference must have a legitimate aim, and there must be effective protection against abuse by the investigators.[61]

It might be argued that any inspection must be approved by a judge if one looks at the case law of the ECtHR. First, in *Niemetz* v. *Germany*, the ECtHR held that the right to private life does not merely encompass private homes but also business premises, when this is necessary to protect the individual against arbitrary interference by public authorities.[62] Secondly, in *Société Colas Est and Others* v. *France*, the ECtHR held that in competition cases, prior judicial authorisation is required when conducting inspections so as to afford adequate and effective safeguards against abuse.[63] However, the European Court of Justice (ECJ) has confirmed that judicial approval is not always necessary.

> **Deutsche Bahn v. Commission, C–583/13 P, CELI:EU:C:2015:404**
>
> 20 Furthermore, although it is apparent from the case-law of the ECtHR that the protection provided for in Article 8 of the ECHR may extend to certain commercial premises, the fact remains that that court did hold

---

[60] *Hoechst AG* v. *Commission*, 46/87 and 227/88, ECLI:EU:C:1989:337, para. 19.

[61] Kerse and Kahn, n. 44 above, 166; *Société Colas Est and Others* v. *France* (2004) 39 EHRR 17.

[62] *Niemetz* v. *Germany* [1993] 16 EHRR 97, para. 31; *Veeber* v. *Estonia (No. 1)* [2004] 39 EHRR 6. See also *Janssen Cilag SAS* v. *France*, No. 33931/12 judgment of 13 April 2017 emphasising the need for proportionality between the inspection and the information obtained.

[63] *Société Colas Est and Others* v. *France* [2002] ECHR 418, para. 49.

that interference by a public authority could go further for professional or commercial premises or activities than in other cases.

22 ... the lack of prior judicial authorisation is only one of the factors borne in mind in the determination of whether Article 8 of the ECHR has been infringed. [In its case law] the ECtHR took into account the extent of the powers held by the national competition authority, the circumstances of the interference and the fact that the system in place at the material time provided for only a limited number of safeguards, all of which differs from the situation under EU law.

23 It must be pointed out in that regard that the Commission's investigative powers under Article 20(2) of Regulation No 1/2003 are restricted to the Commission's agents having the power, *inter alia*, to enter premises of their choosing, to have access to documents they request and make copies thereof, and to have shown to them the contents of pieces of furniture they indicate.

24 It must also be remembered that, under Article 20(6) and (7) of Regulation No 1/2003, authorisation must be sought from a judicial authority where, when the undertaking concerned opposes an inspection, the Member State concerned provides the necessary assistance, requesting where appropriate the assistance of the police or of an equivalent enforcement authority, so as to enable the inspection to be conducted and where such authorisation is required under national law. Authorisation may also be applied for as a precautionary measure. Article 20(8) further provides that although the national judicial authority is to control, *inter alia*, that the coercive measures envisaged are neither arbitrary nor excessive having regard to the subject-matter of the inspection, it may not call into question the necessity for the inspection, and that the decision is subject to review only by the Court of Justice.

The Court continues by stating that the main justification for not requiring prior judicial authorisation is that it is possible to seek judicial review after the event, on the grounds that, in the circumstances, a dawn raid was arbitrary, disproportionate or excessive.[64] It notes that the possibility of *ex post* judicial review is recognised as a criterion to justify intrusions into privacy by the ECtHR. Moreover the powers of inspection are delimited by the inspection decision, the Commission may not seize non-business documents, and the firm may seek legal assistance.[65] If the Court of Justice agrees with the applicant that the Commission abused its powers, then the Commission would be prevented from using, for the purposes of proceeding in respect of an infringement of the competition rules, any documents or evidence which it might have obtained in the course of that investigation.[66] At the same time the legislature acknowledges that in some Member States prior judicial authorisation is required thus Article 20(7) requires the Commission to obtain such authorisation.

However, it has been argued that this falls short of the requirements for derogation stipulated by the ECtHR's case law because a judicial warrant need not be obtained in all cases, and the scope for judicial scrutiny by the national judge in Article 20(8) is limited.[67] Accordingly, dawn raids may be challenged, either at national level, questioning national courts' authorisations of

---

[64] *Dow Chemical Ibérica and Others* v. *Commission*, 97–9/87, ECLI:EU:C:1989:380, para. 16.

[65] *Deutsche Bahn* v. *Commission*, C-583/13 P, EU:C:2015:404, paras. 30–6.

[66] *Roquette Frères* v. *Directeur général de la concurrence, de la consommation et de la répression des fraudes*, C-94/00, ECLI:EU:C:2002:603, para. 49.

[67] A. Riley, 'The ECHR Implications of the Investigation Provisions of the Draft Competition Regulation' (2002) 51 *ICLQ* 55, 76–7.

Commission inspections,[68] or at EU level, for compatibility with the protection of the undertaking's fundamental rights in the absence of judicial authorisation.

(ii) Second Stage: Adjudication

Once the information is gathered, the Commission issues a statement of objections and the parties have access to the Commission's file to see the evidence upon which the allegations are based. Secondly, the parties have the right to a hearing. The rationale for these procedures is to guarantee the parties' right to defend themselves.

(a) Statement of Objections and Access to the File

After proceedings have begun, the Commission must notify the parties of the infringements that it believes have been committed. This document is known as the statement of objections.

Regulation 1/2003, Article 27

(1) Before taking decisions . . . the Commission shall give the undertakings or associations of undertakings which are the subject of the proceedings conducted by the Commission the opportunity of being heard on the matters to which the Commission has taken objection. The Commission shall base its decisions only on objections on which the parties concerned have been able to comment. Complainants shall be associated closely with the proceedings.

As the final sentence of Article 27(1) makes clear, the Commission can only issue a decision on grounds set out in the statement of objections. The right to access the file is enshrined in Regulation 1/2003.[69]

Regulation 1/2003, Article 27

(2) The rights of defence of the parties concerned shall be fully respected in the proceedings. They shall be entitled to have access to the Commission's file, subject to the legitimate interest of undertakings in the protection of their business secrets. The right of access to the file shall not extend to confidential information and internal documents of the Commission or the competition authorities of the Member States. In particular, the right of access shall not extend to correspondence between the Commission and the competition authorities of the Member States, or between the latter. Nothing in this paragraph shall prevent the Commission from disclosing and using information necessary to prove an infringement.

---

[68] As in *Roquette Frères* v. *Directeur général de la concurrence, de la consommation et de la répression des frauds*, C-94/00, ECLI:EU:C:2002:603, appeal against an order of a local judge to empower the Commission to conduct an investigation on the appellant's premises.

[69] And recognised by the ECJ, see e.g. *Aalborg Portland A/S and Others* v. *Commission*, C-204–5/00 P, C-211/00 P, C-213/00 P, C-217/00 P and C-219/00 P, ECLI:EU:C:2004:6, paras. 68–77.

A key principle of EU law is 'equality of arms': the party accused of an infringement has access to the Commission's entire file (save for the documents protected by Article 27(2)) and it is not for the Commission to decide which documents to pass on.[70]

(b) Oral Hearing

Hearings are normally attended by the following: the parties accused, complainants, Commission representatives and representatives of the national competition authorities. They are moderated by a hearing officer. This Commission official is independent of DG Competition and reports directly to the Commissioner for competition. He or she has the task of ensuring 'that the hearing is properly conducted and contributes to the objectivity of the hearing itself and of any decision taken subsequently'.[71] This serves to 'safeguard the effective exercise of procedural rights throughout proceedings before the Commission'.[72]

The hearing is composed of arguments by the Commission and the accused, and is followed by questions from those present.[73] Before the hearing the defendant will have had several exchanges of view with DG Competition. However, it has been said that the hearing is useful because it is the only time for the defendant to set out its case to the national authorities, to the Commission's legal service, and to representatives of other DGs.[74]

After the hearings, the Commission prepares a decision acting as a collegiate body. Draft decisions are reviewed by the Advisory Committee which is composed of representatives of Member States' competition authorities.[75] The Commission must take the 'utmost account' of the Committee's views but is not bound to follow them.[76] For most competition cases, the Commission operates with a 'written procedure' whereby the draft decision is circulated to all Commissioners and is adopted if there are no objections.[77] For controversial cases however, there are debates among the Commissioners, and lobbying is not uncommon.[78] The decisions must be fully reasoned to allow the parties to see which findings of fact and of law led the Commission to its conclusion.[79] This is necessary to afford the parties the opportunity of challenging the Commission's decision in the courts.

(iii) Penalties for Infringement

Once an infringement is established, the Commission has a wide range of powers, which may be divided into two categories. First, the Commission has powers to bring the infringement to a close and to remedy the anti-competitive effects.

---

[70] *Solvay SA* v. *Commission*, T-30/91, ECLI:EU:T:1995:115, paras. 81–3. For a critique see C. D. Ehlermann and B. J. Drijber, 'Legal Protection of Enterprises: Administrative Procedure, in Particular Access to the File and Confidentiality' [1996] *ECLR* 375.

[71] Decision of the President of the European Commission of 13 October 2011 on the function and terms of reference of the hearing officer in certain competition proceedings [2011] OJ L 275/29.

[72] *Evonik Degussa GmbH* v. *European Commission*, C-162/15 P, ECLI:EU:C:2017:205, para. 40.

[73] For detail see Regulation 773/2004 [2004] OJ L 123/18.   [74] Van Bael and Bellis, n. 53 above, 1096.

[75] Regulation 1/2003, Article 14.   [76] *Ibid.* Article 14(5).   [77] Van Bael and Bellis, n. 53 above, 1103.

[78] 'Brussels Braces for a Lobbying Invasion', *Financial Times*, 3 October 2005.

[79] *ACF Chemiefarmia* v. *Commission*, 41/69, ECLI:EU:C:1970:71, paras. 76–81.

> **Regulation 1/2003, Article 7**
>
> (1) Where the Commission, acting on a complaint or on its own initiative, finds that there is an infringement of Article [101 TFEU] or of Article [102 TFEU] ... it may by decision require the undertakings and associations of undertakings concerned to bring such infringement to an end. For this purpose, it may impose on them any behavioural or structural remedies which are proportionate to the infringement committed and necessary to bring the infringement effectively to an end. Structural remedies can only be imposed either where there is no equally effective behavioural remedy or where any equally effective behavioural remedy would be more burdensome for the undertaking concerned than the structural remedy. If the Commission has a legitimate interest in doing so, it may also find that an infringement has been committed in the past.

In a cartel case, for example, the Commission will normally demand that the undertakings bring the agreement to an end so that the damage to competition does not continue. It may also order parties to change their behaviour vis-à-vis competitors, a sanction which has been imposed upon dominant undertakings to oblige them to supply competitors.[80] However, the Commission cannot impose obligations that are not necessary to bring the infringement to an end. In one case the General Court held that requiring members of a cartel to stop fixing prices was legitimate, but asking them to inform customers that they may renegotiate the contracts that had been signed when the cartel inflated prices was unnecessary, because the contracts in question were only of a year's duration and because, if parties to a cartel suffer losses, this is a matter to be addressed in a damages action.[81]

Article 7 adds a novel remedy: empowering the Commission to impose 'structural remedies'. This can entail a demand that a company be broken up into two or more smaller units. This is a draconian remedy for it makes a fundamental change in the way the business is run. It has been imposed once, to require a dominant firm to divest essential infrastructure to allow other firms to compete. However, this is an unusual case where the dominant firm had offered the divestiture and agreed this was a proportional remedy.[82] The final sentence of Article 7 allows the Commission to make decisions against infringements that have occurred in the past but only if there is a legitimate interest: for example, clarifying a point of law or issuing a decision to facilitate follow-on damages claims.[83]

The second category of powers the Commission has is penalising the undertaking for breaching competition law. Fines not exceeding 1 per cent of the undertaking's turnover may be imposed for procedural infringements (e.g. supplying incorrect or misleading information),[84] and fines not exceeding 10 per cent of the undertaking's turnover may be imposed for intentional or negligent infringements of Articles 101 and 102 TFEU.[85] The Commission's approach to fines should be read together with its policy on leniency applications and settlements. In this way, we can gain a sense of the Commission's enforcement strategy as a whole.

[80] See e.g. *Microsoft* v. *Commission*, T-201/04, ECLI:EU:T:2007:289.

[81] *Atlantic Container Line* v. *Commission*, T-395/94, ECLI:EU:T:2002:49, paras. 410–16.

[82] CASE AT.39759 – *ARA foreclosure* 20 September 2016.

[83] *GVL* v. *Commission*, 7/82, ECLI:EU:C:1983:52, para. 24.   [84] Regulation 1/2003, Article 23(1).

[85] *Ibid.* Article 23(2).

(a) Fining Policy

In 1980 the Commission declared that fines would be increased as a means of deterring undertakings,[86] and in 1991, it announced that in appropriate cases it would apply the highest penalty possible: 10 per cent of the undertaking's turnover.[87] The gradual increase can be seen as a sensible policy in that in the early years undertakings were unfamiliar with their obligations under the competition rules, but as the culture of competition spread, and as the deadline for achieving a single market neared, higher fines were justified. The current policy targeting cartels has led to ever-greater fines. Between 2014 and 2017, the Commission imposed fines of nearly €8 billion Euros for twenty-eight cartel infringements.[88] Google has also received very high fines for abusing its dominant position (€6.7 billion for two infringements).[89]

However, the Commission is often criticised for imposing fines arbitrarily, in particular due to the vagueness of Article 23(3) of Regulation 1/2003, which merely provides: 'in fixing the amount of the fine, regard shall be had both to the gravity and duration of the infringement'. In response to calls for greater transparency, the Commission issued Guidelines on the method of setting fines.[90] These reflect the Commission's practice and take into account the rulings of the Court of Justice.[91] They also aim to provide for tougher fines to deter the undertaking in question as well as all undertakings in the market. The Guidelines indicate that the Commission will first determine a 'basic amount' for the fine, which is then adjusted by considering aggravating or mitigating circumstances. We consider these two steps in turn.

The basic amount is set by reference to the value of the sales of the goods to which the infringement relates, having regard to the gravity of the infringement. For 'very serious' infringements (e.g. price-fixing and market-sharing) the basic amount will be up to 30 per cent of the value of the sales. Under the 2006 Guidelines, this figure is then multiplied by the number of years that the undertaking has infringed competition law.[92] Under the 1998 Guidelines, in contrast, an addition was made depending on the duration of the agreement. The change is significant in two respects. First, it places greater emphasis on the duration of the cartel and, secondly, it serves to raise the fine considerably. For example, under the old Guidelines, in a cartel lasting three years where the basic amount was €20 million, the Commission would add 50 per cent for duration, making the total fine €30 million. Under the new Guidelines the same infringement would lead to a fine of €60 million (€20 million x 3). In addition, an 'entry fee' is added to the basic amount (of between 15 and 25 per cent of the value of sales) to cartels that involve price-fixing, market-sharing or output limitation, irrespective of duration.[93]

The basic amount is adjusted both (a) upwards if there are aggravating circumstances (e.g. repeated infringements, for which the fine will be increased by 100 per cent for each previous infringement;[94] refusal to cooperate with the investigation; instigating the

---

[86] *Pioneer* [1980] OJ L 60/21; affirmed in *Musique diffusion française and Others* v. *Commission*, 100–3/80, ECLI:EU:C:1983:158, paras. 105–9.

[87] European Commission, *Twenty-first Report on Competition Policy* (1991), para. 139.

[88] Source: http://ec.europa.eu/competition/cartels/statistics/statistics.pdf.

[89] Commission fines Google €4.34 billion for illegal practices regarding Android mobile devices to strengthen dominance of Google's search engine (Press Release 18 July 2017); CASE AT.39740 *Google Search (Shopping)* 18 December 2017.

[90] Guidelines on the method of setting fines imposed pursuant to Article 23(2)(a) of Regulation 1/2003 [2006] OJ C 210/2.

[91] See further P. Manzini, 'European Antitrust in Search of the Perfect Fine' (2008) 31(1) *World Competition* 3; C. Veljanovski, 'Cartel Fines in Europe: Law, Practice and Deterrence' (2007) 30(1) *World Competition* 65.

[92] 2006 Guidelines, n. 90 above, para. 19.   [93] *Ibid.* para. 25.

[94] *Ibid.* para. 28. See *Groupe Danone* v. *Commission*, C-3/06 P, EU:C:2007:88.

infringement);[95] and (b) downwards in the presence of attenuating circumstances (e.g. a passive role in the infringement; termination as soon as the investigation begins; the existence of reasonable doubt as to the legality of the practice).[96]

Two themes can be detected in the Commission's fining Guidelines. Deterrence features most prominently. The second theme focuses on sales as a proxy for how much each member stood to gain from the cartel, thereby imposing a more accurate fine on each member of the cartel. It can thus be said to lead to fairer fines as between cartel members. This is in response to one frequent ground on which fines are appealed: discrimination between cartel offenders.[97]

The European Courts have upheld the legality of the Commission's general approach to fines in a number of judgments.[98]

Dornbracht v. *Commission*, T–386/10, ECLI:EU:T:2013:450

68   [I]n the first place, it should be noted that in essence, according to the case-law, adoption by the Commission of Guidelines contributes to ensuring observance of the principle that penalties must have a proper legal basis. In that regard, it should be observed that the Guidelines determine, generally and abstractly, the method which the Commission has bound itself to use in setting the amount of fines and, consequently, ensure legal certainty on the part of undertakings.

69   In the second place, as can be seen from point 2 of the 2006 Guidelines, the latter fall within the statutory limits laid down by Article 23(2) and (3) of Regulation No 1/2003 ... [T]hat article meets the requirements deriving from the principle that penalties must have a proper legal basis and the principle of legal certainty.

70   In the third place, it must be held that, in adopting the 2006 Guidelines, the Commission did not exceed the limits of the discretion afforded it by Article 23(2) and (3) of Regulation No 1/2003.

. . .

76   Lastly, in point 35 of the 2006 Guidelines, the Commission provides that, in exceptional cases, the Commission may, for purposes of setting the amount of the fine, take account of an undertaking's inability to pay. Contrary to what is maintained by the applicant, that provision does not give the Commission limitless discretion, since the conditions for reducing the amount of the fine on account of inability to pay are very clearly set out in that point. Thus, it is clearly stated there that no reduction in a fine will be granted on the mere finding of an adverse or loss-making financial situation and also that a reduction can be granted solely on the basis of objective evidence that imposition of a fine would irretrievably jeopardise the economic viability of the undertaking concerned and cause its assets to lose all their value.

77   Also, in point 37 of the 2006 Guidelines, the Commission states that the particularities of a case or the need to achieve deterrence in a particular case may justify departing from the methodology described in the 2006 Guidelines. Since the provisions of that point do not allow the Commission to depart from the principles laid down by Article 23(2) and (3) of Regulation No 1/2003, it must be held that, contrary to what the applicant contends, they do not give the Commission almost limitless discretion and that, hence, point 37 does not derogate from the principle that penalties must have a proper legal basis.

---

[95]   *Shell Petroleum NV* v. *Commission*, T-343/06, EU:T:2012:479, paras. 152–8.
[96]   For an example of the application of the previous Guidelines, see *Commission* v. *SGL Carbon AG*, C-301/04 P, ECLI:EU:C:2006:432.
[97]   E.g. *CD Contact Data GmbH* v. *Commission*, T-18/03, ECLI:EU:T:2009:132. The fine imposed was reduced to ensure compliance with the principle of equal treatment.
[98]   *Dansk Rørindustri and Others* v. *Commission*, C-189/02 P, C-202/02 P, C-205–8/02 P and C-213/02 P, ECLI:EU:C:2005:408.

78 It follows that the adoption by the Commission of the 2006 Guidelines, inasmuch as it fell within the statutory limits laid down by Article 23(2) and (3) of Regulation No 1/2003, contributed to defining the limits within which the Commission exercises its discretion under that provision and did not infringe the principle that penalties must have a proper legal basis but was conducive to observance of it.

The confirmation of the Commission's powers is a boost in its fight against cartels, allowing it to design a fining policy to deter undertakings to create cartels. However, the Commission's wide discretion has led to criticism that the Notice on the method of setting fines does little to increase transparency and consistency.[99] Furthermore, critics have said that the courts do not exercise a sufficiently robust standard of review when fines are appealed.[100] Between 2005 and February 2017 the court has heard 355 appeals: in one-third of these cases the fines were reduced, but often the reduction is less than the cost of the appeal. The most successful pleadings involve the miscalculation of the fine, errors on the duration of the cartel, misapplication of the leniency notice and a failure to state reasons.[101] However it would be unfair to use these statistics as a sign of weak judicial review: often the judgments of the General Court review the Commission decision in quite some detail, and the low rate of success may also be attributed to diligent decision-making by the Commission.

On the other hand, economists consider that the current policy may not do enough to deter. The number of investigations is still too low, so while the fine is high, the probability of being subject to the fine remains low. One study of US antitrust, where discovery and penalties are stronger than those in the Union, estimated that only one in six cartels is detected.[102] A more recent study concluded that fines are at least five times too small to deter.[103] In these circumstances it still pays to engage in restrictive practices because the expected gains are greater than the expected penalties.[104]

(b) Leniency Policy

Pursuant to the Commission's leniency policy, the first undertaking that informs the Commission of the existence of an anti-competitive practice of which it is a member, and whose information allows the Commission to carry out an inspection or find an infringement under Article 101 TFEU, obtains immunity from any fine. If an undertaking collaborates with the Commission

---

[99] L. Solek, 'Administrative and Judicial Discretion in Setting Fines' (2015) 38 *World Competition* 547. E. Barbier de la Serre and E. Lagathu, 'The Law on Fines Imposed in EU Competition Proceedings: Converging Towards Hazier Lines' (2018) 9(7) *Journal of European Competition Law and Practice* 459.

[100] I. Forrester, 'A Challenge for Europe's Judges: The Review of Fines in Competition Cases' (2011) 36 *ELRev* 185; E. Barbier de la Serre and E. Lagathu, 'The Law on Fines Imposed in EU Competition Proceedings: Faster, Higher, Harsher' (2013) 4(4) *Journal of European Competition Law and Practice* 325.

[101] D. Paemen and J. Blondeel, 'Appealing EU Cartel Decisions before European Courts: Winning (and Losing) Arguments' (2017) 18(2) *Business Law International* 155.

[102] P. G. Bryant and E. W. Eckard, 'Price Fixing: The Probability of Getting Caught' (1991) 73 *Review of Economics and Statistics* 531 is the seminal work. Recent research has obtained similar results. E. Combe *et al.*, 'Cartels: The Probability of Getting Caught in the European Union', Bruges European Economic Research Papers, Working Paper No. 12 (2008), http://ssrn.com/abstract=1015061. But see N. H. Miller, 'Strategic Leniency and Cartel Enforcement' (2009) 99 *American Economic Review* 750, suggesting that the probability is now 20–27%, which is reassuring because it means that the leniency policies and the increases in penalties since the early 1990s have had some impact.

[103] J. M. Connor and R. H. Lande, 'Cartels as Rational Business Strategy: Crime Pays' (2012) 34 *Cardozo L Rev* 427.

[104] M. P. Schinkel, 'Effective Cartel Enforcement in Europe' (2007) 30 *World Competition* 539.

during the investigation by providing important evidence that strengthens the Commission's case, this may result in a reduction in the fine of between 20 and 50 per cent, the reduction being more significant for those who collaborate first.[105] The aim of this policy is to give members of a cartel the incentive to bring the existence of cartels to the attention of the Commission.[106] The prize for being the first to do so is designed to encourage cartel members to blow the whistle, which can save Commission resources, as it may be able to rely solely on the evidence supplied by the 'whistleblower' to reach a decision that competition law has been infringed. The policy began in 1996 and has been effective in increasing the number of successful cartel infringement decisions brought by the Commission.[107] A significant proportion of cartel cases have been initiated by a leniency application: over half of the cartel cases decided between 2005 and 2008,[108] and more recently the Commission reports that most cartels come to their attention through this policy,[109] although the Commission stresses that it does not depend solely on leniency applications to uncover cartels.[110] These results match those of a comparable US programme, which has been described as 'the single greatest investigative tool available to anti-cartel enforcers'.[111]

Two factors that may undermine the success of the Commission's leniency policy.[112] First, NCAs can enforce EU competition law, and Member States have different (or no) leniency policies.[113] If an undertaking provides evidence of a cartel to one competition authority, but the cartel is then prosecuted by a competition authority without a leniency programme or one with less generous reductions in fines, the benefits of confessing are reduced.[114] This may deter parties from stepping forward.[115] This has been tackled by the European Competition Network designing a Model Leniency Programme for NCAs to adopt.[116] In 2012 the programme was enhanced in that all leniency applicants who apply for leniency to the Commission may also send a summary leniency application to all Member State competition authorities and the summary form is standardised.[117] Presently a Directive to empower NCAs seeks to harmonise leniency policies.[118]

---

[105] Notice on immunity from fines and reduction of fines in cartel cases [2006] OJ C 298/17. For comment on earlier drafts of this document, see N. Levy and R. O'Donoghue, 'The EU Leniency Programme Comes of Age' (2004) 27 *World Competition* 75.

[106] And some have gone even further, suggesting that the Commission should pay whistleblowers. See A. Riley, 'Beyond Leniency: Enhancing Enforcement in EC Antitrust Law' (2005) 28 *World Competition* 377.

[107] Kerse and Kahn, n. 44 above, 417, report that since 1998 the leniency notice was applied in eighteen out of twenty cartel decisions.

[108] 'Report on Competition Policy 2005', SEC(2006)761 final, para. 174; 'Report on Competition Policy 2006', COM(2007) 358 final, para. 8; 'Report on Competition Policy 2007', COM(2008)368 final, para. 6.

[109] 'Report on Competition Policy 2017', COM(2018)482 final, 3.

[110] 'Report on Competition Policy 2007', COM(2008)368 final, para. 6.

[111] S. D. Hammond, 'When Calculating the Cost and Benefits of Applying for Corporate Amnesty, How Do You Put a Price Tag on an Individual's Freedom?', 8 March 2001, www.usdoj.gov/atr.

[112] For a critical account, see P. Billiet, 'How Lenient is the EC Leniency Policy? A Matter of Certainty and Predictability' (2009) *ECLR* 14.

[113] See L. Brokx, 'A Patchwork of Leniency Programmes' (2001) 2 *ECLR* 35.

[114] *DHL Express (Italy) srl* v. *AGCM*, C-428/14, EU:C:2016:274. The applicant was pursued both by the Commission and the Italian NCA for different infringements. However, his leniency application to the Italian NCA was incomplete.

[115] The Commission suggests this is not a significant problem. S. Blake and D. Schnichels, 'Leniency Following Modernisation: Safeguarding Europe's Leniency Programmes' (2004) 2 *Competition Policy Newsletter* 7.

[116] Commission Staff Working Document, Annex to 'Commission Report on Competition Policy 2007', SEC(2008)2038, para. 449.

[117] Commission Staff Working Document accompanying *Report on Competition Policy* (2012) 8.

[118] This is discussed below at p. 909.

Secondly, leniency policies do not affect the undertaking's liability if the victims of a cartel seek damages. A successful leniency applicant may pay less damages because the Damages Directive provides that a defendant who has benefited from leniency will not be jointly and severally liable for the infringement unless the claimants are unable to secure full compensation from the other cartel members.[119] However, this is a small reduction. As a result, the money saved by confessing to the existence of a cartel (which might otherwise not have come to light) and avoiding the antitrust fine can be lost when the undertaking is sued for damages.[120] This might deter leniency applications. Recently, the Commission has initiated a whistleblower tool whereby employees may contact the Commission with information about restrictive practices. No reward is offered, and it may be that this is a response to the reduced incentives that corporations have to apply for leniency as a result of the damages exposure.[121]

A related policy remains to be mentioned: cartel settlements.[122] Parties secure a discount on the fine up to 10 per cent if they agree not to contest the Commission's proposed infringement findings. The aim is to save resources that go into preparing the case for oral hearing and subsequent appeals. Practitioners report that the Commission gives fairly clear ideas about the estimated fines it proposes to apply so that parties can decide if it is worth settling; however, the discount is not as generous as that found in other legal systems, which may reduce its attractiveness.[123] At the same time 50 per cent of cartel cases are settled.[124] It is of course possible to benefit from both leniency and settlement policies.

(iv) Commitment Decisions

The Commission has frequently used informal means to close certain cases.[125] For undertakings, informality has the obvious advantage that fines and the publicity of an investigation (which may give rise to damages claims) are avoided. The disadvantages, however, are over-enforcement on the one hand (e.g. without a full hearing the Commission may abuse its powers by accusing parties of a non-existent infringement); or under-enforcement on the other (informal closures avoid the imposition of fines and are privately negotiated between parties and Commission).[126] Furthermore, from an enforcer's point of view, if the parties did not comply, the Commission's only solution would be to restart an investigation afresh. In an attempt to increase transparency of its settlements practice, and to strengthen its enforceability, the Council formalised this practice, creating a new category of decisions: commitment decisions.[127]

---

[119] Directive 2014/104/EU on certain rules governing actions for damages under national law for infringements of the competition law provisions of the Member States and of the European Union [2014] OJ L 349/1, Article 11(4).

[120] P. C. Zane, 'The Price Fixer's Dilemma: Applying Game Theory to the Decision of Whether to Plead Guilty to Antitrust Crimes' (2003) *Antitrust Bulletin* 1.

[121] This scheme is explained here: http://ec.europa.eu/competition/cartels/whistleblower/index.html.

[122] Commission Regulation 622/2008 of 30 June 2008 amending Regulation 773/2004, as regards the conduct of settlement procedures in cartel cases [2008] OJ L 171/3.

[123] S.-P. Brankin, 'The First Cases Under the Commission's Cartel Settlement Procedure: Problems Solved?' (2011) 32(4) *ECLR* 5 for an informative insider's perspective. M. P. Schinkel, 'Bargaining in the Shadow of the European Settlement for Cartels' (2011) 56(2) *Antitrust Bulletin* 462.

[124] R. Whish and D. Bailey, *Competition Law*, 9th edn (Oxford University Press, 2018) 273.

[125] I. van Bael, 'The Antitrust Settlement Practice of the EC Commission' (1986) 23 *CMLRev* 61.

[126] For a discussion of these concerns, see G. Bruzzone and G. Boccaccio, 'Taking Care of Modernisation after the Startup: A View from a Member State' (2008) 31 *World Competition* 89.

[127] N. Dunne, 'Commitment Decisions in EU Competition Law' (2014) 10 *Journal of Competition Law and Economics* 399.

> ### Regulation 1/2003, Article 9
>
> (1) Where the Commission intends to adopt a decision requiring that an infringement be brought to an end and the undertakings concerned offer commitments to meet the concerns expressed to them by the Commission in its preliminary assessment, the Commission may by decision make those commitments binding on the undertakings. Such a decision may be adopted for a specified period and shall conclude that there are no longer grounds for action by the Commission.

Proposed decisions to accept commitments must be published, inviting comments from third parties as a way of gaining information about the competitive impact of the commitment[128] and consulting the Advisory Committee.[129] Increased transparency and consultation may lead to more predictable use of commitment procedures; however, a number of concerns have arisen with this new procedure, not least because the Commission uses it in non-cartel cases far more frequently than expected. The first concern is that judicial review appears limited. In *Alrosa*, the Commission was reviewing an agreement by which Alrosa agreed to sell all its diamonds for export to De Beers. After a series of proceedings De Beers offered a commitment to phase out the agreement, which the Commission accepted. Alrosa was dissatisfied with the outcome and argued that the commitment was disproportionate, for less aggressive commitments would have sufficed to resolve the competition concerns.[130]

> ### Commission v. Alrosa, C–441/07 P, ECLI:EU:C:2010:377
>
> **35** . . . Article 9 of the Regulation is based on considerations of procedural economy, and enables undertakings to participate fully in the procedure, by putting forward the solutions which appear to them to be the most appropriate and capable of addressing the Commission's concerns.
>
> **36** As observed by the parties and by the Advocate General . . . the principle of proportionality, as a general principle of European Union law, is . . . a criterion for the lawfulness of any act of the institutions of the Union, including decisions taken by the Commission in its capacity of competition authority . . .
>
> **48** Undertakings which offer commitments on the basis of Article 9 of Regulation No. 1/2003 consciously accept that the concessions they make may go beyond what the Commission could itself impose on them in a decision adopted under Article 7 of the Regulation after a thorough examination. On the other hand, the closure of the infringement proceedings brought against those undertakings allows them to avoid a finding of an infringement of competition law and a possible fine.
>
> **49** Moreover, the fact that the individual commitments offered by an undertaking have been made binding by the Commission does not mean that other undertakings are deprived of the possibility of protecting the rights they may have in connection with their relations with that undertaking.

---

[128] Regulation 1/2003, Article 27(4).

[129] *Ibid.* Article 14(1) (the composition of the committee is described above at p. 887).

[130] There is an added complexity: the Commission had moved against this agreement in two ways: against De Beers for breach of Article 102 TFEU and against both undertakings for breach of Article 101 TFEU. There were ongoing negotiations on the Article 101 commitments when De Beers then proposed to settle under Article 102. The attentive reader will also have noticed that the agreement here looks like a cartel, and Article 9 procedures should not normally apply to such cases, see Regulation 1/2003, recital 13.

50 It must therefore be concluded that the Commission is right to submit that in the judgment under appeal the General Court wrongly considered that the application of the principle of proportionality must be assessed, in the case of decisions taken under Article 9 of Regulation No. 1/2003, by reference to the way in which it is assessed in connection with decisions taken under Article 7 of that Regulation despite the different concepts underlying those two provisions.

Accordingly, in commitment decisions the parties forfeit the accuracy of the Article 7 remedy in favour of a more convenient procedure. The problems with this line of argumentation are many.[131] Principal among these is that the Commission has superior bargaining power and thus can extract significant concessions that go beyond what is strictly necessary, and there is no doubt that the Commission proposes commitments to the parties, contrary to what the Court of Justice intimates.[132] Not only can the Commission threaten a formal procedure with fines, but parties may fear that non-cooperation today damages their future dealings with the Commission. However, a commitment decision does not bind national courts which may still find the conduct infringing competition law.[133] To remedy this critique the Commission has developed a practice of assessing the proportionality of the remedy in detail. Some commitments have been challenged by third parties (who might consider that the commitment is not adequate) with some success at national level.[134] However, further concerns remain. The fact that commitment decisions are not appealed frequently may stimulate the enforcer to use this procedure even for cases where the law is not clear, meaning that rather than exploring in detail the soundness of the competition problem (and risking judicial assessment of that) the Commission can expand the reach of the competition rules. Moreover, many decisions include structural remedies, which are considered exceptional in formal procedures. We show the concrete effects of these risks in Chapter 22.

(v) Commission's Procedures: An Assessment

One theme that emerges from the discussion above is how the significant powers that may be exercised need to be kept in check by reference to the fundamental rights of the parties under investigation. The source of these fundamental rights has evolved: at first these were general principles of EU law, often interpreted by reference to the jurisprudence of the ECtHR, and more recently the source of rights has been the EUCFR. In evaluating the compatibility of EU competition procedures with fundamental rights, one should distinguish two lines of analysis: one is whether the exercise of the various powers noted above is carried out in such a way that fundamental rights are complied with. As discussed above, there is some doubt as to whether this is the case, but it is telling that the European Courts and Commission make genuine attempts to ensure the law evolves to safeguard these rights.[135] The second point is whether the institutional

---

[131] F. Wagner von Papp, 'Best and Even Better Practices in Commitment Procedures After Alrosa' (2012) 49 *CMLRev* 929, offering the most comprehensive critique.

[132] DG Competition, *Antitrust Manual of Procedures* (2012) ch. 16, 7.

[133] *Gasorba SL* v. *Repsol*, C-547/16, EU:C:2017:891.

[134] *Skyscanner Ltd* v. *Competition and Markets Authority* [2014] CAT 16, but so far no success against Commission decisions, see *Morningstar* v. *Commission*, T-76/14, EU:T:2016:481. But see *Groupe Canal +* v. *European Commission*, T-873/16, ECLI:EU:T:2018:904.

[135] See generally I. van Bael, *Due Process in EU Competition Proceedings* (The Hague, Kluwer, 2011).

set-up by which the Commission investigates, prosecutes and reaches a decision is compatible with fundamental rights.[136] We examine this debate here.

Article 6(1) ECHR provides that when persons face criminal charges they are entitled to 'a fair and public hearing by an independent and impartial tribunal established by law'. One might object that Article 23(5) of Regulation 1/2003 provides that fines are administrative in nature, but this is to overlook the case law of the ECtHR which provides that formal classifications are irrelevant and that a wide range of penalties may be described as criminal, by reference to the penalty imposed and whether it aims to sanction and deter the infringer. Accordingly, most assume that Commission procedures are criminal in nature.[137] However, the ECtHR has also held that there are different degrees of criminal charges, and for non-hardcore criminal charges the imposition of penalties by agencies may be appropriate provided that the agency's decisions are subjected to judicial review. In *Menarini Diagnostics* v. *Italy*, the ECtHR ruled that Italy's antitrust procedures, which are similar to those of the Commission, comply with Article 6(1) ECHR in that the decision of the competition authority was susceptible to judicial review by a court that had full jurisdiction.[138] One might thus legitimately assume that the same applies to the Commission, so that undertakings in competition cases do not require the full set of procedural guarantees that are afforded to, say, those accused of theft.[139] If so, the question then is how far the General Court has full jurisdiction. This is where the debate is most heated at the moment, and the Court of Justice has attempted to respond to the *Menarini* judgment in an appeal against a Commission decision imposing fines on members of a cartel.[140]

KME v. *Commission*, C-272/09 P, ECLI:EU:C:2011:810

93 The judicial review of the decisions of the institutions was arranged by the founding Treaties. In addition to the review of legality, now provided for under Article 263 TFEU, a review with unlimited jurisdiction was envisaged in regard to the penalties laid down by regulations.

94 As regards the review of legality, the Court of Justice has held that whilst, in areas giving rise to complex economic assessments, the Commission has a margin of discretion with regard to economic matters, that does not mean that the Courts of the European Union must refrain from reviewing the Commission's interpretation of information of an economic nature. Not only must those Courts establish, among other things, whether the evidence relied on is factually accurate, reliable and consistent but also whether that evidence contains all the information which must be taken into account in order to assess a complex situation and whether it is capable of substantiating the conclusions drawn from it.

---

[136] This is a long-standing debate, see F. Montag, 'The Case for Radical Reform of the Infringement Procedure under Regulation 17' (1998) *ECLR* 428; C. D. Ehlermann and M. Marquis (eds.), *European Competition Annual 2009: The Evaluation of Evidence and its Judicial Review in Competition Cases* (Oxford, Hart, 2011).

[137] *KME* v. *Commission*, C-272/09 P, ECLI:EU:C:2011:63, Opinion of Advocate General Sharpston, para. 64; Editorial Comments, 'Towards a More Judicial Approach? EU Antitrust Fines under the Scrutiny of Fundamental Rights' (2011) 48(5) *CMLRev* 1405, 1408.

[138] *Menarini Diagnostics* v. *Italy* (Application no. 43509/08), Judgment of 27 September 2011.

[139] W. P. J. Wils, 'Antitrust Enforcement Powers and Procedural Rights and Guarantees: The Interplay between EU Law, National Law, the Charter of Fundamental Rights of the EU and the European Convention on Human Rights' (2011) 34 *World Competition* 189.

[140] *Schindler Holding and Others* v. *Commission*, C-501/11 P, EU:C:2013:522, paras. 33-8, citing *Menarini* and stating that judicial review by the ECJ complies with the requirements of the ECtHR.

95   With regard to the penalties for infringements of competition law, the second subparagraph of Article 15(2) of Regulation No. 17 provides that in fixing the amount of the fine, regard is to be had both to the gravity and to the duration of the infringement.

96   The Court of Justice has held that, in order to determine the amount of a fine, it is necessary to take account of the duration of the infringements and of all the factors capable of affecting the assessment of their gravity, such as the conduct of each of the undertakings, the role played by each of them in the establishment of the concerted practices, the profit which they were able to derive from those practices, their size, the value of the goods concerned and the threat that infringements of that type pose to the European Community.

97   The Court has also stated that objective factors such as the content and duration of the anticompetitive conduct, the number of incidents and their intensity, the extent of the market affected and the damage to the economic public order must be taken into account. The analysis must also take into consideration the relative importance and market share of the undertakings responsible and also any repeated infringements.

98   This large number of factors requires that the Commission carry out a thorough examination of the circumstances of the infringement.

99   In the interests of transparency the Commission adopted the Guidelines, in which it indicates the basis on which it will take account of one or other aspect of the infringement and what this will imply as regards the amount of the fine.

100   The Guidelines, which, the Court has held, form rules of practice from which the administration may not depart in an individual case without giving reasons compatible with the principle of equal treatment, merely describe the method used by the Commission to examine infringements and the criteria that the Commission requires to be taken into account in setting the amount of a fine.

101   It is important to bear in mind the obligation to state reasons for Community acts. That is a particularly important obligation in the present case. It is for the Commission to state the reasons for its decision and, in particular, to explain the weighting and assessment of the factors taken into account. The Courts must establish of their own motion that there is a statement of reasons.

102   Furthermore, the Courts must carry out the review of legality incumbent upon them on the basis of the evidence adduced by the applicant in support of the pleas in law put forward. In carrying out such a review, the Courts cannot use the Commission's margin of discretion – either as regards the choice of factors taken into account in the application of the criteria mentioned in the Guidelines or as regards the assessment of those factors – as a basis for dispensing with the conduct of an in-depth review of the law and of the facts.

103   The review of legality is supplemented by the unlimited jurisdiction which the Courts of the European Union were afforded by Article 17 of Regulation No. 17 and which is now recognised by Article 31 of Regulation No. 1/2003, in accordance with Article 261 TFEU. That jurisdiction empowers the Courts, in addition to carrying out a mere review of the lawfulness of the penalty, to substitute their own appraisal for the Commission's and, consequently, to cancel, reduce or increase the fine or penalty payment imposed . . .

106   The review provided for by the Treaties thus involves review by the Courts of the European Union of both the law and the facts, and means that they have the power to assess the evidence, to annul the contested decision and to alter the amount of a fine. The review of legality provided for under Article 263 TFEU, supplemented by the unlimited jurisdiction in respect of the amount of the fine, provided for under Article 31 of Regulation No. 1/2003, is not therefore contrary to the requirements of the principle of effective judicial protection in Article 47 of the Charter.

This judgment leaves something to be desired on two fronts. First, the General Court's power with respect to fines is much more significant than its power when it comes to a review of the facts, which raises questions about whether the Court really has full jurisdiction across the board. Secondly, the Court restates a long-held view that while for factual findings the Court can examine the correctness in detail, in certain complex economic matters it defers to the Commission's judgment (para. 94). Commentators have viewed this approach as unsatisfactory on two grounds: first, it is not always clear which kinds of issue merit more in-depth review and which ones do not; secondly, this passage seems to be evidence that the court lacks full jurisdiction.[141] On the other hand, the judgment has been welcomed because it appears to require the General Court to consider much more closely the grounds of appeal raised by the parties.

The debate on the nature of judicial review has developed in an unsatisfactory manner because no court has yet arrived at a clear conception of what an appropriate level of judicial scrutiny means. This has not been helped by one judge explaining that when faced with the review of complex economic assessments the court applies an 'intense – though marginal – review'.[142]

As a reaction to this it has been argued that a more fruitful approach would be to allow the Court of Justice to retain the present marginal review of delicate economic policy issues (for which the Commission is constitutionally better placed) and instead consider reforming the decision-making organism so that there is a functional separation between prosecution and decision-making. Rendering the decision-maker independent in this way would serve to legitimise the exercise of the Commission's discretionary powers for there would be no confirmation bias.[143] On the other hand, the current dialectic between the Commission and the General Court appears satisfactory in most cases.

C. Harding and J. Joshua, *Regulating Cartels in Europe: A Study of Legal Control of Corporate Delinquency*, 2nd edn (Oxford University Press, 2010) 219–20

[The General Court] has fashioned for itself a distinctive role as a court of review ... Moreover, its review of virtually every aspect of the Commission's procedure has been painstaking. In effect, this has encouraged appeals by undertakings to such an extent that the Court has an almost automatic role in dealing with the Commission's cartel decisions. It would not be an exaggeration to say that it has for practical purposes almost turned itself into a trial court in this context ... In effect, therefore, the separation of powers complaint ... has been addressed. In the majority of cartel cases, the Commission's formal decision has evolved into a summative statement of the case for the prosecution, which is then judicially tested before the [General Court]. Since the dust has settled on this development, from the middle of the 1990s both the Commission and the Court appear to have settled into a comfortable relationship, within which the former prepares its cases carefully, and the latter confirms most of the prosecution case ... the cartels still have their day in court, with the prospect of appeal to the Court of Justice if they wish to continue the legal battle.

---

[141] I. van Bael, *Due Process in Competition Proceedings* (The Hague, Kluwer, 2011) 357–63.

[142] M. Jaeger, 'The Standard of Review in Competition Cases Involving Complex Economic Assessments' (2011) 2(4) *Journal of European Competition Law and Practice* 295, 300. The judge was simply referring to para. 94 in *KME*, noting how this has been the basis for several detailed reviews of the economic evidence brought by the Commission. Yet, the choice of language is rather unfortunate. Likewise, later the learned judge's suggestion that marginal review be limited to matters of 'economic policy' (313) appears too narrow, for what he appears to mean is the application of economic theory by the Commission, its discretion in selecting a theory of harm.

[143] R. Nazzini, 'Administrative Enforcement, Judicial Review and Fundamental Rights in EU Competition Law: A Comparative Contextual-Functionalist Perspective' (2012) 49(3) *CMLRev* 971.

However, Harding and Joshua are concerned with the fact that this legal development has occurred as a result of powerful corporate actors, who have explored the judicial process in the light of clear infringements of EU competition law, and who often make repetitive legal arguments. And while the appeals by these large firms have led to the creation of considerable procedural safeguards for their interests, the Court of Justice has had little opportunity to explain what rights those injured by anti-competitive behaviour have. One possible reaction to this assessment is that the Court's review of the Commission's decisions appears to vary from case to case. In some merger cases the Court appears to be very willing to probe in depth the soundness of the economic theories used,[144] while in cartel and abuse-of-dominance cases the Court appears to be less exacting in its review, although this may be changing.[145]

(vi) Commission's Performance

A further long-standing criticism of the Commission's procedures is the potentially political nature of the decision-making process.

L. Laudati, 'The European Commission as Regulator: The Uncertain Pursuit of the Competitive Market' in G. Majone (ed.), *Regulating Europe* (London, Routledge, 1996) 231, 235–6

The degree of independence of an antitrust enforcement institution is determined by two elements: the structural independence from political authority, and separation of investigatory, prosecutorial and decision-making functions. The Community antitrust enforcement has a low level of independence in both respects . . .

When the Community system was established, it was believed that placing the powers to execute the competition laws in the hands of the Commission would minimize political interference with enforcement by the Member States. The Commission has, however, become a highly political body, and political considerations play a significant role in its competition enforcement decisions. National antitrust officials acknowledge that pressure from national governments may influence the Commission's decisions because the Commission must have the cooperation of national governments in order to fulfil its mission. Thus, the Commission exerts considerable effort to reconcile national policies with Community policy.

Moreover, DG IV [now, DG Competition] cannot act independently of the other DGs since final decisions are made by the full Commission. Political pressure from other DGs is felt constantly, owing to the broad economic implications of competition decisions. Such pressure, in general, runs against the negative decisions by DG IV, particularly with regard to mergers. Moreover, it forces DG IV to take account of policy considerations other than competition policy . . . This type of pressure has grown in recent years owing to the increasingly important role of competition law, and the economic recession and high levels of unemployment throughout the Community.

For instance, DG III (industrial policy) and DG IV (social policy) frequently take positions at odds with those of DG IV. Other DGs likely to intervene regulate specific sectors of the economy – for example DG XIII

---

[144] See e.g. *Commission* v. *Tetra Laval*, C-12/03 P, ECLI:EU:C:2005:87.

[145] See e.g. *Microsoft* v. *Commission*, T-201/04, ECLI:EU:T:2007:289. For discussion see I. Forrester, 'A Challenge for Europe's Judges: The Review of Fines in Competition Cases' (2011) 36 *ELRev* 185; D. Bailey, 'Scope of Review under Article 81 EC' (2004) 41 *CMLRev* 1327; A. Fritzsche, 'Discretion, Scope of Judicial Review and Institutional Balance in European Law' (2010) 47 *CMLRev* 361.

(telecommunications) and DG XVII (energy). This does not mean that all communication among the DGs is contentious. Rather, collaboration and consultation regularly occur between rapporteurs of DG IV and those of other DGs, especially DG III, because of their familiarity with the various sectors. But if DG III staff believe that a merger should be cleared and their counterparts believe the opposite, the staff members of each DG must convince their Commissioner of the merits of their position. Commissioners themselves then resolve the dispute.

Another fault of the system is that it requires Commissioners with no expertise in competition law and severe time constraints to apply complex laws and economic analysis to facts in all cases, then make the final decision. It is doubtful whether all Commissioners are professionally qualified to perform this function. Critics point out that, in practice, most competition decisions are adopted with little or no debate, as written proposed decisions are circulated to each cabinet of each Commissioner and considered to be adopted if no objections are made within a limited period.

An additional problem results from a lack of clarity as to the standards being applied in deciding antitrust cases. As stated above, policy areas other than competition are considered, especially industrial and social policy. However, parties with competition matters before the Commission have no substantive or procedural rules to follow regarding the presentation of evidence on such policy issues, even though these matters could have significant impact on the outcome of their cases. This raises due process concerns.

Laudati's comments strengthen the views of Wesseling (discussed in section 2 of this chapter) by noting how the interference of other EU objectives is inevitable, given the institutional make-up of the Commission and the Commission's own political energies and understanding of how the Community project impacts upon the development of competition law. Of course, not every competition decision is keenly debated by the College of Commissioners – much competition law enforcement is the routine supervision of business practices where wider Community interests are affected marginally, but in significant cases that establish a new precedent or apply to novel markets, other Commissioners' views (whether based upon their portfolio or their national interests) become more prominent. It is fair to say, however, that as a whole, the Commission's enforcement of competition law is like that of any other independent agency: while it must be sensitive to the political context, by and large it exercises its powers autonomously. Indeed, competition enforcement by the Commission is highly regarded worldwide.[146]

4 RESETTLEMENT OF COMPETITION REGULATORY AUTHORITY

(i) Modernisation

Concentrating the task of enforcement in the Commission brought certain advantages: a single regulator, a uniform approach to competition law (although stricter national competition laws could still apply provided the Commission had not acted),[147] and DG Competition gained

---

[146] See generally Monti, n. 3 above.
[147] *Walt Wilhelm* v. *Bundeskartellamt*, 14/68, ECLI:EU:C:1969:4. On the difficulties of this see R. Wesseling, 'Subsidiarity in Community Competition Law over National Law' (1997) 22 *ELRev* 19.

experience in handling disputes. However, there were two drawbacks in concentrating enforcement in the hands of the Commission. The first, as we saw above, is that the Commission could act in a politically motivated manner. In the mid-1990s it was argued that competition enforcement should be delegated to a separate 'European Cartel Office' to enhance the independence of the decision-making process, but this suggestion is now unlikely to be implemented.[148] The second problem is that the Commission considered that its limited resources had become insufficient to deal with all competition problems coming to its attention. This was because parties were able to notify the Commission of their plans and evaluating these proposals was time-consuming and diverted efforts away from a proactive enforcement strategy.[149] This enforcement pattern was neither in the interests of business nor in the interests of the proper enforcement of competition law.

Since the 1970s, the Commission has attempted to ameliorate this, first by developing certain administrative practices that were less time-consuming. It issued comfort letters (informal indications that on the basis of information available there was no competition concern). However, their non-binding character gave parties little legal security where the agreement was challenged in national courts. The second solution was to draft Block Exemption Regulations. These provide that if an agreement meets certain specified criteria, it benefits from automatic exemption, without notification. The weakness of this approach is that it creates a straitjacket effect: the parties use the relevant Block Exemption as the basis for their contractual relations and structure the agreement according to its terms, which might skew their commercial desires. Requiring parties to sacrifice commercial practicality in order to gain legal security seemed to some too high a price to pay.[150]

In the early 1990s the Commission attempted a third solution, often referred to as a programme of decentralisation. It encouraged national competition authorities to enforce EU competition law and invited private parties to use national courts to enforce competition law. The Commission argued that national competition authorities had a common task of protecting competition and the national authorities should use EU competition law to regulate markets, allowing the Commission to take action in cases of particular significance to the Community.[151] However, encouraging decentralised enforcement though soft law failed to galvanise national authorities and courts and the Commission still had a worryingly heavy caseload, and this was due to the 2004 enlargement of the EU, which would prevent it from setting its enforcement priorities. More drastic reforms were needed.[152] This background explains the emergence of Regulation 1/2003.[153]

---

[148] S. Wilks and L. McGowan, 'Disarming the Commission: The Debate Over a European Cartel Office' (1995) 32 *JCMS* 259.

[149] Some 40,000 notifications were received. *Ninth Report on Competition Policy* (1979) 15–16.

[150] The first Block Exemption was implemented in 1967: Regulation 67/67 on exclusive purchase agreements [1967] OJ L 84/67.

[151] Commission Notice on cooperation between national competition authorities and the Commission in handling cases falling within the scope of Articles [101 TFEU] and [102 TFEU] [1997] OJ C 313/1; Commission Notice on cooperation between national courts and the Commission in applying Articles [101 TFEU] and [102 TFEU] [1993] OJ C 39/6.

[152] *White Paper on Modernisation of the Rules Implementing Articles [101 TFEU] and [102 TFEU]* [1999] OJ C 132/1.

[153] Regulation 1/2003 on the implementation of the rules on competition laid down in Articles 81 and 82 of the Treaty [2003] OJ L 1/1.

> **Regulation 1/2003, Article 1**
>
> (1) Agreements, decisions and concerted practices caught by Article [101(1)] of the Treaty which do not satisfy the conditions of Article [101(3)] of the Treaty shall be prohibited, no prior decision to that effect being required.
> (2) Agreements, decisions and concerted practices caught by Article [101(1)] of the Treaty which satisfy the conditions of Article [101(3)] of the Treaty shall not be prohibited, no prior decision to that effect being required.

The implication of Article 1 is profound: parties who before would have submitted a request for exemption and had to wait endlessly for a response must now decide for themselves whether their agreement infringes the competition rules. This represents a switch from an *ex ante* notification-based system of competition enforcement to an *ex post* deterrence-based system. Abolishing the right of parties to notify an agreement means that the Commission is now free to focus on the more serious infringements.

The other plank of the reform is to require national competition authorities to enforce EU competition law, thereby decentralising enforcement of EU competition law.

> **Regulation 1/2003, Article 3**
>
> (1) Where the competition authorities of the Member States or national courts apply national competition law to agreements, decisions by associations of undertakings or concerted practices within the meaning of Article [101(1)] which may affect trade between Member States within the meaning of that provision, they shall also apply Article [101] to such agreements, decisions or concerted practices. Where the competition authorities of the Member States or national courts apply national competition law to any abuse prohibited by Article [102], they shall also apply Article [102].
> (2) The application of national competition law may not lead to the prohibition of agreements, decisions by associations of undertakings or concerted practices which may affect trade between Member States but which do not restrict competition within the meaning of Article [101(1)], or which fulfil the conditions of Article [101(3)] or which are covered by a Regulation for the application of Article [101(3)]. Member States shall not under this Regulation be precluded from adopting and applying on their territory stricter national laws which prohibit or sanction unilateral conduct engaged in by undertakings.
> (3) Without prejudice to general principles and other provisions of Community law, paragraphs 1 and 2 do not apply when the competition authorities and the courts of the Member States apply national merger control laws nor do they preclude the application of provisions of national law that predominantly pursue an objective different from that pursued by Articles [101] and [102].

This provision obliges NCAs to apply Articles 101 and 102 TFEU and to give EU competition law priority over national competition law. 'Enforcement of Articles [101 and 102] is now a shared responsibility, not just in theory but in practice. At both the political and practical level, the modernisation regime requires Member States to adopt a commitment to the enforcement of Community law in this area far in excess of anything to date.'[154] In effect, Regulation 1/2003

---

[154] Kerse and Khan, n. 44 above, 47.

turns the NCA into a Union competition authority. There are three exceptions to the obligation of the NCA to give priority to EU competition law. The first is in the final sentence of Regulation 1/2003, Article 3(2), which allows the authority to apply stricter national competition law that regulates unilateral behaviour. As we will see in the following two chapters, EU competition law only regulates unilateral behaviour when the firm has a dominant position. In contrast, some Member States have competition laws that are wider in scope. The second exception is that national merger law is unaffected. The final exception is that national laws, which pursue non-competition objectives, may be enforced to prohibit a practice which is unobjectionable from a competition perspective, for example consumer protection legislation.

From the perspective of undertakings, Regulation 1/2003 reduces compliance costs because very similar competition rules apply across the Union. Therefore, their practices will be scrutinised uniformly regardless of which competition authority handles the investigation. From the perspective of the Commission, this creates a battalion of competition authorities with ample resources, thereby improving the enforcement of competition law.

(ii) Commission's New Role

The Commission no longer has to review every agreement notified to it. It can now set its own agenda in a legal environment where the majority of competition enforcement will be carried out by national authorities. The Commission has carried out three main tasks.

First, the Commission has increased enforcement against cartels which operate internationally, as well as focusing on industries where a few firms hold market power. This is significant because in the past the Commission was criticised for focusing on harmless business conduct that was notified to it.[155] However, this is somewhat misleading because a closer look at the statistics reveals that the Commission had already begun to focus on cartels around the year 2000, largely because of improved internal working practices, and because Block Exemptions led to fewer notifications. The absence of a significant increase in the Commission's output in the period since 2004 is not easy to explain.[156]

The second task for the Commission is to provide guidance in novel cases to facilitate the work of national competition authorities. The Commission will continue the process of drafting Notices and Guidelines (begun in the late 1990s), which are not binding but are an expression of how the Commission would handle a case and are bound to influence the national authorities. These instruments will be of increasing importance for undertakings because they are now unable to notify agreements to gain exemption and require as much information as possible to determine for themselves whether their planned business practices are lawful. In exceptional circumstances, however, parties may be able to obtain individual guidance from the Commission either informally through guidance letters,[157] or formally.

---

[155] D. Neven, P. Papandropoulos and P. Seabright, *Trawling for Minnows: European Competition Policy and Agreements Between Firms* (London, CEPR, 1998), M. Monti, 'European Competition Policy: Quo Vadis?', 10 April 2003, http://ec.europa.eu/competition/index_en.html.

[156] Monti, n. 3 above, and W. P. J. Wils, 'Ten Years of Regulation 1/2003: A Retrospective' (2013) 4(4) *Journal of European Competition Law and Practice* 1.

[157] Regulation 1/2003, recital 38 and Commission Notice on informal guidance relating to novel questions concerning Articles 81 and 82 of the EC Treaty that arise in individual cases [2004] OJ C 101/78.

> ### Regulation 1/2003, Article 10
>
> Where the Community public interest relating to the application of Articles [101 TFEU] and [102 TFEU] . . . so requires, the Commission, acting on its own initiative, may by decision find that Article [101 TFEU] . . . is not applicable to an agreement, a decision by an association of undertakings or a concerted practice, either because the conditions of Article [101(1) TFEU] . . . are not fulfilled, or because the conditions of Article [101(3) TFEU] . . . are satisfied.
>
> The Commission may likewise make such a finding with reference to Article 82 of the Treaty.

There is a risk that Article 10 could be used for reasons other than merely clarifying the law. The provision is triggered by the need to serve the *Community's public interest*. This is sufficiently wide to allow the Commission to decide that a particular practice does not infringe Article 101 TFEU because of some public policy reason unrelated to competition law. Given the institutional make-up of the Commission, the risk is present, even though the recitals to the Regulation suggest that the purpose of Article 10 is to shed light on areas where the law is unclear.[158] To date, no decision has been issued under Article 10. Instead of using these methods the Commission has used its powers as *amicus curiae* to intervene in cases in national courts to secure harmonised interpretation.[159]

(iii) European Competition Network

To ensure the successful functioning of national enforcement, each Member State must designate the competition authority responsible for the application of Articles 101 and 102 TFEU,[160] and the NCA must be able to impose meaningful remedies, including interim measures, prohibition orders, imposing penalties and accepting commitments.[161] This harmonises the sanctions of all NCAs to guarantee the effective enforcement of EU competition law. However, in addition to empowering each NCA, successful enforcement requires considerable coordination among the NCAs and the Commission. Therefore, as early as 2002 the European Competition Network (ECN) was created, comprising all NCAs and the Commission. The ECN is not a competition authority, but a forum for cooperation for the NCAs. Its principal tasks when it was originally designed were the following: first, to coordinate enforcement so that there is an efficient allocation of cases among the Network; and secondly, to develop mechanisms for cooperation during investigations and means of ensuring consistency in the application of competition rules. In reality the performance of the Network has been even more impressive, if problematic. We chart the performance of the original tasks first.

---

[158] Regulation 1/2003, recital 14.

[159] *Ibid*. Article 15(3) provides for this power (the interventions are available at http://ec.europa.eu/competition/court/antitrust_amicus_curiae.html).

[160] *Ibid*. Article 35(1).   [161] *Ibid*. Article 5.

(a) Case Allocation and Cooperation

Regulation 1/2003 envisaged that each case should be handled by a single authority,[162] but the detailed implementation was left to soft law instruments, setting out in detail how cases may be allocated. Three alternatives are envisaged: enforcement by one NCA, enforcement by several NCAs or enforcement by the Commission.[163] The Network serves as a platform for case reallocation. One agency will initiate a procedure and will inform the others of it. Normally the agency that initiates the case keeps it but other agencies may claim to be better placed. An authority is well placed when the practice in question affects its territory, where it is able to impose effective remedies and when it has access to the information necessary to prove the infringement.[164] Parallel action is envisaged when this might be better for bringing the infringement to an end, or where this might allow for more effective remedies.[165] Finally, the Notice provides that the Commission may be better placed in three scenarios: when the activity affects three or more Member States; when the competition complaint is closely linked to other EU law prohibitions so that it is more efficient for the Commission to intervene; or when the case 'requires the adoption of a Commission decision to develop [EU] competition policy when a new competition issue arises or to ensure effective enforcement'.[166]

Thus far there have been very few reallocations. However, a legal concern arises in instances of parallel proceedings: suppose there is a price-fixing agreement among manufacturers of widgets and prices are fixed in Bulgaria and Hungary. May the two NCAs decide to divide up the case so that each prosecutes it? Arguably this is advantageous because then the two authorities may impose a fine each for the effects of the cartel in their jurisdiction. However, it is arguable that this prosecution infringes the undertakings' right not to be prosecuted twice for the same offence. The Court of Justice has addressed this concern in *Toshiba*: the Commission and the Czech NCA had prosecuted and fined a cartel, but the Czech NCA had done so for activities that had taken place in the Czech Republic before that country's accession to the European Union. In these circumstances, the right not to be prosecuted twice did not arise.[167] Other cartel cases have been divided up among the enforcers.[168] While this may be expedient, it undermines the rights of the firms under investigation: the justifications for prohibiting a second prosecution are in order to discipline the prosecutor so that it has all the evidence before proceeding; a single prosecution also spares the defendant the burdens of defending the issue twice. Furthermore, allowing multiple prosecutions of the same price-fixing cartel misses the key enforcement gap: many NCAs appear to have no power to impose fines for effects that occur outside their Member State.[169] This is particularly problematic because the reason they must apply EU competition law in the first place is that the practice has an effect on trade among Member States.[170]

---

[162] *Ibid.* recital 18.

[163] Commission Notice on cooperation within the Network of Competition Authorities [2004] OJ C 101/43.

[164] *Ibid.* paras. 6–11.   [165] *Ibid.* para. 12.   [166] *Ibid.* para. 15.

[167] *Toshiba Corporation and Others* v. *Úřad pro ochranu hospodářské soutěže*, C-17/10, ECLI:EU:C:2012:72.

[168] G. Monti, 'Galvanising National Competition Authorities in the European Union' in D. Gerard and I. Lianos (eds.), *Reconciling Efficiency and Equity* (forthcoming 2019).

[169] K. Lenaerts, D. Gerard, 'Decentralisation of EC Competition Law Enforcement: Judges in the Frontline' (2004) 27(3) *World Competition* 313

[170] For further discussion, see G. Monti, 'Managing Decentralised Antitrust Enforcement' (2014) 51(1) *CMLRev* 261; G. di Federico, 'EU Competition Law and the Principle of *Ne Bis in Idem*' (2011) 17(2) *EPL* 241.

Once a case is allocated, there are also provisions to assist the NCA: the Commission or any other NCA may transmit information to the NCA in charge, and it is even possible that one NCA carries out investigations in its Member State on behalf of the NCA in charge of prosecuting the case.[171] Some concerns have been expressed that this transmission of information may not contain sufficient safeguards, but so far there have been very few instances where these powers have been exercised.[172]

Finally, before a decision is rendered by an NCA, the Commission may check it.

Regulation 1/2003, Article 11

(6) The initiation by the Commission of proceedings for the adoption of a decision shall relieve the competition authorities of the Member States of their competence to apply Articles [101 TFEU] and [102 TFEU] ... If a competition authority of a Member State is already acting on a case, the Commission shall only initiate proceedings after consulting with that national competition authority.

The article is designed to allow other NCAs to express their views on the decision and, more significantly, it is a way for the Commission to check that the NCA does not use the law in a political manner to favour national industry. As an additional safeguard against national bias in a planned decision, Article 11(6) allows the Commission to remove the case from the NCA and decide it itself. The latter provision is a drastic measure, and the Commission has so far used less drastic (but also less transparent) means of advising NCAs on the approach they should take.[173]

(b) Modernisation in Practice

What has been observed is that the two main tasks for the ECN have not taxed it, but the ECN has been active on other fronts: it appears to be a site where members seek practical advice about how to analyse markets, and where collaborative projects are entered into to improve enforcement. For example, the ECN has surveyed NCAs and issued recommendations on procedural matters like commitment decisions and gathering digital evidence.[174] There has also been one instance where several NCAs coordinated their enforcement efforts when faced with the same concern.[175] In brief, NCAs were alerted to the risks posed by the agreements between booking.com and hotels. The agreements required that the hotel prices on the booking.com website had to be no higher than those that the hotel charged on its own website or on the website of any other platform (a so-called wide price parity clause). NCAs were concerned that this would soften competition for hotel rooms and may also make entry of competitors to booking.com more difficult. The French, Italian and Swedish NCAs took the lead in assessing the competition concerns. This led to three commitment decisions in the three jurisdictions by which booking.com agreed to narrow price parity clauses (that is to say, booking.com could prevent the hotel from charging lower rates on its website but could not prevent the hotel from agreeing to lower rates with other online platforms like Expedia). Nearly all other NCAs then followed this

---

[171] See Regulation 1/2003, Articles 11(3), 12 and 22(4).

[172] D. Reichelt, 'To What Extent Does the Co-operation within the European Competition Network Protect the Rights of Undertakings?' (2005) 42 *CMLRev* 745.

[173] Monti, n. 3 above.   [174] For an overview, see http://ec.europa.eu/competition/ecn/index_en.html.

[175] For an overview, see Monti, n. 168 above.

approach and issued similar commitment decisions. The German NCA however disagreed and issued a decision prohibiting all price parity clauses. In the aftermath of this the Commission facilitated an *ex post* study on the extent to which these actions impacted on the market. Its main conclusions were that more time was needed to test the effects and that many hotels remained unaware of the change in policy.[176] To some, these developments suggest that there is the potential for experimentalist governance.

Y. Svetiev, 'Networked Competition Governance in the EU: Delegation, Decentralization or Experimentalist Governance?' in C. F. Sabel and J. Zeitlin (eds.), *Experimentalist Governance in the European Union: Towards a New Architecture* (Oxford University Press, 2010) 84, 103

[T]he new network has features that can make it an important mechanism for disseminating learning about regulatory interventions by national authorities and the Commission, reviewing such interventions, and using the information gathered so as to advance the identified objectives of competition law and the metrics used to gauge their attainment. Finally, the residual powers of intervention vested in the Commission need not be viewed as instruments of command and control, both because, if exercised, they are checked by requirements for justification and peer review, and because they may play a different role in building up implementation capacity among the network members . . .

Alternatively, the obligation to report initiatives and decisions from specific interventions can provide a key learning tool for members of the network. For example, interventions by authorities considered to have greater implementation capacity and credibility (such as the United Kingdom, France, Germany and Italy) can be used by the smaller and less credible authorities to inform their own decision-making.

This optimistic approach may be challenged by the fact that the booking.com episode remains an isolated example: the vast majority of cases taken by NCAs address national markets, and indeed at times we find cross-border cartels investigated by multiple NCAs which appears inefficient.[177] Moreover, there are those who fear that the system is too informal to work in a legitimate manner. The club-like qualities of the ECN may well ensure better decision-making but at the expense of a transparent forum for deliberation. And opacity brings the risk of domination, whether by the Commission or another NCA, dictating enforcement priorities, thus NCAs work for the European Union's competition policy.[178] Here we have a tension: on the one hand, insiders report that the Network members cooperate amicably and product-ively.[179] But this raises concerns about absence of legitimacy: who actually decides the case, the NCA or the ECN? When does peer review become peer pressure? And who is accountable for the Network's deliberations?

---

[176] European Commission, Report on the monitoring exercise carried out in the online hotel booking sector by EU competition authorities in 2016, http://ec.europa.eu/competition/ecn/hotel_monitoring_report_en.pdf.

[177] *DHL Express (Italy) Srl and Others* v. *Autorità Garante della Concorrenza e del mercato*, C-428/14, ECLI:EU:C:2016:27, where part of the cartel was punished by the Commission and part by the Italian NCA.

[178] S. Wilks, 'Agency Escape: Decentralization or Dominance of the European Commission in the Modernization of Competition Policy?' (2005) 18 *Governance* 431; see Bruzzone and Boccaccio, n. 126 above.

[179] K. Dekeyser and M. Jaspers, 'A New Era of ECN Cooperation' (2007) 30 *World Competition* 3. For a more theoretical analysis, see G. Majone, 'The Credibility Crisis of Community Regulation' (2000) 38(2) *JCMS* 273; I. Maher, 'Regulation and Modes of Governance in EC Competition Law: What is New in Enforcement?' (2007–8) 31 *Fordham Int'l LJ* 1713.

(c) Negative and Positive Harmonisation

It was inevitable, given the incomplete nature of Regulation 1/2003 that the Court of Justice would become involved. What is striking is the vigour with which the Court has tested national arrangements and limited NCAs. This case law is in tension with the flexibility some would like to see develop. The most striking judgment, with far-reaching impact, is *VEBIC*. This was a simple cartel case but the Court was asked to investigate if the Belgian competition procedures were adequate. The legislation designated the Belgian NCA to function like an administrative court, and within it were two bodies: a prosecutor and a decision-maker. This was to ensure compliance with fundamental rights. Parties could appeal, but on such appeals the NCA (which was the lower court) was understandably not allowed to act as respondent. Instead, a Minister responsible for the economy could make written observations in support of the NCA's decision.

VEBIC, C–439/08, ECLI:EU:C:2010:739

57 Although Article 35(1) of the Regulation leaves it to the domestic legal order of each Member State to determine the detailed procedural rules for legal proceedings brought against decisions of the competition authorities designated thereunder, such rules must not jeopardise the attainment of the objective of the Regulation, which is to ensure that Articles 101 TFEU and 102 TFEU are applied effectively by those authorities.

58 In that regard, as the Advocate General has remarked in point 74 of his Opinion, if the national competition authority is not afforded rights as a party to proceedings and is thus prevented from defending a decision that it has adopted in the general interest, there is a risk that the court before which the proceedings have been brought might be wholly 'captive' to the pleas in law and arguments put forward by the undertaking(s) bringing the proceedings. In a field such as that of establishing infringements of the competition rules and imposing fines, which involves complex legal and economic assessments, the very existence of such a risk is likely to compromise the exercise of the specific obligation on national competition authorities under the Regulation to ensure the effective application of Articles 101 TFEU and 102 TFEU.

59 A national competition authority's obligation to ensure that Articles 101 TFEU and 102 TFEU are applied effectively therefore requires that the authority should be entitled to participate, as a defendant or respondent, in proceedings before a national court which challenge a decision that the authority itself has taken . . .

62 Under Article 35(1) of the Regulation, the competition authorities designated by the Member States may include courts. Under Article 35(2), when enforcement of EU competition law is entrusted to national administrative and judicial authorities, the Member States may allocate different powers and functions to those different national authorities, whether administrative or judicial.

63 In that regard, in the absence of EU rules, the Member States remain competent, in accordance with the principle of procedural autonomy, to designate the bodies of the national competition authority which may participate, as a defendant or respondent, in proceedings brought before a national court against a decision that the authority itself has taken, while at the same time ensuring that fundamental rights are observed and that EU competition law is fully effective.

On the facts, this meant that Belgium had to redesign its NCA. The more general point is the Court of Justice's repeated insistence on effectiveness. This may pose significant limits on the possibilities of NCAs to explore alternative means of designing. For example, the Court may challenge the design of leniency policies: in *Schenker* it reminded a national authority that immunity from a fine should be an exceptional reward only when cooperation is 'decisive in detecting and actually suppressing the cartel';[180] in *Donau Chemie*, it found that the criteria to determine whether a plaintiff should be able to have access to the leniency documents must be set at national level having regard to the effectiveness of leniency programmes.[181] It is not clear how far-reaching the judgment in *VEBIC* might be: can one challenge an NCA because its fining policies are not sufficiently high when the NCA imposes fines for the effects of an anti-competitive practice only in its territory?[182] Can it be used to challenge the funding of an NCA, if it is found that insufficient resources are afforded to ensure effective enforcement? Furthermore, the Court of Justice has also eroded some of the powers NCAs may be afforded; for example, an NCA cannot make a decision stating that a given practice does not infringe competition law.[183]

The 'negative' integration that the Court of Justice stimulates (negative because the Court merely prohibits certain procedures of NCAs) is set to be complemented by a Directive to 'empower the competition authorities of the Member States to be more effective enforcers and to ensure the proper functioning of the internal market'.[184] The background to this initiative was the review of ten years of Regulation 1/2003. It reports that decentralised enforcement has worked well with NCAs applying EU competition law to nearly 1,000 cases. At the same time it takes the view that the quality of enforcement would be improved if all NCAs had similar powers. The Directive will therefore align the powers of NCAs with those of the Commission when it comes to powers of inspection, the imposition of fines and limitation periods. Furthermore, it requires States to have a leniency policy which is aligned with that of the Commission. Moreover, it creates a legal requirement that NCAs must be independent and sufficiently well-resourced to carry out their tasks. These added powers have been welcomed by NCAs many of whom had been unsuccessful in lobbying their governments to secure these added powers. However, it is not particularly clear why it is the Commission's powers that serve as the exclusive model for NCAs. (Had no NCA developed some useful procedure for the others to imitate?) Nor does the Directive try and facilitate joint enforcement, save for affording the NCA that has imposed a fine the ability to request that another NCA collect the fine in case this is impossible in the former NCA's territory.[185]

5 PRIVATE ENFORCEMENT

It has been argued that private litigation in competition law should be welcomed for two reasons: first, victims of competition law infringements are compensated (public law enforcement merely prevents further harm); secondly, private litigants increase the number of enforcement actions,

---

[180] *Bundeswettbewerbsbehörde and Bundeskartellanwalt* v. *Schenker & Co. AG and Others*, C-681/11, ECLI:EU:C:2013:404, para. 47.

[181] *Bundeswettbewerbsbehörde* v. *Donau Chemie AG and Others*, C-536/11, ECLI:EU:C:2013:366.

[182] This is a live issue because the practice in many NCAs is to limit fines to local effects, even if the practice is caught by EU competition law. See Monti, n. 168 above.

[183] *Prezes Urzędu Ochrony Konkurencji i Konsumentów* v. *Tele2 Polska sp. z o.o., devenue Netia SA*, C-375/09, ECLI:EU:C:2011:270; see discussion in Ch. 22, p. 944, and the note by S. Brammer (2012) 49(3) *CMLRev* 1163.

[184] Directive (EU) 2019/1 of the European Parliament and of the Council of 11 December 2018 to empower the competition authorities of the Member States to be more effective enforcers and to ensure the proper functioning of the internal market [2019] OJ L11/3.

[185] Directive 2019/1, Article 26. G. Monti, 'The Proposed Directive to Empower National Competition Authorities: Too Little, Too Much, or Just Right?' (2017) 3(3) *Competition Law and Policy Debate* 40.

widening the application of competition law.[186] The Commission has long campaigned for private parties to bring competition cases in national courts.[187] Recently, private enforcement (especially damages claims against undertakings who infringe EU competition law) has been promoted in an effort to complement the Commission's deterrence-based enforcement strategy.

(i) An EU Law Right to Damages

It has long been clear that Articles 101(1) and 102 TFEU have direct effect,[188] opening the way for parties to seek damages. However, there was very little litigation because of uncertainties about the nature of a claim for damages and because a national court could not decide on the application of Article 101(3) (which left it with little room for applying Article 101). The second problem, as we saw above, was resolved by Regulation 1/2003, which establishes the direct effect of Article 101(3), and the first was resolved in 2001 by the Court of Justice in a landmark judgment. Mr Crehan made a contract with Inntrepreneur for the lease of two pubs. The lease contract included a beer tie, providing that Crehan would buy his beer exclusively from Courage. The business was unsuccessful and Crehan abandoned the leases. He sought damages for the loss of a business from Inntrepreneur on the basis that the beer tie prevented him from buying cheaper beer which would have allowed him to make a profit. In the English courts, doubts arose as to whether a party privy to an anti-competitive agreement could claim damages. The Court of Justice enthusiastically affirmed that Crehan could claim damages. When the case returned to the English courts, the Court of Appeal awarded Crehan £131,336 in damages for the losses he suffered, but on appeal to the House of Lords the claim failed.[189]

Courage v. *Crehan*, C–453/99, ECLI:EU:C:2001:465

24 . . . any individual can rely on a breach of Article [101(1) TFEU] before a national court even where he is a party to a contract that is liable to restrict or distort competition within the meaning of that provision.

25 As regards the possibility of seeking compensation for loss caused by a contract or by conduct liable to restrict or distort competition, it should be remembered from the outset that . . . the national courts whose task it is to apply the provisions of Community law in areas within their jurisdiction must ensure that those rules take full effect and must protect the rights which they confer on individuals.

26 The full effectiveness of Article [101 TFEU] and, in particular, the practical effect of the prohibition laid down in Article [101(1) TFEU] would be put at risk if it were not open to any individual to claim damages for loss caused to him by a contract or by conduct liable to restrict or distort competition.

27 Indeed, the existence of such a right strengthens the working of the Community competition rules and discourages agreements or practices, which are frequently covert, which are liable to restrict or distort competition. From that point of view, actions for damages before the national courts can make a significant contribution to the maintenance of effective competition in the Community.

---

[186] *White Paper on Productivity and Enterprise: A World Class Competition Regime*, Cm. 5233 (2001) ch. 8.

[187] European Commission, *Thirteenth Report on Competition Policy* (1983) paras. 217–18; Commission Notice of 23 December 1992 on cooperation between national courts and the Commission in applying Articles 85 and 86 of EEC Treaty [1993] OJ C 39/6.

[188] *BRT* v. *SABAM*, 127/73, ECLI:EU:C:1974:25.

[189] *Crehan* v. *Inntrepreneur* [2004] EWCA Civ 637; *Inntrepreneur Pub Company (CPC) and Others* v. *Crehan* [2006] UKHL 38.

This judgment should be studied from two perspectives. From a narrow perspective focusing on the facts of the case, it should be noted that the English courts had never doubted that a right to damages for breach of competition law was available.[190] Rather, the question that had been referred to the Court of Justice was whether a party privy to an anti-competitive agreement should be able to seek compensation, because the principle of illegality in English law meant that those implicated in an illegal venture lost the right to damages for loss suffered. The Court of Justice paid little attention to this question.[191]

From a wider perspective, the judgment is a general statement establishing an EU law right to damages. This is significant because it gives the European and national courts a shared role in shaping the law. Since then the Court and commentators have helped give shape to the legal implications that Courage has for national tort laws, in particular how the principles of equivalence and effectiveness could be interpreted.[192] For example, in *Manfredi*, the Court of Justice took further steps to explain the right to damages and the role of national courts. This was a damages claim by Italian consumers who had purchased liability insurance for motor vehicles at inflated prices after insurers had colluded. It was a follow-on claim after the Italian competition authority had found a cartel in the sector and the Court explained the damages that may be awarded.

Vincenzo Manfredi and Others v. *Lloyd Adriatico Assicurazioni SpA and Others*, C–295–298/04, ECLI:EU:C:2006:461

93   . . . in accordance with the principle of equivalence, it must be possible to award particular damages, such as exemplary or punitive damages, pursuant to actions founded on the Community competition rules, if such damages may be awarded pursuant to similar actions founded on domestic law.

95   Secondly, it follows from the principle of effectiveness and the right of any individual to seek compensation for loss caused by a contract or by conduct liable to restrict or distort competition that injured persons must be able to seek compensation not only for actual loss (*damnum emergens*) but also for loss of profit (*lucrum cessans*) plus interest.

96   Total exclusion of loss of profit as a head of damage for which compensation may be awarded cannot be accepted in the case of a breach of Community law since, especially in the context of economic or commercial litigation, such a total exclusion of loss of profit would be such as to make reparation of damage practically impossible.

The relevant Italian court rendered a judgment that, among other matters, awards the claimant 'double damages' as a means of giving effect to the Court of Justice's judgment, but it has been suggested that this is not what the Court intended.[193] While the Court of Justice will continue to establish principles to shape private enforcement, these now should be read alongside the Damages Directive.[194]

---

[190] E.g. in the United Kingdom the House of Lords in *Garden Cottage Foods* v. *Milk Marketing Board* [1984] AC 130 assumed damages to be available.

[191] G. Monti, 'Anticompetitive Agreements: The Innocent Party's Right to Damages' (2002) 27 *ELRev* 282.

[192] The key work is A. P. Komninos, *EC Private Antitrust Enforcement* (Oxford, Hart, 2008). See pp. 170–6 therein for a helpful framework.

[193] See P. Nebbia, 'So What Happened to Manfredi?' (2007) *ECLR* 591, for a strong critique of the Italian court's decision.

[194] E.g. *Skanska Industrial Solutions and Others*, C-724/17 P, ECLI:EU:C:2019:204, raises issues about the liability of parent companies.

(ii) The Damages Directive

The journey to this Directive began with the 2005 *Green Paper on Damages Actions*, which was criticised for being too aggressive and creating the risk of US-style over-litigation. The 2008 *White Paper on Damages Actions* addressed this by stating that proposals would be 'balanced measures that are rooted in European legal culture and traditions',[195] but was criticised as not bold enough.[196] This explains the Directive's timid title: Directive on 'certain rules governing actions for damages under national law for infringements of the competition law provisions of the Member States and of the European Union'.[197]

The vast majority of damages claims are the result of follow-on actions. This means that plaintiffs rely on a cartel decision of the Commission or an NCA to bring a damages claim. This is because, as we saw above, the competition authorities have awesome powers to obtain evidence which no individual can equal. In briefest outline the Directive has two main goals: stimulating damages actions by making proof easier for the plaintiff and ensuring consistency among national courts. It begins by stating that plaintiffs have a right to full compensation and then makes provisions to harmonise the following: rules on the evidence that a plaintiff may seek disclosure from the defendant and the NCA (especially important in follow-on claims), rules on passing-on, the quantification of damages, limitation periods and alternative dispute resolution. It also provides for the binding effect of NCA decisions.

Damages Directive, Article 9

(1) Member States shall ensure that an infringement of competition law found by a final decision of a national competition authority or by a review court is deemed to be irrefutably established for the purposes of an action for damages brought before their national courts under Article 101 or 102 TFEU or under national competition law.

(2) Member States shall ensure that where a final decision referred to in paragraph 1 is taken in another Member State, that final decision may, in accordance with national law, be presented before their national courts as at least prima facie evidence that an infringement of competition law has occurred and, as appropriate, may be assessed along with any other evidence adduced by the parties.

It was already clear that decisions of the Commission bind national courts, and many follow-on actions are based on Commission decisions.[198] Notably in *Otis* the plaintiff was the Commission itself: having punished a cartel in the market of escalators and elevators it sought damages for the losses it suffered as a result of purchasing such goods for its offices.[199] This article was controversial for some Member States. Note how in paragraph 1 NCA decisions are not 'binding' – this language would prove too much for States where, from a constitutional perspective, decisions of the administrations cannot bind courts and where judges must remain independent.

---

[195] 'White Paper on Damages Actions for Breach of the EC Antitrust Rules', COM(2008)165, 2.

[196] Editorial Comments, 'A Little More Action Please! The White Paper on Damages Actions for Breach of the EC Antitrust Rules' (2008) 45 *CMLRev* 609.

[197] Directive 2014/104/EU of the European Parliament and of the Council of 26 November 2014 on certain rules governing actions for damages under national law for infringements of the competition law provisions of the Member States and of the European Union [2014] OJ L 349/1.

[198] Regulation 1/2003, Article 16.

[199] The court allowed the claim, see *Commission* v. *Otis NV and Others*, C-199/11, ECLI:EU:C:2012:684.

And while the Commission would have preferred that the decisions of foreign NCAs should have a stronger effect, States objected given the different review standards at national level.[200] However, Article 9(2) probably has little value: as matters stand, most NCAs appear to penalise cartels only for the effects they have in their Member State, so it is unlikely that claimants will find much value in decisions rendered in other Member States.

The right to access documents held by defendants and the NCA is vital in obtaining data on the details of the infringements and on the damage that was caused. A particularly controversial matter is the right to access the leniency application. According to the Court, a plaintiff may access a leniency application when this is necessary to obtain evidence to bring a damages action.[201] However the Commission and the NCAs were concerned that this would create a disincentive for leniency applicants and lobbied hard for a limitation.[202] The Directive provides that leniency documents may not be disclosed and at the same time empowers plaintiffs and courts to secure alternative documents from the files of the NCAs.[203] It remains to be seen if this ban is tested in the courts. As we noted above, leniency applicants are not jointly and severally liable for the harm caused by the infringements. Whether these protections suffice to keep firms interested in making leniency applications remains to be seen.[204]

When it comes to computing loss, the Directive states that courts should be free to estimate loss and should not impose on plaintiffs too high a standard of proof; it establishes a presumption that cartels cause harm, and empowers NCAs to assist the court in estimating damages.[205] These provisions are necessary as the litigation in the UK courts has shown how costly and complex litigation is on quantification of damages.

Finally, the Directive confronts the difficult issue of pass-on.[206] Suppose there is a cartel in the market for industrial paint which raises the price to rise by €2 per unit and the plaintiff wholesaler (the direct purchaser) resells the goods to an automobile manufacturer (the indirect purchaser) at a price that is €1 per unit higher than before the cartel, then the damages to be awarded to the direct purchaser should be only €1 per unit (passing on is a defence), while the indirect purchaser is also entitled to €1 per unit (passing on is the basis for a claim by the indirect purchaser). Under US Federal Law, the courts decided that dividing up a damages claim is so costly and indirect purchasers unlikely to seek compensation for relatively small losses, that it makes more sense, deterrence-wise, to allow the direct purchaser to sue for the entire overcharge and make no deduction for passing on. On the facts above the wholesalers would receive €2 per unit. The over-compensation is an incentive to bring the claim.[207] This approach was rejected by the legislature who believes in full compensation. Accordingly, the defendant wishing to plead a passing on defence has the burden of showing that the plaintiff passed on some or all of the

---

[200] K. Wright, 'The Ambit of Judicial Competence after the EU Antitrust Damages Directive' (2016) 43(1) *LIEI* 15 for comprehensive discussion.

[201] *Bundeswettbewerbsbehörde* v. *Donau Chemie AG*, C-536/11, EU:C:2013:366.

[202] European Competition Network Resolution of the Meeting of Heads of the European Competition Authorities of 23 May 2012, 'Protection of Leniency Material in the Context of Civil Damages Actions'.

[203] Damages Directive, Articles 6–8.

[204] M. C. Buiten, P. van Wijck and J. K. Winders, 'Does the European Damages Directive Make Consumers Better Off?' (2018) 14(1) *Journal of Competition Law & Economics* 91.

[205] Damages Directive, Article 17.

[206] Caro de Sousa, 'EU and National Approaches to Passing on and Causation in Competition Damages Cases: A Doctrine in Search of Balance' (2018) 55 *CMLRev* 1751.

[207] W. M. Landes and R. A. Posner, 'Should Indirect Purchasers Have Standing to Sue under the Antitrust Laws? An Economic Analysis of the Rule in Illinois Brick' (1979) 46 *University of Chicago L Rev* 602.

overcharge.[208] Indirect purchasers may raise a presumption that cartel overcharges were passed on to them, requiring the defendant to disprove that there was a total overcharge.[209]

To really stimulate indirect purchasers, who can at times be final consumers, a class-action regime that allows for a collection of all claims is necessary. However, the European Parliament has three concerns with class actions: the risk of abusive litigation; that opt-out class actions (that is, class actions that are taken on behalf of a large group of consumers, say all those that bought insurance policies at inflated prices because of a cartel among insurers, by a representative of the class and each member is included in the action unless they actively opt out) infringe individual autonomy and are contrary to Article 6 ECHR; and that any class action initiative should cover consumer claims in other fields as well (e.g. product liability).[210] In response, the Commission has issued a communication and a recommendation in an attempt to encourage Member States to adopt analogous procedures for class actions.[211] In the field of consumer law a 'New Deal for Consumers' proposes class actions but it is resisted by the legislature.[212]

(iii) Assessment

Of the fifty-four prohibition decisions issued by the Commission between 2006 and 2012, fifteen have led to follow-on actions: most in three Member States (United Kingdom, Germany and the Netherlands) and almost none were brought by consumers or small or medium-sized firms.[213] There are tensions between Member States that are worried about fomenting a litigation culture and those eager to facilitate claims.[214] It means that Member States will likely be the main players who design procedures to facilitate claims, for example class actions.[215]

Furthermore, one might doubt whether damages actions are desirable in competition law at all. Insofar as the aim of deterrence is concerned, public enforcement is a superior form of deterrence for a number of reasons. First, antitrust authorities have more effective investigatory and sanctioning powers, in particular with the network of NCAs being developed. Secondly, private plaintiffs are motivated by profit and not necessarily motivated to bring claims against practices that injure the public interest, whereas NCAs will tend to bring claims of most value to the economy. Thirdly, private enforcement is more costly than pubic enforcement because NCAs are repeat players, who specialise in competition law and thus the marginal cost of additional actions is lower for them.[216] But this view has, however, come under fire, with the argument that NCAs are superior being questioned on the basis that while private enforcement is imperfect, it is

---

[208] Damages Directive, Article 13. [209] Damages Directive, Article 14.

[210] European Parliament Resolution of 2 February 2012 on 'Towards a Coherent European Approach to Collective Redress' (2011/2089(INI)).

[211] Commission Recommendation of 11 June 2013 on common principles for injunctive and compensatory collective redress mechanisms in the Member States concerning violations of rights granted under Union law [2013] OJ L 201/60.

[212] 'Proposal for a Directive on Representative Actions for the Protection of the Collective Interests of Consumers', COM (2018)184 final. S. Augenhofer, 'Comments on the Proposal for a Directive on Representative Actions for the Protection of the Collective Interests of Consumers' (2018), www.uni-erfurt.de/fileadmin/user-docs/wirtschaftsrecht/ Dies_und_das/Comments_Susanne_Augenhofer_6.10.2018.pdf.

[213] A. Howard, 'Too Little, too Late? The European Commission's Legislative Proposal on Anti-Trust Damages Actions' (2013) Journal of European Competition Law and Practice 455.

[214] J. S. Kortmann and C. R. A. Swaak, 'The EC White Paper on Antitrust Damage Actions: Why the Member States are (Right to Be) Less than Enthusiastic' (2009) 30 ECLR 340.

[215] For discussion, see A. Higgins and A. Zuckerman, 'Class Actions in England? Efficacy, Autonomy and Proportionality in Collective Redress', University of Oxford Legal Research Paper Series No. 93/2013 (2013).

[216] W. P. J. Wils, 'Should Private Antitrust Enforcement Be Encouraged in Europe?' (2003) 26 World Competition 473.

not an argument against allowing those who are able to mount an action to do so, and the risk that private parties will litigate unmeritorious claims is one which affects all private litigation, and which can be tempered by judges striking out worthless claims.[217] The Commission's justification seems to be that the estimated cost to antitrust victims ranges between €25 and €69 billion,[218] and that 'EU-wide infringements are becoming more and more frequent.'[219] However, don't these findings suggest that the Commission should focus on measures to improve public enforcement, for instance by increasing the level of fines?

6 BREXIT

The obligations of the UK to continue to apply competition law under the Withdrawal agreement have been discussed in Chapter 10. The focus here is on what relationship may emerge after the UK exists the EU. Before considering what a bespoke agreement between the United Kingdom and the European Union might look like, we outline the way the Union relates with other third States. The deepest form of cooperation is found in the European Economic Area (EEA) agreement. This establishes an independent agency (the European Free Trade Association (EFTA) Surveillance Authority) which performs a role analogous to that of the Commission for matters that fall within the competence of the EEA. The competition provisions mirror those in the TFEU, so essentially the same rules are applied with similar procedures. The EEA agreement provides for case allocation: if a matter affects trade in the EU and the EEA then the Commission will handle the matter.[220] The Commission may apply EEA law in parallel.[221] There is intensive cooperation between the two sides when cases interest both markets as well as in investigations. Furthermore, the Authority may participate in ECN meetings discussing policy issues, to ensure homogeneous interpretation of EEA and EU rules.[222]

Cooperation agreements with other competition authorities are much less intense: each agency reserves the right to apply their national law (so parallel procedures are common for cartel and merger cases). Increasingly agencies coordinate cartel inspections, but there is no sharing of confidential information between agencies. Comity clauses are frequently inserted so that when one party acts in competition matters it undertakes to take into account the important interests of the other side.

In 2013 the European Union entered into its first 'second generation' bilateral agreement with Switzerland: this includes provisions for coordination of enforcement and exchange of evidence.[223] The Swiss agreement might be of interest to the United Kingdom since, in the Brexit Policy Paper of July 2018, it proposed the following: 'committing to a common rulebook on State aid, to be enforced and supervised in the UK by the Competition and Markets Authority (CMA); maintaining current antitrust prohibitions and the merger control system with rigorous UK enforcement of competition law alongside strong cooperation with EU authorities'.[224] This

---

[217] C. A. Jones, 'Private Antitrust Enforcement in Europe: A Policy Analysis and a Reality Check' (2004) 27 *World Competition* 13.
[218] 'Impact Assessment Report', SEC(2008)405, paras. 42–3.   [219] *Ibid.* para. 32.   [220] EEA Agreement, Article 56.
[221] E.g. COMP/E-1/38.113 – *Prokent-Tomra* (Decision of 23 March 2006) para. 330 where the abuse of dominance occurred in the EU and Norway.
[222] EEA Agreement, Protocol 23 concerning the cooperation between the surveillance authorities (Article 58).
[223] Agreement between the European Union and the Swiss Confederation concerning cooperation on the application of their competition laws (2014) OJ L 347/3.
[224] HM Government, *The Future Relationship between the United Kingdom and the European Union*, Cm. 9593, July 2018, para. 108.

assumes that an *ad hoc*, bilateral agreement would be signed between the two sides, which is less onerous than the EEA, but seeks closer links with the Union than other agreements. We explore what this might entail by considering two issues: the CMA's expected workload and cooperation arrangements.

(i) Workload

Competition law in the United Kingdom is principally enforced by the CMA, which applies both competition law and consumer law (the latter also is largely based on EU law).[225] It is expected that the CMA's workload post-Brexit is set to increase.[226] Pre-Brexit the European Commission would take cases that have EU-wide impact and so the UK market was protected by the interventions of the Commission – consider for instance the infringement action against Google which is intended to benefit all EU markets. Post-Brexit the enforcement action of the Commission will not always serve to protect the UK market and so the CMA will have to act alongside the Commission (both for cases of restrictive practices and mergers). To cope for this expansion, the CMA's budget for 2018–19 was increased by £23.6 million. It is foreseen that 240 additional staff will be recruited to handle consumer and competition issues, of which 150 will handle competition law matters (a 39 per cent increase in staffing).[227]

While it is definitely the case that parties to a merger will notify in the United Kingdom to secure merger clearance (global mergers are notified in multiple transactions), one has to wonder if the forecast that the United Kingdom will have more cases of greater complexity outside of the merger field is realistic. First, the CMA has not shied away from complex cases in the past and there is little evidence to suggest that the Commission presently monopolises the more difficult issues. One may also question whether the volume of cases is really likely to increase. Consider a typical example of a case handled presently by the Commission: a global cartel among large firms. Clearly, if the CMA decides to act then this will be a resource-intensive exercise. However, one has to wonder whether it is in the CMA's interest to take these cases at all. As discussed in this chapter, the aim of public enforcement is deterrence and one has to wonder whether the relatively lower fine that the United Kingdom will set for cartels which will be fined by the Commission can make a meaningful contribution to deterrence. On the other hand, the time-sensitivity of merger cases might mean that the CMA is diverted away from applying antitrust rules and focuses much more on mergers.

(ii) Cooperation

A key to successful management of cross-border cases is cooperation with the Commission. The government indicates that '[r]eciprocal commitments that go beyond those usually made in FTAs will be particularly important to support the breadth and depth of the future UK–EU economic partnership'.[228] In other words, some of the information-sharing facilities found in Regulation

---

[225] For a discussion of the possible impact of Brexit on consumer law see S. Augenhofer, 'Brexit: Marriage "With" Divorce? – The Legal Consequences for Consumer Law' (2017) 40(5) *Fordham Int'l LJ* 1443.

[226] Brexit Competition Law Working Group, para. 8.2.

[227] Comptroller and Auditor General, *Exiting the EU: Consumer Protection, Competition and State Aid*, Session 2017–19, HC 1384, 6 July 2018.

[228] See n. 224 above, para.105.

1/2003 is seen as important for the CMA's enforcement, in particular the ability to obtain confidential information from the Commission when the two are addressing the same offence, each in their jurisdiction. The EU/Switzerland Antitrust Agreement would allow for such cooperation.

In terms of private enforcement, the UK courts are one of the principal sites where damages claims resulting from international cartels are brought. Post-Brexit it is not clear whether follow-on actions based on Commission decisions may still be brought to UK courts. This applies both to decisions taken pre-Brexit ad those afterwards.[229] This could have such a significantly negative impact on the business that British courts bring in that it is expected some arrangements will be sought so that international cartel claims can still be brought in London.

FURTHER READING

G. Amato, *Antitrust and the Bounds of Power* (Oxford, Hart, 1997).

D. Ashton (ed.), *Competition Damages Actions in the EU*, 2nd edn (Cheltenham, Edward Elgar, 2018).

I. van Bael, *Due Process in EU Competition Proceedings* (The Hague, Kluwer, 2011).

M. Bergström, M. Iacovides and M. Strand (eds.), *Harmonising EU Competition Litigation: The New Directive and Beyond* (Oxford, Hart, 2016).

S. Bishop and M. Walker, *The Economics of EC Competition Law*, 3rd edn (London, Sweet and Maxwell, 2010).

S. Brammer, *Co-operation between National Competition Agencies in the Enforcement of EC Competition Law* (Oxford, Hart, 2009).

R. Buch-Hansen and A. Wigger, *The Politics of European Competition Regulation: A Critical Political Economy Perspective* (Abingdon, Routledge, 2011).

N. Dunne, 'Commitment Decisions in EU Competition Law' (2014) 10(2) *Journal of Competition Law & Economics* 399.

D. J. Gerber, *Law and Competition in Twentieth Century Europe* (Oxford University Press, 1998).

D. J. Gerber, 'Two Forms of Modernization in European Competition Law' (2008) *Fordham International Law Journal* 1235.

H. Gilliams, 'Proportionality of EU Competition Fines: Proposal for a Principled Discussion' (2014) 37(4) *World Competition* 435.

C. Heide-Jorgensen *et al.* (eds.), *Aims and Values in Competition Law* (Copenhagen, DJØF Publishing, 2013).

C. S. Kerse and N. Kahn, *EC Antitrust Procedure*, 5th edn (London, Sweet & Maxwell, 2012).

S. B. Völker, 'Rough Justice? An Analysis of the European Commission's New Fining Guidelines' (2007) 44 *Common Market Law Review* 1285.

S. Wilks, 'Agency Escape: Decentralization or Dominance of the European Commission in the Modernization of Competition Policy?' (2005) 18 *Governance* 431.

W. P. J. Wils, 'Ten Years of Regulation 1/2003: A Retrospective' (2013) 4(4) *Journal of European Competition Law and Practice* 1.

W. P. J. Wils, 'Private Enforcement of EU Antitrust Law and Its Relationship with Public Enforcement: Past, Present, Future' (2017) 40 *World Competition* 3.

---

[229] P. Roth, 'Competition Law and Brexit: The Challenges Ahead' [2017] *Competition LJ* 4, 9–10.

Antitrust and Monopolies

CONTENTS

1   INTRODUCTION

In this chapter we review the two principal provisions that implement the competition policy whose aims and enforcement structure were discussed in Chapter 20. Article 101 TFEU declares that agreements between undertakings are void when they restrict competition; Article 102 TFEU applies to dominant undertakings and forbids them from abusing their position. Since the end of the 1990s, the Commission has been engaged in a series of reform initiatives to the application of competition law, in response to criticisms that its approach was insufficiently grounded in economics and was overly aggressive.[1] Explaining and evaluating this process of reform is the central theme of this chapter. In addition, the chapter considers how competition law fares with challenges arising from digital markets.

Section 2 covers three legal issues that are common to both articles: the meaning of an undertaking, the concept of an effect on trade between Member States, and judge-made rules that exclude the application of competition law.

Section 3 is a review of the key issues that have arisen in the application of Article 101. It is divided into three parts. First, we explore how this provision applies to catch cartels, the principal concern of competition authorities today. Secondly, we look at how one determines whether agreements other than cartels may be found to be anti-competitive. Thirdly, we consider how one might justify anti-competitive agreements if they have countervailing beneficial effects.

Section 4 examines Article 102 TFEU by first discussing the concept of abuse in general terms, followed by a case study on predatory pricing and related pricing practices. We trace how far the Commission's attempt to redirect enforcement has fared when reviewed by the European Court of Justice (ECJ).

Section 5 is a brief account of hidden developments. As we noted in Chapter 21, the Commission has the power to issue commitment decisions: it is worth noting that these decisions are increasing in frequency and here the approach appears to deviate from the formal stance the Commission and the Court of Justice take. The implications of this development are that we have two parallel (and not entirely consistent) approaches to competition law.

Section 6 discusses the limited impact that Brexit is likely to have on substantive competition law.

2 SCOPE OF APPLICATION OF EU COMPETITION LAW

(i) Undertakings

EU competition law applies to 'undertakings', a term that 'encompasses every entity engaged in an economic activity, regardless of the legal status of the entity or the way in which it is financed'.[2] Its meaning is independent of any national law definitions of what constitutes a company. Rather, it is effects-based: the question is whether the entity in question, when doing a specific task, has an economic impact on the market by offering goods or services. It means that an economic entity may be treated as an undertaking when it performs certain functions, but fall outside the scope of competition law when pursuing other roles.[3] Inventors,[4] opera

---

[1] The most significant stimulus was a presentation to DG Competition by a distinguished antitrust practitioner: B. E. Hawk, 'System Failure: Vertical Restraints and EC Competition Law' (1995) 32 *CMLRev* 973. For a comprehensive account, see A. C. Witt, *The More Economic Approach to EU Antitrust Law* (London, Bloomsbury, 2016).

[2] *Höfner and Elser* v. *Macrotron GmbH*, C-41/90, ECLI:EU:C:1991:161, para. 21.

[3] E.g. the European Organisation for the Safety of Air Navigation (Eurocontrol) does not act as an undertaking when it controls traffic, but is an undertaking if it abuses its monopsony power when purchasing goods on the market. See *Selex Sistemi Integrati* v. *Commission and Eurocontrol*, C-113/07, ECLI:EU:C:2009:191.

[4] *Reuter/BASF* [1976] OJ L 254/40.

singers,[5] barristers,[6] sporting associations,[7] agricultural cooperatives[8] and multinational corporations can all act as undertakings. Employees acting during the course of employment however, are not undertakings,[9] nor are agents who operate on behalf of their principal and take no financial risk.[10] It follows that the employer is responsible for the anti-competitive conduct of its employees.[11] In recent years, as governments have increasingly contracted out the provision of public services, questions have arisen as to whether entities engaged in the provision of these types of services (e.g. emergency ambulance services and air traffic control) should be regulated by competition law. This issue is discussed in Chapter 24, which is available online.

Subsidiaries may have independent legal personality, but for the purposes of competition law a subsidiary is treated as a single economic entity along with the parent company where the subsidiary has no ability to determine its conduct on the market.[12] Whether parent and subsidiary constitute a single economic entity is a question of fact. Relevant considerations include the number of shares that the parent has in the subsidiary (where a majority shareholding will give rise to a presumption that the parent controls the subsidiary),[13] the composition of the board of directors, and whether the subsidiary carries out the parent's instructions. Whether parent and subsidiary are one undertaking or two has considerable practical implications: first, if they are two undertakings then Article 101 TFEU applies because there is an agreement between them, while if there is one undertaking, it is classified as an intra-firm agreement, to which Article 101 does not apply.

As a result, an undertaking may evade the application of Article 101 by buying firms with whom it would normally contract if it finds that the burden of complying with Article 101 is too onerous. Parker Pen embarked on this strategy, owning all its distributors in certain Member States and orchestrating distribution through them. The effect of this was to partition the market, as each subsidiary was only allowed to sell in the territory allocated to it by Parker Pen. Viho (a Dutch wholesaler) complained because it wished to buy Parker products in Germany for resale in the Netherlands, but was unsuccessful in obtaining the goods from Parker's German subsidiary. Had Parker prohibited an independent distributor in Germany from selling to Viho, this would have constituted an agreement in breach of Article 101, but as it was an internal measure, the Court of Justice held that it was not caught by Article 101 because Parker and its subsidiaries formed a single economic unit.[14] Parker's strategy had been the result of an earlier Commission decision (spurred by an earlier complaint from Viho) that its contracts with an independent distributor in Germany infringed Article 101 by prohibiting the German distributor from exporting Parker products.[15] In response, Parker Pen established its own distribution network, avoiding the finding of an agreement but dividing the market, thereby undermining one central aim of EU competition law.

---

[5] *RAI/UNITEL* [1978] OJ L 157/39.

[6] *Wouters* v. *Algemene Raad van de Nederlandse Orde van Advocaten*, C-309/99, ECLI:EU:C:2002:98.

[7] *The Distribution of Package Tours During the 1990 World Cup* [1992] OJ L 326/31.

[8] *Gøttrup Klim* v. *DLG*, C-250/92, ECLI:EU:C:1994:413.   [9] *Becu*, C-22/98, CLI:EU:C:1999:419.

[10] See Guidelines on Vertical Restraints [2000] OJ C 291/1, paras. 12–20.

[11] *VM Remonts* v. *Konkurences padome*, C-542/14, EU:C:2016:578.

[12] *Viho Europe* v. *Commission*, C-73/95 P, ECLI:EU:C:1996:405.

[13] Cf. *Viho Europe BV* (*ibid.*) (100% shareholding meant the parent and subsidiary was a single economic entity) with *Gosmé/Martell-DMP* [1991] OJ L 185/23 (50% ownership of a joint venture insufficient to treat the two as a single entity) and *Irish Sugar* v. *Commission*, T-228/97, ECLI:EU:T:1999:246 (subsidiary in which Irish Sugar held 51% of the shares held to be a separate undertaking).

[14] *Viho Europe* v. *Commission*, C-73/95 P, ECLI:EU:C:1996:405, paras. 15–18.

[15] *Viho/Parker Pen* [1992] OJ L 233/27; affirmed in *Herlitz* v. *Commission*, T-66/92, ECLI:EU:T:1994:84 and *Parker* v. *Commission*, T-77/92, ECLI:EU:T:1994:85.

A second significant reason for determining whether parents and subsidiaries are a single economic unit is that a parent is responsible for acts by its wholly owned subsidiary. This rule was used in *ICI* v. *Commission* to impose a penalty on foreign parents for a cartel carried out in the Union by subsidiaries even if the parent company had no presence in the European Union.[16] Thirdly, a number of crucial determinations in competition law proceedings depend upon calculating the turnover or market shares of the undertaking concerned. For instance, a fine is calculated in part based upon the turnover of the undertaking (and this figure will include the turnover of the entire economic entity).[17] It means that the fine can be increased significantly because the turnover of the whole corporate group may be taken into account. These two points are particularly important because there is a presumption that the parent and a wholly owned subsidiary are a single undertaking, which parties have challenged regularly.[18]

Schindler Holding Ltd and Others v. Commission, C–501/11 P, ECLI:EU:C:2013:522

108 The presumption that decisive influence is exercised over a subsidiary wholly or almost wholly owned by its parent company is intended, in particular, to strike a balance between, on the one hand, the importance of the objective of combating conduct contrary to the competition rules, in particular to Article [101 TFEU], and of preventing a repetition of such conduct and, on the other hand, the requirements flowing from certain general principles of European Union law such as the principle of the presumption of innocence, the principle that penalties should be applied solely to the offender and the principle of legal certainty as well as the rights of the defence, including the principle of equality of arms. It follows that such a presumption is proportionate to the legitimate aim pursued.

109 Furthermore, first, the aforesaid presumption is based on the fact that, save in quite exceptional circumstances, a company holding all, or almost all, the capital of a subsidiary can, by dint merely of holding it, exercise decisive influence over that subsidiary's conduct and, second, it is within the sphere of operations of those entities against which the presumption operates that evidence of the lack of actual exercise of that power to influence is generally apt to be found. The presumption is, however, rebuttable and the entities wishing to rebut it may adduce all factors relating to the economic, organisational and legal links tying the subsidiary to the parent company that they consider to be capable of demonstrating that the subsidiary and the parent company do not constitute a single economic entity, but that the subsidiary acts independently on the market.

On the facts of this appeal, the Court of Justice also noted that the parent had devised a compliance programme to avoid competition infringements thereby suggesting that it 'did in fact supervise the commercial policy of its subsidiaries'.[19]

---

[16] *ICI* v. *Commission*, 48/69, ECLI:EU:C:1972:70. This approach may be criticised because the Court merely considered whether the parent was able to exercise control over the subsidiary, and not whether it had in fact exercised control. See D. G. Goyder, *EC Competition Law*, 4th edn (Oxford University Press, 2003) 499–500.

[17] Regulation 1/2003 on the implementation of the rules on competition laid down in Articles 81 and 82 of the Treaty, Article 23(2) [2003] OJ L 1/1. Furthermore, damages claims may be brought against parent and subsidiary, and the penalty increases for recidivism may apply if one part of the corporate group has infringed competition law before.

[18] *Akzo Nobel NV* v. *Commission*, C–97/08 P, ECLI:EU:C:2009:536; *Dow Chemical Company* v. *Commission*, C–179/12 P, CLI:EU:C:2013:605, considering parental liability in a 50/50 joint venture and *Alliance One International* v. *Commission*, C–628/10 P, ECLI:EU:C:2012:479.

[19] *Schindler Holding Ltd and Others* v. *Commission*, C–501/11 P, ECLI:EU:C:2013:522, para. 114.

(ii) Effect on Trade between Member States

EU competition law does not apply unless the practice in question has an appreciable effect on trade between Member States. The Court of Justice has set out a wide definition of 'effect on trade', which corresponds to the test deployed in disputes concerning the internal market generally.[20]

Société Technique Minière v. *Maschinenbau Ulm*, 56/65, ECLI:EU:C:1966:17, 249

For this requirement to be fulfilled it must be possible to foresee with a sufficient degree of probability on the basis of a set of objective factors of law or of fact that the agreement in question may have an influence, direct or indirect, actual or potential, on the pattern of trade between Member States. Therefore, in order to determine whether an agreement which contains a clause 'granting an exclusive right of sale' comes within the field of application of Article [101 TFEU], it is necessary to consider in particular whether it is capable of bringing about a partitioning of the market in certain products between Member States and thus rendering more difficult the interpenetration of trade which the Treaty is intended to create.

Two weeks after this judgment the Court of Justice expanded this formula by holding that determining whether an agreement has an effect on trade does not require an evaluation as to whether the effect is positive or negative. Even agreements which increase trade are caught.[21] The aim of the 'effect on trade between Member States' phrase is purely to determine whether EU law applies, and is not used to appraise the agreement. The test is extremely broad: agreements within one Member State may affect trade – for instance a cartel among Dutch roofing-felt manufacturers was held to affect trade between Member States because it restricted the ability of exporters to penetrate the Dutch market;[22] an agreement concerning goods that are not traded across borders may have a potential effect on trade if there is evidence to suggest that cross-border trade could increase;[23] an effect may be indirect when an agreement fixes prices for a raw material which is not exported but which is used in the manufacture of a product which is exported;[24] or when a product is sold with a warranty that is only valid in the Member State where the product is bought.[25] Lastly, an effect on trade may also arise when the agreement relates to trade outside the Union. Thus, a distribution agreement whereby Yves Saint Laurent contracted with a firm to distribute its goods in Russia, Ukraine and Slovenia (at the time not a Member State) and prohibited the distributor from reimporting them into the Union, could have an 'appreciable effect on the pattern of trade between the Member States such as to undermine attainment of the objectives of the common market'.[26]

In 2004, in order to ensure consistency among national authorities in their determination of when to apply EU competition law, the Commission published a Notice on the effect of trade between Member States that establishes the NAAT (no appreciable affectation of trade) test.[27]

---

[20] For an overview, see J. Faull, 'Effect on Trade Between Member States' (1999) 26 *Fordham Corporate Law Institute* 481.
[21] *Consten and Grundig* v. *Commission*, 54 and 58/64, ECLI:EU:C:1966:41.
[22] *Belasco and Others* v. *Commission*, 246/86, ECLI:EU:C:1989:301, paras. 33–8.
[23] *AEG* v. *Commission*, 107/82, ECLI:EU:C:1983:293, para. 60.
[24] *BNIC* v. *Clair*, 123/83, ECLI:EU:C:1985:33, para. 29.   [25] *Re Zanussi SpA Guarantee* [1978] OJ L 322/26.
[26] *Javico International and Javico AG* v. *Yves Saint Laurent Parfums SA*, C-306/96, ECLI:EU:C:1998:173, para. 25.
[27] Commission Notice: Guidelines on the effect on trade concept contained in Articles 81 and 82 of the Treaty [2004] OJ C 101/81, para. 2.4.

According to this test, agreements are incapable of appreciably affecting trade when the parties' aggregate market share does not exceed 5 per cent, and in horizontal agreements the turnover of both parties is less than €40 million, while for vertical agreements the turnover of the supplier does not exceed €40 million. The Commission will not institute proceedings in these cases and the intention of the Notice is to influence national authorities to follow suit. However, agreements below these thresholds may still be caught by national competition law.[28] It has been noted that some national competition authorities (NCAs) under-define the notion of effect on trade and apply solely national competition law.[29]

(iii) Excluded Agreements

All economic activities fall to be regulated by EU competition law, but the Treaty provides for certain exceptions: for example, national security;[30] agriculture;[31] and providers entrusted with the provision of services of general economic interest.[32]

Alongside the economic sectors where exclusion was a matter of legislative choice, the Court of Justice has also identified certain fields where EU competition law is excluded. Agreements resulting from negotiations between employers and workers in the context of collective bargaining are excluded.[33] In the judgment establishing this exclusion, a decision was taken by an organisation representing employers and workers in the wholesale trade of building materials in the Netherlands to establish a single pension fund for all employees in that sector. The fund would be responsible for managing the employees' supplementary pension scheme. The organisation of these supplementary funds was approved by Dutch law but the defendants, undertakings operating in the relevant sector, refused to make the relevant contributions. They had obtained a more advantageous private pension scheme, and considered that the decision by the employers and workers to make affiliation to a fund compulsory was restrictive of competition in two ways: it prevented undertakings from finding alternative pension schemes, and excluded insurers from the relevant market. In spite of the anti-competitive effects, the Court of Justice ruled that the agreement fell outside the scope of Article 101(1). The basis for this was that the Union is tasked with both ensuring competition and also developing a policy in the social sphere, and these two conflicting objectives had to be balanced. The Court found that restrictions of competition would be inherent in collective agreements between organisations representing employers and workers and that the application of competition law would damage collective

---

[28] It is not clear why the Commission invented this test since agreements between operators with little market power are already, in certain circumstances, excluded from the application of Article 101 TFEU when deemed to be of minor importance on the basis that they are incapable of damaging competition substantially. See Commission Notice on agreements of minor importance which do not appreciably restrict competition under Article 81(1) [2001] OJ C 368/13.

[29] M. Botta, M. Bernatt and A. Svetlicinii, 'The Assessment of the Effect on Trade by the National Competition Authorities of the "New" Member States: Another Legal Partition of the Internal Market?' (2015) 52(2) CMLRev 1247.

[30] Article 346 TFEU (ex Article 296 EC) (a provision invoked in mergers in the defence sector).

[31] Article 42 TFEU (ex Article 36 EC) provides that agriculture is covered to the extent that the Council determines, taking into account the aims of the Common Agricultural Policy. See Regulation 26/62 [1959–62] OJ 129. The provisions of the exclusions in this Regulation have been read restrictively, see e.g. *FRUBO* v. *Commission*, 71/74, ECLI:EU:C:1975:61.

[32] Article 106(2) TFEU.

[33] See also *Albany International BV* v. *Stichting Bedrijfspensioenfonds Textielindustrie*, C-67/96, ECLI:EU:C:1999:430, paras. 52–60; *Maatschappij Drijvende Bokken BV* v. *Stichting Pensioenfonds voor de Vervoer- en Havenbedrijven*, C-219/97, ECLI:EU:C:1999:437, paras. 40–7.

attempts to improve the conditions of employment.[34] The judgment can be praised for consistency with the so-called 'European social model'. This imprecisely defined phrase is often used to explain that the European Union's internal market project is not merely about the creation of economic wealth, but also about the safeguard of the interests of employees. However, the Court of Justice does not subject the pension scheme in question to a proportionality test; it does not consider whether this kind of pension arrangement is the least restrictive way of achieving the improvement of working conditions, nor does the Court take into consideration the possibility that Article 101(3) could have exempted these agreements.[35] Instead, the social policy considerations trump the competition policy considerations. Subsequent developments have called into question the validity of this judgment.[36]

A more well-established, and wider, exclusion was designed in *Wouters*. The Dutch Bar Association prohibited partnerships between lawyers and accountants ('multidisciplinary partnerships') by the so-called '1993 Regulation'. The 1993 Regulation (which was characterised as a decision by an association of undertakings) was challenged by lawyers wishing to work for an accountancy firm. It clearly restricted competition by preventing the creation of a new form of business. However, the Dutch Bar Association considered that multidisciplinary practices threatened the obligations of professional conduct because unlike lawyers, accountants had an obligation to audit clients and report their results to interested third parties. Thus the professional obligations of the two professions clashed.

Wouters v. Algemene Raad van de Nederlandse Orde van Advocaten, C–309/99, ECLI:EU: C:2002:98

105 The aim of the 1993 Regulation is therefore to ensure that, in the Member State concerned, the rules of professional conduct for members of the Bar are complied with, having regard to the prevailing perceptions of the profession in that State. The Bar of the Netherlands was entitled to consider that members of the Bar might no longer be in a position to advise and represent their clients independently and in the observance of strict professional secrecy if they belonged to an organisation which is also responsible for producing an account of the financial results of the transactions in respect of which their services were called upon and for certifying those accounts.

106 Moreover, the concurrent pursuit of the activities of statutory auditor and of adviser, in particular legal adviser, also raises questions within the accountancy profession itself . . .

107 A regulation such as the 1993 Regulation could therefore reasonably be considered to be necessary in order to ensure the proper practice of the legal profession, as it is organised in the Member State concerned.

108 Furthermore, the fact that different rules may be applicable in another Member State does not mean that the rules in force in the former State are incompatible with Community law. Even if multi-disciplinary partnerships of lawyers and accountants are allowed in some Member States, the Bar of the Netherlands is entitled to consider that the objectives pursued by the 1993 Regulation cannot, having regard in

---

[34] *Brentjens' Handelsonderneming BV*, C-115–17/97, ECLI:EU:C:1999:434, paras. 55–61.

[35] Advocate General Jacobs in this case (para. 193) had in fact acknowledged that the Court of Justice and Commission had in the past taken employment considerations into account in Article 81(3) (referring to *Metro*, 26/76, [1977] ECR 1875, para. 43; *Remia*, 42/84, [1985] ECR 2545, para. 42; *Synthetic Fibres* [1984] OJ L 207/17, para. 37; and *Ford/ Volkswagen* [1993] OJ L 20/14, para. 23) while the Commission in its submissions insisted that such considerations were irrelevant in deciding on the application of the exemption.

[36] The ECJ refused to apply the principle in the context of the fundamental freedoms (*International Transport Workers' Federation and Finnish Seamen's Union* v. *Viking Line ABP*, C-438/05, ECLI:EU:C:2007:772) and public procurement (*Commission* v. *Germany*, C-271/08, ECLI:EU:C:2010:426).

particular to the legal regimes by which members of the Bar and accountants are respectively governed in the Netherlands, be attained by less restrictive means.

109   In light of those considerations, it does not appear that the effects restrictive of competition such as those resulting for members of the Bar practising in the Netherlands from a regulation such as the 1993 Regulation go beyond what is necessary in order to ensure the proper practice of the legal profession.

The Court of Justice returned to consider the scope of application of competition law in a dispute that arose between two swimmers, on the one hand, and the International Olympic Committee (IOC) and international swimming federation (FINA), on the other. The swimmers were given a two-year ban because a drugs test revealed that they had taken a banned substance, Nandrolone, but they considered the anti-doping rules were too strict and argued that the IOC's decision setting out the doping rules was restrictive of competition.

Meca-Medina and Majcen v. *Commission*, C–519/04 P, ECLI:EU:C:2006:492

42   ... [T]he compatibility of rules with the Community rules on competition cannot be assessed in the abstract. Not every agreement between undertakings or every decision of an association of undertakings which restricts the freedom of action of the parties or of one of them necessarily falls within the prohibition laid down in Article [101(1) TFEU]. For the purposes of application of that provision to a particular case, account must first of all be taken of the overall context in which the decision of the association of undertakings was taken or produces its effects and, more specifically, of its objectives. It has then to be considered whether the consequential effects restrictive of competition are inherent in the pursuit of those objectives and are proportionate to them.

43   As regards the overall context in which the rules at issue were adopted, the Commission could rightly take the view that the general objective of the rules was, as none of the parties disputes, to combat doping in order for competitive sport to be conducted fairly and that it included the need to safeguard equal chances for athletes, athletes' health, the integrity and objectivity of competitive sport and ethical values in sport.

44   In addition, given that penalties are necessary to ensure enforcement of the doping ban, their effect on athletes' freedom of action must be considered to be, in principle, inherent itself in the anti-doping rules.

45   Therefore, even if the anti-doping rules at issue are to be regarded as a decision of an association of undertakings limiting the appellants' freedom of action, they do not, for all that, necessarily constitute a restriction of competition incompatible with the common market, within the meaning of Article [101(1) TFEU], since they are justified by a legitimate objective. Such a limitation is inherent in the organisation and proper conduct of competitive sport and its very purpose is to ensure healthy rivalry between athletes ...

47   It must be acknowledged that the penal nature of the anti-doping rules at issue and the magnitude of the penalties applicable if they are breached are capable of producing adverse effects on competition because they could, if penalties were ultimately to prove unjustified, result in an athlete's unwarranted exclusion from sporting events, and thus in impairment of the conditions under which the activity at issue is engaged in. It follows that, in order not to be covered by the prohibition laid down in Article [101(1) TFEU], the restrictions thus imposed by those rules must be limited to what is necessary to ensure the proper conduct of competitive sport.

48 Rules of that kind could indeed prove excessive by virtue of, first, the conditions laid down for establishing the dividing line between circumstances which amount to doping in respect of which penalties may be imposed and those which do not, and second, the severity of those penalties.

Applying this standard the Court of Justice concluded that banning Nandrolone was justified and that banning athletes whose tests reveal a Nandrolone content higher than 2 nanogrammes per millilitre of urine was a practice that did not go beyond that which was necessary to ensure that sporting events take place and function properly.[37] Conversely, when the Portuguese Accountancy Association (OTOC) imposed procedures that raised entry barriers to undertakings wishing to offer educational services for accountants (and thereby favouring the educational services offered by OTOC) the Court of Justice found that the exclusion in *Wouters* was inapplicable because while ensuring the quality of education was a legitimate objective, exclusion of providers without an appropriate procedure was a disproportionate way of addressing the public policy concern – it would be possible to monitor the performance of different service providers instead, which would not harm competition.[38]

These cases present a puzzle: how widely should they be construed? At its most restrictive, it may be said that these cases are about excluding only ethical rules from the scope of competition law.[39] Alternatively, it has been suggested that these cases identify certain restrictions of competition that are ancillary to the main regulatory function of the body whose decision is being questioned, without being limited to ethical considerations.[40] A third, broader, interpretation is that these judgments exclude certain restrictive agreements when there are valid public policy reasons for so doing.[41] On the latter view, an agreement among pubs to eliminate 'happy hours' when alcohol is cheaper as a means of protecting public health might be justified. This wider interpretation draws legitimacy from the realities of self-regulation in modern society, when private bodies are often encouraged or even required to take the public interest into account when making commercial decisions. Further judicial refinement is required to establish the appropriate limits of this strand of case law, not least because it blurs the line between Article 101(1) and the exemption provision in Article 101(3).[42] However, the cases are problematic: on the one hand, the competition rules are a fundamental building block of the European Union's 'economic constitution' and should only be displaced exceptionally, by primary legislation, not by judges. On the other hand, recent revisions of the Treaty have widened the non-economic interests pursued by the European Union (e.g. environmental protection and the protection of services of general interest) so that the judiciary plays a key role in balancing the relationship between competing values.

---

[37] S. Weatherill, 'Anti-Doping Revisited: The Demise of the Rule of "Purely Sporting Interest"' (2006) 27 *ECLR* 645; another example may be found in a decision of the New Zealand Commerce Commission, Decision 580 New Zealand Rugby Football Union Incorporated, 2 July 2006, www.comcom.govt.nz. For comment, see R. Adhar, 'Professional Rugby, Competitive Balance and Competition Law' (2007) *ECLR* 36.

[38] *Ordem dos Técnicos Oficiais de Contas* v. *Autoridade da Concorrência*, C-1/12, Judgment of 23 February 2013, paras. 95–9.

[39] E. Loozen, 'Professional Ethics and Restraints of Competition' (2006) 31 *ELRev* 28.

[40] R. Whish and D. Bailey, *Competition Law*, 9th edn (Oxford University Press, 2018) 138–42.

[41] G. Monti, *EC Competition Law* (Cambridge University Press, 2007) 110–20.

[42] G. Monti and J. Mulder, 'Escaping the Clutches of EU Competition Law Pathways to Assess Private Sustainability Initiatives' (2017) 42(5) *ELRev* 635.

3 ARTICLE 101 TFEU: RESTRICTIVE PRACTICES

Article 101 TFEU

(1) The following shall be prohibited as incompatible with the common market: all agreements between undertakings, decisions by associations of undertakings and concerted practices which may affect trade between Member States and which have as their object or effect the prevention, restriction or distortion of competition within the common market, and in particular those which:

    (a) directly or indirectly fix purchase or selling prices or any other trading conditions;

    (b) limit or control production, markets, technical development, or investment;

    (c) share markets or sources of supply;

    (d) apply dissimilar conditions to equivalent transactions with other trading parties, thereby placing them at a competitive disadvantage;

    (e) make the conclusion of contracts subject to acceptance by the other parties of supplementary obligations which, by their nature or according to commercial usage, have no connection with the subject of such contracts.

(2) Any agreements or decisions prohibited pursuant to this article shall be automatically void.

(3) The provisions of paragraph 1 may, however, be declared inapplicable in the case of:

- any agreement or category of agreements between undertakings,
- any decision or category of decisions by associations of undertakings,
- any concerted practice or category of concerted practices,

which contributes to improving the production or distribution of goods or to promoting technical or economic progress, while allowing consumers a fair share of the resulting benefit, and which does not:

    (a) impose on the undertakings concerned restrictions which are not indispensable to the attainment of these objectives;

    (b) afford such undertakings the possibility of eliminating competition in respect of a substantial part of the products in question.

We provide a thumbnail sketch of this article before considering it in more detail in the sections that follow. Paragraphs (1) and (3) should be read successively: paragraph (1) declares that agreements which restrict competition are unlawful, subject to the exception in paragraph (3) which provides that anti-competitive agreements that yield certain benefits may be lawful.[43]

If an agreement restricts competition and is not exempted under paragraph (3) then, following paragraph (2), it is automatically void. Under EU law, agreements in breach of Article 101 are prohibited.[44] The Commission may require the undertakings to bring the infringement to an end,[45] and impose fines.[46] In the courts, parties to a void agreement are unable to enforce the

---

[43] See Regulation 1/2003 on the implementation of the rules on competition laid down in Articles 81 and 82 of the Treaty, recital 4, Articles 1, 5 and 6 [2003] OJ L 1/1.

[44] Regulation 1/2003 on the implementation of the rules on competition laid down in Articles 81 and 82 of the Treaty, article 1 [2003] OJ L 1/1.

[45] Regulation 1/2003 on the implementation of the rules on competition laid down in Articles 81 and 82 of the Treaty [2003] OJ L 1/1, Article 7.

[46] Regulation 1/2003 on the implementation of the rules on competition laid down in Articles 81 and 82 of the Treaty, Article 23(2) [2003] OJ L 1/1.

agreement,[47] and may be sued for damages by parties who suffer harm as a result of anti-competitive practices.[48]

(i) Agreements, Decisions and Concerted Practices

Three distinct types of cooperation fall under Article 101 TFEU. An *agreement* represents a consensus between parties to act in a certain manner; it need not be inscribed in a binding contract,[49] and need not be in writing.[50] A *concerted practice* is a term used to catch forms of collusion that fall short of agreement, but where the parties substitute practical cooperation for the risks of competition, affecting the conditions of competition on the market.[51] An example is a situation where undertakings meet to exchange information about the prices they intend to charge and their sales volumes – information which makes coordination of behaviour likely because after the meeting each player takes into consideration what others have disclosed when planning their strategy. There is no agreement because specific conduct has not been determined, but the post-market behaviour of each is influenced by the information received and it is likely that prices are higher and output less than if each had determined their business conduct independently. Often cartels operate over a long period of time and are sustained by a mixture of agreements and concerted practices, whereby targets are agreed upon and then regular meetings are held where key information is disclosed to 'oil' the operation of the agreement.[52] Thus, concerted practices differ in form from agreements because of their intensity, but both are collusive devices having the same effect: coordinating the behaviour of the participants.

A trade association is designed to protect the interests of its members. A *decision* by an association is a provision in the rules of a trade association or a decision reached by a trade association, which affects the members. For example, the Law Society of a Member State may decide to fix the remuneration for lawyers, or an agricultural association may coordinate prices on behalf of its members.[53] In appropriate circumstances, a non-binding recommendation (e.g. on prices to be charged by members of the association) may also constitute a decision where it is likely to affect members' pricing determinations.[54]

(a) Cartels

There are four conditions for a successful cartel: the major suppliers of the product in question take part; they agree on how to coordinate their behaviour (e.g. by agreeing upon how to set prices or allocating geographical markets to each other); there is a mechanism to detect and

---

[47] *Eco Swiss China Time Ltd* v. *Benetton*, C-126/97, ECLI:EU:C:1999:269, a precedent which allows a party in breach to avoid paying damages where the agreement is held to infringe Article 101 TFEU (the so-called 'Euro-defence'). See generally G. Monti, 'EU Competition Law and European Private Law' in C. Twigg-Flesner (ed.), *The Cambridge Companion to European Union Private Law* (Cambridge University Press, 2010).

[48] *Courage Ltd* v. *Crehan*, C-453/99, ECLI:EU:C:2001:465.

[49] See the 'gentlemen's agreement' in *ACF Chemiefarma NV* v. *Commission*, 41/69, ECLI:EU:C:1970:71.

[50] *Polypropylene* [1986] OJ L 230/1, para. 81.

[51] The seminal authorities defining concerted practices are *ICI* v. *Commission (Dyestuffs)*, 48/69, ECLI:EU:C:1972:70, para. 64; *Cooperatiëve Vereniging 'Suiker Unie' UA* v. *Commission*, 40-8, 50, 54-6, 111, 113 and 114/73, ECLI:EU:C:1975:174.

[52] *Polypropylene* [1986] OJ L 230/1, para. 87.

[53] See e.g. *Wouters* v. *Algemene Raad van de Nederlandse Orde van Advocaten*, C-309/99, ECLI:EU:C:2002:98; *Gøttrup-Klim Grovvareforeninger* v. *Dansk Landbrugs Grovvareselskab AmbA*, C-250/92, ECLI:EU:C:1994:413.

[54] *Fenex* [1996] OJ L 181/28, paras. 32–42.

punish cartel members who 'cheat' by cutting prices below the cartel price; there are high entry barriers to prevent competitors entering the market thereby reducing the cartel's profitability.[55] With these factors present, the cartel is able to behave like a monopoly, reducing output and increasing prices. There is evidence that some cartels have broken down because parties were unable to agree or coordinate behaviour,[56] but when there is a high level of trust among members, cartels can last for a considerable length of time.[57] As we saw in Chapter 20, EU competition law creates an additional source of instability for cartels: leniency programmes give incentives for cartel members to expose the existence of a cartel as a way of escaping the Commission's significant penalties.[58] Cartel-busting is a core activity for the Commission (as well as for national competition authorities) and the European Courts have facilitated this task in two ways: first, by setting out wide definitions of the terms 'agreement' and 'concerted practice'; secondly, by allowing the Commission to consider the pattern of collusion by several undertakings over a period of time as being a single infringement characterised in part by agreements and partly by concerted practices.

The Dutch NCA tested the boundaries of the law when it condemned the Dutch mobile phone operators for a single meeting where they exchanged information about the remuneration each provided to their dealers when they sold a post-paid mobile phone subscription. In the aftermath of this meeting each of the four operators reduced the remuneration they paid. This conduct harms competition because by offering higher remuneration, an operator can stimulate dealers to promote their phones, absent this incentive there is less competition for the consumer. It was agreed that the mere exchange of information could constitute a concerted practice (because no specific course of conduct had been stipulated) but could a single meeting result in anti-competitive conduct?

T-Mobile Netherlands BV, KPN Mobile NV, Orange Nederland NV and Vodafone Libertel NV v. Raad van bestuur van de Nederlandse Mededingingsautoriteit, C-8/08, ECLI:EU:C:2009:343

51 As regards the presumption of a causal connection formulated by the Court in connection with the interpretation of Article [101(1)], it should be pointed out, first, that the Court has held that the concept of a concerted practice, as it derives from the actual terms of that provision, implies, in addition to the participating undertakings concerting with each other, subsequent conduct on the market and a relationship of cause and effect between the two. However, the Court went on to consider that, subject to proof to the contrary, which the economic operators concerned must adduce, it must be presumed that the undertakings taking part in the concerted action and remaining active on the market take account of the information exchanged with their competitors in determining their conduct on that market. That is all the more the case where the undertakings concert together on a regular basis over a long period. Lastly, the Court concluded that such a concerted practice is caught by Article [101(1)], even in the absence of anti-competitive effects on the market.

---

[55] On the economics of cartels, see M. Motta, *Competition Policy* (Cambridge University Press, 2004) ch. 4.

[56] See e.g. *Zinc Producer Group* [1984] OJ L 220/27 for a partial breakdown, and D. T. Armentano, *Antitrust and Monopoly: Anatomy of a Policy Failure* (New York, John Wiley and Sons, 1982) ch. 5.

[57] E.g. the first modern cartel case decided by the Commission lasted from 1977 to 1983: *Commission v. Anic Partecipazioni SpA*, C-49/92, ECLI:EU:C:1999:356.

[58] See p. 891.

. . .

59 Depending on the structure of the market, the possibility cannot be ruled out that a meeting on a single occasion between competitors, such as that in question in the main proceedings, may, in principle, constitute a sufficient basis for the participating undertakings to concert their market conduct and thus successfully substitute practical cooperation between them for competition and the risks that that entails.

60 As the Netherlands Government correctly pointed out, together with the Advocate General at points 104 and 105 of her Opinion, the number, frequency, and form of meetings between competitors needed to concert their market conduct depend on both the subject-matter of that concerted action and the particular market conditions. If the undertakings concerned establish a cartel with a complex system of concerted actions in relation to a multiplicity of aspects of their market conduct, regular meetings over a long period may be necessary. If, on the other hand, as in the main proceedings, the objective of the exercise is only to concert action on a selective basis in relation to a one-off alteration in market conduct with reference simply to one parameter of competition, a single meeting between competitors may constitute a sufficient basis on which to implement the anti-competitive object which the participating undertakings aim to achieve.

61 In those circumstances, what matters is not so much the number of meetings held between the participating undertakings as whether the meeting or meetings which took place afforded them the opportunity to take account of the information exchanged with their competitors in order to determine their conduct on the market in question and knowingly substitute practical cooperation between them for the risks of competition. Where it can be established that such undertakings successfully concerted with one another and remained active on the market, they may justifiably be called upon to adduce evidence that that concerted action did not have any effect on their conduct on the market in question.

This judgment confirms that for the purposes of establishing a concerted practice one may presume that parties will act on the information they obtained. When the case was heard again by the Dutch court however, the national court added that this presumption had to be rebuttable to respect the defendants' rights under Article 6 of the European Convention on Human Rights (ECHR). It then quashed the NCA decision because it had not considered the evidence raised by the parties to rebut the presumption.[59]

Parties who meet and obtain information about anti-competitive plans might not wish to follow-up on the information they receive and prefer to compete. However, since there is a presumption that receiving sensitive information is likely to influence one's conduct on the market, how might one escape being found liable under Article 101? This question was addressed in *Eturas*. The Lithuanian NCA found that Eturas operated an online travel booking system to which a number of tour operators subscribed. Each of the travel agencies received a message from Eturas indicating that it planned to reduce the online discount from 4 per cent to anywhere between zero and 3 per cent. Travel agents wishing to retain a higher discount has to enter the system and set a higher discount rate themselves. The NCA considered that, by not rebelling against Eturas's policy, the thirty travel agents and Eturas had engaged in a concerted practice.

---

[59] *College van Beroep voor het bedrijfsleven*, 12–08–2010, AWB 06/657, 06/660 en 06/661, ECLI:NL:CBB:2010:BN3895. For discussion see A. Hans, 'T-Mobile' in P. L. Parcu and G. Monti (eds.), 'European Networking and Training for National Competition Enforcers (ENTraNCE for Judges 2014): Selected Case Notes', EUI Working Papers (RSCAS 2016/20).

While Eturas was not active on the market, it facilitated the collusive outcome.[60] One matter which was disputed was whether the message had indeed been received by all travel agents, but this was a matter of evidence. The question discussed below is how can an undertaking escape liability having received notification of a plan to collude.

'Eturas' UAB and Others v. Lietuvos Respublikos konkurencijos taryba, C–74/14, ECLI:EU:C:2016:42

46 ... [A] travel agency may rebut the presumption that it participated in a concerted practice by proving that it publically distanced itself from that practice or reported it to the administrative authorities. In addition, according to the case-law of the Court, in a case such as that at issue in the main proceedings, which does not concern an anticompetitive meeting, public distancing or reporting to the administrative authorities are not the only means of rebutting the presumption that a company has participated in an infringement; other evidence may also be adduced with a view to rebutting that presumption.

47 As regards the examination of whether the travel agencies concerned publicly distanced themselves from the concertation at issue in the main proceedings, it must be noted that, in particular circumstances such as those at issue in the main proceedings, it cannot be required that the declaration by a travel agency of its intention to distance itself be made to all of the competitors which were the addressees of the message at issue in the main proceedings, since that agency is not in fact in a position to know who those addressees are.

48 In that situation, the referring court may accept that a clear and express objection sent to the administrator of the E-TURAS system is capable of rebutting that presumption.

49 As regards the possibility of rebutting the presumption of participation in a concerted practice by means other than public distancing or reporting it to the administrative authorities, it must be held that, in circumstances such as those at issue in the main proceedings, the presumption of a causal connection between the concertation and the market conduct of the undertakings participating in the practice, referred to in paragraph 33 of the present judgment, could be rebutted by evidence of a systematic application of a discount exceeding the cap in question.

This judgment illustrates the manner by which an undertaking may escape a finding of infringement. Obviously distancing oneself from a cartel is laden with risk for the other members may retaliate.

Finally, in long-running cartels the Commission is allowed to aggregate various rounds of collusion and find that there is a single overall agreement. This was clarified during the polypropylene cartel decision where the Commission found that several undertakings active in the European petrochemical industry had participated in a cartel between 1977 and 1983. The parties had set up a system of target prices and devised a system to limit output to share the market according to agreed quotas. One cartel member, Anic, held a market share between 2.7 and 4.2 per cent and was fined 750,000 ECU. Anic appealed seeking a reduction or an annulment of the decision in its entirety on the basis that, *inter alia*, the Commission had failed to characterise the infringement either as an agreement or as a concerted practice. In affirming the General Court's decision the Court established several important criteria for identifying

---

[60] Liability for cartel facilitators was clarified in *AC-Treuhand AG* v. *Commission*, C-194/14 P, ECLI:EU:C:2015:717.

agreements and concerted practices. These principles have continued to inform the Commission's cartel enforcement strategy since.

Commission v. Anic Partecipazioni SpA, C–49/92, ECLI:EU:C:1999:356

108 The list in Article [101(1)] of the Treaty is intended to apply to all collusion between undertakings, whatever the form it takes. There is continuity between the cases listed. The only essential thing is the distinction between independent conduct, which is allowed, and collusion, which is not, regardless of any distinction between types of collusion. Anic's argument would break down the unity and generality of the prohibited phenomenon and would remove from the ambit of the prohibition, without any reason, certain types of collusion which are no less dangerous than others ...

109 The Court observes first of all that ... the [General Court] held that the Commission was entitled to categorise as agreements certain types of conduct on the part of the undertakings concerned, and, in the alternative, as concerted practices certain other forms of conduct on the part of the same undertakings. The [General Court] held that Anic had taken part in an integrated set of schemes constituting a single infringement which progressively manifested itself in both unlawful agreements and unlawful concerted practices ...

112 Secondly, it must be observed that, if Article [101] of the Treaty distinguishes between 'concerted practices', 'agreements between undertakings' and 'decisions by associations of undertakings', the aim is to have the prohibitions of that article catch different forms of coordination and collusion between undertakings.

113 It does not, however, follow that patterns of conduct having the same anti-competitive object, each of which, taken in isolation, would fall within the meaning of 'agreement', 'concerted practice' or 'a decision by an association of undertakings', cannot constitute different manifestations of a single infringement of Article [101(1)] of the Treaty.

114 The [General Court] was therefore entitled to consider that patterns of conduct by several undertakings were a manifestation of a single infringement, corresponding partly to an agreement and partly to a concerted practice.

In later cases the criteria for finding a single continuous infringement have been clarified. The Commission must show that there is (i) an overall plan with a common objective during the entire period, (ii) that each undertaking contributed intentionally to this plan and (iii) that each undertaking is aware of the offending conduct of the others.[61] This allows the Court to test the quality of the evidence used by the Commission. In BASF for example, the Commission considered that a global price-fixing cartel (1992–4) and an EU-wide cartel (1994–8) were a single infringement but the General Court found no connection between the two: the parties were not the same and there was no overlap in time.[62]

There are several consequences of showing a single infringement. The first is that the Commission is allowed to escape the limitation period of five years, which runs from the day when the infringement ceases.[63] The second consequence is that the Commission's evidentiary

---

[61] *Team Relocations* v. *Commission*, T-204/08, EU:T:2011:286, para. 37.

[62] *BASF AG and UCB SA* v. *Commission*, T-101/05 and T-111/05, ECLI:EU:T:2007:380. See also D. Bailey, 'Single, Overall Agreement in EU Competition Law' (2010) 47 *CMLRev* 473 and J. Joshua, 'Single Continuous Infringement of Article 81 EC: Has the Commission Stretched the Concept Beyond the Limit of its Logic?' (2009) 5(2) *Eur Comp Journal* 451.

[63] Regulation 1/2003 on the implementation of the rules on competition laid down in Articles 81 and 82 of the Treaty, Article 25(1) [2003] OJ L 1/1.

burden is lightened significantly by not having to define each element of coordination as an agreement or a concerted practice. However, the Commission must establish evidence of each instance of collusion and must allow the undertaking to respond and dispute the Commission's finding. The third consequence is that by characterising the infringement as a single conspiracy, a participant is responsible for all of the cartel's actions, even if it did not take part in all of them. This means that a cartel is a 'conspiracy' by its members, and as a result even those with small market shares, whose participation is limited, contribute to the overall conspiracy.[64] Even Anic, with a small market share, contributed to the conspiracy.

In sum, the policy behind the Court of Justice's case law is to send a message to parties to a cartel that once they agree to conspire against the interests of the Union, they will be held responsible for the entirety of the conduct to which they have assented. The aim is to maximise the deterrence of competition law. The only way out for an undertaking is to either make a leniency application confessing the presence of the agreement, or to publicly distance itself from what has been agreed, but then risk retaliation from the undertakings.[65] The sole consolation for a minor participant is that the fact that it has not taken part in all aspects of an anti-competitive agreement, or that it played a minor role, will be taken into consideration when calculating the fine.[66]

So far we have considered the definition of agreements and concerted practices. It is also important to bear in mind the evidence that may be used to establish the existence of cooperation. In the majority of cases, the Commission obtains hard evidence in the form of memoranda or recordings of conversations that prove collusion. However, collusion can be established by inference from the conduct of the parties. The Court approved of this method early on,[67] and the limits upon the use of indirect evidence were set out in the *Wood Pulp* case.[68] The Commission decided that forty producers of wood pulp had colluded to fix prices between 1975 and 1981. For some aspects of the cartel, collusion was proven by documentary evidence of the undertakings' membership to certain trade associations; but, for some, no documentary evidence supported a finding of collusion. The Court ruled that in principle a cartel could be inferred from the way undertakings behave only if their common behaviour has no other explanation than that the parties must have come to an agreement to behave in that way. However, on the facts, two Court-appointed experts reported that the parallel behaviour by the undertakings could be explained by reasons other than a pre-existing agreement to align their commercial strategies and the case failed. Since *Wood Pulp*, the Commission has not used economic evidence to infer the existence of an agreement, but has relied upon tangible evidence seized during searches of the cartel members' premises. While documents are hard to find, it is preferable for the Commission to bring a case based on hard evidence rather than having to argue that it can infer

---

[64] *LR af 1998 A/S* v. *Commission*, T-23/99, ECLI:EU:T:2002:75, where an infringement was found even though the undertaking took no active role.

[65] See D. Bailey, 'Publicly Distancing Oneself from a Cartel' (2008) 32 *World Competition* 177.

[66] *Commission* v. *Anic Partecipazioni SpA*, C-49/92, CLI:EU:C:1999:356, para. 90. In *Fresh Del Monte* v. *Commission*, C-293/13 P, EC:C:2015:416 it was held that a party may escape liability for parts of the infringement it is not aware of.

[67] *ICI* v. *Commission (Dyestuffs)*, 48/69, ECLI:EU:C:1972:70; while the Commission's decision was also based on concrete evidence of collusion the Court focused solely on the circumstances of the market. See also *Züchner* v. *Bayerische Vereinsbank*, 172/80, ECLI:EU:C:1981:178.

[68] *A. Ahlström Osakeyhtiö and Others* v. *Commission (Wood Pulp)*, 89/85, 104/85, 114/85, 116–17/85 and 125–9/85, ECLI:EU:C:1993:120, paras. 70–2; A. Jones, 'Woodpulp: Concerted Practice and/or Conscious Parallelism?' 14 (1993) *ECLR* 273.

an agreement from the way parties behave on the market. This is because it would have to show that the parallel behaviour has no other explanation except prior collusion, and alternative plausible reasons for parallel behaviour can often be found.[69]

(b) Algorithms and Collusion

A contemporary challenge arises with the way undertakings use algorithms to assist them in their commercial strategy. An algorithm is a computer programme that is instructed to analyse a large amount of data and to produce an outcome: for example Amazon offers its third party sellers a feature which always matches the lowest price available on its website.[70] This kind of algorithm benefits consumers because it serves to stimulate competition more quickly than if each seller had to log on every day to adjust its prices. However, pricing algorithms may also facilitate cartels. Again with reference to online sales there have been instances were competitors used a pricing algorithm as a means to implement and monitor a cartel agreement. From the perspective of the cartel, the advantage was that the algorithm was able to monitor the extent to which the parties comply with the agreed price.[71]

An alternative scenario is one where all the firms use a specific algorithm supplied by a third party which uses all the data supplied by the firms to facilitate collusion. This is known as hub-and-spoke collusion and the *VM Remonts* judgment reveals that EU competition law is well-equipped to handle this. A public authority had opened a tender for the supply of food products to schools. The three firms that put in a bid had all subcontracted the preparation of the bid to the same company and the Latvian competition authority suspected that this was done on purpose to generate a collusive outcome. The ECJ was asked under whether by subcontracting the work an undertaking was responsible for the collusion. The Court held that under such circumstances, the tenderer would be liable under three circumstances. First, if in fact, this company was under the control of one of the bidders.

SIA 'VM Remonts', formerly SIA 'DIV un KO' and SIA 'Ausma grupa' v. Konkurences padome, C–542/14, ECLI:EU:C:2016:578

28 It must be stated, secondly, that, assuming the service provider concerned to be genuinely independent (a matter which falls to be determined by the national court), in circumstances such as those in the main proceedings the concerted practice involving that provider may be attributed to the undertaking using that provider's services only under certain conditions.

29 In that regard, it should be recalled that the Court has held that an undertaking may be held liable for agreements or concerted practices having an anti-competitive object when it intended to contribute by its own conduct to the common objectives pursued by all the participants and was aware of the actual conduct planned or put into effect by other undertakings in pursuit of the same objectives or that it could reasonably have foreseen it and was prepared to accept the risk.

---

[69] For a contrary position, see L. Kaplow, *Competition Policy and Price Fixing* (Princeton University Press, 2013) advocating greater use of economic evidence.

[70] Competition and Markets Authority, Pricing algorithms: Economic working paper on the use of algorithms to facilitate collusion and personalised pricing (CMA94, 2018) para. 2.28.

[71] Competition and Markets Authority, Case 50223 – *Online sales of posters and frames*, Decision of 12 August 2016.

30 Accordingly, the concerted practice at issue may be attributed to the undertaking using the services, *inter alia*, if the undertaking was aware of the anti-competitive objectives pursued by its competitors and the service provider and intended to contribute to them by its own conduct. Whilst it is true that such a condition is met when that undertaking intended, through the intermediary of its service provider, to disclose commercially sensitive information to its competitors, or when it expressly or tacitly consented to the provider sharing that commercially sensitive information with them, the condition is not met when that service provider has, without informing the undertaking using its services, used the undertaking's commercially sensitive information to complete those competitors' tenders.

31 The concerted practice at issue may also be attributed to the undertaking using those services if the latter could reasonably have foreseen that the service provider retained by it would share its commercial information with its competitors and if it was prepared to accept the risk which that entailed.

In addition, the ECJ has made it clear that a firm that provides assistance to members of a cartel may be responsible for the infringement of Article 101.[72] It follows that sellers knowingly using a common algorithm supplier through which sensitive data is channelled that helps reach an anti-competitive outcome may be caught by Article 101.

A more complex scenario occurs when the algorithm is itself the decision-maker: it is programmed to take account of all the data available and to reach pricing decisions that, say, maximise profits. In this setting the firm supplying the algorithm may be aware that it can yield cartel-like effects but the users may be unaware of the risk. It is not clear whether EU competition law is able to address such risk.

Biennial Report of the Monopolies Commission (*Competition 2018*) in accordance with Section 44 Paragraph 1 Sentence 1 of the German Act against Restraints of Competition

266 Conversely, liability gaps can open up if the IT service provider brings about a collusive market outcome without the approval of the parties involved. It is possible that several users use pricing algorithms whose use leads to collusive pricing. However, users may not be able to recognize this collusive market outcome themselves – e.g., due to the complexity of the product or the market conditions – and therefore may not form a joint intention necessary to create a cartel. At the same time, however, the IT service provider that provided the pricing algorithms may be well aware of the possibility of collusive pricing and may also approve of it. In such a case, the situation is comparable to that of an external consultant advising several companies in such a way that they act in parallel without the joint intention of all parties involved. Such constellations (the IT service provider acts as an 'indirect perpetrator', so to speak) cannot or only with difficulty be addressed pursuant to Article 101 TFEU.

267 It also does not seem easily possible to base the IT service provider's liability under Article 101 TFEU on the fact that it was the contract for the provision of the respective algorithm that produced the collusive market outcome, and that this contract constitutes an agreement within the meaning of the provision. For the object of the contract is solely the provision of the algorithm, but not the exchange of strategic information or the use of the algorithm to coordinate the users' market conduct. Nevertheless, the fact that the IT service provider is not liable seems unfair, since there is behaviour to which liability could well be attached and which leads to a collusive market outcome.

[72] *AC-Treuhand AG* v. *Commission*, C-194/14 P, ECLI:EU:C:2015:717.

This discussion points to a gap in the application of competition law: a collusive outcome may result without the parties agreeing to reach it. This is not a novel problem: the economics literature had already noted that in an oligopoly market it may be possible for prices to rise to anti-competitive levels absent agreement.[73] Algorithms may make this risk more frequent but the phenomenon points to the same gap as before.

(ii) Object or Effect the Restriction, Distortion or Prevention of Competition

(a) Notion of Restriction of Competition

There is continuing controversy about what it means for an agreement to restrict competition. In *GlaxoSmithKline* (hereinafter *GSK*) we find a clear divergence between the General Court and the Court of Justice on this key question. The dispute arose when GSK, a producer of pharmaceuticals, inserted a clause in its contracts with Spanish wholesalers to ensure that they did not export the medicines to other Member States. The commercial rationale for GSK's practice is that medicines are bought by national health authorities and these buy medicines at different prices: in some, like Spain, the price is low because the government wants to guarantee availability of medicines, while in the United Kingdom the price is higher because the government wishes to reward pharmaceutical firms and encourage future innovation. Given low transport costs, there is a clear incentive for wholesalers in Spain to export to the United Kingdom, and an obvious interest in GSK to prevent these exports because they harm profits in the UK market. The Commission found the agreement had as its object the restriction of competition, a result which was to be expected given that the agreement served to partition the internal market.[74] According to many commentators, the EU competition regime is special because it considers agreements that partition the internal market as restrictive of competition.

From an economic perspective, however, the parallel trader does not bring any benefits to consumers. In fact, by reducing the revenue to the pharmaceutical companies, their research and development strategies are hindered. On this basis, the Commission's policy harms the development of new drugs.[75] On appeal, the General Court ruled that the prevention of parallel trade was not sufficient to find a restriction of competition.

GlaxoSmithKline Services Unlimited v. *Commission*, Case T–168/01, ECLI:EU:T:2006:265

118   In effect, the objective assigned to Article [101(1) TFEU], which constitutes a fundamental provision indispensable for the achievement of the missions entrusted to the Community, in particular for the functioning of the internal market, is to prevent undertakings, by restricting competition between themselves or with third parties, from reducing the welfare of the final consumer of the products in question. At the hearing, in fact, the Commission emphasised on a number of occasions that it was from that perspective that it had carried out its examination in the present case, initially concluding that the General Sales Conditions clearly restricted the welfare of consumers, then considering whether that restriction would be offset by increased efficiency which would itself benefit consumers.

---

[73] G. Monti, 'The Scope of Collective Dominance under Article 82 EC' (2001) 38(1) *CMLRev* 131.

[74] *Glaxo Wellcome* [2001] OJ L 302/1.

[75] For greater detail see P. Rey and J. S. Venit, 'Parallel Trade and Pharmaceuticals: A Policy in Search of Itself' (2004) 29 *ELRev* 176.

119 Consequently, the application of Article [101(1)TFEU] to the present case cannot depend solely on the fact that the agreement in question is intended to limit parallel trade in medicines or to partition the common market, which leads to the conclusion that it affects trade between Member States, but also requires an analysis designed to determine whether it has as its object or effect the prevention, restriction or distortion of competition on the relevant market, to the detriment of the final consumer . . . [T]hat analysis, which may be abridged when the clauses of the agreement reveal in themselves the existence of an alteration of competition, as the Commission observed at the hearing, must, on the other hand, be supplemented, depending on the requirements of the case, where that is not so . . .

121 While it has been accepted since then that parallel trade must be given a certain protection, it is therefore not as such but, as the Court of Justice held, in so far as it favours the development of trade, on the one hand, and the strengthening of competition, on the other hand, that is to say, in this second respect, in so far as it gives final consumers the advantages of effective competition in terms of supply or price. Consequently, while it is accepted that an agreement intended to limit parallel trade must in principle be considered to have as its object the restriction of competition, that applies in so far as the agreement may be presumed to deprive final consumers of those advantages.

However, on appeal, the Court of Justice returned to the position taken by the Commission. The Court ruled that nothing in the case law or in the text of Article 101 supported the position of the General Court.

GlaxoSmithKline Services Unlimited v. *Commission*, C–501/06 P, C–513/06 P, C–515/06 P and C–519/06 P, ECLI:EU:C:2009:610

63 First of all, there is nothing in that provision to indicate that only those agreements which deprive consumers of certain advantages may have an anti-competitive object. Secondly, it must be borne in mind that the Court has held that, like other competition rules laid down in the Treaty, Article [101 TFEU] aims to protect not only the interests of competitors or of consumers, but also the structure of the market and, in so doing, competition as such. Consequently, for a finding that an agreement has an anti-competitive object, it is not necessary that final consumers be deprived of the advantages of effective competition in terms of supply or price.

64 It follows that, by requiring proof that the agreement entails disadvantages for final consumers as a prerequisite for a finding of anti-competitive object and by not finding that that agreement had such an object, the General Court committed an error of law.

The debate between the two courts is illustrative of the current controversy over the standard by which one assesses the anti-competitive nature of agreements. According to the General Court, a consumer welfare standard is preferred. This is in line with the Commission's current policy as well. In contrast, the Court of Justice's position reflects a different understanding of competition. The Court's statement that one is engaged in protecting 'competition as such' is opaque and leads to two competing interpretations.

On the one hand, it may be that the Court is using Article 101(1) to safeguard the economic freedom of market participants.[76] On the other hand, in some of its judgments, the Court

---

[76] This is the view suggested by one of the co-authors of this book. Monti, n. 41 above.

explores the impact of restrictive practices on the market. For example in the *BIDS* judgment the Court held that an agreement among beef slaughterhouses that some of them would cease production was a restriction of competition by object. It then indicated the kinds of anti-competitive effects that would likely result: higher prices as a result of reduced supply and foreclosure of new entrants as a result of the firms exiting the market agreeing to destroy their facilities.[77] The latter approach is preferred by most commentators because it forces the competition authority to explain the reason why competition law should apply. However, it comes at a high cost for competition authorities who need to gather considerable evidence to show the kinds of harm an agreement may cause.

(b) Agreements Restrictive of Competition by Object

Article 101 TFEU distinguishes between agreements whose object is the restriction of competition and those which have as an effect the restriction of competition.[78] In considering infringements by object, there are three policy considerations that justify the power to condemn by reference to the object of an agreement: competition authorities have limited resources to establish the effects of every practice (thus in a price-fixing cartel case it would be wasteful to require the agency to show harmful effects when economics teaches us the negative impact is clear); second, parties benefit from legal certainty if they are aware what conduct is clearly forbidden; third the law at times penalises conduct that creates a risk of harm, without requiring one to show harm.[79]

However, it is not self-evident what agreements are restrictive by object. The Court refers to agreements which 'by their very nature' are 'injurious to the proper functioning of normal competition'.[80] But the application of these standards has proven difficult.

Finally, with decentralised enforcement, there was a concern that national competition authorities might resort to finding agreements restrictive by object as a shortcut to avoid engaging in the more complex approach required to show anti-competitive effects. Some took the view that the Commission was also applying the notion of restriction by object too easily.[81] An attempt to clarify matters occurred in the Cartes Bancaires saga. Cartes Bancaires is an association of the main French banks operating the 'CB' card payment system. This system enabled a CB card issued by a member of the association to be used to make payments to all traders affiliated to the CB system through any other member of the association, and to make withdrawals from ATMs operated by all other members. Under the rules, banks had to pay a higher membership fee if their issuing activities were considerably larger than their acquiring activities. The Commission was concerned that this foreclosed access to new entrants who would be paying a higher fee to enter the market. In its decision it condemned the agreement as restrictive of competition by object and by effect. This afforded the ECJ the occasion to clarify its case law.

---

[77] *Competition Authority* v. *Beef Industry Development Society Ltd*, C-209/07, ECLI:EU:C:2008:643, paras. 37–8.

[78] Agreements may 'restrict, distort or eliminate' competition but the analysis is the same for all three effects. For convenience we will henceforth only refer to 'agreements' but the analysis applies to all forms of cooperation.

[79] Opinion of AG Kokott, *T-Mobile Netherlands BV* v. *Raad van bestuur van de Nederlandse Mededingingsautoriteit*, C-8/08, EU:C:2009:110, paras. 43–7.

[80] *T-Mobile Netherlands BV* v. *Raad van bestuur van de Nederlandse Mededingingsautoriteit*, C-8/08, ECLI:EU:C:2009:343, para. 29.

[81] A. C. Witt, 'The Enforcement of Article 101 TFEU: What Has Happened to the Effects Analysis?' (2018) 55(2) *CMLR* 417.

> ### *Groupement des cartes bancaires (CB) v. Commission*, C–67/13 P, ECLI:EU:C:2014:2204
>
> 49 ... [I]t is apparent from the Court's case-law that certain types of coordination between undertakings reveal a sufficient degree of harm to competition that it may be found that there is no need to examine their effects.
>
> 50 That case-law arises from the fact that certain types of coordination between undertakings can be regarded, by their very nature, as being harmful to the proper functioning of normal competition.
>
> 51 Consequently, it is established that certain collusive behaviour, such as that leading to horizontal price-fixing by cartels, may be considered so likely to have negative effects, in particular on the price, quantity or quality of the goods and services, that it may be considered redundant, for the purposes of applying Article 81(1) EC, to prove that they have actual effects on the market. Experience shows that such behaviour leads to falls in production and price increases, resulting in poor allocation of resources to the detriment, in particular, of consumers.
>
> 52 Where the analysis of a type of coordination between undertakings does not reveal a sufficient degree of harm to competition, the effects of the coordination should, on the other hand, be considered and, for it to be caught by the prohibition, it is necessary to find that factors are present which show that competition has in fact been prevented, restricted or distorted to an appreciable extent.
>
> 53 According to the case-law of the Court, in order to determine whether an agreement between undertakings or a decision by an association of undertakings reveals a sufficient degree of harm to competition that it may be considered a restriction of competition 'by object' within the meaning of Article 81(1) EC, regard must be had to the content of its provisions, its objectives and the economic and legal context of which it forms a part. When determining that context, it is also necessary to take into consideration the nature of the goods or services affected, as well as the real conditions of the functioning and structure of the market or markets in question.
>
> 54 In addition, although the parties' intention is not a necessary factor in determining whether an agreement between undertakings is restrictive, there is nothing prohibiting the competition authorities, the national courts or the Courts of the European Union from taking that factor into account.

The Court followed the advice of its Advocate General closely and suggested that the concept of a restriction of competition by object should be read restrictively. On the facts, the Court held that it was not obvious that this agreement was harmful: the higher fees could be seen as an incentive for banks that only issue cards to invest in building ATMs across France, which could stimulate the growth of the CB system. The case was set back to the General Court to test if the Commission had proven an anti-competitive effect, and the Commission's decision was upheld on that basis.[82]

The judgment raises two issues: on the one hand, it is not completely clear that *Cartes Bancaires* clarifies the case law: some of the passages above suggest that agreements restrictive by object are those where the harm is obvious, but in later passages suggest that a mini-effects analysis should be carried out (considering the economic and legal context of the agreement); on the other, the impact of this lack of clarity forces the Commission to try cases under the object and effect analysis at the same time, which appears to be wasteful. The purposes of creating a category of restrictions by object appears to be frustrated.

---

[82] *Groupement des cartes bancaires (CB) v. Commission*, T-491/07, RENV ECLI:EU:T:2016:379.

(c) Agreements Having an Anti-Competitive Effect

Understanding the methodology for determining whether an agreement has an anti-competitive effect by looking at the Commission's past practice is problematic because in the past the Commission has been too quick to find anti-competitive effects,[83] in spite of the Court of Justice at times reminding the Commission that close analysis is warranted.[84] Before the coming into force of Regulation 1/2003, when parties had the opportunity to notify agreements, some even advised the parties to avoid doing so because the Commission would too easily find a restriction and then take too long to issue an exemption.[85] Others argued that the Commission should apply a more sophisticated approach systematically.[86]

The Commission revised its approach in response to the critiques it received. In 2004 it published Guidelines on the Application of Article 81(3) [now 101(3) TFEU]. These suggest that an economic appraisal will be carried out to determine whether an agreement has the effect of increasing prices or harming consumers in other ways. The intention of the Guidelines is to indicate that henceforth a narrower interpretation of Article 101(1) will be followed.[87] The Court of Justice has shown some support for this in *Maxima Latvija*. The Latvian competition authority took action against a supermarket chain that entered into lease agreements with owners of shopping centres. Of the 119 leases, it was found that 12 contained a clause that gave Maxima Latvija (as the anchor tenant) the right to decide which other shops could have a lease on the same premises. The competition authority considered that this risked excluding competitors of Maxima Latvija. On appeal the Court of Justice confirmed that these facts did not reveal a sufficient degree of harm so that a finding of a restriction by object as uncalled for. It went on to explain how to test for anti-competitive effect.

SIA Maxima Latvija v. Konkurences padome, C–345/14, ECLI:EU:C:2015:784

27 In the present case, the assessment of the impact of the agreements at issue in the main proceedings on competition must take account, in the first place, of all of the factors which determine access to the relevant market, for the purposes of assessing whether, in the catchment areas where the shopping

---

[83] *Télévision par satellite (TPS)* [1999] OJ L 90/6 offers the best example, where an agreement is declared to infringe Article 101(1) but then when considering Article 101(3) the Commission notes that the agreement improves competition.

[84] The leading cases in this respect are *European Night Services* v. *Commission*, T-374–5/94, T-384/94 and T-388/94, ECLI:EU:T:1998:198; *Société Technique Minière* v. *Maschinenbau Ulm GmbH*, 56/65, ECLI:EU:C:1966:38; *Metro SBGroßmärkte GmbH & Co. KG* v. *Commission*, 26/76, ECLI:EU:C:1977:167; *Delimitis* v. *Henninger Bräu AG*, C-234/89, ECLI:EU:C:1991:91.

[85] The *TPS* decision, n. 83 above, is telling: the exemption decision was issued a few months before the agreement was due to expire! See C. Bright, 'EU Competition Policy: Rules, Objectives and Deregulation' (1996) 16 *OJLS* 535; A. Brown, 'Notification of Agreements to the EC Commission: Whether to Submit to a Flawed System' (1992) 17 *ELRev* 323.

[86] R. Joliet, *The Rule of Reason in Antitrust Law: American, German and Common Market Laws in Comparative Perspective* (The Hague, Faculté de Droit and Martinus Nijhoff, 1967). See also V. Korah, 'The Rise and Fall of Provisional Validity: The Need for a Rule of Reason in EEC Antitrust' (1981) *Northwest Journal of International Law and Business* 320; I. Forrester and C. Norall, 'The Laicization of Community Competition Law: Self-Help and the Rule of Reason' (1984) 21 *CMLRev* 11.

[87] J. Bourgeois and J. Bocken, 'Guidelines on the Application of Article 81(3) of the EC Treaty, or How to Restrict a Restriction' (2005) 32 *LIEI* 111.

centres which are covered by those agreements are located, there are real concrete possibilities for a new competitor to establish itself, including through the occupation of commercial premises in other shopping centres located in those areas or by occupying other commercial premises located outside the shopping centres. Accordingly, it is appropriate in particular to take into consideration the availability and accessibility of commercial land in the catchment areas concerned and the existence of economic, administrative or regulatory barriers to entry of new competitors in those areas.

28 In the second place, the conditions under which competitive forces operate on the relevant market must be assessed. In that connection it is necessary to know not only the number and the size of operators present on the market, but also the degree of concentration of that market and customer fidelity to existing brands and consumer habits.

29 It is only if, after a thorough analysis of the economic and legal context in which the agreements at issue in the main proceedings occur and the specificities of the relevant market, it is found that access to that market is made difficult by all the similar agreements found on the market, that it will then be necessary to analyse to what extent they contribute to any closing-off of that market, on the basis that only agreements which make an appreciable contribution to that closing-off are prohibited. To assess the extent of the contribution of each of the agreements at issue in the main proceedings to the cumulative closing-off effect, the position of the contracting parties on the market in question and the duration of the agreements must be taken into consideration.

30 Moreover, according to the settled case-law of the Court, Article 101(1) TFEU does not restrict such an assessment to actual effects alone, it must also take account of the potential effects of the agreement or practice in question on competition.

The significance of this advice is that competition authorities must develop a theory of harm (in this case foreclosure of rivals on the retail market) and then examine if the suspect clauses are able to foreclose rivals. That only 12 out of 119 lease agreement contained the clause allowing Maxima Latvija to exclude rivals, calls into question how this suffices to foreclose rivals. Nor do we know whether rivals have other alternatives to compete against Maxima Latvija, for example we would need to find out what other plots of land are available to build shopping malls. The consequence of an effects-based approach is that the competition agency must review more evidence than in cases of restrictions by object. However, this is not an indeterminate search: the judgment offers a framework to determine what evidence matters based on the theory of harm proposed.

The Commission's new approach was also bolstered by the General Court in a significant judgment that requires the party alleging an infringement of Article 101(1) to provide more refined evidence of the anti-competitive effects than the Commission has provided in some cases to date. At issue was a 'roaming' agreement between O2 and T-Mobile which was designed to help O2 secure a foothold in the German market while it was constructing its own network. The Commission first found that this restricted competition at wholesale and retail level, but when examining the agreement under Article 101(3) it found that the agreement would improve competition in the relevant markets. It exempted the agreement but for a period shorter than that which the parties had originally stipulated, so they sought (and obtained) annulment of the Commission's decision. The significance of this judgment is the legal standard set by the General Court.

O2 (Germany) GmbH & Co. OHG v. Commission, T–328/03, ECLI:EU:T:2006:116

68 [I]n a case such as this, where it is accepted that the agreement does not have as its object a restriction of competition, the effects of the agreement should be considered and for it to be caught by the prohibition it is necessary to find that those factors are present which show that competition has in fact been prevented or restricted or distorted to an appreciable extent. The competition in question must be understood within the actual context in which it would occur in the absence of the agreement in dispute; the interference with competition may in particular be doubted if the agreement seems really necessary for the penetration of a new area by an undertaking.

69 Such a method of analysis, as regards in particular the taking into account of the competition situation that would exist in the absence of the agreement, does not amount to carrying out an assessment of the pro- and anti-competitive effects of the agreement and thus to applying a rule of reason, which the Community judicature has not deemed to have its place under Article [101(1) TFEU].

70 In this respect, to submit, as the applicant does, that the Commission failed to carry out a full analysis by not examining what the competitive situation would have been in the absence of the agreement does not mean that an assessment of the positive and negative effects of the agreement from the point of view of competition must be carried out at the stage of Article [101(1) TFEU]. Contrary to the defendant's interpretation of the applicant's arguments, the applicant relies only on the method of analysis required by settled case-law.

71 The examination required in the light of Article [101(1) TFEU] consists essentially in taking account of the impact of the agreement on existing and potential competition and the competition situation in the absence of the agreement, those two factors being intrinsically linked.

Applied to the facts of the case, the General Court found first that the Commission had failed to examine the competitive effects without the agreement.

O2 (Germany) GmbH & Co. OHG v. Commission, T–328/03, ECLI:EU:T:2006:116

77 Working on the assumption that O2 was present on the mobile communications market, the Commission did not therefore deem it necessary to consider in more detail whether, in the absence of the agreement, O2 would have been present on the 3G market. It must be held that that assumption is not supported in the Decision by any analysis or justification showing that it is correct, a finding that, moreover, the defendant could only confirm at the hearing. Given that there was no such objective examination of the competition situation in the absence of the agreement, the Commission could not have properly assessed the extent to which the agreement was necessary for O2 to penetrate the 3G mobile communications market. The Commission therefore failed to fulfil its obligation to carry out an objective analysis of the impact of the agreement on the competitive situation.

78 That lacuna cannot be deemed to be without consequences. It is apparent from the considerations set out in the Decision in the analysis of the agreement in the light of the conditions laid down in Article [101(3) TFEU] as regards whether it was possible to grant an exemption that, even in the Commission's view, it was unlikely that O2 would have been able, individually, without the agreement, to ensure from the outset better coverage, quality and transmission rates for 3G services, to roll out a network and launch 3G services rapidly, to penetrate the relevant wholesale and retail markets and therefore be an effective competitor (recitals 122 to 124, 126 and 135). It was because of those factors that the Commission considered that the agreement was eligible for exemption.

79   Such considerations, which imply some uncertainty concerning the competitive situation and, in particular, as regards O2's position in the absence of the agreement, show that the presence of O2 on the 3G communications market could not be taken for granted, as the Commission had assumed, and that an examination in this respect was necessary not only for the purposes of granting an exemption but, prior to that, for the purposes of the economic analysis of the effects of the agreement on the competitive situation determining the applicability of Article [101 TFEU].

The key insight from this judgment is that the Commission's evidentiary burden is raised: it is insufficient for it to show that the agreement affects the economic freedom of one of the parties – one has to demonstrate a causal link between the agreement and subsequent restrictions of competition.

M. Marquis, 'O2 (Germany) v. Commission and the Exotic Mysteries of Article 81(1) EC' (2007) *European Law Review* 27, 44–5

[I]t is questionable whether the nature of the counterfactual test is truly different from an analysis that 'weighs' the agreement's pro-competitive and anti-competitive effects ... One could argue that the counterfactual test loses its meaning if the pro-competitive impact of the agreement cannot be weighed against its anti-competitive effects. What is to be compared with the counterfactual, *non-agreement* scenario if it is not the agreement's *net* impact on competition (or more precisely, its net impact on price and output)? If account is not taken of the agreement's pro-competitive effects as well as its restrictive effects, then the comparison becomes distorted and illogical.

The good news is that, regardless of the 'no balancing' doctrine, the CFI appears willing or indeed eager to apply an analysis under Art. 81(1) that is economically rigorous and commercially realistic. Thus, for example, the Commission's view that national roaming agreements restricted competition 'by definition' was rejected as a generalisation that had no specific bearing on the agreement at issue. Furthermore, the Court took very seriously – within the context of Art. 81(1), and consistently with *Société Technique Minière* – the structure of the market and the prospect that roaming could enhance O2's competitive position vis-à-vis the incumbent. This approach has important implications for the network industries, where liberalisation has resulted in lopsided competitive conditions, and above all for rapidly evolving sectors such as electronic communications, where the legacy of a dominant incumbent may potentially distort the development of emerging markets.

In short, the CFI seems to be applying the kind of searching inquiry that it applied in *European Night Services*, and it seems to be carrying out an assessment that looks suspiciously like balancing. Whatever it is called, it is a positive development, and the CFI's judgment provides further confirmation of what the ECJ has often asserted over the last 40 years, namely that there are boundaries to the concept of 'restriction of competition'. To be regretted is the lingering confusion – in the CFI's jurisprudence and in the Commission's Art. 81(3) Guidelines – regarding the division of labour between Art. 81(1) and 81(3). Much clarity could be achieved if the European Courts explicitly embraced the distinction described earlier between a consumer welfare test under Art. 81(1) and an assessment of productive/dynamic efficiency gains under Art. 81(3).

Taking the Guidelines and the judgment together, one may say that in testing for an anti-competitive effect the Commission will be more cautious: first asking if the parties have enough market power to cause harm, then considering the kinds of anti-competitive effects that may result from the agreement (e.g. reduced output or foreclosure), and finally asking whether in the given market context there is a causal link between the agreement and the likely harmful effects. However, as we discuss below, Marquis's suggestion that Article 101(3) is only about efficiencies can be contested.

(iii) Role of Article 101(3) TFEU

When a competition authority or a claimant challenges a restrictive practice, they have the burden of proving that the agreement infringes Article 101(1), and the defendant has the burden to bring evidence to show that its conduct merits an exemption under Article 101(3). Suppose a national competition authority reviews a practice and wishes to issue a decision stating that it may be exempted, can it do so? In *Tele 2*, the Polish competition authority wished to issue a decision that the undertaking whose conduct had been examined had not breached Article 102 TFEU. The Court of Justice held that the authority could not issue such decision.

Prezes Urzędu Ochrony Konkurencji i Konsumentów v. *Tele2 Polska sp. z o.o., devenue Netia SA*, C–375/09, ECLI:EU:C:2011:270

27 Empowerment of national competition authorities to take decisions stating that there has been no breach of Article 102 TFEU would call into question the system of cooperation established by the Regulation and would undermine the power of the Commission.

28 Such a 'negative' decision on the merits would risk undermining the uniform application of Articles 101 TFEU and 102 TFEU, which is one of the objectives of the Regulation highlighted by recital 1 in its preamble, since such a decision might prevent the Commission from finding subsequently that the practice in question amounts to a breach of those provisions of European Union law.

29 It is thus apparent from the wording, the scheme of the Regulation and the objective which it pursues that the Commission alone is empowered to make a finding that there has been no breach of Article 102 TFEU, even if that article is applied in a procedure undertaken by a national competition authority.

30 Consequently, the answer to the first question is that Article 5 of the Regulation must be interpreted as precluding a national competition authority, in the case where, in order to apply Article 102 TFEU, it examines whether the conditions for applying that article are satisfied and where, following that examination, it forms the view that there has been no abuse, from being able to take a decision stating that there has been no breach of that article.

The same reasoning would apply to Article 101 TFEU. It is an awkward ruling because it means the best a competition authority can do is to issue a document stating that the case has been dropped, but it gives little comfort to the undertakings. Furthermore, while the Commission is empowered to declare agreements lawful, it has not yet exercised this power once since the coming into force of Regulation 1/2003. This leaves courts as the sole actors who could consider exemption under Article 101(3). The result of this procedural state of affairs is that since 2004 we have not seen any decisions finding that the conditions for applying this article have been satisfied, only that they have failed. Thus we have shifted from a system where undertakings suffered the results of delayed decisions to one where they suffer from the absence of any decision whatsoever. Having noted this procedural marginalisation of Article 101(3) we turn to interpreting the provision.

(a) Individual Exemptions

Four conditions must be satisfied for an agreement to benefit from an exemption: (1) it must improve the production and distribution of goods or promote technical and economic progress; (2) consumers must receive a fair share of the benefits identified in (1); (3) the restrictions of competition must be necessary to achieve the said benefits; (4) the agreement must not eliminate competition on the market. There is also a fifth implicit requirement by which the benefits outweigh the harm to competition. In theory, all agreements can qualify.[88]

The first condition is the most controversial because its scope is uncertain: does it mean that an agreement is exempted because it yields economic efficiency (the narrow view), or does it also mean that an agreement may be exempted if it makes a contribution to other matters of interest to the Community (the wide view)?[89] For example, can the fact that an agreement enhances employment in a poor European region be a relevant consideration in determining whether it can be exempted? Or an agreement that strengthens a weak European industry against strong rivals from overseas? Neither the decisions of the Commission, nor the European Courts' judgments have provided an unambiguous answer to this question, although most commentators have suggested that non-economic factors play some role in influencing the decision to exempt an agreement, and others have also insisted that this is correct as a matter of law.[90] The Commission has indicated that Article 101(3) can only serve agreements which enhance economic efficiency, and that it is not to be used to exempt agreements that support other interests.[91] This position is somewhat out of line with the approach that has been taken in the past. In a decision concerning the Conseil Européen de la Construction d'Appareils Domestiques (CECED), an association representing manufacturers of domestic appliances, including washing machines, agreed to phase out from the market certain types of washing machines with low energy efficiency. The agreement was found anti-competitive by object because it prevented parties from manufacturing or exporting certain types of washing machines and thus restricted consumer choice. The agreement would also raise production costs for those manufacturers who had not yet developed more energy efficient models. However, the Commission found the following reasons for exempting the agreement.

CECED [2000] OJ L187/47

47 The agreement is designed to reduce the potential energy consumption of new washing machines by at least 15 to 20% (relative to 1994 data on models of washing machines) . . .

48 Washing machines which, other factors being constant, consume less electricity are objectively more technically efficient. Reduced electricity consumption indirectly leads to reduced pollution from electricity

---

[88] *Matra Hachette* v. *Commission*, T-17/93, ECLI:EU:T:1994:89.

[89] For detail on the differences between these two see R. Whish, *Competition Law*, 6th edn (Oxford University Press, 2008) 151–7.

[90] R. B. Bouterse, *Competition and Integration: What Goals Count?* (The Hague, Kluwer Law International, 1994) chs. 1–4; R. Wesseling, *The Modernisation of EC Antitrust Law* (Oxford, Hart, 2000) esp. 105–12; C. Townley, *Article 81 EC and Public Policy* (Oxford, Hart, 2009). Contra, see O. Odudu, 'The Wider Concerns of Competition Law' (2010) 30(3) *OJLS* 599.

[91] Communication from the Commission, Notice: Guidelines on the application of Article 81(3) of the Treaty [2004] OJ C 101/97.

generation. The future operation of the total of installed machines providing the same service with less indirect pollution is more economically efficient than without the agreement . . .

51 CECED estimates the pollution avoided at 3.5 million tons of carbon dioxide, 17,000 tons of sulphur dioxide and 6,000 tons of nitrous oxide per year in 2010, working on the basis of average emission values. Although such emissions are more efficiently tackled at the stage of electricity generation, the agreement is likely to deliver both individual and collective benefits for users and consumers.

(A) Individual Economic Benefits

52 The level at which the minimum performance standard is set provides a fair return within reasonable pay-back periods to a typical consumer for higher initial purchase costs derived from the more stringent standard in fact set out by CECED. Savings on electricity bills allow recouping of increased costs of upgraded, more expensive machines within nine to 40 months, depending mainly on frequency of use and electricity prices . . .

(B) Collective Environmental Benefits

56 The Commission reasonably estimates the saving in marginal damage from (avoided) carbon dioxide emissions (the so-called 'external costs') at EUR 41 to 61 per ton of carbon dioxide. On a European scale, avoided damage from sulphur dioxide amounts to EUR 4,000 to 7,000 per ton and EUR 3,000 to 5,000 per ton of nitrous oxide. On the basis of reasonable assumptions, the benefits to society brought about by the CECED agreement appear to be more than seven times greater than the increased purchase costs of more energy-efficient washing machines. Such environmental results for society would adequately allow consumers a fair share of the benefits even if no benefits accrued to individual purchasers of machines.

This decision gives a wide interpretation of economic efficiency, noting that the considerable environmental benefits which the agreement generates are enough to exempt the agreement. On the one hand, the decision may be read as suggesting that other Union policies affected the decision to exempt (see in particular para. 56). On the other hand, the decision might simply be read as stating that because the agreement reduces energy bills, consumers are better off because, even though the price of washing machines rises, the electricity bills are low enough to compensate for this (see para. 52). Thus it can be read as espousing both the wide and narrow interpretation of Article 101(3). This ambiguity also characterises earlier decisions which suggest that a decision to exempt may be influenced by a range of non-efficiency related competition factors – for example, relieving unemployment,[92] promoting environmental goals[93] and helping the creation of stronger European industry in the face of competition from firms in the United States and Japan.[94]

CECED is also interesting for its interpretation of the second condition in Article 101(3): that consumers should benefit. On the one hand, the benefits should accrue to those who buy the goods, and thus gain directly by the agreement. However, in *CECED* the Commission was willing to consider collective benefits to society as a whole as 'consumer benefits' which is an overly wide interpretation. Another interesting analysis of the consumer benefit criteria was offered by

---

[92] See e.g. *Stichting Baksteen* [1994] OJ L 131/15, paras. 27–8; *Synthetic Fibres* [1984] OJ L 207/17, para. 37.
[93] See e.g. *Philips/Osram* [1994] OJ L 378/37.
[94] See e.g. *Optical Fibres* [1986] OJ L 236/30; *Olivetti/Canon* [1988] OJ L 52/60; *Bayer/BPCL* [1988] OJ L 150/35. See Bouterse, n. 90 above.

the Court of Justice in *Asnef-Equifax* v. *Ausbanc*.[95] Spanish banks agreed to set up an electronic register of credit information that would disclose the credit history of potential customers. The effect was that each bank was aware of each potential client's credit history and took this into account when negotiating further loans. The Court held that it was unlikely that this agreement would restrict competition, but also added some reflections on how one might go about analysing the consumer benefit test in Article 101(3). It suggested that two groups of consumers benefit: those who get loans on better terms, and those who do not get loans because of their bad credit scores, and this is a benefit because it avoids over-indebtedness. That persons who are unable to obtain a service as a result of an anti-competitive agreement can be seen as deriving a benefit requires further reflection: would one say, for example, that a cartel to fix the prices of cigarettes benefits smokers who therefore smoke less? Furthermore, in *GSK*, the Court agreed that a restriction on competition today which would facilitate research and development for future drugs could be exempted.[96]

The third condition is that the agreement must only contain restrictions that are indispensable to achieve the benefits identified by the first two criteria. This means that if the benefits can be achieved in a less restrictive way, then an exemption will not be granted. In *CECED*, for example, the Commission considered whether there were any other ways of reducing energy consumption. One less restrictive alternative could have been for the parties to agree to inform consumers in more detail about the energy costs of each washing machine and allow the consumer to make the choice. This would be less restrictive of competition than withdrawing certain models. However, the Commission decided that informing the consumer would not have been as effective. Thus the restriction agreed by the parties was necessary to achieve the relevant benefits.

The relevance of the final criteria is explained by the Commission: 'Ultimately, the protection of rivalry and the competitive process is given priority over potentially pro-competitive efficiency gains which could result from restrictive agreements.'[97] Therefore, if an agreement were to result in the parties not competing at all, then an exemption will not be granted. In *CECED*, there was no elimination of competition because the parties were able to compete on features like price, brand image and technical performance.[98]

In sum, there remains a tension between the Commission's recent policy of considering that efficiency is the sole basis for exemption, and the Court of Justice insisting that a wider basis for exemption is to be tolerated.[99]

(b) Block Exemptions

Block Exemption Regulations provide that all agreements meeting certain predefined criteria would merit exemption as a group. The 'old style' Block Exemptions defined a type of agreement and provided lists of clauses which parties were allowed to insert in the agreement (white lists) and lists of clauses which if present would deny the agreement the benefit of a Block Exemption (black lists).[100] The advantage of falling within the scope of a Block Exemption was that the

---

[95] *Asnef-Equifax, Servicios de Información sobre Solvencia y Crédito, SL* v. *Asociación de Usuarios de Servicios Bancarios (Ausbanc)*, C-238/05, ECLI:EU:C:2006:734.

[96] *GlaxoSmithKline Services Unlimited* v. *Commission*, C-501/06 P, C-513/06 P, C-515/06 P and C-519/06 P, ECLI:EU:C:2009:610.

[97] Guidelines on Article 81(3), para. 105.   [98] *CECED* [2000] OJ L 187/47, para. 64.

[99] Monti and Mulder, n. 42 above.   [100] See e.g. Regulation 1983/83 on exclusive distribution [1983] OJ L 173/1.

parties did not need to notify the agreement, but this was at the expense of flexibility resulting from long black lists. Moreover, some Block Exemptions were said to be commercially unrealistic and to have been of no use in structuring certain types of agreement. The Commission has now redesigned Block Exemptions to make these more business friendly and more effectively based upon economic analysis. The first Block Exemption to be drafted in this way is that for vertical restraints, and a brief overview is provided below.[101]

Vertical restraints are agreements between undertakings operating at different levels of trade (e.g. a distribution contract between a manufacturer and a retailer), which restrict the parties' behaviour. For example, a manufacturer of plasma TVs may decide to sell these only to a selected type of retail outlet whose staff are competent to give consumers advice. These contracts may restrict the number of outlets selling the plasma TVs (and so stifle intra-brand competition among retail outlets) but their redeeming virtue is that the selected retailers are better placed to satisfy consumer demand by providing valued pre-sale service. Provided there is healthy competition among rival brands of TV sets (inter-brand competition), then vertical restraints will enhance consumer welfare.[102] There may, however, be three anti-competitive risks that materialise with vertical restraints: first, if all manufacturers use similar distribution contracts this may facilitate collusion among them because they can monitor each other's prices more easily; secondly, vertical restraints that encourage unnecessary promotion by retailers may reduce consumer welfare;[103] and thirdly, vertical restraints might foreclose market access for new entrants (say, because the new entrant finds that there are no more outlets willing to distribute his goods).[104]

Anti-competitive risks tend to arise when there is market power, and the Block Exemption Regulation is designed with this in mind.[105] Parties may benefit from the Block Exemption only if they meet the condition specified in Article 3: that the market share held by the supplier and the buyer does not exceed 30 per cent of the relevant market in which the supplier sells or the buyer purchases the contract goods or services. Parties that fall within this threshold are free to enter into whichever distribution contracts they wish save for a small number of 'black-listed' clauses set out in Articles 4 and 5. For instance, the manufacturer cannot impose a minimum price at which distributors may sell the goods (which might facilitate collusion), and the manufacturer cannot prevent the dealer from selling the contract goods in question in another Member State when these are ordered by a customer there (that such 'passive sales' may not be forbidden is based on the crucial importance of the market integration goal). Finally, the Commission (or an NCA) may remove the benefit of the Block Exemption if the benefits to consumers do not materialise.[106] While this has hardly been used, it is a helpful mechanism to

---

[101] The Commission's earlier approach to regulating vertical restraints had been criticised harshly. See Hawk, n. 1 above; D. Neven, P. Papandropolous and P. Seabright, *Trawling for Minnows: European Competition Policy and Agreements Between Firms* (London, CEPR, 1998) 42–3.

[102] For a detailed account of the economics see Motta, n. 55 above, ch. 6; P. W. Dobson and M. Waterson, *Vertical Restraints and Competition Policy* (London, OFT, 1996).

[103] W. S. Comanor, 'Vertical Price-Fixing, Vertical Market Restrictions, and the New Antitrust Policy' (1985) 98 *Harvard L Rev* 983, esp. 991–2 and 100–2.

[104] S. C. Salop, 'Analysis of Foreclosure in the EC Guidelines on Vertical Restraints' (2000) *Fordham Corporate Law Institute* 177, 191–2.

[105] Regulation 330/2010 of 20 April 2010 on the application of Article 101(3) of the Treaty on the Functioning of the European Union to categories of vertical agreements and concerted practices [2010] OJ L 102/1.

[106] Regulation 330/2010, Article 6 empowers the Commission to issue a decision to withdraw the benefit of the exemption in a relevant market, while Regulation 1/2003, Article 29 empowers the Commission and national authorities to withdraw the benefit of exemption from a particular agreement.

regulate vertical restraints that do not live up to their promise. The Regulation is accompanied by Guidelines that explain how the Commission will apply Article 101 TFEU to agreements that fall outside the scope of the Block Exemption (e.g. when the market share threshold is not met) and these provide for an economics-based appraisal of vertical restraints.[107]

(c) Block Exemptions and E-Commerce

This Regulation has been very successful in limiting the intervention of competition law in this field.[108] Most commentators welcome this development because the economics literature suggests that distribution agreements are likely to enhance consumer welfare in particular when there are multiple brands all competing for the buyers' attention. That one brand owner applies more restrictive conditions on its distributors than others does not generally harm competition. Controversies over the application of competition law to distribution agreements have resurfaced recently as a result of the growth of the Internet as a distribution channel. Owners of branded goods are concerned that Internet sales might dilute their brand and are thus entering into distribution agreements that limit the scope for online sales. So far the French and German competition authorities have been the most active.

In *Pierre Fabre*, the Court of Justice held that a selective distribution agreement forbidding distributors in France from selling cosmetics online was a restriction of competition by object.[109] This is in spite of the fact that the undertaking held a 20 per cent share of the market and all other cosmetics manufacturers had already agreed to allow online sales, so it is hard to see what damage Pierre Fabre was likely to cause. It was also held that the agreement could not benefit from the Block Exemption: 'prohibiting *de facto* the internet as a method of marketing, at the very least has as its object the restriction of passive sales to end users wishing to purchase online and located outside the physical trading area of the relevant member of the selective distribution system'.[110] This regulatory approach seems to be more about facilitating online trade than about removing competitive restraints.[111]

In *Coty* the Court appeared to relent somewhat from the position in Pierre Fabre. Coty owns a range of perfume brands: its distributors are selected on the basis of the quality of their outlet and are allowed to sell online provided that their website has certain features that sustain the quality image of the brand. They are forbidden from selling via online platforms (e.g. Amazon). Some distributors challenged this clause as anti-competitive.

Coty Germany GmbH v. Parfümerie Akzente GmbH, C–230/16, ECLI:EU:C:2017:941

36 ... [A] selective distribution system for luxury goods designed, primarily, to preserve the luxury image of those goods complies with that provision to the extent that resellers are chosen on the basis of objective

---

[107] Commission Notice: Guidelines on vertical restraints [2010] OJ C 130/1.

[108] V. Korah and D. O'Sullivan, *Distribution Agreements under the EC Competition Rules* (Oxford, Hart, 2002) ch. 8.

[109] *Pierre Fabre Dermo-Cosmétique SAS* v. *Président de l'Autorité de la concurrence and Ministre de l'Économie, de l'Industrie et de l'Emploi*, C-439/09, ECLI:EU:C:2011:649.

[110] *Ibid.* para. 54.

[111] G. Monti, 'Restraints on Selective Distribution Agreements' (2013) 36(4) *World Competition* 489, reviewing the decision-making practices of the French competition authority.

criteria of a qualitative nature that are laid down uniformly for all potential resellers and applied in a non-discriminatory fashion and that the criteria laid down do not go beyond what is necessary.

. . .

44 With regard, in the first place, to the appropriateness of the prohibition at issue in the main proceedings in the light of the objective pursued, it must be observed, first, that the obligation imposed on authorised distributors to sell the contract goods online solely through their own online shops and the prohibition on those distributors of using a different business name, as well as the use of third-party platforms in a discernible manner, provide the supplier with a guarantee, from the outset, in the context of electronic commerce, that those goods will be exclusively associated with the authorised distributors.

45 Since such an association is precisely one of the objectives sought when recourse is had to such a system, it appears that the prohibition at issue in the main proceedings includes a limitation which is coherent in the light of the specific characteristics of the selective distribution system.

. . .

47 Second, the prohibition at issue in the main proceedings enables the supplier of luxury goods to check that the goods will be sold online in an environment that corresponds to the qualitative conditions that it has agreed with its authorised distributors.

48 Non-compliance by a distributor with the quality conditions set by the supplier allows that supplier to take action against that distributor, on the basis of the contractual link existing between those two parties. The absence of a contractual relationship between the supplier and third-party platforms is, however, an obstacle which prevents that supplier from being able to require, from those third-party platforms, compliance with the quality conditions that it has imposed on its authorised distributors.

49 The internet sale of luxury goods via platforms which do not belong to the selective distribution system for those goods, in the context of which the supplier is unable to check the conditions in which those goods are sold, involves a risk of deterioration of the online presentation of those goods which is liable to harm their luxury image and thus their very character.

50 Third, given that those platforms constitute a sales channel for goods of all kinds, the fact that luxury goods are not sold via such platforms and that their sale online is carried out solely in the online shops of authorised distributors contributes to that luxury image among consumers and thus to the preservation of one of the main characteristics of the goods sought by consumers.

51 Consequently, the prohibition imposed by a supplier of luxury goods on its authorised distributors to use, in a discernible manner, third-party platforms for the internet sale of those goods is appropriate to preserve the luxury image of those goods.

52 With regard, in the second place, to the question of whether the prohibition at issue in the main proceedings goes beyond what is necessary for the attainment of the objective pursued, it must be noted, first, that, in contrast to [*Pierre Fabre Dermo-Cosmétique*], the clause here at issue in the main proceedings does not contain an absolute prohibition imposed on authorised distributors to sell the contract goods online. Indeed, under that clause, the prohibition applies solely to the internet sale of the contract goods via third-party platforms which operate in a discernible manner towards consumers.

53 Consequently, authorised distributors are permitted to sell the contract goods online both via their own websites, as long as they have an electronic shop window for the authorised store and the luxury character of the goods is preserved, and via unauthorised third-party platforms when the use of such platforms is not discernible to the consumer.

When the case returned to the national court it held that the agreement fell within the scope of the Block Exemption as it contained no black-listed clauses, thereby avoiding the need to apply the guidelines issued by the ECJ. This judgment is to be welcomed for understanding the commercial realities faced by sellers of branded goods, and allowing them scope to control the way their goods are marketed online, even if some would want a more aggressive enforcement stance for preserving luxury image can serve to keep prices elevated.[112]

4 ARTICLE 102 TFEU: ABUSE OF A DOMINANT POSITION

Enterprises holding significant market power should receive considerable scrutiny by competition authorities. From an economic perspective, firms that dominate a market have the kind of economic power that normally reduces efficiency because there are no competitive pressures to prevent dominant firms from raising prices and reducing output.[113] Moreover, large firms may exercise market power to consolidate their dominance, or even to expand their influence into the political domain.[114]

> ### Article 102 TFEU
>
> Any abuse by one or more undertakings of a dominant position within the common market or in a substantial part of it shall be prohibited as incompatible with the common market insofar as it may affect trade between Member States.
>
> Such abuse may, in particular, consist in:
> (a) directly or indirectly imposing unfair purchase or selling prices or other unfair trading conditions;
> (b) limiting production, markets or technical development to the prejudice of consumers;
> (c) applying dissimilar conditions to equivalent transactions with other trading parties, thereby placing them at a competitive disadvantage;
> (d) making the conclusion of contracts subject to acceptance by the other parties of supplementary obligations which, by their nature or according to commercial usage, have no connection with the subject of such contracts.

When the Commission seeks to establish an infringement of Article 102 TFEU, it must show the following: that an undertaking is dominant in a given market; that it has abused its dominant position; that the abuse has an effect on trade between Member States; and the absence of any objective justification for the abuse.[115] Four examples of abuse are listed in Article 102 TFEU, but this list is not an exhaustive catalogue. As will be seen, the Commission and Court of Justice have found an ever-increasing number of practices abusive.

Compared to the voluminous case law under Article 101 TFEU, the abuse prohibition has been applied relatively infrequently (approximately seventy decisions by the Commission) but the Commission and the Court's case law has received the most scathing criticism for fettering the

---

[112] M. J. Schmidt-Kessen, 'Selective Distribution Systems in EU Competition and EU Trademark Law: Resolving the Tension' (2018) 9(5) *Journal of European Competition Law & Practice* 304.

[113] See Ch. 20 for a review of the economic analysis underlying this.

[114] See R. A. Posner, 'The Social Costs of Monopoly and Regulation' (1975) 83 *Journal of Political Economy* 807; R. Pitofsky, 'The Political Content of Antitrust' (1979) 127 *U Penn L Rev* 105; G. Amato, *Antitrust and the Bounds of Power* (Oxford, Hart, 1997) ch. 7.

[115] The interpretation of the requirement of an effect on trade between Member States is considered at p. 922 and the same approach is taken in Article 102 TFEU.

economic freedom of dominant firms unnecessarily and for being incoherent.[116] In response to this criticism, and in line with the more economics-oriented approach of contemporary competition law, the Commission embarked on a controversial reform process.[117] We start by considering the current law and the criticisms it has elicited before turning to examine the main traits of the new approach and how far the ECJ has approved of the Commission's new line.

(i) Dominance

A dominant undertaking need not monopolise the entire market. Such an extreme degree of dominance is possible when an undertaking is given a monopoly by the Member State, for instance if the State grants the right to operate job centres exclusively to one undertaking.[118] But the concept of dominance is much wider than that.[119]

> ### J. Temple Lang, 'Some Aspects of Abuse of a Dominant Position in EC Antitrust Law' (1979) 3 *Fordham International Law Forum* 1, 9–12
>
> A dominant position exists when the dominant enterprise is able to use its economic power to obtain benefits or to practise behaviour which it could not obtain or practise in conditions of reasonably effective competition, i.e., that dominant power is power of which unfair advantage can be taken, or power which is great enough to be 'abused' . . . This principle also implies a link between the concept of dominance and the concept of abuse . . .
>
> It is the ability to contain competition, not the ability to ignore it, which is characteristic of dominance. Dominant firms can overcome competition, but very few of them can disregard it. The power to plan and choose a controlled response to competitors' efforts, sufficient to ensure no significant long term loss of market share, is typical of dominant firms. As market leader a dominant firm is often able to adopt a strategy advantageous to itself and disadvantageous for the rest of the industry, without using overtly exclusionary practices, which will maintain its market in spite of some competition. Such a strategy may be adopted on the dominant firm's own initiative or in response to competitors' actions. Since dominance does not mean absence of competition, or even absence of effective competition, clearly it does not mean freedom to disregard competition. It follows that dominance can exist even if the dominant firm is compelled to react to its competitors' activities.

Accordingly, dominance means that an undertaking has the power to harm the competitive process, either by harming consumers (e.g. through higher prices) or by harming competitors (e.g. by offering discounts to customers who would otherwise buy the competitor's goods). From this perspective, it can be said that there are different degrees of dominance: some undertakings are so powerful that they face no competitive constraint, while some dominant undertakings may

---

[116] B. Sher, 'The Last of the Steam Powered Trains: Modernising Article 82' (2004) 25 *ECLR* 243; C.-D. Ehlermann and M. Marquis (eds.), *European Competition Law Annual 2007: A Reformed Approach to Article 82 EC* (Oxford, Hart, 2008).

[117] P. Lowe, 'DG Competition's Review of the Policy on Abuse of Dominance' (2003) *Fordham Corporate Law Institute* 163.

[118] *Höfner and Elser* v. *Macrotron GmbH*, C-41/90, ECLI:EU:C:1991:161.

[119] The Court's definition is: 'A position of economic strength enjoyed by an undertaking which enables it to prevent effective competition being maintained on the relevant market by giving it the power to behave to an appreciable extent independently of its competitors, customers and ultimately of its consumers.' *United Brands* v. *Commission*, 27/76, ECLI:EU:C:1978:22, para. 65.

face competition from others, but are strong enough to keep the smaller competitors at bay. Dominance is measured in two steps: first, by considering the undertaking's market share; and secondly, by other factors used to confirm the undertaking's position vis-à-vis its competitors, customers and consumers.[120]

(a) Market Shares

Market shares are used as a preliminary filter to determine whether there is dominance.[121] A market share of 50 per cent can give rise to a presumption of dominance.[122] In many cases the dominant firm has held market shares in excess of 50 per cent while its competitors all have had considerably smaller market shares.[123] However, a market share between 40 and 50 per cent has also been sufficient to identify a dominant position once other factors were taken into consideration.[124]

(b) Additional Factors

Dominance does not exist if entry is easy. A firm with a 90 per cent share of the market is not dominant if, as soon as it raised the price of its goods, other firms would enter its market and sell their goods at more competitive prices. As a result, a definition of dominance requires an analysis of whether there are any barriers to entry. But this notion is not without controversy. Economists have been divided between those who take a wide conception of entry barriers (any factor that allows the existing company to raise price), and a narrower conception of entry barriers (only those costs that a new entrant must incur that were not faced by the existing firms).[125] The wider the concept used, the more likely it is that one finds dominance. However the application of this debate in competition law has been criticised: '[w]hat matters . . . is not what might happen in some year far off in the future but what will actually happen now and in the near future. Rather than focusing on whether an "entry barrier" exists according to some definition, analysts should explain how the industry will behave over the next several years'.[126] In this light, the wide range of factors identified by the Court of Justice as indicators of dominance can be explained by the Court's concern about whether in the relatively short term other firms can enter to compete against the dominant undertaking. In *Michelin*, the Court approved the Commission's decision that Michelin held a dominant position in the market for new tyres for certain types of vehicles. It found that this position was abused because Michelin entered into distribution agreements with tyre retailers in the Netherlands which restricted the retailer's freedom to source tyres from competitors because it was given financial incentives in the form of quantity rebates if it purchased more Michelin tyres. In this passage the appellant's challenge against the finding of dominance was rejected by the Court.

---

[120] *Nederlandsche Banden-Industrie Michelin NV* v. *Commission*, 322/81, ECLI:EU:C:1983:313, para. 31.

[121] *Hoffmann-La Roche & Co. AG* v. *Commission*, 85/76, ECLI:EU:C:1979:36, paras. 39–41.

[122] *AKZO* v. *Commission*, 62/86, ECLI:EU:C:1991:286, para. 60.

[123] See e.g. *Nederlandsche Banden-Industrie Michelin NV* v. *Commission*, 322/81, ECLI:EU:C:1983:313, dominant firm with a market share of approximately 57–60% and the others with market shares between 4 and 8%.

[124] *United Brands* v. *Commission*, 27/76, ECLI:EU:C:1978:22, paras. 109–10; *British Airways* v. *Commission*, T-219/99, ECLI:EU:T:2003:343, paras. 211–24.

[125] R. Schmalensee, 'Ease of Entry: Has the Concept been Applied Too Readily?' (1987) 56 *Antitrust LJ* 41; P. Geroski and A. Jacquemin, 'Industrial Change, Barriers to Mobility and European Industrial Policy' (1985) 1 *Economic Policy* 170, 182–3.

[126] D. E. Carlton, 'Why Barriers to Entry and Barriers to Understanding' (2004) 94 *American Economic Review* 466, 469.

Nederlandsche Banden-Industrie Michelin NV v. *Commission*, 322/81, ECLI:EU:C:1983:313

55 ... it should first be observed that in order to assess the relative economic strength of Michelin NV and its competitors on the Netherlands market the advantages which those undertakings may derive from belonging to groups of undertakings operating throughout Europe or even the world must be taken into consideration. Amongst those advantages, the lead which the Michelin group has over its competitors in the matters of investment and research and the special extent of its range of products, to which the Commission referred in its Decision, have not been denied. In fact in the case of certain types of tyre the Michelin group is the only supplier on the market to offer them in its range.

56 That situation ensures that on the Netherlands market a large number of users of heavy-vehicle tyres have a strong preference for Michelin tyres. As the purchase of tyres represents a considerable investment for a transport undertaking and since much time is required in order to ascertain in practice the cost-effectiveness of a type or brand of tyre, Michelin NV therefore enjoys a position which renders it largely immune to competition. As a result, a dealer established in the Netherlands normally cannot afford not to sell Michelin tyres.

57 It is not possible to uphold the objections made against those arguments by Michelin NV, supported on this point by the French government, that Michelin NV is thus penalized for the quality of its products and services. A finding that an undertaking has a dominant position is not in itself a recrimination but simply means that, irrespective of the reasons for which it has such a dominant position, the undertaking concerned has a special responsibility not to allow its conduct to impair genuine undistorted competition on the common market.

58 Due weight must also be attached to the importance of Michelin NV's network of commercial representatives, which gives it direct access to tyre users at all times. Michelin NV has not disputed the fact that in absolute terms its network is considerably larger than those of its competitors or challenged the description, in the Decision at issue, of the services performed by its network whose efficiency and quality of service are unquestioned. The direct access to users and the standard of service which the network can give them enables Michelin NV to maintain and strengthen its position on the market and to protect itself more effectively against competition.

59 As regards the additional criteria and evidence to which Michelin NV refers in order to disprove the existence of a dominant position, it must be observed that temporary unprofitability or even losses are not inconsistent with the existence of a dominant position. By the same token, the fact that the prices charged by Michelin NV do not constitute an abuse and are not even particularly high does not justify the conclusion that a dominant position does not exist. Finally, neither the size, financial strength and degree of diversification of Michelin NV's competitors at the world level nor the counter poise arising from the fact that buyers of heavy-vehicle tyres are experienced trade users are such as to deprive Michelin NV of its privileged position on the Netherlands market.

The judgment provides an extensive list of factors that contributed to give Michelin a competitive advantage over its rivals. In addition, the Court of Justice has found that a dominant position might be protected by ownership of intellectual property rights (which prevent others from duplicating the dominant undertaking's products);[127] by access to capital; by considerable costs of entry; by economies of scale necessary to penetrate the market;[128] or by

---

[127] See e.g. *Hugin Kassaregister AB* v. *Commission*, 22/78, ECLI:EU:C:1979:138; *Hilti* v. *Commission*, T-30/89, ECLI:EU:T:1991:70.
[128] *United Brands* v. *Commission*, 27/76, ECLI:EU:C:1978:22.

a well-organised distribution system, advertising and brand recognition.[129] The criticism that by considering these factors one is merely describing the efficiency of the dominant firm, and using those efficiencies as a means to determine dominance, is rejected by the Court at paragraph 57 of *Michelin*: dominance is not unlawful, but dominant undertakings have a special responsibility not to hinder competition. But this has not assuaged those who think that the too-wide definition of dominance, combined with this passage, places a Damoclean sword over dominant undertakings whose commercial freedom is detrimentally affected by this obligation, paradoxically restricting the very kind of competition that dominant firms are said to endanger.[130]

(ii) Abuse of Dominance: General Principles

The types of abuse may be classified in two categories: exploitative and exclusionary. The first includes abuses that aim to harm the customer of the dominant undertaking (e.g. excessive prices). However, the Commission has shown little interest in punishing exploitative abuses. In any market where an undertaking has *some* market power, prices are higher than marginal cost.[131] However, if EU competition law were to apply to all prices above marginal cost, virtually all undertakings would be subject to scrutiny. Clearly, only exorbitantly high prices require regulation, although the Court's case law has provided little clear guidance to identify what constitutes an excessive price. In *United Brands*, the Court of Justice suggested that a price is excessive when it bears no reasonable relation to the economic value of the product in question. This could be measured by comparing the selling price with the cost of production.[132] This standard suggests that dominant firms are entitled to sell at a price somewhat above the cost of production, but not excessively beyond it. Quite how the line between a reasonably high and an unreasonably high price is to be drawn is not explained. As a result, the Commission has not prioritised exploitative abuses in its enforcement plans.[133] That said, the Commission has initiated investigations over excessive prices in economic sectors that have only recently been liberalised, these have often resulted in commitment decisions and price adjustments monitored by national regulators.[134]

The second category of abuse, exclusionary, covers abuses that are designed to impact negatively on rivals. There are two justifications for extending the application of Article 102 TFEU to exclusionary abuses.[135] On the one hand, these abusive practices are designed to safeguard the undertaking's dominant position and to facilitate subsequent exploitation of dominance.[136] For instance, United Brands, dominant in the market for bananas, fought to exclude other banana manufacturers from the European market as a way of maintaining its power over customers. Another justification for treating exclusionary abuses as anti-competitive

---

[129] *Michelin* v. *Commission*, T-203/01, ECLI:EU:T:2003:250.

[130] S. Turnbull, 'Barriers to Entry, Article 86 and the Abuse of a Dominant Position' (1996) 2 *ECLR* 96.

[131] See S. Bishop and M. Walker, *The Economics of EC Competition Law*, 2nd edn (London, Sweet and Maxwell, 2002) ch. 2, 43–4.

[132] *United Brands* v. *Commission*, 27/76, ECLI:EU:C:1978:22, paras. 250–2.

[133] European Commission, *XXIVth Report on Competition Policy* (1994) para. 207.

[134] See Case COMP/39.388, *German Electricity Wholesale Market*, Decision of 26 November 2008; Case COMP/39.402, *RWE Gas Foreclosure*, Decision of 19 March 2009.

[135] But some see no good reason for applying Article 102 TFEU to exclusionary abuses, notably R. Joliet, *Monopolization and Abuse of Dominant Position* (Université de Liège, 1970).

[136] T. G. Kattenmaker and S. C. Salop, 'Anticompetitive Exclusion: Raising Rivals' Costs to Achieve Power Over Price' (1986) 96 *Yale LJ* 20.

is that by eliminating or weakening competitors, the dominant firm denies the opportunities of other economic actors to participate on the market. These rivals may have been capable of bringing new goods into the market or developing the market in other ways. The risk with this second justification of penalising exclusionary conduct is that it gives the appearance that the Commission protects smaller undertakings rather than consumers. This is so for two reasons: the first is that a finding of an infringement is made very easy by the Court of Justice's case law (there is no need to show likely consumer harm, nor indeed a need to show that the exclusionary tactic was or will be successful); and the second is that the undertakings under scrutiny find it difficult to justify their actions once these have been judged to constitute an abuse.

The controversial judgment in *British Airways* serves as a clear example of what many see as the overly aggressive approach adopted by the Union.[137] The Commission had condemned BA's strategy of offering travel agents extra commissions when they promoted BA tickets on the basis that this was discriminatory, designed to induce loyalty and served to exclude competing airlines.[138]

British Airways plc v. *Commission*, C-95/04 P, ECLI:EU:C:2007:166

Criteria for Assessing Exclusionary Effects

68 It follows that in determining whether, on the part of an undertaking in a dominant position, a system of discounts or bonuses which constitute neither quantity discounts or bonuses nor fidelity discounts or bonuses within the meaning of the judgment in *Hoffmann-La Roche* constitutes an abuse, it first has to be determined whether those discounts or bonuses can produce an exclusionary effect, that is to say whether they are capable, first, of making market entry very difficult or impossible for competitors of the undertaking in a dominant position and, secondly, of making it more difficult or impossible for its co-contractors to choose between various sources of supply or commercial partners.

69 It then needs to be examined whether there is an objective economic justification for the discounts and bonuses granted. In accordance with the analysis carried out by the [General Court] . . . an undertaking is at liberty to demonstrate that its bonus system producing an exclusionary effect is economically justified.

70 With regard to the first aspect, the case-law gives indications as to the cases in which discount or bonus schemes of an undertaking in a dominant position are not merely the expression of a particularly favourable offer on the market, but give rise to an exclusionary effect.

71 First, an exclusionary effect may arise from goal-related discounts or bonuses, that is to say those the granting of which is linked to the attainment of sales objectives defined individually . . .

73 It is also apparent from the case-law that the commitment of co-contractors towards the undertaking in a dominant position and the pressure exerted upon them may be particularly strong where a discount or bonus does not relate solely to the growth in turnover in relation to purchases or sales of products of that undertaking made by those co-contractors during the period under consideration, but extends also to the whole of the turnover relating to those purchases or sales. In that way, relatively modest

---

[137] For strong critique of the policy towards these practices, see J. Kallaugher and B. Sher, 'Rebates Revisited: Anticompetitive Effects and Exclusionary Abuse under Article 82' (2004) 25 *ECLR* 263; for a defence of these cases see L. Gyselen, 'Rebates: Competition on the Merits or Exclusionary Practice?' in C.-D. Ehlermann and I. Atanasiu (eds.), *European Competition Law Annual: What is an Abuse of a Dominant Position?* (Oxford-Portland, Hart, 2006).

[138] *Virgin/British Airways* [2000] OJ L 30/1; affirmed by the CFI *British Airways* v. *Commission*, T-219/99, [2003] ECR II-5917. See further Monti, n. 41 above, 162–72; and O. Odudu, 'Case Note on BA v. Commission' (2007) 44 *CMLRev* 1781.

variations – whether upwards or downwards – in the turnover figures relating to the products of the dominant undertaking have disproportionate effects on co-contractors . . .

75 Finally, the Court took the view that the pressure exerted on resellers by an undertaking in a dominant position which granted bonuses with those characteristics is further strengthened where that undertaking holds a very much larger market share than its competitors. It held that, in those circumstances, it is particularly difficult for competitors of that undertaking to outbid it in the face of discounts or bonuses based on overall sales volume. By reason of its significantly higher market share, the undertaking in a dominant position generally constitutes an unavoidable business partner in the market. Most often, discounts or bonuses granted by such an undertaking on the basis of overall turnover largely take precedence in absolute terms, even over more generous offers of its competitors. In order to attract the co-contractors of the undertaking in a dominant position, or to receive a sufficient volume of orders from them, those competitors would have to offer them significantly higher rates of discount or bonus.

Applying these standards to the facts of the case, the Court of Justice confirmed that BA had abused its dominant position: the bonuses were drawn up individually for each travel agent; they were based upon the total number of tickets sold, and not on those sold over a given level, so selling a few extra BA tickets meant a significant increase in bonus payments, so that it was often more worthwhile selling a few extra BA tickets rather than selling some other airlines' tickets; BA's size was such that other competitors lacked 'a sufficiently broad financial base to allow them effectively to establish a reward scheme similar to BA's.[139] It may be argued that this is insufficient to sustain a finding of abuse; for instance, there was no evidence that BA's scheme meant that its prices were below cost, in which case BA was simply more efficient than its rivals, or at least lucky to have been the first on the market and benefited from a statutory monopoly for several years giving it a significant advantage over new entrants.

The Court of Justice's approach in this case did little to reduce the criticisms that EU competition law protects competitors, and not competition,[140] but there is a rational basis for this approach, as Professor Fox has indicated:

It is a principle of freedom of non-dominant firms to trade without artificial obstacles constructed by dominant firms, and carries an assumption that preserving this freedom is important to the legitimacy of the competition process and is likely to inure to the benefit of all market players, competitors and consumers.[141]

The reader should note the similarity between the Court of Justice's appraisal here and the approach it takes in Article 101 cases like *GlaxoSmithKline* discussed earlier: in both instances, the Court is committed to safeguarding the competitive process, not solely competitive outcomes.

---

[139] *British Airways plc* v. *Commission*, C-95/04 P, ECLI:EU:C:2007:166 para. 76.

[140] But see H. Schweitzer, 'Parallels and Differences in the Attitudes Towards and Rules regarding Market Power: What Are the Reasons?' in C.-D. Ehlermann and M. Marquis (eds.), *European Competition Law Annual 2007: A Reformed Approach to Article 82 EC* (Oxford, Hart, 2008).

[141] E. M. Fox, 'What Is Harm to Competition? Exclusionary Practices and Anticompetitive Effect' (2002) 70 *Antitrust LJ* 37, 395.

(iii) Predatory Pricing

The tension between penalising dominant firms because of the possible harm they might cause to the competitive process and the possible benefits of certain forms of behaviour by dominant undertakings is particularly relevant in the context of below-cost pricing, often referred to as predatory pricing. Below-cost pricing can be a benevolent strategy to enter a market, by reducing prices so as to invite customers, but it may also constitute a predatory strategy designed to drive other competitors out of the market, whereby the predator endures losses until the prey exits the market. Below-cost pricing is often practised selectively, targeting those customer groups where the benefits of below-cost pricing is greatest. The seminal predatory pricing case concerns Akzo, a dominant manufacturer of benzonyl peroxide (a chemical used in two lines of business, flour additives and plastics). It became concerned that one of its competitors, ECS, who had originally sold benzonyl peroxide in the flour sector, was expanding its sales in the plastics sector. Intent on safeguarding its profits, Akzo threatened ECS with retaliation and sold benzonyl peroxide at very low prices to ECS's customers in the flour market while maintaining a higher price for its regular customers, and engaged in other commercial tactics designed to woo customers away from ECS in an effort to persuade ECS to abandon the plastics sector. The Court of Justice established the parameters to determine when low prices are to be deemed predatory.

AKZO Chemie BV v. Commission of the European Communities, 62/86, [1991] ECR I-3359

69 It should be observed that, as the Court held in its judgment in Case 85/76 *Hoffmann-La Roche v. Commission* [1979] ECR 461, paragraph 91, the concept of abuse is an objective concept relating to the behaviour of an undertaking in a dominant position which is such as to influence the structure of a market where, as a result of the very presence of the undertaking in question, the degree of competition is weakened and through recourse to methods which, different from those which condition normal competition in products or services on the basis of the transactions of commercial operators, has the effect of hindering the maintenance of the degree of competition still existing in the market or the growth of that competition.

70 It follows that Article [102] prohibits a dominant undertaking from eliminating a competitor and thereby strengthening its position by using methods other than those which come within the scope of competition on the basis of quality. From that point of view, however, not all competition by means of price can be regarded as legitimate.

71 Prices below average variable costs (that is to say, those which vary depending on the quantities produced) by means of which a dominant undertaking seeks to eliminate a competitor must be regarded as abusive. A dominant undertaking has no interest in applying such prices except that of eliminating competitors so as to enable it subsequently to raise its prices by taking advantage of its monopolistic position, since each sale generates a loss, namely the total amount of the fixed costs (that is to say, those which remain constant regardless of the quantities produced) and, at least, part of the variable costs relating to the unit produced.

72 Moreover, prices below average total costs, that is to say, fixed costs plus variable costs, but above average variable costs, must be regarded as abusive if they are determined as part of a plan for eliminating a competitor. Such prices can drive from the market undertakings which are perhaps as efficient as the dominant undertaking but which, because of their smaller financial resources, are incapable of withstanding the competition waged against them.

While complex economic theories of predatory pricing suggest that price predation is possible, the Court of Justice's approach appears too wide-ranging.[142] First, it does not take into account that below-cost pricing can be a pro-competitive strategy when a firm is entering a new product market, where low prices are necessary to generate initial sales.[143] Secondly, the judgment may dent dominant firms' competitive edge: why should Akzo not be entitled to increase its market share? Thirdly, intention was inferred by internal memoranda indicating the desire to undercut ECS, but the desire to undermine competitors is the prime instinct of any company, dominant or not, so the probative value of this approach to intention is unclear. Fourthly, the judgment requires no showing that the predatory pricing campaign is likely to be successful:[144] for prices below average variable cost the Court appears to assume that the predator will be able to recover the lost profits it suffers because it will later be able to raise prices, but there is no showing that this is a likely effect; for prices above average variable cost but below average total cost, the Court finds harm by assuming that this pricing behaviour, coupled with a plan to exclude rivals, will most likely injure a rival as efficient as the dominant undertaking and so harm the competitive process.

In a subsequent application of the *Akzo* test by the Commission, WIN (Wanadoo Interactive which, following a merger, was at that time a part of France Télécom) was found to have set predatory prices 'as part of a plan to pre-empt the market in high-speed Internet access during a key phase in its development'.[145] On appeal to the Court of Justice, the parties claimed that a finding of predatory pricing should only succeed if there was proof that the predator would be able to recoup the losses incurred during the predatory pricing campaign. While the Advocate General was sympathetic, the Court confirmed that there was no need to establish recoupment.[146]

(iv) Reform

Practitioners have regularly criticised the jurisprudence under Article 102: first, the abuse case law has arisen pragmatically in response to individual disputes and without a systematic enforcement policy. As a result, the Commission and European Courts in individual cases have operated without 'any clear general analytical or intellectual framework'.[147] Secondly, the influence of economic thinking, which has increasingly affected other areas of competition law, has not had the same impact on the application of Article 102. Instead the case law is (according to economists) based on formalistic distinctions, like the notion of loyalty rebates, and simple price-cost tests. These criticisms apply at two levels: first, each case is judged poorly; secondly, the function of Article 102 is distorted because the Commission can protect competitors without considering the likely effects of the practices it prohibits. However, reviewing the case law from a historical perspective, David Gerber suggests that the jurisprudence is not without wealth or value.

---

[142] See P. Bolton, J. F. Brodley and M. H. Riordan, 'Predatory Pricing: Strategic Theory and Legal Policy' (2000) 88 *Georgetown LJ* 2239; A. Kate and G. Niels, 'On the Rationality of Predatory Pricing' (2002) 47 *Antitrust Bulletin* 1.

[143] The point was recognised in theory in *Tetra Pak* v. *Commission*, T-83/91, ECLI:EU:T:1994:246, para. 147, but the scope for justification is very narrow.

[144] *Tetra Pak* v. *Commission*, C-333/94 P, ECLI:EU:C:1996:436, para. 44.

[145] Case COMP/38.233, *Wanadoo Interactive*, Decision of 16 July 2003, Article 1.

[146] *France Télécom SA* v. *Commission*, C-202/07 P, ECLI:EU:C:2009:214 paras. 110–12.

[147] J. T. Lang and R. O'Donoghue, 'Defining Legitimate Competition: How to Clarify Pricing Abuses under Article 82 EC' (2002) 26 *Fordham Int'l LJ* 83.

D. J. Gerber, 'Law and the Abuse of Economic Power in Europe' (1987) 62 *Tulane Law Review* 57, 100–5

A Conceptual Structure

In Community law the broad principle of competitive distortion is the central mechanism for giving content to the abuse concept. It is generally applied, however, according to a developing set of case-law principles fashioned to protect particular interests. These application principles protect, for example, the interests of consumers and small and medium-sized firms. They also protect dominant enterprises by providing that conduct which otherwise would be a violation of Article 86 may be justified under certain circumstances. Analysis generally begins, therefore, with the issue of whether conduct 'distorts competition' and then turns to case law to determine whether the competitive distortion harms interests whose protection is required under existing guidelines . . .

B The Application of Abuse Law Concepts

Both systems [German and European] have also identified competitive unfairness as a category of abuse. Here the abuse concept is used to prevent dominant firms from using their power to achieve an unfair advantage in competition with other firms, such as, for example, through predatory pricing. In German law competitive unfairness is included within the concept of impediment abuse, whereas the European Commission applies Article 86 to such conduct because it distorts competition to the detriment of smaller competitors and, in the long run, consumers.

Both systems have encountered, however, significant difficulties in conceptualizing competitive unfairness for purposes of judicial application. Each has turned primarily to the intuitively appealing idea of competition on the merits in order to provide a fairness standard, but this method of giving content to the abuse concept has not been finally accepted in either system, and there are many who doubt its viability. These doubts relate to whether the merit competition notion has sufficient analytical power to make justifiable and reasonably predictable distinctions among the various types of conduct available to economically powerful firms. Neither system has yet had sufficient experience with this concept to warrant final conclusions about its effectiveness. Nevertheless, the fact that both systems have chosen to rely on it in using the abuse concept to combat competitive unfairness means that the future of the idea of unfairness as part of abuse law may well depend on the amenability to judicial application of the concept of merit competition.

A third category of practices that are considered abusive in both systems includes those by which dominant producers exercise control over firms that distribute their products. In both systems loyalty rebates, exclusive dealing contracts, and similar control measures may be abusive . . . Under Community law, such control mechanisms are found abusive when they distort competition to the detriment of consumers and interfere with the freedom of small and medium-sized firms. This analysis refers directly to the power that a dominant producer may have over distributors as well as to its effects. The result has been the development of flexible and judicially applicable principles to guide business behavior . . .

C Methods of Interpretation

In Community law the decision in *Continental Can* to interpret abuse teleologically – i.e., by reference to the objectives of the Community – has determined the structure and development of abuse law, because it established the concept of competitive distortion as the analytical starting point. In addition, the court often fashions its application principles according to its perception of the systemic needs of the Community. For example, the court's application of the abuse concept to loyalty rebates is based on the perceived need to protect the structure of competition by protecting the competitive freedom of small and medium-sized firms. Although the court occasionally also finds guidance by analogizing to the examples provided in Article 86, the teleological method has been the dominant means of ascribing meaning to abuse in Community law.

Despite criticism for failure fully to utilize more predictable methods of interpretation, the European Court has fashioned a body of legal principles with sufficient integrity and coherence to have achieved general acceptance. Its success in doing so is clearly related, however, to a general consensus concerning the basic objectives of Articles 85 and 86 – principally, the elimination of barriers to trade within the Community – as well as to the articulation of Community objectives in the governing treaty . . .

D The Process of Legal Development

. . . Although basic principles of analysis in Community abuse law were provided through the authority of outside experts,[148] the subsequent development of the law has been primarily the product of adjudication by the European Court. The court has established a basic framework for giving content to the abuse concept and has consistently applied this framework and the ideas generated thereby to new fact situations. Consequently, it is the court's central role that has dominated the developmental process.

The Commission has shaped this development through both policy and enforcement decisions. Its identification and articulation of Community policy goals has been particularly influential because of the court's focus on using the abuse concept to achieve the fundamental objectives of the Community. Moreover, not only has the Commission's enforcement policy determined the fact situations which would reach the court, but its decisions have also established lines of conceptual development which the court has later adopted.

One helpful lesson which we might draw from Gerber's analysis is that to understand the law in this field, less attention should be paid to legal nuances and to economic edicts. Instead, greater focus should be placed upon matching the abuse doctrine to EU policies, with an understanding that the Commission has regularly used Article 102 TFEU as a tool to achieve a vast array of EU objectives, and the Court of Justice gave this approach unstinting support in the early years but has since the 1990s exercised a more stringent form of judicial review.[149] From this angle, a richer synthesis of abuse might be attained by matching the decisions with Community policies: cases which support the aims of safeguarding small and medium-sized undertakings and of market integration are both seen as engines for developing, in the long term, the interests of consumers.

However, the reformers were eager to intervene. In late 2005, DG Competition published a Discussion Paper on Exclusionary Abuse which indicated that it sought to redirect its policy by using a more economics-oriented framework.[150] This stimulated a lively debate.[151] The outcome

---

[148] This alludes to a report prepared by academics for the Commission: 'Memorandum sur le problème de la concentration dans le Marché Commun' (1 December 1965), repr. (1966) *Revue trimestrelle de droit européen* 651.

[149] See generally A. Arnull, *The European Union and Its Court of Justice* (Oxford University Press, 1999) noting a general trend whereby the Court of Justice supports the expansion of EU competition law doctrines in the early years but applies a stricter approach from the mid-1980s.

[150] Discussion Paper on the Application of Article 82 of the Treaty to Exclusionary Abuses (December 2005), http://ec.europa.eu/comm/competition/antitrust/art82/index.html.

[151] See e.g. C.-D. Ehlermann and I. Atanasiu (eds.), *European Competition Law Annual 2003: What Is an Abuse of a Dominant Position?* (Oxford, Hart, 2004); Ehlermann and Marquis, n. 140 above; J. Vickers, 'Abuse of Market Power' (2005) 115 *Economic Journal* F244. See also EAGCP, 'An Economic Approach to Article 82' (July 2005), http://ec.europa.eu/dgs/competition/economist/eagcp_july_21_05.pdf.

of these reflections was a paper issued in 2009 entitled *Guidance on the Commission's Enforcement Priorities in Applying Article 82 of the EC Treaty [now Article 102 TFEU] to Abusive Exclusionary Conduct by Dominant Undertakings.*[152] This paper should be studied from two angles.[153]

First, it is designed to set the tone for the Commission's overall enforcement strategy, which will focus on behaviour likely to harm consumers and indicates a shift away from merely protecting competition as such. This is a major change of position and sets the Commission on a collision course with the Court of Justice, as only the latter can determine the scope of Article 102 TFEU. However, the way the Commission avoids this clash is not by denying the correctness of the case law, but by saying that while potentially more abuse cases could be brought, the Commission will exercise its prosecutorial discretion by only taking those cases where, in addition to establishing abuse under the legal parameters set out by the Court, the Commission also finds that the abuse is likely to result in consumer harm. From this perspective, the title of the Guidance is telling, if a little misleading: in contrast to other soft law notices, which usually contain guidelines, this one simply indicates enforcement priorities. In this way the Commission does not appear to be rewriting the case law. This is a very astute move from the Commission: incapable of overruling the Court of Justice's case law, it supplements the current elements of abuse (harm to the competitive process) with new ones (likely foreclosure of competitors and likely consumer harm). In the long run, the European Courts may feel compelled to endorse these new elements and so incrementally a novel abuse doctrine will materialise. It is less easy to see a scenario where the Court of Justice will be asked to reject the enforcement standard being proposed by the Commission. Parties who are condemned will more likely question the evidence of consumer harm, and the victims of those dominant undertakings who escape conviction are unlikely to be able to use the Court to require the Commission to ascertain an infringement absent likely consumer harm given the Commission's wide prosecutorial discretion. That said, national courts may continue to follow the precedents set by the Court of Justice and so there may be a tension between the interpretation of abuse at national and EU level. Finally, one must pause and consider why a successful competition authority should publish a document by which it makes it more difficult for it to prosecute abuse cases. This shows how sensitive certain members of DG Competition are to stakeholder criticism and to ensuring that the Commission utilises 'best practices' in applying competition law.

The second perspective through which to study the Guidance Paper is to test how the current tests for abuse are affected. For instance, in considering predatory pricing abuses, one might reasonably conclude that the new approach would hinge on proving that the predator will be able to gain from this strategy by raising prices, and so insist on recoupment. However, the Commission's approach is somewhat broader.

---

[152] [2009] OJ C 45/7.
[153] G. Monti, 'Article 82 EC: What Future for the Effects-Based Approach?' (2009) 1(1) *Journal of European Competition Law and Practice* 2; H. Schweitzer, 'Recent Developments in EU Competition Law (2006–2008): Single-Firm Dominance and the Interpretation of Article 82' (2009) *European Review of Contract Law* 175.

Guidance on the Commission's Enforcement Priorities in Applying Article 82 of the EC Treaty [now Article 102 TFEU] to Abusive Exclusionary Conduct by Dominant Undertakings [2009] OJ C45/7

68 . . . [T]he Commission will generally investigate whether and how the suspected conduct reduces the likelihood that competitors will compete. For instance, if the dominant undertaking is better informed about cost or other market conditions, or can distort market signals about profitability, it may engage in predatory conduct so as to influence the expectations of potential entrants and thereby deter entry. If the conduct and its likely effects are felt on multiple markets and/or in successive periods of possible entry, the dominant undertaking may be shown to be seeking a reputation for predatory conduct. If the targeted competitor is dependent on external financing, substantial price decreases or other predatory conduct by the dominant undertaking could adversely affect the competitor's performance so that its access to further financing may be seriously undermined.

69 The Commission does not consider that it is necessary to show that competitors have exited the market in order to show that there has been anticompetitive foreclosure. The possibility cannot be excluded that the dominant undertaking may prefer to prevent the competitor from competing vigorously and have it follow the dominant undertaking's pricing, rather than eliminate it from the market altogether. Such disciplining avoids the risk inherent in eliminating competitors, in particular the risk that the assets of the competitor are sold at a low price and stay in the market, creating a new low cost entrant.

70 Generally speaking, consumers are likely to be harmed if the dominant undertaking can reasonably expect its market power after the predatory conduct comes to an end to be greater than it would have been had the undertaking not engaged in that conduct in the first place, that is to say, if the undertaking is likely to be in a position to benefit from the sacrifice.

71 This does not mean that the Commission will only intervene if the dominant undertaking would be likely to be able to increase its prices above the level persisting in the market before the conduct. It is sufficient, for instance, that the conduct would be likely to prevent or delay a decline in prices that would otherwise have occurred. Identifying consumer harm is not a mechanical calculation of profits and losses, and proof of overall profits is not required. Likely consumer harm may be demonstrated by assessing the likely foreclosure effect of the conduct, combined with consideration of other factors, such as entry barriers. In this context, the Commission will also consider possibilities of re-entry.

These passages indicate that the Commission will consider the likely effect of predatory pricing on consumer welfare, but without requiring proof that prices will rise allowing the predator to recover the costs incurred. Instead, the major difference between the case law and the Guidance Paper is that, in the latter, the Commission is aware that mere proof of below-cost pricing is insufficient, and it identifies a number of scenarios where predation is more likely to prove a successful exclusionary strategy: predation by reputation, or disciplining rivals; these have been discussed by economists as plausible scenarios for exclusion.[154] Thus in the future the Commission plans to only condemn below-cost pricing in a scenario where it is realistic to expect that such prices foreclose rivals.

The proposed change in rebate cases like *British Airways* or *Michelin* would be more profound, however. The Commission proposes to apply a standard similar to that for predatory pricing cases, with a slight difference which is best illustrated by an example. Suppose a retailer of car

---

[154] C. Fumagalli, M. Motta and C. Calcagno, *Exclusionary Practices* (Cambridge University Press, 2018) ch. 1.

tyres sells a hundred units a week, and without rebates they know that sixty consumers will buy Michelin. This means that of the hundred sales, sixty are non-contestable (the retailer must stock at least sixty Michelin branded tyres). It means that rivals of Michelin can only, at best, sell forty tyres (this is the contestable part of the market, where there can be competition). Now, suppose Michelin offers the retailer a discount if they buy eighty Michelin tyres. The Commission will apply the amount of the discount to the twenty extra tyres and work out what the 'effective price' for those twenty tyres is. (This makes sense because the retailer would have bought the first sixty tyres even at the usual price, so the discount only affects his decision to buy the additional twenty.) If this 'effective price' is below Michelin's costs then it will be taken as a sign that the discounts are exclusionary because a firm as efficient as Michelin cannot afford to sell tyres at such a price.[155] This approach (in the jargon, known as the as-efficient-competitor test) is significantly more attentive to trying to infer likely exclusionary effects, but it is also more resource-intensive.[156]

(v) Response by the Court of Justice

The Court's response has been mixed.[157] *Post Danmark 1* approves the general approach of the Commission's initiative.[158] The question that the Court confronted was whether above-cost discounts offered by the dominant firm to its three largest clients could be characterised as an abuse. The judgment is significant for the general approach: the Court accepts that not every exclusionary effect harms competition, and that less-efficient rivals should not be protected by competition law.[159] Moreover the Court is sceptical about whether above-cost discounts can really serve to exclude rivals as efficient as the dominant firm.[160]

The same defendant was later challenged again, this time for setting rebates to exclude rivals in the market for bulk advertising mail. The Danish court asked whether the as-efficient-competitor test should be applied to rebates granted by the dominant firm. The strategy behind asking this question is clear: to test whether the approach suggested in the Guidance Paper is supported by the ECJ.

Post Danmark A/S v. *Konkurrencerådet*, C-23/14, ECLI:EU:C:2015:651

57　It is not possible to infer from Article [102 TFEU] or the case-law of the Court that there is a legal obligation requiring a finding to the effect that a rebate scheme operated by a dominant undertaking is abusive to be based always on the as-efficient-competitor test.

58　Nevertheless, that conclusion ought not to have the effect of excluding, on principle, recourse to the as-efficient-competitor test in cases involving a rebate scheme for the purposes of examining its compatibility with Article [102 TFEU].

---

[155] Guidance Paper, n. 152 above, paras. 37–45.

[156] This approach was applied for the first time in Case COMP/C-3/37.900, *Intel*, Decision of 13 May 2009. However, this is an awkward one: first the Commission established the anti-competitive nature of rebates applying the established case law; secondly, it also applied the methodology in the Guidance Paper. We discuss this case below.

[157] An early judgment went against the trend of the more recent case law, *Konkurrensverket* v. *TeliaSonera Sverige AB*, C-52/09, ECLI:EU:C:2011:83.

[158] E. Rousseva and M. Marquis, 'Hell Freezes Over: A Climate Change for Assessing Exclusionary Conduct under Article 102 TFEU' (2012) *Journal of European Competition Law and Practice* 32.

[159] *Post Danmark A/S* v. *Konkurrencerådet*, C-209/10, ECLI:EU:C:2012:172, para. 22.　　[160] *Ibid.* paras. 36–9.

59 On the other hand, in a situation such as that in the main proceedings, characterised by the holding by the dominant undertaking of a very large market share and by structural advantages conferred, *inter alia*, by that undertaking's statutory monopoly, which applied to 70% of mail on the relevant market, applying the as-efficient-competitor test is of no relevance inasmuch as the structure of the market makes the emergence of an as-efficient competitor practically impossible.

60 Furthermore, in a market such as that at issue in the main proceedings, access to which is protected by high barriers, the presence of a less efficient competitor might contribute to intensifying the competitive pressure on that market and, therefore, to exerting a constraint on the conduct of the dominant undertaking.

61 The as-efficient-competitor test must thus be regarded as one tool amongst others for the purposes of assessing whether there is an abuse of a dominant position in the context of a rebate scheme.

This judgment stands in stark contrast to *Post Danmark I*: on the specific question addressed above (does the as-efficient-competitor test apply?) the court is hesitant. In the remainder of the judgment the court takes the view that it is not necessary to look into the actual effects of the conduct in question, suggesting that mere likelihood suffices to show an abuse and that the effects need not be serious or appreciable. Such an approach is in contrast with the spirit of the Guidance Paper insofar as it places less emphasis on testing the effects of an abuse in a robust way.

In *Intel* the Court of Justice returned to discuss rebates and introduced a small but significant qualification to the existing case law. The Commission's Intel decision was taken during the period that the Commission was reviewing Article 102 and, as a way of showing what the as-efficient-competitor test meant, the Commission's decision contains a detailed discussion on whether Intel's rebates would exclude rivals as efficient as it, but it stated that this was not part of the decision.[161] The Commission maintained that existing precedents sufficed to condemn rebates. The Court had other ideas.

Intel Corporation Inc. v. *Commission*, C–413/14 P, ECLI:EU:C:2017:632

138 However, that case-law must be further clarified in the case where the undertaking concerned submits, during the administrative procedure, on the basis of supporting evidence, that its conduct was not capable of restricting competition and, in particular, of producing the alleged foreclosure effects.

139 In that case, the Commission is not only required to analyse, first, the extent of the undertaking's dominant position on the relevant market and, secondly, the share of the market covered by the challenged practice, as well as the conditions and arrangements for granting the rebates in question, their duration and their amount; it is also required to assess the possible existence of a strategy aiming to exclude competitors that are at least as efficient as the dominant undertaking from the market.

140 The analysis of the capacity to foreclose is also relevant in assessing whether a system of rebates which, in principle, falls within the scope of the prohibition laid down in Article 102 TFEU, may be objectively justified. In addition, the exclusionary effect arising from such a system, which is disadvantageous for competition, may be counterbalanced, or outweighed, by advantages in terms of efficiency which also benefit the

---

[161] Case COMP/C-3/37.900, *Intel*, Decision of 13 May 2009, para. 916.

consumer. That balancing of the favourable and unfavourable effects of the practice in question on competition can be carried out in the Commission's decision only after an analysis of the intrinsic capacity of that practice to foreclose competitors which are at least as efficient as the dominant undertaking.

Applied to the facts of the case, the Court held that since the Commission had applied the as-efficient-competitor test and the defendant contested the approach taken, that it was necessary for the Court to test review the application of that test.[162] The change in the law brought by *Intel* is significant: it gives defendants two opportunities to challenge the findings of a competition authority: first it can challenge the finding of exclusionary potential and require that the authority carries out a burdensome set of tests to determine the likely effect of the agreement. Secondly, if this proves unsuccessful, the defendant may bring evidence to establish that rebates are efficient. Many welcome this as a move away from the formalistic approach that had characterised the rebates case law in the past. The old approach was likely to yield Type 1 errors (i.e. erroneous convictions) which places unnecessary liability on dominant firms. However, the greater costs of the new approach will yield Type 2 errors (i.e. erroneous findings that there is no abuse) because competition authorities will be extra cautious before finding an abuse.[163]

5 THE HIDDEN SIDE OF COMPETITION LAW ENFORCEMENT

In Chapter 20 we noted that Regulation 1/2003 formalised a procedure by which parties subject to an investigation could offer commitments to the Commission to vary their conduct and thereby eliminate the Commission's competition concerns. There we addressed the procedural concerns with this decision: absence of meaningful judicial review; the Commission's relatively stronger bargaining position, with the concomitant risk that parties make unnecessary commitments; and the doubtful precedential value of these decisions. Here we suggest that the procedural weaknesses have allowed the Commission to develop an alternative enforcement strategy by applying new and possibly questionable theories of anti-competitive conduct, and solving cases with far-reaching remedies.[164] This applies in particular to cases involving Article 102 TFEU.

The approach of commitments in energy markets provides a good case study. The Commission has tried to liberalise electricity and gas markets for some twenty years, but with little result: all EU markets remain dominated by the former State monopolist who remains vertically integrated, and this makes it hard for new entrants.[165] Commitments have been used to complement the deregulatory efforts. In Italian gas markets (where all supply is imported), ENI is dominant in the transmission markets (pipelines that take gas into Italy) as well as the wholesale and retail gas markets. The Commission accused ENI of making access to the transmission market for new

---

[162] *Intel Corporation Inc.* v. *Commission*, C413/14 P, ECLI:EU:C:2017:632, paras. 141–7.

[163] For a lively exchange of views, see W. P. J. Wils, 'The Judgment of the EU General Court in Intel and the So-Called "More Economic Approach" to Abuse of Dominance' (2014) 37(4) *World Competition* 405 and P. Rey and J. Venit, 'An Effects-Based Approach to Article 102 – A Response to Wouter Wils' (2015) 38 *World Competition* 1.

[164] Y. Botteman and A. Patsa, 'Towards a More Sustainable Use of Commitment Decisions in Article 102 TFEU Cases' (2013) 1(2) *Journal of Antitrust Enforcement* 347.

[165] 'Communication from the Commission: Inquiry Pursuant to Article 17 of Regulation 1/2003 into the European Gas and Electricity Sectors', COM(2006)851 final. This summarises the remaining barriers to open markets and was the basis of all subsequent investigations.

entrants more difficult by the following strategies: refusing to offer capacity on its pipelines; making some capacity available on inconvenient terms; and strategically choosing to under-invest in increasing transmission capacity, all to protect its monopoly in the downstream markets. ENI then agreed to divest some of its transmission capacity and the Commission approved this remedy because the new owner would have no interest in protecting downstream profits and their incentives would be to use the transmission capacity in the most efficient way.[166] Note that the Commission has never attempted to secure a structural remedy in prohibition decisions, while they are frequently found in commitment decisions; furthermore, some of the suspected abuses are not well settled in the case law (e.g. under-investment). Similarly, in the German market the Commission managed to secure structural remedies so that E.ON (one of the major electricity players in Germany) agreed to divest generation capacity because it was suspected that it was under-exploiting these to create scarcity in the market and so raise prices of its electricity. It was also suspected of deterring new entrants in the market for electricity generation, *inter alia*, by offering shares in E.ON's generation projects. The Commission considered these to be individual abuses of a collective dominant position.[167] Again, a far-reaching remedy is imposed on theories of abuse that are not too well-established in the case law. However, these two decisions serve the Union's energy policy well because they open the two national markets to new entrants.

The criticisms that are made of this style of intervention are that the Commission uses commitments to advance a range of policy goals that are regulatory in nature; moreover, that the Commission completes the liberalisation of the sector that had not been agreed to politically by the Member States.[168] Furthermore, it has been noted that these decisions are 'a new phenomenon, a peculiar "negotiated antitrust" characterised by weak cases with extensive remedies'.[169] Against this concern about overly aggressive enforcement, it has been argued that this kind of approach may be justified because it is more appropriate as a method of regulating markets well.

D. A. Crane, 'Antitrust Antifederalism' (2008) 96(1) *California Law Review* 1, 32

To be sure, there are good reasons to treat the monopolist who built a better mousetrap more favorably than the one who blew up the competitor's factory. But most monopolists do not fall neatly into one category or the other. Most secured and maintained their position through some complex combination of skill, foresight, industry, accident, luck, shrewdness, strategic behavior, manipulation, and interrelated industry features such as government-sponsored entry barriers, first-mover advantages, network effects, entrenched customer preferences due to risk-aversion and switching costs, and so forth. Even if one could define the monopolization offense in a conceptually satisfying way, one lacks the tools to apply the standard reliably given the complexity of industrial markets.

---

[166] Case COMP/39.315, *ENI*, Decision of 29 September 2010.

[167] Case COMP/39.388, *E.ON: German Electricity Wholesale Market*, Decision of 26 November 2008.

[168] H. von Rosenberg, 'Unbundling Through the Back Door . . . the Case of Network Divestiture as a Remedy in the Energy Sector' (2009) 30 *ECLR* 237.

[169] M. Sadowska, 'Energy Liberalization in an Antitrust Straitjacket: A Plant Too Far?' (2011) 34(3) *World Competition* 449, 471.

Rather than think of monopolization as a criminal and tortious affront to some competition norm, one could think about how to manage the behavior and structure of dominant corporations so as to capture the efficiencies inherent in large aggregations of capital while minimizing the inefficiencies attendant to market power ... The crime-tort model is comparatively ill-suited for advancing consumer welfare and economic efficiency. Many commercial practices can simultaneously help and hurt consumers. For example, tying contracts that require a customer to purchase a patented product together with an unpatented product can be good for some sets of consumers but not for others since they can entail raising the price to some consumers and lowering the price to others. Asking after the fact whether such price discrimination conformed to some ephemeral legal norm and awarding damages if it did is unhelpful. What is needed is a technical appraisal of the practice and expertly designed rules to make its implementation as efficient and consumer-friendly as possible.

Crane is not writing to advocate commitment decisions, but notes the comparative advantage of the regulatory style they embody. A further feature of commitment is that in sensitive cases the time to reach a decision can be quite extensive.[170] For example, Gazprom's commercial practices which served to raise the prices of gas to certain East European countries gave rise to concerns in 2012 but it took until 2018 to agree on a set of measures which are hoped to bring gas prices down.[171] This can reduce the impact of competition law enforcement.

6 BREXIT

Brexit will have a minor impact on the matters discussed in this chapter. The substantive rules in the Treaty were taken as the model for the new UK competition regime in the Competition Act 1998 (CA98): the so-called Chapter 1 and Chapter 2 prohibitions found in this Act reproduce Articles 101 and 102 respectively, except that the effect on trade has to be felt in the United Kingdom and not the European Union. Ironically, this statute was passed to align EU and UK law to facilitate compliance. Membership of the European Economic Area would entail the application of substantive rules that are identical to the EU rules.

Insofar as a bespoke agreement is designed, the government signals that its position would be to make no changes: '[t]he UK legal system already has the key components the EU expects ... it will be important to ensure that competition decisions are compatible.'[172] Under the present legislation this compatibility is ensured by section 60 which provides a duty to interpret UK competition law in line with developments at EU level including a duty to act consistently with the EU Courts. However, with Brexit it is likely that this section will be removed. If so, however, it is not clear how this may be reconciled with the government's wish to ensure that the CMA decisions are compatible with those of the Union. Moreover, it has been suggested that judgments of the ECJ are likely to continue to bind for matters that the CMA investigates that took place pre-Brexit, so complete substantive independence may be some years away.[173]

---

[170] M. Marinello, 'Commitments or Prohibition? The EU Antitrust Dilemma', Bruegel Policy Brief 2014/01.
[171] Case AT.39816, *Upstream Gas Supplies in Central and Eastern Europe*, 24 May 2018.
[172] HM Government, *The Future Relationship between the United Kingdom and the European Union*, Cm. 9593, July 2018, paras. 114 and 115 respectively.
[173] P. Roth, 'Competition Law and Brexit: The Challenges Ahead' [2017] *Competition LJ* 4, 11, and see Article 92 of the Withdrawal Agreement.

Even without any agreement, however, matters will change only slightly. A Brexit briefing note provides that the Block Exemption Regulations will be preserved with minor amendments to ensure they apply to the United Kingdom.[174] This would retain the present system of parallel exemptions (whereby agreements benefiting from an EU Block Exemption are automatically deemed to comply with UK competition law). Other minor adjustments to CA98 will be needed, for example removing section 60 (discussed above) and section 10(1) which makes Commission decisions binding on national courts.

It has been suggested that Brexit affords the CMA the opportunity to develop competition law in a manner that improves upon what is found in the European Union. For example, some have suggested that the CMA and the British courts have tended to adopt a more sophisticated economic approach.[175] However, as indicated in this chapter, the Commission and the European Courts are also moving to a more economics-oriented approach.

FURTHER READING

D. Bailey, 'Reinvigorating the Role of Article 101(3) under Regulation 1/2003' (2016) 81 *Antitrust Law Journal* 111.

E. Deutscher and S. Makris, 'Exploring the ordoliberal paradigm: the competition-democracy nexus' (2016) 11(2) *Competition Law Review* 181.

C.-D. Ehlermann and M. Marquis (eds.), *European Competition Law Annual 2007: A Reformed Approach to Article 82 EC* (Oxford, Hart, 2008).

A. Ezrachi and M. Stucke, *Virtual Competition: The Promise and Perils of the Algorithm-Driven Economy* (Harvard University Press, 2016).

P. Ibanez Colomo, *The Shaping of EU Competition Law* (Cambridge University Press, 2018).

L. Kjølbe, 'The New Commission Guidelines on the Application of Article 81(3): An Economic Approach to Article 81' (2004) *ECLR* 566.

G. Monti and J. Mulder, 'Escaping the Clutches of EU Competition Law Pathways to Assess Private Sustainability Initiatives' (2017) 42(5) *European Law Review* 635.

M. Motta, *Competition Policy* (Cambridge University Press, 2004).

R. Nazzini, *The Foundations of European Competition Law: The Objective and Principles of Article 102* (Oxford University Press, 2011).

R. O'Donoghue and A. J. Padilla, *The Law and Economics of Article 102 TEU*, 2nd edn (Oxford, Hart, 2012).

O. Odudu, *The Boundaries of EC Competition Law* (Oxford University Press, 2006).

P. Rey and J. Venit, 'An Effects-Based Approach to Article 102 – A Response to Wouter Wils' (2015) 38 *World Competition* 1.

E. Rousseva, *Rethinking Exclusionary Abuses in EU Competition Law* (Oxford, Hart, 2010).

C. Townley, *Article 81 EC and Public Policy* (Oxford, Hart, 2009).

J. Vickers, 'Abuse of Market Power' (2005) 115 *Economic Journal* F244.

A. Witt, 'The Commission's Guidance Paper on Abusive Exclusionary Conduct: More Radical than it Appears?' (2010) 35(2) *European Law Review* 214.

---

[174] Department for Business, Energy and Industrial Strategy, Merger review and anti-competitive activity if there's no Brexit deal (13 September 2018).

[175] J. Vickers, 'Consequences of Brexit for Competition Law and Policy' (2017) 33 (supplement 1) *Oxford Review of Economic Policy* S70.

CONTENTS

1 INTRODUCTION

As we noted in Chapter 16, one of the results of economic and monetary union is that the European Union has considerable influence in national budgets. In this chapter we consider a specific power that the Union has had since the very beginning to control State spending: those rules that prohibit Member States from granting economic advantages to firms. In trade law, these forms of intervention go under the name of subsidies. In contrast, the European Union refers to State aids because, as we show below, this term allows one to control a wider range of State intervention, for example tax exemptions or loans on preferential terms. These powers are controversial because they control the way States use their budgets to pursue their economic and social policies.

In section 2 we summarise the State aid rules and place them in context. Here we note that the rules make little sense when seen as part of the competition law family and make more sense if they are seen as complementing the provisions of the Treaty pertaining to the internal market. However, even then the rationale for State aid law is perhaps best explained either by paternalism or by political considerations. We also identify the key policy considerations that have informed the Commission, in particular the State Aid Action Plan of 2005 and State Aid Modernisation of 2012 that are designed to strengthen State aid enforcement, on the one hand, and enhance the European Union's industrial policy, on the other.

In section 3 we look at the most contested aspect of State aid law, the definition of State aid. We note that in determining the boundaries of this concept the Court of Justice is torn between a wide approach whereby all harmful effects of national policies are caught and a narrower approach whereby some space is left for Member States to implement national policy. It is a matter of regret that this delicate policy-balancing exercise is carried out in defining the meaning of certain words and phrases and not more openly.

In section 4 we consider the structure of enforcement and supervision in State aid law. We explain the notification procedures and note the limited powers that the Commission has to enforce the law on State aid, both when it comes to discovering infringements of EU law and when it comes to punishing Member States which have infringed the rules. The limited scope for private enforcement suggests that a more effective system is necessary and we examine how far recent policy proposals may go in this respect.

In section 5 we explore what State aid may be allowed. Since 2005, the Commission has sought to reconsider its approach to ensure State assistance was provided where it was most effective. In 2008 this reflection was affected by the banking crisis which led to the unprecedented need for States to rescue banks, and by the subsequent economic crisis, which led the Commission to rethink its State aid policy further. The upshot is that there is now a more coherent framework for State aid regulation, with the result that national expenditure is channelled to safeguard the interests of the Union. Issues pertaining to financing for services of general interest are explored in Chapter 24, which is available online.

Section 6 explores what State aid law may look like after Brexit, considering legal and policy aspects.

2 ROLE OF STATE AID LAW IN THE EUROPEAN UNION

In brief, the rules on State aid provide (in Article 107(1) TFEU) that aid is forbidden when it restricts competition and has an effect on trade between Member States. However, the Commission may authorise certain types of State aid if these fall within the exemptions provided in Article 107(2)–(3) TFEU. These rules are enforced by imposing on Member States an obligation to notify State aid and on the Commission a duty to assess these measures once notified (Article 108 TFEU).

(i) Justifications for State Aid Control

As we will discuss in section 3 below, neither the Commission, nor the European Courts, has placed much emphasis on explaining the precise anti-competitive effects of State aids. After all, if Member State A grants a subsidy to its steel industry, Member State B should say 'thank you' and encourage Member State A to grant that subsidy for as long as possible.[1] This is because the other States may respond by reallocating resources away from steel production into other markets. Everyone appears to be better off.

However, there are situations where the cross-border externalities are negative and this can make an economic case for State aid. First, turning again to the example above, if Member State A did not have a comparative advantage in the steel industry, then the subsidy is inefficient: producers in other States should be making steel and State A should focus on producing goods where it has a comparative advantage. This suggests that State aids can reduce efficiency. In particular by granting State aid to firms that are inefficient and should be wound down State aid reduces dynamic efficiency by reducing the firm's incentive to modernise.[2] But these effects are not distortive of competition in an antitrust sense, they are just inefficiencies. It has also been suggested that State aid rules prevent subsidy wars whereby Member States compete to give more and more subsidies to their firms. Again, this is undesirable because it is wasteful, but it is not necessarily anti-competitive. Moreover, this justification of State aid control is odd within the context of the Union because there is no coordination of corporate taxation, so merely closing off the State aid route does not remove all attempts to subsidise industries.[3]

A competition-law-based explanation for forbidding State aid is that it can be used to finance a predatory pricing campaign to exclude other rivals, or can be used to weaken rivals. However, this harm depends on specific market configurations (i.e. that the beneficiary has market power which is enhanced by the State aid such as to allow it to harm rivals). Doubtless some would welcome the requirement that the Commission develop a theory of anti-competitive harm before applying the State aid rules, because this would render them much less widely applicable. For instance, some have suggested that State aid should only be caught if it is likely to harm a competitor as efficient as the beneficiary.[4] Applying this test, few measures would fall within Article 107 TFEU: although in most cases the beneficiary is in a better position, this is not likely to allow it to reduce consumer welfare.[5]

Another line of argument that supports State aid rules is paternalism: States are likely to spend money unwisely at times, so a regime that keeps some external check on the ways Member States use their budget may be desirable. Research has shown that the allocation of State aid is largely determined by political factors as opposed to economic ones.[6] According to some this may be the better way to explain the institutional design of the EU State aid rules: they are forbidden unless they genuinely confer a benefit.[7]

---

[1] A. O. Sykes, 'The Questionable Case for Subsidies Regulation: A Comparative Perspective' (2010) 2(2) *Journal of Legal Analysis* 473.

[2] J. Kavanagh and N. Robins, 'Introduction to State Aid Law and Policy' in K. Bacon (ed.), *European Union Law of State Aid*, 3rd edn (Oxford University Press, 2017) paras. 1.17–1.19.

[3] D. Spector, 'State Aids: Economic Analysis and Practice in the European Union' in X. Vives (ed.), *Competition Policy in the EU: Fifty Years on from the Treaty of Rome* (Oxford University Press, 2009) 183. However, as we see below, EU State aid law increasingly controls national tax regimes. See C. H. Panayi, 'State Aid and Tax: The Third Way?' (2004) 32 *Intertax* 283.

[4] C. Ahlborn and C. Berg, 'Can State Aid Control Learn from Antitrust?' in A. Biondi, P. Eeckhout and J. Flynn (eds.), *The Law of State Aid in the European Union* (Oxford University Press, 2004).

[5] See e.g. *Commission v. The Netherlands*, C-279/08 P, [2011] ECR I-07671, para. 132, agreeing that a mere strengthening of the position of the beneficiary suffices to show harm to competition.

[6] D. J. Neven, 'The Political Economy of State Aids: Econometric Evidence for the Member States' in D. J. Neven and L. H. Röller (eds.), *The Political Economy of Industrial Policy: Does Europe Have an Industrial Policy* (Berlin, Sigma, 2000).

[7] See Spector, n. 3 above.

This overview supports the view that State aid law should not be examined through the lens of conventional competition law, because it has closer affinities to the internal market rules in the EU Treaties. In other words, the harm that the rules cause is to the normal functioning of the market. One disadvantage of this approach to State aid control is that almost any aid can be prohibited, leading to the Commission intervening in many minor aspects of national policy.

(ii) Commission's State Aid Policy

It was not until the 1990s that the Commission began to prioritise State aid enforcement.[8] This was part of a broader 'public turn' in competition law enforcement, as the Commission also tackled undertakings that had been provided privileged positions by the State, thereby deregulating a number of economic sectors, like telecommunications and energy.[9] Having secured a legitimate space for State aid policy, and having had its approach supported but also circumscribed by the Court of Justice, the Commission was well placed to move to a second phase where it would give its enforcement policy more coherence. To the extent that data is available, it appears to demonstrate a correlation between increased State aid enforcement and a reduction of State aid: there has been a downward trend since the 1980s (when aid was 2 per cent of GDP), down to 1 per cent of GDP in the 1990s, down to 0.5 per cent of GDP since 2004, and in recent years (excluding assistance for banks) it has not gone above 0.7 per cent of GDP. In 2016 total State aid granted was €102.8 billion.[10] Since 2007 States have also intervened to rescue banks as a result of the financial crisis and these measures have entailed much more significant amounts of aid granted (approximately €1,800 billion between 2008 and 2016).[11] However the new regulatory framework for banks (the so-called Banking Union) is expected to reduce the need to resort to State aid for future bank failures.

In addition to securing a reduction in State aid, the Commission has also been active in steering State expenditure. In 2005 it launched a major policy document, the State Aid Action Plan. Its key theme is found in its subtitle: 'less and better targeted state aid'.[12] The first prong entails stronger enforcement powers, while the second suggests that State aid should not be banned entirely but redirected towards projects that benefit the European Union as a whole. The reorientation of national State aid policy to serving the EU agenda is even more pronounced in the subsequent reform programme.

Communication from the Commission, 'State Aid Modernisation', COM(2012)209 final

12 Modernised State aid control should facilitate the treatment of aid which is well-designed, targeted at identified market failures and objectives of common interest, and least distortive ('good aid'). This shall ensure that public support stimulates innovation, green technologies, human capital development, avoids environmental harm and ultimately promotes growth, employment and EU competitiveness. Such aid will best contribute to growth when it targets a market failure and thereby complements, not replaces, private

---

[8] M. G. Ross, 'State Aids: Maturing into a Constitutional Problem' (1995) 15 *YEL* 79.

[9] D. J. Gerber, *Law and Competition in Twentieth Century Europe* (Oxford University Press, 1998) ch. 10.

[10] European Commission, 'State Aid Scoreboard', COM(2017) final, 2.   [11] *Ibid.* 20–1.

[12] Commission State Aid Action Plan, 'Less and Better Targeted State Aid: A Roadmap for State Aid Reform 2005–2009', COM(2005)107 final.

spending. State aid will be effective in achieving the desired public policy objective only when it has an incentive effect, i.e. it induces the aid beneficiary to undertake activities it would not have done without the aid. And State aid will have the greatest impact on growth only when it is designed in a way which limits competition distortions and keeps the internal market competitive and open. Therefore State aid control is crucial in order to improve the efficiency and effectiveness of public spending taking the form of State aid, with the overarching objective of spurring more growth in internal market, for which a necessary condition is developing competition. State aid which does not target market failures and has no incentive effect is not only a waste of public resources but it acts as a brake to growth by worsening competitive conditions in the internal market.

13   State aid control already underpins the Europe 2020 flagships. For example, the broadband guidelines provide conditions for efficient State support to broadband rollout, supporting the achievement of the objectives of 'Digital agenda for Europe'. Public support to develop infrastructure is also instrumental to the achievement of smart, upgraded and fully interconnected transport and energy networks as foreseen by 'Resource efficient Europe'. The framework for State aid to research, development and innovation facilitates the achievement of 'Innovation Union' as well as 'An industrial policy for the globalisation era' objectives. The enforcement of 'polluter pays' principle as well as a possibility to provide aid in order to encourage companies to go beyond mandatory EU environmental standards or to promote energy efficiency provided for in the Environmental aid guidelines are one of the tools to implement 'Resource efficient Europe' flagship. The possibility to support training with State funds contributes to the goals of 'An agenda for new skills and jobs'. Rescue and restructuring aid guidelines allow State aid to ailing companies only under strict conditions and if it results in their return to long-term viability, encouraging thereby exit of inefficient firms and bracing the companies for global competition, contributing to 'An industrial policy for a globalised era'. The link between the Europe 2020 objectives and flagship initiatives on the one hand, and State aid rules on the other, should be further developed to streamline the Commission's instruments and to encourage Member States to direct scarce public resources to common priorities.

14   By putting an emphasis on the quality and the efficiency of public support, State aid control can also help Member States to strengthen budgetary discipline and improve the quality of public finances – resulting in a better use of taxpayers' money. It is particularly important in order to achieve smart fiscal consolidation, reconciling the role of targeted public spending in generating growth with the need to bring budgets under control. There is therefore also a need to embed State aid control and more general competition concerns in the EU Semester procedure.

15   Robust State aid control is also essential to ensure a well functioning single market. Such robust control goes hand in hand with the effective implementation of EU internal market rules and is of particular relevance in markets that have only recently been opened and where large incumbents aided by the State still play a major role, such as transport, postal services or, in more limited cases, energy. State aid modernisation can improve the functioning of the internal market through a more effective policy aimed at limiting distortions of competition, preserving a level playing field and combating protectionism. This role of State aid becomes more important now as we need to mobilise the full potential of the internal market for growth.

This stance is quite different from the early days of State aid enforcement when the frameworks for assessing which aid should be authorised 'emerged directly from Member State preferences'.[13] The most recent *State Aid Scoreboard*, which records all State aid expenditures that

[13] M. P. Smith, 'Autonomy by the Rules: The European Commission and the Development of State Aid Policy' (1998) 36(1) *JCMS* 55, 59.

have been approved, reveals that this policy has had an impact on State spending. For instance, the largest tranche of State aid (54 per cent of all aid) is granted to environmental and energy savings which help achieve the Energy Union strategy of a low gas, secure and competitive energy network.[14] While each Member State has its own policy priorities, these largely tally with the kinds of policies favoured by the Union.[15]

Having noted the Commission's entrepreneurship, it must be recalled that other stakeholders can also act as policy entrepreneurs. One telling example is how the Assembly of European Regions steered the agenda over State support for regional airports (which came up in the context of the *Ryanair/Charleroi* case discussed below) and appeared to have secured a policy change that favoured the use of State aid to support regional development.[16] Lobbying and high-level politics are an inextricable feature of State aid enforcement.[17] Having said that, the strategies of Member States change as State aid law becomes institutionalised: whereas resistance against the Commission was once possible, now that the legitimacy of State aid control is much more well-established, Member States must channel their strategies through the prism of the Commission's policy. This strengthens the enforcement hand of the Commission even its the formal powers are weak.[18]

3 MEANING OF STATE AID

The definition of what measures constitute State aid is highly contested. This is for procedural and substantive reasons. At a procedural level, once a measure is found to be State aid, then the Member State must notify it to the Commission and wait for approval; moreover, the Commission may determine that the aid cannot be given or may only be granted if modified, and the Member State must report to the Commission on the implementation of the aid.[19] It should also be borne in mind that national courts play a central role in the definition of State aid: the only segment of the State aid rules to have direct effect is Article 108(3) TFEU (the duty to notify aid), and parties will seek to enforce this obligation as a means of securing a remedy (whether repayment of tax, or damages). This gives the Court of Justice a key role in determining the contours of the notion of State aid through preliminary rulings.

---

[14] European Commission, n. 10 above, 2–3.

[15] This is also revealed by the increased grant of State aid that benefits from the General Block Exemption Regulation discussed below: 97% of new measures reported in 2016 fell under this Regulation. *Ibid.* 14.

[16] D. C. Christopoulos, 'Relational Attributes of Political Entrepreneurs: A Network Perspective' (2006) 13(5) *JEPP* 757, 763–6.

[17] W. Bishop, 'From Trade to Tutelage: State Aid and Public Choice' in I. Govaere, R. Quck and M. Brockners (eds.), *The European Union in Trade and Competition Law in the EU and Beyond* (Cheltenham, Edward Elgar, 2011).

[18] For an absorbing account, see P. Le Galès, 'Est Maître Celui Qui Les Organise: How Rules Change when National and European Policy Domains Collide' in A. Stone Sweet, W. Sandholts and N. Fligstein (eds.), *The Institutionalisation of Europe* (Oxford University Press, 2004).

[19] This reporting obligation was used to determine that a Member State could appeal even against a Commission Decision that had found that a measure was State aid but had authorised it. The Member State's interest in having the decision quashed on the definition of aid is that it relieves it from having its measures reviewed by the Commission, *Commission* v. *Netherlands*, C-279/08 P, ECLI:EU:C:2011:551.

> ### Article 107 TFEU
>
> (1) Save as otherwise provided in the Treaties, any aid granted by a Member State or through State resources in any form whatsoever which distorts or threatens to distort competition by favouring certain undertakings or the production of certain goods shall, in so far as it affects trade between Member States, be incompatible with the internal market.

At a substantive level, the precise boundaries of this provision have been contested. Since the early days the Court has maintained the view that its approach to interpreting this provision is by considering the effects of the measures in question.[20] However, as we will see from the case law below, this approach has been tempered by the recognition that certain national policy considerations justify a narrower approach. The search for a balance between regulating all measures that affect the market and the respect for national policy characterises the case law.[21]

Looking at the case law in the round, the following elements must be shown for this provision to apply: (i) intervention by the Member State and through State resources; (ii) the intervention gives the recipient an advantage; (iii) the intervention is selective (e.g. it is available only for specific companies or industry sectors, or to companies located in specific regions); (iv) an effect on trade and a restriction of competition.[22]

(i) Intervention by the Member State and through State Resources

(a) Necessary Involvement of State Resources

The first criterion is potentially very broad, for the test reads that the Member State may intervene either by committing resources, or in some other way (recall Article 107(1) TFEU speaks of intervention by the State *or* through State resources). This literal interpretation was rejected by the Court of Justice. In one of the key cases, a German law provided that national labour law protections were not applicable to ships registered in Germany but employing non-EU crew members. It is obvious that this measure is a form of State intervention that gives the ship owners who recruit non-EU workers a competitive advantage over those who recruit EU nationals because they face lower costs. However, the Court held that the measure did not require the expenditure of State resources and so was not State aid.

> ### *Firma Sloman Neptun Schiffahrts AG* v. *Seebetriebsrat Bodo Ziesemer der Sloman Neptun Schiffahrts AG*, C–72–3/91, ECLI:EU:C:1992:130
>
> 19 ... only advantages which are granted directly or indirectly through State resources are to be regarded as State aid within the meaning of Article [107(1) TFEU]. The wording of this provision itself and the procedural rules laid down in Article [108 TFEU] show that advantages granted from resources other than those of the

---

[20] *Italy* v. *Commission*, 173/73, [1973] ECR 709.

[21] *Amministrazione delle finanze dello stato* v. *Denkavit*, 61/79, ECLI:EU:C:1974:71 where the Court recognised this consequence.

[22] Commission, Notice on the notion of State Aid as referred to in Article 107(1) TFEU [2016] OJ C 262/1 provides detailed technical guidance.

State do not fall within the scope of the provisions in question. The distinction between aid granted by the State and aid granted through State resources serves to bring within the definition of aid not only aid granted directly by the State, but also aid granted by public or private bodies designated or established by the State ...

21 The system at issue does not seek, through its object and general structure, to create an advantage which would constitute an additional burden for the State or the abovementioned bodies, but only to alter in favour of shipping undertakings the framework within which contractual relations are formed between those undertakings and their employees. The consequences arising from this, in so far as they relate to the difference in the basis for the calculation of social security contributions, mentioned by the national court, and to the potential loss of tax revenue because of the low rates of pay, referred to by the Commission, are inherent in the system and are not a means of granting a particular advantage to the undertakings concerned.

This approach has also served to exclude Italian legislation that exempted the post office from the statutory duty to grant its employees contracts of indefinite duration,[23] and the exclusion of small and medium-sized undertakings from the national laws of unfair dismissal.[24] In a further controversial development, the Court of Justice also excluded the provisions of a German electricity law. This required electricity distributors to purchase (at a fixed minimum price) electricity generated from renewable sources. In addition, generators of electricity from conventional sources had to pay extra to the distributors for the costs incurred. The effect of this measure was certainly to benefit the generators of renewable energy, but the Court nevertheless held that this was not State aid.

PreussenElektra AG v. Schleswag AG, C-379/98, ECLI:EU:C:2001:160

59 In this case, the obligation imposed on private electricity supply undertakings to purchase electricity produced from renewable energy sources at fixed minimum prices does not involve any direct or indirect transfer of State resources to undertakings which produce that type of electricity.

60 Therefore, the allocation of the financial burden arising from that obligation for those private electricity supply undertakings as between them and other private undertakings cannot constitute a direct or indirect transfer of State resources either.

61 In those circumstances, the fact that the purchase obligation is imposed by statute and confers an undeniable advantage on certain undertakings is not capable of conferring upon it the character of State aid within the meaning of Article [107(1) TFEU].

62 That conclusion cannot be undermined by the fact, pointed out by the referring court, that the financial burden arising from the obligation to purchase at minimum prices is likely to have negative repercussions on the economic results of the undertakings subject to that obligation and therefore entail a diminution in tax receipts for the State. That consequence is an inherent feature of such a legislative provision and cannot be regarded as constituting a means of granting to producers of electricity from renewable energy sources a particular advantage at the expense of the State.

---

[23] *Epifanio Viscido* v. *Ente Poste Italiane*, C-52-4/97, ECLI:EU:C:1998:209, [1998] ECR I-2629.
[24] *Kirsammer-Hack* v. *Nurhan Sidal*, C-189/91, ECLI:EU:C:1993:907.

In both of the cases above the Commission had argued in favour of a wide interpretation under which both measures would have fallen within the scope of Article 107 TFEU.[25] There are two responses to these judgments: one is that the Court of Justice showed some sensitivity to national policy measures and so tempered the breadth of the State aid rules. This is particularly convincing in the context of labour relations, for had the Court ruled otherwise it would have meant that the Commission would become competent to evaluate 'the entire social and economic life of a Member State'.[26] The second is that the case law risks undermining the rules on State aid, for it seems quite easy to circumvent the application of Article 107(1), and this is especially so after *Preussen Elektra* since one can force private parties to pay the beneficiary and omit the deployment of State resources.

Moreover, the definition leads to some odd results. Another energy scheme operated in France where energy suppliers had an obligation to buy certain amounts of wind-generated electricity at a high price, which was financed by final consumers of electricity. However, the funds were collected by the Caisse des dépôts et consignations (a French public long-term investment group), before being received by the undertakings.

***Association Vent De Colère! Fédération nationale and Others** v. **Ministre de l'Écologie, du Développement durable, des Transports et du Logement, and Ministre de l'Économie, des Finances et de l'Industrie**, C-262/12, ECLI:EU:C:2013:851*

34 All those factors taken together serve to distinguish the present case from that which gave rise to the judgment in *PreussenElektra*, in which the Court held that an obligation imposed on private electricity supply undertakings to purchase electricity produced from renewable sources at fixed minimum prices could not be regarded as an intervention through State resources where it does not lead to any direct or indirect transfer of State resources to the undertakings producing that type of electricity.

35 As the Court has already had occasion to point out in the case which gave rise to the judgment in *PreussenElektra*, the private undertakings had not been appointed by the Member State concerned to manage a State resource, but were bound by an obligation to purchase by means of their own financial resources.

36 Consequently, the funds at issue [in Preussen Elektra] could not be considered a State resource since they were not at any time under public control and there was no mechanism, such as the one at issue in the main proceedings in the present case, established and regulated by the Member State, for offsetting the additional costs arising from that obligation to purchase and through which the State offered those private operators the certain prospect that the additional costs would be covered in full.

The distinction between this and *Preussen Elektra* is not persuasive.[27] The economic effect of the two schemes is the same, and all hinges on how the State has designed its regulatory scheme. An alternative suggestion is to ask if there is a sufficiently direct connection between the advantage and the commitment of State resources.[28] On this basis the judgment in *Preussen Elektra* is

---

[25] *Firma Sloman Neptun Schiffahrts AG v. Seebetriebsrat Bodo Ziesemer der Sloman Neptun Schiffahrts AG*, C-72-3/91, ECLI:EU:C:1993:97.

[26] *Epifanio Viscido v. Ente Poste Italiane*, C-52-4/97, ECLI:EU:C:1998:209, [1998] ECR I-2629, Opinion of Advocate General Jacobs, para. 16.

[27] See generally K. Talus, *EU Energy Law and Policy: A Critical Account* (Oxford University Press, 2013) 142–4.

[28] F. de Cecco, *State Aid and the European Economic Constitution* (Oxford, Hart, 2013) 114; and *Commission v. Netherlands*, C-279/08 P, ECLI:EU:C:2011:551, paras. 109–12 and *Eventech Ltd v. The Parking Adjudicator*, C-518/13, ECLI:EU:C:2015:9, paras. 34–44.

explained because while the financial burden to buy electricity at a higher price would reduce the revenue of the buyers and thus lead to lower taxes, this impact on the national budget was too remote from the State policy. However, this does not seem to help to explain why the measures in *Preussen Elektra* and *Vent de Colère*, which have the same effect, are treated differently.

(b) State Involvement

As observed above, measures are State aid if the Member State's resources are engaged. However, this is not sufficient. It must also be shown that the State is involved in the adoption of the measure in question. This is not a problem when the advantage is allocated by central or local government, but State involvement must be proven when a third party is responsible for the measure. In *Pearle*, an association of opticians in the Netherlands asked the Central Industry Board for Skilled Trades (a trade association) to finance a collective advertising campaign for opticians' businesses. The Board did this by imposing a levy on all opticians. The plaintiffs considered this levy was illegal State aid and sought their money back.

> ### *Pearle BV, Hans Prijs Optiek Franchise BV and Rinck Opticiëns BV* v. *Hoofdbedrijfschap Ambachten*, C-345/02, ECLI:EU:C:2004:448
>
> 36 Even if the Board is a public body, it does not in the circumstances of the case appear that the advertising campaign was funded by resources made available to the national authorities. On the contrary, the judgment making the reference makes it clear that the monies used by the Board for the purpose of funding the advertising campaign were collected from its members who benefited from the campaign by means of compulsory levies earmarked for the organisation of that advertising campaign. Since the costs incurred by the public body for the purposes of that campaign were offset in full by the levies imposed on the undertakings benefiting therefrom, the Board's action did not tend to create an advantage which would constitute an additional burden for the State or that body.
>
> 37 Furthermore, the file clearly shows that the initiative for the organisation and operation of that advertising campaign was that of the NUVO, a private association of opticians, and not that of the Board. As the Advocate General pointed out . . . the Board served merely as a vehicle for the levying and allocating of resources collected for a purely commercial purpose previously determined by the trade and which had nothing to do with a policy determined by the Netherlands authorities.

Establishing the role of the State is particularly difficult in cases where the funds are in the hands of a company where the State is a shareholder. Here the question of whether the State is responsible for an investment made by the company hinges on the degree of control the State has in the company's activities.[29]

(ii) Intervention Gives the Recipient an Advantage

In determining whether the Member State's financing confers an advantage, one asks whether under 'normal market conditions' that undertaking would have secured a comparable advantage.[30] One way of testing for this is to ask if the measures taken by the State are like those which

---

[29] See *France* v. *Commission (Stardust Marine)*, C-482/99, ECLI:EU:C:2002:294.
[30] *Spain* v. *Commission*, C-342/96, ECLI:EU:C:1999:210, para. 412.

would have been taken by a private investor. If so, then the State has made an economically rational investment and so there is no advantage because the undertaking would likely have secured a similar funding from the private sector. This test was first developed in cases where the State invests in a company: would a private investor have taken the same kind of risk, considering the likely returns of this investment? This test is controversial: the State will often invest in its companies for reasons other than profit, but which may make economic sense – saving a company is better than having to deal with the social fallout from insolvency, for example. However the Court of Justice has insisted that when one compares public and private investors, the only criterion is the expected economic gains from the investment.[31]

Applying this standard, arguments that reducing social security contributions to hotel operators in Venice are designed as compensation because they face higher operating costs being on an island and because their presence serves to safeguard the centre of Venice are irrelevant: the firms getting a tax break secure an advantage.[32] The one exception is when State measures compensate firms that the State has entrusted with a provision of services of general interest, for instance operating a regional bus service.[33]

In determining whether the State has not offered an advantage one asks whether the State has acted like a 'private investor' would have. For example, loans and the terms of the loan can be analysed by considering whether a private investor would have made the loan, and if so whether on terms similar to those set by the State. It is even applicable when the State is owed money but does not clam it because it considers it more prudent to allow the undertaking to keep the money and invest it.[34] There are practical difficulties in applying this test, and in many instances the Commission has been criticised for failing to take into account all the evidence.[35] An interesting illustration is the *Ryanair/Charleroi* decision. Here, the Walloon region in Belgium (the owner of Charleroi airport) and Brussels South Charleroi Airport (BSCA, a public undertaking controlled by the Walloon region) offered a number of inducements for Ryanair to land its planes at Charleroi. The Walloon region offered reduced landing charges, while BSCA offered payments for (among others) hotel costs, training staff and bonuses for new routes that Ryanair opened from Charleroi. The commercial logic of the transaction was that by giving Ryanair incentives to invest in the airport, there would be benefits to both the airport and the region. The Commission took the view that the measures of the two actors should be assessed separately. It held that the measures taken by the Walloon region were carried out in the exercise of its public functions, and so could not be assessed using the private investor test. BSCA's activities were instead assessed using the private investor test and the Commission ruled that the risk taken by BSCA was excessive. Some of the aid was authorised, but some was to be recovered. On appeal, the General Court quashed the decision. First, it held that the two entities should have been regarded as a single actor because of the close legal and

---

[31] *Italy* v. *Commission*, C-303/88, ECLI:EU:C:1991:136; *Spain* v. *Commission*, C-278/92, ECLI:EU:C:1994:325.

[32] *Comitato 'Venezia Vuole Vivere' and Others* v. *Commission*, C-71/09 P, C-73/09 P and C-76/09 P, ECLI:EU:C:2011:368, paras. 84–100.

[33] *Altmark Trans*, C-280/00, EU:C:2003:415 sets out the framework for this kind of case.

[34] *Frucona* v. *Commission*, C-73/11, EU:C:2013:32.

[35] See e.g. *Commission* v. *France*, C-483/99, ECLI:EU:C:2002:327 and *Linde* v. *Commission*, T-98/00, ECLI:EU:T:2002:248. For a clear account of methods that may be used see G. Conte and J. Kavanagh, 'Advantage' in P. Werner and V. Verouden (eds.), *EU State Aid Control: Law and Economics* (Alphen aan den Rijn, Kluwer Law International, 2017).

economic links between them. Then the Court turned to the question of how to assess the measures taken by the Walloon region.

Ryanair Ltd v. *Commission*, T–196/04, ECLI:EU:T:2008:585

85 While it is clearly necessary, when the State acts as an undertaking operating as a private investor, to analyse its conduct by reference to the private investor principle, application of that principle must be excluded in the event that the State acts as a public authority. In the latter event, the conduct of the State can never be compared to that of an operator or private investor in a market economy . . .

88 Contrary to what is stated by the Commission . . . it must be held that the actions of the Walloon Region were economic activities. The fixing of the amount of landing charges and the accompanying indemnity is an activity directly connected with the management of airport infrastructure, which is an economic activity.

89 On that point, the airport charges fixed by the Walloon Region must be regarded as remuneration for the provision of services within Charleroi airport, notwithstanding the fact . . . that a clear and direct link between the level of charges and the service rendered to users is weak . . .

91 Accordingly, the provision of airport facilities by a public authority to airlines, and the management of those facilities, in return for payment of a fee the amount of which is freely fixed by that authority, can be described as economic activities; although such activities are carried out in the public sector, they cannot, for that reason alone, be categorised as the exercise of public authority powers. Those activities are not, by reason of their nature, their purpose or the rules to which they are subject, connected with the exercise of powers which are typically those of a public authority.

92 The fact that the Walloon Region is a public authority and that it is the owner of airport facilities in public ownership does not therefore in itself mean that it cannot, in the present case, be regarded as an entity exercising an economic activity . . .

98 When examining the measures at issue, the Commission should have differentiated between the economic activities and those activities which fell strictly under public authority powers. In addition, whether the conduct of an authority granting aid complies with national law is not a factor which should be taken into account in order to decide whether that authority acted in accordance with the private investor principle or granted an economic advantage in contravention of Article 87(1) EC. It does not follow from the fact that an activity represents in legal terms an exemption from a tariff scale laid down in a regulation that that activity must be described as non-economic . . .

101 The mere fact that, in the present case, the Walloon Region has regulatory powers in relation to fixing airport charges does not mean that a scheme reducing those charges ought not to be examined by reference to the private investor principle, since such a scheme could have been put in place by a private operator.

It follows that excessive formalism is unhelpful: States are hybrid entities, sometimes performing State functions but increasingly they are also market actors. Furthermore, the decision also contains a flaw that the judgment did not cure: as noted earlier, the deal made commercial sense, and had any other airline offered similar traffic to any other airport it would have received similar treatment by the authorities. It follows that the anti-competitive impact is not that one airline has an edge over the others. Rather, competition among airports is distorted by one region spending to enhance its airport at the expense of others.[36]

---

[36] F. Gröteke and W. Kerber, 'The Case of Ryanair: EU State Aid Policy on the Wrong Runway', Marburger volkswirtschaftliche Beiträge No. 2004 /13.

In cases where the State does act as a public authority, the private investor test is not applicable but then the advantage is shown when, but for the State's intervention, there is no other way that the undertaking would have benefited in the same way.[37]

(iii) Intervention Is Selective

Applying the selectivity test requires one to distinguish between general measures of economic policy (not State aid) and measures that benefit certain undertakings at the expense of others in a comparable situation (State aid). For instance, if the rate of company taxation is cut for everyone, this is a general measure, even if it confers on all firms in that country a comparative advantage over firms located elsewhere. On the other hand, if a tax exemption is given to doctors then this is selective and qualifies as State aid.[38] The Court of Justice goes beyond appearances and looks at the operation of schemes. For example, in *Kimberly Clark* the Court ruled that a scheme, which appeared generally applicable, was in fact selective because of the wide discretion enjoyed by the body in charge of administering it, so that certain undertakings would receive advantages and others not.[39] It is convenient to distinguish two scenarios: geographical selectivity and material selectivity.

(a) Geographical Selectivity

What happens when the local government of a region takes a measure designed to benefit those doing business there? The legislature of the Azores archipelago, for example, decided to support the local economy by imposing a lower rate of tax on firms in the Azores than on firms elsewhere in Portugal. Was this a general measure because it was determined by the government of a region? In answering this question the Court of Justice distinguished three scenarios.

Portugal v. *Commission* , C–88/03, ECLI:EU:C:2006:511

64 In the first situation, the central government unilaterally decides that the applicable national tax rate should be reduced within a defined geographic area. The second situation corresponds to a model for distribution of tax competences in which all the local authorities at the same level (regions, districts or others) have the autonomous power to decide, within the limit of the powers conferred on them, the tax rate applicable in the territory within their competence. The Commission has recognised, as have the Portuguese and United Kingdom Governments, that a measure taken by a local authority in the second situation is not selective because it is impossible to determine a normal tax rate capable of constituting the reference framework.

65 In the third situation described, a regional or local authority adopts, in the exercise of sufficiently autonomous powers in relation to the central power, a tax rate lower than the national rate and which is applicable only to undertakings present in the territory within its competence.

---

[37] Determining whether the State acts as an investor or acts as a public authority can be controversial. The ECJ has held that waiving a tax claim in a State-owned company was done by the State in its capacity as the firm's shareholder and thus was comparable to a capital injection: the market economy investor test applied, *Commission* v. *EDF*, C-124/10, ECLI:EU:C:2012:318.

[38] *Wolfgang Heiser* v. *Finanzamt Innsbruck*, C-172/03, ECLI:EU:C:2005:130.

[39] *France* v. *Commission*, C-241/94, ECLI:EU:C:1996:353.

66 In the latter situation, the legal framework appropriate to determine the selectivity of a tax measure may be limited to the geographical area concerned where the infra-State body, in particular on account of its status and powers, occupies a fundamental role in the definition of the political and economic environment in which the undertakings present on the territory within its competence operate.

67 As the Advocate General pointed out in paragraph 54 of his Opinion, in order that a decision taken in such circumstances can be regarded as having been adopted in the exercise of sufficiently autonomous powers, that decision must, first of all, have been taken by a regional or local authority which has, from a constitutional point of view, a political and administrative status separate from that of the central government. Next, it must have been adopted without the central government being able to directly intervene as regards its content. Finally, the financial consequences of a reduction of the national tax rate for undertakings in the region must not be offset by aid or subsidies from other regions or central government.

68 It follows that political and fiscal independence of central government which is sufficient as regards the application of Community rules on State aid presupposes, as the United Kingdom Government submitted, that the infra-State body not only has powers in the territory within its competence to adopt measures reducing the tax rate, regardless of any considerations related to the conduct of the central State, but that in addition it assumes the political and financial consequences of such a measure.

In the first scenario, the power to tax is in the hands of central government so its decision to impose a different tax in one region is selective. In the second the power to tax is in the hands of a region and that region's decision to charge tax is not selective. The third category requires a case-by-case analysis. On the facts, the case fell under the third heading and the Court of Justice found that the measures were in effect subsidised by the central government, so the measure was selective.[40] This approach is relatively clear but constitutionally controversial.[41] In particular, it requires the Court of Justice or national courts to investigate on questions that are deeply sensitive, such as whether the Basque Country is sufficiently autonomous that its corporation tax is a general measure.[42] Nevertheless the judgment in *Azores* is to be welcomed, especially given that in some Member States we have asymmetric devolution (that is, some regions have greater independence than others) so that a fact-intensive inquiry is appropriate.

(b) Material Selectivity

If the measures apply to the whole territory of a Member State, selectivity is normally easier to ascertain when some undertakings are excluded. Measures that benefit only small or only large undertakings are selective.[43] Measures benefiting only certain manufacturers, or public undertakings, are also selective.[44] It should be noted that there is no requirement that the beneficiaries of the measure and those that are excluded are actual or potential competitors. However, in some

---

[40] *Portugal* v. *Commission*, C-88/03, ECLI:EU:C:2006:511, paras. 71–9.
[41] R. Greaves, 'Autonomous Regions, Taxation and EC State Aid Rules' (2009) 34 *ELRev* 779.
[42] *Unión General de Trabajadores de La Rioja (UGT-Rioja) and Others* v. *Juntas Generales del Territorio Histórico de Vizcaya and Others*, C-428-34/06, ECLI:EU:C:2008:488.
[43] Respectively, see *Spain* v. *Commission*, C-409/00, ECLI:EU:C:2003:92 2003 and *Ecotrade* v. *Altiforni e Ferriere di Servola*, C-200/97, CLI:EU:C:1998:579.
[44] Respectively, see *Germany* v. *Commission*, 248/84, ECLI:EU:C:1987:437, and *Cassa di Risparmio di Firenze and Others*, C-222/04, ECLI:EU:C:2006:8.

instances the measures might harm competitors in other Member States: tax measures favouring Italian road hauliers, or a reduction in Belgian social security contributions for employers in determined sectors, are both examples of selective measures.[45] The concern, however, is that it becomes very difficult to implement any advantage-conferring policy that is not selective in scope. This would mean that a considerable amount of national legislation should be reviewed by the Commission: for example, most tax legislation contains exemptions of one sort or another but it cannot be that every such exemption is a State aid.

The precise test for identifying material selectivity is unclear from the case law. One might suggest that there is a three-stage test: first, identifying the normal system of State action; secondly, to ask if the measure that is suspected to be State aid discriminates in favour of certain undertakings in a manner that is not justified by public policy considerations; thirdly, to consider if this differentiation may be justified by reasons inherent in the regulatory policy.[46] In *Adria-Wien Pipeline*, Austrian legislation granted an energy tax rebate to goods manufacturers, to the exclusion of service providers. Applying stage 1, we find that the reference framework is the energy tax system. Appling stage 2 we can see that the rebate discriminated in favour of certain undertakings. The question then arises whether this might be justified.

Adria-Wien Pipeline GmbH and Wietersdorfer and Peggauer Zementwerke GmbH v. Finanzlandesdirektion für Kärnten, C-143/99, ECLI:EU:C:2001:598

42 According to the case-law of the Court, a measure which, although conferring an advantage on its recipient, is justified by the nature or general scheme of the system of which it is part does not fulfil that condition of selectivity.

49 . . . [A]ny justification for the grant of advantages to undertakings whose activity consists primarily in the production of goods is not to be found in the nature or general scheme of the taxation system established under the Strukturanpassungsgesetz of 1996.

50 For one thing, undertakings supplying services may, just like undertakings manufacturing goods, be major consumers of energy and incur energy taxes above 0.35% of their net production value – the threshold above which undertakings manufacturing principally goods are eligible for the energy tax rebate.

51 There is nothing in the national legislation at issue to support the conclusion that the rebate scheme restricted to undertakings which primarily manufacture goods is a purely temporary measure enabling them to adapt gradually to the new scheme because they are disproportionately affected by it, as the Austrian Government maintains.

52 For another thing, the ecological considerations underlying the national legislation at issue do not justify treating the consumption of natural gas or electricity by undertakings supplying services differently than the consumption of such energy by undertakings manufacturing goods. Energy consumption by each of those sectors is equally damaging to the environment.

---

[45] See *Italy* v. *Commission*, C-6/97, ECLI:EU:C:1999:251; *Belgium* v. *Commission*, C-75/97, ECLI:EU:C:1999:311. For an example of indirect selectivity, see *Italy* v. *Commission*, 173/73, ECLI:EU:C:1974:71. For discussion, B. Kurcz and D. Vallindas, 'Can General Measures Be . . . Selective? Some Thoughts on the Interpretation of a State Aid Definition' (2008) 45 *CMLRev* 159, suggesting that there seems little real scope for general measures.

[46] M. Honoré, 'Selectivity' in P. Werner and V. Verouden (eds.), *EU State Aid Control: Law and Economics* (Alphen aan den Rijn, Kluwer Law International, 2017).

53 It follows from the foregoing considerations that, although objective, the criterion applied by the national legislation at issue is not justified by the nature or general scheme of that legislation, so that it cannot save the measure at issue from being in the nature of State aid.

54 Besides, as the Commission has rightly observed, the statement of reasons for the bill which led to the enactment of the national legislation at issue indicates that the advantageous terms granted to undertakings manufacturing goods were intended to preserve the competitiveness of the manufacturing sector, in particular within the Community.

While the arguments were unsuccessful in this case, the point to note is that the answer to whether a measure is selective or not hinges on the policy objectives of the measure.[47] This test is quite difficult to apply: neither the temporary protection afforded to some undertakings, nor the environmental considerations pleaded were proven on the facts.[48]

Stage 3 offers the State a further chance to justify selective measures, but here the pleading is limited to trying to show that selectivity is designed to ensure the regulatory system in question works. For example, in *GIL Insurance*, British tax legislation imposed a higher tax rate on insurance sold together with certain goods or services. The Court of Justice found that this was driven by the concern that many sellers in this market were manipulating the price of the insurance and that the higher tax rate was designed to deter this. Accordingly the selectivity was justified to preserve the functioning of the tax system.[49]

In applying the notion of selectivity there is a balance to be struck: ensuring harmful State aid is caught on the one hand and allowing States to conduct legitimate policies on the other. In *Gibraltar* the corporate tax system was based on a tax on employees and on property – the effect was that offshore companies paid very little tax irrespective of their profits. The European Court of Justice (ECJ), however, held that the tax system was selective even if there was no derogation from the reference framework that benefited offshore firms because 'in practice' the tax system discriminated in favour of offshore tax companies.[50] The risk of such a wide sweeping approach is that State aid law seems to become an instrument to regulate harmful tax practices rather than focusing on anti-competitive effects. This risk is further evidenced in the Commission's pursuit of tax regimes that are perceived to be too beneficial for certain corporations leading to tax avoidance and unfair tax competition. One controversial strand of cases involves the taxation regime for multinational corporations, and we use the *Luxembourg/Fiat* decision as an illustrative example.[51] FTT is a Luxembourg-based subsidiary of Fiat and provides financial services to affiliates of the Fiat group. The question arose about how to calculate the revenue that FTT made as a result of these services so that its tax liabilities in Luxembourg could be calculated. As a result of discussion between FTT and the Luxembourg tax authorities the latter issued a tax

[47] Although at times the Court of Justice also appears to take a narrower approach in *Commission* v. *Netherlands*, C-279/08 P, ECLI:EU:C:2011:551. See the excellent discussion in W. Sauter and H. Vedder, 'State Aid and Selectivity in the Context of Emissions Trading: Comment on the NOx Case' (2012) 37(3) *ELRev* 327, noting that when the EU legislates on emissions trading it can balance a range of factors, but such balancing is not allowed when the Member State implements that policy.

[48] See also *British Aggregates Association* v. *Commission*, T-210/02 RENV, ECLI:EU:T:2012:110 where the General Court was not satisfied with the view that the tax exemption would achieve environmental objectives.

[49] *GIL Insurance Ltd and Others* v. *Commissioners of Customs and Excise*, C-308/01, ECLI:EU:C:2004:252.

[50] *Commission and Spain* v. *Government of Gibraltar and United Kingdom*, C-106–7/09 P, EU:C:2011:732, para. 101.

[51] Case SA.38375, *Luxembourg/Fiat* [2016] OJ L 351/1 (On appeal, T-759/15 and T-755/15).

ruling to set out how the fees for these operations would be calculated. The Commission took objection to this arrangement: it felt that too much revenue was transferred to Luxembourg from other branches. In technical language, the concern of the Commission was that the transfer pricing rules applied by the tax authorities did not conform with the arm's length principle, according to which the price FTT should charge subsidiaries for its branches should be equivalent to that which would have been charged by an independent firm. As a result Fiat paid too little tax across the EU. The Commission applied the three-stage test: first, the reference framework was that for levying corporate income tax; secondly, the Commission found that the tax ruling issued to FTT was a departure from that framework because the tax authority had overestimated the amount that FTT profited from these services; and, thirdly, there was no justification for the tax ruling. The Commission bolstered these findings by noting that this tax ruling was not consistent with similar tax rulings issued by Luxembourg. The advantage of applying State aid law to these settings is that multinational firms that try and avoid paying tax in certain jurisdictions can be regulated.

> **US Department of the Treasury,** *White Paper on the European Commission's Recent State Aid Investigations of Transfer Pricing Rulings* **(24 August 2016) 10**
>
> Now, the Commission can find advantage if it disagrees with the Member State's application of the arm's length principle . . . The Commission's new approach therefore reduces a State aid inquiry to whether the Commission believes that a transfer pricing ruling satisfies its view of the arm's length principle. This shift in approach appears to expand the role of the Commission's Directorate-General for Competition . . . beyond enforcement of competition and State aid law under the TFEU in to that of a supranational tax authority that reviews Member State transfer price determinations.

One possible way out could be for State aid law enforcement to focus on those measures that cause the most damage to other trading partners, thus using selectivity as a proxy for anti-competitive effects.[52] But as we see below, the Court has also favoured a wide interpretation of the restrictive effects of State aid.

(iv) Effect on Trade and Restriction of Competition

We can examine the final requirements together, because the Court of Justice applies very low standards for both elements. This position harks back to the discussion in section 2 above as to the nature of the State aid prohibition. As noted there, the role of State aid law has less to do with the anti-competitive impact of a measure (i.e. it does not look to whether the aid gives the beneficiary market power to harm its rivals) and more to do with ensuring a level playing field or preventing costly subsidies.

(a) Overly Broad Standards

In order to show harm to competition it suffices that an undertaking is put in a better position than its competitors, so the competitive conditions on the market are not vital. Similarly, an

---

[52] Honoré, n. 46 above.

effect on trade may be shown merely by proof that the beneficiary operates across borders, or where the beneficiary does not export, but the increased production that results from State aid means there are less imports. And the effects of trade may also be potential. In *Heiser*, the Court of Justice considered whether small amounts of aid to medical practitioners in Austria could affect competition and trade.

Wolfgang Heiser v. Finanzamt Innsbruck, C–172/03, ECLI:EU:C:2005:130

30 The Austrian Government also submits that the effect of the measure at issue in the main proceedings on trade between Member States is not very marked given the particular nature of medical care which is primarily provided locally.

31 However, those arguments do not establish that the second condition [relating to the effect on trade] is not fulfilled.

32 According to the Court's case-law, there is no threshold or percentage below which it may be considered that trade between Member States is not affected. The relatively small amount of aid or the relatively small size of the undertaking which receives it does not as such exclude the possibility that trade between Member States might be affected ...

35 Accordingly, since it is not inconceivable ... that medical practitioners specialising in dentistry, such as Mr Heiser, might be in competition with their colleagues established in another Member State, the second condition for the application of Article [107(1) TFEU] must be considered to be fulfilled ...

55 As regards the fourth condition ... that the intervention by the State must distort or threaten to distort competition, it must be borne in mind that aid, that is to say aid which is intended to release an undertaking from costs which it would normally have had to bear in its day-to-day management or normal activities, distorts the conditions of competition.

56 The argument of Mr Heiser and the Austrian Government that the fourth condition is not fulfilled on the ground that the medical practitioners who benefit from a measure such as that at issue in the main proceedings do not face competition based on prices, cannot be upheld.

57 Even if, as Mr Heiser and the Austrian Government point out, the choice of a medical practitioner by patients may be influenced by criteria other than the price of the medical treatment, such as its quality and the confidence placed in the medical practitioner, the fact none the less remains that that price is liable to have an influence, or even a substantial influence, on the choice of medical practitioner by the patient. That is so where, *inter alia*, as is clear from the case-file put before the Court, in the case of medical practitioners not under contract such as Mr Heiser, the patient has to pay more than 50% of the cost of the treatment out of his own pocket.

The case law does not exclude a finding that these two criteria are not met,[53] so that a decision that does not explain how a measure can affect trade and competition may be quashed. However, the very expansive approach has two adverse effects: first, it makes it harder for the Commission to focus on the more harmful State measures; and, secondly, it should be in the context of these two criteria that the policy debate about the appropriate scope of the State aid rules should be carried out rather than in the definition of advantage and selectivity where instead we see policy debates hidden behind formalistic distinctions.

---

[53] *Italy and Sardegna Lines* v. *Commission*, C-15/98 and C-105/99, ECLI:EU:C:2000:570, where the Commission failed to take into account that the market had not been opened to competition.

(b) *De Minimis* Aid

The Court of Justice's refusal to entertain a *de minimis* rule in State aid law also means that the Commission would be unable to prioritise its enforcement strategies. In 1998 an Enabling Regulation was agreed, which empowers the Commission to establish that certain types of State aid are exempted from the notification requirement.[54] This served as the legal basis for a *de minimis* Regulation, which sets the *de minimis* threshold at €200,000 to a single undertaking over three years.[55]

The legality of this Regulation may be questioned.[56] In particular, the Court of Justice has exclusive competence to define the notion of aid. Even though the Court appears to have approved of the Commission's approach, this was when the threshold was only €100,000.[57] It might have been simpler had it been declared that *de minimis* measures may be State aid but that, given their limited impact, they are exempted automatically. However, with this approach one would then have to adopt a more sophisticated analysis of the effects of all State aid.

4 ENFORCEMENT AND SUPERVISION

(i) Commission Supervision

In the beginning the Commission was not provided with a procedural regulation to formalise how it could exercise its competences. Nevertheless, the Commission, accompanied by the Court of Justice, developed a set of procedural practices in a piecemeal fashion. These were codified in 1999,[58] and today procedures are governed by the Procedural Regulation adopted in 2015.[59] However, this is incomplete, and the rights of third parties, for example, are still largely governed by the case law of the Court of Justice.[60]

The Commission procedure has two phases. In phase 1 (based on Article 108(3) TFEU) the Commission considers the measure in question in a relatively brief span of time, and at the end of its inquiry it may reach three conclusions: the measure is not aid; the measure is State aid, but it is compatible with the Treaty; the measure is State aid and raises serious concerns as to its compatibility such that closer inquiry is warranted. Phase 2 (based on Article 108(2) TFEU) is a longer procedure with no formal time limits. At the end of its inquiry the Commission may reach one of three decisions: authorising the measure (either because it turns out not to have been State aid at all or because it is compatible with the Treaty); authorising the aid subject to certain conditions or a negative decision holding that the aid may not be granted.

The Regulation identifies four different kinds of situations and sets out procedures for each: (i) new aid, which consists of measures a Member State has notified to the Commission prior to

---

[54] Commission Regulation 1407/2013 on the application of Articles 107 and 108 of the Treaty on the Functioning of the European Union to de minimis aid. Text with EEA relevance [2013] OJ L 352/1.

[55] Commission Regulation 1998/2006 on the application of Articles 87 and 88 of the Treaty to *de minimis* aid [2006] OJ L 379/5.

[56] M. Berghofer, 'The New De Minimis Regulation: Enlarging the Sword of Damocles?' (2007) *EstAL* 11.

[57] *Spain* v. *Commission*, C-351/98, ECLI:EU:C:2002:530.

[58] A. Sinnaeve and P. J. Slot, 'The New Regulation on State Aid Procedures' (1999) 36 *CMLRev* 1153.

[59] Council Regulation 2015/1589 laying down detailed rules for the application of Article 108 of the Treaty on the Functioning of the European Union [2015] OJ L 248/9.

[60] K. Norlander and D. Went, 'Checks and Balances in EU State Aid Procedures: Should More Be Done to Protect the Rights of Aid Recipients and Third Parties?' (2010) 11(3) *ERA Forum* 361.

granting the aid; (ii) existing aid (e.g. aid that has already been approved); (iii) unlawful aid (aid which is implemented without notification, or before notification or in breach of a condition set by the Commission); (iv) misused aid (where the beneficiary misuses the aid). It may come as a surprise that the Commission may authorise both new aid and unlawful aid. While in the context of unlawful aid the Commission also has powers to require the Member State to submit information, to put an end to the aid pending the Commission's review, or even issue a recovery order when the measure in question is clearly State aid, these powers are too weak to serve as an adequate deterrent. Likewise the procedure for misuse of aid is weak, because it requires a formal investigation and provisional recovery is not available. In contrast, when the Member State is diligent it finds that it has a duty to cooperate with the Commission and review all existing aid measures, and discuss any changes. The more a State cooperates, the greater the burdens.

It is not surprising that the Commission was eager to use the current State Aid Modernisation initiative to strengthen enforcement. However, the outcome still falls short of what is necessary.[61] Its principal new powers are the following. First, it may request information from other Member States or undertakings when assessing complex cases, and it may impose fines on undertakings that furnish incorrect or misleading information.[62] However, no penalties are available for Member States who fail to cooperate, only the tacit threat that the decision will be made irrespective of their cooperation. Secondly, it may launch EU-wide inquiries where certain measures or certain instruments appear to distort competition across the EU or where certain existing aids are no longer compatible.[63] This replicates the procedure for sector inquiries in antitrust law, which have been successful in allowing the Commission to identify priority sectors for intervention. Thirdly, also replicating antitrust rules, it formalises the cooperation between national courts and the Commission, allowing the courts to request information and the Commission to send written or oral comments.[64]

One significant gap in the rules is that increasingly aid is implemented via lawful channels that do not require notification. The Commission found that roughly 85 per cent of aid granted to industry and services is granted on the basis of previously approved aid schemes or under Block Exemption. As a result, in 2006 Directorate General (DG) Competition stepped up its monitoring efforts: in 2017 it reviewed a sample of fifty aid schemes from most Member States and examined how far they complied with the procedures for preferential treatment. While data on non-compliance is not available, the Commission states that there were some irregularities, which States agreed to resolve voluntarily – for example, by amending national legislation or recovering the excess aid granted.[65]

(ii) Enforcement

(a) Recovery

The major power that the Commission has to enforce the State aid rules is to order recovery of unlawful aid. This power had originally been identified by the Court of Justice,[66] and is now

---

[61] For a critique, see A. Bartosch, 'The Procedural Regulation in State Aid Matters: A Case for Profound Reform' (2007) 6 *European State Aid Law Quarterly* 474.

[62] Regulation 2015/1589, Article 7.   [63] *Ibid.* Article 25.   [64] *Ibid.* Article 29.

[65] Commission Staff Working Document Accompanying the document Report on Competition Policy (2017) SWD(2018)349 final, 35.

[66] *Commission* v. *Germany*, 70/72, ECLI:EU:C:1973:87.

codified in the Regulation. Recovery means that the Member State takes back (with interest) the advantage it has meted out. While this obligation will frustrate the State's policy and may cause some degree of political embarrassment, the delays between the grant of the aid and the time recovery is ordered may well mean that the measure achieves its desired effect anyway, even if only in part. Moreover, the Member State loses little since money is returned to its coffers. This leads one to be somewhat sceptical about the value of this kind of remedy. Finally, recovery of State aid is in the hands of the Member State, and national procedures to organise such recovery are not always in place to cover this eventuality, nor are State organs particularly eager to prioritise measures that harm national policy. In spite of these structural weaknesses, the rate of recovery by Member States has improved considerably: in 2004, 75 per cent of illegal or incompatible aid had yet to be recovered, but this was down to 25 per cent by December 2012.[67] More recently statistics give total amounts of aid instead of percentages: by the end of 2017, 'the sum of illegal and incompatible aid recovered from beneficiaries amounted to EUR 13.3 billion. At the same time, the outstanding amount pending recovery was EUR 18.4 billion.'[68]

Recovery does not deter Member States from granting State aid, but it is said that it re-establishes the *status quo ante*. That is to say, the beneficiary is put back in the position before the aid was awarded.[69] This may be so in some cases, but not always: there remains the risk that the advantage has led to even greater benefits accruing to the beneficiary, or to losses for its competitors that the recovery order cannot cover. These further harms may be addressed by private enforcement, but as we discuss below this is not well developed. As a result, it seems necessary for the remedy to be reformed substantially if it should serve to deter and restore the *status quo ante*. A provocative set of suggestions was made by Sir Jeremy Lever: the State aid should be paid back to the Union, not to the Member State, and the Union should then use these sums to recompense the undertakings that were harmed by the grant of the State aid. This might be costly to implement and politically impossible to obtain, but it serves to show the massive gap that exists between the current rules on recovery and a system that would, in reality, secure optimal enforcement.[70]

The Commission must issue a recovery decision if it adopts a negative decision in relation to unlawful or misused aid,[71] and while the specific implementation is left to national procedures, these must allow for 'immediate and effective execution of the Commission's decision'.[72] While it is for the Member State to identify the beneficiaries and the amount to be recovered,[73] the Commission tends to do this in its decisions.[74] Given the multifarious ways in which State aid might be granted, recovery has to be adapted. For example, when the aid is in the form of a State guarantee, recovery is the difference between the interest rate on the loan that would have been

---

[67] European Commission, *Staff Working Document accompanying the Commission on Competition Policy 2012*, SWD(2013)159 final, 5.

[68] European Commission, *Staff Working Document Accompanying the document Report on Competition Policy* (2017) SWD(2018)349 final, 35.

[69] *Begium* v. *Commission (Tubemuse)*, 142/87, ECLI:EU:C:1990:125.

[70] J. Lever, 'The EC State Aid Regime: The Need for Reform' in A. Biondi, P. Eeckhout and J. Flynn (eds.), *The Law of State Aid in the European Union* (Oxford University Press, 2004).

[71] Regulation 2015/1589, Article 16.   [72] *Ibid.* Article 16(3).

[73] *Commission* v. *France*, C-441/06, ECLI:EU:C:2007:616 and *Spain* v. *Commission*, C- 480/98, ECLI:EU:C:2000:559, paras. 25 and 26.

[74] Notice from the Commission – Towards an effective implementation of Commission decisions ordering Member States to recover unlawful and incompatible State aid (Recovery Notice) [2007] OJ C 272/4 32, 37.

paid absent the guarantee and that which was paid as a result of the guarantee. In cases where no loan would have been made absent the guarantee, this means the loan itself is invalid.[75] When the aid is a tax exemption then the beneficiary should be ordered to repay the equivalent of the tax exemption received.[76]

Attempts by Member States to escape the obligation to recover aid have been unsuccessful: national procedures cannot stand in the way of the duty to recover;[77] insolvency does not extinguish the duty to recover (the State should register its claim in insolvency proceedings);[78] and the transfer of the beneficiary's assets means that the buyer may be the new beneficiary and duty bound to repay the aid. This is particularly so when it appears that the divestiture of assets was designed specifically to avoid repayment.[79] Nor have Member States fared any better in pleading that principles of EU law nullify the recovery decision. In a number of cases it was argued that the beneficiary's legitimate expectations would be harmed by the recovery order. However, the Court of Justice has not been sympathetic, ruling that a diligent businessman would be able to determine whether the State had followed the correct procedures to ensure that aid was lawful under EU law.[80] The plea of legitimate expectations only works when the Commission (or another EU Institution) gave the beneficiary reason to believe the aid is lawfully granted, it cannot work when the Member State reassures the beneficiary. The Commission has, in some cases, decided not to impose recovery orders when it considered that the case law of the Court of Justice led the beneficiary to consider that the measure in question was not State aid.[81]

(b) Private Enforcement

As indicated above, the only part of the State aid rules that has direct effect is the final sentence of Article 108(3) TFEU which provides that Member States may not grant State aid until the Commission has authorised it, and this obligation is also applicable to State aid that has not been notified at all.[82] Moreover, the breach of EU law that results from the failure to notify before granting the aid remains even if, at a later date the Member State notifies the aid and this is approved by the Commission.[83]

But what can national courts do? First, they are empowered to issue declarations that a certain measure is State aid. This empowers them to strike down national legislation.[84] Secondly, the court may order that aid that has been paid out is recovered. The view taken is that recovery restores the *status quo ante*, so it is plausible that a competitor who is injured by the aid has

---

[75] Decision 2005/786 [2005] OJ L 296/19, para. 107.

[76] *Finanzamt München III* v. *Mohsche*, C-193/91, ECLI:EU:C:1993:203, para. 17.

[77] *Commission* v. *Germany*, 94/87, ECLI:EU:C:1989:46.

[78] *Commission* v. *Poland*, C-331/09, ECLI:EU:C:2011:250; Recovery Notice, n. 74 above, paras. 63–7.

[79] *Commission* v. *Greece*, C-415/03, ECLI:EU:C:2005:287. In contrast,when shares are sold, then normally the seller of the shares remains the person liable for the recovery order. See generally, G. Monti, 'Recovery Orders in State Aid Proceedings: Lessons from Antitrust?' (2011) 10(3) *European State Aid Law Quarterly* 415.

[80] *Commission* v. *Germany*, C-5/89, ECLI:EU:C:1990:320.

[81] See e.g. Decision 2005/565 on an aid scheme implemented by Austria for a refund from the energy taxes on natural gas and electricity in 2002 and 2003, [2005] OJ L 190/13, para. 66 (on the basis of the *Adria Wien* judgment discussed above).

[82] *Lorenz* v. *Germany*, 120/70, ECLI:EU:C:1973:152. [83] *SFEI* v. *La Poste*, C-39/94, ECLI:EU:C:1996:285.

[84] This is how the notorious *British Aggregates* litigation began: *R (on the Application of BAA)* v. *HM Treasury* [2002] EWHC 926 (Admin).

standing to seek recovery to protect their interests.[85] However, to date the majority of claims have been beneficiaries or States litigating to oppose recovery.[86] Claims by those who claim they have overpaid tax when other corporations have benefited from a selective tax exemption have been rejected as these would simply increase the amount of State aid.[87] Thus, private enforcement to date does not complement private enforcement.

One reason for this is the continuing uncertainty over the meaning of State aid which also hampers the effective use of national courts. Perhaps the most dramatic illustration is the *CELF* saga. This concerned subsidies granted between 1980 and 2002 to an exporter in order to promote the sale of French books abroad. The question of whether this measure was State aid and, if so, if it merited exemption, was the subject of several exchanges between the Commission and the General Court. By 2009 CELF was insolvent, and to add to its woes, a recovery order was issued at the request of the original complainant. The Court of Justice was asked to advise (twice) on the duties of the national courts in light of the tortuous and lengthy path the measure had pursued, and both times it confirmed the duty of the courts to secure repayment of the aid: the uncertainty over the Commission's position did not constitute an exceptional circumstance to prevent enforcement of the duty to notify. This can serve to deter the Member State, because the notification process cannot be circumvented, and recovery prevents the expected benefits of the aid from maturing.[88]

There remains uncertainty over the role of national courts pending Commission procedures over the same State aid: how much autonomy do national courts retain at this stage? In *Lufthansa* the plaintiff sought a remedy for benefits that it felt a rival low-cost airline had received. The question the national court faced was what was the relevance of the Commission having started a formal investigation procedure on the same facts.

Deutsche Lufthansa AG v. *Flughafen Frankfurt-Hahn GmbH*, C-284/12, ECLI:EU:C:2013:755

37 While the assessments carried out in the decision to initiate the formal examination procedure are indeed preliminary in nature, that does not mean that the decision lacks legal effects.

38 It must be pointed out in that regard that, if national courts were able to hold that a measure does not constitute aid within the meaning of Article 107(1) TFEU and, therefore, not to suspend its implementation, even though the Commission had just stated in its decision to initiate the formal examination procedure that that measure was capable of presenting aid elements, the effectiveness of Article 108(3) TFEU would be frustrated.

39 On the one hand, if the preliminary assessment in the decision to initiate the formal examination procedure is that the measure at issue constitutes aid and that assessment is subsequently confirmed in the final

---

[85] Recovery Notice, n. 74 above, para. 30 and see *CELF and ministre de la Culture et de la Communication*, C-1/09, ECLI:EU:C:2010:136, where the competitor made a request that aid be recovered.

[86] Study on the Enforcement of State Aid Law at National Level (2006, updated 2009), http://ec.europa.eu/competition/court/state_aid_info.html.

[87] *Air Liquide Industries Belgium SA* v. *Ville de Seraing and Province de Liège*, C-393/04 and C-41/05, [2006] ECR I-5293, paras. 41–6.

[88] *CELF and ministre de la Culture et de la Communication*, C-1/09, [2010] ECR I-02099, and for discussion see T. Jaeger, 'CELF II: Settling into a Weak *Effet Utile* Standard for Private State Aid Enforcement' (2010) 1(4) *Journal of European Competition Law and Practice* 319.

decision of the Commission, the national courts would have failed to observe their obligation under Article 108(3) TFEU and Article 3 of Regulation No 659/1999 to suspend the implementation of any aid proposal until the adoption of the Commission's decision on the compatibility of that proposal with the internal market.

40 On the other hand, even if in its final decision the Commission were to conclude that there were no aid elements, the preventive aim of the State aid control system established by the TFEU and noted in paragraphs 25 and 26 of the present judgment requires that, following the doubt raised in the decision to initiate the formal examination procedure as to the aid character of that measure and its compatibility with the internal market, its implementation should be deferred until that doubt is resolved by the Commission's final decision.

41 It is also important to note that the application of the European Union rules on State aid is based on an obligation of sincere cooperation between the national courts, on the one hand, and the Commission and the Courts of the European Union, on the other, in the context of which each acts on the basis of the role assigned to it by the Treaty. In the context of that cooperation, national courts must take all the necessary measures, whether general or specific, to ensure fulfilment of the obligations under European Union law and refrain from those which may jeopardise the attainment of the objectives of the Treaty, as follows from Article 4(3) TEU. Therefore, national courts must, in particular, refrain from taking decisions which conflict with a decision of the Commission, even if it is provisional.

42 Consequently, where the Commission has initiated the formal examination procedure with regard to a measure which is being implemented, national courts are required to adopt all the necessary measures with a view to drawing the appropriate conclusions from an infringement of the obligation to suspend the implementation of that measure.

43 To that end, national courts may decide to suspend the implementation of the measure in question and order the recovery of payments already made. They may also decide to order provisional measures in order to safeguard both the interests of the parties concerned and the effectiveness of the Commission's decision to initiate the formal examination procedure.

44 Where they entertain doubts as to whether the measure at issue constitutes State aid within the meaning of Article 107(1) TFEU or as to the validity or interpretation of the decision to initiate the formal examination procedure, national courts may seek clarification from the Commission and, in accordance with the second and third paragraphs of Article 267 TFEU, as interpreted by the Court, they may or must refer a question to the Court for a preliminary ruling.

When the national court and Commission are in agreement on whether there is State aid, this approach has its advantages for it allows for an immediate enforcement of State aid law to safeguard the interest of competitors. However, if the national court considers that there is no State aid, the procedure recommended appears to prolong matters and duplicate resources as the ECJ might also see an appeal against the Commission decision on the same issue, but perhaps with a different factual context after its investigation.

5 EXEMPTIONS

(i) Overview

Not all State aid is forbidden.

Article 107 TFEU

(2) The following shall be compatible with the internal market:

  (a) aid having a social character, granted to individual consumers, provided that such aid is granted without discrimination related to the origin of the products concerned;

  (b) aid to make good the damage caused by natural disasters or exceptional occurrences;

  (c) aid granted to the economy of certain areas of the Federal Republic of Germany affected by the division of Germany, in so far as such aid is required in order to compensate for the economic disadvantages caused by that division. Five years after the entry into force of the Treaty of Lisbon, the Council, acting on a proposal from the Commission, may adopt a decision repealing this point.

(3) The following may be considered to be compatible with the internal market:

  (a) aid to promote the economic development of areas where the standard of living is abnormally low or where there is serious underemployment, and of the regions referred to in Article 349, in view of their structural, economic and social situation;

  (b) aid to promote the execution of an important project of common European interest or to remedy a serious disturbance in the economy of a Member State;

  (c) aid to facilitate the development of certain economic activities or of certain economic areas, where such aid does not adversely affect trading conditions to an extent contrary to the common interest;

  (d) aid to promote culture and heritage conservation where such aid does not affect trading conditions and competition in the Union to an extent that is contrary to the common interest;

  (e) such other categories of aid as may be specified by decision of the Council on a proposal from the Commission.

The distinction between these two subsections is that aid must be authorised if it fulfils the criteria of Article 107(2), while the Commission retains discretion when it comes to measures considered under Article 107(3).

The first two grounds in Article 107(2) are designed to address extreme scenarios – for example, allowing the State to issue food or travel vouchers to disadvantaged consumers, or to assist firms affected by floods, earthquakes or even acts of terrorism. The key concern of the Commission in these settings is to ensure the proportionality of the aid so that the Member State does not misuse these provisions to support the growth of the industries benefiting from the assistance, but only resolves the concerns caused by an exceptional event.[89] The final basis is construed narrowly: it only applies to the kinds of disadvantages suffered by the former East Germany that were the result of the geographical division of Germany. Therefore, the mere fact that the regions of the former East Germany are less economically developed as a result of different economic policies is not a basis for authorising aid under this provision.[90]

It is in the domain of discretionary exemptions (Article 107(3) TFEU) where most of the aid has been granted and authorised. Already in the *Philip Morris* judgment in 1980, the Court of Justice had recognised that the Commission's assessment was to be carried out in the context of the

---

[89] *Greece* v. *Commission*, C-278/00, ECLI:EU:C:2004:239, where there was no connection between the Chernobyl nuclear disaster and the assistance given to settle debts owed by agricultural cooperatives.

[90] See *Germany* v. *Commission*, C-156/98, ECLI:EU:C:2000:467.

Union as a whole.[91] Here the Court endorsed the compensatory justification principle that had been developed by the Commission: aid is authorised if the beneficiary makes a contribution to the interests of the EU over and above that which it would have made absent the State aid.[92]

However, one of the main criticisms of the Commission's approach to determining State aid exemptions under Article 107(3) has been that the approach lacks structure and is also subject to lax scrutiny by the Court of Justice. This means that sometimes aid may be granted when it makes no contribution to the interests of the EU, while at other times it may be denied even if it yields benefits.[93] If we recall the decision-making context, whereby the College of Commissioners takes decisions to authorise aid, one can legitimately fear that decisions to authorise State aid may be more based on political considerations than a systematic assessment of the expected benefits of State intervention.[94] In response to this criticism the Commission launched a series of reforms to improve its assessment. We turn to the substantive reform in (ii), and to the procedural reform in (iii).

(ii) Better Targeted Aid and Europe 2020

The Commission now operates a new framework to test whether State aid should be authorised, which is one of the main results of the State Aid Modernisation policy. We take research and development as an example; similar frameworks apply for other kinds of aid.

Communication from the Commission – Framework for State aid for research and development and innovation [2014] OJ C198/1

35 To assess whether a notified aid measure can be considered compatible with the internal market, the Commission generally analyses whether the design of the aid measure ensures that the positive impact of the aid towards an objective of common interest exceeds its potential negative effects on trade and competition.

36 The communication on State aid modernisation of 8 May 2012 called for the identification and definition of common principles applicable to the assessment of compatibility of all the aid measures carried out by the Commission. For this purpose, the Commission will consider an aid measure compatible with the Treaty only if it satisfies each of the following criteria:

(a) *contribution to a well-defined objective of common interest:* a State aid measure must aim at an objective of common interest in accordance with Article 107(3) of the Treaty;

(b) *need for State intervention:* a State aid measure must be targeted towards a situation where aid can bring about a material improvement that the market cannot deliver itself, for example by remedying a market failure or addressing an equity or cohesion concern;

(c) *appropriateness of the aid measure:* the proposed aid measure must be an appropriate policy instrument to address the objective of common interest;

---

[91] *Philip Morris Holland BV* v. *Commission*, 730/79, ECLI:EU:C:1980:209.

[92] Thus, for aid under Article 107(3)(a) TFEU one looks at the impact in the EU: *Spain* v. *Commission*, C-114/00, ECLI:EU:C:2002:508, para. 81; for aid under Article 107(3)(b) the aid must complement some sort of transnational European programme: *Exécutif regional wallon* v. *Commission*, 62/87 and 72/87, ECLI:EU:C:1988:132.

[93] L. Hancher, T. Ottervanger and P.-J. Slot (eds.), *EU State Aids*, 4th edn (London, Sweet & Maxwell, 2012) 146–7.

[94] S. Bishop, 'State Aids: Europe's Spreading Cancer' (1995) *ECLR* 331.

(d) *incentive effect:* the aid must change the behaviour of the undertaking(s) concerned in such a way that it engages in additional activity, which it would not carry out without the aid or would carry out in a restricted or different manner or location;

(e) *proportionality of the aid (aid to the minimum):* the amount and intensity of the aid must be limited to the minimum needed to induce the additional investment or activity by the undertaking(s) concerned;

(f) *avoidance of undue negative effects on competition and trade between Member States:* the negative effects of aid must be sufficiently limited, so that the overall balance of the measure is positive;

(g) *transparency of aid:* Member States, the Commission, economic operators, and the public, must have easy access to all relevant acts and to pertinent information about the aid awarded thereunder.

This approach sets out a 'social welfare' standard for assessing State aid, which is open to exploring all positive and negative effects of State aid policy.[95] Before assessing it, we first explain how this test operates in practice. We compare two decisions: *SABRE*, where a grant of £50 million to develop a new rocket engine was authorised;[96] and *CEATF*, where State aid of €358 million to fund the construction of a testing facility for high-speed trains (with speeds of up to 520 km/h) was not authorised.[97]

In *SABRE* all the conditions were met: (a) the project would serve to stimulate ancillary research and development activities by other firms in the EU in the value chain in question (the development of facilities to launch satellites); (b) State aid was necessary to stimulate the remaining £70 million of private investment because private investors feared entering into a project where the benefits were so far into the future but were reassured by the State's involvement; (c) State aid in the form or a grant was appropriate: a loan would have been problematic because the R&D activity was very far from the market (the products would only appear in 2021) making repayment tricky; (d) there was an incentive effect because while the risks were high the possibilities for healthy returns in the long run were present but no investment would be made without the State aid; (e) the amount of aid was proportionate because it was below what the firm was entitled to under the guidelines and the United Kingdom would monitor progress and provide findings in tranches against progress; (f) there were no negative effects either in increasing concentration (the market was growing) or in crowding out other research initiatives.

In *CEAFT*, in contrast, none of the conditions were met: (a) there was no demand for a track to test trains that go as fast as the track would allow; while jobs might be created this benefit would be only for the construction of the track and it is anyway irrelevant when looking for R&D benefits; (b) Spain gave no evidence that there was a market failure (e.g. it was not shown that a private investor would not carry out this project because of uncertainties about the future); (c) Spain did not show that it considered any other policy option to assist in financing this project; (d) there was no incentive effect insofar as there was no evidence that the project would stimulate R&D activity by the beneficiary; (e) according to the Commission guidelines the beneficiary was

[95] P. Lowe, 'Some Reflections on the European Commission's State Aid Policy' (2006) 2(2) *Competition Policy International* 67. P. Nicolaides and I. Rusu, 'The "Binary" Nature of the Economics of State Aid Law' (2010) 37(1) *LIEI* 25.

[96] Case SA.39457 (2015/N), *United Kingdom: SABRE – Aid to Reaction Engines Limited* (14/8/2015).

[97] Case SA.37185, *Funding of the Centro de ensayos de alta tecnología ferroviaria de Antequera (CEATF)* [2017] OJ L 9/8135.

only entitled to 60 per cent of the costs, whereas here the aid would finance the totality of the project, so the aid was disproportionate; (f) while there were no positive effects there was a possible negative effect because the new track would compete against the three other testing tracks in the EU: 'the measure is designed to subsidise the entry on the market of a new competitor entirely through State resources and is liable to significantly distort competition on that market as a result'.[98]

One striking aspect of this approach is that while as we saw above with the definition of State aid, no detailed economic assessment is done at the stage of defining the harm caused by the State aid, considerable effort is spent looking for the benefits of State aid intervention.[99] It has led one economist to conclude that 'aid not solving a well-defined market failure should be banned, even in the absence of any distortion'.[100] The Commission acts more like an auditor, asking how far the State's money is well spent. Furthermore, it is not yet apparent how this approach can properly be said to balance positive and negative effects: in most cases it seems as if the effects are either overwhelmingly positive or the aid is unnecessary so one does not need to carry out the balance at all.[101] In *SABRE* for instance, there were no negative effects to speak of and only gains.

These concerns have led some to raise the more fundamental argument that the Commission lacks the competence to steer State aid policy in this direction: the economic tools do not fit the Treaty provisions, and the policy of less aid is not selected in a democratic manner.[102] Moreover, the State Aid Modernisation programme also entails certain policy choices about the kinds of spending that is perceived to be most useful for the European Union. The Commission is particularly eager to promote State expenditure in projects that help meet the targets set out in the Union's industrial policy, the so-called Europe 2020 programme, for example, to facilitate developments in electronic communications. The Court has played little role in testing the substantive policy choices made in the guidelines, the case law merely checks that the Commission applies the guidelines properly.[103] However, the response is that State aid law has always been applied by the Commission in such a way as to consider the EU interest: the modernised approach is just a more sophisticated way of finding out whether the aid yields benefits for the Union as a whole.

M. Blauberger, 'Of Good and Bad Subsidies: European State Aid Control through Soft Law and Hard Law' (2009) 32(4) *West European Politics* 719

Two factors have been responsible for the Commission's ability to act as a supranational entrepreneur of positive integration: vague Treaty rules and heterogeneous Member State interests. EC Treaty rules reflect the conflicting policy goals in the field of state aid and they entrust the Commission to balance them in concrete cases. The ECJ has limited the scope of European state aid control and checks the Commission's

---

[98] *Ibid.*

[99] For this important criticism see Monopolkommission, *The More Economic Approach in European State Aid Control* (8 July 2008), www.monopolkommission.de/haupt_17/chapteriv_h17.pdf.

[100] Spector, n. 3 above, 200.   [101] Nicolaides and Rusu, n. 95 above.

[102] C. Kaupa, 'The More Economics Approach: A Reform Based on Ideology?' (2009) 2 *European State Aid Law Quarterly* 311.

[103] E.g. *Smurfit Kappa Group* v. *Commission*, T-304/08, ECLI:EU:T:2012:351.

practices for procedural correctness, but it largely follows a policy of 'judicial self-restraint' with regard to the underlying assessment of admissible state aid. Member states' conflicting views on national state aid policies meant that they were initially unwilling to agree upon secondary rules, and later were unable to counter the Commission's increasingly complex and detailed vision of 'good' state aid policy. Essentially, the Commission's strategy can be described as one of 'lesser evil' from the Member States' perspective. Compared to case-by-case control, state aid soft law has improved legal certainty, and, rather than being exclusively oriented toward competition, it left some scope for the design of national state aid policies. Compared to the remaining uncertainties under soft law, particularly those arising from lengthy Commission investigations, directly applicable Block Exemption Regulations further clarify the remaining possibilities of national policy makers and relieve them from burdensome notification procedures. In exchange, the Commission gains influence on national state aid policies.

Obviously, there are limits to the Commission's entrepreneurship: some stem from the fact that within the Commission there are competing visions on the role of State aid law, others from the reality that when Member States are relatively united in opposing a Commission initiative, then the Commission will back down. It is also plausible that the new rules facilitate creative compliance: that is, Member States appear to follow the Commission's line but, in reality, use the aid for other reasons.[104] Moreover critics suggest that the current approach intimates that without State aid control Member States would succumb to political pressures and misspend resources, while the Commission can be more wise in directing State expenditures. The benevolence of the Commission may be questioned, however: it too is a political organ which may be lobbied and where Member States may do deals to secure policies that benefit their interests.[105]

(iii) Better Targeted Aid Enforcement

As we have seen, one efficient way of handling recurring and unproblematic scenarios is to issue Block Exemptions. Powers to apply this tool in State aid were conferred on the Commission in 1998.[106] Ten years later the Commission consolidated all existing Block Exemptions in a single legal instrument, which undergoes regular updates: the General Block Exemption Regulation (GBER). The current version is in force from 2014 to 2020.[107]

The GBER applies to a very wide category of measures (including regional aid: aid for environmental protection and for research and development; and aid for local infrastructure, ports and for the recruitment of disabled or disadvantaged workers). It is divided into three chapters. Chapter I identifies categories of aid that are covered and those that are excluded. Aid is

---

[104] Evidence for this is found by M. Nicolini, C. Scarpa and P. Valbonesi, 'Aiding Car Producers in the EU: Money in Search of a Strategy' (2013) 13 *Journal of Industry Competition and Trade* 67.

[105] K. Mause and F Gröteke, 'The Economic Approach to European State Aid Control: A Politico-Economic Analysis' (2017) 17 *Journal of Industry Competition and Trade* 185.

[106] There is judicial support for the Commission's Block Exemptions, see *Belgium* v. *Commission*, C-110/03, ECLI:EU:C:2005:223.

[107] Commission Regulation (EU) No. 651/2014 of 17 June 2014 declaring certain categories of aid compatible with the internal market in application of Articles 107 and 108 of the Treaty OJ L 187 26.6.2014, 1 (General Block Exemption Regulation). It was amended by Commission Regulation (EU) 2017/1084 of 14 June 2017 [2017] OJ L 156/1. This amplifies the scope of certain provisions, but the regulatory approach is unchanged. For a useful assessment see Werner and Veoruden n. 35 above, chs. 6 and 7.

only exempted if it meets the following conditions: first, the aid must be below a given threshold (e.g. for investment aid to small and medium-sized enterprises, the maximum is €7.5 million per undertaking per investment project).[108] Secondly, the aid must be transparent (which serves to exclude aid in the form of a capital injection, i.e. cash in exchange for equity).[109] Thirdly, there must be an incentive effect. One of the main innovations of the current GBER is to deem that there is an incentive effect for many types of aid, thus requiring a verification of the incentive effect only in cases of large amounts going to one beneficiary.[110] Finally, a summary of each State aid measure benefiting from GBER must be published: this is designed to allow third parties to monitor misuse. Chapter III then contains specific conditions to be satisfied for each type of aid measure.

For State aid schemes that exceed €150 million, Member States must provide the Commission an evaluation plan. For example, the Czech Republic's Law on investment incentives created a scheme to which companies in the manufacturing industry could apply to obtain tax relief or financial support for training employees. To secure the benefit of GBER the State submitted a plan by which it would take stock, *ex post*, of whether the scheme achieved its objectives and what lessons could be learned. The Commission, while expressing some reservations on the methodology proposed, authorised the plan.[111]

Chapter II provides for means to monitor the State: requiring annual reports and the retention of information. It also provides for the withdrawal of the benefit of GBER.

Article 10 Commission Regulation (EU) No. 651/2014 of 17 June 2014 declaring certain categories of aid compatible with the internal market in application of Articles 107 and 108 of the Treaty OJ L 187 26.6.2014, 1

Where a Member State grants aid allegedly exempted from the notification requirement under this Regulation without fulfilling the conditions set out in Chapters I to III, the Commission may, after having provided the Member State concerned with the possibility to make its views known, adopt a decision stating that all or some of the future aid measures adopted by the Member State concerned which would otherwise fulfil the requirements of this Regulation, are to be notified to the Commission in accordance with Article 108(3) of the Treaty. The measures to be notified may be limited to the measures granting certain types of aid or in favour of certain beneficiaries.

The provision is said to be a proportionate penalty for the Member State now has to undergo the onerous notification procedure.[112] Note that in addition, unlawful aid will be subject to investigation and recovery.

The Commission expects that the majority of State aid (90 per cent) will be channelled through the GBER: this tallies with the desire to focus on specific kinds of projects and with a focus on economic growth. It also places more responsibility on Member States to ensure that funds are spent wisely. However, rather than requiring that States monitor this *ex ante* by testing if the aid has an incentive effect, this is now carried out *ex post* by requiring States to assess how successful aid has been. This might be a change in regulatory strategy, but some see it as a

---

[108] General Block Exemption Regulation, n. 107 above, Article 4(1)(c).   [109] *Ibid.* Article 5.   [110] *Ibid.* Article 6.
[111] Case SA.38751, *Czech investments incentives scheme* (10 December 2014).
[112] K. Bacon (ed.), *European Union Law of State Aid*, 3rd edn (Oxford University Press, 2017) ch. 5.

political trade-off: loosening the incentive effect allowed the Commission to tightened up segments of the GBER to exclude certain forms of aid that the Commission was against (e.g. regional aid and aid to firms in economic difficulty).[113] The enforcement role of the Commission following GBER is designed to allow it to focus on larger, more problematic State aid falling outside the regulation, but some attention should also be paid to monitoring compliance with GBER.

(iv) Rescuing Banks

Between October 2008 and October 2011, the volume of financial support to the financial sector was €4.5 trillion (36.7 per cent of EU GDP).[114] Compared to the high of 2 per cent of GDP spent on State aids in the 1980s, the involvement of Member States in rescuing banks is astonishing. It is impossible to address all the details here, but the key elements of the Commission's approach can be set out briefly.

First, the Commission agreed that the measures taken to save banks merited exemption on the basis of Article 107(3)(b): they remedied a serious disturbance in the economy of the Member States in question. However, it also indicated that it would apply, by analogy, the kinds of criteria that it had developed in situations where the Commission monitored aid to rescue other kinds of struggling firms. In practice, this meant that the Commission authorised the State aid quickly (and so reassured the financial markets) but only on the condition that the Member State would later on explain what measures would be taken to mitigate the effects of the State aid. This two-stage procedure is unusual but wise: it gave the right market signals (banks would be saved) and allowed the Member State (and the Commission) some time to explore how the negative effects of the aid could be dealt with. However, a counter-argument is that if the legal basis for rescuing aid is Article 107(3)(b) then there is no good reason why there should be any conditions attached to the measure: the reason the State must act is that it faces an emergency and so the aid should not have any strings attached.

Secondly, the Commission, in cooperation with governments and the European Central Bank, learned about the kinds of measures that were necessary to rescue banks and created legal frameworks that allowed for the measures to be implemented and monitored. For example, in early 2009 one of the issues that surfaced is that a number of banks held so-called 'toxic assets'. That is to say, some of the assets held by banks had no value, and this hindered their capacity to trade. Governments agreed to buy these assets at a price higher than the market price so as to relieve the banks of them. The guidance from the Commission set out principles by which this procedure should be carried out to qualify for exemption: (i) the costs of handling these assets should be shared between the State and the bank; (ii) the identification of the impaired assets must be done in a transparent manner and validated by the national supervisory authority; (iii) for banks that are in distress or have already received some other forms of aid, then there must be a restructuring plan following the exit of the toxic assets.[115] Almost all requests for State aid to

---

[113] V. Verouden, 'EU State Aid Control: The Quest for Effectiveness' (2015) *European State Aid Law Quarterly* 459.

[114] International Monetary Fund, *European Union: Publication of Financial Sector Assessment Program Documentation – Technical Note on Progress with Bank Restructuring and Resolution in Europe*, IMF Country Report No. 13/67 (March 2013) 7.

[115] Communication from the Commission on the treatment of impaired assets in the Community banking sector [2009] OJ C 72/1.

banks were approved. This might raise concerns about whether the Commission implemented its policies robustly, but it is likely that the Member States consulted the Commission prior to notification, to avoid any objections.[116] As the Commission gained more experience with State aid to banks, it issued soft law documents to explain how it would assess new State aid requests. In 2013 the general Banking Communication was redrafted.[117] In addition to recommending early contact with the Commission and the importance of a restructuring plan (discussed below), it requires that before the State bails out a bank, that bank's investors transfer some of their resources into bailing in the bank. The bail-in will hurt shareholders and subordinated debtors who will contribute to rescuing the bank. While the bail-out socialised the State's debts, making society pay for this through higher taxes and reduced public spending, the bail-out targets a discrete group of individuals who were quick to challenge the bail-in tool. In *Kotnik* the investors challenged the use of bail-in in the Slovenian Constitutional Court. Their challenge was against Slovenia: in brief, national law had integrated the Banking Communication into national law so that before notifying a State aid request to the Commission the banks had to agree to bail in some of the losses. Thus at first blush it is not clear how the ECJ could help the Slovenian court: the communication is soft law, not a Directive to be transposed. The question thus posed was whether the Commission could require a bail-in at all. The Court followed its Advocate General.

Kotnik and Others v. *Državni zbor Republike Slovenije*, C–526/14, ECLI:EU:C:2016:102, Opinion of Advocate General Wahl

53 According to settled case-law, aid can be declared compatible only when it is necessary to achieve one of the objectives set out in Article 107(3) TFEU. Aid which goes beyond what is strictly necessary to achieve the objective pursued gives rise to an unjustified competitive advantage granted to the beneficiary of the aid. Such an aid cannot, consequently, be considered compatible with the internal market.

54 Clearly, a requirement that a bank in difficulty mobilise its internal resources to cover at least part of the losses before any public support is granted and that, where necessary and appropriate, investors in that bank also contribute to its recapitalisation, appears apt to limit the aid to the essential minimum. Therefore, the raison d'être of points 40 to 46 of the Banking Communication [which generally require a bail-in] would seem to be consistent with the principles underlying the Treaty provisions on State aid.

. . .

57 For the reasons which follow, I do not find it unreasonable that, first, the exceptional nature of the situations governed by the Banking Communication requires a particularly rigorous assessment of whether the notified aid is truly reduced to the essential minimum; and, second, that such a rigorous assessment is carried out, in principle, in all similar cases notified to the Commission.

58 Financial services, and banking services in particular, constitute activities which should be considered – at least from the State aid angle – in the same way as any other economic activity. It is an activity which several (privately-held or publicly-held) companies carry out in an open and competitive market. As for any other economic activity, individuals invest in undertakings active on that market, with the aim, normally, to realise a profit on their investment. It is in the nature of any economic activity that some undertakings –

---

[116] D. Zimmer and M. Blaschczok, 'The Role of Competition in European State Aid Control during the Financial Markets Crisis' (2011) 32(1) *ECLR* 9.

[117] [2013] OJ C 216/1.

generally the most poorly performing – will fail and leave the market, and their investors, consequently, lose all or part of their investments.

59 At the same time, however, financial services play a very distinct role in modern economic systems. Banks and other credit institutions are a vital source of finance for (most) undertakings active on any given market. Furthermore, banks are often closely interconnected and many of them operate at an international level. That is why the crisis of one or more banks risks quickly spreading to other banks (both in the home State and in other Member States) and that, in turn, risks producing negative spill-over effects in other sectors of the economy (often referred to as the 'real economy'). This effect of contagion is liable, ultimately, to severely affect the lives of private individuals.

60 Accordingly, during a financial crisis, public authorities face the challenging task of having to act, often within great urgency, in order to strike a delicate balance between different competing interests. On the one hand, authorities need to ensure the stability of their financial system and avoid, or reduce, any contagion to 'healthy' banks and to the real economy. On the other hand, however, the authorities need to limit, as much as possible, the public resources involved, since the costs for the public budget to ensure that stability may be considerable. A too large exposure of the State may in fact contribute to turn a financial crisis into a sovereign debt crisis, with possible repercussions also on the whole Economic and Monetary Union ('EMU'). Moreover, as pointed out by the Slovenian Government, a massive public intervention, providing for full and unconditional support to ailing banks, may provoke serious distortions of competition and compromise the integrity of the internal market: well-run companies may be penalised by the aid granted to less-performing competitors. Furthermore, moral hazard may be encouraged: credit institutions might be induced to make more risky investments, with the hope of realising larger profits, since in case of financial troubles the public authorities appear ready to step in and save them with public money.

61 There is, furthermore, a good argument for the Commission to require burden-sharing measures generally. The Commission would be actually un-levelling the playing field for banks if it required such measures only when the Member State concerned would be unable to add the extra funds necessary to replace those measures. Indeed, banks should not be treated differently depending on the size of, and economic conditions prevailing in, the Member State in which they are established.

A third, controversial approach in the State aid decisions is that the Commission made the grant of State aid to banks subject to a duty on banks to restructure. This had been known to the beneficiaries from the start but it was only in July 2009 that the precise framework was established to guide banks.[118] This provides that the banks must present a strategy for restructuring their business to ensure that they are viable, and should pay the costs themselves (which is achieved mostly by restricting the dividend payments banks make to their shareholders). The aim is twofold: first, making sure that the banks are viable in the long term and can sustain further shocks; secondly, that the State aid that has been granted does not create a moral hazard risk – that is to say, the risk that banks may make imprudent transactions in the future again, knowing that they will be saved by the Member States. Having to suffer the costs and the burdens of restructuring is a means of deterring risk-taking. The restructuring measures include the requirement to sell off some assets to allow for the emergence of new banks or the entry of new competitors. This is an imaginative and

---

[118] Commission Communication on the return to viability and the assessment of restructuring measures in the financial sector in the current crisis under the state aid rules [2009] OJ C 195/9.

controversial remedy: it is not clear that by granting State aid to a bank in difficulty that this foreclosed market access to other firms. On the contrary, given the perilous state of the market it is not clear that anyone would take the risk of entering the market. The measure requested by the Commission thus serves to create competition that was not there before. This is a desirable effect, but it is also open to the criticism that it goes further than necessary to reverse the anti-competitive effects. Finally, the Commission also requires the beneficiary from using the State aid to make better offers to customers as this would distort competition further. Some examples will serve to illustrate how these principles have been applied.

First, we consider the restructuring of the Royal Bank of Scotland (RBS).[119] This bank received State aid in a variety of forms (recapitalisations, guarantees, impaired assets assistance). It was required to divest a business that accounts for 5 per cent of banking services for retail and small and medium-sized customers, which included 318 branches and 6,000 staff. The aim of this divestiture was to create a new player in the British market that would compete seriously with the four leading banks. The purchaser cannot have a market share above 14 per cent on that market, thus preventing one of the other large British banks from acquiring it. As indicated above, this kind of remedy is remarkable for two reasons. First, there was no indication that the State aid had in fact prevented the emergence of competition: the reason the British market was highly concentrated had more to do with banking policy over the past twenty years than with the State aid. Secondly, the remedy interferes with the British regime for merger control, by forbidding certain acquirers from buying the assets. In addition, RBS also undertook to sell off a number of other assets, so as to reduce its balance sheet. This was designed to address the moral hazard concern. Furthermore, RBS also undertook not to acquire competitors, or use the State aid benefits to gain any advantage on the market (e.g. advertising that its products are supported by a State guarantee). And, finally, RBS undertook to adhere to the remuneration code of the Financial Services Authority.

Secondly, we look to the restructuring plan for Bayern LB.[120] This bank received State aid in the form of a capital injection, a risk shield and a number of State guarantees. The restructuring plan included a reduction of the balance sheet by 50 per cent (as compared with the bank's size in 2008) and the reduction of risky activities abroad (e.g. international project finance and real estate). The Commission considered that these measures would be likely to ensure that the bank will be viable in the long term, and will focus on lending to the real economy in its region. It also considered that the plan, which included a repayment schedule for the aid received, ensured that the regional savings banks that own Bayern LB, would make a sufficient contribution to the repayment.

The Commission took stock of the impact of its decisions between 2008 and 2011. It concluded that its policies were on the right track: banks had become gradually less reliant on State aid, and markets had become less unstable. However, it also noted that there may still be the need for State aid, so that the processes and procedures that it had established needed to be extended.[121] It also noted that the measures implemented by States and banks under the Commission's supervision were no substitute for wider legislative measures to regulate financial markets in the

---

[119] *RBS Restructuring Plan*, N422/2009, [2010] OJ C 119/1.

[120] Decision 2015/657 on State aid granted by Germany and Austria to Bayerische Landesbank [2015] OJ L 109/1.

[121] Communication from the Commission on the application, from 1 August 2013, of state aid rules to support measures in favour of banks in the context of the financial crisis ('Banking Communication') [2013] OJ C 216/1.

European Union.[122] However, not everyone is convinced of the wisdom of the Commission's State aid policy.

A. Heimler and F. Jenny, 'The Limitations of European Union Control of State Aid' (2012) 28(2) *Oxford Review of Economic Policy* 347, 364

[T]hese behavioural measures unnecessarily constrain the market-response possibilities of aid-receiving banks and effectively reduce competition, instead of enhancing it. In particular, mergers and aggressive pricing benefit consumers and should not be prohibited unless they lead to violation of the antitrust laws. In some way, the Commission, instead of protecting competition (i.e. asking what would happen to the market if a particular bank were not granted the aid) is making sure that the bank would not need more aid in the future, forgetting that this is the objective of the once-and-for-all clause. Furthermore, just prohibiting mergers or aggressive pricing is hardly likely to affect ex ante moral hazard in corporate strategies . . .

As for other ex post measures taken to reduce moral hazard on the part of the managers of the aided financial institutions, the Commission is equally ineffective. Through behavioural constraints affecting the action of managers, the Commission is trying to ensure stability over excessive risk-taking. The approach is in some way simplistic and a bit naive. For example, in the Commerzbank case the Commission imposed limitations on managers' compensation and severance packages. The reason for this cap is unclear. If the constraint imposed by the Commission is binding, then good managers of subsidized institutions would leave for better jobs elsewhere, leading to worse results overall and to a slower recovery of the aided company. If the constraint is not binding it is, of course, useless. As a result, capping managers' pay does not lead to speedier recovery; on the contrary.

In addition to the effectiveness of these measures, others have also doubted their legal soundness, and criticise the Commission for a 'market structuring tendency'.[123] Others, however, have been more supportive, indicating that the Commission pragmatically adjusted to the crisis by adapting existing frameworks in a manner that was flexible enough to allow banks to be rescued, but also ensured that State aid control was exercised.[124] Whether the measures taken are a success will require evaluation at a later time. It is not, however, particularly clear by what benchmark success should be measured. The sole consideration should be to ask if the banking industry has been stabilised, but as we noted above, a number of other policies have been pursued: ensuring lending to small and medium-sized businesses, addressing moral hazard considerations and enhancing competition in concentrated markets.

The emergency measures just discussed led the European Union to propose a Banking Union: a set of supranational measures to supervise banks more attentively and uniformly. Of particular salience is the Bank Resolution and Recovery Directive. Banks that are failing or likely to fail will be put under a special resolution regime which is designed to prevent failure. Rather than the State bailing out a bank, it will be up to shareholders and subordinated debt-holders to suffer losses so that the bank's equity can be replenished. Thus, investors will 'bail in' the banks. As discussed in *Kotnik*, there is a good justification for requiring investors to bear the costs of bank

---

[122] European Commission Staff Working Paper, *The Effects of Temporary State Aid Rules Adopted in the Context of the Financial and Economic Crisis* (October 2011).

[123] Zimmer and Blaschczok, n. 116 above.

[124] H. Gilliams, 'Stress Testing the Regulator: Review of State Aid to Financial Institutions after the Collapse of Lehman' (2011) 36(1) *ELRev* 3.

failure: subordinated debtors are normally institutional investors who buy this debt because it is risky and they expect that their superior financial knowledge will allow them to assess such risk well enough and reap higher interest rates that this debt pays. If the State (i.e. taxpayers) bail out these investors, it appears unfair and gives the investors a reward they do not deserve. It should be noted that the transition to a more comprehensive bail-in that phases out the need for State aid is still not fully settled: some States have found wriggle-room to continue to grant State aid in some delicate cases.[125]

6 STATE AID AND BREXIT

(i) State Aid Policy

The United Kingdom is often seen as a Member State that has complied with State aid law and has also used the flexibility afforded by the rules in a smart way. It has also played an important role in shaping the existing regulatory framework.[126] However, the inability to rescue certain industries can lead to some scepticism of the value of EU State aid control.[127] In its White Paper charting the United Kingdom's industrial policy, the government indicates that 'sector deals' between firms and the State can be a helpful means to stimulate economic sectors. Does this signal that, liberated from the European Union's State aid discipline the United Kingdom might grant more subsidies? This would be too hasty a conclusion: the government remains set against subsidies but takes the view that State intervention should occur in consultation with interested stakeholders and industry rather than dictated top-down.[128] This could mean that the United Kingdom decides to place more emphasis on granting certain types of aid that the European Union may not favour under GBER, but not abandoning a system for targeting money in a smart way. It would be parties on the left who may see Brexit as an opportunity to augment spending significantly, in the national interest.[129]

The approach of today's government is easily aligned with any Brexit scenario as a matter of policy, because it appears that the United Kingdom wishes to be cautious about how to invest State resources. This would also serve to ensure compliance with World Trade Organisation Law. Furthermore, given that spending has been in part devolved, a central controller of State aid spending would be desirable to ensure coherence in the way State support to firms is provided.[130]

---

[125] M. Bodellini, 'Greek and Italian "Lessons" on Bank Restructuring: Is Precautionary Recapitalisation the Way Forward? (2017) 19 *CYELS* 144.

[126] A. Biondi, 'State Aid, Government Spending and the Virtue of Loyalty' in P. J. Brikinshaw and A. Biondi (eds.), *Britain Alone! The Implications and Consequences of United Kingdom Exit from the EU* (Alphen aan den Rijn, Kluwer Law International, 2016) 305–8; HM Government, *The Future Relationship between the United Kingdom and the European Union*, Cm. 9593, July 2018, para. 109.

[127] A. Biondi, 'Brexit and State Aid Control: Our Quartets' (2018) 17(1) *Competition LJ* 3, discussing the failed rescue of Port Talbot and the impact on the Brexit referendum vote.

[128] HM Government, *Industrial Strategy: Building a Britain Fit for the Future*, Cm. 9528, November 2017, 192–207 discussing sector deals.

[129] E.g. the current Labour Party leader suggests that his government may favour more spending. Speech by Jeremy Corbyn MP, 26 February 2018.

[130] G. Perez and K. Bacon, 'Paper on Post-Brexit Options for State Aid' (2016), http://uksala.org/paper-on-post-brexit-options-for-state-aid/.

(ii) State Aid Law

Unlike competition law, State aid rules have no corresponding national legislation. Members of the European Economic Area (EEA) are subject to a State aid regime which is modelled on the European Union's: there is little variation and all of the hard law and soft laws discussed above are generally transplanted into the EEA system. Accordingly, if the United Kingdom were to join the EEA this policy domain would be left relatively unchanged. If the United Kingdom secures a bilateral trade agreement, it would find some obligations akin to State aid law, with more flexibility on how to implement it than if it became a member of the EEA. However, even absent a trade agreement, the present government is of the view that some form of State aid law will be applied and little will hinge on whether there is a trade agreement or not.[131]

The White Paper produced in July 2018 (written foreseeing a trade agreement) provides that the Competition and Markets Authority (CMA), responsible for applying competition and consumer law, would take on the State aid supervisory work carried out by the Commission, and it would apply 'a common rule book with the EU on state aid'.[132] A practical consideration is that this has entailed a budget of £3.3 million for State aid for 2018–19 and the CMA plans to recruit forty-six new staff to manage the State aid regime and questions have been raised if these can be recruited. However, these estimates are done with some uncertainty as to the actual workload that State aid will bring.[133] The alignment with the Union would appear to be important for the Union wishes to ensure a level playing field in any agreement.

At the same time that regulatory alignment is proposed, the government cautions that it may depart from this shared approach, in particular when it comes to: (i) payments to farmers and other land managers for environmental benefits and (ii) the United Kingdom's future public procurement policy. Moreover, the government indicates that any relationship with the European Union 'would not fetter its sovereign discretion on tax, including to set direct or indirect tax rates, and to set its own minimum tax rates'.[134] It remains to be seen how these reservations are implemented. Insofar as the United Kingdom remains bound to the pre-Brexit case law, we have seen that tax legislation may fall to be controlled by a State aid regime, which may limit the scope of action for the United Kingdom. In the longer term, however, there would be concerns from the Union if these reservations give the United Kingdom too much latitude to offer State support that Member States are unable to grant.

Little detail is available at this time on how the CMA would handle its new functions. It appears that primary law would transpose the EU Treaty rules (with adequate modification, e.g. without requiring an effect on trade) as well as the Regulations. This raises two issues: first, given the criticisms noted above when it comes to the Commission's procedural framework, it would be desirable to implement an improved framework.[135] Secondly, the CMA will have to determine

---

[131] Department for Business, Energy and Industrial Strategy, 'Guidance: State Aid if there's No Brexit Deal' (23 August 2018), www.gov.uk/government/publications/state-aid-if-theres-no-brexit-deal/state-aid-if-theres-no-brexit-deal.

[132] HM Government, n. 126 above, para. 111.

[133] National Audit Office, Report by the Comptroller and Auditor General, *Exiting the EU: Consumer Protection, Competition and State Aid* (July 2018) paras. 4.10–4.13.

[134] HM Government, n. 126 above, paras. 111–12.

[135] UK State Aid Law Association written submission to the House of Lords' EU Internal Market Sub-Committee on Brexit and Competition and State aid (18 September 2017); House of Lords' Report, Brexit: Competition and State Aid (2 February 2018) (see esp. paras. 37–42).

how to evaluate State aid that does not fall within the Block Exemption Regulation. It is likely that that the substantive assessment would be broadly aligned with that operated by the Commission. A tricky issue constitutionally is that the CMA, while exercising its State aid law powers, may be empowered to challenge national legislation, which would test the boundaries of parliamentary sovereignty from the inside. In the context of competition law, the CMA does on occasion provide advocacy briefs to the legislature, noting the anti-competitive risks of planned legislation. This might prove satisfactory for domestic polices, but it would likely not be accepted as part of an EU–UK trade agreement where the European Union would wish for the CMA to have greater powers.[136] Moreover, the risk of political pressure on the CMA in the context of State aid is likely to be much more pronounced than in the enforcement of competition law.

Another issue which would require discussion in a bilateral trade agreement is how far the negative externalities caused by a grant of State aid by a Member State or the United Kingdom on the other party are taken into account. For instance, if Italian State aid is approved for having a positive effect in the Union, but it has a negative effect in the United Kingdom, how will this be managed, if at all? The EEA agreement contains provisions for addressing such disputes, commencing with an exchange of views to find a commonly agreed solution, absent which a solution is sought via the EEA Joint Committee, and if this does not materialise the injured party may take measures to remedy matters unilaterally. Whether a formal dispute resolution system outside of the ECJ (e.g. arbitration) may be devised remains uncertain. Having said that, it has so far been rare for a Member State to seek judicial review of a Commission decision to authorise aid that benefits another Member State, so while building a system of dispute settlement is important, it will likely be invoked rarely.[137]

FURTHER READING

C. Ahlborn and D. Piccinin, 'The Application of the Principles of Restructuring Aid to Banks during the Financial Crisis' (2010) *European State Aid Law Quarterly* 47.

K. Bacon (ed.), *European Community Law of State Aid*, 2nd edn (Oxford University Press, 2013).

A. Bartosch, 'The Procedural Regulation in State Aid Matters: A Case for Profound Reform' (2007) *European State Aid Law Quarterly* 474.

A. Bartosch, 'Is there a Need for a Rule of Reason in European State Aid Law? Or How to Arrive at a Coherent Concept of Material Selectivity' (2010) 47 *Common Market Law Review* 729.

A. Biondi, 'State Aid Is Falling Down, Falling Down: An Analysis of the Case Law on the Notion of Aid' (2013) 50 *Common Market Law Review* 1719.

A. Biondi, P. Eeckhout and J. Flynn (eds.), *The Law of State Aid in the European Union* (Oxford University Press, 2004).

M. Blauberger, 'Of Good and Bad Subsidies: European State Aid Control through Soft Law and Hard Law' (2009) 32(4) *West European Politics* 719.

F. de Cecco, *State Aid and the European Economic Constitution* (Oxford, Hart Publishing, 2012).

D. Ferri, 'The New General Block Exemption Regulation and the Rights of Persons with Disabilities: Smoke without Fire' (2015) *European State Aid Law Quarterly* 465.

---

[136] A possible compromise might be that the CMA can issue a declaration of incompatibility of primary law (like those it issues under the Human Rights Act 1998), but even this does not compel Parliament.

[137] However, recently Austria challenged the Commission's approval of £61 billion of State aid to a nuclear power facility in the United Kingdom: *Austria* v. *Commission*, T-356/15, ECLI:EU:T:2018:439.

C. Kaupa, 'The More Economics Based Approach: A Reform Based on Ideology?' (2009) 3 *European State Aid Law Quarterly* 311.

P. Nicolaides, 'The Incentive Effect of State Aid: Its Meaning, Measurement, Pitfalls and Applications' (2009) *World Competition* 579.

F. Pastor-Merchante, *The Role of Competitors in the Enforcement of State Aid Law* (Oxford, Bloomsbury, 2017).

J. J. Piernas López, *The Concept of State Aid under EU Law* (Oxford University Press, 2015).

M. P. Smith, 'Autonomy by the Rules: The European Commission and the Development of State Aid Policy' (1998) 36(1) *Journal of Common Market Studies* 55.

D. Spector, 'State Aids: Economic Analysis and Practice in the European Union' in X. Vives (ed.), *Competition Policy in the EU: Fifty Years on from the Treaty of Rome* (Oxford University Press, 2009).

P. Werner and V. Verouden, *EU State Aid Control: Law and Economics* (Alphen aan den Rijn, Kluwer Law International, 2017).

D. Zimmer and M. Blaschczok, 'The Role of Competition in European State Aid Control during the Financial Market Crisis' (2011) *European Competition Law Review* 9.

Index